CASES, PROBLEMS AND MATERIALS

Security Interests in Personal Property

FOURTH EDITION

by

Steven L. Harris
Professor of Law
Chicago-Kent College of Law

Charles W. Mooney, Jr.
Charles A. Heimbold, Jr. Professor of Law
University of Pennsylvania Law School

Foundation Press

2006

THOMSON
—————∗—————™
WEST

© 2006 By FOUNDATION PRESS

    395 Hudson Street
    New York, NY 10014
    Phone Toll Free 1–877–888–1330
    Fax (212) 367–6799
    foundation-press.com

Printed in the United States of America

ISBN–13: 978–1–58778–893–2

ISBN –10: 1–58778–893–4

 *TEXT IS PRINTED ON 10% POST CONSUMER RECYCLED PAPER*

To Jacob and Molly, with love.

S.L.H.

To Carla, Mia and Natasha, with love.

C.W.M.

*

PREFACE

The focus of this book is the law governing secured transactions. This law is a direct and conscious response to the desire of debtors and creditors to structure their relationships in particular ways. Because this law cannot be understood without an understanding of the transactions it governs, we have designed the book to give students an understanding not only of the governing law but also of the transactions themselves. To this end, the book consists in large part of Problems that are tailored to focus attention on both the language of the relevant statutes and its application to common patterns of secured financing. The two Prototypes—one on wholesale and retail automobile financing and the other on financing of accounts and other receivables—introduce the student to many of these patterns. The Problems range from those that ask the student to predict the outcome of a dispute to those that ask the student to give advice to clients, to structure transactions, and to draft certain provisions of documents. In this way, the book helps students develop counseling, planning, drafting, and litigation skills. While many of the Problems have been adapted from the Third Edition, some are entirely new.

Most of this book is concerned with the application of Revised Article 9 of the Uniform Commercial Code ("UCC"). The revised Article has been in effect in every state since January 1, 2002 and in all but four states since July 1, 2001. Even after Revised Article 9's effective date, its predecessor (which we refer to as "Former Article 9") has remained relevant. However, in recognition of the limitations inherent in teaching a one-semester course on secured transactions, we have kept discussion of Former Article 9 to a minimum.

One reason for revising Article 9 was to resolve ambiguities in, and unanswered questions under, Former Article 9. Many of these ambiguities arose from reported cases, whose relevance is reduced, if not altogether eliminated, by the revision.

As did the Third Edition, the Fourth Edition contains numerous explanatory Notes, designed to draw the student's attention to the applicable legal principles, the policies that underlie them, and the process by which the policies became reflected in the statute. Many of the Notes reflect insights we gained during a decade of service as Reporters, first to the Study Committee on Article 9 and then to the drafting committee to revise Article 9.

Although the organization of the Fourth Edition has changed somewhat from the Third Edition, it remains essentially the same. Before turning to secured financing in earnest, Chapter 1 outlines the rights of unsecured creditors and the state-law collection process. It considers the *in rem* rights of a seller of goods to withhold delivery, stop goods in transit, and reclaim delivered goods as against the buyer and as against third parties. Chapter 1 covers basic conveyancing principles for goods, including voidable title and good faith purchase, reclamation, and entrustment. It also introduces good faith purchase of negotiable instruments, other rights to payment, and documents of title.

Chapter 2 provides an introduction to secured financing that describes the differing treatment afforded unsecured and secured debt, canvasses prevailing consumer and business financing patterns, and explains the diverse roles of lawyers in secured financings. In addition, Chapter 2 contains an overview of Revised Article 9, to which the student and the instructor can refer throughout the course.

The remaining Chapters address the details of secured financing. They focus on the scope and fundamental concepts of Article 9, the rights of the parties to a secured transaction between themselves, the rights of Article 9 secured parties against the holders of competing claims, and the treatment of Article 9 security interests in bankruptcy. Note that Chapter 3, Section 6, of the Third Edition now is incorporated into a separate, new Chapter 4 covering priorities. The other chapters have been renumbered accordingly.

We wish to thank our colleagues and the many law librarians, secretaries, and students whose encouragement and support have made the Fourth Edition possible. In particular, Mr. Yan Yuan (University of Pennsylvania Law School, J.D. Class of 2007) provided helpful research assistance. Thanks also are owed to the late Professor Allan Farnsworth for the use of cases and notes developed in connection with materials on which he and Professor John Honnold collaborated.

We owe a great debt to John Honnold. Although this book no longer bears his name, these materials still bear the stamp of his creativity and thoughtfulness. We hope we have succeeded in maintaining the high standard he set.

The study of law can be interesting and challenging. We hope this book to be both.

STEVEN L. HARRIS
Chicago
October 2005

CHARLES W. MOONEY, JR.
Philadelphia
October 2005

NOTE ON SOURCES AND CITATION CONVENTIONS

We appreciate the kindness of the authors and publishers who have permitted us to reproduce portions of the following copyrighted works:

- Baird & Jackson, Possession and Ownership: An Examination of the Scope of Article 9, 35 Stanford Law Review 175 (1983).
- Braucher, The Repo Code: A Study of Adjustment to Uncertainty in Commercial Law, 74 Washington University Law Quarterly 549 (1997).
- Clark, The Law of Secured Transactions under the Uniform Commercial Code (rev. ed. 2005)
- Frisch, Buyer Status Under the U.C.C.: A Suggested Temporal Definition, 72 Iowa Law Review 531 (1987).
- Gilmore, The Commercial Doctrine of Good Faith Purchase, 63 Yale Law Journal 1057 (1954).
- Gilmore, Security Interests in Personal Property (1965).
- Harris, The Interaction of Articles 6 and 9 of the Uniform Commercial Code: A Study in Conveyancing, Priorities, and Code Interpretation, 39 Vanderbilt Law Review 179 (1986).
- Harris, The Interface Between Articles 2A and 9 Under the Official Text and the California Amendments, 22 Uniform Commercial Code Law Journal 99 (1989).
- Harris, A Reply to Theodore Eisenberg's *Bankruptcy Law in Perspective*, 30 UCLA Law Review 327 (1982).
- Harris & Mooney, How Successful Was the Revision of UCC Article 9?: Reflections of the Reporters, 74 Chicago-Kent Law Review 1357 (1999).
- Harris & Mooney, A Property-Based Theory of Security Interests: Taking Debtors' Choices Seriously, 80 Virginia Law Review 2021 (1994).
- Hillman, McDonnell & Nickles, Common Law and Equity Under the Uniform Commercial Code (1985). Reprinted with the permission of Warren Gorham Lamont, a division of Research Institute of America, 210 South Street, Boston, MA 02111. All rights reserved.
- Jackson & Kronman, A Plea for the Financing Buyer, 85 Yale Law Journal 1 (1975).

- Kripke, Should Section 9-307(l) of the Uniform Commercial Code Apply Against a Secured Party in Possession?, 35 The Business Lawyer 153 (1977).
- Kupfer, Accounts Receivable Financing—A Legal and Practical Look–See, The Practicing Lawyer, November 1956.
- Mooney, Beyond Negotiability: A New Model for Transfer and Pledge of Interests in Securities Controlled by Intermediaries, 12 Cardozo Law Review 305 (1990).
- The Philadelphia Inquirer, "They're the Night Stalkers" (November 20, 1988).
- Plumb, Legislative Revision of the Federal Tax Lien, 22 The Business Lawyer 271 (1967).
- Report of the American Bar Association Stock Certificate Committee (1975).
- Revised Uniform Commercial Code Article 9 (draft of March, 1998).
- Restatement (Third) Suretyship and Guaranty (1996).
- Schill, An Economic Analysis of Mortgagor Protection Laws, 77 Virginia Law Review 489 (1991).
- Scott, The Truth About Secured Financing, 82 Cornell Law Review 1436 (1997).
- A Second Look at the Amendments to Article 9 of the UCC, 29 The Business Lawyer 973 (1974).
- Shupack, Solving the Puzzle of Secured Transactions, 41 Rutgers Law Review 1067 (1989).
- Turner, Barnes, Kershen, Noble & Shumm, Agricultural Liens and the U.C.C.: A Report on Present Status and Proposals for Change, 44 Oklahoma Law Review 9 (1991).
- Uniform Commercial Code, 2000 Official Text. Copyright 2000 by The American Law Institute and the National Conference of Commissioners on Uniform State Laws. Reprinted with the permission of the Permanent Editorial Board for the Uniform Commercial Code.
- Wittie, Review of Recent Developments in U.C.C. Article 8 and Investment Securities, 52 The Business Lawyer 1575 (1997).

In editing the foregoing works and the principal cases, we have taken the liberty of making minor adjustments to style and deleting footnotes and authorities without indication. We have retained the original footnote numbers for footnotes that remain. Editorial interpolations, including additional footnotes, have been bracketed.

Citations to Revised UCC Article 9 and to other Articles of the UCC generally are to the 2001 Official Text, which includes Revised Article 1. They are preceded by "UCC" (e.g., UCC 9–320(a), UCC 2–502). Earlier Official Texts of Article 9 are referred to as "Former Article 9." Citations to Former Article 9 are preceded by "F" (e.g., F9–307(1)), as are citations to pre–2001 Article 1 (e.g., F1–201(37)). The 2003 amendments to Articles 2, 2A, 3, and 4, and the 2003 revision of Article 7, which have not been widely adopted, are referred to as "Revised" (e.g., Revised 2–702); citations to them are preceded by the letter "R" (e.g., R2–702). Citations to the United States Code are current through July 1, 2005, and include the amendments to the Bankruptcy Code ("BC") that took effect in October, 2005.

Because Revised Article 9 did not enter into effect until July 1, 2001, nearly all of the principal cases were decided under Former Article 9. For each such case, we indicate in a footnote whether the opinion applies a pre–1972 version of Former Article 9 or a post–1972 version.

The Notes and Problems contain many business, financial, and legal terms that lawyers often use. When these terms first appear, they are printed in bold-face type and are explained briefly. A useful source for those who wish more detailed explanations is J. Dolan, Commercial Law: Essential Terms and Transactions (2d ed. 1997).

*

SUMMARY OF CONTENTS

*

DETAILED TABLE OF CONTENTS

*

TABLE OF CASES

Principal cases are in bold type. Non-principal cases are in roman type.
References are to Pages.

*

General Introduction

(A) Scope

The dominant theme of this book is the extension of credit. The fascination of the subject results in part from its astonishing variety: complex financings in corporate merger and acquisition settings, involving millions (even billions) of dollars; short-term credit extended in business settings by sellers of goods and providers of services; credit given to consumers who wish to buy automobiles, furniture, and many other kinds of goods. This enormous variety places heavy strain on both the rules of law and the ingenuity of counselors and lawmakers.

Chapter 1 covers the fundamentals of the legal rights of creditors. It also addresses the resolution of a variety of conflicting claims to personal property—tangible and intangible—among owners, buyers, sellers, and creditors. For example, goods are delivered to the buyer on credit. To protect against the risk that the buyer may fail to pay, can the seller who is financing the sale obtain a claim to the goods that will permit the seller to recapture them from the buyer or from the buyer's other creditors?

With the fundamentals in tow, the remainder of this book centers on legal arrangements that give a creditor powers over personal property of the debtor. It embraces an enormous variety of financing transactions, some of which have little or nothing to do with the distribution of goods. For example, a business needs more cash in order to operate profitably. Can a loan at an acceptable interest rate be arranged if the borrower agrees that the lender will have a claim on the borrower's equipment, inventory of goods held for sale, accounts receivable, and other personal property that will survive attack by other creditors? What is the impact of this arrangement on the borrower's suppliers and other creditors? Will courts permit the lender to enforce against the borrower the full range of rights that lenders write into credit agreements? If the debtor defaults, may the creditor seize and resell the borrower's personal property and, if the loan is not satisfied, recover any shortfall?

(B) Development of Commercial Law

The history of commercial law is important not only for insight into the past but also for understanding of the present. In spite of recent reformulations of commercial law, it would be crippling to know nothing of the roots from which this branch of the law has grown. As we shall see, old issues keep coming back. The following outline highlights the origins of commercial law.

(1) Mercantile Custom and Nationalization. Until the seventeenth century a large share of commercial law was merchants' law—a body of customs made and administered by the merchants themselves. Some of the rules were international in scope: maritime insurance policies still bear the marks of customs from Genoa and Antwerp. These pie poudre (dusty foot) courts also decided controversies that developed at the fairs that were the centers for much of early trade; important staple commodities (such as wool) were governed by specialized courts with a jury of merchants presided over by a "mayor of the staple," skilled in mercantile practice.

In the seventeenth century the merchants' courts were shouldered to one side by the King's judges, who in 1666 proclaimed that "the law of merchants is the law of the land"[1]—a hollow claim, but one that later was in part fulfilled by the work of a renowned Scotsman, William Murray. In 1756 Murray was made Chief Justice of the King's Bench and was given the title of Lord Mansfield. In controversies between merchants, Mansfield made it a point to ascertain and apply the customs of the trade. One of his tools for this work was a special group of merchants who acted as a jury in commercial cases and gave him advice on commercial practice.[2]

(2) Nineteenth Century Codification. In the nineteenth century codification was in the air. In 1804, in the aftermath of revolution and under Napoleon's firm hand, conflicting local rules and customs in France were supplanted by the Civil Code. Napoleon carried the Code to much of Europe. Even after his armies were driven out, the Code remained. It also was followed in most of Latin America and in substantial parts of Africa and Asia.

Jeremy Bentham argued the case for codification in England. In 1811 he wrote to President Madison volunteering personally to write a code of law for use in the United States. In New York, the constitution of 1846 called for the codification of the entire body of law of the state. Under the leadership of David Dudley Field, New York adopted the first Code of Civil Procedure and prepared a code of substantive law which, although rejected in New York, was adopted in 1872 in California, and in the Dakotas, Idaho, and Montana. For the most part, proposals for general codification were rejected.

(3) Federal Courts and the "General Commercial Law." In the early nineteenth century United States, the law "received" from England after the Revolution prevailed among the settled states along the Eastern seaboard. Maintaining uniformity of commercial law among those states was difficult enough. The problem became wholly unmanageable as new states were carved out of the wilderness. Frontier law was rough and ready, marked by a shortage of law books and legal education, and a cheerful willingness to improvise. The rapidly developing commerce lacked uniform, or even ascertainable, rules of law.

---

1.   Woodward v. Rowe, 2 Keb. 132, 84 Eng. Rep. 84 (1666).

2.   Mansfield's Scottish background is not irrelevant, for it may explain his receptiveness to civil law doctrines prevalent in Scotland. (Like the Civil Code, described below, Scottish law derived from Roman law.)

In 1821 Joseph Story, speaking in his home state of Massachusetts, called for codification of some aspects of commercial law. This call went unanswered. In 1842 Story wrote the opinion in Swift v. Tyson, holding that federal courts, unhampered by divergent state court decisions, could declare uniform rules for "general commercial law." Indeed, the opinion opened up wider vistas: Lord Mansfield and Cicero were cited for the proposition that commercial law was "in a great measure, not the law of a single country only, but of the commercial world."[3] The federal courts continued to declare rules of "general commercial law," in a sporadic manner and with decreasing effectiveness, until 1938. In that year such federal law-making was held unconstitutional in Erie Railroad Co. v. Tompkins.[4]

(4) Specialized Statutes in Britain and America. A development like Swift v. Tyson was not needed in England. Royal judges already had established a common law.[5] But towards the end of the century pressure for certainty led to statutory enactments in specific fields of commercial law. In 1882 Parliament enacted the Bills of Exchange Act and in 1893 enacted the Sale of Goods Act—laws that still are in force in various parts of the world as part of the British legacy of empire.

Enactment of these two important laws in Britain was soon followed by similar legislation in the United States. The National Conference of Commissioners on Uniform State Laws ("NCCUSL")[6] in 1895 requested John J. Crawford to draft a Uniform Negotiable Instruments Law ("NIL"). Within one year the NIL was completed; by 1924 it had been enacted by every state. By 1906 the Uniform Sales Act ("USA") had been drafted by Professor Samuel Williston and approved by the Commissioners. The USA was eventually adopted in over thirty states; the principal exceptions were in the South.

3. Swift v. Tyson, 41 U.S. (16 Pet.) 1, 10 L.Ed. 865 (1842).

4. 304 U.S. 64, 58 S.Ct. 817, 82 L.Ed. 1188 (1938).

5. As noted above, however, Scotland held to Roman law. In 1855, a Royal Commission brought in an important and fascinating report on ways in which "the Mercantile Laws in the different parts of the United Kingdom of Great Britain and Ireland may be advantageously assimilated." Second Report of the Commissioners on Mercantile Laws of the United Kingdom, 354 Parliamentary Papers (1855). In 1856 Parliament enacted legislation to deal with some of these divergences. Mercantile Law Amendment Act, Scotland, 1856, 19 & 20 Vict. c. 60; Mercantile Law Amendment Act, 1856, 19 & 20 Vict. c. 97.

6. NCCUSL was formed through enactment of legislation, by each state, to create a uniform state law commission for that state. The number of Commissioners and the method of their selection are provided by each state's law. The Commissioners of all the states meet annually in a Conference of Commissioners, a meeting that typically lasts eight working days. Between annual meetings, drafting committees made up of Commissioners and aided by Reporters prepare drafts for submission at an annual meeting. Under NCCUSL procedures, no act can be approved unless it has been "read" and debated at two annual meetings.

The NIL and the USA were patterned closely after the British Bills of Exchange Act and Sale of Goods Act. Those Acts had been based on case-law doctrine developed in the nineteenth century. The legislative goals were stability, clarity, and uniformity, rather than reform. The NIL and the USA were followed by more specialized uniform laws on warehouse receipts (1906), bills of lading (1909), conditional sales (1918), and trust receipts (1933).

(C) THE UNIFORM COMMERCIAL CODE

(1) Development of the Uniform Commercial Code. In 1936 the New York Merchants' Association launched a movement to modernize sales law; it proposed that Congress adopt a Federal Sales Act to govern foreign and interstate trade. In part to avoid the problems that could be posed by separate federal law, NCCUSL in 1940 started work on a Revised Sales Act to supplant the Uniform Sales Act. The scope of revision was expanded to the other areas of commercial law that had been addressed in uniform acts, and beyond. The American Law Institute ("ALI")[7] joined with NCCUSL to sponsor this ambitious project. The Chief Reporter and overall architect of the project was Professor Karl Llewellyn. The result of this enormous effort was the Uniform Commercial Code ("UCC").

The original UCC contained nine substantive Articles. Articles 2 and 3 supplanted the Uniform Sales Act and the Negotiable Instruments Law, respectively. In other respects, the UCC created positive commercial laws for which there were no historic statutory counterparts. Article 9 on secured transactions was the most innovative of these creations.

The story of subsequent modification and enactment of the UCC is complex. For now it is sufficient to note the highlights. The first version of the UCC's Official Text was released in 1952 and promptly enacted in Pennsylvania. Further enactments were deferred pending action by New York. Studies by the New York Law Revision Commission led to substantial revisions that were embodied in the 1957 and 1958 Official Texts. Thereafter, for over a decade, the UCC's sponsors held the line against proposals for change; only a few serious errors were corrected in the Official Texts of 1962 and 1966.

By 1968 the UCC had been adopted by all states except Louisiana, where integration with the Civil Code presented difficulties. (Since then, Louisiana has enacted Articles 1, 3, 4, 4A, 5, 8, and 9.) The UCC has been enacted by Congress for the District of Columbia and also by Guam, Puerto Rico, and the Virgin Islands.

The perceived need for further revision eventually eclipsed the extraordinary success of the original UCC supplemented by the New York revision. Article 9 (Secured Transactions), in which the original drafters had gone well beyond existing law, was modified substantially in 1972.

---

7.   The ALI is a membership organization that probably is best known for producing Restatements of the Law.

Responding to the perceived need for certificateless securities, the UCC's sponsors made important changes centering on Article 8 (Investment Securities) in 1977.

(2) Ongoing Revision. In the 1980's the UCC's sponsors, NCCUSL and the ALI, launched a program of major additions and revisions that continues to the present day.

Two new Articles were added in the late 1980's—Article 2A (Leases) (1987 with 1990 amendments) and Article 4A (Funds Transfers) (1989). In 1988, the sponsors of the UCC recommended that states repeal Article 6 (Bulk Sales). For those states reluctant to repeal, the sponsors prepared a substantially revised Article 6. A major revision of Article 3 (Negotiable Instruments), with related changes in Article 4 (Bank Deposits and Collections), was concluded in 1990.[8] A revised Article 8 (Investment Securities) was completed in 1994, and a revised Article 5 (Letters of Credit) was completed the following year. The former has been enacted in all states, and the latter in most.

The last decade has seen a flurry of activity. Of particular importance to this course is the complete revision of Article 9 that was promulgated in 1998. To minimize the problems that would attend the transition from Former Article 9 to the revised Article, the sponsors recommended a uniform effective date of July 1, 2001. By that date all the states had enacted Revised Article 9 and it was in effect in all but four. By January 1, 2002, the revised Article was effective in all fifty states.

In 2001 Revised Article 1 (General Provisions) was promulgated, and the revision of Article 7 (Documents of Title) was completed in 2003.

The process of revising Article 2 has proven particularly difficult. In 1991 a drafting committee was appointed to revise the Article. That step followed the completion of a major report by a study committee on Article 2. The draft revisions of Article 2 proved to be controversial. In 1999 NCCUSL reconstituted the drafting committee and narrowed substantially the scope of the project. Amendments to Articles 2 and corresponding amendments to Article 2A were completed in 2003. They have not yet been enacted by any state, and prospects for enactment in the next few years are slim.[9]

This book affords you the opportunity to study portions of several Articles of the UCC. Chapter 1 begins by addressing transactions in goods, which are governed by UCC Article 2 (Sales). It then considers rights to receive payment, including rights to payment evidenced by negotiable instruments governed by Article 3 (Negotiable Instruments). Finally, Chapter 1 deals with the right to control goods through paper documents,

---

8.   More modest revisions to Articles 3 and 4 were completed in 2002. These revisions were intended to keep the articles consistent with new technologies and practices in payments systems.

9.   The revision of Article 2 has drawn substantial criticism, particularly from manufacturers of durable consumer goods.

which are governed by Article 7 (Documents of Title). Much of the remainder of this book concentrates on Article 9 (Secured Transactions). However, reference is made to certain provisions of other Articles, as well.

Students studying commercial law following these important changes have an obvious problem and a significant opportunity. For parts of the UCC, two versions of the text and Comments must be considered.[10] Inasmuch as uniform enactment of revisions and additions takes several years to complete, both the new and old versions of the UCC will be in force in different states. Inevitably, the UCC will not be "uniform" for some years.[11] This may be unsettling to someone looking merely to learn what the law "is." But considering a major body of statutory law in the midst of policy debates is a unique opportunity to gain the deeper understanding that comes from evaluating the perceived weaknesses in older texts and considering whether the new changes will be better.[12]

A practicing lawyer must, of course, work from the version enacted in the state whose law governs a particular aspect of a particular transaction. Judicial decisions, including cases in this book, are governed by the version of the UCC in effect in the jurisdiction whose law governs the transaction in question. (As we shall see in Chapter 3, determining the applicable law sometimes can be a daunting exercise.)

(3) Consumer Transactions. In many countries the "Commercial Code" is applicable only when one (or both) of the parties is a merchant. Lawyers schooled in such a legal setting are startled to learn that the "Uniform Commercial Code" extends to transactions among ordinary consumers and that (with a few exceptions) the rules are the same for both commercial and consumer transactions.

It must quickly be added that these general rules may lead to different results in commercial and in consumer settings. One example is the rule of UCC 2–315 that gives special protection to a buyer who relies "on the seller's skill or judgment"; similar flexibility is inherent in the UCC's rules on "good faith" and "unconscionability." The point is that the applicability of these rules does not depend on placing the parties or the transaction in a "commercial" or "consumer" category, although the results may differ.

(4) Reference Materials. A most useful tool for intensive research on the UCC is the Uniform Commercial Code Reporting Service and Case Digest. This service includes the UCC and Comments, including local

---

10.   Current statutory supplements of the UCC published for student use contain both recently superseded versions of the text and Comments as well as the most recent Official Text promulgated by NCCUSL and the ALI.

11.   Over the years the UCC as proposed has not been adopted uniformly by state legislatures. Hundreds of changes (usually minor) were made by various states in enacting the UCC.

12.   Current students may find that their up-to-date knowledge of the emerging UCC is an asset that prospective employers will value, as happened four decades ago when very few practicing lawyers had studied the UCC as initially promulgated.

variations. It also reproduces all the cases that cite the UCC and provides a digest that arranges the cases according to the UCC sections they cite. Another helpful research guide is the Uniform Laws Annotated. Useful insights into the drafting history of the UCC are provided by the twenty-three volumes of Uniform Commercial Code Drafts (E. Kelly ed. 1984) (hereinafter cited as "Kelly, Drafts") and the ten volumes of Uniform Commercial Code: Confidential Drafts (E. Kelly & A. Puckett ed. 1995).

On the UCC as a whole, see J. White & R. Summers, Uniform Commercial Code (5th ed. 2000) (hereinafter cited as "White & Summers"). For good descriptions of many patterns and structures of commercial transactions, including many illuminating charts and forms, see J. Dolan, Commercial Law: Essential Terms and Transactions (2d ed. 1997) (hereinafter cited as "Dolan, Commercial Law"). The myriad intersections between the UCC and other law are thoroughly developed in R. Hillman, J. McDonnell & S. Nickles, Common Law and Equity Under the UCC (1985 & Supp. 1991) (hereinafter cited as "Hillman, McDonnell, & Nickles, Common Law"). In view of the rapid evolution of laws regarding consumer protection, loose-leaf services are useful. See, e.g., Consumer Credit Guide (CCH).

A comprehensive and frequently updated treatment of Article 9 is B. Clark, The Law of Secured Transactions under the Uniform Commercial Code (rev. ed.) (hereinafter cited as "Clark, Secured Transactions"). In addition, chapters 21–25 of White & Summers deal incisively with the essential issues raised by Article 9. A clear and thorough explanation of many of the transactional patterns in secured financing, with numerous examples of documentation, is found in Dolan, Commercial Law 91–214.

The field of secured transactions has been blessed by a book that belongs on the short list of classics in legal literature: G. Gilmore, Security Interests in Personal Property (1965) (cited herein as "Gilmore, Security"). Those of you who wish to probe deeply should consult this work for perspective and for intensive examination of the history of personal property security law as well as the policies and provisions of Article 9 (and when you are in the mood for the refreshment offered by writing that combines charm with insight). Although portions are quite dated (the book deals with the 1962 Official Text of the UCC), Professor Gilmore's treatise remains an important resource.

Counsel for banks and finance companies that operate on a multi-state basis need current and readily accessible material on developments in each state. The CCH Secured Transactions Guide can be helpful in this regard. In addition, the Uniform Commercial Code Reporting Service (U.C.C. Rep. Serv.), mentioned above, tracks adoptions of both the official text of, and nonuniform amendments to, the UCC on a state-by-state basis. For many of the difficult issues posed by secured financing under Article 9, the most thorough treatment will be found in legal periodicals.

(D) COMMERCIAL LAW OUTSIDE THE UCC

(1) Other Recent Uniform Laws. For a number of years, the sponsors of the UCC worked on developing a new Article governing licenses of software and information. The Article was designated tentatively as UCC Article 2B. In April, 1999, the sponsors decided that this law should not be incorporated into the UCC. The project was renamed the Uniform Computer Information Transactions Act ("UCITA") and was approved by NCCUSL later that year. The ALI had no role in UCITA's promulgation.

UCITA contemplates that many transactions in information will be electronic. Likewise, each of the recently revised Articles of the UCC has made appropriate provision for electronic commerce. For other fields of law, NCCUSL promulgated the Uniform Electronic Transactions Act ("UETA") in 1999. We shall have occasion to consider select provisions of UETA as well as of the federal legislation that derives from it, the Electronic Signatures in Global and National Commerce Act ("E–SIGN").

(2) Consumer Law. One of the striking legal developments of the past four decades has been the enactment of legislation designed to give special protection to ordinary consumers, individuals who engage in transactions for personal, family, or household purposes. Consumer-protection legislation has been enacted at both the state and federal levels.

The federal government created a substantial body of consumer-protection law. In 1960 Senator Paul Douglas introduced his first legislative proposal for "Truth in Lending." In 1968 Congress passed the Consumer Credit Protection Act, 15 U.S.C. §§ 1601–1693r, which includes the Truth in Lending Act (Title I), the Fair Credit Reporting Act (Title VI), the Equal Credit Opportunity Act (Title VII), and the Fair Debt Collection Practices Act (Title VIII). Sweeping regulation of some seller's warranties in the interests of consumers first became effective on July 4, 1975, under the federal Magnuson–Moss Warranty Act, 15 U.S.C. §§ 2301–2312. In addition, the Federal Trade Commission has issued important regulations for the protection of consumers. See, e.g., 16 C.F.R. part 433 (preserving consumers' claims and defenses); 16 C.F.R. part 444 (regulating unfair credit practices).

Senator Douglas's proposal stimulated countermeasures for state enactment, including the preparation by NCCUSL of a Uniform Consumer Credit Code ("U3C"). The U3C, as promulgated in 1968, provided the basis for legislation in a number of states; a revised version was issued in 1974.

(3) Bankruptcy Law. In all commercial transactions, the possibility exists that one (or both) of the parties to the transaction will become insolvent. The consequences for the parties to exchange transactions are likely to be significant, particularly for those parts of transactions that are executory (unperformed). Credit transactions are especially vulnerable when debtors cannot pay.

Some insolvent persons file a petition for bankruptcy under the federal Bankruptcy Code ("BC"), 11 U.S.C. §§ 101–1532. A person's entry into bankruptcy gives rise to important and potentially adverse consequences for the person's secured creditors. The effects of bankruptcy on secured creditors is discussed in Chapter 7, infra.

(E) UNIFORM LAWS FOR INTERNATIONAL TRANSACTIONS

Economic activity of all kinds is increasingly becoming globalized. In the absence of international commercial law, the law governing an international transaction will be the domestic law of one nation. Important steps have been and are being taken to unify the law applicable to international commercial transactions.

(1) Sales. One field for unification is the law applicable to the international sale of goods. Because earlier unification efforts had met with only limited success, in 1966 the General Assembly of the United Nations provided for the creation of the United Nations Commission on International Trade Law ("UNCITRAL"). UNCITRAL's membership, limited to 36 States, is allocated among the regions of the world: Africa, 9; Asia, 7; Eastern Europe, 5; Latin America, 6; Western Europe and Others, 9. This last region (the industrial West) extends to Australia, Canada, and the United States. The United States has been a member from the outset and has played an active role in UNCITRAL's work.

After several years of effort, in 1980 a diplomatic conference of 62 States, at the end of five weeks of intensive work, approved the United Nations Convention on Contracts for the International Sale of Goods ("CISG"). The Convention went into force on January 1, 1988, following ratification (or similar implementation) by eleven nations. The United States was one of those nations. The Convention has now been ratified by over 60 nations, including nations on each continent and with diverse legal and economic systems. The United Nations Convention on the Limitation Period of the International Sale of Goods specifies the limitations period applicable to actions under CISG.

(2) Negotiable Instruments and Credit Transfers. A second field for unification involves the rules governing the principal instruments used in international payments—bills of exchange, promissory notes, checks, and letters of credit. In this field, UNCITRAL developed uniform rules that led in 1988 to the United Nations Convention on International Bills of Exchange and International Promissory Notes; an unusual feature of this Convention, which has yet to enter into force, is that its rules apply only to a special international instrument that states it is issued under the Convention. In 1992 UNCITRAL promulgated a Model Law on International Credit Transfers (i.e., funds transfers). Its Convention on Independent Guarantees and Stand-by Letters of Credit entered into force in five nations in 2000. The United States is not a party to either of these conventions and neither the United States nor any of its states has adopted the model law.

(3) Financing Transactions. Two international conventions sponsored by the International Institute for the Unification of Private Law

("UNIDROIT") that cover important areas of international financing were adopted in 1988 at a diplomatic conference in Ottawa. They are the UNIDROIT Convention on International Financial Leasing and the UNIDROIT Convention on International Factoring. The United States is not a party to either of these conventions.

Two other projects in the field of international finance have been completed in recent years. The Convention on International Interests in Mobile Equipment and the Protocol thereto on Matters specific to Aircraft Equipment were completed at a diplomatic conference in Cape Town, South Africa in 2001. The texts submitted to the conference were prepared under the auspices of UNIDROIT and the International Civil Aviation Organization. The convention and protocol govern the financing of large civil aircraft. The United States ratified the convention and protocol in 2004, and the convention has entered into force. Additional protocols are being negotiated for the financing of railroad rolling stock and space stations and satellites. In 2001 UNCITRAL completed work on the United Nations Convention on the Assignment of Receivables in International Trade, which addresses the international assignment of receivables. The United States has signed but has not ratified this convention.

Finally, work is proceeding on the Preliminary Draft Convention on Harmonised Substantive Rules Regarding Intermediated Securities. This draft convention emerged from a first meeting of governmental experts, held in Rome in 2005 under the auspices of UNIDROIT. The draft convention addresses the secured financing of intermediated securities as well as a broad swath of other issues arising out of the crediting of securities to securities accounts maintained with financial intermediaries (e.g., banks and securities firms).

(4) Other Fields. In 1994 UNIDROIT promulgated, and in 2004 it expanded and revised, a set of contract principles, the UNIDROIT Principles of International Commercial Contracts. These principles enunciate rules that are common to most existing domestic legal systems, but that are best adapted to the special requirements of international trade. They deal with a number of matters that are either completely excluded from CISG or not sufficiently covered in that Convention. The principles can be applied when contracting parties have agreed to be governed by them, but are also offered as guides to solving issues when tribunals cannot ascertain the relevant rule of the applicable law.

Because of the vital part that sea transport plays in international trade, UNCITRAL developed new rules that govern the responsibility of ocean carriers for cargo. Despite the active opposition of the carriers, the United Nations Convention on Carriage of Goods by Sea came into force in 1991.

Other examples of the rapidly growing body of uniform law for international commerce include the 1976 UNCITRAL Arbitration Rules, which become effective by a reference in a contractual arbitration clause, and the 1985 UNCITRAL Model Law on International Commercial Legislation. Judicial enforcement of arbitration awards is covered by the

United Nations Convention on the Recognition and Enforcement of Foreign Arbitral Awards, commonly known as the "New York Convention."

(F) INTERPRETATION OF THE UNIFORM COMMERCIAL CODE

Much of this book deals with the examination and interpretation of the texts of state statutory law, primarily Article 9 of the Uniform Commercial Code. The objective is to find the meaning of the text as applied to factual circumstances found in reported decisions or posed in problem situations, many of which are set out in these materials. Given the central importance of this task, it is useful at the outset to consider how to go about it.

(1) Two Polar Approaches to Statutory Interpretation. Four hundred years ago, during the reign of Elizabeth I, one of the greatest common-law judges, Lord Coke, proposed a maxim for statutory interpretation: Identify the "mischief . . . for which the common law did not provide [a remedy]," and then identify precisely the "remedy the Parliament hath resolved."[13] Lord Coke's maxim posits that statutes are corrective measures, enacted from time to time to overcome particular deficiencies in the common law. On this view, each statute is only a patch on the broad cloth of common law and its meaning can be ascertained by examining the nature of the hole the legislature sought to mend.

When the statute to be construed is a large, integrated work, such as a code, a quite different approach is to seek the meaning of its various provisions in light of the overarching purposes and policies that animate the whole work. A piecemeal, mischief-correction reading would not take adequate account of the greater set of principles envisioned by the legislature. Gaps in the text of a code can be filled by interpolating provisions that serve the code's general policies.

(2) General Provisions; Definitions. Like most codes, the UCC contains a number of important provisions that are applicable generally. These include a statement of the purposes and policies of the UCC, see UCC 1–103(a) [F1–102] , as well as a provision linking the UCC to other bodies of law. See UCC 1–103(b) [F1–103].

The UCC has a large number of definitions and contains ingenious devices to aid in finding them. Some of the Articles provide a fast and easy way to find many of these definitions: "Definitional Cross References" are found at the end of the Official Comments to each section. However, a careful lawyer will not rely on the completeness of these cross-references. For a thorough job, one will check Article 1, which contains important provisions applicable to the UCC as a whole; UCC 1–201(b) [F1–201] contains the definitions of several dozen terms used throughout the UCC. In addition, one should check the definitions contained in, and specially applicable to, a particular Article. See, e.g., UCC 2–103 (which contains

---

13.   Heydon's Case, 3 Co. Rep. 7a, 7b, 76 Eng. Rep. 637, 638 (1584).

definitions, an index of definitions inserted in the text of the Article, and an index of applicable definitions in other Articles).

It would be useful for you to skim through the sections of Article 1 at this time. You should pay particular attention to UCC 1–103 and UCC 1–304 [F1–203].

(3) The Comments to the UCC: Uses and Hazards. A hazard for the lazy mind, and a help for the responsible lawyer, are the Official Comments that follow each section of the UCC. We should note some of the troublesome problems concerning the role of the Comments in the UCC scheme.

The most obvious point about the Comments is the one that, curiously enough, is most often overlooked: The text to the UCC was enacted by the legislature; the Comments were not. One is tempted to ignore this point because the Comments, written in an explanatory and non-statutory style, are easier to read. Facilis est descensus Averno.

But the tempter will whisper: The drafters wrote these Comments, didn't they? If they say what the UCC does, that's bound to be right, isn't it? Why bother then with this prickly statutory language? (You may find it easier to resist these temptations if you put yourself, in your mind's eye, in the role of a judge to whom this argument has been made and then imagine your response to that hapless attorney.)

The problem of the force of the Comments is sufficiently important to justify some background. Versions of the UCC prior to 1957 included a significant provision about the Comments in the general provisions of Article 1. Section 1–102, Purposes; Rules of Construction, stated in subsection (3)(f):

> The Comments of the National Conference of Commissioners on Uniform State Laws and the American Law Institute may be consulted in the construction and application of this Act but if text and Comment conflict, text controls.

In 1956 the sponsoring organizations released the 1956 Recommendations of the Editorial Board for the Uniform Commercial Code, recommending widespread revisions (many of which were adopted by the sponsors). These recommendations called for the deletion of the above-quoted UCC 1–102(3)(f) and did not substitute any new provision on the status of the Comments.[14] The question immediately arises: Does this deletion imply the rejection of the idea behind the deleted provision so that reference to the Comments has become illegitimate?

An answer appears in the Comments to the 1956 Recommendations. The reasons for this and other changes were only briefly stated; the explanation for this change was as follows: "paragraph (3)(f) was deleted because the old Comments were clearly out of date and it was not known when new ones

---

14.   1956 Recommendations of the Editorial Board for the Uniform Commercial Code (hereinafter cited as 1956 Recommendations), 18 Kelly, Drafts 27.

could be prepared."[15] Revised Comments accompanied the 1957 and subsequent versions of the UCC, but without any statutory provision referring to them.

Embarrassing questions arise if one subjects the Comments to the standards often imposed for recourse to legislative history. In some states the revised Comments had not yet been drafted at the time of the UCC's adoption. In others it is highly doubtful that the Comments were laid before the legislators in the form of a committee report explaining the legislation that the legislators were asked to adopt. Moreover, some of the Comments were not even written by those who drafted the Official Text. Nor are the Comments approved by the sponsors of the UCC. The practice for some Articles has been for the Reporter to draft Official Comments in consultation with the Chair of the drafting committee after the sponsors have approved the text. In recent years draft Comments to other Articles were available to aid the sponsors in their consideration of the text (as well as to the public on the Internet). The final versions were approved by a relatively small number of persons entrusted with this task by the sponsors.

It would be very wrong, however, to conclude that the Comments are without value to lawyers and to courts. Professor Williston's treatise on Sales was given heavy weight by courts in construing the Uniform Sales Act on the ground that it reflected the intent of the drafter although it was written subsequent to the drafting of the Act; as you will see, courts repeatedly have quoted the Comments in construing the UCC and often have given the Comments substantial weight in their reasoning.

Surely the Comments may be given at least as much weight as an able article or treatise construing the UCC. It is equally clear that the Comments do not approach the weight of legislation. If the statutory provisions adopted by the legislature contradict or fail to support the Comments, then the Comments must be rejected.

The point is significant, for we shall see instances, easily understood in the light of the Comments' bulk and the many successive revisions of the UCC, where the Comments have been less than faithful to the statute. More frequent are instances of enthusiastic discussion of significant problems on which the statute is silent.

A thorough job of construing the UCC calls for using the Comments to make sure one has found the pertinent language of the statute, as a double-check on a tentative construction, and as a secondary aid where the language of the statute is ambiguous. However, we warn you that we sternly reject any reference to Comments until after the pertinent statutory language has been carefully examined in the light of the statutory definitions and the statutory structure.

One additional development necessitates yet another warning. Pursuant to its resolution of March 14, 1987, the Permanent Editorial Board for the

---

15. Id. Perhaps we face here an engineering problem: How high can the Comments lift themselves by their own boot-straps? Are the authors violating their own principles in quoting this Comment?

Uniform Commercial Code ("PEB") has issued (and continues to issue) PEB Commentaries. The PEB Commentaries (and the cited resolution) are set out in full in most statutory supplements published for student use. The PEB Commentaries have necessitated supplemental changes to the Comments. Although the Comments refer to the relevant PEB Commentaries, in some cases portions of the Comments have been deleted and replaced by entirely new language. Because the Comments have been relied upon by legislators, courts, and counsel alike, one hopes that the UCC's sponsors will find a way to preserve the Comments intact as supplemented by the PEB Commentaries.

CHAPTER 1

RIGHTS OF CREDITORS, OWNERS, AND PURCHASERS

SECTION 1. THE RIGHTS OF UNSECURED CREDITORS

Much of law school is devoted to determining whether one person is legally obligated to another and, if so, the amount of damages recoverable or other appropriate remedy. The course in secured transactions is one of the few that generally assumes the defendant's liability and explores how the aggrieved party can turn its claim into cash.

Consider a simple case: Bank lends Dana $1,000, which Dana agrees to repay, together with stated interest, in one year. At the end of the year, Dana fails to pay. What can Bank do to recover its claim?

Above all, and particularly when the claim is very small, Bank wishes to avoid incurring the expense and delay inherent in legal proceedings. Accordingly, it strongly prefers to encourage Dana to pay voluntarily. Bank's first approach is likely to be informal. It may write one or more **dunning letters** to Dana, in which it demands payment and threatens suit if payment is not forthcoming immediately. The letter may suggest that failure to pay will adversely affect Dana's ability to obtain credit in the future. It may suggest also that, if Dana cannot make full payment, Bank would be willing to enter into an arrangement for Dana to pay in installments. Rather than attempt to collect the claim itself, Bank may refer the claim to a **collection agency**, which, for a fee, will attempt collection. The collection agency's first approach also is likely to be informal.

Employees of Bank or its collection agency may be tempted to induce Dana to pay by "making an offer you can't refuse." The criminal law, the common law of tort, and federal and state statutes regulating debt collection provide some check against the overexuberance of those who wish to collect what is due and owing, particularly when the debtor is a consumer. For example, the Fair Debt Collection Practices Act, 15 U.S.C. §§ 1692–1692o, affords remedies to persons who are subjected to harassment, misrepresentations, and certain other unfair practices by collection agencies. Some states have extended similar protection against abuses by creditors themselves, as well as by collection agencies. See, e.g., Wis. Stat. Ann. §§ 427.104, 427.105.

It is worth noting what may be obvious to some: Bank has a right to be paid; however, it has no interest whatsoever in any particular property that

Dana may own. Bank may not simply send its agents to Dana's house to take whatever they can find. To collect a claim in this way would be to engage in both tortious and criminal conduct. If Dana does not pay voluntarily, Bank is relegated to the judicial process. Its lawyers will prepare a complaint and summons, which they will file with the clerk of the court and cause to be served upon Dana. Dana will have a period of time in which to respond. In many cases of this kind, where the facts are simple and the defenses are likely to be few, the debtor may fail to respond at all. If so, the creditor will be able to obtain the entry of a **default judgment** upon an ex parte showing that the debt is owed. If the debtor does respond, then the case will proceed through the motion and discovery stages and, if settlement is not forthcoming, to trial and the entry of judgment.

Assume that, whether by default or after trial, Bank obtains judgment in the amount of $1,000 plus interest and costs. Dana, the **judgment debtor**, ignores the entry of the judgment and continues to fail to pay. What can Bank do? Is Dana in contempt of court for failing to pay?

A judgment is an adjudication that the judgment debtor owes a particular amount to the **judgment creditor**. It is not an order requiring the judgment debtor actually to pay. Even so, a judgment is not without value. Without a judgment, a creditor must rely on persuasion and other informal techniques to induce a debtor to pay. A judgment entitles the judgment creditor in addition to invoke the "long arm of the law" to dispossess the debtor from property (other than property that is exempt from the reach of creditors[1]) and cause the property to be applied toward the satisfaction of the claim.

We leave to courses in creditors' rights a detailed examination of the collection of judgments. For our purposes, the following, highly simplified overview should suffice. Collecting a judgment through the judicial process typically involves two steps. The first is to obtain a **judicial lien** on particular property of the judgment debtor. The second is to turn the lien into cash.[2]

---

1.   All states have laws providing that certain property of individuals (as opposed to partnerships or corporations) is **exempt** from the reach of creditors. These laws vary widely: some award liberal **exemptions** and other afford only meager protection. Exempt property typically includes the home, household and personal effects, and tools of the trade. Often, the extent to which property is exempt is limited to a specified dollar amount (e.g., up to $750 in jewelry; up to $10,000 of the value of one's home).

2.   Although the following discussion focuses on postjudgment liens, most states make some provision for prejudgment liens under limited circumstances, e.g., upon a showing that the defendant is about to abscond from the jurisdiction or hide property otherwise available to creditors. Many of the restrictions on the availability of prejudgment remedies, including those affording the debtor notice of the exercise of the remedy and an opportunity to be heard, reflect cases decided under the due process clause of the fourteenth amendment. See, e.g., North Georgia Finishing, Inc. v. Di–Chem, Inc., 419 U.S. 601, 95 S.Ct. 719, 42 L.Ed.2d 751 (1975) (discussing constitutional requirements surrounding prejudgment garnishment of corporate debtor's bank account). See also Note (3) on Wrongful Repossession, p. 590, infra. Prejudgment liens are similar

A lien is a property interest of a particular kind. The holder of the lien (the **lienor**) may use the property subject to the lien for only one purpose, to apply toward satisfaction of the debt it secures. Although state laws and procedures governing postjudgment liens vary, generally speaking a judgment creditor acquires a lien in one of two ways. The creditor may obtain from the clerk of the court a **writ of execution**, instructing the sheriff to **levy** upon (seize) assets of the judgment debtor located within the sheriff's bailiwick (usually a county). In the majority of states, the creditor acquires an **execution lien** on whatever property the sheriff levies upon before the writ expires. In a minority of states, an **inchoate** execution lien arises on all property of the judgment debtor within the bailiwick when the writ is delivered to the sheriff; however, the inchoate lien cannot be enforced against specific property until the sheriff levies upon the property and the lien becomes **consummate**. If the sheriff fails to levy before the writ expires, the inchoate lien is discharged.[3]

In most states, a judgment creditor may obtain a **judgment lien** simply by recording a memorandum or abstract of the judgment in the real estate records or (depending on local law) having the court clerk enter the judgment in the docket book. Upon the recordation or docketing, a judgment lien arises on all of the debtor's interests in real property in the county. In only a few states does the judgment lien extend to personal property. See, e.g., Cal. Code Civ. Proc. § 697.530 (judgment lien arises on most nonexempt personal property upon filing a notice with the Secretary of State). Because this book is concerned almost exclusively with personal property, we shall have no more to say about judgment liens.

An execution lien affords two important advantages to the judgment creditor. First, it provides a means for applying the judgment debtor's property to satisfaction of the judgment. To turn the lien into cash, the judgment creditor usually looks to the sheriff, who will sell the property at a **sheriff's sale**.[4] Because the sale usually is poorly advertised (often in a legal newspaper), because the sheriff makes no warranty of title, and because the judgment debtor is an unwilling seller, the price paid at a

---

in many ways to the postjudgment liens discussed below. The principal difference is that the creditor ordinarily cannot cause the former to be turned into cash until judgment is entered against the defendant-debtor.

3.   While levy may be a suitable means for acquiring a lien upon **tangible** personal property, a different method is necessary when the creditor seeks to acquire a lien on a debtor's **intangible** personal property, which, by its very nature, cannot be seized. A common example of intangible property is a claim against a third party. Suppose, for example, that Bank has reason to know that Kerry owes Dana $100. Bank could cause the clerk of the court to issue a **writ of garnishment** directed to Kerry, instructing Kerry to inform the court whether Kerry is indebted to Dana and, if so, for how much. In most jurisdictions, a **garnishment lien** on Kerry's debt to Dana arises when the writ is served upon Kerry.

4.   To turn a garnishment lien into cash, the court will order the **garnishee** (Kerry, in the example in footnote 3) to pay the debt to Bank, either directly or through a judicial officer.

sheriff's sale rarely, if ever, approaches the price that the property would command in the marketplace. The first two reasons also explain why few, if any, buyers appear at the sale other than the judgment creditor. Inasmuch as the judgment creditor is entitled to the proceeds of the sale (less the costs of sale), the judgment creditor need not pay cash. Rather, the creditor may **bid in the judgment**, i.e., simply reduce the amount of the judgment debt by the amount it wishes to pay for the property. If the judgment creditor is the successful bidder, it becomes the owner of the property and must thereafter resell the property to obtain cash.

An execution lien enables the judgment creditor not only to apply particular property toward the satisfaction of its claim against the debtor but also to reach the property to the exclusion of other, competing creditors who have not obtained liens. Although more than one execution lien may attach to particular property, liens generally rank in temporal order; that is, the holder of the debt secured by the earliest lien is entitled to be paid first from the proceeds of the sale of the property. Thus, by winning the "race of diligence" and obtaining a lien on specific assets, Bank generally acquires not only a property interest in those assets but also **priority** over other, subsequently arising liens.

Any consideration of the judicial collection system should take into account its costs. These include Bank's out-of-pocket expenses as well as the cost of delay. How much would it cost to obtain and collect a judgment against Dana? How long would it take? What risks attend the delay?

All things being equal, Bank would be in a better position if it could acquire a lien without first having to obtain a judgment and invoke the power of the sheriff. At the time Bank extended credit, or at any time thereafter, Bank and Dana could have *agreed* that Bank would have a limited interest in particular property. The nature of this interest could be such that if Dana failed to pay, Bank could cause the property to be sold and apply the proceeds to the satisfaction of its claim without the need to incur the costs and delay attendant to obtaining a judgment and collecting it through the judicial process. When the property concerned is personal property, this kind of **consensual lien**, which arises by the agreement of the parties, is called a **security interest**. (A consensual security interest must be distinguished from a **judicial lien**, which arises through the exercise of judicial process, and a **statutory lien**, which arises by operation of law in favor of certain suppliers of goods and services.) A security interest affords yet another benefit to the holder that a judicial lien does not. Whereas the law governing judicial liens differs from state to state, the law governing security interests, including the rights and duties of the immediate parties (debtor and creditor) and the rights of third parties, is found largely in UCC Article 9. Security interests under UCC Article 9 are the principal focus of this book.

SECTION 2.   SELLER'S POWER OVER THE GOODS AS AGAINST BUYER

As Section 1 suggests, unless the borrower agrees to grant the lender a security interest, the lender must resort to the judicial process if the borrower does not repay the debt voluntarily. Is a seller of goods in any better position with respect to a buyer?

Generally, the answer is "no." If the seller delivers goods on credit to the buyer and the buyer, having received a conforming tender, fails to pay, the law affords the seller exactly what the seller bargained for: the right to recover the price from the buyer. See UCC 2–709. The seller ordinarily has no right to recover the goods themselves (except, of course, if it can do so through **execution** or other judicial remedy). See generally UCC 2–703.

Suppose that the seller advances the following argument: Buyer promised to pay for the goods and broke that promise. For such a serious (indeed, fundamental) breach I should have a right to **rescind** (undo) the transaction and recover the goods by a possessory remedy, such as **replevin**.[1]

This argument is consistent with a common misunderstanding. Many people believe that if they don't pay for a purchase, the seller can "take it back." This argument may be sound in some civil-law legal systems, but it is not supported by the common law. Any attempt by a seller to replevy goods sold on credit would have failed under the English common law, which was codified in the (British) Sale of Goods Act, which in turn was followed in the Uniform Sales Act. The drafters of the UCC did not dream of overturning the basic common-law approach. The catalogue of the seller's remedies in UCC 2–703 does not mention recovery of the goods,[2] and the seller's limited rights to recover goods under UCC 2–507 and UCC 2–702 (discussed below in Section 2(C)) do not extend to the buyer's failure to pay for goods delivered on credit.

Although a credit seller ordinarily may not recover goods delivered to the buyer and must instead enforce the buyer's promise to pay, the following materials suggest that the law does afford to a seller of goods certain rights that a lender of funds does not enjoy.

(A) THE RIGHT TO WITHHOLD DELIVERY

Problem 1.2.1. On January 3, Seller and Buyer entered into a contract for the sale of a garden tractor, which Buyer agreed to pay for and take

---

1.   Replevin, like sequestration and claim and delivery, is a judicial remedy to recover possession of personal property. Replevin statutes are procedural: They do not create the right to possession but rather aid those who are entitled to possession under other law.

2.   Note that Revised 2–703(2)(d) and (3)(c) do refer to reclamation rights under Revised 2–507(2) and Revised 2–702(2), respectively.

away by January 30. The agreement specified that "title" passed to Buyer on January 3. On January 30, Buyer demands the tractor but declines to pay. Is Seller justified in denying Buyer possession of "Buyer's" goods? May Seller close out the transaction by reselling "Buyer's" tractor to another customer? See UCC 2–401; UCC 2–511(1); UCC 2–703; UCC 2–706.

Problem 1.2.2. On January 3, Seller and Buyer entered into a contract for the sale of a power lathe. Seller agreed to deliver the lathe on January 30, and Buyer agreed to pay for the lathe within 30 days thereafter. On January 15, Seller received an updated credit report, showing that Buyer recently had become extremely slow in paying its debts. Seller is concerned that Buyer will take delivery and will not pay. What can Seller do? See UCC 2–609; UCC 2–702(1); UCC 1–201(b)(23) [F1–201(23)].

(B) THE RIGHT TO STOP DELIVERY

In many transactions, the seller ships the goods to the buyer on a truck, railroad, or other common carrier. A seller who wishes to prevent the buyer from obtaining the goods from the carrier without first paying for them can structure the transaction accordingly. (One of these structures is discussed briefly in the Introductory Note to Section 5, infra.) Often, however, a seller ships goods to the buyer on **open account**, with the expectation that the buyer will pay for them at a specified time after delivery. What happens under these circumstances if, while the goods are in transit, the seller becomes concerned about the buyer's ability to pay? Who has the better claim to goods in transit, the seller or the buyer? Even if the seller has the better claim, what, if anything, can the seller do to stop the carrier from delivering the goods to the buyer?

A seller is entitled to stop delivery of goods in transit if the seller discovers that the buyer is insolvent. UCC 2–702(1); UCC 2–705(1); UCC 1–201((b)(23) [F1–201(23)]. In addition, in the case of a "carload, truckload, planeload or larger shipments," a seller may stop delivery if the buyer repudiates, fails to make a payment due before delivery of the goods, or if the seller otherwise is entitled to withhold or reclaim the goods. Under R–705(1), the "carload," etc. requirement has been eliminated; repudiation, nonpayment, and the right to withhold or reclaim provide a basis for stopping delivery in all sales transactions. Under UCC 2–705(2), the seller's right to stop delivery expires when the buyer receives the goods and in certain other circumstances.

To exercise its right to stop delivery, a seller must notify the carrier in time for the carrier to prevent delivery by exercising "reasonable diligence." UCC 2–705(3)(a). After proper notification the carrier must "hold and deliver the goods according to the directions of the seller." UCC 2–705(3)(b). But, if a **negotiable document of title** was issued for the goods the carrier is not obligated to obey a seller's instructions until the document is surrendered to the carrier. (Negotiable documents of title are addressed in Section 5 of this Chapter, infra.) Once a seller effectively exercises its right to stop delivery the carrier is relieved of its duty to deliver the goods to a "person entitled under the document." UCC 7–403(1)(d), (4) [R7–403(a)(4); R7–102(a)(9)].

Would you advise a seller to ship on credit to a shaky buyer in view of the seller's stoppage rights? Would sellers often hear of insolvency during the time required for shipment? On the other hand, an attorney would probably be liable for malpractice if a client presented facts requiring immediate action to stop delivery and the attorney could think of no course of action other than taking a day or so to research the point.

(C) THE RIGHT TO RECOVER DELIVERED GOODS

Problem 1.2.3. Boris Bilk, who only recently entered business and has no credit history, went to Seller's place of business with a forged letter of introduction. Relying upon the letter, which showed Bilk to be Sterling Worth, a merchant with well-established credit, Seller delivered cotton valued at $100,000 to Bilk on credit. Before payment became due, Seller discovered the fraud and consults you to determine the remedies that might be available. In particular, Seller would prefer not to wait for the outcome of a lawsuit and instead recover the goods immediately (assuming Bilk can be found). What is your advice? See UCC 2–703; UCC 1–103; Note on the Defrauded Seller's Right to Reclaim, infra.

NOTE ON THE DEFRAUDED SELLER'S RIGHT TO RECLAIM

In this area, the drafting style of Article 2 is especially incomplete and allusive. We need to be aware of this approach; one who assumes that the UCC lays down the basic rules on the seller's right to reclaim goods will come to odd and unintended consequences. Indeed, one who searches the UCC for Seller's remedies against Bilk will be disappointed. True, one could not expect a statute on the sale of goods to repeat the general rule of torts allowing Seller to recover damages for deceit. In any event, such an *in personam* claim for damages would be scarcely more useful than Seller's action against Bilk for the price (UCC 2–709). Neither action would be of practical use, since, after the delay involved in obtaining judgment, a sheriff trying to execute on the judgment is not likely to find any substantial assets of someone like Bilk (i.e., Bilk is likely to be or become **judgment proof**).

On the other hand, one might expect that a "Code" on "Sales" would say something about Seller's possessory or *in rem* rights to the goods. May Seller **replevy** the goods from Bilk? If Bilk is hiding the goods, may Seller obtain an equity decree ordering Bilk to return the goods? In more conventional terms, how do we know whether Seller has a *property* remedy to recover the goods?

The drafters of the 1906 Uniform Sales Act and the UCC may well have assumed that "everyone knows" that one who is induced by fraud to enter into a contract may rescind the contract. The drafters may have assumed, as well, that "everyone knows" that one who rescinds for fraud has effective remedies to recover the assets obtained by fraud—by seizure through replevin and, in case of need, by the coercive command of an equity decree. In the dim past, advanced law-school courses (and codifying statutes) could build safely on the students' knowledge of these principles. But today's curriculum seems to pass these principles by.

Moreover, sustained exposure to detailed statutory regimes may foster the impression that if an idea is not set forth in the UCC, then it doesn't exist. This assumption is not only contrary to the UCC (see UCC 1–103) but also dangerous. Important parts of the UCC (especially Article 2) are characterized by provisions addressed to specific problems that had proved troublesome at common law. What one misses is a statement of the basic principles for which the narrow rules provide a fringe or border.

Prior to the UCC, the sharpest controversy over reclamation of goods by the seller grew out of attempts to base reclamation not on overt fraud by the buyer but on an implied false representation of an intent to pay. See Keeton, Fraud—Statements of Intention, 15 Tex. L.Rev. 185 (1937) (decisions in Illinois, Missouri, Indiana, Pennsylvania and Vermont refused to base fraud remedies on such an "implied" misrepresentation). As the following Problem suggests, the drafters of the UCC addressed this controversy directly. (One wonders whether the drafters were so bemused by this vexing question that they failed to set their solution to this narrow question in a wider context. Perhaps that approach to drafting statutes is in the "common-law tradition.")

Problem 1.2.4. Buyer induced Seller to deliver goods on credit by fraudulently promising to pay for them in 30 days. (What is a "fraudulent promise"?) Shortly after delivering the goods, Seller discovered that, when Buyer promised to pay, Buyer was hopelessly insolvent. Seller seeks to recover the goods. May Seller do so? See UCC 2–702(2) [R2–702(2)]. What difference, if any, would it make if:

(a) Two months prior to delivery Seller had received Buyer's **financial statement** showing Buyer to be solvent? Would your answer depend on when the sales contract was formed?

(b) Seller had been delivering goods to Buyer for several months; most of Buyer's checks were good, but one or two were dishonored (i.e., "bounced")? See Theo. Hamm Brewing Co. v. First Trust & Savings Bank, 103 Ill.App.2d 190, 242 N.E.2d 911 (1968) (check may constitute representation of solvency if seller relied upon it as such).

(c) Two months prior to delivery Seller had received a report from a credit reporting agency erroneously showing Buyer to be solvent?

Problem 1.2.5. On June 1 Seller and Buyer tentatively agreed on a sale to Buyer of a load of cotton; the price was $4,000. Buyer then said, "I hope you can give me a week to pay." Seller replied, "I'm afraid I'll have to ask for cash." Buyer said, "I'll arrange for my driver to bring my check for the price tomorrow." The next day (June 2) Buyer's driver gave Seller a $4,000 check drawn by Buyer to Seller's order on Firstbank, and removed the cotton. Seller deposited the check in an account with Secondbank. Five days later

(June 7) Secondbank notified Seller that Buyer's check had been returned because of insufficient funds. Seller immediately brings a replevin action for the cotton.

(a) What result? See UCC 2–507 [R2–507]; UCC 2–511; Note on the Cash Seller's Right to Reclaim, infra.

(b) Would the result in part (a) change if Seller waits until June 15 to take any action? See UCC 2–507, Comment 3 [R2–507]; PEB Commentary No. 1.

NOTE ON THE CASH SELLER'S RIGHT TO RECLAIM

UCC 2–507(2) deals with transactions in which sellers have not agreed to extend credit. By custom, these transactions are called "cash sales," and the sellers are called "cash sellers." In these transactions, "tender of payment is a condition to the seller's duty to tender and complete any delivery." UCC 2–511(1). What relief, if any, is available to a cash seller who has delivered the goods but has not received the price?

In stark contrast to UCC 2–702(2), which expressly grants a credit seller the right to reclaim goods under certain circumstances, UCC 2–507(2) refers cryptically to the buyer's "right as against the [cash] seller to retain or dispose of" the goods as being "conditional upon his making the payment due."[3] Nevertheless, courts routinely have concluded that the unpaid cash seller enjoys a right to reclaim goods from the buyer. One court has referred to the cash seller's reclamation right as "judicially-confected." In re Samuels & Co., 526 F.2d 1238 (5th Cir.) (en banc), cert. denied 429 U.S. 834 (1976). Is this a fair characterization? Can you articulate a statutory basis for the cash seller's reclamation right? Does it help to characterize reclamation as a remedy for enforcing a statutory right to possession of the goods? Is the fact that the seller enjoyed such a right under pre-UCC law relevant? Revised Article 2 addresses the issue directly by providing an explicit right to reclaim goods in a cash sale when payment is not made. R2–507(2)

Assuming that the UCC affords a reclamation right to cash sellers, does it also impose a time limit on the exercise of that right? The time limit, if any, for reclamation under UCC 2–507 has been litigated most often under facts like the following: Buyer and Seller agree for payment on delivery. Buyer tenders its check (see UCC 2–511(2)), which Seller deposits and Buyer's bank dishonors ("bounces"). Having not received payment (see UCC 2–511(3)), Seller seeks to reclaim the goods.

All probably would agree that even a seller who exchanges goods for an **NSF check** (drawn on insufficient funds) or who is the victim of active

---

3. Originally drafted in the 1940's and 1950's, the UCC has followed then-prevailing English usage and has utilized the masculine pronoun to signify antecedents of indefinite gender. See UCC 1–106(2) [F1–102(5)(b)]. Recent revisions to articles of the UCC have taken account of changes in English usage and no longer follow this practice.

fraud should not have an unlimited time for reclamation.[4] One approach to filling the gap of silence as to timing in UCC 2–507, suggested by UCC 1–103, is to turn to the common-law rule. At common law an attempt to reclaim after excessive delay would be defeated by doctrines such as waiver, estoppel, or ratification of the buyer's property interest. See, e.g., Frech v. Lewis, 218 Pa. 141, 67 A. 45 (1907). The PEB adopted this approach in PEB Commentary No. 1 and it revised Comment 3 to UCC 2–507 accordingly. Is the revised comment any more or less binding on a court than the original Comment? Comment 3 to UCC 2–507 rejects any analogical extension of the time limits in UCC 2–702 and fills the gap with "delay causing prejudice to the buyer, waiver, estoppel, or ratification of the buyer's right to retain possession." Under R 2–507(2), demand for reclamation must be made "within a reasonable time after the seller discovers or should have discovered that payment was not made."

Problem 1.2.6. Buyer acquired goods under circumstances giving Seller a right to reclaim. Before Seller could exercise its rights, Buyer resold the goods to Purchaser, who took delivery in good faith and without notice of Seller's rights. Buyer extended credit to Purchaser, who has not yet paid Buyer. Assume for now that Purchaser cuts off Seller's property right in the goods. (Purchaser's rights are discussed in Section 3, which follows.) Does Seller's property (reclamation) right against the goods shift to the property received by Buyer upon resale of the goods—Buyer's claim against Purchaser for the price? (Although it is intangible, a right to payment is property and can be transferred.)

Neither UCC 2–507 nor UCC 2–702 refers to a seller's claim against what the buyer receives upon disposition of the goods (the **proceeds** of the goods). Does the absence of a statutory reference to proceeds necessarily mean that Seller has no claim to them? Or, should a court validate such a claim by reference to the common law or by analogy? The cases are divided, but the majority do not permit sellers with reclamation rights to reach proceeds. Compare, e.g., United States v. Westside Bank, 732 F.2d 1258 (5th Cir.1984) (credit seller who complies with all the requirements of UCC 2–702 retains claim against traceable proceeds from the sale of the goods) with, e.g., In re Coast Trading Co., Inc., 744 F.2d 686 (9th Cir.1984) (UCC 2–702 does not in and of itself create a right to reclaim proceeds). The Article 2 Study Group's "tentative conclusion is that a reclaiming seller

---

4.   From the 1951 Official Text of the UCC until 1990, Comment 3 to UCC 2–507 provided that "[t]he provision of this Article for a ten-day limit within which the seller may reclaim goods delivered on credit to an insolvent buyer is also applicable here." The UCC itself, however, imposed no such limitation. Some courts followed Comment 3 and permitted a seller to reclaim only when demand was made within the ten-day period. See, e.g., Szabo v. Vinton Motors, 630 F.2d 1 (1st Cir.1980) ("Comment 3 does not contradict, but merely complements and explains the Code."). Others, observing that the text of the UCC itself contains no time limit, refused to apply the limit contained in the Comment. See, e.g., Burk v. Emmick, 637 F.2d 1172 (8th Cir.1980) ("the only limitation imposed upon the seller's [reclamation] right is a reasonableness requirement").

should not have a right to proceeds." PEB Article 2 Report 200. Do you agree? Revised Article 2 follows this conclusion inasmuch as it is silent concerning the right of a reclaiming seller to proceeds of a disposition.

SECTION 3.   SELLER'S POWER OVER THE GOODS AS AGAINST THIRD PARTIES

The Problems in Section 2, supra, deal with the seller's power over goods when only two parties (Seller and Buyer) are involved. Often, however, a third party claims an interest in the goods. This third party may claim an interest through Seller (e.g., one of Seller's creditors may levy upon the goods while they are in transit) or through Buyer (e.g., Buyer may contract to resell the goods, as in Problem 1.2.6, supra). The rights of secured creditors of Seller are discussed below in Chapter 4, Section 2. This section discusses the rights of those who claim through Buyer.

(A) TRANSFER OF INTERESTS IN GOODS: THE BASIC RULES

INTRODUCTORY NOTE

A paradigmatic sequence of events, which we shall see recur in various settings, is as follows: A is the owner of goods. B acquires the goods under circumstances that give A the right to recover the goods from B. B, voluntarily (e.g., by sale or by grant of a security interest) or involuntarily (e.g., by sheriff's levy), purports to transfer (or suffer to be transferred) an interest in the goods to C. A seeks to recover the goods from C, or to hold C liable for **conversion**.[1]

For such cases, the traditional rule is this: B can convey to C, and C can acquire from B, whatever rights B had in the goods.[2] Two different, but interrelated, ideas are packed into this rule. First, the rule enables B to dispose of any and all rights that B has. Thus, if B acquires goods free and clear of all third-party claims, B will be able to convey the goods to C free and clear. Were the rule otherwise, the value of the goods to B would be substantially reduced in many cases. When the rule is applied to enable C

---

1.   The Restatement (Second) of Torts defines conversion of personal property as "an intentional exercise of dominion or control over a chattel which so seriously interferes with the right of another to control it that the actor may justly be required to pay the other the full value of the chattel." Restatement (Second) of Torts § 222–A(1) (1965). As with A's replevin suit to recover the cotton, C will be liable to A in conversion only if A's right to control the cotton is paramount to C's right.

2.   The principle that the transferee of property acquires all rights that the transferor had applies not only to goods (see UCC 2–403(1) (1st sentence)) but also to negotiable instruments (see UCC 3–203(b)), documents of title (see UCC 7–504(1)), and investment securities (see UCC 8–302(a)). The conveyancing rules governing negotiable instruments and securities are discussed in Section 4, infra; those governing documents of title, in Section 5.

to defeat a third party's claim on the ground that B could have done so, it sometimes is referred to as a "shelter" or "umbrella" rule.

The second idea is that B cannot transfer any greater rights than B has; that is, B may convey whatever rights B has and no more. This aspect of the rule, which sometimes is referred to by the Latin phrase *nemo dat quod non habet* (one cannot give what one does not have), appears to flow from the broader principle that, in a regime of private property, the law should keep property rights secure.[3] Security of property means that a person may not be deprived of property rights without the person's consent. It means, for example, that a thief cannot transfer the real owner's property interest to a third party. A rule of law contrary to *nemo dat*, one that would enable a person to convey rights that the person did not have, would enable the person to deprive another person of the other's rights and would violate the security of property principle.

The security of property principle is far from ironclad; in fact, the law often enables a person to convey greater rights to personal property than the person has. Because those to whom the law affords greater rights than their transferors had often are good faith purchasers for value, the exceptions to *nemo dat* often are termed "good-faith-purchase" rules. As you work through the following materials, try to articulate the reasons underlying the various good-faith-purchase rules and to assess the validity of those reasons. You may also wish to consider whether *nemo dat* no longer is the baseline rule but rather has become the exception.

Before turning to the primary focus of this Section—the rights of a reclaiming seller (A) against a person (C) who claims through the buyer (B)—we examine the application of the basic rules in another setting.

Problem 1.3.1. A's bales of cotton worth \$5,000 were stored in A's warehouse. B broke into the warehouse and stole the cotton. B resold the cotton to C, who paid B \$5,000, not suspecting the cotton was stolen.

(a) C is in possession of the cotton. A brings a replevin action against C. What result? See UCC 2–403; Note (1) on the Basic Conveyancing Rules, infra.

(b) Assume that C, before learning of A's interest resold the cotton to D. Does A have a cause of action against C? On what theory?

(c) Does A have any rights against D?

(d) If A recovers from D, does D have a right of recourse against C? See UCC 2–312; Note (5) on the Basic Conveyancing Rules, infra.

Problem 1.3.2. B, who only recently entered business and has no credit history, went to A's place of business with a forged letter of introduction. Relying upon the letter, which showed B to be Sterling Worth, a merchant with well-established credit, A delivered cotton valued at \$100,000 to B on credit. (These are the facts of Problem 1.2.3, supra.) B resold the cotton to

---

3.   For this reason, sometimes the principle is referred to as "security of property."

C, who paid $100,000 for it and took delivery, not suspecting the fraud. *A* sues *C* to replevy the cotton.

(a) What result? See UCC 2–403; Note (1) on the Basic Conveyancing Rules, infra. What result if *A* sues *C* in conversion?

(b) Would any of the following make any difference?

(i) *C* is in business.

(ii) *C* is in the cotton business.

(iii) *C* is a cotton dealer who never dealt with *B* previously and took no measures to check on *B*'s background. (It is customary for cotton dealers in the area to purchase only from growers or from other dealers whom they know.)

See UCC 1–201(b)(20) [F1–201(20)]; UCC 2–103(1)(b); UCC 2–104(1).

(c) What result if *C* had paid *B* only $60,000? Cf., e.g., Funding Consultants, Inc. v. Aetna Casualty and Surety Co., 187 Conn. 637, 447 A.2d 1163 (1982) (trier of fact may reasonably consider whether an instrument was purchased in good faith if a party pays an amount considerably less than face value).

(d) Would it make any difference if *C* had promised to pay $100,000 but has not yet paid anything? See UCC 1–204 [F1–201(44)]. Under these circumstances, should the law award the goods to a person who has not paid for them? Does this transaction pose the same risks to *C* as does *C*'s payment of cash to *B*? Does this transaction jeopardize *A*'s interests as much as *C*'s payment of cash? Consider the possibility of an equity action by *A* against *B* and *C*, invoking the doctrine that *A* can follow its property interest in the cotton into its proceeds. (Do not confuse this *in rem* action with *A*'s garnishment of *C*'s debt to *B* to satisfy an *in personam* claim or judgment. In garnishment, *A* may need first to obtain a judgment against *B*; in any event, *A*'s garnishment may be subordinate to earlier garnishments by *B*'s other creditors, who may be numerous and hungry.)

(e) Would it make any difference if *C* paid *B* $100,000 but had not yet taken delivery when *A* notified *C* of the fraud? See Note (6) on the Basic Conveyancing Rules, infra.

NOTES ON THE BASIC CONVEYANCING RULES

(1) Void Title and Voidable Title. The first sentence of UCC 2–403(1), which embodies the *nemo dat* principle, takes one only so far. To determine what the purchaser (*C*) acquires, one needs to know what rights the transferor *(B)* has or has power to convey. What rights does a thief have? The traditional rule, which still is dominant in Anglo–American law, is that a thief has no rights or "void title."

The "void title" of a thief is to be distinguished from the "voidable title" referred to in the second sentence of UCC 2–403(1). The seminal case in the voidable title area is the English case of Parker v. Patrick, 101 Eng. Rep. 99 (1793), which was followed in Mowrey v. Walsh, 8 Cow. 238

(N.Y.Sup.Ct.1828). The latter posed the question: "where the goods are obtained by fraud from the true owner [A], and fairly purchased of, and the price paid to the fraudulent vendee [B], without notice, by a stranger [C], which is to sustain the loss, the owner or the stranger?" The court's answer: "the innocent purchaser for valuable consideration must be protected." The only reason mentioned by the New York court for distinguishing fraud from theft was the one given by the English court in its one sentence, per curiam opinion-the existence of a statute as to theft. By the time of White v. Garden, 10 Common Bench, 919, 138 Eng. Rep. 364 (Q.B. 1851), however, doctrine had developed to the point that the court could write that where fraud was involved, "the transaction is not absolutely void, except at the option of the seller; that he may elect to treat it as a contract, and he must do the contrary before the buyer has acted as if it were such, and re-sold the goods to a third party."

Professor Gilmore's summary of the historical development deserves an extended quotation:

> The initial common law position was that equities of ownership are to be protected at all costs: an owner may never be deprived of his property rights without his consent. That worked well enough against a background of local distribution where seller and buyer met face to face and exchanged goods for cash. But as the marketplace became first regional and then national, a recurrent situation came to be the misappropriation of goods by a faithless agent in fraud of his principal. Classical theory required that the principal be protected and that the risks of agency distribution be cast on the purchaser. The market demanded otherwise.

> The first significant breach in common law property theory was the protection of purchasers from such commercial agents. The reform was carried out through so-called Factor's Acts, which were widely enacted in the early part of the 19th century. Under these Acts any person who entrusted goods to a factor—or agent—for sale took the risk of the factor's selling tem beyond his authority; anyone buying from a factor in good faith, relying on his possession of the goods, and without nice of the limitations on his authority, took good title against the true owner. In time the Acts were expanded to protect people, i.e., banks, who took goods from a factor as security for loans made to the factor to be used in operating the factor's own business. The Factor's Acts, as much in derogation of the common law as it is possible for a statute to be, were restrictively construed and consequently turned out to be considerably less than the full grant of mercantile liberty which they had first appeared to be. Other developments in the law gradually took the pressure off the Factor's Acts, which came to be confined to the narrow area of sales through commission merchants, mostly in agricultural produce markets.

> Even while they were cutting the heart out of the Factor's Acts, the courts were finding new ways to shift distribution risks. Their happiest discovery was the concept of "voidable title"—a vague idea, never

defined and perhaps incapable of definition, whose greatest virtue, as a principle of growth, may well have been its shapeless imprecision of outline. The polar extremes of theory were these: if *B* buys goods from *A*, he gets *A*'s title and can transfer it to any subsequent purchaser; if *B* steals goods from *A*, he gets no title and can transfer none to any subsequent purchaser, no matter how clear the purchaser's good faith. "Voidable title" in *B* came in as an intermediate term between the two extremes: if *B* gets possession of *A*'s goods by fraud, even though he has no right to retain them against *A*, he does have the power to transfer title to a good faith purchaser.

The ingenious distinction between "no title" in *B* (therefore true owner prevails over good faith purchaser) and "voidable title" in *B* (therefore true owner loses to good faith purchaser) made it possible to throw the risk on the true owner in the typical commercial situation while protecting him in the noncommercial one. Since the law purported to be a deduction from basic premises, logic prevailed in some details to the detriment of mercantile need, but on the whole voidable title proved a useful touchstone.

The contrasting treatment given to sales on credit and sales for cash shows the inarticulate development of the commercial principle. When goods are delivered on credit, the seller becomes merely a creditor for the price: on default he has no right against the goods. But when the delivery is induced by buyer's fraud-buyer being unable to pay or having no intention of paying-the seller, if he acts promptly after discovering the facts, may replevy from the buyer or reclaim from buyer's trustee in bankruptcy. The seller may not, however, move against purchasers from the buyer, and the term "purchaser" includes lenders who have made advances on the security of the goods. By his fraudulent acquisition the buyer has obtained voidable title and purchasers from him are protected.

Gilmore, The Commercial Doctrine of Good Faith Purchase, 63 Yale L.J. 1057, 1057–60 (1954).

Why do you suppose the UCC neither explains that a thief has void title nor sets forth a definition of voidable title? Perhaps the drafters thought that their project—codifying the law of sales—did not require codification of all the basic common-law rules of personal property conveyancing. Even if so, it remains puzzling that Article 2 contains some of the "building block" rules (e.g., the "shelter" principle in the first sentence of UCC 2–403(1)) but not others. Note that Revised Article 2 generally did not expand on the basic conveyancing rules. Should it have done so?

(2) Conflicting Rules on Good Faith Purchase: Unification. Consider the observations of the Ontario Law Reform Commission:

It is necessary in every legal system to reconcile the conflict that arises when a seller purports to transfer title of goods that he does not own, or that are subject to an undisclosed security interest, to a person who buys them in good faith and without notice of the defect in title. The alternative means of resolving this conflict are usually stated in terms of a policy favouring security of ownership, as opposed to a policy that favours the safety of commercial transactions. Few, if indeed any, legal systems have committed themselves fully to the adoption of one or the other solution. Between these extremes there lies a, range of compromise solutions that depend on the nature of the goods, the persons involved, and the type of transaction.

2 Ontario Law Reform Commission, Report on Sale of Goods 283 (1979).

As we have seen, the common law begins with the principle that a buyer acquires no better title to goods than the seller had. To this principle the common law admits a number of exceptions, the most significant of which has been the doctrine of voidable title for cases of fraud.

The civil law (including the law of France and Germany) begins with a very different principle under which the good faith purchaser of goods generally is protected against the original owner, a principle expressed in the phrase *possession vaut titre* (possession is the equivalent of title). Civil law systems therefore have no need for a doctrine of voidable title for cases of fraud. But many such systems make an exception for cases of theft, allowing the original owner of stolen goods to reclaim them from a good faith purchaser within a statutory period. Some of these systems, however, require the good faith purchaser who has acquired stolen goods at a fair or a market or from a merchant who deals in similar goods to return the goods to the original owner only on reimbursement of the purchase price. This rule has particular significance when the goods have special value to the true owner or when the purchaser has "snapped up" the goods at a cheap price but the true owner has difficulty proving that the purchaser did not act in good faith.

What accounts for the variety of approaches to the universal problem raised by good faith purchasers of stolen property? One author links the variety to "the difficulty of discerning the best solution to a hard question. Societies may share the goal of minimizing the costs associated with the theft of property but may disagree over the way to achieve this goal." Levmore, Variety and Uniformity in the Treatment of the Good–Faith Purchaser, 16 J. Legal Stud. 43, 45 (1987). In this regard, consider Problem 1.3.1, supra. As between the two innocent parties, A and C, the more efficient rule would allocate the loss to the party who could have avoided the loss at lower cost. Who is that party? Is it less costly for A to protect the goods from theft (e.g., by hiring more guards or building a stronger fence) than for C to protect itself from acquiring stolen goods (e.g., by investigating the circumstances under which B acquired the goods)?

Although the lower-cost loss avoidance analysis projects an aura of simplicity, its application can be enormously difficult. A complete analysis would take into account not only the costs of preventing the loss but also a variety of other costs, including the costs to A (the owner) and C (the good faith purchaser) of insuring against the loss and the litigation costs attendant to determining the foregoing costs. And even when efficiency analysis can be applied with some degree of assurance, other normative concerns may override it. Judge Posner, for example, assumes that A would be the lower-cost loss avoider, but he explains that A is the winner under current law (in the U.S.) because allowing C to win would encourage theft and "[w]e do not want an efficient market in stolen goods." R. Posner, Economic Analysis of Law 91 (5th ed. 1998). See also Weinberg, Sales Law, Economics, and the Negotiability of Goods, 9 J. Legal Stud. 569, 592 (1980) (concluding that the "efficiency criterion has proved useful in explaining the pattern of protection for legally innocent purchasers of goods that exists under American law," but recognizing that other issues, such as "costs of a rule change" and "public and private costs of alternative regimes," should be considered before deciding to change the legal rules).

International traffic in ill-gotten goods, like other types of international trade, seems to be accelerating; even the newspapers report on international traffic in stolen paintings and other art objects. A 1986 article contained an estimate that "around $1 billion a year in cultural property is stolen from around the world." N.Y. Times, October 19, 1986, at C25. More recently, heightened concerns have been expressed about stolen goods that are important cultural property. And recent years also have seen increased attention given to artwork that may have been looted in Europe immediately prior to and during World War II.

The variations in national rules, and the difficulty of determining which law governs, have led to efforts at international unification of the law governing the rights of owners of stolen goods. See International Institute for the Unification of Private Law (UNIDROIT), Draft Uniform Law on the Protection of the Bona Fide Purchaser of Corporeal Movables with Explanatory Report (1968). The Report contains (at 5–11) a helpful review of the varying national rules in the field. Article 10(2) of the Draft adopted the principle of *possession vaut titre* in the case of stolen goods that were bought in good faith "under normal conditions from a dealer who usually sells goods of the same kind." A committee of governmental experts studied this draft and prepared a 1974 revision, which receded from this extreme position because a majority feared that it might encourage trafficking in stolen goods, particularly works of art. The revised text therefore provides that the "transferee of stolen moveables cannot invoke his good faith." Uniform Law on the Acquisition in Good Faith of Corporeal Moveables art. 11, in Uniform Law Review (UNIDROIT), No. I, at 79 (1975). The draft Uniform International Law was prepared on the assumption that it would be submitted to a diplomatic conference and the final text submitted to governments for ratification, but the diplomatic conference never was held.

UNIDROIT has prepared another convention relating to stolen goods. See UNIDROIT Convention on Stolen or Illegally Exported Cultural Objects (1995). Article 2 of the convention defines "cultural objects" as "those which, on religious or secular grounds, are of importance for archaeology, prehistory, history, literature, art or science" and which fall within one of 12 categories, including products of archaeological excavations, antiquities more than one hundred years old, property of artistic interest, and rare specimens of fauna, flora, minerals, and anatomy. Although more limited in scope, the new effort has been somewhat better received than the earlier draft uniform law. At the time of publication,, it had been ratified by 26 nations. See http://www.unidroit.org/english/implement/i–95.pdf (visited Oct. 21, 2005).

Even within a given legal system, efforts have been made to adjust the tension between *nemo dat* and *possession vaut titre*. See, e.g., (English) Law Reform Committee, Twelfth Report (Transfer of Title to Chattels) Cmnd. 2958 (1966); Ontario Law Reform Commission, Report on Sale of Goods (1979). The major recommendations of each of these reports have yet to be enacted. The PEB Article 2 Report did not address these issues.

(3) Statute of Limitations. Understandably, it generally is very difficult to locate stolen goods. Even when they are found, a considerable time may have elapsed since the theft occurred. For this reason, some courts have sought to resolve the timeliness of property claims of aggrieved owners against innocent possessors by using conventional statute–of–limitations principles. The owners' claims are cut off after the passage of a statutory period. When is the original owner of stolen goods barred by the statute of limitations from reclaiming them? The answer depends in large part on when the statute of limitations starts to run, i.e., when the owner's cause of action accrues. The few reported cases reflect a variety of views on this issue. See, e.g., O'Keeffe v. Snyder, 83 N.J. 478, 416 A.2d 862 (1980) (cause of action accrues when the owner first knew, or reasonably should have known through the exercise of due diligence, of the cause of action, including the identity of the possessor of the paintings); Kunstsammlungen Zu Weimar v. Elicofon, 678 F.2d 1150 (2d Cir.1982) (applying New York law) (where owner's demand for return of stolen goods and purchaser's refusal to return them are requisite elements of the cause of action the statute of limitations begins to run only after such demand and refusal); Solomon R. Guggenheim Foundation v. Lubell, 77 N.Y.2d 311, 567 N.Y.S.2d 623, 569 N.E.2d 426 (1991) (owner's failure to exercise due diligence does not cause the statute of limitations to begin running before owner demands and is refused return of stolen goods; however, owner's diligence could be considered in connection good faith purchaser's defense of laches).

(4) Good Faith Purchase and Notice or Knowledge of Conflicting Claims. During the past decades the UCC has contained two definitions of "good faith." In the 1962 Official Text, the term meant "honesty in fact," although UCC 2–103(1)(b) provided a narrower definition in the case of a merchant: honesty in fact and the observance of reasonable commercial standards of fair dealing. As UCC Articles were revised, they generally incorporated the broader, "merchant" standard as the generally applicable standard. See UCC 3–103(a)(4); UCC 4–104(c); UCC 4A–105(a)(6); UCC 9–102(a)(43). But see UCC 5–102(a)(7) (retaining the "honesty in fact" standard). The recent revisions of Articles 1, 2, and 2A also incorporated the broader standard. See UCC 1–201(b)(20); R2–103(1)(j); R2A–103(1)(m).

Both formulations of good faith are silent concerning the effect of *C*'s (a putative good faith purchaser from *B*) knowledge or notice of *A*'s claim to the goods (e.g., that *B* had only voidable title). Despite this silence, no one would doubt that *C* would not have acted in good faith if it purchased goods with actual knowledge of *B's* fraud. Aside from the relatively easy case of actual knowledge, however, there is a wide range of possible application of the "good faith" requirement, depending on the facts. Of what relevance is the fact that purchasers under other UCC articles must act not only in good faith but also without notice of claims in order to benefit from good-faith purchase rules? See UCC 3–302(a)(2)(ii) and (v); UCC 7–501(4); F9–206(1); UCC 9–403(b)(3). Of what relevance is the pre-UCC law? "Both case law and commentators agree that subjective knowledge of the original seller's claim was not necessary to disqualify a purchaser from the protection of the voidable-title or estoppel concepts. Reason to know or circumstances that would put a reasonable man on inquiry were, sufficient." McDonnell, The Floating Lienor as Good Faith Purchaser, 50 S.Cal.L.Rev. 429, 442 (1977). UCC 8–303(a)(2) is *sui generis*. Good faith is not an explicit requirement for achieving the status of a "protected purchaser," although the somewhat elaborate description of "notice of adverse claim" (UCC 8–105) can be viewed as a proxy for good faith.

(5) Warranty of Title. Assume that *C* must return the goods to *A* either because *C*'s seller, the wrongdoing *B*, stole the goods from *A* or because *B* defrauded *A* and *C* fails to qualify as a good faith purchaser for value. Does *C* have a claim against *B*? UCC 2–312(1) provides an affirmative answer in most cases: "there is in a contract for sale a warranty by the seller that . . . the title conveyed shall be good, and its transfer rightful." An exception in UCC 2–312(2) provides that the warranty of title can be "excluded or modified only by specific language or by circumstances which give the buyer reason to know that the person selling does not claim title in himself or that he is purporting to sell only such right or title as he or a third person may have." One easily can imagine a case in which *C*'s actual knowledge of *B's* theft or fraud would constitute "circumstances" that would exclude *B's* warranty of title; however, in many other cases in which *B* has void or voidable title, *C* would have a valid warranty claim. Whether *B* can be found and the warranty claim turned into cash is, of course, another (not insignificant) matter.

(6) Delivery and Bona Fide Purchase. The role of delivery in good faith purchase presents an awkward, unsolved problem under Article 2 of the UCC. As we shall see in Section 6(B), similar problems arise under Article 9. In contrast, Articles 3, 7, and 8 face the issue. Articles 3 and 7 confer protection on the "holder" of instruments and documents, which UCC 1–201((b)(21) [F1–201(20)] defines as a person "in possession." See UCC 3–305 (defenses); UCC 3–306 (claims); UCC 7–502.[4] Article 8 makes clear

---

4.   A transfer of a negotiable instrument from a holder to a non-holder can vest the non-holder transferee with the right to enforce the instrument. See UCC 3–203(b).

when possession of an investment security (by the transferee itself or by a third party acting on its behalf) is a necessary condition to becoming a "protected purchaser" and when it is not. See UCC 8–303(a).

In analyzing the solicitude the law should pay to a buyer (C) who pays before delivery, consider whether it is usual and necessary for a buyer to pay before receiving the goods. In most cases of payment before delivery, is it difficult for the buyer (C) to take precautions against misconduct by the seller (B)? Would it be easier for the original owner (A) to take precautions?

Should it make any difference whether C has a right to possession as against its seller, B? If C has no right to recover the goods from B, the malefactor, it would be surprising if C could recover them from A, who also is a victim of B's wrongdoing. Article 2 provides pre-delivery possessory rights to a buyer only under very limited circumstances. See UCC 2–502(1)(b) (reclamation right with respect to consumer goods if at least part of the price is paid and the seller repudiates or fails to deliver; reclamation right with respect to all goods "if the seller becomes insolvent within ten days after receipt of the first installment on their price"); UCC 2–716(1) (right to specific performance of the sale contract "where the goods are unique or in other proper circumstances"); R2–716(3) (right to replevin of goods identified to the contract in two limited circumstances). This approach would answer Problem 1.3.2(e) in favor of A in all but a few cases.

The problem extends beyond "buyers" to a wider category—called "purchasers"—that, as we shall see, includes financers who extend credit on the security of goods. When (in our model sequence) B gives C a security interest in goods to secure a loan, B usually needs to keep the goods for B's personal or business use. Accordingly, B usually will not deliver the goods to C. In this setting, perhaps the public filing of a "financing statement," indicating that C may have a security interest in the goods, is a substitute for delivery. But this public filing has been conceived with concern for the creditors of B and other "purchasers" from B—not prior owners of the goods. Consider as well that a secured party with a nonpossessory security interest in goods *does* have a possessory right to the goods—albeit one that is contingent on the debtor's default. UCC 9–609(a).

Should Article 2 be revised to answer clearly the question whether delivery, or at least possessory rights to goods, is necessary for protection as a good-faith purchaser?

(B) RIGHTS OF RECLAIMING SELLER AS AGAINST THIRD PERSONS

Problem 1.3.3. Assume that instead of buying the cotton in Problem 1.3.2, supra, C acquired a judgment against B and caused the sheriff to levy on the cotton pursuant to a writ of execution. Before the sheriff sells the goods, A discovers the fraud.

(a) Who has the better claim to the goods? See UCC 2–403; Oswego Starch Factory v. Lendrum, infra; UCC 1–201(b)(29), (30) [F1–201(32), 33)]; UCC 1–204 [F1–201(44)]; Notes on Reliance and Nonreliance Parties, infra.

(b) What result if the sheriff sells the cotton to D before A discovers the fraud? See Mazer v. Williams Bros., 461 Pa. 587, 337 A.2d 559 (1975) (buyer at sheriff's sale not "bona fide purchaser" under F1–201(32), (33), F8–302).

Problem 1.3.4. What result in Problem 1.3.2 if, instead of buying the cotton, C took it as security for a loan that C had extended to B six months earlier? See UCC 1–201(b)(29), (30) [F1–201(32), 33)]; UCC 1–204 [F1–201(44)]; Notes on Reliance and Nonreliance Parties, infra.

Problem 1.3.5. On June 1 Seller and Buyer tentatively agreed on a sale to Buyer of a load of cotton; the price was $4,000. Buyer then said, "I hope you can give me a week to pay." Seller replied, "I'm afraid I'll have to ask for cash." Buyer said, "I'll arrange for my driver to bring my check for the price tomorrow." The next day (June 2) Buyer's driver gave Seller a $4,000 check drawn by Buyer to Seller's order on Firstbank, and removed the cotton. Seller deposited the check in an account with Secondbank. Five days later (June 7) Secondbank notified Seller that Buyer's check had been returned because of insufficient funds. Seller immediately brings a replevin action for the cotton. (These are the facts of Problem 1.2.5, supra.)

(a) Would the result in Problem 1.2.5(a) change if, in the meantime, Buyer had sold and delivered the goods to C, who did not suspect Buyer's wrongdoing? See UCC 2–507 [R2–507]; UCC 2–511; UCC 2–403.

(b) Would the result in Problem 1.2.5(a) change if, in the meantime, Buyer had granted a security interest in the cotton to secure an antecedent debt to C, who did not suspect Buyer's wrongdoing? See UCC 2–507 [R2–507]; UCC 2–511; UCC 2–403.

Problem 1.3.6. Suppose, in Problem 1.3.5, when Buyer asked for a week to pay for the cotton, Seller had replied, "I'm afraid I'll have to have your check within three days after delivery, with the understanding that you won't dispose of the cotton until the check clears." Buyer agreed. Buyer took delivery on June 2 and sent Seller the check on June 5. On June 10, Seller received word that the check had "bounced." On June 12, Seller brings a replevin action to recover the cotton.

(a) What result? What, if any, additional facts are needed? See Problem 1.2.4, supra; Note on the Cash Seller's Right to Reclaim, p. 23, supra; UCC 2–702 [[R2–702]]; UCC 1–201(b)(23 [F1–201(23)); UCC 2–401(1).

(b) Would the result in part (a) change if Seller waits until June 15 to take any action? See UCC 2–702 [R2–702].

(c) Would the result in part (a) change if, in the meantime, Buyer had sold and delivered the goods to C, who did not suspect Buyer's wrongdoing? Does Buyer have the "right" to sell the goods? The "power"?

(d) Would the result in part (a) change if, in the meantime, Buyer had granted a security interest in the cotton to secure an antecedent debt to C, who did not suspect Buyer's wrongdoing?

(e) Compare the results in Problem 1.3.5 with those in this Problem. What, if anything, remains of the common-law distinction between the cash seller and the credit seller? Should any distinction be preserved?

Oswego Starch Factory v. Lendrum

Supreme Court of Iowa, 1881.
57 Iowa 573, 10 N.W. 900.

Action of replevin by Oswego Starch against sheriff Lendrum. Plaintiff's petition alleged that plaintiff had sold and shipped goods to Thompson & Reeves, and that this firm prior to the purchase was knowingly insolvent and intended to defraud plaintiff of the purchase price. Defendant Lendrum levied on the goods for creditors of Thompson & Reeves and thereafter plaintiff elected to rescind the sale because of fraud.

Lendrum demurred on the ground, inter alia, that he and the attaching creditors had no knowledge of the alleged fraud and that therefore the contract could not be rescinded after the levy. From a decision for Lendrum, plaintiff appealed.

■ BECK, J.

. . . [T]he point of contest involves the rights of an attaching creditor without notice.

The title of the property was not divested by the attachment, but remained in the vendees. The seizure conferred upon the creditors no right to the property as against plaintiff other or different from those held by the vendee. The sole effect of the seizure was to place the property in the custody of the law, to be held until the creditors' execution. They parted with no consideration in making the attachment, and their condition as to their claims were in no respect changed. Their acts were induced by no representation or procurement originating with plaintiff which would in law or equity give them rights to the property as against plaintiff. Plaintiff's right to rescind the sale inhered in the contract and attached to the property. It could not be defeated except by a purchaser for value without notice of the fraud. . ..

Our position is simply this, that as an attaching creditor parts with no consideration, and does not change his position as to his claim, to his prejudice, he stands in the shoes of the vendee. . . . The innocent purchaser for value occupies a different position, and his rights are, therefore, different. [Reversed.]

NOTES ON RELIANCE AND NONRELIANCE PARTIES

(1) The Position of a Creditor Who Levies. The *Oswego Starch* decision represents the preponderant view of the pre-UCC case law. See *3 Williston, Sales § 620 (1948)*. Is it persuasive? What is the basis of the distinction the court draws between a judicial lien creditor, against whom the right to rescind may be exercised, and a "purchaser for value," who would defeat this right? Is the court correct that "an attaching creditor parts with no consideration"? If so, then how can the creditors in *Oswego Starch* obtain judgment against Thompson & Reeves, the debtor?

Does UCC 2–403(1) change the pre-UCC result? *B's* rights to the goods are subject to *A's* right to rescind the transaction and recover the goods. See Problem 1.2.3, supra. But does *B* have *power* to convey greater rights? Even if *B* has "voidable title" (see Note (1) on the Basic Conveyancing Rules, supra), the answer is "no," unless the lien creditor is a "good faith purchaser for value."

A lien creditor is likely to meet the good faith and value requirements. See UCC 1–201(b)(19) [F1–201(20)]; UCC 1–204 [F1–201(44)]. Is the lien creditor a "purchaser"? The UCC defines "purchase" (UCC 1–201(b)(29) [F1–201(32)]) to include "taking by sale, discount, negotiation, mortgage, pledge, lien, security interest, issue or re-issue, gift or any other voluntary transaction creating an interest in property." One will note that the list of transactions includes "taking by . . . lien," and a judgment creditor who levies execution on property often is called a *"lien* creditor." See UCC 9–102(a)(52). But the word "lien" is a chameleon; prior to the UCC voluntary transactions creating mortgages and similar security interests were often said to create a "lien." In the setting of the types of transactions listed in the definition of "purchase" and the concluding characterization that the list applies to "any other *voluntary* transaction," it seems fairly clear that the drafters did not mean to say that the seizure of a debtor's property by a sheriff acting for a creditor makes the creditor a "purchaser." This conclusion becomes inescapable in the light of UCC sections that distinguish between, on the one hand, lien creditors and, on the other, transferees or purchasers. See, e.g., UCC 9–317(a), (b). As to the judgment debtor, the judicial lien obtained by a judgment creditor appears to be *in*voluntary creation of an interest in property.

Does any policy justify distinguishing between a judicial lien creditor and a buyer? Consider some of the ways in which the two are different. Unlike a buyer, who contracts to purchase all of the rights to the goods, a lien creditor acquires only a limited interest in (i.e., a **lien** on) the goods. And unlike a buyer, whose rights arise by virtue of its contract, a judicial lien creditor acquires its rights through the judicial process (a overview of which appears in Section 1, supra). Finally, whereas a buyer typically acquires its rights in exchange for new consideration (current payment or a promise to pay), a lien creditor's extension of credit is divorced from the property on which it subsequently obtains a lien. Is any of these distinctions relevant?

(2) The Position of an Article 9 Secured Party. Like the lien creditor, the Article 9 secured party can be expected ordinarily to meet the good faith and value requirements.[5] Is the secured party a "purchaser"?

---

5.   The most serious challenge to a secured party's good faith is likely to arise from its knowledge or notice of competing claims. See Note (4) on the Basic Conveyancing Rules, supra.

Interestingly, until it was revised in conjunction with the recent revision of Article 9, the definition of "purchase" did not specifically include taking by "security interest." However, there was general agreement that the creation of an Article 9 security interest was an "other voluntary transaction creating an interest in property," if not a "lien."

Together with Note (1), supra, the foregoing paragraph suggests that one might read the UCC to provide that a judicial lien creditor is not a "purchaser," and thus takes subject to A's right to rescind the transaction and recover the goods, whereas an Article 9 secured party (like a buyer) is a "purchaser," and thus may cut off A's rights. Can one justify this distinction?

Although most of the remainder of this book is devoted to the rights of a secured party, for present purposes one can draw several comparisons with buyers and judicial lien creditors. An Article 9 secured party is like a buyer, in that its rights in the goods (a security interest, defined in UCC 1–201(b)(35) [F1–201(37)]) arise by contract. See UCC 9–109(a)(1). It is like a judicial lien creditor in that it acquires only a limited interest in the goods. This limited interest entitles the secured party, upon its debtor's (B's) default, to repossess the goods, sell them, and apply the proceeds to its claim against the debtor.

Sometimes, an Article 9 secured party takes a security interest in specific goods owned by the debtor at the time the loan is made or acquired by the debtor in conjunction with the extension of credit.[6] In this respect a secured party is like a buyer, exchanging new consideration for an interest in goods. Other times, as in Problem 1.3.4, supra, an Article 9 secured party takes a security interest to secure an antecedent debt, i.e., a debt owed before the security interest is taken. This secured party seems to be analogous to a judicial lien creditor—it has extended credit on an unsecured basis, and its acquisition of rights in particular property is not a *quid pro quo* for the loan (although it may have taken the security interest in exchange for its forbearance in exercising its remedies).

Sometimes a secured party takes a security interest in both property existing at the time credit is extended as well as **after-acquired property,** i.e., property the debtor may acquire after the loan is made. See UCC 9–204. A security interest covering both existing and after-acquired property (often referred to as a **"floating lien")** is particularly common when the collateral is inventory (goods held for sale) or accounts receivable (rights to payment, often for goods sold or services rendered). The rights of a reclaiming seller

---

6.   Two variations of this paradigm are common. In one, the seller of goods retains a security interest to secure the purchase price. In the other, a lender takes a security interest in goods acquired with the borrowed funds. A security interest arising under either of these circumstances is called a "purchase-money security interest" ("PMSI") and receives special treatment under both the UCC and the Bankruptcy Code. See, e.g., UCC 9–103 (explanation of "purchase-money security interest"); UCC 9–324 (priority rules for PMSI's); BC 547(c)(3) (protecting certain PMSI's that otherwise would be avoidable as preferences). PMSI's are discussed in Chapter 4, Section 1(B), infra.

as against a buyer's secured creditor who claims a "floating lien" are considered in Chapter 4, Section 4, infra.

(3) The Role of Reliance in Resolving Competing Claims. Personal property law often distinguishes among third-party claimants on the basis of whether they gave value in reliance upon the transferor's (in our case, *B*'s) apparent ownership of particular property. This distinction is reflected in Oswego *Starch,* supra, as well as in Mowrey v. Walsh, 8 Cow. 238, 245 (N.Y.Sup.Ct.1828) ("The judgment creditor had not advanced money upon these goods, and his loss placed him in no worse situation than he was in before the fraud.") It also underlies the delivery requirement in the third sentence of UCC 2–403(1).

We shall have occasion throughout the remainder of the book to consider how the UCC resolves competing claims. In that connection, you may wish to think about the following questions:

(i) Is a third party's reliance at all relevant to whether that party's claim to goods should prevail?

(ii) If reliance is relevant, should the strength of a person's claim to goods turn on whether the person actually relied, or should it turn on (i) whether the person belongs to a class that generally relies and on (ii) whether, had the person investigated, it would have uncovered facts that would have formed the basis for reasonable reliance upon the debtor's ownership (e.g., the goods in question were located in the debtor's warehouse in boxes addressed to the debtor)?

(iii) As an empirical matter, do buyers generally give value in reliance upon their seller's ownership of particular property? Do judicial lien creditors? Do Article 9 secured parties?

(C) THE BASIC CONVEYANCING RULES IN OTHER SETTINGS

Problem 1.3.7. On January 3, Seller (*A*) and Buyer *(B)* entered into a contract for the sale of a garden tractor, which *B* agreed to pay for and take away by January 30. The agreement specified that "title" passed to *B* on January 3. (These are the facts of Problem 1.2.1, supra.) On January 15, *B* contracted to sell the tractor to *C*. *B* told *C* that the tractor was in storage with A and was ready for immediate delivery. *C* had no reason to doubt *B's* honesty and paid $5,000 to *B*.

That afternoon *C* went to *A*'s place of business to take delivery of the tractor. *A* said that the tractor would be released to *C* only on payment of the $5,000 that *B* had agreed to pay. May *C* replevy the tractor from *A*? May *C* recover from *A* for conversion of the tractor?

(a) Which sentence of UCC 2–403(1) applies to these facts? Did the transaction of January 3 give *B* a property interest in the tractor? See UCC

2–401(1).[7] If so, was *B's* interest most analogous to (1) the "void" title of a thief, (2) a "voidable title" of one who acquires goods through fraud, or (3) the "good title" of an owner?

Consider in this regard the relevance, if any, of the fact that *A* retained possession of the goods. This fact necessarily implies that neither *B* nor *C* took delivery of the goods.

With respect to *B's* failure to take delivery:

(i) does the reference in the third sentence of UCC 2–403(1) to goods that "have been delivered under a transaction of purchase" suggest that delivery generally is a condition to obtaining voidable title? Paragraphs (a)-(d) of UCC 2–403(1) describe situations in which transfers from *A* to *B,* according to some pre-UCC cases, had given *B* only a "void" title. Is the sentence in which these paragraphs appear designed only to settle the "void-voidable" question for "a number of specific situations that have been troublesome under prior law," or does it have broader application? See Comment 1 to UCC 2–403.

(ii) is there any reason to construe the concept of "voidable title" in UCC 2–403(1) so broadly as to eliminate the requirement of possession, which the common law imposed? See Dolan, The Uniform Commercial Code and the Concept of Possession in the Marketing and Financing of Goods, 56 Tex.L.Rev. 1147, 1172–73 (1978) ("The doctrine of voidable title manifests the law's concern that possession not mislead").

With respect to *C's* failure to take delivery, is *C* disqualified from being a "good faith purchaser for value" by the fact that *C* had not taken delivery when it learned of *A's* claim to the tractor? Does the definition of "purchase" in UCC 1–201(b)(29) [F1–201(32)] require delivery? Is it implicit in UCC 2–403? If so, then what are the implications for a secured party who seeks to qualify as a good faith purchaser for value of collateral that its debtor acquired by fraud? See Problem 1.3.2(e), supra; Note (6) on the Basic Conveyancing Rules, supra; Problem 1.3.4, supra; Note (2) on Reliance and Nonreliance Parties, supra.

(b) Is it conceivable that the drafters of UCC 2–403 failed to face the question whether delivery is necessary for protection as a good faith purchaser of goods? Do the Comments give any indication of attention to this question? Is it appropriate to resolve the problem by applying the basic conveyancing principle, *nemo dat*? If so, who prevails?

(c) A buyer in ordinary course of business ("BIOCOB") is one type of good faith purchaser. In construing UCC 2–403(1), is it relevant that, in conjunction with the revision of Article 9, the definition of "buyer in ordinary course of business" was revised to make clear that a person does not qualify as a BIOCOB unless the person "takes possession of the goods

---

7. *B* also received a "special property and an insurable interest" upon identification of the tractor to the contract. UCC 2–501(1). But only in limited circumstances do those interests give a buyer a possessory right to goods or protection against claims to the goods by the seller's creditors. See UCC 2–402(1); UCC 2–502; UCC 2–716.

or has a right to recover the goods from the seller under Article 2"? UCC 1–201((b)(9) [F1–201(9)].

(d) If the law were to protect *C* in this Problem, how would this rule affect the way transactions between *A* and *B* would be conducted? What could *A* have done to avoid the loss of both the tractor and its value? Would the precautions necessary to protect *A* be consistent with the efficient conduct of business?[8]

Problem 1.3.8. *A* owned cotton worth $100,000. *A* placed it in storage with *B*, who not only stores cotton but also regularly buys and sells it. *B* wrongfully sold and delivered the cotton to *C*, who did not suspect *B's* wrongdoing, for $100,000. *A* sues *C* to replevy the cotton.

(a) What result? See UCC 2–403; UCC 1–201(b)(9) [F1–201(9)]; Notes on Entrustment, infra.

(b) What result in part (a) if *C* had promised to pay $100,000 but has not yet paid it when *A* claims the cotton?

(c) What result in part (a) if *C*, instead of buying the cotton from *B*, had taken it as security for a loan that *C* had extended to *B* six months earlier. Compare Problem 1.3.4, supra.

(d) What result if *B* had wrongfully delivered the cotton to *C* who is in the cotton business, as security for a loan that *C* had extended to *B* six months earlier, and *C* had sold the cotton to *D*, who suspected nothing, for $100,000? Cf. Canterra Petroleum, Inc. v. Western Drilling & Mining Supply, 418 N.W.2d 267 (N.D.1987) (buyer in ordinary course of business can cut off rights of true owner who entrusts goods to merchant-dealer when employees of merchant-dealer transfer goods to "dummy corporation," which then sells to the buyer). See also PEB Article 2 Report 130 ("[I]t should be made clear that if the goods are entrusted to Merchant #1, who sells to non-BIOCB [non-buyer in ordinary course of business] Merchant #2, who

---

8.   Delivery of the goods may affect the rights of good faith purchasers in another context, that of the seller's right to stop delivery under UCC 2–705. (This right is discussed in Section 2(B), supra.). Unlike UCC 2–702, and like UCC 2–507, UCC 2–705 does not address the circumstances, if any, in which a good faith purchaser from the buyer takes free of the seller's right to stop delivery. The few reported cases have refused to afford good faith purchase rights to persons who have not taken delivery. In In re Murdock Machine & Engineering Co., 620 F.2d 767 (10th Cir.1980), the court observed that the "old equitable right of stoppage *in transitu* has been repeatedly held to defeat rights of good faith purchasers for value," and that "if the drafters of the Code had intended to give third party purchasers greater rights than under previous law, we believe that the official comments to the Code provisions on stoppage in transit would reflect that intention. Instead, the official comments do not indicate a change from prior law. *See* U.C.C. § 1–103." (The case also suggests that delivery of the goods to the "subpurchaser" (i.e., the purchaser from the buyer) does not cut off the seller's right to stop delivery unless the seller acquiesced in the transfer from its buyer to the subpurchaser). See also Ceres Inc. v. ACLI Metal & Ore Co., 451 F.Supp. 921 (N.D.Ill.1978) (holding that under UCC 2–403, a good faith purchaser prevails over a seller seeking to stop delivery but that "without delivery, the buyer did not obtain power under § 2–403 to confer good title upon the bona fide purchaser").

sells to BIOCB, the BIOCB takes 'all rights' or takes 'free' of a security interest."). Would the result be different if *B* had wrongfully delivered the cotton to *C* for temporary storage purposes and not as security?

NOTES ON ENTRUSTMENT

(1) The Historical Development of the Law of "Entrusting." UCC 2–403(2) represents a sharp break with the traditional law of good faith purchase. Under facts similar to those in Problem 1.3.8, the common law usually favored the original owner. Merely entrusting possession to a dealer was not sufficient to clothe the dealer with the authority to sell. "If it were otherwise people would not be secure in sending their watches or articles of jewelry to a jeweller's [sic] establishment to be repaired, or cloth to a clothing establishment to be made into garments." Levi v. Booth, 58 Md. 305 (1882).

During the nineteenth century, however, many states enacted "Factor's Acts" under which an owner of goods who entrusted them to an agent (or "factor") for sale took the risk that the agent might sell them beyond the agent's authority. A good faith purchaser from the agent, relying on the agent's possession of the goods and having no notice that the agent's sale was unauthorized, took good title against the original owner. (See the discussion by Professor Gilmore in Note (1) on the Basic Conveyancing Principles, supra.) But the Factor's Acts did not protect the good faith purchaser where, as in Problem 1.3.8, the owner entrusted the goods to another for some purpose other than that of sale. A mere **bailee** could not pass good title, even to a good faith purchaser for value.

In this regard UCC 2–403(2) goes well beyond the Factor's Acts, since it applies to "[a]ny entrusting," i.e., "any delivery" under UCC 2–403(3), regardless of the purpose. The section gives protection, however, only to a "buyer," not to all those who give value and take in good faith from the person to whom the goods are entrusted. Contrast the narrow scope of "buyer in ordinary course" under UCC 1–201(b)(9) [F1–201(9)] with the definitions of "purchase" and "purchaser" in UCC 1–201(b)(29) and UCC 1–201(b)(30) [F1–201(32) and F1–201(33)]. See Comment 3 to UCC 2–403.[9]

---

9.   According to Professor Gilmore: "For some reason, the security transferees who were protected in the voidable title subsection by the use of the term 'purchaser' do not qualify for protection under the entrusting section. I have no idea why the draftsmen chose thus to narrow the protected class." Gilmore, The Good Faith Purchase Idea and the Uniform Commercial Code: Confessions of a Repentant Draftsman, 15 Ga. L. Rev. 605, 618 (1981). The Ontario Law Reform Commission was "attracted to the distinction":

> The supporting theory is, presumably, grounded on either of the following premises: namely, that commerce will not be impeded if lenders are required to assume the risk of a merchant-borrower exceeding his actual authority; or, that lenders are in as good a position as are entrusters, or perhaps even better, to protect themselves against a dishonest merchant.

2 Ontario Law Reform Commission, Report on Sale of Goods 314–15 (1979).

(2) Testing the Limits of UCC 2–403(2): Porter v. Wertz. Despite its apparent simplicity, UCC 2–403(2) contains a number of wrinkles, several of which came to light in Porter v. Wertz, 68 A.D.2d 141, 416 N.Y.S.2d 254 (1979), affirmed mem., 53 N.Y.2d 696, 439 N.Y.S.2d 105, 421 N.E.2d 500 (1981), a case with particularly interesting facts:

Samuel Porter, an art collector, owned Utrillo's painting "Chateau de Lion-sur-Mer," but lost the painting through the machinations of one Harold "Von" Maker—sometimes operating under the name of Peter Wertz, a junior collaborator over whom, the trial judge observed, Von Maker "cast his hypnotic spell . . . and usurped his name, his signature and his sacred honor."

Von Maker had engaged in several transactions as an art dealer. (Other activities had led to arrests for possession of obscene literature and theft of checks, and to conviction for transmitting a forged cable in connection with a scheme to defraud the Chase Manhattan Bank.) Von Maker (alias "Wertz"), in his capacity as art dealer, approached Porter and expressed an interest in the Utrillo. Porter, unaware of Von Maker's illegal activities, permitted Von Maker to hang the Utrillo temporarily in Von Maker's home pending a decision as to purchase.

Without Porter's knowledge, Von Maker's junior collaborator, the true Peter Wertz, sold the Utrillo to an art dealer, Feigen Galleries. Feigen sold the painting to Brenner, who resold it to a third party, who took the painting to South America.

Porter brought actions for conversion against Wertz and Von Maker and also against the purchasers, Feigen and Brenner. Defendant Feigen argued that Porter "entrusted" the painting to Von Maker and as a consequence: (1) Feigen was protected under UCC 2–403(2) as a "buyer in ordinary course of business," and (2) Porter's claim as owner was barred by equitable estoppel.

The trial court rejected Feigen's defense based on UCC 2–403(2) but concluded that Porter was barred by equitable estoppel and dismissed his action. The Appellate Division reversed the trial court and held that neither statutory estoppel (UCC 2–403(2)) nor equitable estoppel barred recovery. It found that Feigen was not a buyer in ordinary course because Wertz, from whom Feigen bought the Utrillo, was not an art dealer ("[i]f anything, he was a delicatessen employee") and because Feigen did not act in good faith (good faith, as defined in UCC 2–103(1)(b) "should not—and cannot—be interpreted to permit, countenance, or condone commercial standards of sharp trade practice or indifference as to the 'provenance', *i.e.*, history of ownership or the right to possess or sell an object d'art, such as is present in the case before us.").

Feigen appealed to the Court of Appeals, which affirmed the Appellate Division. The court wrote (421 N.E.2d at 501):

> It also has been suggested that transfers for security are transfers "in which the price or consideration received for the goods . . . is likely to be considerably less than the amount normally received in a sale of the same goods in other transactions." Leary & Sperling, The Outer Limits of Entrusting, 35 Ark.L.Rev. 50, 65 (1981).

Because Peter Wertz was not an art dealer and the Appellate Division has found that Feigen was not duped by Von Maker into believing that Peter Wertz was such a dealer, subdivision (2) of section 2–403 of the Uniform Commercial Code is inapplicable for three distinct reasons: (1) even if Peter Wertz were an art merchant rather than a delicatessen employee, he is not the same merchant to whom Porter entrusted the Utrillo painting; (2) Wertz was not an art merchant; and (3) the sale was not in the ordinary course of Wertz' business because he did not deal in goods of that kind [F 1–201(9)].[10]

Would it have made any difference if Feigen had bought the Utrillo from Von Maker rather than from Wertz? Why?

What is the relevance, if any, of the knowledge of either the entruster or the buyer? Does it make a difference under UCC 2–403(2) if the original owner of the goods does not know that the person to whom the owner entrusts them is a merchant who deals in goods of that kind? See Atlas Auto Rental Corp. v. Weisberg, 54 Misc.2d 168, 281 N.Y.S.2d 400 (Civ.Ct.1967) (knowledge of dealer-merchant status is necessary element of entrusting). Accord, Leary & Sperling, The Outer Limits of Entrusting, 35 Ark. L. Rev. 50, 83–85 (1981) (relying on *Atlas Auto*). But cf. Antigo Co-op. Credit Union v. Miller, 86 Wis.2d 90, 271 N.W.2d 642 (1978) (knowledge by secured party that debtor was a dealer-merchant not necessary for applicability of analogous provision in F9–307(1)).

Suppose Feigen had been duped by Von Maker into believing that Wertz was an art dealer. Suppose that Feigen had been duped by Wertz, who held himself out as an art dealer. Compare UCC 2–104(1) with UCC 2–403(2). In Sea Harvest, Inc. v. Rig & Crane Equipment Corp., 181 N.J.Super. 41, 436 A.2d 553 (1981), the court said: "A buyer's misunderstanding that the seller was in the business of selling does not improve the former's position." Do you agree with this reading of the UCC?

SECTION 4. GOOD FAITH PURCHASE OF RIGHTS TO PAYMENT

One of the concerns that occupy a secured party is the status of the debtor's title to the property subject to the security interest (the "collateral"). As the previous Section explains, a secured party who takes a security interest in goods ordinarily acquires no better rights than its transferor (the "debtor") has. The creation of a security interest does not, of itself, normally cut off third-party claims to the goods. In a few, narrowly circumscribed situations, however, a secured party who qualifies as a "good faith

---

10. Although it received amicus briefs on the "good faith" question from both the New York State Attorney General (arguing that good faith among art merchants requires inquiry as to ownership) and the Art Dealers Association of America, Inc. (arguing that a duty of inquiry would cripple the art business), the court found no need to reach the question.

purchaser for value" takes free of otherwise valid third-party claims and thereby acquires greater rights than the debtor had. As we shall see in this Section and the one following, the two primary conveyancing principles discussed in Section 3—security of property and good faith purchase—apply not only to goods but also to other kinds of personal property that may serve as collateral.

Problem 1.4.1. The Atlas Co. was the owner of a negotiable promissory note, made by Merchant, who promised "to pay on demand to the order of The Atlas Co. $100,000." In preparation for a proposed sale of the note to Hometown Bank, Atlas's president indorsed the company's name on the back of the note. That night, Atlas's bookkeeper (Bates) arranged to work late and took the note from the vault. The following day Bates delivered the note to Crispy Bank to secure a loan for $80,000 and promptly disappeared.

(a) Who has the better claim to the note? See UCC 3–306; UCC 3–302; UCC 1–201(b)(21) [F1–201(20)]; UCC 3–201; UCC 3–109; UCC 3–205; UCC 3–303; UCC 3–103(a)(4); UCC 1–202 [F1–201(25)]; Note (1) on Competing Claims to Negotiable Instruments and Certificated Securities, infra.

(b) What result if the note had not been indorsed? See UCC 3–306; UCC 3–201; UCC 3–203(c).

Problem 1.4.2. What result in the preceding Problem if the property at issue is not a note but rather one of a series of 500 Class A Bonds (debt obligations) issued by the I Corporation? (You may assume that The Atlas Co. was the registered owner.) See UCC 8–102(a)(4); R8–302; R8–301; UCC 8–303; UCC 8–106(b); Note (2) on Competing Claims to Negotiable Instruments and Certificated Securities, infra.

NOTES ON COMPETING CLAIMS TO NEGOTIABLE INSTRUMENTS AND CERTIFICATED SECURITIES

(1) Negotiable Instruments. Negotiable instruments (most commonly, checks and promissory notes) have a long history—one that is best left to courses in Commercial Paper or Payment Systems. For our purposes, it is sufficient to recognize that rights to payment that are embodied in a writing in a particular form constitute a different kind of property from rights to payment that are not so embodied.

UCC Article 3 applies to "negotiable instruments."[1] UCC 3–104(a), which defines the term, preserves the tradition that form triumphs over substance in negotiable instruments law. The term includes only a "promise" (defined in UCC 3–103(a)(9)) or an "order" (defined in UCC 3–103(a)(6)) to pay a fixed sum of "money" (defined in UCC 1–201(b)(24) [F1–201(24)]).[2] Succeeding sections explain the requirements that the

---

1.   Article 3 was revised in 2002. Unless otherwise noted in these materials, however, the substance of the provisions discussed here was not modified.

2.   An instrument is a "note" if it is a promise and a "draft" if it is an order. UCC 3–104(e).

promise or order be "unconditional" (UCC 3–106); that it be for a fixed amount of money, with or without "interest" (UCC 3–112(b)); that it be "payable to bearer or to order" (UCC 3–109); and that it be "payable on demand" or "at a definite time" (UCC 3–108). Other sections in Part 1 of the Article are devoted to other aspects of the form of negotiable instruments.

The "formal requisites" of negotiability now found in UCC 3–104 were based initially on commercial practice and case law. They were embodied in the pre–1990 version of UCC Article 3 and its predecessors, the Negotiable Instruments Law of 1896 (which was adopted in each of the United States) and the (British) Bills of Exchange Act of 1882. The continued emphasis on form may seem an anachronism, but perhaps it serves a purpose. As we shall see, one who becomes a party to a negotiable instrument assumes special risks. The formal requisites, like the fence and warnings around high voltage equipment, arguably confine and identify the danger areas. Of course, the formalities afford no warning to one who is unfamiliar with this specialized branch of the law.

In the commercial setting, negotiable notes rarely are used to evidence an obligation to pay for goods sold on credit.[3] When negotiable notes are used, it is typically in connection with a loan of money. Nevertheless, in either case, the person to whom the note is payable (The Atlas Co., in Problem 1.4.1) may sell the note or use it to secure a loan. Like Articles 2 and 9, Article 3 contains both security of property and good-faith-purchase rules governing the extent to which a purchaser (buyer or secured party) takes a negotiable instrument free from competing claims. Unless a person has the rights of a holder in due course ("HDC"), the person takes the instrument subject to any existing claim of a property or possessory right in the instrument or its proceeds. A person having rights of a holder in due course takes free of the claim to the instrument. UCC 3–306. The freedom from "claims" is analogous to the protection from outstanding ownership interests that Article 2 affords to the good faith purchaser of goods. See UCC 2–403 and Section 3, supra.

The typical commercial note is payable to the order of an identified person (the payee). Although a note may be transferred or negotiated many times, most negotiable notes are transferred or negotiated once (if at all), from the payee to a purchaser. The risk that the transferor acquired the note through theft or fraud and that the true owner will claim it from the

---

3.   This has been true for some time. Writing more than sixty years ago, Karl Llewellyn observed:

> I shall not undertake to explain how or why the commercial system of a century ago lost the use of notes to evidence the credit-price of freshly delivered goods. It is enough here that the practice went into decline, and that between merchants goods are now delivered typically on purely "open" credit (resulting in a "book account," and "account receivable"), often with the buyer, if he is financially strong, paying within ten days against a large "cash discount." The giving of a commercial note between dealers has come to be the gesture with which a stale account, long overdue, is promised *really* to be met next time. Such a note smells.

Llewellyn, Meet Negotiable Instruments, 44 Colum.L.Rev. 299, 321–22 (1944).

purchaser, as in Problem 1.4.1., is negligible. A greater risk, but one that is still rather small, is that the note is encumbered with a security interest. As we shall see in Chapter 6, Section 2, infra, a purchaser who takes possession of a note is likely to prevail over competing secured parties. See UCC 9–330(d). But even when the purchaser would be junior under the normal Article 9 priority rules, the purchaser will take free of competing claims to the note if it can establish that it is an HDC. See UCC 9–331(a); UCC 3–306.

The Holder in Due Course. "Holder in due course" is the name given to good faith purchasers for value of negotiable instruments under Article 3. UCC 3–302(a) defines the term. Observe that not every person who takes an instrument in good faith[4] and for value[5] qualifies as an HDC. One also must be without notice of any of a variety of claims, defenses, and irregularities. (You may recall that notice of competing claims may be relevant to a putative good faith purchaser's "good faith" under Article 2.)

Two other requirements for becoming a holder in due course are less obvious. First, one must be the holder of an "instrument," which UCC 3–104(b) defines as a "negotiable instrument." Second, the person must be a "holder." When the instrument is payable to an identified person and the identified person is in possession of the instrument, the person is the holder. Alternatively, when the instrument is payable to bearer, the person in possession is the holder. See UCC 1–201(b)(21) [F1–201(20)].

Merchant's note in Problem 1.4.1, like the overwhelming majority of negotiable promissory notes, is payable to the order of an identified person (Atlas) and not payable to bearer. To become a holder, Crispy Bank not only must take possession but also must obtain the indorsement (signature) of The Atlas Co., the payee. Custom dictates that Atlas will indorse the note on the back. Atlas's indorsement may identify Crispy Bank as a person to whom the instrument is payable (e.g., Atlas's signature may be accompanied by the words "Pay to Crispy Bank") or it may identify no such person (e.g., it may consist only of Atlas's signature), thereby making the note payable to bearer. See UCC 3–205(a), (b). In either case, Crispy Bank will become a holder upon taking possession of the note. If it meets the other requirements of UCC 3–302(a), then Crispy Bank will become a holder in due course and take free of all claims, including Atlas's ownership claim.

(2) Certificated Securities. Some rights to payment, such as the corporate **bonds** in Problem 1.4.2, are traded on securities exchanges or securities markets. These rights to payment often are used as collateral. The UCC distinguishes between securities, which by definition are, or are of a type, dealt in or traded on securities markets or exchanges, and negotiable

---

4.   In Article 3, " 'Good faith' means honesty in fact and the observance of reasonable commercial standards of fair dealing." UCC 3–103(a)(4).

5.   UCC 3–303(a)(2) expressly provides that an instrument is transferred for value if the transferee acquires a security interest in it. This is consistent with the definition of "value" in UCC 1–204 and F1–201(44).

instruments. Compare UCC 8–102(a)(15) (defining "security") with UCC 3–104(a) (defining "negotiable instrument"). The transfer of interests in securities—i.e., the mechanisms by which a person becomes the owner of a security—is governed by Article 8 and not by Article 3. See UCC 8–103(d); UCC 3–102(a). (The federal securities laws, which are discussed in courses on Business Organizations, Corporations, and Securities, are regulatory and anti–fraud statutes.)

Bonds, stocks, and other securities frequently are represented by a piece of paper, which Article 8 calls a "security certificate". UCC 8–102(a)(16) (defining "security certificate").

To fall within the scope of Article 8, a "certificated security" (i.e., a security represented by a security certificate) must be in bearer or registered form. See UCC 8–102(a)(15) (defining "security"), (a)(2) (defining "bearer form"), (a)(13) (defining "registered form"). This requirement is somewhat analogous to the requirement that a negotiable instrument be payable to bearer or order. See UCC 3–104(a)(1); UCC 3–109.

Like the purchaser of a negotiable instrument, a purchaser (buyer or secured party) of a certificated security may acquire greater rights than the transferor. Qualifying good faith purchasers for value of a security, whether or not the security is represented by a certificate, are called "protected purchasers." UCC 8–303(a). A protected purchaser takes free of any adverse claim to the security. UCC 8–303(b). The requirements for becoming a protected purchaser of a security are similar to those for becoming an HDC of a negotiable instrument. Compare UCC 8–303(a) with UCC 3–302(a). The differences are attributable largely to the fact that, unlike negotiable instruments, securities are traded in markets, where the parties to a transaction are unknown to each other. Buyers under these circumstances are unable to investigate the title of their sellers; they need comfort that they will be able to enjoy what they paid for without having to defend against the claims of third parties.

––––––––

When the collateral consists of an obligation of some kind (e.g., the debtor's right to payment for goods sold), the secured party is concerned not only with taking the collateral free from the *claims* of third parties but also, and usually more so, with its ability to enforce the obligation free of the obligor's *defenses*.

Problem 1.4.3. *B* manufactures and sells auto parts on credit to wholesale dealers. To secure a **line of credit** from *C* finance company, *B* granted to *C* a security interest in "all *B*'s existing and after-acquired rights to payment for goods sold ('accounts') and all notes and other instruments representing such rights to payment." *B* defaults on its obligations to *C*, and *C* demands payment from each of *B*'s customers. One customer, *A*, contracted to pay $60,000 for a shipment of goods but now is willing to pay only $40,000 because the goods were seriously nonconforming. See UCC 2–714; UCC 2–717. *C* brings suit against *A*.

(a) What result? See UCC 9–404(a); Note (1) on Defenses to Payment Obligations, infra.

(b) What result if *A* refused to pay for the goods because *B* had failed to repay a $20,000 loan from *A*? Does it matter when *B*'s default occurred? See UCC 9–404(a). Cf. Restatement (Second) of Contracts § 336(2).[6]

(c) Assume the contract of sale contained the following provision: "Buyer [*A*] understands and acknowledges that Seller [*B*] may assign Seller's rights under this Agreement for collateral purposes or otherwise. Buyer agrees that, in the event of any such assignment, Buyer will not assert against any assignee any claims or defenses that Buyer may have against Seller arising under this Agreement or otherwise." What result in parts (a) and (b)? See UCC 9–403(a)–(c); UCC 3–305.

(d) Why would anyone sign a contract that contains the provision set forth in part (c)?

Problem 1.4.4. *B* manufactures and sells auto parts on credit to wholesale dealers. To secure a line of credit from *C* finance company, *B* granted to *C* a security interest in "all *B*'s existing and after-acquired rights to payment for goods sold ('accounts') and all notes and other instruments representing such rights to payment." *B* undertakes to deliver, and does deliver, each such instrument to *C* immediately upon its receipt by *B*. *B* defaults on its obligations to *C*, and *C* demands payment from each of *B*'s customers. One customer, *A*, signed a negotiable promissory note, in which *A* agreed to pay $60,000 "to the order of *B*" for a shipment of goods. *A* now is willing to pay only $40,000 because the goods were seriously nonconforming. *C* brings suit against *A*.

(a) What result if *B* had indorsed the note, "pay to *C*, [signed] *B*" before delivering it? See UCC 3–412; UCC 3–104; UCC 3–301; UCC 3–305(a), (b); UCC 3–302; UCC 1–201(20); UCC 3–205; UCC 3–303; UCC 3–103(a)(4); UCC 1–202 [F1–201(25)]; Note (2) on Defenses to Payment Obligations, infra.

(b) What result if *B* delivered the note without having indorsed it? Can *C* even bring suit against *A*? See UCC 3–412; UCC 3–301; UCC 3–203; UCC 3–305. Would *C* improve its position by obtaining *B*'s indorsement before bringing suit?

(c) Assume that *B* delivered the note without having indorsed it. What result if *A* refused to pay for the goods because *B* had failed to repay a loan from *A*? Does it matter when *B*'s default occurred? See UCC 3–203(c); UCC 3–305(a) and Comment 3 (last paragraph).

---

6.   Restatement (Second) of Contracts § 336(2) provides: "The right of an assignee is subject to any defense or claim of the obligor which accrues before the obligor receives notification of the assignment but not to defenses or claims which accrue thereafter except as stated in this Section or as provided by statute."

NOTES ON DEFENSES TO PAYMENT OBLIGATIONS

(1) Rights to Payment. Problem 1.4.3 represents a typical commercial transaction with which you will become increasingly familiar. Seller (B) sells goods to Buyer (A) on **open account**, i.e., Buyer's unsecured obligation is not represented by a negotiable promissory note but simply by a purchase order or other writing that, perhaps taken together with other writings, creates a contract. Finance Company (C) finances Seller's rights to payment (accounts) by advancing funds against the accounts as they arise. In this way, Seller obtains cash immediately, without having to wait for the credit period to expire. (Accounts receivable financing is quite complicated; it is discussed in detail in Chapter 6, Section 1, infra.)

Upon Seller's default on its obligation to Finance Company, and even before if Seller agrees, Finance Company may collect from Buyer on Buyer's obligation. See UCC 9–607(a)(1) (in Article 9 terminology, Finance Company is the "secured party" and Buyer is an "account debtor"). Whether Finance Company will succeed in collecting from Buyer depends in large part on whether Buyer is able to pay and whether it is legally obligated to do so. Finance Company may be concerned about the credit risk, i.e., the risk that, when the obligation is enforced, Buyer will be unable or unwilling to pay. Finance Company may choose to investigate the creditworthiness of Buyer. Or, if Finance Company is receiving an assignment of a large number of receivables, then it may elect to investigate the creditworthiness of Seller's customers *generally* before it agrees to take Seller's accounts as collateral. In addition, Finance Company can take steps to minimize the risk that Buyer can assert valid defenses to its obligation. These steps may include determining Seller's reputation for performing its contracts before Finance Company extends credit.

When Finance Company calls upon Buyer to pay, Buyer may raise a defense to its obligation to pay for the goods. For example, if the goods never were delivered, Buyer would have a defense of failure of consideration. If the goods were delivered and accepted but were nonconforming, as in Problem 1.4.3, Buyer would have the right to deduct from its obligation for the price (UCC 2–709) its damages for breach of warranty (UCC 2–714). See UCC 2–717. The right to deduct sometimes is called **recoupment**. See Note (2), infra. Under some circumstances, Buyer may be able to revoke its acceptance of the goods. See UCC 2–608. Are these defenses (or claims in recoupment) available to defeat Finance Company?

UCC 9–404(a) contains a provision that protects parties to contracts, like Buyer, from unexpected inroads on their contractual relationships—another example of the "security of property" principle discussed in Section (3)(A), supra. Under this provision, the assignee of a right to payment, like the purchaser of goods, ordinarily acquires no better rights than the assignor had.[7] Thus, the assignment of Seller's right to

---

7.   With respect to transactions not covered by Article 9, see Restatement (Second) of Contracts §§ 336(1), (2), which contain rules that are similar to UCC 9–404(a).

payment does not ipso facto deprive Buyer of its right to defend against the claim.[8] On the other hand, UCC 9–403(b) contains a good-faith-purchase rule: A **waiver-of-defense clause**, whereby Buyer agrees not to assert against an assignee any claim or defense that Buyer may have against Seller, is enforceable by an assignee (i.e., a secured party) who takes the assignment for value, in good faith, and without notice of any claim or defense.[9]

The implications of the preceding sentence may not be readily apparent. Buyer buys goods on credit from Seller pursuant to an agreement containing a waiver-of-defense clause. Seller borrows from Finance Company and uses Buyer's obligation (and the obligations of Seller's other customers) as collateral. The goods prove to be defective. If *Seller* were to demand payment from Buyer, Buyer would have a defense. But *Finance Company* may enforce the agreement and take free of that defense if it acquired its security interest for value, in good faith, and without notice of any claims or defenses. In short, Buyer is legally obligated to pay Finance Company for the defective goods.

Of course, even if Buyer must pay the price to Finance Company, Buyer still has a claim against Seller. The following considerations, which are particularly striking in consumer transactions (discussed below in Note (4)), suggest that Buyer is in a stronger position if can assert a defense against Finance Company: (1) *The inertia of litigation.* Setting up a defense as a defendant is easier than starting an action, even though the "burden of proof" with regard to Seller's breach may fall on Buyer in either case. In practice, this consideration has its greatest impact on the settlement value of Buyer's claim, since a reduction in price is much easier to negotiate than a cash refund. (2) *The strain of current cash outlay.* Buyer may not have the resources to pay the full amount for defective goods and wait (perhaps for years) until a legal action against Seller can reach trial and finally be converted into a judgment. (3) *The risk of Seller's insolvency.* Seller may be insolvent or **judgment proof**. Seller may have been a fly-by-night operator, or driven into sharp practice by financial pressure, or forced to the wall by keen competition, poor management, or a business recession.

Conversely, these advantages to Buyer in preserving defenses against an action for the price suggest the importance to Finance Company of freeing itself from these defenses. Finance Company's interest is magnified to the extent that buyers interpose spurious defenses in an attempt to scale down or avoid their obligation to pay for what they buy.

---

8.   UCC 9–404(a) subjects the assignee to a buyer's claims as well as its defenses. A buyer who pays the contract price for defective goods has a claim against the seller for damages. See UCC 2–714. A buyer may assert this claim against the seller's assignee (here, Finance Company) only to reduce the amount the buyer owes; the buyer may not recover from Finance Company any payments already made. UCC 9–404(b).

9.   The agreement is not enforceable with respect to defenses that may be asserted against a holder in due course unless other law would give it effect. UCC 9–403(c), (f). These few defenses are set forth in UCC 3–305(a)(1). See UCC 3–305(b).

(2) Negotiable Instruments. Like accounts, negotiable instruments are used as collateral. If the payee-debtor defaults on its obligation to the secured party, the secured party has a right (as against the debtor) to collect on the note from the maker (here, Buyer). See UCC 9–607(a). However, the secured party normally must have possession of the instrument as a condition to enforcing it. See UCC 3–412; UCC 3–301.

As is the case with claims, Article 3 contains both a security of property rule (shelter) and a good-faith-purchase rule with respect to defenses. The former is found in UCC 3–203(b): "Transfer of an instrument . . . vests in the transferee any right of the transferor to enforce the instrument. . . ." The right to enforce the obligation of a party to an instrument ordinarily is subject to the claims and defenses set forth in UCC 3–305(a). These include "a defense of the obligor that would be available if the person entitled to enforce the instrument were enforcing a right to payment under a simple contract," UCC 3–305(a)(2), as well as certain "claim[s] in recoupment." UCC 3–305(a)(3). A holder in due course (UCC 3–302(a)) takes free of most defenses and claims in recoupment. See UCC 3–305(b). A person having the rights of an HDC can transfer those rights, even to a person who does not itself qualify as an HDC (e.g., because it is not a holder or did not give value for the instrument). Under those circumstances, the transferee acquires the rights of the HDC and takes free of most defenses and claims in recoupment. See UCC 3–203(b).

The UCC does not define "recoupment." Generally speaking, it means the right of a defendant to reduce its liability for damages by deducting damages caused by the plaintiff's failure to comply with its obligations under the *same contract*. Consider the facts of Problems 1.4.4(a) and (b). By accepting nonconforming goods, Buyer becomes liable for their price under UCC 2–709; however, the nonconformity gives rise to a claim for damages against Seller under UCC 2–714. UCC 2–717 affords Buyer a right of recoupment: "The buyer on notifying the seller of his intention to do so may deduct all or any part of the damages resulting from any breach of the contract from any part of the price still due under the contract." Ordinarily, Finance Company will take subject to this right of recoupment.[10]

Not uncommonly, as in Problem 1.4.4(c), Buyers seek to **set off** against their obligation to pay for goods, a claim against the Seller arising from an *unrelated* transaction.[11] In some jurisdictions, Buyer's right to set off would

---

10.   Buyer may use its claim for breach of warranty "only to reduce the amount owing on the instrument at the time the action is brought." UCC 3–305(a)(3). Buyer may not use this claim to recover from Finance Company amounts previously paid. Article 9 takes the same approach to rights to payment that have not been embodied in a negotiable instrument. See note 8, supra.

11.   Setoff is not restricted to merchants and other commercial parties. Suppose Jack and Jill go out to dinner and a movie. Jack pays $9 for Jill's dinner and Jill pays $6 for Jack's movie ticket. Rather than give Jack $9 for dinner and then collect $6 from Jack for the movie, Jill will set off her $6 claim against her $9 obligation and pay Jack the difference, $3.

be a good defense against Seller's action for the price. Regardless of whether Buyer enjoys setoff rights against Seller, the drafters of Article 3 apparently intended that Buyer not be permitted to set off against Seller's transferees, such as Finance Company. They accomplished this result through the negative implicit in UCC 3–305(a)(3): The right to enforce *is* subject to "a claim in recoupment . . . if the claim arose from the transaction that gave rise to the instrument." The right to enforce *is not* subject to claims in recoupment that arise from other transactions. See UCC 3–305, Comment 3 (last paragraph).

Enabling the transferee of a note to take free of the maker's rights of setoff may result in the anomaly that a transferee who gives no value for the note (e.g., Buyer's donee) acquires better rights than a person who gives value for an assignment of an obligation that is not represented by a note (e.g., *C* in Problem 1.4.3(b)), supra. See UCC 9–404(a). Can this anomaly be justified, especially given that UCC 9–403 analogizes good-faith purchasers of rights to payment with holders in due course of negotiable instruments?

Other Consequences. Although waiver-of-defense clauses and negotiable notes may accomplish the same primary objective—insulation of the secured party from the buyer's defenses—the negotiable note can have legal consequences that reach beyond a contractual "cut-off" clause. For example, a person who has executed a negotiable note cannot safely make payment without obtaining the instrument and seeing that the payment is noted on it. The reason is that the instrument might be negotiated thereafter to a holder in due course, who, under the basic rules of UCC 3–305, takes free of the maker's defenses, including payment. See also UCC 3–601(b) (discharge is not effective against a person acquiring rights of an HDC without notice of the discharge). (A railroad or warehouse that has issued a negotiable document of title—bill of lading or warehouse receipt—runs a similar risk if it delivers the goods without surrender of, or notation on, the document. See Section 5, infra.) Revised Article 3 substantially ameliorates this result for obligors on notes, although it leaves the text of UCC 3–601(b) intact. Revised 3–602(d) deems a transferee, even a holder in due course, to have notice of a payment that discharges an obligor's obligation under Revised 3–602(b). Revised 3–602(b) provides that a note is discharged to the extent that a payment is made to a person formerly entitled to enforce a note unless the obligor has received adequate notification that the note has been transferred and that payments are to be made to the transferee.

(3) "Transferable Records." To qualify as a negotiable instrument under UCC Article 3, a note must be written. See UCC 3–104(a); UCC 3–103(a)(9). In the 1990's business transactions increasingly became evidenced by electronic rather than paper records. We have seen that one of the major benefits of negotiability—the ability to acquire a right to

---

In many jurisdictions, setoff differs from recoupment: the former relates to claims unrelated to the contract upon which the defendant is being sued, whereas the latter relates to claims based upon the same contract. Often, however, the term setoff is used to encompass both concepts.

payment free of the claims and defenses of the person obligated to pay—can be acquired by obtaining the obligated person's agreement to that effect. See UCC 9–403(b). Other benefits, including the ability to acquire the right to payment free of third-party claims, cannot be achieved readily (if at all) by contract. To enable businesses to acquire the benefits of negotiability in an electronic environment, in 1999 the National Conference of Commissioners on Uniform State Laws ("NCCUSL") promulgated section 16 of the Uniform Electronic Transactions Act ("UETA"). As of this writing (October, 2005), UETA has been enacted in 46 states, the District of Columbia, and the U.S. Virgin Islands.

UETA 16(a) provides for the creation of a "transferable record"—an electronic record that would be a note under UCC Article 3 if it were in writing.[12] An electronic record can qualify as a transferable record only if the issuer agrees that it is a transferable record. UETA 16(a)(2). A person can become the holder of a transferable record and acquire the same rights as a holder of a negotiable note under Article 3 by having "control" of the electronic record. UETA 16(d). As Comment 3 to UETA 16 explains, "Under Section 16 acquisition of 'control' over an electronic record serves as a substitute for 'possession' in the paper analog. More precisely, 'control' under Section 16 serves as the substitute for delivery, indorsement and possession of a negotiable promissory note." A person who has control and also satisfies the requirements of UCC 3–302(a) acquires the rights of a holder in due course. UETA 16(d).

UETA 16 establishes a general standard for control: "A person has control of a transferable record if a system employed for evidencing the transfer of interests in the transferable record reliably establishes that person as the person to which the transferable record was issued or transferred." UETA 16(b). It also provides, in UETA 16(c), "a safe harbor list of very strict requirements for such a system." UETA 16, Comment 3. Neither the general standard nor the safe harbor mandates the use of particular technology; rather, any system that accomplishes the purpose of "control"—to reliably establish the identity of the person entitled to payment—is sufficient.

Federal law also contemplates the creation of negotiable, "transferable records." See Electronic Signatures in Global and National Commerce Act ("E–SIGN"), Pub. L. No. 106–229, § 201, 114 Stat. 464 (2000) (codified at 15 U.S.C. § 7021). Section 201 of E–SIGN generally tracks UETA 16, but the federal rule applies only to an electronic record that "relates to a loan secured by real property." Id. § 201(a)(1)(C). The transfer of mortgage notes is discussed in more detail in Chapter 8, Section 3(B), infra.

Although systems for control of electronic notes are still being developed and refined, at least one system that is up and running describes its services as follows:

---

12.   The term "transferable record" also encompasses an electronic record that would be a document under UCC Article 7 if it were in writing. See Section 5, infra.

The eOriginal eCore Business Suite . . . fully complies with E-Sign, UETA, and UCC Revised Article 9 legislation requirements for the creation and management of electronic negotiable instruments (e.g., bills of lading, promissory notes, chattel paper, etc.). It . . . provides the means for establishing ownership and control of Electronic Original documents, allowing for the transfer of ownership of those documents within a secure and trusted environment, among multiple parties instantaneously.

http://www.eoriginal.com/products/product_overview.html (visited Apr. 4, 2005).

(4) Good Faith Purchase in Consumer Transactions. Permitting *commercial* buyers to waive their right to assert defenses against third parties, whether by a waiver-of-defense clause or a negotiable note, for the most part has been uncontroversial. Consumer buyers have been thought to present a special problem. For several decades, opposing interests struggled over whether a financing agency should be permitted to insulate itself from defenses that a consumer buyer would have had against the seller. The result was a substantial revision of the traditional concept of good faith purchase as applied to consumer transactions.

The first victories for the consumer-oriented view came in the courts, which began to hold by the early 1950's that a financing agency that was closely connected with a retailer could not be an HDC and was not protected by a waiver-of-defense clause. (The Article 9 provision that generally validated waiver-of-defense clauses was expressly "[s]ubject to any statute or decision which establishes a different rule for buyers or lessees of consumer goods." F9–206(1). UCC 9–403(f) is similar in effect. However, some of the cases invalidating these clauses involved goods that were not consumer goods—i.e., not bought or leased for personal, family, or household purposes.) In the teeth of statutory language designed to protect the negotiability of notes, a substantial number of courts found legal grounds to place the burden of adjustment for the seller's default upon the secured party.

Inasmuch as buyers had to show a sufficiently close connection between the seller and the financing agency in each case, judicial decisions fell short of giving the buyer optimum protection. By the early 1970's, however, most states had enacted statutes applicable to consumer transactions prohibiting negotiable instruments and waiver-of-defense clauses, limiting their effectiveness, or depriving them of effect altogether. Under these statutes, some of which derive from 1974 version of the Uniform Consumer Credit Code ("U3C") 3.307, 3.404, it is no longer necessary to show that the financing agency and the seller were closely connected.

The 1974 U3C also dealt with a developing practice, known as "dragging the body," whereby the seller refers the buyer to a financing agency that makes a direct loan to the buyer. The loan is secured by an interest in the goods purchased by the buyer, and the financing agency makes sure that the loan proceeds are applied to purchase the goods by making its check payable jointly to the buyer and the seller. Should the buyer refuse payment of the loan on the ground of a defense against the seller, the financing agency responds that its contract with the buyer is entirely separate from the seller's contract with the buyer and was fully performed when it gave the buyer the money. Statutes protecting consumers in the case of direct loans include a requirement that there be a sufficient connection between the seller and the lender; for this reason they tend to be complex.

In 1976, Federal Trade Commission Rule 433 took effect, making it an "unfair and deceptive trade practice" for the seller to fail to incorporate in a contract of sale to a consumer a legend that will preserve the buyer's defenses against the financing agency. In addition, if the seller receives the proceeds from a direct loan made to the buyer by a financing agency to which the seller "refers consumers" or with whom the seller "is affiliated . . . by common control, contract, or business arrangement," the loan contract must include a similar legend. 16 C.F.R. 433.1(d); 433.2. Placing the required legend on a note does not of itself destroy the note's negotiability; however, there cannot be an HDC of the note, even if the note otherwise is negotiable. UCC 3–106(d).

Staggering numbers of sellers and lenders, large and small, fall within the terms of the FTC Regulation. Suppose that sellers and lenders are not inclined to obey the Regulation and fail to use the prescribed provision. How effective are the FTC's tools to compel compliance? The FTC is authorized to bring civil actions against persons who violate FTC cease and desist orders and (more importantly) against persons who violate FTC rules respecting "unfair or deceptive acts or practices." See 15 U.S.C. § 57b.

Suppose a seller or lender nevertheless fails to include the prescribed formula in a contract and that, under state law, negotiable notes and waiver-of-defense clauses are effective to bar buyers from asserting defenses against transferees. Will the FTC Regulation override state law and allow the buyer to assert a defense or claim a refund? A substantial body of case law holds that FTC regulations do not ipso facto modify private rights or confer private rights of action. However, Revised Article 9 provides that the rights of an assignee of a contract that fails to include the required formula are the same as if the contract had included the formula. See UCC 9–403(d); UCC 9–404(d).

SECTION 5.   GOOD FAITH PURCHASE OF DOCUMENTS OF TITLE

INTRODUCTORY NOTE

Another type of personal property that may serve as collateral for a secured loan is a "document of title." As the definition of the term suggests (UCC 1–201(b)(16) [F1–201(15)]), documents of title purport to cover goods in the possession of a **bailee**. The two major types of documents of title are the "bill of lading" (UCC 1–201(b)(6) [F1–201(6)]), as to which the bailee is in the business of transporting or forwarding goods (e.g., a railroad), and the "warehouse receipt" (UCC 1–201(b)(42) [F1–201(45)]), as to which the bailee is engaged in the business of storing goods for hire (e.g., a warehouse).

A description of the common uses for the bill of lading and the warehouse receipt will aid in understanding the rights of secured parties whose collateral consists of documents of title and the rights of transferees of documents generally.

Bills of Lading. A bill of lading (originally, "bill of loading") is a document of title that a railroad or other **carrier** issues when goods are delivered to it for shipment. See UCC 1–201(b)(6), (16) [F1–201(6), (15)]. The UCC's rules governing bills of lading are collected in Article 7.[1] However, bills of lading in interstate shipments and exports are governed by the federal law, 49 U.S.C. §§ 80101–16, and not by the UCC. For present purposes, however, the differences are not crucial.

The bill of lading, in part, embodies a contract between the carrier and the shipper (often termed the "consignor," see UCC 7–102(1)(c)). This contract sets forth, inter alia, the consignor's obligations to pay freight and other charges and the carrier's obligations with respect to the transportation and delivery of the goods. It also addresses the carrier's liability in the event of casualty to the goods or failure to deliver.

Control of the bill of lading can be used to control delivery of the goods. In this regard, one must distinguish between the nonnegotiable (or **straight**) bill of lading and the negotiable one. As is true with instruments, see supra Section 4, the form of the paper is determinative. See UCC 7–104. Under the nonnegotiable bill of lading, the carrier undertakes to deliver the goods to a stated person (the "consignee"). See UCC 7–102(1)(b); UCC 7–104(2). For example, if the bill of lading runs "to Buyer & Co.," then the carrier discharges its delivery obligation by delivering the goods to Buyer & Co. Because the carrier can perform its contract by delivering to the named person (Buyer & Co.), Buyer need not present the bill of lading or even have taken possession of it. See UCC 7–403; UCC 7–404. Cf. Section 2(B), supra.

Buyer may have bought the goods for resale (to, say, *C*). If *C* contracts to buy the goods before Buyer takes delivery, Buyer will give written instructions to the carrier to deliver the goods to *C*, thereby entitling *C* to enforce the carrier's delivery obligation. See UCC 7–403. In this way, Buyer can transfer control over the goods without taking possession of them. Note, however, that although notification of the carrier entitles *C* to obtain delivery, the carrier nevertheless may honor Seller's instruction to stop delivery if it wishes to do so. See UCC 7–403(1)(d); UCC 2–705.

---

1.   Not all of Article 7 applies to bills of lading; Part 2 contains special provisions applicable only to warehouse receipts. Article 7 was revised in 2003, primarily in order to accommodate electronic documents of title and to modernize the article to take account of federal and international developments. Revised Article 7, Prefatory Note. Unless otherwise noted in these materials, however, the substance of the provisions discussed here was not modified.

Under the *negotiable* bill of lading, the carrier agrees to deliver the goods to the order of a stated person, e.g., "to the order of Seller & Co.," or occasionally to "bearer." The carrier's delivery obligation runs to the holder of the document. See UCC 7–403; UCC 1–201(b)(21) [F1–201(20)]. If the document runs to the order of Seller but the person to receive the goods is someone other than Seller (say, Buyer or *C*), then Seller must indorse and deliver the bill of lading to that person so that the person becomes a holder.

One of the important practical consequences of shipping under a negotiable bill of lading is that the carrier will deliver the goods only to one who surrenders the bill of lading. See UCC 7–403(3). If Seller wants to be sure of being paid before Buyer gets the goods, Seller may use a negotiable bill of lading, consign the shipment to the order of Seller, and thereby maintain control over the goods until Buyer pays. When Seller (or, more often, its local agent) receives payment, the agent will deliver the indorsed bill of lading to Buyer. At that point Buyer can take the bill of lading to the carrier and receive the goods.

Warehouse Receipts. Warehouse receipts (receipts issued by a person in the business of storing goods for hire, see UCC 1–201(b)(42) [F1–201(45)]) function much like bills of lading: They serve as a receipt for goods delivered to a bailee, set forth the terms of the contract between the bailor and bailee (warehouse), and enable parties to transfer control over goods without the need to take possession of them. Like bills of lading, warehouse receipts may be negotiable or nonnegotiable, depending upon their form. See UCC 7–104.

Nature delivers great crops at annual harvests, while consumption is gradual throughout the year. Consequently, commodities of enormous value must be kept in storage pending processing, distribution, and use. Other commodities—like fuel oil—are stored in large quantities because their use is seasonal. In other instances, storage is a significant part of preparation for use. Seasoning for years in charred oak barrels is of the essence in making good whiskey. Warehouse receipts may be employed as a means for traders to deal in these goods without the inconvenience of physical delivery. A slightly different use arises when a concern, such as a brewer or a mill, needs to hold commodities that tie up more capital than it can spare. Using warehouse receipts as collateral may facilitate a low-interest loan that otherwise would not be available.

A negotiable warehouse receipt and a nonnegotiable warehouse receipt are reproduced below on pages 60 through 63.

Purchasers of Documents of Title. A creditor who takes a warehouse receipt or bill of lading to secure a loan wishes to be sure that it takes both the document and the goods free from the claims of third parties, including other secured parties. The first three Problems below address some of the risks that the secured party runs in this regard. A secured party also wishes to take free of any defenses the issuer (warehouse or carrier) may raise to its delivery obligation. Notes (1) and (2) on the Scope of the Warehouse's Responsibility When Goods Disappear, *infra*, address three of these potential defenses as they apply to warehouse receipts: non-receipt (the warehouse never received the goods); misdescription (the goods actually received were not as described in the receipt); and disappearance (the goods disappeared). As for misdelivery (delivery of goods by the issuer to the wrong person), the UCC generally imposes absolute liability on a bailee who delivers goods to one other than a "person entitled under the document." See UCC 7–403(1).

Electronic Documents of Title. Although UCC Article 7 contemplates only written documents of title, the storage and transportation industries have begun to use electronic documents. For this reason, Revised Article 7 explicitly contemplates the use of electronic documents of title as well as tangible documents of title. See Revised Article 7, Prefatory Note; R1–201(b)(16) (defining "document of title" and explaining the meaning of "electronic document of title" and "tangible document of title"). The first statutory basis for electronic documents appeared in the United States Warehouse Act, which authorizes the use of electronic warehouse receipts covering cotton and contains provisions specifically addressing security interests in cotton covered by an electronic receipt. See 7 U.S.C. § 259(c) (repealed 2000). In 2000 the Act was amended to authorize the use of electronic documents covering other agricultural products as well. See 7 U.S.C. § 241 et seq.

We saw in Section 4, supra, that the Uniform Electronic Transactions Act provides a statutory framework for the transfer of an electronic record that would be a note under UCC Article 3 if it were in writing. The same framework applies to an electronic record that would be a document under Article 7 if it were in writing. As with electronic notes, an electronic document (warehouse receipt or bill of lading) is a "transferable record" under UETA only if the issuer of the electronic record expressly agrees that the record is to be considered a "transferable record." See UETA 16(a). A person can become the holder of a transferable record and acquire the same rights as a holder of an equivalent document under Article 7 by having "control" of the electronic record. Id. A person who has control and also satisfies the requirements of UCC 7–501 acquires the rights of a holder to whom a negotiable document of title has been duly negotiated ("HTWANDOTHBDN"). UETA 16(d). Revised Article 7 borrowed from the UETA structure and concepts. It provides explicitly that due negotiation of an electronic document of title can be effected through the voluntary transfer of "control." See R1–201(b)(15) (defining "delivery); R7–501(b) (due negotiation of electronic document of title); 7–106 (control of electronic document of title).

AMERICAN WAREHOUSE COMPANY
A PUBLIC WAREHOUSE
2121 AMERICAN AVENUE   •   AMERICA

Date of Issue __January 20, 1976__   Consecutive No. __432__

THIS IS TO CERTIFY that we have received in Storage Warehouse _____

situated at __2121 American Avenue__ _____

for the account of __O Company, Inc.__

in apparent good order, except as noted hereon (contents, condition and quality unknown) the following described property, subject to all the terms and conditions contained herein and on the reverse hereof, such property to be delivered to (His) (Their) (Its) order, upon payment of all storage, handling and other charges and the surrender of this Warehouse Receipt properly endorsed,

LOT NO.	QUANTITY	SAID TO BE OR CONTAIN	STORAGE PER MONTH		HANDLING IN AND OUT	
			RATE	PER	RATE	PER
3628	250 bales	Cotton	¢	bale	¢	bale

NEGOTIABLE

Quantities subject to deliveries noted below.

Advances have been made and liability incurred on such goods, as follows:

_____
_____
_____

The property covered by this receipt has NOT been insured by this company for the benefit of the depositor against fire or any other casualty.

(This clause to be omitted from forms used in those states where warehousemen are required by law to insure goods.)

American Warehouse Company claims a lien for all lawful charges for storage and preservation of the goods; also for all lawful claims for money advanced, interest, insurance, transportation, labor, weighing, coopering and other charges and expenses in relation to such goods.

AMERICAN WAREHOUSE COMPANY

By __John Jones__

John Jones, Vice President

THE GOODS MENTIONED BELOW ARE HEREBY RELEASED FROM THIS RECEIPT FOR DELIVERY FROM WAREHOUSE. ANY UNRELEASED BALANCE OF THE GOODS IS SUBJECT TO A LIEN FOR UNPAID CHARGES AND ADVANCES ON THE RELEASED PORTION.

DELIVERIES

DATE	LOT NUMBER	QUANTITY RELEASED		SIGNATURE	QUANTITY DUE ON RECEIPT
2/25/76	3628	50	bales	Henry Smith	200 bales

This Receipt Is Valid Only When Signed by an Officer of the Company.

NEGOTIABLE WAREHOUSE RECEIPT
[Front—Printed on Green Paper—Reduced in Size]

ORIGINAL
NON-NEGOTIABLE WAREHOUSE RECEIPT

AMERICAN WAREHOUSE COMPANY STREET ADDRESS • CITY & AMERICA 00000 TELEPHONE: (312) – 123-4567	

AMERICAN WAREHOUSE COMPANY claims a lien for all lawful charges for storage and preservation of the goods, also for all lawful claims for money advanced, interest, insurance, transportation, labor, weighing, coopering and other charges and expenses in relation to such goods, and for the balance on any other accounts that may be due. The property covered by this receipt has NOT been insured by this Company for the benefit of the depositor against fire or any other casualty.

DOCUMENT NUMBER	1046
DATE	Jan. 20, 1976
CUSTOMER NUMBER	8919
CUSTOMER ORDER NO.	
WAREHOUSE NO.	1046

O Company, Inc.
200 State Street
Statesville, New York

THIS IS TO CERTIFY THAT WE HAVE RECEIVED the goods listed hereon in apparent good order, except as noted herein (contents, condition and quality unknown). SUBJECT TO ALL TERMS AND CONDITIONS INCLUDING LIMITATION OF LIABILITY HEREIN AND ON THE REVERSE HEREOF. Such property to be delivered to THE DEPOSITOR upon the payment of all storage, handling and other charges. Advances have been made and liability incurred on these goods as follows.

O Company, Inc.
200 State Street
Statesville, New York

DELIVERING CARRIER	CARRIER NUMBER	PREPAID COLLECT	... NUMBER
PC	PC 458632	Prepaid	

QUANTITY	SAID TO BE OR CONTAIN (CUSTOMER ITEM NO., WAREHOUSE ITEM NO., LOT NUMBER, DESCRIPTION, ETC.)	WEIGHT	RATE	STORAGE RATE	HANDLING RATE	DAMAGE & EXCEPTIONS
250	bales cotton 500 lbs.	125,000		¢CS ¢CS		None
	TOTALS					

NO DELIVERY WILL BE MADE ON THIS RECEIPT EXCEPT ON WRITTEN ORDER.

AMERICAN WAREHOUSE COMPANY	
BY	John James
	AUTHORIZED SIGNATURE

(B2875)

NONNEGOTIABLE WAREHOUSE RECEIPT
[Front—Printed on White Paper—Reduced in Size]

The property described on this receipt is stored and handled in accordance with the terms and conditions of the Contract and Rate Quotation approved by the American Warehousemen's Association. These Contract and Rate Quotation terms and conditions are repeated below for the convenience of the storer and others having an interest in the property.

STANDARD CONTRACT TERMS AND CONDITIONS FOR MERCHANDISE WAREHOUSEMEN

(APPROVED AND PROMULGATED BY THE AMERICAN WAREHOUSEMEN'S ASSOCIATION, OCTOBER 1968)

ACCEPTANCE – Sec. 1

(a) This contract and rate quotation including accessorial charges endorsed on or attached hereto must be accepted within 30 days from the proposal date by signature of depositor on the reverse side of the contract. In the absence of written acceptance, the act of tendering goods described herein for storage or other services by warehouseman within 30 days from the proposal date shall constitute such acceptance by depositor.

(b) In the event that goods tendered for storage or other services do not conform to the description contained herein, or conforming goods are tendered after 30 days from the proposal date without prior written acceptance by depositor as provided in paragraph (a) of this section, warehouseman may refuse to accept such goods. If warehouseman accepts such goods, depositor agrees to rates and charges as may be assigned and invoiced by warehouseman and to all terms of this contract.

(c) This contract may be cancelled by either party upon 30 days written notice and is cancelled if no storage or other services are performed under this contract for a period of 180 days.

SHIPPING – Sec. 2

Depositor agrees not to ship goods to warehouseman as the named consignee. If, in violation of this agreement, goods are shipped to warehouseman as named consignee, depositor agrees to notify carrier in writing prior to such shipment, with copy of such notice to the warehouseman, that warehouseman named as consignee is a warehouseman and has no beneficial title or interest in such property and depositor further agrees to indemnify and hold harmless warehouseman from any and all claims for unpaid transportation charges, including undercharges, demurrage, detention or charges of any nature, in connection with goods so shipped. Depositor further agrees that, if it fails to notify carrier as required by the next preceding sentence, warehouseman shall have the right to refuse such goods and shall not be liable or responsible for any loss, injury or damage of any nature to, or related to, such goods. Depositor agrees that all promises contained in this section will be binding on depositor's heirs, successors and assigns

TENDER FOR STORAGE – Sec. 3

All goods for storage shall be delivered at the warehouse properly marked and packaged for handling. The depositor shall furnish at or prior to such delivery, a manifest showing marks, brands, or sizes to be kept and accounted for separately, and the class of storage and other services desired.

STORAGE PERIOD AND CHARGES – Sec. 4

(a) All charges for storage are per package or other agreed unit per month.

(b) Storage charges become applicable upon the date that warehouseman accepts care, custody and control of the goods, regardless of unloading date or date of issue of warehouse receipt.

(c) Except as provided in paragraph (d) of this section, a full month's storage charge will apply on all goods received between the first and the 15th, inclusive, of a calendar month; one-half month's storage charge will apply on all goods received between the 16th and last day, inclusive, of a calendar month, and a full month's storage charge will apply to all goods in storage on the first day of the next and succeeding calendar months. All storage charges are due and payable on the first day of storage for the initial month and thereafter on the first day of the calendar month.

(d) When mutually agreed by the warehouseman and the depositor, a storage month shall extend from a date in one calendar month to, but not including, the same date of the next and all succeeding month. All storage charges are due and payable on the first day of the storage month.

TRANSFER, TERMINATION OF STORAGE, REMOVAL OF GOODS – Sec. 5

(a) Instructions to transfer goods on the books of the warehouseman are not effective until delivered to and accepted by warehouseman, and all charges up to the time transfer is made are chargeable to the depositor of record. If a transfer involves rehanding the goods, such will be subject to a charge. When goods in storage are transferred from one party to another through issuance of a new warehouse receipt, a new storage date is established on the date of transfer.

(b) The warehouseman reserves the right to move, at his expense, 14 days after notice is sent by certified or registered mail to the depositor of record or to the last known holder of the negotiable warehouse receipt, any goods in storage from the warehouse in which they may be stored to any other of his warehouses; but if such depositor or holder takes delivery of his goods in lieu of transfer, no storage charge shall be made for the current storage month. The warehouseman may, without notice, move goods within the warehouse in which they are stored.

(c) The warehouseman may, upon written notice to the depositor of record and any other person known by the warehouseman to claim an interest in the goods, require the removal of any goods by the end of the next succeeding storage month. Such notice shall be given to the last known place of business or abode of the person to be notified. If goods are not removed before the end of the next succeeding storage month, the warehouseman may sell them in accordance with applicable law.

(d) If warehouseman in good faith believes that the goods are about to deteriorate or decline in value to less than the amount of warehouseman's lien before the end of the next succeeding storage month, the warehouseman may specify in the notification any reasonable shorter time for removal of the goods and in case the goods are not removed, may sell them at public sale held one week after a single advertisement or posting as provided by law.

NEGOTIABLE OR NONNEGOTIABLE WAREHOUSE RECEIPT

[Back—Printed on Same Color Paper as Front]

(e) If as a result of a quality or condition of the goods of which the warehouseman had no notice at the time of deposit the goods are a hazard to other property or to the warehouse or to persons, the warehouseman may sell the goods at public or private sale without advertisement on reasonable notification to all persons known to claim an interest in the goods. If the warehouseman after a reasonable effort is unable to sell the goods he may dispose of them in any lawful manner and shall incur no liability by reason of such disposition. Pending such disposition, sale or return of the goods, the warehouseman may remove the goods from the warehouse and shall incur no liability by reason of such removal.

HANDLING — Sec. 6

(a) The handling charge covers the ordinary labor involved in receiving goods at warehouse door, placing goods in storage, and returning goods to warehouse door. Handling charges are due and payable on receipt of goods.

(b) Unless otherwise agreed, labor for unloading and loading goods will be subject to a charge. Additional expenses incurred by the warehouseman in receiving and handling damaged goods, and additional expense in unloading from or loading into cars or other vehicles not at warehouse door will be charged to the depositor.

(c) Labor and materials used in loading rail cars or other vehicles are chargeable to the depositor.

(d) When goods are ordered out in quantities less than in which received, the warehouseman may make an additional charge for each order or each item of an order.

(e) The warehouseman shall not be liable for demurrage, delays in unloading inbound cars, or delays in obtaining and loading cars for outbound shipment unless warehouseman has failed to exercise reasonable care.

DELIVERY REQUIREMENTS — Sec. 7

(a) No goods shall be delivered or transferred except upon receipt by the warehouseman of complete instructions properly signed by the depositor. However, when no negotiable receipt is outstanding, goods may be delivered upon instructions by telephone in accordance with a prior written authorization, but the warehouseman shall not be responsible for loss or error occasioned thereby.

(b) When a negotiable receipt has been issued no goods covered by that receipt shall be delivered, or transferred on the books of the warehouseman, unless the receipt, properly indorsed, is surrendered for cancellation, or for indorsement of partial delivery thereon. If a negotiable receipt is lost or destroyed, delivery of goods may be made only upon order of a court of competent jurisdiction and the posting of security approved by the court as provided by law.

(c) When goods are ordered out a reasonable time shall be given the warehouseman to carry out instructions, and if he is unable because of act of God, war, public enemies, seizure under legal process, strikes, lockouts, riots and civil commotions, or any reason beyond the warehouseman's control, or because of loss or destruction of goods for which warehouseman is not liable, or because of any other excuse provided by law, the warehouseman shall not be liable for failure to carry out such instructions and goods remaining in storage will continue to be subject to regular storage charges.

EXTRA SERVICES (SPECIAL SERVICES) — Sec. 8

(a) Warehouse labor required for services other than ordinary handling and storage will be charged to the depositor.

(b) Special services requested by depositor including but not limited to compiling of special stock statements; reporting marked weights, serial numbers or other data from packages; physical check of goods, and handling transit billing will be subject to a charge.

(c) Dunnage, bracing, packing materials of other special supplies, may be provided for the depositor at a charge in addition to the warehouseman's cost.

(d) By prior arrangement, goods may be received or delivered during other than usual business hours, subject to a charge.

(e) Communication expense including postage, teletype, telegram, or telephone, will be charged to the depositor if such concern more than normal inventory reporting or if, at the request of the depositor, communications are made by other than regular United States Mail.

BONDED STORAGE — Sec. 9

(a) A charge in addition to regular rates will be made for merchandise in bond.

(b) Where a warehouse receipt covers goods in U. S. Customs bond, such receipt shall be void upon the termination of the storage period fixed by law.

MINIMUM CHARGES — Sec. 10

(a) A minimum handling charge per lot and a minimum storage charge per lot per month will be made. When a warehouse receipt covers more than one lot or when a lot is in assortment, a minimum charge per mark, brand, or variety will be made.

(b) A minimum monthly charge to one account for storage and/or handling will be made. This charge will apply also to each account when one customer has several accounts, each requiring separate records and billing.

LIABILITY AND LIMITATION OF DAMAGES — Sec. 11

(A) THE WAREHOUSEMAN SHALL NOT BE LIABLE FOR ANY LOSS OR INJURY TO GOODS STORED HOWEVER CAUSED UNLESS SUCH LOSS OR INJURY RESULTED FROM THE FAILURE BY THE WAREHOUSEMAN TO EXERCISE SUCH CARE IN REGARD TO THEM AS A REASONABLY CAREFUL MAN WOULD EXERCISE UNDER LIKE CIRCUMSTANCES AND WAREHOUSEMAN IS NOT LIABLE FOR DAMAGES WHICH COULD NOT HAVE BEEN AVOIDED BY THE EXERCISE OF SUCH CARE.

(B) GOODS ARE NOT INSURED BY WAREHOUSEMAN AGAINST LOSS OR INJURY HOWEVER CAUSED

(C) THE DEPOSITOR DECLARES THAT DAMAGES ARE LIMITED TO _____ . PROVIDED, HOWEVER, THAT SUCH LIABILITY MAY AT THE TIME OF ACCEPTANCE OF THIS CONTRACT AS PROVIDED IN SECTION I BE INCREASED ON PART OR ALL OF THE GOODS HEREUNDER IN WHICH EVENT A MONTHLY CHARGE OF _____ WILL BE MADE IN ADDITION TO THE REGULAR MONTHLY STORAGE CHARGE.

NOTICE OF CLAIM AND FILING OF SUIT — Sec. 12

(a) Claims by the depositor and all other persons must be presented in writing to the warehouseman within a reasonable time, and in no event longer than either 60 days after delivery of the goods by the warehouseman or 60 days after depositor of record or the last known holder of a negotiable warehouse receipt is notified by the warehouseman that loss or injury to part or all of the goods has occurred, whichever time is shorter.

(b) No action may be maintained by the depositor or others against the warehouseman for loss or injury to the goods stored unless timely written claim has been given as provided in paragraph (a) of this section and unless such action is commenced either within nine months after date of delivery by warehouseman or within nine months after depositor of record or the last known holder of a negotiable warehouse receipt is notified that loss or injury to part or all of the goods has occurred, whichever time is shorter.

(c) When goods have not been delivered, notice may be given of known loss or injury in the goods by mailing of a registered or certified letter to the depositor of record or to the last known holder of a negotiable warehouse receipt. Time limitations for presentation of claim in writing and maintaining of action after notice begin on the date of mailing of such notice by warehouseman

[B2874]

NEGOTIABLE OR NONNEGOTIABLE WAREHOUSE RECEIPT
[Back—Printed on Same Color Paper as Front]

A warehouse receipt embodying the obligation of the bailee to deliver goods has some similarity to a promissory note embodying the obligation of the maker to pay money. After you have worked through the following three Problems, consider the following: To what extent are the rules applicable to the transfer of warehouse receipts similar to those applicable to the transfer of negotiable instruments calling for the payment of money? To what extent are they similar to those applicable to the transfer of the goods themselves? To what extent must a person acquire the status of HTWANDOTHBDN in order to take free of claims to the goods and defenses of the warehouse? To what extent does such a holder enjoy the same freedom from claims and defenses as a holder in due course?

Problem 1.5.1. A warehouse receipt covering 600 barrels of whiskey was issued to "Old Soak Beverage Company or order." In preparation for a proposed sale of the whiskey to another company, the president of Old Soak (*A*) indorsed the Company's name on the receipt. That night, Sal Sly (*B*), an ambitious bookkeeper, arranged to work late and took the receipt from the vault. Sly delivered the receipt to a friend in the liquor business (*C*), who sold and delivered the receipt to DT Beverage Company (*D*) for $120,000 cash (the fair market value). Both Sly and the friend disappeared.

(a) Who has the better claim to the whiskey? See UCC 7–104; UCC 7–502; UCC 7–501.

(b) Suppose *D* is Downtown Bank, which took the receipt to secure a new $25,000 loan. Is *A*'s claim of ownership of the whiskey superior to *D* 's security interest in it? Would the answer change if *D* took the warehouse receipt to secure a preexisting, unsecured loan?

(c) What result if *B*, rather than *C*, sold and delivered the warehouse receipt to DT Beverage Company? See UCC 7–501(4) and Comment 1; UCC 7–504. Does the statutory text adequately support the Comment?

(d) Suppose that *A*'s president had not endorsed the document, but that *B* supplied a clever imitation of the president's signature. Is *A* or *D* entitled to the whiskey? See UCC 7–502(1) ("negotiated"); UCC 7–501(1) ("*his* indorsement"); UCC 7–504.

(e) Suppose that the warehouse receipt ran "for the account of Old Soak Beverage Company." Is *A* or *D* entitled to the whiskey? See UCC 7–504.

Problem 1.5.2. Old Soak Beverage Company (*A*) instructed Dale Driver (*B*), one of its truck drivers, to haul 100 barrels of whiskey from Old Soak's warehouse to the bottling works. Instead, Driver hauled the whiskey to Waiting Warehouse Company, stored the whiskey, and took a warehouse receipt deliverable to "Dale Driver or order." Driver then indorsed and delivered the warehouse receipt to Creative Finance Company (*C*) to secure a previously unsecured note. Driver is unable to pay the note, and both Creative Finance and Old Soak claim the whiskey.

(a) Who prevails? See UCC 7–502; UCC 7–503; UCC 7–504; Note on Authority and Power of Disposition, infra.

(b) What result if Driver had negotiated the receipt to a friend in the liquor business, who had negotiated it to Creative Finance?

Problem 1.5.3. While its own warehouse was being refurbished, Old Soak Beverage Company (*A*) temporarily stored several hundred barrels of whiskey with *B*, a competitor. Without Old Soak's consent, *B* delivered the goods to Waiting Warehouse Company, which issued a negotiable warehouse receipt to "*B* or order."

(a) *B* indorsed and delivered the receipt to DT Beverage Company (*C*), which promised to pay fair value for the whiskey in 30 days and did not suspect *B*'s wrongdoing. Who has the better claim to the whiskey, *A* or *C*? Would the answer change if the warehouse receipt were nonnegotiable?

(b) What result if *B* indorsed and delivered the negotiable warehouse receipt to Downtown Bank, which took the receipt to secure a new loan and did not suspect *B*'s wrongdoing? Would the answer change if the warehouse receipt were nonnegotiable?

(c) Compare your answers to this Problem with your answers to Problem 1.3.8, supra. Can you account for the differences in result?

NOTE ON AUTHORITY AND POWER OF DISPOSITION

Problem 1.5.2 invites you to consider, inter alia, whether Driver had "actual or apparent authority to ship, store or sell" the whiskey. UCC 7–503(1)(a). The Restatement (Second) of Agency (1958) does not use the term "actual authority," preferring instead the term "authority," which section 7 defines as "the power of the agent to affect the legal relations of the principal by acts done in accordance with the principal's manifestations of consent to him." The proposed Restatement (Third) of Agency (Tentative Draft No. 2, 2001) provides that "[a]n agent acts with actual authority when, at the time of taking action that has legal consequences for the principal, the agent reasonably believes, in accordance with the principal's manifestations to the agent, that the principal wishes the agent so to act." What is the least authority that would empower Driver to pass good title under UCC 7–502 and 7–503? Consider: (i) authority to transport the whiskey to Old Soak's warehouse; (ii) authority to transport the whiskey to Waiting Warehouse; (iii) authority to deliver the whiskey to a named purchaser; (iv) authority to complete a sale to a named purchaser at a named price.

The near demise of law school courses in Agency makes it desirable to underline the limited applicability of the term "apparent authority" in UCC 7–503(1)(a). According to comment *a* to section 8 of the Restatement (Second) of Agency, "[a]pparent authority results from a manifestation by a person that another is his agent, the manifestation being made to a third person and not, as when authority is created, to the agent." The illustrations to that section give this example:

P writes to A directing him to act as his agent for the sale of Blackacre. P sends a copy of this letter to T, a prospective purchaser. . . . [I]n the letter to A, P adds a postscript, not included in the copy to T, telling A to make no sale until after communication with P. A has no authority to sell Blackacre but, as to T, he has apparent authority.

The proposed Restatement (Third) of Agency (Tentative Draft No. 2, 2001) provides that "[a]pparent authority is the power held by an agent or other actor to affect a principal's legal relations with third parties when a third party reasonably believes the actor has authority to act on behalf of the principal and that belief is traceable to the principal's manifestations."

Does the notion of "apparent authority" extend to the situations covered by the "entrusting" provision of UCC 2–403(2), discussed in Section 3(C), supra? Even if it does not, "power of disposition" under UCC 2–403 affords an alternative ground for depriving a person of its ownership interest or security interest in the goods when that interest comes in conflict with a claim of a HTWANDOTHBDN. UCC 2–403(2) affords a merchant to whom goods have been entrusted and who deals in goods of that kind the "power to transfer all rights of the entruster to a buyer in ordinary course of business." As the Notes on Entrustment, pp. 41 ff., supra, suggest, the merchant does not enjoy the power to transfer the entruster's rights to other (non-buyer) purchasers. Does UCC 7–503(1)(a) expand this "power of disposition"? Should it?

Note that even if *B* (in Problems 1.5.2 and 1.5.3) has "actual or apparent authority" or "power of disposition," Old Soak is not necessarily out of luck. See UCC 7–501(4).

NOTES ON THE SCOPE OF THE WAREHOUSE'S RESPONSIBILITY

(1) Non–Receipt and Misdescription of Goods. What risks does a secured party take when its collateral consists of goods covered by a document of title? The problems in this section address the risk of competing claims to documents of title and priority conflicts. But there are other risks. For example, what if the warehouse never received the goods that the document purports to cover (called "non-receipt")? What if the goods are not as described in the warehouse receipt (called "misdescription")? Under UCC 7–203, a warehouse is liable in damages to a party to a warehouse receipt or to a good faith purchaser for value of the warehouse receipt in the case non-receipt or misdescription. Note that UCC 7–203 works in favor of all good faith purchasers for value, whether or not the purchaser takes by due negotiation and even if the warehouse receipt is nonnegotiable.

What UCC 7–203 gives may easily be taken away. UCC 7–203 provides that the warehouse is not liable to the extent that the warehouse receipt "conspicuously indicates that the issuer does not know whether any part or all of the goods in fact were received or conform to the description," but only if "such indication be true." The section also provides examples of such conspicuous indications, including "'contents, condition, and quality unknown'." These disclaimers are standard. For example, examine again the front pages of the warehouse receipts on pages 60 and 61 and note the exculpatory language. Damages also will not be available if the party or purchaser "otherwise has notice" of the non-receipt or misdescription.

To the extent a warehouse makes a conspicuous disclaimer on the warehouse's receipt that is effective under UCC 7–203, and the disclaimer is true, a party or purchaser cannot recover from the warehouse. As an alternative to seeking recovery from the warehouse, a purchaser can seek damages from its transferor for breach of warranty under UCC 7–507. Of course, if the transferor is insolvent or judgment-proof, that claim may have little value.

In many situations, the *liability* of a warehouse may be much less of an issue than the effectiveness of a limitation in the warehouse receipt on the *amount* for which A may be liable. See, e.g., Section 11(C) of the form of warehouse receipt (p. 62). Typically, damages are limited to amounts that are nominal in comparison with the value of stored goods. However, such limitations are not "effective with respect to the warehouseman's liability for conversion to his own use." UCC 7–204(2) (2d sentence).

(2) Liability When Goods "Disappear": I.C.C. Metals v. Municipal Warehouse. Under UCC 7–204, a warehouse is liable for loss of (or injury to) the goods caused by its failure to exercise reasonable care but is not liable for damages that could not have been avoided by the exercise of such care. Observe that this section does not limit the universe of potential plaintiffs to holders to whom negotiable warehouse receipts have been duly negotiated or even to holders of negotiable warehouse receipts. Note as well that the standard of care imposed by UCC 7–204(1) cannot be disclaimed. UCC 1–302 [F1–102(3)].

Although the burden of going forward with evidence normally rests on the plaintiff (here, the bailor), a number of cases applying UCC 7–204 have imposed this burden on the defendant warehouse. Of particular interest is I.C.C. Metals, Inc. v. Municipal Warehouse Co., 50 N.Y.2d 657, 431 N.Y.S.2d 372, 409 N.E.2d 849 (1980), in which a commercial warehouse informed the bailor, an international metals trader, that it was unable to locate three lots (845 pounds) of an industrial metal called indium that it had taken for storage. The bailor commenced an action in conversion, seeking to recover the value of the indium, $100,000. The warehouse contended that the metal had been stolen through no fault of its own and that, in any event, the terms of the warehouse receipt limited the bailor's potential recovery to a maximum of $50 per lot, or $150. (The limitation complied with UCC 7–204(2).)

The trial court granted summary judgment for the bailor for the full value of the metal. It found that the bailor had made out a prima facie case of conversion by proffering undisputed proof that the indium had been delivered to the warehouse and that the warehouse had failed to return it upon a proper demand. The court concluded that the warehouse's contention that the metal had been stolen was completely speculative and that the warehouse had failed to raise any question of fact sufficient to warrant a trial on the issue. Finally, the trial court held that the contractual limitation upon liability was inapplicable to a conversion action. The Appellate Division affirmed, as did the Court of Appeals.

The Court of Appeals observed that UCC 7–204 contemplates that "a warehouse which fails to redeliver goods to the person entitled to their return upon a proper demand, may be liable for either negligence or conversion, depending upon the circumstances." Moreover, "although the merely careless bailee remains a bailee and is entitled to whatever limitations of liability the bailor has agreed to, the converter forsakes his status as bailee completely and accordingly forfeits the protections of such limitations." See UCC 7–204(2).

In negligence cases, the established rule in New York is that once the plaintiff proffers proof of delivery to the defendant warehouse, of a proper demand for its return, and of the warehouse's failure to honor the demand, then "the warehouse must come forward and explain the circumstances of the loss of or damage to the bailed goods upon pain of being held liable for negligence." For the first time, the court unambiguously applied the same burden-shifting rule to conversion cases. Thus, unless the warehouse comes forward with "an explanation supported by evidentiary proof in admissible form," the plaintiff will not be required to prove that the warehouse converted the goods.

Applying this rule to the explanation presented by the warehouse, the court stated the following in a footnote:

> Viewed most favorably to defendant, this evidence would indicate at most that theft by a third party was one possible explanation for the defendant's failure to redeliver the indium to plaintiff. This is simply insufficient, since the warehouse is required to show not merely what might conceivably have happened to the goods, but rather what actually happened to the goods. Defendant proved only that theft was possible, and presented no proof of an actual theft. Hence, the proffered explanation was inadequate as a matter of law.

409 N.E.2d at 853 n.3. The bailor having made a prima facie case of conversion and the warehouse having failed to present an adequate explanation, the bailor was entitled to summary judgment. Inasmuch as judgment was entered for conversion, rather than for negligence, the contractual limitation of damages became ineffective, see UCC 7–204(2) (2d sentence), and the bailor became entitled to recover the actual value of the missing indium.

A dissenting opinion accused the majority of "eras[ing] the critical distinction between negligence and conversion" and "doing violence to the law, without rhyme or reason." What policy considerations support imposing on the warehouse the burden of going forward with an explanation of what happened to the goods when *negligence* is alleged? Do these considerations support the two principal rulings in *I.C.C. Metals* : (i) permitting a plaintiff to sustain a *conversion* action without proving any intentional wrongdoing by the defendant and (ii) rendering ineffective a contractual limitation on liability entered into between two commercial parties? In practical effect, how far removed is the approach in *I.C.C. Metals* from the imposition of absolute liability on the warehouse? Is the result consistent with the standard of "care" in UCC 7–204(1)? Judicial response to *I.C.C. Metals* has been mixed.

(3) The Great "Salad Oil Swindle." Questions of warehouse responsibility *in excelsis* arose in connection with the 1963 disappearance from **field warehouse** tanks in Bayonne, New Jersey, of over a billion pounds of vegetable oils—one of the great commercial frauds of modern times. Leading banks in the United States and Britain had made loans totaling $150 million "secured" by warehouse receipts for oil for which the bailee was unable to account. See Procter & Gamble Distrib. Co. v. Lawrence American Field Warehousing Corp., 16 N.Y.2d 344, 266 N.Y.S.2d 785, 213 N.E.2d 873 (1965); N. Miller, The Great Salad Oil Swindle (1965); Brooks, Annals of Finance: Making the Customer Whole, The New Yorker, Nov. 14, 1964, at 160.

(4) Warehouses, Carriers, and Statutory Interpretation. An interesting (and puzzling) contrast is presented by the UCC's language on the responsibility of warehouses (UCC 7–204) and the provision on the responsibility of carriers (UCC 7–309). Subsection 4 of UCC 7–204 states: "This section does not impair or repeal . . ." and leaves a blank for the preservation of *named* statutes that may impose a higher responsibility on the warehouse. On the other hand, UCC 7–309(1) on the responsibility of carriers, after articulating the "reasonably careful man" test, adds: "This subsection does not repeal or change any law *or rule of law* which imposes liability upon a common carrier for damages not caused by its negligence" (emphasis added). The phrase "rule of law" (as contrasted with the reference to specific statutes in UCC 7–204) provides access to (and possibly development of) the broad common-law liability of carriers as insurers of goods.[2] Do the reasons that led to the absolute liability of carriers apply to warehouses? Does the difference between the approaches of these two sections of the UCC bar the extension by analogy of absolute liability to warehouses? Would the failure of a warehouse to carry insurance protecting both itself and the owner constitute a default in the "reasonable care" standard? If so, should the net result be simplified by a change in the language of the UCC?

In the drafting of statutory provisions like those of Article 7, who are likely to be more vocal—warehouses or those who may store goods with warehouses? In construing statutes that are reasonably susceptible to two interpretations, should courts give voice to those who are less vocal during the legislative process? Cf. Restatement (Second) of Contracts § 206 (1981) ("In choosing among the reasonable meanings of a promise or agreement or

---

2.   Federal law codifies the common-law liability of certain carriers for loss or injury to goods in interstate shipments, imports, and exports. See 49 U.S.C. §§ 11706, 14706 (imposing liability for "actual loss or injury to the property caused by" certain carriers). For certain carriers, the remedies provided "are in addition to remedies existing under another law or common law." 49 U.S.C. § 13103.

a term thereof, that meaning is generally preferred which operates against the party who supplies the words or from whom a writing otherwise proceeds."). Or should courts assume that the squeaky wheel got the grease and construe the statute to favor the "prevailing" interests?

CHAPTER 2

INTRODUCTION TO SECURED FINANCING

The remainder of this book deals primarily with consumers and businesses that need credit and the lenders and credit sellers who extend credit to them. In particular, the focus is on transactions in which creditors obtain consensual liens—"security interests"—on personal property (both goods and intangibles). Chapter 1's treatment of basic precepts of personal property law—security of property and good faith purchase, in particular—considers the rights of secured creditors as purchasers of personal property. This Chapter takes a broader and more systematic view of secured credit. Section 1 describes the contexts in which extensions of credit take place and the patterns and participants involved. Section 2 provides an overview of the principal statute that regulates security interests, Article 9 of the Uniform Commercial Code. Finally, Section 3 considers the variety of roles lawyers play in secured transactions.

SECTION 1. SECURED FINANCING IN CONTEXT

(A) UNSECURED AND SECURED CREDIT

Although the following materials focus primarily on the legal regulation of secured credit, the legal regime can be understood only by approaching secured credit as a subset of credit extensions generally. Why is credit sought and given? The likely intuitive answer of most North American consumers would be essentially correct: Both consumers and businesses need funds, goods, or services *now*, not later, and often they choose to enjoy the fruits of credit while paying over time. Creditors extend credit not only to increase profit directly, by earning interest, but also indirectly, by increasing the sale of their goods and services.

Many of the problems in this part of the book focus on the Prototype transaction described in Chapter 3, Section 1, infra. As you will see, the Prototype includes detailed examples of both consumer and business credit transactions. In the Prototype, Lee Abel purchased a new car from Main Motors under an **installment purchase** arrangement. After making a down payment (consisting of a trade-in), Abel signed an agreement containing a promise to pay the balance of the purchase price, plus **carrying charges** (comparable to interest charges on a loan) and certain other charges. Main Motors, on the other hand, itself required financing in order to buy the car that it sold to Abel as well as the other automobiles in its inventory. On average, Main Motors maintains an inventory of automobiles that cost (wholesale) about $3,500,000; it does not have capital sufficient to enable it to invest that much money for extended periods. Consequently, Main buys automobiles with funds that it borrows from Firstbank.

In the Prototype, Lee Abel granted a security interest in the new car to Main Motors in order to secure the obligations under the installment purchase contract. Similarly, Main Motors granted a security interest in its automobile inventory to Firstbank in order to secure its obligation to repay the loan. Although it is clear enough why Abel and Main Motors needed credit, why was the credit given to Abel and Main *secured,* as opposed to *unsecured,* credit? Before venturing an answer to that question, one must consider three aspects of secured and unsecured credit: (i) enforcement against the borrower or buyer (the "debtor"), (ii) priorities among creditors and buyers competing to satisfy their claims from the same property of the debtor, and (iii) enforcement of the security interest in a bankruptcy proceeding of the debtor.

We saw in Chapter 1 that a secured creditor with an Article 9 security interest has the right to satisfy its claim against the debtor from the collateral (the property subject to the security interest). The Article 9 secured party's rights include the right to take possession of the collateral upon the debtor's default in payment or performance of the obligation secured. See UCC 9–609. We also considered the more limited rights of unsecured creditors; unsecured creditors have *no* property rights in the debtor's property. Their remedies generally depend on first obtaining a judgment against the debtor and subsequently obtaining a lien through the judicial process. Only at that time would a formerly unsecured creditor become secured by the **judicial lien**. See Chapter 1, Section 1, supra.[1]

In general, an Article 9 secured party can acquire rights in the debtor's personal property that are senior to later-in-time secured creditors (including judicial lien creditors) and buyers. (Note, however, that much of Article 9—and consequently much of these materials—is concerned with conditions, qualifications, and exceptions to this generalization.) An unsecured creditor, on the other hand, is subject to the "race of diligence"—it generally is junior to earlier-in-time secured creditors and must obtain a judicial lien in order to take priority over later-in-time secured creditors. See Chapter 1, Section 1, supra.

How does a debtor's bankruptcy affect security interests and other liens? Bankruptcy law is complex and interesting enough to be the subject of a separate course. Although the following brief overview of bankruptcy is

---

1. The rights of other kinds of secured creditors, such as holders of **statutory liens** and mortgagees of real property (land and buildings), vary enormously according to the law of each state. Those creditors may enforce some of their rights against the debtor's property only through judicial proceedings.

greatly simplified, it will suffice for our immediate purposes. Chapter 7 details many of the ways in which a debtor's bankruptcy affects Article 9 secured parties.

The substantive law of bankruptcy is contained in the federal Bankruptcy Code (title 11, U.S. Code). Enacted in 1978, the Bankruptcy Code superseded the Bankruptcy Act of 1898, which had been amended many times and substantially overhauled in 1938. The filing of a petition by or against a debtor commences a bankruptcy case (see BC 301; BC 302(a); BC 303(b)), and creates an "estate" comprised of all the legal and equitable interests of the debtor in property as of the commencement of the case. BC 541(a). When the petition is filed under Chapter 7 of the Bankruptcy Code, which contemplates liquidating the debtor's nonexempt assets and distributing the proceeds to creditors, the United States trustee[2] appoints an interim trustee, who will continue to serve as *the* trustee in bankruptcy unless the creditors elect another person to the position. See BC 701; BC 702.

The bankruptcy trustee is a representative of creditors, primarily unsecured creditors. The trustee is charged with the duty, inter alia, of collecting and reducing to money the property of the estate and distributing the money to creditors. See BC 704. The Bankruptcy Code affords to the trustee the power to avoid (i.e., undo) certain valid prebankruptcy transactions, including those that have the effect of improperly preferring one creditor to another and those that are fraudulent. See generally BC 544–548; Chapter 7, infra.

Chapter 11 cases contemplate that the debtor's enterprise will be reorganized; that is, the enterprise will continue and the claims against the debtor will be scaled down or extended or both. In Chapter 11, the debtor's management ordinarily remains in control of the enterprise as the "debtor in possession." A trustee normally is appointed only when management has been guilty of fraud, dishonesty, incompetence, or gross mismanagement. See BC 1104(a). The debtor in possession enjoys the avoiding powers of a trustee. See BC 1107(a).

One important, and immediate, effect of a bankruptcy filing is the automatic stay of virtually all activities of creditors directed toward collection of their debts. See BC 362(a). This means that the state law "race of diligence" for unsecured creditors ends when the debtor enters bankruptcy.

Except for some special priority rules for certain types of claims, unsecured creditors share pro rata in their common debtor's bankruptcy. In contrast, federal bankruptcy law generally respects a secured creditor's

---

2.   The Attorney General appoints one United States trustee and one or more assistant United States trustees for each of 21 regions. See 28 U.S.C. §§ 581; 582. The United States trustee serves for a term of five years and, like the assistants, is subject to removal by the Attorney General. Id.

claim to the value of its collateral. The following example may assist in comparing the treatment of secured and unsecured claims in bankruptcy:[3]

> A debtor in a bankruptcy case has three creditors, each owed $100, for a total of $300 of debt. One creditor is secured by $100 of assets (i.e., fully secured), and the other two creditors are unsecured. The debtor's trustee in bankruptcy sells all the assets for cash and, after payment of all fees and expenses, $150 in cash (of which $100 is attributable to the property that was subject to the security interest) remains. What result? The fully secured creditor would have its claim satisfied in full, leaving $50 to be distributed between the two remaining creditors, each of which claims $100. Each unsecured creditor, then, would receive a distribution of $25 or "25 cents on the dollar," i.e., $50 (assets) ÷ $200 (claims).

Given these obvious advantages of secured credit for creditors, it is easy to see why in the Prototype Main Motors and Firstbank preferred to have a security interest in collateral. Because Abel's purchase of a new automobile and Main Motors' automobile inventory purchases represent very large dollar amounts when compared with their respective net worths and incomes, they had little choice but to agree to give collateral as a condition to obtaining the credit. Virtually all consumer automobile installment financing and automobile dealer inventory financing is done on a secured basis. Even if unsecured credit had been available, the absence of collateral could have resulted in a much higher interest rate to compensate the extenders of credit for the additional risk.

These observations lead to yet other questions: Why do some creditors extend unsecured credit? By conferring senior status (in and out of bankruptcy) on Firstbank, would Main Motors' unsecured creditors charge higher interest rates that would offset any reductions in interest rates paid by Main Motors to Firstbank as a result of providing collateral? Suffice it to observe, for now, that factors such as disparities in bargaining power and information, profit margins of sellers of goods and providers of services on unsecured credit, the relative size and duration of credit extensions, the costs of creating secured financings, disparities among creditors in their ability to monitor the debtor's financial activities and use of collateral, and market competition all serve to explain current financing patterns, to be addressed shortly, which involve a mix of secured and unsecured credit.

A related question should be raised here, although its answer must be deferred. A positive explanation of why debtors sometimes give and creditors sometimes take secured credit under current law does not provide a normative justification for the advantages the current legal regime affords to secured claims. Secured credit imposes costs, particularly on the hapless unsecured creditors of a financially distressed debtor. As we shall see, whether and how the social benefits conferred by secured credit can justify those costs has inspired a lively scholarly debate. See Chapter 8, Section 5, infra.

---

3. The treatment of secured claims in bankruptcy is dealt with in detail in Chapter 7, infra.

Although collateral provides important advantages for a creditor, its significance in the extension of credit should not be overemphasized. For example, a lawyer who thinks that the security interest is the most important part of a credit transaction will be corrected quickly by a banker or merchant. From the point of view of a lender or seller, the most important safeguard for the credit is the likelihood that the debtor will pay voluntarily. Evaluation of this likelihood requires mature judgment of the debtor's character, ability, and financial status, and sometimes of the business outlook generally. Recourse to the most ironclad security interest is sure to be costly. Executives and lawyers must spend valuable time to enforce the security interest (perhaps fighting off claims of other creditors in the process) and dispose of such diverse collateral as steel, oil, cattle, and blouses—unwieldy merchandise for a banker, whose stock in trade is money. Indeed, enforcement of a security interest in collateral represents a serious breakdown of the financing operation, whose profit depends on a rapid and routine flow of money. Creditors regard the opportunity to enforce a security interest with something of the zest with which a merchant regards the opportunity to file a claim under an insurance policy.

This does not suggest that security arrangements are without value or that bankers and merchants so regard them. The most canny banker or credit manager makes errors in judgment; business conditions shift. While recourse to security ranks far below voluntary payment, it stands well above loss of the entire claim or receipt of a small dividend at the conclusion of extended bankruptcy proceedings. In addition, in consumer transactions the security device often is used as leverage against the debtor. The threat of depriving the debtor of goods that he or she needs or prizes (such as a refrigerator or an automobile) often encourages "voluntary" payment, even though the used goods would realize little for the creditor upon sale. In 1985 the Federal Trade Commission sought to limit the "hostage value" of certain consumer collateral by prohibiting as an unfair trade practice the taking of security interests in household goods unless the secured party maintains possession of the collateral or has extended the credit that enabled the debtor to acquire it. See FTC Rule on Credit Practices, 16 C.F.R. § 444.2(a)(4).

(B) PATTERNS OF FINANCING

Recent decades witnessed profound changes in the patterns of consumer and business financing and in the financial services industry generally. Nonetheless, some useful generalizations about financing patterns remain possible.

Unsecured Consumer Credit. "Consumer credit" generally refers to credit extended to natural persons for personal, family, or household purposes. Much consumer credit is unsecured. Examples are credit extended pursuant to bank and other **lender credit card** arrangements,[4] credit extended by department stores and gasoline companies under **seller credit cards** or charge accounts,[5] and personal or **signature loans** extended by finance companies, banks, thrift institutions, and credit unions. Consumer credit usually is extended with the expectation that it will be repaid from the consumer's future earnings, an expectation often based on satisfactory credit reports obtained from private credit reporting services.

Unsecured Business Credit; Trade Credit. Many business borrowers also obtain unsecured credit. The most creditworthy corporations issue short-term (i.e., 30–to 90–day) debt instruments known as **commercial paper**. Holders of these instruments who wish to dispose of them before they become due can trade (sell) them in a secondary market. As long as the issuer's credit remains satisfactory (according to **rating agencies** such as Moody's and Standard & Poor's), the debt typically is repaid by issuing and selling new commercial paper as the old paper matures. Corporations also issue longer-term debt securities (**bonds** or **debentures**), many of which are publicly traded.

Creditworthy business borrowers obtain both medium-and long-term financing from commercial banks, as well. Bank credit is extended in a variety of forms. Arrangements known as **revolving credits** ("revolvers") allow a borrower to borrow, repay, and reborrow amounts as needed during an agreed time period, provided that the aggregate unpaid amount of loans does not at any time exceed the agreed cap. Some revolvers obligate the bank to extend loans (a **committed credit facility**), subject to certain conditions precedent (such as the absence of any default by the borrower). Others create a **line of credit**, pursuant to which the lending bank is not obligated to lend. The line of credit agreement ("line letter") governs the terms and conditions of the loans that the borrower requests and the lender, in its discretion, elects to make from time to time. Loans outstanding under lines of credit often are to be repaid on the lender's demand or within a relatively short time following demand. Under other credit arrangements, known as **term loans**, the loan advances are to be paid back in installments over a period of time.[6] Some revolvers automatically convert into term loans after a specified period of time, such as two or three years.

---

4. Charges made pursuant to lender credit cards constitute loans by the card issuer to the cardholder. The loans are advanced when the card issuer pays, or becomes obligated to pay, the merchant who accepts the credit card in connection with the sale of goods or services.

5. Some "private label" credit cards nominally issued by sellers of goods actually are issued by third-party lenders who may or may not be affiliated with the seller. Also, some credit cards and charge account arrangements provide that the seller receives a security interest in goods sold to secure the price.

6. Many term loans also are made by insurance companies, although the transactions usually are structured as a purchase of a note by the insurance company—a "private placement."

Bank credit agreements typically contain provisions dealing with (i) the amount of credit, interest rate, commitment fee, repayment terms, and the like; (ii) conditions precedent to lending (in committed facilities); (iii) affirmative covenants (e.g., the borrower will comply with the law, pay all taxes, give financial statements to the lender periodically); (iv) negative covenants (e.g., the borrower will not incur debt or create security interests except within agreed limits, will not merge with another entity, will not sell substantially all of its assets); (v) events of default (e.g., bankruptcy, nonpayment of the loan when due, default on debt owed to another lender); and (vi) remedies (e.g., acceleration of entire amount of loan).

For most businesses, the banks, finance companies, and other professional lenders are not the most significant source of short-term credit. Instead, the most important providers of short-term credit are other businesses that typically give extended terms (usually 30 to 90 days) for payment for goods and services—**trade credit**.[7] Most businesses not only receive trade credit in their purchases of goods and services but also grant trade credit in connection with sales of their own goods and services. Principal advantages of trade credit are its general availability and the absence of costly negotiations or formalities associated with longer-term arrangements such as bank credits. From the standpoint of the trade creditor, the credit extensions facilitate the sales of goods and services to those who are not in a position to pay cash or who otherwise would patronize a competitor.

Secured Financing of Sales of Goods. As we have seen, unsecured credit is common and important in both the consumer and the business environments. We shall see, next, that the same can be said of secured credit. We turn first to secured financing in its most familiar (at least to consumers) and historically significant role—secured credit extended to buyers of goods (including consumer goods, equipment used in business, and inventory held for sale or lease).

Consumer Goods. Lee Abel was not unique in entering into a secured installment purchase of a car; most automobiles are sold on a secured, installment basis. Consider the volume of consumer credit extended in the United States. By year-end 1999, outstanding consumer credit obligations stood at over $1,460 billion, with more than one-half of that amount being automobile and other installment credit.[8] This staggering figure is even more startling when compared with $4.5 billion in 1939, $15 billion in 1951,

---

7.   Of course, many consumers also receive short-term, unsecured credit from businesses such as the electric company, lawn care service, plumber, cable TV company, and newspaper delivery service.

8.   Fed. Res. Stat. Rel. G19 (August 7, 2000). The figure includes both secured and unsecured credit; however, consumer automobile financing typically involves secured credit. Also, the figure includes installment credit extended in connection with services; it is not limited to goods-related credit.

and $750 billion in 1990.[9] Increases in these figures reflect both inflation and the expansion of the economy.[10] For example, annual disposable income rose from $226.1 billion in 1951 to $6.775 trillion in 1999, an increase of more than 2,900%.[11] But in 1951 installment credit was equal to approximately 6.6% of disposable income; and in 1999 the percentage was 21%.[12] United States consumers obviously have been increasingly willing to encumber their future earnings.

In the case of consumer goods, secured credit commonly is extended by the seller (dealer), who retains a security interest in the goods to secure payment of the purchase price (or the balance of the price remaining after a down payment). Because dealers usually prefer to obtain the sale price immediately after the sale, rather than in installments over time, dealers commonly enter into an arrangement with a provider of secured financing, such as a bank or finance company, whereby the dealer assigns to the provider the buyer's payment obligation and the security interest and the provider pays the dealer the unpaid portion of the purchase price for the goods. To facilitate this arrangement, which is similar to the automobile chattel paper financing discussed in Chapter 3, Section 1, infra, the financing party usually supplies the dealer with the form of credit application and retail installment sale-security agreement and often approves the consumer's credit before the dealer makes the sale. The Prototype transaction presents the entire operation (secured sale by the dealer and assignment to the provider of financing) in greater detail in the concrete setting of automobile financing. When expensive consumer goods, such as motor vehicles and boats, are involved, it is not unusual for a third-party lender to make a secured loan directly to the buyer to cover a substantial portion of the purchase price. For example, instead of obtaining credit from Main Motors, Abel might have obtained a secured purchase-money loan from Abel's regular bank: the bank would have provided funds for the specific purpose of enabling Abel to pay for the new car, and Abel would have secured the repayment obligation by giving the bank a security interest in the new car.

An increasingly varied group of creditors holds consumer installment credit obligations. Probably the most significant trend during the last several decades has been the growing dominance of commercial banks in the installment credit market. More recently, deregulation has permitted savings institutions to enter the consumer installment credit market.

---

9. 77 Fed. Res. Bull., May, 1991, at A38, A53; 42 Fed. Res. Bull., Dec., 1956, at 1352, 1370.

10. The dollar amounts mentioned in this paragraph have not been adjusted to take account of inflation, but nonetheless suffice to illustrate substantial increases and expansion.

11. Bur. of Econ. Anal., Surv. of Curr. Bus. 46 (August 2000); 42 Fed. Res. Bull., Dec., 1956, at 1352, 1370.

12. 86 Fed. Res. Bull. 624, Sept., 2000, at 624; 42 Fed. Res. Bull., Dec., 1956, at 1352, 1370.

Perhaps the most striking aspect of Table 2.1 is the amount of the installment credit obligations held in "pools of securitized assets."[13] By 1990 almost 10% of the obligations were held in these "pools," although this category of holdings was not even listed in the 1982 figures. And by 2004 that share had grown to almost 30%. The following table reflects the shifting market shares in the consumer installment credit market.[14]

TABLE 2.1

Type of Institution	Credits Outstanding (In Millions)						
	1950	1960	1970	1982	1990	2000	2004
Commercial Banks	5798	16672	45398	152069	351695	554000	697400
Finance Companies	5315	15435	27678	94322	136154	220500	365600
Credit Unions	590	3923	12986	47253	91203	184400	215400
Retail Outlets/ Non-financial Business	2898	6295	13900	51154	46858	82300	65, 900
Savings Institutions					49594	64800	91300
Pools of Securitized Assets					75437	521300	606600

The legal regulation of consumer credit is extensive and complex enough to warrant a separate course at many law schools. Special consumer protection rules are discussed in several Chapters of this book.

Business Equipment. When consumer goods are bought on credit the financing necessarily anticipates that the debtor will earn income from other sources, usually wages or salary. Business equipment (taxicabs, trucks, computers, commercial refrigerators), however, is intended to assist in generating income that will help repay the credit and even leave a profit for the user. The installment financing of sales of business equipment does not match the mammoth scope of consumer financing, but it has played an important role in aiding productive activity—particularly by small businesses.[15] The financing patterns for buyers of business equipment are similar in many respects to those for consumer buyers. Both dealer-arranged financing, in which the dealer takes the security interest and assigns it to a provider of financing, and third-party direct secured lending to buyers are common.

---

13. Securitization is discussed below in this Section.

14. Fed. Res. Stat. Rel. G19 (May 6, 2005); 77 Fed. Res. Bull., May, 1991, at A38; 69 Fed. Res. Bull., Nov., 1983, at A40; 60 Fed. Res. Bull., May, 1974, at A50.

15. Secured financing has been significant in aiding smaller business enterprises to buy a wide range of equipment, such as printing presses, laundry equipment, mining and oil field equipment, drink dispensing and bar equipment, commercial refrigerators, machine tools, power shovels, cranes, road-building equipment of all types, agricultural equipment, bottling machines, electronic data processing equipment, dental and medical equipment, hairstyling equipment, trucks, diesel engines, and generators. This list can only suggest the wide variety of equipment involved.

Inventory. Sellers of goods extend secured credit routinely to wholesalers and dealers who hold the goods for sale as their inventory; however, seller-financed sales of inventory are much less common than seller-financed sales of consumer goods and business equipment. Sellers of expensive items that will become the buyer's inventory (e.g., the manufacturers of construction equipment and automobiles) normally insist on cash payment of the purchase price upon delivery. Other sellers, as we have seen, typically extend unsecured, short-term trade credit to buyers of inventory. Dealers and wholesalers who need longer-term inventory financing typically look to third-party secured lenders, much as Main Motors looked to Firstbank for inventory financing in the Prototype.

Other Secured Financing. Much secured credit is extended for purposes other than to finance buyers' purchases of consumer goods, business equipment, and inventory. Many business, large and small, must supplement their capital by borrowing, in order to obtain adequate funds to remain in operation. Funds borrowed under **working capital** or **operating capital** lending arrangements may be used for payment of salaries, rent, utilities, and other expenses of operation as well as for the purchase of equipment, supplies, and inventory. Many of these financings are secured, especially in cases of small-to medium-sized borrowers. These loans frequently are structured as uncommitted lines of credit or as revolving credit arrangements that, at some point, convert into term loans, not unlike the unsecured credit arrangements discussed above. Other secured financings are highly specialized and bear little resemblance to traditional unsecured lending arrangements.

Following are descriptions of some typical financing patterns that, although common, are particularly complex. They are included here with a view toward giving you a "taste" for the diverse contexts in which secured financing plays a central role and introducing you to some transactions about which you may have heard or read and in which you someday may play a role. We do not expect you to memorize these materials, or even to understand them fully at first reading. As will become apparent, the descriptions present only the basics; important details and qualifications have been omitted in the interest of brevity and comprehensibility. Please remember that while the essential elements of many transactions conform to these descriptions, the variations in terms, structure, collateral, and purposes of these secured financings are infinite.

Inventory and Receivables Financings. Consumer goods and business equipment, both of which are purchased for use, must be contrasted with goods held for sale. Goods held for sale include not only inventory, such as cars, trucks, and refrigerators in a dealer's showroom or warehouse, but also raw materials and components awaiting or in the course of manufacture: nuts and bolts to be used for assembly and bales of cotton held by a spinner or going through the spindles. The distinctive fact about inventory, and one that creates complex and fascinating legal problems, is that all parties hope for rapid turnover and liquidation of the goods into cash. The goods often will be (re)sold on credit, thereby creating an account receivable to which the secured creditor's security interest may be transferred.

In many cases creditors who make loans secured by inventory and receivables rely heavily on the collateral as their "way out"—their source of repayment. The current jargon used to refer to transactions in which the lender relies heavily on the value of its collateral is **asset-based financing**. In a typical arrangement a borrower would be required to maintain at all times a **borrowing base** value of inventory and qualifying (not in default) receivables that is at least equal to the outstanding loan balance. Normally the borrowing base would be a percentage (say, 60%) of the book value of inventory plus a percentage (say, 75%) of the face amount of receivables. The excess of collateral value over the outstanding loan balance provides the lender with a "cushion" that offers protection if the borrower defaults. Reporting requirements and, in some cases, inspections of inventory put the lender in a position to monitor the collateral and act to protect its interests if the borrower experiences a financial downslide. In many instances a borrower's receivables, which usually represent its most liquid assets (other than cash), are the principal collateral on which secured lenders rely.[16] The receivables financing Prototype in Chapter 6, Section 1(B), provides a detailed illustration of a "borrowing base" financing secured by accounts and inventory.

"All Assets" Secured Financing. A pattern has emerged in certain credit markets whereby lenders routinely take a security interest in all of a borrowers assets.[17] A typical example is a commercial bank loan to a small business. The individual controlling shareholders of a closely-held corporate borrower generally are required to give a guaranty of payment as additional security. Compared to asset-based lenders, these "all assets" lenders may place relatively slight reliance on the collateral's value and the individuals' guaranties as a source of repayment. Instead, they tend to rely heavily on the borrower's predicted cash flow and overall ability to pay. Like those extenders of credits who take consumer goods collateral for its hostage value instead of its market value, the "all asset" lenders probably look to the collateral and guaranties primarily as a tool for obtaining power over the borrower so as to inhibit business decisions and investments that could undermine their position.[18]

Acquisition Financing: Leveraged Buyouts. Another financing pattern involves obtaining a security interest in virtually all of a debtor's assets, but

16.   The general setting for receivables financing is developed in detail in Chapter 6, Section 1, infra.

17.   The borrower's real property may or may not be taken as collateral, depending on its value and the attendant costs.

18.   Professor Robert Scott has dubbed these lenders "relational" creditors because the value of the collateral seems to lie primarily in its impact on the relationship between the borrower and the lender. See Scott, A Relational Theory of Secured Financing, 86 Colum.L.Rev. 901 (1986).

that is its only similarity to the "all assets" financings just mentioned. The "takeover" phenomenon of the 1980's fueled demand for secured credit to finance acquisitions of controlling interests in publicly held corporations. Although the transaction structures were and remain quite varied, these **leveraged buyouts** ("LBO's") exhibit certain common patterns. Usually a substantial percentage of the purchase price of the corporate stock of the entity to be acquired (the "target") is borrowed (hence, the **leverage**); those borrowings typically are secured by substantially all of the assets of the *target*, once it is acquired.[19] Many of these secured loans, usually made by **syndicates** of commercial banks, have involved hundreds of millions of dollars and, in some cases, billions. The LBO secured lenders typically rely heavily on collateral value. In many cases unsecured debt also is incurred in order to fund a portion of the purchase price. Because of the high leverage and the dominant position of the secured lender, this unsecured debt became known as **junk bonds** (or, even more bluntly, "junk").[20]

"Special Purpose Vehicle" Financing: Leveraged Leasing. Some very innovative forms of receivables financings involve the use of a type of borrower called a **special purpose vehicle** ("SPV"). In these financings the SPV, which may be a corporation, partnership, or trust, is organized for the specific purpose of participating in the financing.[21] **Leveraged leasing** is one such form of financing.

A business entity may choose to lease equipment instead of buying it for a variety of reasons (often including its inability to use the tax benefits of ownership, such as accelerated depreciation, because it lacks sufficient taxable income). For example, long-term leasing is a typical means by which airlines obtain the use of commercial aircraft. The lessor often will be an SPV (typically a trust) formed by "equity" investors who (through the SPV) invest in the equipment and lease it to the lessee. These investors often wish to obtain, through the SPV, the tax benefits of ownership that the lessee cannot use. The investors capitalize the SPV with only a portion (say, 20%) of the funds necessary to purchase the equipment. The SPV then borrows the additional necessary funds, pays for the equipment, and enters into a lease with the lessee. By causing the SPV to borrow a substantial portion of the purchase price (i.e., "leveraging" the investment), the investors achieve 100% of the tax benefits of ownership by putting up only a fraction of the cash necessary to buy the equipment. As collateral for its borrowing, the SPV grants to the lender a security interest in the equipment (subject to the lessee's rights under the lease, of course) and in the lease itself (including the rental stream, payable over time by the lessee).

---

19. Because the assets of the target are used as collateral, these transactions have long been known as "bootstrap" transactions, reflecting the notion that the target seems to be "buying itself." The vanities of the 1980's investment bankers being what they were, the "bootstrap" label was replaced by the "LBO" nomenclature.

20. The investment bankers, of course, prefer another term: "high-yield securities."

21. Hence the "vehicle" denomination, reflecting the SPV's role as an tool or implement necessary for the financing structure.

Because the equipment and the lease are the SPV's only assets, the lender must be satisfied with the value of the equipment and the creditworthiness of the lessee.[22] The lessee is instructed to make the lease payments directly to the lender, as assignee of the lease, and those payments are applied by the lender against the SPV's secured debt. If for any reason (such as the lessee's default combined with unanticipated obsolescence of the equipment) the equipment and the lease are not adequate to satisfy the SPV's debt, then the lender will suffer a loss. It will have no recourse against any of the investors. If the lessee does not default and the secured debt is satisfied, then the SPV (and, indirectly, the investors) will be entitled to the **residual value** of the equipment at the end of the lease. The investors expect that value (combined with any tax savings arising out of the SPV's ownership of the equipment, which are passed on to the investors) to be sufficient for them to recover their investments and enjoy a return thereon. Depending on the value of the equipment at the end of the lease term, however, that expectation may or may not be realized. Because the lender's repayment turns on its ability to collect the rental stream from the lessee and on the value of the equipment, the lender must be assured that its security interest will withstand attack by any creditor of, or trustee in bankruptcy for, the SPV, any investor, or the lessee.

"Special Purpose Vehicle" Financing: Securitization. **Securitization** transactions (sometimes called "structured finance") are similar in some respects to leveraged leasing transactions, but there are some important distinctions. First, securitization involves the creation of debt securities that are backed by "pools" of receivables (rights to payment); traditional leveraged leasing transactions involve one or more equipment leases to the same lessee. Almost any kind of receivable can support securitization financings; the types seem to increase daily. For example, the future royalties of David Bowie and other recording artists have been securitized, and leveraged leases themselves have been pooled for this purpose. Second, whereas professional lenders (usually banks and finance companies) typically engage in leveraged leasing transactions, securitization involves the issuance of debt securities that can be sold to other kinds of investors. Third, the receivables involved in a securitization transaction initially are owned by a non-SPV operating company, whereas in a leveraged lease the SPV-lessor normally is the original lessor.

A typical securitization transaction begins with a business entity that originates receivables. For example, the originator could be a bank that holds consumer installment sale contracts (as Firstbank holds Lee Abel's

---

22.   In some transactions the lessor is not an SPV but is an operating company that has other assets and other liabilities. In those transactions the debt of the lessor to the lender normally is **limited recourse** debt. That is, the lending agreement provides that the lender is entitled to look only to the collateral—the equipment and the lease—for satisfaction of the debt. The lender is not entitled to satisfy the debt out of other assets of the lessor.

contract in the Prototype) or it could be a financial institution that generates credit card receivables (rights to payment from holders of credit cards issued by the institution). The first receivables used in securitization transactions were home mortgage loans secured by residential real estate. These transactions probably remain the most commercially significant securitizations as measured by dollar volume.

> The first structured financing came in 1970 when the newly created Government National Mortgage Association began publicly trading "pass-through" securities. In a mortgage pass-through security, the investor purchases a fractional undivided interest in a pool of mortgage loans, and is entitled to share in the interest income and principal payments generated by the underlying mortgages. Mortgage lenders originate pools of mortgages with similar characteristics as to quality, term, and interest rate. The pool is placed in a trust. Then, through either a government agency, a private conduit, or direct placement, certificates of ownership are sold to investors. Income from the mortgage pool passes through to the investors.[23]

A similar pattern is followed in most other securitizations: The originator transfers a large number of receivables (usually referred to as a "pool") to an SPV, and the SPV issues debt securities. As in the leveraged leasing transaction, because the SPV's only assets are the receivables, collections of the receivables are the only source of payment of interest on, and repayment of principal of, the securities. The funds generated by the sale of the securities are used to pay the originator for the receivables it sells to the SPV. (The financial intermediaries that arrange the transaction take their shares of the funds as well.) Although the investors are not necessarily knowledgeable enough to evaluate, on their own, the quality of the receivables, disclosure documents provide information concerning the quality of the receivables (e.g., past history of collections of similar receivables, nature and quality of the collateral (if any) securing the assigned receivables) and the risks that the investors are undertaking. Investors in publicly traded securities also may be guided by a rating agency's ratings of the securities.

Before making their investment, the investors must be assured that neither the SPV's nor the originator's insolvency will interfere with the collection of the receivables and the application of those collections to payments to the investors. But, the fact that the receivables originally were owned by the originator, an operating company with liabilities, creates a problem that the lender in a typical leveraged lease transaction does not encounter: making sure that the SPV and the operating company are not linked and that the transfer of the receivables to the SPV will be effective against creditors of the operating company (i.e., making sure that the SPV is **bankruptcy remote** from the originator). Indeed, in securitization transactions it is not unusual for the SPV's obligations to the investors, on

---

23. S. Schwarcz, Structured Finance: A Guide to the Principles of Asset Securitization § 1:2 (3d ed. 2003).

the securities, to be *un*secured. It is the transfer of the receivables from the originator to the SPV that is of particular concern.[24]

Securitization can provide an originator with a lower cost of funds than a conventional loan secured by the receivables. Even the fully secured, conventional secured lender faces a variety of risks in the event of a borrower's bankruptcy or other financial distress. By removing the receivables entirely from the asset base of the originator, however, securitization of the receivables may produce less risk and, consequently, lower financing costs for the originator.

Agricultural Financing. The agricultural industry, including the proverbial "family farmers," the large, corporate "agri-business" concerns, and the myriad other businesses in the chain of production, processing, and distribution, depends heavily on secured credit. Farms, like many other businesses, need expensive equipment; what has been observed above about financing sales of business equipment applies as well to farm equipment. Agricultural financing also presents some unique characteristics:

> Like Caesar's Gaul, agricultural lending is divided into three parts: (1) long-term credit to finance the purchase or improvement of real estate by a farmer or rancher; (2) intermediate production credit to finance the purchase of equipment and livestock; and (3) short-term loans to cover current operating expenses, including annual crop production. . ..
>
> The variety of collateral put up by farmers and ranchers as security for loans is very broad; it includes the farmland itself, fixtures, growing and future crops (including those pledged to landowner-lessors), products of crops (such as harvested grain), livestock, equipment, and a wide assortment of intangibles, including accounts receivable and U.S. Department of Agriculture "entitlements."[25]

Article 9 and a wide variety of other statutes, both state and federal, contain rules specifically addressing some perceived special problems of agricultural financing.

Secured Financing in the Securities Markets. Secured financing plays an indispensable role in modern securities markets. The transactional patterns vary widely, and most cannot be explained and understood in the absence of a broad and deep treatment of the operations of securities markets. However, some very general examples follow:

> • An individual investor who has physical possession of a stock certificate registered in the investor's own name with the issuing corporation wishes to borrow from a local bank and **pledge** (i.e., grant a security interest in) the stock certificate to the bank.

---

24. As we shall see in Chapter 6, Section 1(D), infra, applicable law may characterize the transfer as a sale or transfer for security.

25. B. Clark, The Law of Secured Transactions Under the Uniform Commercial Code ¶ 8.01, at 8–1 to 8–2.

- An individual investor who has a securities account with a stockbroker wishes to borrow from a local bank and pledge to the bank stocks and bonds "in" the investor's account.

- In order to buy securities on **margin**, an individual investor who has a securities account with a stockbroker wishes to obtain credit from the stockbroker and pledge to the stockbroker the securities to be purchased.

- A stockbroker wishes to obtain an "overnight" secured loan from a bank in order to obtain funds needed to settle (pay) its end-of-day payment obligations to other professional securities industry participants.

In the securities markets, secured financing, including **repo** financing,[26] involves truly staggering amounts each day, especially in the United States government securities markets. In late 1999 primary dealers reported approximately \$1.2 trillion in repos on their balance sheets.[27] The legal and operational aspects of taking collateral in the third and fourth examples mentioned above are likely to be encountered only by securities market professionals and their specialized counsel; however, lenders and their lawyers confront the first two examples with great frequency. We shall consider them in Chapter 6, Section 3, infra.

(C) REAL PROPERTY COLLATERAL, GUARANTIES OF PAYMENT, AND OTHER CREDIT ENHANCEMENTS

Although the focus here is on personal property collateral, one must keep in mind that both consumers and businesses also obtain credit on the strength of real property collateral, e.g., through home mortgage loans, second mortgage "home equity" loans, construction loans, long-term

---

26. "Repurchase agreements," or "repos," are an important means of financing, especially for government securities dealers.

In a repo, a seller of a security (a funds borrower) transfers the security to a buyer (a funds lender) under an arrangement whereby the securities seller agrees to repurchase the security on a specified date (often the next day) at a specified price, and the securities buyer agrees to resell the security back to the seller. From the perspective of the buyer, the transaction is a reverse repurchase agreement (reverse repo). Repos serve the function of secured borrowings and loans, although they are denominated as sales and resales. The economics of the transaction are such that when the seller (funds borrower) pays the repurchase price (i.e. repays the loan), the buyer (funds lender) receives a profit (a return on the money loaned). The legal characterization of repos . . . is not clear.

Mooney, Beyond Negotiability: A New Model for Transfer and Pledge of Interests in Securities Controlled by Intermediaries, 12 Cardozo L. Rev. 305, 324 n. 51 (1990).

27. 85 Fed Res. Bull, Dec., 1999, at 797. This figure double-counts the transactions by adding both sides of each trade. Nevertheless, because it includes figures only for primary dealers, it probably approximates the aggregate volume. See M. Stigum, The Repo and Reverse Markets 7–8 (1989).

"permanent" mortgage loans, etc. Moreover, there are other means of supporting an extension of credit, such as a third-party's guaranty of payment or a bank's letter of credit. In many cases personal property collateral is taken in a transaction that also involves real property collateral, guaranties of payment, or other credit enhancements. The interplay between the law governing security interests in personal property (Article 9) and that governing the other aspects of the transaction can give rise to some interesting problems. See Chapter 8, Section 3, infra; Chapter 9, Section 3(A), infra.

SECTION 2.   A ROADMAP TO SECURED TRANSACTIONS UNDER UNIFORM COMMERCIAL CODE ARTICLE 9

(A) BACKGROUND

Article 9 of the Uniform Commercial Code substantially rewrote the law of secured transactions; it was the most revolutionary of the Articles of the UCC. By virtually abandoning the concept of "title," UCC Article 2 required a drastic change in the focus of legal thinking about sales. But Article 9 even more sharply changed the focus of legal thought about secured transactions.

Prior to the UCC, a creditor seeking security had to choose among a bewildering variety of legal "devices"—pledge, chattel mortgage, conditional sale, trust receipt, assignment of accounts receivable, factor's lien. Each "device" operated within complex (and often unclear) rules governing its scope and the procedures for its validation and enforcement; the choice of the wrong "device" was subject to perils reminiscent of common-law pleading.

The UCC swept away the separate security "devices." The old names (pledge, conditional sale) may still be used, but the label does not control the result. Instead, Article 9 prescribes general rules for all secured transactions, with some variations depending on the type of transaction. The decision to establish a unitary approach to secured transactions was one of the UCC's most important contributions to the legal system. The important questions that remain relate, for the most part, to whether the maximum possible benefit has been gained from what most agree was a brilliant idea.

Article 9 was the first part of the UCC to undergo significant revision by the UCC's sponsors. Although for a time the UCC's sponsors held the line against most proposed improvements in the UCC, by 1966 the pressure to modify Article 9 became irresistible. The work of the Article 9 Review Committee began in 1967; its efforts culminated in the 1972 Official Text. Without affecting the basic structure of Article 9, the 1972 revisions effected numerous changes (some of them very important) to the Article. The 1978 Official Text made additional material changes to Article 9 as it dealt with securities and other investment property. Article 9's treatment of investment property was overhauled in conjunction with the revision of

Article 8 in 1994; its treatment of letters of credit was adjusted in conjunction with the revision of Article 5 in 1995.

In 1999 the UCC's sponsors approved Revised Article 9. Revised Article 9 is the product of nearly a decade of work—first by a Permanent Editorial Board study committee, which in December, 1992, issued a report recommending revision, and then by a drafting committee that met fifteen times from 1993 to 1998. Even after Revised Article 9 was officially promulgated, the work continued: As interested persons stumbled across stylistic and other minor errors and occasionally spotted an error that was more substantive, the sponsors responded by correcting the Official Text and Comments. Following an intensive and unprecedented effort, Revised Article 9 was enacted in all 50 states and the District of Columbia. It became effective in all but four of the enacting jurisdictions on July 1, 2001, and in the remaining jurisdictions within six months thereafter.

Like the early drafting efforts and the 1972 revision, Revised Article 9 is informed by commercial practice. The conflicting interests affected by Article 9 have had able and alert representatives who invested time and energy to participate in the drafting and otherwise work toward improving the legal regulation of those interests. (Comparatively speaking, very few worry about sales law under Article 2; at least between commercial parties, the problems usually can be solved by contract.)

We turn now to an overview of the substance of Revised Article 9. You should read through this overview several times, to glean a general understanding of the principal terms and concepts. As the course progresses and the details mount up, reference to the overview may restore a needed perspective.

(B) SCOPE OF ARTICLE 9; SECURITY INTERESTS IN COLLATERAL

Article 9 "applies to . . . a transaction, regardless of its form, that creates a security interest in personal property or fixtures by contract." UCC 9–109(a)(1). This provision makes sense only if we consult UCC 1–201(b)(35) [F1–201(37)], which defines the term "security interest," in pertinent part, as "an interest in personal property or fixtures which secures payment or performance of an obligation."[1] The broad reach of Article 9 is limited by various exclusions set forth in UCC 9–109(c) and (d). The scope of Article 9 is discussed in Chapter 5, infra.

Article 9 tells us nothing about the obligation that is secured, leaving that to other law. Although we usually think of the obligation as being a contractual promise to repay a loan or to pay the price of goods bought, in

---

1.   Certain other transactions—consignments and sales of accounts, chattel paper, payment intangibles, and promissory notes—also are embraced by the definition of "security interest" and by Article 9's basic scope provision, UCC 9–109(a). We shall defer consideration of those transactions for now and focus on interests that secure obligations.

theory a security interest could secure virtually any obligation—liquidated or unliquidated, contingent or noncontingent.

"[T]he property subject to a security interest" is the "collateral." UCC 9–102(a)(12). Property can be "carved up" in many ways. Two or more persons might own property "in common," as owners of undivided fractional interests. Or, property can be divided temporally, as in a lease, where the lessee owns the right to use and possession during the lease term and the lessor owns the residual interest that remains at the end or the term. See UCC 2A–103(1)(m), (1)(q) [R2A–103(1)(s), (1)(w)] (defining "leasehold interest" and "lessor's residual interest"). A security interest that secures an *metrics for a* obligation, however, can be measured in two dimensions at any given point *security interest* in time: the *value of the collateral* and the *amount of the obligation secured*.

The following figure illustrates these two dimensions:

Figure 2.1

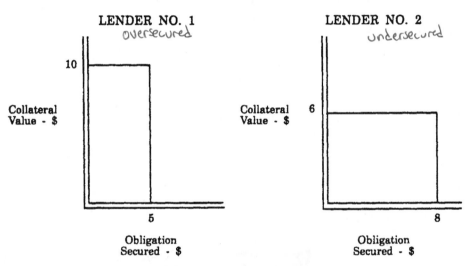

As you can see, Lender #1 has a security interest in collateral valued at $10 and is owed $5; at this point in time Lender #1 is **oversecured**. Lender #2, on the other hand, is owed $8 but its security interest extends only to collateral with a value of $6; Lender #2 is **undersecured**. Keep in mind that the value of collateral securing an obligation can change (e.g., by appreciation, depreciation, or the acquisition of additional collateral), as can the amount of the obligation secured (e.g., by additional borrowings, the accrual of interest, and repayments).

(C) THE CAST OF CHARACTERS

The chief protagonists in a secured transaction are the "debtor" and the "secured party." The secured party is "a person in whose favor a security interest has been created." UCC 9–102(a)(72). The debtor is the "person having an interest, other than a security interest or other lien, in the collateral." UCC 9–102(a)(28). Usually, the debtor is the sole owner of the collateral as well as the only person who owes the obligation that the collateral secures. However, there are many possible variations from this straightforward scenario. For example, a corporation might grant a security interest in collateral it owns to secure the indebtedness of its subsidiary. In this situation, the corporation is the debtor; the subsidiary, which owes the secured debt, is a non-debtor "obligor." See UCC 9–102(a)(59) (defining "obligor"). Or, parents might cosign a promissory note with their child, thereby becoming obligated for the same debt as the child, while the child gives a security interest in collateral that he or she owns. Here, the child, who owns the collateral, is the debtor; each parent is an obligor, as is the child. See UCC 9–102, Comment 2.a.

The UCC also deals with the rights of some, but not all, third parties who may claim an interest in collateral covered by a security interest. We already have considered priority contests between a secured party, as a good faith purchaser, and a seller seeking to reclaim goods from a debtor-buyer who has voidable title. See Chapter 1, Section 3, supra. We also have taken note of the trustee in bankruptcy—often a significant player in secured credit when the debtor becomes financially distressed. Other third parties whose rights Article 9 addresses will be mentioned shortly in the discussion of priorities.

(D) CREATION OF A SECURITY INTEREST: ATTACHMENT

The creation of a security interest under Article 9 is embodied in the concept of "attachment." "A security interest attaches to collateral when it becomes enforceable against the debtor with respect to the collateral." UCC 9–203(a). UCC 9–203(b) sets forth three conditions to enforceability, and thus to attachment. These conditions may be met in any order. First, "value" (UCC 1–204 [F1–201(44)]) must have been given. Second, the debtor must have "rights in the collateral." Third, the debtor must agree that a security interest will attach *and* either the collateral must be in the secured party's possession or control or the debtor must have signed a security agreement (UCC 9–102(a)(73)) containing a description of the collateral (UCC 9–108). Until all these elements have been satisfied, a security interest does not attach and is not enforceable against the debtor or third parties with respect to the collateral. See UCC 9–203(a), (b). See generally Chapter 3, Section 2, infra.

Although not mentioned as a condition to attachment, the debtor's agreement must address the obligation that is secured by collateral—otherwise one of the two dimensions that mark the borders of a

prerequisites for enforceability

security interest would be missing. Article 9 affords the parties considerable freedom to determine which obligations are secured: "A security agreement may provide that collateral secures . . . future advances or other value." UCC 9–204(c). In addition, "a security agreement may create or provide for a security interest in after-acquired collateral." UCC 9–204(a).[2] But recall that no security interest can attach to the collateral under UCC 9–203(b) until the debtor has "rights" in it.

(E) TYPES OF COLLATERAL

Although Article 9's "unitary" approach to security interests generally treats all security interests the same, different types of collateral receive different treatment in several respects. Before mentioning some of those differences, which derive primarily from differences in the nature of the collateral and in the related financing patterns, it will be useful to identify the various "types" of Article 9 collateral. "Goods" are subdivided into "consumer goods," "equipment," "farm products," and "inventory." Intangible collateral includes "accounts," "deposit accounts," and "general intangibles." Types of paper representing or embodying intangible rights include "chattel paper," "documents," and "instruments," although "chattel paper" may be electronic rather than paper-based. Likewise, "investment property" such as stocks and bonds may be evidenced by paper or may be intangible. Goods affixed to real estate can become "fixtures," although Article 9 leaves to real estate law the determination of what constitutes fixtures. See generally Chapter 8, Section 3, infra. Property acquired by a debtor upon the exchange or disposition of collateral, such as the account (right to payment) that arises when inventory is sold on unsecured credit, constitutes "proceeds." See generally Chapter 3, Section 5, infra.

Although we shall revisit the various types of collateral later in these materials (most of them on several occasions), it would be useful for you to review the statutory definitions in UCC 9–102(a) at this point in your reading. The Comments to UCC 9–102, particularly Comments 4, 5, and 6, contain additional explanations of the terms.

(F) PERFECTION AND PRIORITY

A secured party who wishes to rely on the benefits of a security interest in collateral will be concerned about whether conflicting claims to the collateral could come ahead of its security interest. A baseline rule of Article 9 can be found in UCC 9–201: "Except as otherwise provided in [the *general rule* Uniform Commercial Code], a security agreement is effective according to its terms between the parties, against purchasers of the collateral, and against creditors." That (somewhat awkward) statement generally is understood to mean that an attached security interest in collateral will be

---

2. UCC 9–204(b) limits security interests in after-acquired consumer goods and commercial tort claims.

senior to conflicting claims unless a provision in the UCC provides otherwise. Much of the remainder of this book is devoted to an examination of the substantial number of provisions otherwise.

PERFECTION

In many cases a security interest's priority over other conflicting claims to collateral will depend on whether the security interest is "perfected." Perfection occurs when a security interest has attached and when the applicable steps specified in Article 9, Part 3 (specifically, UCC 9–310 through UCC 9–316) have been taken. UCC 9–308(a). If those steps are taken before attachment, perfection occurs upon attachment. Id. Although there are some specialized means of perfection, the two principal means are (i) the filing of a "financing statement" and (ii) the secured party's taking possession of the collateral. A security interest in some types of collateral can be perfected by either filing or possession (e.g., goods); other types can be perfected only by filing (e.g., accounts) or only by possession (e.g., money). See generally Chapter 3, Section 3, infra.

Part 5 of Article 9 deals with filing. Of particular importance are UCC 9–502 (dealing with what to file—the contents of a financing statement) and UCC 9–501 (dealing with where to file). See also UCC 9–301 through UCC 9–307 (dealing with what state's law governs perfection and the effect of perfection or non-perfection). See generally Chapter 3, Section 4, infra.

Article 9 includes several important priority rules. For example, under UCC 9–317 certain non-ordinary course, good-faith buyers of collateral take free of an attached but unperfected security interest. Perhaps more important, the same section provides that an attached but unperfected security interest is subordinate to the rights of a "lien creditor." (A "lien creditor" is a creditor with a judicial lien. See UCC 9–102(a)(52). We shall see in Chapter 7 that a debtor's trustee in bankruptcy can assume the seniority of a judicial lien creditor and set aside security interests that are unperfected when the debtor enters bankruptcy.) Under Article 9's priority rules, even perfected security interests are not perfect. For example, they usually are subordinate to competing Article 9 security interests under the first-in-time rule of UCC 9–322(a)(1), which, however, is subject to long list of exceptions. See generally Chapter 4, Section 1, infra. Also, perfected security interests in goods can be cut off by a "buyer in ordinary course of business." UCC 1–201(b)(9) [F1–201(9)]; UCC 9–320(a). See generally Chapter 4, Section 2, infra.

Notwithstanding the apparent breadth of the baseline priority rule in UCC 9–201 and the large number of priority rules found elsewhere in the Article, many priority contests between Article 9 security interests and competing claimants to collateral are not addressed in Article 9 (or elsewhere in the UCC). Examples are priority contests with federal tax liens and a growing variety of other statutory liens. See generally Chapter 8, Section 4, infra.

(G) ENFORCEMENT

The right and ability of a secured party to satisfy its claim out of the collateral already has been mentioned in general terms. Part 6 of Article 9 regulates in detail a secured party's enforcement rights. See generally Chapter 9, infra. These rights arise upon a debtor's "default." Just as Article 9 is silent concerning the nature and scope of the obligation secured by a security interest, so Article 9 does not define what constitutes a default in that obligation. Defining default is left primarily to the agreement of the debtor and secured party. In addition to failure to make a payment when due, sometimes with a grace period, typical defaults include the debtor's insolvency, bankruptcy, and breach of a loan covenant, and the existence of a conflicting lien on the collateral.

A menu of the rights and remedies of secured parties and debtors after default appears in UCC 9–601. Notwithstanding the UCC's general deference to freedom of contract, see UCC 1–103(a) [F1–102], Article 9 prohibits debtors from waiving certain of their rights before default. UCC 9–602. As an empirical matter, the secured party's most important *enforcement tools* enforcement tools are its rights (i) to collect on intangible collateral, such as accounts, from the obligors (called "account debtors"), (ii) to take possession of collateral on default, and (iii) to dispose of collateral (typically, by sale or lease). UCC 9–102(a)(3) (defining "account debtor"); UCC 9–607 (secured party's collection rights); UCC 9–609 (secured party's right to take possession); UCC 9–610 (disposition of collateral). In the case of collections and dispositions, the secured party is entitled to apply funds received to the obligation secured, leaving an obligation for a "deficiency" should the funds be insufficient. UCC 9–608(a)(4); UCC 9–615(d). The debtor is entitled to any "surplus" that remains after satisfaction of the secured obligation and certain junior security interests. Id. In addition, a secured party may propose to accept collateral in full or (except in consumer transactions) partial satisfaction of the secured debt, but the debtor and certain junior secured parties are entitled to object to that proposal, thereby forcing the secured creditor to turn to another remedy, such as disposition. UCC 9–620.

To increase the likelihood that a fair price will be obtained upon the disposition of collateral, the secured party must give advance notice of the disposition to the debtor and certain junior secured parties, see UCC 9–611(b), and every aspect of the disposition must be "commercially reasonable." UCC 9–610(b). Similarly, collections on intangible collateral must be undertaken in a commercially reasonable manner. UCC 9–607(c).

A debtor is entitled to "redeem" collateral at any time before the secured *redemption* party disposes (or contracts to dispose) of the collateral, collects upon the collateral, or accepts the collateral in satisfaction of the secured obligation. UCC 9–623. This redemption right derives from the "equity of redemption" developed by the English courts of equity with respect to real estate. It recognizes that at some point the debtor's equitable right must be "foreclosed." Even today, people commonly use the term "debtor's equity" to refer to the positive remainder obtained when the amount of the secured obligation is subtracted from the value of the collateral and usually speak of "foreclosure" as the means of enforcing a lien. These terms can be traced historically to the foreclosure of a debtor's equity of redemption.

Depending on the circumstances, a secured party who fails to comply with Article 9 can be held liable to a debtor in damages, deprived of some or all of its claim for a deficiency, or subjected to judicial restraint. UCC 9–625; UCC 9–626. In consumer and consumer-goods transactions, noncomplying secured parties may be subjected to losses that bear no relationship to the amount of actual harm or damage (if any) caused by the noncompliance. See UCC 9–625(c)(2); UCC 9–626(b).

SECTION 3. THE ROLES OF LAWYERS IN SECURED TRANSACTIONS

We have met tax lawyers, litigators, securities lawyers, and patent lawyers, but we have never met a self-styled "secured transactions" lawyer. To be sure, we have met many who held themselves out as experts on secured transactions (and most of them really were). But the law governing secured transactions never represents more than one slice of any pie, significant and complex as that slice may be.

Consider, for example, a large, syndicated bank financing, in which several banks in a "syndicate" are extending credit to a corporation under the same credit agreement. The lawyers who represent each of the parties in such a large, sophisticated transaction well might refer to themselves as "financing lawyers" or "commercial lawyers," but would be just as likely, perhaps, to observe that they are "corporate lawyers" who "do deals." As counsel for the lenders and the borrower, they would be expected to prepare and negotiate the wording of the documentation and render formal, written legal opinions on the enforceability of the documentation and on various other aspects of the transaction. Counsel would consult frequently with their clients and advise them concerning legal risks. Counsel almost certainly would need not only a sound understanding of business matters, such as how the banks obtain funds to make their loans and the accounting principles featured in various covenants, but also expertise in diverse areas of the law: regulations affecting the bank lenders, restrictions on interest rates that can be charged, rights of setoff against bank accounts, liens arising out of the Employee Retirement Income Security Act ("ERISA"), federal and state tax liens and a variety of other federal and state lien statutes, securities regulation laws affecting the borrower, conflict of laws, equitable principles that limit the enforceability of agreements, tort law relating to the behavior of lenders, the effects of the borrower's or lender's insolvency, etc. (the list could go on and on). The collateral may be an indispensable part of the transaction and may occupy much of the time of the lawyers involved, but it is only one part of the deal.

Assume now that the borrower in our syndicated bank financing becomes financially distressed; it is in default under that financing, as well as under various other financings, and is behind in paying its trade debt. If the borrower is not in bankruptcy, counsel for many of the creditors and counsel for the debtor might undertake negotiations (usually called a **workout**) leading to a restructuring of credit extensions. Much of the same expertise and many of the same lawyering skills brought to bear in the original financings will be called upon in the workout context. If the borrower becomes a debtor under the Bankruptcy Code, the nature of the work of many of the lawyers will be essentially the same as in the out-of-court workout. However, some disputes or claims may require litigation, in which case lawyers skilled in trial practice will be utilized.

Now consider an individual consumer's purchase of an automobile financed by a commercial bank. The bank will present several "forms" to the individual borrower for signature (e.g., credit application, promissory note, security agreement). It would be quite rare for the bank's loan officer or the borrower to retain and consult counsel to assist in this financing. Indeed, it is unlikely that the bank would agree to one-time changes to its forms under any circumstances. Although the parties need not worry about securities laws that apply to the borrower or about complicated financial covenants, it would be a serious mistake to think that lawyers had not played an essential role in this consumer transaction. Federal and state regulation of consumer credit (including disclosure requirements and mandatory and prohibited practices and terms) is so complex and pervasive that only highly specialized and knowledgeable counsel are equipped to prepare and approve consumer credit forms.[1]

If the consumer buyer defaults in the monthly payments or files for bankruptcy, the bank may retain a "collection" lawyer who specializes in collections of consumer debts. The lawyer might resort to legal proceedings or, if the debtor is in bankruptcy, might assist the bank in obtaining possession of the collateral or in working out a mutually acceptable resolution between the borrower and the bank. At that stage, the borrower also might have retained a lawyer (if the borrower could afford the cost); the borrower's lawyer would be sure to examine closely the transaction with the bank to uncover potential attacks on the validity of the bank's claim and security interest and any possible counterclaim against the bank arising out of regulatory noncompliance or otherwise.

In sum, the roles of legal counsel in financings, including secured financings, involve much more than the ex post analysis of facts for the purpose of predicting (or advocating) an appropriate judicial resolution (i.e., A sues B; who wins?). As you work your way through the following materials, from time to time you will be asked to identify problems and propose ex ante solutions. You will also have an opportunity to consider how you might counsel your client in a variety of circumstances.

---

1.   We have seen the FTC's anti-holder in due course rule in Chapter 1, Section 4, supra, and its rule prohibiting nonpossessory, non-purchase-money security interests in household goods in Section 1 of this Chapter.

CHAPTER 3

ESTABLISHMENT AND PERFECTION OF SECURITY INTERESTS

SECTION 1.   FINANCING AUTOMOBILES: A PROTOTYPE

The preceding Chapter briefly mentioned some aspects of the automobile financing transactions illustrated in this Section. The following Prototype portrays in more detail the legal and related business practices employed in financing the marketing of automobiles.[1] This picture may suggest ways to avoid legal pitfalls through proper handling of business transactions generally; it also provides a good setting for dealing with the legal problems that arise in this and other important types of financing. You should read this Section quickly at this point to get an overview of the basic transactions. We shall return to this Prototype at various points later in these materials when dealing with specific problems.

The following pages present a typical example of automobile financing at two levels: (i) while the dealer holds the automobiles (in this case, cars and light trucks) as inventory (financing the acquisition of a dealer's inventory of durable goods sometimes is called **floorplanning**) and (ii) upon the sale of one of the automobiles to an individual consumer who buys the automobile "on time." The dealer is Main Motors, Inc., a Chevrolet dealer; credit for the dealer's inventory financing is supplied by a lending institution named Firstbank. The consumer buyer is Lee Abel; secured credit for Abel's purchase also is provided by Firstbank, but in a transaction that is separate and distinct from the inventory financing for Main Motors.

(A) FINANCING THE DEALER'S INVENTORY: THE SETTING

Main Motors sells about 700 new Chevrolets each year at a retail value of close to $14,750,000; Main's sales of used automobiles (most taken by Main as "trade-ins" on new automobiles) come to about one-third of this amount. To meet varied tastes for model, color, and combinations of accessories, and to facilitate sales to eager buyers, Main carries an inventory averaging 175 new automobiles, with a wholesale cost to Main of

---

1.   This Prototype was prepared with the generous assistance of William B. Solomon, Jr., and Thomas J. Buiteweg of General Motors Acceptance Corporation. It does not necessarily describe the practices of any particular bank, automobile dealer, or automobile manufacturer.

about $3,500,000. Main has a physical plant (land and buildings, including showroom, service facility, and parking lots; tools and other equipment; etc.) valued at $2,800,000, and carries about $400,000 worth of parts and accessories required for its service department. More than one-half of Main's sales of new automobiles are installment credit sales; for used automobiles the proportion is greater. Most of the installment contracts for new automobiles run 48 months, and for used automobiles 30 months. Consequently, without financing assistance, Main's investment in new automobiles would be tied up for extended periods even after their sale. Like most automobile dealers, Main lacks capital to meet all of these needs and relies heavily on financing.

Firstbank has field representatives who solicit dealers to establish financing arrangements. One of them contacts Main Motors and proposes terms on which the bank will (i) finance (floorplan) Main's inventory of new automobiles, thereby enabling Main to acquire automobiles on credit, and (ii) purchase the consumer installment contracts generated by Main's installment sales, thereby eliminating Main's burden of waiting for payment until each installment comes due.

Finding the terms of Firstbank's proposal more attractive than Main's existing financing arrangements with another lender, Main's management indicates its willingness to accept Firstbank's terms.

(B) CREATING AND PERFECTING FIRSTBANK'S SECURITY INTEREST

At this point, Firstbank prepares several documents, including a *financing statement* and a *security agreement*.

The Financing Statement. Firstbank will file a financing statement (Form 3.1) in the appropriate filing office;[2] the completed form is designed to meet the requirements of UCC 9–502. Unlike many of the other transaction documents, this one does not require Main's signature.

The Security Agreement. You will recall that perfection of a security interest requires, in addition to filing a financing statement, that the security interest attach. UCC 9–308(a). Recall as well that one element of attachment is that the debtor sign (or otherwise authenticate) a security agreement describing the collateral. UCC 9–203(b)(3)(A). The security agreement signed by Main Motors is a detailed, **blanket lien** (i.e., very broad coverage) agreement, the "Dealer Inventory Security Agreement" (Form 3.2). This comprehensive contract between the parties includes language not only evidencing the bank's continuing security interest in Main's inventory and related collateral (see ¶ 5), but also authorizing the bank to endorse notes and sign financing statements on behalf of Main (see ¶ 6). It also contains provisions relating to the terms of the lending

2.   For the place of filing within a state, see UCC 9–501(a); as to the applicability, here, of Pennsylvania law, see UCC 9–301(1) and Section 4, infra. Firstbank will file with the Secretary of State of the Commonwealth of Pennsylvania, in Harrisburg.

arrangements (see ¶ ¶ 1, 2, and 8), defining the "Events of Default" (see ¶ 12), and setting forth Firstbank's remedies (see ¶ 13).

FORM 3.1
FINANCING STATEMENT

UCC FINANCING STATEMENT
FOLLOW INSTRUCTIONS (front and back) CAREFULLY

A. NAME & PHONE OF CONTACT AT FILER [optional]
P. A. SYSTEM, ESQ. - 800-111-2222

B. SEND ACKNOWLEDGMENT TO: (Name and Address)

SYSTEM LAW OFFICES
125 SPRAWL OFFICE PARK
MALVERN, PA 19355

THE ABOVE SPACE IS FOR FILING OFFICE USE ONLY

1. DEBTOR'S EXACT FULL LEGAL NAME - insert only one debtor name (1a or 1b) - do not abbreviate or combine names

1a. ORGANIZATION'S NAME				
MAIN MOTORS, INC.				
OR 1b. INDIVIDUAL'S LAST NAME	FIRST NAME	MIDDLE NAME		SUFFIX
1c. MAILING ADDRESS	CITY	STATE	POSTAL CODE	COUNTRY
237 NORTH SEVENTH STREET	PHILADELPHIA	PA	19116	USA

1d. TAX ID #: SSN OR EIN	ADD'L INFO RE ORGANIZATION DEBTOR	1e. TYPE OF ORGANIZATION	1f. JURISDICTION OF ORGANIZATION	1g. ORGANIZATIONAL ID #, if any	
1234567		CORP	PENNSYLVANIA	PA12345	NONE

2. ADDITIONAL DEBTOR'S EXACT FULL LEGAL NAME - insert only one debtor name (2a or 2b) - do not abbreviate or combine names

2a. ORGANIZATION'S NAME				
OR 2b. INDIVIDUAL'S LAST NAME	FIRST NAME	MIDDLE NAME		SUFFIX
2c. MAILING ADDRESS	CITY	STATE	POSTAL CODE	COUNTRY

2d. TAX ID #: SSN OR EIN	ADD'L INFO RE ORGANIZATION DEBTOR	2e. TYPE OF ORGANIZATION	2f. JURISDICTION OF ORGANIZATION	2g. ORGANIZATIONAL ID #, if any	
					NONE

3. SECURED PARTY'S NAME (or NAME of TOTAL ASSIGNEE of ASSIGNOR S/P) - insert only one secured party name (3a or 3b)

3a. ORGANIZATION'S NAME				
FIRSTBANK, N.A.				
OR 3b. INDIVIDUAL'S LAST NAME	FIRST NAME	MIDDLE NAME		SUFFIX
3c. MAILING ADDRESS	CITY	STATE	POSTAL CODE	COUNTRY
BROAD & SPRUCE STREETS	PHILADELPHIA	PA	19116	USA

4. This FINANCING STATEMENT covers the following collateral:

ALL OF THE FOLLOWING, WHETHER NOW OWNED OR HEREAFTER ACQUIRED: ACCOUNTS; CHATTEL PAPER; GENERAL INTANGIBLES; INSTRUMENTS (INCLUDING PROMISSORY NOTES); INVENTORY; LETTER-OF-CREDIT-RIGHTS; PAYMENT INTANGIBLES; SUPPORTING OBLIGATIONS; CONTRACTS OF LEASE, SALE, RENTAL OR OTHER DISPOSITIONS OF INVENTORY; BOOKS AND RECORDS; RIGHTS IN CONNECTION WITH THE RESIDUAL VALUE OF INVENTORY LEASED, RENTED, SOLD, OR OTHERWISE DISPOSED OF, INCLUDING PROCEEDS OF ANY THIRD PARTY'S EXERCISE OF AN OPTION TO PURCHASE; REPLACEMENTS OR SUBSTITUTIONS OF ANY OF THE FOREGOING, CASH PROCEEDS AND NONCASH PROCEEDS THEREOF, AND PROCEEDS OF PROCEEDS.

5. ALTERNATIVE DESIGNATION [if applicable]: | LESSEE/LESSOR | CONSIGNEE/CONSIGNOR | BAILEE/BAILOR | SELLER/BUYER | AG. LIEN | NON-UCC FILING

6. This FINANCING STATEMENT is to be filed [for record] (or recorded) in the REAL ESTATE RECORDS. Attach Addendum [if applicable] | 7. Check to REQUEST SEARCH REPORT(S) on Debtor(s) [ADDITIONAL FEE] [optional] | All Debtors | Debtor 1 | Debtor 2

8. OPTIONAL FILER REFERENCE DATA

FILING OFFICE COPY — NATIONAL UCC FINANCING STATEMENT (FORM UCC1) (REV. 07/29/98)

FORM 3.2
DEALER INVENTORY SECURITY AGREEMENT

FIRSTBANK, N.A., a national banking association with a place of business located at Broad & Spruce Streets, Philadelphia, Pennsylvania

("Bank"), and ___Main Motors, Inc.___ a ___Pennsylvania corporation___ whose principal place of business is

___237 North Seventh Street, Philadelphia, PA 19116___ ("Dealer"), intending to be legally bound, hereby agree as follows:

1. BACKGROUND.

Dealer hereby requests Bank from time to time to make loans and advances to Dealer ("Loan(s)") acceptable to Bank to finance the purchase of Inventory, as that term is defined herein, from suppliers thereof ("Suppliers") for sale or lease in the ordinary course of Dealer's business. Subject to the terms and conditions of this agreement ("Agreement"), Bank expects to finance Dealer's purchase of Inventory, but reserves in its sole discretion, the right to decline to make any Loan(s) requested by Dealer for any reason. Loan(s) may be disbursed either directly to Dealer, to Dealer's demand deposit account at Bank, or by Bank's paying, at Dealer's request and for Dealer's account, drafts of, or other demands for payment by, a Supplier properly presented to Bank when accompanied by the manufacturer's invoice or bill of sale and adequate documentation of proper ownership.

2. LOAN(S) AND NOTE.

Subject to the terms and conditions hereof, and Bank's continuing satisfaction with the financial and other conditions of Dealer, Bank will from time to time during the continuance of the Agreement make Loan(s) to Dealer, as Dealer may from time to time request, on not less than five (5) days prior notice, by submitting to Bank a properly completed Loan Request Form in the form attached hereto ("Loan Request Form") (or by complying with any other means of requesting Loans as may be agreed upon by Bank and Dealer in writing), to finance Dealer's purchase of Inventory, provided, however, the aggregate principal amount outstanding of such Loan(s) shall not, at any one time, exceed the sum of ___$3,500,000.___ ("Loan Limit"). Bank may, from time to time, raise or lower the Loan Limit upon five (5) days' written notice to Dealer. Bank expressly reserves, in its sole discretion, the right to decline to make any Loan(s) requested by Dealer for any reason. Dealer agrees to execute and deliver to Bank a demand note in an amount equal to the Loan Limit, in the form attached hereto ("Note(s)") and, at Bank's request, to execute from time to time such additional or substituted Note(s) as are necessary to evidence any change in the Loan Limit. The actual amount due under the Note(s) shall be that amount as shown on the Bank's books and records. Bank will from time to time render to Dealer statements of all amounts due Bank under the Note(s) which statements shall be deemed conclusive and irrefutable evidence of the actual amounts due Bank, unless Dealer notifies Bank in writing to the contrary within fifteen (15) days of Bank's sending such statements to Dealer.

3. INVENTORY.

For purposes of this Agreement, "Inventory" means any new or used inventory (as that term is defined in the Pennsylvania Uniform Commercial Code (the "UCC"), Article 9) that is owned or possessed by Dealer and shall include all tangible personal property held by Dealer for sale or lease or to be furnished under contracts of service, tangible personal property that the Dealer has so leased or furnished, tangible personal property held by others for sale on consignment for the Dealer, tangible personal property sold by the Dealer on a sale or return or consignment basis, tangible personal property returned to the Dealer or repossessed by the Dealer following a sale thereof by Dealer, and tangible personal property represented by a document of title, including, but not limited to, automobiles, parts and accessories, together with all materials, additions, equipment, accessions, accessories and parts installed in, related, attached or added thereto or used in connection therewith and all substitutions and exchanges for and replacements thereof whether installed prior to receipt or after receipt by Dealer. An item of Inventory financed hereunder is an "Item".

4. FINANCING TERMS.

The percentage of the purchase price of any Item that Bank, in its discretion, elects to lend to Dealer to finance the purchase thereof pursuant to this Agreement will be established by Bank from time to time by prior written notice to Dealer ("Financing Terms").

5. GRANT OF SECURITY INTEREST.

As security for the prompt and punctual payment and performance of all liabilities and obligations of Dealer to Bank, including, but not limited to, the Note(s), and the performance by Dealer of all of Dealer's obligations as set forth herein and/or in any and all documents and instruments executed or delivered in conjunction herewith, and the complete satisfaction of all existing and future liabilities and obligations of Dealer to Bank or of Dealer and others to Bank of any nature whatsoever, whether matured or unmatured, absolute or contingent, direct or indirect, sole, joint or several, and any extensions, modifications or renewals thereof, including, but not limited to, all of Bank's expenses incurred in connection with the collection and performance of Dealer's liabilities and obligations hereunder, Bank's reasonable attorney's fees and the costs of curing any Event of Default (as specified below in paragraph 12) that Bank elects to cure, all of which Dealer hereby agrees to pay (collectively, "Dealer's Liabilities to Bank"), Dealer hereby grants and conveys to Bank a ~~continuing lien upon and~~ security interest in all of Dealer's property described below now owned or hereafter acquired:

(a) Inventory;

(b) Accounts, chattel paper, general intangibles, and instruments (each as defined in the Pennsylvania UCC, Article 9) and all obligations of sureties and guarantors for the payment and satisfaction thereof;

(c) Contracts of lease, sale, rental or other disposition of Inventory in which Dealer has an interest;

(d) Books and Records (herein defined to mean all books and records of original or final entry, including, without limitation: invoices; receipts; instruments; documents; account ledgers and journals (both due and payable); minutes; resolutions; correspondence with regard to the Collateral; tax returns; bank checks, receipts and financing statements; contracts; agreements; and any other books and records maintained by Dealer in the normal course of Dealer's business, including all such books and records as have been photocopied, reduced to film images or otherwise, or encoded into electronic or mechanical impulses in or upon computer tapes, programs, software, and data banks associated therewith, or accounting or recording machines or the like, and without regard to whether such books and records are maintained at Dealer's place of business or elsewhere);

(e) Rights in connection with the residual value of any of Dealer's Inventory leased, rented, sold or otherwise disposed of, including but not limited to the proceeds of any third party's option to purchase any portion of Dealer's Inventory;

(f) Balances on deposit with or held in any capacity by Bank at any time and any other property of any nature of Dealer that Bank may at any time have in its possession wherever located, now or hereafter acquired; and

(g) All replacements and substitutions of all or any of the foregoing, all cash and non-cash proceeds thereof, proceeds of proceeds thereof, all insurance thereon, and all proceeds of such insurance, including, but not limited to trade-ins, returned, and/or repossessed goods.

Bank's rights in all of the above property (collectively, "Collateral") shall be independent of any right of set-off or appropriation that Bank may have or acquire under paragraph 13 hereof or otherwise.

6. POWER OF ATTORNEY.

Dealer hereby appoints any employee, officer or agent of Bank as Dealer's true and lawful attorney-in-fact, with power:

(a)   To endorse the name of Dealer upon:

    (i)   Any Note(s), security agreement, UCC financing statement and continuations thereof, certificates of origin and certificates of title to any motor vehicle or other property evidenced by such a certificate and any other instrument or document required by Bank to perfect or continue perfection of the liens and security interests granted to Bank hereunder or otherwise in connection with Loan(s);

    (ii)   Any and all other notes, checks, drafts, money orders or other instruments of payment;

    (iii)   Instruments received by Dealer in connection with the sale or other disposition of any Collateral;

    (iv)   Any check that may be payable to Dealer on account of returned or unearned premiums or the proceeds of insurance (and any amount so collected may be applied by Bank toward satisfaction of any of Dealer's Liabilities to Bank).

(b)   To sign and endorse the name of Dealer upon any: drafts against all persons obligated to pay, directly or indirectly any account, chattel paper, general intangible, or instrument ("Account Debtors"); assignments, verifications and notices in connection with any Collateral; and invoices, freight or express bills, bills of lading, and storage or warehouse receipts relating to any Collateral;

(c)   To give written notices in connection with accounts, chattel paper, general intangibles, or instruments;

(d)   To give written notices to officers and officials of the United States Postal Service to effect a change or changes of address so that all mail addressed to Dealer may be delivered directly to Bank (Bank will return all mail not related to the Dealer's Liabilities to Bank or the Collateral to Bank); and

(e)   To open all such mail.

Dealer hereby grants unto said attorney full power to do any and all things necessary to be done with respect to the above as fully and effectively as Dealer might or could do with full power of substitution and hereby ratifies and confirms all its said attorney or its substitute shall lawfully do or cause to be done by virtue hereof. This power of attorney shall be deemed to be coupled with an interest and irrevocable until all of Dealer's Liabilities to Bank are paid or performed in full, and shall survive any dissolution, termination or liquidation of Dealer.

7. DOWN PAYMENT; ASSIGNMENT OF TITLE.

Dealer agrees that on or before accepting delivery of any Item it will pay Supplier, in cash and not by credit whether extended by Supplier or any other person, the amount(s) required pursuant to the Financing Terms. Dealer hereby requests and authorizes Bank to pay the proceeds of the Loan(s) to Supplier. Dealer acknowledges that it acquires each Item subject to Bank's lien and security interest therein and Dealer hereby irrevocably authorizes Supplier to deliver to Bank, upon Bank's written request, a certificate of origin, certificate of title or other evidence of ownership evidencing a first perfected security interest in favor of Bank in or unencumbered title to each Item and all other documents and certificates necessary to evidence the same.

8. DEALER'S PAYMENTS TO BANK.

Without Bank's prior written consent, Dealer will not sell any Item for a price less than the then outstanding principal balance of the Loan(s) plus accrued and unpaid interest thereon made to enable Dealer to acquire that Item ("Release Price"). When Dealer sells an Item it will promptly pay to Bank the Release Price of such Item.

Dealer agrees to make such payments to Bank from time to time to reduce the principal balance of any Loan(s) made hereunder to enable Dealer to purchase an Item that Dealer has not sold as Bank and Dealer shall agree to, in writing, from time to time.

Provided, however, that nothing herein shall be construed to amend in any way the terms of the Note(s) which is, and is intended to remain, payable ON DEMAND, it being understood that Bank may demand payment at any time of the Note(s). Without first paying Bank in full the Release Price, Dealer will not return for credit, exchange or consign any Item.

9. INVENTORY RISKS.

Bank assumes no responsibility for the existence, character, quality, quantity, condition, value and/or delivery of any Item. Dealer shall not be relieved of any of Dealer's Liabilities to Bank because any Item fails to conform to the manufacturer's, Supplier's, or Dealer's warranties, or because any Item may be lost, stolen destroyed or damaged. Dealer will promptly notify Bank of the loss, theft or destruction of or damage to any Item and will forthwith pay to Bank the Release Price of such Item.

10. INDEMNIFICATION.

Dealer agrees to comply with all requirements of the federal Truth in Lending Act and the federal Equal Credit Opportunity Act, and Regulations Z and B of the Board of Governors of the Federal Reserve System, Trade Regulation Rules of the Federal Trade Commission, the federal Fair Debt Collection Practices Act and Fair Credit Reporting Act, the Pennsylvania Model Act for the Regulation of Credit Life Insurance and Credit Accident and Health Insurance, the Pennsylvania Unfair Trade Practices and Consumer Protection Law, the Motor Vehicle Sales Finance Act, the Goods and Services Installment Sales Act, and all regulations promulgated by all governmental units and agencies thereunder, and all other applicable state, federal and local laws, regulations and ordinances regulating the credit sale of goods and/or services by Dealer and at all times to carry on its business in a lawful manner. Dealer hereby agrees to indemnify, defend and hold Bank harmless from and against all liability and claims asserted against Bank by any person in connection with:

    (a)   any sale, lease, enforcement or other disposition of any Collateral;

    (b)   any alleged violation of any law, regulation or ordinance by Dealer or Bank in connection with this Agreement or any other contract between Dealer and Bank;

    (c)   any personal injury alleged to have been suffered by any person in connection with any sale, lease, enforcement or other disposition of any Collateral;

    (d)   any claim by any person arising out of Dealer's breach of warranty or failure to perform any of Dealer's obligations under any contract regarding the sale, lease, enforcement or disposition of any Collateral; or

    (e)   any claim by any person arising from a claim made by a consumer under the Federal Trade Commission's Trade Regulation Rule to Preserve Consumer Defenses on any loan made by Bank to said consumer, whether referred to Bank by Dealer or not.

Dealer further agrees to reimburse Bank for all interest, counsel fees and costs expended by Bank in connection with the foregoing, including, but not limited to, those incurred in any bankruptcy or insolvency proceedings, and any subsequent proceedings or appeals from any order or judgment entered therein. This indemnification shall survive termination of this Agreement.

11. WARRANTIES, REPRESENTATIONS AND COVENANTS.

To induce Bank to enter into this Agreement and to extend credit, Dealer warrants, represents and covenants (which warranties, representations and covenants shall survive termination of this Agreement) that:

    (a)   Dealer will keep complete and accurate Books and Records and make all necessary entries thereon to reflect all transactions respecting the Collateral. Dealer will keep Bank informed as to the location of all Books and Records and will permit Bank, its officers, employees and agents, to have access to all Books and Records and any other records pertaining to Dealer's business and financial condition that Bank may request and, if deemed necessary by Bank, permit Bank, its officers, employees and agents, to remove them from Dealer's places of business or any other places where the same may be found for the purposes of examining, auditing and copying same. Any Books and Records so removed by Bank will be returned to Dealer by Bank as soon as Bank shall have completed its inspection, audit or copying thereof.

    (b)   Dealer's jurisdiction of organization (if any), the location of Dealer's chief executive office, all of Dealer's offices where it keeps its Books and Records concerning the Collateral, all locations at which it keeps its Inventory, and all locations at which it maintains a place of business are listed in Schedule A attached hereto. Dealer will not change its jurisdiction of organization (if any) unless it gives Bank at least 30 days' prior written notice. Dealer will promptly notify Bank in writing of any change in the locations of its chief executive office, Books and Records, of the Collateral, of any place of business or of the closing or establishment of any new place of business. If any of the Collateral or any Books and Records are at any time to be located on premises leased by Dealer or on premises owned by Dealer subject to a mortgage or other lien, Dealer will obtain and deliver or cause to be delivered to Bank, prior to delivery of any Collateral or Books and Records to such premises, an agreement, in form and substance satisfactory to Bank, waiving the landlord's, mortgagee's or lienholder's rights to enforce any claim against Dealer for monies due under the landlord's lien, mortgagee's mortgage, or other lien by levy or distraint, or other similar proceedings against the Collateral or Books and Records and assuring Bank's ability to have access to the Collateral and Books and Records in order to exercise Bank's rights to take possession thereof and to remove them from such premises.

    (c)   Dealer has, and at all times will have, good, marketable and indefeasible title to the Collateral, free and clear of all liens or encumbrances (except for taxes not in default or contested in good faith, for which adequate reserves have been set aside, and Bank's liens and security interests). All accounts, chattel paper, general intangibles, and instruments included in the Collateral arose in the ordinary course of Dealer's business and are not subject to any defense, set-off, or counterclaim.

    (d)   Dealer will, at its sole cost and expense, preserve the Collateral and Dealer's rights against Account Debtors free and clear of all liens and encumbrances, except those created pursuant hereto, and take such further actions as may be necessary to maintain the perfection and first priority of Bank's security interest in the Collateral. Dealer will not grant to anyone other than Bank any lien upon or security interest in the Collateral nor allow any person other than Bank to obtain a lien upon the Collateral. At Dealer's sole expense, Dealer will keep the Collateral in good condition and repair at all times.

    (e)   Dealer will at all times keep itself and the Collateral insured against all hazards in such amounts and by such insurers as are satisfactory to Bank together with full casualty and extended coverage in amount not less than one hundred ten percent (110%) of the Loan Limit. Dealer will cause Bank's security interests in the Collateral to be endorsed on all policies of insurance thereon in such manner that all payments for losses will be paid to Bank as loss payee and Dealer will furnish Bank with evidence of such insurance and endorsements. Such policies shall be payable to Dealer and Bank as their respective interests appear and shall contain a provision whereby they cannot be cancelled except after ten (10) days' written notice to the Bank. In the event that Dealer fails to pay any such insurance premiums when due, Bank may, but is not required to, pay such premiums and add the costs thereof to the amounts due Bank by Dealer under the Note(s), which costs Dealer hereby agrees to pay to Bank with interest at the rate specified in the Note(s). Dealer hereby assigns to Bank any returned or unearned premiums that may be due Dealer upon cancellation of any such policies for any reason whatsoever and directs the insurers to pay Bank any amounts so due.

    (f)   Dealer will promptly notify Bank if there is any change in the status or physical condition of any Collateral or the ability of any Account Debtor to pay or preserve the Collateral, or of any defense, set-off, or counterclaim asserted by any person. If any Collateral is sold, leased, rented, released for demonstration, transferred or otherwise moved from the place where such Collateral is normally kept by Dealer, Dealer will notify Bank forthwith.

(g)   Dealer will permit Bank to inspect and audit the Collateral at all reasonable times. In the event that Bank and Dealer cannot agree within seventy-two (72) hours as to what shall be a reasonable time to inspect and audit Collateral, Bank's decision shall be controlling, and upon oral notice, Dealer will permit such inspection and audit.

(h)   Dealer hereby irrevocably assigns to Bank all of its rights of stoppage in transit with respect to any Item sold on credit to any Account Debtor, which rights shall be paramount to Dealer's.

(i)   Dealer will, at such intervals as Bank may require, submit to Bank:

    (i)   a schedule reflecting, in form and detail satisfactory to Bank, the names and addresses of all Account Debtors together with the amounts due for all of Dealer's outstanding accounts; and

    (ii)   copies of all invoices evidencing the sale or lease of any Item or Items to Account Debtors pertaining to any or all of its accounts, with evidence of shipment of the Item or Items, the sale or the leasing of which have given rise to such accounts.

(j)   Dealer will file all tax returns that Dealer is required to file and pay when due all taxes and license and other fees with respect to the Collateral and Dealer's business, except taxes contested in good faith and for which adequate reserves have been established by Dealer.

(k)   If a certificate of title is required to be issued for any Item, Dealer will file all documents necessary to obtain such a certificate from the appropriate governmental authority within three (3) days after the date of the Loan made to enable the Dealer to purchase that item. Dealer will cause a notation of the Bank's lien and security interest to be made and noted on such certificate at Dealer's sole expense. If Dealer fails or refuses to so file such document or note Bank's liens and security interests thereon, Bank may, at Dealer's expense, file such documents as Bank, in its sole discretion, deems appropriate to perfect its lien and security interest.

(l)   The proceeds of each Loan will be used solely to finance the purchase price of Inventory in accordance with the Financing Terms.

(m)   Dealer, if a corporation, is duly organized, validly existing and in good standing under the laws of the state of its incorporation, has the power and authority to make and perform this Agreement, and is duly qualified in all jurisdictions in which it conducts its business or where such qualification is required. The execution, delivery and performance of this Agreement, and the execution and delivery of the Note(s) and all other documents required hereunder have been duly authorized and will not violate any provision of law or regulation or of the articles of incorporation, by-laws or partnership agreement of Dealer or of any agreement, indenture or instrument to which Dealer is a party, or result in the creation or imposition of any security interest, lien or encumbrance in any of the Collateral. This Agreement, the Note(s) and all other documents related hereto, when executed and delivered by Dealer, will be valid and binding obligations of Dealer, enforceable against Dealer in accordance with their terms.

(n)   Within ninety (90) days after the end of each fiscal year of Dealer, Dealer will furnish Bank with annual financial reports relating to the financial condition of Dealer and its affiliates (including but not limited to consolidated and consolidating balance sheets, earnings or profit or loss statements and surplus statements), each in reasonable detail and prepared by an independent certified public accountant ("CPA") in accordance with generally accepted accounting principles consistently applied. In addition, Dealer will obtain from such independent CPA and deliver to Bank, within ninety (90) days after the close of each fiscal year, such CPA's written statement that in making the examination necessary to the certification, the CPA has obtained no knowledge of the occurrence or imminent occurrence of any Event of Default (as specified in paragraph 12 below) by Dealer hereunder, or disclosing all Events of Default of which such CPA has obtained knowledge; provided, however, that in making the examination such CPA shall not be required to go beyond the bounds of generally accepted auditing procedures for the purposes of certifying financial statements. Bank shall have the right, from time to time, to discuss Dealer's affairs directly with Dealer's independent CPA after notice to Dealer and opportunity for Dealer to be present at any such discussions. Dealer agrees that the CPA selected by Dealer shall be acceptable to Bank, it being agreed that Bank will not unreasonably withhold its consent of the accountants selected by Dealer.

(o)   On or before the fifteenth (15th) day of each month Dealer will furnish to Bank (in form satisfactory to Bank) unaudited statements of the financial condition and operations of Dealer and its affiliates for the preceding calendar month.

(p)   Dealer will furnish Bank promptly with such information in addition to that specified in subparagraphs (n) and (o) above respecting the financial condition and affairs of Dealer and its affiliates as Bank may, from time to time, reasonably require.

(q)   No Event of Default, as specified in paragraph 12 below, has occurred or is about to occur and no event has occurred or is about to occur that, with the passage of time or giving of notice or both, could be an Event of Default.

(r)   There are no suits in law or equity or proceedings before any tribunal or governmental instrumentality now pending or, to the knowledge of Dealer, threatened against Dealer or any guarantor or surety for Dealer's Liabilities to Bank, the adverse result of which would in any material respect affect the property, finances or operations of Dealer or of any surety or guarantor for Dealer, or their ability to satisfy Dealer's Liabilities to Bank.

(s)   No statement, warranty, representation, covenant, information, document or financial statement made, presented or asserted by Dealer to Bank in connection with this Agreement or as an inducement to Bank to make Loan(s) hereunder was or is incorrect, incomplete, false or misleading in any material respect nor has Dealer failed to advise Bank of any information affecting materially Dealer's business, operations or financial condition.

(t)   In the event that Bank, for any reason, determines that the value of the Collateral is insufficient to secure adequately the actual amount due Bank under the Note(s), Dealer will, upon ten (10) days' written notice:

    (i)   deliver or cause to be delivered to Bank additional Collateral in an amount sufficient, in Bank's sole discretion, to secure adequately such amounts due Bank; or

    (ii)   reduce the outstanding aggregate balance of Loan(s) by an amount satisfactory to Bank.

(u)   Dealer will not permit:

    (i)   any of the Collateral to be levied or distrained upon under any legal process;

    (ii)   any of the Collateral to become a fixture unless that fact has been disclosed to Bank in advance in writing; or

(iii)   any Item to be subject to any lease or rental agreement if the Account Debtor's obligations thereon have not been assigned to Bank pursuant to the provisions hereof, unless Dealer has paid Bank in full the Loan made to enable Dealer to purchase that Item.

12. EVENTS OF DEFAULT.

Dealer shall be in default hereunder upon the occurrence of any one or more of the following ("Events of Default"):

(a)   The failure of Dealer at any time to observe or perform any of its agreements, warranties, representations, covenants or obligations contained in this Agreement, the Note(s) or any other document related hereto, or if any statement, warranty, representation, covenant, signature or information made herein or contained in any application, exhibit, schedule, statement, certificate, financial statement or other document executed or delivered pursuant to or in connection with this Agreement or the Note(s), was or is incorrect, incomplete, false or misleading;

(b)   The failure of Dealer to furnish promptly to Bank such financial or other information as Bank may reasonably request;

(c)   The failure to pay the outstanding balance of Loan(s) and all accrued interest thereon to Bank UPON DEMAND by Bank or the nonpayment when due of any amount payable on any of Dealer's Liabilities to Bank of whatsoever nature;

(d)   The failure of Dealer to observe or perform any agreement of any nature whatsoever with Bank or any other party; or the occurrence of any event of default, or any event that, with the passage of time or giving of notice or both, would be an event of default by Dealer under any other agreement;

(e)   Dealer, or any surety or guarantor for Dealer's Liabilities to Bank, becomes insolvent, or makes any assignment for the benefit of creditors, or any petition is filed by or against Dealer, or any surety or guarantor for Dealer's Liabilities to Bank, under the federal Bankruptcy Code or under any provision of any other law or statute alleging that Dealer, or any surety or guarantor for Dealer's Liabilities to Bank, is insolvent or unable to pay debts as they mature;

(f)   The entry of any judicial or tax lien against Dealer, or any surety or guarantor for Dealer's Liabilities to Bank, or against any of their respective properties, whether such lien is junior or senior to Bank's security interest, or the appointment of any receiver, trustee, conservator or other court officer over the Dealer, or any surety or guarantor for Dealer's Liabilities to Bank, or against any of their respective properties, for any purpose, or the occurrence of any change in the financial condition of Dealer or any surety or guarantor for Dealer's Liabilities to Bank, which, in the sole judgment of Bank, is materially adverse;

(g)   The Collateral or any rights therein shall be subject to or threatened with any judicial process, condemnation or forfeiture proceedings;

(h)   The dissolution, merger, consolidation or reorganization of Dealer;

(i)   A substantial change, as determined by Bank in its sole judgment, in the identity, ownership, control or management of Dealer;

(j)   The cancellation, termination or other loss of any franchise held by Dealer, or any restriction on such franchise that affects adversely, as determined by Bank in its sole judgment, Dealer's continued existence, operations or financial condition;

(k)   The borrowing of any money by Dealer from any source other than Bank, whether or not subordinate to this Agreement or the Note(s) executed in conjunction herewith, without Bank's prior written consent;

(l)   Bank believes, in good faith, subject only to its own business judgment, that the prospect of any payment or performance of any obligation hereunder is or may become impaired.

13. BANK'S RIGHTS UPON DEFAULT.

Upon the occurrence of any Event of Default, Bank may, without notice and at its option, do any or all of the following:

(a)   Exercise from time to time any and all rights and remedies available to Bank under the UCC or otherwise available to Bank, including the right to collect, settle, compromise, adjust, sue for, foreclose or otherwise realize upon any of the Collateral and to dispose of any of the Collateral at public or private sale(s) or other proceedings, and Dealer agrees that Bank or its nominee may become the purchaser at any such public sale(s) and that ten (10) days' prior notice of any such disposition constitutes reasonable notification. The proceeds of any Collateral shall be applied to the payment of Dealer's Liabilities to Bank, in such order as Bank may, in its sole discretion, elect. Dealer waives and releases any right to require Bank to collect any of Dealer's Liabilities to Bank from any other Collateral under any theory of marshaling of assets or otherwise, and specifically authorizes Bank to apply any Collateral in which Dealer has any right, title or interest against any of Dealer's Liabilities to Bank in any manner that Bank may determine.

(b)   Declare all of Dealer's Liabilities to Bank to be immediately due and payable.

(c)   Reduce Dealer's Liabilities to Bank to judgment.

(d)   Appropriate, set-off, and apply, on account of any of Dealer's Liabilities to Bank, all balances of Dealer on deposit with, or held in any capacity by Bank at any time, and any other property of any nature of Dealer that Bank may at any time have in its possession, including but not limited to, certificates of deposit and savings, demand and other deposit accounts, securities and personal property.

(e)   Take possession of all or any Collateral with or without legal process, for the purpose of which Bank through its representatives may enter any premises wherein the Collateral may be found and Dealer, on Bank's request, will assemble the Collateral and make it available to Bank at a place designated by Bank that is reasonably convenient to both Dealer and Bank.

(f)   Bank may send notices in Dealer's name or instruct Dealer to send notices and Dealer agrees to send such, advising any and all Account Debtors that the accounts have been assigned to Bank and that all payments thereon are to be made directly to Bank.

14. MISCELLANEOUS.

(a) This Agreement shall inure to the benefit of and is and shall continue to be binding upon the parties, their successors, representatives, receivers, trustees, heirs and assigns, but nothing contained herein shall be construed to permit Dealer to assign this Agreement or any of Dealer's rights or obligations hereunder without first obtaining Bank's express written approval.

(b) Until all of Dealer's Liabilities to Bank are paid in full and all of Dealer's obligations hereunder are satisfactorily performed in full, all obligations, representations, warranties, covenants, undertakings and agreements of Dealer hereunder and under the Note(s) and all other documents executed in connection herewith or related hereto shall remain in full force and effect.

(c) This Agreement and the Note(s) have been executed pursuant to, delivered in and shall be governed by and construed under the laws of the Commonwealth of Pennsylvania. The parties acknowledge the jurisdiction of the state, federal and local courts located within the Commonwealth of Pennsylvania over controversies arising from or relating to this Agreement.

(d) If any provision of this Agreement shall for any reason be held to be invalid or unenforceable, such invalidity or unenforceability shall not affect any other provision hereof.

(e) All rights, powers and remedies of Bank hereunder or under any other obligation are cumulative and not alternative and shall not be exhausted by any single assertion thereof. The failure of Bank to exercise any such right, power or remedy will not be deemed a waiver thereof nor preclude any further or additional exercise of such right, power or remedy, now or in the future, upon any obligation of Dealer. The waiver of any default hereunder shall not be a waiver of any subsequent default. This paragraph shall be applicable to Dealer and any person liable with respect to any of Dealer's obligations.

(f) All notices provided for herein shall be deemed to have been given:

  (i) if by Bank to Dealer, when deposited in the mail or delivered to a reputable courier addressed to:

MAIN MOTORS, INC.
237 NORTH SEVENTH STREET
PHILADELPHIA,   PA   19116

; and

  (ii) if by Dealer to Bank upon receipt by Bank at:

FIRSTBANK, N.A.
DEALER FINANCE DEPARTMENT
BROAD AND SPRUCE STREETS
PHILADELPHIA, PA 19116

(g) This Agreement:

  (i) is the complete written Agreement of the parties hereto, supersedes any prior understandings or written agreement; and

  (ii) cannot be varied, changed or otherwise modified except by written permission of Bank; and no oral promises, conditions or representations made by either party shall vary the terms and conditions herein.

(h) This Agreement:

  (i) may be executed in any number of counterparts and all of such counterparts taken together shall be deemed to constitute one and the same document; and

  (ii) shall become effective when each of the parties hereto shall have signed a copy hereof (whether the same or different copies) and shall have delivered the same to Bank or shall have sent to Bank a facsimile or electronic message stating that the same has been signed and mailed to it. Complete sets of counterparts shall be lodged with Dealer and with Bank.

IN WITNESS WHEREOF, the parties have hereunto caused this Agreement to be executed and sealed by their proper and duly authorized representatives as of this___19th___day of_____March_____20_06___.

FIRSTBANK, N.A.

By:_____
    Vice President

NAME OF DEALER____MAIN MOTORS, INC._____

By:____G. S. Gessell_____
        G. S. Gessell, President

(Name and Title)

Attest:____Stacey Stribe_____
        Stacey Stribe, Secretary

(Name and Title)

(If a corporation, Dealer's corporate seal must be affixed and its Secretary, Assistant Secretary, Treasurer or Assistant Treasurer must sign on the line marked "Attest".)

The Dealer's Line of Credit; The Demand Note. A "Demand Note" (Form 7.3) is issued in conjunction with the Dealer Inventory Security Agreement (see ¶ 2). This note evidences the obligation of Main Motors to repay loans made to it under the **line of credit** arrangement (Firstbank makes each advance in its discretion, not pursuant to a commitment). The maximum amount of the line of credit set by the bank and reflected in the Dealer Inventory Security Agreement and the Demand Note is $3,500,000. Main executes only one note throughout the course of this business relationship with Firstbank. However, should the principal amount of Firstbank's loans to Main Motors rise above the stipulated principal amount, the Demand Note (second paragraph) and the Dealer Inventory Security Agreement (¶ 2) protect Firstbank by virtue of Main's promise therein to repay the actual amount of the loans "as shown on the bank's books and records."[3]

"Picking Up" a Floor Plan. Main Motors decided to change its financing relationship from its current lender (Old Bank) to Firstbank. When this happens, Firstbank is said to "pick up a floor plan."

Before picking up the floor plan Firstbank performs a physical inspection of Main Motors' premises. The bank's representative checks all units in stock by listing the vehicle identification number of each unit and examining all invoices held by the dealer. These invoices reflect the wholesale price that has been paid for each unit. Old Bank will send Firstbank a list of all units upon which Main has an outstanding indebtedness, and Firstbank will compare this list with the list compiled by its own representative. When the two lists match dollar for dollar and cent for cent, Main completes a "Loan Request Form" (Form 3.4). Firstbank requires this document only when it refinances an outstanding indebtedness of a dealer; the form functions as a record of those units in which Firstbank initially takes a security interest.

---

3.   Firstbank and other lenders require borrowers to execute and deliver promissory notes largely by custom. For most purposes Firstbank's position would be identical if it were to rely only on a borrower's agreement to repay contained in a Dealer Inventory Security Agreement.

FORM 3.3
DEMAND NOTE

<u> March 19, 2006 </u>
Philadelphia, Pennsylvania

$<u> * * * 3,500,000.00 * * * </u>

FOR VALUE RECEIVED AND INTENDING TO BE LEGALLY BOUND HEREBY, the undersigned (each jointly and severally if more than one and jointly and severally referred to as "Dealer") promises to pay to the order of FIRSTBANK, N.A., Philadelphia, Pennsylvania ("Bank") in lawful money of the United States of America, at any of its banking offices, the principal sum of

THREE MILLION FIVE HUNDRED THOUSAND AND NO/100

Dollars ("Loan Limit") to be repaid ON DEMAND, but until such time as demand is made by Bank, to be repaid in accordance with the terms and conditions of a certain Dealer Inventory Security Agreement between Dealer and Bank dated   March 19, 2002   ("Agreement") together with interest on the outstanding principal balance hereof payable monthly, as billed, at a fluctuating rate per annum equal at all times to   one percent (1)   % per annum over the rate of interest announced by the Bank publicly, from time to time, in Philadelphia, Pennsylvania, as the Bank's base rate, but in no event in excess of the maximum rate permitted by applicable law. Each change in the fluctuating rate shall take effect simultaneously with such change in the Bank's base rate. Interest shall be calculated hereunder for the actual number of days that the principal balance is outstanding, based on a year of three hundred sixty (360) days, unless otherwise specified in writing.

The principal balance due hereunder plus all accrued interest due thereon at any time and from time to time shall be that amount as shown on the Bank's books and records and the statements submitted to Dealer by Bank in accordance with paragraph 2 of the Agreement, which shall, if no timely objection is made, be conclusive and irrefutable evidence of the amount of principal and interest due Bank.

THE AGREEMENT. This Note is the Note(s) referred to in and is issued in conjunction with and under and subject to, the terms and conditions of the Agreement, and is secured by, among other things, the Collateral, as that term is defined in the Agreement and a mortgage on all the real property of   N/A   . Upon the happening of an Event of Default, as specified in the Agreement, Bank will be entitled to all of Bank's Rights Upon Default as specified in the Agreement.

PREPAYMENT. The principal sum due under this Note may be repaid by Dealer in whole or in part without penalty at any time.

MISCELLANEOUS. Dealer hereby waives protest, notice of protest, presentment, dishonor and notice of dishonor. In addition to all other amounts due hereunder, Dealer agrees to pay to Bank all costs (including reasonable attorney's fees) incurred by Bank in connection with the enforcement hereof. The rights and privileges of Bank under this note shall inure to the benefit of Bank's successors and assigns forever. All obligations shall bind Dealer's heirs, successors and assigns forever. If any provision of this Note shall be held to be invalid or unenforceable, such invalidity or unenforceability shall not affect any other provision hereof, but this Note shall be construed as if such invalid or unenforceable provision had never been contained herein. This Note has been delivered in, shall be construed in accordance with, and shall be governed by the laws of the Commonwealth of Pennsylvania. The waiver of any default hereunder shall not be a waiver of any other or subsequent default.

Dealer has duly executed this Note the day and year first above written and has hereunto set hand and seal.

IF INDIVIDUAL(S), SIGN BELOW

_____

_____

_____

IF GENERAL OR LIMITED PARTNERSHIP,
SIGN BELOW

_____(SEAL)

_____(SEAL)

_____(SEAL)

IF A CORPORATION, SIGN BELOW

NAME OF CORPORATION: _MAIN MOTORS, INC._

BY: _G. S. Gessell_____(SEAL)   (AFFIX CORPORATE SEAL HERE)
   G. S. Gessell, President

(NAME AND TITLE)

ATTESTED:_____*Stacey Scribe*_____
   Stacey Scribe, Secretary

(SIGNATURE AND TITLE)

Upon completion of the Loan Request Form, Firstbank will pay Old Bank (by check or electronic funds transfer) for the total debt on all listed units. In return, Old Bank will sign a release, by which it releases all interest in the units listed, and will provide for filing a *termination statement* (see UCC 9–513) to the effect that it no longer claims a security interest in connection with its financing statement.

FORM 3.4
LOAN REQUEST FORM

March 19   , 20 06
(Date)

MAIN MOTORS, INC.
(Dealer Name)

237 North Seventh Street
(Street Address)

Philadelphia   PA   19116
(City or Town)   (State)

Dealer hereby requests FIRSTBANK, N.A., Philadelphia, Pennsylvania ("Bank") to make the following Loan(s), as the term Loan(s) is defined in a certain Dealer Inventory Security Agreement and Power of Attorney between Dealer and Bank dated   March 19, 2002 ("Agreement"), in accordance with and under and subject to the terms and conditions of the Agreement. Pursuant to the Agreement, Dealer confirms that it has granted to Bank and hereby affirms and grants to Bank a lien and security interest in the Items of Inventory described below together with all materials, additions, equipment, accessions, accessories and parts installed in, related, attached or added thereto or used in connection therewith and all substitutions and exchanges for and replacements thereof as security for all of "Dealer's Liabilities to Bank".

Loan No.	Description of Item	VIN.	New or Used	Dealer Cost	Less Down Payment	Loan Amount
871	Chevrolet	903399	New	16,123.22	None	16,123.22
871	Chevrolet	803821	New	15,839.44	None	15,839.44
871	Chevrolet	921874	New	25,256.12	None	25,256.12
871	Chevrolet	804745	New	18,740.20	None	18,740.20
871	Chevrolet	800215	New	23,839.44	None	23,839.44
871	Chevrolet	907704	New	21,252.50	None	21,252.50

TOTAL   121,049.92

This Loan Request Form is the Loan Request Form referred to in Paragraph 2 of the Agreement and is issued in conjunction with and under and subject to the terms and conditions of the Agreement. All terms used herein shall be defined as such terms are defined in the Agreement. The Loan(s) requested hereunder are the Loan(s) referred to in Paragraph 2 of the Agreement and the Items of Inventory described herein are the Items of Inventory referred to in the Agreement, which is part of the Collateral as that term is defined in the Agreement.

As an inducement to Bank to make the Loan(s) requested hereby, Dealer hereby reaffirms and restates all of Dealer's agreements, liabilities, representations, warranties, covenants and obligations under the Agreement and further covenants that if the Loan(s) requested hereunder are made by Bank they are and will be received by Dealer under and subject to all the terms and conditions of the Agreement.

IF INDIVIDUAL(S), SIGN BELOW

_____

_____

_____

IF GENERAL OR LIMITED PARTNERSHIP,
SIGN BELOW

_____(SEAL)

_____(SEAL)

_____(SEAL)

IF A CORPORATION, SIGN BELOW

NAME OF CORPORATION: <u>MAIN MOTORS, INC.</u>

BY: _G. S. Gessell_____(SEAL)   (AFFIX CORPORATE SEAL HERE)
     G. S. Gessell, President

          (NAME AND TITLE)

ATTESTED:__Stacey Scribe_____
      Stacey Scribe, Secretary

          (SIGNATURE AND TITLE)

Figure 3.1 diagrams the documentation and payment involved when Firstbank picks up Main Motors' floor plan from Old Bank.

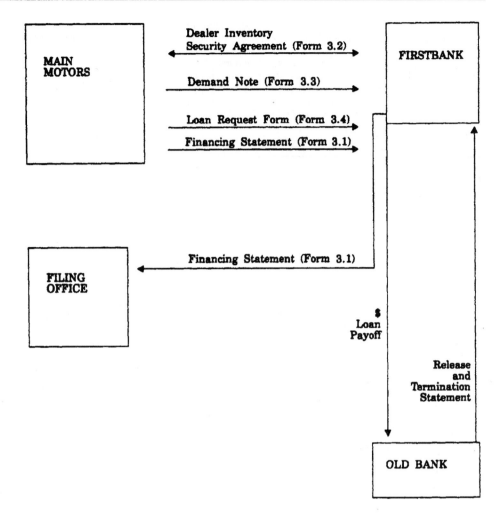

Figure 3.1

Financing of New Deliveries. Firstbank will make loans to finance new deliveries of automobiles from the Chevrolet Motor Division of General Motors Corporation by advancing the wholesale price of each automobile directly to General Motors. The details of that procedure are addressed below.

(C) DELIVERY OF AUTOMOBILES: ASSURING THE MANUFACTURER OF PAYMENT

General Motors, like all other automobile manufacturers, does not extend credit to automobile dealers in connection with the purchase of automobiles. Consequently, General Motors must either be paid or be assured of payment before delivery.

At one time it was customary to ship new automobiles by rail, and to send a **sight draft** (instruction to pay upon presentment), accompanied by a negotiable bill of lading, to a local bank that would release the bill of lading to the dealer upon the dealer's payment of the draft. Today, new automobiles usually are delivered by highway trailer. These vehicle haul-away carriers, unlike the railroads, typically do not have facilities to store automobiles during periods of delay that may occur when negotiable bills of lading, with sight drafts attached, pass through banking channels into the hands of the dealer. This relatively cumbersome method of controlling delivery until payment is unnecessary because of the assurance of payment that Firstbank's letter of credit (described next) affords General Motors.

Bank Letter of Credit; Dealer Inventory Security Agreement. In order to provide assurance of payment, Firstbank issues a **letter of credit** in favor of General Motors. The letter of credit provides that from time to time, subject to a stated limitation on amount per week, upon receipt of General Motors' (paper or electronic) draft drawn on Firstbank accompanied by an automobile invoice for the automobiles being shipped, Firstbank will pay to General Motors the amount of the invoice. Of course, under the Dealer Inventory Security Agreement, Main Motors agrees to reimburse Firstbank for all amounts advanced to General Motors under the letter of credit and further agrees that all such amounts constitute loans made under the line of credit established under the Dealer Inventory Security Agreement (Form 3.2) and the Demand Note (Form 3.3).

On receipt of an order for new automobiles from Main Motors, General Motors sends the automobiles and the related manufacturer's certificates of origin[4] directly to Main Motors and, through the bank collection system, sends to Firstbank information describing the shipment (giving models, vehicle identification numbers, and prices of automobiles) and its draft calling on Firstbank to pay under the letter of credit. Upon receipt of these documents, Firstbank pays General Motors by sending funds to General Motors' bank, for credit to General Motors' account. Under an alternative arrangement, General Motors would maintain a bank account with Firstbank and, upon receipt of the documents, Firstbank would credit that account.

Figure 3.2 diagrams the documentation and payment involved each time Firstbank makes an advance for a new delivery of automobiles by General Motors to Main Motors.

---

4.   The function of the manufacturer's certificates of origin is explained below in connection with financing sales to consumers.

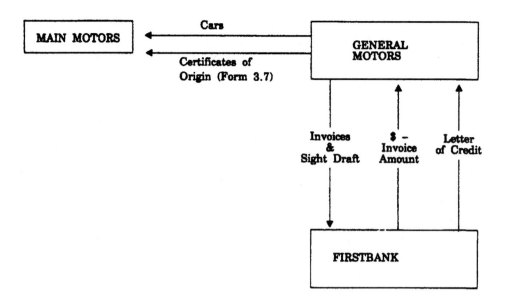

Figure 3.2

Option to Repurchase. Although the letter of credit arrangement just described provides General Motors with assurance of payment, General Motors also has an interest in protecting its reputation and its products in the marketplace. Specifically, General Motors wishes to ensure that new General Motors automobiles are sold only by authorized dealers who maintain certain standards. Consequently, General Motors requires its dealers to obtain secured financing from lenders who enter into an agreement affording General Motors a repurchase option. Under that agreement (which is not to be confused with securities "repos," discussed on page xxr, supra), if Main Motors defaults and Firstbank takes possession of its inventory of automobiles, then General Motors will have an *option* to repurchase the automobiles for the original wholesale price. Firstbank is not averse to that arrangement; General Motors' exercise of its option to repurchase would provide a convenient means for Firstbank to recover the principal amount of its outstanding loans on new automobiles. General Motors is unique in this respect; financial institutions, like Firstbank, which finance automobile inventory typically insist on and receive a repurchase *obligation* from other automobile manufacturers.

(D) DIAGRAM OF AUTOMOBILE DEALER INVENTORY FINANCING

Figure 3.3 diagrams all of the transactions and documentation involved in the Prototype automobile dealer inventory financing.

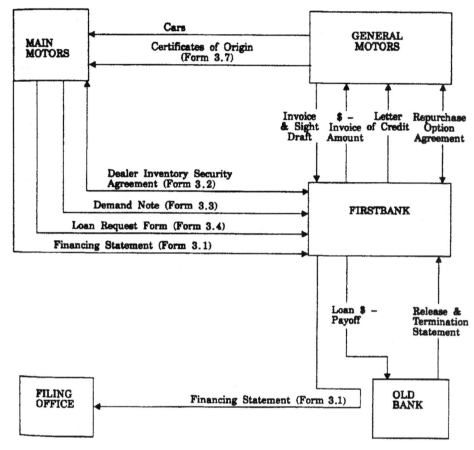

Figure 3.3

(E) SALES TO CONSUMERS

Lee Abel drives a 1995 Mazda Miata to Main's showroom and, after negotiating a $10,556 trade-in allowance for the used car, reaches an agreement with one of Main's salespersons for the purchase of a 2006 Chevrolet Blazer for a cash price of $27,056. (Actually, the negotiations focused on the amount by which the cash price would exceed the trade-in allowance for the Miata; Abel was satisfied with the difference of $16,500, making the trade-in allowance and cash price generally irrelevant to Abel.) Like most automobile buyers, Abel will buy on credit.

The Credit Decision. The relationship between Firstbank and Main Motors concerning consumer installment sales agreements is developed in detail below. For the moment, recall that Main Motors is not in a position to wait for Abel to pay for the new automobile over 48 months. It follows that Main's decision to sell to Abel on credit depends on whether a third party (here, Firstbank) is willing to purchase Abel's installment obligation from Main, thereby putting Main in funds at the inception of the transaction.

Main Motors asks Abel to fill out an "Instalment Credit Application" supplied by Firstbank. That form calls for information concerning Abel's place and length of employment, salary, number of dependents, banking relationships, and other credit outstanding, as well as other information relevant to Firstbank's credit decision. Main Motors then faxes the application to Firstbank's consumer credit department. Firstbank's staff reviews the application, obtains information about Abel's credit history and creditworthiness from a centralized **credit reporting agency**, and (within a matter of hours) reaches a decision about whether to extend credit to Abel.

Typically Firstbank's credit investigation shows that the prospective buyer is a satisfactory risk for the amount of credit requested. If so, Firstbank agrees to purchase the installment contract, provided that the amount of the down payment and other terms meet its standard requirements. One typical requirement is that the down payment reduce the amount owing for the automobile to not more than the dealer's cost. In this case, the trade-in allowance of $10,556 for Abel's used car reduces the unpaid balance to $16,500—comfortably less than the $25,256 wholesale cost of the new Chevrolet. Nevertheless, the present case does deviate from the customary pattern in that the credit investigation shows that Abel, although honest and reliable, occasionally has been slow in meeting installment obligations.

Alternative Assignment Plans. The method for dealing with this problem depends in part upon the underlying arrangement between a dealer and a purchaser of installment paper for the allocation of the risk of default by buyers. There are five common forms of agreements between a dealer and an assignee of installment credit contracts: (1) without recourse, (2) repurchase, (3) partial guaranty, (4) limited repurchase, and (5) full guaranty. The details of each of these alternatives are found in an "Assignment and Repurchase Agreement" (Form 3.5).

Note that Form 3.5 refers to an arrangement called the "Firstbank Retail Plan." That arrangement consists of a set of standard provisions that Firstbank and Main Motors (and Firstbank's other dealer customers) have agreed will apply to all purchases of consumer installment contracts. It contemplates that in the normal case Firstbank would purchase contracts of buyers on a **non-recourse** basis (i.e., Firstbank will not look to the dealer-assignor in the event of a buyer's nonpayment), thereby relieving Main Motors of liability or risk by reason of a buyer's failure to pay. In this case, however, because of the "slow pay" reports on Abel, Firstbank and Main Motors agree to allocate the risk of default differently. Firstbank requests Main to execute the "repurchase" portion of the Assignment and Repurchase Agreement.

FORM 3.5
ASSIGNMENT AND REPURCHASE AGREEMENT

A. For value received, the undersigned does hereby sell, assign and transfer to Firstbank, N.A. his, its or their entire right, title and interest in and to the attached contract, herewith submitted to Firstbank, N.A. for acceptance, and the property covered thereby, described as follows:

DESCRIPTION OF CONTRACT

Type of Contract	Date of Contract	Customer's Name
Motor Vehicle Installment Sales Contract	7/09/06	Lee Abel

Covering the following property

Year	Make	New or Used	Model	Vehicle Identification No.
2001	Chevrolet	New	Blazer	1FMES24VS2921874

and authorizes Firstbank, N.A. to do every act and thing necessary to collect and discharge obligations arising out of or incident to said contract and assignment. In order to induce Firstbank, N.A. to accept assignment of the contract, the undersigned warrants that: the contract arose from the sale of the within described property; the contract was complete in all respects and the undersigned made all disclosures required by law, including all disclosures required by Title 1 of the Consumer Credit Protection Act of 1968, as amended, and by local law, prior to execution thereof by the Customer; the Customer is not a minor and has capacity to contract; the contract and personal guaranty by third party, if any, are genuine, legally valid and enforceable and comply with all applicable requirements of state and federal law; title to the contract is vested in the undersigned free of all liens and encumbrances and the undersigned has the right to assign the contract; the property is as represented to the Customer by the undersigned; statements made by the Customer in the contract are true to the best of the undersigned's knowledge and belief, and the undersigned has no knowledge of any fact that would impair the validity or value of the contract; the down payment paid by the Customer and received by the undersigned was as stated in the contract; a certificate of title to the property showing the lien or encumbrance for the benefit of Firstbank, N.A. or the undersigned has been or will be applied for forthwith, if permitted by law. If there is a breach of any such warranty, without regard to the undersigned's knowledge or lack of knowledge with respect thereto or Firstbank, N.A.'s reliance thereon, the undersigned hereby agrees unconditionally, notwithstanding the numbered paragraph below executed by the undersigned, to purchase said contract from Firstbank, N.A., upon demand, for the full amount then unpaid whether said contract shall then be, or not be, in default. The undersigned further agrees that in the event the Customer or any other person or governmental agency makes a claim against Firstbank, N.A. alleging facts which, if true, would constitute a breach of any of the foregoing warranties or representations, the undersigned shall assume the defense of such claim and shall indemnify and save Firstbank, N.A. harmless from all loss, cost and expenses arising therefrom, and, at Firstbank, N.A.'s option, the undersigned will repurchase the contract for the full amount then unpaid. Liability of the undersigned arising out of or incident to this assignment shall not be affected by any indulgence, compromise, settlement, extensions, or variations of terms of said contract effected with, or by, the discharge or release of the obligation of the Customer or any other person interested, by operation of law or otherwise. The undersigned waives notice of acceptance of this assignment and notices of non-payment and non-performance of the contract. The acceptance or approval of the contract by Firstbank, N.A. shall not constitute an agreement, representation or warranty by Firstbank, N.A. as to the legal sufficiency thereof or of the disclosures therein contained or a waiver of Firstbank, N.A.'s right to rely on the foregoing warranties or representations with respect thereto.

B. As part of the foregoing assignment, the undersigned's obligations are further defined in the particular numbered paragraph below executed by the undersigned, and signature of any such numbered paragraph shall constitute signature of the entire assignment.

---

1. "Without Recourse" (See paragraphs A and B above)
   The assignment of said contract is and shall be without recourse against the undersigned, except as otherwise provided above and by the terms of the Firstbank, N.A. Retail Plan in effect at the time this assignment is accepted.

Seller Signs _____ By _____
                                          (If corporation or partnership) (Title)

---

2. "Repurchase" (See paragraphs A and B above)
   The undersigned guarantees payment of the full amount remaining unpaid under said contract, and covenants if default be made in payment of any instalment thereunder to pay the full amount then unpaid to Firstbank, N.A., upon demand, except as otherwise provided by the terms of the Firstbank, N.A. Retail Plan in effect at the time this assignment is accepted.

Main Motors, Inc.

Seller Signs *G.S. Gessell* _____ By G. S. Gessell, President _____
                                          (If corporation or partnership) (Title)

---

3. "Partial Guaranty" (See paragraphs A and B above)
   Notwithstanding the terms of the Firstbank, N.A. Retail Plan, the undersigned unconditionally guaranties payment of the full amount remaining unpaid under said contract, and agrees to purchase said contract from Firstbank, N.A. upon demand for the full amount then unpaid whether said contract shall then be, or not be, in default, provided, however, at the time of any such demand by Firstbank, N.A. the undersigned may, at his election, pay to Firstbank, N.A. the sum of $ _____ in consideration of being released from such guaranty obligation, and in such event, the assignment of said contract is without recourse against the undersigned, except as otherwise provided above and by the terms of the Firstbank, N.A. Retail Plan in effect at the time this assignment is accepted.

Seller Signs _____ By _____
                                          (If corporation or partnership) (Title)

---

4. "Limited Repurchases" (See paragraphs A and B above)
   The undersigned guaranties payment of the full amount remaining unpaid under said contract, and covenants if default be made in payment of any instalment thereunder to pay the full amount then unpaid to Firstbank, N.A. upon demand, except as otherwise provided by the terms of the Firstbank, N.A. Retail Plan in effect at the time this assignment is accepted provided, that if the Customer satisfactorily pays each of the first _____ installments coming due under the within contract, this assignment shall thereafter be without recourse against the undersigned, except as otherwise provided above and by the terms of the Firstbank, N.A. Retail Plan in effect at the time this assignment is accepted.

Seller Signs _____ By _____
                                          (If corporation or partnership) (Title)

---

5. "Full Guaranty" (See paragraphs A and B above)
   Notwithstanding the terms of the Firstbank, N.A. Retail Plan, the undersigned unconditionally guaranties payment of the full amount remaining unpaid under said contract, and agrees to purchase said contract from Firstbank, N.A., upon demand, for the full amount then unpaid, whether said contract shall then be, or not be, in default.

Seller Signs _____ By _____
                                          (If corporation or partnership) (Title)

NOTE: If a corporation, assignment must be executed in the name of the corporation by an officer having proper authority from the Board of Directors. If a partnership, assignment must be executed by a partner.

Under the "repurchase" terms, if a default occurs under Abel's contract, Main Motors agrees to repurchase the contract from Firstbank by paying the entire unpaid amount thereunder. Although not reflected in the Assignment and Repurchase Agreement, the terms of the Firstbank Retail Plan provide that Main would not be required to repurchase the contract until after Firstbank takes possession of the car from Abel. Thus this arrangement divides the burdens and risks of default between Firstbank and Main Motors: Firstbank assumes the burden of repossession and also the risk of loss in the event the automobile cannot be located for repossession; Main Motors assumes the burdens and losses involved in any foreclosure proceedings and in collecting any deficiency from Abel.

The Dealer's Contract With the Consumer. With financing arrangements completed, Main Motors is in a position to make delivery to Abel. As we have seen, Main Motors and Abel have agreed on a cash price of $27,056 for the Chevrolet. Main has agreed to take Abel's 1995 Miata for a trade-in credit of $10,556, leaving a balance of $16,500. In addition, Abel must pay state sales taxes ($1,036.50) and fees ($29.00) and a documentation fee to Main Motors ($40.00). Abel also has elected to purchase an extended warranty contract ($775.00). These costs bring Abel's unpaid obligation for the car to $18,380.50.

Abel also must pay a finance charge. In this instance, Abel agrees to pay an Annual Percentage Rate of 9.5% on the amount financed, which amounts to $3,784.74 for the four years the contract is to run. This finance charge brings the total of payments to $22,165.24, payable in 48 installments of $461.79. Main Motors and Abel sign an "Instalment Sale Contract" (Form 3.6) that evidences this obligation. Certain provisions of Form 3.6, such as disclosure of the Total Sale Price and the Annual Percentage Rate, are included in order to comply with the Truth In Lending Act, 15 U.S.C. §§ 1601–1667f. (Form 3.6 would not be used in an actual transaction in Pennsylvania because it does not contain certain disclosures required under Pennsylvania law. We have assumed away these provisions of Pennsylvania law in order to simplify the Prototype).

In addition to providing for Abel's payment obligations, the Instalment Sale Contract also contains a security agreement in which Abel grants a security interest in the new car to Main Motors to secure those payment obligations. When the assignment by Main to Firstbank is effected, Firstbank becomes Abel's creditor and is the new secured party in the transaction.[5] (Accordingly, as discussed below, Firstbank will promptly send Abel a notification of the assignment and instruct Abel to make all payments under the Instalment Sale Contract directly to Firstbank.)

---

5.   You may note that at the bottom of the face of the Instalment Sale Contract there is a brief assignment form that refers to the Firstbank Retail Plan agreement, as does the Assignment and Repurchase Agreement (Form 3.5). Because the parties elected the "repurchase" option in Form 3.5, Main Motors has signed the "without recourse or with limited recourse" form of assignment on the Instalment Sale Contract.

FORM 3.6
RETAIL INSTALMENT SALE CONTRACT

RETAIL INSTALMENT SALE CONTRACT

Dealer Number	Contract Number

Buyer (and Co-Buyer) - Name and address (include county and zip code)	Creditor (Seller name and address)
LEE ABEL 123 EAST 10TH STREET PHILADELPHIA, PA 19116	MAIN MOTORS, INC. 237 NORTH 7TH STREET PHILADELPHIA, PA 19116

You, the Buyer (and Co-Buyer, if any), may buy the vehicle described below for cash or on credit. The cash price is shown below as "cash price." The credit price is shown below as "Total Sale Price." By signing this contract, you choose to buy the vehicle on credit under the agreements on the front and back of this contract. You agree to pay us, the Creditor, the Amount Financed and Finance Charge according to the payment schedule shown below.

New or Used	Year	Make and Model	Vehicle Identification No.	Primary Use for Which Purchased
NEW	2006	CHEVROLET BLAZER	1FMES23VS292187	X personal, family, or household ☐ agricultural ☐ business ☐

Your trade-in is a: Year _____   Make _____   Model _____

FEDERAL TRUTH-IN-LENDING DISCLOSURES

ANNUAL PERCENTAGE RATE The cost of your credit as a yearly rate.	FINANCE CHARGE The dollar amount the credit will cost you.	Amount Financed The amount of credit provided to you or on your behalf.	Total of Payments The amount you will have paid after you have made all payments as scheduled.	Total Sale Price The total cost of your purchase on credit, including your downpayment of $10556 is
9.50 %	$3784.74	$18380.50	$ 20277.60	$ 30833.60

Your Payment Schedule Will Be:

Number of Payments	Amount of Payments	When Payments Are Due	Or as Follows
48	$461.79	Monthly beginning 8/24/06	N/A

Late Charge. If a payment is not received in full within 10 days after it is due, you will pay a late charge of 5% of the part of the payment that is late, with a minimum charge of $1.

Prepayment. If you pay off all your debt early, you may be entitled to a refund of part of the finance charge.

Security Interest. You are giving a security interest in the vehicle being purchased.

Additional Information: See this contract for more information including information about nonpayment, default, any required repayment in full before the scheduled date, prepayment refunds and security interest.

ITEMIZATION OF AMOUNT FINANCED

1 Cash price (including any accessories, services, and taxes)	$ 27056.00	(1)
2 Total downpayment = (If negative enter "0" and see line 4H below)		
Gross trade-in $ 10556 – payoff by seller $ 0		
= net trade-in $ 10556 – cash $ 0		
+ other (describe) $	$ 10556.00	(2)
3 Unpaid balance of cash price (1 minus 2)	$ 16500.00	(3)
4 Other charges including amounts paid to others on your behalf (Seller may keep part of these amounts.):		
A Cost of optional credit insurance paid to the insurance company or companies.		
Life $		
Disability $	$ N/A	
B Other insurance paid to the insurance company	$ N/A	
C Official fees paid to government agencies	$ 5.00	
D Taxes not included in cash price	$ 1036.50	
E Government license and/or registration fees (identify)	$ 4.00	
F Government certificate of title fees	$ 20.00	
G Other charges (Seller must identify who is paid and describe purpose)		
to CMI 60 mos/60,000 mi for	$ 775.00	
to Main Motors for Doc Fee	$ 40.00	
to for	$	
H Net trade-in payoff to	$	
Total other charges and amounts paid to others on your behalf	$ 1880.50	(4)
5 Amount financed (3 + 4)	$ 18380.50	(5)

Insurance. You may buy the physical damage insurance this contract requires (see back) from anyone you choose who is acceptable to us. You are not required to buy any other insurance to obtain credit.

If any insurance is checked below, policies or certificates from the named insurance companies will describe the terms and conditions.

Check the insurance you want and sign below:

Optional Credit Insurance.

☐ Credit Life: ☐ Buyer   ☐ Co-Buyer   ☐ Both
☐ Credit Disability (Buyer Only)
Premium:
     Credit Life $ _____
     Credit Disability $ _____

_____
(Insurance Company)

_____
(Home Office Address)

Credit life insurance and credit disability insurance are not required to obtain credit. They will not be provided unless you sign and agree to pay the extra cost. Credit life insurance and credit disability insurance are for the term of this contract unless a different term for the insurance is shown below.

Other insurance.

☐ _____
         Type of Insurance   Term
Premium $ _____

_____
(Insurance Company)

_____
(Home Office Address)

I want the insurance checked above.

_____
Buyer Signature   Date

_____
Co-Buyer Signature   Date

ANY INSURANCE REFERRED TO IN THIS CONTRACT DOES NOT INCLUDE COVERAGE FOR PERSONAL LIABILITY AND PROPERTY DAMAGE CAUSED TO OTHERS.

HOW THIS CONTRACT CAN BE CHANGED. This contract contains the entire agreement between you and us relating to this contract. Any change to the contract must be in writing and we must sign it. No oral changes are binding. Buyer (and any Co-Buyer) initials _____.

If any part of this contract is not valid, all other parts stay valid. We may delay or refrain from enforcing any of our rights under this contract without losing them. For example, we may extend the time for making some payments without extending the time for making others.

See back for other important agreements.

You agree to the terms of this contract and confirm that you received a completely filled-in copy when you signed it.

Buyer Signs *Lee Abel*   Date 7/9/06   Co-Buyer Signs _____   Date _____

Co-Buyers and Other Owners – A co-buyer is a person who is responsible for paying the entire debt. An other owner is a person whose name is on the title to the vehicle but does not have to pay the debt. The co-buyer or other owner knows that we have a security interest in the vehicle and consents to the security interest.

Other owner signs here _____   Address _____

Creditor Signs MAIN MOTORS, INC Date 7/9/2006 By *B. Fold*   Title Sales Manager

Seller assigns its interest in this contract to Firstbank, N.A. under the terms of the Firstbank, N.A. Retail Plan agreement.	
Assigned with recourse	MAIN MOTORS, INC. assigned without recourse or with limited recourse Sales Manager *B. Fold*
Seller By Title	Seller By Title

Notice: See Other Side

(FACE)

OTHER IMPORTANT AGREEMENTS

1. YOUR OTHER PROMISES TO US

a. If the vehicle is damaged, destroyed, or missing. You agree to pay us all you owe under this contract even if the vehicle is damaged, destroyed, or missing.

b. Using the vehicle. You agree not to remove the vehicle from the U.S. or Canada, or to sell, rent, lease, or transfer any interest in the vehicle or this contract without our written permission. You agree not to expose the vehicle to misuse, seizure, confiscation, or involuntary transfer. If we pay any repair bills, storage bills, taxes, fines, or charges on the vehicle, you agree to repay the amount when we ask for it.

c. Security interest. You give us a security interest in:
1. The vehicle and all parts or goods installed in it;
2. All money or goods received (proceeds) for the vehicle;
3. All insurance or service contracts we finance for you; and
4. All proceeds from insurance or service contracts we finance for you. This includes any refunds of premiums.

This secures payment of all you owe on this contract. It also secures your other agreements in this contract. You will make sure the title shows our security interest (lien) in the vehicle.

d. Insurance you must have on the vehicle. You agree to have physical damage insurance covering loss or damage to the vehicle for the term of this contract. The insurance must cover our interest in the vehicle. If you do not have this insurance, we may, if we decide, buy physical damage insurance. If we decide to buy physical damage insurance, we may either buy insurance that covers your interest and our interest in the vehicle, or buy insurance that covers only our interest. If we buy either type of insurance, we will tell you which type and the charge you must pay. The charge will be the premium for the insurance and a finance charge at the highest rate the law permits.

If the vehicle is lost or damaged, we agree that we may use any insurance settlement to reduce what you owe or repair the vehicle.

e. What happens to returned insurance or service contract charges. If we obtain a refund of insurance or service contract charges, we will apply the refund and the unearned finance charges on the refund to as many of your payments as they will cover beginning with the final payment. We will tell you what we do.

2. YOU MAY PREPAY IN FULL

You may prepay all of your debt and get a refund of part of the Finance Charge.

How we will calculate your Finance Charge refund. We will figure the refund by the Rule of 78's if the term of this contract is 61 months or less. If the term of this contract is more than 61 months, we will figure the refund by the Actuarial Method using the payment dates in this contract. We will not pay you a refund if it is less than $1.

3. IF YOU PAY LATE OR BREAK YOUR OTHER PROMISES

a. You may owe **late charges.** You will pay a late charge on each payment we receive more than ten days late. The charge is on the front. Acceptance of a late payment or late charge does not excuse your late payment or mean that you may keep making late payments. If you pay late, we may also take the steps described below.

b. You may have to pay all you owe at once. If you break your promises (**default**), we may demand that you pay all you owe on this contract at once. Default means:
1. You do not pay any payment on time;
2. You start a proceeding in bankruptcy or one is started against you or your property; or
3. You break any agreements in this contract.

In figuring what you owe, we will give you a refund of part of the Finance Charge as if you had prepaid in full.

c. You may have to pay collection costs. If we hire an attorney to collect what you owe, you will pay the attorney's fee and court costs, as the law allows.

d. We may take the vehicle from you. If you default, we may take (repossess) the vehicle from you if we do so peacefully and the law allows it. If your vehicle has an electronic tracking device, you agree that we may use the device to find the vehicle. If we take the vehicle, any accessories, equipment, and replacement parts will stay with the vehicle. If any personal items are in the vehicle, we may store them for you at your expense. If you do not ask for these items back, we may dispose of them as the law allows.

e. How you can get the vehicle back if we take it. If we repossess the vehicle, you may pay to get it back (redeem). We will tell you how much to pay to redeem. Your right to redeem ends when we sell the vehicle.

f. We will sell the vehicle if you do not get it back. If you do not redeem, we will sell the vehicle. We will send you a written notice of sale before selling the vehicle.

We will apply the money from the sale, less allowed expenses, to the amount you owe. Allowed expenses are expenses we pay as a direct result of taking the vehicle, holding it, preparing it for sale, and selling it. Attorney fees and court costs the law permits are also allowed expenses. If any money is left (surplus), we will pay it to you. If money from the sale is not enough to pay the amount you owe, you must pay the rest to us. If you do not pay this amount when we ask, we may charge you interest at the highest lawful rate until you pay.

g. What we may do about optional insurance or service contracts. This contract may contain charges for optional insurance or service contracts. If we repossess the vehicle, you agree that we may claim benefits under these contracts and cancel them to obtain refunds of unearned charges to reduce what you owe or repair the vehicle.

4. WARRANTIES SELLER DISCLAIMS

Unless the Seller makes a written warranty, or enters into a service contract within 90 days from the date of this contract, the Seller makes no warranties, express or implied, on the vehicle, and there will be no implied warranties of merchantability or of fitness for a particular purpose.

This provision does not affect any warranties covering the vehicle that the vehicle manufacturer may provide.

5. Used Car Buyers Guide.
The information you see on the window form for this vehicle is part of this contract. Information on the window form overrides any contrary provisions in the contract of sale.

Spanish Translation:
Guía para compradores de vehículos usados. La información que ve en el formulario de la ventanilla para este vehículo forma parte del presente contrato. La información del formulario de la ventanilla deja sin efecto toda disposición en contrario contenida en el contrato de venta.

6. APPLICABLE LAW

Federal and Pennsylvania law apply to this contract.

NOTICE: ANY HOLDER OF THIS CONSUMER CREDIT CONTRACT IS SUBJECT TO ALL CLAIMS AND DEFENSES WHICH THE DEBTOR COULD ASSERT AGAINST THE SELLER OF GOODS OR SERVICES OBTAINED PURSUANT HERETO OR WITH THE PROCEEDS HEREOF. RECOVERY HEREUNDER BY THE DEBTOR SHALL NOT EXCEED AMOUNTS PAID BY THE DEBTOR HEREUNDER.

The preceding NOTICE applies only to goods or services obtained primarily for personal, family, or household use. In all other cases, Buyer will not assert against any subsequent holder or assignee of this contract any claims or defenses the Buyer (debtor) may have against the Seller, or against the manufacturer of the vehicle or equipment obtained under this contract.

(REVERSE)

Figure 3.4 diagrams the documentation and deliveries involved when Main Motors sells the new car to Lee Abel and assigns Abel's Instalment Sale Contract to Firstbank.

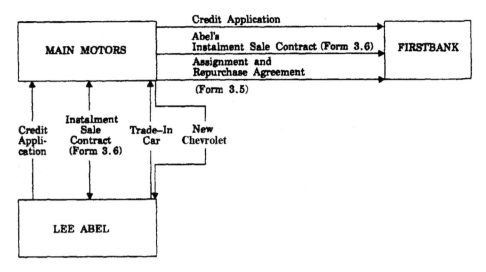

Figure 3.4

(F) PERFECTING THE SECURITY INTEREST IN THE NEW CAR; THE CERTIFICATE OF TITLE

One of the terms of Firstbank's purchase of Abel's Instalment Sale Contract is that the security interest in Abel's Chevrolet is to be perfected. (This is a warranty that Main Motors makes under the Firstbank Retail Plan agreement.) All states now have "certificate of title" laws; although these laws vary materially, in general they provide that the normal method of perfecting a security interest in an automobile (or other vehicle required to be titled) is by causing the security interest to be reflected on the certificate of title issued by a central state office (e.g., in Pennsylvania, the Bureau of Motor Vehicles). An exception is made for vehicles in a dealer's inventory, as to which the usual financing statement filing rules apply. See UCC 9–311(d).

Certificates of Origin and Control Over Dealer Operations. For each new vehicle, the manufacturer issues a manufacturer's certificate of origin (Form 3.7) (sometimes referred to as an "MCO").

In most states, because a certificate of title for a new vehicle cannot be issued without presenting a certificate of origin, the latter document is a useful device to ensure that a dealer is operating in conformity with its financing agreement. For this reason, some lenders hold certificates of origin in their own files until they receive word from a dealer that a particular automobile has been sold. Firstbank, like many other lenders, has decided that holding each certificate of origin for each automobile would be too cumbersome; Firstbank also is satisfied with the integrity of Main Motors' operation. Consequently, Firstbank has notified General Motors that these documents are to be delivered directly to Main Motors.

At least once a month Firstbank does a floorplan check at each dealership it finances. During the check the bank's representative looks at every new automobile listed on the invoices it has received from the manufacturer (i.e., all of the automobiles it has financed). After checking the collateral, the representative matches the serial numbers of the units with the serial numbers printed on the certificates of origin kept in the dealer's files. This is done to make sure that each automobile on the floorplan financing remains untitled. If either a certificate of origin or a automobile is missing, Firstbank probably should have been paid by the dealer.[6]

---

6.   Under the terms of the Dealer Inventory Security Agreement (Form 3.2, ¶ 8), a dealer is required to repay immediately the amount loaned to finance an automobile (here, the wholesale price) when an automobile is sold. The absence of an automobile or a certificate of origin would be an indication that a sale may have occurred.

FORM 3.7
MANUFACTURER'S CERTIFICATE OF ORIGIN

(*FACE*)

Each undersigned seller certifies to the best of his knowledge, information and belief under penalty of the law that the vehicle is new and has not been registered in this or any state at the time of delivery and the vehicle is not subject to any security interests other than those disclosed herein and warrant title to the vehicle. FOR VALUE RECEIVED I TRANSFER THE VEHICLE DESCRIBED ON THE FACE OF THIS CERTIFICATE TO:

DISTRIBUTOR-DEALER ASSIGNMENT NUMBER 1

NAME OF PURCHASER(S) _____

ADDRESS _____

I certify to the best of my knowledge that the odometer reading is _____ No Tenths

DEALER _____ BY _____
NAME OF DEALERSHIP   DEALER'S LICENSE NUMBER

Being duly sworn upon oath says that the statements set forth are true and correct. Subscribed and sworn to me

State of _____ before this _____ day of _____ 19___

County of _____ Notary Public

USE NOTARIZATION ONLY IF REQUIRED IN TITLING JURISDICTION

DISTRIBUTOR-DEALER ASSIGNMENT NUMBER 2

NAME OF PURCHASER(S) _____

ADDRESS _____

I certify to the best of my knowledge that the odometer reading is _____ No Tenths

DEALER _____ BY _____
NAME OF DEALERSHIP   DEALER'S LICENSE NUMBER

Being duly sworn upon oath says that the statements set forth are true and correct. Subscribed and sworn to me

State of _____ before this _____ day of _____ 19___

County of _____ Notary Public

USE NOTARIZATION ONLY IF REQUIRED IN TITLING JURISDICTION

DISTRIBUTOR-DEALER ASSIGNMENT NUMBER 3

NAME OF PURCHASER(S) _____

ADDRESS _____

I certify to the best of my knowledge that the odometer reading is _____ No Tenths

DEALER _____ BY _____
NAME OF DEALERSHIP   DEALER'S LICENSE NUMBER

Being duly sworn upon oath says that the statements set forth are true and correct. Subscribed and sworn to me

State of _____ before this _____ day of _____ 19___

County of _____ Notary Public

USE NOTARIZATION ONLY IF REQUIRED IN TITLING JURISDICTION

DISTRIBUTOR-DEALER ASSIGNMENT NUMBER 4

NAME OF PURCHASER(S) _____

ADDRESS _____

I certify to the best of my knowledge that the odometer reading is _____ No Tenths

DEALER _____ BY _____
NAME OF DEALERSHIP   DEALER'S LICENSE NUMBER

Being duly sworn upon oath says that the statements set forth are true and correct. Subscribed and sworn to me

State of _____ before this _____ day of _____ 19___

County of _____ Notary Public

USE NOTARIZATION ONLY IF REQUIRED IN TITLING JURISDICTION

ODOMETER DISCLOSURE FOR RETAIL SALE

Federal law requires you to state the odometer mileage in connection with the transfer of ownership. Failure to complete or provide a false statement may result in fines and / or imprisonment.

I certify to the best of my knowledge that the odometer reading is the actual mileage of the vehicle unless one of the following statements is checked. Odometer Reading _36_ NO Tenths. ☐ The mileage stated is in excess of its mechanical limits ☐ The odometer reading is not the actual mileage. **WARNING-ODOMETER DISCREPANCY**

Signature(s) of Seller(s) _B Cold , Sales Mgr_

Printed Name(s) of Seller(s) **Main Motors, Inc.** Dealer's No. _6075_

Date of Statement _7/9/06_ Date of Sale _7/9/06_

Being duly sworn upon oath says that the statements set forth are true and correct. Subscribed and sworn to me

Signature of Purchaser(s) _Lee Abel_

before this _____ day of _____ 19___

Printed Name of Purchaser(s) _Lee Abel_ Notary Public

Company Name (if Applicable) _____ State of _____

Address of Purchaser(s) _123 E. 10th, Phila. PA 19116_ County of _____

USE NOTARIZATION ONLY IF REQUIRED IN TITLING JURISDICTION

LIENHOLDER

1st lien in favor of _Firstbank, NA_

whose address is _Broad & Spruce Streets, Philadelphia, PA 19116_

2nd lien in favor of _____

whose address is _____

GM521 REV. 3-91

In the event that Firstbank finances a dealer with serious financial problems, Firstbank will be particularly careful to see that it gets paid for each automobile sold. Firstbank's physical inventory checks will be more frequent—perhaps even daily. In protecting its interests, one of the first things that Firstbank will do is take possession of all certificates of origin. Because a dealer cannot title automobiles it sells without such certificates, Firstbank thereby achieves some comfort that it will be paid upon a dealer's sale of each vehicle.

Issuance of the Certificate of Title. Main Motors, as seller, executes an assignment of the Certificate of Origin to Abel, indicating that Firstbank is to have a lien (security interest) in the new car (see the reverse side of Form

3.7). (If Main were going to retain the contract it would list itself as lienholder.) Main Motors then sends the Certificate of Origin to the Bureau of Motor Vehicles, which, in turn, issues a Certificate of Title (Form 3.8). Here, the Certificate of Title is issued in the name of Lee Abel, and it states that the vehicle is subject to an encumbrance in favor of Firstbank. The Certificate of Title is then forwarded to Firstbank.[7]

---

7. In some states the certificate of title is forwarded to the owner, not the lienholder, and in others a duplicate is forwarded to the owner.

FORM 3.8
CERTIFICATE OF TITLE

COMMONWEALTH OF PENNSYLVANIA
DEPARTMENT OF TRANSPORTATION
CERTIFICATE OF TITLE FOR A VEHICLE

10,098

9620400180002692-001

1FMES24VS2921874	06	CHEVROLET	49895484201 MO
VEHICLE IDENTIFICATION NUMBER	YEAR	MAKE OF VEHICLE	TITLE NUMBER

SW	D		07/27/06	000036	D
BODY TYPE	DUP / SEAT CAP	PRIOR TITLE STATE	ODOM PROCD DATE	ODOM MILES	ODOM STATUS
07/27/06	07/27/06				
CATE PA TITLED	DATE OF ISSUE	UNLADEN WEIGHT	GVWR	GCWR	TITLE BRANDS

ODOMETER STATUS
0 = ACTUAL MILEAGE
1 = MILEAGE EXCEEDS THE MECHANICAL UNITS
2 = NOT THE ACTUAL MILEAGE
3 = NOT THE ACTUAL MILEAGE-ODOMETER TAMPERING VERIFIED
4 = EXEMPT FROM ODOMETER DISCLOSURE

TITLE BRANDS
A = ANTIQUE VEHICLE
C = CLASSIC VEHICLE
F = OUT OF COUNTRY
G = ORIGINALLY MFGD FOR NON-U.S. DISTRIBUTION
H = AGRICULTURAL VEHICLE
L = LOGGING VEHICLE
P = FORMERLY A POLICE VEHICLE
R = RECONSTRUCTED
S = STREET ROD
T = RECOVERED THEFT VEHICLE
V = VEHICLE CONTAINS RE-ISSUED VIN
W = FLOOD VEHICLE
X = FORMERLY A TAXI

REGISTERED OWNER(S)
LEE ABEL
123 EAST 10TH STREET
PHILADELPHIA, PA 19116

FIRST LIEN FAVOR OF

FIRSTBANK, N.A.

SECOND LIEN FAVOR OF

FIRST LIEN RELEASED _____ DATE

BY _____ AUTHORIZED REPRESENTATIVE

If a second lienholder is listed upon satisfaction of the first lien, the first lienholder must forward this Title to the Bureau of Motor Vehicles with the appropriate form and fee

SECOND LIEN RELEASED _____ DATE

BY _____ AUTHORIZED REPRESENTATIVE

MAILING ADDRESS
FIRSTBANK, N.A.
BROAD & SPRUCE STREETS
PHILADELPHIA, PA 19116

I certify as of the date of issue the official records of the Pennsylvania Department of Transportation reflect that the person(s) or company named herein is the lawful owner of the said vehicle.

BRADLEY L MALLORY

Secretary of Transportation

D. APPLICATION FOR TITLE AND LIEN INFORMATION

TO BE COMPLETED BY PURCHASER WHEN VEHICLE IS SOLD AND THE APPROPRIATE SECTIONS ON THE REVERSE SIDE OF THIS DOCUMENT ARE COMPLETED

SUBSCRIBED AND SWORN TO BEFORE ME

	MO	DAY	YEAR

SIGNATURE OF PERSON ADMINISTERING OATH

When applying for title with a co-owner, other than your spouse, check one of these blocks. If no block is checked, title will be issued as "Tenants in Common"
A ☐ Joint Tenants with Right of Survivorship (on death of one owner, title goes to the surviving owner)
B ☐ Tenants in Common (on death of one owner, interest of deceased owner goes to his or her heirs or estate)

LIEN DATE		IF NO LIEN CHECK BOX ☐
FIRST LIENHOLDER		
NAME		
STREET		
CITY		
STATE		ZIP

SEAL

The undersigned hereby makes application for Certificate of Title to the vehicle described above subject to the encumbrances and other legal claims set forth here.

SIGNATURE OF APPLICANT OR AUTHORIZED SIGNER

LIEN DATE		IF NO LIEN CHECK BOX ☐
SECOND LIENHOLDER		
NAME		
STREET		
CITY		
STATE		ZIP

SIGNATURE OF CO-APPLICANT/TITLE OF AUTHORIZED SIGNER

STORE IN A SAFE PLACE — IF LOST APPLY FOR A DUPLICATE — ANY ALTERATION OR ERASURE VOIDS THIS TITLE

THE FACE OF THIS DOCUMENT HAS A COLORED BACKGROUND ON WHITE PAPER

06444053

(FACE)

(REVERSE)

Figure 3.5 diagrams the assignment of the certificate of origin and the issuance of the certificate of title.

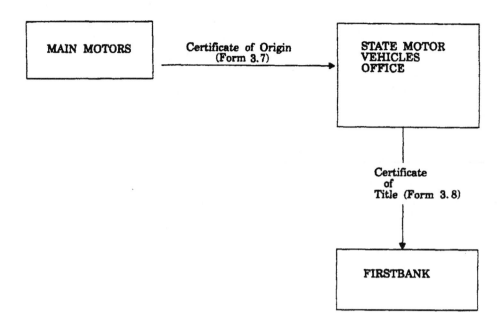

Figure 3.5

(G) REPAYMENT OF INVENTORY LOAN AND ASSIGNMENT OF CONSUMER PAPER; NOTIFICATION OF ASSIGNMENT AND PAYMENT INSTRUCTIONS

In the Dealer Inventory Security Agreement (Form 3.2, ¶ 8) Main Motors agreed that when it sells one of the automobiles in which Firstbank holds a security interest, it will pay the amount advanced by Firstbank for that automobile. Main's cost for Abel's Chevrolet, advanced by Firstbank, was $25,256. Had Abel paid cash for the car, Main Motors would send its check for $25,256 to Firstbank. In the more typical situation, as in this sale to Abel, Main Motors has sold the automobile under an Instalment Sale Contract.

In order to obtain funds to pay Firstbank, Main has assigned the contract to a purchaser. Main well might have obtained funds by assigning Abel's contract to a purchaser *other* than Firstbank (e.g., a finance company or another bank). However, Main "just happens" to have assigned the contract to Firstbank, and Firstbank "just happens" to be the lender that financed the inventory and is owed payment upon the sale of the car. For this reason, Firstbank can make entries in Main's bank account with Firstbank to effectuate both *Firstbank's payment of the purchase price of Abel's contract* and *Main's repayment to Firstbank of the inventory loan.* Main sends Abel's contract to Firstbank, and Firstbank credits Main's account with the price it is to pay for the contract. The $10,556 allowance given for Abel's trade-in reduced the Unpaid Balance of Cash Price for the car to $16,500. That amount, plus the amount of the state taxes and fees, documentation fee, and extended warranty contract (a total of $18,380.50) approximates the amount that Firstbank will pay to Main as the purchase price for Abel's contract, inasmuch as Firstbank expects to earn the finance charges that Abel is to pay. After crediting Main's account in that amount, the Bank then debits the account for the amount due on the inventory loan. Note that the amount of the debit ($25,256, which Firstbank advanced to Main against the car) substantially exceeds the amount Firstbank pays for an assignment of the contract. Under these circumstances Main will be expected to enclose its check, or authorize Firstbank to debit its account, for the difference.

Main has not yet received as much cash for the Chevrolet sold to Abel as it has paid for that car. It is evident that Main's profit on this transaction will depend in part on the price it gets from the sale of Abel's 1995 Miata, which Main took in trade. Not so obvious is the opportunity for further profit that Main Motors enjoys. Competition among banks and finance companies to purchase installment sale contracts leads to arrangements with a dealer that enhance the dealer's return. The reasons for this competition become evident when one considers the relatively high finance charges that can be charged on consumer automobile installment paper (9.5% on Abel's contract).

Firstbank may make an informal arrangement for sharing this return with Main Motors. The portion of the finance charges returned to Main (**dealer participation**) will depend on factors such as the level of interest rates generally, the level of the dealer's residual liability, the volume of business provided by the dealer, the bank's cost of funds, and the degree of competition to obtain financing arrangements with Main. Now we can see that it was not a pure coincidence that Firstbank purchased Abel's contract and also provided Main Motors with inventory financing. Many banks and finance companies provide inventory financing, sometimes even as a "loss leader," in order to get the first opportunity to acquire the lucrative retail installment contract financing.

On receipt of Abel's contract, Firstbank writes to Abel and directs that payments are to be made to Firstbank; along with the letter is a coupon book containing coupons to be enclosed with each of the 48 installment payments. When (and if) Abel completes the payments, Firstbank will return the Certificate of Title, marked "encumbrance satisfied."

Figure 3.6 diagrams (i) Firstbank's payment to Main Motors for Abel's Instalment Sale Contract; (ii) Main's payment to Firstbank of the amount of the inventory loan made against the Chevrolet;[8] (iii) Firstbank's communication to Abel, notifying Abel that the contract has been assigned to Firstbank, instructing Abel to make all payments to Firstbank, and enclosing payment coupons; and (iv) Abel's monthly payments.

---

8.   As the text observes, Firstbank and Main Motors effect payments to one another by debits and credits to the bank account Main Motors maintains with Firstbank.

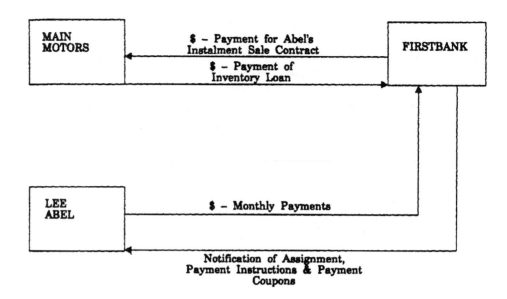

Figure 3.6

(H) DIAGRAM OF AUTOMOBILE INSTALMENT SALE CONTRACT FINANCING

Figure 3.7 diagrams all of the transactions and documentation featured in the Prototype installment sale contract financing.

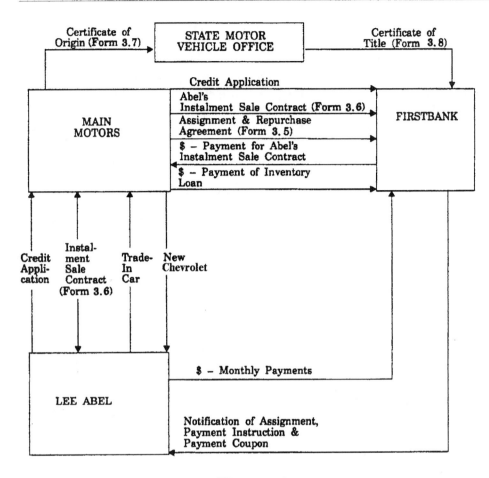

Figure 3.7

(I) THE CONSUMER FAILS TO PAY

At this point the transaction with Lee Abel departs from the typical pattern, in which the buyer makes the payments when due. We now shall assume that after 12 months Abel is unable to keep up the monthly payments.

Collection Efforts. If Abel does not respond to one or two dunning letters from Firstbank, a collector calls Abel on the telephone to encourage prompt payment; if letters and telephone calls fail, the collector may demonstrate Firstbank's seriousness of purpose by making a house call. (In special circumstances, the creditor and debtor may execute a new contract (a **refinancing agreement**) that reduces the amount of each monthly payment by extending the payments over a longer period.)

Repossession. In this case we shall assume that there is no hope for prompt improvement in Abel's financial position; Firstbank takes steps to repossess the Chevrolet. Often debtors voluntarily surrender collateral upon the secured creditor's request. If a debtor is uncooperative, the creditor may resort to self help or to judicial proceedings such as a replevin action. In most cases creditors employ self help as the faster and less expensive method. An employee of the secured creditor or of a third-party collection service normally will be able to locate the automobile and take it away.

After Abel's car is repossessed, Firstbank sends Abel a notification to the effect that Firstbank has taken the car. The notification also informs Abel of the right to redeem the car upon payment of the balance due (including any late fees, costs of repossession, and expenses of making the car ready for disposition) and of a proposed disposition of the car if that amount is not forthcoming. This letter follows as Form 3.9. (As in the case of the Instalment Sale Contract (Form 3.6), for simplicity Form 3.9 omits several items required under Pennsylvania law.)

FORM 3.9
NOTIFICATION OF REPOSSESSION AND DISPOSITION

FIRSTBANK, NA.
Broad & Spruce Streets
Philadelphia, PA 19116

September 10, 2007

NOTICE OF OUR PLAN TO SELL PROPERTY

Lee Abel
123 East 10th Street
Philadelphia, PA 19116

Subject: Contract Number 81347

We have your vehicle (a 2001 Chevrolet Blazer with VIN 1FMES24VS292187), because you broke promises in our agreement.

We will sell your vehicle at private sale sometime after September 25, 2007. A sale could include a lease or license.

The money that we get from the sale (after paying our costs) will reduce the amount you owe. If we get less money than you owe, you will still owe us the difference. If we get more money than you owe, you will get the extra money, unless we must pay it to someone else.

You can get the property back at any time before we sell it by paying us the full amount you owe (not just the past due payments), including our expenses. To learn the exact amount you must pay, call us at 215-800-0000.

If you want us to explain to you in writing how we have figured the amount that you owe us, you may call us at 215-800-0000 or write us at Broad & Spruce Streets, Philadelphia, PA 19116 and request a written explanation. [We will charge you $10.00 for the explanation if we sent you another written explanation of the amount you owe us within the last six months.

If you need more information about the sale call us at 215-800-0000 or write us at Broad & Spruce Streets, Philadelphia, PA 19116.

We are sending this notice to the following other people who have an interest in your vehicle or who owe money under your agreement:

None.

FIRSTBANK, N.A.

L. Null

L. Null
Consumer Lending Department

At this point Firstbank calls upon Main Motors to repurchase the contract as Main agreed to do under the terms of the assignment. Main then assumes the rights and duties of a secured party. After the specified notice period expires, Main will sell the automobile. The rights of parties in these situations are developed more fully in Chapter 9, infra.

SECTION 2.   ATTACHMENT OF SECURITY INTERESTS

Problem 3.2.1. The transaction followed precisely the steps described in the Prototype. Main Motors defaults on its obligations under the Demand Note (Form 3.3, supra). What are Firstbank's remedies? See UCC 9–203(b); UCC 9–601(a); Chapter 1, Section 1, supra; UCC 9–609(a), (b); UCC 9–610(a), (b); UCC 9–607(a); Dealer Inventory Security Agreement (Form 3.2, supra) ¶¶ 12(a), 13.

Problem 3.2.2. Assume that the only document signed by Main Motors was the Demand Note (Form 3.3, supra) and that the note made no reference to collateral. Firstbank paid General Motors for a trailerload of new cars delivered to Main. Main's president, G.S. Gessell, orally agreed that Firstbank had a security interest in the cars.

(a) If Main defaults on its obligations under the note, may Firstbank enforce its security interest by seizing the cars and selling them? See UCC 9–203(b); UCC 9–102(a)(73); UCC 1–201(b)(3) [F1–201(3)]; UCC 1–201(b)(35) [F1–201(37)] (1st sentence); UCC 9–102(a)(7); UCC 1–201(b)(37) [F1–201(39)]; UCC 9–102(a)(69); Notes (1) and (2) on Attachment, infra.

(b) Would Firstbank have an enforceable security interest if the promissory note signed by Main contained the notation: "Collateral: Motor Vehicles"? See In re In re Cheqnet Systems, Inc., infra.

(c) Would Firstbank have an enforceable security interest if Main's oral agreement that Firstbank had a security interest the cars was recorded on Firstbank's voice messaging system ("voice mail")? If so, would you advise Firstbank to extend credit to Main in reliance on this agreement?

(d) Would Firstbank have an enforceable security interest if Gessell sent Firstbank an e-mail message stating, "This confirms that you have a security interest in our existing and future inventory"? Below the message, Gessell's e-mail program automatically inserted the following:

G.S. Gessell, President
Main Motors, Inc.
gsgessell@mainmotorsinc.com

Would you advise Firstbank to extend credit to Main in reliance on this message? Would your answer change if the e-mail program inserted, instead, the following?

G.S. Gessell

Problem 3.2.3. Assume that, in the course of negotiating the financing arrangements, Firstbank and Main Motors signed a letter that described the terms and conditions under which Firstbank expressed its intention (but not its obligation) to extend a line of credit to Main. Included among the terms was that the credit would be secured by "Collateral," which was defined to include Main's inventory. The letter also provided that "Firstbank is authorized to pre-file financing statements with respect to all of the Collateral, including 'all-assets' filings, if applicable, naming Firstbank as secured party." Firstbank promptly filed the Financing Statement in the proper filing office.

Thereafter, Main signed the Demand Note (Form 3.3, supra), and Firstbank paid General Motors for a trailerload of new cars delivered to Main. Does Firstbank have an enforceable security interest in the cars? (Assume that the note made no reference to collateral.) See UCC 9–203(b)(3)(A); UCC 1–201(b)(3) [F1–201(3)]; UCC 9–102(a)(73); UCC 9–102(a)(7); Note (2) on Attachment, infra. Why would anyone authorize the filing of a financing statement without intending to create a security interest? See UCC 9–502(d); UCC 9–322(a)(1).

Problem 3.2.4. Assume that by error a new Chevrolet Cavalier was omitted from the Loan Request Form (Form 3.4, supra), and that this form and the Demand Note (Form 3.3, supra) were the only documents executed by Main. Also assume that the note made no reference to collateral.

(a) Does Firstbank have an enforceable security interest in the omitted Cavalier, for which it has paid Old Bank? See UCC 9–108; UCC 9–203(b)(3); Note (3) on Attachment, infra.

(b) Would the Dealer Inventory Security Agreement cover the slip-up? See Dealer Inventory Security Agreement (Form 3.2, supra) ¶ 5.

(c) Would your answer to part (b) be the same if paragraph 5 of the Dealer Inventory Security Agreement contained no subparagraphs and covered only "all Dealer's personal property, of every kind and nature whatsoever"? See UCC 9–203(b)(3); UCC 9–108.

(d) Would your answer to part (b) be the same if paragraph 5 of the Dealer Inventory Security Agreement contained no subparagraphs and covered only "certain motor vehicles"? Note that Article 9 classifies goods into four types: consumer goods, equipment, farm products, and inventory. See UCC 9–102, Comment 4.a. See generally Note (3) on Attachment, infra.

Problem 3.2.5. Assume that Firstbank "picked up" the floorplan financing for Main Motors as described in the Prototype. Subsequently, Firstbank paid General Motors for a new shipment of cars to Main Motors. Does Firstbank have an enforceable security interest in the newly arrived cars? See UCC 9–203(a), (b); UCC 9–204(a); Dealer Inventory Security Agreement ¶ 5. Would it make any difference if the only references to collateral in the Dealer Inventory Security Agreement and the Financing Statement were to "all inventory"? See UCC 9–108 & Comment 3; Note (3) on Attachment, infra.

Problem 3.2.6. The facts are as in the Prototype, except that paragraph 5 of the Dealer Inventory Security Agreement (Form 3.2, supra) covered only "Inventory."

(a) Does Firstbank's security interest in the cars in Main's inventory extend to the vast array of software used to keep major systems (e.g., exhaust, brakes) in the cars operating properly? Or does Firstbank's security interest attach only to the frames, engines, and other tangible aspects of the cars? See UCC 9–102(a)(48), (a)(44), (a)(75); Dealer Inventory Security Agreement ¶ 3.

(b) Does Firstbank's security interest in Main's inventory extend to electronic repair manuals, car-racing computer games, and other computer software that Main sells as a sideline? If not, how should the security agreement describe this kind of property? See UCC 9–108; UCC 9–102(a)(42), (a)(44), (a)(48), (a)(75).

(c) Does Firstbank hold a security interest in Main's "loaners" (cars that Main Motors allows its customers to use while their cars are being serviced)? See UCC 9–102(a)(33), (a)(23), (a)(34), (a)(48); Dealer Inventory Security Agreement ¶ 3.

(d) Does Firstbank hold a security interest in the Chevrolet Monte Carlo that Main owns but allows Main's president, G.S. Gessell, to use as part of his compensation?

Problem 3.2.7. Main Motors leases from Office!Office! a variety of sophisticated office equipment on a three-year lease. Main may terminate the lease without penalty, for any reason, upon giving 30 days' advance notice to Office!Office!.

(a) Can Main create an enforceable security interest in the equipment? See UCC 9–203(b); Note (1) on Attachment, infra. If so, would you advise a lender to extend credit to Main in reliance on a security interest in the equipment?

(b) The lease contains the following provision: "Lessee [Main] agrees not to assign this lease or its rights hereunder. Any purported assignment shall be void and shall constitute a default resulting in the immediate termination of this lease." Does this provision affect your answers to part (a)? See UCC 9–401(a); UCC 9–407; Note (1) on Attachment, infra. (Note: We shall return to the question of the alienability of a debtor's interest in collateral and the relationship, in this context, between Article 9 and non-Article 9 law in Chapter 6, Sections 1(F) and 6.)

In re Cheqnet Systems, Inc. [*]

United States Bankruptcy Court, Eastern District of Arkansas, 1998.
227 B.R. 166.

■ SCOTT, BANKRUPTCY JUDGE. This cause is before the Court upon a motion for summary judgment filed by Citizens First Bank of Fordyce on July 7, 1998. Prior to filing a chapter 7 case, the debtor was in the business of check collection. The debtor contracted with merchants to pursue recovery of returned and uncollected checks and remit a portion of the recovery to the merchants. On June 18, 1993, and again on July 24, 1994, the debtor signed

---

[*]   [The court's citations are to Former Article 9.]

promissory notes in favor of Citizens Bank of Fordyce ("the bank").[1] The note granted the bank "a…security interest in the property described in the documents executed in connection with the note as well as other property designated as security for the loan now or in the future. Assignment of Contract with Walmart Stores, Inc., and Second Mortgage on Commercial Building More Particularly Described on Mortgage Dated 6-18-93." Other documents, including the mortgage but not including the financing statement referenced in the motion for summary judgment, were executed with the notes. It was not until nearly three years after the first note was signed that the debtor and the bank executed and filed a UCC-1 financing statement listing other collateral. The financing statements were filed with the Secretary of State on April 9, 1996, and with the Pulaski County Circuit Clerk on April 10, 1996.

On January 31, 1997, the debtor filed a case under chapter 7 of the Bankruptcy Code. On February 12, 1998, the trustee filed this adversary proceeding alleging that the bank does not enjoy a perfected security interest in property of the estate because the security documents do not properly reference the collateral. The bank moves for summary judgment, Fed. R. Bankr. P. 7056, on the grounds that, as a matter of law, it holds a perfected security interest in accounts and contract rights of the debtor as of the date of the filing of the petition.

While federal bankruptcy law determines the effect of legal or equitable interests in property, N.S. Garrott & Sons v. Union Planters National Bank (In re N.S. Garrott & Sons), 772 F.2d 462, 466 (8th Cir. 1985), the Court looks to state law to determine the nature and extent of the interest, Butner v. United States, 440 U.S. 48, 59 L. Ed. 2d 136, 99 S. Ct. 914 (1979); In re N.S. Garrott & Sons, 772 F.2d at 466.

[handwritten margin note: determines • state law defines interest]

Under Arkansas law, in order to have a perfected security interest, the secured party must demonstrate that (1) the debtor has rights in the collateral; (2) the debtor signs a security agreement in favor of the secured party which contains a description of the collateral; (3) value is given by the secured party to the debtor; and (4) a valid financing statement is properly recorded. Ark. Code Ann. § 4-9-203 (Michie Supp. 1997); In re Hot Shots Burgers & Fries, Inc., 169 B.R. 920 (Bankr. E.D. Ark. 1994). In the instant case, the parties do not dispute the first, third and fourth elements. Rather, the parties dispute whether there is a valid security agreement containing a description of the property in which the bank claims to be secured. The bank argues on alternative grounds that the note constitutes a security agreement, that the financing statement constitutes a security agreement, and that, under the composite document rule, the note and financing statement taken together constitute a security agreement.

[handwritten margin note: perfected sec. int?]

The Arkansas Code defines a security agreement as an agreement which creates or provides for a security interest. Ark. Code Ann. § 4-9-203(1) (Mitchie Supp. 1997). Whether a security interest exists is generally considered to be a question of fact, Gibson Co. Farm Bureau Cooperative

---

1.   Two other notes were also signed by the debtor granting security interests.

Assoc. v. Greer, 643 N.E.2d 313, 319, 320 (Ind. 1994), because it is the intent of the parties that determines the existence and nature of a security interest.

The Note as Security Agreement

The bank first argues that the note itself constitutes a security agreement such that it is perfected in the debtor's property. The note may constitute a security agreement because it grants a security interest, contains a description of the collateral, and is signed by the debtor. However, if the note is the security agreement, the bank's security is that collateral described in the agreement -- the note. Neither the composite document rule nor the parole evidence rule apply to expand the items of collateral securing the note or to correct any error in the granting language of the security agreement. In re Kevin W. Emerick Farms, Inc., 201 B.R. 790 (Bankr. C.D. Ill. 1996). If the note is the security agreement, the financing statement, a mere notice document, does not serve to extend the bank's rights to other collateral. See id.; cf. General Electric Credit Corp. v. Bankers Commercial Corp., 244 Ark. 984, 429 S.W.2d 60 (Ark. 1968) (describing notice nature of financing statement). In light of the discussion below, the Court can not rule as a matter of law that the bank is limited in its security interest to the collateral described in the note, but it also cannot grant the motion for summary judgment to the extent the bank asserts it is secured by collateral not specifically listed in the note.

The Financing Statement as Security Agreement

The bank also argues that the financing agreement constitutes a security agreement. Although there is some limited authority in other jurisdictions, see, e.g., In re Amex-Protein Development Corp., 504 F.2d 1056 (9th Cir. 1974), the majority of jurisdictions, including Arkansas, hold to the rule that [HN4] a financing statement, standing alone, does not create a security interest in the debtor's property. General Electric Credit Corp. v. Bankers Commercial Corp., 244 Ark. 984, 429 S.W.2d 60 (Ark. 1968). Accord Gibson v. Resolution Trust Corporation, 51 F.3d 1016, 1022 (11th Cir. 1995); In re Colortran, Inc., 218 B.R. 507, 35 U.C.C.R. Serv. 2d(Callaghan) 300 (B.A.P. 9th Cir. 1997); In re Center Auto Parts, 6 U.C.C. Rep. Serv. (Callaghan) 398 (C.D. Cal. 1968). Accordingly, the motion for summary judgment is denied to the extent the bank asserts that the financing statement constitutes a security agreement.

The Composite Document Rule

Finally, the bank asserts that the composite document rule applies to create a perfected security interest in all of the collateral described in all the documents. The composite document rule provides that there need not be a separate document labeled "security agreement," but that all relevant loan documents may be examined to determine whether a security agreement exists and what collateral is covered. Id; Hoffman v. Schlegel (In re S.O.M.B., Inc.), 1995 Bankr. LEXIS 1267, 1995 WL 542512, 28 U.C.C.R. Serv. 2d(Callaghan) 363 (Bankr. D. Conn. Aug. 21, 1995). The documents need not contain any particular words, but there must be language in the instrument(s) that lead to the conclusion that the parties intended that a security interest be created. In re Ace Lumber Supply, Inc., 105 B.R. 964 (Bankr. D. Mont. 1989). That is, the language must meet the requirements of U.C.C. § 9-203 and objectively indicate that the parties intend to create a security interest. Id. Thus, in applying the composite document rule, the court looks to the transaction as a whole to determine if there are writings signed by the debtor which describe the collateral and which demonstrate an intent to create a security interest in particular collateral. In re Bollinger Corp., 614 F.2d 924, 928 (3d Cir. 1980).

Although there does not appear to be any case authority in Arkansas as to whether the composite document rule exists under Arkansas law, the majority of jurisdictions apply such a rule. Maddox v. FDIC (In re Maddox), 92 B.R. 707 (Bankr. W.D. Tex. 1988); Gibson Co. Farm Bureau Cooperative Assoc. v. Greer, 643 N.E.2d 313, 319 (Ind. 1994). The Court believes that the Arkansas courts would apply such a rule, which would not only be consistent with the extensive authority in other jurisdictions but would also comport with the policies and language of the Uniform Commercial Code, codified in the Arkansas Statutes under title 4, subtitle 1.

Although the Court believes that the composite document rule may be applied under Arkansas law, summary judgment based upon an application of the rule to the facts of this case is inappropriate. The trustee has raised numerous issues which preclude summary judgment, including, but not limited to, the question of what documents were executed "in conjunction with the July 28, 1994, note," and more specifically, what collateral the parties intended would secure the note. Vagueness in the affidavits of the debtor's principals raises concern and highlights the need for an opportunity for cross-examination. Even the authority ardently asserted by the bank indicates that the contemporaneous nature of the execution of the documents may be a factor in the application of the composite document rule. See In re Center Auto Parts, 6 U.C.C. Rep. Serv. (Callaghan) 398 (1968). Inasmuch as documents other than the financing statement were signed contemporaneously with the first note, the fact that the financing statement was so belatedly filed is not only relevant but it raises questions as to which other documents constitute the security agreement and what collateral secures the debt. Accordingly, it is

ORDERED that the motion for summary judgment filed by Citizens First Bank of Fordyce on July 7, 1998, is Denied.

NOTES ON ATTACHMENT

(1) The Conditions for Attachment. "Attachment" is one of the fundamental concepts in Article 9. When the conditions giving rise to an enforceable security interest are satisfied, then a security interest attaches. See UCC 9-203(a), (b). A security interest is an interest in property. See UCC 1-201(b)(35) [F1-201(37)]. Unless and until a security interest attaches to particular property, the secured party has no enforceable

sec. int = prop. int.

security interest—and thus no enforceable property right—in the collateral. That is, until the security interest attaches, the secured party is, as a practical matter, unsecured.

UCC 9–203(b) provides that "a security interest is enforceable against the debtor or third parties with respect to the collateral only if" the three conditions specified in therein occur. They may occur in any order, but until all occur, a security interest is not enforceable.

Value. One condition for attachment is that "value has been given." UCC 9–203(b)(1). By definition, a security interest "secures payment or performance of an obligation." UCC 1–201(b)(35) [F1–201(37)]. Before a security interest can attach, there must be an obligation (usually a money debt) to secure. The "value" condition normally is satisfied easily; that the secured party extended credit usually is clear. See UCC 1–204 [F1–201(44)] (defining "value" to include not only present consideration but also antecedent debt). Any issue that arises with respect to the "value" condition is likely to concern *which* debt is secured rather than whether *any* debt is outstanding. See Problem 3.2.8, infra.

Rights in Collateral. A second condition for attachment is that "the debtor has rights in the collateral or the power to transfer rights in the collateral to a secured party." UCC 9–203(b)(2). The first aspect of this condition ("rights in the collateral") is best conceptualized and understood as a specialized aspect of the familiar principle of *nemo dat quod non habet* (one cannot give what one does not have): A debtor can give a security interest in collateral only if it has rights in that collateral. See Chapter 1, Section 3(A), supra. Straightforward as this may seem, more than a few courts and commentators have confounded the application of the "rights in the collateral" condition in the context of Former Article 9's basic conveyancing principles.

One source of the confusion has been the first sentence of Former 9–201: "Except as otherwise provided by this Act a security agreement is effective according to its terms between the parties, against purchasers of the collateral and against creditors." (This sentence appears almost verbatim as UCC 9–201(a).) This principle often has been paraphrased to the effect that a security interest in collateral is "good as against the world" except as the UCC provides otherwise. Broad as this statement may be, it is important to mind its limitations. We discuss below, particularly in Chapter 4, many of the specific instances where the UCC expressly limits the operation of UCC 9–201. For present purposes you should realize that *UCC 9–201 generally operates only with respect to the debtor's rights in collateral—however limited or expansive they might be.* For example, assume that Debtor is the owner of a 25% undivided interest in an item of equipment. Having "rights in the collateral," Debtor can cause a security interest to attach to that item of equipment. Assume further that Debtor signs a security agreement purporting to grant a security interest in the equipment to Bank to secure a loan. Does UCC 9–201 afford Bank a security interest "good against the world" in the 75% interest that Debtor does not own as well as the 25% interest owned by Debtor? Of course not. The "collateral" addressed by UCC 9–201 consists only of the debtor's rights in the equipment. Again, the *nemo dat* principle applies; Debtor cannot give more than it has.

We have seen that sometimes the law affords a person the power to transfer greater rights than the person has. See Chapter 1, supra. If the transferee of these rights can be a secured party, then one condition for attachment and enforceability of a security interest would be satisfied. We shall see examples of how this rule works in Chapter 5, Section 1(B) (consignments) and Chapter 6, Section 1(D) (sales of receivables).

Applicable law sometimes restricts a person from transferring its interest in property or makes an attempted transfer ineffective. Article 9 generally does not override non-Article 9 law to the effect that property is inalienable; a security interest cannot be created in otherwise inalienable property merely because security interests in that type of property are within the scope of the Article. See UCC 9–401(a). UCC 9–401(a) specifies exceptions, however. One exception is found in subsection (b). For an example and discussion of the operation of subsection (b) in a typical setting, see UCC 9–401, Comment 5. Other specified exceptions are UCC 9–406 through R–9–409. See Chapter 6, Sections 1(F) and 6.

Debtor's Agreement. A third condition to attachment is the debtor's agreement that a security interest be created. See UCC 9–203(b)(3). The following Note examines this condition.

(2) Article 9's "Statute of Frauds." A security interest cannot attach in the absence of the debtor's security agreement. See UCC 9–203(b)(3); UCC 9–102(a)(73) (defining "security agreement" as "an agreement that creates or provides for a security interest"). Because the attachment of a security interest is a transfer—a conveyance—of a property interest from the debtor to the secured party, the necessity for the debtor's agreement is apparent (at least in a system that respects private property). However, not every agreement that provides for a security interest satisfies the requirements of UCC 9–203(b)(3). That section requires that the requisite agreement be manifested in one of four specified ways. The Comments refer to these as "evidentiary requirement[s] in the nature of a Statute of Frauds"—i.e., formal requisites that both enhance the veracity of claims to secured party status and serve to caution a debtor. UCC 9–203, Comment 3; see E.A. Farnsworth, Contracts § 6.1, at 356 (4th ed. 2004) (discussing functions of Statute of Frauds).

In the vast proportion of secured transactions, the requirements of UCC 9–203(b)(3) are satisfied when the debtor signs a written security agreement describing the collateral. It is not difficult to satisfy this requirement in the usual case; nonetheless, slip-ups do occur. The courts generally have applied the (relatively forgiving and broad) definition of "signed" in UCC 1–201(b)(37) [F1–201(39)] in cases where the debtor's signature on a security agreement has been called into question. As to how an inanimate business entity may sign a security agreement, one must resort to non-UCC law of partnerships, corporations, or agency. See UCC 1–103(b) [F1–103]. Normally, such an organization signs through a individual, e.g., an officer of a corporate debtor or the general partner of a partnership debtor. Good lawyers avoid litigation over the sufficiency of the debtor's signature in these circumstances by making sure that the security agreement identifies the organization as the debtor and the individual as its agent. See, e.g., Main Motors' signature on Forms 3.2, 3.3, and 3.4, supra. They also make sure that the individual purporting to sign on behalf of the debtor is in fact authorized by the debtor to do so.

"Authenticate"

Article 9 does not require that a security agreement be in writing. UCC 9–203(b)(3)(A) is satisfied when "the debtor has *authenticated* a security agreement." The definition of "authenticate" in UCC 9–102(a)(7) means not only to "sign" (which requires a writing, see UCC 1–201(b)(37) [F1–201(39)] (defining "signed")) but also "to execute or otherwise adopt a symbol . . . with the present intent of the authenticating person to identify the person and adopt or accept a *record*." Thus, a security agreement may be in any authenticated "record," i.e., it may be "inscribed on a tangible medium or . . . stored in an electronic or other medium," provided that the information is "retrievable in perceivable form." See UCC 9–102(a)(69). This definition is very broad, but it excludes information in unrecorded oral communications. Can you think of another type of information that is not a "record"? We can anticipate that the case law will develop the outer reaches of the concepts of "record" and "authentication" as they apply to security agreements that are not in writing.[1]

Under UCC 9–203(b)(3)(B), (b)(3)(C), and (b)(4)(D), even an oral security agreement is sufficient if the secured party has possession or control of the collateral pursuant to that agreement. A secured creditor who fails to obtain an authenticated security agreement, but has possession or control of the collateral, nonetheless must provide evidence that its possession or control is "pursuant to the debtor's security agreement." As used in the UCC, "control" has a technical meaning. See UCC 9–104 (deposit accounts); UCC 9–105 (electronic chattel paper); UCC 9–106 (investment property), discussed below in Chapter 6, Sections 4, 2, and 3, respectively.

Printed forms of security agreements are readily available; when properly completed and signed they easily satisfy the minimal requirements of UCC 9–203(b)(3)(A). Moreover, a security agreement need not contain any "magic words" to create a security interest. The courts generally have been generous to secured parties who have used inartful language. Nevertheless, the debtor's failure to sign or otherwise authenticate an "agreement that

---

1. Some of the case law may arise under UETA or E–SIGN (discussed in Chapter 1, Section 4, supra), each of which contains a definition of "record" that is virtually identical to the definition in Article 9. See UETA 2(13); 15 U.S.C. § 7006(9). However, UETA does not apply to a transaction to the extent it is governed by Article 9, and the provisions of E–SIGN validating electronic signatures and electronic contracts do not apply to a contract or other record to the extent it is governed by Article 9. UETA 3(b)(2); 15 U.S.C. § 7003(a)(3).

creates or provides for a security interest" normally will be fatal to the assertion of an attached (enforceable) security interest. For example, many cases decided under Former Article 9 have held that a debtor's signature on a financing statement alone does not satisfy Former 9–203(1)(a) when the financing statement meets only the minimum requirements for a financing statement (see Former 9–402) and does not contain additional language constituting an appropriate "agreement." See UCC 1–201(b)(3) [F1–201(3)] (defining "agreement" as "the bargain of the parties in fact as found in their language or by implication from other circumstances").

Does a debtor's written authorization of the filing of a financing statement create an "implication" that the debtor has agreed to create a security interest? A "technical" answer is found in UCC 9–502(d): "A financing statement may be filed before a security agreement is made or a security interest otherwise attaches." Why else would a debtor authorize the filing a financing statement if not to create a security interest? As a practical matter, prospective secured parties frequently file before a secured loan or sale is consummated (i.e., they "pre-file") so that a filing office search report reflecting the filed financing statement can be obtained before value is given. That a financing statement is filed does not necessarily mean that any security interest has been or will be created. See UCC 9–502, Comment 2.

Why do putative secured parties sometimes fail to take the relatively simple step of requiring a debtor to sign a security agreement? The reported decisions, at least, indicate that inadvertence and clerical or administrative errors are most often to blame (although examples of mistakes by truly "amateur" creditors also can be found). In the slightly altered words of a famous bumper sticker: "It happens."

Compliance with the requirement that a debtor sign or otherwise authenticate a security agreement is easy enough when a modest amount of care is taken or properly-completed, well-drafted forms are employed. When mistakes are made, however, the results can be disastrous for a putative secured party, even when the debtor's subjective intention to grant a security interest is apparent. The failure of secured creditors to use standard-form security agreements has engendered scores of reported decisions under Former Article 9. In many of these cases the creditors have argued successfully that a group of writings, taken together, are sufficient to comprise a security agreement. See the discussion of the "composite document rule" in In re Cheqnet Systems, Inc., supra. Those arguments sometimes have failed, however.

The following summaries of reported cases will give you a sense of the factual settings in which the issue has been litigated.

- a board of directors' resolution recognizing that an agreement existed and a financing statement itemizing collateral satisfied the Statute of Frauds and identification of collateral functions and, together, comprised adequate security agreement.

- an adequate security agreement consisted of a signed financing statement, loan application, and promissory note.
- a promissory note that recited "this note is secured by" specified collateral was held to be an adequate security agreement.
- an adequate security agreement was composed of a loan agreement and funding advance voucher containing a description of the collateral.
- an application for an automobile certificate of title that named the putative secured party as lienholder was analogized to a financing statement and, when considered with other insufficient documents (including a promissory note), did not constitute a security agreement.
- the debtor's execution of a note and financing statement was held insufficient to constitute a security agreement; the secured party had prepared a security agreement, and the note made reference to a security agreement, but the debtor did not sign it.
- a composite of documents indicating that collateral included inventory and accounts was held not to create a security interest in those assets when the "Security Agreement" executed by the debtor covered only "machinery, equipment, furniture and fixtures."
- a reference to after-acquired collateral in a financing statement was held not sufficient to expand coverage of a security agreement that made no such reference.

These cases are important not only for their specific outcomes but also as a reminder of how easy it would have been for the secured parties involved to have avoided the problem. The fact that a filed financing statement can be effective under Revised Article 9 without the debtor's signature makes it less likely that a careless secured party will have any collateral-related record authenticated by the debtor.

Finally, consider the situation where *A* grants a security interest in *A*'s property to secure the indebtedness of *B*. (This transaction often is referred to as a **hypothecation**.) Who is the "debtor" whose security agreement is required? UCC 9–102(a)(28) provides that the "debtor" is "a person having an interest, other than a security interest or other lien, in the collateral," regardless of whether the person owes the obligation that the collateral secures. There is little doubt that the debtor is *A*—the owner of the collateral. If collateral is jointly owned, each co-owner would be a debtor with respect to that owner's interest in the collateral.

(3) Description of the Collateral; After–Acquired Property. A security agreement authenticated by the debtor must "provide[ ] a description of the collateral" to satisfy UCC 9–203(b)(3)(A). UCC 9–108(a) contains the general rule: "[A] description of personal or real property is sufficient, whether or not it is specific, if it <u>reasonably identifies</u> what is described." Comment 2 to UCC 9–108 indicates that a description in a security agreement must "do the job assigned to it: *make possible* the identification of the collateral described," while rejecting the notion that a description must be "exact and detailed (the so-called 'serial number' test)" as applied in pre-UCC chattel mortgage cases. UCC 9–108, Comment 2 (emphasis added). As the Comment explains, a security agreement provides evidence that a security interest *in fact* has been created in certain collateral. (The identification function also is served by the alternative of possession or control by the secured party; these alternatives serve as evidentiary proxies for a security agreement that describes the collateral.)

Is it necessary for a description to identify the collateral itself? Or, is a description sufficient if it provides enough information so that someone, by *additional* investigation or with *additional* information, *could* identify it? Whether a security interest in fact has been created may become relevant in the event that the debtor disputes the secured party's claim of a security interest in particular property. The description requirement helps minimize the likelihood of such a dispute. The debtor and secured party may not be the only interested persons; the creation of a security interest may be relevant also to a third party (e.g., a buyer, competing secured party, or judicial lien creditor) who claims an interest in the property. Under these circumstances, the debtor and secured party may have an incentive to extend the coverage of the security agreement beyond their original agreement. The description requirement helps protect the third party from such after-the-fact collusion.

One should place the risk of a collusive "reinterpretation" of a security agreement in proper perspective. As a general matter, third parties are ill-advised to rely on information contained in a security agreement. Any comfort drawn from that information could be illusory, and any protection might be fleeting. Other security agreements covering additional collateral or securing other indebtedness might then exist or thereafter be entered into, and it is the date of *filing a financing statement*—not the date of a security agreement—that generally determines priorities. See Chapter 4, Section 1(A), infra.

UCC 9–108(b) indicates a variety of ways in which a description might "reasonably identif[y]" collateral. Subsection (b)(3) follows the prevailing interpretation under Former Article 9 and expressly validates descriptions by Article 9 "type," such as "equipment" or "inventory." The case law under Former Article 9 was divided over the question whether "super-generic" collateral descriptions, such as "all personal property" and "all assets," are sufficient for purposes of a security agreement. Although generally such "super-generic" descriptions have been held to be sufficient (see White & Summers § 22–3, at 760), UCC 9–108(c) follows those cases that held them to be insufficient. When it is determined that the bargain-in-fact of the parties is that the security agreement covers all personal property of the debtor, why should it be necessary to resort to more detail? In nearly *every* case where attachment is in dispute it will be necessary to determine that a debtor has "rights in the collateral." UCC 9–203(b)(2). If all personal property is to be covered, then, the distinguishing factor between collateral and non-collateral is the existence of those rights.

Why do you suppose the drafters opted for invalidating "super-generic" descriptions? Perhaps the drafters subscribed to the view that, absent overreaching or the debtor's failure to appreciate the full implications of an agreement to encumber everything the debtor has, no one would enter into such an agreement. If so, do you agree with that view? Another possible explanation is that UCC 9–108(c) is designed to increase the likelihood that a debtor actually appreciates that the security agreement creates a security interest in all the debtor's personal property. Which do you think is more likely to drive this point home—an agreement that provides for a security interest in "all debtor's personal property," or an agreement that provides for a security interest in "all Collateral," defined as "accounts, chattel paper, general intangibles, documents, inventory, equipment, deposit accounts, letter-of-credit rights, instruments, and investment property"? Might the drafters have intended to induce secured parties to consider carefully the collateral they take, rather than relying on boilerplate "all assets" collateral descriptions? A more cynical possibility is that some supporters of UCC 9–108(c) simply hoped that secured parties might omit a category or two from the collateral descriptions, thereby making it more likely that property would remain unencumbered.

UCC 9–108 does not resolve one important issue that arose often under Former Article 9: does a description such as "all of debtor's equipment" cover not only equipment of the debtor at the time the security agreement is entered into but also equipment subsequently acquired by the debtor? The question is not whether Article 9 gives effect to a security agreement that encumbers after-acquired property; clearly, it does: "a security agreement may create or provide for a security interest in after-acquired collateral." UCC 9–204(a). Rather the question is whether a particular security agreement that does not expressly refer to after-acquired property nevertheless creates a security interest in that property. Whether conceptualizing the issue as one concerning the adequacy of the collateral description or as one concerning whether the parties agreed to cover after-acquired collateral, some courts have refused to uphold claims to after-acquired property in the absence of an explicit reference in the security agreement. Others have been more generous, especially when the collateral concerned has been accounts or inventory, which turn over continually and for which it would make little commercial sense for the parties to limit the collateral to that on hand at the inception of the transaction. Comment 3 to UCC 9–108 explains: "This question is one of contract interpretation and is not susceptible to a statutory rule (other than a rule to the effect that it is a question of contract interpretation). Accordingly, this section contains no reference to descriptions of after-acquired collateral."

More generally, should courts apply ordinary principles of contract interpretation to discern the meaning of a description in a security agreement? Is there anything special about a security agreement that would justify special treatment? See UCC 1–103(b) [F1–103] (unless displaced, principles of law supplement the UCC); UCC 1–201(b)(3) [F1–201(3)] (defining "agreement");UCC 1–303 [F1–205] (roles of course of dealing, usage of trade, and express terms in construing an agreement); Shelby County State Bank v. Van Diest Supply Co., 303 F.3d 832 (7th Cir.2002) (ambiguity in security agreement as to coverage of after-acquired property construed against the drafter under the rule of contract interpretation that "ambiguous language is to be 'strictly construed against the drafter'").

Problem 3.2.8. Several months after Firstbank and Main Motors established the inventory financing arrangements as described in the Prototype, Main fell behind in payments to its unsecured trade creditors. Main requested a short-term (60–day) loan from Firstbank in the amount of $100,000. Firstbank agreed and advanced that sum to Main. The only documentation was a promissory note signed by Main. The note contained no reference to any of the inventory financing documentation. Main failed to pay the note when due and also defaulted under the inventory financing arrangement. Subsequently, Lean, a judgment creditor of Main, caused the sheriff to levy on Main's automobile inventory.

As counsel for Lean, you conclude that Lean's execution lien is junior to Firstbank's security interest. It appears that the value of the automobile inventory probably is sufficient to satisfy all amounts outstanding on Main's inventory loans from Firstbank, with surplus value available for Lean. However, if the automobile inventory secures not only the inventory loans but also the $100,000 term loan, there would be little, if anything, left for Lean.

(a) What are the best arguments that the automobile inventory does not secure the $100,000 loan? See UCC 9–204(c) & Comment 5; Dealer Inventory Security Agreement (Form 3.2, supra) ¶ 5; Note on Obligations (Including Future Advances) Covered by Security Agreements, infra.

(b) Assuming that the $100,000 loan would be secured, what result if Main's $100,000 obligation to Firstbank arose not out of a loan but out of an accident in which one of Main's tow-trucks ran through Firstbank's plate glass window, into its lobby, and over its president?

(c) As Firstbank's counsel, how could you draft the Dealer Inventory Security Agreement so as to ensure that the collateral would secure Main's obligations to Firstbank in both of these circumstances?

NOTE ON OBLIGATIONS (INCLUDING FUTURE ADVANCES) COVERED BY SECURITY AGREEMENTS

The term "security interest" is defined in UCC 1–201(b)(35) [F1–201(37)] to include "an interest in personal property or fixtures which secures payment or performance of an obligation." The UCC leaves it to the parties to agree as to what obligations are secured by a security interest. Although the UCC does not define or regulate generally the obligations that are secured, UCC 9–204(c) does address one aspect of the obligations that may be secured by a security interest: "A security agreement may provide that collateral secures . . . future advances or other value, whether or not the advances or value are given pursuant to commitment." This provision might seem superfluous, were it not for the pre-UCC treatment of future advance provisions in the courts. Comment 5 to Former 9–204 noted that "[a]t common law and under chattel mortgage statutes there seems to have been a vaguely articulated prejudice against future advance agreements comparable to the prejudice against after-acquired property interests." The following passage reveals the source and flavor of at least some of that prejudice:

> **Validity of future advance arrangements under pre-Code law: The "dragnet" cases.** A convenient starting point will be the type of situation which regularly calls down the thunderings of judicial wrath: the lender's claim that obligations of the mortgagor [debtor] which are in no sense related to the financing transaction which the mortgage [security interest] was given to secure are, nevertheless, covered by the mortgage. Cases of this type, which often are indistinguishable from cases of outright fraud, keep coming along in numbers just sufficient to keep fresh in the judicial mind the ease with which the future advance device can be exploited by the overreaching mortgagee [secured party] to crush the impoverished but no doubt honest debtor.

> A standard boiler-plate clause provides in substance: the mortgaged property [collateral] shall stand as security for any indebtedness of any sort which may now or hereafter be owing by mortgagor to mortgagee. In polite society this is sometimes referred to as a "cross-security" clause; it can serve many useful and legitimate purposes. A court which proposes to invalidate a claim asserted under such a clause will refer to it less politely as a "dragnet" clause, with the remark that such clauses "are not highly regarded in equity. They should be 'carefully scrutinized and strictly construed.' " Or as the Arkansas court [Berger v. Fuller, 180 Ark. 372, 21 S.W.2d 419, 421 (1929)] put it in a colorful passage:

>> Mortgages of this character have been denominated "Anaconda mortgages" and are well named thus, as by their broad and general terms they enwrap the unsuspecting debtor in the folds of indebtedness embraced and secured in the mortgage which he did not contemplate . . .

> What often happens in dragnet cases is that a mortgagee who holds a mortgage given to secure a small claim on an otherwise impoverished debtor's one valuable piece of property—which may be his homestead—buys up, no doubt at a large discount, other claims against the mortgagor and adds these to the mortgage debt. A variant is that the mortgagee, after his debt has been largely paid, will assign the mortgage to another creditor, who asserts that his previously unsecured claim is now, by virtue of the dragnet clause, the debt secured.

2 Gilmore, Security § 35.2, at 917–18.

It is clear enough that the UCC itself legitimizes future advance provisions and puts no restrictions on what obligations can be secured. Yet Professor Gilmore argued that the pre-UCC law survived the enactment of

Former Article 9, at least to the extent that only future advances that are similar and related to an initial, principal obligation should be given the benefit of broad future advance and "all obligations" provisions. Id. § 35.5, at 932. Numerous cases have taken the approach urged by Professor Gilmore. See, e.g., Community Bank v. Jones, 278 Or. 647, 566 P.2d 470 (1977) (citing, inter alia, Gilmore, Security; applying "general test" of whether indebtedness was of same class as primary obligation); In re Fassinger, 246 B.R. 513 (Bkrtcy.W.D.Pa.2000). In *Fassinger* the bankruptcy court refused to enforce "dragnet clauses" contained in separate security agreements, because the agreements failed the "Four-Part Test" applicable to determine whether they violated the "relatedness" doctrine. The court quoted earlier case law for the "Four-Part Test":

> "(1) Whether the other indebtednesses allegedly covered by the . . . [security agreement containing said dragnet clause] are [specifically expressed] therein . . .; (2) Whether the other indebtednesses allegedly covered are 'of the same class' as the debt referenced in the . . . [security agreement] . . .; (3) Whether the other indebtednesses were intended to be separately secured . . .; and (4) Whether the . . . [secured party] relied on the clause in making further loans. . . .."

Id. at 269 (bracketed language in original).

If the bargain-in-fact of the parties is that a security agreement is to secure all of a debtor's obligations, should that bargain be disregarded merely because a putative secured obligation is somehow dissimilar or unrelated to earlier obligations? (See part (2) of the "Four–Part test," just quoted.) If so, the result would offend the freedom-of-contract principle that the UCC appears to respect in the context of what obligations are to be secured. Cf. UCC 1–103(a) [F1–102(2)(b)] (providing that an underlying purpose and policy of the UCC is to permit the continued expansion of commercial practices through agreement of the parties); UCC 1–302 [F1–102(3)] (affording parties substantial freedom to vary UCC provisions and to agree on standards of performance).

As may be the case when determining what collateral is covered by a security agreement, a better approach might be to apply conventional rules of contract interpretation to the task at hand. See, e.g., In re Public Leasing Corp., 488 F.2d 1369 (10th Cir.1973) (parol evidence should not have been admitted to construe a "cross-collateralization clause" that was "clear and unambiguous"). Comment 5 to UCC 9–204 adopts this approach:

> Determining the obligations secured by collateral is solely a matter of construing the parties' agreement under applicable law. This Article rejects the holdings of cases decided under former Article 9 that applied other tests, such as whether a future advance or other subsequently incurred obligation was of the same or a similar type or class as earlier advances and obligations secured by the collateral.

Although experience has shown that the courts' distrust of broad cross-collateralization agreements may die slowly, notwithstanding this clear instruction in Comment 5, one court recently embraced the comment:

As the Official Comment to new § 9–204(c) unequivocally states, the drafters of Revised Article Nine clearly intended its language to countermand the "same kind and character" and "close relatedness" tests implied by courts into the Uniform Commercial Code from real estate cases . . .. In the absence of any statute or case law under Revised Article 9 to the contrary, this Court must conclude that the dragnet clauses questioned here are effective and enforceable.

In re Christy, 2004 Bankr. LEXIS 1733, at *23–*24 (Bkrtcy.D.Kan. Oct. 27, 2004). See also Pride Hyundai, Inc. v. Chrysler Fin. Co., L.L.C., 369 F.3d 603, 614-15 (1st Cir.2004) ("We think that the [Massachusetts Supreme Judicial Court] would adopt the approach to dragnet clauses in the Article Nine context that is contained in the Official Commentary [5] to [9–204 of] the revised Code.")

SECTION 3.   PERFECTION OF SECURITY INTERESTS

We saw in Section 2 that a security interest is not enforceable against the debtor or third parties, and does not attach, until the three conditions in UCC 9–203(b) are satisfied. In this Section we shall see that even if a security interest is enforceable, the secured party does not necessarily prevail over holders of competing claims to the collateral.

(A) PERFECTION BY FILING

Problem 3.3.1. Firstbank established the financing arrangement with Main Motors as described in the Prototype. Subsequently, Secondbank became interested in providing floorplan financing to Main Motors. Secondbank asks you, its counsel, to check the public record to discover whether, and to what extent, Main's assets may be subject to security interests.

What does the public record reveal? Does it show whether any motor vehicles in fact are subject to Old Bank's or Firstbank's security interest and, if so, which ones? Does it show whether Main is obligated to Old Bank or Firstbank and, if so, the amount of the obligation? See Financing Statement (Form 3.1, supra); UCC 9–502(a); UCC 9–522(a); UCC 9–515(a), (c).

Problem 3.3.2. The transaction followed precisely the steps described in the Prototype in Section 1, supra. Lean, the holder of a judgment against Main Motors, subsequently caused the sheriff to levy on the cars in Main's inventory. Is Lean's execution lien senior or junior to Firstbank's security interest in the cars? See UCC 9–201; UCC 9–203(a), (b); UCC 9–317(a)(2); UCC 9–308(a); UCC 9–102(a)(52); UCC 9–310; UCC 9–502(a); UCC 9–102(a)(48); UCC 9–501(a); UCC 9–311(d); Notes (1) and (2) on Perfection by Filing, infra.

Problem 3.3.3. The transaction followed precisely the steps described in the Prototype, except that one of Firstbank's clerks neglected to file the Financing Statement (Form 3.1, supra). On May 1, 2002, Lean, the judgment creditor, caused the sheriff to levy on Main's inventory of cars. Is Lean's execution lien senior or junior to Firstbank's security interest? See UCC 9–317(a)(2); UCC 9–310.

Problem 3.3.4. The transaction followed precisely the steps described in the Prototype, except that, instead of filing the Financing Statement with the Pennsylvania filing office as required by UCC 9–301(1) and UCC 9–501(a)(2), one of Firstbank's clerks mistakenly filed the Financing Statement in the New Jersey filing office. Lean, the judgment creditor, caused the sheriff to levy on Main's inventory of cars. Is Lean's execution lien senior or junior to Firstbank's security interest? See UCC 9–317(a)(2); UCC 9–310. (The proper place of filing is considered in more detail in Section 4, infra.)

Problem 3.3.5. Firstbank obtained the documentation and followed the procedures in the Prototype. However, after Firstbank delivered the Financing Statement to the proper filing office, an error in the process of inputting data into a computer resulted in the Financing Statement's being erroneously indexed so as to reflect Firstbank as *debtor* and Main Motors as *secured party*. This error was reflected in a receipt mailed to Firstbank by the filing office, but none of Firstbank's staff noticed the error.

(a) Secondbank becomes interested in providing floorplan financing to Main Motors and wishes to learn whether Main's inventory may be subject to a security interest. Would Secondbank be able to discover the Financing Statement? See UCC 9–519(c); UCC 9–523(c).

(b) Was the filing effective to perfect Firstbank's security interest? See UCC 9–516(a); UCC 9–517; In re Flagstaff Foodservice Corp., 16 B.R. 132 (Bkrtcy.S.D.N.Y.1981) (filing officer's complete failure to index financing statement did not impair effectiveness of filing under Former Article 9, notwithstanding that three years after the filing the secured party had not yet received a copy of the filed financing statement and its check for the filing fee had not cleared). But cf. In Re Enos, 185 B.R. 388 (Bkrtcy.D.Mass.1995) (under Former Article 9, burden of proof that financing statement was presented to filing office was not satisfied by evidence of mailing and the presumption of receipt; proof of actual delivery is required). What result better promotes the purposes of the filing system?

(c) If Secondbank were to extend financing to Main Motors secured by Main's existing inventory, and if Secondbank failed to "pick up" Firstbank's floor plan by satisfying Main's indebtedness to Firstbank, would Secondbank's security interest in the cars be senior or junior to Firstbank's security interest? See UCC 9–322(a)(1); Note (2) on Perfection by Filing, infra.

(d) Do creditors or lienholders who may be damaged by the erroneous indexing have any recourse other than to attack the effectiveness of the security interest? See UCC 9–519(c); UCC 9–523(c); Mobile Enterprises, Inc.

v. Conrad, 177 Ind.App. 475, 380 N.E.2d 100 (1978) (complaint against Indiana's Secretary of State and Director of the UCC Division for negligent failure to disclose to plaintiff the existence of a filed financing statement was sufficient to withstand a motion to dismiss); see generally Murray, Liability of the State and Its Employees in the Mishandling of Security Interests Under Commercial Codes and Motor Vehicle Laws, 51 U. Miami L. Rev. 1109 (1997).

Problem 3.3.6. On March 19 Main executed and delivered the documents described in the Prototype and Firstbank advanced funds to General Motors for a trailer-load of new cars. The new cars were delivered to Main on March 23; that same day Lean levied on the newly-delivered cars. On March 26 Firstbank filed the Financing Statement in the proper office. Is Lean's execution lien senior or junior to Firstbank's security interest? See UCC 9–317(a)(2); UCC 9–317(e); UCC 9–103(b), (a); Note (2) on Perfection by Filing, infra.

NOTES ON PERFECTION BY FILING

(1) The Concept of Perfection. We have seen in our discussion of attachment that, as a general matter, "a security agreement is effective according to its terms between the parties, against purchasers of the collateral, and against creditors." UCC 9–201(a). We also have seen that even if a security interest has been created, it is enforceable against the debtor and third parties only if the three conditions for attachment—value, rights in the collateral, and the debtor's security agreement—have been satisfied. UCC 9–203(b). But even an enforceable (attached) security interest is unlikely to be effective against third parties claiming an interest in the collateral unless it is "perfected."

A security interest is "perfected" when the security interest has attached *and* "all of the applicable requirements for perfection in Sections 9–310 through 9–316 have been satisfied." UCC 9–308(a). For the most part, these "applicable requirements" consist of methods by which a secured party gives public notice of its security interest. The filing of a financing statement is the most common method—so common, in fact, that UCC 9–310(a) provides that "[a] financing statement must be filed to perfect all security interests," with certain specified exceptions. The following chart summarizes the methods of perfection that are discussed in this book. For now, three things are worthy of note:

- A security interest in virtually all types of collateral may be perfected by filing a financing statement.
- For many types of collateral, more than one method of perfection is available.
- Certain security interests are perfected "automatically," i.e., when they attach.

TABLE 3.1
METHODS OF PERFECTION

Method	Collateral	UCC §	Discussed
Filing	All except deposit accounts and letter-of-credit rights taken as original collateral and money	9–310(a); 9–312(b)	Chapter 3, Section 3(A)
Possession	Goods, instruments, tangible chattel paper, tangible negotiable documents, money	9–313	Chapter 3, Section 3(B)
Delivery	Certificated securities	9–313	Ch. 6, Sec. 3
Control	Investment property	9–314; 9–106	Ch. 6, Sec. 3
	Deposit accounts	9–314; 9–104	Ch. 6, Sec. 4
	Letter-of-credit rights	9–314; 9–107	n/a
	Electronic chattel paper	9–314; 9–105	pp. 425–26
	Electronic documents	R7–106; R9–314	p. 418
Automatic	Consumer goods (purchase-money security interests)	9–309(1)	Chapter 3, Section 3(B)
	Sale of payment intangibles or promissory notes	9–309(3), (4)	Chapter 6, Section 1(D)
	Assignment of insignificant part of debtor's accounts or payment intangibles	9–309(2)	Chapter 6, Section 1(E)
	Supporting obligation	9–308(d)	pp. 226–27
	Lien securing a right to payment	9–308(e)	n/a
Temporary	Proceeds	9–315(c)	Ch. 3, Sec.5
	Certain collateral taken for new value	9–312(e)	pp. 428, 434 n3
	Certain collateral made available to debtor	9–312(f), (g)	p. 434 n3
Compliance with non-UCC statute[1]	Goods covered by a certificate of title (e.g., automobiles)	9–311	Chapter ,3 Sec. 3(B)
	Collateral as to which federal law preempts perfection		Chapter 5, Sec. 4
Document issued in SP's name or Notification of bailee	Goods in possession of issuer of tangible nonnegotiable document	9–312(d)	n/a

---

1.   Compliance "is equivalent to the filing of a financing statement."

The various elements of perfection and attachment can occur in any order. For example, a secured party first might comply with UCC 9–310 by filing a financing statement. (Firstbank did so in the Prototype.) Next, the debtor might sign a security agreement describing collateral (say, inventory) in which the debtor already has rights. Finally, the secured party might give value (e.g., by making a loan) to the debtor. In this example, upon the occurrence of the last step, the giving of value, the security interest simultaneously would attach and become perfected. Now assume that, subsequent to the initial attachment and perfection as to the debtor's existing inventory, the debtor acquires a new item of inventory. If the security agreement covers "after-acquired" as well as existing collateral, e.g., "all inventory now owned or hereafter acquired," then immediately upon the debtor's acquisition of rights in the new inventory, the security interest would attach and become perfected in the new inventory. As to the after-acquired inventory, the last step giving rise to a perfected security interest would be the debtor's acquisition of "rights in the collateral."

(2) Priority Rules and Conveyancing Principles. For practical purposes, a secured party who fails to take the "applicable steps" for perfection is likely to be no better off than one whose security interest did not attach. Although an attached but unperfected security interest is enforceable against the debtor, such a security interest may be defeated by the claims of several different types of claimants. In particular, an unperfected security interest is vulnerable to the rights of a "lien creditor," such as a creditor who obtains an execution or other judicial lien. See UCC 9–317(a)(2) (unperfected security interest is subordinate to lien creditor); UCC 9–102(a)(52) (defining "lien creditor"). Even worse, from the secured party's perspective, is that an unperfected security interest will not be effective when it is needed most—in the debtor's bankruptcy. See BC 544(a)(1); UCC 9–317(a)(2); UCC 9–102(a)(52); Chapter 7, Section 2(A), infra.[2]

The priority rule of UCC 9–317(a)(2) constitutes an important exception to the general rule of UCC 9–201(a) (a security agreement is effective against creditors). It also represents an exception to the *nemo dat* principle. Although the debtor already has conveyed an enforceable (attached) security interest to an unperfected secured party, a lien creditor can achieve rights that are senior to those of the secured party, thereby receiving greater rights than those of the debtor!

UCC 9–317(e) provides an exception to UCC 9–317(a)(2). Under limited circumstances, a secured party who files a financing statement *after* a lien has attached to the collateral may achieve priority over the lien creditor. UCC 9–317(e) creates a grace period for purchase-money security interests, whereby a security interest perfected by filing "before or within 20 days after the debtor receives delivery of the collateral" is senior to the interest

---

2.   An unperfected security interest also is subordinate to a conflicting perfected security interest, UCC 9–322(a)(2), as well as to the rights of certain good-faith buyers and other transferees. UCC 9–317(1)(b)–(d); see Chapter 4, Section 2, infra.

of a person who becomes a lien creditor (or buyer or lessee) "between the time the security interest attaches and the time of filing." UCC 9–103 defines "purchase-money security interest" to include a security interest retained by a seller to secure the price of collateral sold, such as Main's security interest (which subsequently was assigned to Firstbank) in the car sold to Lee Abel in the Prototype. That term also embraces a security interest taken by a third-party lender who advances funds to enable a debtor to acquire the collateral, such as Firstbank's advances to General Motors for cars bought by Main in the Prototype.

The priority rule in UCC 9–317(e) balances the interests of extenders of purchase-money credit, who may find it inconvenient or impossible to file before the debtor receives possession of collateral, against those of (presumably) nonreliance lien creditors. Is the balance struck an appropriate one? (The rights of a purchase-money secured party when the debtor's bankruptcy intervenes before the secured party has filed a financing statement are considered in Chapter 7, Section 2, infra.)

Consideration of another priority rule rounds out this overview of the effect of perfection on priority. Assume that *SP*–1 extends credit to Debtor and receives a security interest in Debtor's equipment pursuant to a written security agreement, and further assume that *SP*–1 fails to perfect its security interest by filing or otherwise. Next, assume that, for whatever reason, Debtor grants an enforceable security interest in its equipment to another secured party (*SP*–2); *SP*–2 perfects its security interest by a proper filing. Under the "first-to-file-or-perfect" rule that generally applies among conflicting Article 9 security interests, *SP*–2's security interest is senior to that of *SP*–1, even though *SP*–1's security interest was created and attached first and even if *SP*–1 eventually files a financing statement. See UCC 9–322(a)(1). Like UCC 9–317(a)(2), which subordinates unperfected security interests to subsequent lien creditors, the subordination of *SP*–1's security interest under UCC 9–322(a)(1) reflects an exception to the general rule of UCC 9–201 as well as to the *nemo dat* principle. Although Debtor's rights in its equipment were subject to *SP*–1's (unperfected) security interest, Debtor conveyed greater rights to *SP*–2.

Chapter 4, Section 1, infra, focuses in detail on priorities among conflicting Article 9 security interests, including the baseline, first-to-file-or-perfect rule of UCC 9–322(a)(1). In that connection, we shall see that a secured party who acquires a purchase-money security interest (as defined in UCC 9–103) may qualify for priority over earlier-filed secured parties. See UCC 9–324; Chapter 4, Section 1(B), infra.

(3) Fraud, Ostensible Ownership, and Filing. Why does the filing of a proper (UCC 9–502(a)) financing statement play such an important role in resolving conflicts between an Article 9 secured party and a lien creditor? What purpose or purposes motivated the UCC drafters to impose a filing system? Do the actual benefits of that system outweigh the costs? The answers to these and related questions are complex and uncertain, as the following brief exploration of the historical background of the filing system suggests.

Retention of Possession and the "Fraud in Law" Doctrine. Consider the following facts:

> *P* was indebted both to *C* and *T*. *C* brought an action on the debt against *P*. In the meantime, *P* transferred all of *P*'s personal property to *T* in full satisfaction of *P*'s debt to *T*. However, *P* retained possession of the personal property and continued to use it and treat it as *P*'s own, with *T*'s acquiescence. Subsequently, *C* obtained a judgment against *P* and the sheriff attempted to levy on *P*'s property. *P*'s friends resisted the levy, claiming that the property had been transferred to *T* for good consideration.

TWYNE'S CASE

These are the facts of Twyne's Case, 76 Eng. Rep. 809 (Star Ch. 1601), in which *T* (Twyne) was held convicted of a violation of the Statute of 13 Elizabeth, ch. 5 (1571). That statute provided that transfers made with the "intent[] to delay, hinder or defraud creditors and others" were void, provided for the recovery from the transferee of the "whole value of . . . goods and chattels" transferred, and also provided for criminal sanctions against the parties to the transfer. *Twyne's Case* is best known for setting forth what have become known as "badges of fraud"—in particular, a seller's retention of possession of personal property after its sale. The court in *Twyne's Case* simply could not believe that *P* (Pierce) and Twyne really contemplated the general transfer of all of Pierce's personal property ("without exception of his apparel"—underwear, toothbrush, and all) to Twyne; in short, the transaction was a sham.

The Statute of 13 Elizabeth was either received into the common law or expressly adopted by statute in most jurisdictions in the United States. See, e.g., Sturtevant v. Ballard, 9 Johns. 337 (N.Y.Sup.Ct.1812) ("[A] voluntary sale of chattels, with an agreement . . . that the vendor may keep possession, is, except in special cases, and for special reasons, to be shown to and approved of by the court, fraudulent and void, as against creditors."). Subsequent to the *Sturtevant* case, New York law (after various vicissitudes) became more favorable to buyers who could establish their good faith. See 2 Williston, Sales § 385 (rev. ed. 1948). Several other states, however, continued to articulate the view that a seller's retention of tangible personal property constituted "fraud *per se.*" Other jurisdictions rejected this "fraud in law" approach in favor of a more lenient, "fraud in fact" version of the vendor-in-possession doctrine. Modern "fraudulent conveyance" or "fraudulent transfer" law, epitomized by the Uniform Fraudulent Transfer Act (UFTA), adopts the "fraud in fact" approach. Under this approach, the seventeenth-century "badges of fraud" retain their vitality. UFTA 4(b)(2) provides that, in determining whether a transfer is made "with actual intent to hinder, delay, or defraud any creditor of the debtor" and, thus, whether an aggrieved creditor may be able to set the transfer aside, the court may consider various factors, including "whether . . . the debtor retained possession or control of the property transferred after the transfer."

UFTA

Common-law courts typically viewed a transfer for security purposes, such as a mortgage, as a species of sale, which was to be scrutinized for fraud and possibly avoided (set aside) based upon the debtor-transferor's continued possession. Clow v. Woods, 5 Serg. & Rawle 275 (Pa.1819), is an early example. Relying on the rule of the Statute of 13 Elizabeth, the court held a mortgage of all of a tanner's equipment and inventory to be "fraudulent and void" where, under the terms of the mortgage, the debtor (tanner) was to remain in possession of the goods in the absence of default. The court was concerned primarily with the potential for such a transaction to be used for dishonest purposes: "I do not suppose the parties had in fact a fraudulent view, but as such a transaction might be turned to a dishonest use, it was their duty, as far as in their power, to secure the public against it."

Cases like *Clow* proved to be most inconvenient for debtors and secured parties. To be absolutely sure that a creditor could not obtain a judicial lien senior to its interest in the collateral, the creditor could have taken the collateral into its possession; however, for many kinds of collateral (e.g., the bark, tools, skins, and unfinished leather in *Clow*) a possessory security interest (**pledge**) would have been most impractical. Do you see why?

The Problem of "Ostensible Ownership." The potential for a sham transaction—perhaps a conveyance by the debtor that the transferee (a friendly relative or creditor) would assert only if creditors attempted to levy on the debtor's assets—is but one aspect of the fraud that concerned judges from *Twyne's Case* through the early twentieth century. During the same period, reported decisions and commentary dealing with a seller's or debtor's retention of possession typically intermixed expressions of concern about bogus transactions with apprehension about another perceived problem—"ostensible ownership." The ostensible ownership problem involves the risk that a debtor's retention of possession will deceive its creditors into believing that the debtor owns the property free of conflicting claims.

[handwritten margin note: problem: possession indicates ownership]

A sham transaction presents a problem distinct from that engendered by ostensible ownership. In the former, the debtor "really" owns the goods free and clear but attempts to deceive creditors into believing that the goods have been conveyed to a third party; in the latter, a third party really has an interest in the goods, but the debtor's continued possession deceives creditors into believing that the debtor owns the goods free and clear.[3]

---

3. The distinction can be seen particularly clearly when intangibles, rather than chattels, are the subject of the challenged transfer. For example, in Benedict v. Ratner, 268 U.S. 353, 45 S.Ct. 566, 69 L.Ed. 991 (1925), the Court struck down as fraudulent a financing arrangement involving the assignment of accounts receivable, pursuant to which the debtor-assignor was permitted to collect the receivables and use the proceeds in the usual course of its business without accounting to the lender-assignee. The Court held that the fraud consisted of "the reservation [by the debtor] of dominion inconsistent with the effective disposition of title and the creation of a lien." In other words, as in *Twyne's Case*, the perceived inconsistency between what the debtor *did* and what the

Notwithstanding this distinction, the courts and commentators frequently failed to draw a clear line between the two aspects of fraud, often referring to them interchangeably when determining that a secured transaction constituted a fraudulent conveyance.

Consider, on the one hand, the points made by two judges in *Clow v. Woods*: "In every case where possession is not given, the parties must leave *nothing* unperformed, within the compass of their power, to secure third persons from the consequences of the apparent ownership of the vendor." (Gibson, J.) "There is no way of coming at the knowledge of who is the owner of goods, but by seeing in whose possession they are." (Duncan, J.). On the other hand, the court indicated that it would have approved an arrangement whereby the mortgagee would have bought the goods and leased them to the mortgagor:

> The object of the parties might have been attained without any (at least with less) risk to the public, by the landlord [mortgagee] himself becoming the purchaser in the first instance, and permitting the tenant [mortgagor] to have the use of the property: in which case, the transaction would have been a safe and fair one; and that course should have been pursued.

5 Serg. & Rawle at 280 (Gibson, J.). Thus, Justice Gibson would have been content with the **sale-leaseback** arrangement, even though it would have created the same problem of ostensible ownership as the "secret" mortgage created.[4] Perhaps leases and other bailments, which already had become established commercial devices, seemed a less hospitable environment for sham transactions.

The judiciary's concern for unsecured creditors and hostility toward nonpossessory security devices (i.e., devices in which the debtor remains in possession of the collateral) extended beyond ostensible ownership and

---

debtor *said* it was doing, led the Court to conclude that the purported financing arrangement was a sham. Much to the chagrin of the District Court (L. Hand, J.), whose decision was reversed, the Court specifically denied that the fraud rested "upon seeming ownership because of possession retained." Indeed, any fraud concerning assignments of intangibles, which by their nature cannot be possessed or observed, could not derive from misleading appearances. An analogous genre of deception could result, however, when a debtor's books do not reflect an earlier assignment.

4.   Commentary likewise failed to come to grips fully with the sham-ostensible ownership dichotomy. For example, Garrard Glenn argued that the relationship between the English reputed ownership doctrine—never widely adopted by statute in the United States—and the avoidance of fraudulent conveyances based on the vendor-in-possession doctrine, was grounded in estoppel. See 1 G. Glenn, Fraudulent Conveyances and Preferences §§ 346–48, at 606–07 (rev. ed. 1940). But Glenn was forced to concede that the courts, in their application of the vendor-in-possession doctrine, were less than faithful to the ostensible ownership rationale. For a brief account of the development of filing statutes and their relationship to fraud and ostensible ownership concerns, see Mooney, The Mystery and Myth of "Ostensible Ownership" and Article 9 Filing: A Critique of Proposals to Extend Filing Requirements to Leases, 39 Ala. L. Rev. 683, 725–38 (1988).

fraud (more generally). At least some courts feared that, rather than facilitate commerce, the widespread use of these devices would wreak economic havoc, depriving debtors of their ability to pay unsecured claims and, perhaps, of their ability to obtain credit in the first instance.[5]

We will never know the extent to which nonpossessory security devices actually posed serious risks to creditors. We do know that, more than a century and a half ago, one court expressed skepticism about the empirical basis for the doctrine of ostensible ownership and concern over the impediments to commerce that the doctrine itself might impose:

> The truth is, there is something rather loose and indefinite in the idea of a delusive credit gained by the possession of personal property. Such inconvenience may spring from this source, to be guarded against by prudent enquiries on the part of those concerned, and to some extent by legislative enactments, tending to a degree of notoriety in regard to the title. More than this seems to me a remedy worse than the disease; and it is obvious that to prohibit altogether the separation of the title from the possession of personal property, would be incompatible with an advanced state of society and commerce, and productive of much inconvenience and injustice in the pursuits and business of life.

Davis v. Turner, 45 Va. (4 Gratt.) 422, 441 (1848).

Dispelling Fraud Through "Public Notice." Although the judiciary's approach to nonpossessory security interests was somewhat muddled, the legislative responses have been abundantly clear. Beginning with the chattel mortgage statutes in the early nineteenth century and culminating with UCC Article 9, state legislatures enacted statutes that legitimized a wide variety of personal property security devices, including chattel mortgages, conditional sales, accounts receivable financings, and trust receipt financings. These statutes generally imposed (under penalty of ~public notice~ avoidance or subordination) an obligation of what came to be known as "public notice," requiring the secured creditor to make a filing or recording in a public office as a substitute, or proxy, for taking possession of the collateral. Article 9's provision for perfection by filing (UCC 9–310(a)) is a direct descendant of these earlier statutes.

The Role of Public Notice in the New Millennium. Perhaps it is of no great moment (but surely it is of historical interest) whether the judicial hostility toward nonpossessory security interests and the demonstrated legislative bias toward "public notice" were motivated primarily by general fraud concerns or by more narrowly focused concerns about ostensible

---

5.   See, e.g., Zartman v. First Nat'l Bank of Waterloo, 189 N.Y. 267, 82 N.E. 127 (1907) (refusing to give effect to chattel mortgage on after-acquired inventory "if the result would deprive the general creditors . . . of their only chance to collect debts"; observing that "[i]f it is understood that a corporate mortgage given by a manufacturing corporation may take everything except accounts and debts, such corporations, with a mortgage outstanding, will have to do business on a cash basis or cease to do business altogether.").

ownership (even if such motivations actually could be identified). However, for those who would evaluate the Article 9 scheme and for those who must interpret and live with that scheme, it is important to obtain the broadest possible understanding of what Article 9's "public notice" requirements actually achieve and fail to achieve. Professors Baird and Jackson see the Article 9 filing system as little more than a solution to the problem of "ostensible ownership." Their somewhat narrow view leads them to argue for an expanded reach of the Article 9 filing regime:

> [O]nce one realizes that these [ostensible ownership] problems have a common source, simple solutions to them become apparent. In proposing these simple solutions to problems that have consumed hundreds of pages of law review commentary, we are not advocating a radical departure from established wisdom. Rather, we are urging only that rulemakers apply more generally the principle that has shaped the law of security interests in personal property for four hundred years: A party who wishes to acquire or retain a nonpossessory interest in property that is effective against others must, as a general matter, make it possible for others to discover that interest.
>
> . . . An ostensible ownership problem . . . exists whenever there is a separation of ownership and possession. Article 9's treatment of the ostensible ownership problem created by secured credit naturally leads one to ask whether the ostensible ownership problem created by leases or other bailments is different. We believe the answer is simple: The two ostensible ownership problems are not different in any relevant respect. They impose the same costs on third parties, and if a filing system is an appropriate response to the first problem, it is an equally appropriate response to the second.

Baird & Jackson, Possession and Ownership: An Examination of the Scope of Article 9, 35 Stan.L.Rev. 175, 178, 186 (1983). As you ponder the attributes of the Article 9 filing system, addressed next, consider whether this "simple" analysis is a useful, or sufficient, normative baseline. Does it expose all of the costs and benefits? On what empirical assumptions does it depend?

The Attributes of Article 9 Filing. A brief consideration of the operation of the Article 9 filing regime may provide useful insight into the "theory" and "purpose" of that system. Benefits that tend to justify or explain the filing system derive from the following attributes:

(i) The system *provides useful information to prospective purchasers* of personal property—both buyers and secured parties. For example, a prospective non-ordinary course buyer of an item of equipment[6] or a prospective secured lender can, by searching the proper files, determine

---

6.   See UCC 9–315(a)(1) (security interest normally continues notwithstanding sale); UCC 9–317(b)(2) (buyer not in ordinary course of business sometimes takes free of unperfected security interest); UCC 1–201(b)(9) [F1–201(9)] (defining "buyer in ordinary course of business").

whether a security interest in the equipment may have been perfected by filing. The absence of a filing thereby allows the prospective transferor to offer some evidence tending to establish a negative—that no (perfected) security interest has been given to another party. Even if no filing is found, however, the prospective purchaser of tangible personal property also must ascertain that the property is not in the possession of a secured party. See UCC 9–313. Moreover, even a "clean" search does not provide comfort that the prospective transferor owns the equipment or that it acquired its title free of claims that would be senior to those of the prospective purchaser. Finally, the UCC filing records generally cover only security interests; they do not reveal many other claims to the property, including tax and most other statutory liens that may be senior to the rights of the prospective purchaser.

(ii) The filing system also *provides information to existing and prospective creditors generally*. This attribute is related to the preceding one; the filing system reduces the costs of obtaining information. (And, if one believes that prospective creditors and purchasers are misled by a debtor's possession of personal property, the information provided by filing can be viewed as reducing the "problem of ostensible ownership.") That unsecured creditors somehow are "entitled" to accessible information concerning claims of secured creditors may explain, in part, the priority rule that subordinates unperfected security interests to judicial liens. See UCC 9–317(a)(2). Yet no one really knows the extent to which unsecured creditors use or rely upon the filing system. The position of unsecured creditors is unlike that of purchasers, who normally take steps to ensure their seniority to later-arising claims to the purchased property. Ascertaining that there is no filing against a debtor would not provide an existing or prospective unsecured creditor with any protection against the debtor subsequently encumbering some or all of its assets.[7] Unsecured creditors sometimes may be interested in whether there are filings against a debtor for other reasons, however. For debtors in some lines of business a filing against receivables or inventory may be seen by trade creditors as a signal of financial distress, whereas a filing against equipment would be viewed differently. On the other hand, debtors in other lines of business may be expected to give a security interest in "all assets" as a routine matter. The market for secured loans is somewhat stratified, with some secured lenders catering to less creditworthy borrowers. The unexpected filing of a financing statement that names such a secured party may prompt trade creditors to reconsider their credit policy with respect to the debtor. Interestingly, reports issued by business credit reporting agencies such as Dun & Bradstreet frequently include information concerning Article 9 filings.

---

7.   An unsecured creditor might bargain for the debtor's agreement not to create security interests in its property; however, any security interest created in violation of this agreement ordinarily will be valid. Cf. UCC 9–401(b).

(iii) Article 9's priority rules based on the time of filing also *reduce evidentiary costs and disputes in connection with determination of security interest priorities.* The public office filing system memorializes the time of filing and constitutes a visible and (generally) reliable "scoreboard."

(iv) Article 9's filing rules *create a hurdle that a secured party must clear in order to justify its entitlement to collateral at the expense of a debtor's unsecured creditors.* It is arguable that, as a normative matter, the benefits of security should not be easily obtained. However, this "hurdle" argument is a poor justification for a filing requirement; most would endorse the Article 9 provisions that make compliance with filing requirements less difficult and costly than it had been under Former Article 9.

(v) No matter how simple Article 9's requirements may have become, secured parties from time to time will fail to comply with the filing rules—either by failing to file in the proper location or by filing a defective financing statement. In many cases this noncompliance results in the subordination of security interests to lien creditors or, more often, to trustees in bankruptcy. Consequently, the Article 9 filing rules *enable unsecured creditors to capture assets that otherwise would be allocated to secured parties.* This distributional attribute of the filing regime is related to the "hurdle" rationale just mentioned; seniority to unsecured creditors requires that a secured party "play the game according to the rules." Although those who benefit from the inevitable instances of noncompliance undoubtedly would oppose the abolition of filing requirements, it seems wrong to characterize the inevitability of noncompliance and resulting subordination as a "benefit" of filing. Similar results could be obtained more directly, e.g., by requiring that each debtor maintain a pool of unencumbered assets.[8]

Please continue to ponder the rationale and effects of the Article 9 filing rules as you consider, next, issues concerning the adequacy of financing statements and other issues of compliance and noncompliance with those rules.[9]

Problem 3.3.7. Firstbank established the financing arrangement with Main Motors as described in the Prototype. As in Problem 3.3.1, supra, Secondbank became interested in providing floorplan financing to Main Motors.

(a) If the only reference to collateral were "inventory," would the Financing Statement (Form 3.1, supra) be adequate to perfect a security interest in the automobiles in Main's inventory as of the time the Financing

---

8. Exemption laws are intended to preserve a pool of assets for individual (i.e., human) debtors; however, otherwise exempt property ordinarily may be encumbered by a purchase-money security interest.

9. The characteristics of filing rules also are considered in the context of what transactions are and ought to be subjected to those rules. See Chapter 5, infra.

Statement was filed? Would it be adequate to perfect a security interest in   S ᴋ ᵢ ᴘ
inventory that Main acquired after the Financing Statement was filed? See
UCC 9–502(a)(3); UCC 9–504; UCC 9–108. If so, how can an interested
party such as Secondbank discover the relevant facts? See UCC 9–210. (Do
not overlook the obvious while pondering this question!)

(b) Would the Financing Statement be adequate to perfect a security
interest in Main's inventory of automobiles if the only reference were to
"certain motor vehicles"? Is "certain motor vehicles" a "description" of the
collateral? See Problem 3.2.4(d), p. 133, supra. If not, would "certain motor
vehicles" nevertheless satisfy the requirements of UCC 9–502(a)(3)? See
UCC 9–504, Comment 2; Note (4) on the Adequacy of Financing Statements,
infra. If "certain motor vehicles" is not a sufficient "description" for a
security agreement but is a sufficient "indication" for a financing statement,
what policy explains the difference in result?

(c) Should the UCC require more complete information to appear in the
public record? Should the answer turn on the purpose(s) of Article 9 filing?
See Note (3) on Perfection by Filing, p. 153, supra. Should the answer turn
on the type of collateral involved? Would it be feasible to require more
detailed filing in the setting of inventory financing like that involved in the
Prototype? See UCC 9–502, Comment 2.

On the other hand, insofar as filing is intended to alert interested
parties to the possibility that the secured party may claim a security
interest, how could anyone be misled by a filing covering "all debtor's
personal property, of every kind and nature"? Would such an indication of
collateral be sufficient? See UCC 9–504. Would it suffice as a description of
collateral for a security agreement? See Problem 3.2.4(c), p. 133, supra.
What policy explains the difference?

Problem 3.3.8. The documentation and procedures in the Prototype
were followed, except that the Financing Statement filed by Firstbank set
forth the name of the debtor as "Main Motors"; Main's exact corporate name
is "Main Motors, Inc." Lean, Main's judgment creditor, caused the sheriff to
levy on all the cars. Is Lean's execution lien senior or junior to Firstbank's
security interest? See UCC 9–317(a)(2); UCC 9–502; UCC 9–503(a)(1); UCC
9–102(a)(70); UCC 9–102(a)(50); UCC 9–506(a)–(c); Note (2) on the
Adequacy of Financing Statements, infra.

Problem 3.3.9. In the context of the Prototype, assume that Main's
business is operated (i.e., signs, letterhead, business forms, telephone
listing, advertising) under the **trade name** "Center City Chevrolet Sales
and Service." Would the filing against "Main Motors, Inc." be sufficient to
perfect Firstbank's security interest? Would a filing against "Center City
Chevrolet Sales and Service" be sufficient? See UCC 9–502(a); UCC
9–503(a)–(c); Note (2) on the Adequacy of Financing Statements, infra.

Problem 3.3.10. In the context of the Prototype, assume that
Firstbank's operations are carried out under the trade name "Phirst of
Philly" and that the Financing Statement set out that trade name in the box
for the secured party's name. Is the Financing Statement sufficient? See

UCC 9–102(a)(72); UCC 9–502(a); UCC 9–506(a) & Comment 2; Note (3) on the Adequacy of Financing Statements, infra.

Problem 3.3.11. Assume that the line of credit in the Prototype was extended to Main Motors not by Firstbank alone but by a group (**syndicate**) of banks, including Firstbank, and that the Dealer Inventory Security Agreement (Form 3.2, supra) named all of these banks as secured parties. As part of an **intercreditor agreement**, the banks agreed among themselves that the Financing Statement would show only Firstbank as secured party and that Firstbank would act as agent for the banks in its capacity as the secured party of record. Is the Financing Statement sufficient? See UCC 9–503(d) and Comment 3; Note (3) on the Adequacy of Financing Statements, infra.

Problem 3.3.12. The Financing Statement filed by Firstbank appears on the "uniform form" set forth in UCC 9–521. Would the Financing Statement be legally sufficient if it lacked the information requested in boxes 1.c. through 1.g. and 3.c.? If so, would you advise Firstbank to adopt a cost-saving policy of leaving those boxes blank? See UCC 9–502(a); UCC 9–520(a); UCC 9–516(b)(4), (b)(5); 9–520(c); Note (6) on the Adequacy of Financing Statements, infra.

Problem 3.3.13. Most other documents placed in the public record, including financing statements filed under Former Article 9 (see Former 9–402(1)) and mortgages, are ineffective unless they are signed (or otherwise authenticated). However, a financing statement is sufficient under Revised Article 9 even without any authentication. See UCC 9–502(a).

(a) Why does Revised Article 9 eliminate the signature requirement? See UCC 9–502 & Comment 3; UCC 9–510(a); UCC 9–509(a); Note (5) on the Adequacy of Financing Statements, infra.

(b) What course of action would you recommend to a client against whom a financing statement had been filed (purportedly by a secured party named "SpongeBob SquarePants") for the purpose of impairing the client's ability to obtain secured credit? See UCC 9–510(a); UCC 9–509(a); UCC 9–625(e)(3); UCC 9–509(d); UCC 9–102(a)(72), (a)(79); UCC 9–513(c), (d); UCC 9–518; UCC 9–625(e)(4), UCC 9–511.

(c) Do you suppose the elimination of the signature requirement has increased the use of the filing system by malefactors to impair the ability of others to get secured credit? See UCC 9–625(b), (e)(3). Consider, in this regard, the deterrent effect of the signature requirement of Former 9–402(1).

Problem 3.3.14. Firstbank obtained the documentation and followed the procedures in the Prototype, except that the Dealer Inventory Security Agreement (Form 3.2, supra) did not include paragraph (5)(b).

(a) Lean, the holder of a judgment against Main Motors, caused the sheriff to serve a garnishment summons on G.S. Gessell, who had borrowed $10,000 from Main. Under applicable law, the service of the garnishment summons gave Lean a judicial lien on Main's right to payment from Gessell.

Who has a better claim to the right to payment, Lean or Firstbank? See UCC 9–317(a)(2); UCC 9–203(b). (The right to payment is a "general intangible." See UCC 9–102(a)(42).)

(b) Lean, the holder of a judgment against Main Motors, subsequently caused the sheriff to levy on the cars in Main's inventory. Is Lean's lien junior to Firstbank's security interest in the cars? Or, does the fact that Main did not authorize the filing of a financing statement covering accounts, chattel paper, or general intangibles render the filed financing statement ineffective? See UCC 9–317(a)(2); UCC 9–510(a) & Comment 2; UCC 9–509(a), (b).

NOTES ON THE ADEQUACY OF FINANCING STATEMENTS

(1) The Formal Requisites. UCC 9–502(a) sets forth the three formal requisites for a sufficient financing statement. Except with respect to filings covering collateral related to specific real property, "a financing statement is sufficient only if it (1) provides the name of the debtor; (2) provides the name of the secured party or a representative of the secured party; and (3) indicates the collateral covered by the financing statement." This seemingly straightforward system of "notice filing" derives from the notice filing system of Former Article 9, which was borrowed in large part from the Uniform Trust Receipts Act, promulgated in 1933. It is surprising, perhaps, that determining the adequacy of financing statements under Former Article 9 proved perplexing to courts, commentators, and practitioners alike. In an effort to reduce the uncertainty that developed under the case law and commentary construing Former 9–402(1), UCC 9–503 expounds upon the first two requirements (the names of the parties), and UCC 9–504 expounds upon the third (the indication of the collateral). UCC 9–506 provides additional guidance with respect to errors.

[handwritten note in right margin: REQUIREMENTS FOR A FINANCING STATEMENT]

Note (3) on Perfection by Filing, page 153, supra, summarizes several plausible positive explanations for what the filing system actually does and does not do. The courts, however, generally have measured the adequacy of financing statements under Former Article 9 against a narrow paradigm consisting of an interested person who wishes to discover whether there are filings against a debtor and, if there are filings, the collateral that they cover. Can an interested person find the financing statement in question? Is the information contained in the financing statement sufficiently complete and meaningful? Revised Article 9 likewise adopts this general approach.

(2) Debtor's Name. Filing officers index financing statements "according to the name of the debtor." UCC 9–519(c)(1). Consequently, whether an interested person can find a financing statement is a function of (i) the debtor's name as it appears on the financing statement, (ii) the name against which the interested person requests a search of the filing office's records, and (iii) the financing statements disclosed by the filing office as a result of that search request.

UCC 9–503(a) explains how to satisfy the requirement that a financing statement provide "the name of the debtor." UCC 9–502(a)(1). If the debtor is a corporation or other "registered organization" (as defined in UCC 9–102(a)(70)), a financing statement sufficiently provides the name of the debtor "only if the financing statement provides the name of the debtor indicated on the public record of the debtor's jurisdiction of organization which shows the debtor to have been organized." UCC 9–503(a)(1). These public records are readily available, often on the Internet. For example, you can conduct a free search of the records concerning Iowa corporations at http://sos.state.ia.us/corp/corp_search.asp.

Errors in a Debtor's Name. If past practice is any indication, secured parties will make errors even in corporate names. Minor errors ordinarily do not render a financing statement ineffective, unless the error makes the financing statement seriously misleading. See UCC 9–506(a). However, when it comes to errors in debtors' names, Revised Article 9 generally is unforgiving: Any name that does not comply with the requirements of UCC 9–503(a) ordinarily is seriously misleading as a matter of law, see UCC 9–506(b), unless "a search of the records of the filing office under the debtor's correct name, using the filing office's standard search logic, if any, would disclose a financing statement." UCC 9–506(c). Cases decided under Former Article 9 reveal many errors in the debtor's name that seem trivial and harmless. See, e.g., In re Tyler, 23 B.R. 806 (Bkrtcy.S.D.Fla.1982) (filing against "Tri–State Mo*u*lded Plastics, Inc." (emphasis added); correct corporate name was "Tri–State Molded Plastics, Inc."); In re Raymond F. Sargent, Inc., 8 U.C.C. Rep. Serv. 583 (Bkrtcy.D.Me.1970) (filing against "Raymond F. Sargent *Co.*, Inc." (emphasis added); correct corporate name was "Raymond F. Sargent, Inc."). Would the financing statements in these cases be effective under Revised Article 9? Do you need more information to answer this question?

Assuming the names implicated in the question just posed do not comply with the requirements of UCC 9–503(a) (i.e., are inaccurate), UCC 9–506(b) requires one bit of necessary additional information—whether a search under the correct name would have uncovered the financing statements "using the filing office's standard search logic, if any." Despite advances in technology, some filing offices still process search requests manually; individuals search the files for filings against the name(s) submitted by a party requesting a search. In such a system, whether a search request for filings against "A.B.C. Corp." (the "real" name) would result in identification of filings against other variations (e.g., "ABC Corp.," "A. B. C. Corp.," "ABC," "A.B.C. Systems") will depend on the formal or informal procedures adopted by that office and, perhaps, the judgment of the particular employee conducting the search.

Because all filing systems now are "computerized" to some extent, one cannot determine whether a financing statement benefits from UCC 9–506(b) without taking into account the filing office's search logic. Many states have adopted the search logic (or a variant thereof) promulgated by the International Association of Corporate Administrators ("IACA"), an organization of administrators responsible for statewide corporate and UCC filings. For example, the Arizona Secretary of State explains the state's basic rules for searching by name as follows:

- Case insensitive
- Punctuation and Accents discarded
- Ignore
  - Spacing
  - The word "The" at the beginning of names
  - Ending "noise words" as defined by IACA[10]
- Organizational Name or Individual Last Name must be exact
- Individual First Name and Middle Name - optional and more fuzzy logic
  - A single initial matches fields as a wildcard
  - A "name" in field matches all exact names and names where it is just an initial and first letter of "name" matches
    - Names may be additionally filtered on address, city or postal code
    - Address fields are matched "begins with 'criteria'"

http://www.azsos.gov/business_services/ucc/UCC_Search_Instr.htm (visited Aug. 19, 2005).

Even without knowing the precise search logic of a given filing office, one can determine whether the search logic will uncover a given financing statement by searching under the debtor's correct name and seeing the results of the search. The UCC filings in more than half the states are searchable on the Internet, sometimes at no cost. For example, one can search the Arizona UCC filings at http://www.azsos.gov/business_services/ UCC.htm.

Trade Names. Apart from inaccuracies in the debtor's name, there is the problem of "trade names," under which individuals, partnerships, and corporations may choose to conduct business. (For example, the Chicago National League Ball Club, Inc., has adopted the trade name "Chicago Cubs.") Although Former Article 9 does not provide for this result explicitly, a majority of the reported cases indicate that use of a trade name instead of a "real" name is insufficient. See, e.g., Greg Restaurant Equipment & Supplies, Inc. v. Valway, 144 Vt. 59, 472 A.2d 1241 (1984) (filing against trade name ("Ricardo's") that differed materially from debtor's actual name ("Richard M. Valway") was ineffective); In re Covey, 66 B.R. 459 (Bkrtcy.D.N.H.1986) (filing against debtor's trade name ("RBF Industries") instead of actual name ("George R. Covey") was ineffective because a third party searching the files against the actual name would not discover the trade name filing). Other courts have reached a different conclusion. See, e.g., In re Glasco, Inc., 642 F.2d 793 (5th Cir.1981) (applying Florida law)

---

10. [IACA's list of ending "noise words" includes "Corporation," "Co," "Partnership," and other words and abbreviations indicating that the debtor is an organization. The list appears at http://www.iaca.org/sts/busend.pdf.]

(filing against "Elite Boats, Division of Glasco, Inc." was effective to perfect security interest notwithstanding that debtor's correct corporate name was "Glasco, Inc.," because a "reasonably prudent creditor" would have searched against "Elite Boats," the debtor's trade name).

UCC 9–503(c) addresses the issue explicitly: a financing statement that provides only the debtor's trade name does not sufficiently provide the name of the debtor. Nevertheless, under some circumstances a financing statement may be sufficient even if it provides only a trade name for the debtor; however, the sufficiency of a trade name is determined by the same rules for determining the sufficiency of any other incorrect name. See UCC 9–506(b), (c). How would the cases in the preceding paragraph be decided under Revised Article 9?

Searching the Public Records. One might assume from the foregoing discussion that a person searching the public records need only search under a debtor's correct name and can safely disregard other names that the debtor might use. A potential lender may find it prudent, however, to search more broadly for several reasons. First, a potential lender may wish to discover *all* financing statements filed against the debtor, even financing statements that may be ineffective. Second, a small number of financing statements filed before the effective date of Revised Article 9 may remain effective if they provide a name that was sufficient under Former Article 9, even if it is incorrect (and thus insufficient under Revised Article 9). Third, in some states notices of judicial liens and federal tax liens are filed and indexed in the UCC filing offices. The law governing those liens, and not Article 9, controls the adequacy of a debtor's name in a filing. See, e.g., In re Spearing Tool and Manufacturing Co., 412 F.3d 653 (6th Cir.2005) (notice of tax lien providing a debtor's name that would be ineffective for a financing statement held to be an effective tax lien filing nonetheless). (*Spearing Tool* is reproduced and discussed beginning on page 537, infra.). Finally, as the following discussion explains, a broad search may be warranted when the debtor is an individual.

One way to search more broadly than the debtor's correct name is, of course, to search under additional names that a filer may have used to identify the debtor. Another way is to search under the debtor's correct name but use a search logic that is more flexible, and thus likely to recover more "hits" than the standard search logic. Private search firms typically offer this option, as do some filing offices. For example, the New York Secretary of State offers three search engines in addition to the standard search logic. See http://appsext4.dos.state.ny.us/pls/ucc_public/web_search.main_frame (visited Aug. 19, 2005).

Names of Individuals. Names of individual (human) debtors are particularly problematic: Consider an individual whose birth certificate refers to Kelly Livingston Jones, who normally goes by "K. Livingston Jones" for personal affairs and "K. L. Jones" for professional and business purposes, and who is called "Kelly Jones" by friends. What is the "individual . . . name" of this person, as the phrase is used in UCC 9–503(a)(4)(A)? Can a single debtor have more than one name for purposes of UCC 9–502(a)(1) and UCC 9–503(a)(4)(A)? Is a filing that names "Kelly Jones" sufficient?

Professor Julianna Zekan proposed that Article 9 require filings against the "legal name" of a debtor, which she would define as "the official name (appellation) of an individual . . . as stated on an official document such as the birth certificate, passport, registration . . . as modified, supplemented or amended of record with the appropriate judicial or other governmental authorities." Zekan, The Name Game—Playing to Win Under § 9–402 of the Uniform Commercial Code, 19 Hofstra L. Rev. 365, 440–41 (1990). Revised Article 9 does not adopt this proposal. Should it have done so? Are there situations in which an individual debtor could have more than one "legal" name? Although UCC 9–503 substantially clarifies the analysis for names of registered organizations and certain other entities, it preserves the perplexing issues surrounding individual names that existed under Former Article 9.

Under these circumstances, what should a court do? If a financing statement fails to provide "the individual . . . name of the debtor" as required by UCC 9–503(a)(4), then the standard search logic of the filing office is relevant to whether the financing statement is sufficient. See UCC 9–506(b). If, for example, the debtor's name is K. L. Jones, then the search logic will determine whether a search under that name will disclose a filing against K L Jones, KL Jones, K. Livingston Jones, or Kelly Jones; any financing statement that the search discloses satisfies the debtor's-name requirement. But one cannot apply UCC 9–506(b) without first knowing "the individual . . . name of the debtor" under UCC 9–503(a)(4), and UCC 9–503(a)(4) gives no guidance in determining which name (or names) is "the individual . . . name of the debtor." UCC 9–503(a)(4). Should courts treat as "the individual . . . name of the debtor" *every* name under which a *reasonable searcher* would search? Some courts took this approach under Former Article 9. Is this approach circular: Can one know the names under which a reasonable searcher would search without first knowing which names are sufficient under UCC 9–503? Revised Article 9 rejects the "reasonable-searcher" approach with respect to the name of registered organizations. Does this mean that imposing such a burden on searchers with respect to individual debtors conflicts with the policy of UCC 9–503 and UCC 9–506?

The Bankruptcy Appellate Panel of the Tenth Circuit recently confronted this very issue in In re Kinderknecht, 308 B.R. 71 (10th Cir.B.A.P.2004). The financing statement named the debtor as "Terry J. Kinderknecht." It was undisputed that the debtor's legal name was "Terrance Joseph Kinderknecht" and that the debtor was known informally as "Terry." The bankruptcy petition was signed "Terry Kinderknecht," but was filed under "Terrance J. Kinderknecht."

The bankruptcy court held that the financing statement was sufficient. The Bankruptcy Appellate Panel reversed, holding that, "For a financing statement to be sufficient under Kansas law, the secured creditor must list an individual debtor by his or her legal name, not a nickname." 308 B.R. at

73. Following is the core of the court's discussion (with some footnotes omitted):

Although § 84-9-503 specifically sets parameters for listing a debtor's name in a financing statement when the debtor is an entity, it does not provide any detail as to the name that must be provided for an individual debtor—it simply states that the "name of the debtor" should be used. This could be construed, as it was by the bankruptcy court, as allowing a debtor to be listed in a financing statement by his or her commonly-used nickname. But, we do not agree with that interpretation because the purpose of § 84-9-503, as well as a reading of that section as a whole, leads us to conclude that an individual debtor's legal name must be used in the financing statement to make it sufficient under § 84-9-502(a)(1).

As discussed above, § 84-9-503 is new, and it was enacted to clarify the sufficiency of a debtor's name in financing statements. The intent to clarify when a debtor's name is sufficient shows a desire to foreclose fact-intensive tests, such as those that existed under the former Article 9 of the UCC, inquiring into whether a person conducting a search would discover a filing under any given name. Requiring a financing statement to provide a debtor's legal name is a clear cut test that is in accord with that intent.

Furthermore, § 84-9-503, read as a whole, indicates that a legal name should be used for an individual debtor. In the case of debtor-entities, § 84-9-503(a) states that legal names must be used to render them sufficient under § 84-9-502(a). Trade names or other names may be listed, but it is insufficient to list a debtor by such names alone. A different standard should not apply to individual debtors. The more specific provisions applicable to entities, together with the importance of naming the debtor in the financing statement to facilitate the notice filing system and increase commercial certainty, indicates that an individual debtor must be listed on a financing statement by his or her legal name, not by a nickname.

Our conclusion that a legal name is necessary to sufficiently provide the name of an individual debtor within the meaning of § 84-9-503(a) is also supported by four practical considerations. First, mandating the debtor's legal name sets a clear test so as simplify the drafting of financing statements. Second, setting a clear test simplifies the parameters of UCC searches. Persons searching UCC filings will know that they need the debtor's legal name to conduct a search, they will not be penalized if they do not know that a debtor has a nickname, and they will not have to guess any number of nicknames that could exist to conduct a search.[16] Third, requiring the debtor's legal name will avoid

16. We note that in the current case, Terrance and Terry are closely aligned; however we believe that it sets an unsatisfactory precedent to allow the use of nicknames in filing. See Harry C. Sigman, *The Filing System Under Revised Article 9*, 73 Am. Bankr.L.J. 61, 73 (1999) (use of a legal name "does not burden searchers with the

litigation as to the commonality or appropriateness of a debtor's nickname, and as to whether a reasonable searcher would have or should have known to use the name. Finally, obtaining a debtor's legal name is not difficult or burdensome for the creditor taking a secured interest in a debtor's property. Indeed, knowing the individual's legal name will assure the accuracy of any search that creditor conducts prior to taking its secured interest in property.

Additionally, we note that although use of the Official Forms is not mandated, the language in the Financing Statement Form set forth in § 84-9-521 expressly states that the preparer should include the "DEBTOR'S EXACT FULL LEGAL NAME." This Form, which is meant to "reduce error," indicates to us an intent to increase certainty in the filing of financing statements by requiring a debtor's legal name. Our holding in this case will foster that intent.

... Included in the record before us are the results of a UCC search conducted by Deere's counsel in Kansas's official and unofficial UCC search systems. Under both systems, she found no matches for the debtor's legal name "Terrance," but numerous matches for his nickname "Terry" and the initial "T." Thus, a search of the debtor's "correct name" did not disclose a financing statement, and therefore, § 84-9-506(c) does not apply. The result of Deere's UCC searches underscores the need for a clear-cut method of searching a debtor's name in UCC filings. The logical starting point for a person searching records would be to use the debtor's legal name. When a UCC search of the debtor's legal name does not provide any matches, parties in interest should be able to presume that the debtor's property is not encumbered, and they should not be charged with guessing what to do next if the legal name search does not result in any matches. Deere's financing statements, being seriously misleading, do not perfect its interest in the debtor's property[.]

308 B.R. at 75-77.

The parties in *Kinderknecht* did not dispute whether "Terrance" was the debtor's legal name and "Terry" his nickname, nor did the court explain how to determine which name is an individual debtor's "legal name." How would you advise a lender to make that determination with reasonable certainty?

As the *Kinderknecht* court acknowledged, UCC 9-503(a)(4) does not expressly require the use of an individual debtor's "legal name" or even (to the extent it is different) the debtor's "full name" or "formal name." Rather, it requires the use of the debtor's "individual . . . name." The court in In re Erwin, 50 UCC Rep. Serv. 2d 933 (Bkrtcy.D.Kan.2003), concluded that, absent a statutory provision stating that a legal name is required, the word "name" should be given its common and ordinary meaning, which, according

obligation to dream up every potential error and name variation and perform searches under all possibilities. Revised Article 9 allows a searcher to rely on a single search conducted under the correct name of the debtor and penalizes filers only for errors that result in the nondisclosure of the financing statement in a search under the correct name.")[.]

to the seventh edition of Black's Law Dictionary, includes the debtor's nickname. (*Black's* defines "name" as any "word or phrase identifying or designating a person and distinguishing that person . . . from others.") What, if anything, would be wrong if an individual debtor's "correct name" included a nickname that was free from error?

To what extent should Article 9 place the risks and burdens of investigating and listing the exact name of a debtor on the secured party who files? To what extent should the risks of investigating and searching against trade names and names similar to a debtor's "real" name lie with those who search? Is it possible to generalize about which class of parties—secured parties who file or searchers—can protect themselves better against these risks and burdens? For which class of parties is such protection less costly? In answering the foregoing questions, is the frequency with which filings and searches occur relevant?

Who is the "Debtor"? Finally, in considering the adequacy of a debtor's name on a financing statement, it is worth remembering the need to ascertain the identity of the debtor. UCC 9–102(a)(28) defines "debtor" to include "a person having a [non-security interest or non-lien] interest in the collateral, whether or not the person is an obligor." This, of course, makes perfect sense in the present context. The filing system is designed to provide publicity about possible claims against a debtor's property.

(3) Secured Party's Name; Secured Party of Record. The second formal requirement for a sufficient financing statement is that it must "provide[] the name of the secured party or a representative of the secured party." UCC 9–502(a)(2). The person whose name is provided is the "secured party of record." UCC 9–511(a). The secured party of record has the power to authorize certain amendments to a filed financing statement, including the power to terminate the financing statement's effectiveness. See UCC 9–509(d)(1).

When there is one secured party, the financing statement usually provides the secured party's name. That is, the "secured party" and the "secured party of record" are the same person. An error in this name will not render the financing statement ineffective. See 9–506, Comment 2. In large loans, it is not uncommon for several financial institutions to provide funds that are secured by a security interest. Sometimes each lender is a "secured party," i.e, "a person in whose favor a security interest is created or provided for under a security agreement." UCC 9–102(a)(72). Sometimes a security interest is created in favor of one of the lenders, who serves as the **collateral agent** and holds the security interest for the benefit of itself and the other lenders, usually for a fee. This lender is the "secured party." Sometimes the secured party is a non-lender third party who serves as collateral agent for a fee. Where many lenders are involved, Article 9 affords considerable flexibility in satisfying UCC 9–502(a)(2). Providing the name of all the secured parties is sufficient and will create multiple secured parties of record, each of which has the power to affect its own rights. In the alternative, a financing statement may provide the name of a "representative" (as defined in UCC 1–201(b)(33) [F1–201(35)]) of the secured parties. A financing statement that provides the name of the collateral agent or other representative satisfies UCC 9–502(a)(2), even if it fails to indicate that the name provided is that of a representative and not that of the secured party itself. UCC 9–503(d). A secured party should choose its representative carefully. As the secured party of record, the representative has the power to impair the secured party's rights, e.g., by terminating the effectiveness of the financing statement and thereby rendering the security interest unperfected. See UCC 9–509(d)(1).

The flexibility and margin for error that Article 9 affords with respect *more forgiveness re* to names of secured parties provides a dramatic contrast with the *secured parties' names* considerable precision that Article 9 requires with respect to debtors' names. Article 9's treatment of post-filing changes makes this contrast even starker. Post-filing changes in the secured party's name do not affect perfection, whereas in certain circumstances a financing statement becomes ineffective to perfect a security interest unless it is amended to reflect a change in the debtor's name. See UCC 9–507(b), (c); Problems 3.3.16 and 3.3.17, pp. 176–77, infra; Note on Post–Filing Changes, infra.

Why is Article 9 so much more exacting with respect to debtors' names? The principal explanation is that Article 9 filing systems normally provide no system for searching against a *secured party's* name. See UCC 9–519(c); UCC 9–523(c). Rather, the secured party's name must be provided so that notices can be sent to the secured party. See, e.g., UCC 9–324(b). In addition, the secured party's name provides a potential source of information concerning the transaction.

(4) References to <u>Collateral</u>. A secured party must do more than ensure that a financing statement correctly states the debtor's name and provides its own name or the name of its representative. A financing statement also must "indicate the collateral covered by the financing statement." UCC 9–502(a)(3). As Comment 2 explains:

> This section adopts the system of "notice filing." What is required to be filed is not, as under pre-UCC chattel mortgage and conditional sales acts, the security agreement itself, but only a simple record providing a limited amount of information (financing statement). . . .

> The notice itself indicates merely that a person may have a security interest in the collateral indicated. Further inquiry from the parties concerned will be necessary to disclose the complete state of affairs.

UCC 9–502, Comment 2.

As a general matter, "[a]n indication is sufficient if it satisfies the purpose of conditioning perfection on the filing of a financing statement, i.e., if it provides notice that a person may have a security interest in the collateral indicated." UCC 9–504, Comment 2. UCC 9–504 provides two safe harbors. First, a "description" of collateral under UCC 9–108–i.e., an indication that "reasonably identifies" the collateral—is a sufficient "indication" of collateral for purposes of UCC 9–502(a)(3). See UCC 9–504(1). In particular, a financing statement that lists the items of collateral (e.g., "two Techno A–32 power lathes, serial numbers 54–0958–98 and 54–0921–98"), identifies the collateral by category (e.g., "motor vehicles"), or refers to collateral by a defined UCC type (e.g., "all equipment") provides a sufficient indication. See UCC 9–108(b). Second, an indication that a financing statement covers all assets or all personal property is a sufficient indication of collateral for a financing statement. See UCC 9–504(2). In this respect, UCC 9–504 rejects the overwhelming majority of cases decided under Former Article 9 which refused to uphold financing statements containing only "super-generic" indications. Is anyone likely to be misled by the use of a "super-generic" indication? Given how little information is conveyed by a financing statement and the permissible use of generic terms, is the informational value of filing reduced by the use of "super-generic" indications that clearly include *all* types of personal property?[11]

Super-generic okay for financing statements

Although they suffice as an indication of collateral for purposes of a financing statement, "all debtor's assets" and words of similar import are insufficient as a "description" in a security agreement. See UCC 9–108(c); Note (3) on Attachment, p. 142, supra. In this respect, UCC 9–108 rejects the view of those cases decided under Former Article 9 which held that such an indication could "reasonably identify" the collateral. Is there an inherent conflict between the rules in UCC 9–504(a)(2) and UCC 9–108(c)? Even if not, is there a need for two different standards for referring to collateral? If different standards are appropriate, who chose the right standards—the drafters of Revised Article 9 or the judges whose opinions the drafters rejected?

(5) Authorization. A debtor has a strong interest in the content of the public records that disclose possible claims against the debtor's property. To protect this interest, Former 9–402(1) required that a financing statement be "signed by the debtor." In considering ways in which to facilitate electronic filing of financing statements, the drafters of Revised Article 9 realized that the debtor's interest could be protected by requiring that the debtor authorize the filing of a financing statement, even if the authorization itself (the debtor's signature) does not appear in the public record. Thus a financing statement need not be signed to be sufficient. See UCC 9–502(a). However, a financing statement is not effective unless the filing is authorized by the debtor in an authenticated record. See UCC 9–509(a).

---

11.   In the words of Judge William Hillman:

One of the basic words in English is "all." It is actually easier to understand "all" than a compilation of all of the U.C.C. generics. Why must a security document state 1 + 1 + 1 when 3 is easily understood?

In re Legal Data Systems, Inc., 135 B.R. 199, 201 (Bkrtcy.D.Mass.1991). In a footnote, Judge Hillman observed: "There is a T-shirt available in resort areas with the legend: 'What part of NO don't you understand?'." Judge Hillman served on the Drafting Committee to Revise Article 9.

A debtor's authorization of a filing is easy enough to understand in the case of a debtor who is a natural person. When another entity (e.g., a corporation or partnership) is involved, agency law and the law regulating acts taken by the particular entity (e.g., corporate law or partnership law) determine whether the entity authorized a filing. See UCC 1–103(b) [F1–103]; UCC 9–502, Comment 3; UCC 9–509, Comment 3.

A person who creates a security interest ordinarily does not object to the filing of a financing statement covering the collateral. Indeed, the person may even covenant to take whatever steps may be necessary to perfect, and maintain the perfected status of, the security interest. UCC 9–509(b) reflects this phenomenon by providing that the debtor's authentication of a security agreement *ipso facto* constitutes the debtor's authorization of the filing of a financing statement covering the collateral described in the security agreement. See UCC 9–509(b)(1).

Many unauthorized filings are made in good faith, as when a lender files a financing statement with respect to a transaction that being negotiated with the potential debtor. Others, however, are filed maliciously, to interfere with the ability of the purported debtors to obtain credit. Individuals and organized groups that use UCC filing system to express their displeasure with judges, sheriffs, legislators, and other public officials present a particularly visible problem. (For example, an unauthorized financing statement was filed against the Governor of Hawaii.) Article 9 responds to the problem of bogus financing statements in two ways. First, it requires a secured party to provide (or, in the case of consumer goods, to file) a termination statement for a financing statement whose filing the putative debtor did not authorize. See UCC 9–513(a), (c).[12] If the secured party fails to comply with this requirement, the debtor itself may authorize the filing of termination statement; however, a debtor-authorized termination statement must indicate that the debtor authorized the filing. See UCC 9–509(d). Second, the person named as debtor may file a correction statement, which sets forth the basis for the person's belief that the financing statement was wrongfully filed. See UCC 9–518.

Article 9 provides an incomplete solution to the problem. A debtor-authorized termination statement is not effective unless the debtor was entitled to file it. A debtor who actually was entitled to file may have difficulty proving the entitlement to the satisfaction of a potential lender. And unlike an authorized termination statement, which amends the public record and terminates the effect of the wrongfully-filed financing statement, a correction statement has no legal effect. Comment 3 to UCC 9–518 observes that, "A summary judicial procedure for correcting the public record and criminal penalties for those who misuse the filing and recording systems are likely to be more effective and put less strain on the filing system than provisions authorizing or requiring action by filing and

---

12.   A secured party is required to file (or send) a termination statement also if there is no obligation secured by the collateral covered by the financing statement and no commitment to extend value in the future. See UCC 9–513(a), (c).

recording offices." IACA currently is developing a model law along those lines.

(6) Additional Information. Former Article 9 required that a financing statement give the addresses of the debtor and secured party in addition to their names. The courts generally have imposed a less exacting standard for addresses than they have with respect to debtors' names and identifications of collateral. Indeed, although contrary authority exists, there is support for upholding the sufficiency of financing statements even when addresses are missing entirely. Revised Article 9 adopts this approach and provides that a financing statement may be sufficient even if it does not provide addresses. See UCC 9–502(a).

Although they did not think that providing addresses in a financing statement should be a condition of perfection, the drafters of Revised Article 9 recognized that the addresses serve a useful function. The debtor's address helps a searcher eliminate from consideration financing statements filed against debtors (in particular, individual debtors) whose names are the same as the person against whom the search was conducted. The actual usefulness of an address in eliminating "false positives" depends on the circumstances. For example, an address may be of great assistance to one who is searching against the name "John Smith," and considerably less so to one searching against, say, Phineas T. Bluster or Microsoft Corporation. As for the address of the secured party, Article 9 contemplates circumstances in which one secured party will send notification to the holder of a conflicting security interest. See, e.g., UCC 9–324(b); UCC 9–610(b), (c). A financing statement that provides the secured party's address substantially increases the likelihood that the notification will reach the right person. Sometimes interested third parties seek information, or seek confirmation of information provided by the debtor, from secured parties who have filed. The secured party's address helps direct the seeker to the appropriate person. (Of course, a secured party who receives a request for information from a third party should resolve any confidentiality concerns before responding. See UCC 9–210, Comment 3.)

Revised Article 9 reflects the drafters' appreciation of the utility that addresses may provide. It supplies a strong incentive for a filer to provide the relevant addresses: The filing office is required to reject a financing statement that does not provide an address for each of the parties. See UCC 9–520(a); UCC 9–516(b)(4), (b)(5)(A). Other information that might help distinguish the debtor from another person having the same or a similar name is treated the same way. Thus, UCC 9–520(a) and UCC 9–516(b) require the filing office to reject a financing statement that does not indicate whether the debtor is an individual or an organization. If the financing statement indicates that the debtor is an organization, the filing office must reject the filing unless it provides for the debtor a type of organization (e.g., corporation or partnership), a jurisdiction of organization, and an organizational identification number (or indicates that the debtor has none). See UCC 9–520(a); UCC 9–516(b)(5)(B), (b)(5)(C).

What is the legal effect, if any, of a financing statement that the filing office is obligated to reject but nevertheless files? If the financing statement satisfies the formal requirements of UCC 9–502(a) and the filing is authorized under UCC 9–509(a), then the filed financing statement is effective. See UCC 9–520(c).

NOTE ON FILING SYSTEMS

Personal property filing systems based upon an index of debtor names have been utilized at least since the time of the chattel mortgage laws of the nineteenth century. The "modern" system of "notice filing" embraced by Article 9 dates back more than seventy years, to the Uniform Trust Receipts Act of 1933. Although "computerized" systems became common under Former Article 9, there developed a consensus that the filing systems generally did not work well and failed to take full advantage of the benefits of existing technology. See Report of the Uniform Commercial Code Article 9 Filing System Task Force to the Permanent Editorial Board's Article 9 Study Committee 6–10 (1991) (reporting results of an empirical study of the Article 9 filing system and finding many filing offices to be unacceptably slow and inaccurate and to impose unnecessary costs on users.)

One of the principal goals of Revised Article 9 was to improve the operations of the filing offices. To this end, the revision makes clear that, should it choose to do so, a filing office may accept filings only in electronic form. To date, no state has accepted this invitation. However, one now can file a financing statement electronically in around half the states and search electronically in even more. In addition, as we explain elsewhere:

> Revised Article 9 contains several provisions that promote efficiency and uniformity in the operations of filing offices. For example, Revised sections 9–516 and 9–520 underscore that filing offices serve a ministerial, rather than regulatory, function. Taken together, they contain an exclusive list of grounds for rejecting a financing statement or other record that is communicated to a filing office and require a filing office that rejects a record to promptly inform the filer of the fact of and reason for the rejection. To further insure that filers of written financing statements are not burdened by idiosyncratic requirements imposed by individual filing offices, Revised section 9–521 contains forms for initial financing statements and amendments which each filing office must accept (assuming it accepts written records). Revised section 9–519(f) facilitates searches of the public records by requiring a filing office to be capable of retrieving an initial financing statement and all amendments and other filed records relating to it either by the debtor's name or by the file number assigned to the initial financing statement. Revised section 9–523 increases the utility of responses to search requests by requiring a filing office to respond to requests promptly and with current and complete information.

The Drafting Committee realized that dictating the minimum services a filing office must provide and setting the minimum performance standards for providing those services are appropriate subjects for legislation, but specifying the details of day-to-day filing-office operations is not. Detailed procedures specified in statutes cannot be changed easily enough to enable filing offices to adjust to changes in filing load, personnel, and technology. Particularly given the substantial differences among Article 9 filing offices (in their current operations, in the quantity of filings processed, and in the number of employees who do the processing), imposing absolute uniformity of practices and procedures would be both unnecessary and unwise. Yet, because filers and searchers often deal with many filing offices, great value would come from having filing-office practices and procedures be harmonious with one another. Revised section 9–526 is a useful step toward realizing that value. This section requires the adoption and publication of filing-office rules after consultation with other filing offices and after consideration of the rules and practices of, and technology used by, other Article 9 filing offices. Revised section 9–526 requires the rule-adopting official or agency also to consult the Model Rules promulgated by [IACA].

Harris & Mooney, How Successful Was the Revision of UCC Article 9?: Reflections of the Reporters, 74 Chi.–Kent L. Rev. 1357, 1382–84 (1999).

Early indications are that Revised Article 9 has increased the speed, accuracy, and uniformity of the UCC filing system. Those filing offices that accept electronic filings generally have experienced a reduced need for personnel. A good deal of information about the operation of each state's filing office, including the number of filings annually and the availability of electronic filing and searching, can be found in the annual reports compiled each year by IACA and posted on its website, http://iaca.org.

Problem 3.3.15. Firstbank established the financing arrangement with Main Motors as described in the Prototype. Subsequently, Secondbank became interested in providing floorplan financing to Main Motors. A search of the UCC filings revealed Firstbank's financing statement. Notwithstanding both Main's and Firstbank's assurances that Firstbank has been paid in full and has made no commitment whatsoever to extend more credit to Main, Secondbank refuses to advance funds to Main Motors in the face of the financing statement filed in favor of Firstbank,. (We shall see below in Chapter 4 that Secondbank is not acting unreasonably.) What would you advise Main to do? See UCC 9–513(c) and (d).

Problem 3.3.16. Assume that Firstbank "picked up" the floorplan financing for Main Motors, on September 3, 2001, as described in the Prototype, and that, effective October 1, 2001, Main changed its corporate name from "Main Motors, Inc." to "Center City Chevrolet Sales and Service, Inc." Main received new shipments of cars on November 15 and December 20, 2001, and on February 14, 2002. Firstbank took no action to perfect its security interest subsequent to filing the original Financing Statement (Form 3.1, supra). Lean, Main's judgment creditor, caused the sheriff to levy on all the remaining cars in Main's inventory on February 20, 2002. Is

Lean's execution lien senior or junior to Firstbank's security interest? See UCC 9–507(b), (c); Note on Post–Filing Changes, infra. Does the answer depend on whether Firstbank knew that Main had changed its name? Should it?

Problem 3.3.17. You are an attorney in Firstbank's office of legal counsel. Two years after the transactions described in the Prototype, the general counsel informs you that Firstbank plans to change its name to Phirst of Philly, N.A., and asks whether the bank risks becoming unperfected on all its secured loans if it fails to amend each of the several thousand filed financing statements that show the bank's name as Firstbank, N.A. What advice do you give? See UCC 9–507(b); Note on Post–Filing Changes, infra.

Problem 3.3.18. In the context of the Prototype, assume that Firstbank assigned its security interest and the obligations of Main Motors that it secures to Secondbank, but nothing indicating the assignment is filed with the filing office (i.e., the financing statement naming Firstbank as secured party remains unchanged).

(a) Does the Financing Statement remain sufficient to perfect the security interest (now) held by Secondbank? See UCC 9–310(c); UCC 9–507(b).

(b) Assume further that one of Firstbank's clerks, having become aware that Firstbank no longer has any outstanding loans to Main on its books, sends a termination statement to the filing office. What is the effect, if any, on Secondbank's security interest? See UCC 9–513(d); UCC 9–514(b); UCC 9–511; UCC 9–509(d); Note (3) on the Adequacy of Financing Statements, p. 170, supra.

NOTE ON POST–FILING CHANGES

The world is always changing. As Problems 3.3.16 through 3.3.18 suggest, information in a financing statement that is correct when the financing statement is filed may become incorrect thereafter. How do post-filing changes affect the legal sufficiency of the financing statement?

Consider the case of a debtor whose name changes after a financing statement is filed. One can imagine a legal regime in which the financing statement becomes ineffective, and the security interest unperfected, immediately upon the name change. Such a rule would impose upon the secured party the burden of discovering the change and amending the financing statement to reflect the debtor's new name. The opposite rule—a financing statement containing correct information remains effective notwithstanding that the information becomes incorrect—is equally imaginable. This rule would impose a risk upon a searcher who fails to ascertain not only the debtor's current name but also its past names.

The debtor's name is not the only information whose change might be relevant to the continued utility of a filed financing statement. For example, the collateral might be put to a different use. A computer dealer might take a computer from inventory and use it in the business. Should a financing statement covering "inventory" remain effective to perfect a security interest in collateral that has become "equipment"?

Article 9 generally imposes no burden to correct information in a filed financing statement. See UCC 9–507(b). However, a secured party who fails to amend a financing statement to reflect a change in the debtor's name risks being unperfected with respect to some collateral. See UCC 9–507(c). What accounts for imposing a greater burden with respect to the debtor's name than with respect to the secured party's name or indication of collateral?

Observe that the rule in UCC 9–507(c) takes an intermediate position between the two extreme positions described above. As to certain collateral, the "old name" financing statement remains effective, whereas it is ineffective as to other collateral. Professor Jay Westbrook thought the predecessor of this rule (to the extent a secured party is absolved indefinitely from providing the debtor's new name in the public record) and of the rule that appears in UCC 9–507(a) created a "loophole" that is "inconsistent with the entire statutory scheme." See Westbrook, Glitch: Section 9–402(7) and the U.C.C. Revision Process, 52 Geo. Wash. L. Rev. 408, 411, 416–17 (1984). UCC 9–507(a) is considered in Chapter 4, Section 2(A), infra. Professor Stephen Knippenberg, on the other hand, has argued that the provision may be grounded on the assumption that there are very few second-in-time searchers who would be misled by "old name" financing statements and many first-in-time secured parties whose perfection would be jeopardized by a system that requires them to monitor name changes. See Knippenberg, Debtor Name Changes and Collateral Transfers Under 9–402(7): Drafting From the Outside–In, 52 Mo.L.Rev. 57, 113–115 (1987).

Does UCC 9–507(c) strike an appropriate balance between the burden imposed on the filer and the burden imposed on the searcher? What reasons can you think of for imposing more diligence on a secured party at the time a filing is made (i.e., get the debtor's name *right*) than is imposed on a secured party subsequently?

We shall have occasion to consider the way in which Article 9 deals with other changes that affect the utility of a financing statement. See, e.g., Problems 3.4.3 and 3.4.4, p. 198, infra (concerning a debtor who relocates and thereby changes the jurisdiction in which a financing statement should be filed); Note (2) on Authorized and Unauthorized Dispositions, p.276, infra (discussing situations in which collateral is sold to a new owner).

(B) PERFECTION BY MEANS OTHER THAN FILING

Problem 3.3.19. Lee Abel purchased a Chevrolet from Main Motors and executed a motor vehicle Instalment Sale Contract (Form 3.6, supra). Main assigned to Firstbank its rights under this contract, and the parties followed the other procedures described in the Prototype. Note that no financing statement naming Abel as debtor was filed with respect to Abel's new Chevrolet.

(a) Friendly Finance, a judgment creditor of Abel's, caused the sheriff to levy on the car. Is Friendly's execution lien senior or junior to Firstbank's security interest? See UCC 9–317(a)(2); UCC 9–310(a), (b)(2); UCC 9–309(1); UCC 9–103(b)(1), (a); UCC 9–102(a)(23); UCC 9–311(a), (b); Uniform Certificate of Title Act §§ 25, 26, 3. Is the result consistent with the policy of requiring public notice as a condition to prevailing over judicial liens and the claims of many other third parties?

(b) The facts are the same, except that Abel purchased a tractor for use on a farm that Abel operates. Under the applicable Motor Vehicle Code, the tractor is not a motor vehicle that must be licensed, registered, or covered by a certificate of title. Again, no financing statement was filed, and Friendly caused the sheriff to levy on the tractor. Is Friendly's execution lien senior or junior to Firstbank's security interest in the tractor? See UCC 9–317(a)(2); UCC 9–310(a), (b)(2); UCC 9–309(1); UCC 9–103(b)(1), (a); UCC 9–102(a)(23), (a)(33); UCC 9–311(a).

(c) The facts are the same as in part (b), except that Abel, who lives in a house surrounded by several acres of rolling lawn, bought the tractor to pull a lawn mower. Is Friendly's execution lien senior or junior to Firstbank's security interest? See UCC 9–317(a)(2); UCC 9–310(a), (b)(2); UCC 9–309(1); UCC 9–103(b)(1), (a); UCC 9–102(a)(23); UCC 9–311(a). Can you reconcile the result with the result in part (b)? With Article 9's policy in favor of public notice? Are Abel's other creditors likely to assess the tractor differently under the facts of part (c) than under the facts of part (b)? Federal law views nonpossessory, non-purchase-money security interests in consumer goods with disfavor. See FTC Rule on Credit Practices, 16 C.F.R. 444.2(a)(4) (taking a nonpossessory, non-purchase-money security interest in household goods constitutes an "unfair act or practice" under Federal Trade Commission Act § 5); BC 522(f) (nonpossessory, non-purchase-money security interests in certain consumer goods can be avoided in bankruptcy).

(d) The facts are the same as in part (c), except that after having used the tractor around the house for a few months, Abel decided that it could be put to better use at the farm. Thereafter, Abel used the tractor exclusively for farming operations. As in part (b), the sheriff levied on the tractor at the farm. Is Friendly's execution lien senior or junior to Firstbank's security interest? See UCC 9–317(a)(2); UCC 9–310(a), (b)(2); UCC 9–309(1); UCC 9–103(b)(1), (a); UCC 9–102(a)(23); UCC 9–311(a). When is the use of collateral determined for purposes of classifying collateral? See UCC 9–102(a)(23) ("used or bought for use"). What is the effect of a change in use? Cf. UCC 9–507(b). See also UCC 9–628(c) (nonliability of secured party that reasonably relies on debtor's or obligor's representation concerning use of collateral or purpose for which obligation incurred).

Problem 3.3.20. Dooley, an amateur numismatist, applied to Castle Finance Company for a loan. In response to Castle's request for security, Dooley delivered to Castle a valuable coin collection and received a loan for $25,000.

(a) Lean, a judgment creditor of Dooley, levies on the coin collection held by Castle. Who has priority? Does Castle even have an interest in the coins? See UCC 9–201; UCC 9–317(a)(2); UCC 9–308(a); UCC 9–203(a), (b); UCC 9–310(a), (b)(6); UCC 9–313(a); UCC 1–201(b)(24) [F1–201(24)]; UCC 9–102(a)(44).

(b) What result if Castle filed a financing statement conforming to UCC 9–502(a) but did not take delivery of the coins? See UCC 9–312(b); UCC 1–201(b)(24) [F1–201(24)]; UCC 9–102(a)(44); UCC 9–203(b).

(c) What result if Castle itself did not take delivery of the coin collection but instead appointed Dooley its agent for the purpose of holding the coins on its behalf? Dooley's lawyer? See UCC 9–313(a) & Comment 3; In re Copeland & Notes following, infra; Note (2) on Perfection by Possession, infra.

Problem 3.3.21. Assume that Dooley's coin collection in the preceding Problem consisted of coins issued by the 18th century Republic of Vermont and was on display at the Money Museum. Advise Castle on the steps it should take to protect its security interest in the coins, given the size of the transaction (a $25,000 loan). Assume alternatively that the museum is cooperative and that the museum is uncooperative. In particular, consider:

(i) How should Castle perfect its security interest while the coins are on display and thereafter? See UCC 9–312(b); UCC 9–313(a), (c), (d), (f).

(ii) How will Castle be able to enforce its security interest if Dooley defaults on its obligation? See UCC 9–609; UCC 9–610; UCC 9–313(g).

Problem 3.3.22. Recall that in the Prototype, Firstbank filed a financing statement (Form 3.1, supra) to perfect its security interest in Main's inventory of automobiles. Given that Firstbank took possession of the manufacturer's certificates of origin (Form 3.7, supra), was the filing unnecessary? See In re Haugabook Auto Co., 9 U.C.C. Rep. Serv. 954 (Bkrtcy.M.D.Ga.1971) (possession of certificates of origin held not to constitute possession of motor vehicles); cf. Lee v. Cox, 18 U.C.C. Rep. Serv. 807 (M.D.Tenn.1976) (possession of registration papers for Arabian horses held not to constitute possession of horses). If the filing perfects Firstbank's security interest, then what purpose, if any, is served by Firstbank's taking possession of the certificates of origin? See Section 1(F), supra; Note (3) on Perfection by Possession, infra.

Problem 3.3.23. Equipco is in the business of selling construction equipment. It sells to its very best customers on unsecured credit: the customer pays 20 percent down and gives a negotiable promissory note for the balance. To secure a line of credit, Firstbank took a security interest in "all Equipco's existing and after-acquired rights to payment in every form whatsoever, whether or not represented by a writing, and including, without limitation, accounts receivable, general intangibles, chattel paper, and instruments." The security agreement obligates Equipco to deliver to Firstbank all writings evidencing rights to payment within seven days after Equipco receives them. Firstbank filed a financing statement containing the same description of the collateral. On July 1, Equipco files a bankruptcy petition.

(a) On June 15 Equipco sold and delivered a backhoe to Butcher, a customer. Though inadvertence, the only document Butcher signed was a purchase order (i.e., a form in which Butcher offers to buy the backhoe from Equipco). Is Firstbank's security interest in Equipco's right to payment perfected as of the commencement of the bankruptcy case? See UCC 9–310(a); UCC 9–102(a)(2). (Do not assume that, if the security interest is perfected, it necessarily will be valid in bankruptcy. The ability of the trustee in bankruptcy to avoid security interests, both perfected and unperfected, is discussed in Chapter 7, Section 2, infra.)

(b) Also on June 15 Equipco received a promissory note from Baker, another customer, but neglected to turn over the note to Firstbank. Is Firstbank's security interest perfected as of the commencement of the bankruptcy case? See UCC 9–310(a); UCC 9–312(a); UCC 9–102(a)(47).

(c) On June 19 Equipco sold some equipment to Chandler on secured credit: Chandler paid 10 percent down, signed a promissory note for the balance, and signed a security agreement covering the equipment. Again, Equipco failed to deliver the note and security agreement to Firstbank. Is Firstbank's security interest perfected as of the commencement of the bankruptcy case? See UCC 9–310(a); UCC 9–312(a); UCC 9–102(a)(11).

(d) What answer in the preceding parts if the financing statement had not been filed? See UCC 9–310(a), (b)(5); UCC 9–312(e); UCC 9–102(a)(57). Would it make any difference if the transaction documents entered into between the buyers and Equipco had been delivered to Firstbank? See UCC 9–310(a), (b)(6); UCC 9–313(a).

Problem 3.3.24. Diggins Construction Company entered into a contract to build a small office building for Realty for a total price of $10,000,000. The contract called for step-by-step progress payments to Diggins as the building reached specified stages of completion. Firstbank is willing to lend Diggins $8,000,000, to be secured by a security interest in the contract with Realty and the payments due and to become due under the contract.

Diggins prefers not to reveal this transaction to the public, and so it suggests to Firstbank that no financing statement be filed. It proposes instead that (i) the security agreement be entitled "Pledge of Contract," (ii) the original signed contract with Realty be delivered to Firstbank by way of pledge, and (iii) upon Diggins's default, Firstbank would have the right to notify Realty to make payments directly to Firstbank.

As counsel to Firstbank, how would you respond to this suggestion? See UCC 9–102(a)(2), (a)(47), (a)(11), (a)(61), (a)(3), (a)(42) & Comment 5.a.–d.; UCC 9–310(a), (b)(6); UCC 9–313(a); UCC 9–607.

Problem 3.3.25. Delgado imports whiskey in large quantities, which Delgado stores in storage tanks at a warehouse bonded by the U.S. Customs Service. (Under applicable law, the whiskey may remain in a bonded warehouse for up to five years before Delgado is obligated to pay the import duty. See 19 U.S.C. § 1557(a).) Each time Delgado stores a quantity of whiskey, Delgado receives a written warehouse receipt running "to the order of Delgado."

(a) Firstbank is willing to take the whiskey as collateral for a loan and asks you for advice on how to perfect its security interest. Among the possibilities are (i) filing a financing statement; (ii) taking delivery of the warehouse receipts; and (iii) notifying the warehouse of Firstbank's security interest. What do you recommend? See UCC 9–102(a)(30); UCC 1–201(b)(16) [F1–201(15)]; UCC 9–312(c), (a); UCC 9–313(a), (c); UCC 7–502(1); UCC 9–331; UCC 9–312(e), (f).

One way to approach this question is to begin by determining which, if any, of the possibilities would satisfy the requirements of UCC 9–310. Next, consider the potential advantages and disadvantages of each course of action. For example, does one approach afford Firstbank the most protection against claims of third parties? Does one approach enhance Delgado's ability to obtain needed access to the whiskey, e.g., when Delgado wishes to bottle some of it?

(b) Assume that Firstbank decides to perfect its security interest by filing a financing statement. How should Firstbank indicate the collateral?

(c) Assume that Firstbank decides to perfect its security interest by taking delivery of the warehouse receipt. Should Firstbank require Delgado to indorse the warehouse receipt before delivery? See UCC 7–502; UCC 7–501; UCC 7–504. If Delgado delivers the warehouse receipt to Firstbank but neglects to indorse it, is Firstbank perfected? See UCC 9–312(c); UCC 9–313(a). If Firstbank wishes to take possession of the whiskey upon Delgado's default, see UCC 9–609, will the warehouse permit Firstbank to remove the whiskey without Delgado's indorsement? See UCC 7–403; R7–102(a)(9). If Firstbank makes the loan and later wishes to obtain Delgado's indorsement, what can Firstbank do? See UCC 7–506.

In re Copeland[*]

United States Court of Appeals, Third Circuit, 1976.
531 F.2d 1195.

■ SEITZ, CHIEF JUDGE.

This is a consolidated appeal from two separate orders of the district court in a Chapter XI bankruptcy proceeding instituted by Lammot duPont Copeland, Jr. (hereinafter "Copeland" or "debtor"). The appeals are united by a common factual basis. In July of 1967, Copeland personally guaranteed payment on a $2,700,000 loan by Pension Benefit Fund, Inc. ("Pension Benefit") to two corporations and entered into an agreement which required him to pledge as collateral security 18,187 shares of Christiana Securities Co. stock. An "escrow agreement" was simultaneously executed between Copeland, Pension Benefit and Wilmington Trust Company ("Wilmington

---

[*]   [The court's citations are to the applicable pre–1972 version of the UCC.]

Trust") which designated Wilmington Trust as escrow holder of the pledged stock. [The stock was thereupon delivered to Wilmington Trust.]

Nearly three years later, in April, 1970, there was a default on the loan. Following written demand upon the principal corporations for payment, Pension Benefit notified Copeland and Wilmington Trust by letter of September 11, 1970 of the uncured default and of its intention to demand the surrender of the escrowed stock in accordance with the pledge agreement. Copeland did not respond to this letter, but on October 20, 1970, filed a petition for an arrangement under Chapter XI of the Bankruptcy Act, 11 U.S.C. §§ 701 et seq., and an application to stay enforcement of Pension Benefit's lien on the Christiana stock. Thereafter, Copeland withdrew his objection to the delivery of the stock to Pension Benefit, and the stock was turned over by Wilmington Trust on December 1, 1970. . . .

[D]ebtor filed an independent application for an order requiring Pension Benefit to surrender the stock itself and dividends received with respect thereto. Debtor's application was denied by the district court, sitting as a bankruptcy court, by order dated February 3, 1975. Debtor and the Statutory Creditors' Committee appealed.

I. DEBTOR'S APPEAL

We shall consider first the issues raised in debtor's appeal since, if he is successful in recovering the stock, Pension Benefit's appeal will be rendered moot.

Copeland asserts a superior right to possession of the stock by virtue of his status as debtor-in-possession which enables him to exercise all the powers of a trustee in bankruptcy, Bankruptcy Act § 342 [the predecessor to Bankruptcy Code § 1107], and specifically, to avail himself of all rights and remedies of any creditor—real or hypothetical—who had or could have obtained a lien on the debtor's property on the date of bankruptcy. Bankruptcy Act § 70c [the predecessor to Bankruptcy Code § 544(a)]. The rights of a lien creditor must be determined by reference to state law. Pertinent here is § 9–301(1)(b) of the Uniform Commercial Code as enacted in Delaware, 6 Del. C. § 9–301(1)(b), which provides:

"(1) Except as otherwise provided in subsection (2), an unperfected security interest is subordinate to the rights of

"(b) a person who becomes a lien creditor without knowledge of the security interest and before it is perfected."

Since under § 70c of the Bankruptcy Act the trustee has all rights of an ideal lien creditor under § 9–301(1)(b) of the Code, his rights in the stock are superior to Article 9 claimants whose interests were unperfected as of the date of bankruptcy. *[handwritten: Bankruptcy T'ee = Lien creditor]*

Copeland contends that Pension Benefit's security interest in the Christiana stock was unperfected on the date of bankruptcy. He asserts that the district court therefore erred in denying his application for an order requiring Pension Benefit to surrender the stock and dividends received with respect thereto.

A. Attachment

Copeland first argues that Pension Benefit's security interest was unperfected because it had not attached as of October 20, 1970, the date on which debtor filed his Chapter XI petition. The district court determined to the contrary.

Section 9–303 provides that a "security interest is perfected when it has attached and when all of the applicable steps required for perfection have been taken." Attachment occurs under § 9–204 [UCC 9–203(1)] when there is an agreement that the security interest attach, value is given, and the debtor has rights in the collateral. A security interest attaches immediately upon the happening of these events "unless explicit agreement postpones the time of attaching." § 9–204(1) [UCC 9–203(2)]. Although the aforementioned prerequisites to attachment had been fulfilled on the date the pledge agreement was executed in 1967,[3] Copeland contends that the parties explicitly agreed to postpone the time of attachment. In support of this contention, he relies upon paragraph 8 of the pledge agreement which states:

> "8. In the event there is a default by the Pledgor in the performance of any of the terms of this Agreement, or if there is a default in the payment of the loan as provided in the note and if such default continues for a period of fifteen (15) days, the Pledgee shall have the right, upon fifteen (15) days notice, sent by registered mail to the Pledgor, to call upon The Wilmington Trust Company to forthwith deliver all of the stock and stock powers which it is holding as security hereunder to Pledgee, or such other party as Pledgee may designate, and thereupon, without any liability for any diminution in price which may have occurred, and without further consent by the Pledgor, the said Pledgee may sell all or part of the said stock in such manner and for such price or prices as the said Pledgee may be able to obtain. At any bonafide public sale, the Pledgee shall be free to purchase all or any part of the pledged stock. Out of the proceeds of any sale, the Pledgee shall retain an amount equal to the entire unpaid principal and interest then due on the loan plus the amount of the actual expenses of the sale and shall pay the balance to the Pledgor. In the event that the proceeds of any sale are insufficient to cover the entire unpaid principal and interest of the loan plus the expenses of the sale, the Pledgor shall be liable for any deficiency."

Copeland argues that by the terms of this paragraph, Pension Benefit's security interest did not attach until each of the following events had occurred: (1) the debtor had defaulted; (2) default had continued for fifteen days; (3) fifteen days written notice by registered mail had been sent to the

---

3.   The pledge and escrow agreements together constituted the requisite agreement. Value was given by Pension Benefit's binding commitment to extend credit. § 1–201(44). The debtor had rights in the collateral in that he remained owner of record and was empowered to vote the shares and receive the dividend income even after the stock was transferred to Wilmington Trust.

debtor by Pension Benefit; (4) proper demand had been made upon Wilmington Trust to deliver the stock and stock powers; and (5) the stock and stock powers had been delivered to Pension Benefit. Since the stock was not turned over to Pension Benefit until December 1, 1970, he maintains that the security interest had not attached, and consequently was not perfected, on the pivotal date of bankruptcy, October 20, 1970.

We believe that the relevant language of paragraph 8 which debtor urges postpones the date of attachment merely establishes an orderly procedure for enforcement of the security interest upon default. It is understandable that debtor would seek to protect his stock to the fullest extent possible from hasty and premature foreclosure attempts by Pension Benefit. Indeed, § 9–501 of the Code, with exceptions not here relevant, specifically recognizes the right of parties to a security agreement to agree among themselves as to the duties and responsibilities of a secured party when default occurs. To read paragraph 8 as anything other than an attempt to safeguard debtor's interest in the valuable pledged stock against unwarranted claims of default and improper attempts to enforce the security interest would distort the nature of the transaction envisioned by the parties and would render Pension Benefit's security for repayment of the loan largely meaningless. We say this because Pension Benefit's interest in the stock would be subordinate to any intervening creditors who had obtained and perfected a security interest in the stock after Pension Benefit but before bankruptcy, a result clearly not intended by either party. We therefore conclude that the pledge agreement was not intended to delay the date of attachment of Pension Benefit's security interest, but rather was designed to protect debtor's interest in the stock from improper attempts by Pension Benefit to obtain its possession in the event there was a claim of default.

B. Perfection

Relying on § 9–304(1) and § 9–305, Copeland next argues that even assuming the security interest had attached, it was not properly perfected on the date of bankruptcy. Section 9–304 provides that a security interest in instruments, defined in § 9–105(g) and § 8–102 to include corporate securities such as the Christiana stock, can only be perfected by the secured party's taking possession. Section 9–305 modifies this rule by permitting a secured party to perfect his security interest through the possession of his bailee. Section 9–305 states in pertinent part:

"A security interest in letters of credit and advices of credit (subsection (2)(a) of Section 5–116), goods, instruments, negotiable documents or chattel paper may be perfected by the secured party's taking possession of the collateral. If such collateral other than goods covered by a negotiable document is held by a bailee, the secured party is deemed to have possession from the time the bailee receives notification of the secured party's interest. . . ."

Debtor maintains that Pension Benefit's security interest was not perfected by Wilmington Trust's possession of the stock because Wilmington Trust was the agent of both parties. He asserts that this position is inconsistent with the degree of possession needed to perfect under the "bailee with notice" provision of § 9–305. To satisfy the requirement of this section, he urges, possession must be maintained by an agent under the sole control of the secured party.

In support of this contention, debtor places considerable emphasis upon what would have been the nature of the relationship between the parties at common law. Since the stock was held by Wilmington Trust as agent for both parties, he argues that the arrangement must be characterized as an escrow, rather than a perfected pledge which requires possession by the pledgee or an agent under his absolute dominion and control. Citing In re Dolly Madison Industries, Inc., [351 F.Supp. 1038 (E.D.Pa.1972) aff'd mem., 480 F.2d 917 (3d Cir.1973),] he further stresses that the simultaneous existence of an escrow and a pledge is a legal impossibility. Since the transaction fails as a common law pledge for lack of possession by the pledgee or his agent, and since the Code, he asserts, has incorporated the requirement of the common law pledge that the pledgee or an agent under his absolute control maintain possession of the collateral, Pension Benefit's security interest was unperfected under § 9–304 and § 9–305 on the date of bankruptcy.

Although concluding that Wilmington Trust was an escrow agent at common law and hence incapable of becoming Pension Benefit's agent for the purpose of perfecting the pledge, the district court held that the provision of § 9–305 permitting perfection by a "bailee with notice" had been satisfied, and that the security interest was consequently perfected under the Code. The court rejected debtor's argument that § 9–305 had incorporated the restrictive possession requirement of the common law pledge, finding that an acceptance of this proposition would frustrate the parties' intent to collateralize the loan as against third party creditors, would be in disregard of the policy considerations underlying both the law of pledge and the Code, and would unduly restrict the use of the escrow device.

We find it unnecessary to consider the parties' rights at common law because we believe that the language and policy underlying § 9–305 support the district court's conclusion that Pension Benefit's security interest was perfected upon delivery of the stock to Wilmington Trust in July, 1967. While it is true that the Code does not wholly displace the common law, § 1–103, nor abolish existing security devices, Official Comment 2, § 9–102,[4] Article 9 simplifies pre-Code secured financing by providing for the unitary treatment of all security arrangements. It eliminates many of the antiquated distinctions between various security devices in favor of a single "security interest", §§ 9–102, 1–201(37), and a single set of rules regarding

---

4.   While Delaware has not adopted the Official Comments prepared by the drafters of the Uniform Commercial Code, these comments are nevertheless useful in interpreting the Code, as it is to be applied in Delaware, in view of the Code's expressed purpose of making uniform the law among the various jurisdictions. § 1–102(2)(c). . . .

creation and perfection, designed to govern "any transaction (regardless of its form) which is intended to create a security interest in personal property or fixtures including goods, Documents, Instruments. . .." § 9–102. Since neither party denies that the pledge and escrow agreements were intended to create a security interest in the stock within the meaning of the Uniform Commercial Code, we attach no particular significance to the common law distinctions between the pledge and the escrow which debtor stresses, except insofar as they bear on the question of whether Pension Benefit's security interest was properly perfected under § 9–305 of the Code through Wilmington Trust's possession of the stock.

It is to that question which we now turn. Historically and prior to the Code, possession of collateral by a creditor or third party has served to impart <u>notice</u> to prospective creditors of the possessor's possible interest therein. The Code carries forward the notice function which the creditor's possession formerly provided. Notice to future lenders is furnished under the Code by a filed financing statement, § 9–302, or by the possession of the property subject to the security interest by a secured party or his agent, §§ 9–304, 9–305, depending upon the nature of the collateral.

who must possess to give notice?

Where the Code requires perfection by possession of the secured party or his bailee, it is clear that possession by the debtor or an individual closely associated with the debtor is not sufficient to alert prospective creditors of the possibility that the debtor's property is encumbered. See, In re Black Watch Farms, Inc., 9 UCC Rep.Serv. 151 (Ref. Dec. S.D.N.Y.1974). Thus, Official Comment 2 to § 9–305 states:

> "Possession may be by the secured party himself or by an agent on his behalf: it is of course clear, however, that the debtor or a person controlled by him cannot qualify as such an agent for the secured party. . . ."

It does not follow from this statement or from the policy underlying § 9–305, however, that possession of the collateral must be by an individual under the sole dominion and control of the secured party, as debtor urges us to hold. Rather, we believe that possession by a third party bailee, who is not controlled by the debtor, which adequately informs potential lenders of the possible existence of a perfected security interest satisfies the notice function underlying the "bailee with notice" provision of § 9–305.

In the case presently before us, the collateral was held by Wilmington Trust pursuant to the terms of both the pledge and escrow agreements. Regardless of whether Wilmington Trust retained the stock as an escrow agent or as a pledge holder, its possession and the debtor's lack of possession clearly signaled future creditors that debtor's ownership of and interest in the stock were not unrestricted. As an independent, institutional entity, Wilmington Trust could not be regarded automatically as an instrumentality or agent of the debtor alone. There was consequently no danger that creditors would be misled by its possession.

The fact that debtor remained owner of record and was empowered to vote the shares and receive current income does not compel a different finding. The location of title to collateral is immaterial with respect to the rights and obligations of the parties to a security transaction. § 9–202; Barney v. Rigby Loan & Investment Co., 344 F.Supp. 694 (D.Idaho 1972).

Nor do we believe our summary affirmance of the district court's decision in *In re Dolly Madison Industries, Inc.*, supra, dictates a contrary conclusion. In reversing a decision by the referee denying the trustee's application for a turnover order, the district court in *Dolly Madison* rested its decision on a finding that the security agreement . . . postponed the attachment of the security interest asserted by a creditor of the bankrupt until after bankruptcy. In support of this decision, the court noted that the parties had evidenced their intent to delay attachment by placing the collateral in the neutral custody of an escrow agent pending payment or default. Statements by the court indicating that the simultaneous existence of an escrow and a pledge is a legal impossibility were merely intended to underscore the parties' deliberate choice of the escrow device rather than a pledge in order to assure that attachment would be postponed. Since the district court found that attachment had been delayed by specific agreement of the parties, it was not called upon to determine whether an attached security interest had been perfected. Hence, any statements suggesting that the placement of collateral in escrow precludes a creditor from perfecting his security interest for lack of sufficient possession under § 9–305 are mere uncontrolling dicta.

Having found that Wilmington Trust's possession of the stock afforded the requisite notice to prospective creditors, we conclude that it was a "bailee with notice" within the meaning of § 9–305 and that its possession therefore perfected Pension Benefit's security interest. Hence, perfection occurred in July, 1967, more than three years in advance of bankruptcy, on the date the stock was delivered to Wilmington Trust with notification of Pension Benefit's interest therein. For this reason, the district court correctly concluded that debtor's interest in the stock as debtor-in-possession was subordinate to that of Pension Benefit and properly denied debtor's application for a turnover order.

NOTES ON *IN RE COPELAND*

(1) **The Role of Pre–UCC Law.** Counsel for Copeland "placed considerable emphasis on what would have been the nature of the relationship between the parties at common law." They argued that the escrow would have failed as a common-law pledge "for lack of possession by the pledgee or his agent." Does the court disagree with this assessment? Assuming that counsel's assertions about the common-law rules were correct, what justifies the court's departure from the common law? See UCC 1–103(a) [F1–102]; UCC 1–103(b) [F1–103]; UCC 9–205(b) (substantially similar to Former 9–205).

(2) **The Effect of Post-*Copeland* Amendments to the UCC.** The rules governing security interests in investment property (e.g., stocks and bonds) have changed several times since *Copeland* was decided. The Notes

on Security Interests in Investment Property, page 413, infra, discuss these rules in some detail. For present purposes, please observe that, under Revised Article 9, possession of a security certificate by or on behalf of the secured party remains an effective method by which to perfect a security interest in securities represented by a certificate. See UCC 9–313(a); UCC 8–301(a). Thus, *Copeland*'s discussion of perfection by possession remains "good law." See UCC 9–313(a), Comment 6 ("The second sentence of subsection (a) reflects the traditional rule for perfection of a security interest in certificated securities.").

Revised Article 9 carries forward the rule, first introduced to the UCC in 1994, that perfection of a security interest in certificated securities may be achieved also by filing a financing statement. See UCC 9–310(a). As we shall see, filing and taking possession each has its advantages, as does perfecting by having control. See Chapter 6, Sections 3 and 4.

NOTES ON PERFECTION BY POSSESSION

(1) The Pledge. Under UCC 9–313(a), a security interest in most tangible collateral, including goods, may be perfected by the secured party's taking possession of the collateral. The possessory security interest, or **pledge**, was the prototypical common-law security device. In contrast to nonpossessory arrangements, where the debtor remained in possession of the collateral, the pledge was thought not to give rise to significant ostensible ownership or other fraud problems. Possession by the secured party put to rest any notion that the debtor owned the property free and clear; it also was consistent with the secured party's assertion that it was relying on the collateral for repayment of its claim against the debtor. See generally Note (3) on Perfection by Filing, supra.

(2) Possession by Agents and Bailees. It is not much of a stretch to conclude that if possession by the secured party is sufficient for an effective pledge, then possession by its agent would suffice as well. Article 9 apparently adopts this common-law view. See UCC 9–313, Comment 3 ("In determining whether a particular person has possession, the principles of agency apply."). See also UCC 1–103(b) [F1–103](unless displaced by particular provisions of the UCC, principles of principal and agent apply). Of course, possession by certain agents—most notably, the debtor itself—would not alleviate one's concerns that the purported secured transaction is a sham or that other creditors might mistakenly rely on the debtor's possession as an indication that the debtor's ownership rights were unencumbered. See UCC 9–313, Comment 3; Restatement of Security § 11 & Comment *b* (1941).

UCC 9–313, Comment 3, indicates that:

under appropriate circumstances, a court may determine that a person in possession is so closely connected to or controlled by the debtor that the debtor has retained effective possession, even though the person may have agreed to take possession on behalf of the secured party. If so, the person's taking possession would not constitute the secured party's taking possession and would not be sufficient for perfection. See also Section 9–205(b). In a typical escrow arrangement, where the escrowee has possession of collateral as agent for both the secured party and the debtor, the debtor's relationship to the escrowee is not such as to constitute retention of possession by the debtor.

Consider what happens when the collateral consists of property that a third party (Bailee) holds for the debtor.[13] The secured party may wish to perfect a security interest by taking possession of the collateral but without dispossessing Bailee. One way to accomplish this result is for Bailee to become the secured party's agent. Another is for Bailee to authenticate a record acknowledging that it holds possession of the collateral for the secured party's benefit.[14] As UCC 9–313, Comment 4, suggests:

> [i]n some cases, it may be uncertain whether a person who has possession of collateral is an agent of the secured party or a non-agent bailee. Under those circumstances, prudence might suggest that the secured party obtain the person's acknowledgment to avoid litigation and ensure perfection by possession regardless of how the relationship between the secured party and the person is characterized.

In what way is Bailee's acknowledgment akin to possession by the secured party? Does the acknowledgment adequately allay concerns that the purported security interest is a sham? The fact that a (presumably disinterested) third party has been informed of a secured transaction would seem to lend credence to the secured party's assertion that the parties actually contemplated one. The acknowledgment makes it less likely that the parties are engaging in after-the-fact fabrication.

Does Bailee's acknowledgment address the ostensible ownership problem? Does it make the debtor less of an ostensible owner than does the original bailment? Suppose Lender wishes to extend credit to the debtor and seeks to determine whether the debtor owns the bailed goods free and clear. Lender could ask the debtor, but the perfection rules of Article 9 are designed to afford creditors a means to obtain information without having to rely solely on the debtor's honesty. (In fact, the drafters of Former Article 9 rejected an early proposal to scrap public files and introduce appropriate safeguards to protect people misled by false or incomplete financial statements. See 1 Gilmore, Security § 15.1, at 464–65.) Lender could ask Bailee. Does Bailee's acknowledgment that it holds possession for the benefit of the secured party impose upon Bailee a legal duty to confirm the acknowledgment to third parties with whom it has not contracted? Not unless Bailee agrees or law other than Article 9 provides. See UCC 9–313(g).

---

13.   Recall from Chapter 1, Section 5, supra, that a bailee is a person rightfully in possession of goods owned by another. Chapter 5, Section 1, infra, contains a detailed discussion of leases, consignments, and other bailments.

14.   UCC 9–313(c) does not apply to certificated securities or goods covered by a document of title. Instead, UCC 8–301 applies to the former, and UCC 9–312(c) and (d) apply to the latter.

If Bailee has no legal duty to confirm the acknowledgment, does it have a duty to refrain from affirmatively misleading third parties, e.g., by denying the fact that it has acknowledged? If not, would it be a sufficient solution to the ostensible ownership problem that most bailees tell the truth most of the time, even if they are not legally bound to do so?

A secured party is concerned not only about achieving perfection but also about <u>maintaining the perfected status</u> of its security interest. If Bailee delivers the collateral to the debtor, then the security interest will become unperfected unless it was perfected also by a method other than possession. UCC 9–313(g)(2) makes clear that Bailee's acknowledgment imposes upon Bailee no duty to the secured party, unless Bailee agrees otherwise or law other than Article 9 imposes a duty. Thus, there may be major practical differences between actual possession by the secured party (or its agent) and "deemed" possession by Bailee: Unless the secured party voluntarily relinquishes the collateral in its actual possession, the debtor cannot retake it without engaging in theft; however, Bailee's acknowledgment does not ipso facto deprive the debtor of its right to take possession of, and dispose of, the bailed property. Rather, the debtor may maintain control over the goods notwithstanding Bailee's acknowledgment. Conversely, if the debtor defaults and the secured party demands that Bailee relinquish the collateral, Bailee may be under no duty to obey the secured party's demand.

[margin note: achieve & maintain perfection]

Does the foregoing lead inexorably to the conclusion that only a foolish secured party would rely upon perfection through a bailee under UCC 9–313(c)? Or, do you see a way in which the secured party could reduce substantially the risk that the bailee will deliver the goods to the debtor or ignore the secured party's instructions?

(3) Other Benefits of Taking Possession of Collateral; Field Warehouses. A secured party can perfect a security interest in all types of tangible collateral, except "money" (as defined in UCC 1–201(b)(24) [F1–201(24)]), by a method other than taking possession. Even when a security interest is perfected by another method, e.g., by filing a financing statement, a secured party may insist upon taking possession of collateral. One reason for doing so is to facilitate enforcement in the event of the debtor's default. Although a secured party has a right to take possession of collateral after default, the secured party may not breach the peace in doing so. See UCC 9–609(a). If the debtor remains in possession and refuses to turn over the collateral to the secured party after default, the secured party must resort to the judicial process to recover any value from the collateral. Taking possession before default reduces this risk.

A more important reason for the secured party's taking possession of collateral is that taking possession (or, more accurately, depriving the debtor of possession) prevents the debtor from disposing of the collateral, either outright or to the holder of a senior security interest. On the other hand, the collateral may have much greater value being used by the debtor than sitting in storage with the secured party. For example, a secured party will not take possession of machinery used in the debtor's manufacturing operations. Not only is the risk of the debtor's wrongfully disposing of the collateral normally very small, but also the benefit to the debtor of retaining possession is quite high. (Without the equipment, how would the debtor earn funds with which to satisfy the secured obligation?) A secured party is much more likely to take possession of a negotiable instrument. Because negotiable instruments are so liquid, the risk of the debtor's wrongful disposition may be substantial, and the benefit to the debtor of retaining possession of the collateral often is negligible.

What can a secured party do if it is concerned that the debtor will wrongfully dispose of collateral, but taking possession of the collateral would impair the debtor's ability to pay the secured obligation? For example, although filing can perfect a security interest in inventory, it does not prevent the debtor from selling the inventory and absconding with or dissipating the proceeds. The lender may not have the skills and resources needed to keep a close watch on the assets of a borrower of questionable financial standing or integrity. Under such circumstances, the secured party may contract with a specialist in watching over the ebb and flow of inventory. Historically, these specialists established a complex and colorful "pledge" arrangement known as a "field warehouse."

Field warehouses developed under the common law, in response to the law's requirement that a secured party take possession of collateral in order to enjoy a property right that was valid against other creditors. The notion of a field warehouse derives from the creative application of the principle that a secured party may take possession of collateral through its agent, which might be a warehouse. Rather than suffer the adverse consequences of moving the debtor's inventory to a warehouse, inventory lenders moved the warehouse to the inventory. Typically, the debtor's inventory was placed in a fenced area (the "warehouse") within its premises. The "warehouse" usually was the debtor's stockroom, but might be a tank of oil or whiskey with a padlock on the outlet vale or a fenced-in pile of coal; there have been an astonishing variety of settings. More recent uses have included "field warehouse feedlots," in which cattle are held, and leased rooms for warehousing a variety of "instruments," as to which possession was the exclusive means of perfection under Former Article 9.

Under the traditional arrangement, a specialized field warehouse company leased the premises from the debtor for a nominal amount, posted signs indicating that the goods in the fenced area were in the custody of the warehouse, and administered the flow of goods in and out of warehouse. Typically, the company issued non-negotiable warehouse receipts naming the secured party as the person entitled to delivery. As such, the secured party could cause the warehouse to release inventory by issuing written delivery orders (or a single, standing delivery order). See UCC 7–403; R7–102(a)(9).

Neither Former nor Revised Article 9 relaxes the common-law rules on the degree and extent of possession that are necessary to constitute a valid field warehouse. See UCC 9–205(b). Nevertheless, the UCC has had an indirect, but basic, impact on field warehousing. By providing for the perfection of security interests in fluctuating assets by the filing of a simple financing statement, Former Article 9 undercut the principal reason for the establishment of the field warehouse. Thus, in 1963, Lawrence Systems, then the leading operator of field warehouses, in a dramatic reversal of policy, began to encourage lenders holding its receipts to file under Article 9. The basic reason was the danger that the holder of a competing security interest who filed would have a prior claim to new assets. See Former 9–312(5)(a); UCC 9–322(a)(1). (The rules governing priority of competing security interests will be examined more fully in Chapter 4, Section 1, infra.)

Widespread adoption of Former Article 9 deprived the field warehouse of a significant "perfection" function; however, there was still a need for "certified (or 'verified') inventory control." "Certified inventory control" eliminates the bailment trappings, such as the fence and signs. It replaces the warehouse receipt with a certificate or statement to the lender that certifies to the value of the inventory on the borrower's premises; the certifier by contract engages to comply with the lender's delivery instructions and also accepts liability for any loss that may result from reliance on the certificates or from failure to observe the lender's delivery instructions. Day-to-day administration of the program is conducted by a "custodian" on the borrower's premises—usually a former employee of the debtor who was placed on the payroll of the field warehouse (subject, of course, to reimbursement by the debtor).

(4) Rights and Duties of Secured Party in Possession of Collateral. UCC 9–207 affords certain rights to, and imposes certain duties upon, a secured party who perfects a security interest by possession. The most significant of these duties is a requirement to "use reasonable care in the custody and preservation of collateral in the secured party's possession." UCC 9–207(a). As with all obligations of care in the UCC, that duty "may not be disclaimed by agreement." UCC 1–302(b) [F1–102(3)].

SECTION 4. MULTIPLE–STATE TRANSACTIONS: LAW GOVERNING PERFECTION AND PRIORITY

One generally acknowledged purpose of the Article 9 filing system is to provide information to third parties. See Note (3) on Perfection by Filing, p. 153, supra. A well-fashioned system affords prospective purchasers of the collateral (including prospective secured parties) the opportunity to discover, with relative ease, whether the debtor may have encumbered particular property with a security interest. But a prospective purchaser or other searcher will be unable to commence a search of the public records to determine whether a financing statement has been filed against a debtor without first knowing which records to search.

The UCC is state law; each state maintains its own filing offices. Thus, before starting to search, a searcher must determine not only the state in which a financing statement would have been filed but also the particular office within that state in which a financing statement would have been filed. And because a financing statement that is filed in the wrong place is insufficient to perfect a security interest, a secured party who attempts to perfect by filing likewise must make the same determinations. The following materials address Article 9's answers to the problems of where to file and search.

(A) WHERE TO FILE A FINANCING STATEMENT

NOTES ON CHOICE OF LAW

(1) The Need for Choice–of–Law Rules. Owner sells or mortgages Blackacre to Purchaser. Owner lives in State *X*; Blackacre is in State *Y*; Purchaser lives in State *Z*. Where should the transaction be placed on the public record? What law governs perfection of Purchaser's interest against third persons? The answer is clear: the law of the place where Blackacre is (*lex rei sitae*). See Restatement (Second) of Conflict of Laws § 223 (1969). This rule is so firmly established that it may seem to be "in the nature of things," but its strength lies in its practicality. Even if Owner and Purchaser move, Blackacre stays. The rules and the records at the place where Blackacre is located provide a reliable point of reference.

For personal property the answer is not so easy or intuitive. Debtor sells goods on credit to Buyer; to secure a loan, Debtor assigns the account (right to payment) to Secured Party. Debtor is in State *X*, Buyer is in State *Y*, and Secured Party is in State *Z*. Where should notice of the transaction be filed? Which law applies? Those used to thinking about transactions in land may say, "wherever the *res* is." But where is the debt that Buyer owes Debtor? In State *X* with Debtor, the obligee? In State *Y* with Buyer, the obligor? Or in State *Z* with Secured Party, the assignee? The questions multiply when each of the three parties is a corporation with offices in several states.

Even tangible goods—cotton, furniture, railroad cars—present vexing problems. The goods may be moving from state to state at the time of the transaction, or they may be moved after the transaction. They may be resold to a buyer in another, possibly distant, state. And goods usually leave no trail, in the public records or elsewhere, that will disclose where they have been or what has happened.

These problems carry us into a large field (known as conflict of laws, choice of law, and private international law) where, for the most part, solutions must be sought in an amorphous and evolving body of case law. However, statutes on substantive rules sometimes deal with "conflicts" problems by specifying when the statute's rules are applicable to transactions that have contacts with other states. Even after general adoption of "uniform" laws, these conflicts rules are useful because of the proclivity of both legislatures and courts to develop local variations in the "uniform" law.

UCC 1–105(1) contains two general choice-of-law rules: the parties enjoy the right to agree that the law of any state bearing a "reasonable relation" to the transaction shall govern their rights and duties; absent such agreement, the UCC as enacted by the state in which the litigation is brought "applies to transactions bearing an appropriate relation to [such] state." These general rules may be suitable for controversies between the debtor and creditor, e.g., to determine which state's version of Article 9 applies to the exercise of the secured party's rights on default. They are wholly unsuitable for controversies concerning the effectiveness of a security interest against third parties, i.e., controversies whose outcome depends on whether a security interest is perfected. For the Article 9 filing system to work effectively, <u>searchers</u> must be able to determine where to search. Enabling the parties to the transaction to agree between themselves as to the applicable law would be foolhardy. How could a searcher discover whether any such agreement had been made? And even if a searcher could assure itself of the absence of such an agreement, how could the searcher predict which state's law a court would apply in the event of litigation?

Recognizing that the debtor and secured party should not be able to choose the applicable law so as to affect the rights of third parties, the UCC's drafters created a special set of rules that determine the law applicable to perfection and the effect of perfection or non-perfection of security interests. These rules are in UCC 9–301 through UCC 9–307, whose provisions govern notwithstanding an agreement of the parties to the contrary. See UCC 1–105(2). *[handwritten: 3d party choice of law]*

UCC 1–301(g) follows Former 1–105(2) in preventing the debtor and secured party from choosing the law governing perfection of security interests. However, it changes both of the two general choice-of-law rules found in Former 1–105(1). First, in business-to-business transactions, the revision generally expands upon the parties' freedom to choose the governing law. UCC 1–301(c) ordinarily gives effect to the parties' agreement that their rights and obligations will be determined by the law of a designated jurisdiction, even if the jurisdiction bears *no* relationship to the transaction in question. However, it does not give automatic effect to an agreement designating the law of a foreign country in a "domestic transaction" (i.e., one that does not bear a "reasonable relationship" to a country other than the United States, see UCC 1–301(a)(1)). Second, in the absence of an effective choice-of-law agreement, the court must apply its non-UCC choice-of-law principles to determine the governing law. UCC 1–301(d). *[handwritten: Ignore §1-301 not adopted anywhere]*

Although the advocates of "party autonomy" prevailed in the promulgation process, as yet they have not succeeded in the legislative process. Of the fourteen states and one territory that have enacted Revised Article 1, only the U.S. Virgin Islands has adopted UCC 1–301.

(2) An Approach to Solving Choice–of–Law Problems. Thinking about choice-of-law problems under the UCC is subject to a subtle trap. In the classroom we have in our hands only one statute—the "uniform" UCC. We can easily forget that the conflicts rules we see in our version of UCC 9–301 may invoke "perfection" rules that are quite different from those we see in our version of Article 9. State legislatures routinely have made the

UCC nonuniform, and Revised Article 9 was no exception. Some of the nonuniform provisions are intended to square Article 9 with other, non-UCC state laws; other nonuniform provisions seek to implement a particular policy of the enacting state. Moreover, we may not safely forget that all the world does not have Article 9: Goods may move into the UCC domain from foreign countries that have a wide variety of rules governing what we (but not they) call the "perfection" of "security interests"; debtors may be owed money by persons located in foreign jurisdictions whose law invalidates the assignment of the right to payment.

In short, having only one "uniform" code in our hands can seduce us into forgetting what we are doing in this area—working with *two* legal systems. In law practice we would not fall into this trap, for we would work with at least two different statutes on our desks: (1) one with the conflicts rules of UCC 9–301 through UCC 9–307 and (2) a second with the "perfection" rules (e.g., UCC 9–310, UCC 9–501) of the jurisdiction whose law is made applicable by the conflicts rules of the first statute. In the classroom it may help those of us who are visually-minded to imagine that (as in practice) we are working with these two statutes.

Applying Article 9's conflicts rules is not easy, even when one has recourse to two statutes. Thinking about the relationship between two legal systems requires some intellectual strain, as we shall see again in Chapter 7 and Chapter 8, Section 4(E), when we try to mesh state property law with the federal bankruptcy law and the federal tax lien law, respectively.

The Problems in this Section examine the UCC's approach to multiple-state problems in a variety of settings. They will help you appreciate the crucial importance of the UCC's choice-of-law rules both to planning a secured transaction and to litigating over perfection and priority.[1]

Problem 3.4.1. Binary Bits, Inc. (BB), borrowed $50,000,000 from EZ Credit Co. BB is a conglomerate that is incorporated in Indiana, has plants and offices in 21 states, and has its headquarters in Cleveland, Ohio. EZ is incorporated in Delaware but has its headquarters in New Jersey and has representatives in all 50 states. The security agreement, which is governed by the law of California, covers and adequately describes all BB's existing and after-acquired personal property.

(a) In which office(s) should EZ file a financing statement to perfect its security interest? See UCC 9–301; UCC 9–307; UCC 9–102(a)(70); UCC

---

1.   Although the Problems do not address them, the choice-of-law rules in Former 9–103 remain relevant notwithstanding that Revised Article 9 has taken effect. See UCC 9–705(c) (financing statements filed pursuant to Former Article 9 may remain effective until June 30, 2006). The rules differ in many important respects from those of Revised Article 9. Accordingly, a potential secured party may wish to search the filings in the office(s) specified in the "old" choice-of-law rules as well as those specified in the revised Article. For a discussion of these and other transition issues, see Edwin E. Smith & Harry Sigman, *Revised UCC Article 9's Transition Rules: Insuring a Soft Landing* (pts. 1 & 2), 55 Bus. Law. 1065, 1763 (2000).

1–201(b)(25) [F1–201(28)]; UCC 1–301(g) [F1–105(2)]; UCC 9–501(a). (Recall that, for certain kinds of collateral, the filing of a financing statement does not perfect a security interest. See UCC 9–311(a); UCC 9–312(b)(1); Problem 3.3.20, p. 179, supra. See also UCC 9–109.).

(b) Assume that BB is a general partnership. In which office(s) should EZ file a financing statement to perfect its security interest? See UCC 9–301; UCC 9–307; UCC 9–102(a)(70); UCC 1–201(b)(25) [F1–201(28)]; UCC 9–501(a).

(c) Assume that BB is a German corporation. Does U.S. law apply to this transaction? See UCC 1–301 [F1–105]. If so, in which office(s) should EZ file a financing statement to perfect its security interest? See UCC 9–301; UCC 9–307; UCC 9–102(a)(70); UCC 9–501(a). What result if BB's headquarters are in Hamburg, Germany, and not Cleveland, Ohio?

(d) Assume that BB is incorporated under both the law of Delaware and the law of Germany. In which office(s) should EZ file a financing statement to perfect its security interest? See UCC 9–301(1); UCC 9–307; UCC 9–102(a)(70); UCC 9–501(a).

(e) Assume that BB is Bobby Baker, who owns (as a sole proprietor) Mustard's Last Stand. BB lives in Hammond, Indiana, and the hot dog stand is in South Chicago, Illinois. In which office(s) should EZ file a financing statement to perfect its security interest? (The collateral includes both business assets and property held for personal use.) See UCC 9–301; UCC 9–307; UCC 9–501(a).

Problem 3.4.2. The facts are as in the preceding Problem (i.e., BB is an Indiana corporation). EZ "prefiled" a proper financing statement in the Ohio filing office on July 15, 2001. BB authenticated the security agreement and funds were advanced on July 24. Thereafter, on July 28, Lean, a judgment creditor of BB's, acquired an execution lien on the manufacturing equipment in BB's plant in Taylor, Michigan.

(a) Which state's law governs priority between Lean's lien and EZ's security interest? See UCC 9–301. This question may become important if different versions of Article 9 are in force in different states or if different states have different priority rules for nonconsensual liens. See UCC 9–301, Comment 7.

(b) Is EZ's security interest senior or junior to Lean's lien? Assume the state whose law governs priority has enacted UCC 9–317(a)(2), so that the answer turns on whether EZ filed in the proper filing office. Did EZ file in the proper filing office? Which state's law dictates the filing office in which to file? See UCC 9–301; UCC 9–307.

––––––––

The preceding Problems required you to apply the choice-of-law rules in a static situation. In the two Problems that follow, the facts that determine the applicable law change as time passes: Upon the debtor's relocation, a financing statement that was filed in the "right" jurisdiction becomes a financing statement filed in the "wrong" jurisdiction.

We have seen analogous situations in which the utility of a properly filed financing statement is compromised because of post-filing changes. See, e.g., Problem 3.3.16, p. 176, supra. As the Note on Post–Filing Changes, page 177, supra, explains, to the extent that Article 9 removes from the filer the burden to update the public record immediately, Article 9 imposes a corresponding burden on potential searchers to discover the facts not only as they are but also as they were, and to search accordingly. After working the following Problems, consider this question: When the debtor relocates, does Article 9 appropriately allocate risk between the secured party who filed in the old location and a subsequent searcher?

Problem 3.4.3. The facts are as in Problem 3.4.1, except that BB is a general partnership. EZ filed a proper financing statement in the Ohio filing office on July 15, 2001. In June, 2002, without EZ's knowledge or consent, BB moved its headquarters from Cleveland to Los Angeles. On November 19, 2002, Buyer bought and took delivery of certain used manufacturing equipment from BB in Taylor, Michigan.

(a) Which state's law governs perfection of EZ's security interest? See UCC 9–301.

(b) Which state's law governs priority between Buyer and EZ's security interest? See UCC 9–301; UCC 9–307.

(c) It is now December 1, 2002, and EZ has yet to discover the removal of BB's headquarters or the sale of the equipment. Does Buyer take free of or subject to EZ's security interest? See UCC 9–316(a), (b). (The rights of buyers are discussed in Chapter 4, Section 2, infra. For purposes of this Problem, you may assume that a buyer takes free of unperfected security interests but subject to perfected security interests.) What could the losing party have done to protect itself?

(d) What result in part (c) if Buyer bought and took delivery of the equipment on July 20, 2002? What could the losing party have done to protect itself?

(e) What result in part (c) if Buyer bought and took delivery of the equipment on May 15, 2002? What could the losing party have done to protect itself?

(f) Does the result in any of the preceding parts change if BB is a Delaware corporation and EZ filed in the Delaware filing office? If so, how? Will the passage of time affect the rights of EZ and Buyer? See UCC 9–316(a)(3).

Problem 3.4.4. The facts are as in Problem 3.4.1, except that BB is a general partnership. EZ filed a proper financing statement in the Ohio filing office on July 15, 2001. In June, 2002, without EZ's knowledge or consent, BB moved its headquarters from Cleveland to Los Angeles. On July 20, 2002, Elsie, who held a judgment against BB, acquired an execution lien on certain manufacturing equipment at BB's plant in Taylor, Michigan.

(a) It is now August 1, 2002, and EZ has yet to discover the removal of BB's headquarters. Is EZ's security interest senior or junior to Elsie's lien? See UCC 9–317(a)(2); UCC 9–316(a).

(b) It is now December 1, 2002, and EZ has yet to discover the removal of BB's headquarters. Is EZ's security interest senior or junior to Elsie's lien? See UCC 9–317(a)(2); UCC 9–316(a), (b); UCC 1–201(b)(30), (29) [F1–201(33), (32)]. What could the losing party have done to protect itself?

(c) Can you reconcile UCC 9–316's treatment of Elsie with the treatment it affords to Buyer in the preceding Problem?

(d) Does the result in part (a) change if BB acquired the manufacturing equipment in early July, after the relocation of its headquarters? When was the security interest in the equipment "perfected"? See UCC 9–316(a) & Comment 2; UCC 9–308(a); UCC 9–203(b)(2).

(e) Does the result in part (a) or (b) change if BB is a Delaware corporation and EZ filed in the Delaware filing office? If so, how?

NOTE ON THE PROSPECTS FOR A NATIONWIDE FILING SYSTEM

Many of the problems associated with determining where to file and whether and when to refile could be solved by scrapping state filing systems and adopting a single, nationwide system. One way to establish a nationwide system would be through preemptive federal legislation. A less intrusive (and probably more feasible) route would be through developments in the private sector: one or more corporations might provide search and filing systems and services to states pursuant to contract. Even if several such nongovernmental systems were to be developed, a de facto nationwide system might emerge if the systems were to share their information. UCC 9–523(f), which requires states to offer to sell or license to the public on a nonexclusive basis, in bulk, copies of all Article 9 filings, may be the first step in that direction.

Why do you suppose the UCC's sponsors did not propose a national filing system?

(B) MOTOR VEHICLES AND CERTIFICATES OF TITLE   See handout – skip

INTRODUCTORY NOTE

We have seen that a security interest in automobiles and other goods covered by a certificate of title normally may not be perfected by filing a financing statement; rather, it may be perfected only by compliance with a certificate-of-title statute. See UCC 9–311(a), (b); Problem 3.3.19, p. 178, supra. But which jurisdiction's certificate-of-title statute must be complied with? UCC 9–303(c) answers this question. The answer should not surprise you: the law of the jurisdiction under whose certificate of title the goods are covered. For example, in the Prototype, Lee Abel's Chevrolet was covered by a Pennsylvania certificate of title. For this reason, Firstbank perfected its security interest in Lee Abel's Chevrolet by compliance with the Pennsylvania certificate-of-title statute. See Form 3.8, supra.

Just as the basic choice-of-law rules become more complicated when the debtor changes its location, so the choice-of-law rules applicable to goods covered by a certificate of title become more complicated when the goods are re-titled in another jurisdiction. Further complications may arise when the debtor engages in fraud. As Comment 6 to UCC 9–303 notes:

> Ideally, at any given time, only one certificate of title is outstanding with respect to particular goods. In fact, however, sometimes more than one jurisdiction issues more than one certificate of title with respect to the same goods. This situation results from defects in certificate-of-title laws and the interstate coordination of those laws, not from deficiencies in [Revised Article 9]. As long as the possibility of multiple certificates of title remains, the potential for innocent parties to suffer losses will continue. At best, [Revised Article 9] can identify clearly which innocent parties will bear the losses in familiar fact patterns.

UCC 9–303, Comment 6.

The following Problems present some "familiar fact patterns" that feature duplicitous debtors. To what extent does Revised Article 9 "identify clearly which innocent parties will bear the losses"? Are losses imposed on the "right" innocent parties?

Please assume that, unless otherwise specified, each jurisdiction in the following Problems has enacted the Uniform Certificate of Title Act (2005) ("UCTA").

Problem 3.4.5. On March 1, Bilk, a resident of New Mexico, purchased a car in Arizona with money loaned by Firstbank. The following week, the State of Arizona issued a certificate of title noting Firstbank's security interest and sent the certificate to Firstbank. On March 15 Bilk, by means of a fraudulent affidavit, obtained a clean Arizona certificate. On June 16 Bilk moved to California, driving the car, which still had Arizona license plates.

(a) On August 1, Lean, the holder of a judgment against Bilk, acquires an execution lien on the car.

(i) Which state's law governs priority between Lean's lien and Firstbank's security interest? See UCC 9–303; UCC 9–102(a)(10).

(ii) Is Firstbank's security interest senior or junior to Lean's lien? See UCC 9–317(a)(2); UCC 9–311. See UCTA § 26.

(iii) What could the losing party have done to protect itself?

(b) What result in part (a) if Lean acquires the execution lien on November 15?

(c) Using the clean Arizona certificate, on July 15, Bilk sold the car to Bushing, a used car dealer. Does Bushing take free of or subject to Firstbank's security interest? (The rights of buyers are discussed in Chapter 4, Section 2, infra. For purposes of this Problem, you may assume that a buyer takes free of unperfected security interests but subject to perfected security interests.) What could the losing party have done to protect itself?

(d) What result in part (c) if Bilk moved to California on June 15 but did not sell the car to Bushing until November? What could the losing party have done to protect itself?

(e) Would it make any difference in part (c) if Bilk sold the car to Broom, a laborer, who bought the car for personal use in November? What could the losing party have done to protect itself?

Problem 3.4.6. On June 1, Bilk purchased a car in Arizona with money loaned by Firstbank. The following week, the State of Arizona issued a certificate of title noting Firstbank's security interest and sent the certificate to Firstbank. On July 1, Bilk registered the car in Pennsylvania, obtained Pennsylvania license plates for the car, and, using a false affidavit, applied for a clean Pennsylvania certificate of title. Under Pennsylvania law, a security interest in a motor vehicle is perfected when the Commonwealth issues a certificate of title showing the security interest. On July 15, the clean Pennsylvania certificate of title was issued.

Luciano, the holder of a judgment against Bilk, acquires an execution lien on the car on July 5.

(a) Which state's law governs priority between Luciano's lien and Firstbank's security interest? See UCC 9–303.

(b) Is Firstbank's security interest senior or junior to Luciano's lien? See UCC 9–317(a)(2); UCC 9–316(d), (e); UCC 1–201(b)(30), (29) [F1–201(33), (32)].

(c) What could the losing party have done to protect itself?

(d) Would the result in part (b) change if Luciano acquires the execution lien on December 5? If so, how?

Problem 3.4.7. The facts are as in the preceding Problem, except that Luciano did not acquire a lien. On July 5, Bilk sold the car to Broucher, a used car dealer.

(a) Does Broucher take free of or subject to Firstbank's security interest? You may assume that the general rule is that a buyer takes free of unperfected security interests but subject to perfected security interests. See UCC 9–311; UCC 9–316(d), (e); UCC 1–201(b)(30), (29) [F1–201(33), (32)]; UCC 9–337.

(b) What could the losing party have done to protect itself?

(c) What result if the sale to Broucher occurred on November 1? What could the losing party have done to protect itself? In this setting, is Broucher more or less deserving of protection than was Bushing in Problem 3.4.5? Is Firstbank more or less deserving?

(d) Would it make any difference in part (a) or (c) if the Pennsylvania certificate of title stated that the car may be subject to other liens not noted on the certificate?

(e) Would it make any difference in part (a) or (c) if Bilk had sold the car to Brice, a laborer, who bought the car for personal use? Assume that Brice and Firstbank litigate their rights in Pennsylvania. Would the same result obtain if litigation proceeds in Arizona?

Problem 3.4.8. The facts are as in Problem 3.4.6, except that Luciano did not acquire a lien. On July 5, Bilk created a security interest in the car in favor of Secondbank, which perfected its security interest shortly thereafter by notation on a replacement Pennsylvania certificate of title.

(a) Which security interest, Firstbank's or Secondbank's, has priority in the car? See UCC 9–322(a); UCC 9–311; UCC 9–316(d), (e); UCC 1–201(b)(30), (29) [F1–201(33), (32)]; UCC 9–337. What could the losing party have done to avoid the loss?

(b) Would the result in part (a) change if Bilk created the security interest in favor of Secondbank on May 1, but Secondbank did not perfect its security interest until July?

SECTION 5. PROCEEDS OF COLLATERAL

INTRODUCTORY NOTE

Creditors who have ongoing relationships with business debtors often secure their loans with interests in the debtor's inventory. The Prototype automobile financing transaction that opened this Chapter is an example. When, as both parties hope and expect, the inventory is sold, the creditor's security interest rarely can be asserted against the buyer. See UCC 9–320(a); Chapter 4, Section 2(A), infra. Instead, the secured party must enforce its security interest against the "proceeds" of its collateral—whatever is received upon the sale. See UCC 9–102(a)(64); UCC 9–315(a)(2).

Creditors who finance inventory and accounts expect that their collateral will be sold or collected. For them, the creation of proceeds is a normal—indeed, desirable—aspect of the financing; proceeds are the means by which the debtor will be able to repay the loan. In contrast, for those who finance the acquisition of equipment, the creation of proceeds may signal a breakdown in the financing relationship; it may mean that the debtor has disposed of the collateral in violation of the security agreement. Even though the security interest in the equipment may survive the sale, see UCC 9–315(a)(1) (discussed in Chapter 4, Section 2, infra), the secured party may be unable to locate the collateral to enforce its security interest. Under those circumstances, the secured party's only remaining hope for protection may lie in the proceeds.

The problem of wrongful dispositions is not confined to security interests. In a wide variety of settings in which B wrongfully disposes of A's property, basic remedial principles have accorded A a property interest in traceable proceeds—not only proceeds held by B but also those held by third persons who do not have a strong claim for protection, e.g., persons who lack the reliance interest of a good faith purchaser. For a discussion of the legal tools used to protect A's interest, including the doctrines of "constructive trust" and "equitable lien," see Restatement of Restitution § 202 (1937); D. Dobbs, Remedies §§ 4.3, 5.18 (1993).

As you work through the following materials, it will be useful to consider the extent to which the detailed "proceeds" rules of Article 9 (UCC 9–315) constitute particularized responses to a basic and pervasive remedial problem and the extent to which the rules serve to fill gaps in the articulated bargain between the debtor and the secured party.[1]

Problem 3.5.1. In the setting of the Prototype transaction, a new Chevrolet financed by Firstbank was traded by Main Motors for a Lincoln. Subsequently, Main traded the Lincoln for a Cadillac.

(a) Does the Dealer Inventory Security Agreement (Form 3.2, supra) create a security interest in the Cadillac in favor of Firstbank? If so, is the security interest perfected? See UCC 9–204(a); Financing Statement (Form 3.1, supra); UCC 9–310(a); UCC 9–311(d).

(b) Suppose that both the Security Agreement and the Financing Statement covered only the motor vehicles financed by Firstbank (here, the Chevrolet). Does Firstbank have a security interest in the Cadillac? If so, is it perfected? See UCC 9–203(f); UCC 9–102(a)(64); UCC 9–315(a), (c).

Problem 3.5.2. Firstbank financed the purchase of new cars by Main Motors in the manner described in the Prototype transaction, except that the financing statement referred to the collateral as "Motor Vehicles." On June 1 Main sold to Computer Storehouse, Inc. (CSI), a computer dealer, a new Chevrolet that had been financed by Firstbank. CSI paid for the Chevrolet, in part, by delivering to Main certain computer equipment; CSI installed the equipment in Main's office.

(a) On June 25 one of Main's trade creditors, LC Co., had the sheriff levy on all of Main's office equipment, including the computer equipment. Does Firstbank's security interest extend to the computer equipment? If so, is Firstbank's security interest senior to LC's execution lien? See UCC 9–315(a), (c); UCC 9–102(a)(64); UCC 9–317(a)(2); Notes on Security Interests in Proceeds, infra.

(b) Now assume that instead of swapping the computer equipment for a portion of the price of the Chevrolet, CSI paid cash for the Chevrolet. The next day, June 2, Main Motors used a portion of the cash to purchase the computer equipment. Firstbank took no further action to perfect a security interest in the computer equipment. LC then had the sheriff levy on June 25. Do the results in part (a) change? See UCC 9–315(d).

(c) The facts are as in part (b), except that LC levied ten days earlier, on June 15. Is Firstbank's security interest senior to LC's execution lien? Are the relative rights of LC and Firstbank fixed as of the date of levy, or can they change as time passes? Cf. UCC 9–515(c) (security interest that

---

1.   Bankruptcy and other insolvency proceedings pose special risks and afford special protection for claims to proceeds. Those matters are addressed in Chapter 7, Section 2(B), infra. This section focuses on the treatment of claims to proceeds outside of insolvency proceedings.

becomes unperfected upon lapse is deemed never to have been perfected as against a purchaser for value); UCC 9–316(b) (security interest that becomes unperfected after debtor changes location is deemed never to have been perfected as against a purchaser for value).

Howarth v. Universal C.I.T. Credit Corp.[*]

United States District Court, Western District of Pennsylvania, 1962.
203 F.Supp. 279.

■ MARSH, DISTRICT JUDGE. The plaintiff, trustee in bankruptcy of Spohn Motor Company, Inc. (Spohn), brought this action, pursuant to § 60 of the Bankruptcy Act, as amended March 18, 1950, 11 U.S.C.A. § 96 (1961 Supp.), to recover from the defendant, Universal C.I.T. Credit Corporation (UCIT) the value of property transferred to UCIT from Spohn within four months of filing the petition in bankruptcy.

The underlying facts stipulated by the parties are adopted by the court. From these facts it appears that an involuntary petition in bankruptcy was filed against Spohn on January 6, 1958, and it was adjudicated a bankrupt on February 13, 1958.

On February 5, 1957, pursuant to a Loan Agreement (Ex. H), UCIT advanced to Spohn the sum of $75,000. On the same day, Spohn executed a Chattel Mortgage (Ex. I) covering certain chattels. Shortly thereafter UCIT perfected a security interest therein by properly filing a Financing Statement (Ex. J) under the provisions of the Uniform Commercial Code—Secured Transactions, Act of April 6, 1953, P.L. 3, § 9–101 et seq. . . .(hereinafter referred to as U.C.C.).

Prior to September 28, 1957, Spohn also executed in favor of UCIT used car Trust Receipts (Ex. D) and assigned to UCIT certain Bailment Leases (Ex. E).

During August of 1957, and for some months prior thereto, UCIT had advanced to Spohn, or to Ford Motor Company for the benefit of Spohn pursuant to an Agreement for Wholesale Financing (Ex. A), dated December 13, 1954, the principal sum of $437,972.84 for 201 new motor vehicles, each secured under the terms of new car Trust Receipts (Ex. G). On March 3, 1955, UCIT perfected a security interest in, inter alia, new and used motor vehicles, equipment, accessories or replacement parts, and proceeds by properly filing a Financing Statement (Ex. B).

Prior to September 28, 1957, 110 of the new motor vehicles had been sold out of trust by Spohn, leaving 91 new vehicles which UCIT repossessed and sold for $188,268.32, leaving a remainder of $249,704.52 due by Spohn to UCIT for new vehicles sold out of trust.

Between September 28, 1957 and October 31, 1957, Spohn being thus indebted to UCIT, transferred to it the following items, to which the plaintiff-trustee concedes he has no claim: the proceeds of the sale of 15

[*] [The court's citations are to the applicable pre–1972 version of the UCC.]

vehicles subject to bailment leases; office furniture, fixtures and equipment; shop equipment; accounts receivable from UCIT; accounts receivable from Ford Motor Company for wholesale incentive; warranty and policy claims receivable from Ford Motor Company; and other receivables from Ford Motor Company. The facts show conclusively that UCIT had a perfected security interest in each of these items.

In addition to these items, during the same period, Spohn transferred to UCIT, either voluntarily or involuntarily the following: bank cash, shares of stock, customers receivables, 70 used vehicles, and motor parts and accessories. These transfers were made by Spohn for its antecedent debts, at a time when Spohn was insolvent and UCIT had reason to so believe. The plaintiff-trustee contends that these transfers constituted preferences within the meaning of § 60 of the Bankruptcy Act, since their effect was to enable UCIT to obtain a greater percentage of its debt that Spohn's unsecured creditors, except as to those items in which UCIT held a perfected security interest.

proceeds or preferential transfer

We take up the disputed items seriatim.

BANK CASH

Spohn's bank account in the Peoples First National Bank & Trust Company in the sum of $6,734.21 was garnisheed and transferred to UCIT pursuant to a writ of attachment execution issued on a judgment in favor of UCIT in the sum of $75,000. The lien against the bank cash obtained by the attachment within four months of bankruptcy and while Spohn was insolvent is null and void. Section 67 of the Bankruptcy Act, 11 U.S.C.A. § 107.

Spohn's bank account was not under the control of UCIT, and the source of this money has not been identified. Apparently UCIT has not been able to trace any of the money in the bank to proceeds from the sales of collateral on which it held a security interest. The defendant argues that the money must have come from the sale of property in which it had a security interest. This is an unwarranted assumption for all of it could have come from services rendered, sale of Spohn's common stock, or loans to Spohn.

The court may not assume the source of the money in the bank. The burden is upon UCIT to trace cash proceeds received by Spohn from the disposition of secured collateral into the bank deposits. This it has not done. This cash was received by Spohn, the debtor, and deposited more than 10 days prior to the bankruptcy proceeding (cf. U.C.C. § 9–306(2) [UCC 9–315(a)]); it is not identifiable cash proceeds received from the sale or disposition of any collateral. Thus it is free from any security interest of UCIT and is subject to the claims of general creditors represented by the plaintiff-trustee.

Creditor must be able to trace proceeds.

We hold the bank cash garnisheed by UCIT is a voidable preference and the plaintiff-trustee is entitled to recover $6,734.21.

ACCOUNTS RECEIVABLE

Spohn collected customers receivables by cash and checks in the sum of $10,847.75 and transferred this amount to UCIT within four months of bankruptcy. Of this sum $1,100.00 was identified as cash proceeds from the sale of two new vehicles on which UCIT held a perfected security interest, leaving in dispute the sum of $9,747.75. This remainder comprises commingled cash proceeds arising from the sale of motor vehicles, parts and services.

From the Stipulated Facts and Exhibit L, it cannot be ascertained whether any of the articles sold were covered by a perfected security interest in favor of UCIT. Exhibit L gives only the name of the person owing the account, the amount paid, and the date the money was transferred to UCIT. Moreover, even if it were to be assumed that some of the accounts arose from the sale of parts and vehicles, it still could not be ascertained whether or not any portion of any account arose from services performed by Spohn. As UCIT did not hold a security interest in proceeds received from the sale of services, it is not entitled to retain proceeds which may have come from this source.

Furthermore, as we understand the Uniform Commercial Code, in insolvency proceedings the secured creditor is only entitled to commingled cash when it is received as proceeds of collateral within ten days of the filing of the petition.

For these reasons, we hold that the plaintiff-trustee is entitled to $9,747.75.

17 USED VEHICLES

These 17 used vehicles were taken in trade by Spohn toward the purchase price of 17 new vehicles. On each of the new vehicles sold, UCIT held a perfected security interest by virtue of the Agreement for Wholesale Financing (Ex. A), new car Trust Receipts (Ex. G), and Financing Statement (Ex. B). The 17 new vehicles were sold out of trust by Spohn.[**] . . .

The plaintiff-trustee contends that according to the Motor Vehicle Code no lien can be obtained on a "trade-in" unless the lien is noted on the title certificate. It is the opinion of the court that a finance company such as UCIT engaging in wholesale financing of new and used vehicles held for resale by a dealer, and having obtained a security interest in new vehicles and the proceeds thereof, may perfect its security interest in the proceeds by filing in compliance with § 9–302(1) of the U.C.C. [UCC 9–310(a)], and,

---

[**] [Selling inventory "out of trust" is an expression frequently used in financing circles, perhaps because of appealing connotations that the sale was a breach of "trust" that should invoke the powerful remedies available against defalcating trustees. (The debtor actually was denominated a "trustee" under the Uniform Trust Receipts Act, which governed much pre-UCC inventory financing. See generally 1 Gilmore, Security ch. 4.) However, as you probably surmised, there was nothing wrong with the *sale* of the cars; the only thing that went wrong was that the *dealer failed promptly to pay* the debt to UCIT attributable to the vehicles that it sold.]

in view of § 207(c) of the Motor Vehicle Code, need not require the dealer to procure title certificates for each "trade-in" on which to show its lien. . ..

The security interest of UCIT in these proceeds was created at the times the Agreement and the Trust Receipts were executed and perfected by the filing of the Financing Statement in March, 1955. Pursuant to § 9–306(1) of the U.C.C. [UCC 9–315], this security interest continued up to the time UCIT took possession, within four months of bankruptcy, of the 17 "trade-ins", i.e., identifiable proceeds. In our opinion § 9–306(1) is not in conflict with § 60 of the Bankruptcy Act, and the perfected security interest of UCIT in these proceeds is enforceable.

We hold that UCIT is entitled to retain the money received from the sale of the 17 used vehicles.

42 USED VEHICLES

These 42 used vehicles were taken in trade for new vehicles, which had been financed by UCIT, under the terms of the Agreement for Wholesale Financing (Ex. A) and the Trust Receipts (Ex. G). These vehicles must also be regarded as identifiable proceeds in which, as previously shown, UCIT had perfected a security interest by filing the Financing Statement (Ex. B).

It was not stipulated that the new vehicles were sold out of trust by Spohn. However, as we interpret the pertinent security agreements, UCIT created a security interest in *all proceeds*, which would include these 42 "trade-ins", until *all the indebtedness* due by Spohn to UCIT was paid. As heretofore quoted, the Agreement for Wholesale Financing (Ex. A) provided that until payment in full, Spohn would hold all proceeds separately and in trust for UCIT. Likewise, the Trust Receipts (Ex. G), after providing that UCIT could accelerate all indebtedness then owing to it by Spohn in the event of insolvency, further provided that UCIT "may require the respective amount on any chattel to be paid to it in cash. Until such payment we [Spohn] will hold *all proceeds* of sale separately and in trust for * * * Universal C.I.T." (Emphasis supplied.) Since Spohn owed UCIT upwards of $400,000 on all the chattels which it had financed at the time of the transfers, we think these 42 used cars were proceeds to which UCIT is entitled.

The other arguments advanced by the plaintiff-trustee to recover the value of these used vehicles have been disposed of in the preceding section of this opinion.

We hold that UCIT is entitled to retain the money received from the sale of the 42 used vehicles. . ..

NOTES ON SECURITY INTERESTS IN PROCEEDS

(1) "Automatic," Perfected Security Interests. Article 9 affords the secured party an automatic right to proceeds. See UCC 9–203(f). A claim to proceeds of the collateral is considered so basic that (like implied warranties) this understanding "goes without saying." See Former 9–306, Reasons for 1972 Change, Uniform Commercial Code, 1999 Official Text with Comments, App. II, at 1032 ("automatic right to proceeds" based on the "theory that this is the intent of the parties, unless otherwise agreed"). Moreover, Article 9 treats a filing against the original collateral as a filing against the proceeds. See UCC 9–315(c). The drafters apparently thought the absence of a claim to proceeds in a financing statement would not mislead third persons; however, they recognized some limits to this principle, as the following Note explains.

(2) Security Interests in Proceeds and in After–Acquired Property: A Comparison. In many cases a perfected security interest in proceeds could be achieved simply by covering after-acquired property of the appropriate type in the security agreement and financing statement. For example, the security agreement of an inventory lender might (and often does) cover after-acquired accounts. However, the "automatic right to proceeds" affords additional benefits to a secured party if after-acquired property qualifies as "proceeds." As explained in the preceding Note, a secured party has an automatic security interest in proceeds even if (through oversight or otherwise) the security agreement does not cover the proceeds as original collateral. Does this benefit represent more than statutory generosity? In addition to rescuing some secured parties from careless omissions, might the "automatic" approach save the costs of extended negotiations? Might it also inhibit abuse and overreaching by some secured parties who, if it were necessary to protect one's claim to proceeds in the security agreement, might use unnecessarily broad language?

As to perfection, UCC 9–315(c) provides that "[a] security interest in proceeds is a perfected security interest if the security interest in the original collateral was perfected." This is good news for a secured party who has perfected against the original collateral. The bad news is that the security interest in proceeds becomes unperfected "on the 21st day after the security interest attaches to the proceeds," subject to three exceptions.

The first exception, UCC 9–315(d)(1), is very helpful to a secured party who has perfected against the original collateral by filing. This exception generally makes it unnecessary for a financing statement to cover the collateral that proceeds represent (except when proceeds are acquired with cash proceeds). For example, a filing covering inventory is sufficient to ensure continued perfection in proceeds consisting of accounts, as long as financing statements covering inventory and accounts are to be filed in the same office, which they are. See UCC 9–301; UCC 9–501(a); Section 4, supra. Of course, when proceeds are of a type in which a security interest can be perfected by filing, a secured party could achieve the same result as that provided by UCC 9–315(c) and (d)—continued long-term perfection—merely by filing a financing statement covering that type of collateral. If authorized by the debtor, such a filing may be made in advance. Even if not authorized, it ordinarily may be made after the security interest attaches to the proceeds. See UCC 9–509(b)(2).

The second exception to the 20–day limitation on automatic perfection against proceeds applies to "identifiable cash proceeds." UCC 9–315(d)(2).

A security interest in "cash proceeds" (UCC 9–102(a)(9)) consisting of an instrument (for example, a checks) may be perfected by filing; however, a filing does not perfect a security interest in other types of cash proceeds as original collateral. Specifically, a security interest in a non-consumer deposit account (as original collateral) may be perfected only by control, and consumer deposit accounts are excluded from Article 9 (as original collateral) altogether. See UCC 9–312(b)(1); UCC 9–109(d)(13). A security interest in money may be perfected only by taking possession. See UCC 9–312(b)(3). It follows that the continued perfection conferred by UCC 9–315(d)(2) provides greater protection for cash proceeds, as such, than would be available under the after-acquired property approach.

The third exception, UCC 9–315(d)(3), permits continued perfection beyond the 20–day period if the security interest in proceeds is perfected (other than automatically under UCC 9–315(c)) before the period expires. A security interest in after-acquired property other than proceeds also can be perfected following the debtor's acquisition of the property; but the temporary perfection provided by UCC 9–315(d)(3) can be important for purposes of priority. See, e.g., UCC 9–317(b), UCC 9–322(b)(1). If a secured party acts within the 20–day period, there will be no "gap" during which the security interest is unperfected. Again, to the extent proceeds consist of property not excluded from the scope of Article 9, and in which a security interest can be perfected by filing, the same advantage could be had by an initial filing covering the after-acquired property. Moreover, unless the debtor cooperates or the secured party monitors the debtor's activities closely, the secured party is not likely to discover the need to perfect in proceeds prior to the expiration of the 20–day period.

The distinction between proceeds and after-acquired, non-proceeds collateral can be particularly important if the debtor enters bankruptcy. Generally speaking, a security interest in property acquired during a bankruptcy case is not subject to a security interest created by a pre-bankruptcy security agreement; however, property that constitutes proceeds (or the like) of pre-bankruptcy collateral is subject to the security interest. See BC 552; Chapter 7, Section 2(B), infra.

(3) Tracing Proceeds to Original Collateral. The *Howarth* case, supra, illustrates the consequence of a secured party's inability to demonstrate that the collateral it claims constitutes "identifiable proceeds": loss of a security interest. As the following excerpt makes clear, a secured party faces particular difficulty when the proceeds are cash, or its equivalent, deposited in the debtor's bank account.

> GECC sought to establish its security interest in deposited funds by establishing that (1) ninety-two of Machinery's customers made lease payments to Machinery during January, February, and March 2001, (2) those customers leased GECC-financed inventory, and (3) the funds paid by those customers were deposited in the parent account [i.e., one of Machinery's bank accounts]. The funds paid by a lessee of inventory are proceeds of that inventory under Missouri law, and GECC's security

interest in the inventory therefore continued in those proceeds. But GECC's evidence was weak. Audit records indeed revealed that the ninety-two customers had leased GECC-financed inventory. And cancelled checks that had been deposited in Machinery's parent account established the amounts paid by the ninety-two customers to Machinery. But no leases, invoices, or other evidence tying the payments to the collateral was presented. GECC nonetheless argued that the audit records and cancelled checks showed that the funds paid by the ninety-two lessees and deposited in the parent account were proceeds of GECC-financed inventory because those customers were likely making payments on their leases of GECC-financed inventory.

proof of proceeds

UPB countered with testimony establishing that twenty-three of the ninety-two customers also leased equipment in which GECC had no security interest. The district court concluded that GECC had not proven that those twenty-three customers' payments were proceeds of GECC-financed inventory because the inference upon which GECC relied—that such customers were likely making payments on their leases of GECC-financed inventory—was no longer valid given UPB's evidence. The court therefore excluded those twenty-three customers' payments from its deposit calculations and held that GECC had proven that the remaining sixty-nine customers' payments were proceeds of GECC-financed inventory that was deposited in the parent account. We agree with the district court. Including the twenty-three customers' payments requires speculation, and although GECC's evidence was scant, we see no clear error in the district court's finding with regard to the remaining sixty-nine customers' payments.

General Electric Capital Corp. v. Union Planters Bank, 409 F.3d 1049, 1054-55 (9th Cir.2005).

The court noted that:

one of [GECC's] many arguments borders on frivolity. GECC argues that the district court clearly erred because GECC should be excused from presenting competent evidence on the issue—i.e., through an analysis of Machinery's leases, accounts, invoices, and deposits. According to [GECC's Reply Brief], "the record was clear that such an attempted reconstruction would have taken weeks of professional time and cost hundreds of thousands of dollars, something obviously unreasonable in this case, with less than $500,000 in controversy." The amount of money at stake in litigation is relevant only to our diversity jurisdiction; it does not excuse a plaintiff from offering evidence that proves its claim.

Id. at 1055 n.3.

Problem 3.5.3. Continental Construction Co. bought a new backhoe; Palmetto Bank loaned Continental the purchase price, and perfected a security interest in the backhoe by filing.

(a) An employee of Iceberg Masonry, Inc., negligently dropped a load of bricks on the backhoe at a job site; the damaged backhoe was beyond repair. Continental's insurer, Everystate Insurance Co., sent its check covering the value of the backhoe ($100,000) to Continental. Does Palmetto's security interest extend to the check? See UCC 9–315(a); UCC 9–102(a)(64); UCC 9–102(a)(13). If so, is it perfected? See UCC 9–315(c), (d).

(b) Would the result in part (a) be the same if the $100,000 check had been sent by *Iceberg's* liability insurance carrier? What result if the check had been sent by Iceberg itself?

(c) Suppose instead that the backhoe malfunctioned and that Continental pressed a claim against Manufacturer for damages resulting from negligent design and breach of implied warranty; the claim included evidence of damage resulting from the malfunctions and loss of profits resulting from loss of use of the backhoe. Manufacturer settled for $50,000 and sent a check to Continental for that sum. Palmetto Bank claims the check as proceeds of its collateral. What result? See Note on What Constitutes Proceeds, infra.

(d) Now suppose that the backhoe was not damaged. Instead, a sluggish economy reduced Continental's business and its equipment needs. Continental leased the backhoe to Deep Dig Corp. for a one-year term pursuant to a written lease. Does Palmetto's security interest extend to the lease? To checks sent to Continental by Deep Dig as lease payments? Would the answers be different if the lease had been an oral one, not reduced to writing? Would it matter if the lease were for a day or a month instead of a year?

Problem 3.5.4. United Entertainment Group, Inc. (UEG), operates coin-operated music and entertainment machine "routes." UEG supplies coin-operated jukeboxes, video games, pool tables, and the like to establishments (called "joints," in the trade) such as restaurants, taverns, and clubs. The operators of the joints receive no interest in the machines (other than the right to possession) and pay nothing for the machines. However, once or twice each week, an employee of UEG stops by each joint. The joint manager and the UEG employee "rob" the machine and, together, count the money. The joint keeps one half of the money and UEG takes the other half. Either party can terminate the arrangement for any reason upon five-days' notice.

Firstbank has a security interest in UEG's existing and after-acquired equipment, inventory, and accounts, perfected by filing. Does Firstbank acquire a security interest in the funds obtained from the machines? If so, is the security interest perfected?

Problem 3.5.5. Busy Bee Co. operates an interstate bus company. Firstbank has a security interest in Busy's existing and after-acquired equipment, inventory and accounts, perfected by filing. Every day, thousands of riders pay Busy and independent travel agents for tickets. Does Firstbank acquire a security interest in these payments? If so, is the security interest perfected? What could Firstbank have done to improve its position? See UCC 9–312(a); UCC 9–102(a)(49).

Problem 3.5.6. On June 1, Dale Bookbinder obtained a short-term (six-month) loan from Firstbank in the amount of $25,000. Bookbinder delivered to Firstbank, as collateral, a certificate for 2,000 shares of General Motors Corporation (GMC) common stock. On June 3 GMC declared (i.e., undertook to pay) a stock dividend: each stockholder became entitled to receive one additional share of stock for each four shares owned. Because Bookbinder remained the registered owner of the shares, GMC mailed a new certificate for 500 shares directly to Bookbinder, who received it on July 15. Does Firstbank acquire a security interest in the new certificate? If so, is the security interest perfected? See UCC 9–315(a); UCC 9–102(a)(64) & Comment 13.a.; Note on What Constitutes Proceeds, infra; UCC 9–315(c), (d). What could Firstbank have done to improve its position?

NOTE ON WHAT CONSTITUTES PROCEEDS: EXCHANGE AND REPLACEMENT; PROPERTY CLOSELY ASSOCIATED WITH ORIGINAL COLLATERAL

The definition of proceeds is transactional. Each of the triggering events specified in UCC 9–102(a)(64) contemplates that proceeds are to some extent acquired in place of and in substitution for the original collateral, which has been disposed of or reduced in value (such as by collections). This "replacement" standard is most clear in the case of dispositions, such as sales, leases, licenses, and exchanges under subsection (a)(64)(A).[2] But it also is apparent with respect to the other triggering events as well.

Another plausible way to conceptualize what are or should be proceeds of collateral does not depend on the exchange concept. Instead, one can view proceeds as property that is so necessarily and obviously associated with an interest in the original collateral that a security agreement and financing statement ought not to be required to mention them explicitly. After all, "automatic" attachment and perfection are the principal effects that flow from classifying property as proceeds. If the debtor, by virtue of its interest in the original collateral, is necessarily entitled to additional property, then a secured party likewise would be entitled to the additional property as proceeds. Claims for damage or loss of collateral seem to fit this characterization. The same could be said for all forms of distributions on account of securities, partnership interests, and other intangibles (which may or may not be covered as "collections" proceeds), certain government subsidies, and other rights that do not, technically, involve an "exchange" or disposition.

Former 9–306(1) defined proceeds to include "whatever is received upon the sale, exchange, collection or other disposition of collateral or proceeds." It also included "insurance payable by reason of loss or damage to collateral." Arguably, the former definition could have been construed to include all proceeds covered by the current definition, UCC 9–102(a)(64), but in some cases the "exchange" and "collection" formulations probably

---

2.   Although the proceeds may replace the original collateral, in many cases the security interest continues to exist in the original collateral as well. See UCC 9–315(a)(1).

were too narrow to support that construction. Even when the formulations were ample, courts occasionally were reluctant to construe them as broadly as they might have. The current definition more easily accommodates and more clearly mandates a <u>broad view of proceeds</u>.

Of course, even the more explicit and broader definition of proceeds has limits. Can you imagine the acquisition of assets by a debtor, due in part to a disposition or diminution in value of collateral, to be too attenuated to be considered proceeds of that collateral? For example, would anyone think that accounts generated by a construction contractor would (or should) be considered proceeds of the contractor's construction equipment, even though the equipment depreciates as a result of its use in earning the accounts? Similarly, would (or should) inventory fabricated by a debtor's factory equipment be considered proceeds of that equipment? What about cash earned from music or video machines? Has the equipment merely provided a service, or is the better analogy that of a short-term rental? Should the result turn on whether the equipment user has acquired a *property* interest in the machine under non-UCC law?

Problem 3.5.7. Firstbank has a security interest, perfected by filing, in all of the restaurant equipment of The Bus Corp., the operator of a small restaurant. The Bus wrongfully sold a used oven to the operator of another restaurant, The Light Dog Co. (Because the sale by The Bus was not authorized, Firstbank's security interest in the oven continued and The Light Dog's interest remains subject to that security interest. See UCC 9–315(a)(1); Chapter 4, Section 2, infra.) Light Dog then resold the oven to another restaurant operator, The New Neck, Inc. In payment, New Neck gave Light Dog its check for $1,500.

(a) Does Firstbank have a security interest in the $1,500 check? See UCC 9–315(a); UCC 9–102(a)(64); UCC 9–102(a)(12). UCC 9–102(a)(64)(A) is one of the few places in which Revised Article 9 uses the passive voice ("whatever is acquired"). Why didn't the drafters use the active voice to identify the acquirer? See UCC 9–102, Comment 13.d.; Former 9–306(2).

(b) Assuming an affirmative answer in part (a), is Firstbank's security interest perfected? See UCC 9–315(c), (d).

(c) Now assume that the collateral involved was not an oven but was a delivery van, in which Firstbank perfected its security interest by complying with the relevant motor vehicle certificate of title law. Does Firstbank have a perfected security interest in the $1,500 that New Neck paid for the van? See UCC 9–315(d); UCC 9–311(b).

––––––

The problem of security interests in proceeds of collateral takes new twists when the proceeds are cash, or its equivalent, that is deposited in the debtor's bank account. The deposited funds may be paid to third parties, commingled with other funds, or both. The next portion of this Section explores these twists.[3]

Problem 3.5.8. Finco extended a line of credit to Lappin Leather Ltd. Lappin secured its obligations to Finco with all its existing and future accounts. Finco perfected its security interest by filing. Under the transaction documents, Lappin is obligated to deposit all checks received in payment of accounts into a special "proceeds" deposit account maintained with Local Bank.

(a) Does Finco have a perfected security interest in the bank account, which contains nothing but proceeds of Lappin's accounts? See UCC 9–102(a)(64); UCC 9–315(a), (c), (d), (e).

(b) Lappin draws a $2500 check to Supplier, and Local properly pays the check from the bank account. May Finco recover the payment or hold Supplier liable for money had and received? See UCC 9–332; General Electric Capital Corp. v. Union Planters Bank, infra; Note (1) on Cash Proceeds, infra.

(c) Lappin draws a $500 check as a charitable contribution to the United Way. Local properly pays the check from the bank account. May Finco recover the payment or hold the United Way liable for money had and received? Is the United Way deserving of protection even if it did not give value or otherwise act in reliance on receipt of the funds? See UCC 9–332 & Comment 3.

Problem 3.5.9. In the setting of the automobile financing Prototype, assume that Firstbank's security interest in Main's inventory was perfected by a filed financing statement that referred to the collateral only as "Motor Vehicles" (as in Problem 3.5.2, p. 203, supra). Moreover, the security agreement covered only new motor vehicles financed by Firstbank, not used vehicles.

Main deposited cash received from the sale of new and used cars and from its repair department into a checking account maintained with Firstbank. As in the Prototype, when financed cars were sold, Main promptly sent Firstbank a check covering the amount Firstbank had advanced to the manufacturer for those cars. However, in June, when Main owed $1,500,000 to Firstbank, Main became short of cash and used proceeds from the sale of financed cars to meet payroll, rent, utilities, and other pressing obligations. On June 1 Main had a balance of $1000 in its checking account. The following table shows the deposits (+) and withdrawals (-) for the first few days of June; "PC" indicates proceeds of collateral subject to Firstbank's security interest.

---

3.   The issue raised by Problem 3.5.8 arises not only with respect to deposit accounts containing proceeds but also with respect to deposit accounts serving as original collateral. For a detailed discussion of security interests in deposit accounts, see Chapter 6, Section 4, infra.

June		Deposit or Withdrawal	Balance
1			$ 1,000.
2	+ $15,000.	Sale of one new Chevrolet (PC)	16,000.
3	+ 9,000.	Sale of one new Chevrolet (PC)	25,000.
4	− 4,000.	Rent on off-site storage lot	21,000.
5	− 12,000.	Payroll	9,000.
6	− 2,000.	Fuel oil	7,000.
7	− 1,000.	Telephone; electricity	6,000.
8	+ 2,000.	Collections for body repairs	8,000.
9	+ 6,000.	Sale of used cars (Not PC)	14,000.
10	+ 12,000.	Loan from relative	26,000.

During this period Main made no payments to Firstbank.

On June 12 Caesar, a creditor of Main with a judgment for $50,000, garnished the checking account by serving a garnishment summons on Firstbank. Is Caesar's garnishment lien senior to Firstbank's security interest in Main's checking account? If so, to what extent? See UCC 9–315(b) & Comment 3; General Electric Capital Corp. v. Union Planters Bank, infra; Note (2) on Cash Proceeds, infra. (Ignore, for now, any right of setoff that Firstbank may enjoy. Setoffs are considered in Chapter 8, Section 4(D), infra.)

General Electric Capital Corporation v. Union Planters Bank, NA*

United States Court of Appeals, Ninth Circuit, 2005.
409 F.3d 1049.

■ BEAM, CIRCUIT JUDGE.

This diversity case involves a dispute between two creditors—General Electric Capital Corporation (GECC), the plaintiff, and Union Planters Bank (UPB), the defendant—about funds UPB received from their common debtor— Machinery, Inc. (Machinery). The district court granted GECC's motion for summary judgment on liability, and held a bench trial to determine damages. Ultimately, the court entered judgment against UPB for $62,818. GECC appeals the damages determination, and UPB cross-appeals the liability ruling. We affirm in part, reverse in part, and remand the case for further proceedings.

I. BACKGROUND

Machinery was in the business of renting, selling, and servicing aerial manlift equipment. Machinery financed the purchase of its manlift inventory with GECC, UPB, and various other lenders, and it gave those creditors security interests in the inventory they financed. UPB was also Machinery's lender on an operating note, secured by a blanket lien on all of

---

* [Unless otherwise indicated, the court's citations are to the applicable version of Former Article 9.]

Machinery's property, and it was Machinery's depository bank. In March 2000, GECC and UPB entered into a subordination agreement in which UPB subordinated its security interest in GECC-financed inventory to the interest of GECC, as well as its interest in "all cash, rents and non-cash proceeds" arising from that same property.

In April 2000, UPB and Machinery set up a cash management system. Under this system, Machinery maintained three demand deposit accounts with UPB: a parent account and two operating accounts. Machinery would deposit the funds it had collected from equipment rentals, sales, and service into the parent account and write checks on the operating accounts to cover expenses. Each day, when Machinery's checks were presented for payment, UPB would transfer funds from the parent account to the operating accounts to cover the checks. If the parent account balance was inadequate to cover the operating-account expenditures, a revolving line of credit covered the shortfall. And, if an excess existed in the parent account after the items drawn on the operating accounts were paid, UPB would automatically "sweep" the funds from Machinery's parent account to pay down the balance owing on the line of credit. . . ..

From April 2000, Machinery deposited its revenue in the parent account without identifying which items of inventory, if any, generated the funds it was depositing. UPB swept funds from the parent account and provided funds to the operating accounts regularly and automatically. The system operated in this manner until the beginning of March 2001, when Machinery's affairs began to fall apart. Machinery fell into default with UPB, and UPB terminated the automatic feature of the cash management system. Ultimately, Machinery filed for bankruptcy on March 29, 2001.

GECC filed suit against UPB claiming that UPB wrongfully swept proceeds of GECC-financed inventory from Machinery's parent account in January, February and March 2001. GECC asserted causes of action for wrongful setoff, breach of the subordination agreement, conversion, tortious interference with contract, and unjust enrichment. GECC moved for partial summary judgment on its conversion claim, arguing that UPB converted funds in which GECC had a superior interest when UPB swept the account. UPB cross-moved for summary judgment on all of GECC's claims. The district court granted GECC's partial motion, holding that UPB was liable for conversion, but reserved the question of damages for trial. The court dismissed the remaining counts with prejudice because they all sought relief for the same injury.

Evidence of damages was presented at a bench trial. The district court concluded that UPB converted $62,818 of funds in which GECC had a superior interest when it swept Machinery's account in January, February, and March.

GECC appeals the damages ruling, and UPB cross-appeals the district court's entry of summary judgment on liability. . . ..

II. DISCUSSION

In diversity cases, we apply the substantive law of the state in which the district court sits. Erie R.R. Co. v. Tompkins, 304 U.S. 64, 58 S.Ct. 817, 82 L.Ed. 1188 (1938). Here, that is Missouri, and we review the district court's interpretation of Missouri law de novo.

Under Missouri law,

[c]onversion is the unauthorized assumption of the right of ownership over the personal property of another to the exclusion of the owner's rights. . . . . [A] plaintiff must show title to, or a right of property in, and a right to the immediate possession of the property concerned at the alleged date of conversion.

This case involves a conflict over funds generated by leases of inventory in which GECC held a security interest. Those proceeds were deposited in Machinery's parent account with UPB. This was typical of Machinery's operations and there is no evidence that GECC objected to the deposit of those funds in that account. GECC's conversion theory is based on what happened after those funds were deposited.

GECC claimed that UPB converted GECC's property when it swept funds from Machinery's parent account under the cash management system in January, February, and March 2001. GECC premised this claim on its security interest in the proceeds of GECC-financed inventory. Specifically, it sought to establish that it had a "right of property in, and a right to the immediate possession of," the funds UPB received. Because GECC's rights were premised on its security interest, GECC had to prove that it had a security interest in the funds UPB received from the parent account. To do that, GECC was faced with two tasks. First, it had to prove that proceeds in which it held a security interest were deposited in Machinery's parent account. If GECC established that fact, then GECC's security interest in the funds that were deposited continued in the deposit account to the extent of the amount of such deposits. GECC's second task, then, was to prove that the funds UPB received through its sweeps were encumbered by GECC's security interest in the deposit account. We address these two aspects of GECC's claim in turn.

A. GECC's Security Interest in Machinery's Deposits

The district court determined that GECC had a security interest in certain funds that were deposited by Machinery in its parent account. It made this determination at the bench trial, and its conclusion is a finding of fact. [The court of appeals saw no clear error in the district court's finding on this issue. Its discussion is reproduced in Note (3) on Security Interests in Proceeds, supra, and is omitted here.]

B. GECC's Security Interest in the Funds UPB Received

1. Ordinary Course Payments: When To Use Equitable Tracing

GECC, however, did not object to the deposit of these funds. Its conversion claim rests on UPB's sweeps. So GECC had the burden of proving that the funds UPB swept were traceable to the funds deposited—funds in which it had a security interest. But proving that link is quite difficult, if not impossible, when funds from numerous sources are deposited and credited to a single account, from which the depositor makes withdrawals and orders payments. Equitable tracing principles ease this difficulty. The question *how* such tracing works in this case is addressed below. But because equitable tracing principles cannot be used unless equity calls for it, and because there are "good commercial reasons" for not using such principles to impose liability, we must initially "determine *when* [a court] should trace proceeds through a commingled account." Harley-Davidson Motor Co. v. Bank of New England, 897 F.2d 611, 622 (1st Cir.1990).

[Under Former Article 9, o]ne UCC provision has been used to delineate when a debtor's payee will be deemed a recipient of encumbered proceeds through the use of equitable tracing principles. That provision provides the following:

> Where cash proceeds are covered into the debtor's checking account and paid out in the operation of the debtor's business, recipients of the funds of course take free of any claim which the secured party may have in them as proceeds. What has been said relates to payments and transfers in ordinary course. The law of fraudulent conveyances would no doubt in appropriate cases support recovery of proceeds by a secured party from a transferee out of ordinary course or otherwise in collusion with the debtor to defraud the secured party.

Mo. Ann. Stat. § 400.9-306, cmt. 2(c).

We agree with the district court that Missouri, like most other states confronted with this issue, would recognize this official comment as law. The current version of Missouri's Uniform Commercial Code supports this result. *See* Mo. Ann. Stat. § 400.9-332(b) (West 2003) (ending a security interest in a deposit account upon the transfer of funds "unless the transferee acts in collusion with the debtor in violating the rights of the secured party").[**] And we agree with those courts that have held that this comment effectively delineates those circumstances when tracing is appropriate [under Former Article 9]: when the payee receives funds "out of ordinary course or otherwise in collusion with the debtor." Here, the district court held that the subordination agreement meant that UPB, as a matter of law, did not receive the funds swept from the parent account in the ordinary course of Machinery's business. We disagree.

In Orix Credit Alliance, Inc. v. Sovran Bank, 4 F.3d 1262 (4th Cir.1993), the court was faced with a factually similar situation. The depository bank and the debtor/depositor had set up a "cash collateral account" in which all

----

**   [Missouri adopted the revised version of Article 9, effective July 1, 2001. However, the court applies Former Article 9 because all events in question occurred before the revisions became effective. See UCC 9–708(a) (Revised Article 9 determines the priority of conflicting claims to collateral; however, if relative priorities were established before Revised Article 9 takes effect, then Former Article 9 determines priority).]

of the debtor's customers' payments were deposited. Routinely, and pursuant to an agreement, the balance of that account was applied to the depositor's line of credit with the depository bank. The transaction that gave rise to the lawsuit involved the depository bank's application of the balance of the deposit account to reduce the balance on the outstanding line of credit just after the proceeds of a crane had been deposited in the debtor's cash collateral account. Both the plaintiff—another lender—and the depository bank had a security interest in the crane and the generated proceeds that were deposited. The depository bank had subordinated its interest in the crane to the competing lender's interest in the crane. And the court assumed that the bank knew the proceeds of the crane had been deposited in the account.

The court in *Orix* held that the depository bank took the funds free of the plaintiff's superior security interest under Official Comment 2(c). As to the plaintiff's claim that the depository bank knew that encumbered proceeds had been deposited, the court said, "[A] transferee's knowledge of a prior security interest in proceeds does not, by itself, indicate that the transfer of these proceeds occurred outside the ordinary course of the debtor's business." We agree with that statement and, like the court in *Orix*, we conclude that the phrase "in the ordinary course," means that the plaintiff must establish more than a defendant's knowledge of a superior security interest: It must establish either a lack of good faith or that the payee "knows . . . that the [payment] is in violation of some term in the security agreement not waived by the words or conduct of the secured party." Mo. Ann. Stat. § 400.9-307, cmt. 2 [cf. UCC 9–320, Comment 3]; *accord Orix*, 4 F.3d at 1266-67; ITT Commercial Fin. Corp. v. Bank of the West, 166 F.3d 295, 307-08 (5th Cir.1999) (collecting and discussing authorities).

GECC's claim is weaker than the plaintiff's claim in *Orix*. In *Orix*, the balance of the cash collateral account was applied only to the line of credit and there was some evidence that the depository bank knew that the deposit at issue contained proceeds. Thus, there was at least an inference (albeit an insufficient inference for liability purposes) of the depository bank's knowledge that proceeds of a secured party's collateral had been deposited, and there was no question that the account balance was created by such funds. Here, there is no evidence that UPB knew that proceeds of GECC-financed inventory had been deposited. And, more importantly, there is no evidence that UPB knew that the account balance after all other expenses had been paid was created by such deposits. Even GECC's trial evidence shows that only about four or five percent of Machinery's $4 million in total deposits were proceeds of GECC-financed inventory, while UPB swept an amount that equaled 37.6% of the total deposits. UPB should not be charged with knowing that the remaining account balance was created by the small portion of proceeds of GECC-financed inventory that had been deposited.

If UPB did not know that the remaining account balance was traceable to the encumbered deposits, then as a matter of law it did not know that its sweeps violated the terms of GECC's security agreement with Machinery because it did not know GECC's interests were implicated. And even if UPB knew that proceeds of GECC-financed inventory had been deposited in the account and that the remaining balance had been created by the deposits, as in *Orix,* that knowledge is not enough. Given Machinery's apparent ability to deposit those funds and use the account to pay creditors, UPB surely did not know, and should not be expected to know, that its sweeps would violate a term in Machinery and GECC's security agreement that GECC had not waived.

The district court concluded that the subordination agreement "unlock[ed] the mystery to this case," holding UPB could not avoid liability by claiming it did not know that the funds it swept were encumbered by GECC's security interest. UPB argued that GECC should have required Machinery to segregate the lease payments on GECC-financed inventory from Machinery's other revenue, and that without such segregation, there was no way for UPB to know that it was being paid with proceeds of GECC-financed inventory. The court responded: "When . . . [UPB] gave up its rights to whatever [GECC] had, it should have been the party responsible for making sure that it did not violate its contractual obligations." GECC takes this to mean that the district court held that the subordination agreement imposed upon UPB an implicit contractual duty to find and segregate any funds that were deposited in which GECC may claim a security interest, and that in the face of that duty, UPB could not claim a lack of knowledge. If that is what the district court meant, it erred. First, as explained below, UPB did not give up all of its rights. Second, we will not imply a duty to segregate a debtor's deposits. Sophisticated lenders like GECC and UPB are fully able to bargain for such duties, and they know the risks associated with allowing debtors to commingle funds in a single account that is used to pay various creditors in the ordinary course of the debtor's business.

Apparently, the district court concluded that the subordination agreement meant that UPB agreed that it would not accept payment from Machinery if the funds Machinery used were produced by leasing GECC-financed inventory. The terms of the subordination agreement, however, are not that broad. UPB claimed that the sweeps from the cash management system were the conduit through which Machinery paid UPB on the line of credit. GECC did not present any evidence to the contrary, and Machinery does not appear to have paid UPB on the line of credit in any other way. Thus, UPB sufficiently established that the sweeps were payments.

Therefore, the question becomes whether the subordination agreement barred UPB from accepting such payments in the ordinary course of business if they were traceable to funds in which GECC could have claimed an interest. It did not. While UPB limited its ability to look to its security to satisfy Machinery's indebtedness by subordinating its "security interest" to GECC's, it did not promise to forego Machinery's payment of the substantial debt that Machinery owed. The cases GECC cites do not support a contrary conclusion. In the *Orix* dissent, Chief Judge Ervin based his analysis on the bank's express subordination of "any interest[]" it had in the crane and its proceeds, not simply the bank's subordination of its security interest. In Safeco Credit Co. v. U.S. Bancorp Leasing & Fin., Inc., 833 F.Supp. 833 (D.Or.1993), the court based its conclusion on the bank's express subordination of "any security interest, lien, claim or right, now or hereafter asserted . . . with respect to the [loader] or the cash or non-cash proceeds of the [loader]." And in HCC Credit Corp. v. Springs Valley Bank & Trust, 712 N.E.2d 952, 958 (Ind.1999), the court was describing a situation in which a secondary lender subordinates its *debt* to the secured party or otherwise excludes "the debtor's obligations to the secured lender in computing the debtor's borrowing base." All are inapposite.

At most, the subordination agreement in this case ensured that UPB was a junior secured creditor[4] and firmly established that UPB knew of GECC's security interest in some of Machinery's inventory and its proceeds. But even a junior secured creditor that knows of its junior status can be paid in the ordinary course of business. GECC had to show more.

We conclude the district court erred in holding that the payments from Machinery to UPB were not in the ordinary course of Machinery's business. We decline, however, to direct the district court to enter summary judgment in UPB's favor. The district court based its conclusion on the subordination agreement, and we have concluded that agreement does not carry the day. And while we have strong doubts as to whether any other evidence establishes the requisite wrongdoing for January and February, March is a closer question. . . . . Because GECC may be able to prevail at trial, at least for the March sweeps, we vacate the district court's grant of summary judgment and remand the case for further proceedings.

2. How Equitable Tracing Works in this Case

As indicated, GECC may be able to establish that some of UPB's sweeps occurred outside of the ordinary course of business, enabling it to use equitable tracing principles to establish that the funds UPB received were identifiable proceeds of GECC-financed inventory. Because the district court ruled on how GECC may trace deposited funds to UPB's sweeps, and because the parties have briefed the issue, we address the matter.

When funds from multiple sources are deposited to the same account and subsequent payments are made from the account, it becomes difficult, if not impossible, to determine whether the subsequent payments are

---

4.   The subordination agreement also does not clearly make UPB junior with regard to the funds at issue. For example, the language does not bind UPB to subordinate future security interests it may obtain in the property or its proceeds. The agreement was executed in March 2000, and GECC appears to claim that UPB subordinated the security interest it obtained the next month in conjunction with the line of credit. Also, despite an artful quotation by GECC—"cash . . . and non-cash proceeds," App. Reply Br. at 2 (alteration in original)—the phrase, "cash, rents and non-cash proceeds" from the subordination agreement does not use "cash" as an adjective to modify "proceeds." It appears as a noun, like "rents."

traceable to the initial deposits. Equity, though, can serve as a means of attributing rights in such a commingled account by tracing the subsequent payments to particular deposits. And, as the district court held, Missouri law recognizes the use of equitable tracing principles to identify a secured party's interest in a commingled deposit account.

As an initial matter, we reject GECC's attempt to characterize the use of equitable tracing principles as a way of measuring damages. The measure of damages in a conversion action "is generally the fair market value of the property at the time and place of the conversion." Equitable tracing, on the other hand, allows a plaintiff to establish that the credit created by the deposit of encumbered funds was used to make a payment or a withdrawal. While tracing is a "tool to permit the calculation of damages at the time of conversion," Meyer v. Norwest Bank Iowa, 112 F.3d 946, 951 (8th Cir.1997), it is not a measure of damages. It is the primary means of demonstrating the plaintiff's rights, and therefore the defendant's liability, in cases involving commingled accounts. This case illustrates that premise. Without equitable tracing, GECC cannot make out a claim for conversion because it cannot establish that the funds allegedly converted were identifiable proceeds in which it had a security interest.

In its summary-judgment order, the district court held that the lowest intermediate balance rule could be applied to Machinery's parent account. But at the damages trial, it concluded that a pro-rata methodology based on the total deposits, withdrawals, and sweeps over the relevant period was more appropriate because the lowest intermediate balance rule yielded a result of zero. Under its pro-rata rationale, the district court concluded that GECC could recover 37.6% of the total GECC proceeds deposited because UPB swept 37.6% of the total deposits.

The parties have cited no Missouri cases utilizing a pro-rata tracing methodology like that employed in this case, and we have found none. Thus, we conclude that the lowest intermediate balance rule is the only tracing method available in this litigation.

But the district court erred in concluding that a proper application of the lowest intermediate balance rule yielded a result of zero. Because UPB received the funds at different times over the course of the three months, and GECC's conversion claim is based on UPB's sweeps, the analysis must look to those transactions. "Under the lowest intermediate balance rule, it is assumed the traced proceeds are the last funds withdrawn from a contested account. Once the traced proceeds are withdrawn, however, they are treated as lost, even though subsequent deposits are made into the account." Id. at 951 (citation omitted). The district court concluded that because the account was zeroed out by UPB sweeps and other payments, the traced proceeds were therefore gone. That conclusion would be appropriate if GECC's claim were based on the account balance *after* UPB swept the account. But GECC's claim is based on UPB's sweeps. Thus, Machinery's account balance *at the time* UPB swept it is the relevant account balance. By the very occurrence of the sweep, we know the balance of the account was not zero at that time. An appropriate application of the lowest intermediate balance rule would therefore focus on attributing the account balance at that time to preceding deposits of GECC proceeds.

Of course, a zero balance in the parent account after a deposit of GECC proceeds but before a UPB sweep would mean all of the credit that resulted from the deposit of GECC proceeds had been exhausted and, thus, lost. So the time frame the court must look to ends with a UPB sweep and begins with the immediately preceding zero balance. If GECC proceeds were deposited after the immediately preceding zero balance, they may be traced to UPB's sweep through an ordinary application of the lowest intermediate balance rule. Thus, the funds UPB swept on a given day will be deemed identifiable proceeds of GECC-encumbered deposits to the extent post-deposit withdrawals that precede the sweep didn't reduce the account balance below the amount of those encumbered deposits.

A hypothetical explains this proposition. If UPB swept the account on March 16 and received $20,000, then the court should look back to the immediately preceding zero balance. If that event occurred on March 15 (either through a transfer to the operating accounts or a previous UPB sweep), the court begins its application of the lowest intermediate balance rule there. After the preceding zero balance, assume that (1) $10,000 in GECC proceeds were deposited, (2) then $50,000 of other funds were deposited, (3) then $55,000 were transferred to the operating accounts to cover expenses, and (4) then $15,000 of other funds were deposited. The following chart represents the deposits, withdrawals, and account balances during the relevant time frame.

GECC Proceeds Deposits	Other Deposits	Withdrawals	Account Balance
$ 10,000			$ 10,000
	$ 50,000		$ 60,000
		($ 55,000)	$ 5,000
	$ 15,000		$ 20,000

On these facts, GECC would be able to trace $5,000 of deposited proceeds in which it had a security interest, through the account, to the funds UPB received. Its other $5,000 interest in the account would be lost because after the $10,000 of GECC proceeds were deposited, the account balance dropped to $5,000 when $55,000 were transferred to the operating accounts. The subsequent deposit of $15,000 did not replenish GECC's interest in the account.

We recognize that the facts upon which this analysis must proceed could be difficult to establish. But that problem does not entitle a plaintiff to recover on a conversion claim without establishing what property was converted.

. . .

NOTES ON CASH PROCEEDS

(1) Transferees of Cash Proceeds. In General Electric Credit Corp. v. Union Planters Bank, supra, the court grapples with the question whether certain payments that UPB received from Machinery's bank account were encumbered by GECC's security interest. The answer turns in part on whether GECC's proceeds actually were deposited into the bank account. (Some of them were. See Note (3) on Security Interests in Proceeds, supra.) Inasmuch as GECC's proceeds were commingled with other deposits, it also turns on whether the particular funds that were paid to UPB were encumbered by GECC's security interest. The following Note discusses how equitable tracing principles may be used to determine whether proceeds or non-proceeds have been withdrawn from a commingled bank account.

Part II.B.1 of the *GECC* opinion recognizes that certain (indeed, most) recipients take payments free of security interests; as against these recipients, any attempt to use equitable tracing principles to establish a security interest in the funds would be unavailing. You may have noticed that the "UCC provision" on which the court relies is not a statutory provision at all; rather, it is a comment to Former 9–306. Courts may have been attracted to the comment because it squared with their intuition that a creditor who has been paid normally should be able to keep the payment. See Restatement of Restitution §§ 172 (acquirer of property for value and without notice of circumstances that would subject property to constructive trust does not take subject to constructive trust); 173 (transfer of property in satisfaction of pre-existing debt is for value) (1937). (Indeed, the text of Former Article 9 may be silent on whether recipients of cash proceeds take free of a security interest because the drafters thought the answer—that "recipients of the funds *of course* take free" of any security interest—was obvious.)

As the *GECC* court observes, the text of the UCC now addresses this question; resort to the comments no longer is necessary. See UCC 9–332. To what extent does UCC 9–332 follow the case law under Former Article 9? Courts generally have construed Former Article 9 to be quite protective of those who receive funds from deposit accounts containing proceeds: A recipient of funds take free of a security interest unless the secured party establishes that the recipient lacks good faith or knows that the payment violates the security agreement. Is a recipient who lacks good faith or who knows that the payment violates a security agreement eligible for protection under UCC 9–332?

More specifically, would UCC 9–332 have afforded UPB more or less protection than Former Article 9? Consider, in this regard, the court's discussion of the March payment:

> [W]hile we have strong doubts as to whether any other evidence establishes the requisite wrongdoing for January and February, March is a closer question. In March, Machinery was in default on its obligation to UPB, GECC contacted UPB and demanded that UPB turn over all proceeds of GECC-financed inventory (albeit without

mentioning the amount or any way of identifying particular proceeds), and UPB had taken a much more active role in Machinery's operations, requiring Machinery to justify its expenses to UPB and sweeping a larger percentage of deposited funds in that month than in either of the two preceding months. See Barber-Greene Co. v. Nat'l Bank of Minneapolis, 816 F.2d 1267, 1272 (8th Cir.1987) (concluding that a depository bank's total control over the account from which payment was made took the transfer out of the ordinary-course language of Official Comment 2(c)).

409 F.3d at 1058. Had UCC 9–332 been in effect, would the court have been able to conclude (as it did under Former Article 9) that "GECC may be able to prevail at trial, at least for the March sweeps"?

Although the court characterizes the action of UPB in "sweeping" the account as a "payment," it might well have treated it as a "setoff." Setoffs are discussed in Chapter 8, Section 4(D), infra.

(2) Tracing and Commingled Cash Proceeds. We have seen that a security interest attaches to "any *identifiable* proceeds" of collateral and remains perfected in *"identifiable* cash proceeds" beyond the 20–day period. UCC 9–315(a)(2) & (d)(2). Problems 3.5.1 through 3.5.8 involved proceeds (or putative proceeds)—goods, intangibles, and cash proceeds such as money or checks—that clearly were "identifiable." Problem 3.5.9 and the *GECC* case, however, considered deposit accounts in which proceeds and non-proceeds had been commingled. As you know, a depositor has no property interest in specific coins or currency deposited in a bank or other depositary institution. Clearly, then, once cash proceeds are deposited in a deposit account containing non-proceeds, the cash proceeds are not "identifiable" in the same sense as the proceeds considered earlier in this section. They become even less "identifiable" as the debtor makes withdrawals from, and deposits into, the deposit account.

Former Article 9, under which *GECC* was decided, did not explain exactly what it meant for proceeds to be "identifiable." Like many others, the *GECC* court reached for a legal fiction—the "lowest intermediate balance rule" ("LIBR")—to identify what otherwise would not have been identifiable. Courts have developed tracing rules, including LIBR, in an effort to afford an equitable, restitutionary remedy to victims of wrongdoing. For example, LIBR applies to trust funds that are commingled with a trustee's individual funds. To prevent the trust from being dissipated, the rule presumes that payments from the commingled account were made from the trustee's individual contribution and not from the trust funds. See Restatement (2d) of Trusts § 202 (1959). Is the case for tracing as strong in the context of proceeds of a secured creditor's collateral as it is when a trustee has misappropriated trust funds? Might the courts easily have concluded that cash proceeds lose their identity upon commingling?[4]

---

4.   Although there is some early authority supporting the position that proceeds cease to be identifiable upon deposit in a commingled bank account, since 1973 the reported cases uniformly have allowed a secured party to employ tracing principles in

Application of LIBR in the commingled deposit account context has provoked considerable scholarly debate. In general, the commentary gives the approach mixed reviews. Notwithstanding their abundance, the scholarly critiques seem to have had little, if any, influence on the judiciary; nor have there been other indications of dissatisfaction with the current state of the law. Unlike Former Article 9, Revised Article 9 specifically addresses the question of commingled funds. See UCC 9–315(b)(2) & Comment 3. What, exactly, does UCC 9–315(b)(2) mean? When *may* a court use LIBR? When *must* it do so?

Commingled cash proceeds in deposit accounts is not the only example of commingling that can affect Article 9 security interests. The identity of goods can be lost through manufacturing or production (e.g., flour that has become part of baked goods) as well as by commingling with other goods from which they cannot be distinguished (e.g., ball bearings). UCC 9–336 explains the extent to which a security interest attaches to the product or mass into which "commingled goods"—whether original collateral or proceeds—have been commingled.

_____

Problem 3.5.10. In the setting of the Prototype, assume that Lee Abel had just turned 18 and had never applied for credit before. As a condition of extending purchase-money credit, Main and Firstbank required that a person with a good credit history undertake the obligation to repay the debt secured by the Chevrolet. Lee Abel's aunt, Bea, signed a guaranty, in which she agreed to perform Lee's obligations under the Instalment Sale Contract (Form 3.6, supra).

(a) Why did Main and Firstbank require a guaranty? Wouldn't the security interest in the Chevrolet insure the full repayment of Abel's debt? See Note on Supporting Obligations, infra.

(b) Why do you suppose Bea Abel agreed to sign the guaranty?

(c) Does Firstbank have a security interest in Main's rights under the guaranty? If so, is the security interest perfected? See UCC 9–102(a)(77), (a)(71); UCC 9–203(f); UCC 9–308(d).

NOTE ON SUPPORTING OBLIGATIONS

As in Problem 3.5.10, extenders of credit not infrequently require, as a condition of extending credit, that a financially responsible third party guaranty payment of the debt. Apparently Abel's credit rating and income were not adequate to justify the extension of $18,380.50 credit, even though the credit was secured by a Chevrolet having a retail price of $27,056. Do

_____

order to claim a continuing perfected security interest in a commingled deposit account. The case law all seems to be directly or indirectly traceable to Universal C.I.T. Credit Corp. v. Farmers Bank of Portageville, 358 F.Supp. 317 (E.D.Mo.1973), and the cases generally have invoked LIBR as the tracing principle.

you see why? In business settings, the shareholders and officers of a closely-held corporation typically are required to guaranty loans made to the corporation. In many cases this is not so much to have a "deep pocket" to which the lender may turn if the debtor becomes insolvent; the fortunes of the shareholders and officers are likely to rise and fall with that of the corporation. Instead, it is an effective and persuasive mechanism to keep the individuals on the job and interested in the success of the venture.

In Article 9 terminology, a third-party guarantor is a "secondary obligor."[5] A secondary obligor's secondary obligation is a "supporting obligation" if it supports one of the types of collateral specified in the definition of the term. UCC 9–102(a)(77).[6] For example, in the setting of the Prototype and Problem 3.5.10, the secondary obligation of Lee Abel's Aunt Bea is a supporting obligation because it supports Lee Abel's payment and performance obligations under the Instalment Sale Contract, which is chattel paper. Recall that in the Prototype Firstbank advanced funds against the chattel paper, the collateral. Naturally, Firstbank expects that its perfected security interest in the chattel paper will extend to collections from Lee Abel; these collections would be proceeds of the chattel paper. But what are Firstbank's rights with respect to collections from Aunt Bea? As UCC 9–203, Comment 8, explains, "Under subsection (f), a security interest in a 'supporting obligation'... automatically follows from a security interest in the underlying, supported collateral." Moreover, if the security interest in the underlying collateral is perfected, then the security interest in the supporting obligation is perfected as well. UCC 9–308(d). In short, Firstbank's perfected security interest in the Instalment Sale Contract (chattel paper) carries with it a perfected security interest in collections on Aunt Bea's guaranty.[7]

5.   Secondary obligors and the law of suretyship, which governs secondary obligations, are addressed in more detail in Chapter 9, Section 3(A), infra.

6.   A letter-of-credit right (defined in UCC 9–102(a)(51)) also may be a supporting obligation.

7.   Former Article 9 did not specifically address supporting obligations for collateral. However, most would agree that collections from Aunt Bea under her guaranty of Abel's obligations under the chattel paper would have been proceeds of the chattel paper itself under Former Article 9. See UCC 9–203, Comment 8 (the treatment of supporting obligations under UCC 9–203(f) "was implicit under former Article 9").

CHAPTER 4

CONFLICTING CLAIMS TO COLLATERAL

The preceding Chapter dealt primarily with whether a security interest is enforceable against the debtor and would withstand attack from judicial lien creditors. This Chapter deals with other claims to the collateral, primarily claims by holders of conflicting security interests and by buyers and lessees of the collateral from the debtor. Sections 3 and 4 expand upon earlier discussions of judicial liens and reclaiming sellers, respectively.

SECTION 1. COMPETING SECURITY INTERESTS

INTRODUCTORY NOTE

Prior to enactment of the UCC, conflicts between security interests had to be resolved under circumstances that approached anarchy. Only some of the security "devices" (chattel mortgage, conditional sale, trust receipt, assignment of accounts, factor's lien) had the benefit of statutory priority rules; even these rules almost invariably were rudimentary and were confined to conflicts between security interests created by the same "device." When separate security worlds would collide (e.g., conditional sale vs. trust receipt; assignment of accounts vs. factor's lien), the outcome was wildly unpredictable. The total effect was bearable only for one who had a taste for case-law improvisation or for chaos.

In bringing all personal property security under one roof, the UCC exposed the wide variety of priority problems that had been lurking in the crannies among the various types of chattel security; the drafters met a scene that makes one think of Noah when he came to the room in the Ark reserved for snakes.

Even in the initial version of Article 9, by a happy marriage of theory and practical experience, the drafters developed a priority system that created a kind of order. Experience and further thought during the UCC's first two decades produced significant refinements that were reflected in the 1972 revision of Former Article 9. The priority rules of Revised Article 9 reflect yet additional refinements.[1]

---

1. Revised Article 9 also carries forward, with minor changes, the special priority rules governing security interests in investment property which accompanied the 1994 revision of UCC Article 8. These rules were adapted to govern the priority of security

Interestingly, Article 9 does not define or explain (at least not directly) the concept of "priority." What does it mean to say that one claim has "priority" over another or that one claim is "senior" or "junior" to another? One answer is that the claimant with priority, the senior claimant, is entitled to have its claim satisfied first from the value of the collateral involved. The junior claimant, then, could look to the remaining value, if any. However, as we shall consider in Chapter 9, Section 3(B), even in the absence of any action or participation by a senior claimant, a junior claimant sometimes can enforce its security interest by collecting or disposing of collateral after the debtor's default.

(A) THE FIRST–TO–FILE–OR–PERFECT RULE

Problem 4.1.1. On June 1 *D*, a dealer in mink pelts, obtained a $50,000 loan from *SP*–1 and as security delivered to *SP*–1 pelts of equivalent value. *SP–1* did not file a financing statement.

On July 1 *D* obtained a $50,000 loan from *SP*–2 and authenticated a security agreement granting to *SP*–2 a security interest in all mink pelts owned by *D*. *SP*–2 immediately filed a financing statement covering "mink pelts."

(a) *D* defaults on the debts to *SP*–1 and *SP*–2. *D*'s principal assets are the pelts delivered to *SP*–1. Do both *SP*–1 and *SP*–2 have a security interest in the pelts? Is each security interest perfected? Whose security interest is senior? See UCC 9–322(a)(1) & Comment 4; UCC 9–310(a), (b)(6); Notes (1) and (2) on the First-to-File-or-Perfect Rule, infra. What could the losing party have done to avoid the loss?

(b) Reverse the order of the transactions in part (a): The transaction with *SP*–2 (including filing) occurred on June 1, and the transaction with *SP*–1 occurred on July 1. In this setting whose security interest is senior? What could the losing party have done to avoid the loss?

(c) Now assume that *SP*–2 filed the financing statement on June 1 but did not make the loan or obtain a security agreement at that time. On July 1 the transaction with *SP*–1 occurred (including the loan and delivery of the pelts). On August 1 *SP*–2 made the loan to *D* and *D* signed the security agreement. Whose security interest is senior? What could the losing party have done to avoid the loss? See UCC 9–513(c), (d); UCC 9–339.

Problem 4.1.2. On June 1 *D*, a dealer in soybeans, borrowed $200,000 from *SP*–1. *D* granted to *SP*–1 a security interest in all soybeans that *D* then owned or might thereafter acquire, to secure the $200,000 loan and any other indebtedness of *D* to *SP*–1 that might arise in the future. *SP*–1 filed a financing statement covering "soybeans, now owned or hereafter acquired." On June 1 *D* owned and held in its granaries approximately 50,000 bushels of soybeans with a market price of $5.00 per bushel (i.e.,

interests in deposit accounts. See Chapter 6, Sections 3 and 4, infra (discussing priority of security interests in investment property and deposit accounts).

with an aggregate value of $250,000). During the summer and fall D made many purchases and sales of soybeans, but the amount held in the granaries remained in the vicinity of 50,000 bushels; also, the price remained in the neighborhood of $5.00 per bushel.

By September 1 D's payments to SP–1 had reduced the debt from $200,000 to $25,000. On that date D applied to SP–2 for a loan and showed SP–2 cancelled checks showing payments to SP–1 and current statements from SP–1 to D that accurately reported the current balance of $25,000 owing to SP–1. SP–2 thereupon loaned D $150,000, took a written security agreement covering D's soybeans, and filed a financing statement.

On September 15 SP–1 made a further loan to D of $175,000; SP–1's financing statement of June 1 remained on file throughout.

(a) On October 1 D defaulted on the loans to both SP–1 and SP–2. Who has the senior security interest in the 50,000 bushels of soybeans in D's granaries? See UCC 9–204(c); UCC 9–322(a)(1); UCC 9–323(a) & Comment 3; Note (3) on the First-to-File-or-Perfect Rule, infra. What should the losing party have done to protect itself? See UCC 9–339; UCC 9–513(c), (d); UCC 9–514(b); UCC 9–511(b).

(b) Would the result in part (a) change if, on September 1, SP–2 gave written notice of its transaction to SP–1? See UCC 9–322(a)(1); UCC 9–323(a).

(c) Would the result in part (a) change if, on September 1, when SP–2 made the loan of $150,000 to D, D's debt to SP–1 had been reduced to zero? (As above, the financing statement remained on file, and on September 15 SP–1 made a further loan of $175,000.) See UCC 9–322(a)(1); UCC 9–323(a).

(d) Would the result in part (a) change if SP–1's security agreement secured payment of "all amounts due and to become due under D's promissory note in the amount of $200,000 of even date herewith" and SP–1's September 15 loan was evidenced by a new promissory note in the amount of $175,000? If so, what should the losing party have done to protect itself?

(e) In preparing to apply for a loan from SP–2, D presented to SP–1 on September 1 a signed "request regarding a statement of account" under UCC 9–210. The request indicated what D believed to be the aggregate amount of unpaid obligations secured by collateral on September 1 of $25,000 and reasonably identified the transaction. D requested that SP–1 approve or correct the statement and return it to D. SP–1 wrote "approved" on the statement, signed it, and returned it to D. D showed this statement to SP–2 in applying for the $150,000 loan that SP–2 thereupon extended to D. On September 15 SP–1 extended to D a further loan of $175,000, as described above. On D's default on October 1, who has the senior security interest in D's 50,000 bushels of soybeans? What should the losing party have done to protect itself?

NOTES ON THE FIRST–TO–FILE–OR–PERFECT RULE

(1) Article 9's Basic Rule on Priority Among Competing Security Interests: A Complex Excursus to Explain a Basic Rule. UCC 9–322(a)(1) gives legal priority to a security interest that is prior in time with respect to either "filing or perfection." It may seem odd, at first glance, that legal priority is given to the interest that is first in time with respect to *either* filing *or* perfection. Wouldn't the party who *files* first also be first as to *perfection* of a security interest? If so, why not omit the reference to perfection? To state the basic rule solely in terms of who files first would not be adequate, since in some situations security interests can be perfected without filing. See UCC 9–310(b); Chapter 3, Section 3, supra.

A more complex question is this: Why doesn't Article 9 simply say that legal priority is given to the security interest that is *perfected* first? Why is there also a reference to filing? For most ordinary security transactions, the simpler first-to-perfect rule would be adequate. But in many common commercial transactions, particularly those in which the collateral includes after-acquired property (see, e.g., Problem 4.1.2, supra), filing may precede "perfection."

This distinction between filing and perfection results from the interplay of UCC 9–308 and UCC 9–203. Consider the following example: Bank files a financing statement on June 1 and makes a secured loan to Debtor on July 1. UCC 9–308(a) provides that a security interest is not "perfected" unless it has "attached." UCC 9–203(b) lays down a series of requirements for enforceability and thus for "attachment": (a) authentication of a security agreement (or the secured party's possession or control of the collateral pursuant to a security agreement); (b) the giving of value by the secured party; and (c) the debtor's having rights in the collateral. UCC 9–203(b) tells us that Bank's security interest did not "attach" until July, when Bank gave "value" and took an authenticated security agreement. And we have just learned from UCC 9–308(a) that a security interest must "attach" before it is "perfected." Thus, "perfection" did not occur until July 1, although filing took place a month earlier.

Why does Article 9 go to such lengths to provide that "perfection" of a security interest, in some circumstances, will not occur at filing? Was all this designed to lead to the result that a security interest that is filed before any other security interest will be subordinate to a security interest that is filed later but is the first to reach "perfection"? Quite the contrary. Let us return to the basic priority rule in UCC 9–322(a)(1): "Conflicting perfected security interests . . . rank according to priority in time of filing *or* perfection." Suppose that *A* files on June 1, that *B* files and makes a secured loan on June 15, and that *A* makes a secured loan on July 1. Under the basic rule of UCC 9–322(a)(1), the prevailing security interest is the one that is first *either* to file *or* to perfect. *A* filed before *B* either filed *or* perfected. Consequently, *A*'s security interest prevails over *B*'s. See UCC 9–322, Comment 4, Example 1.

The drafters thought these intricacies necessary to address the setting of continuing financing arrangements where credits and collateral ebb and flow—the "floating lien." (The financing of Main Motors' inventory in the Prototype is an example of the "floating lien." This type of financing is discussed in detail in Chapter 7, Section 2(B), infra.) Moreover, in many ordinary financings the creditor extends "value" at a time when the other elements of "attachment" (UCC 9–203) and "perfection" (UCC 9–308) already have been satisfied. When filing and perfection occur together, there is no occasion to distinguish between the separate elements in the basic rule of UCC 9–322(a)(1): filing *or* perfection. Perhaps it would have been better to state Article 9's basic rule on priority in a way so that it could be applied to simple financing transactions without worrying about the significance of language that was designed for more complex (albeit not uncommon) situations. Be that as it may, the current rule affords secured parties the opportunity to fix their place in line by filing a financing statement even before the details of a secured loan have been finalized.

(2) Guarding Against Prior Security Interests: The Two–Step Ideal. Assume that Bank is considering making a loan to Debtor, and that the loan will be extended only if secured by certain assets of Debtor. How can Bank be sure that there is no outstanding security interest that will take priority? As we have seen from Chapter 3, Section 3(B), supra, and from UCC 9–310(b), checking the public records will not, alone, give Bank the assurance it desires. But let us suppose that the cautious Bank takes two steps: (1) It ascertains that Debtor is in possession of the collateral; and (2) it checks the public records and finds that no other creditor has filed a financing statement.[2] Under these circumstances is Bank safe from outstanding security interests? The answer is: Yes—in most situations, but not in all. For instance, a creditor who wants to be sure there is no outstanding security interest that will receive priority also will need to consider whether the collateral, or the situation, is of a type that might fall within one of the other exceptions from the filing requirement that are listed in UCC 9–310(b). Happily, most of these exceptions are limited either as to type of collateral or as to the period of temporary perfection.

(3) Future Advances. As we have seen, collateral may secure future as well as past or present advances if the parties so agree. See UCC 9–204(c); Chapter 3, Section 2, supra. A strict application of the first-to-file-

---

2. Checking the public record may prove to be easier said than done. We have seen several Article 9 provisions under which financing statements remain effective even though the facts governing the location of the filing and the content of the statement have changed. See, e.g., UCC 9–316(a) (financing statement remains effective after debtor changes its location) (discussed in Chapter 3, Section 4, supra); UCC 9–315(d) (financing statement covering one type of collateral may be effective to perfect a security interest in another type of collateral constituting proceeds) (discussed in Chapter 3, Section 5, supra); UCC 9–507(c) (financing statement remains effective as to certain collateral even after debtor's name changes) (discussed in Chapter 3, Section 3(A), supra, and Chapter 8, Section 1, infra).

or-perfect rule of UCC 9–322(a)(1) would seem to leave no room for determining priority of security interests based on the time that value is given, except when a financing statement was not filed and the advance is the giving of value as the last step for attachment and perfection. (Of course, if a first-filed secured party *never* gives value, it will not be entitled to any of the benefits of a security interest.)

As a general matter, then, all advances securing a security interest enjoy the same priority under UCC 9–322(a)(1). However, UCC 9–323(a) sets forth certain narrow circumstances under which the priority of an advance does not date from the time of filing or perfection:

> when the security interest is perfected only automatically under Section 9–309 or temporarily under Section 9–312(e), (f), or (g), and the advance is not made pursuant to a commitment entered into while the security interest was perfected by another method. Thus, an advance has priority from the date it is made only in the rare case in which it is made without commitment and while the security interest is perfected only temporarily under Section 9–312.

UCC 9–323, Comment 3.[3]

As we have seen, some courts evidenced a hostility to future advance clauses by construing them narrowly. See Note, p. 145, supra. This hostility also was evidenced in decisions denying priority to future advances, even if made by the first–filed secured party. Consider an example:

> On March 1, 2002, D entered into a security agreement granting to *SP*–1 a security interest in an item of equipment to secure a new $100,000 loan. *SP*–1 perfected by filing on March 2 a financing statement covering "all equipment now owned or hereafter acquired." By December 1, 2002, D paid the loan in full. There was no commitment by *SP*–1 to give further value, and the entire transaction between *SP*–1 and D came to an end. On February 3, 2003, D obtained a $500,000 loan from *SP*–2 and entered into a security agreement granting to *SP*–2 a security interest in all of D's equipment. *SP*–2 perfected by filing a financing statement on the same day. On January 15, 2006, D obtained another $100,000 loan from *SP*–1 and entered into a new security agreement granting to *SP*–1 a security interest in all of D's equipment.

Whose security interest has priority? Both UCC 9–322(a) and its predecessor, Former 9–312(5), could not be more clear on this point. By virtue of having the first-filed financing statement, filed back in 2002, *SP*–1 holds the senior security interest. That the parties' intention and motivation for the filing arose in connection with a long-since completed transaction under a security agreement that did not secure future advances has no impact on application of the first-to-file-or-perfect rule. Nonetheless, some

---

3.   As we shall see, the timing of advances can be relevant to sorting out priorities between secured parties and certain buyers (see UCC 9–323(d), considered in Section 2, infra), lien creditors (see UCC 9–323(b), considered in Section 3, infra), and the United States (see Chapter 8, Section 4(E), infra).

early cases refused to give *SP*–1 its due priority. In one notorious opinion, the court expressed concern that affording priority to *SP*–1 "places a lender in an unusually strong position, vis-a-vis, the debtor and any subsequent lenders. In fact, it gives the lender a throttle hold on the debtor." Coin–O–Matic Service Co. v. Rhode Island Hospital Trust Co., 3 U.C.C. Rep. Serv. 1112, 1116 (R.I.Super.Ct.1966). Was that a legitimate concern? Most later cases were to the contrary. What went wrong for *SP*–2 was not the harshness of the first-to-file-or-perfect rule. It was, instead, either *SP*–2's careless failure to search the filing office or its foolishness in proceeding in the face of *SP*–1's filing. Observe that had *SP*–2 insisted that *SP*–1's filing be terminated, *SP*–1 would have been obliged to terminate the financing statement had D made an authenticated demand on *SP*–1 to do so. See UCC 9–513(c).

Problem 4.1.3. *SP*–1 perfected a security interest in certain collateral by filing a financing statement in May, 2002. It is now July, 2007.

(a) In April, 2007, the debtor created a security interest in the same collateral in favor of *SP*–2, who immediately perfected the security interest by filing. *SP*–2 had actual knowledge of *SP*–1's security interest. Which security interest is senior? See UCC 9–515(a), (c) & Comment 3. What, if anything, could the holder of the junior security interest have done to prevent the loss? See UCC 9–515(c), (d); UCC 9–102(a)(27); UCC 9–521(b).

(b) Should one inclined toward the "good faith" principle, discussed in the *Shallcross* and *Lowry* cases, infra, apply that principle to preserve *SP*–1's priority over *SP*–2 notwithstanding UCC 9–515(c)? Cf. Frank v. James Talcott, Inc., 692 F.2d 734 (11th Cir.1982) (lapse of first-filed financing statement rendered secured party unperfected and subordinate to second-to-file secured party; the latter's knowledge of the earlier-in-time security interest was not relevant) (decided under 1962 lapse provisions); School Board of Broward County v. J.V. Construction Corp., 2004 U.S. Dist. LEXIS 9815 (S.D.Fla. Apr. 23, 2004) (citing *Frank* and reaching the same conclusion on effect of lapse under UCC 9-515(c)). Has *SP*–2 acted dishonestly, violated reasonable commercial standards of fair dealing, or otherwise misbehaved in any way that would warrant continued subordination of *SP*–2's security interest notwithstanding the lapse of *SP*–1's financing statement? See UCC 1–304 [F1–203]; UCC 9–102(a)(43).

(c) The facts are as in part (a). In March, 2007, Elsie acquired an execution lien on the collateral. How should the three competing claims be ranked? See UCC 9–317(a)(2); UCC 9–515(c) & Comment 3; UCC 1–201(b)(29) [F1–201(32)]; Note (4) on the Role of Knowledge in Priority Contests, infra.

Problem 4.1.4. John Brown owns, as a sole proprietor, a shoe store. Brown created a security interest in the store's inventory in favor of Lender, who filed a financing statement covering "inventory." Due to a clerical error by one of Lender's paralegals, the financing statement indicated that Brown's mailing address was "2425 Chicago Ave., Springfield IL." The correct address was "2425 Springfield Ave., Chicago, IL." Sometime thereafter, Brown approached Finco for inventory financing. Before closing the loan, Finco sought and received from the filing office information concerning all financing statements naming "Brown, John" as debtor. See UCC 9–523(c). The filing office provided information concerning dozens of such financing statements, including the one filed by Lender. After reviewing the information provided by the filing office, Finco proceeded to close the inventory loan.

(a) Is Lender's security interest perfected? See UCC 9–502(a).

(b) Which security interest has priority? See UCC 9–338.

(c) Would the results in parts (a) and (b) change if Lender's financing statement had failed to provide any mailing address for the debtor? See UCC 9–520(c), (a); UCC 9–516(b)(5)(A); UCC 9–502(a).

(d) Would the results in parts (a) and (b) change if Finco had requested information concerning financing statements naming "Brown, John" of 2425 Springfield Ave., Chicago, IL, as debtor? See UCC 9–338; UCC 9–523(c).

––––––––

The following two cases test whether a secured party's knowledge or conduct may deprive the secured party of the benefits of the first-to-file-or-perfect rule under Former 9–312(5). Although the cases were decided under Former Article 9, the discussions remain relevant to the first-to-file-or-perfect rule of UCC 9–322(a)(1).

Shallcross v. Community State Bank & Trust Co. [*]

Superior Court of New Jersey, Law Division, 1981.
180 N.J.Super. 273, 434 A.2d 671.

■ LONG, J. S. C.

This case involves a novel issue arising out of a priority dispute between two secured creditors. The facts are as follows:

Plaintiff is Lawrence Shallcross, the president of Shallcross and Pace Sheet Metal Works. In February 1977 Shallcross had a discussion with Raymond Dunphey, president of R. Dunphey Sheet Metal Works, Inc., concerning a Wysong shear owned by Shallcross and an RAS shear owned by Dunphey. According to Shallcross, Dunphey wanted to purchase plaintiff's shear but could not then afford it. It was agreed that Shallcross would deliver the Wysong shear to Dunphey, and if Dunphey paid the purchase price of $13,500 within six months, Shallcross would transfer title to him. It was also agreed that if Dunphey sold its RAS shear within the six-month period, Shallcross was to be paid at that time. Dunphey took possession of the Wysong shear on or about February 25, 1977 and the terms of the above oral agreement were set forth in a letter dated March 4, 1977.

––––––

[*]   [The court's citations are to the applicable pre–1972 version of the UCC.]

In January 1978 Dunphey sold its RAS shear and Shallcross sought payment for the Wysong shear. In June, 1978, Shallcross and Dunphey renegotiated the price of the Wysong shear downward to $11,250 when Dunphey indicated that only $10,000 had been received for its RAS shear. Dunphey agreed to make monthly payments of $356.95. On June 29, 1978 a bill of sale, promissory note, financing statement and security agreement were signed by plaintiff and Dunphey, and on July 12, 1978 the financing statement was filed. Dunphey made three of the monthly payments and then defaulted.

In the interim, defendant Community State Bank and Trust Company (hereinafter, the bank) entered into a loan transaction and security agreement with Dunphey on June 19, 1978. The Wysong shear was listed as one of the items of collateral for the loan, and the security agreement contained an after-acquired property clause. Pursuant to this agreement the bank loaned Dunphey $50,000 on the date of the agreement and an additional $40,000 on December 15, 1978, in accordance with the provision for future advances. This security agreement was filed on June 23, 1978. Dunphey defaulted in the payment of the loan and the shear was sold by the bank to offset the debt under the terms of this security agreement. When Shallcross attempted to satisfy Dunphey's obligation to him by obtaining possession of the shear, he found that the collateral was no longer available. Shallcross has sued the bank for wrongful conversion of the shear. The bank now moves for summary judgment, claiming that there are no genuine issues of fact and that it clearly had priority in the collateral under the provisions of Article 9 of the Uniform Commercial Code, N.J.S.A. 12A:9–101 et seq.

Article 9 lays out the framework upon which competing security interests can be evaluated and priorities established. In this regard, N.J.S.A. 12A:9–312(5) provides in relevant part that

> In all cases not governed by other rules stated in this section (including cases of purchase money security interests which do not qualify for the special priorities set forth in subsections (3) and (4) of this section), priority between conflicting security interests in the same collateral shall be determined as follows: (a) in the order of filing if both are perfected by filing, regardless of which security interest attaches first under 12A:9–204(1) and whether it attaches before or after filing. . ..

Here, it is undisputed that the bank filed first in time and therefore perfected its security interest prior to Shallcross. Shallcross maintains that this provision does not establish the relative positions of the parties, for several reasons which will be discussed serially.

Shallcross must . . . proceed under the general priority rules of N.J.S.A. 12A:9–312(5). As has previously been noted, that statute clearly provides that the priority is to be determined by the order of filing when both security interests are perfected by filing. In order to avoid the effect of the statute, Shallcross has suggested that the bank's knowledge of his prior interest in the collateral prevents the bank from obtaining a priority. Factually,

Shallcross asserts that the bank knew of his interest in the shear before it loaned Dunphey the money and accordingly took the shear as collateral subject to his interest. In support of this position, Shallcross claims that he was present in Dunphey's shop when a representative of the bank came to inspect the shop and equipment, and that he personally heard Dunphey inform the representative that he still owed Shallcross money on the shear.

Although no New Jersey court has yet to pass on this issue, a review of the statute, decisions from other jurisdictions and the Official Code Comments adopted by the New Jersey Study Commission leads to the conclusion that knowledge of a prior interest does not affect the priority provisions of the act.

First, it should be noted that there is no suggestion in the language of N.J.S.A. 12A:9–312(5) that knowledge or notice of a prior interest is a bar to the invocation of the priorities established therein. The absence of a notice provision in this section of the act is particularly significant since the drafters of the act saw fit to specifically include knowledge or notice provisions in other sections of it. One such example is N.J.S.A. 12A:9–301(1)(b), dealing with the priority between an unperfected security interest and a lien creditor.

> Except as otherwise provided in subsection (2), an unperfected security interest is subordinate to the rights of . . . (b) a person who becomes a lien creditor without knowledge of the security interest and before it is perfected.

[The 1972 amendments to Former Article 9 eliminated the knowledge test from Former 9–301(1)(b).]

Obviously, the drafters contemplated that, in certain cases, knowledge of another interest would bar the subsequent interest from obtaining priority. Had they intended that this be an element of N.J.S.A. 12A:9–312(5), they would have specifically provided so. Even in N.J.S.A. 12:9–312(3), which governs a purchase money security interest in inventory collateral, there is a notice provision. There is, however, no such provision in clause (5). Hence, it seemed clear that the failure to set forth a "knowledge" or "notice" provision in 9–312(5) was intentional and that such a provision is not to be implied. This conclusion is consistent with the weight of decisional authority. First Nat'l Bank and Trust Co. v. Atlas Credit Corp., 417 F.2d 1081 (10 Cir.1969); In re Smith, 326 F.Supp. 1311 (D.Minn.1971); National Bank of Sarasota v. Dugger, 335 So.2d 859 (Fla.App.1976); Madison Nat'l Bank v. Newrath, 261 Md. 321, 275 A.2d 495 (Ct.App.1971); Bloom v. Hilty, 427 Pa. 463, 234 A.2d 860 (Sup.Ct.1967); Noble Co. v. Mack Financial Corp., 107 R.I. 12, 264 A.2d 325 (Sup.Ct.1970).

The leading out-of-state case on the subject is *In re Smith*, supra, where the court discussed these issues at length. There, Smith purchased an automobile, and a conditional sales contract was executed by the dealer and subsequently assigned to the First National Bank of Minneapolis. No financing statement was filed. A few months later Community Credit Co. lent Smith money and Smith executed a chattel mortgage on the automobile and a financing statement was filed. Community Credit Corp. had actual knowledge of the unperfected security interest held by First National in the automobile. Id. at 1312. The court concluded that prior knowledge was irrelevant for several reasons equally applicable here. First, the court discussed the integrity of the filing system, a point raised by Professor Gilmore in his treatise, Security Interests in Personal Property, § 34.2 (1965). The court commented:

> It is desirable that perfection of interests take place promptly. It is appropriate then to provide that a secured party who fails to file runs the risk of subordination to a later but more diligent party. In this regard it should be pointed out that filing is of particular importance with respect to notice to other parties. It is agreed that where the later party has actual notice there is no need to rely upon a filing to notify him of a prior interest. The problem, however, cannot be analyzed in this narrow context. Some parties may rely on the record in extending credit and obtaining a security agreement in collateral. Although they will prevail over the unperfected prior interest in time if a dispute arises, it is entirely possible that they wanted to avoid the dispute altogether. In other words, they may not have relied in ultimately prevailing in the event of a dispute but they may have relied on the complete absence of a prior interest perfected or otherwise out of which a dispute could arise. The only way this kind of record expectation can be protected is by prompt perfection of all security interests. [326 F.Supp. at 1313–1314].

In conjunction with this, the *Smith* court also recognized the evidentiary problems created by a knowledge requirement, which is subjective and is much more difficult to establish than an objective criterion such as the date of filing. Id. at 1314. Finally, the court in *Smith* analyzed the Official Comments accompanying the Code and determined that they supported the view that knowledge is not an element for consideration in this connection.

The official comments to § 9–312 contain several examples which illustrate the resolution of priority disputes under clause (5). These examples, adopted by the New Jersey Study Commission in its comment to the section, comport with the conclusion in *Smith*. Example 2 is perhaps closest in point.

> A & B [make] non-purchase money advances against the same collateral. The collateral is in the debtor's possession and neither interest is perfected when the second advance is made. Whichever secured party first perfects his interest (by taking possession of the collateral or by filing) takes priority and *it makes no difference whether he knows of the other interests at the time he perfects his own.* [Emphasis supplied]

The language of this example is clear—it makes no difference whether the secured party knows of the other's interest at the time he perfects his own. The point of the example and the statutory scheme itself is to encourage the prompt perfection of security interests as an unequivocal method of establishing priorities with certainty and without opening the flood gates of litigation, no more or no less.

Nothing in this interpretation can be considered to controvert the good faith requirement of N.J.S.A. 12A:1–203. For this record is devoid of any evidence to show a leading on, bad faith or inequitable conduct on the part of the bank which would justify what in essence is estoppel against the assertion of a priority. This is not to say that the priorities established under N.J.S.A. 12A:9–312(5) would never be affected by a showing of bad faith. That is simply not the question presented here.

For the foregoing reasons the motion for summary judgment is hereby granted.

General Insurance Co. v. Lowry[*]
United States District Court, Southern District of Ohio, 1976. 412 F.Supp. 12.
Affirmed 570 F.2d 120 (6th Cir.1978).

■ CARL B. RUBIN, DISTRICT JUDGE.

This is an action to compel specific performance of an agreement. It was heard on June 20, 1975, for purposes of a preliminary injunction and on the merits on February 2, 1976. In accordance with Rule 65(a)(2), evidence presented at the hearing for preliminary injunction was deemed to be evidence on the merits as well and has been considered by the Court in reaching its determination. Pursuant to Rule 52 of the Federal Rules of Civil Procedure the Court does submit herewith its findings of fact and conclusions of law.

FINDINGS OF FACT

1. Prior to January 14, 1972, plaintiff General Insurance Company of America issued surety bonds on which George A. Hyland, Edward F. Lowry and C. M. Dingledine were indemnitors. Pursuant to obligations credited by such bonds the plaintiff paid out various sums of money for which it sought indemnity from the named indemnitors.

2. On January 14, 1972, a cognovit note in the sum of $564,566.79 was executed by the three named indemnitors. Twelve items of collateral security were given to secure such promissory note. For purposes of this litigation, only one such is of any significance. Item III in the list of collateral securities is stated to be "shares of common stock owned by Edward F. Lowry in Pico, Inc., an Ohio corporation." On the same date the above indemnitors executed a Memorandum Agreement (Plaintiff's Exhibit 1) which contained the following language:

> Hyland, Lowry and Dingledine each agree that he will do no act which will reduce or impair the security listed and that each will cooperate in the preparation and execution of the instruments necessary to perfect the security.

---

[*]   [The court's citations are to the applicable pre–1972 version of the UCC.]

3. Subsequently on October 12, 1972, and on July 3, 1973, other notes were executed by the indemnitors and in each instance Item III of the collateral security was a pledge of shares of common stock owned by Edward F. Lowry in Pico, Inc. (Plaintiff's Exhibits 2 and 3). At no time were the shares of stock ever delivered to the plaintiff and no further written agreement regarding such shares was ever executed by the defendant.

4. Throughout these proceedings defendant was represented by attorney Jacob Myers, both as an individual practitioner and as President and sole shareholder in Kusworm & Myers Company, LPA. Mr. Myers attended the meeting of January 14, 1972, examined the documents signed by his client and actively represented defendant Lowry throughout the time involved in this litigation. Subsequent meetings of the parties were held in July, 1972, September, 1972, and May, 1973. Mr. Myers attended the meetings of September 27, 1972, and May 8, 1973, but did not attend the meeting in July of 1972. Other than a letter in January of 1972 from counsel for plaintiff to Mr. Myers requesting delivery of the shares of stock, no other written demand for such shares was ever made by plaintiff's counsel.

5. On January 8, 1974, Edward Lowry executed a promissory note to Kusworm & Myers Company, LPA, in the sum of $12,555.65 (Joint Exhibit I). To secure such note defendant Lowry likewise signed an agreement pledging 19 shares of stock in Pico Development Company, Inc. to Kusworm & Myers Company, LPA, (Joint Exhibit IV) and endorsed at the appropriate place Certificate No. 4 of Pico Development Company (Joint Exhibit II). The stock was subsequently transferred on the books of such company to the name of Kusworm & Myers Company, LPA, and Jacob Myers individually had knowledge of the agreements that had been signed, the reference to the stock in Pico Development Company and the fact that such shares had not been transmitted to plaintiff. The note signed by Edward Lowry to Kusworm & Myers Company, LPA, was given for valuable consideration, to-wit: attorney fees rendered and to be rendered by both Kusworm & Myers Company, LPA, and Jacob Myers.

6. Pursuant to preliminary injunction issued by this Court on June 26, 1975, physical possession of 19 shares of Pico Development Company still remain with Jacob A. Myers, conditioned upon an injunction against sale, assignment, transfer, hypothecation or other disposition without prior approval of this Court.

OPINION

Were it not for the unusual circumstances surrounding this case, its resolution would be a simple matter. The Memorandum of Agreement and the list of collateral which it incorporates by reference from the note fulfill the requirements of a binding security agreement. . . .. General Insurance Company gave value for this security interest. Lowry had rights in the stock and accordingly the security interest did attach under [Former 9–204]. But since this was a security interest in an instrument as defined in [Former 9–105], and General Insurance never took possession of the Pico stock, the security interest was never perfected under [Former 9–304].

By taking possession of Lowry's stock pursuant to its 1974 pledge agreement, Kusworm & Myers, LPA, did perfect their security interest. Under [Former 9–312] defendants' rights in the stock prevail over the plaintiff's unperfected security interest, even though they had knowledge of the plaintiff's interest. In re Smith, 326 F.Supp. 1311 (D.Minn.1971).

If the integrity of the concept of "good faith" is to be maintained, we do not believe that such a result can be tolerated. Defendant Myers is not merely a disinterested creditor who attempted to protect his commercial interests. He is the [defendant's] attorney and he and his client as witness and obligor respectively signed the memorandum of agreement. Under the circumstances herein, when the parties signed that agreement and executed the note, the plaintiff obtained an equitable lien against the 19 shares of Pico stock superior in priority to the later perfected security interest held by Kusworm & Myers, LPA.

Although courts should hesitate to invoke equity powers to disturb the operation of a statute, nothing in the Uniform Commercial Code precludes the imposition of an equitable lien in narrowly-circumscribed situations. Aetna Casualty & Surety Co. v. Brunken & Son, Inc., 357 F.Supp. 290 (D.S.D.1973); Warren Tool Company v. Stephenson, 11 Mich.App. 274, 161 N.W.2d 133 (1968); see [F1–103; UCC 1–103(b)].

All of the prerequisites to the establishment of an equitable lien by plaintiff are present here: all of the parties intended that the Pico stock then in Lowry's possession be given to the plaintiff as security for the debt; an instrument was signed by the parties memorializing this intent; and the present holder of the stock, Mr. Myers, had knowledge of the agreement. The defendants may not use their own dereliction in failing to turn over the stock to the plaintiffs as a defense of their actions.

Faced with facts similar to the instant case, the Supreme Court of Ohio imposed an equitable lien on stock which a defendant failed to deliver according to its agreement with the plaintiff stating that:

> *What good conscience requires, equity should require*, and while we are able to find no adjudicated case upon parallel facts, we are persuaded from the nature of the transaction, the relations and rights of the parties, good conscience and sound morals among men in every-day business, that Klaustermeyer should have his lien for his loan. (emphasis added)

Klaustermeyer v. Cleveland Trust Company, 89 Ohio St. 142, 105 N.E. 278 (1913).

The Court finds this reasoning sound and adopts it *in toto*.

CONCLUSIONS OF LAW

A. This Court has jurisdiction in accordance with 28 U.S.C. § 1332.

B. Where defendant Edward F. Lowry as first party for consideration agrees to secure a bond issued by plaintiff General Insurance Company of America as second party with collateral security and agrees further not to impair such security, he creates an equitable lien on such collateral in favor of such second party.

C. The Uniform Commercial Code does not preclude the imposition of an equitable lien under appropriate circumstances.

D. Defendants Jacob A. Myers and Kusworm & Myers, LPA, as third party with full knowledge of the agreements referred to in Conclusion of Law B and occupying an attorney-client relationship to first party may not under the circumstances of this case obtain by pledge under the U.C.C. a security interest superior to the equitable lien of second party General Insurance Company of America.

E. The prayer of the amended complaint should be and is hereby GRANTED. Defendant Edward F. Lowry is hereby ordered to pledge the shares of Pico, Inc., referred to herein to Plaintiff. Defendant Jacob A. Myers and Kusworm & Myers, LPA, are hereby directed to endorse, transfer and deliver to plaintiff the shares of Pico, Inc.

Costs to be assessed against defendants.

Let Judgment Issue in Accordance With the Foregoing.

[The opinion of the United States Court of Appeals, affirming the District Court, included the following]:

■ PHILLIPS, CHIEF JUDGE.

The issue in this diversity suit is whether the priority provision of the Ohio Uniform Commercial Code, Ohio Rev.Code Ann. § 1309.31 [Former 9–312], precludes the imposition of an equitable lien under the unusual facts of the present case. In comprehensive findings of fact and conclusions of law, District Judge Carl B. Rubin allowed an equitable lien under the "narrowly-circumscribed" situation here presented. General Insurance Company of America v. Lowry, 412 F.Supp. 12 (S.D.Ohio 1976). Reference is made to the reported decision of the district court for a detailed recitation of pertinent facts.

In diversity cases, federal courts must apply the law of the State as pronounced by its highest court. See Erie R. R. v. Tompkins, 304 U.S. 64, 58 S.Ct. 817, 82 L.Ed. 1188 (1938). We conclude that because of the peculiar circumstances involved in this case, the Supreme Court of Ohio would uphold the imposition of an equitable lien notwithstanding the priority provisions of [Former 9–312]. We reach this conclusion based upon two considerations.

First, § 1301.09 (UCC 1–203) provides: "Every contract or duty within [Chapter 1309] of the Revised Code, imposes an obligation of good faith in its performance of enforcement." Section 1301.01(S) defines good faith as "honesty in fact in the conduct or transaction concerned." See In re Samuels & Co., 526 F.2d 1238, 1243–44 (5th Cir.1976) (en banc), cert. denied, Stowers v. Mahon, 429 U.S. 834, 97 S.Ct. 98, 50 L.Ed.2d 99 (1976). In Thompson v. United States, 408 F.2d 1075, 1084 (8th Cir.1969), the Eighth Circuit held that the good faith provision of the UCC "permits the consideration of the lack of good faith . . . to alter priorities which otherwise would be determined under Article 9."

The district court emphasized that this case involves the attorney for one of the parties, not a disinterested creditor attempting to protect his commercial interests. We agree with the district court that the record discloses facts which do not meet the good faith standards of the Uniform Commercial Code.

Second, an equitable lien was created by appellants in favor of appellee. In 1913, the Supreme Court of Ohio dealt with facts strikingly similar to the present suit. In Klaustermeyer v. The Cleveland Trust Co., 89 Ohio St. 142, 105 N.E. 278 (1913), each member of the Board of Directors of Euclid Avenue Trust Company loaned $5,000 to the company when the trust company began having financial difficulties. Stock owned by the company was to be delivered to the directors as security for each member of the Board of Directors of Euclid Avenue Trust for the benefit of creditors to the Cleveland Trust Company before the stock was delivered to Klaustermeyer, one of the board members. The Supreme Court of Ohio held that Klaustermeyer had an "equitable lien on the securities in the possession of the Euclid Avenue Trust Company, which were assigned and transferred to The Cleveland Trust Company. . . ." 89 Ohio St. at 144, 105 N.E. at 279. In holding that the trust company had a duty to deliver the securities to Klaustermeyer, the court said:

> In modern times the doctrine of equitable liens has been liberally extended for the purpose of facilitating mercantile transactions, and in order that the intention of the parties to create specific charges may be justly and effectually carried out. Bispham's Principles of Equity (8 ed.), Section 351.

> What good conscience requires, equity should require, and while we are able to find no adjudicated case upon parallel facts, we are persuaded from the nature of the transaction, the relations and the rights of the parties, good conscience and sound morals among men in everyday business, that Klaustermeyer should have his lien for his loan. 89 Ohio St. at 153, 105 N.E. at 282.

We disagree with appellants' argument that the enactment of the Uniform Commercial Code overruled *Klaustermeyer* and eliminated equitable liens in all situations. Section 1301.03 (UCC 1–103) states in pertinent part: "Unless displaced by the particular provisions of [Chapter 1309] of the Revised Code, the principles of law *and equity* . . . shall supplement its provisions." (emphasis added).

Discussing the doctrine of equitable liens and citing *Klaustermeyer*, the Ohio Court of Appeals held in Syring v. Sartorious, 28 Ohio App.2d 308, 309–10, 277 N.E.2d 457, 458 (1971):

> The doctrine may be stated in its most general form that every express executory agreement in writing whereby a contracting party sufficiently indicates an intention to make some particular property, real *or personal*, or fund, therein described or identified, *a security for*

a debt or other obligation, or whereby the party promises to convey, assign, or transfer the property as security, creates an equitable lien upon the property so indicated, which is enforceable against the property in the hands not only of the original contractor, but of his purchasers or encumbrancers with notice. Under like circumstances, a merely verbal agreement may create a similar lien upon personal property. The doctrine itself is clearly an application of the maxim "equity regards as done that which ought to be done." Cf. Klaustermeyer v. Cleveland Trust Co., 89 Ohio St. 142, 105 N.E. 278. (emphasis added).

This court has recognized the continuing validity of *Klaustermeyer*. See In re Easy Living, Inc., 407 F.2d 142, 145 (6th Cir.1969). See also In re Troy, 490 F.2d 1061, 1065 (6th Cir.1974).

Construing Texas law, the Fifth Circuit implicitly found that the existence of an equitable lien does not conflict with Article Nine of the UCC. See Citizens Co–Op Gin v. United States, 427 F.2d 692, 695–96 (5th Cir.1970). Other Circuits construing various state laws have recognized the doctrine of equitable liens. See Casper v. Neubert, 489 F.2d 543, 547 (10th Cir.1973); Arkwright Mutual Insurance Co. v. Bargain City, U.S.A., Inc., 373 F.2d 701 (3d Cir.1967); Cherno v. Dutch American Mercantile Corp., 353 F.2d 147, 151–53 (2d Cir.1965). But cf. Shelton v. Erwin, 472 F.2d 1118 (8th Cir.1973).

We, therefore, are convinced that the Ohio Supreme Court, if it were deciding this case, would follow its earlier opinion in *Klaustermeyer* holding that General Insurance Company is entitled to an equitable lien on the Pico stock in possession of appellant Myers.

Affirmed.

NOTES ON THE ROLE OF KNOWLEDGE IN PRIORITY CONTESTS

(1) The "Pure Race" Priority Rule of UCC 9–322(a)(1). In holding that knowledge of an earlier, unperfected security interest is irrelevant to a priority contest governed by the first-to-file-or-perfect rule of Former 9–312(5)(a), the *Shallcross* case is in accord with the majority of reported decisions that have considered the issue. The commentary also generally supports that reading of the statute. Like the first-to-file-or-perfect rule of Former 9–312(5)(a), the first-to-file-or-perfection rule of UCC 9–322(a)(1) is silent concerning the effect, if any, of knowledge; however, the Examples in Comment 4 to UCC 9–322 suggest that knowledge is irrelevant to a priority contest governed by UCC 9–322(a). A recording system (such as UCC 9–322(a)(1)) that awards priority to the first party to file irrespective of that party's knowledge of an unfiled, earlier-in-time interest is called a "pure race" system. The priority rule of UCC 9–317(a)(2), which affords priority to a person who becomes a lien creditor before a competing security interest is perfected and before a financing statement is filed, whether or not the lien creditor knows of the security interest, is another "pure race" rule.

(2) "Notice" and "Race–Notice" Priority Systems. Some of Article 9's priority rules are not "pure race" rules, but are more accurately described as "notice," or perhaps "race-notice," rules. In a "notice" system, a subsequent purchaser who takes with notice of an earlier-in-time claim is subordinated to that claim even if the earlier-in-time claimant has failed to give any public notice, such as by filing. As we have seen, UCC 9–337(1) affords priority to certain buyers of goods covered by a certificate of title only if they act "without knowledge of the security interest." See Chapter 3, Section 4(B), supra. In a similar vein, UCC 9–317(b), (c), and (d) give certain non-secured party transferees priority over an unperfected security interest only if the transferees do not have "knowledge of the security interest" at the specified relevant time. See Section 2(B), infra.

In a "race-notice" system, a subsequent claimant becomes senior to an earlier, unperfected security interest only if the subsequent party takes its interest without notice (or knowledge) of the earlier interest and *also* is the first to perfect its interest. If one conceptualizes the "delivery" requirement in UCC 9–317(b) and (c) as a form of compliance with a "public notice" requirement, then those provisions arguably fall within the "race-notice" category.

(3) Non–temporal Priority Systems. As we shall see, a number of the priority rules in Revised Article 9 are non-temporal, i.e., they afford priority without regard to whether a security interest was perfected before or after a competing claim to the collateral. Most of these rules relate to specialized collateral, such as deposit accounts and investment property, and are discussed in Chapter 6, infra. With respect to goods, we have seen that purchase-money security interests are eligible for non-temporal priority. See UCC 9–317(e); Problem 3.3.6, p. 150, supra. Purchase-money security interests are discussed in greater detail in Section 1(B), infra.

(4) Circular Priority. Peculiar priority problems may arise when more than two creditors claim an interest in particular collateral. Assume, for example, that under the applicable priority rules, C–1 takes priority over C–2 and C–2 takes priority over C–3. One might be tempted to jump to the conclusion that C–1 takes priority over C–3. One ought not yield to this temptation. The transitive law of mathematics (i.e., if $A > B$ and $B > C$, then $A > C$) does not necessarily apply to priority rules. It is possible that C–1 prevails over C–2, C–2 prevails over C–3, and C–3 prevails over C–1! This unhappy state of affairs is called a "circular priority."

Circular priorities can arise under Revised Article 9. Consider, for example, the facts of Problem 4.1.3(c), supra. SP–2's security interest is senior to SP–1's because the effectiveness of SP–1's financing statement lapsed. See UCC 9–515(c). SP–1's security interest was perfected before Elsie became a lien creditor, and so is senior to Elsie's execution lien. UCC 9–317(a)(2). (UCC 9–515(c) is of no assistance to Elsie, who is not a "purchaser." See UCC 1–201(b)(29) [F1–201(32)]; Chapter 1, Section 3(B), supra.) However, Elsie's lien is senior to SP–2's security interest under UCC

9–317(a)(2). *SP*–2 beats *SP*–1, *SP*–1 beats Elsie, and Elsie beats *SP*–2 (who beats *SP*–1, who beats Elsie, who beats *SP*–2 . . .).

"Race-notice" and "notice" systems are particularly likely to generate circular priorities because they can enable a later claimant to take priority over some, but not all, earlier claims. UCC 9–338 presents a similar possibility. Suppose, for example, that in the setting of Problem 4.1.4, supra, Bank took and perfected a security interest after Lender filed but before Finco. If Bank did not reasonably rely on the incorrect information in Lender's financing statement, then Lender would be senior to Bank under the first-to-file-or-perfect rule. See UCC 9–322(a)(1). Likewise, Bank would be senior to Finco. See id. However, Finco would be senior to Lender if Finco reasonably relied on the incorrect mailing address in Lender's financing statement. See UCC 9–338. Lender beats Bank, Bank beats Finco, and Finco beats Lender.

Although Article 9 creates circular priority puzzles, it provides no solution for them. In the absence of a controlling statutory rule, how should a court determine the priority? Possibilities might include allocating the value of the collateral pro rata and subordinating the party (or parties) that the court deems least deserving (because of carelessness or some other reason that the court finds compelling).

(5) Certainty, Good Faith, and Extra–UCC Principles. A few commentators have called for tempering the "pure race" rule of Former 9–312(5)(a) with some sort of knowledge qualification. See Felsenfeld, Knowledge as a Factor in Determining Priorities Under the Uniform Commercial Code, 42 N.Y.U.L.Rev. 246 (1967); Nickles, Rethinking Some U.C.C. Article 9 Problems, 34 Ark. L. Rev. 1, 72–103 (1980). Professors Baird and Jackson, on the other hand, have defended the "pure race" rule. Baird & Jackson, Information, Uncertainty, and the Transfer of Property, 13 J. Legal Stud. 299 (1984).

Baird and Jackson argue that judicial inquiries into the question of knowledge would be costly and would cause delay. Among the costs of "notice" systems are the costs of determining whether and when a person acquired knowledge of a competing claim and the uncertainty costs arising from the possibility that a court would make an erroneous determination. Baird and Jackson also argue that knowledge of an earlier-in-time interest is not equivalent to bad faith. In their view, parties should not be penalized for obtaining knowledge; acquiring knowledge should be encouraged. They point out that "notice" systems do not provide any incentive for a knowledgeable second-in-time party to cause the public records to be corrected so as to reflect the earlier, unfiled security interest.

By way of contrast, Professor Carlson's study offers the harshest critique of the "pure race" rule. Carlson, Rationality, Accident, and Priority Under Article 9 of the Uniform Commercial Code, 71 Minn.L.Rev. 207 (1986). To Carlson, a knowledgeable second-in-time party who achieves seniority under Former 9–312(5)(a)'s first-to-file-or-perfect rule is much like a thief. Carlson explains that cost-benefit analyses such as those of Baird and Jackson fail to consider all of the pertinent costs, including the costs to the parties who are subordinated and the social costs of a rule that is inconsistent with well-accepted morality. Moreover, his analysis of the drafting history suggests that the drafters of Former 9–312(5) may not have intended to create a strict "pure race" rule!

Interestingly, Carlson stops short of proposing a modification of what generally has been construed to be a "pure race" statutory scheme. Instead, he seems satisfied that courts can import, through Former 1–103 [UCC 1–103(b)], extra-UCC doctrine that is sufficient to deprive the truly bad-faith actors of the fruits of their wrongful actions. The *Lowry* case is an example.

One hopes that case-by-case application of extra-UCC doctrines to a "pure race" reading of UCC 9–322(a)(1) will result in a just, workable, and sufficiently predictable system of priorities. To a considerable extent, the success of the system depends on the ability of judges to override the first-to-file-or-perfect rule judiciously, i.e., only in appropriate cases and only with appropriate techniques. In the *Lowry* case, the court resorted to the doctrine of "equitable lien" to justify subordinating the perfected security interest of Kusworm & Myers's. That doctrine carries with it a considerable amount of baggage, including a set of priority rules that may have been appropriate for the case at bar but inappropriate in another Article 9 case. (See the excerpt from Syring v. Sartorious quoted in the opinion of the Sixth Circuit.) Rather than giving the unperfected secured party an additional property right (an "equitable lien") that took priority over Kusworm & Myers's perfected security interest, could the court have reached the same result by applying the good faith requirement of Former 1–203 [UCC 1–304] to subordinate Kusworm & Myers's perfected security interest? Would that approach have created fewer potential problems?

As Baird and Jackson point out, acting with knowledge that an earlier-in-time interest exists is not *necessarily* equivalent to bad faith. Indeed, what Carlson condemns is acting with the knowledge that achieving seniority over that interest is *wrongful* as to the earlier-in-time claimant. The knowledgeable second-in-time secured party may be exposed to liability for tortious interference with the contractual relations between the earlier-in-time secured party and the common debtor. See First Wyoming Bank v. Mudge, 748 P.2d 713 (Wyo.1988) (imposing liability for tortious interference on bank that took security interest with knowledge that transaction caused debtor to violate a covenant in agreement between debtor and another creditor). Well-drafted credit agreements typically contain provisions requiring debtors to maintain the perfection and priority of security interests and prohibiting debtors from giving senior interests (and often *any* competing interests) to other parties. For an example, see ¶ 11(d), Form 3.2, supra. In most cases, then, one might argue that knowledge of the earlier, unperfected interest is essentially equivalent to knowledge that subordination of the earlier party's interest is wrongful. Does this argument give knowledge too great a role to play in rearranging the "pure race" priorities of UCC 9–322(a)(1)?

We will return to these issues again when we consider the special priority rules applicable to buyers of goods in ordinary course of business (see Section 2(A), infra), and purchasers of chattel paper and instruments (see Chapter 6, Section 2, infra). These rules regulate priority in part on the basis of whether a buyer or other purchaser acts "without knowledge" that the transaction "violates the rights" of the secured party. See UCC 1–201(b)(9) [F1–201(9)]; UCC 9–330(b), (d).

(B) PURCHASE–MONEY SECURITY INTERESTS

Problem 4.1.5. On June 1 D, a construction company, obtained a $100,000 loan from SP–1, and executed in favor of SP–1 a security agreement covering "all construction equipment now owned or hereafter acquired" by D. D owned construction equipment such as bulldozers, cranes and trucks. SP–1 immediately filed a financing statement covering "construction equipment."

(a) On July 1 D told SP–2 of the need for a loan to buy a new Cletrac bulldozer from the manufacturer, M. SP–2 then made a loan to D in the form of a $90,000 check payable jointly to D and M; D then endorsed the check to M and paid M the remaining $10,000 of the price. On July 2 M delivered the bulldozer to D. SP–2 filed a financing statement covering the new bulldozer (bulldozers are not subject to the relevant certificate-of-title act) on July 8. D defaulted on the loans from SP–1 and SP–2. Who has priority as to the new bulldozer? See UCC 9–322(a)(1), (f)(1); UCC 9–324(a); UCC 9–103(a), (b). What, if anything, could the losing party have done to avoid the result?

(b) Suppose that on July 1 D bought a new Cletrac bulldozer from M, and paid M the price of $100,000. On July 2 D obtained a $90,000 loan from SP–2, and executed to SP–2 a security agreement covering the new bulldozer. SP–2 promptly filed a financing statement. D defaulted on the loans to SP–1 and SP–2. Who has priority as to the new bulldozer? See UCC 9–322(a)(1); UCC 9–324(a), (f)(1); UCC 9–103(a), (b); Note (3) on Purchase–Money Priority and the Definition of "Purchase–Money Security Interest," infra. What, if anything, could the losing party have done to avoid the result?

(c) What policy considerations underlie the legal rules that decide parts (a) and (b)? See UCC 9–324, Comment 4; Note (2) on Purchase–Money Priority and the Definition of "Purchase–Money Security Interest," infra.

(d) Would the results in parts (a) and (b) change if the security agreement in favor of SP–1 contained the following provision?

> Debtor shall not create or suffer to exist any security interest (including any purchase-money security interest) in any collateral that is, at any time, covered by this agreement, and any such prohibited security interest that Debtor may attempt to create shall be null and void.

See UCC 9–401.

Problem 4.1.6. The facts are as in part (a) of the preceding Problem. In August, SP–2 made an additional $25,000 loan to D. The loan agreement, signed by D, provided that the new loan was secured by the Cletrac bulldozer. Is SP–1's security interest in the bulldozer senior to SP–2's? If so, to what extent? See UCC 9–103(b), (f); Note (4) on Purchase–Money Priority and the Definition of "Purchase–Money Security Interest," infra.

Problem 4.1.7. The facts are as in Problem 4.1.5(a). By August, *D* was having difficulty making the monthly payments on the loan from *SP*–2. *SP*–2 agreed to extend a new loan to *D* to be secured by the Cletrac bulldozer. The new loan was in the amount of $70,000, which was sufficient to pay off the remaining balance of the original $90,000 loan and give *D* an additional $10,000. By the end of November, *D* had reduced the loan balance to $65,000. Is *SP*–1's security interest in the new bulldozer senior to *SP*–2's? If so, to what extent? See UCC 9–103(b), (f), (e); Note (4) on Purchase–Money Priority and the Definition of "Purchase–Money Security Interest," infra.

Problem 4.1.8. The facts are as in Problem 4.1.5(a). By August, *D* was having difficulty making the monthly payments on the loan from *SP*–2. *SP*–3 agreed to extend a new loan in the amount of $70,000 to *D*, to be secured by the Cletrac bulldozer. The loan was for the purpose of paying off the balance of the original $90,000 loan from *SP*–2 and affording *D* some additional working capital. After using the loan proceeds to pay off the loan from *SP*–2, $10,000 remained for *D*'s use. By the end of November, *D* had reduced the loan balance to $65,000.

(a) Is *SP*–3's security interest in the new bulldozer senior to *SP*–1's? If so, to what extent?

(b) Would the result in part (a) differ if *SP*–2 had assigned to *SP*–3 *SP*–2's loan balance and security interest?

(c) Would the result in part (a) differ if *SP*–3 had paid $60,000 of the loan proceeds directly to *SP*–2?

(d) Would the result in part (a) differ if *SP*–3 had made a working capital loan to *D* and *D* used the loan proceeds to pay off the loan from *SP*–2?

Problem 4.1.9. *D*, a wholesaler, sells textiles to retail stores from substantial stocks of textiles maintained in *D*'s warehouse.

On June 1 *D* obtained a $100,000 loan from *SP*–1 and authenticated a security agreement granting a security interest to *SP*–1 in all the textiles that *D* then owned or might thereafter acquire. *SP*–1 immediately filed a financing statement covering "textiles."

Late in June *D* needed to purchase $20,000 worth of additional textiles from the manufacturer, *M*. *M* would not sell to *D* on credit. *D* lacked the necessary cash and *SP*–1 refused to enlarge the existing $100,000 loan.

Because of these difficulties, on July 1 *D* applied to *SP*–2 for a loan to pay *M* for the textiles. *SP*–2 agreed and made out a check for $20,000 payable jointly to *D* and *M*; *D* endorsed the check to *M*. On July 2 *SP*–2 filed a financing statement. On July 5 *M* delivered the textiles to *D*, who placed them in the warehouse.

Shortly after the $20,000 shipment of textiles arrived, *D* defaulted on the loans to *SP*–1 and *SP*–2. Whose security interest is senior as to this shipment of textiles? See UCC 9–322(a)(1); UCC 9–324(b), (c); UCC 9–103(a), (b). What, if anything, could the losing party have done to improve its position?

NOTES ON PURCHASE–MONEY PRIORITY AND THE DEFINITION OF "PURCHASE–MONEY SECURITY INTEREST"

(1) Relevance of the Distinction Between "Purchase–Money Security Interests" and Non–purchase–money Security Interests. Whether a security interest meets the definition of "purchase–money security interest" ("PMSI") in UCC 9–103 is important in several contexts. We saw above in Chapter 3, Section 3(A), that a PMSI perfected by filing "before or within 20 days after the debtor receives delivery of the collateral" receives priority over the interests of lien creditors which arise "between the time the security interest attaches and the time of filing." UCC 9–317(e). Observe also that UCC 9–317(e) also subordinates to a PMSI the interests of buyers and lessees whose interests arise during the "gap" between attachment and filing. We also saw that PMSI's in most consumer goods are "automatically" perfected without filing or possession by the secured party. See UCC 9–309(1) (discussed in Chapter 3, Section 3(B), supra).

This Section of the materials addresses the priority of PMSI's as against competing security interests. In particular, it looks at priority rules that provide exceptions to the first-to-file-or-perfect rule of UCC 9–322(a)(1), thereby allowing qualifying PMSI's to achieve seniority over security interests perfected by earlier-in-time filings. See Note (2), infra. In Chapter 8, Section 3, infra, we shall see that Article 9 affords a similar "super-priority" to PMSI's in fixtures. See UCC 9–334(d).

(2) Purchase–Money Priority Under UCC 9–324. A set of PMSI priority rules in UCC 9–324 overrides the otherwise-applicable first-to-file-or-perfect rule of UCC 9–322(a)(1). To qualify for these special rules, a PMSI must meet the definition in UCC 9–103, which is discussed more fully in the following Notes. In addition, PMSI priority is conditioned on the satisfaction of certain procedural requirements, discussed below in this Note. When these requirements are not met, UCC 9–322(a) governs the priority of a PMSI.

Eligible Collateral. A PMSI can arise in only two types of collateral, goods and software. See UCC 9–103(b), (c). However, in many cases a "second-in-time" secured party can achieve priority in "paper collateral" (such as documents, instruments, and chattel paper) and other intangible collateral (such as investment property and deposit accounts) under other special priority rules. See, e.g., UCC 9–312(c)(2); UCC 9–327; UCC 9–328;

UCC 9–330; UCC 9–331. See generally Chapter 1, Sections 4 and 5, supra; Chapter 6, Sections 2, 3 and 4, infra.

Timing of Perfection. Each of the PMSI priority rules establishes a temporal standard for perfection. For goods other than inventory and livestock, the security interest must be "perfected when the debtor receives possession of the collateral or within 20 days thereafter." UCC 9–324(a). The standard for inventory collateral is less flexible. An inventory PMSI must be "perfected when the debtor receives possession of the inventory"; there is no 20–day period of grace. UCC 9–324(b)(1). The same requirement applies to livestock. See UCC 9–324(d)(2).

[handwritten margin note: generally 20 day grace period]

[handwritten margin note: not for livestock or inventory]

Notification to Competing Secured Parties. For inventory collateral, UCC 9–324(b) provides a detailed scheme that requires a secured party holding a PMSI to give a written notification to certain competing secured parties (see UCC 9–324(c)).[4] The notification must be received by those parties before (but not more than five years before) the debtor receives possession of the inventory (see paragraph (b)(3)). Finally, the notification must state that the person giving the notification has or may obtain a PMSI in specified items or types of inventory (see paragraph (b)(4)). You should study these notification requirements with care.

Comment 4 to UCC 9–324 explains the rationale for the notification requirement of subsections (b) and (c) as follows:

The arrangement between an inventory secured party and its debtor typically requires the secured party to make periodic advances against incoming inventory or periodic releases of old inventory as new inventory is received. A fraudulent debtor may apply to the secured party for advances even though it has already given a purchase-money security interest in the inventory to another secured party. For this reason, subsections (b)(2) through (4) and (c) impose a second condition for the purchase-money security interest's achieving priority: the purchase-money secured party must give notification to the holder of a conflicting security interest who filed against the same item or type of inventory before the purchase-money secured party filed or its security interest became perfected temporarily under Section 9–312(e) or (f). The notification requirement protects the non-purchase-money inventory secured party in such a situation: if the inventory secured party has received notification, it presumably will not make an advance; if it has not received notification (or if the other security interest does not qualify as purchase-money), any advance the inventory secured party may make ordinarily will have priority under Section 9–322. Inasmuch as an arrangement for periodic advances against incoming goods is unusual outside the inventory field, subsection (a) does not contain a notification requirement.

Do you find this explanation of the notification requirement persuasive? Should that requirement be extended to other collateral, such as

---

4.   The rules applicable to PMSI's in livestock are similar to those applicable to PMSI's in inventory. See UCC 9–324(d), (e).

equipment? See Baird & Jackson, Possession and Ownership: An Examination of the Scope of Article 9, 35 Stan.L.Rev. 175, at 194–96 (1983), where the authors argue that a notification requirement should be added to Former 9–312(4) for non-inventory PMSI's. Apparently they believe that the reliance of secured creditors on after-acquired equipment warrants a notification requirement. Although they base their argument on ostensible ownership grounds, they fail to address the empirical question of whether secured creditors typically are aware of debtors' possession of after-acquired equipment. For a different view of reliance on after-acquired equipment, see Harris, A Reply to Theodore Eisenberg's *Bankruptcy in Law Perspective*, 30 UCLA L. Rev. 327, at 338 n.66 (1982) (defending the application of the two-point test in BC 547(c)(5) only to accounts and inventory):

> [T]hose who take equipment as collateral typically expect the original collateral to remain in the debtor's possession so that he can use it to generate income that will enable him to repay the loan. Although they may easily take a security interest in after-acquired equipment, ordinarily these lenders do not expect to rely upon it and would be protected without it.

Why Purchase–Money Priority? The most commonly advanced justification for PMSI priority is that it provides a means for a debtor to obtain additional secured financing when the first-to-file secured party is unwilling to provide it. In this sense, PMSI priority ameliorates the "situational monopoly" of a first-to-file secured creditor who has the benefit of an after-acquired property clause. See Jackson & Kronman, Secured Financing and Priorities Among Creditors, 88 Yale L.J. 1143, at 1167 (1979) ("Although the after-acquired property clause saves costs, it also creates what economists call a 'situational monopoly,' in that a creditor with a security interest in after-acquired property enjoys a special competitive advantage over other lenders in all his subsequent dealings with the debtor.").

It is understandable that a debtor might prefer the flexibility that purchase-money financing affords. What price does the first-to-file secured party (and, indirectly, the debtor) pay for this flexibility? Do the PMSI priority rules place a substantial risk on the first-to-file secured creditor? If so, does the first-to-file secured creditor react to the risk by charging higher rates (in effect, discounting the value of collateral) to offset the risks? In fact, several safeguards are available to first-to-file lenders who might otherwise perceive that the PMSI priority rules present material risks to their positions. For example, we already have seen that inventory lenders are entitled to notification from later secured parties who hold a PMSI. That notification puts the inventory lender in a position to protect itself by not relying on the PMSI-financed collateral. Also, creditors who are the first to file can bargain for covenants and events of default that restrict or prohibit the debtor from obtaining PMSI financing. Although these contractual obligations and remedies do not entirely eliminate the risk (see UCC 9–401(b)), they are considered important nonetheless in the credit markets.

There is a more fundamental reason why PMSI priority does not seriously impair the position of first-to-file secured creditors. The PMSI holder contributes new value that *in fact is used by the debtor to acquire a new asset.* The debtor's balance sheet reflects both a new debt and a new asset. Neither the first-to-file secured creditor's existing collateral nor its overall position are affected. (This rationale also assumes that non-notified, first-to-file secured creditors do not rely materially to their detriment on after-acquired, non-inventory collateral.) This explanation highlights the importance of the tracing requirement in UCC 9–103(b)'s definition of PMSI, discussed below in Note (3). Consider the effect of a rule to the contrary, under which a debtor could borrow funds, fail to acquire a new asset, and confer on the lender a super-priority in a first-to-file secured creditor's existing collateral: it would undercut the core basis of secured credit. Would the result of that sort of "last-in-time" priority rule be that no one would go the trouble of obtaining collateral? Would all credit be unsecured credit? An affirmative answer to each of these questions is developed in Jackson & Kronman, Secured Financing and Priorities Among Creditors, 88 Yale L.J. 1143, at 1162–64 (1979).

(3) Definition of "Purchase–Money Security Interest"; The Tracing Requirement. UCC 9–103(b)(1) contains the basic definition of a PMSI in goods: "A security interest in goods is a purchase-money security interest . . . to the extent that the goods are purchase-money collateral with respect to that security interest." Working through the definitions of "purchase-money collateral" and "purchase-money obligation," one finds that UCC 9–103(b)(1) provides for two types of PMSI's in goods: those held by a seller to secure "an obligation . . . incurred as all or part of the price of the collateral," and those taken by a lender to secure "an obligation . . . incurred . . . for value given to enable the debtor to acquire rights in or the use of the collateral if the value is in fact so used." UCC 9–103(a)(2).

For a security interest taken by a lender to qualify as a PMSI, the value (i.e., the loan—or **enabling loan** as it often is called) (i) must be given for the purpose of enabling the debtor to acquire the collateral and (ii) must actually be used for that purpose. It follows from the second component of this rule that, to achieve PMSI status, a secured lender must trace the loaned funds and establish that they actually were used to pay the purchase price for the collateral. The secured lender typically accomplishes this by advancing the loaned funds directly to the seller of the collateral or by issuing a check payable jointly to the seller and the buyer-debtor. Does the rationale of the purchase–money priority rules, considered above in Note (2), explain this strict tracing requirement? Normally there is no tracing problem when a PMSI is created in favor of a seller.

A few courts have relaxed the strict tracing requirement when the value given is sufficiently "closely allied" with the acquisition of the collateral. See, e.g., General Electric Capital Commercial Automotive Finance, Inc. v Spartan Motors, Ltd., 246 App.Div.2d 41, 675 N.Y.S.2d 626 (1998). The *Spartan Motors* court held that a PMSI was created when the secured party reimbursed the debtor for the purchase prices of goods earlier acquired with the debtor's own funds. The court reasoned that (i) the debtor's expectation of obtaining the loans was a factor in the debtor's negotiation of the purchases of the collateral, (ii), the PMSI lender's reimbursements were only six and two days after the purchases, (iii) the post-acquisition reimbursement was typical the particular trade and routine in the debtor's dealings with the PMSI lender, and (iv) the debtor could not have afforded to purchase the collateral without the loans. For a more conventional approach, see, e.g., Wade Credit Corp. v Borg-Warner Acceptance Corp., 83 Or.App. 479, 732 P.2d 76 (1987) (because debtor had already acquired title and possession of collateral before the putative PMSI lender advanced funds for payment of the price of the collateral, lender's security interest was not a PMSI).

Does PMSI status require a close temporal connection between the incurrence of purchase-money obligation and the attachment and perfection of the security interest? Suppose, for example, that a seller sells goods on unsecured credit (an **open account**) or a lender makes an unsecured enabling loan. Sometime (months, or even years) later, the buyer gives the seller (or the enabling lender) a security interest in the goods to secure the balance of the purchase price (or unpaid balance of the loan). Is the security interest a PMSI? Comment 3 to UCC 9–103 indicates that it is not: "a security interest does not qualify as a purchase-money security interest if a debtor acquires property on unsecured credit and subsequently creates the security interest to secure the purchase price." Is the Comment consistent with the text of UCC 9–103? Even if the security interest is a PMSI, in many cases the delay would disqualify the security interest from enjoying purchase–money *priority* under UCC 9–324. See Note (2), supra; Note, p. 263, infra.

(4) The "Transformation" and "Dual Status" Rules. UCC 9–103(b)(1) provides that a security interest in goods is a PMSI "to the extent" that the goods are purchase-money collateral, i.e., to the extent that they secure a purchase-money obligation incurred with respect to those goods. The implication of the quoted phrase is that a security interest in the PMSI-financed collateral is *not* a PMSI "to the extent" that it also secures debt other than the price or an enabling loan. Likewise, that language suggests that a security interest in collateral other than the PMSI-financed collateral is not a PMSI even though it secures a purchase-money obligation with respect to other collateral.

The words "to the extent" in UCC 9–103(b) derive from the definition of "purchase money security interest" in Former 9–107. Several cases construing Former 9–107 have supported the retention of PMSI status for a security interest in PMSI-financed collateral when that collateral also secures obligations other than the purchase-money obligation. Those cases recognize security interests having a "dual status": they are part PMSI (i.e., to the extent that they secure the price or an enabling loan) and part non-PMSI (i.e., to the extent that they secure other indebtedness). However, there is a substantial body of Former Article 9 case law holding that what otherwise would be a PMSI is "transformed" into a non-PMSI whenever the PMSI-financed collateral secures any obligations other than the price or an enabling loan or whenever other collateral, in addition to the PMSI-financed collateral, secures the purchase-money obligation.

A number of cases construing Former 9–107 also have applied this "transformation" rule to deny PMSI status when the purchase-money obligation (the price or an enabling loan) has been **refinanced** (i.e., extended or combined with other indebtedness), even when the secured party could identify a portion of the collateral as PMSI-financed collateral and a portion of the remaining secured indebtedness as the price or as an enabling loan for that collateral. In re Matthews, 724 F.2d 798 (9th Cir.1984), is typical of those cases. In *Matthews*, the debtors owed $3,902.64 to Transamerica. The debt was secured by a PMSI in a piano and a stereo. The parties agreed to refinance the loan: the term was extended and the monthly payment was reduced in amount. Transamerica's books showed a new secured loan to the debtors in the amount of $4,245.01, of which $3,902.64 was applied to pay off the old delinquent loan. The court observed that the debtors did not use the proceeds of the new loan to acquire rights in or the use of the piano or stereo; they already owned them. "The new security interest in the piano and stereo taken by Transamerica at the time of the refinancing was therefore not a 'purchase money security interest' as [Former Article 9] has defined it."

Which approach—transformation or dual-status—is more consistent with the policies that underlie Article 9? Consider two important principles of the Article 9 scheme that seem to be well-accepted. First, parties are given great flexibility to agree as to what collateral (any combination of now-owned and after-acquired property) will secure what obligations (any combination of now-existing or later-arising debt). See UCC 9–204. But see UCC 9–204(b)(1) (limiting the effect of an after-acquired property clause with respect to consumer goods). Second, PMSI's are given favored treatment. See, e.g., UCC 9–317(e); UCC 9–309(1); UCC 9–324. Should parties to a secured transaction be forced to sacrifice flexibility for PMSI treatment or PMSI treatment for flexibility? Should consensual refinancing and restructuring of debt, including secured debt, be discouraged by the threat of losing PMSI status? See In re Billings, 838 F.2d 405 (10th Cir.1988) (transformation rule discourages creditors holding PMSI's from helping their debtors work out of financial problems without the need to enter bankruptcy or surrender collateral); In re McAllister, 67 B.R. 614 (Bkrtcy.N.D.Iowa 2001) (approving the dual status doctrine and noting that "[t]he new Article 9 revision adopts the dual status doctrine" in UCC 9–103(f)).

For non-consumer-goods transactions, UCC 9–103(f) straightforwardly rejects the "transformation" rule. In those transactions, a PMSI does not lose its status as such, even if the purchase-money collateral also secures an obligation that is not a purchase-money obligation, collateral that is not purchase-money collateral also secures the purchase-money obligation, or the purchase-money obligation has been renewed, refinanced, consolidated, or restructured. UCC 9–103(f). Most cases that have confronted the issue under Former Article 9, including *Matthews*, supra, have concerned consumer goods. Revised Article 9's treatment of PMSI's in consumer-goods transactions are discussed in the Notes on page 259, infra.

The "dual status" rule, which UCC 9–103(f) adopts, can prove troublesome to apply. For example, suppose Bank holds a PMSI in an item of equipment to secure an enabling loan of $50,000 and all present and future obligations of Debtor to Bank. When the loan is reduced to $35,000, Bank extends an additional $10,000 to Debtor. To what extent is the security interest a PMSI? The answer is easy to intuit: to the extent of $35,000. Gleaning the answer from the statute is a bit more difficult. The security interest is a PMSI only to the extent the equipment is purchase-money collateral. UCC 9–103(b)(1). The equipment is purchase-money collateral if it secures a purchase-money obligation with respect to the equipment. See UCC 9–103(a)(1). Of the obligations secured by the equipment, only $35,000 is a purchase-money obligation. See UCC 9–103(a)(2). To the extent that the equipment secures the $10,000 non-purchase-money obligation, the security interest is not a PMSI.

Now suppose that Debtor pays Bank $5,000, leaving a balance of $40,000 secured by the equipment. To what extent is the security interest a PMSI? The answer depends on the amount of the purchase-money obligation, which in turn depends on how much, if any, of the $5,000 payment was applied towards satisfaction of the $35,000 purchase-money obligation and how much, if any, was applied towards satisfaction of the $10,000 non-purchase-money obligation. Cases decided under Former Article 9 generally required the secured party to prove that amount. In non-consumer-goods transactions, UCC 9–103(g) adopts this approach. (Consumer-goods transactions are discussed in the Notes on p. 259, infra.) To assist the secured party in meeting this burden, UCC 9–103(e) permits the parties in non-consumer-goods cases to agree to an allocation formula and provides rules of allocation applicable in the absence of an agreement.

(5) Purchase–Money Security Interests in Software. A PMSI may be created only in goods and, in limited circumstances, software. See UCC 9–103. To be eligible to be the subject of a PMSI, software must be associated with goods in the manner specified in UCC 9–103(c): the debtor must acquire an interest in the software in an integrated transaction in which the debtor acquires an interest in the goods, and the debtor must acquire an interest in the software for the principal purpose of using the software in the goods. This rule permits a person who finances a debtor's acquisition of the goods and related software to take a PMSI in both. (Take care not to confound this approach with the concept of a computer program "embedded" in goods; such an "embedded" program actually is a part of the goods under UCC 9–102(a)(44). See Problem 3.2.6, p. 133, supra.) The priority of a PMSI in software is the same as that of the goods in which the software was acquired for use. See UCC 9–324(f).

Problem 4.1.10. *D* is a wholesale distributor of toys. On June 1 *D* obtained a $100,000 loan from *SP–1* and signed a security agreement covering "all inventory now owned or hereafter acquired." On June 2 *SP–1* properly filed a financing statement.

On July 1 *D* signed a security agreement in favor of *SP–2*, a toy marble manufacturer, covering "all marbles that SP–2 sells to Customer from time to time" and securing "the purchase price of marbles sold from time to time by SP–2 to Customer." That same day *SP–2* properly filed a financing statement and sent a notice to *SP–1* in compliance with the requirements of UCC 9–324(b).

On July 15, at *D*'s request, *SP–2* shipped 100,000 marbles to *D* in 1,000 bags containing 100 marbles each, and sent *D* an invoice for $1,000 (a unit price of 1 cent per marble). On July 30 *SP–2* filled another order from *D* by shipping another 100,000 marbles, packaged in 100 boxes of 1,000 marbles each. *SP–2* then sent to *D* an invoice for another $1,000.

After making three payments in the aggregate amount of $700, *D* failed to make further payments to *SP–2*. It is now September 1 and *D* is in possession of 350 bags of marbles from the first order and 25 boxes of marbles from the second order—the other marbles having been sold and the proceeds dissipated.

Is *SP–2*'s perfected security interest in the marbles senior to the security interest of *SP–1*? If so, to what extent? Does it matter if *SP–2* and *D* agreed that the entire $700 is allocable to the price of the bags rather than to the price of the boxes? See UCC 9–103(b) & Comment 4; UCC 9–324(b), (c); Note (4) on Purchase–Money Priority and the Definition of "Purchase–Money Security Interest," supra; Note on "Cross–Collateralization" and Purchase–Money Financing of Inventory, infra.

NOTE ON "CROSS–COLLATERALIZATION" AND PURCHASE–MONEY FINANCING OF INVENTORY

Problem 4.1.10, supra, presents a common fact pattern: Debtor creates a security interest in all its inventory, existing and after-acquired, in favor of a lender (*SP–1*). Thereafter, *SP–2* periodically sells inventory to Debtor on secured credit (or, *SP–2* might be another lender, who makes a series of secured loans that enable Debtor to acquire inventory). Debtor and *SP–2* also enter into a **cross-collateral** agreement; that is, they agree that each item of inventory secures not only its own price but also the aggregate unpaid price of all other inventory financed by *SP–2*.

As we have seen, the fact that an item of inventory secures not only its own price but also other obligations does not destroy the purchase–money status of a security interest. See UCC 9–103(f). However, under UCC 9–103(b)(1), *SP–2* has a PMSI in each item of inventory only to the extent that the item secures a purchase-money obligation incurred with respect to that item of collateral. This rule may present serious practical problems for *SP–2*. Suppose that some of the *SP–2*–financed inventory has been sold and some of the debt to *SP–2* has been paid. To establish its PMSI under UCC 9–103(b)(1), and thus its priority under UCC 9–324(b), *SP–2* would have to allocate each payment towards a particular purchase-money obligation incurred with respect to particular collateral. When inventory is financed in bulk, as when *D* acquired 1,000 bags of marbles in Problem 4.1.10, must *SP–2* work this calculation shipment by shipment? Bag by bag? Marble by marble? And, when *SP–2* has financed multiple shipments of fungible inventory, how is *SP–2* to determine which inventory has been sold and which remains?

When *SP–2* has sold all the marbles to Debtor on a purchase-money basis, *should* the extent of its priority depend on which inventory has been sold and how payments have been allocated? In Southtrust Bank v. Borg–Warner Acceptance Corp., 760 F.2d 1240 (11th Cir.1985), the Fifth Circuit answered "yes" to this question under Former Article 9. In *Southtrust*, a secured party claimed a purchase-money priority in all the inventory that it financed, without regard to payments made by the debtors. It urged the court to limit the transformation rule to consumer cases because, it argued, "applying the transformation rule to inventory financiers would require them to police inventory constantly and to see that inventory corresponds on an item-by-item basis with debt." The court refused to limit the transformation rule in this way. Acknowledging that other courts have applied the dual status rule where there were contractual or legislative guidelines for allocating particular collateral to the related purchase-money obligation, the court refused to do so under the facts of *Southtrust* because neither the parties nor the legislature had provided any such guidelines and the court was unwilling to provide them itself. Thus, having failed to agree with the debtors upon a method for determining the extent to which each item of collateral secures its purchase-money obligation, the secured party effectively gave up its purchase-money status altogether.

A number of institutional lenders disagreed with the outcome in *Southtrust* and sought to prevent it from arising in the future by contract. They entered into an **intercreditor agreement** affording priority to each purchase-money secured party in the inventory that it had financed. Revised Article 9 adopts this approach. UCC 9–103(b)(2) provides that, if inventory subject to a PMSI secures not only its own price (or enabling loan) but also the price of (or enabling loan with respect to) other purchase-money inventory, then the security interest in the inventory is a PMSI not only to the extent the inventory secures its own price but also the price of the other inventory. In other words, by cross-collateralizing PMSI's in inventory, the parties create a PMSI in each item of inventory that secures the aggregate of the purchase-money obligations. See UCC 9–324, Comment 4.

––––––––

In the commercial setting, the purchase–money secured party's concerns relate primarily to priority under UCC 9–324. In the consumer setting, a series of transactions between the debtor and a purchase-money secured party may implicate perfection under UCC 9–309(1) and also raise the consumer-protection issues discussed below in the Notes following Problem 4.1.11.

Problem 4.1.11. You represent Bigstore Co., which owns and operates a national chain of appliance stores. Bigstore frequently sells appliances to its customers (mainly for personal and household use) on the basis of installment sale agreements that grant a security interest to Bigstore to secure the price. (For an example of such an agreement in another setting, see the Instalment Sale Contract, Form 3.6, supra.) Bigstore never files financing statements against its customers. Often a single customer will enter into multiple installment sale agreements at different times in connection with different sales transactions. The manager of Bigstore's credit department consults you about a proposed modification of its standard form of installment sale agreement. The manager would like the agreement to provide that the collateral it covers will secure all indebtedness of the customer to Bigstore, including any debt owed in connection with the customer's *other* installment sales agreements. The manager believes that the modified version will be especially useful for Bigstore in connection with customers who fall behind on their payments and request an extension or "refinancing" of their obligations under multiple agreements.

Bigstore's general counsel has heard that Revised Article 9 is much more friendly to purchase-money financings than was Former Article 9. In particular, the general counsel has asked you for advice about (i) the agreements and procedures necessary to implement the proposed modification and (ii) the procedures for consolidating multiple agreements of a customer into a single refinancing arrangement. What advice do you give the general counsel? See UCC 9–103(a), (b), (e)–(h) & Comments 7 & 8; Note (4), p. 254, supra; Notes on Purchase–Money Security Interests in the Consumer Context, infra.

NOTES ON PURCHASE–MONEY SECURITY INTERESTS IN THE CONSUMER CONTEXT

(1) The "Transformation" and "Dual Status" Rules. As Note (4) on page 254, supra, indicates, UCC 9–103(f) rejects the "transformation" rule for non-consumer-goods transactions. Most of the cases that raised the issue under Former Article 9 have concerned consumer goods. They have arisen largely under BC 522(f), which permits the avoidance (nullification) in bankruptcy of certain non-purchase-money security interests in, inter alia, certain consumer goods,[5] or under BC 544(a), which permits the avoidance

---

5.   BC 522(f)(1)(B) permits debtors to avoid "nonpossessory, nonpurchase-money security interest[s]" in certain types of exempt property. The significance of this avoidance power is limited by the FTC's Rule on Credit Practices, which restricts the taking of certain nonpossessory, non-PMSI's and is discussed in the following Note.

in bankruptcy of unperfected security interests.[6] Despite the salience of the issue, Revised Article 9 is aggressively agnostic concerning the "dual status" rule in consumer-goods transactions. See UCC 9–103(h) & Comment 8.[7] Absent subsection (h), would there be any statutory basis for the application of one rule or the other? See UCC 9–103(b)(1), (b)(2) ("to the extent"). Does subsection (h) create a statutory basis for the "transformation" rule where none would exist otherwise? Do you think a court confronted with the issue will rely on cases decided under Former 9–107, or will it consider the issue anew? Do you think the revision of Article 9—i.e. its rejection of the "transformation" rule for non-consumer-goods transactions and its agnosticism with respect to consumer-goods transactions—will affect the outcome in cases construing the term "purchase money security interest" in BC 522(f)? Should it? See UCC 9–103, Comment 8.

(2) The FTC Rule on Credit Practices. The Federal Trade Commission's Rule on Credit Practices makes it an unfair practice for a lender or retail installment seller to obtain from a consumer a nonpossessory, non-PMSI in household goods. See 16 C.F.R. 444.2(a)(4). This Rule, like that of BC 522(f), recognizes that used home furnishings and other used consumer goods bring relatively little at liquidation sales when compared with their use value to the installment buyer. Both the Rule and BC 522(f) reduce the "hostage value" aspect of collateral consisting of consumer goods. As the FTC explained it, the Rule seems to reject the "transformation" rule, at least with respect to refinancing and consolidations:

> When a purchase money loan is refinanced or consolidated, we intend that, for purposes of this rule, the security collateralizing the prior loan can continue to secure the new loan, even if the new loan is for a larger amount or is in other respects a non-purchase money loan.

49 Fed. Reg. 7740, 7767 (March 1, 1984). To what extent, if any, is the FTC's construction of the concept of a PMSI relevant to the construction of the Bankruptcy Code or the UCC? The FTC informs us that, "In enunciating our intent for purposes of this rule, we intimate no opinion with respect to

---

6. Recall that a security interest in consumer goods is automatically perfected upon attachment. See UCC 9–309(1); Former 9–302(1)(d). Automatic perfection is lost, and the security interest can be avoided, if a PMSI is transformed into a non-PMSI and no perfection step (e.g., filing) is taken. BC 544(a) is discussed in Chapter 7, Section 2(A), infra.

7. A transaction is a "consumer-goods transaction" if the secured obligation is incurred primarily for personal, family, or household purposes and the collateral includes consumer goods. The fact that some of the obligations secured or some of the collateral is acquired for a business purpose does not prevent a transaction from being a "consumer-goods transaction." See UCC 9–102(a)(24) & Comment 7.

different approaches taken by various jurisdictions in analogous questions raised under the Bankruptcy Code." Id.[8]

(3) Payment Allocation Formulas. We saw in the preceding Note that the FTC Rule appears to prohibit **cross-collateral** provisions—agreements whereby each item of collateral secures not only its own price (and, absent application of the transformation rule, would be subject to a PMSI to that extent) but also the price of other items of collateral sold by the PMSI holder (to that extent, a non-PMSI). However, the FTC's explanation of the Rule, quoted above, seems to point in the opposite direction. Moreover, the FTC has taken the position that, for purposes of the FTC Rule, state law should govern the determination of the extent of the purchase-money security interest. If under applicable state law an interest is in part a purchase-money security interest at the time a contract is signed, the FTC has stated that the contract does not violate the Rule, even if the purchase-money portion of the security interest is exhausted before the end of the contract.

Assuming that applicable state law is Article 9 and that the "dual status" rule applies in consumer-goods transactions, on what basis are payments allocated? As we saw in Note (4) on page 254, supra, UCC 9–103(e) contains rules concerning the allocation of payments between PMSI's and non-PMSI's in non-consumer-goods transactions. Yet, as with the "dual status" rule itself, Article 9 is agnostic on the issue of application of payments. See UCC 9–103(h).

In leaving the court free to fashion the applicable legal rule, UCC 9–103(h) permits the court to "apply established approaches." Cases decided under Former Article 9 approved different methods for determining the extent of purchase-money obligations. For a case upholding the parties' agreement on a formula for allocating payments, see In re Breakiron, 32 B.R. 400 (Bkrtcy.W.D.Pa..1983). In some jurisdictions there is a statutory method of allocation. See, e.g., Pristas v. Landaus of Plymouth, Inc., 742 F.2d 797 (3d Cir.1984) (applying formula provided by Pennsylvania's Goods and Services Installment Sales Act to a dual-status security interest). In the absence of explicit agreement or statutory guidance, some courts have devised a method of allocation. See, e.g., In re Conn, 16 B.R. 454 (Bkrtcy.W.D.Ky.1982) (allocation based on first-in, first-out method). Others have been less generous. See, e.g., In Re: Oszajca, 199 B.R. 103 (1996) ("[W]ithout an agreement containing a method for allocating payments . . . [w]e are simply unable to determine the extent of any potential Sears' liens

---

8.   The FTC further explains:

   We intend that, for purposes of this rule, when a loan is consolidated or refinanced, a creditor can retain an existing purchase money security interest in collateral which would otherwise come within the rule's definition of household goods. Thus, analogous "transformation" rules in bankruptcy decisions will have no bearing in determining, for purposes of the rule, the basic character of the collateral at the time of the refinancing or consolidation.

49 Fed. Reg. 7740, 7767 n.97.

because we do not know if the . . . [payment] in fact did release a lien by paying off an individual balance."). Which approach should a court apply? Uniform Consumer Credit Code (U3C) 3.303, which has not been widely enacted, deals with this problem by providing that payments shall be "applied first to the payment of the debts arising from the sales first made." Is this a reasonable and appropriate regulation of the parties' freedom to contract?

Secured parties may be able to preserve much of the leverage that comes from the threat of repossessing many of the debtor's most valued consumer goods without violating the FTC regulations, if each item secures only its own price but the system of allocating installment payments among a series of purchases means that the debt for none of the goods is paid until all debts are paid. For example, a consumer buyer and a secured seller (or secured enabling lender) could agree that each payment made by the buyer would be allocated proportionately among the outstanding balances for all items purchased. In this way, any default in payment would constitute a default under each transaction, and the secured creditor would be entitled to take possession of all of the items of collateral.

This type of arrangement with a consumer debtor was attacked as "unconscionable" in the famous case of Williams v. Walker–Thomas Furniture Co., 350 F.2d 445 (D.C.Cir.1965) (remanded to trial court for factual determinations on issue of unconscionability). The court in In re Breakiron, supra, held that this kind of allocation agreement did not transform PMSI's into non-PMSI's, for purposes of BC 522(f), because each item secured only its own price. The court was influenced by a Pennsylvania statute that contains a similar allocation formula. See 69 Pa. Cons. Stat. Ann. § 1802.

Why do you suppose UCC 9–103(h) leaves to courts the decision whether to apply the allocation rules in subsection (f), or other rules, or no rules at all (e.g., to hold that cross-collateralization results in the loss of PMSI status, thereby obviating any need to allocate payments between PMSI's and non-PMSI's)? Does the continued absence of a clear statutory rule help or hurt consumers?

Problem 4.1.12. Lee is in the data processing business. *SP–1* has a perfected security interest in "all equipment now owned or hereafter acquired" by Lee. On June 1, 2002, Lee and Lor entered into a "true lease" of a computer for a three-year term. The lease agreement provides that Lee, as lessee, has an option to purchase the computer at the end of the lease term for its "fair market value." In accordance with the lease, on May 1, 2005, Lee notified Lor of Lee's intention to exercise that option. Thereafter Lee and Lor reached agreement that the fair market value of the computer—and therefore the sale price—is $1,000.

Lee requests financing from your client, *SP–2*, for Lee's purchase of the leased computer. Your search of the records uncovers *SP–1's* financing statement covering "all equipment." Lee is reluctant to ask *SP–1* to subordinate its security interest to that of *SP–2* because Lee does not want to pay the fees that *SP*–1's lawyers will charge for drawing up the subordination agreement. However, Lee has assured your client that Lee's agreement with *SP*–1 permits Lee to give PMSI's in equipment to other creditors.

How can you assure *SP*–2 that it will achieve purchase–money priority? See UCC 9–102(a)(28), (a)(12); UCC 9–103(a), (b); UCC 9–324(a) & Comment 3; Note on Debtor's Receipt of Possession of Collateral, infra.

NOTE ON DEBTOR'S RECEIPT OF POSSESSION OF COLLATERAL

We have seen that a PMSI does not qualify for purchase–money priority under UCC 9–324(b) unless it is perfected "when the debtor receives possession of the inventory." Likewise, purchase–money priority in collateral other than inventory and livestock under UCC 9–324(a) depends on perfection of the PMSI "when the debtor receives possession of the collateral or within 20 days thereafter." The UCC does not define "possession" for these purposes, nor does the text of Article 9 explain what it means for the debtor to "receive[ ] possession of the collateral." Cf. UCC 9–313 (explaining when secured party takes possession of collateral).

Delivery of various components of a product to a buyer, over a period of time, is one circumstance in which the determination of the beginning of the 20–day period can be perplexing. This is especially so when the seller is required to assemble and test the goods before the buyer becomes obligated to accept them. Courts have reached differing results in these situations under Former 9–312(4), which likewise measured the timeliness of perfection from "when the debtor receives possession." Compare In re Ultra Precision Industries, Inc., 503 F.2d 414 (9th Cir. 1974) (period did not begin to run until testing of machines was completed and financing arrangements were made, because those events were conditions precedent to buyer's obligation to buy) and In re Galbreath Clearing & Grading,, Inc., 258 B.R. 859 (Bkrtcy. S.D.Ga. 2000) (debtor did not receive possession *as a debtor* until consummation of financing transaction at the expiration of a five month term of a true lease to debtor) with In re Vermont Knitting Co., 98 B.R. 184 (Bkrtcy.D.Vt.1989) (period began when machines were delivered to buyer and was not delayed until after machines had been set up by seller's technician) and In re Michaels, 156 B.R. 584 (Bkrtcy.E.D.Wis.1993) (period began when equipment came under the recipient's "physical control"). Comment 3 to UCC 9–324 attempts to give guidance under this circumstance. Is Comment 3 persuasive? Is it an appropriate use of the Comments?

The courts also have struggled with the scenario presented by Problem 4.1.12, supra, in which a prospective debtor in a PMSI transaction is *already* in possession of collateral in a capacity other than that of buyer-owner. Comment 3 to UCC 9–324 addresses this issue, as well. Relying on the reference in UCC 9–324(a) to the debtor's receiving "possession of the *collateral*," Comment 3 indicates that "the 20–day period in subsection (a) does not commence until a the goods become 'collateral' (defined in Section

9–102), i.e., until they are subject to a security interest." The result urged by Comment 3—that the 20–day period starts to run only once the debtor has created a security interest—is consistent with cases decided under Former Article 9; however, the Former Article 9 cases were decided based on whether the person in possession was a "debtor" as defined in Former 9–105(1)(d). See, e.g., Color Leasing 3 v. FDIC, 975 F.Supp. 177 (D.R.I.1997). Does delaying the commencement of the 20–day period undercut the policy of favoring public notice and the policy against "secret" liens? Or, is this approach better characterized as being consistent with current law that does *not* require public notice in the case of leases and various other bailments? We shall see in Chapter 5, Section 1, infra, that there is disagreement over whether some of those transactions should be subjected to Article 9's filing regime. But, inasmuch as filing is not required, isn't it appropriate to delay commencement of the 20–day period until the relationship of the parties falls within the scope of Article 9?

Does the statutory argument presented in Comment 3 prove too much? Consider the following case: A seller sells equipment to a buyer on unsecured credit, or an enabling lender extends unsecured credit that enables the buyer to acquire equipment. Subsequently—say, one year later—a security agreement is signed covering the equipment and, within 20 days thereafter, a financing statement is filed. Does the secured party enjoy purchase–money priority status under UCC 9–324(a)? If the 20–day period does not start running until the debtor receives possession of the "collateral," and the equipment is not "collateral" as defined in UCC 9–102(a)(12) until the security agreement is authenticated, then arguably the secured party enjoys priority under UCC 9–324(a).

Is this result consistent with the underlying purposes and policies of purchase-money priority? If not, can one fairly read Article 9 to yield a different result? The special priority in UCC 9–324 applies only to PMSI's. One never reaches the priority issue if the security interest in question is not a PMSI. As mentioned in Note (3) on page 253, supra, Comment 3 to UCC 9–103 states definitively that the security interest would not be a PMSI in the case under discussion; however, the cases decided under Former Article 9 go both ways. Compare In re Cerasoli, 27 B.R. 51 (Bkrtcy.M.D.Pa.1983) (security interest taken to secure enabling loan several months after enabling loan was made, held a PMSI) with In re Brooks, 29 U.C.C. Rep. Serv. 660 (Bkrtcy.D.Me.1980) (security interest taken several months after the making of enabling loans, held not a PMSI) and In re Carter, 169 B.R. 227 (Bkrtcy. M.D.Ga. 1993) (seller's security interest taken five months after a credit sale of the collateral, held not a PMSI). Although there are few cases, the results in *Brooks* and *Carter* appear to reflect the prevailing view.

(C) PROCEEDS

Problem 4.1.13. The facts are as in Problem 4.1.5(a), supra: *SP*–1 holds a security interest in present and future construction equipment; *SP*–1 filed on June 1. *SP*–2 holds a security interest in the new Cletrac bulldozer purchased in July with the loan from *SP*–2. *SP*–2 filed on July 8.

Late in July *D* found that, to meet the special requirements of a new construction job, *D* needed a bulldozer with a power attachment that the Cletrac bulldozer lacked. On August 1, without consulting *SP*–1 or *SP*–2, *D* traded the Cletrac bulldozer for a used Caterpillar bulldozer that met *D*'s needs.

Shortly thereafter *D* ran out of cash and defaulted on the debts to *SP*–1 and *SP*–2. Who has priority as to the Caterpillar bulldozer? See UCC 9–322(a), (b); UCC 9–315(a); UCC 9–102(a)(64); UCC 9–324(a).

Problem 4.1.14. *D* is a wholesaler of textiles whose business is like that described in Problem 4.1.9, supra. *D* makes many sales on credit to retail stores. The retail stores, in a period of recession, began to take more and more time to pay, with the result that *D* ran short of operating funds.

On June 1, when accounts receivable due *D* from retail stores amounted to $60,000, *D* applied to *SP*–1 for a loan. *SP*–1 extended *D* a loan of $50,000, and *D* executed a security agreement covering "all present and future accounts." *SP*–1 promptly filed a financing statement covering "accounts receivable currently existing or arising hereafter."

On July 1, finding itself in need of additional funds, *D* applied to *SP*–2 for a loan. *D* offered its inventory as collateral. *SP*–2 searched the files and found only *SP*–1's financing statement covering accounts, not inventory. *SP*–2 made a loan of $20,000 to *D*, and *D* executed a security agreement covering "all inventory now owned or hereafter acquired." *SP*–2 promptly filed a financing statement covering "inventory."

In September *D* defaulted on the loans to *SP*–1 and *SP*–2. At that time there were on hand (i) inventory valued at $5,000; (ii) accounts (that arose out of the sale of inventory) valued at $25,000; and (iii) a bank account containing $5,000 that came from the collection of accounts.

(a) Who has the senior security interest in each of these three groups of property? See UCC 9–322(a), (b); Note on Conflicting Security Interests of Accounts Lenders and Inventory Lenders, infra. What, if anything, could the losing party have done to improve its position?

(b) Now assume that *SP*–2 was the first to file a financing statement. What result?

NOTE ON CONFLICTING SECURITY INTERESTS OF ACCOUNTS LENDERS AND INVENTORY LENDERS

Before concluding that the answers to Problem 4.1.14 are the result of accident or whimsy, read the following excerpts from a 1973 panel discussion by some of the drafters of the 1972 revisions to section 9–312 of the 1962 UCC.[9]

PROFESSOR KRIPKE: . . . A prospective debtor goes to the bank and asks, "Will you lend me $1,000,000 on my accounts receivable?" The bank asks its counsel to check the filings against the debtor. He finds no filings of any kind against this debtor, and the bank is prepared as a matter of credit to make the loan, but it says to its counsel, "Are you sure that we'll have a first security interest on these accounts?" and counsel says, "Yes, of course, there's nothing on file against this debtor. You will therefore be first." Then the counsel says, "On second thought I don't know, because even though you now file first on accounts, I don't know what the answer will be if someone else later files on inventory and claims the accounts as proceeds." That problem exists today under the Code and we think we have a very serious problem if counsel can't give that opinion. . . . From my point of view, next to the fixture problem which was causing a great deal of public difficulty, the solution to this problem before it got into the cases was the principal reason for undertaking this amendment process. It was not a purely theoretical question. Sitting in New York as I do where a number of the commercial lenders are situated, every time they get a difficulty under the Code they call me up and bawl me out for it. This was one of the particular problems that they constantly came back to—this whole group of problems as to the relationship between inventory financing and accounts receivable financing.

The first step to solve it was to do something about the two different rules for priority problems which are contained in the existing [1962] Code in Section 9–312(5). One of those rules is the first to file rule and the other is the first to perfect rule. One can never see ahead to the answers to priority problems unless he can visualize what the rules of the game are going to be. Here are two different rules of the game and you don't know which game you're going to play. . . .

We collapsed the effect of filing and the effect of perfection, and the basic principle is that the priority ranks from the time at which either of these events occurs. . . . Applying this to the simple fact situation that I have suggested, if the accounts receivable secured party lends on accounts and files before anything else happens, he will win even though someone else enters the chain of production earlier and files on inventory and its proceeds. Similarly, if someone files on inventory and has through it a claim to proceeds, he will have the first right to accounts even though someone else later comes along and claims accounts. In that latter case the inventory financer has it because he gets there first by perfecting a claim to inventory through possession or through filing. We rejected the notion that I think caused this difficulty and which is implied in certain writings under the Code that the person

9.   A Second Look at the Amendments to Article 9 of the UCC, 29 Bus. Law. 973, 1001–03 (1974).

who handles inventory has a prior claim simply because inventory precedes accounts in the cycle of a business. We thought that if we recognized such a principle we could never give an accounts financer any certainty as to his position. It was important to give him certainty so we make the inventory right depend on his first filing or perfection and not on the fact that inventory comes ahead of accounts in the cycle of a business.

. . . It's more important to have a clear rule that everyone can accommodate to than it is to have a vague rule that no one is sure of even though you might argue that some different rule is theoretically correct.

MR. COOGAN: I would stress again that this is a purely empirical answer. I think everybody said that if one could practically protect the financer who furnishes new inventory, without cutting the heart out of accounts financing, we would have been willing to do it, but the difficulty is that if you protected the inventory financer you make the accounts financing so problematical that you cut off the most likely source of cash that is going to be used to pay the inventory financer.

MR. HAYDOCK: It does seem unfair to some people where an inventory financer comes in later with a purchase money security interest to have him defeated, when we have adopted a different rule with respect to other types of collateral.

SOMEONE IN AUDIENCE: In the case of an inventory financer would you ever go into inventory financing if you had checked the records and knew that there was an accounts receivable financing statement on file?

MR. HAYDOCK: No.

PROFESSOR KRIPKE: I think there are people who do that.

AUDIENCE: Is it normal business procedure? Would you ever advise your client to do inventory financing without getting a waiver on it? When they do it they take a credit risk.

PROFESSOR KRIPKE: They take a credit risk. That raises a point that I think is worth mentioning and which was the subject of a quite vehement attack on our drafting on the floor of the American Law Institute. A gentleman from Massachusetts said in substance: "When we agreed to the Code, we understood that there could be purchase money priorities as to inventory, and I took it for granted that the priority would flow through to the receivables. My orientation is in favor of unsecured trade creditors, but it was on this assumption that I was willing to go along with the Code. Now you say that the inventory security interest does not carry through to receivables." His ultimate point was just like yours: "What good is the inventory financing if it doesn't carry through to the receivables." Now Bob Braucher and I answered him on the floor of the Institute, and I think the answer is still applicable and is sound. The answer is: "If you were right that your inventory financing carried through to the receivable, there wouldn't be any receivables financing and you wouldn't get paid until the receivable was paid. You'd have to extend your credit a great deal longer. By permitting receivables financing to occur, you're going to get paid when the sale occurs. You'll get paid a lot earlier, you're a trade creditor, you're not in the financing business, you need your own working capital, and you want to limit the duration of your own extensions of credit." Now, if the inventory parties are seriously concerned about the problem, they can, of course, insist on some kind of an arrangement with the receivables party that he pay them, or they'll refuse to do the inventory financing. I recall another meeting at which this question was thrashed out. Persons presently actively engaged in financing said that a number of Japanese trading companies are doing substantial amounts of inventory financing in the United States on the goods which they ship over here, knowing that others will be picking up the receivables financing and being content to lose their security interest when the goods are sold.

MR. HAYDOCK: I see that our time is up. Thank you very much.

Problem 4.1.15. *D* is a wholesaler of textiles whose business is like that described in Problems 4.1.9 and 4.1.14.

On June 1, when *D* had difficulty obtaining textiles on credit from its suppliers, *D* applied to *SP*–1 for a loan. *SP*–1 extended *D* a loan of $50,000, and *D* executed to *SP*–1 a security agreement covering "all inventory now owned or hereafter acquired." *SP*–1 promptly filed a financing statement covering "inventory now owned or hereafter acquired."

On July 1 *D* wanted to purchase $20,000 worth of additional stocks of textiles from manufacturer *M*. In response to *D*'s request *SP*–2 made a $20,000 loan to *D* by a check payable jointly to *D* and *M*; *D* indorsed the check to *M*. *D* executed a security agreement covering the new shipment. *SP*–2 immediately filed a financing statement covering "textiles, now owned or hereafter acquired." In addition, *SP*–2 immediately gave *SP*–1 written notice of the transaction. Shortly thereafter *M* delivered the textiles to *D*.

In September *D* defaulted on the loans to *SP*–1 and *SP*–2. In the meantime, textiles purchased from *M* under the July transaction had been sold to retail stores, generating (i) unpaid accounts of $15,000; (ii) a separate deposit collateral account containing $5,000, which came from payments by retail stores of such accounts; and (iii) a check for $4,000 received as an advance payment for an order of textiles that were subsequently shipped to the buyer.

Who has priority with respect to (i) the unpaid accounts of $15,000; (ii) the $5,000 in the deposit account; (iii) the $4,000 check? See UCC 9–322(a), (b); UCC 9–324(a)–(c); UCC 9–102(a)(9). What explains the result?

It may help to take the following steps: (a) Is the purchase-money priority under UCC 9–324(a) applicable to this case? (b) Does the purchase-money priority for inventory under UCC 9–324(b) carry through to proceeds in the form of accounts? (Note: "identifiable *cash* proceeds.") (c) As to the identifiable cash received from the payments of accounts, note the language of UCC 9–324(b): "cash proceeds . . . received *on or before* the delivery of the inventory to a buyer." (d) Is any of the "special" rules in UCC 9–322(c)–(f) applicable to these proceeds? If not, what result follows from the general rules of UCC 9–322(a) and (b)?

SECTION 2.   BUYERS OF GOODS

INTRODUCTORY NOTE

We have seen that UCC 9–201(a) provides secured lenders with powerful words of comfort: "Except as otherwise provided in [the Uniform Commercial Code], a security agreement is effective . . . against *purchasers* of the collateral, and against creditors." Of course, Article 9 does "otherwise provide[ ]" if a security interest is not perfected; certain buyers of goods (and instruments, documents, tangible chattel paper, and security certificates) can prevail under UCC 9–317(b). See Section 2(B), infra. But when the security interest *is* perfected (usually by filing), then UCC 9–201, especially when read in conjunction with UCC 9–315(a)(1), stands as a serious threat to buyers. In many circumstances a buyer who fails to check the public records will have only itself to blame if its ownership interest is encumbered by a security interest.

(A) PERFECTED SECURITY INTERESTS AND BUYERS OF GOODS

We deal first with priority contests between buyers of goods and secured parties with *perfected* security interests.

Problem 4.2.1. Gadget Construction Co. is in the road construction business. Gadget has a line of credit with Wowsers State Bank ("Bank"), secured by all of Gadget's construction equipment. Bank's security interest is perfected by filing. The security agreement signed by Gadget strictly prohibits Gadget from selling, leasing, or otherwise disposing of any of the collateral without first obtaining Bank's written permission.

Gadget's business was slow during the winter months. On February 1 Gadget sold two of its front-end loaders to Penny, Inc., another construction company. Penny did not check the UCC records and had no knowledge of Bank's security interest or Gadget's agreement not to dispose of the equipment. Gadget used the funds received from Penny to pay various unsecured creditors.

Gadget is in default, and Bank has made demand on Penny to deliver the two loaders to Bank.

(a) Is Bank's security interest senior to Penny's interest in the loaders? See UCC 9–315(a)(1). If so, is the security interest of any practical value to

Bank? See Notes (1) and (2) on Authorized and Unauthorized Dispositions, infra.

(b) Assume that Bank's security interest continued in the loaders following the sale to Penny (i.e., that Penny bought the loaders *subject to* Bank's security interest).

(i) Does Bank's security interest continue to be perfected as against creditors of Penny? Is Bank under a duty to file a new financing statement against Penny? Should it be? If Bank is under no duty to refile, how can Penny's creditors discover that Penny owns the loaders subject to Bank's "secret" security interest? See UCC 9–507(a) & Comment 3; PEB Commentary No. 3; Note (2) on Authorized and Unauthorized Dispositions, infra.

(ii) If Bank's security interest continues to be perfected, for how long does the perfected status last? See UCC 9–316(a), (b). What additional information do you need to answer the preceding question?

(c) What result in part (a) if the security agreement permits Gadget to sell collateral free of the security interest "on the condition that, immediately following any such sale, Gadget remits the net proceeds of the sale to Bank." See UCC 9–315(a)(1) & Comment 2; National Livestock Credit Corp. v. Schultz, infra; Notes on Authorized and Unauthorized Dispositions, infra. Would your answer be different if Penny had *known* about the foregoing "condition"?

(d) What result in part (a) if the security agreement permits Gadget to sell collateral on the condition that Bank's security interest will continue in the collateral (i.e., sales are to be *subject to*, instead of *free of*, the security interest)? See UCC 9–315(a)(1) & Comment 2; PEB Commentary No. 3; Note (1) on Authorized and Unauthorized Dispositions, infra.

(e) What result in part (a) if, during the last two years, Gadget has sold unneeded equipment on several occasions, and Bank, which was aware of those dispositions, raised no objection with Gadget? What difference, if any, would it make if Penny had been a party to several of these sales? See UCC 1–103(b) [F1–103]; UCC 1–303 [F 1–205]; Note (3) on Authorized and Unauthorized Dispositions, infra.

Problem 4.2.2. The facts are as in the preceding Problem. Assume that Bank's security interest continued in the loaders following the sale to Penny and that, on February 1 (the date of Penny's purchase), $25,000 was outstanding on the line of credit. Unaware of the sale, Bank extended an additional $5,000 on the line of credit on March 1 and an additional $10,000 on April 1.

(a) Can Bank enforce its security interest in the loaders to recover the entire $40,000? See UCC 9–322(a); UCC 9–323(d), (e). (The equitable doctrine of "marshaling," discussed in Chapter 9, Section 3(B), infra, may affect the result.)

(b) What result in part (a) if Bank had learned of the sale to Penny on February 15?

This Problem concerns the priority of "future advances." Problem 4.1.2, supra, raises a similar priority dispute; however, the competing claimant in that Problem is not a buyer, but another secured party. Compare your answers to this Problem with your answer to Problem 4.1.2. Can you explain any differences in result? (The 45–day periods in UCC 9–323(b), (d), and (f) derive from the Federal Tax Lien Act. See Chapter 8, Section 4(E), infra.)

National Livestock Credit Corp. v. Schultz[*]

Court of Appeals of Oklahoma, 1982.
653 P.2d 1243.

■ BRIGHTMIRE, JUDGE.

The major question raised by this appeal is whether the terms of a cattle security agreement regarding sale of the cattle, designed for perfected lender's protection, were waived by the creditor's long-term course of conduct inconsistent with the protective provisions. A secondary issue is whether a secured party is estopped to deny authorization of the sale in a suit for conversion against the buyer based upon a detrimental reliance theory. The trial court resolved both issues against the loan company. We affirm.

I

The facts are not disputed. G.W. "Bill" Schultz and his son were the general and limited partners of Schultz Cattle Co., that ran and grazed cattle until 1973 when it began a so-called "fat cattle" operation.[1] Beginning in April 1964, Schultz Cattle Co. financed its operation with funds from loans obtained through National Livestock Credit Corporation. The financial arrangement was such that in April 1964 a note was executed in excess of $400,000 payable to National in one year. In each of the succeeding years a new note was executed representing the carry over indebtedness of the cattle company from the preceding year's operations. The last such note, and the one that forms the basis of the present suit, was executed on July 27, 1973, in the principal sum of $586,639.02, payable on July 1, 1974. G.W. Schultz signed the note as co-maker with Schultz Cattle Co. and both executed a security agreement to National giving it a security interest in the herd, including after-acquired cattle and proceeds. Also executed was a loan agreement that, among other things, allowed Schultz to draw whatever money he needed over the course of the year to operate his business. Through this type of arrangement there would be no need for Schultz to retain any portion of the proceeds received from sales of cattle to meet business expenses.

The security agreement also provided: "The Debtor will care for and maintain the crops and property herein described in a good and

---

[*]   [The court's citations are to the applicable pre–1972 version of the UCC.]

[1]   That is, cattle were raised and fed at a feedlot and sold for slaughter at a higher rate of return.

husbandlike manner and will not further encumber, conceal, remove or otherwise dispose of the same without the written consent of the Secured Party; however, permission is granted for the Debtor to sell the property described herein for the fair market value thereof, providing that payment for the same is made jointly to the Debtor and to the Secured Party. . .."

The loan agreement contained no conditional consent provision, but did say that "Borrower agrees to remit all funds from sale of secured property directly to National" to apply toward the indebtedness.

Between 1973 and 1974, Schultz sold portions of the collateral cattle to various packers without the prior written consent or knowledge of National. In every instance, the check was made payable to Schultz Cattle Co. only. Schultz, in turn, either mailed the check to National or deposited the packer's check into the Cattle Co.'s account and then issued a new check to National to pay off the note indebtedness. National concedes that it never rebuked Schultz for ignoring the terms of the security agreement relating to sales of secured cattle. As a matter of fact, it admits this procedure was customarily followed by all its loan account clients and by the industry as a whole.

In 1974 and 1975, Schultz, along with the entire cattle industry, began experiencing severe financial problems. By a letter dated April 19, 1974, National's then manager, Harley Custer, informed Schultz that several loans would have to be "shaken down fairly well," including the Schultz Cattle Co. loan and that this loan would be discussed at the next board meeting. On June 20, 1974, Custer again wrote Schultz saying there would be no renewal of the loan, due July 1, 1974, because National's bank would approve no more loans and National could not carry the loan unless it were discounted. Custer told Schultz that the loan could be extended an additional 60 to 90 days if Schultz could reduce the loan amount by $200,000. National, however, agreed to a plan by Schultz to liquidate the herd as "fat cattle" over a period of several months instead of immediately selling the cattle as feeders—the expectation was that this plan would increase the value of the herd by $100,000.

It was anticipated, said Custer, that under this program cattle would be sold out of the feedlot to a packer buyer beginning in September 1974 and that National was leaving it solely up to Schultz to decide to whom he would sell the cattle. And, according to Custer, the procedure for handling the proceeds of the sales was to be the same as it had been in the past, i.e., packer would send check to Schultz Cattle Co. in its or Schultz' name and then the cattle company would forward the check to National.

Schultz could not sell the cattle during the fall of 1974 and this spawned weekly calls from Custer to Schultz expressing the lender's concern that no sales had been made. "We had fulfilled our part of the plan in advancing this money [additional money for feed, and extending the note's due date]," he once said, "and we did want him to get to selling these cattle. . . ."

Eventually, some sales were made to a small processing plant owned by Schultz (Schultz Farms), and the proceeds of these sales were remitted to National in the usual manner. On January 5, 1975, Wilson and Company bought 34 steers and 42 heifers from Schultz on a grade and yield basis[2] for a total fair market value of $29,089. Wilson acquired 42 more heifers on January 6 for which it paid a grade and yield price of $14,609. On January 8, Schultz sold 140 heifers to Iowa Beef Processors (IBP) for $50,330.24 and on January 19 sold another 148 head to IBP for $51,121.73. With the exception of the last draft paid by IBP,[3] all of the checks were made payable to Schultz Cattle Co. or Schultz Industries, as directed by Schultz. The proceeds, however, were not transmitted to National, but rather to some of Schultz' feed suppliers.

Upon learning of the sales and Schultz' application of the proceeds to grain bills, National liquidated the remaining herd and otherwise attempted to salvage what it could to reduce the loan balance. National also made demand of Wilson and IBP for payment, which demand, of course, was refused. Schultz, in the meantime, had filed bankruptcy. On March 3, 1976, National filed this action against Wilson and IBP claiming the unauthorized sales to them were in derogation of its security interest and filed financing statements and constituted conversion.

Defendants in their answer admitted the respective purchases of cattle and that they rejected National's demand for the purchase price, but denied they had converted the cattle. IBP also raised the affirmative defenses of waiver and estoppel. Wilson alleged, among other things, "that a pattern and practice of dealing was developed over many years whereby [National] allowed . . . Schultz . . . to keep possession of all [secured] cattle," sell them without National's knowledge or consent and remit the proceeds of the sale to National; therefore, National waived the consent terms in the security agreement, relinquished its security interest in the cattle and is estopped to assert any claim against Wilson. Both defendant buyers specifically asked for reasonable attorney's fees.

Cross-motions for summary judgment were filed by plaintiff and defendants. By letter order dated July 10, 1980, the trial court granted summary judgment in favor of the defendants after finding that National waived the sale restriction terms of the security agreement through a "course of performance" that allowed Schultz to remit only the proceeds of such sales to National. "Thus," the court said, "National authorized Schultz to sell the cattle to IBP and Wilson without restriction and they took title free and clear of National's security interest." Moreover, the court concluded, National was estopped to demand literal compliance with the payment provisions of its security agreement on a detrimental reliance

---

2.   The sales price for cattle bought on a grade and yield basis as opposed to live weight basis is not determined until after the cattle are slaughtered.

3.   At this point in time, National had learned of the sales and Schultz' failure to pay it the proceeds. National instructed IBP to make the last check jointly payable to Schultz Cattle Co. and National, and IBP complied.

theory on the authority of Poteau State Bank v. Denwalt, Okl., 597 P.2d 756 (1979). Finally, the trial judge denied the defendants' prayer for attorney's fees upon the theory that 12 O.S.1979 Supp. § 940(A) does not apply to conversion of property causes of action.

National timely filed its petition in error challenging the judgment. . . .

II

The arguments raised by National in its voluminous brief boil down to this: only the provisions of general Article One of the Uniform Commercial Code and of secured transactions Article Nine govern security agreements, and therefore, the trial court erred in finding that the course of performance and waiver provisions of Article Two can be invoked to undermine express terms of a security agreement. It further argues there were no transactions between National and defendant packing companies that could act to estop National from asserting its security interest in the cattle.

Since we affirm the trial court's order as to the waiver issue, it becomes unnecessary to address the detrimental reliance theory.

National concedes, as it must, that the uniform code expressly provides that its provisions shall be supplemented by principles of law and equity unless these principles have been displaced by particular provisions of the act. 12A O.S.1981 § 1–103. The code, too, explicitly provides that it is to be liberally construed and applied to promote its underlying purposes and policies, one of which is "to permit the continued expansion of commercial practices through custom, usage and *agreement of the parties.*" 12A O.S.1981 § 1–102(1) & (2)(b) (emphasis added).

The principal code provision having application to the present appeal is 12A O.S.1981 § 9–306, which provides in part:

"(2) Except where this Article otherwise provides, a security interest continues in collateral, notwithstanding sale, exchange or other disposition thereof, *unless the disposition was authorized by the secured party in the security agreement or otherwise,* and also continues in any identifiable proceeds including collections received by the debtor." (emphasis added)

Clearly, the statute continues the secured party's security interest both in the collateral in the hands of a buyer as well as the proceeds received by the borrower from the unauthorized sale of the collateral. The security interest can be lost, however, and is lost if the sale is authorized by the secured party in the "security agreement or otherwise."

The trial court found the undisputed facts to be that National's prior conduct and its actions in regard to the sales at issue here constituted a waiver of its contractual rights. While National does not deny the facts are undisputed, it does disagree with the court's conclusion on the ground that the doctrine of waiver cannot be applied to a U.C.C. security agreement. More specifically National contends that the court impermissibly applied an Article Two concept to an Article Nine transaction, and in advancing this thesis it assumes that the only statutory basis for the decision is 12A O.S.1981 § 2–208.[5]

We think National misapprehends the basis of the trial court's decision and the effect the separate articles of the uniform code have on one another as well as the effect supplemental principles of law and equity have on commercial transactions. Another provision in Article One, which is applicable to all sections of the code, amply supports the trial court's legal conclusions.

As at least one court has quite correctly pointed out, the definitions in Article One (12A O.S.1981 § 1–201) are automatically made a part of each article in the code and thus a "security agreement" must first be an "agreement" as defined in § 1–201. And, since an agreement is defined by the code as "the bargain of the parties in fact as found in their language or by implication from other circumstances including . . . course of performance as provided in this Act (Section . . . 2–208)," this has to include security agreements. Therefore, a certain course of performance can result in the waiver of an express term in a security agreement.[**]

There is yet another U.C.C. basis for the invocation of the waiver theory. Section 9–306(2) contemplates extinguishment of a security interest if disposition of collateral is authorized by a secured party "in the security agreement *or otherwise*." The italicized language cannot be considered as mere surplusage and, in fact, the connective "or" gives it at least as much substantive value as the express terms of a security agreement. National's course of conduct certainly has to be considered as an "otherwise" authorization of the sale that resulted in defendant purchasers taking the cattle free from National's security interest.

Finally, apart from the interconnections among the various articles and sections of the code, the previously mentioned §§ 1–103 and 1–102—which allow for supplementation of the code with principles of law and equity in determining rights of the parties—require the court to look not only at the words used by the parties but to analyze their conduct as well in determining what agreement they actually made and what the equities should be. Certainly the facts of this case lend themselves to the application

---

5.   This section, entitled "Course of Performance or Practical Construction," provides:

"(1) Where the contract for sale involves repeated occasions for performance by either party with knowledge of the nature of the performance and opportunity for objection to it by the other, any course of performance accepted or acquiesced in without objection shall be relevant to determine the meaning of the agreement.

. . .

"(3) Subject to the provisions of the next section [2–209] on modification and waiver, *such course of performance shall be relevant to show a waiver* or modification *of any term inconsistent with such course of performance*." (emphasis added)

**   [Revised Article 1 reformulates somewhat the UCC provisions concerning "course of performance" and moves them to UCC 1–303. As a consequence, they apply directly to security agreements.]

of one time honored maxim of equity: "Where one of two innocent persons must suffer by the act of a third, he who has enabled such third person to occasion the loss must suffer." Pettis v. Johnston, 78 Okl. 277, 190 P. 681 (1920).

Assuming National is an innocent party, it made no effort to alter the customary financial practices of prosperous times after the cattle business turned sour. This "business as usual" attitude made it possible for Schultz to misapply the funds in question and, therefore, from an equitable standpoint National should bear the loss.

[Judgment affirmed.]

NOTES ON AUTHORIZED AND UNAUTHORIZED DISPOSITIONS

(1) "Authorized" Dispositions. UCC 9–315(a)(1) provides that "a security interest . . . continues in collateral notwithstanding sale, lease, license, exchange, or other disposition thereof unless the secured party authorized the disposition free of the security interest." Thus a disposition of the collateral causes a security interest to terminate if the secured party has authorized the disposition *free and clear* of the security interest, but the security interest survives a disposition of the collateral if the secured party has authorized the disposition *subject to* the security interest. Is this a sensible rule? Is it reasonable to require a transferee to investigate the details of any authorization given by its transferor's secured party? (Keep in mind that the transferee normally will be able to identify the secured party by searching the appropriate public records.)

(2) Consequences of an Unauthorized Disposition: Remedies Against Collateral and Proceeds; Continued Perfection. A secured party whose security interest survives an unauthorized disposition is entitled to exercise its rights against the collateral, such as the right to take possession from the debtor, the purchaser, or any other junior party following the debtor's default. See UCC 9–609; see generally Chapter 9, infra. (Note that in the typical case the unauthorized disposition itself would constitute a default.) This is, of course, the clear implication of the continuation of the security interest. UCC 9–315(a)(2) also makes it clear that the secured party is entitled not only to the continued security interest in the original collateral *but also* to the identifiable proceeds of that collateral. Does this give the secured party a "windfall"? A "double recovery"? Keep in mind that the secured party will be entitled to only one satisfaction of the secured debt.

A secured party's continuing security interest following an unauthorized disposition also will be effective against the purchaser's creditors and transferees. Under UCC 9–507(a) a financing statement continues to be effective following a disposition of collateral "even if the secured party knows of or consents to the disposition." UCC 9–507(a). (Of course, if a secured party "consents" to a disposition *free of* the security interest, the security interest will not continue and the effectiveness of the financing statement will not matter. See Note (1), supra.) It follows that when a security interest is perfected by filing and continues following a disposition, the security interest may remain perfected until and unless the financing statement lapses. The secured party is not obliged to file a new financing statement, even though no one searching against the buyer's name would discover the filing against the original debtor. Earlier in these materials we noted Professor Westbrook's criticism of this rule and the operation of the second sentence of Former 9–402(7) (insofar as a secured party need not refile against a new name following a debtor's name change.) See Westbrook, Glitch: Section 9–402(7) and the U.C.C. Revision Process, 52 Geo. Wash. L. Rev. 408 (1984); Chapter 3, Section 3(A), supra. See also Chapter 8, Section 1, infra (considering some troublesome priority contests arising from the operation of UCC 9–507(a)).

Article 9's choice-of-law rules may temper the effects of UCC 9–507(a) to some extent. As we saw in Chapter 3, Section 4, supra, when collateral is sold or otherwise transferred to a person who becomes an Article 9 debtor, how long the security interest retains its perfected status depends on where the buyer or other transferee is located (within the meaning of UCC 9–307). If the buyer is located in the jurisdiction in which the financing statement has been filed, then the security interest remains perfected until lapse. But if the buyer is located in another jurisdiction, the security interest becomes unperfected one year after the transfer, unless the security interest is perfected under the law of the transferee's jurisdiction before the year expires. UCC 9–316(a), (b). When a security interest becomes unperfected under these circumstances, not only third parties are affected; the buyer, too, may benefit. If within the year the secured party fails to file (or otherwise perfect) in the jurisdiction where the buyer is located, the security interest is "deemed never to have been perfected as against a purchaser of the collateral for value." UCC 9–316(b). Thus, a buyer who bought subject to a security interest that was perfected normally will take free of the security interest, which becomes unperfected. See UCC 9–316(b); UCC 9–317(b); Problems 3.4.3 and 3.4.4, p. 198, supra; Section 2(B), infra.

(3) Waiver, Estoppel, Course of Performance, and Course of Dealing. UCC 9–315(a)(1) does not prescribe the manner by which a secured party must authorize the disposition of collateral free of its security interest. The statutory silence on this point invites a buyer of goods covered by a perfected security interest to assert that the disposition was "authorized" by the secured party. Even in the absence of UCC 9–315(a)(1), a buyer could attempt to prove that the secured party had waived or subordinated its security interest. Cf. UCC 9–339. In many situations, however, the buyer will be unable to marshal evidence sufficient to establish, through UCC 1–103(b) [F1–103], a common-law waiver. See, e.g., Weidman v. Babcock, 241 Va. 40, 400 S.E.2d 164 (1991) (" 'Waiver is the voluntary, intentional abandonment of a known legal right, advantage, or privilege.' Essential elements of the doctrine are both knowledge of the facts basic to the exercise of the right and the intent to relinquish that right. A waiver of legal rights will be implied only upon clear and unmistakable proof of the intention to waive such rights; the essence of waiver is voluntary choice.").

In a proper case a secured party also might be estopped from asserting that its security interest continues in collateral following a disposition. But, as with waiver, buyers often cannot prove the reasonable reliance on the secured party's actions or omissions that is necessary to establish an estoppel. "A well-established principle of estoppel doctrine provides that in order for silence and inaction to estop a person from pressing some right or claim, there must have been a timely opportunity for the person to speak or act and, in addition, an obligation to do so." Hillman, McDonnell & Nickles, Common Law ¶ 22.04[2][d], at 24–54 to 24–55 (citing 3 J. Pomeroy, Equity Jurisprudence § 808a (S. Symons 5th ed. 1941)).

Because buyers usually lack the clear evidence necessary to establish a true waiver or an estoppel, they often argue that an authorization should be inferred from a secured party's conduct. (Keep in mind that a buyer asserting that a disposition was authorized typically will not have known, at the time of sale, about the facts relevant to the issue of authorization; rather, the buyer will be making the assertion "after the fact.") Indeed, an alternative holding in the *Schultz* case, supra, is that the secured party's conduct—repeatedly failing to insist on the debtor's compliance with a requirement that checks for livestock sold be made jointly payable to the debtor and the secured party—constituted an authorization under Former 9–306(2) (UCC 9–315(a)(1)). The *Schultz* court also pointed to the secured party's conduct as evidence of a "course of performance" sufficient to constitute a waiver of the offended provisions of the security agreement, citing UCC 2–208 (now UCC 1–303). The cases that have inferred authorizations from the secured party's conduct reflect the following common-sense approach: "A secured party deserves no protection from the terms of a security agreement that he himself ignores." Hillman, McDonnell & Nickles, Common Law ¶ 22.02[1][b][iv], at 22–27.

A "course of dealing" may provide another rationale for finding an authorization. See UCC 1–303(b) ("A 'course of dealing' is a sequence of conduct concerning previous transactions between the parties to a particular transaction that is fairly to be regarded as establishing a common basis of understanding for interpreting their expressions and other conduct."). (Former 1–205(1) is to the same effect.) But when a course of dealing and the "express terms of an agreement" cannot reasonably be construed "as consistent with each other," the express terms prevail. UCC 1–303(e) [F1–205(4)]. Consequently, some courts have declined to allow a course of dealing to overcome an inconsistent provision of a security agreement, especially if the security agreement provides that a consent to a disposition must be in writing.

What seems to be missing in the UCC, the case law, and the commentary is a principled approach to putative authorizations. Should a court stretch to find an authorization, thereby diluting the value of a security interest, or should it practice a contrary bias? It is important to note, here, that the case law construing Former 9–306(2) may be contaminated by the over-representation of cases in which the buyer was a *buyer in ordinary course of business* ("BIOCOB") of *farm products*. See F1–201(9) (definition of "buyer in ordinary course"); F9–109(3) (definition of "farm products"). Buyers of inventory in ordinary course of business take free of security interests granted by their sellers. See F9–307(1); UCC 9–320(a) (considered in more detail in Problem 4.2.3, p. 284, and the Note on p. 285, infra). However, buyers of farm products—even if in the ordinary course—are exempted from the cleansing benefits of Former 9–307(1) and UCC 9–320(a). See Note (5), infra. To the extent that reported cases involve sales of farm products in the ordinary course of business (excluded from the benefits of Former 9–307(1)), they may not provide useful precedents for non-ordinary course dispositions of other types of collateral.[10]

(4) Conditional Authorization of Sales. Recall that the security agreement in the *Schultz* case gave the debtor permission "to sell [collateral] . . . for the fair market value thereof, providing that payment for the same is made jointly to the Debtor and to the Secured Party." Implicit in the court's opinion is the belief that when a debtor fails to comply with the condition, a buyer acquires the goods subject to the security interest. Otherwise, the court's reliance on the secured party's conduct as authorizing the sale would not have been necessary.

The effectiveness (as against the debtor's transferee) of these "conditional authorizations" also was upheld in Southwest Washington Production Credit Association v. Seattle–First National Bank, 92 Wn.2d 30, 593 P.2d 167 (1979) (sale was not authorized because debtor failed to comply with condition of authorization requiring debtor to pay over proceeds of disposition to secured party). Consider the following critique of the result and reasoning of that case:

> The reasoning of the court in *Southwest* is problematic, however. First, the only unauthorized aspect of the debtor's disposition in such a case is the failure to remit the sale proceeds. The sale itself is authorized. Moreover, even if such a disposition is properly deemed unauthorized, the reasoning in *Southwest* runs counter to well-established principles of agency law that should apply directly to cases such as *Southwest*. The secured party's consent never is required for a debtor to sell his own rights in collateral. The true significance, therefore, of authorizing a debtor to dispose of collateral is to empower him to sell the secured party's own interest in the property. The debtor in effect becomes the secured party's agent for this purpose. When an agent acts for his principal, the rights acquired by one who deals with the agent are unaffected by the agent's failure to follow secret instructions of his principal even though the principal is disclosed. Further, the law is clear that when an agent is authorized to deal with

---

10.   Most buyers of inventory from merchants need not rely on UCC 9–320(a) alone: Creditors secured by inventory often expressly authorize the debtor's ordinary-course sales of inventory free of the security interest. Agricultural lenders, however, normally insist on restricting the debtor's authority to sell farm products collateral.

chattels, the "interests of the principal are affected by an unauthorized transaction of the same kind as that authorized."[132] Professor Seavey wrote that for this reason, if an agent's authority to sell is conditioned on the agent holding the proceeds for his principal, "the rights of a transferee can not, of course, be taken away by his [the agent's] failure to perform the condition subsequent."[133]

The court's reasoning in the *Southwest* case also ignores the predicament of the debtor's transferee. As observed by the court in *First National Bank v. Iowa Beef Processors*,[134] when a secured party consents to a sale of collateral in the debtor's own name provided the debtor remits the proceeds to the secured party,

> such a condition makes the buyer an insurer of acts beyond its control. The . . . [secured party] has made performance of the debtor's duty to remit proceeds . . . a condition of releasing from liability a third party acting in good faith. [The buyer from the debtor] could not ascertain in advance whether this condition would be met . . .; nor did [this buyer] . . . have any control over the performance of the condition, as long as it paid . . . [the debtor].[135]

These considerations led to the conclusion in *Iowa Beef* that "even though the secured party conditions consent on receipt of the proceeds, failure of this condition will not prevent that consent from cutting off the security interest under [Former] Section 9–306(2)."[136]

Hillman, McDonnell & Nickles, Common Law ¶ 22.02[2], at 22–28 to 22–29. A majority of the cases, like *Iowa Beef*, do not give effect to similar conditions placed on authorizations to dispose of collateral; they treat dispositions as being authorized even when the conditions are not satisfied.

The facts surrounding the "conditional authorization" may be determinative. Consider, for example, Baker Production Credit Association v. Long Creek Meat Co., 266 Or. 643, 513 P.2d 1129 (1973), which involved more than $88,000 of proceeds of the sale by a debtor, Cattle Feeders, of livestock from a large herd in which Baker PCA held a security interest. The court stated, "[t]he evidence is clear and undisputed that Baker PCA was aware that Cattle Feeders was selling cattle to Meat Company and had no objection to those sales"; however, the PCA's consent was "on condition that payment was received when the cattle left the feed lot for delivery to Meat Company." Both Meat Company and its lender, Bank, knew about the arrangement between Cattle Feeders and Baker PCA; specifically, both knew that the PCA's consent to disposition of the cattle was conditional.

---

132. [Restatement (Second) Agency] §§ 175(2) (disclosed principal), 201(2) (undisclosed principal) [1958].

133. W. Seavey, Handbook of the Law of Agency § 66 at 115 (1964).

134. 626 F.2d 764 (10th Cir. 1980).

135. Id. at 769.

136. Id.

Bank refused to honor drafts that Meat Company drew on Bank to pay Cattle Feeders for the cattle; instead, Bank applied the proceeds in the account to overdue debt that Meat Company owed to Bank. The court concluded (i) that the sale of the cattle by Cattle Feeders was not authorized because the condition for authorizing the sale was broken by nonpayment and (ii) that Bank was liable to Baker PCA for conversion of the funds.

In the above-quoted passage, Professors Hillman, McDonnell, and Nickles express concern about "the agent's [i.e., the debtor's] failure to follow secret instructions of his principal." Nevertheless, they would reach a different result where the debtor's transferee *knows* of the conditional authorization and, consequently, is in a position to ensure compliance (such as by remitting proceeds directly to the secured party). For this reason, they approve of the result in the *Baker PCA* case. Hillman, McDonnell & Nickles, Common Law ¶ 22.02[2], at 22–30 n. 141.

Comment 2 to UCC 9–315 indicates that Revised Article 9 does not "address the frequently litigated situation in which the effectiveness of the secured party's consent to a disposition is conditioned upon the secured party's receipt of the proceeds. In that situation, subsection (a) leaves the determination of authorization to the courts, as under Former Article 9." Does UCC 9–315(a)(1) admit of a construction that would render a conditional authorization effective to cut off a security interest when the transferee does not know of the condition but ineffective when the transferee knows of the condition? Would it be reasonable to insist instead that prospective transferees identify secured creditors (by searching the financing statement records) and confirm the existence or nonexistence of (and any conditions on) the secured party's authorization of dispositions? (Again, the "ordinary course" nature of sales of farm products may engender additional sympathy for the plight of the farm products transferee.)

(5) Farmers and Farm Products: Amendments to Former 9–307(1); The Food Security Act; UCC 9–320(a). We mentioned above that farm products were excluded from the general rule of Former 9–307(1) that protected buyers in ordinary course of business. Responding to a large volume of litigation and widespread dissatisfaction with the farm products exception in Former 9–307(1), several states repealed (or limited) the farm products exception. Mr. Clark's withering barrage of questions, quoted below, offers some insight into the nature and extent of the criticisms of the farm products exception.

> The farm products rule was something of an anomaly. Marketing agents, auctioneers, and packers argued with force that Article 9 gives unusual protection to agricultural financers at the expense of buyers in the ordinary course of business. If buyers of automobile inventory take free of a security interest, why should not the same rule apply to ordinary course buyers of cattle and crops? Is this not a case where the urban-oriented drafters of Article 9 mistakenly viewed farmers and ranchers as other than sophisticated borrowers? Does the farm products exception not encourage lack of diligence on the part of lenders in

policing their loans, because they can always collect from the auctioneer or packer if their debtor defaults and fails to turn over proceeds from the sale of farm products collateral? Is it fair that an innocent auctioneer, selling as a mere agent for the debtor, should be liable in conversion under the farm products exception? . . . Is it right for the courts to allow agricultural financers to ignore so often the "prior written consent" boilerplate in their security agreements? Instead of enforcing these restrictions, is it not the custom to trust the debtor to sell the cattle or crops, collect the proceeds, and remit them to the secured party? Should the buyers in ordinary course assume the risk of the debtor's default, or is this a risk that agricultural lenders are in a better position to assume and distribute by adjusting the cost of credit? Is not the lender adequately protected in that its security interest carries over to the proceeds? Has the farm products exception not led some courts to invoke too stingily the common-law concepts of implied consent, waiver, and estoppel? Should the purchaser have to show an express consent in order to carry the day? Why should the law protect a secured party who knows that the debtor is selling cattle or crops without prior written consent, but who does not object to the practice?

Clark, Secured Transactions ¶ 8.08[4][a], at 8–105 to 8–106.

In 1985 Congress intervened. Section 1324 of the Food Security Act of 1985, Pub. L. No. 99–198, § 1324, 99 Stat. 1535 (1985) (codified at 7 U.S.C. § 1631) preempts the farm products exception of Former 9–307(1) and UCC 9–320(a). Under the federal statute, ordinary course buyers take free of security interests in farm products—subject to two significant exceptions. (The Act also protects commission merchants and selling agents.)

The first exception applies when (i) a buyer has received a notification that contains certain details (specified in the statute) concerning a security interest, including "any payment obligations imposed on the buyer by the secured party as conditions for waiver or release of the security interest" and (ii) "the buyer has failed to perform the payment obligations." 7 U.S.C. § 1631(e)(1)(A)(v), (e)(1)(B). For example, if a buyer has received a conforming notification stating that a security interest will be released upon a buyer's delivery to the debtor of a check that is jointly payable to the debtor and the secured party, and the buyer fails to comply with that "payment obligation," then the buyer will take its interest subject to the security interest. To take advantage of this exception, agricultural lenders typically require their debtors to provide a list of prospective buyers and send a notification to each of those prospective buyers.

The second exception applies to certain buyers who buy "a farm product produced in a State that has established a central filing system." 7 U.S.C. § 1631(e)(2). (Nineteen states have established such a system.) The statute specifies the attributes of a qualifying "central filing system." 7 U.S.C. § 1631(c)(2). In general, a "central filing system" involves two lists. One list relates to "effective financing statements" that are filed by secured parties and that contain certain information (specified in the statute) concerning security interests in farm products. (Inasmuch as the "central filing system" is wholly separate from the regular UCC filing system, filing an "effective financing statement" has nothing to do with "perfection" of a security interest.) The other list contains information concerning prospective buyers of farm products who have registered by filing a form in the system. To qualify, the system must require a state's Secretary of State to match up, on a regular basis, buyers whose forms have named particular debtors and the effective financing statements filed against those debtors, and to send to the registered buyers information concerning the relevant effective financing statements. Id. Under the operative priority rule, the buyer will take subject to a security interest if (i) the buyer has failed to register in the system and the secured party has filed an "effective financing statement," or (ii) the buyer has received a notice from the Secretary of State concerning that security interest and the buyer has not complied with the requirements for a waiver or release of the security interest. 7 U.S.C. § 1631(e)(2), (e)(3).

Why does the priority rule for buyers of farm products collateral warrant such a complicated (some might say, convoluted), federally imposed system? Why, as Mr. Clark's questions suggest, cannot agricultural lenders live with the same rules applicable to inventory financing generally? One answer is suggested by the inherent characteristics of agricultural production and marketing. Unlike inventory generally, many farm products are marketed only a few times each year—e.g., at harvest-time or after cattle are fattened. Moreover, sales frequently may involve a large proportion (sometimes all) of the farm products owned by a debtor at the time. These factors indicate that the prospects for a secured lender to be left "high and dry" are materially greater in the case of agricultural financing. (UCC Article 6, which regulates "bulk sales" of a large proportion of a merchant's inventory, reflects similar concerns; however, Article 6 is primarily for the benefit of unsecured creditors. See generally Notes, p. 293, infra.)

In the face of nonuniform state approaches to the problem, it is understandable that buyers of farm products would seek a federal solution. A well-drafted statute easily could deal with the principles embraced by the Food Security Act. However, as written, the statute is fraught with problems. It contains internal inconsistencies and appears to have been drafted without the benefit of an understanding of past and present systems of public notice and secured financing. It fails to acknowledge or deal with many matters that are adequately dealt with by the UCC. For example, it largely ignores the issues and problems raised by multi-state transactions. It also makes possible circular priorities that otherwise would not appear. Consequently, it is not surprising that its detractors hold it up as a prime example of the dangers of creeping federal encroachment on commercial law. For another example, see 7 U.S.C. § 196, which protects cash sellers of livestock to packers by imposing a trust for the benefit of the sellers.

UCC 9–320(a) protects buyers in ordinary course of business in much the same fashion as did Former 9–307(1). Yet despite the fact that several states repealed or limited the farm products exception to Former 9–307(1), and despite the enactment of the Food Security Act, UCC 9–320(a) carries forward the farm products exception. That UCC 9–320(a) retains the approach to farm products taken by Former 9–307(1) does not necessarily reflect widespread satisfaction. Instead, it probably indicates the absence of a strong consensus for change and the realization that achieving uniformity among the states on this issue is unlikely in any event.

Problem 4.2.3. The Diapason Music Company is a retail store that sells electric organs, grand pianos, and other expensive musical instruments. Diapason's inventory has been purchased with the aid of loans from Castle Finance Company. Diapason has executed in Castle's favor a security agreement covering its inventory, both existing and after-acquired. Castle filed a financing statement that described the collateral as "organs, pianos and other musical instruments."

(a) Diapason, without consulting Castle, sold and delivered an organ to Customer, a consumer, for $4,000 cash, and used the money to pay rent, utilities, and other pressing bills. Promptly upon learning the facts, Castle brings a replevin action for the organ against Customer. What result? See UCC 9–315(a)(1); UCC 9–320(a); UCC 1–201(b)(9) [F1–201(9)]. (If you are not sure whether subsection (a) or subsection (b) of UCC 9–320 applies to this Problem, see UCC 9–320, Comment 5.) What considerations underlie the UCC's rule on this point? Whose expectations does the rule reflect?

(b) Suppose that the security agreement in part (a) included the following covenant: "Diapason agrees that, under no circumstances, will it complete a sale of any of its inventory without Castle's prior approval. In the event of such approval, Diapason will immediately turn over to Castle any cash, chattel paper or other proceeds resulting from such sale." Suppose also that the financing statement added the sentence, "Sale of collateral not authorized without Castle's prior approval." Would the result change? See UCC 9–320(a); UCC 9–401(b). Does the UCC's rule make sense?

(c) Would the result in part (a) change if Diapason delivered the organ to Customer under a month-to-month lease? See UCC 9–321(c); UCC 2A–103(1)(o) [R2A–103(1)(u)].

(d) Clef, a similar music store in the same city, needed a particular model of organ in order to make prompt delivery to a customer. Diapason had such an organ in stock. In accordance with past arrangements between the two firms, Diapason sold the organ to Clef for $3,000 cash, which was slightly more than wholesale cost. Clef knew that Diapason had inventory financing with Castle. As in part (a), Diapason dissipated the cash received for the organ. Castle brings a replevin action against Clef. What result? See UCC 9–315(a)(1); UCC 9–320(a); UCC 1–201(b)(9) [F1–201(9)]. What difference, if any, would it make if the past arrangements between Clef and Diapason were highly unusual among music stores?

(e) Diapason owed $4,000 to Creditor, who was pressing for payment. Diapason delivered one of the organs in the store to Creditor in satisfaction of the debt. Castle brings a replevin action against Creditor. What result? What could the losing party have done to protect itself?

(f) Assume that, in part (e), Creditor also was in the business of selling organs. Before Castle learned that Creditor was in possession of the organ,

Creditor sold and delivered the organ to Bass, who had no idea how Creditor acquired the organ. Castle brings a replevin action against Bass. What result? What could the losing party have done to protect itself?

(g) What result in part (f) if, several weeks before Creditor sold the organ to Bass, Castle had learned that Creditor was in possession of the organ but had raised no objection with Diapason or Creditor? See UCC 9–320(a) ("A buyer in ordinary course of business . . . takes free of a security interest *created by the buyer's seller*") & Comment 3, Example 2; UCC 2–403(2), (3); UCC 2–402(3); Note on the "Buyer's Seller" Rule and the Interplay Between UCC 2–403(1) and UCC 9–320(a), infra.

NOTE ON THE "BUYER'S SELLER" RULE AND THE INTERPLAY BETWEEN UCC 2–403(1) AND UCC 9–320(a)

UCC 9–320(a) contains a curious limitation: a buyer in ordinary course of business takes free only of security interests that are "created by the buyer's seller." This means that an inventory lender takes the risk that *its own debtor* will cut off the security interest by selling to a buyer in ordinary course of business, but does not risk losing its security interest if the collateral is sold by some other merchant. For example, assume that *A*, a merchant dealer in goods of that kind, sells inventory to *B*, another merchant, and that *B* is *not* a buyer in ordinary course of business (say, because the sale was in "bulk" and not in "ordinary course"). *B* then sells to *C*, who *is* a BIOCOB. *C* would cut off *SP–B*, who holds a security interest in *B*'s inventory, but not *SP–A*, *A*'s inventory secured party.

UCC 9–320(a) seems to be an analogue to UCC 2–403(2) in that a creditor secured by inventory typically can be said to have "entrusted" the collateral to the merchant-dealer. But what result obtains if *C,* in the example, could show that *SP–A* entrusted the goods to *B*? See UCC 2–403(3) (" 'Entrusting includes . . . any acquiescence in retention of possession[.]' "). As the most straightforward example, imagine that a secured party takes possession of inventory after the debtor's default (UCC 9–609) and then delivers an item of the inventory to another merchant dealer for repairs. The non-debtor merchant dealer then sells to a BIOCOB. If the sale would cut off the rights of an *owner*-entruster—and it would under UCC 2–403(2)—why should the secured party's rights remain intact?

Courts reached conflicting results under Former Article 9. Revised Article 9 leaves no doubt as to the appropriate resolution: UCC 9–315(a) makes clear that UCC 2–403(2) is an exception to the general rule that a security interest survives disposition of the collateral. Under the facts in the example above, *C* would take free of the security interest, even though *SP–A* did not authorize the disposition to *C* free of the security interest. See UCC 9–315, Comment 2; UCC 9–320, Comment 3, Example 2. The "[e]xcept" clause in R2–402(3) underscores this point.

Problem 4.2.4. Manufacturer delivered manufactured homes to Dealer on credit and, by filing, perfected a security interest in that inventory. Buyer agreed in writing to purchase one of the manufactured homes, for Buyer's business use, and Buyer made a substantial down payment to Dealer. Before Buyer took possession, Dealer defaulted on its debt to Manufacturer and Manufacturer repossessed the manufactured homes held by Dealer, including the one that Buyer had agreed to purchase.

(a) Does UCC 9–320(a) protect Buyer? See UCC 1–201(b)(9) [F1–201(9)]; UCC 2–502; UCC 9–320(e); Notes on Buyers Who Do Not Take Possession, infra.

(b) Would the result in part (a) change if the manufactured home had been "specially" constructed to Buyer's specifications, such that if Buyer were to order a similar, specially constructed manufactured home from another dealer, delivery to Buyer would be delayed at least six months? See UCC 1–201(b)(9) [F1–201(9)]; UCC 2–716. Assuming that Buyer's right to take delivery (as against Dealer) is contingent on Buyer's payment of the remaining balance of the purchase price, could Buyer become a BIOCOB before making the payment?

Problem 4.2.5. The facts are as in the preceding Problem, except Buyer agreed in writing to purchase one of the manufactured homes for Buyer's personal use as a residence.

(a) Does UCC 9–320(a) protect Buyer? See UCC 1–201(b)(9) [F1–201(9)]; UCC 2–502; UCC 9–320(e); Notes on Buyers Who Do Not Take Possession, infra. Can Buyer prevail despite UCC 9–320(e) and Comment 8? (Hint: Did Buyer become a BIOCOB *before* Manufacturer took possession?)

(b) Is there a basis other than Manufacturer's security interest for Manufacturer to attack Buyer's interest? See UCC 2–402(2); Uniform Fraudulent Transfer Act §§ 4(a)(1), 4(b)(2), 7, 8(a); Note (6) on Buyers Who Do Not Take Possession infra.

(c) Suppose that Buyer made a substantial down payment to Dealer for a manufactured home to be ordered from Manufacturer. The manufactured home was delivered to Dealer but was seized by Manufacturer before Buyer took possession. Should this modification of the facts change the result?

NOTES ON BUYERS WHO DO NOT TAKE POSSESSION

(1) In General. In Chapter 1, Section 3(A), we considered whether taking possession was necessary for protection, under UCC 2–403(1), as a good faith purchaser for value from a seller with voidable title. In that setting, the interest at risk was the general (or "beneficial") ownership interest of a person who enjoyed a right to reclaim goods that the person had sold to the seller. We saw that the significance of taking possession has been the subject of doubt and contention. Our current concern is with a putative BIOCOB under UCC 9–320(a) as against a secured party with a security interest in the goods. In particular, we consider the role of possession in determining when a buyer achieves the status of "buyer in ordinary course of business" under UCC 1–201(b)(9) [F1–201(9)].

(2) "Temporal Definition" of "Buyer in Ordinary Course of Business." The stage of a sale transaction at which a buyer becomes eligible to be a BIOCOB was a primary issue raised in both the commentary and the cases interpreting Former 9–307(1) and Former 1–201(9). A variety of views were expressed, each of them purportedly flowing from the text of the UCC and grounded in sound policy. Revised Article 9 goes a long way towards resolving this issue: "Only a buyer that takes possession of the goods or has a right to recover the goods from the seller under Article 2 may be a buyer in ordinary course of business." UCC 1–201(b)(9) [F1–201(9)]. This approach adopts the resolution proposed by Professor Frisch in the following passage (references to UCC 2–502 and UCC 2–716 do not reflect the amendments accompanying Revised Article 9 or reflected in Revised Article 2):

V. A Suggested Temporal Definition

This Article has looked at the several contemporary views of when buyer status attaches and has found that each lacks a persuasive justification for its adoption. But the separate criticisms heaped upon each fail to suggest a convincing alternative. It is only when the deficiency common to all accepted definitions is realized that the necessary materials for constructing a theoretically sound temporal definition become apparent.

Kwikset Division of Emhart Industries v. Mohawk Industrial Design Enterprises (In re Pennsylvania Conveyor Co.)[243] may clarify the problem. Kwikset had contracted to purchase a customized press from Mohawk Industrial Design Enterprises, for a price of $69,375.25. When the press was substantially completed and after Kwikset had paid $54,377.25 toward the purchase price, the press was repossessed by Mohawk's secured creditor, PennBank. Kwikset brought suit seeking possession of the press upon payment of the remainder of the purchase price. PennBank argued that Kwikset had no right of possession because the stringent prerequisites of section 2–502 had not been satisfied.

The bankruptcy court found for Kwikset. In so doing, it drew a sharp distinction between rights under section 2–502 and rights under section 9–307(1) [UCC 9–320(a)]. Acknowledging Kwikset's inability to recover from its seller under section 2–502, the court concluded that if Kwikset were to pay the balance of the purchase price it would qualify for buyer in ordinary course protection under section 9–307(1).

The *Kwikset* approach illustrates how courts and commentators have consistently failed to perceive the anomaly that one can be a buyer in ordinary course absent the availability of a possessory remedy against the immediate seller. Had Mohawk remained in possession of the press, Kwikset, because it failed to meet the requirements of section 2–502, would have been relegated to that hapless class of unsecured creditors for whom full recovery is seldom a reality. Instead, because of the

---

243.   31 Bankr. 680 (Bankr.W.D.Pa.1982).

fortuitous circumstance of PennBank's repossession, Kwikset was assured the benefit of its original bargain.

Another version of the same objection to the separability of a possessory remedy from the rights of a buyer in ordinary course views the situation from the secured party's perspective. Before the repossession, PennBank, not Kwikset, had a property interest in the press. And PennBank, not Kwikset, had the legal right of possession. But all this changed once the right of possession was exercised. When PennBank exercised its exclusive right to repossess the printing press, the exclusivity of that right was destroyed. In other words, once a secured party with the sole and exclusive right of possession repossesses the collateral, its right to retain possession is lost. This is not only bad policy, but also logically inconsistent and linguistically incoherent.

A second argument in favor of defining buyer status in terms of buyer remedies is that such a definition, more than any other, comports with the scope and purpose of the good faith purchase doctrine embodied in the Code. Because the doctrine seeks to facilitate market trading by reducing title uncertainty, its application is premised on the implicit assumption that a point in the sales transaction has been reached at which the buyer has a title expectation needing protection. In assessing where that point lies, it is helpful to think of a sale as the movement of a variety of property sticks from seller to buyer. Absent a stick in the buyer's bundle that give the right to take possession of the goods, the state of the seller's title is immaterial. If the seller breaches, the buyer's expectations are satisfied by an award of monetary damages. If there is no breach, more sticks will come and the cleansing of the seller's title can wait. The buyer's title concerns crystallize, however, once the buyer obtains the legally cognizable right to compel the seller's performance. It is with this stick in hand that the buyer's legitimate claim to good faith purchase treatment materializes.

To see why this is so, one need only understand the Code's approach to buyer's remedies. A central assumption of Article 2 is the homogeneity of goods. If the seller does not deliver the goods, the buyer will, most often, be able to obtain similar goods elsewhere. As a result, the buyer's expectation interest is fully vindicated by a damages award based on an imagined or actual substitute purchase. There are, however, situations, sufficiently out of the ordinary, in which protection of the buyer's expectation demands that the remedy be the right to obtain possession of the goods from the seller. Thus, the buyer has the limited right to recover the goods in certain insolvency situations under section 2–502, the right to specific performance under section 2–716(1), and the right to replevin under section 2–716(3).

Observe the similarity of purpose between the good faith purchase doctrine and the Code's possessory remedies. The essence of both is the perceived utility of protecting the buyer's expectation interest. As a matter of logical consistency, it is impossible to square this common goal with a decision to withhold buyer in ordinary course status until some time after the buyer becomes legally entitled to the goods. Odd indeed would be a legal regime that bestows a possessory right to protect the expectation interest but, at the same time, leaves that right unprotected because of the inapplicability of a doctrine specifically designed to protect that very same interest. Conversely, if one is unwilling to say that the buyer, not the seller, has the superior right of possession, what justification is there for terminating, in favor of that same buyer, third party claims to the goods? It is this constant interplay between remedies and expectations that calls for a definition of buyer status based on remedies. Only when the buyer's expectation interest requires, for its satisfaction, an award of a possessory remedy, should buyer status be recognized.

Frisch, Buyer Status under the U.C.C.: A Suggested Temporal Definition, 72 Iowa L. Rev. 531, 568–572 (1987).

To understand more fully the thinking behind UCC 1–201(b)(9) [F1–201(9)], consider the implications of permitting a putative buyer (*B*) of goods to become a buyer in ordinary course of business from Seller (*S*) *before B* obtains possessory rights against *S*. That approach normally would produce the anomalous result that *B* could cut off the rights of *S*'s secured party (*SP*) under UCC 9–320(a) even though *B* has no right to possession of the goods as against *S*! As discussed more fully in Note (3), infra, Article 2 would provide pre-delivery possessory rights to *B* only under the limited circumstances set forth in UCC 2–502 and UCC 2–716. Even *S*'s *unsecured* creditors can obtain rights in the goods (e.g., by execution lien) that are senior to those of *B* until such time as *B* obtains possessory rights against *S*. See UCC 2–402(1). *SP*, on the other hand, does have a right to possession as against *S* (albeit a right that normally is contingent on *S*'s default). See UCC 9–609.

Consider also the implications of permitting a buyer to become a BIOCOB and take free of a security interest when the seller (Article 9 debtor) remains in possession of the goods. Can one reconcile such a result with one of Article 9's principal themes: that a secured party ordinarily must give public notice of its interest in order to prevail over competing claimants to the collateral? Should the UCC have been revised to provide that a buyer becomes a BIOCOB only if it either removes the goods from the seller-debtor's possession or notifies the secured party of its purchase? The answer would seem to turn, at least in part, on whether inventory secured parties actually rely on the debtor's possession of particular items of inventory.

(3) Buyer's Right to Recover Goods from Seller. The temporal aspect to the definition of BIOCOB in UCC 1–201(b)(9) [F1–201(9)] compels one to focus on the circumstances under which a disappointed buyer has an *in rem* rather than an *in personam* remedy against a defaulting seller. UCC 2–716(1) affords a right to specific performance of the sale contract "where the goods are unique or in other proper circumstances." R2–716(1) also would authorize a court to decree specific performance of a nonconsumer contract if the parties have agreed to that remedy. UCC 2–716(3) affords a right to replevin of goods identified to the contract in two limited circumstances: the buyer is unable to effect cover for the goods (or the circumstances reasonably indicate that such effort will be unavailing) or the goods have been shipped under reservation and satisfaction of the security interest in them has been made or tendered.

What are the rights of a buyer who actually has paid for the goods? The secured party has a claim to the payment as proceeds of its collateral. Moreover, if the sale is in the seller's (debtor's) ordinary course of business, the secured party fully expects that the goods will be replaced by the proceeds. As between the prepaying buyer and the seller's secured party, shouldn't the buyer be entitled to the goods? The answer may surprise you: Until the recent revision of Article 9, the fact that a buyer prepaid for goods would appear to have been legally relevant to the buyer's right to recover the goods in only a narrow band of cases. Former 2–502 afforded a reclamation right "if the seller becomes insolvent within ten days after receipt of the first installment on their price," and then only if the buyer made and kept good a tender of any unpaid portion of the price. If the seller became insolvent before, or more than ten days after, receipt of the first installment, then this reclamation right was unavailable. In practice, however, prepaying buyers may have fared much better. Following is Professor Frisch's analysis:

> Consider *Proyectos Electronicos, S.A. v. Alper*.[266] Proyectos had ordered certain electronics equipment from Ram Manufacturing. The full purchase price was paid and the equipment was segregated from the rest of Ram's inventory. Unfortunately for Proyectos, Ram's bankruptcy occurred before the equipment was shipped. Recognizing Proyectos' right to recover the goods from the trustee in bankruptcy, the district court specifically considered the cumulative effect of prepayment and insolvency:
>
> > In this case Proyectos has already paid the debtor the full price for the goods. To require Proyectos to cover would require it to pay for identical goods a second time and then stand in line with other unsecured creditors of the debtor, now bankrupt, with the illusory hope that it would get reimbursed for the difference between the cost of cover and the original contract price, plus the money already paid to debtor. Such a result would not be in keeping with the purpose of the Commercial Code to make a non-breaching party whole.
>
> If it were possible to characterize the opinion in *Proyectos* as typical, the inquiry would be at an end and one would be a bit wiser for having made the effort. One would know that a buyer can establish a right to possession, at least against an insolvent seller, by showing a substantial prepayment. The buyer in ordinary course cases could then be viewed as a reaffirmation and extension of this principle, despite the

---

266.   37 Bankr. 931 (E.D.Pa.1983).

dissimilarity of rhetoric, to similar situations distinguishable only as to the identity of the party contesting the buyer.

Although this logic deduces a pervasive judicial bias in favor of the prepaying buyer, the deduction is premised on the typicality of *Proyectos*. Yet, the majority of courts continue to couch their opinions on possessory remedies in the traditional orthodoxy of uniqueness or peculiarity. The fact remains, however, that prepayment and insolvency are recurrent factual themes in most cases in which the buyer is, for some other stated reason, awarded possession; and prepayment and insolvency are absent in most cases in which possession is withheld. Because this alignment of result is not inevitable, the proposition that the buyer in ordinary course and the right to possession cases are readily explicable as a consequence of a preexistent bias is only tentatively offered. Yet, until courts articulate the relevancy, if not the determinacy, of prepayment and insolvency, intuition suggests that these facts have a part to play in determining buyer status, and that the best guess is that they play the leading role.

Frisch, Buyer Status under the U.C.C.: A Suggested Temporal Definition, 72 Iowa L. Rev. 531, 573–74 (1987).

The conflict between the paltry rights that the UCC affords to a prepaying buyer on one hand and what Professor Frisch describes as "a pervasive judicial bias in favor of the prepaying buyer" on the other has been resolved in part. As revised in conjunction with the revision of Article 9, UCC 2–502 affords considerably greater protection to prepaying buyers of consumer goods: a buyer of consumer goods who has paid a part or all of the price of goods identified to the contract has a right to recover the goods from a seller who repudiates or fails to deliver, if the buyer makes and keeps good a tender of any unpaid portion of the price. UCC 2–502(1)(a). As a consequence, such a consumer buyer is eligible to be a BIOCOB and take from any security interest created by the seller. Should the same protection have been afforded to buyers of all types of goods?

(4) The *Tanbro* Debate. One of the most controversial cases concerning the right of a BIOCOB to take free of a security interest under Former 9–307(1) (the predecessor to UCC 9–320(a)) is Tanbro Fabrics Corp. v. Deering Milliken, Inc., 39 N.Y.2d 632, 385 N.Y.S.2d 260, 350 N.E.2d 590 (1976). The case concerned unfinished textile fabrics ("greige goods") manufactured by Deering Milliken. Deering sold these goods and others to Mill Fabrics on a "bill and hold" basis; i.e., the goods would be paid for but remain in Deering's warehouse to be delivered as Mill Fabrics instructed. Mill Fabrics agreed that the goods, even if paid for, would secure the obligations of Mill Fabrics to Deering. Mill Fabrics (the Article 9 debtor) resold the goods to Tanbro, also on a bill and hold basis. Deering (the secured party) refused to deliver the goods (Deering's collateral) to Tanbro on Tanbro's instruction because, although these goods had been paid for, there was an open account balance due Deering from Mill Fabrics, which had become insolvent. Tanbro brought an action in conversion against Deering.

The New York Court of Appeals affirmed the judgment for Tanbro. It found that Mill Fabrics' sale to Tanbro was in the ordinary course of business, and that, as a buyer in ordinary course of business, Tanbro took free of Deering's security interest. The court also found, on an alternative analysis, that such a sale by Mill Fabrics was impliedly authorized under the UCC if its indebtedness to Deering was to be liquidated. The court concluded by saying, "All [Former 9–307(1)] requires is that the sale be of the variety reasonably to be expected in the regular course of an on-going business. . . .. This was such a case." 39 N.Y.2d at 637, 385 N.Y.S.2d at 262-63, 350 N.E.2d at 593.

The *Tanbro* case became a *cause celebre* that generated dispute among specialists in secured financing. Professor Kripke argued strenuously that the case was wrongly decided and that the buyer (Tanbro) should bear the risk that inventory is encumbered with a possessory security interest:

> It is irrelevant to argue that it is not commercially feasible for the law to require buyers to inspect the goods and ascertain that the seller has them, and that therefore the secured party as the person best able to bear the risk should bear it. Of course, I do not contend that every buyer should inspect the goods. Trust in fair dealing and honesty is the foundation of all forms of business, but when there is a mistaken reliance on the seller to have unseen goods, it is obvious that there is not always a likely victim to bail out the buyer who thinks that he is in ordinary course of business. As we have seen, the buyer who thinks that he is in ordinary course is out of luck if the seller never had the goods or if he has sold them or if a secured party has repossessed them and thus taken title in himself or another. Why should a secured party who has done everything that he could, namely, taken them into his possession and eliminated any apparent ownership by the merchant, be the one victim required to bail out the improvident or unlucky buyer?

> When a secured party has taken possession in himself, he has done everything he could to preclude the existence of a buyer in ordinary course. In my opinion, the Code should not make it impossible to have a loan on goods which are not in fact available for exhibition, sale and delivery by the merchant, without running the risk of losing the security through sales to purported buyers in ordinary course, just because the goods are classified as inventory. The fact that the goods are not in the buyer's possession, but are held by the secured party under an adverse claim of right, makes them very different from ordinary inventory.

Kripke, Should Section 9–307(1) of The Uniform Commercial Code Apply Against a Secured Party in Possession?, 33 Bus.Law. 153, 159 (1977). Both the *Tanbro* opinion and Professor Kripke's article provoked others to address the issue at some length.

Revised Article 9 resolves the debate by rejecting *Tanbro*. UCC 9–320(e) provides expressly that the "BIOCOB-takes-free" rule of UCC 9–320(a) "do[es] not affect a security interest in goods in the possession of the secured party under Section 9–313."[11]

(5) Buyer's Nonpayment in Cash Sale. Assume that *B*, in a *cash sale* transaction, has a right to specific performance under UCC 2–716(1). Notwithstanding *B*'s right to specific performance, does *B* actually have a possessory right against *S* before *B* pays the price? See UCC 2–511(2); UCC 2–511(1). If not, and if *B*'s interest is (consequently) subordinate to *S*'s inventory lender, *SP*, what remedy does *B* have against *S*? See UCC 2–711; UCC 2–713.

(6) Fraudulent Transfer Implications of Seller's Retention of Possession; UCC 2–402(2). Recall the discussion of *Twyne's Case* and the "Fraud in Law" doctrine in Note (3) on page 153, supra). We noted there that modern fraudulent transfer law adopts the "fraud in fact" approach, whereby a seller's retention of possession of goods is merely a factor to be considered in determining whether the seller has made the transfer "with actual intent to hinder, delay, or defraud any creditor." Uniform Fraudulent Transfer Act §§ 4(a)(1), 4(b)(2). The UCC generally leaves the matter of fraudulent transfers to non-UCC law. However, UCC 2–402(2) does provide a safe harbor for "retention of possession in good faith and current course of trade by a merchant-seller for a commercially reasonable time after a sale or identification." Detailed treatment of fraudulent transfers is beyond the scope of these materials.

NOTES ON BULK SALES

(1) Regulation of Bulk Sales. According to the definition of "buyer in ordinary course of business," "a person that acquires goods in a transfer in bulk" is not a buyer in ordinary course of business. UCC 1–201(b)(9) [F1–201(9)]. Pre–1988 Article 6 governed certain transfers in bulk. That Article defined "bulk transfer" as "any transfer in bulk and not in the ordinary course of the transferor's business of a major part of the materials, supplies, merchandise or other inventory . . . of an enterprise subject to this Article." UCC 6–102(2) (pre–1988). "The enterprises subject to this Article are all those whose principal business is the sale of merchandise from stock, including those who manufacture what they sell." UCC 6–102(3) (pre–1988).

In 1988, the sponsors of the UCC recommended that Article 6 be repealed and not replaced. The following excerpt from the Prefatory Note to the Repealer of Article 6 explains the history of bulk sales legislation and the reasons for eliminating Article 6 from the UCC:

11.   The revised definition of "buyer in ordinary course of business," under which only a buyer who takes possession of the goods or has a right to recover the goods from the seller under Article 2 may be a BIOCOB, drastically limits the significance of the *Tanbro* debate. See UCC 1–201(b)(9) [F1–201(9)]. However, it does not resolve the debate entirely. For example, *B* might have a pre-delivery possessory right in goods by way of an entitlement to specific performance under UCC 2–716(1) even though *SP* is in possession of the goods.

Background. Bulk sale legislation originally was enacted in response to a fraud perceived to be common around the turn of the century: a merchant would acquire his stock in trade on credit, then sell his entire inventory ("in bulk") and abscond with the proceeds, leaving creditors unpaid. The creditors had a right to sue the merchant on the unpaid debts, but that right often was of little practical value. Even if the merchant-debtor was found, in personam jurisdiction over him might not have been readily available. Those creditors who succeeded in obtaining a judgment often were unable to satisfy it because the defrauding seller had spent or hidden the sale proceeds. Nor did the creditors ordinarily have recourse to the merchandise sold. The transfer of the inventory to an innocent buyer effectively immunized the goods from the reach of the seller's creditors. The creditors of a bulk seller thus might be left without a means to satisfy their claims.

To a limited extent, the law of fraudulent conveyances ameliorated the creditors' plight. When the buyer in bulk was in league with the seller or paid less than full value for the inventory, fraudulent conveyance law enabled the defrauded creditors to avoid the sale and apply the transferred inventory toward the satisfaction of their claims against the seller. But fraudulent conveyance law provided no remedy against persons who bought in good faith, without reason to know of the seller's intention to pocket the proceeds and disappear, and for adequate value. In those cases, the only remedy for the seller's creditors was to attempt to recover from the absconding seller.

State legislatures responded to this perceived "bulk sale risk" with a variety of legislative enactments. Common to these statutes was the imposition of a duty on the buyer in bulk to notify the seller's creditors of the impending sale. The buyer's failure to comply with these and any other statutory duties generally afforded the seller's creditors a remedy analogous to the remedy for fraudulent conveyances: the creditors acquired the right to set aside the sale and reach the transferred inventory in the hands of the buyer.

Like its predecessors, [pre–1988] Article 6 . . . is remarkable in that it obligates buyers in bulk to incur costs to protect the interests of the seller's creditors, with whom they usually have no relationship. Even more striking is that Article 6 affords creditors a remedy against a good faith purchaser for full value without notice of any wrongdoing on the part of the seller. The Article thereby impedes normal business transactions, many of which can be expected to benefit the seller's creditors. For this reason, Article 6 has been subjected to serious criticism.

In the legal context in which [pre–1988] Article 6 . . . and its nonuniform predecessors were enacted, the benefits to creditors appeared to justify the costs of interfering with good faith transactions. Today, however, creditors are better able than ever to make informed decisions about whether to extend credit. . . . A search of the public real estate and personal property records will disclose most encumbrances on a debtor's property with little inconvenience.

In addition, changes in the law now afford creditors greater opportunities to collect their debts. ... Moreover, creditors of a merchant no longer face the choice of extending unsecured credit or no credit at all. Retaining an interest in inventory to secure its price has become relatively simple and inexpensive under Article 9.

Finally, there is no evidence that, in today's economy, fraudulent bulk sales are frequent enough, or engender credit losses significant enough, to require regulation of all bulk sales, including the vast majority that are conducted in good faith. ...

Recommendation. The National Conference of Commissioners on Uniform State Laws and the American Law Institute believe that changes in the business and legal contexts in which sales are conducted have made regulation of bulk sales unnecessary. The Conference and the Institute therefore withdraw their support for Article 6 of the Uniform Commercial Code and encourage those states that have enacted the Article to repeal it.

The Conference and the Institute recognize that bulk sales may present a particular problem in some states and that some legislatures may wish to continue to regulate bulk sales. They believe that [pre–1988] Article 6 has become inadequate for that purpose. For those states that are disinclined to repeal Article 6, they have promulgated a revised version of Article 6. The revised Article is designed to afford better protection to creditors while minimizing the impediments to good-faith transactions.

As of this writing, 46 states are without a bulk sales law; four states and the District of Colombia have adopted revised Article 6.

(2) Does a Buyer's Compliance With Article 6 Affect Its Rights?
Bulk sales legislation was enacted primarily for the benefit of *unsecured* creditors of the seller. But for this legislation, these unsecured creditors would have no right to satisfy their claims against the seller from the property of the buyer (i.e., from the inventory sold in bulk). See generally Chapter 1, Section 3, supra (discussing the *nemo dat* principle).

In contrast, the seller's secured party (inventory lender) would seem to have little need for the protection Article 6 affords. Inasmuch as a "person that acquires goods in a transfer in bulk" is not a "buyer in ordinary course," UCC 1–201(b)(9) [F1–201(9)], a person who buys the seller's inventory at a bulk sale would not take free of perfected security interests in the inventory. See UCC 9–315(a)(1); UCC 9–320(a). Nevertheless, one court suggested repeatedly, albeit in dictum, that compliance with the notice and other requirements of pre–1988 Article 6 would enable a non-ordinary course buyer to take free of perfected security interests. In re McBee, 714 F.2d 1316 (5th Cir. 1983). For strong criticism of this, and other, aspects of the case, see Harris, The Interaction of Articles 6 and 9 of the Uniform Commercial Code: A Study in Conveyancing, Priorities, and Code Interpretation, 39

Vand.L.Rev. 179 (1986). For a somewhat less disapproving view of *McBee*, see Carlson, Bulk Sales Under Article 9: Some Easy Cases Made Difficult, 41 Ala. L. Rev. 729, 736–48 (1990).

Problem 4.2.6. Lender obtained a perfected security interest in all existing and after-acquired inventory of Poss.

(a) Poss is now in the process of assembling components into a finished widget that Nonposs has agreed to buy. Nonposs has made advance payments to Poss under the written sale contract. Is Lender's security interest in the components senior to the interest claimed by Nonposs? Can a judgment creditor of Poss acquire an execution lien on the components? If so, is the lien senior to the interest claimed by Nonposs in the goods? What, if anything, could Nonposs have done to ensure its seniority? See generally Notes, p. 287, supra.

(b) Would the results in part (a) change if Nonposs had loaned funds to Poss, the seller, in order to enable Poss to acquire the components and complete the manufacture of the widget? See Note on the "Financing Buyer," infra.

(c) Instead of agreeing to buy a widget from Poss, Nonposs agrees to buy, directly from third-party suppliers, all of the raw materials and components necessary to build a widget. Under the terms of the purchase orders, Nonposs will advance funds directly to the suppliers of the materials and components, although the goods are to be delivered directly to Poss's factory. Poss and Nonposs enter into a "service agreement" under which Poss is to manufacture the widget using the supplies "bought and paid for" by Nonposs. Is there an economic difference between this arrangement and Nonposs's prepayment under a contract of sale and the use of those funds by Poss to buy the components? Would each transaction appear in the same fashion on Poss's balance sheet? Should the result here differ from the results in (a) and (b) above? See Notes, pp. 348, infra.

NOTE ON THE "FINANCING BUYER"

We have seen that a prepaying buyer is in a precarious position until it takes delivery or obtains pre-delivery possessory rights against a seller. See Notes, p. 286, supra; UCC 2–402(1), (2); UCC 2–502; UCC 2–716.

There are many reasons why one who contracts to buy goods might be called upon to pay before delivery. The seller may require a down payment (or even prepayment of the price in full) to offset the risk that the seller will acquire or manufacture the goods only to discover that the buyer cannot or will not pay. But what of the situation where the buyer prepays to "finance" the seller's costs of manufacturing the goods to be sold to the buyer? (Among these costs might be the costs of labor, materials, rent, and utilities.) The buyer could achieve priority over subsequent lien creditors by taking and perfecting a security interest in the seller's relevant materials and in the work in process as manufacturing proceeds. The security interest could be made to secure all of the seller's obligations under the sales contract. But, assuming that there is an earlier-filed financing statement made by the seller's inventory lender (as often is the case), the buyer is left with two choices. One choice is to seek to obtain a subordination agreement from the seller's inventory lender. See UCC 9–339. The other alternative is to ensure that the security interest is a purchase-money security interest ("PMSI") and that all of the steps necessary for PMSI priority under UCC 9–324(b) are taken.

In many transactions the time and expense of obtaining a subordination agreement may make that alternative infeasible. Obtaining a PMSI also may be impractical; in addition, the PMSI may not provide the buyer with the protection it desires. For example, to comply with the strict tracing requirement of UCC 9–103(a)(2), the buyer would be required to advance funds directly to the seller's suppliers. Even then, PMSI status would be available only to the extent of the cost of the raw components, and buyer's damages for the seller's non-delivery could exceed that amount. See generally Section 1(B), supra. Problems also could arise from the commingling of PMSI-financed goods with other supplies and materials of the seller-debtor. See UCC 9–336.

Professors Jackson and Kronman recognized that the purchase-money secured party and the financing buyer perform a similar economic function and that Article 9 affords scant protection to the latter. The following excerpt reflects their proposed solution:

> The financing buyer may be elevated to parity with the purchase money lender in two ways. The first would simply be to abolish the strict tracing requirement of § 9–107(1)(b) [UCC 9–103(a)(2)] by deleting the words "if such value is in fact so used." Although the elimination of the § 9–107(b) tracing requirement may be desirable, it is also certain to be controversial.

> A more conservative solution would be to add a new subsection (c) to § 9–107 . . ., which would read as follows:

A security interest is a "purchase money security interest" to the extent that it is . . .

(c) taken by a buyer who makes advances to a seller to enable the seller to manufacture, assemble or process goods for the buyer during the period of one year following the advance, and the collateral securing the advance consists of (i) materials acquired after the advance has been made which are necessary for the manufacture, assembly or processing of the contract goods, and (ii) goods manufactured, assembled, or processed after the advance has been made which could be used to satisfy the contract (whether or not in a deliverable state).[147]

---

147. The proposed section limits the priority to materials received or manufacturing steps taken after the advance of the money. This is to ensure that the financing buyer is, indeed, a "financing," and not merely a prepaying, buyer. The ordinary prepaying buyer does nothing to allow the manufacturer to move forward in the completion of the contract, and should not receive a special priority in the completed goods.

No further change in the Code would be necessary; the new subsection would give the financing buyer a purchase money security interest in the goods he had contracted for, thereby making him eligible for the special priority of § 9–312(3) [UCC 9–324(b)]. In this way, the financing buyer would be endowed with the rights and charged with the duties, of a purchase money lender.

Although the latter approach lacks simplicity and elegance, it achieves the same result, so far as the financing buyer is concerned, as the abolition of the strict tracing requirement. Whichever approach is preferred, the time has come to improve the status of the financing buyer. Indeed, as we have suggested, the elevation of the financing buyer is dictated by the Code's own policy of giving new money priority protection over old. By promoting the financing buyer to parity with the purchase money lender, the Code can cure a longstanding anomaly in commercial law and effectuate the fair and uniform application of one of its own underlying policies.

Jackson & Kronman, A Plea for the Financing Buyer, 85 Yale L.J. 1, 36–37 (1975).

Professors Jackson and Kronman apparently have recanted as to the plausibility of eliminating generally the tracing requirement for PMSI's. See Jackson & Kronman, Secured Financing and Priorities Among Creditors, 88 Yale L.J. 1143, 1176 (1979) (arguing that eliminating the tracing requirement would result in a "last-in-time" priority rule leading to all credit being unsecured credit); Note (3), p. 253, supra.

Does their proposed UCC 9–107(c) have merit? Although it solves some of the commingling and tracing problems, it elevates the "new money" above the interest of the first-to-file secured party as to *all* of the qualifying goods. Those goods might be of a value considerably in excess of the amount of the financing buyer's advances, thereby giving the financing buyer a greater "equity cushion" than the normal holder of a PMSI. Would this "last-in-time" priority rule have deleterious effects on the utility of secured credit similar to (even if not so significant as) those that the authors later argued would follow from generally eliminating the tracing requirements for PMSI's? Would the proposed solution exacerbate the problem of commingling in cases of multiple financing buyers who claim the same collateral? Is the plight of the financing buyer limited to so few transactions

The relevant test should be, not the strict tracing requirement itself, but rather a test that looks to see if the financing money has actually been used in a manner that arguably enabled the debtor to progress towards completion of its contract with the financing buyer. This test is, itself, a kind of "tracing" requirement. It looks to any manufacturing steps taken after the receipt of the money from the financing buyer that further the production of goods that are for, or arguably could be for, the financing buyer. The existence of such a continuing manufacturing process signals that the money has been used in an "enabling" sense for that contract. The equities that attach to the purchase money lender, as a consequence, also attach here.

that the alternative of obtaining subordination agreements is more cost-effective than creating additional complexity in the statute?

(B) UNPERFECTED SECURITY INTERESTS AND BUYERS OF GOODS

Problem 4.2.8. On June 1 *SP* loaned $50,000 to *D*. On the same day, to secure the loan, *D* granted a security interest to *SP* by signing a security agreement covering "all equipment now owned or hereafter acquired." *SP* inadvertently failed to file a financing statement.

On July 1 *D* sold an item of equipment (a used backhoe) to *B*–1, a competitor, for $5,000 cash. That same day *B*–1 came to *D*'s place of business and picked up the backhoe and took it away. *B*–1 knew nothing of *SP*'s security interest.

(a) On July 15 *SP* discovered the error and demanded that *B*–1 deliver the backhoe to *SP*. Advise *B*–1. See UCC 9–317(b); UCC 9–310(a), (b).

(b) On July 15 *SP* discovered the error and filed the financing statement in the proper office. On August 1, *B*–1 sold the backhoe to *B*–2. Whose rights are senior, *SP*'s or *B*–2's? See UCC 2–403(1).

(c) Now assume that *SP* did not file a financing statement. However, *SP* found out about the sale to *B*–1 as well as the imminent sale to *B*–2. On August 1, while *B*–2 was at *B*–1's place of business preparing to load the backhoe on *B*–2's truck, *SP* showed up and said to *B*–2, "Don't go through with that sale. I want the backhoe; I have a security interest in it!" *B*–2 ignored the demand and took the backhoe away. Whose rights are senior, *SP*'s or *B*–2's?

Problem 4.2.9. On June 1 *SP*, with *D*'s authorization, filed a financing statement covering "equipment." The following day *D* sold an item of equipment (a used backhoe) to *B*, a competitor, for cash. That same day *B* came to *D*'s place of business, picked up the backhoe, and took it away. *B* did not conduct a UCC filing search. On June 15 *SP* loaned $50,000 to *D*. On the same day, to secure the loan, *D* granted a security interest to *SP* by signing a security agreement covering "all equipment now owned or hereafter acquired."

(a) On July 15 *SP* discovered the sale to *B* and demanded that *B* deliver the backhoe to *SP*. Advise *B*. See UCC 9–317(b); UCC 9–308(a).

(b) Would your advice to *B* change if *D* had signed the security agreement on June 1 and *SP* made the $50,000 loan two days thereafter?

(c) Under the facts of part (b), would your advice to *B* change if on June 1 *SP* also had made the $50,000 loan to *D* and then made another $50,000 loan on June 15? See UCC 9–323(d), (e). Do you need additional facts to answer this question?

Problem 4.2.10. Your client, *B*, is interested in buying, for cash, a large quantity of used construction equipment from *S*, a contractor that is going out of business. What precautions would you take to ensure that your client gets good title to the equipment free of all Article 9 security interests? How would you structure the closing of the transaction (i.e., payment and delivery of the equipment)? See UCC 9–317(b), (e).

NOTES ON UNPERFECTED SECURITY INTERESTS AND BUYERS OF COLLATERAL

(1) The "Delivery" Requirement. UCC 9–317(b) conditions a buyer's taking free of an unperfected security interest on both the giving of value and the receipt of delivery of the property "without knowledge of the security interest . . . and before it is perfected." How can a buyer ensure its seniority? Consider the prospective buyer who searches, turns up no filed financing statements against the seller (or its predecessors in interest), and then pays the seller. What result if the buyer learns of the unperfected security interest, or if the secured party files, during the gap (which might be very short) between payment and delivery? What result if the security interest is a purchase-money security interest and the financing statement is filed shortly after the buyer pays for the goods and takes delivery?

(2) Buyers of Certain Intangible Collateral. UCC 9–317(d) applies to licensees of general intangibles and buyers of certain types of intangible collateral. For the most part, the subsection parallels UCC 9–317(b). Observe, however, that subsection (d) contains no "delivery" requirement. Unlike the collateral covered by subsection (b), the types of collateral covered by subsection (d) (i.e., accounts, electronic chattel paper, general intangibles, and investment property other than a certificated security) cannot be delivered or possessed.

SECTION 3.   LIEN CREDITORS

In Chapter 3, Section 3, supra, we saw a few fact patterns in which a security interest came in conflict with a judicial lien. This Section considers a few other fact patterns.

Problem 4.3.1. In the setting of the Prototype (Chapter 3, Section 1, supra), Lean, the holder of a judgment against Main, caused the sheriff to levy on Main's inventory of cars. Lean obtained the writ of execution and the sheriff levied after the parties had executed the Dealer Inventory Security Agreement (Form 3.2) and the Financing Statement (Form 3.1) had been filed. After the levy, Firstbank "picked up" the floorplan financing by advancing funds to Old Bank pursuant to Loan Request Form (Form 3.4), as described in the Prototype.

(a) Who has a better claim to the cars, Lean or Firstbank? See UCC 9–317(a)(2); UCC 9–203(a), (b); UCC 9–308(a); UCC 1–204 [F1–201(44)]; Dealer Inventory Security Agreement ¶ 5. What could the losing party have done to avoid the loss?

(b) Would the answer to part (a) change if the deal "cratered" because of the levy (i.e., if Firstbank never provided financing to Main)?

(c) What result in part (a) if the parties executed the Dealer Inventory Security Agreement after the sheriff levied? What could the losing party have done to avoid the loss?

Problem 4.3.2. On March 19 Main Motors executed and delivered to Firstbank the Dealer Inventory Security Agreement and Demand Note (Forms 3.2 and 3.3) described in the Prototype (Chapter 3, Section 1, supra). Immediately thereafter, pursuant to paragraph 2 of the Dealer Inventory Security Agreement, Main gave to Firstbank a Loan Request Form, requesting that Firstbank advance funds to General Motors for a trailerload of new cars. Should Firstbank make the loan as requested, even though the Financing Statement has not been filed? See UCC 9–317(a)(2); UCC 9–317(e); UCC 9–103(b), (a).

Problem 4.3.3. Using the proceeds of a loan from Credit Union, on March 1 Dombrowski, a resident of Delaware, purchased and took delivery of a car. The loan was secured by a security interest in the car. Dombrowski's application for a Pennsylvania certificate of title arrived at the Pennsylvania department of motor vehicles on March 3. The application indicated Credit Union's security interest. On March 22, the certificate of title, which indicated Credit Union's security interest, was mailed to Credit Union. Assume that under both Delaware and Pennsylvania law, a security interest in a motor vehicle is perfected when the state issues a certificate of title showing the security interest. In the meanwhile, on March 15, Eck, a judgment creditor of Dombrowski's, acquired an execution lien on the car.

(a) Which state's law governs priority between Eck's lien and Credit Union's security interest? See UCC 9–301; UCC 9–303.

(b) Is Credit Union's security interest senior or junior to Eck's lien? See UCC 9–311(b); UCC 9–317(e) & Comment 8.

Problem 4.3.4. To secure a line of credit, Party Press, a printer, created a security interest in all its inventory and equipment, existing and after-acquired, in favor of Carton Credit Co. Carton perfected the security interest by filing. On February 1 Elsie, who held a judgment against Party, caused the sheriff to levy on two of Party's presses. At the time of the levy, $250,000 was outstanding on the line of credit. Unaware of the levy, Carton extended an additional $50,000 on the line of credit on March 1 and an additional $100,000 on April 1.

(a) Who has the senior claim to the presses, Carton or Elsie? See UCC 9–317(a)(2); UCC 9–323(a), (b).

(b) What result in part (a) if Carton had learned of the levy on February 15?

This Problem concerns the priority of "future advances." Problems 4.1.2 and 4.2.2, pages 229 and 270, supra, raise similar priority disputes in which the competing claimant is a competing secured party and a buyer, respectively. Compare your answers to this Problem with your answers to the others. Can you explain any differences in result? (Hint: See UCC 9–323, Comment 4.)

SECTION 4. RECLAIMING SELLERS

In Chapter 1, Section 3, supra, we considered the rights of a reclaiming cash seller and a reclaiming credit seller as against third parties—lien creditors of, buyers from, and secured creditors of the buyer. Now that we have seen how after–acquired–property clauses facilitate lending against inventory, accounts, and other collateral that "turns over," it is useful to revisit the priority contest between a reclaiming seller and a buyer's secured creditor claiming the sold goods as after-acquired collateral.

Problem 4.4.1. In the setting of the Prototype (Chapter 3, Section 1, supra), Main Motors bought replacement parts and accessories on unsecured credit from several sources, including Supplier. A few days after making an unusually large delivery, Supplier learned that Main had stopped paying its debts. Supplier immediately sent Main a written demand to return the goods and filed an action in replevin.

Firstbank intervenes in Main's replevin action, claiming that its security interest is senior to Supplier's reclamation right.

What result? See UCC 2–702; UCC 2–403; Note on the Priority of a Reclaiming Seller, infra. Would the result change if Firstbank knew that Main routinely acquired inventory on unsecured credit? See UCC 1–201(b)(20) [F1–201(19)].

NOTE ON THE PRIORITY OF A RECLAIMING SELLER

In Chapter 1, Section 3(B), supra, we saw that the second sentence of UCC 2–403(1) distinguishes between a "good faith purchaser for value," who takes good title from a person with voidable title, and a "lien creditor," who does not. We examined in some detail whether the position of a secured party whose debtor has voidable title to goods more closely resembles that of a prototypical good faith purchaser (i.e., buyer) or that of a lien creditor. We also examined the role of reliance in resolving competing claims to goods acquired by wrongdoers. See Notes, p. 36, supra. We now return to these inquiries in the context of the "floating lien."

As you know, unless an inventory lender takes a security interest in future inventory (and accounts), its collateral base will erode and the loan may become less and less secured. Sometimes a lender agrees to make recurring advances as the debtor continues to acquire inventory and generate accounts; sometimes not. In the former case, the secured party with an after-acquired property clause acts more like a buyer, giving value in exchange for an interest in particular property; in the latter, less so. But even when after-acquired property secures an antecedent debt, the secured party usually bargains for a security interest in the after-acquired property at the time it extends the credit. In this respect it is unlike a judicial lien creditor, who extends unsecured credit and acquires its lien only in conjunction with judicial collection procedures.

UCC 2–702, which creates a reclamation right for credit sellers, provides explicitly that the right to reclaim is "subject to the rights of a . . . good faith purchaser under this Article (Section 2–403)." Under the definitions in Part 1 of the UCC, a secured party who holds a floating lien is eligible to be a good faith purchaser for value and take free of a credit seller's reclamation right. See UCC 1–201(b)(29) [F1–201(32)] ("purchase" includes taking by security interest); UCC 1–204(2) [F1–201(44)(b)] (one who acquires rights as security for a preexisting claim gives value). Although the definition of "purchase" was less explicit before the amendment accompanying Revised Article 9 (see p. 38, supra), most courts have subordinated reclamation claims of sellers based on fraud or UCC 2–702 to claims of creditors under after-acquired property clauses in security agreements. The courts generally have treated secured creditors as "good faith purchasers for value" without inquiring whether the secured creditor extended credit subsequent to or in exchange for the property that the seller delivered to the buyer.

Most courts have reached the same result with regard to cash sellers, although the route to the result is somewhat more circuitous. Unlike UCC 2–702, UCC 2–507 does not even explicitly provide for reclamation, let alone purport to address priorities. Moreover, unlike a misrepresentation of solvency, which was considered a fraud at common law and gave rise to "voidable title," failure to abide by an agreement to pay for goods upon delivery was sometimes treated as theft, giving the buyer "void title." In protecting secured parties against reclaiming cash sellers, courts have looked to UCC 2–507, Comment 3. That Comment suggests that UCC 2–507(2) addresses a cash seller's rights only as against the buyer, not against third parties who may be protected under "the bona fide purchase sections of this Article." Among those sections, clause (b) of UCC 2–403(1) supports the view that, at least when a cash seller takes a "rubber check" upon delivery, the voidable title rule applies to cash sales. See also clause (d) (applying the voidable title rule to buyers who procure delivery through fraud punishable as larcenous under the criminal law). (The recent amendments to Article 2 arguably would solidify the floating lien against cash sellers. R2–507(2) dispels any doubt that an unpaid cash seller enjoys the right to reclaim the goods from the buyer; however, new subsection (3) expressly provides that the cash seller's reclamation right is "subject to the rights of a . . . good-faith purchaser for value" under UCC 2–403.)

Some critics have opposed giving good-faith-purchase protection to all security interests in after-acquired property. They argue that a secured party should not always be entitled to increase its collateral at the expense of suppliers who deliver inventory to the debtor on unsecured credit. Rather, they would afford good-faith-purchase protection to a secured party only to the extent it extends credit against particular items of inventory (or, in other contexts, particular accounts). Do you agree with this approach? Would a statutory change be necessary to implement it, given that a secured party does not take free of a reclamation right unless it acts in good faith?

CHAPTER 5

THE SCOPE OF ARTICLE 9

The discussion in Chapter 3 of the law governing attachment, perfection, and priorities was premised upon the assumption that Article 9 applies to the transactions. Article 9 does not, however, apply to *all* secured transactions. And some of its provisions apply to transactions that do not create security interests. This Chapter examines more closely the scope of Article 9.

Substance, rather than form, controls whether a transaction is within the scope of Article 9. Article 9 applies "to a transaction, *regardless of its form*, that creates a security interest in personal property or fixtures by contract." UCC 9–109(a)(1). What exactly is the substance of a "security interest"? When does a transaction that the parties consider not to be for security nevertheless create a security interest?

To understand which transactions give rise to a "security interest," one must consult the definition of the term in UCC 1–201(b)(35) [F1–201(37)]. The first sentence explains that a security interest is "an interest in personal property . . . which secures payment or performance of an obligation." As Professor Gilmore pointed out, "[t]his, like most definitions of basic terms, is essentially a declaration of faith." 1 Gilmore, Security § 11.1, at 334.

Declarations of faith, however, are not meaningless. Section 1 of this Chapter focuses on interests in goods; it explores how courts have attempted to discern the line between security interests, as to which Article 9 applies, and other, similar property interests that are not security interests and as to which Article 9 generally is inapplicable. It not only attempts to refine the definition of "security interest" but also examines the legal treatment of nonpossessory interests in goods that are not "security interests." Section 2 addresses briefly transactions in rights to payment (receivables): accounts, chattel paper, payment intangibles, and promissory notes. (A fuller discussion of rights to payment appears in Chapter 6, Sections 1 and 2, infra.) As we shall see in each of the first two Sections, the definition of "security interest" and the scope of Article 9 extend beyond interests that secure an obligation; that is, certain interests in goods and receivables are "security interests" governed by Article 9 even though they do not "secure[ ]" payment or performance of an obligation." See UCC 1–201(b)(35) (2d sentence) [F1–201(37)]; UCC 9–109(a)(3); UCC 9–109(a)(4).

Whereas the scope of Article 9 generally is limited to interests created by contract, Article 9 nevertheless applies to statutorily-created "agricultural liens." See UCC 9–109(a)(2); UCC 9–102(a)(5). Section 3 introduces you to these liens, which are discussed more fully in Chapter 8, Section 4(C), infra. Finally, Section 4 looks at transactions that Article 9 excludes from its scope, even though they do create security interests.

Section 1.   Bailments

INTRODUCTORY NOTE

Much of Article 9 addresses problems that may arise when one person claims an interest in goods in the possession of another. Secured transactions are not the only occasion for nonpossessory interests in goods. These interests arise in a wide variety of settings. Individuals often leave goods with third parties: watches are repaired; clothing is cleaned; tools are loaned to neighbors; film is developed. Commercial transactions, too, often give rise to nonpossessory interests: grain is stored and milled; cattle are fattened in feed lots and sold; metals are refined; construction equipment is leased.

Many of these interests may pose problems similar to those posed by nonpossessory security interests: they may be sham transactions; they may create "ostensible ownership" problems. See generally Chapter 3, Section 3(A), supra. The priority rules contained in Part 3 of Article 9 provide the Article's "solution" to the problems of nonpossessory security interests. As you know, security interests as to which no public notice has been given generally are unperfected, see UCC 9–308(a), and unperfected security interests generally are subordinate to the rights of third parties who claim an interest in the collateral. See, e.g., UCC 9–317(a)(2), (b); UCC 9–322(a)(2). See also Chapter 4, supra. To what extent does the UCC impose this solution on transactions that create nonpossessory interests in goods but that are not for security? To what extent should it do so? These are two of the questions that are the focus of this Section.

The law applicable to most nonpossessory interests in goods contains no public notice requirement akin to the Article 9 perfection rules. Rather, third parties take subject to a nonpossessory interest even if the holder of that interest does not publicize it. But see, e.g., UCC 2–403(2) (buyer in ordinary course takes rights of entruster of goods) (discussed in Chapter 1, Section 3(C), supra). Debtors and secured parties desirous of avoiding the application of Article 9's filing and priority rules may be tempted to document a secured transaction in another way (say, as a lease). Similarly, a secured party who has failed to perfect a security interest may argue in retrospect that the transaction does not create a security interest and so the failure to perfect (e.g., file) was irrelevant.

The law distinguishes between security interests and most other nonpossessory interests in goods not only with respect to perfection and priority rules but also with regard to the enforcement rights of the person not in possession. Article 9 affords debtors certain rights and imposes upon secured parties certain duties that cannot be waived. See UCC 9–602; Chapter 9, infra. The law applicable to other, similar transactions may afford no such protection to the person in possession of the goods. This disparity, too, may prompt secured parties to assert that their interests are not security interests.

The scope provisions of Article 9 preclude debtors and secured parties from overriding the substantive provisions of the Article (whether relating to the secured party's remedies or the relative rights of competing claimants to the collateral) by characterizing what is in essence a security interest as something else. To determine whether to reject the parties' characterization of a particular transaction, however, one must have an idea of what a security interest is.

Many of the transactions that create nonpossessory interests in goods are bailments. A commonly used definition of "bailment" is that of Justice Story: "a delivery of a thing in trust for some special object or purpose, and upon a contract express or implied, to conform to the object of the trust." J. Story, Commentaries on the Law of Bailments § 2 (6th ed. 1856). Professor Williston defined bailment even more broadly as "the rightful possession of goods by one who is not the owner." 4 Williston & Thompson, Law of Contracts § 1032 (rev. ed. 1936). This Section examines several common types of bailments with a view toward determining (i) whether the transaction creates a "security interest" and (ii) if not, what law regulates the nonpossessory interest.

(A) LEASES

INTRODUCTORY NOTES

(1) The Role of Personal Property Leasing. A firm that wishes to acquire equipment may be reluctant (or unable) to pay with cash on hand. One option is to acquire the equipment on secured credit. Even a firm with strong credit may prefer, however, to acquire the use of the equipment by entering into a lease. The following are among the reasons that prompt firms to lease goods: the lessor may be able to purchase equipment in large quantity at advantageous rates and may have efficient outlets for disposing of used equipment; the lessor (Xerox and IBM are examples) may have special skill in servicing technical equipment; a leasing arrangement may give the lessee a higher tax deduction than the rate of depreciation on equipment that it purchases; the lessee may have promised other creditors (e.g., in a credit agreement or bond indenture) that it would not grant security interests in its property. In some situations leasing has tax advantages for the lessor, who is able to pass a portion of the tax savings along to the lessee. For example, a lessor who has substantial income from other sources may wish to take advantage of tax deductions for accelerated depreciation.

These various factors have produced in recent decades a tremendous growth in equipment leasing. For example, during the 1990's business investment in leased equipment in the United States nearly doubled—from 388 billion dollars in 1990 to an estimated 738 billion dollars in 1999. The annual volume of equipment leases in the United States rose during that period from 124 billion dollars in 1990 to an estimated 226 billion dollars in 1999. Of the new equipment currently accepted for delivery in the United States, nearly one-third is leased. Leasing also plays an important role in the acquisition of consumer goods. These transactions range from week-to-week "rent to own" leases of television sets to long-term leases of expensive automobiles.

(2) The Legal Consequences of Distinguishing Leases From Secured Transactions. One might argue that the lessor's interest under a lease "secures payment or performance of an obligation" and is therefore always a "security interest" within the meaning of UCC 1–201(b)(35) [F1–201(37)]: If the lessee fails to comply with its obligations under the lease, e.g., fails to pay rent, then the lessor may retake the goods. Despite this potentially broad reading of "security interest," the last sentence of the definition makes clear that not every lease creates a security interest. See UCC 1–201(b)(35) ("Whether a transaction in the form of a lease creates a 'security interest' is determined pursuant to Section 1–203."). F1–201(37) is to the same effect.

How does one determine whether Article 9 applies to a particular transaction that has been documented as a lease? Before answering this important question, it is useful to have in mind some of the consequences of the distinction between putative leases that are within the scope of Article 9, and other ("true") leases.

A lease for security is nothing other than an Article 9 secured transaction dressed up in lease terminology. The "lessee," who is obligated to make periodic payments, is an Article 9 "debtor." The "lessor," who is entitled to payment and who enjoys the right to recover the leased goods upon the "lessee's" default, is an Article 9 secured party. The attachment, perfection, priority, and remedial rules of Article 9 apply to the transaction, just as if the parties had used the secured transaction form and terminology. In contrast, a "true lease" is not an Article 9 transaction. Article 2A governs the rights of the lessor and lessee in a true lease transaction. To some extent, Article 2A also governs the rights of third parties.

The need to distinguish between a lease for security and a true lease arises in a variety of contexts. Of primary importance is that the "lessor's" interest in goods under a lease for security is an Article 9 security interest. To protect its interest against the claims of third parties, the "lessor" must file a financing statement; otherwise, the "lessor's" security interest will be unperfected and the competing claimant probably will take priority over the "lessor." See UCC 9–317(a)(2), (b); UCC 9–322(a)(1). (Perfecting by taking possession of the goods is an alternative to filing, but it is of virtually no practical use in a transaction, like a lease for security, which is characterized by the debtor ("lessee") using the goods.) In contrast, absent a statute to the contrary, filing is irrelevant as to true leases.

If the "lessee" under a lease for security enters bankruptcy, the "lessor's" failure to file a financing statement will result in the avoidance (nullification) of the "lessor's" interest by the bankruptcy trustee. See BC 544(a)(1) (discussed in Chapter 7, Section 2(A), infra). The failure of a lessor under a true lease to file a financing statement will not affect the lessor's rights in bankruptcy.

Another consequence of the application of Article 9 to leases for security is that the "lessor" under such a lease must comply with Part 6 of Article 9 upon the "lessee's" default. (Part 6 is discussed in Chapter 9, infra.) In contrast, the rights and obligations of a lessor under a true lease upon the lessee's default are described in UCC 2A–523 to 2A–532.

UCC 1–201(b)(35) and UCC 1–203 afford some guidance on the question whether a particular lease is a security interest subject to Article 9 or is a lease (i.e., a "true lease") subject to Article 2A. (These substance of these provisions appeared in F1–201(37).) Please read them carefully as you work through the following Problems.

Problem 5.1.1. Smith and Jones entered into a written agreement concerning a machine having a useful life of ten years. No financing statement was filed with respect to the machine. Six months after Jones took possession, Lean, one of Jones's creditors, acquired an execution lien on the machine. Under which of the following scenarios, if any, is Lean's lien senior to Smith's interest? In any case where Lean's lien is senior, what, if anything, could Smith have done to avoid the loss?

(a) Smith agreed to sell the machine to Jones for $120,000, payable $10,000 monthly. Smith retained title until Jones made all 12 payments. See UCC 1–201(b)(35) [F1–201(37)]; UCC 1–203 [F1–201(37)]; UCC 9–109(a)(1); UCC 9–317(a)(2); UCC 9–310(a); UCC 2A–307(1).

(b) Smith agreed to lease the machine to Jones for one year at $10,000 per month. The lease gives Jones the option to buy the machine at the end of the year for $10.

(c) Smith agreed to lease the machine to Jones for one year at $1,200 per month. The lease gives Jones the option to buy the machine at the end of the year for $110,000.

(d) Smith agreed to lease the machine to Jones for ten years at $1,200 per month. At the end of the lease term, Jones must return the goods to Smith.

(e) Smith agreed to lease the machine to Jones for one year at $10,000 per month, with an option to renew the lease at $1 per month for each of the following nine years. At the end of the lease term, Jones must return the goods to Smith.

(f) Smith agreed to lease the machine to Jones for ten years at $10,000 per month for the first year and $1 per month thereafter. At the end of the lease term, Jones must return the goods to Smith.

Problem 5.1.2. Grace agreed to lease a bread wrapping machine to Royer's Bakery for one year at $10,000 per month. Royer's has the option to purchase the machine at the end of the lease term for $1. Royer's also has the right to terminate the lease at any time without penalty, provided it gives thirty days' advance notice to Grace. No financing statement was filed with respect to the machine.

(a) At the end of the first month of the lease, Lean acquired an execution lien on Royer's interest in the machine. Is the execution lien senior or junior to Grace's interest?

(b) Assume that the transaction creates a security interest in favor of Grace and that Royer's defaults after making only one monthly payment. If the property is sold pursuant to UCC 9–610 for $110,000, how are the proceeds of the sale to be allocated? (Under UCC 9–615(d)(1), the debtor is entitled to any surplus after satisfaction of the secured obligation and any related costs of sale. What is the size of the secured obligation?)

(c) Would your answer to part (a) change if Lean acquired the lien during the eleventh month?

(d) If you believe that Grace's interest is junior in part (a) or part (c), what could Grace have done to avoid the loss?

Problem 5.1.3. Manufacturer agreed to lease a $6 million aircraft to Airline for three years at $2.3 million a year. Airline has the option to purchase the aircraft at the end of the lease term for $500,000.

(a) Is Manufacturer an Article 9 secured party?

(b) Assume that the transaction creates a security interest in favor of Manufacturer and that Airline defaults after making the payment for year two.

(i) If the property is sold pursuant to UCC 9–610 for $4 million, how are the proceeds of the sale to be allocated? (Under UCC 9–615(d)(1), the debtor is entitled to any surplus after satisfaction of the secured obligation and any related costs of sale. What is the size of the secured obligation?)

(ii) If the property is sold pursuant to UCC 9–610 for $2.2 million, what is the size of Manufacturer's deficiency claim; i.e., how much more, if anything, does Airline owe Manufacturer? See UCC 9–615(d)(2) (obligor is liable for any deficiency).

Problem 5.1.4. Developer was constructing a new office building. A local ordinance required Developer to install sprinklers throughout the building. Developer agreed to lease a sprinkler system from Wetco for three years at $1,000 per month. No financing statement was filed with respect to the sprinkler system. Developer has the option to purchase the system at the end of the lease term for $10,000. If Developer does not exercise the purchase option, then it must return the system to Wetco. To remove the system from the building, Developer would incur costs (including the costs of repairing the damage to the building caused by the removal) totaling approximately $50,000.

Lean acquires an execution lien on Developer's interest in the sprinkler system.

(a) Is the execution lien senior or junior to Wetco's interest?

(b) If you believe that Lean's lien is senior in part (a), what, if anything, could Wetco have done to avoid the loss?

In re: Pillowtex, Inc.[*]

United States Court of Appeals, Third Circuit, 2003.
349 F.3d 711.

■ FUENTES, CIRCUIT JUDGE

Duke Energy Royal LLC ("Duke") appeals from an order of the District Court denying a motion to compel Pillowtex Corporation ("Pillowtex" or "debtor") to make lease payments owing under the Master Energy Services Agreement ("MESA"), an agreement its predecessor entered into with Pillowtex. The District Court denied Duke's motion on the grounds that the MESA was not a true lease, but rather a secured financing arrangement. The sole issue in this appeal is whether the District Court correctly determined that the MESA entered into between Pillowtex and Duke prior to Pillowtex's bankruptcy filing was a secured financing arrangement rather than a true lease. We affirm because we agree with the District Court that, based on the economic realities of the underlying transaction, the MESA was a secured financing arrangement.

I. Facts and Procedural Background

Because the nature of the MESA is at issue, we first turn to its provisions and the transaction underlying the agreement. Pillowtex and Duke entered into the MESA on June 3, 1998. Pursuant to the MESA, Duke agreed to install certain equipment "for the purpose of improving the efficiency of energy consumption or otherwise to reduce the operating costs" incurred by Pillowtex at its facilities. (MESA § 2.5). The MESA covered two different sets of energy services projects, one involving production equipment and the other energy-savings equipment. The production equipment was provided to Pillowtex by Duke pursuant to separate stand-alone agreements, which were recorded as true leases on Pillowtex's books, and which the parties agree constituted true leases. Therefore, only the nature of the parties' arrangements concerning the energy-savings equipment is at issue in this appeal.

The energy-savings equipment included certain lighting fixtures, T8 lamps and electronic ballasts (collectively the "lighting fixtures"), which were installed in nine of Pillowtex's facilities and a new wastewater heat recovery system that included hot water heating equipment (the "wastewater system" and together with the lighting fixtures, the "energy fixtures"), which was installed at Pillowtex's Columbus, Georgia plant. The

---

[*]   [The court's citations are to Former Article 9.]

lighting fixtures were selected, and the wastewater system was constructed, specifically for Pillowtex's facilities.

In order to induce Pillowtex to enter into the energy services projects, Duke offered to originate funding for the production equipment "on a two-to-one basis (i.e., for every $ 1 million of energy projects Duke would originate $ 2 million for funding of equipment) with a minimum of $ 28 million in funding for equipment leasing or financing." Another incentive Pillowtex had for entering into the agreement was "that the energy projects would be cost neutral to Pillowtex for the term of the agreement; that is, Pillowtex's payments to Duke would be equivalent to Pillowtex's actual savings . . . and Pillowtex would then reap the benefits from the cost savings after the end of the term of the project." In keeping with this arrangement, Pillowtex accounted for its payments to Duke under the MESA as a utility expense.

The MESA provided that the cost of acquiring and installing the energy fixtures would be paid by Duke, which incurred total costs of approximately $ 10.41 million. (MESA § 5). Of this amount, approximately $ 1.66 million was for material and labor costs for the wastewater system. Approximately $ 4.46 million was for labor to install the lighting fixtures and $ 4.29 million was for material costs for the lighting fixtures, which is to say that the cost of labor to install the fixtures was higher than the cost of the actual materials themselves. Also, Duke paid approximately $ 223,000 to dispose of light fixtures and related equipment that it removed from Pillowtex's facilities.

In exchange, Pillowtex was to pay Duke on a monthly basis one-twelfth of Pillowtex's annual energy savings, in an amount the parties agreed to in advance, until the end of the MESA's 8 year term. (MESA § 7.0). In addition, the parties agreed that the simple payback of all of Duke's costs was not to exceed 5 years. (MESA § 4.1(f)). "Simple payback" is synonymous with "payback period," an accounting term which refers to "the length of time required to recover a venture's initial cash investment, without accounting for the time value of money." BLACK'S LAW DICTIONARY 1150 (7th ed. 1999). In other words, the payments were structured to ensure that Pillowtex would make predetermined, equal monthly payments and that Duke would recover its costs 3 years prior to the end of the term of the MESA. Although the MESA was for an 8 year term, the parties agree that the useful life of the energy fixtures was 20–25 years.

It is undisputed that Duke and Pillowtex intended to structure the MESA to have the characteristics of a lease and that the parties were trying to create a true lease. Indeed, Pillowtex's counsel conceded during oral argument before the District Court, "I don't disagree that [the MESA] was structured to have those characteristics for tax purposes and, you know, to [the] extent they could, the parties were trying to create a true lease, I would admit that." The parties intended for the MESA to be structured as a true lease, in large part, because Pillowtex was subject to capital expenditure limitations under its senior credit facility and did not wish to have the energy-savings equipment count as capital expenditures under that facility. Nevertheless, the MESA is not labeled a lease and it does not refer to the parties as lessee and lessor. Also, Duke alleges that the parties were concerned with structuring the MESA's provisions relating to energy-savings equipment in accordance with the requirements of Financial Accounting Standard 13, which sets the standards for financial accounting and reporting for leases. However, the MESA fails to qualify as a true lease under P 7 of that standard because the present value of the total payments due under the MESA exceeds the value of the original cost of the energy fixtures.

In keeping with their intent to structure the transaction as a lease, the MESA provides that title to the equipment would remain with Duke. (MESA § 11.0, App. at 308). Also, Pillowtex agreed not to claim ownership of the equipment for income tax purposes, (MESA § 9.13(ii)), and Pillowtex was not obligated to purchase the equipment at the end of the term of the MESA. Rather, the MESA provided the following four options to Duke at the conclusion of its term, if Pillowtex was not then in default:

> (i) remove the Equipment installed and replace those [sic] Equipment with equipment comparable to those originally in place, provided that no such replacement shall be required with respect to Production Equipment; or,
>
> (ii) abandon the Equipment in place; or,
>
> (iii) continue this Agreement until the expiration of the term hereof and then extend the term of this Agreement for such additional period(s) and payment terms as the parties may agree upon; or,
>
> (iv) give the Customer the option of purchasing all (but not less than all) of the Equipment at a mutually agreed upon price.

(MESA § 8.3). If Duke elected to exercise option (i), it was bound to "be responsible for all costs and expenses in removing such Equipment, including costs to repair any damage to [Pillowtex's] Facility caused by such removal." (Id.)[2] Despite the existence of the option for Duke to repossess the equipment, Pillowtex's Vice President for Engineering, Michael Abba, testified that in his understanding, there was no chance of that option being exercised:

> It was clearly my understanding that Duke would abandon the Lighting Fixtures and the Wastewater System at the conclusion of the MESA and in fact statements were made to me by Duke sales personnel to that effect. Moreover, because the energy projects were of no economic benefit to Pillowtex until the end of the term when Pillowtex would reap the energy savings going forward, I would not have signed off on the projects if the Lighting Fixtures and Wastewater System were not to be abandoned. I also believe that, based on the prohibitive cost of removing and replacing the Lighting

---

2.   In the event of a default by Pillowtex, Duke would have the right to remove the equipment at Pillowtex's expense, without being obligated to replace it, and could terminate the MESA. (MESA § 13.2).

Fixtures and the Wastewater System for Pillowtex, Duke [had] no choice but to abandon the Lighting Fixtures and the Wastewater System at the end of the term of the MESA.

Abba Affidavit at P 6.

After Duke and Pillowtex executed the MESA, Duke entered into a Master Lease Agreement ("Master Lease") with General Electric Capital Corporation ("GECC"), dated August 2, 1999, pursuant to which GECC agreed to finance the lighting fixtures for four of the nine Pillowtex facilities in which Duke was to install new fixtures pursuant to the MESA. Concurrently with the execution of the Master Lease and the execution of an equipment schedule listing lighting fixtures subject to the Master Lease, Duke and GECC entered into a Collateral Assignment Agreement through which Duke granted GECC a security interest in all of Duke's rights and interests in the MESA, including Duke's right to payment under the MESA, as security for Duke's obligations under the Master Lease. Also, in connection with the Master Lease transaction, Pillowtex executed an Acknowledgment Letter which provides that its interest in the MESA and equipment covered by it "is subject and subordinate to [GECC's] rights under . . . the Master Lease Agreement . . . between GECC and Duke." Shortly after Duke and GECC entered into the Master Lease, on August 12, 1999, GECC and SouthTrust Bank executed a Master Assignment Agreement, pursuant to which GECC assigned all of its rights and interests in the Master Lease and the Collateral Assignment it had with Duke, as well as the MESA and certain other documents, to SouthTrust. Therefore, with respect to the lighting fixtures, SouthTrust holds the rights and interests under the MESA for the lighting fixtures at four of Pillowtex's facilities and Duke holds the rights and interests under the MESA for the lighting fixtures at the other five facilities.

On November 14, 2000, Pillowtex and certain of its subsidiaries filed petitions for relief under Chapter 11 of the Bankruptcy Code. Thereafter, Pillowtex stopped making payments due under the MESA. On February 21, 2002, Duke filed a motion under section 365(d)(10) of the Bankruptcy Code to compel Pillowtex to make lease payments on the equipment it had provided to Pillowtex under the MESA. . . . In response to Duke's motion, Pillowtex filed an objection in which it argued that Duke was not entitled to payment of post-petition monthly obligations, which Pillowtex represented amounted to $ 1.8 million, because the MESA was not a true lease. After a hearing on the matter, the District Court, sitting in Bankruptcy, denied Duke's motion. n4 Duke timely appealed.

II. Jurisdiction and Standard of Review

The District Court had subject matter jurisdiction over Duke's motion to compel pursuant to 28 U.S.C. § 1334(a), which provides district courts with subject matter jurisdiction over bankruptcy cases. This Court has jurisdiction to review the District Court's order of June 4, 2002 pursuant to *28 U.S.C. § 1291.*

Our standard of review over the District Court's bankruptcy decision is the same as that exercised by the District Court. E.g., In re Woskob, 305 F.3d 177, 181 (3d Cir. 2002). Accordingly, we review the Bankruptcy Court's findings of fact for clear error and exercise plenary review over the Bankruptcy Court's legal determinations. Id.

III. *Analysis*

Whether an agreement is a true lease or a secured financing arrangement under the Bankruptcy Code is a question of state law. In re Continental Airlines, Inc., 932 F.2d 282, 294 (3d Cir. 1991) (citing H.R. Rep. No. 95–595, at 314 (1978), reprinted in 1978 U.S.C.C.A.N. 5963, 6271). In this case, the parties agreed that the MESA would be interpreted, performed, and enforced in accordance with the laws of the State of New York. (MESA, Appendix A, § 17.7). Accordingly, we turn to New York law in order to resolve whether the MESA constitutes a secured financing arrangement or a lease. Under New York law, because Pillowtex is seeking to characterize the MESA as a secured financing arrangement rather than a lease, Pillowtex bears the burden of proof on that issue. In re Owen, 221 B.R. 56, 60 (Bankr. N.D.N.Y. 1998).

Article 2A of the New York Uniform Commercial Code explains that a lease is "a transfer of the right to possession and use of goods for a term in return for consideration, but a sale . . . or retention or creation of a security interest is not a lease." N.Y. U.C.C. § 2–A–103(1)(j) (McKinney 2002). Thus, the definition of a lease expressly excludes security interests. The exclusion of security interests from the definition of a lease requires that we turn to the U.C.C. definition of a security interest.[7]

Section 1–201(37) of the U.C.C. provides that a security interest "means an interest in personal property or fixtures which secures payment or performance of an obligation." U.C.C. § 1–201(37). After defining the term "security interest," section 1–201(37) sets out a test for determining whether a transaction creates a lease or a security interest. Section 1–201(37) begins by noting that whether a transaction creates a lease or a security interest is to be determined on a case-by-case basis. After indicating that courts are to examine the facts of each case in order to characterize a transaction, the statute sets out a bright-line test, sometimes referred to as a per se rule, for determining whether a transaction creates a security interest as a matter of law. Specifically, section 1–201(37) provides:

(a) Whether a transaction creates a lease or security interest is determined by the facts of each case; however, a transaction creates a security interest if the consideration the lessee is to pay the lessor

---

7. See U.C.C. § 1–201(37), Official Cmt. ("Lease is defined in Article 2A as a transfer of the right to possession and use of goods for a term, in return for consideration. Section 2–A–103(1)(j). The definition continues by stating that the retention or creation of a security interest is not a lease. Thus, the task of sharpening the line between true leases and security interests disguised as leases continues to be a function of this section").

for the right to possession and use of the goods is an obligation for the term of the lease not subject to termination by the lessee, *and*:

(i) the original term of the lease is equal to or greater than the remaining economic life of the goods,

(ii) the lessee is bound to renew the lease for the remaining economic life of the goods or is bound to become the owner of the goods,

(iii) the lessee has an option to renew the lease for the remaining economic life of the goods for no additional consideration or nominal additional consideration upon compliance with the lease agreement, *or*

(iv) the lessee has an option to become the owner of the goods for no additional consideration or nominal additional consideration upon compliance with the lease agreement.

N.Y. U.C.C. § 1–201(37) (emphasis added). Thus, under the two-part test set out in New York's U.C.C., if Pillowtex did not have the right to terminate the MESA prior to the end of its term, *and* any of the four factors set out in section 1–201(37)(a)(I)–(iv) are met, then the MESA would be considered to create a security interest as a matter of law. See In re Owen, 221 B.R. at 60–61. If, on the other hand, it is determined that "the transaction is not a disguised security agreement per se, [we] must then look at the specific facts of the case to determine whether the economics of the transaction suggest such a result." In re Taylor), 209 B.R. 482, 484 (Bankr. S.D. Ill. 1997. See also In re Murray, 191 B.R. 309 (Bankr. E.D. Pa. 1996); In re American Steel Prod., 203 B.R. 504, 506–07 (Bankr. S.D. Ga. 1996) (describing the standards for determining whether a disguised security arrangement exists). In this case, the District Court went directly to the economic realities of the transaction memorialized in the MESA. In doing so the Court seems to have implicitly held that the MESA was not a disguised security agreement under the bright-line test of section 1–201(37). We agree.

On appeal, Pillowtex argues that the MESA is a secured financing agreement both under this bright-line test and also based on the economics of the MESA transaction. Specifically, Pillowtex argues that the second and fourth factors set out in the second part of the statutory two-part test are present: (1) that at the end of the MESA's term Pillowtex was bound to become the owner of the energy fixtures and (2) that it was bound to become the owner of the fixtures for no or nominal additional consideration upon compliance with the terms of the MESA. Duke concedes that the first part of the two-part test is satisfied: that the MESA prohibits Pillowtex from terminating its obligation to pay Duke the full cost of the energy fixtures before the termination of the MESA's term. However, Duke maintains that none of the four factors in section 1–201(37)(a)(I)–(iv) are present. These factors are hereafter referred to as "residual value factors" because they relate to whether residual value will remain for the purported lessor, Duke, at the end of the term of the MESA. See E. Carolyn Hochstadter Dicker and John P. Campo, FF&E and the True Lease Question: Article 2A and

Accompanying Amendments to UCC Section 1–201(37), 7 Am. Bankr. Inst. L. Rev. 517, 552 (1999).

As an initial matter, we note that the first and third residual value factors are not satisfied. The first factor is whether "the original term of the lease is equal to or greater than the remaining economic life of the goods." N.Y. U.C.C. § 1–201(37)(a)(i). Here, the term of the MESA is eight years and Pillowtex concedes that the expected useful life of the equipment is 20–25 years. Thus, the economic life of the equipment exceeds the term of the MESA by a factor of three and the first residual value factor set out in section 1–201(37) is not met. The third factor indicative of a security interest is met where "the lessee has an option to renew the lease for the remaining economic life of the goods for no additional consideration or nominal additional consideration upon compliance with the lease agreement." N.Y. U.C.C. § 1–201(37)(a)(iii). This factor is not met because the terms of the MESA do not give Pillowtex the option to renew the lease for the remaining life of the equipment for no or nominal consideration.

As to the second factor, Pillowtex argues that it was bound, if not formally then in a de facto sense, to become the owner of the energy fixtures because the only way that the fixtures would be removed from Pillowtex's facilities is if Duke paid millions of dollars to acquire and install replacements. Along the same lines, Pillowtex argues with respect to the fourth residual value factor that, although the MESA does not expressly give it the option to become the owner of the energy fixtures for no or nominal consideration, in effect it has this option because it can compel Duke to abandon the energy fixtures by refusing to negotiate an extension of the MESA or a purchase of the energy fixtures at the end of the MESA's term.

We agree with Duke that neither the second nor the fourth residual value factors are present here because Pillowtex is not contractually bound to become the owner of the energy fixtures, nor does the MESA provide Pillowtex with the option to become the owner of the energy fixtures for no or nominal consideration. Rather, the existing options as to how to proceed at the end of the term of the MESA were to be exercised only by Duke. Pillowtex provides no authority for the proposition that a de facto arrangement is enough to satisfy the requirements of section 1–201(37)(a)(ii) and (iv). If anything, the relevant caselaw points us to the opposite conclusion. See *Edison Bros.*, 207 B.R. at 810 ("If the lease agreement *explicitly* provides that the lessee has an option to purchase the leased goods for nominal consideration (e.g., for $ 1), the agreement is presumed to be a disguised security agreement") (emphasis added). Accordingly, we conclude that none of the four residual value factors set forth in N.Y. U.C.C. § 1201(37)(a)(i)–(iv) are met.

The parties agree that, where none of the four factors set out in section 1–201(37) are present, courts are to consider the economic reality of the transaction in order to determine, based on the particular facts of the case, whether the transaction is more fairly characterized as a lease or a secured financing arrangement. They also agree that the District Court applied the correct standard for evaluating the economic reality of their transaction. As the District Court explained:

> Under relevant case law, courts will look to various factors in evaluating the "economic reality of the transaction . . . in determining whether there has been a sale or a true lease," Pactel Fin. v. D.C. Marine Serv. Corp., 136 Misc. 2d 194, 518 N.Y.S.2d 317, 318 (N.Y. Dist. Ct. 1987), including the following: "[a] whether the purchase option is nominal; [b] whether the lessee is required to make aggregate rental payments having a present value equaling or exceeding the original cost of the leased property; and [c] whether the lease term covers the total useful life of the equipment." In re Edison Bros. Stores , 207 B.R. 801, 809–10 and n.8, 9, 10 (Bankr. D. Del. 1997). See also [N.Y. U.C.C.] § 1–201(37) (McKinney Supp. 1996). "In this regard, courts are required to examine the intent of the parties and the facts and circumstances which existed at the time the transaction was entered into." In re Edison Bros. Stores, 207 B.R. at 809.

In re Pillowtex, Inc. et al., Nos. 00–4211 to 00–4234, slip op. at 5–6 (Bankr. D. Del. June 4, 2002) ("Dist. Ct. Op.") (footnote omitted). The District Court found that the MESA was substantively better characterized as a security agreement than a true lease because the second *Edison Bros.* factor clearly weighed in Pillowtex's favor, and the first and third factors were largely neutral. We agree with the District Court's conclusion in this regard.

Specifically, with respect to the second factor, Duke concedes that the aggregate rental payments owing by Pillowtex under the MESA had a present value equal to or exceeding the cost of the energy fixtures. The Edison Bros. court cogently explained the importance of such a fact in showing the existence of a security agreement:

> The rationale behind this second factor is that if the alleged lessee is obligated to pay the lessor a sum equal to or greater than the full purchase price of the leased goods plus an interest charge over the term of the alleged lease agreement, a sale is likely to have been intended since what the lessor will receive is more than a payment for the use of the leased goods and loss of their value; the lessor will receive a consideration that would amount to a return on its investment.

Edison Bros., 207 B.R. at 814 (quoted in *Owen*, 221 B.R. at 61–62). Applying that logic to this case, Duke has already been well-compensated for the transferral of the lighting fixtures to Pillowtex, undercutting the proposition that the fixtures were merely leased.

Like the District Court, we are unpersuaded by Duke's attempt to rely on the first and third *Edison Bros.* factors. With respect to the first factor, Duke points out that the MESA provides that it "has the option to . . . give [Pillowtex] the option of purchasing all (but not less than all) of the Equipment at a *mutually agreed price*." (emphasis added). Based on this provision of the MESA, Duke asserts that "Pillowtex does not have the option to purchase the Equipment unless Duke offers it such option, and even then only if Pillowtex agrees on a satisfactory price with Duke." Duke concludes that, therefore, the first economic realities factor weighs in favor of a finding that the MESA is a lease. We agree, however, with Pillowtex's contention that, although the MESA nominally required Pillowtex to bargain for an option price, Pillowtex could essentially ensure a nominal option price by refusing to bargain. This refusal would "effectively compel Duke to abandon the energy fixtures to avoid the exorbitant expense of acquiring and installing replacements. Thus, as an economic reality the option price at the end of the MESA was illusory, nullifying the weight of this factor.

With respect to the third factor, Duke observes that the useful life of the energy fixtures is longer than the term of the MESA, and cites to *Edison Bros.* for the proposition that the long life of the fixtures is indicative of a true lease. In relevant part, the *Edison Bros.* court explained that

> An essential characteristic of a true lease is that there be something of value to return to the lessor after the term. Where the term of the lease is substantially equal to the life of the lease property such that there will be nothing of value to return at the end of the lease, the transaction is in essence a sale. Conversely, if the lessor expected a remaining useful life after the expiration of the lease term, it can be reasonably inferred that it expected to retain substantial residual value in the leased property at the end of the lease term and that it therefore intended to create a true lease.

207 B.R.. We agree that under certain circumstances, the fact that transferred goods have a useful life extending beyond the term of the transferring agreement could reveal the transferor's expectation of retaining residual value in those goods. Such an inference would only be proper, however, where the evidence showed a plausible intent by the transferor to repossess the goods.

The economic realities of the particular transaction in this case belie any such intent. Although the useful life of the lighting fixtures is 20–25 years, eclipsing the MESA's 8–year term, it would be unreasonable for Duke to incur the high costs necessary to repossess the fixtures: namely, the costs associated with removing, scrapping, and replacing the fixtures. Also, the uncontroverted evidence in this case establishes that there is little (if any) market value for used lighting fixtures. In short, it would have made no economic sense for Duke to spend large amounts of money to reclaim the fixtures, especially in the face of poor resale prospects. We therefore conclude that the District Court did not err by discounting the significance of the useful life of the lighting fixtures as compared to the length of the MESA when conducting its analysis of the economic realities of the transaction underlying the MESA. On balance, then, applying the three *Edison Bros.* factors to this case leads us to conclude that the MESA was not a true lease.

Beyond reiterating its arguments on the three factors, Duke argues that (1) the mutual subjective intent of the parties was to structure the MESA as a lease; (2) Pillowtex's accounting for the MESA payments as a utility expense is evidence that it did not treat the MESA as a repayment of debt incurred to purchase the energy fixtures; (3) it is of no consequence that the MESA is not labeled a lease; and (4) Duke maintained a meaningful reversionary interest in the fixtures at the end of the MESA's term. None of these arguments is persuasive to us.

First, Duke argues that the District Court erred by failing to analyze the intent of the parties. Duke asserts that the record shows that the parties structured the MESA so that it would qualify as a lease under relevant accounting standards. That way, Pillowtex would not reduce the amount of credit available to it under its senior credit facility. Duke also cites a statement that counsel for Pillowtex made to the District Court, which Duke characterizes as a concession: "I don't disagree that it was structured to have that, those characteristics for tax purposes and, you know, to the extent that they could, the parties were trying to create a lease, I would admit that."

Duke's intent argument fails, however, because the New York U.C.C. no longer looks to the intent of the drafting parties to determine whether a transfer is a lease or a security agreement. Specifically, the 1992 version of § 1–201(37) directed courts to determine "whether a lease *is intended* as security" (emphasis added); this language was amended in 1995 to read "whether a transaction *creates* a lease or security interest" (emphasis added). In this way, the reference to parties' intent was explicitly omitted. The Official Comment to the amended version confirms the importance of the changed language:

> Prior to this amendment, section 1–201(37) provided that whether a lease was intended as security (i.e., a security interest disguised as a lease) was to be determined from the facts of each case . . . Reference to the intent of the parties to create a lease or security agreement has led to unfortunate results. In discovering intent, courts have relied upon factors that were thought to be more consistent with sales or loans than leases. Most of these criteria, however, are as applicable to true leases as to security interests . . . Accordingly, amended section 1–201(37) deletes all references to the parties' intent.

U.C.C. § 1–201(37), Official Cmt; accord In re Murray, 191 B.R. at 314 (stating that "judicial opinions construing U.C.C. § 1–201(37) and the Official Uniform Commercial Code Comments . . . clearly place the focus of the inquiry under the revised statute on the economics of the transaction rather than on the intent of the parties as had been the emphasis previously").

Duke relies on *Edison Bros.*, 207 B.R. at 809, for the proposition that "courts are required to examine the intent of the parties and the facts and circumstances which existed at the time the transaction was entered into." *Edison Bros.*, however, explicitly relied on the 1992 version of the statute in looking at intent, and therefore has been superseded by the 1995 version of the U.C.C. Indeed, Judge Walsh, the author of *Edison Bros.*, noted in a later opinion: "I am persuaded by the clear weight of authority that the intent of the parties, no matter how clearly spelled out in the parties' representations within the agreement, can not control the issue of whether the agreement constitutes a true lease or a security agreement." In re Homeplace Stores, 228 B.R. 88, 94 (Bankr. D. Del. 1998). Judge Walsh observed that the shift away from intent had been remarked upon by various commentators. Id. (citing Richard L. Barnes, Distinguishing Sales and Leases: A Primer on the Scope and Purpose of UCC Article 2A, 25 U. Mem. L. Rev. 873, 882 (1995) ("What had been a test of intention has become a test of economic realities; that is, intention has been dropped from section 1–201(37). . . Thus, the parties to a transaction may create a secured transaction under the revised definition even though their every intention was to create a lease")).

Based on the foregoing authority, we are unwilling to characterize the MESA as a lease on the basis that the parties intended it to appear to be one for tax purposes. Duke admonishes the Court in its brief that "equipment leasing between sophisticated commercial entities dealing at arms length for their mutual benefit is an important commercial activity and one that should not be lightly recharacterized." This admonition rings hollow in the context of bankruptcy cases, however, because every dollar that is used to pay a purported lessor depletes the pool of assets available to pay other constituencies of the estate. In other words, refusing to defer to the intent of contracting parties in resolving whether their agreement is a lease is particularly appropriate in bankruptcy, as otherwise the costs of the agreement would be externalized to third-party creditors.

Duke's accounting argument is similarly meritless. Duke argues that the District Court erred by attaching significance to the fact that Pillowtex did not account for the energy projects under the MESA as true leases. Duke argues that Pillowtex's accounting for the MESA payments as a utility expense should instead be viewed as evidence that it did not treat the MESA as a repayment of debt incurred to purchase the energy fixtures. We disagree. Pillowtex's accounting for the MESA payments as utility expenses seems to us to be consistent with the parties' agreement that Pillowtex's payments to Duke under the MESA would be equivalent to Pillowtex's actual savings. Moreover, as the District Court noted in its opinion, Pillowtex "entered into separate Production Equipment leases, each of which was recorded as a true lease on Pillowtex's books." We agree with the District Court that it is significant that, while payments for the energy fixtures were treated as utility expenses by Pillowtex, the agreements with respect to manufacturing and production equipment (which are not at issue in this case) were recorded on Pillowtex's books as true leases. This distinction suggests that Pillowtex did not find it appropriate to record its MESA payments as leases, which bolsters our conclusion that they were not in fact true leases.

Next, Duke argues that the District Court erred by taking into consideration that the MESA was not labeled a lease. The District Court merely observed in passing, however, that "the MESA is not labeled a lease," and that there is no indication that the court relied heavily on this observation. Even if it did rely to some extent on this fact, this reliance was harmless since the economic realities independently dictate that the MESA was in fact not a lease. Accordingly, we do not believe that the District Court committed reversible error by mentioning the labeling of the MESA.

Duke goes on to insist that it had a "meaningful residual interest" in the fixtures, such an interest being "the fundamental characteristic distinguishing a lease from a security interest." E.g., In re Thummel, 109 B.R. 447, 448 (Bankr. N.D. Okla. 1989). As discussed earlier, however, Duke only has a nominal residual interest, not a *meaningful* one: the combination of the cost of retrieving the fixtures and their poor market value renders the residual interest negligible. Duke claims that we should not "speculate" as to what it might do for economic reasons at the end of the MESA's term, and instead look to the parties' intent at the time of drafting the agreement. As we have mentioned above, however, Duke's argument is backwards: the Court must subordinate the parties' intent to the economic reality that Duke would not have plausibly reclaimed the fixtures at the end of the MESA's term. This is not mere speculation on our part. The uncontroverted evidence shows that removal of the fixtures would be prohibitively expensive, and that the fixtures' value on the market would not make it worth Duke's while to reclaim them. In short, the economic realities analysis not only permits, but *requires* us to examine the state of affairs at the end of the MESA's term.

Finally, Duke asserts that the District Court erred by characterizing the Master Lease between Duke and SouthTrust as a secured financing agreement, as opposed to a lease. The Master Lease applies only to the lighting fixtures that were SouthTrust's collateral and SouthTrust did not elect to appeal the District Court's order. Therefore, the District Court's holding that the Master Lease was a secured financing is not before us on appeal.

IV. Conclusion

After carefully considering the arguments discussed above and all other arguments advanced by appellant, we conclude that the District Court correctly determined that the MESA was not a lease and, therefore, that Duke was not entitled to lease payments under 11 U.S.C. § 365(d)(10). We will remand this case to the District Court so that it may determine whether Duke is entitled to adequate protection.

NOTES ON DISTINGUISHING LEASES FROM SECURED TRANSACTIONS[1]

(1) The "Factors" Approach. Few commercial law issues have spawned as much litigation and provided as much uncertainty as the determination whether a purported lease of goods creates a security interest or a true lease. The pre–1987 version of UCC 1–201(37) gave relatively little

---

1.   These Notes are drawn substantially from Harris, The Interface Between Articles 2A and 9 Under the Official Text and the California Amendments, 22 UCC L.J. 99, 104–110 (1989).

guidance on the issue. It stated that "[w]hether a lease is intended as security is to be determined by the facts of each case. . ..." Although the courts usually took cognizance of the facts of the cases before them, they often exhibited great difficulty in determining which facts are relevant and which are not. The scores of reported cases on the subject identified no fewer than two dozen factors that courts have used in drawing the lease/security interest distinction. Most of these factors are consistent with both a lease and a secured transaction.

UCC 1–203, which derives from the 1987 amendments to F1–201(37), goes a long way toward clarifying the distinction between the two transactions.[2] It does not draw a precise line between true leases and security interests. Instead, it continues to state that whether a transaction creates a lease or security interest is determined by the facts of each case. See UCC 1–203(a). Nevertheless, UCC 1–203 makes a major contribution by stating unequivocally that some of the factors upon which courts have relied in holding that a transaction creates a security interest *do not, of themselves, create a security interest*. These factors, which appear in UCC 1–203(c) [F1–201(37) (second a)–(e)], are:

• the discounted present value of the rental stream equals or exceeds the fair market value of the goods at the time the lease is entered into (often known as a "full-payout" lease);

• provisions whereby the lessee assumes risk of loss of the goods, or agrees to pay taxes, insurance, filing, recording, or registration fees, or service or maintenance costs with respect to the goods (these provisions are commonly found in "net" leases);

• an option for the lessee to renew the lease, including an option for a fixed rent that equals or exceeds the reasonably predictable fair market rent at the time the option is to be performed; and

• an option for the lessee to become the owner of the goods, including an option for a fixed price that equals or exceeds the reasonably predictable fair market value of the goods at the time the option is to be performed.

(2) The Irrelevance of the Parties' Subjective Intent. A second major contribution of UCC 1–203 is the substitution of the term "security interest" for the phrase "intended as security." That phrase prompted some courts to distinguish between leases and security interests by reference to the subjective intentions of the parties rather than by analysis of the economics of the transaction. For example, in Carlson v. Tandy Computer Leasing, 803 F.2d 391 (8th Cir.1986) (construing Missouri law), the court relied in part on the "intent of the parties, as expressed in the written document, to create nothing more than a lessor-lessee relationship." The court noted that the document "consistently uses 'lease language'" and "states in clearest terms that the agreement is only a lease." Id. Because the

---

2.   The provisions of UCC 1–203 track closely F1–201(37), starting with the last sentence of the first paragraph of the latter. For ease of explication, many references to UCC 1–203 in these Notes do not include cross-references to F1–201(37).

characterization of the transaction may affect the rights of third parties, reliance upon the subjective intentions of the parties to the lease transaction is inappropriate. Rather, the economic substance of the transaction should determine its characterization. (In *Carlson*, the "lessee" was obligated to pay an amount substantially in excess of the purchase price and had the right to use the property for its entire economic life. As the following Notes suggest, these facts are indicative of a secured transaction.)

(3) **The Importance of the Lessee's Contractual Obligation.** In explaining the difference between a lease and a security interest, UCC 1–203 focuses on economic realities. Subsection (b) [F1–201(37) (2d paragraph)] sets forth four specific cases in which a transaction creates a security interest. Each case is characterized by two elements, the first of which is the existence of a debt owed by the "lessee" to the "lessor." Without a debt to secure, there can be no security interest. The statute states this point as follows: "the consideration that the lessee is to pay the lessor . . . is an obligation for the term of the lease and is not subject to termination by the lessee." Although the Uniform Conditional Sales Act contained a similar requirement, pre–1987 UCC 1–201(37) contained none. The better cases have recognized that an obligation of this kind is a necessary but not sufficient condition to the existence of a secured transaction; however, some courts have failed to grasp this important principle. See, e.g., In re J.A. Thompson & Son, Inc., 665 F.2d 941 (9th Cir.1982) (holding that a nominal purchase option establishes conclusively that a transaction is a secured transaction, even if the "lessee" unilaterally may terminate its obligation to pay the "lessor").

(4) **The Importance of a Meaningful Residual Interest for the Lessor.** In addition to an unconditional obligation to pay, each secured transaction described in UCC 1–203(b) [F1–201(37) (2d paragraph)] includes a second element—the absence of a meaningful residual interest for the lessor. In a true lease, the lessor is the owner of the goods. The lessee acquires the right to use the goods for a limited period of time. When the lease term ends, the lessor expects the property to be returned so that the lessor can use it, relet it, or otherwise dispose of it. The lessor's interest in the goods after expiration, cancellation, or termination of the lease is called the "lessor's residual interest." See UCC 2A–103(1)(q) [R2A–103(1)(w)]. In contrast, if the lease affords the lessee the right to use the goods for their entire economic life, then the lessee (and not the lessor) is in effect the owner of the goods. The goods have been sold to the lessee, and the lessor does not expect to recover them unless the lessee fails to pay for them. In other words, the lessor has only a security interest.

Determining whether the lessor retains a meaningful residual interest in the goods can be difficult. UCC 1–203(b) [F1–201(37) (2d paragraph)] sets forth four specific cases in which the lessor lacks a meaningful residual interest and that, therefore, create security interests if the lessee has a noncancellable obligation to pay. These cases are:

• the original term of the lease equals or exceeds the remaining economic life of the goods;

• the lessee is bound to renew the lease for the remaining economic life of the goods or is bound to become the owner of the goods;

• the lessee has an option to renew the lease for the remaining economic life of the goods for no additional consideration or nominal additional consideration upon compliance with the lease agreement; and

• the lessee has an option to become the owner of the goods for no additional consideration or nominal additional consideration upon compliance with the lease agreement.

In the first two cases the lessee acquires the right to use the goods until the goods have no further economic life. At the end of the lease term or renewal term, the goods will have no value to the lessor, who therefore is a secured party.

The third and fourth cases address an issue with which the courts have grappled, with varying degrees of success, under pre–1987 UCC 1–201(37): the effect of renewal and purchase options. The fourth case follows pre–1987 UCC 1–201(37), and the third case is a variation on the same theme. But rather than refer to an option to become the owner, the third case refers to its equivalent—an option to renew the lease for the remaining economic life of the goods.

Although not specifically mentioned in UCC 1–203 [F1–201(37)], the remedies that a "lease" affords to the "lessor" upon the "lessee's" default may deprive the "lessor" of its residual and thus be indicative of a secured transaction. Consider a lease that requires the lessor to sell the property upon the lessee's default and to apply the proceeds of sale to the lessee's obligation under the lease. The proceeds of the sale represent the value of the use of the goods for their entire useful life. The useful life consists of two portions—the portion covered by the lease term, for which the lessee bargained, and the portion commencing with the expiration of the lease, which the lessor retains as the lessor's residual interest. A lessor who credits to the lessee the entire amount of the proceeds received upon a sale following the lessee's default has, in effect, allocated none of the value of the property to its residual interest. This suggests that the lessor never enjoyed a residual interest (businesses rarely give away property for other than eleemosynary purposes), which, in turn, suggests that the transaction was not really a lease to begin with. Cf. In re Tulsa Port Warehouse Co., 690 F.2d 809 (10th Cir.1982) (lease held to be security interest where termination and default provisions provided for (i) sale of automobile by lessor, (ii) application of proceeds of sale to "agreed depreciated value," and (iii) lessee's liability for any deficiency and entitlement to any surplus).

(5) The Meaning of "Nominal Consideration." In determining whether consideration is "nominal," UCC 1–203 follows the better-reasoned case law under pre–1987 UCC 1–201(37). Subsection (d) [F1–201(37)(x)] provides that "[a]dditional consideration is nominal if it is less than the lessee's reasonably predictable cost of performing under the lease agreement if the option is not exercised." "Reasonably predictable" costs are to be "determined with reference to the facts and circumstances at the time the transaction is entered into." UCC 1–203(e) [F1–201(37)(y)]. In other words, if it would appear to the parties at the outset of the lease that it would cost the lessee less to exercise the option than not to exercise it, one reasonably can assume that the lessee will exercise the option and become the owner of the goods, leaving no meaningful residual for the lessor.

UCC 1–203(d) [F1–201(37)(x)] also gives two examples of when additional consideration is not nominal:

• when the consideration for an option to renew is stated to be the fair market rent for the use of the goods for the term of the renewal, determined at the time the option is to be performed; and

• when the consideration for an option to become the owner of the goods is stated to be the fair market value of the goods determined at the time the option is to be performed.

A lessee faced with either of these "fair-market" options cannot necessarily be expected to exercise them and deprive the lessor of a residual interest. For a well-reasoned case analyzing an option to purchase at fair market value, see In re Celeryvale Transport, Inc., 44 B.R. 1007 (Bkrtcy.E.D.Tenn.1984), affirmed per curiam 822 F.2d 16 (6th Cir.1987).

(6) Dealing With Uncertainty. Detailed as it is, UCC 1–203 does not eliminate all uncertainty over the distinction between security interests and leases. This uncertainty derives not only from unavoidable infelicities of drafting but also from the decision of the drafters not to draw a precise line between security interests and leases, to create safe harbors for transactions that meet certain requirements, or to consider all possible variations and combinations of factors. See UCC 1–203, Comment 2 [F1–201, Comment 37] (penultimate paragraph).

Consider the unusual but interesting facts of *Pillowtex*, supra. The arrangement between Duke and Pillowtex was denominated a "Master Energy Savings Agreement," not a "lease." Duke supplied certain energy savings equipment to Pillowtex, and Pillowtex agreed to pay to Duke agreed-upon monthly payments (equivalent to one-twelfth of Pillowtex's annual energy savings) over a term of eight years. The useful life of the equipment was found to be 20 to 25 years, suggesting that, as a lessor, Duke would enjoy a meaningful residual at the expiration of the 8–year term. Ordinarily, a lessor's retention of a meaningful residual would indicate that the transaction is a true lease (or at least that the transaction would not create a security interest as a matter of law). See UCC 1–203(b)(1) (Former 1–201(37)(first a)). However, the court observed that Duke's cost of removing the equipment coupled with the very thin market for such used equipment meant that, in actuality, Duke would be unlikely to capture any meaningful residual value at the end of the term. Focusing primarily on the lack of any meaningful residual value in fact, the court concluded from the economic realities that the transaction was a security interest. The court's analysis of the residual value issue is a mirror image of the UCC's approach to nominal value: Consideration is nominal if it is less than the cost of returning the goods to the lessor. See UCC 1–203(d) (Former 1–201(37)(x)). In *Pillowtex*, Duke's cost of taking back the goods would have exceeded their value.

The *Pillowtex* court was faced with a situation in which all four of the criteria that would have compelled secured transaction treatment were absent. See Former 1–201(37) (2d paragraph) [UCC 1–203(b)(1)]. It reasoned that the absence of these secured-transaction criteria did not necessarily compel the conclusion that the transaction was a true lease. Is this an appropriate reading of the statute?

Curiously, the *Pillowtex* court cited with apparent approval a factor that, under the holding in In re Edison Bros. Stores, 207 B.R. 801 (Bankr.D.Del.1997), indicates a secured transaction—that the lease was a "full-payout" lease, in which the lessor recovered its entire investment. But, as the *Pillowtex* court itself pointed out, *Edison Bros. Stores* applied an earlier version of Former 1–201(37) which emphasized the intention of the parties. Moreover, under UCC 1–203(c)(1), a transaction "does not create a security interest merely because" it is a full-payout lease—although the *Pillowtex* court failed even to cite the predecessor of that provision. See note (1), supra. Is it appropriate for a court to rely on any of the "factors" listed in UCC 1–201(c) as indicative of a secured transaction even though it may not base its characterization "merely" on that factor? Or, should subsection (c) be read to mean that the factors it lists should play no role whatsoever in the analysis?

In re Marhoefer Packing Co., 674 F.2d 1139 (7th Cir.1982), concerned another interesting transaction—a "lease" containing a renewal option for a term that did not extend to or beyond the economic life of the goods *coupled* with a nominal purchase option at the end of the renewal term. The court quite appropriately held that the nominal purchase option did not conclusively require secured transaction treatment because the lessee was not entitled to exercise the purchase option at the end of the initial term but only at the end of the renewal term. But there is one weak link in the otherwise sound reasoning of *Marhoefer*. The *Marhoefer* court did not explore whether the renewal option rentals were "nominal." Nominal renewal rentals would indicate an economic compulsion on the lessee to renew the lease and thereby become entitled to the one dollar purchase option, resulting in a lease for security.

Close cases will continue to arise in which, for example, reasonable people might differ over whether the lessee enjoys an option to become the owner of the goods for "nominal consideration." The extensive case law construing the pre–1987 version provides another source of uncertainty, as does the fact that many of the reported opinions emanate from bankruptcy courts, where the economics of litigating sometimes results in issues not being briefed as fully as they otherwise might be.

A cautious lessor may wish to plan in advance for the possibility that a court will recharacterize what the lessor believes to be a "lease" as a secured transaction. The lessor's principal concern in this regard is that, if its interest in the goods is held to be a security interest, then its failure to file a financing statement would render the security interest unperfected. The lessor might be reluctant to file a financing statement using the terms "debtor" and "secured party"; a court might consider the use of those terms as evidence that the transaction creates a security interest. UCC 9–505 suggests the solution: File a precautionary financing statement using the terms "lessee" and "lessor" instead of "debtor" and "secured party." The fact of filing "is not of itself a factor in determining whether the collateral secures an obligation." However, "[i]f it is determined for another reason that the collateral secures an obligation, a security interest held by the . . . lessor . . . which attaches to the collateral is perfected by the filing. . .." UCC 9–505(b). Box 5 on the uniform financing statement form accommodates this practice. See UCC 9–521(a).

NOTE ON LEASES AND "OSTENSIBLE OWNERSHIP"

One way to eliminate much of the litigation over the lease/security interest distinction would have been to create a set of rules under which third parties take free of a lessor's interest as to which there had been no public notice (e.g., by filing a financing statement). Indeed, the imposition of a filing requirement for leases has been urged by prominent members of the current generation of Article 9 scholars as well as by some of those who were present at the creation of Article 9. These commentators generally have argued that a lessor's nonpossessory interest in leased goods gives rise to the same problems of "ostensible ownership" as does a nonpossessory security interest. From the perspective of third parties, goods held subject to lease appear identical to goods held subject to a security interest. Creditors of the lessee, like creditors of an Article 9 debtor, may be misled into thinking that the person in possession of the goods owns them free and clear. Why, then, should the rights of third parties differ, depending on whether the holder of the nonpossessory interest enjoys a meaningful residual interest and the unconditional right to receive payment for the goods?

The Article 2A drafting committee was not moved by this strong support for the imposition of a filing requirement for leases. Rather, Article 2A generally reflects the longstanding common-law rule that creditors of, and other transferees from, the lessee take subject to the lessor's interest in the goods, regardless of whether the lessor's interest has been publicized. See, e.g., UCC 2A–307(1) (creditors); UCC 2A–305 (buyers and sublessees).

Can one develop a principled justification of the drafting committee's decision? Is it simply a response to pressures brought by the leasing industry, or perhaps the reflection of unthinking conservatism? Consider the premise of those who would extend the filing system to leases: Do leases and secured transactions present equivalent problems of ostensible ownership? Were the Article 9 filing system to be abolished, would it be as difficult to determine whether a person in possession of goods in fact is the owner as it would be to determine whether the person owns them free of a security interest? The absence of an outcry from creditor groups suggests that the secret interests held by lessors of personal property have not resulted in losses to third parties claiming through lessees.

Imposing a filing requirement is easier than articulating the consequences that would flow from a failure to file. For example, would the non-filing lessor lose its residual interest, which it may never have agreed to convey and which may be of substantial value relative to the lessee's rights under the lease? To the extent that the consequences of failing to file with respect to a true lease would differ from those with respect to a security interest, parties will retain the incentive to litigate over the characterization of the transaction, and a major incentive for imposing a filing requirement would be lost.

(B) CONSIGNMENTS

INTRODUCTORY NOTE

The preceding part of this Chapter explored leases—bailments in which the bailee was to *use* the goods. As we saw, these bailments bear a resemblance (sometimes a very close resemblance) to purchase-money security interests in *equipment*. This part of the Chapter addresses consignments—bailments in which the bailee is to *sell* the goods. These bailments resemble purchase-money security interests in *inventory*. As you work through the following materials, you will see that the UCC's treatment of consignments differs considerably from its treatment of leases. Should the drafters have afforded the same treatment to both consignments and leases? If so, what should that treatment have been?

Problem 5.1.5. The Corona Company has just developed what it believes to be its crowning achievement: Cal–Trak, a portable instrument that can measure and record calories as they are expended. Corona wishes to market this product to joggers and others concerned with fitness. It entered into the following agreement with Spartners: Corona will deliver a specified quantity of Cal–Traks to Spartners "on consignment." Title will remain in Corona. Spartners will use best efforts to sell the Cal–Traks to retail stores. Spartners has no obligation to pay for the Cal–Traks until they are sold, at which time Spartners will remit the sale price, less its commission. Spartners may return unsold Cal–Traks at any time without penalty and must return them upon Corona's demand.

Two months later, one of Spartners' judgment creditors caused the sheriff to levy upon all its inventory, including 10,000 Cal–Traks. Corona seeks to recover the Cal–Traks from the sheriff, arguing that they are not property of the judgment debtor's (i.e., of Spartners').

(a) What result? See UCC 1–201(b)(35) [F1–201(37)] (2d & 5th sentences); UCC 9–109(a)(1), (4); UCC 9–102(a)(20), (21), (72), (19), (28); UCC 9–319; UCC 9–317(a)(2); In re Zwagerman, infra; Notes on

Consignments, infra. What could the loser have done to avoid the loss? See UCC 9–310(a); UCC 9–505.

(b) Suppose that, prior to taking delivery of the Cal–Traks, Spartners had granted a security interest in all its inventory, existing and after-acquired, to Bank. Would Bank's security interest attach to the Cal–Traks (which, recall, are still owned by Corona)? See UCC 9–319; UCC 9–203(b). (Do not assume that, if Bank's security interest attaches then Bank necessarily defeats Corona. See Note (1), p. 137, supra (discussing "rights in the collateral"). As to the relative priority of Corona's ownership interest and Bank's security interest, see UCC 9–103(d); UCC 9–324(b); Note (4) on Consignments, infra.)

(c) What result in part (a) if Spartners were required to obtain Corona's approval of the terms of each sale?

(d) What result in part (a) if Spartners were free to determine the price at which the Cal–Traks were sold?

(e) What result in part (a) if Spartners had agreed to pay Corona the wholesale price of the Cal-Traks 30 days after delivery, but also had the right to return for a refund any goods that Spartners had been unable to sell after three months?

(f) What result in part (e) if, instead of giving Spartners the right to return Cal-Traks, the agreement provided that Corona could demand return of the goods if Spartners failed to pay the wholesale price 30 days after delivery?

Problem 5.1.6. Crispin is a stereophile who acquires new speakers every six months or so. Crispin leaves the old speakers with Dealer, who agrees to try to sell them on commission. Acting pursuant to an execution writ issued at the request of one of Dealer's judgment creditors, the sheriff levies on the speakers. Is the levy effective against Crispin? If so, then the sheriff's sale would cut off Crispin's ownership interest.

In Chapter 1, Section 3(C), supra, we saw that Factor's Acts and UCC 2–403(2) empower Dealer to make even an unauthorized sale of the speakers free of Crispin's ownership interest. Is Crispin a consignor? See UCC 9–102(a)(21). Is Crispin's ownership interest also subject to the claims of Dealer's creditors? See UCC 9–109(a)(4); UCC 9–102(a)(20); Note (4) on Consignments, infra.

––––––––

As the Notes on Consignments, infra, explain in some detail, Revised Article 9 applies to certain transactions in which goods are delivered to a merchant "for the purpose of sale," even if the goods do not secure a debt or other obligation. UCC 9–102(a)(20) (defining "consignment"). The quoted phrase derives from Former 2–326(3), which likewise described a set of transactions (referred to as "consignments") in which goods are delivered to a person "for sale." The *Zwagerman* case, which follows, reveals how courts have attempted to distinguish transactions in which goods have been delivered "for sale" from those in which they have been delivered other than "for sale." Under Former 2–326, the owner's interest in goods delivered to a person "for sale" was vulnerable to claims of the person's creditors unless the owner takes a specified step (which might be the filing of a financing statement) to publicize its ownership interest.

In re Zwagerman[*]

United States Bankruptcy Court, W.D. Michigan, 1990.
115 B.R. 540, affirmed 125 B.R. 486 (W.D.Mich.1991).

OPINION

■ DAVID E. NIMS, JR., BANKRUPTCY JUDGE.

This case comes before the court on the complaint filed by James D. Robbins, the Trustee in this estate, for a determination as to the respective interests in proceeds from the sale of cattle present on the farm of Gordon and Joan Zwagerman, doing business as Zwagerman Farms, the Debtors herein, at the time of the filing of the petition. . ..

FACTS

Gordon and Joan Zwagerman filed their Chapter 7 bankruptcy petition on December 30, 1985. Other than at a 341 Meeting held on February 5, 1986, the Debtors have refused to testify, claiming their privilege against self-incrimination. David Bradley claims that all proceeds belong to him because he owned the cattle on the Debtors' farm. Comerica Bank–Detroit, the Bank herein, argues that based on their properly perfected security interest in the cattle, they are entitled to the proceeds.

Since approximately 1969, the Debtors operated a farm at which they fattened hogs and cattle and then sold them for slaughter. Originally, the Debtors fattened livestock which they personally owned. At some point in the early 1980's the Debtors apparently had a cash flow problem and started to bring some cattle into their feedlots[1] in which they did not have an ownership interest. Those cattle were furnished by David Bradley, a man the Debtor met while buying cattle out of the South. Bradley agreed to deliver cattle to the Zwagerman farm in order for the cattle to be fattened. The first delivery to the Debtors was on or about November 27, 1981. Both the number of head per shipment and the number of shipments per month were sporadic. Each shipment was accompanied by a contract, generally including the following pertinent provisions:

1. That Red River will deliver a specified number of cattle on a specified date, with the expense of hauling to be paid by Red River.

2. Zwagerman agrees to feed such cattle and to be paid fifty-five (55) cents per pound for the poundage the cattle gain after being delivered.

---

*   [The court's citations are to Former Article 9.]

1.   A "feed lot" is an area where the operator keeps his cattle while fattening them. A "custom feed lot" physically appears the same, but the operator does not own the cattle.

3. Any loss of cattle by death shall be borne by Zwagerman.

4. Zwagerman agrees to feed the cattle until the weights reach approximately one thousand one hundred (1,100) pounds and when sold, the proceeds will be delivered to Red River. Red River will send to Zwagerman its check for the number of pounds gained by the cattle from time of delivery to Zwagerman to time of sale.

5. The parties agree that should any dispute arise in this agreement that the forum for settling such dispute will be Sumner County, Tennessee.

. . .

Bradley never visited the farm, but called the Debtor two to six times a week to discuss the best time to sell based on the market and cattle conditions. Although no amount of time was set for the fattening of the cattle, Bradley estimated that it took 90–140 days. The purchasers made checks out to the Debtor who then deposited the check into one of his personal checking accounts. Pursuant to the contract, the Debtor was supposed to send a check to Bradley for the full amount of the sale. Once Bradley received a check for the sale of cattle, he would send a weight gain check in return to the Debtor. . . .

In the spring of 1983, the Debtor contacted Phillip Roberts, an agricultural loan officer at Comerica Bank, to pursue the refinancing of his debt to P.C.A. and F.M.B. The cattle on the farm were to be part of the security for the Comerica loan, just as they were for the existing P.C.A. loan. In deciding to recommend to the loan committee that a revolving credit loan for $1,300,000.00 and a term loan for $200,000.00 be given to the Debtor, Roberts testified that he took many things into consideration. He went out to the farm and saw cattle which the Debtor referred to as "my cattle." Parties mentioned on the various documents were contacted for verification, including Michigan Livestock Exchange which informed the Bank that Zwagerman bought cattle through them. Lien searches were done at the Register of Deeds. Various financial records, including bank statements and tax returns, were reviewed. A balance sheet paralleling statements dated 12/31/82 and 3/31/83, accompanied by an earnings work sheet, was submitted by the Debtor. Production of the Bills of Sale for the cattle was not required since Comerica was refinancing a debt owed to P.C.A.

The balance sheet bearing dates of 12/31/82 and 3/31/83 indicated in the assets section an increase of 715 cattle in three months and a decrease in liabilities. Roberts commented that it is typical for banks to have problems interpreting the figures submitted by farmers, particularly those who do a large amount of buying and selling, as farmers are usually poor bookkeepers. Therefore, it was left up to an analyst to reconcile the figures. The accompanying earnings work sheet showed "custom cattle" as an entry separate from "cattle" in the amount of $208,232.00 for the period ending 3/31/83. Roberts admitted that in 1983 he knew the term "custom cattle" meant that the farmer didn't own the cattle, but rather would be compensated for feed and care of the cattle pursuant to an agreement with the owner. Furthermore, he stated that he would have red flagged any documents with such an entry to require more information regarding ownership. The only explanation Roberts proffered to the Court was that when the loan application was being reviewed in 1983, no one from the Bank, including himself, caught the entry.

On November 10, 1983, a note and security agreement were signed. The security agreement purportedly gave the Bank a security interest in the livestock. The following paragraph was also contained within that document,

> 2.4 At the time any Collateral becomes subject to a security interest in favor of Bank, Debtor shall be deemed to have warranted that (i) Debtor is the lawful owner of such Collateral and has the right and authority to subject the same to a security interest in Bank . . .

A financing statement was filed by the Bank on November 17, 1983.

. . .

On December 3, 1985, Bradley received a call from Gordon Zwagerman who disclosed that many Bradley cattle had been sold without accounting for them to Bradley. . . . The 90–140 day turnaround period had become a 13–14 month turnaround period. No cattle were shipped and no checks were sent or received by Bradley after that December 3, 1985, telephone call. A few days later, the Zwagermans' attorney told Bradley that approximately 458 cattle were on the farm. In contrast, Bradley's records showed that 3,141 cattle should have been on the farm.

On December 11, 1985, Comerica was contacted by the Zwagermans' attorney who relayed that the Zwagermans had encountered financial difficulties due to losses in the commodity futures market, the number of cattle presently on the farm was much lower than the Bank records reflected, and a David Bradley owned at least some of the cattle. Two days later the Bank "took possession" of the cattle, but actually left them on the farm and paid Gordon Zwagerman $500.00 a week to take care of them.

. . .

DISCUSSION

Bradley contends that because he retained ownership in the cattle and the relationship between himself and the Debtor was only a bailment, the proceeds are held for his benefit by constructive trust. Comerica claims that the Bradley/Debtor relationship was not a bailment, but rather a consignment subject to [Former 2–326], and therefore their properly perfected security interest gives them an interest in the proceeds which has priority over Bradley. The Trustee argues that the nature of Bradley's interest is either a consignment subject to [Former 2–326] or a security interest, and not a bailment. Thus, the Trustee asserts that Comerica has a superior interest in the proceeds, or in the alternative, based on his status as hypothetical lien creditor under 11 U.S.C. § 544,[**] the proceeds are

---

** [BC 544 is discussed in Chapter 7, Section 2(A), infra.]

property of the estate; and all the payments the Debtors made to Bradley for cattle sales within ninety days of the bankruptcy are preferences.

Although Count I of the Complaint suggested that the contract between Zwagerman and Bradley created a security interest under Article 9 of the U.C.C., I assume that such a claim has been abandoned since there were no arguments at trial advancing that position. In addition, the evidence does not indicate that there was any intent between the contracting parties that Bradley would retain a security interest in the cattle.

Bailment

. . .

A bailment is nothing more than a delivery of goods for some purpose, upon a contract, express or implied, to be redelivered to the bailor upon fulfillment of the purpose or to be dealt with according to the bailor's direction. Similarly, an agency is a relationship arising from a contract, express or implied, by which one of the parties confides to the other the transaction or management of some business or other activity in his name, or on his behalf, and whereby the other party assumes so to act and to render an account thereof. Thus in both situations, the title to the property remains in the bailor or principal, and the bailee or the agent holds the property under the bailment or agency for the owners' benefit. Consequently, it became well settled under the Bankruptcy Act that absent state statutory enactment to the contrary, if property was in a debtor's hands as bailee or agent, the trustee held it as such, and the bailor or principal could recover the property or its proceeds.

4 Collier on Bankruptcy § 541.08[2] (15th ed. 1990). Bradley has suggested in his briefs that Zwagerman was an agister and the contract was an agistment. The term agistment is an ancient one derived from the old Germanic word *giest* meaning guest. The Random House Dictionary of the English Language (1973) indicates agistment as being an obsolete word meaning the act of feeding or pasturing for a fee. Black's Law Dictionary 61 (5th ed. 1979) defines agistment as:

Agistment. A contract whereby a person, called an agister, has control of animals and retains possession of land. The taking in and feeding or pasturing of horses, cattle, or similar animals for a reward and is a species of bailment.

Delivery of animals pursuant to a contract of agistment has been held to be a bailment of the animals.

"Bailment," in its ordinary legal signification, imports the delivery of personal property by one person to another in trust for a specific purpose, with a contract, express or implied, that the trust shall be faithfully executed and the property returned or duly accounted for when the special purpose is accomplished.

The contracts and the practice of the parties seem to clearly indicate their intent. Bradley had cattle to be fed. Zwagerman had good feed. Not only was Michigan grass superior to Tennessee grass but also Zwagerman had access to good silage and even discarded cookies. Bradley delivered the cattle to Zwagerman who fed them until they reached a certain weight. Then, by mutual agreement they were sold at an agreed price. Zwagerman, as a bailee or agister, never had title to the cattle.

Effect of U.C.C. § 2–326

The Bank and Trustee claim that because of Bradley's failure to give notice under Uniform Commercial Code (U.C.C.) § 2–326, his interest is subordinate to theirs. The written contracts seem to imply that Tennessee law will apply. However, both Tennessee and Michigan have adopted the U.C.C. and I find no material differences between Tenn. Code Ann. § 47–2–326 (1989) and Mich. Comp. Laws § 440.2326 (1989). . . .

. . .

Section 2–326(1) is limited to transactions where delivered goods may be returned by the buyer even though they conform to the contract. There was never any intent that Zwagerman could return the cattle to Bradley. Costs, together with the shrinkage loss, would have made a return economically unfeasible.

In this case, delivery was never made to a buyer. U.C.C. § 2–103(1)(a) provides: "(1) In this article unless the context otherwise requires (a) 'Buyer' means a person who buys or contracts to buy goods." The U.C.C. does not seem to define "buy." Black's Law Dictionary 181 (5th ed. 1979) defines "buy" as "to acquire the ownership of property by giving an accepted price or consideration therefor; or by agreeing to do so; to acquire by the payment of a price or value; to purchase."

There was no agreement between Bradley and Zwagerman that Zwagerman would acquire ownership in the cattle. No price was agreed upon. Sale was not to take place until sometime in the future at which time Zwagerman would sell as agent for Bradley, at a price agreeable to Bradley, and the entire proceeds of the sale would be sent to Bradley less a shrinkage fee.

Section 2–326(1)(b) would restrict the operation of § 2–326 "Sale or return" transactions to those instances where the goods were delivered "primarily" for resale. The word "primarily" is not defined in the U.C.C. XII The Oxford English Dictionary 472 (2d ed. 1989) defines "primarily" as "[w]ith reference to other temporal order: In the first place, first of all, pre-eminently, chiefly, principally; essentially."

In this case I find that delivery was not primarily for resale. The cattle were shipped for feeding and fattening. If it were primarily for resale, it would have been much more reasonable to sell them in Tennessee and avoid the expense of transporting, shrinkage, and other loss unless an unusual market condition existed in the Southwestern Michigan area; and there were no proofs to that effect.

Thus, for all the reasons stated, the court finds that this case does not involve a "sale or return" under § 2–326(1).

This brings us to [former] § 2–326(3). Undisputedly, the exclusions found in subsections 2–326(3)(a), (b), and (c) do not affect this case. No applicable sign law exists, the Debtors were not known by their creditors to be engaged in selling the goods of others, and Bradley stipulated that he did not file a financing statement. Therefore, a determination must be made as to whether or not the facts of this case fall within the parameters of U.C.C. § 2–326(3).

The court finds that the goods were not delivered to Zwagerman "for sale." It is not clear whether "for sale" refers to the sale to the buyer or resale by the buyer to third parties. But, delivery was not "for sale" in either event. As stated above, the delivery was for the care, feeding, and fattening the cattle. It would have been far more economical for Bradley to sell or to have someone in Tennessee sell the cattle and save shipping and shrinkage costs.

. . .

I do not find a definition of consignment in the code. A "consignment contract" is defined in Black's Law Dictionary 278 (5th ed. 1979) as "[c]onsignment of goods to another (consignee) for sale under agreement that consignee will pay consignor for any sold goods and will return any unsold goods." A consignment contract, as defined above, is common. This type of consignment has not given courts a lot of trouble, and is the subject of many of the cases cited to by the Trustee and the Bank. I have read and agree with the conclusion of those cases.

BFC Chemicals, Inc., v. Smith–Douglas, Inc., 46 Bankr. 1009 (E.D.N.C.1985) is slightly different from the cases noted above. A certain chemical was placed by BFC, the creditor, in a large storage tank from which the debtor withdrew its needs from time to time to formulate agricultural chemicals for resale to its customers. The debtor then paid BFC for chemical taken. The debtor filed under Chapter 11. BFC filed what was treated by the bankruptcy judge as a motion for relief from stay [in order to recover the chemicals]. This was denied. The district judge held that N.C.G.S. § 25–2–326 was applicable because the goods were delivered "for sale" and the matter was remanded for reconsideration and a determination whether BFC complied with N.C.G.S. 25–2–326(3)(a). While this is somewhat different than the above cited consignment cases, I believe I would be inclined to agree with the district judge.

In Simmons First National Bank v. Wells, 279 Ark. 204, 650 S.W.2d 236 (1983), the bank had a perfected security interest in inventory and after acquired property of Western Rice Mills. Western defaulted on its loan and a receiver was appointed. Wells intervened. Until about four months prior to the receivership, Wells sold his rice to Western which milled and resold it. But, because of Western's financial inability to buy the rice outright, Wells had orally agreed that Western would mill for a certain price, market at an agreed price, and turn over the proceeds less Western's charge for milling. The trial court held for Wells. The state supreme court held that here was a clear consignment but remanded to determine whether Wells was protected by the state statute pertaining to grain warehousemen. This case differs from our case in that Western marketed the rice at an agreed minimum price. It could be said that in the Wells case delivery was primarily for resale.

O'Brien v. Chandler, 765 P.2d 1165 (N.M.1988) involved an oral agreement between McCoy, a cattle dealer, and Chandler, a cattle broker, whereby McCoy agreed to ship cattle to a feedlot for delivery to Chandler. Delivery was made and McCoy furnished invoices to Chandler which set out the sales price. Without knowledge to McCoy, Chandler obtained a loan from a bank and pledged the cattle as security. This security interest was perfected. The bank claimed that it had no knowledge of any interest of McCoy. McCoy sued to recover the cattle. The trial court held that the bank had a perfected security interest superior to any rights of McCoy. The New Mexico Supreme Court affirmed, holding that the contract was a sale. This case differs from ours in two important facts. First, a price was set, and secondly, invoices were furnished. If the bank had requested proof of ownership, Chandler had the proof in the invoices. In our case, if any creditor had requested proof of ownership, all Zwagerman could have furnished would have been contracts that indicated that he had no interest in the cattle.

. . .

In Eastman Kodak Co. v. Harrison (In re Sitkin Smelting & Refining, Inc., 639 F.2d 1213 (5th Cir.1981), reh'g en banc denied, 645 F.2d 72 (1981)), Sitkin entered into an agreement with Eastman by which it would process film waste and purchase the silver content recovered. Sitkin filed under Chapter XI. Eastman filed an adversary proceeding against the trustee in bankruptcy and C.I.T. Corp., a secured creditor. The bankruptcy referee held that possession should be entrusted to the [sic] C.I.T. The court of appeals reversed, concluding that the agreement between Kodak and Sitkin provided for a bailment of the unprocessed waste, and therefore, Kodak was entitled to reclaim possession. The court stated:

> The transaction between Kodak and Sitkin is not a sale or return within the meaning of section 2–326, since the goods were not delivered for resale with an option to return. C.I.T., then, fails to overcome the presumption against the application of section 2–326.

Id. at 1218. I would agree with the result reached in Sitkin but not on the basis for the decision. Even if this was a "sale or return," the print waste was not "delivered primarily for resale."

In Union State Bank of Hazen v. Cook (In re Cook), 63 Bankr. 789 (Bankr.D.N.D.1986), parents, a son and his wife, and a partnership of which the father and son were partners filed petitions under Chapter 11. These debtors operated a family farm on which they raised Angus cattle and maintained a custom feed lot. Another son, Tom, did not stay on the farm but cattle he had raised as part of a 4–H project were left on the farm. He spent about one week each year on the farm. The court found that the business relationship between Tom and the debtors was quite loose. Tom's cattle were not separated from the debtors' cattle. The debtors were allowed to cull and market Tom's cattle, and even retain some of the proceeds of his cattle, but he never gave them authority to mortgage his cattle. The plaintiff bank was granted a security interest by the debtors in all livestock owned by them, including the increase thereof. The bank was not aware of Tom's interest until the bankruptcy was filed. Partnership schedules indicated 36 head were held for Tom, valued at approximately $22,000.00. While there were other issues before the court in determining ownership, the court noted that the cattle were all branded with the partnership brand. Although North Dakota has a branding statute, a brand is only prima facie evidence of ownership. N.D. Cent. Code § 36–09–19 (1980). The testimony of Tom and his brother was found to be convincing and supported by the fact that some of the cattle were registered by the American Angus Association in Tom's name. The court held that the parties' intent was crucial, and the intent was that Tom retain ownership. The burden was on the bank to demonstrate that the debtors possessed sufficient rights in Tom's cattle for the security interest to attach. The debtors' authority to sell Tom's cattle did not give them the authority to encumber the cattle.

In *Cook*, as in our case, the bank was casual about its loan. Although the bank representative made inspections of the operation, he never counted the cattle. The bank's officer admitted that other cattle besides debtors' could have been on the ranch and that he relied only on the financial statements submitted. The court held that Tom's cattle were not subject to the bank's lien.

In First National Bank of Blooming Prairie v. Olsen, 403 N.W.2d 661 (Minn.Ct.App.1987), Olsen owned and operated a feedlot for which the bank provided financing. The bank had a perfected security interest in Olsen's farm property including livestock. There were approximately 2,500 cattle on the farm, all of which were owned by third-party investors. The owner-investors did not perfect under § 2–326. The bank filed a replevin action and the trial court held that § 2–326 did not apply because the cattle were not delivered for sale. The court of appeals held that the § 2–326 did apply, relying on the official comment that "Subsection (3) resolves all reasonable doubts as to the nature of the transaction in favor of the general creditors of the buyer." However, the court found for the investors because the bank had actual knowledge that Olsen custom-fed a substantial number of cattle.

. . .

In Walter E. Heller & Co. S.E. v. Riviana Foods, Inc., 648 F.2d 1059 (5th Cir.1981) Riviana entered into a warehouse agreement with Amos Brokerage Company to store and eventually deliver the goods to Riviana's customers. Amos was not permitted to sell these goods but did maintain a place where it sold like goods under another name. Heller and Amos entered into an inventory security agreement and accounts financing security agreement. Subsequently, Amos filed bankruptcy. The court held that the goods were not delivered "for sale" as required by U.C.C. § 2–326 for a "sale and return." It drew a comparison to Allgeier v. Campisi, 117 Ga.App. 105,

159 S.E.2d 458 (1968), where the plaintiff entrusted her car to a dealer who was authorized to receive offers but lacked authority to sell without the approval of the plaintiff. The defendant, a security interest holder in the plaintiff dealer's inventory, sought possession of the car. The court held for the plaintiff since the car was not delivered "for sale" under U.C.C. § 2–326.

As can be noted from the cases mentioned above, there has been little uniformity in the court decisions on § 2–326. There is much to be said for extension of the section to situations that were not anticipated or intended by the drafters of the law. If I could interpret the law as I think it should be written, I would probably hold that 2–326 should be applied to every situation where there may be secret interests in property which would be harmful to those dealing with the person having possession. One of the purposes of Article 9 was to eliminate the secret lien, and an aim of 2–326 was to protect third parties in consignment cases. However, cattle cases are not as serious as some of the situations faced by courts in the cases above. Any prudent, prospective lender or purchaser is well aware that cattle may be custom fed or cows may be leased. More disturbing are the inventory cases in which it is not common practice to deliver goods while retaining title.

I am well aware of the provision in § 1–102 of the U.C.C. which provides that, "This Act shall be liberally construed and applied to promote its underlying purposes and policies." Nevertheless, radical changes in the unambiguous provisions of the law should not be made by judicial interpretation. The result would be to uproot the drafters' intent to promote uniformity and certainty. It is much better that such changes be brought about by legislation after much discussion both inside and outside the legislative bodies concerned. It was no accident that the Michigan U.C.C. Act of 1962, 1962 Mich. Pub. Acts 174, did not become effective until over a year later on January 1, 1964. Those of us who were around at that time can recall the many seminars which were held for lawyers, accountants, financial institutions, trade associations, and many others to prepare the commercial world for this new law. Because the U.C.C. was so superior to what it replaced it was not surprising that some lawyers and jurist expected a miraculously all-encompassing statute. However, the U.C.C. has been amended many times and I am sure it will be amended many more times in the future.

R. Anderson, Anderson on the Uniform Commercial Code § 1–102:20–21 (1981) states:

> When a section of the code is clear and unambiguous there is "no occasion" to engage in statutory construction.

> Contrary to the rule of liberal construction stated in the preceding sections, there is some authority that the Code is to be strictly construed where in derogation of the common law, and a statute should be construed in harmony with the common law unless there is a clear legislative intent to abrogate the common law. In many states there are special statutory construction acts that expressly repudiate this

principle of statutory construction, so that it is extremely doubtful whether strict construction should be made solely because of conflict with the common law.

A better reason for strict construction is that if the court does not adhere to the letter of the Code, the objective of certainty will be defeated. Thus where the Code is unambiguous, it should be applied according to its letter, as to do otherwise would merely produce confusion in the business world.

When the provisions of the Code are unambiguous they are to be followed by the courts. . ..

A court should adhere strictly to the provisions of the Code in order to achieve stability, consistency, and predictability. And an "overly" liberal interpretation of the Code should be avoided as creating uncertainty among businessmen and their legal advisors who believe themselves to be entering into transactions on the basis that the Code means what it says.

Loose construction of the Code cannot be justified on the basis of the direction to construe the Code liberally as a mandate for liberal construction is not a "license to legislate."

Later Anderson continues:

The certainty of commercial practices and relations is essential to furthering trade. Consequently as a variant of the objective of furthering trade, a court should so interpret the Code as to further certainty in commercial dealings.

The dangers of expanding the boundaries of § 2–326 cannot be better illustrated than the case before us. Bradley, at the time of trial, was an 80 year old man who had been in the cattle business his entire life except for a few years in service during World War II. He had also served as a vice president of a local bank. While he was aware of the practice of custom feeding of cattle, he never actually engaged in it before his arrangement with the Debtors. He then did what any prudent businessman should do—he visited his lawyer who "was good," according to Bradley, because he subsequently became a judge. His lawyer set up a group of forms to be used and instructed Bradley as to the procedure to be followed, but he never instructed Bradley to perfect his transaction by filing with a register of deeds. Bradley had never heard of requiring the filing of a financing statement as to these transactions. Testimony during the trial indicated that there was little custom feeding going on in Michigan at the time Zwagerman and Bradley entered into their joint undertaking. In the fall of 1986, Michigan Livestock, a large cattle dealer, commenced delivering their cattle for feeding in an operation similar to that of Bradley and Zwagerman. It is possible they may have heard of Bradley's operation and problems by this time. Before that, most of the custom lots were carried out by the big lots out West. Michigan Livestock filed a sort of financing statement; the form used did not comply with the U.C.C. but did give notice. However, testimony indicated that most persons delivering cattle for custom feeding did not file financing statements.

Twenty states have branding laws and dispose of title matters as to cattle through these laws. Neither Michigan or Tennessee have adopted such a statute.

From the clear terms of § 2–326, related sections of the U.C.C., the general commercial practice, and the fact that a number of states have felt that control in this area should be by a separate branding statute outside of the U.C.C., I find that the transaction with which we are concerned is not a "sale or return" under the meaning of § 2–326 and that the title to the cattle delivered to the Zwagermans by Bradley remained in Bradley.

[In the remainder of the opinion, the court determined which cattle were Bradley's and whether certain pre-bankruptcy payments from Zwagerman to Bradley were recoverable as preferences under BC 547. Preferences are discussed in Chapter 7, Section 2(B), infra.

The District Court affirmed on both the consignment issue and the preference issue. Its conclusion as to the former was as follows: "While the question is a close one, the factual finding that the delivery was not 'for sale' is not clearly erroneous and will not be upset on appeal."]

NOTES ON CONSIGNMENTS

(1) **Consignments Under Pre–UCC Law.** The delivery of goods on "consignment" has an ancient and honorable history. A consignee (sometimes called a "factor") was a selling agent who did not undertake entrepreneurial risks. To the extent consigned goods were sold, the consignee received a commission or a margin above a stated price; unsold goods could be returned to the owner.

The agreement between consignor and consignee clearly provided that the consignor remained the owner of the goods; when the consignee, as selling agent, effected a sale to a buyer, title passed from the consignor to the buyer. Under this arrangement, creditors of the *consignor* could, of course, levy on the goods while they were held by the consignee. By the same token, most courts held that creditors of the *consignee* had no right to levy on the consignor's goods. Possession often did not imply ownership. On the other hand, courts usually would rebel when an agreement made the "consignee" an entrepreneur rather than a selling agent, as when the agreement required the consignee to pay for the goods even though the consignee was unable to sell them. See 1 Gilmore, Security § 3.5.

(2) **Consignments Under the UCC: "True" Consignments versus Consignments for Security.** Does Article 9 govern an orthodox ("true") consignment, where the consignee has no obligation to pay for the goods? It is difficult to conclude that the consignor's ownership of the goods is an "interest in personal property . . . which secures payment or performance of an obligation." UCC 1–201(b)(35) [F1–201(37)]. The duty of a bailee to return bailed goods is not the kind of obligation that supports a security

interest. If it were, then *all* bailments would create security interests; we know this is not the case.

The drafters of the UCC recognized, however, that *some* "consignments" might secure payment or performance of an obligation, i.e., that the parties to inventory financing might describe the transaction in their documents as a "consignment." You have seen that the common law provided an incentive to do so: By retaining title, a consignor immunized the goods from the reach of the consignee's creditors.[3] The UCC follows pre-UCC law in treating as secured transactions those "consignments" that are for security. UCC 9–109(a)(1). For example, a "consignment" that requires the "agent-consignee" to pay for goods that the consignee is unable to sell is likely to be characterized as securing an obligation. If so, then the transaction creates an Article 9 security interest and is subject to Article 9 in its entirety; the rules concerning attachment, perfection, priority, and remedies all apply. For example, in In re Oriental Rug Warehouse Club, Inc., 205 B.R. 407 (Bkrtcy.D.Minn.1997), a rug manufacturer put rugs in retailer's possession under a "consignment agreement." The court held that the manufacturer actually retained only a security interest because (i) the retailer was entitled to set its own prices, (ii) the manufacturer billed the retailer upon shipment of the rugs, not on the sale of the rugs by the retailer, (iii) the retailer commingled both the rugs and the proceeds of sale with its own property, and (iv) the retailer was entitled to obtain a profit on its sales instead of a commission.

(3) "True" Consignments before the 1999 Revision of Article 9. For true consignments, the drafters of the UCC rejected the common-law rule, which provides that creditors of the consignee cannot reach the consignor's (owner's) interest in the consigned goods. They concluded instead that, even in true consignments, creditors of a consignee deserve protection from a consignor's undisclosed interest in goods. This protection now appears in Article 9; before the 1999 revision of Article 9, protection was found in Article 2.

Former 2–326(3) specified circumstances where consigned goods were "deemed to be on sale or return," i.e., where the creditors of the consignee (who held only the limited interest of a bailee) could reach the consignor's ownership interest. That section afforded the three methods by which a cautious consignor could have shielded the goods from the reach of the consignee's creditors. One was a litigator's nightmare: "establish [cf. F1–201(8) (definition of 'burden of establishing')] that [the consignee] is *generally* known by his creditors to be *substantially* engaged in selling the

---

3. In addition, because the consignor remained the owner of the consigned goods, the consignor was free to set the resale price charged to the ultimate consumer. However, a consignor who sets the resale price should be aware that if a court later determines that there was not a genuine consignment relationship between the consignor and consignee, the consignor could be liable for violating antitrust laws against price fixing. Simpson v. Union Oil Co., 377 U.S. 13, 84 S.Ct. 1051, 12 L.Ed.2d 98 (1964).

goods of others." Former 2–326(3)(b). Would you have advised a client to rely on this subsection?

A second method by which a consignor could have protected its ownership interest against creditors of the consignee under Former Article 9 was to comply with "an applicable law providing for a consignor's interest or the like to be evidenced by a sign." Former 2–326(3)(a). Resort to this method was likely to be futile: There is authority to the effect that the phrase "applicable law" refers only to a statute and not to a common-law rule, see, e.g., Vonins, Inc. v. Raff, 101 N.J.Super. 172, 243 A.2d 836 (App.Div.1968), and "there are few states if any that have enacted a sign law that would protect a consignor." Clark, Secured Transactions ¶ 1.06[1], at 1–105.

The only realistic alternative for a consignor under Former Article 2 was to "compl[y] with the filing provisions of the Article on Secured Transactions (Article 9)." Former 2–326(3)(c). Former Article 9 permitted a consignor to file a financing statement showing itself as "consignor" and the party in possession as "consignee" without prejudicing the determination whether the transaction was a consignment or a security interest. See Former 9–408. For purposes of priority, Former Article 9 treated a perfected consignment (i.e., one where the consignor had filed a financing statement) much like a purchase-money security interest. See Former 9–114.

(4) "True" Consignments under Revised Article 9. The drafters of Revised Article 9 found favor with most of the results of the pre–1999 approach to consignments; however, they took exception to the drafting approach. Revised Article 9 replaces the consignment provisions of Former 2–326 with Article 9 provisions intended to have much the same effect.

Scope of Revised Article 9; "Consignment." We have seen that Article 9 applies to a consignment for security, which is a garden-variety security interest. See Note (2), supra. Article 9 also applies to a "consignment." UCC 9–109(a)(4). This term, which is defined in UCC 9–102(a)(20) and discussed below, includes many, but not all, "true" consignments and excludes purported consignments where the goods secure an obligation. See UCC 9–102(a)(20)(D). The term "security interest" now includes the ownership interest of a consignor in a transaction that is subject to Article 9. UCC 1–201(b)(35) [F1–201(37)] (2d sentence). Thus the term "security interest" encompasses a true consignment, where the consignor is a bailor whose ownership interest does not secure payment or performance of an obligation, as well as a purported consignment that secures an obligation.

In the case of a (true) consignment under Article 9, the consignor is a "secured party," and the consignee is a "debtor." See UCC 9–102(a)(72)(C), (a)(28)(C). A consignment is not enforceable against the consignee unless the requirements for attachment in UCC 9–203(b) are satisfied, and the consignor must give public notice to insulate its ownership interest from claims of the consignee's creditors. The primary purpose of subjecting true consignments to Article 9 is to regulate the relative rights of a consignor and creditors of the consignee. Because consigned goods do not secure an obligation owed by the consignee to the consignor, it would make no sense to apply Article 9's remedial scheme to a consignee's breach of a consignment agreement. Accordingly, law other than Article 9 governs a consignor's remedies against the consignee. See UCC 9–601(g); Note (4), p. 324, supra.

The (true) consignments to which Article 9 applies are to some extent the same as those described in Former 2–326(3): transactions in which a person delivers goods to a merchant for the purpose of sale, and the merchant deals in goods of that kind under a name other than the name of the person making delivery. See UCC 9–102(a)(20) (defining "consignment"). As the *Zwagerman* case, supra, indicates, courts construing Former 2–326(3) have had difficulty determining whether a particular transaction meets this description: Were the goods delivered "for the purpose of sale"? Does the person in possession (the putative consignee) deal in goods of that kind "under a name other than the name of the person making delivery"?

What purpose do these phrases serve? Comment 2 to Former 2–326(3) suggested that public notice is required for transactions where creditors of the consignee may reasonably be deemed to have been misled by the secret reservation of title in the consignor. Did the *Zwagerman* court, which professed to be sympathetic to "ostensible ownership" concerns, construe these requirements too narrowly?

The Article 2 Study Group recommended that the phrase "delivered to a person for sale" in Former 2–326(3) "should be expanded to include all deliveries of goods pursuant to which the parties expect the consignee ultimately to sell to others, even though further processing or prior consent to sale is required." PEB Article 2 Report 122. Does UCC 9–102(a)(20) (delivered "for *the purpose of* sale") accomplish this result? Would the italicized words have changed the result in *Zwagerman*? Comment 14 to UCC 9–109 appears to capture the Article 2 Study Group's recommendation. Is the Comment consistent with the statutory text? Would it have changed the result in *Zwagerman*?

Relying on pre-Revised Article 9 case law, Comment 14, and policy grounds, one court has given an expansive reading to the definition of "consignment" in UCC 9–102(a)(20). In re Georgetown Steel Co., 318 B.R. 352 (Bkrtcy.D.S.C.2004), involved a firm that delivered hot briquetted iron (HBI) to a steel manufacturer for use in the manufacture of steel that, in due course, was to be sold by the manufacturer. The bankruptcy court held that the manufacturer delivered the HBI "for the purpose of sale" and that the manufacturer "deal[t] in goods of that kind," notwithstanding that the HBI was merely a component of the steel manufacturing process and that the manufacturer did not sell or deal with HBI itself as a commodity. The court also noted that "[t]he purpose of [UCC 9–102(a)(20) and UCC 9–319(a)] is to protect creditors of the consignee from claims of consignors that have undisclosed consignment agreements with the consignee that create secret and undisclosed competing interests in the inventory held by a consignee." 318 B.R. 362. Is this a correct reading of UCC 9–102(a)(20)?

Of Comment 14? Does the result in *Georgetown Steel* necessarily follow from the analysis in *Zwagerman*, supra? Could *Georgetown Steel* have been decided under the fifth sentence of UCC 1–201(b)(35) [F1–201(37)], concerning retention of title by a seller of goods?

As mentioned above in Note (3), Former 2–326(3) protected a consignor from claims of creditors of a consignee who is generally known by its creditors to be substantially engaged in selling the goods of others. Although this rule may present problems of interpretation and proof, Revised Article 9 retains it. See UCC 9–102(a)(20)(A)(iii). However, Revised Article 9 has reversed the burden of proof. Under Former 2–326(3), a consignor seeking to avoid the presumption of "sale or return" status had the burden of establishing that debtor was known by its creditors to be substantially engaged in selling the goods of others. Under the revision, however, the person asserting that a transaction *is* a consignment has that burden, inasmuch as the "substantially engaged" issue is a component of the definition of "consignment. For a case pointing out this change, see In re Valley Media, Inc., 279 B.R. 105, 131 & n.54 (Bkrtcy.D.Del.2002). In addition, Revised Article 9 is inapplicable (and the common-law rule favoring the consignor applies) to goods delivered to auctioneers and goods having a value of less than $1,000. See UCC 9–109(a)(20)(A), (a)(20)(B). What justifies these exclusions?

The definition of "consignment," and thus the scope of Article 9, also excludes true consignments of consumer goods. Although Former 2–326, literally applied, subjected consumer consignors, like Crispin in Problem 5.1.6, supra, to the risk that their goods would be used to satisfy debts owed by their consignees, Professor John Dolan has observed that the cases generally protect the consumer consignor. See Dolan, The UCC Consignment Rule Needs an Exception for Consumers, 44 Ohio St. L.J. 21 (1983). Professor Dolan approves of the results of those cases but not their reasoning, which does not depend on the fact that the consignor was a consumer. He argues that contemporary credit practices no longer justify rules based on ostensible ownership concerns. Whatever validity remains in requiring consignors to file financing statements derives from antifraud concerns not present when consumers are the consignors: There is little risk that a consumer is cloaking what is essentially inventory financing in the guise of a consignment. Are you persuaded by Professor Dolan's argument? Even if not, can you justify Revised Article 9's exclusion of consumer-goods consignments?

Conflicting Claims to Consigned Goods. Like pre–1999 Article 2, Revised Article 9 contains a rule that violates the *nemo dat* principle and enables creditors of the consignee (who has a bailee's limited interest in the goods) to reach the consignor's (ownership) interest in the goods: "while the goods are in the possession of the consignee, the consignee is deemed to have rights and title to the goods identical to those the consignor had or had power to transfer." UCC 9–319(a). Thus, if the consignor's security interest is unperfected, creditors of the consignee may acquire a senior judicial lien on the consigned goods. See UCC 9–317(a)(2). Similarly, the consignee may create an enforceable security interest not only in its own (bailee's) interest but also in the consignor's (ownership) interest. See UCC 9–203(b)(2) (debtor has power to transfer a security interest in the collateral to a third party).

A consignor may perfect its security interest by filing. Like a lessor (see Note (6), p. 326, supra), a consignor may file a financing statement showing itself as "consignor" and the party in possession as "consignee" without prejudicing the determination whether the transaction is actually a consignment. See UCC 9–505. If the consignor's security interest is perfected and has priority over a conflicting claim to the goods, then law other than Article 9 determines the rights and title of the consignee. UCC 9–319(b). For example, at common law a true consignee was merely a bailee-agent of goods owned by the consignor-principal. See R. Brown, The Law of Personal Property at 247–48 (Raushenbush ed., 3d ed. 1976).

In determining whether a consignor's security interest has priority over a conflicting claim to the goods, do not ignore the teaching of UCC 9–103(d): A consignor's security interest in consigned goods is a purchase-money security interest in inventory. In some settings, purchase-money status may be advantageous. See UCC 9–317(e) (PMSI takes priority over the rights of a lien creditor that arise between the time the security interest attaches and the time of filing, if filing occurs before or within 20 days after the debtor receives delivery of the collateral); Chapter 3, Section 3(A), supra; Chapter 4, Section 3, supra. On the other hand, to enjoy priority over the holder of a "floating lien" on the consignee's inventory, the consignor must comply with the notification requirement of UCC 9–324(b). See Note (2), p. 250, supra.

Most people would agree that, in their pre–1999 incarnation, "[t]he Uniform Commercial Code's provisions regarding consignments are not models of draftsmanship." In re State Street Auto Sales, Inc., 81 B.R. 215 (Bkrtcy.D.Mass.1988). Are the consignment provisions of Revised Article 9 an improvement?

(5) "Sale or Return" Transactions. What is the effect of filing a financing statement against a buyer in a transaction that is a "sale or return," i.e., a transaction where goods are delivered to a buyer primarily for resale, which goods the buyer may return even though they conform to the contract? See UCC 2–326(1). Unlike a true consignment, where the person in possession of the goods is a bailee, a "sale or return" is a sale to a buyer. Is a "sale or return" simply an unsecured sale that provides an alternative method (i.e., return of the goods) by which the buyer can discharge its obligation for the price? If so, then the filing of a financing statement would be irrelevant. On the other hand, does the buyer's privilege of returning unsold goods for credit against its obligation for the purchase price create an interest in the goods in favor of the seller? If so, what is the nature of that interest? Can it be anything more than a security interest, given UCC 2–401(1) (second sentence) and UCC 1–201(b)(35) [F1–201(37)] (fifth sentence)?

(C) BAILMENTS FOR PROCESSING

The UCC directly addresses two prototypical types of bailments: leases and consignments. But many transactions in which one person is in possession of goods "owned" by another do not fit within these prototypes. Among these are arrangements whereby the person in possession is to return the goods (or something extracted from them) to the owner—or deliver them to a third party—only after the goods are repaired, processed, refined, fabricated, or similarly dealt with. Regardless of the form these arrangements take (and they may take an infinite variety of forms), if the "owner's" interest in the goods "secures payment or performance of an obligation" (UCC 1–201(b)(35) [F1–201(37)]), then the "owner" holds a security interest subject to Article 9. See UCC 9–109(a)(1). As observed above, if the *only* performance that the goods secure is the obligation to return them to the owner, then the transaction would not be a security interest; otherwise, all bailments would be Article 9 transactions.

As the following materials suggest, drawing the lines among secured transactions, consignments, and other bailments is quite difficult.

Problem 5.1.7. Grower delivers rice to Miller. Miller agrees to pay for the rice in three installments. Concerned about Miller's ability to make the payments, Grower retains title to the rice.

(a) Is this transaction a security interest or a bailment?

(b) The sheriff levies on the rice pursuant to an execution writ procured by Elsie, a judgment creditor of Miller's. Whose rights are senior, Grower's or Elsie's? Recall that a judicial lien creditor ordinarily acquires no better rights to the goods than its debtor enjoyed, see Chapter 1, Section 3(B), supra; however, under UCC 9–317(a)(2) an unperfected security interest often will be subordinate to the rights of a person who becomes a lien creditor.

Problem 5.1.8. Grower delivers rice to Miller. Miller agrees to mill it for a fee and return it to Grower.

(a) Is this transaction a security interest or a bailment?

(b) While Miller is in possession of the rice, the sheriff levies on it pursuant to an execution writ procured by Elsie, a judgment creditor of Miller's. Whose rights are senior, Grower's or Elsie's?

(c) Assume that Lender holds a security interest in all Miller's existing and after-acquired inventory and equipment. Will the security interest attach to the rice? See UCC 9–203(b); Note (1), p. 137, supra. If so, will Lender be able to cut off Grower's interest in the rice? See UCC 2–403(1) (1st sentence); Note on Bailments for Processing, infra.

(d) Assume that, in addition to agreeing to mill the rice for a fee, Miller agrees to deliver it at Grower's direction to Grower's customers. The customers are to pay Miller, who will deduct the milling fee and remit the balance to Grower. Would the results in parts (a), (b), and (c) change?

(e) What results in parts (a), (b), and (c) if Miller delivers the rice to its own customers, rather than Grower's? See Simmons First National Bank v. Wells, 279 Ark. 204, 650 S.W.2d 236 (1983) (holding arrangement whereby miller was obligated to sell at an agreed minimum price to be subject to Former 2–326(3); this case was described, and distinguished, in *Zwagerman*, supra).

NOTE ON BAILMENTS FOR PROCESSING

Article 9 applies to secured transactions; it does not apply to bailments (other than certain consignments).[4] Two important consequences follow from this observation. First, if the person in possession of goods claimed by another is a bailee, then the bailor's ownership interest in the goods generally is enforceable against third parties even in absence of public notice. See UCC 2–403(1) (1st sentence) (*nemo dat* principle). But see UCC 2–403(2) (entrustment rule). See also Chapter 1, Section 3, supra (discussing these rules).[5] If, however, the person in possession is an Article 9 debtor, then the secured party must file a financing statement to protect its security interest against most third parties. See, e.g., UCC 9–317(a)(2), (b) (lien creditors, certain buyers); UCC 9–322(a)(2) (perfected secured parties).[6] Second, a bailor's remedies against the bailee and the bailed goods are determined by common law and scattered statutes, whereas Article 9 governs a secured party's remedies against the debtor and the collateral.

As we have seen, the UCC expounds at length about the distinction between leases ("bailments for hire" at common law) and security interests, see UCC 1–203 [F1–201(37) (last three paragraphs)], and it singles out certain types of consignments (bailments for sale) for special treatment. See UCC 9–109(a)(4); UCC 9–102(a)(20). The UCC does not, however, give any other guidance for distinguishing between bailments and security interests. Some cases are easy to characterize: No one would seriously contend that a security interest is created when, for example, Lee Abel brings the Chevrolet to Jiffy Lube for an oil change or Benny Stulwicz brings Arnie Becker's suits to the cleaners. But as one moves away from the "pure"

---

4. The possessory security interest (**pledge**), whereby a debtor's property is delivered to a secured party to secure an obligation, is a bailment that is subject to Article 9; however, the pledge differs from the bailments under consideration in this Chapter. Unlike a pledge, if any of the "bailments" discussed here creates a security interest, the person in possession of the goods would be the debtor, not the secured party.

5. In some cases, the common law of accession and confusion may operate to subordinate the rights of the bailor to claims of creditors of, and purchasers from, the bailee. See R. Brown, The Law of Personal Property ch. VI (Raushenbush ed., 3d ed. 1976).

6. Of course, if a putative bailment is a secured transaction, the secured party will have no enforceable security interest unless the requirements for attachment are met. See UCC 9–203(a), (b) (discussed in Chapter 3, Section 2, supra).

bailment, characterizing the transactions becomes more difficult and the results become harder to predict.

As with the lease/security interest distinction, courts have looked to a variety of factors when distinguishing between a bailment for processing and a secured transaction. Two of these factors seem particularly irrelevant. First, some courts appear to have been influenced by the perception that creditors of the bailee (including Article 9 secured parties) may rely to their detriment on the bailee's possession of bailed goods. Although one might argue, as some commentators have, that public notice of bailments *should* be required as a prerequisite for protection against creditors and purchasers, the law simply is not to that effect: Bailors generally are not required to cure any "ostensible ownership" problems by filing or otherwise. It follows that the "ostensible ownership" of the goods provides no illumination whatsoever concerning the lease/security interest distinction.

Second, courts may become concerned with the subjective intentions, or purposes, of the parties. The learning in the context of leases is relevant here: Because the characterization of the transaction affects not only the rights of the parties but also the rights of third parties, subjective intentions should be irrelevant. See Note (2), p. 323, supra. Nevertheless, some reported decisions attempt to divine the "intention," "motivation," or "purpose" of the parties.

Rohweder v. Aberdeen Production Credit Association, 765 F.2d 109 (8th Cir. 1985), is a fine example of this phenomenon. The facts of *Rohweder* were described in the *Zwagerman* opinion, supra, as follows:

> . . . Rohweder turned over certain cows to Bellman with an option to purchase for an agreed price. Bellman bred the cows with his bulls, calved them out, pastured, and cared for all of the cows and calves. Bellman was to receive 40% of calf crop and Rohweder was to retain the rest. The Rohweder cattle were pastured with Bellman's. Bellman branded some of the cows with his brand and ear tagged the calves. Rohweder instructed Bellman to sell off some of the older and poorer cows. Some sale barns paid Bellman, who then paid Rohweder, and others paid Rohweder directly. Bellman had given PCA a security interest in all of his cattle and after acquired cattle. Bellman then filed under Chapter 11. PCA seized all of the cattle, resulting in Rohweder suing PCA for conversion. The district court ruled that Bellman had sufficient rights for attachment of a security interest and granted a directed verdict at the close of plaintiff's proofs.

115 B.R. at 552.

In dismissing the judgment and remanding the proceedings for trial by jury, the Eighth Circuit concluded that Rohweder was entitled to the cattle only if he was a bailor, not if he was a secured party.

> The crucial question in this regard is the parties' intent. If Rohweder intended to make a conditional sale when he delivered the cows to Bellman, he retained only a security interest and Bellman had sufficient rights for PCA's security interest to attach. On the other hand, if the

parties intended to create a bailment, with Rohweder retaining complete ownership of the cows and relinquishing only possession, Bellman would not have sufficient rights for attachment of PCA's lien and, in the absence of an estoppel, Rohweder should prevail. While the factors of control over the cattle, including the right of sale, and the option to purchase do not necessarily constitute "rights in collateral," they are relevant evidence for the jury in determining the parties' intent to transfer an ownership interest to Bellman.

765 F.2d at 113.[7]

What can a putative bailor do to protect itself against the risk that a court will determine its interest in the goods to be a security interest? The easiest step is to file a financing statement; in the event the arrangement is held to be a secured transaction, the security interest will be perfected. (Under some loan agreements, the filing of a financing statement against the debtor is a default; if the bailee is a debtor under such an agreement, a bailor who files a financing statement without the bailee's authorization would face liability to the bailee.) Will the fact that a financing statement has been filed affect the court's characterization of the transaction? To reduce this risk, a bailor might file a financing statement referring to itself as "bailor" and to the person in possession as "bailee." See UCC 9–505.

A filed financing statement will protect the "bailor's" interest against lien creditors of the "bailee" and, as we shall see in Chapter 7, Section 2(A), against the "strong arm" of the "bailee's" bankruptcy trustee. But, as Chapter 4, Section 1(A), supra, makes clear, perfection of a security interest does not guarantee priority over conflicting security interests. The bailment-security interest issue often is litigated between a putative bailor and the "bailee's" inventory lender. In that setting, if the arrangement is characterized as a secured transaction rather than a bailment, the "bailor's" security interest may be subordinate to that of the inventory lender. See UCC 9–324(b) (discussed in Chapter 4, Section 1(B), supra).

---

7.   The *Rohweder* court's concern with the subjective intentions of the parties is not its only error. The court mistakenly assumed that PCA's security interest cannot attach to bailed goods because bailees do not have "rights in the collateral" within the meaning of Former 9–203(1). Unfortunately, the court is not unique in this regard. See, e.g., In re Sitkin Smelting & Refining, Inc., 639 F.2d 1213 (5th Cir.1981); In re Zwagerman, 125 B.R. 486 (W.D.Mich.1991) (quoting *Rohweder*). Of course bailees have rights in bailed goods! At a minimum they have the right to possession as against the entire world, other than the owner.

Note that to challenge the court's assumption is not necessarily to disagree with its conclusion. Even if Bellman had rights in the cattle, PCA ordinarily would acquire no greater rights than Bellman had. See UCC 2–403(1) (1st sentence). Thus the court was correct that resolution of the conflicting claims turned on whether Rohweder was a bailor or an Article 9 secured party.

Section 2.   Sales of Rights to Payment

As we have seen, questions as to the applicability of Article 9 to transactions in goods are dominated by the concept of "security interest." This unitary approach is expressed in the basic rule of UCC 9–109(a)(1): Article 9 applies "to a transaction, regardless of its form, that creates a *security interest*." We also have seen that the term "*security* interest" can be misleading. It encompasses not only an interest that "*secures* payment or performance of an obligation" but also "any interest of a consignor . . . in a transaction that is subject to Article 9." UCC 1–201(b)(35) [F1–201(37)]. See UCC 9–109(a)(4); Section 1(B), supra.

Article 9 also applies to certain transactions in rights to payment that do not secure payment or performance of an obligation. Specifically, "[t]he term ['security interest'] also includes any interest of . . . a buyer of accounts, chattel paper, a payment intangible, or a promissory note in a transaction that is subject to Article 9." Article 9 applies to most sales of these rights to payment. See UCC 9–109(a)(3) (Article 9 applies to "a sale of accounts, chattel paper, payment intangibles, or promissory notes"). But see UCC 9–109(d)(4) though (7) (excluding certain sales of rights to payment from Article 9).

The implications of Article 9's including sales of rights to payment are discussed more fully in Chapter 6, Section 1(D), infra.

Section 3.   Agricultural Liens and UCC Liens

Article 9 is designed primarily for consensual transactions: transactions that create a security interest by contract, including consignments and sales of receivables. See UCC 9–109(a)(1), (a)(3), (a)(4). However, Article 9 also applies to liens arising under other articles of the UCC. See UCC 9–109(a)(5), (a)(6). The application of Article 9 to security interests arising under Article 4 (in favor of a bank that takes an item for collection) and Article 5 (in favor of an issuer of, or nominated person with respect to, a letter of credit) is limited by UCC 4–210 and UCC 5–118, respectively. The application of Article 9 to security interests arising under Article 2 (in favor of a seller or buyer of goods) or 2A (in favor of a lessee of goods) is limited by UCC 9–110.

Notwithstanding its general inapplicability to statutory liens, Article 9 also governs the perfection, priority, and enforcement of a large variety of statutorily-created "agricultural liens" on farm products. See UCC 9–109(a)(2); UCC 9–102(a)(5) (defining "agricultural lien"). Non–Article 9 law governs the creation of agricultural liens, and the circumstances giving rise to the liens vary widely from state to state. We discuss agricultural liens in Chapter 8, Section 4(C), infra.

Section 4.   Exclusions From Article 9 or its Filing Provisions

We have seen that Article 9 applies not only to interests that "secure[ ] payment or performance of an obligation," UCC 1–201(b)(35) [F1–201(37)], but also to many sales of accounts, chattel paper, payment intangibles, and promissory notes and to agricultural liens. See UCC 9–109(a)(2), (3); Sections 2 and 3, supra. And, as we saw in Section 1(B), supra, Article 9's attachment, perfection, and priority provisions apply to true consignments.

This Section discusses two other aspects of the scope of Article 9: transactions that create security interests, but as to which Article 9 nevertheless is inapplicable in whole or in part; and transactions that create security interests covered by Article 9, but as to which public notice is given by filing or recording in a non-Article 9 system.

UCC 9–109 excludes certain types of transactions from Article 9. Many of the exclusions follow directly from the basic scope provision, UCC 9–109(a)(1). For example, Article 9 applies to "a transaction . . . that creates a security interest in personal property or fixtures." UCC 9–109(d)(11) reflects the converse: Article 9 generally "does not apply to . . . the creation or transfer of an interest in or lien on real property" other than fixtures. Security interests in real property (i.e., mortgages and trust deeds) are governed by real property law. We shall consider fixtures and the applicability of Article 9 to other real property-related collateral in Chapter 8, Section 3, infra.

In a similar fashion, UCC 9–109(a)(1) provides that Article 9 applies to security interests created "by contract,"[1] and UCC 9–109(d) specifically excludes from the applicability of Article 9 two types of nonconsensual liens: landlord's liens, see UCC 9–109(d)(1), and liens given by statute or other rule of law for services or materials (other than agricultural liens). See UCC 9–109(d)(2). The creation, priority, and enforcement of most nonconsensual, nonagricultural liens is governed by the statutory and common law of each jurisdiction. However, Article 9 contains a provision governing priority contests between an Article 9 security interest and a nonagricultural lien for services or materials. This provision, UCC 9–333, is discussed in Chapter 8, Section 4(B), infra. When UCC 9–333 does not apply, non-UCC law governs priorities; that law often is not well developed.

Another exclusion that one might think to be self-evident is that of UCC 9–109(c)(1): Article 9—state law—does not apply "to the extent that a statute, regulation, or treaty of the United States preempts this article." The phrase "to the extent that" is a signal that the provision creates delicate problems of meshing state and federal law. The federal statutes that touch on security interests—e.g., those governing copyrights, patents, ships, and

---

1.   Recall that Article 9 also applies to statutory "agricultural liens" on farm products and to security interests arising under Articles 2, 2A, 4, and 5. See UCC 9–109(a)(2), (a)(5), (a)(6); UCC 9–102(a)(5); Section 3, supra.

aircraft—do not contain a complete set of rules governing creation, perfection, priority, and enforcement. (For a recent list of such statutes, see White & Summers § 21–11.) The courts must determine the extent to which any particular federal statute touching upon a secured transaction governs the specific issue in question. Suppose the statute, as often is the case, is not explicit. Courts choosing to apply Former Article 9 typically have justified their decision on one of two grounds: They have concluded that Congress did not (or constitutionally could not) preempt the field, so that state law governs. See, e.g., Johnston v. Simpson, 621 P.2d 688 (Utah 1980) (Federal Aviation Act has preempted field of recordation of conveyances of aircraft but not validity of conveyances or determination of title or ownership). Or they have concluded that Congress did intend to preempt the field but did not enact a rule governing the issue before them, in which case they have created a federal rule modeled after Article 9. See, e.g., Interpool Ltd. v. Char Yigh Marine (Panama) S.A., 890 F.2d 1453 (9th Cir.1989), modified and rehearing denied 918 F.2d 1476 (1990) (UCC is taken as indicative of federal law of admiralty). However, at least one case holds that, under Former 9–104(a), Article 9 ceded the field to the United States. See In re Peregrine Entertainment, Ltd., 116 B.R. 194 (C.D.Cal.1990) (Former 9–104 provides for "voluntary step back" of Article 9 to the extent federal law governs the rights of the parties). The reference to preemption in UCC 9–109(c)(1) is intended to reject this view and make clear that Revised Article 9 "steps back" *only to the extent required by the Constitution.*

A more detailed discussion of UCC 9–109(c)(1) would require greater familiarity with particular federal statutes. Two points nevertheless are worthy of note. First, the integration of Former Article 9 with federal statutes often has been confused and unpredictable. For example, the cases hold that a security interest in patents and trademarks may be perfected without recording in the Patent and Trademark Office. See, e.g., City Bank & Trust Co. v. Otto Fabric, Inc., 83 B.R. 780 (D.Kan.1988) (patents); In re Roman Cleanser Co., 43 B.R. 940 (Bkrtcy.E.D.Mich.1984), affirmed 802 F.2d 207 (6th Cir.1986) (trademarks). But a secured party seeking to perfect a security interest in registered copyrights must record in the Copyright Office. See In re Peregrine Entertainment, Ltd., 116 B.R. 194 (C.D.Cal.1990). As to *un*registered copyrights, however, see In re World Auxiliary Power Co., 303 F.3d 1120 (9th Cir.2002) (limiting *Peregrine* to registered copyrights; holding that a security interest in an unregistered copyright can be perfected under Article 9).

Second, many of the federal statutory recording schemes are not designed to accommodate contemporary financing. For example, the records of the Copyright Office are arranged by copyrighted work. A secured party who wishes to perfect a security interest in, say, the film library of a motion picture studio, must make a separate filing against each title in the Copyright Office. In contrast, a single financing statement filed in the appropriate Article 9 filing office would suffice to perfect a security interest in unregistered copyrights, which are not subject to the federal statute. Efforts at making federal intellectual-property law more conducive to contemporary patterns of commercial finance began in the mid–1980's. The American Bar Association Joint Task Force on Security Interests in Intellectual Property, comprised of lawyers from the Sections of Business Law and Intellectual Property Law (formerly the Section of Patent, Trademark and Copyright Law), prepared drafts of acts that would govern security interests in all federally regulated intellectual property, including copyrights, patents, and trademarks. More recently, the Commercial Finance Association, an international trade association for financial institutions engaged in commercial secured lending and factoring, supported the enactment of the Security Interests in Copyrights Financing Protection Act. As the name implies, this was a more modest reform effort than that of the ABA Task Force. To date, however, reform has been elusive.

Related, but not identical, to the exclusion from the *applicability* of Article 9 in UCC 9–109(c) and (d) is the exclusion from the Article 9 *filing system* in UCC 9–311(a)(1). The filing of a financing statement under Article 9 is unnecessary and ineffective to perfect a security interest in property subject to "a statute, regulation, or treaty of the United States whose requirements for a security interest's obtaining priority over the rights of a lien creditor with respect to the property preempt Section 9–310(a)." Rather, perfection under Article 9 is to be accomplished by compliance with the requirements of the federal statute, regulation, or treaty. UCC 9–311(b). Which federal requirements must be complied with? The "requirements . . . for obtaining priority over the rights of a lien creditor." Id. Even if federal law governs perfection, Article 9 would continue to apply to questions other than perfection (unless, of course, UCC 9–109 excludes the transaction to a greater extent).

UCC 9–109 excludes certain transactions the drafters thought were governed adequately by other law. (Others, who must find, and make decisions based on, this other law, sometimes disagree.) Subsections (c)(2) and (3) exclude security interests *granted* by a government or governmental subdivision or agency, but only to the extent that another statute expressly governs the creation, perfection, priority, or enforcement of the security interest.[2] In adopting Revised Article 9 a number of states enacted

---

2.   Federal law governs the rights of the United States as *creditor*, including as secured party. In United States v. Kimbell Foods, Inc., 440 U.S. 715, 99 S.Ct. 1448, 59 L.Ed.2d 711 (1979), the Supreme Court adopted Former Article 9, as enacted by the appropriate state, as the federal law applicable to security interests held by the Small Business Administration and the Farmers Home Administration. The opinion left room for the adoption, in appropriate cases, of a federal rule of law that is not borrowed from Article 9, e.g., when the federal program in question by its nature must be uniform in character throughout the nation or when application of state law would frustrate specific objectives of the federal program in question. Some courts have taken advantage of this leeway, most notably in cases involving the Department of Defense. See, e.g., In re American Pouch Foods, Inc., 769 F.2d 1190 (7th Cir.1985), cert. denied 475 U.S. 1082, 106 S.Ct. 1459, 89 L.Ed.2d 716 (1986) (refusing to apply Former 9–301(1)(b) [UCC 9–317(a)(2)] to the government's interest, which would have been an unperfected security interest under state law).

nonuniform changes to subsections (c)(2) and (3), perhaps reflecting the diversity of state regimes dealing with public finance. Subsection (d) excludes security interests in wages, salary, or other compensation; they "present important social issues that other law addresses." UCC 9–109(d)(3), Comment 4. (Since 1984, most wage assignments have been prohibited by the Federal Trade Commission. See FTC Rule on Credit Practices, 16 C.F.R. § 442.2(3).)

Comment 7 to Former 9–104 observed that "[r]ights under life insurance and other policies . . . are often put up as collateral." Nevertheless, security interests in this type of property were excluded from Former Article 9, except insofar as the property constituted proceeds of other collateral. See Former 9–104(g); Chapter 3, Section 5, supra (discussing proceeds). With one exception, discussed below, the exclusion continues in Revised Article 9. See UCC 9–109(d)(8). As a consequence, a lender who takes a consensual lien on the debtor's rights under an insurance policy must consult non-UCC law to determine whether its lien has attached and is protected against the competing claims of third parties. Non–UCC law also regulates the enforcement of these liens. The law applicable to these transactions may be difficult to find; it is likely to be incomplete.

Can one justify the exclusion of security interests in insurance policies from Article 9, especially given the UCC's goals of simplifying, clarifying, and modernizing the law governing commercial transactions, and of making uniform the law among the various jurisdictions? See UCC 1–103(a)(1), (3) [F1–102(2)(a), (c)]. Comment 7 to Former 9–104 explained that "[s]uch transactions are often quite special, do not fit easily under a general commercial statute and are adequately covered by existing law." Do you find that explanation persuasive? Is a more cogent, albeit equally unsatisfying, explanation, that the drafters bowed to pressure from the insurance industry to exclude these transactions? See 1 Gilmore, Security § 10.7, at 315 (the exclusion of insurance policies "was politically inspired"). Professor Gilmore recalled that the attitude of counsel for the insurance companies "was not that any provision of the Article was incorrect, harmful, or disadvantageous to their clients, but was rather that they were disinclined to flee to evils that they knew not of." Id.

Insurers that make payments under their policies understandably do not want to face liability for paying the wrong party; in particular, they do not want to be caught in the cross-fire between their customers and their customers' secured parties. In what ways, if any, do the concerns of insurers differ from those of other persons who owe a debt to an Article 9 debtor? Would it be possible to incorporate insurance policies into Article 9 in a manner that facilitates their use as collateral but still affords appropriate protection for the insurers?

The Article 9 Drafting Committee was inclined to answer the question just posed in the affirmative. As the following excerpt explains, the Drafting Committee ultimately decided not to proceed along these lines:

[Former] Article 9 excluded transfers of "an interest in or claim in or under any policy of insurance," except as proceeds of other collateral. Consistent with the [Article 9 Study Committee] Report's recommendation, early drafts of Revised Article 9 narrowed the exclusion substantially. Certain sectors of the insurance industry, most notably the life insurance industry, objected to the potential inclusion of insurance as original collateral. [As Reporters, we] met with representatives of the life insurance industry to discuss their concerns, nearly all of which related to the insurer's status as an obligor. In essence, the insurers wanted to be able to determine with certainty whom to pay to discharge their obligations under their policies, and they wanted to continue making that determination in accordance with existing procedures. The Drafting Committee agreed with us that some of these concerns were unwarranted (*e.g.*, the concern that an insurer would need to consult the UCC filings before deciding whom to pay) and that others (*e.g.*, the concern that the insurer would be obligated to pay the secured party upon receipt of a notification of assignment) could be addressed with special rules that would not require insurers to change their way of doing business. At is meeting in June, 1996, the Drafting Committee voted 5–3 in favor of including insurance within the scope of Revised Article 9.

Immediately following the vote, we asked for guidance on the substance of some of the special rules that might be needed. These preliminary discussions highlighted the complexity that might be necessary to bring insurance-related collateral into Revised Article 9 without upsetting current practices and prompted the Drafting Committee to reconsider its decision. On reconsideration, apparently motivated by the substantial thought required to address this complex subject properly and the limited time in which to do so, the Drafting Committee voted 9–0 in opposition to including insurance policies within the scope of Revised Article 9. We were asked, however, to consider any special scope or other provisions that might be necessary to facilitate the financing of what Revised Article 9 now calls "health-care-insurance receivables," *i.e.*, rights to payment for health-care goods or services which arise under an insurance policy.

Harris & Mooney, How Successful was the Revision of UCC Article 9?: Reflections of the Reporters, 74 Chi.-Kent L. Rev. 1357, 1374–75 (1999).

As the excerpt intimates, Revised Article 9 has narrowed the insurance exclusion somewhat, by bringing within Article 9's scope any assignment of "health-care-insurance receivables" by or to a health-care provider. See UCC 9–109(d)(8); UCC 9–102(a)(46) (defining "health-care-insurance receivable"). Thus, Article 9 applies to assignments of health insurance policy benefits by a patient to a doctor, hospital, or other health-care provider; however, these assignments are automatically perfected. See UCC 9–309(5). Article 9 applies as well as to assignments of these receivables from the health-care provider to its lender. From the perspective of the health-care provider, these receivables are the equivalent of traditional accounts—rights to payment for goods sold or services rendered. For this reason, Article 9 classifies "health-care-insurance receivables" as "accounts." See UCC 9–102(a)(2). But see UCC 9–408 (special rules governing assignments of otherwise non-assignable health-care-insurance receivables).

Insurers are not the only institutions that often owe debts to a large number of claimants; a bank may owe a debt to tens of thousands of depositors. Former Article 9 did not apply to security interests in deposit accounts. The Comments explained this exclusion on the same ground offered for the exclusion of insurance policies. See Former 9–104, Comment 7. As we shall see in Chapter 6, Section 4, the drafters expanded the scope of Revised Article 9 to encompass deposit accounts as original collateral in transactions other than consumer transactions. See UCC 9–109(d)(13). This change has been controversial; some believe that the expansion of Article 9's scope is ill-advised, whereas others contend that it did not go far enough (i.e., that Article 9 should govern security interests in all deposit accounts, even those in consumer transactions).

Former 9–104, Comment 8, explained that Former Article 9 did not apply to security interests in certain "types of claims which do not customarily serve as commercial collateral: judgments . . ., set-offs . . . and tort claims." UCC 9–109(d)(9) retains the exclusion of judgments (other than judgments taken on a right to payment that itself was collateral under Article 9). UCC 9–109(d)(12) narrows somewhat the broad exclusion of transfers of tort claims under Former 9–104(k). Revised Article 9 applies to assignments of "commercial tort claims" as well as to security interests in tort claims that constitute proceeds of other collateral (e.g., a right to payment for negligent destruction of the debtor's inventory). As defined in UCC 9–102(a)(13), "commercial tort claim" includes all tort claims held by a corporation, partnership, or other organization, and those tort claims of individuals that arise in the course of the individual's business or profession (except claims for damages arising out of personal injury or death). UCC 9–109(d)(10) retains and clarifies the exclusion of setoffs. We discussed the ability of an assignee of a right to payment to take free of the obligor's right to set off in Note (2), p. 52, supra. In Chapter 8, Section 4(D), infra, we consider the exercise of setoff rights by banks against funds on deposit.

The foregoing exclusions relate to the scope provision in UCC 9–109(a)(1): transactions that create a security interest by contract. Two limitations of the other scope provisions are worthy of mention. First, the definition of "consignment" excludes from Article 9 certain "true" consignments, such as consignments of consumer goods. See UCC 9–102(a)(20); Section 1(B), supra. Second, although Article 9 applies to most sales of receivables, UCC 9–109(d)(4)–(7) excludes from Article 9 "certain sales . . . of receivables that, by their nature, do not concern commercial financing transactions." UCC 9–109, Comment 12. See generally Chapter 6, Section 1(D) (discussing sales of receivables).

CHAPTER 6

SECURITY INTERESTS IN RIGHTS TO PAYMENT, INVESTMENT PROPERTY, AND OTHER INTANGIBLES

This Chapter is concerned with security interests in intangible property, including rights to payment of various kinds (referred to colloquially as "receivables"), investment property (such as stocks and bonds), and deposit accounts (such as checking and savings accounts). Although the extension of credit secured by goods goes back to ancient times, the use of intangible property as collateral is largely a product of the twentieth century. Over the past fifty years, the relative importance of intangible property as a source of wealth has grown substantially. This dramatic change is reflected in Revised Article 9; the revised Article contains many new provisions applicable only to one or more types of intangible collateral.

The secured financing of intangible property raises many of the same considerations as the financing of goods, and many of the same legal rules apply. The secured party must insure that its security interest is enforceable, i.e., that the conditions for attachment in UCC 9–203 have been met. See Chapter 3, Section 2, supra. To prevail over subsequent judicial lien creditors and secured parties, the security interest must be perfected, often by filing a financing statement. See UCC 9–317(a)(2); UCC 9–322(a)(1); UCC 9–310(a); Chapter 3, Section 3, supra. We have seen that Article 9 contains special rules governing security interests in goods. See, e.g., UCC 9–324; (governing PMSI's). That Article 9 likewise contains special rules governing security interests in various forms of intangible property should come as no surprise. One also would expect that the Article would contain provisions that reflect the vast array of types of intangible property. While a franchisee's rights under a franchise agreement, a stockholder's rights against the corporation, and a merchant's right to payment for goods sold share certain attributes, they are in many ways dissimilar; Article 9 reflects some of these dissimilarities. Even rights to payment come in a variety of forms. Rights secured by personal property (as evidenced by the Instalment Sale Contract, Form 3.6), rights secured by real property (as evidenced by a mortgage), bank accounts, negotiable and nonnegotiable promissory notes, and rights to insurance proceeds are just a few examples.

SECTION 1.   FINANCING RECEIVABLES

(A)   BACKGROUND

The following bird's-eye-view of accounts receivable financing was written, on the basis of first-hand practical experience, shortly after the completion of the UCC. As you might imagine, some details have become dated and some new practices have developed during the nearly 50 years since the following was written; however, the terminology retains its vitality, and the discussion of the mechanics of receivables financing, including the allocation of risks between the assignor and assignee, retains its utility as an introduction to the field.

Kupfer, Accounts Receivable Financing: A Legal and Practical Look–See

Prac. Law., Nov. 1956, at 50, 50–65.

Less than half a century ago, a mere moment of transit in our Anglo–Saxon legal and economic history, accounts receivable financing was virtually unknown. It now approximates an annual volume of ten billion dollars. The office of this paper will be to dissect the economic structure of the mechanism and to analyze the details of the legal blueprints that make it tick. . . .

Purposes of Accounts Receivable Financing. A borrower normally will first seek unsecured credit to the extent to which he can obtain it. But the overwhelming majority of our industrial and commercial units constitute "small business," and require accommodation for which unsecured credit is not readily available. They may require liquid funds for more working capital; or for expansion purposes; or to take discounts on merchandise purchased. For these needs, they will usually resort to their most liquid asset other than cash—their accounts receivable.

Generally speaking, because of its inherently self-liquidating and revolving nature, accounts receivable financing is not an apt permanent source of capital, although it is frequently so employed on a temporary basis. . . .

The greater part of accounts receivable financing covers sales of manufacturers and merchants, and, historically, it was confined, in its early development, to that area. In recent years, however, its operation has been expanded into much wider, and at times greener, fields. Illustrations are the financing of deferred-payment sales and the leasing plans of commercial and industrial equipment; the financing, for department stores, of retail budget-instalment and charge accounts; the rediscounting of the paper of small-loan companies and the smaller consumer-finance companies; and even the financing of mergers and acquisitions of businesses. Its operation in the purely service field is by no means unknown, although the author has yet to hear of lawyers' accounts receivable being accepted as collateral! It could, however, happen, and probably will before we know it.

The Different Types of Accounts Receivable Financing:

The Parties. To every accounts receivable operation there are necessarily three parties: (1) the lender upon, or purchaser of, the accounts; (2) the borrower upon, or seller of, them; and (3) the debtor upon the accounts assigned. For semantic uniformity and brevity, these three parties will be respectively called the "*assignee,*" the "*assignor,*" and the "*account-debtor,*" unless the context otherwise indicates. (Occasionally, the words "*lender*" or "*secured creditor*" will connote the assignee, and the word "*borrower,*" the assignor. Only exceptionally—and then obviously—will there be any departure from the use of "*account-debtor.*")

The Two Basic Forms. There are two essential requirements to the payment of any account receivable. First, the assignor must comply with the terms of his agreement with, or the order of, the account-debtor, and secondly, the latter must be financially able and willing to pay. The first requirement is called the "merchandise risk," and the second, the "credit risk." And out of this dichotomy arise the two basic forms of accounts receivable financing. These are respectively known as "*recourse*" and "*non-recourse*" financing, and the terminology in itself differentiates them.

In *both,* the assignor necessarily retains the *merchandise* risk, because the fabrication of the goods or the rendition of the service in accordance with his commitment to the account-debtor at all times rests solely within his control.

In *recourse* financing, the *assignor* also retains the *credit* risk; he guarantees to the assignee that the account will be paid at its maturity. Therefore, both in economics and in law, the financing transaction, however the contract may be set up, constitutes a loan upon the security of the assigned accounts.

In the *non-recourse* operation, the *assignee* assumes the *credit* risk, and, in legal consequence, the operation constitutes a purchase. (Non-recourse financing is sometimes called "*factoring.*" Historically, factoring was first associated solely with inventory financing. When accounts receivable financing—usually on a non-recourse basis—developed as an adjunct to inventory financing, the term was originally applied to the combined operation. Latterly, it is occasionally used to cover both recourse and non-recourse accounts receivable financing, with or without a precedent inventory loan. Therefore, except to the highly initiated and in the context of a specific operation, the use of the term is only apt to confuse, and will be eschewed in this paper.)

The distinction between recourse and non-recourse financing is of great importance in the application of interest and usury laws.

Combining With Inventory Financing. Inventory financing can be combined with either the non-recourse or recourse financing of accounts;

traditionally, it was more intimately associated with the former, although it may, but need not, be employed in connection with either type, as the economic "lead line" which ultimately becomes solely the accounts receivable operation. When inventory financing is absent, the operation is called "pure" accounts receivable financing, and this is the more usual form that it takes.
. . .

Function of Banks. The function of banks in accounts receivable financing is also a matter of considerable interest. In the first place they constitute the wholesalers of credit to the account receivable companies. Secondly, a number of them are engaged directly in the accounts receivable field. The competition is not at all unwelcome to finance companies, although, from the standpoint of the banks, it presents both advantages and disadvantages which are beyond the ambit of this paper. And finally, the banks frequently participate with finance companies in specific operations because it minimizes the risk and puts at their disposal the specialized know-how of accounts receivable companies, thus reducing the overall cost of the lending operation. . . .

Implementation of the Operation:

The Underlying Contract and the Assignments. Every accounts receivable operation starts with the execution of an underlying contract between the assignor and the assignee. It spells out in detail the rights of the parties, and its contents have become more or less standard.

When the accounts to be assigned have been created by the assignor, they are listed on assignment forms or "schedules." Since the assigned accounts constitute the very lifeblood of the assignee's security, all the material documents pertaining to the assigned accounts must accompany the assignment schedule and be contemporaneously delivered to the assignee at the time when it makes its advance to the assignor upon them. These documents vary with the nature of the assigned accounts but must always include copies of the relevant invoices; the original bills of lading or express receipts evidencing the delivery of the merchandise or (where applicable) proof of the rendition of the service; and all other papers necessary to effect collection of the assigned accounts. It is vital that the assignee satisfy himself as to the authenticity and legal competence of these documents.

The assignment-schedules as a rule must cover specific accounts; in most jurisdictions [prior to the UCC], blanket assignments [were] of little, if any, legal value. See, illustratively, State Factors Corp. v. Sales Factors Corp., 257 App.Div. 101, 12 N.Y.S.2d 12 (1st Dep't 1939). However, under the so-called "floating lien" provisions of the Uniform Commercial Code ([Former] §§ 9–108 and 9–204 [UCC 9–204]) . . . general, or blanket, assignments are permitted and recognized. . . .

Indirect and Direct Collections. There are two methods—indirect or direct, so-called, for the actual collection of the assigned accounts.

In the indirect collection program, the account-debtors are not notified of the assignments, and remittances are made to the assignor, who is obligated promptly to endorse and transmit them in specie to the assignee—customarily on the day of their receipt. If it has not already become apparent, we shall, a little later, appreciate the economic and legal necessity [prior to the UCC] for the imposition of this requirement.

In the direct collection program, the account-debtors are forthwith notified of the assignments, and are instructed to make their remittances directly to the assignee.

Indirect collection is much more frequently found in recourse financing, and direct collection in non-recourse financing, but the association is by no means inevitable. Indeed, one of the larger and most respected financing agencies has recently instituted a non-notification, non-recourse program, for assignors whose operations and standing make it adaptable to their business.

In all accounts receivable programs, the assignee, at periodic intervals (usually monthly) makes an audit of the assignor's books and operations, through one of the members of its own staff. In addition, when the collection program is indirect, the assignee causes periodic spot verification to be made of the existence of the assigned accounts and the amounts due upon them. This is accomplished by direct correspondence between an auditing concern and a random selection of the account-debtors.

Causes of Loss. Experience has demonstrated that the incidence of loss in an accounts receivable operation is minimal, almost to the vanishing point, if: the adaptability of the assignor's business to accounts receivable financing has been soundly analyzed and conceived; the credit standing of the account-debtors has been sensibly evaluated at the time when the assignments are tendered for advances upon them; and the operation is properly conducted within the framework above outlined. Of course, losses do take place, but, when they do, they are attributable, largely, if not solely, to what, in air-travel, would be called "pilot failure" in one of three aspects:

(1) Over-concentration. The first such cause, over-concentration, is purely economic and is by no means indigenous to the accounts receivable field. It is basic (a) that the assignee should diversify, as among the types and selection of assignors whose business he finances, and (b) that the accounts receivable of any one assignor should be diversified as much as the nature of its business permits. If the author were charged with operational responsibility (which none of his clients has ever "threatened" to entrust to him), he would view, with a highly piscatorial eye, financing a borrower who had only three large customers, however, financially "good" these customers might be. All of this is purely an economic matter, but a very important one.

(2) Fictitious Accounts. The second cause of loss—the assignment of fictitious accounts—brings us into the legal area. Obviously, if an assignor ships goods on consignment or, worse yet, purports to assign "accounts" against "account-debtors" to whom no merchandise has been shipped at all,

the assignee has no security for his advances. Neither the nature of the operation nor the rates charged for it permit the assumption of any such hazard, and it is this signpost which points the path to the importance of checking the shipping and other documents adverted to above. . . .

One final feature of this whole matter is so obvious as merely to require mention. If the account-debtor, without notice of either of the duplicate assignments, pays the assignor or either of the assignees, he is fully protected and naturally need not pay any of them, all over again.

(3) Conversions. The last cause of loss is the conversion by the assignor of the proceeds of assigned accounts. It can occur only when the collection method is indirect. . . .

Although there is no substitute for watchfulness, relatively simple techniques exist to guard against and obviate the hazard of over-concentration, fictitious accounts and duplicate assignments, and conversions. Assuming the original soundness of the assignor's business operation, no financing assignee who makes a reasonable realistic check of the account-debtor's credit is apt to sustain any serious loss if he will just watch these three matters.

(B)   FINANCING RECEIVABLES: A PROTOTYPE

You have seen many examples of how Article 9 reflects prevailing patterns of financing. One of the basic patterns is receivables financing. The following Prototype portrays in some detail the legal and related business practices employed in the financing of receivables arising from both the retail sale of inventory and the provision of services.[1] In reviewing the Prototype, consider the ways in which the practices and documentation differ from those in the Prototype on financing automobiles in Chapter 3, Section 1, supra. To what extent do these differences appear to stem from differences in the nature of the collateral? To what extent from differences in the applicable law? To what extent from custom in the industry?

Carguys, Inc., is a Delaware corporation that is a nationwide retail and wholesale seller of automobile parts. Carguys sells auto parts from stores in all 50 states; it also operates full-service automobile repair facilities at each of its store locations.

Most of Carguys' customers are consumers. However, many commercial customers also patronize Carguys. Some utilize Carguys' repair and maintenance services; they include taxi and limousine operators, car and truck rental companies, delivery services, and corporate employers that provide automobiles to their employees. Other commercial customers, who operate their own repair and maintenance operations, buy auto parts from

---

1.   This Prototype was prepared with the generous assistance of Edwin E. Smith of Bingham McCutchen LLP. It does not necessarily describe the practices of any particular finance company or seller of auto parts.

Carguys. These customers also buy and lease sophisticated automobile diagnostic equipment from Carguys.

Carguys' consumer customers pay for goods and services at the time they are received. They use cash, checks, and credit cards. Unlike its arrangements with consumer customers, Carguys extends credit to its commercial customers. It provides repair and maintenance services and sells parts and equipment on **open account**—i.e., on unsecured credit. Carguys sends bills (**invoices**) to its commercial customers monthly for services and parts purchased during the preceding month. The credit terms require the customers to pay the outstanding charges within 30 days after the date of the invoice.

Not unlike Main Motors in the Prototype on financing automobiles, Chapter 3, Section 1, supra, Carguys requires financing. It lacks the capital necessary to extend credit to its commercial customers while also meeting its operating expenses and other current obligations, including its obligations to suppliers, employees, and landlords.

Revolving Credit Agreement; Revolving Credit Note. Effective July 2, 2006, Carguys established a new credit relationship with Eastinghome Credit Corporation. The essential aspects of the relationship are embodied in a Revolving Credit Agreement (Form 6.1), which is reproduced below (with some provisions omitted and summarized).

FORM 6.1
REVOLVING CREDIT AGREEMENT

This **REVOLVING CREDIT AGREEMENT** (this "Agreement") is made as of July 1, 2006, by and between CARGUYS, INC. (the "Borrower"), a Delaware corporation having its principal place of business at 1313 West Rosannadanna Boulevard, Los Angeles, California, and EASTINGHOME CREDIT CORPORATION (the "Lender"), a New York corporation having its office at 94 Wintershire Drive, Territown, New York.

1. DEFINITIONS:

Certain capitalized terms are defined below:

Accounts: All rights of the Borrower to any payment of money for goods sold, leased or otherwise marketed in the ordinary course of business or for services rendered in the ordinary course of business, whether evidenced by or under or in respect of a contract or instrument, and all proceeds thereof.

Agreement: This Agreement as amended and in effect from time to time.

Base Accounts: Those Accounts (net of any finance charges, late charges, credits, commissions, contras or other offsets or counterclaims) (i) that the Borrower reasonably determines to be collectible, (ii) the account debtors in respect of which purchased the goods or services from Borrower at arms' length, are deemed creditworthy by the Lender, are solvent, and are not affiliated with the Borrower, (iii) that are not outstanding for more than sixty (60) days past the earlier to occur of (A) the date of invoice and (B) the date of shipment (as to goods) or of provision (as to services), (iv) in which the Lender has a valid and perfected first-priority security interest, and over which there is no other lien, (v) that are in payment of fully performed and undisputed obligations, and (vi) that are payable in U.S. currency from an office within the United States.

Base Inventory: Inventory (i) that is owned, possessed and held for sale or lease by the Borrower within the United States but not yet shipped, (ii) that is not held on land leased by, or in a warehouse of a warehouseman other than, the Borrower, absent delivery to the Lender of a waiver of the lien of the lessor or warehouseman in form an substance satisfactory to the Lender, (iii) as to which a valid and perfected first-priority security interest in favor of the Lender has been created and on which there is no other lien, and (iv) that the Lender deems neither obsolete nor unmarketable.

Base Rate: The annual rate of interest announced from time to time by Firstbank, N.A., at its office as the that bank's "base rate."

Borrower: See preamble.

Borrowing Base: An amount equal to the sum of 75% of the Base Accounts and 60% of the Base Inventory.

Borrowing Base Report: A report, in form and with supporting details satisfactory to the Lender, setting forth the Borrower's computation of the Borrowing Base.

Business Day: Any day on which banks in New York, New York, are open for business generally.

Collateral: All of the property, rights and assets of the Borrower that are or are intended to be subject to the security interest created by the Security Documents.

Commitment: The obligation of the Lender to make Loans to the Borrower up to an aggregate outstanding principal amount not to exceed Twenty-Five Million Dollars ($25,000,000), as such amount may be reduced from time to time or terminated under this Agreement.

Default: An event or act which with the giving of notice and/or the lapse of time, would become an Event of Default.

Drawdown Date: In respect of any Loan, the date on which such Loan is made to the Borrower.

Event of Default: Any of the events listed in §7 hereof.

Indebtedness: In respect of any entity, all obligations, contingent and otherwise, that in accordance with generally accepted accounting principles should be classified as liabilities, including without limitation (i) all debt obligations, (ii) all liabilities secured by liens, (iii) all guarantees, and (iv) all liabilities in respect of bankers' acceptances or letters of credit.

Inventory: All goods now owned or hereafter acquired by the Borrower which are held for sale or lease.

Lender: See preamble.

Loan: Any loan made or to be made to the Borrower pursuant to §2 hereof.

Loan Documents: This Agreement, the Note, and the Security Documents, in each case as from time to time amended or supplemented.

Loan Request: See §2.1.

Margin: Two percent (2%) per annum.

<u>Materially Adverse Effect</u>: Any materially adverse effect on the financial condition or business operations of the Borrower or material impairment of the ability of the Borrower to perform its obligations under this Agreement or under any of the other Loan Documents.

<u>Maturity Date</u>: July 1, 2009, or such earlier date on which all Loans may become due and payable pursuant to the terms hereof.

<u>Note</u>: See §2.1.

<u>Obligations</u>: All indebtedness, obligations and liabilities of the Borrower to the Lender, existing on the date of this Agreement or arising thereafter, direct or indirect, joint or several, absolute or contingent, matured or unmatured, liquidated or unliquidated, secured or unsecured, arising by contract, operation of law or otherwise, arising or incurred under this Agreement or any other Loan Document or in respect of any of the Loans or the Note or other instruments at any time evidencing any thereof.

<u>Security Documents</u>: The Security Agreement dated as of the date hereof between the Lender and the Borrower, pursuant to which the Borrower grants to the Lender a security interest in the Borrower's existing and after-acquired personal property and fixture assets, the Perfection Certificate dated as of the date hereof and executed and delivered by the Borrower, all financing statements authorized by the Borrower under the Security Agreement, and any other documents delivered by Borrower in connection with the Security Agreement.

2. REVOLVING CREDIT FACILITY.

2.1. Commitment to Lend.

(a)   Upon the terms and subject to the conditions of this Agreement, the Lender agrees to lend to the Borrower such sums that the Borrower may request, from the date hereof until but not including the Maturity Date, <u>provided</u> that the sum of the outstanding principal amount of all Loans (after giving effect to all amounts requested) shall not exceed the lesser of (i) the Commitment and (ii) the Borrowing Base. Loans shall be in the minimum aggregate amount of Two Hundred Fifty Thousand Dollars ($250,000) or an integral multiple thereof.

(b)   The Borrower shall notify the Lender in writing or telephonically not later than 12:00 noon New York time on the day of the Drawdown Date (which must be a Business Day) of the Loan being requested and of the principal amount of the Loan (a "Loan Request"). Subject to the foregoing, so long as the Commitment is then in effect and the applicable conditions set forth in §5 hereof have been met, the Lender shall advance the amount requested to the Borrower's Lender account no.

081347-012060 at Firstbank, New York, New York, in immediately available funds not later than the close of business on the Drawdown Date.

(c)   The obligation of the Borrower to repay to the Lender the principal of the Loans and interest accrued thereon shall be evidenced by a promissory note (the "Note") in the maximum aggregate principal amount of Twenty-Five Million Dollars ($25,000,000) executed and delivered by the Borrower and payable to the order of the Lender, in form and substance satisfactory to the Lender.

2. 2. Interest. So long as no Event of Default is continuing, the Borrower shall pay interest on the Loans at a rate per annum which is equal to the sum of (i) the Base Rate, and (ii) the Margin, such interest to be payable in arrears on the first day of each calendar month for the immediately preceding calendar month, commencing with the first such day following the date hereof. While an Event of Default is continuing, amounts payable under any of the Loan Documents shall bear interest (compounded monthly and payable on demand in respect of overdue amounts) at a rate per annum which is equal to the sum of (i) the Base Rate, and (ii) three percent (3%) above the Margin until such amount is paid in full or (as the case may be) the Event of Default has been cured or waived in writing by the Lender (after as well as before judgment).

2.3. Repayments and Prepayments. The Borrower agrees to pay the Lender on the Maturity Date the entire unpaid principal of and interest on all Loans. The Borrower may elect to prepay the outstanding principal of all or any part of any Loan, without premium or penalty, in a minimum amount of Two Hundred Fifty Thousand Dollars ($250,000) or an integral multiple thereof, upon written notice to the Lender given by 10:00 a.m. New York time on the date of the prepayment, of the amount to be prepaid. The Borrower shall be entitled to reborrow before the Maturity Date such amounts, upon the terms and subject to the conditions of this Agreement. Each repayment or prepayment of principal of any Loan shall be accompanied by payment of the unpaid interest accrued to date on the principal being repaid or prepaid. If at any time the outstanding principal amount of the Loans shall exceed the lesser of (i) the Commitment and (ii) the Borrowing Base, the Borrower shall immediately pay the amount of the excess to the Lender for application to the Loans. The Borrower may elect to reduce or terminate the Commitment by a minimum principal amount of Two Hundred Fifty Thousand Dollars ($250,000) or an integral multiple thereof, upon written notice to the Lender given by 10:00 a.m. New York time at least two (2) Business Days prior to the date of such reduction or termination. The Borrower shall not be entitled to reinstate the Commitment following the reduction or termination.

3. FEES AND PAYMENTS.

Contemporaneously with execution and delivery of this Agreement, the Borrower shall pay to the Lender a closing fee in the amount of Twenty-Five Thousand Dollars ($25,000). The Borrower shall pay to the Lender, on the first day of each calendar quarter hereafter, and upon the Maturity Date or the date upon which the Commitment is no longer in effect, a commitment fee calculated at a rate per annum which is equal to one and one-half percent (1-1/2%) of the average daily difference by which the Commitment amount exceeds the aggregate of the outstanding Loans during the preceding calendar quarter or portion thereof. All payments to be made by the Borrower under this Agreement or under any of the other Loan Documents shall be made in U.S. dollars in immediately available funds at the Lender's office at 94 Wintershire Drive, Territown, New York, without set-off or counterclaim and without any withholding or deduction whatsoever. If any payment under this Agreement is required to be made on a day which is not a Business Day, it shall be paid on the immediately succeeding Business Day, with interest and any applicable fees adjusted accordingly. All computations of interest or of the commitment fee payable under this Agreement shall be made by the Lender on the basis of actual days elapsed and on a 360-day year.

4. REPRESENTATIONS AND WARRANTIES.

The Borrower represents and warrants to the Lender on the date hereof, on the date of any Loan Request, and on each Drawdown Date that:

> [This section of the Agreement sets forth various facts as to which the Borrower makes representations and warranties. The "reps and warranties" relate to matters such as the Borrower's due organization and good standing, its power and authority to enter into the Loan Documents, the validity and enforceability of the Loan Documents, various aspects of the Borrower's business, the Borrower's financial condition and the absence of a Materially Adverse Effect, legal proceedings affecting the Borrower, the Borrower's compliance with various agreements, corporate restrictions, and laws, and the perfection and priority of the Lender's security interest.]

5. CONDITIONS PRECEDENT.

In addition to the Borrower's foregoing representations and warranties and the delivery of the Loan Documents and such other documents and the taking of such actions as the Lender may require at or prior to the time of executing this Agreement, the obligation of the Lender to make any Loan to the Borrower under this Agreement is subject to the satisfaction of the following further conditions precedent:

(a)   each of the representations and warranties of the Borrower to the Lender herein, in any of the other Loan Documents or any documents, certificate or other paper or notice in connection herewith shall be true and correct in all material respects as of the time made or deemed to have been made;

(b)   no Default or Event of Default shall be continuing;

(c)   all proceedings in connection with the transactions contemplated hereby shall be in form and substance satisfactory to the Lender, and the Lender shall have received all information and documents as it may have reasonably requested; and

(d)   no change shall have occurred in any law or regulation or in the interpretation thereof that in the reasonable opinion of the Lender would make it unlawful for the Lender to make such Loan.

6. <u>COVENANTS</u>.

6.1. <u>Affirmative Covenants</u>. The Borrower agrees that until the termination of the Commitment and the payment and satisfaction in full of all the Obligations, the Borrower will comply with its obligations as set forth throughout this Agreement and to:

> [This section of the Agreement sets forth various affirmative covenants, including the Borrower's obligation to provide the Lender with audited financial statements and other reports, to keep accurate books and records, to maintain its existence and lines of business, to comply with the law, to use the proceeds of the Loans for specified purposes, and to insure the Collateral and keep it free of competing liens.]

6.2. <u>Negative Covenants</u>. The Borrower agrees that until the termination of the Commitment and the payment and satisfaction in full of all the Obligations, the Borrower will not:

> [This section of the Agreement sets forth various negative covenants, including restrictions on the Borrower's incurrence of Indebtedness, creation of liens, investments, distributions of capital (e.g., dividends), and combinations (e.g., mergers) with other entities.]

6.3. <u>Financial Covenants</u>. The Borrower agrees that until the termination of the Commitment and the payment and satisfaction in full of all the Obligations, the Borrower will not:

[This section of the Agreement sets forth various covenants relating to the financial condition of the Borrower. They include a restriction on capital expenditures and an obligation to maintain specified minimum or maximum levels of certain indicators of financial health, e.g., the ratio of total liabilities to tangible net worth, the amount of tangible net worth, the ratio of current assets to current liabilities, and the ratio of operating cash flow to total debt service. Credit agreements normally contain detailed definitions of the financial terms used in financial covenants. However, these definitions have been omitted here.]

7. <u>EVENTS OF DEFAULT; ACCELERATION.</u>

If any of the following events ("Events of Default") shall occur:

(a)   the Borrower shall fail to pay when due and payable any principal of the Loans when the same becomes due;

(b)   the Borrower shall fail to pay interest on the Loans or any other sum due under any of the Loan Documents within two (2) Business Days after the date on which the same shall have first become due and payable;

(c)   the Borrower shall fail to perform any term, covenant or agreement contained in [here the Agreement lists certain important covenants contained in Section 6, such as those relating to reporting requirements, use of Loan proceeds, and the negative and financial covenants];

(d)   the Borrower shall fail to perform any other term, covenant or agreement contained in the Loan Documents within fifteen (15) days after the Lender has given written notice of such failure to the Borrower;

(e)   any representation or warranty of the Borrower in the Loan Documents or in any certificate or notice given in connection therewith shall have been false or misleading in any material respect at the time made or deemed to have been made;

(f)   the Borrower shall be in default (after any applicable period of grace or cure period) under any agreement or agreements evidencing Indebtedness owing to the Lender or any affiliates of the Lender or any other Indebtedness in excess of Twenty-Five Thousand Dollars ($25,000) in aggregate principal amount, or shall fail to pay such Indebtedness when due, or within any applicable period of grace;

(g)   any of the Loan Documents shall cease to be in full force and effect,

(h)   the Borrower (i) shall make an assignment for the benefit of creditors, (ii) shall be adjudicated a bankrupt or insolvent, (iii) shall seek the appointment of, or be the subject of an order appointing, a trustee, liquidator or receiver as to all or part of its assets; (iv) shall commence, approve or consent to, any case or proceeding under any bankruptcy, reorganization or similar law and, in the case of an involuntary case or proceeding, such case or proceeding is not dismissed within forty-five (45) days following the commencement thereof, or (v) shall be the subject of an order for relief in an involuntary case under federal bankruptcy law;

(i)   the Borrower shall be unable to pay or generally shall cease to pay its debts as they mature;

(j)   there shall remain undischarged for more than thirty (30) days any final judgment or execution action against the Borrower that, together with other outstanding claims and execution actions against the Borrower exceeds Twenty-Five Thousand Dollars ($25,000) in the aggregate;

THEN, or at any time thereafter:

(1)   In the case of any Event of Default under clause (h) or (i), the Commitment shall automatically terminate, and the entire unpaid principal amount of the Loans, all interest accrued and unpaid thereon, and all other amounts payable under this Agreement and under the other Loan Documents shall automatically become forthwith due and payable, without presentment, demand, protest or notice of any kind, all of which are hereby expressly waived by the Borrower; and

(2)   In the case of any Event of Default other than under clause (h) or (i), the Lender may, by written notice to the Borrower, terminate the Commitment and/or declare the unpaid principal amount of the Loans, all interest accrued and unpaid thereon, and all other amounts payable under this Agreement and under the other Loan Documents to be forthwith due and payable, without presentment, demand, protest or further notice of any kind, all of which are hereby expressly waived by the Borrower.

No remedy herein conferred upon the Lender is intended to be exclusive of any other remedy and each and every remedy shall be cumulative and in addition to every other remedy under this Agreement, now or hereafter existing under the other Loan Documents, at law or in equity, or otherwise.

8. <u>SETOFF</u>.

Regardless of the adequacy of any collateral for the Obligations, any sums credited by or due from the Lender to the Borrower may be applied to or set off against any principal, interest and any other amounts due from the Borrower to the Lender at any time without notice to the Borrower, or compliance with any other procedure imposed by statute or otherwise, all of which are hereby expressly waived by the Borrower.

9. <u>MISCELLANEOUS</u>.

The Borrower agrees to indemnify and hold harmless the Lender and its officers, employees, affiliates, agents, and controlling persons from and against all claims, damages, liabilities and losses of every kind arising out of the Loan Documents, including without limitation, against those in respect of the application of environmental laws to the Borrower absent the gross negligence or willful misconduct of the Lender. The Borrower shall pay to the Lender promptly on demand all costs and expenses (including any taxes and reasonable legal and other professional fees and fees of its commercial finance examiner) incurred by the Lender in connection with the preparation, negotiation, execution, amendment, administration, or enforcement of any of the Loan Documents. Any communication to be made under this Agreement shall (i) be made in writing, but unless otherwise stated, may be made by telex, facsimile transmission or letter, and (ii) be made or delivered to the address of the party receiving notice which is identified with its signature below (unless such party has by five (5) days written notice specified another address), and shall be deemed made or delivered, when dispatched, left at that address, or five (5) days after being mailed, postage prepaid, to such address. This Agreement shall be binding upon and inure to the benefit of each party hereto and its successors and assigns, but the Borrower may not assign its rights or obligations under this Agreement. This Agreement may not be amended or waived except by a written instrument signed by the Borrower and the Lender, and any such amendment or waiver shall be effective only for the specific purpose given. No failure or delay by the Lender to exercise any right under this Agreement or any other Loan Document shall operate as a waiver thereof, nor shall any single or partial exercise of any right, power or privilege preclude any other right, power or privilege. The provisions of this Agreement are severable and if any one provision hereof shall be held invalid or unenforceable in whole or in part in any jurisdiction, such invalidity or unenforceability shall affect only such provision in such jurisdiction. This Agreement expresses the entire understanding of the parties with respect to the transactions contemplated hereby. This Agreement and any amendment hereto may be executed in several counterparts, each of which shall be an original, and all of which shall constitute one agreement. In proving this Agreement, it shall not be necessary to produce more than one such counterpart executed by the party to be charged. **THIS AGREEMENT AND THE OTHER LOAN DOCUMENTS ARE CONTRACTS UNDER THE LAWS OF THE STATE OF NEW YORK AND SHALL BE CONSTRUED IN**

ACCORDANCE THEREWITH AND GOVERNED THEREBY. THE BORROWER AGREES THAT ANY SUIT FOR THE ENFORCEMENT OF ANY OF THE LOAN DOCUMENTS MAY BE BROUGHT IN THE COURTS OF THE STATE OF NEW YORK OR ANY FEDERAL COURT SITTING THEREIN. The Borrower, as an inducement to the Lender to enter into this Agreement, hereby waives its right to a jury trial with respect to any action arising in connection with any Loan Document.

IN WITNESS WHEREOF, the undersigned have duly executed this Revolving Credit Agreement as a sealed instrument as of the date first above written.

CARGUYS, INC., a Delaware corporation
1313 West Rosannadanna Boulevard
Los Angeles, California 90210
Attention: Angie Boombox, President
Tel: 999-674-1022
Fax: 999-674-1023

By: _Angie Boombox_
    Name: Angie Boombox
    Title: President

EASTINGHOME CREDIT
CORPORATION, a New York corporation
94 Wintershire Drive
Territown, New York 10156
Attention: Tabb Collar, III, President
Tel: 666-785-2133
Fax: 666-785-2134

By: _Tabb Collar, III_
    Name: Tabb Collar, III
    Title: Vice-President

As you can see, the Revolving Credit Agreement creates a **committed credit facility** in favor of Carguys—i.e., Eastinghome has made a binding agreement to lend an amount up to its "Commitment" (see the definition in § 1 of the Agreement and the commitment to lend in § 2.1) of $25,000,000. (This arrangement is to be contrasted with the discretionary **line of credit** that Firstbank provided to Main Motors in the automobile financing Prototype in Chapter 3.) However, under § 2.1, Eastinghome's commitment is further limited to the *lesser* of the Commitment and the "Borrowing Base," which is the sum of 75% of the "Base Accounts" and 60% of the "Base Inventory" (see § 1 for the definitions of these terms and "Accounts" and "Inventory"). Under this structure, Eastinghome is not required to lend more than its Commitment and, depending on the value of the Base Accounts and Base Inventory, may be obligated to lend only a smaller amount. In any event, Eastinghome is assured that it will have a **collateral value cushion** over and above the amount of its Loans of 25% in the case of Base Accounts and 40% in the case of Base Inventory. The Agreement also contains another set of important lender protections. Eastinghome is obliged to make a Loan only if the Conditions Precedent (pronounced preh-SEE-dent, and not to be confused with a PREH-seh-dent) specified in § 5 are satisfied.

This arrangement is called a **revolving credit facility** or **revolver** because Carguys is entitled to borrow, repay, and reborrow throughout the term of the facility, so long as the aggregate outstanding loan balance does not exceed the lesser of the Commitment or the Borrowing Base at any time (see § 2.3). However, on the Maturity Date, July 1, 2009 (three years after the Agreement became effective), Carguys is obliged to repay the Loans in full. In reality, however, Eastinghome is likely to renew the arrangement for an additional term if Carguys remains a viable and creditworthy enterprise and continues to need financing. In the alternative, Carguys might arrange for a new facility with a new lender that would **take out** Eastinghome (not unlike the situation in the automobile financing Prototype in Chapter 3, in which Firstbank "picked up the floor plan" from Main Motors' earlier lender, Old Bank).

The Note (see § 2.1(c) of the Agreement) evidences the outstanding Loans under the Revolving Credit Agreement. A "grid" or table attached to the Note is designed to reflect the various advances and repayments of Loans. In the Note, Carguys authorizes Eastinghome to make the relevant notations on the grid, which Carguys agrees will be *prima facie* evidence of the various Loans and repayments. With respect to each Loan and repayment, Eastinghome will enter on the grid the date and amount, the resulting outstanding principal balance, and the name of the person making the notation. In actuality, of course, the grid is redundant; Eastinghome will have computerized business records of all transactions with respect to the Loans. Nevertheless, as a general matter a note is customary but not necessary.

In addition to interest charges on outstanding Loans (see § 2.2 of the Agreement), Carguys has agreed to pay certain fees to Eastinghome. The fees consist of a one-time "closing fee" of $25,000 and a "commitment fee" of one and one-half percent (1–1/2%) per annum on the unused portion of Eastinghome's Commitment (see § 3). The commitment fee reflects the principle that Eastinghome should be compensated for its ongoing obligation to extend credit.

The Revolving Credit Agreement also specifies "Events of Default" in § 7(a)–(j). Upon the occurrence of certain Events of Default Eastinghome's obligation to extend credit will be terminated and the Loans and all other amounts owed by Carguys automatically become due and payable (i.e., these amounts will be automatically **accelerated**). See § 7(1). Other Events of Default provide Eastinghome with the option to terminate its obligations and to accelerate the payment obligations of Carguys. See § 7(2). Finally, in § 4 Carguys makes various representations and warranties of fact and law, and in § 6 it makes certain covenants (promises).

Security Agreement; Perfection Certificate. The Security Documents, including a Security Agreement, are among the Loan Documents to be delivered by Carguys as a condition precedent to the making of Loans. See §§ 1 and 5 of the Revolving Credit Agreement. Pertinent portions of the Security Agreement are set forth below:

FORM 6.2
SECURITY AGREEMENT

This **SECURITY AGREEMENT** (this "Agreement") is made as of July 1, 2006, by and between CARGUYS, INC. (the "Company"), a Delaware corporation having its principal place of business at 1313 West Rosannadanna Boulevard, Los Angeles, California, and EASTINGHOME CREDIT CORPORATION (the "Lender"), a New York corporation having its office at 94 Wintershire Drive, Territown, New York.

WHEREAS, the Company has entered into a Revolving Credit Agreement dated as of July 1, 2001 (as amended and in effect from time to time, the "Credit Agreement"), with the Lender, pursuant to which the Lender, subject to the terms and conditions contained therein, is to make loans to the Company; and

WHEREAS, it is a condition precedent to the Lender's making any loans to the Company under the Credit Agreement that the Company execute and deliver to the Lender a security agreement in substantially the form hereof; and

WHEREAS, the Company wishes to grant a security interest in favor of the Lender as herein provided;

NOW, THEREFORE, in consideration of the promises contained herein and for other good and valuable consideration, the receipt and sufficiency of which are hereby acknowledged, the parties hereto agree as follows:

1. **Definitions.** All capitalized terms used herein without definitions shall have the respective meanings provided in the Credit Agreement. The term "State", as used herein, means the State of New York. All terms defined in the Uniform Commercial Code of the State and used herein shall have the same definitions herein as specified therein; provided, however, that the term "instrument" shall be such term as defined in Article 9 of the Uniform Commercial Code of the State rather than Article 3. The term "Obligations", as used herein, means all of the indebtedness, obligations and liabilities of the Company to the Lender, individually or collectively, whether direct or indirect, joint or several, absolute or contingent, due or to become due, now existing or hereafter arising under or in respect of the Credit Agreement, this Agreement, any promissory notes or other instruments or agreements executed and delivered pursuant thereto or in connection therewith or this Agreement, or any other Loan Documents.

2. **Grant of Security Interest.** The Company hereby grants to the Lender, to secure the payment and performance in full of all of the Obligations, a security interest in and so pledges and assigns to the Lender the following properties, assets and rights of the Company, wherever located, whether now owned or hereafter acquired or arising, and all proceeds and products thereof (all of the same being hereinafter called the "Collateral"): all personal and fixture property of every kind and nature including without limitation all goods (including inventory, equipment and any accessions thereto), instruments (including promissory notes), documents, accounts (including health-care-insurance receivables), chattel paper (whether tangible or electronic), deposit accounts, letter-of-credit rights (whether or not the letter of credit is evidenced by a writing), commercial tort claims,

securities and all other investment property, supporting obligations, any other contract rights or rights to the payment of money, insurance claims and proceeds, tort claims, and all general intangibles including, without limitation, all payment intangibles, patents, patent applications, trademarks, trademark applications, trade names, copyrights, copyright applications, software, engineering drawings, service marks, customer lists, goodwill, and all licenses, permits, agreements of any kind or nature pursuant to which the Company possesses, uses or has authority to possess or use property (whether tangible or intangible) of others or others possess, use or have authority to possess or use property (whether tangible or intangible) of the Company, and all recorded data of any kind or nature, regardless of the medium of recording including, without limitation, all software, writings, plans, specifications and schematics.

3. **Authorization to File Financing Statements.** The Company hereby irrevocably authorizes the Lender at any time and from time to time to file in any Uniform Commercial Code jurisdiction any initial financing statements and amendments thereto that (a) indicate the Collateral (i) as all assets of the Company or words of similar effect, regardless of whether any particular asset comprised in the Collateral falls within the scope of Article 9 of the Uniform Commercial Code of the State or such jurisdiction, or (ii) as being of an equal or lesser scope or with greater detail, and (b) contain any other information required by part 5 of Article 9 of the Uniform Commercial Code of the State for the sufficiency or filing office acceptance of any financing statement or amendment, including (i) whether the Company is an organization, the type of organization and any organization identification number issued to the Company and, (ii) in the case of a financing statement filed as a fixture filing or indicating Collateral as as-extracted collateral or timber to be cut, a sufficient description of real property to which the Collateral relates. The Company agrees to furnish any such information to the Lender promptly upon request.

4. **Other Actions.** Further to insure the attachment, perfection and first priority of, and the ability of the Lender to enforce, the Lender's security interest in the Collateral, the Company agrees, in each case at the Company's own expense, to take the following actions with respect to the following Collateral:

4.1.   **Promissory Notes and Tangible Chattel Paper.** If the Company shall at any time hold or acquire any promissory notes or tangible chattel paper, the Company shall forthwith endorse, assign and deliver the same to the Lender, accompanied by such instruments of transfer or assignment duly executed in blank as the Lender may from time to time specify.

4.2.   **Deposit Accounts.** For each deposit account that the Company at any time opens or maintains, the Company shall, at the Lender's request and option, pursuant to an agreement in form and substance satisfactory to the Lender, either (a) cause the depositary bank to agree to comply at any time with instructions from the Lender to such depositary bank directing the disposition of funds from time to time credited to such deposit account, without further consent of the Company, or (b) arrange for the Lender to become the customer of the depositary bank with respect to the deposit account, with the Company being permitted, only with the consent of the Lender, to exercise rights to withdraw funds from such deposit account. The Lender agrees with the Company that the Lender shall not give any such instructions or withhold any withdrawal rights from the Company, unless an Event of Default has occurred and is continuing, or, after giving effect to any withdrawal not otherwise permitted by the Loan Documents, would occur. The provisions of this paragraph shall not apply to (i) any deposit account for which the Company, the depositary bank and the Lender have entered into a cash collateral agreement specially negotiated among the Company, the depositary bank and the Lender for the specific purpose set forth therein and (ii) deposit accounts specially and exclusively used for payroll, payroll taxes and other employee wage and benefit payments to or for the benefit of the Company's salaried employees

4.3.   Investment Property. If the Company shall at any time hold or acquire any certificated securities, the Company shall forthwith endorse, assign and deliver the same to the Lender, accompanied by such instruments of transfer or assignment duly executed in blank as the Lender may from time to time specify. If any securities now or hereafter acquired by the Company are uncertificated and are issued to the Company or its nominee directly by the issuer thereof, the Company shall immediately notify the Lender thereof and, at the Lender's request and option, pursuant to an agreement in form and substance satisfactory to the Lender, either (a) cause the issuer to agree to comply with instructions from the Lender as to such securities, without further consent of the Company or such nominee, or (b) arrange for the Lender to become the registered owner of the securities. If any securities, whether certificated or uncertificated, or other investment property now or hereafter acquired by the Company is held by the Company or its nominee through a securities intermediary or commodity intermediary, the Company shall immediately notify the Lender thereof and, at the Lender's request and option, pursuant to an agreement in form and substance satisfactory to the Lender, either (i) cause such securities intermediary or (as the case may be) commodity intermediary to agree to comply with entitlement orders or other instructions from the Lender to such securities intermediary as to such securities or other investment property, or (as the case may be) to apply any value distributed on account of any commodity contract as directed by the Lender to such commodity intermediary, in each case without further consent of the Company or such nominee, or (ii) in the case of financial assets or other investment property held through a securities intermediary, arrange for the Lender to become the entitlement holder with respect to such investment property, with the Company being permitted, only with the consent of the Lender, to exercise rights to withdraw or otherwise deal with such investment property. The Lender agrees with the Company that the Lender shall not give any such entitlement orders or instructions or directions to any such issuer, securities intermediary or commodity intermediary, and shall not withhold its consent to the exercise of any withdrawal or dealing rights by the Company, unless an Event of Default has occurred and is continuing, or, after giving effect to any such investment and withdrawal rights not otherwise permitted by the Loan Documents, would occur.

4.4.   Collateral in the Possession of a Bailee. If any goods are at any time in the possession of a bailee, the Company shall promptly notify the Lender thereof and, if requested by the Lender, shall promptly obtain an acknowledgement from the bailee, in form and substance satisfactory to the Lender, that the bailee holds such Collateral for the benefit of the Lender and shall act upon the instructions of the Lender, without the further consent of the Company. The Lender agrees with the Company that the Lender shall not give any such instructions unless an Event of Default has occurred and is continuing or would occur after taking into account any action by the Company with respect to the bailee.

4.5.   Electronic Chattel Paper and Transferable Records. If the Company at any time holds or acquires an interest in any electronic chattel paper or any "transferable record," as that term is defined in Section 201 of the federal Electronic Signatures in Global and National Commerce Act, or in §16 of the Uniform Electronic Transactions Act as in effect in any relevant jurisdiction, the Company shall promptly notify the Lender thereof and, at the request of the Lender, shall take such action as the Lender may reasonably request to vest in the Lender control under Uniform Commercial Code §9-105 of such electronic chattel paper or control under Section 201 of the federal Electronic Signatures in Global and National Commerce Act or, as the case may be, §16 of the Uniform Electronic Transactions Act, as so in effect in such jurisdiction, of such transferable record. The Lender agrees with the Company that the Lender will arrange, pursuant to procedures satisfactory to the Lender and so long as such procedures will not result in the Lender's loss of control, for the Company to make alterations to the electronic chattel paper or transferable record permitted under Uniform Commercial Code §9-105 or, as the case may be, Section 201 of the federal Electronic Signatures in Global and National Commerce Act or §16 of the Uniform Electronic Transactions Act for a party in control to make without loss of control, unless an Event of Default has occurred and is continuing or would occur after taking into account any action by the Company with respect to such electronic chattel paper or transferable record.

4.6.   Letter-of-credit Rights. If the Company is at any time a beneficiary under a letter of credit now or hereafter issued in favor of the Company, the Company shall promptly notify the Lender thereof and, at the request and option of the Lender, the Company shall, pursuant to an agreement in form and substance satisfactory to the Lender, either (i) arrange for the issuer and any confirmer of such letter of credit to consent to an assignment to the Lender of the proceeds of any drawing under the letter of credit or (ii) arrange for the Lender to become the transferee beneficiary of the letter of credit, with the Lender agreeing, in each case, that the proceeds of any drawing under the letter to credit are to be applied as provided in the Credit Agreement.

4.6.   Commercial Tort Claims. If the Company shall at any time hold or acquire a commercial tort claim, the Company shall immediately notify the Lender in a writing signed by the Company of the brief details thereof and grant to the Lender in such writing a security interest therein and in the proceeds thereof, all upon the terms of this Agreement, with such writing to be in form and substance satisfactory to the Lender.

4.8.   Other Actions as to any and all Collateral. The Company further agrees to take any other action reasonably requested by the Lender to insure the attachment, perfection and first priority of, and the ability of the Lender to enforce, the Lender's security interest in any and all of the Collateral including, without limitation, (a) executing, delivering and, where appropriate, filing financing statements and amendments relating thereto under the Uniform Commercial Code, to the extent, if any, that the Company's signature thereon is required therefor, (b) causing the Lender's name to be noted as secured party on any certificate of title for a titled good if such notation is a condition to attachment, perfection or priority of, or ability of the Lender to enforce, the Lender's security interest in such Collateral, (c) complying with any provision of any statute, regulation or treaty of the United States as to any Collateral if compliance with such provision is a condition to attachment, perfection or priority of, or ability of the Lender to enforce, the Lender's security interest in such Collateral, (d) obtaining governmental and other third party consents and approvals, including without limitation any consent of any licensor, lessor or other person obligated on Collateral, (e) obtaining waivers from mortgagees and landlords in form and substance satisfactory to the Lender and (f) taking all actions required by any earlier versions of the Uniform Commercial Code or by other law, as applicable in any relevant Uniform Commercial Code jurisdiction, or by other law as applicable in any foreign jurisdiction.

5. Relation to Other Security Documents.

* * *

6. Representations and Warranties Concerning Company's Legal Status.

* * *

7. Covenants Concerning Company's Legal Status.

* * *

8. Representations and Warranties Concerning Collateral, Etc. The Company further represents and warrants to the Lender as follows: (a) the Company is the owner of the Collateral, free from any adverse lien, security interest or other encumbrance, except for the security interest created by this Agreement, (b) none of the Collateral constitutes, or is the proceeds of, "farm products" as defined in §9-102(a)(34) of the Uniform Commercial Code of the State, (c) none of the account debtors or other persons obligated on any of the Collateral is a governmental authority subject to the Federal Assignment of Claims Act or like federal, state or local statute or rule in respect of such Collateral, (d) the Company holds no commercial tort claim except as indicated on the Perfection Certificate, (e) the Company has at all times operated its business in compliance with all applicable provisions of the federal Fair Labor Standards Act, as amended, and with all applicable provisions of federal, state and local statutes and ordinances dealing with the control, shipment, storage or disposal of hazardous materials or substances and (f) all other information set forth on the Perfection Certificate pertaining to the Collateral is accurate and complete.

9. Covenants Concerning Collateral, Etc.. The Company further covenants with the Lender as follows: (a) the Collateral, to the extent not delivered to the Lender hereunder, will be kept at those locations listed on the Perfection Certificate and the Company will not remove the Collateral from such locations, without providing at least 30 days prior written notice to the Lender, (b) except for the security interest herein granted, the Company shall be the owner of the Collateral free from any lien, security interest or other encumbrance, and the Company shall defend the same against all claims and demands of all persons at any time claiming the same or any interests therein adverse to the Lender, (c) the Company shall not pledge, mortgage or create, or suffer to exist a security interest in the Collateral in favor of any person other than the Lender, (d) the Company will keep the

Collateral in good order and repair and will not use the same in violation of law or any policy of insurance thereon, (e) the Company will permit the Lender, or its designee, to inspect the Collateral at any reasonable time, wherever located, (f) the Company will pay promptly when due all taxes, assessments, governmental charges and levies upon the Collateral or incurred in connection with the use or operation of such Collateral or incurred in connection with this Agreement, (g) the Company will continue to operate, its business in compliance with all applicable provisions of the federal Fair Labor Standards Act, as amended, and with all applicable provisions of federal, state and local statutes and ordinances dealing with the control, shipment, storage or disposal of hazardous materials or substances, and (h) the Company will not sell or otherwise dispose, or offer to sell or otherwise dispose, of the Collateral or any interest therein except for (i) sales and leases of inventory in the ordinary course of business and (ii) so long as no Default or Event of Default has occurred and is continuing, use of cash proceeds.

10. **Insurance.**

    10.1. **Maintenance of Insurance.**

    * * *

    10.2. **Insurance Proceeds.**

    * * *

    10.3. **Notice of Cancellation, etc.**

    * * *

11. **Collateral Protection Expenses; Preservation of Collateral.**

    11.1. **Expenses Incurred by Lender.** In its discretion, the Lender may discharge taxes and other encumbrances at any time levied or placed on any of the Collateral, make repairs thereto and pay any necessary filing fees. The Company agrees to reimburse the Lender on demand for any and all expenditures so made. The Lender shall have no obligation to the Company to make any such expenditures, nor shall the making thereof relieve the Company of any default.

    11.2. **Lender's Obligations and Duties.** Anything herein to the contrary notwithstanding, the Company shall remain liable under each contract or agreement comprised in the Collateral to be observed or performed by the Company thereunder. The Lender shall not have any obligation or liability under any such contract or agreement by reason of or arising out of this Agreement or the receipt by the Lender of any payment relating to any of the Collateral, nor shall the Lender be obligated in any manner to perform any of the obligations of the Company under or pursuant to any such contract or agreement, to make inquiry as to the nature or sufficiency of any payment received by the Lender in respect of the Collateral or as to the sufficiency of any performance by any party under any such contract or agreement, to present or file any claim, to take any action to enforce any performance or to collect the payment of any amounts which may have been assigned to the Lender or to which the Lender may be entitled at any time or times. The Lender's sole duty with respect to the custody, safe keeping and physical preservation of the Collateral in its possession, under §9-207 of the Uniform Commercial Code of the State or otherwise, shall be to deal with such Collateral in the same manner as the Lender deals with similar property for its own account.

12. Securities and Deposits. The Lender may at any time following and during the continuance of a Default or Event of Default, at its option, transfer to itself or any nominee any securities constituting Collateral, receive any income thereon and hold such income as additional Collateral or apply it to the Obligations. Whether or not any Obligations are due, the Lender may following and during the continuance of a Default or Event of Default demand, sue for, collect, or make any settlement or compromise which it deems desirable with respect to the Collateral. Regardless of the adequacy of Collateral or any other security for the Obligations, any deposits or other sums at any time credited by or due from the Lender to the Company may at any time be applied to or set off against any of the Obligations.

13. Notification to Account Debtors and Other Persons Obligated on Collateral. If a Default or an Event of Default shall have occurred and be continuing, the Company shall, at the request of the Lender, notify account debtors and other persons obligated on any of the Collateral of the security interest of the Lender in any account, chattel paper, general intangible, instrument or other Collateral and that payment thereof is to be made directly to the Lender or to any financial institution designated by the Lender as the Lender's agent therefor, and the Lender may itself, if a Default or an Event of Default shall have occurred and be continuing, without notice to or demand upon the Company, so notify account debtors and other persons obligated on Collateral. After the making of such a request or the giving of any such notification, the Company shall hold any proceeds of collection of accounts, chattel paper, general intangibles, instruments and other Collateral received by the Company as trustee for the Lender without commingling the same with other funds of the Company and shall turn the same over to the Lender in the identical form received, together with any necessary endorsements or assignments. The Lender shall apply the proceeds of collection of accounts, chattel paper, general intangibles, instruments and other Collateral received by the Lender to the Obligations, such proceeds to be immediately credited after final payment in cash or other immediately available funds of the items giving rise to them.

14. Power of Attorney.

    14.1. Appointment and Powers of Lender.

    * * *

    14.2. Ratification by Company.

    * * *

14.3. <u>No Duty on Lender</u>.

* * *

15. <u>Remedies</u>. If an Event of Default shall have occurred and be continuing, the Lender may, without notice to or demand upon the Company, declare this Agreement to be in default, and the Lender shall thereafter have in any jurisdiction in which enforcement hereof is sought, in addition to all other rights and remedies, the rights and remedies of a secured party under the Uniform Commercial Code of the State or of any jurisdiction in which Collateral is located, including, without limitation, the right to take possession of the Collateral, and for that purpose the Lender may, so far as the Company can give authority therefor, enter upon any premises on which the Collateral may be situated and remove the same therefrom. The Lender may in its discretion require the Company to assemble all or any part of the Collateral at such location or locations within the jurisidction(s) of the Company's principal office(s) or at such other locations as the Lender may reasonably designate. Unless the Collateral is perishable or threatens to decline speedily in value or is of a type customarily sold on a recognized market, the Lender shall give to the Company at least ten (10) Business Days prior written notice of the time and place of any public sale of Collateral or of the time after which any private sale or any other intended disposition is to be made. The Company hereby acknowledges that five (5) Business Days prior written notice of such sale or sales shall be reasonable notice. In addition, the Company waives any and all rights that it may have to a judicial hearing in advance of the enforcement of any of the Lender's rights hereunder, including, without limitation, its right following an Event of Default to take immediate possession of the Collateral and to exercise its rights with respect thereto.

16. <u>Standards for Exercising Remedies</u>. To the extent that applicable law imposes duties on the Lender to exercise remedies in a commercially reasonable manner, the Company acknowledges and agrees that it is not commercially unreasonable for the Lender (a) to fail to incur expenses reasonably deemed significant by the Lender to prepare Collateral for disposition or otherwise to complete raw material or work in process into finished goods or other finished products for disposition, (b) to fail to obtain third party consents for access to Collateral to be disposed of, or to obtain or, if not required by other law, to fail to obtain governmental or third party consents for the collection or disposition of Collateral to be collected or disposed of, (c) to fail to exercise collection remedies against account debtors or other persons obligated on Collateral or to remove liens or encumbrances on or any adverse claims against Collateral, (d) to exercise collection remedies against account debtors and other persons obligated on Collateral directly or through the use of collection agencies and other collection specialists, (e) to advertise dispositions of Collateral through publications or media of general circulation, whether or not the Collateral is of a specialized nature, (f) to contact other persons, whether or not in the same business as the Company, for expressions of interest in acquiring all or any portion of the Collateral, (g) to hire one or more professional auctioneers to assist in the disposition of Collateral, whether or not the collateral is of a specialized nature, (h) to dispose of Collateral by utilizing Internet sites that provide for the auction of assets of the types included in the Collateral or that have the reasonable capability of doing so, or that match buyers and sellers of assets, (i) to dispose of assets in wholesale rather than retail markets, (j) to disclaim disposition warranties, (k) to purchase insurance or credit enhancements to insure the Lender against risks of loss, collection or disposition of Collateral or to provide to the Lender a guaranteed return from the collection or disposition of Collateral, or (l) to the extent deemed appropriate by the Lender, to obtain the services of other brokers, investment bankers, consultants and other professionals to assist the Lender in the collection or disposition of any of the Collateral.   The Company acknowledges that the purpose of this §16 is to provide non-exhaustive indications of what actions or omissions by the Lender would not be commercially unreasonable in the Lender's exercise of remedies against the Collateral and that other actions or omissions by the Lender shall not be deemed commercially unreasonable solely on account of not being indicated in this §16. Without limitation upon the foregoing, nothing contained in this §16 shall be construed to grant any rights to the Company or to impose any duties on the Lender that would not have been granted or imposed by this Agreement or by applicable law in the absence of this §16.

17. No Waiver by Lender, etc.

* * *

18. Suretyship Waivers by Company.

* * *

19. Marshaling.

* * *

20. Proceeds of Dispositions; Expenses.
The Company shall pay to the Lender on demand any and all expenses, including reasonable attorneys' fees and disbursements, incurred or paid by the Lender in protecting, preserving or enforcing the Lender's rights under or in respect of any of the Obligations or any of the Collateral. After deducting all of said expenses, the residue of any proceeds of collection or sale of the Obligations or Collateral shall, to the extent actually received in cash, be applied to the payment of the Obligations in such order or preference as the Lender may determine, proper allowance and provision being made for any Obligations not then due. Upon the final payment and satisfaction in full of all of the Obligations and after making any payments required by Sections 9-608(a)(1)(C) or 9-615(a)(3) of the Uniform Commercial Code of the State, any excess shall be returned to the Company, and the Company shall remain liable for any deficiency in the payment of the Obligations.

21. Overdue Amounts.
Until paid, all amounts due and payable by the Company hereunder shall be a debt secured by the Collateral and shall bear, whether before or after judgment, interest at the rate of interest for overdue principal set forth in the Credit Agreement.

22. Governing Law; Consent to Jurisdiction.

* * *

23. Waiver of Jury Trial.

* * *

24. **Miscellaneous.**

* * *

IN WITNESS WHEREOF, intending to be legally bound, the Company has caused this Agreement to be duly executed as of the date first above written.

CARGUYS, INC., a Delaware corporation

By: *Angie Boombox*

Name: Angie Boombox
Title: President

EASTINGHOME CREDIT CORPORATION, a New York corporation

By: *Tabb Collar, IV*

Name: Tabb Collar, III
Title: Vice-President

Note the broad range of collateral covered by the granting language in § 2 of the Security Agreement—it covers virtually all types of personal property. Contrast the Revolving Credit Agreement's much narrower definitions of Accounts and Inventory, and its still narrower definitions of Base Accounts and Base Inventory. Under the Borrowing Base formulation, Loans must be supported by the relevant percentages of the Base Accounts (75%) and Base Inventory (60%), but Eastinghome has required Carguys to provide additional collateral beyond those components of the Borrowing Base.

In the terminology used by Kupfer in the foregoing excerpt, the Eastinghome–Carguys facility reflects a **recourse** financing, inasmuch as Carguys is fully liable to repay the Loans, whether or not Eastinghome makes any recovery from the collateral. Moreover, the transaction involves the **indirect collection** of receivables—until a Default or Event of Default has occurred, Carguys is entitled to collect receivables from the various account debtors. See UCC 9–607(a); § 13 of the Security Agreement. In some transactions, a "lockbox" or "cash collateral agreement" is entered into by the borrower-assignor, a depositary bank, and the lender-assignee. See § 4.2. Account debtors are instructed to send all remittances on receivables to a post office box address controlled by the bank (usually, the post office box is listed as the borrower-assignor's address on its invoices); the receipts are then deposited in a deposit account maintained for this purpose (a **cash collateral account**). In this way, the lender-assignee may gain control over all receipts without the necessity of undertaking an actual **direct collection** from account debtors in is own name.

For present purposes we are interested primarily in the collateral consisting of accounts and inventory (as defined in Revised Article 9; see § 1 of the Security Agreement). Perfection of Eastinghome's security interest in that collateral is straightforward—filing a financing statement in the jurisdiction in which Carguys is located, Delaware. See UCC 9–310; UCC 9–301(1); UCC 9–307(e). (Perfection of Eastinghome's security interest in other types of collateral requires further analysis. See Sections 2, 3, 4, and 6, infra. See also § 4 of the Security Agreement.) To make sure that it has all of the relevant facts necessary for determining the steps required for perfection and priority, Eastinghome requires Carguys to deliver a Perfection Certificate, which contains representations concerning these facts (e.g., the exact corporate name and place of incorporation of Carguys, the mailing address of Carguys, the location of Carguys' chief executive office, the locations of tangible collateral, etc.). Note that during the transition from Former Article 9 to Revised Article 9, Eastinghome is interested in facts related to the applicable law for perfection under Former Article 9 as well as Revised Article 9. The possibility always exists that a financing statement has been filed against Carguys in the filing office designated by Former 9–103 and Former 9–401.

(C) PROBLEM UNDER THE PROTOTYPE

The following Problem focuses primarily on the business terms of the Prototype and how they relate to both legal issues and Eastinghome's credit analysis.

Problem 6.1.1. (a) Why are the definitions of "Accounts," "Inventory," "Base Accounts," and "Base Inventory" in the Revolving Credit Agreement so narrow in comparison with the broad definitions of the terms "accounts" and "inventory" in UCC 9–102 and in the Security Agreement? See Revolving Credit Agreement §§ 1, 2.1(a); Security Agreement § 1.

(b) Why do you suppose that Eastinghome has insisted on limiting its obligation to make Loans to an amount equal to the *lesser* of the Commitment and the Borrowing Base? See Revolving Credit Agreement § 2.1(a).

(c) If Carguys sells diagnostic equipment on a secured basis, is the right to payment included in the Borrowing Base? See Revolving Credit Agreement § 1. Cf. UCC 9–102(a)(2), (a)(11).

(d) What are the purposes of the conditions precedent listed in § 5 of the Revolving Credit Agreement? What is the significance of the dates on which Carguys makes its representations and warranties? See Revolving Credit Agreement § 4. What is the relationship among the conditions precedent and Carguys' representations and warranties? See Revolving Credit Agreement §§ 4, 5, 6.

(e) What is the relationship among the Events of Default and Carguys' representations and warranties and covenants? See Revolving Credit Agreement §§ 4, 5, 6, 7.

(f) Why does the Revolving Credit Agreement distinguish between a "Default" and an "Event of Default"? See Revolving Credit Agreement §§ 1, 5(b), 7; Security Agreement § 15.

(g) Why does the Revolving Credit Agreement distinguish between payments of principal and payments of interest and other sums? See § 7(a), (b).

(h) Why does the Revolving Credit Agreement distinguish between breach of certain covenants and breach of others? See § 7(c), (d).

(i) Why does Revolving Credit Agreement § 7(e) cover only a representation and warranty that is inaccurate at the time that it is made or deemed made?

(j) Why does the Revolving Credit Agreement distinguish between Events of Default under § 7(h) and (i) and other Events of Default? See § 7(1), (2).

(k) Why is the description of collateral in § 2 of the Security Agreement so long? Wouldn't a list of UCC-defined types of collateral have been sufficient? See UCC 9–108(b)(3).

(l) What purpose is served by § 3 of the Security Agreement, given that Carguys' authentication of the security agreement ipso facto authorizes Eastinghome to file a financing statement? See UCC 9–509(b).

(D) SALES OF RECEIVABLES

Problem 6.1.2. In the setting of the Prototype on receivables financing, Carguys approaches a representative of Lax Factor Co., a specialist in the nonrecourse factoring of receivables. (As Kupfer explained, these are transactions in which the "*assignee* assumes the *credit* risk"—i.e., the risk that an account debtor will not pay its debt to the debtor/assignor.) Factor proposes a financing arrangement that would replace the Eastinghome revolving credit facility. Under the proposal, Carguys would sell and Factor would buy, on a nonrecourse basis, accounts generated by Carguys. Factor would pay 85% of the face amount of each account that it buys. The accounts that Factor would be willing to buy are essentially those that would be "Base Accounts" under the Eastinghome facility. Carguys sees certain advantages to the Factor arrangement. Significantly, because of the nonrecourse structure, Carguys would not incur any debt on its balance sheet—the accounts would simply be replaced with cash. Of course, Carguys would be required to warrant to Factor that the accounts are genuine and that none of the account debtors has a defense to payment (i.e., Carguys would retain the "merchandise risk," as Kupfer explained).

Carguys accepted Factor's proposal and satisfied its obligations to Eastinghome, which filed a termination statements for its financing statement. Carguys and Factor entered into a sale agreement under which Factor agreed to buy Carguys' qualifying accounts from time to time up to an aggregate of $25,000,000 face amount at any time outstanding and unpaid. Factor failed to file a financing statement in the appropriate filing office in Delaware.

(a) Lean, a judgment creditor of Carguys', served a **garnishment** summons on three of Carguys' biggest customers. The summons instructs each **garnishee** to inform the court of the amount it owes to Carguys; service of the summons gives rise to a lien in favor of the judgment creditor (here, Lean) in that amount. If a garnishee answers that it is indebted to Carguys, the court will enter judgment in that amount in favor of Lean, and the customer will be obligated to pay Lean instead of Carguys. Prior to the entry of judgment, Factor intervenes, asserting that it is the owner of the accounts, that Carguys retains no interest in them, that the customers owe Carguys nothing, and that Lean is not entitled to payment from the customers. What result? See UCC 9–109(a)(3); UCC 1–201(b)(35) [F1–201(37) (2d sentence)]; UCC 9–318; UCC 9–317(a)(2); UCC 9–310(a); Note (1) on Sales of Receivables, infra.

(b) Would the result in part (a) change if, before service of the garnishment summons, Factor had notified Carguys' customers that it had purchased their accounts? If Factor had taken possession of the contracts that gave rise to the accounts (i.e., the contracts pursuant to which Carguys provided repair and maintenance services and sold auto parts and diagnostic equipment)?

(c) Would the result in part (a) change if Carguys had retained purchase-money security interests in the auto parts and diagnostic equipment and sold Factor the secured rights to payment? See UCC 9–102(a)(11); UCC 9–109(a)(3); UCC 1–201(b)(35) [F1–201(37) (2d sentence)].

(d) Assume that instead of obtaining a judicial lien pursuant to a garnishment summons, Lean (i) bought the accounts from Carguys on terms similar to those under which Factor bought them and (ii) filed a financing statement against Carguys covering the accounts in the appropriate filing office in Delaware. Who has the better claim to the accounts? See UCC 9–318(b) & Comment 3; UCC 9–322(a).

Problem 6.1.3. CC Bank issues credit cards to consumers. To raise capital, CC periodically sells its portfolio of credit-card receivables (rights to payment from its credit-card customers). When cardholders use their cards to buy merchandise, CC advances the purchase price to the merchants. The receivables consist in part of the cardholders' obligations to repay those advances, some of which obligations are unsecured and others of which are secured by the merchandise purchased. The receivables also include cardholders' obligations to repay cash advances. Lax Factor agreed to buy the receivables at a discount. What steps, if any, should Factor take to protect its ownership interest against CC's creditors? See UCC 9–102(a)(2), (11); UCC 9–109(a)(3); UCC 1–201(b)(35) [F1–201(37) (2d sentence)]; UCC 9–318; UCC 9–317(a)(2); UCC 9–310(a); Note (2) on Sales of Receivables, infra.

Problem 6.1.4. In the setting of the Prototype on financing automobiles, Chapter 3, Section 1, supra, the outstanding principal balance owed by Main Motors to Firstbank under the line of credit is $2,400,000. Unlike the facts of that Prototype, however, assume that the documentation did not include the Demand Note (Form 3.3). To reduce its risk, Firstbank enters into a written Participation Agreement with Secondbank, pursuant to which Firstbank sells to Secondbank a 25% undivided interest in the loan for $600,000. In exchange, Secondbank is entitled to receive 25% of all principal and interest payments made by Main under the line of credit. Secondbank also agrees to advance 25% of all future loans made by Firstbank under the line of credit.

(a) What steps, if any, should Secondbank take to protect its ownership interest in the loan against lien creditors of Firstbank? See UCC 9–109(a)(3); UCC 9–102(a)(61), (42); UCC 1–201(b)(35) [F1–201(37) (2d sentence)]; UCC 9–318; UCC 9–317(a)(2); UCC 9–310(a), (b)(2); UCC 9–309(3).

(b) The facts are as in part (a), except that Main's obligation to repay the loan is evidenced by the Demand Note, and Secondbank bought a 25% undivided interest in the Demand Note. What steps, if any, should Secondbank take to protect its ownership interest in the note against lien creditors of Firstbank? See UCC 9–102(a)(65), (47); UCC 9–109(a)(3); UCC 1–201(b)(35) [F1–201(37) (2d sentence)]; UCC 9–318; UCC 9–317(a)(2); UCC 9–310(a), (b)(2); UCC 9–309(4). Does the definition of "promissory note" in UCC 9–102(a)(65) include a negotiable note payable to order? What steps should Secondbank take if the note were payable "to Firstbank"? (Do not assume that a security interest having priority over subsequent lien creditors also has priority over subsequent purchasers. See Chapter 1, Section 4, supra; Section 2, infra.)

(c) Both this Problem and the preceding one concern the sale by a bank of its right to repayment of a loan. Can you reconcile the results in this Problem with those in the preceding Problem? See Note (2) on Sales of Receivables, infra.

NOTES ON SALES OF RECEIVABLES

(1) The Broad Scope of Former Article 9: Sales of Accounts and Chattel Paper. Consider the variation on the receivables financing Prototype presented in Problem 6.1.2: Carguys provides goods and services on unsecured credit to a variety of customers. Carguys needs cash to continue to operate. Rather than wait for payment, Carguys approaches Factor, who agrees to buy Carguys' rights under its contracts with its customers. Inasmuch as Factor has become the owner of the accounts (rights to payment), one might jump to the conclusion that Article 9 is irrelevant to the transaction. In doing so, one would be making a serious mistake.

As we have seen, most questions as to the applicability of Article 9 are dominated by the concept of "security interest." We also have seen that although a "security interest" often secures an obligation, the framers of the

UCC concluded that other transactions had features that made it unwise to limit the application of Article 9 to transfers of "an interest . . . which secures payment or performance of an obligation." UCC 1–201(b)(35) [F1–201(37) (2d sentence)]. Thus, "security interest" includes, and Article 9 applies to, consignments. See Chapter 5, Section 1(B), supra.

The term also includes "any interest of a buyer of accounts, chattel paper, a payment intangible, or a promissory note in a transaction that is subject to Article 9." UCC 1–201(b)(35) [F1–201(37) (2d sentence)]. Article 9 applies broadly to "a *sale* of accounts, chattel paper, payment intangibles, or promissory notes." UCC 9–109(a)(3). But, as we shall see below in Note (3), the sweep of the provision bringing "a sale" of rights to payment (receivables) within Article 9 is slightly narrowed by a set of exclusions from Article 9, see UCC 9–109(d)(4)–(7), as well as by a set of exemptions from the filing requirement. See UCC 9–310(b)(2) and UCC 9–309(2)–(5). (The sharply different treatment of property other than receivables is illustrated by the specific provision in UCC 1–201(b)(35) [F1–201(37) (3d sentence)] that the property interest of a buyer of *goods* "is not a 'security interest'.")

Revised Article 9 is not the first statute on secured transactions to include outright sales of rights to payment. For most purposes, Former Article 9 abandoned the distinction between an assignment of accounts or chattel paper for collateral purposes and an outright sale.[2] Why? According to Comment 2 to Former 9–102, "[c]ommercial financing on the basis of accounts and chattel paper is often so conducted that the distinction between a security transfer and a sale is blurred, and a sale of such property is therefore covered by [Article 9] whether intended for security or not[.]"

As Kupfer's description indicates, accounts are used as a source of current capital through two primary types of arrangements. (1) One arrangement is a loan, with repayment secured by the assignment of accounts. This transaction may be expressed as a sale of the account (at a discount), with recourse by the "buyer" against the "seller" to the extent that any obligor (account debtor) fails to pay. (2) A second arrangement provides for the sale of the accounts without a right of recourse; however, even in a "non-recourse" sale (sometimes called **factoring**), the assignor is responsible if an obligor (account debtor) has a claim for breach of warranty or for some other reason returns the goods for credit. Between these two prototypical arrangements lies a range of transactions, tailored to suit the appetite of the parties for accepting (or sharing) the credit risk—the risk that the account debtor will be financially unable to pay the entire amount of the account in a timely manner.

When goods are sold on *secured* credit and the resulting *chattel paper* is sold, as in the case of the automobile financing Prototype in Chapter 3, the parties must agree to allocate not only the credit risk but also the risks attendant to enforcing the security interest that the seller (assignor of the

---

2. The distinction may affect the assignee's remedies against the assignor. See F9–502(2); F9–504(2); UCC 9–601(g); UCC 9–607(c); UCC 9–615(d); Chapter 9, Section 5, infra.

chattel paper) has retained in the goods and assigned to the buyer (assignee/secured party). For an example of some of the ways in which this risk may be allocated, see Form 3.5, supra.

Suppose the drafters of Article 9 had divided the world of accounts and chattel paper financing in two: (1) "recourse" arrangements that would be treated like security interests and would be subject to Article 9 and (2) "non-recourse" arrangements that would be excluded from the Article. A sharp eye would be needed to distinguish between the two arrangements; a fair amount of time and money would be expended on classifying ambiguous arrangements after the fact. The number of ambiguous arrangements might increase, since parties planning these transactions would have incentives to camouflage the substance in order to pull themselves in or out of Article 9.

Indeed, non-UCC law sometimes provides these incentives, adding to the confusion. Even where the transaction in substance clearly is a loan, the lender may wish to make the transaction look like a sale: The lender's return for the loan may exceed the statutory limit for "interest." Usury statutes do not, of course, regulate the *price* for *sales* of accounts. And such a "sale" at a discount coupled with a "warranty" by the "seller" that the account is "good" and will be paid at maturity might conceivably lead a sympathetic (or dull) judge to conclude that the transaction really was a sale and not a usurious loan.

Against this background, it is less surprising that not only Former Article 9 but even the pre-UCC statutes on the assignment of accounts covered not only assignments for security but also outright sales. See 1 Gilmore, Security § 8.7.

(2) Crafting the Even Broader Scope of Revised Article 9: Sales of Payment Intangibles and Promissory Notes. Former Article 9 applied to sales of certain types of receivables—accounts and chattel paper. As defined in Former 9–106, "accounts" included rights to payments only "for goods sold or leased or for services rendered." Not all rights to payment are accounts or chattel paper as defined under Former Article 9; some are instruments, others are general intangibles. Like accounts and chattel paper, instruments and general intangibles have been the subject of both secured financings and outright sales. For example, to increase its liquid assets (and for regulatory accounting purposes, the details of which are beyond the scope of this discussion), a bank may wish to utilize its portfolio of **credit-card receivables**—obligations of its cardholders to pay for credit they received through the use of the card. See Problem 6.1.3. The reason for including outright sales of payment streams in a law governing secured transactions applies equally to virtually all rights to payment, regardless of the nature of the transaction under which the right arises. However, if these credit-card receivables were "accounts" under Former Article 9, then the Article would have applied regardless of whether the receivables were sold or were used to secure a loan. On the other hand, if the receivables were general intangibles, then Former Article 9 would have applied to the financing only if the receivables secured an obligation.

The exclusion of sales of general intangibles from Former Article 9 gave rise to several problems. The most obvious is that exclusion from Former Article 9 excused assignees from compliance with the public notice (filing) provisions of the Article. See Former 9–302; Note (1), p. 403, infra.

The excluded transactions were governed by non-UCC law, typically the common law dealing with the assignment of choses in action. This law may be both hard to find and unclear. (Some of these transactions would have been governed by pre-UCC statutes dealing with assignments of accounts receivable; however, those statutes were repealed in the course of enacting the UCC. See UCC 10–102.) This non-UCC law may include the doctrine of Benedict v. Ratner, 268 U.S. 353, 45 S.Ct. 566, 69 L.Ed. 991 (1925), which held that the grant of a security interest in accounts receivable was fraudulent where the assignor retained unfettered dominion over the proceeds, and which Former 9–205 repealed insofar as it might have applied to Article 9 transactions (security interests in all kinds of collateral and sales of accounts and chattel paper). For discussions of *Benedict*, see pages 155, note 3, supra, and 471, note 3, infra.

Moreover, as Note (1), supra, suggests, determining whether a transaction should be characterized as a true sale or as a secured transaction often is difficult. In making this determination, courts have used a number of factors, including the existence and nature of recourse against the assignor. According to one writer, the cases addressing the dichotomy "are not easily harmonized, and different readers can argue as to which factors are relevant and which are entitled to the greater weight." S. Schwarcz, Structured Finance § 4:1 (3d ed. 2003). As a result of this uncertainty, prudent parties proceeded on alternative assumptions, thereby further complicating transactions and increasing costs. In a similar vein, classifying certain types of property as accounts, chattel paper, general intangibles, or instruments may be difficult. (Recall Problem 3.3.24, p. 181, supra, concerning a construction contract.)

The drafters of Revised Article 9 set out to solve these problems. One easy fix—adding sales of general intangibles to the scope of Article 9—would have been disastrous. Many general intangibles (e.g., a franchisee's rights under a franchise agreement) do not consist primarily of rights to payment; sales of these types of property typically are not financing transactions. Accordingly, Revised Article 9 distinguishes "payment intangibles"—i.e., general intangibles "under which the account debtor's principal obligation is a monetary obligation"—from other general intangibles. UCC 9–102(a)(61). Revised Article 9 applies to sales of payment intangibles, but not to sales of other general intangibles. See UCC 9–109(a)(3).

During the drafting process the idea of bringing payment intangibles into Revised Article 9 proved to be popular with those departments of banks and other financial institutions that handle sales of credit-card receivables and other financing transactions. Whether an institution is on the selling or buying side of a given transaction, this change would enable the transaction to proceed with greater certainty, less risk, and less cost. However, other departments of some of the same financial institutions feared that bringing sales of payment intangibles into Revised Article 9 would wreak havoc in the market for **loan participations** and adamantly opposed revising Article 9 along those lines. A loan participation is created when the originator of a loan (the original lender) sells an undivided interest in the loan (and any security for the loan) to a third party, usually another financial institution. See Problem 6.1.4, supra. Banks and other institutional lenders enter into participation agreements with regularity. Often they do so to limit their risk. By selling an interest in certain of its loans, an originator can reduce the amount of credit outstanding to a particular borrower or group of related borrowers, industry, or market sector. The sale of a participation interest may have another advantage: it moves an asset (the right to payment of the loan) off the originating bank's balance sheet and thereby reduces the amount of capital that the originator is required to set aside. (The sale gives rise to this accounting treatment even if, as typically is the case, the participation agreement provides that the originator-assignor retains the exclusive power to enforce the borrower's obligation and that the participant has no direct contractual relationship with the borrower.) Buyers and sellers argued that applying the perfection provisions of Revised Article 9 to sales of loan participations would impose unnecessary delay and costs upon this well functioning, high velocity market.

The Drafting Committee considered and rejected a variety of approaches for distinguishing between sales of loan participations, which would remain outside the scope of Revised Article 9, and sales of other receivables, which would be subject to Revised Article 9. Ultimately the drafters realized that the concern of participants in the loan-participation markets was less with the abstract question of inclusion or exclusion from Revised Article 9 than with the practical impediments that might arise from conditioning perfection on the filing of a financing statement. The elegant solution to this problem was to provide that sales of loan participations are perfected automatically upon attachment. See UCC 9–309(3). To accomplish this result, the Drafting Committee still needed to distinguish sales of loan participations, which were perfected automatically, from sales of other rights to payment, which require some act to perfect. It did so not by defining "loan participation" (a task that proved futile) but rather by defining as an "account" nearly every type of payment stream the Drafting Committee could think of, other than payment streams represented by chattel paper or instruments. Treating all these rights to payment as accounts had the effect of imposing a filing requirement for both outright sales and assignments that secure obligations. It also had the effect of leaving in the residual category of "payment intangibles" the right to repayment of a loan (other than credit-card cash advances, which are accounts, and loans evidenced by chattel paper or an instrument).[3]

Having extended the scope of Revised Article 9 to include sales of accounts (as broadly defined), chattel paper, and payment intangibles, the Drafting Committee decided to extend Revised Article 9 to sales of promissory notes. See UCC 9–109(a)(3). Like sales of payment intangibles, and for the same reason (so as not to interfere with the loan-participation market, inasmuch as many loans in which participations are sold are evidenced by notes), sales of promissory notes are perfected upon attachment. See UCC 9–309(3). For a discussion of whether the exemption of sales of payment intangibles and promissory notes from Article 9's filing requirement offends the Article's public-notice policy, see Note (2), p. 403, infra.

(3) Narrowing the Scope Through Exclusions. From the outset, the UCC's drafters recognized that the inclusion of all sales of accounts and chattel paper would go too far, in that it would include transactions that, "by their nature, have nothing to do with commercial financing transactions." F9–104(f), Comment 6. Former Article 9 excluded these transactions in accounts and chattel paper; Revised Article 9 contains the same exclusions and extends them to sales of payment intangibles and promissory notes. Excluded transfers include the assignment of a right to payment as part of a sale of the business out of which the receivable arose, the assignment to an assignee who is also obligated to perform under the contract, and the assignment of a single account, payment intangible, or promissory note to an assignee in full or partial satisfaction of a preexisting indebtedness. UCC 9–109(d)(4), (6), and (7). (The term "assignment," used in UCC 9–109(d)(4), (6), and (7), among other provisions, embraces both outright sales of receivables as well as security interests that secure an indebtedness. See UCC 9–102, Comment 26.)

Although these and other exclusions reintroduce the problem of line-drawing that the inclusion of "a sale" eliminates, as a practical matter the problem has not proven to be particularly difficult one under Former Article 9. The amount of litigation on this issue is trivial; it is dwarfed by that concerning the lease/sale distinction and the other ambiguous transactions in goods discussed in Chapter 5, Section 1, supra.

---

3.   Changing the classification of certain receivables, discussed above in Note (2), has resulted in some headaches during the years of transition from Former Article 9 to the revised Article. For example, if the term "account" is used in a security agreement entered into before Revised Article 9 takes effect, will the term be given the expanded meaning after Revised Article 9's effective date? Will "general intangible" be given the narrowed meaning? See UCC 9–703, Comment 3. The transition rules in Part 7 of Revised Article 9 are designed to minimize these headaches, but they do not eliminate them. However, because the revised Article has been effective in all the states for several years, we do not address the details of the transition rules here. (Recall as well that knowledge of the choice-of-law rules of Former Article 9 was essential to advising clients properly under Revised Article 9. See Chapter 3, Section 4, supra.)

(4) Securitization Transactions: Additional Considerations.
Chapter 2, Section 1, supra, provides a thumbnail sketch of secured
transactions in a variety of contexts, one of which is "securitization" or
"structured finance" transactions. Please review that description of
securitization transactions (p. 83) now. The principal issues and concerns
in the secured financing of receivables are generally of concern in
securitization transactions—i.e., perfection and priority of the SPV's
interest in the receivables that it buys from the originator-seller of the
receivables. However, in order to ensure that the value of the SPV's interest
is unaffected by the originator's financial status, investors in securities
issued by the SPV on the strength of the receivables also must have
assurances that the purchase by the SPV will be treated as a "true sale" in
any bankruptcy proceeding involving the originator. Otherwise, were the
purchased receivables to remain property of the originator, and thus
property of the originator's bankruptcy estate, the SPV's access to the
receivables could be interrupted or delayed. As we shall see, such an
interruption or delay could occur even if the SPV's non-ownership security
interest in the receivables were perfected. See Chapter 7, Section 1, infra.
The investors (through rating agencies assessing the SPV's securities) also
seek assurance that any insolvency proceeding of the originator would not
be "substantively consolidated" with that of the SPV (i.e., that the debts and
assets of the originator would not be combined with those of the SPV as if
the two were a single entity).

The necessary assurances on the true sale and substantive consolidation
issues (as well as perfection and other important issues) typically are
provided by an opinion of counsel. Because the applicable legal standards
are general and the outcome depends heavily on the court's judgment in
weighing a variety of facts, opinions issued in connection with securitization
transactions are extensive, often running in excess of 25 pages. The opinion
typically is in the form of a letter addressed to the parties; the letter not
only sets forth the opinion itself but also describes the transaction, discusses
the applicable law, provides a long list of assumed facts, and applies the law
to the facts. Following are examples of the "bottom line" of a substantive
consolidation opinion and a true sale opinion of a major law firm:

> *Substantive Consolidation:* Based on the foregoing facts, and subject to
> the assumptions, qualifications and discussions contained herein and
> the reasoned analysis of analogous case law (although there is no
> precedent directly on point), it is our opinion that a United States
> bankruptcy court, in the event of a case under the Bankruptcy Code
> involving the Originator as debtor, would not disregard the separate
> corporate existence of the Buyer so as to consolidate the Buyer's assets
> and liabilities with those of the Originator.

> *True Sale:* Based on the foregoing facts, and subject to the qualifications
> and discussion contained herein and the reasoned analysis of analogous
> case law (although there is no precedent directly on point), it is our
> opinion that, a court, under the Bankruptcy Code or similar state
> insolvency law, would hold that the assignment of the Receivables from

the Originator to the Buyer pursuant to the Transfer Agreement (even if the purchase price for such Receivables is funded through proceeds of a capital contribution by the Originator) constitutes a true sale, and therefore such Receivables would not constitute property of the estate of the Originator under Section 541(a) of the Bankruptcy Code.

Each of the preceding is followed immediately by the following sentence:

Our opinion is subject to the further qualifications that (i) the assumptions set forth herein are and continue to be true in all material respects, (ii) there are no additional facts that would materially affect the validity of the assumptions and conclusions set forth herein or upon which this opinion is based and (iii) such case is properly presented and argued.

(E) PUBLIC NOTICE OF SECURITY INTERESTS IN RECEIVABLES

Problem 6.1.5. You are partner at a law firm (Firm). One of Firm's clients (Client) owes Firm several hundred thousand dollars, most of which is past due. Client has been manufacturing some custom equipment under one of its larger contracts; it expects to pay Firm once its buyer pays for the equipment. Firm is willing to wait (it has little choice), but it wants to be sure that when Client is paid, Firm will be paid. You prepare a security agreement for Client to sign.

(a) From your past representation of Client, you suspect that Client would be reluctant to have a financing statement filed against it. Do you inform client that Client's authentication of the security agreement ipso facto authorizes Firm to file a financing statement covering the collateral? See UCC 9–509(b)(1).

(b) Assume that the security agreement expressly authorizes the filing of a financing statement against the collateral and that Client is reluctant to have a financing statement filed against it. How would you respond to each of the following alternative suggestions?

(i) Client could sell the account to Firm, instead of granting a security interest in it. See UCC 9–109(d)(7).

(ii) Firm does not need to file a financing statement to protect its security interest. See UCC 9–310(a), (b)(2); UCC 9–309(2) & Comment 4; In re Vigil Bros., infra; Note (1) on Public Notice of Transfers of Receivables, infra.

(c) Other than taking the security agreement and filing the financing statement, are there any other steps you would advise Firm to take to bolster its position? See UCC 9–406(a); Note (3), p. 406, infra.

The following case grapples with Former 9–302(1)(e) and Comment 5. The language that the court finds troublesome ("significant part," "casual or isolated") appears in UCC 9–309(2) and Comment 4.

In re Vigil Bros. Construction, Inc.*

United States Bankruptcy Appellate Panel, Ninth Circuit, 1996.
193 B.R. 513.

■ JONES, Bankruptcy Judge.

I. FACTS

Joe E. Woods, Inc., ("Woods") a general contractor, entered into a construction contract with Arizona State University. In order to fulfill the terms of the contract, Woods subcontracted with Vigil Bros. Construction, Inc. ("Vigil"). Vigil in turn subcontracted with Concrete Equipment Co., Inc. ("CECO") whereby CECO was obligated to provide equipment and labor necessary for pumping concrete. CECO fulfilled its obligations under the contract and billed Vigil. . . . Vigil executed an assignment to CECO of the Woods' account receivable not to exceed $49,385.56. CECO did not file a financing statement.

On November 13, 1990, an involuntary chapter 7 petition n1 was filed against Vigil and an Order of Relief was entered on February 11, 1991. CECO filed a proof of claim in the amount of $49,385.56. The trustee objected to the claim on the grounds that CECO failed to produce evidence of a security agreement and failed to perfect its security interest. CECO responded by claiming that the assignment was an absolute assignment or in the alternative a valid security interest. Before trial, the trustee collected $35,000 on the Woods account in a full settlement between Vigil and Woods. The bankruptcy court approved this settlement by order dated September 8, 1992.

The bankruptcy court conducted an initial hearing on the trustee's objection to CECO's proof of claim on April 4, 1994, after which the court entered a pre-trial order on July 15, 1994. In the pretrial order, the court made findings of fact and conclusions of law that: the assignment was not an outright assignment, but rather a security interest governed by Article 9 of the Uniform Commercial Code ("U.C.C.") as adopted by the State of Arizona; CECO did not perfect its interest in the Woods account receivable by filing a financing statement; and perfection of a security interest required the filing of a financing statement except for an assignment of accounts which does not transfer a significant portion of the outstanding accounts of the assignor.

Trial was held on August 2, 1994 on the issue of whether Vigil assigned only an insignificant portion of its accounts, thereby excusing CECO from the requirement to file a financing statement. . . . In a published memorandum decision dated December 9, 1994 (amended April 19, 1995), the bankruptcy court found that Vigil had approximately $125,000 in accounts receivable and assigned $49,385.56 to CECO. In its decision, the court found that Vigil assigned a significant amount (40%) of its accounts to CECO and thus CECO was required to file a financing statement. CECO appeals this decision.

---

*   [The court's citations are to Former Article 9.]

II. ISSUES

1. Did the bankruptcy court err by holding that Article 9 of the Uniform Commercial Code as adopted by the state of Arizona governs the assignment of an account receivable?

2. Did the bankruptcy court err by holding that the assignment assigned a significant part of Woods' outstanding accounts and thus required a filed financing statement for perfection?

III. STANDARD OF REVIEW

Factual findings of the bankruptcy court are reviewed under the clearly erroneous standard. Clear error exists when, after examining the evidence, the reviewing court is left with a definite and firm conviction that a mistake has been committed. The determination as to whether Article 9 governs the assignment of accounts receivable and whether an exception to the filing requirement is met are legal conclusions interpreting statutory construction which is reviewed de novo.

IV. DISCUSSION

A. *The Assignment of the Woods Account was not an Absolute Conveyance, but Instead Created a Security Interest in CECO.*

. . .

The official comments to the U.C.C., persuasive case law from Arizona and other jurisdictions, and the fact that an assignment of accounts is listed in subsection (1)(b) [of UCC § 9-102] rather than subsection (1)(a) which speaks to intent, clarify that intention of the parties is irrelevant. Therefore, the bankruptcy court was correct in finding that the assignment of the Woods account created a security interest in CECO, the assignee.

B. *CECO was Required to Perfect Its Security Interest.*

Because Article 9 applies to assignments of accounts, the perfection requirements of Article 9 govern these transactions. James J. White & Robert S. Summers, Uniform Commercial Code § 30-9 (4th ed. 1995). The assignee must file a financing statement to perfect its security interest. A.R.S. § 47-9302 (Supp. 1995). The official comments to the 1962 and 1972 official text of the U.C.C. state that Article 9 adopts the filing requirements "on the theory that there is no valid reason why public notice is less appropriate for assignments of account than for any other type of non-possessory interest." Many parties buy accounts outright without recourse. Given these practices, if account buyers are to have priority against other creditors of the borrower who might assume that the borrower has not sold or encumbered his accounts, the account buyer must publicize his claim by filing a financing statement. White & Summers, Uniform Commercial Code § 30-9 (4th ed. 1995). Even though not all assignments are of a financing nature, the official comments state that Article 9 applies to all assignments to avoid "difficult problems of distinguishing between transactions intended for security and those not so intended."

There is an exception, however, to the filing requirements for "an assignment of accounts which does not alone or in conjunction with other assignments to the same assignee transfer a significant part of the outstanding accounts of the assignor." A.R.S. § 47-9302(A)(5) (Supp. 1995). Such assignments enjoy automatic perfection. White & Summers, Uniform Commercial Code § 31-10 (4th ed. 1995). The assignee has the burden of proving "insignificance." Black, Robertshaw, Frederick, Copple & Wright, P.C. v. United States, 130 Ariz. 110, 634 P.2d 398, 402 (Ariz. Ct. App. 1981).

Courts have recognized three tests in determining significance: (1) a percentage of accounts test; (2) a "casual and isolated transaction" test; and (3) a combination of (1) and (2). The court in *Black* cited as persuasive authority White & Summers, Uniform Commercial Code, § 23-8 (1972), which favored the percentage test because it would produce a comparatively certain and reliable rule on which parties could rely.[4] The court in Black, however, did not select a specific test for Arizona because there was no evidence presented as to "significance." Id. at 402.

The bankruptcy court in this case decided to use the percentage of accounts test based upon the reasoning of White & Summers. CECO argues that the bankruptcy court erred by not using the casual and isolated test. CECO argues that if the creditor satisfies one test, the transaction must, as a matter of law be excluded. In order to determine whether the bankruptcy court erred in choosing the percentage of accounts test, it is necessary that we analyze case law on both tests and the interaction between the two tests.

1. The percentage of accounts test

Under the percentage of accounts test, a court asks only what percentage of the total accounts of the assignor were assigned and whether that percentage constitutes a "significant" part of the whole. White & Summers, Uniform Commercial Code, § 31-10 (4th ed. 1995). Courts have attempted to define what percentage constitutes a significant part of the assignor's account receivables. An assignment of an account which represented 16% of the assignor's accounts receivable has been held not to be a significant part and thus fell within the exception to filing. Standard Lumber Co. v. Chamber Frames, Inc., 317 F. Supp. 837, 840 (E.D. Ark. 1970). However, an assignment representing 20% of the assignor's accounts receivable has been held to be significant, thus requiring a filed financing statement for perfection. Miller v. Wells Fargo Bank Int'l Corp., 406 F. Supp. 452, 477 (S.D.N.Y. 1975), aff'd, 540 F.2d 548 (2d Cir. 1976). In In re Klein Glass & Mirror, Inc., 155 Bankr. 718, 721 (Bankr. S.D. Tex. 1992), the court held that an assignment of 40% of the assignor's accounts was significant, requiring the filing of a financing statement.

In this case, the bankruptcy court made a factual finding that as of the time of the assignment of $49,385.56 to CECO, Vigil's had outstanding

---

4. White & Summers, Uniform Commercial Code, § 31-10 (4th ed. 1995), no longer favors either the percentage test or the "casual and isolated" test, but instead states "certainty in this setting is no more than a will o' the wisp." However, this change initiated after the Black court's reliance on White & Summer's.

accounts of $125,000. Although there is some question as to the certainty of the $125,000 figure because of loss of Vigil's records, we do not find that the bankruptcy court's finding of outstanding accounts of $125,000 was clearly erroneous. The bankruptcy court then concluded that the assignment of 40% of Woods' accounts receivable to CECO was significant. In light of the above analyzed case law, we find that the court did not err by determining that 40% was a significant percentage. However, we still must determine whether the court erred by adopting the percentage test by analyzing the "casual and isolated" test.

2. The "casual and isolated" test

The "casual and isolated" test was extrapolated from the official comments to the 1962 and 1972 official text of the U.C.C. § 9-302 dealing with the "significant" exception, which states:

> The purpose of the subsection (1)(e) exemption is to save from ex post facto invalidation casual or isolated assignments: some accounts receivable statutes were so broadly drafted that all assignments, whatever their character or purpose, fell within their filing provisions. Under such statutes many assignments which no one would think of filing might have been subject to invalidation.

"The totality of the circumstances surrounding the transaction determines whether an assignment was casual or isolated." In re Tri-County Materials, Inc., 114 Bankr. 160, 164 (C.D. Ill. 1990). Under this test, a court may consider whether the assignee or assignor is in the business of commercial financing and whether the assignee regularly takes assignment of any debtor's accounts as part of its business. Even if the assignee is not in the business of accepting assignments, or had not done so in the past, an assignment still may fail the "casual and isolated" test if it is a "classic secured transaction." Tri-County, 114 Bankr. at 165. *Tri-County* was a case involving facts similar to the facts in this case. Ladd Construction Company ("Ladd") was a general contractor who entered into a contract in which Tri-County would act as a subcontractor. Tri-County then entered into a contract with KMB to provide equipment to Tri-County. Tri-County then assigned part of its account with Ladd to KMB for purposes of securing rental charges which Tri-County owed to KMB. Although the assignment of the account only represented 12% of Tri-County's total accounts, the court found that despite the "isolated" nature of the transaction, it was a "classic secured transaction" thus failing to fall within the "casual and isolated" exception. Id. at 165. The court reasoned that this was "not the type of 'casual' transaction in which reasonable parties would fail to see the importance of filing." Id. The court considered that the assignment was evidenced by a formal written agreement between two corporations, notice was sent to Ladd, the general contractor, and other conduct engaged in by KMB indicated the degree of formality attached to the assignment. Id. The court then stated "this is the type of transaction for which the U.C.C. requires filing in order to perfect." Id.

The Tri-County decision is also important for its interaction between the percentage test and the "casual and isolated" test. The Tri-County court held that both the percentage test and the "casual and isolated" test must be met, reasoning that the statutory language specifically requires that the assignment be of an insignificant part, which must at the very least be met in every case. Id. at 164. Thus, "[a] showing of a casual or isolated assignment of a significant part of outstanding accounts would not be entitled to the exemption given this clear statutory requirement." Id. However, pursuant to the comments to the U.C.C., if a case involves an insignificant part but the assignee is one whose regular business is financing, the exception should not apply. Id. This logic was also used in In re Klein Glass & Mirror, Inc., 155 Bankr. 718, 722 (Bankr. S.D. Tex. 1992), in which the court stated that in light of the plain language of the statute, the percentage of accounts assigned must be considered as part of the casual and isolated analysis. The court reasoned that "if the legislature had intended that all 'casual and isolated' transactions regardless of the proportion of accounts assigned be exempt from the filing requirement, it could have, and no doubt would have, stated so in the statute." Id. The court further stated that any other interpretation would allow a debtor to assign 100% of its accounts in a casual and isolated transaction, without requiring the assignee to give notice to other creditors, which would be "totally inconsistent with the plain meaning of the language of the statute." Id.

We agree with the rationale of these two cases and find that the plain language of A.R.S. § 47-9302(A)(5) governs. The term "casual and isolated" was included in the official comment as an interpretation of the purpose of the statute. However, the plain language of the statute only exempts from the filing requirement an assignment of accounts which does not assign a significant part of the outstanding accounts of the assignor. Thus, an assignment of a significant part of outstanding accounts is not a casual and isolated transaction, and a financing statement must be filed to give notice to other creditors. We find that the bankruptcy court did not err by choosing the percentage of accounts test. We **HEREBY AFFIRM** the bankruptcy court's decision that the assignment of 40% of outstanding accounts was significant and that CECO was required to file a financing statement in order to perfect its security interest.

. . .

V. CONCLUSION

Article 9 governs all assignments of accounts receivable. The assignment of the Woods account by Vigil to CECO is thus subject to the perfection requirements of Article 9. The bankruptcy court did not err in finding that the assignment did not enjoy automatic perfection pursuant to A.R.S. § 47-9302 because it was an assignment of a significant portion of Vigil's outstanding accounts receivable. The bankruptcy court was correct in holding that CECO was required to file a financing statement in order to perfect its interest. CECO failed to file a financing statement and thus holds the position of an unsecured creditor. The bankruptcy court properly sustained the trustee's objection to CECO's proof of claim. For these reasons, we **HEREBY AFFIRM.**

NOTES ON PUBLIC NOTICE OF TRANSFERS OF RECEIVABLES

(1) Construing UCC 9–309(2). As the *Vigil Bros.* case indicates, courts have disagreed over the meaning of Former 9–302(1)(e), which exempted certain transfers of accounts from the general rule that filing is necessary to perfect a security interest. The range of opinions is even broader than *Vigil Bros.* suggests. See, e.g., Park Avenue Bank v. Bassford, 232 Ga. 216, 205 S.E.2d 861 (1974) (dollar amount of assigned accounts "significant" without regard to percentage); Architectural Woods, Inc. v. Washington, 88 Wn.2d 406, 562 P.2d 248 (1977) (en banc) (applying only "casual and isolated" test).

One way to evaluate the proper scope of the exemption is to determine which types of transfers do not implicate the need for public notice. This, in turn leads one to examine the reason or reasons underlying the general rule. Note (3), p. 153, supra, explores a number of these reasons. Please review it now. Do the reasons justifying a filing requirement for security interests in tangible collateral apply equally to secured parties (including buyers, see UCC 9–102(a)(72)(D)) whose collateral consists of intangible property, such as accounts? If so, does any of these reasons support an exemption for a transfer of accounts having insubstantial value? Insubstantial value relative to the assignor's total accounts? Does any of these reasons support an exemption for "casual or isolated assignments"? Assignments as to which "no one would think of filing"? UCC 9–309, Comment 4. Assignments as to which only professionals would think of filing?

Do you suppose the drafters of Revised Article 9 were familiar with the problem of statutory construction raised in *Vigil Bros.* and elsewhere? If so, how do you explain the fact that the drafters did absolutely nothing to solve it? See UCC 9–309(2) & Comment 4. Will the problem be more or less likely to arise under Revised Article 9 than it did under Former Article 9? Consider, in this regard, that the exception in UCC 9–309(2) applies to assignments of payment intangibles as well as to assignments of accounts and that the definition of "account" has itself been expanded.

(2) "Automatic" Perfection of Sales of Payment Intangibles and Promissory Notes. We have seen that, largely in response to the concerns of participants in the loan-participation market, the sale of payment intangibles and promissory notes is perfected upon attachment, without the need for an additional public-notice step. See UCC 9–309(3), (4) (discussed in Note (2), p. 392, supra). Does this approach undermine the integrity of the filing system and the need for public notice? Arguably not. Every potential buyer of a loan participation from a bank knows that the bank sells participations. The filing of a financing statement covering "general intangibles" or "loan" gives no information. Even a financing statement that describes a particular loan is unlikely to give sufficient information to justify the delay that might result if sales of participations routinely were preceded by a search of the files against the seller. Under Former Article 9, a prospective buyer of a loan participation had no way to insure that it was buying something that had not been sold before. Participants took this risk and were forced to rely on the honesty of the seller (typically the originating bank that made the loan to the borrower) to minimize it.

Revised Article 9's automatic-perfection rule applicable to sales of payment intangibles does not exacerbate the situation. Moreover, by expanding the category of accounts to include many rights to payment other than those for goods sold or leased or services rendered, *Revised Article 9 actually increases the sale transactions in which filing is required as a condition of perfection.* In some cases, doubt may arise concerning whether the collateral is a payment intangible or an account or, if the collateral is a payment intangible, whether the transaction a sale or an assignment that secures an obligation. The parties most likely to engage in the assignment of rights to payment are likely to be sophisticated and to file in doubtful cases. By doing so, for very little cost they can protect against the possibility that the collateral is an account or that the transaction is the assignment of a payment intangible to secure an obligation.

(F) COLLECTION OF RECEIVABLES

Problem 6.1.6. Assume the facts in Problem 6.1.2, p. 388, supra, in which Carguys sold its accounts to Factor. (Ignore the facts in paragraphs (a)-(d), dealing with Lean.) Assume also that Factor perfected its security interest by filing and that the agreement between Factor and Carguys gives Factor the right to notify Carguys's customers to make payment directly to Factor.

(a) Two weeks after its account is sold to Factor, Customer #1 pays Carguys in full. Is Factor out of luck? See UCC 9–406(a); Note (3) on Rights and Obligations of Account Debtors and Persons Obligated on Promissory Notes, infra.

(b) Would the result in part (a) change if, prior to paying Carguys, Customer #1 received a letter from Factor stating as follows: "You are hereby advised that all amounts owing from yourself to Carguys, Inc., have been sold to the undersigned. Kindly remit all future payments to the undersigned at the address shown on the letterhead."?

(c) Would the result in part (a) change if the letter described in part (b) did not contain the second sentence? Compare Vacura v. Haar's Equipment, Inc., 364 N.W.2d 387 (Minn.1985) (notification of assignment will not cut off account debtor's right to pay assignor unless it contains explicit direction that payment is to be made to assignee) with First National Bank of Rio Arriba v. Mountain States Telephone & Telegraph Co., 91 N.M. 126, 571 P.2d 118 (1977) (unconditional language of assignment, which was accepted in writing by account debtor, was notice that payment was to be made to assignee). Courts often have read Former 9–318(3), the predecessor to UCC 9–406(a), strictly, to protect account debtors from having to pay twice.

(d) Customer #2 received the letter described in part (b) but refuses to pay Factor, citing a provision of its contract with Carguys stating that "this contract is not assignable." Is Factor out of luck? See UCC 9–406(d).

(e) Would the result in part (d) change if Carguys had retained a purchase-money security interest in the diagnostic equipment purchased by Customer #2 and had sold Factor the secured rights to payment? See UCC 9–406(d).

(f) Customer #3 received the letter described in part (b) but refuses to pay Factor, claiming that it doesn't believe Carguys has stooped so low as to "hock its receivables." What, if anything, can Factor do? See UCC 9–406(c). What can Customer #3 do if it remains dubious?

(g) Customer #4 received the letter from Factor. In response it informed Factor that, two weeks before it received the letter, the equipment it bought from Carguys malfunctioned. A manufacturing defect caused sparks to fly from the equipment; these sparks set off a fire causing damage to Customer's repair facility, which damage required Customer to close the facility for three days. Accordingly, Customer #4 not only refuses to pay for the equipment (which does not operate) but also seeks compensation from Factor for property damage and loss of profits.

(i) Is Customer obligated to pay for the equipment? See UCC 9–404(a); Note (4) on Rights and Obligations of Account Debtors and Persons Obligated on Promissory Notes, infra.

(ii) Is Customer entitled to compensation from Factor for its loss? See UCC 9–404(b); Note (4) on Rights and Obligations of Account Debtors and Persons Obligated on Promissory Notes, infra.

(h) Would the result in part (g) change if Customer #4 had paid in full for the equipment that malfunctioned and the account that Factor was assigned was for the sale of a different item of equipment? See UCC 9–404(a).

(i) Would the result in part (h) change if the equipment malfunctioned three days *after* Customer #4 received the letter? See UCC 9–404(a); UCC 2–725 (regarding when a cause of action for breach of warranty accrues). Would it make any difference in part (h) if both items of equipment were the subject of a single contract between Carguys and Customer? If there was a master agreement containing general terms, supplemented by separate agreements containing the specifications for each item of equipment?

NOTES ON RIGHTS AND OBLIGATIONS OF ACCOUNT DEBTORS AND PERSONS OBLIGATED ON PROMISSORY NOTES

(1) "Account Debtor"; Person Obligated on a Promissory Note. The value of a receivable as collateral depends upon the likelihood that the person obligated to pay actually will perform its obligation in full, in a timely manner. The Notes that follow address matters that go to the heart of a receivable's value: the rights and obligations of persons who are obligated to pay. Before turning to those matters, a few words about terminology: Not every person obligated to pay a receivable is an "account debtor." Rather the term is limited to "a person obligated on an account, chattel paper, or general intangible." UCC 9–102(a)(3). Thus it excludes persons obligated on a promissory note or other instrument. In one respect, the definition of "account debtor" distinguishes between negotiable and nonnegotiable promissory notes: It excludes "persons obligated to pay a negotiable instrument, even if the instrument constitutes part of chattel paper," but includes persons obligated to pay a nonnegotiable note that constitutes part of chattel paper. Id. Try to keep these distinctions in mind as you study the following Notes.

(2) Secured Party's Right to Notify Obligated Persons. As the excerpt from Kupfer, supra, suggests, some receivables financing is done on a notification basis, i.e., the obligated persons are notified to remit payment directly to the assignee (secured party). Not surprisingly, Article 9 provides that such an agreement is effective against the debtor. See UCC 9–607(a)(1). When receivables financing is done on a non-notification basis, upon the debtor's (assignor's) default the secured party is entitled to require obligated persons to make payment to the secured party, regardless of whether the debtor has not agreed to the procedure. See id.

Chapter 9, Section 5, infra, discusses the duties of a secured party and rights of a debtor with respect to the secured party's collection of receivables. The Notes that follow address the rights and obligations of an account debtor or other obligated person.

(3) The Obligated Person's Problem: Whom to Pay? Whereas UCC 9–607(a) governs the secured party's *right*, as against the debtor, to notify a person obligated on a receivable, it does not govern the *obligation* of the person receiving the notification.

Account debtors. When the receivable is an account, chattel paper, or payment intangible, and the secured party is entitled to notify the account debtor, UCC 9–406 sets forth the circumstances under which the account debtor must pay the secured party, who may be a stranger to the transaction, rather than the assignor (debtor), with whom the account debtor has dealt. Knowing the proper party to pay is (or should be) a major concern for the account debtor. If an account debtor pays the wrong party, the account debtor does not discharge its obligation on the contract and will have to pay again—this time to the proper party. (Although the mistaken account debtor will be entitled to recover its payment from a party who is not entitled to it, see Restatement of Restitution § 17 (1937), the account debtor would prefer not to litigate the issue, particularly against a person who wrongfully kept funds to which it was not entitled.) UCC 9–406(a) contains what sometimes is referred to as the "notification" rule: An account debtor becomes obligated to pay an assignee upon receipt of a notification "that the amount due or to become due has been assigned and that payment is to be made to the assignee." UCC 9–406(a). Subsections (b) and (c) help protect the account debtor from having to pay twice.

The account debtor on a contract may wish to avoid entirely the risk of paying the wrong party by simply making the contract non-assignable, or by conditioning assignment on its advance consent. However, UCC 9–406(d)(1) generally makes provisions of this kind, which are not terribly common, "ineffective." An "ineffective" prohibition on assignment will not prevent the assignment from taking effect; that is, the prohibition will not prevent a security interest from attaching to the receivable. The account debtor and assignor might be tempted to circumvent this rule by agreeing that the assignor's violation of the prohibition on assignment constitutes a default under the contract, excusing the account debtor from its contractual obligations. Were this agreement to be given effect, the value of the receivable as collateral would be substantially impaired. Does Article 9 give effect to this agreement? See UCC 9–406(d)(2).

UCC 9–406(d) is one of several UCC rules promoting the free alienability of rights to payment and other (primarily intangible) property. These rules, which appear in UCC 9–406 through UCC 9–409, enable a debtor to create (and, in some cases, a secured party to enforce) a security interest in certain property that otherwise is non-assignable, either by operation of law or by contract. Cf. UCC 9–401(b) (debtor's rights in collateral may be transferred notwithstanding a prohibition in the security agreement). The rules apply to accounts, chattel paper, promissory notes, payment intangibles, letter-of credit rights, rights under leases of personal property, and the lessor's residual interest in leased goods. The assignability of property not covered by UCC 9–406 through UCC 9–409 is governed by law other than Article 9. See UCC 9–401(a).

The rules in UCC 9–406 through UCC 9–409 are very complex and must be read with unusual care. The complexity is the direct consequence of the diversity of intangible property and the drafters' decision not to interfere with existing transaction patterns. For example, the borrower of a large sum may seek the lender's agreement not to assign, or sell participation interests in, the loan. The borrower may be motivated by a concern that, if a dispute arises or the loan goes into default, the assignee, who usually is a stranger, will be less accommodating than the originator, with whom the borrower typically has a pre-existing relationship. Even if the originator is unwilling to restrict its ability to assign the loan, the originator may have reason to agree with the borrower that the borrower need not make payment to an assignee: An originator may be concerned that an assignee (participant) will establish its own business relationship with the originator's customer. For this reason, among others, participation agreements typically provide that the originator–assignor retains the exclusive power to enforce the borrower's obligation and that the participant has no direct contractual relationship with the borrower.

Article 9 balances the policy of free alienability of rights to payment with respect for these practices in the loan and loan-participation market. When a payment intangible has been *sold* and the seller and account debtor so agree (and the agreement is enforceable under law other than Article 9), even an account debtor who has received a notification under UCC 9–406(a) may discharge its obligation by paying the seller-assignor. See UCC 9–406(b)(2). To the same end, UCC 9–406(d), which renders ineffective a contractual restriction on assignment of a payment intangible, does not apply to sales of payment intangibles. See UCC 9–406(e). UCC 9–408 applies instead. Like UCC 9–406(d), which applies to security interests that secure an obligation, UCC 9–408(a) overrides a contractual restriction on the sale of a payment intangible. But whereas UCC 9–406(d) overrides contractual restrictions for all purposes, including for purposes of enforcement against the account debtor (here, the borrower), UCC 9–408 is much more solicitous of the bargain between the lender and borrower. When a payment intangible is sold and law other than Article 9 would give effect to the contractual restriction on assignment but Article 9 does not, then the buyer's security interest in the payment intangible may not be enforced against the borrower. See UCC 9–408(d). Under these circumstances, the borrower may ignore the assignment (sale) and render performance to the lender with whom it dealt.

Persons Obligated on a Promissory Note. We have seen that UCC 9–406(a) provides that whether an account debtor has received a notification determines whether the account debtor must pay the assignor-debtor or assignee-secured party. But UCC 9–406(a) applies only to account debtors; it does not apply to persons obligated on a promissory note or other instrument. What law does apply? If the promissory note is negotiable, then UCC Article 3 determines whom the maker (or other person obligated on the instrument) must pay to discharge its obligation: "[A]n instrument is paid to the extent payment is made . . . to a person entitled to enforce the instrument." UCC 3–602(a). A person normally must be in possession of an instrument to qualify as a person entitled to enforce. See UCC 3–301. If the promissory note is not negotiable, then law other than the UCC determines whom a person obligated on the instrument must pay to discharge its obligation.

Recent amendments to UCC Article 3 would change the rules governing discharge of the obligation to pay a negotiable note. R3–602(b) adopts a rule analogous to that of UCC 9–406(a). A note is paid, and the obligation to pay the note is discharged thereby, not only to the extent payment is made to a person entitled to enforce the instrument at the time of payment but also to the extent payment is made to a person that *formerly* was entitled to enforce the instrument (e.g., a former holder who no longer has possession of the note). Payment to a former holder does not effect a discharge if, before making the payment, the party obliged to pay had received notification that the note had been transferred and that payment was to be made to the transferee. R3–602(b), (c).

Like an account debtor, the maker of a nonnegotiable promissory note may wish to avoid entirely the risk of paying the wrong party by making the note non-assignable, or by conditioning assignment on its advance consent.

Article 9 deals with provisions of this kind, which are very unusual,[4] in the same way it deals with restrictions on the assignment of payment intangibles: They are ineffective to prevent a security interest (whether securing an obligation or arising from a sale) from attaching to the promissory note, and they are ineffective to cause the assignor's violation of the prohibition to constitute a default under the note, excusing the maker (or other obligated person) from its obligation to pay. See UCC 9–406(d), (e); UCC 9–408(a), (b). However, when a promissory note is sold and law other than Article 9 would give effect to the contractual restriction on assignment but Article 9 does not, then the buyer's security interest in the promissory note may not be enforced against the maker. See UCC 9–408(d). Under these circumstances, the maker may ignore the assignment (sale) and render performance to the lender with whom it dealt.

(4) The Secured Party's Problem: Claims and Defenses of the Obligated Person.

Account debtors. As we explored to some extent in Chapter 1, Section 4, UCC 9–404(a) generally reflects the *nemo dat* principle. The assignee (secured party) generally takes its interest in the account subject to defenses of the account debtor. If, for example, the account debtor has a defense to payment, it may assert the defense against the assignee. By notifying the account debtor of the assignment, the assignee may deprive the account debtor of certain defenses that may arise in the future. See UCC 9–404(a)(2). And, as we also saw in Chapter 1, Section 4, an assignee may take free of nearly all defenses if the account debtor agrees. See UCC 9–403(b). (Of course, the account debtor retains its rights against the assignor.)

Suppose an account debtor makes payments to the assignee and then discovers that the goods are worth only half what the account debtor has paid for them. The account debtor seeks to recover the overpayment from the assignee. Had the account debtor known of the defense before payment, it could have asserted a defense to the assignee's demand for payment. Do the legal positions of the account debtor and assignee change simply because the account debtor discovers the goods are defective after it has paid for them?

Yes, according to UCC 9–404(b). Although UCC 9–404(a) provides that an assignee takes subject to an account debtor's "claims" as well as "defenses," "the claim of an account debtor against an assignor may be asserted against an assignee under subsection (a) only to reduce the amount the account debtor owes." UCC 9–404(b). What explains this result, which comports with the pre-UCC common law? See Restatement of Restitution § 14(2) (1937) ("An assignee of a non-negotiable chose in action who, having paid value therefor, has received payment from the obligor is under no duty to make restitution although the obligor had a defense thereto, if the

---

4.   Negotiable notes containing a restriction on assignment are rare as hen's teeth. Do you understand why?

transferee made no misrepresentation and did not have notice of the defense.").

The First Circuit had occasion to address some of these issues under Former Article 9 in Michelin Tires (Canada) Ltd. v. First National Bank of Boston, 666 F.2d 673 (1st Cir.1981). Michelin entered into a contract for the design and installation of a carbon black handling and storage system, which was to form part of a Michelin tire factory in Nova Scotia. Michelin agreed to pay the contractor, JCC, periodic progress payments. JCC granted a security interest in its rights under the contract to FNB. FNB notified Michelin of the assignment, and Michelin paid FNB a total of $724,197.60. Thereafter, Michelin discovered that JCC had submitted fictitious invoices and fraudulent sworn statements showing that JCC had paid its subcontractors. JCC filed a bankruptcy petition, and Michelin sued to recover the payments from FNB.

The majority found that Michelin was not entitled to recover under principles of restitution and that Former 9–318(1), despite providing that an assignee takes subject to "claims," did not create affirmative rights of recovery against an assignee who did not actively participate in the fraudulent transactions. (Former Article 9 contained no analogue to UCC 9–404(b), which expressly limits an account debtor's rights of recovery.) The court found this result to be consistent with sound policy:

> While it is our judgment that analysis of the statutory language, taken in context, indicates that no affirmative right was contemplated and further that those cases that have permitted such a right are factually inapposite, we also believe it would be unwise to permit such suits as a matter of policy. [A]llowing affirmative suits would "make every Banker, who has taken an assignment of accounts for security purposes, a deep pocket surety for every bankrupt contractor in the state to whom it had loaned money."

> We are unwilling to impose such an obligation on the banks of the Commonwealth without some indication that this represents a considered policy choice. By making the bank a surety, not only will accounts receivable financing be discouraged, but transaction costs will undoubtedly increase for everyone. The case at hand provides a good example. In order to protect themselves, FNB would essentially be forced to undertake the precautionary measures that Michelin attempted to use, independent observation by an intermediary and sworn certifications by the assignor. FNB would have to supervise every construction site where its funds were involved to ensure performance and payment. We simply do not believe that the banks are best suited to monitor contract compliance. The party most interested in adequate performance would be the other contracting party, not the financier. Given this natural interest, it seems likely to us that while the banks will be given additional burdens of supervision, there would be no corresponding reduction in vigilance by the contracting parties, thus creating two inspections where there was formerly one. Costs for everyone thus increase, without any discernible benefit. It is also

difficult to predict the full impact a contrary decision would have on the availability of accounts receivable financing in general.

Our holding, of course, is not that § 9–318 *prohibits* claims against the assignee. We hold merely that § 9–318 concerns only the preservation of defenses to the assignee's claims and, as such, is wholly inapposite in an affirmative suit against an assignee.

666 F.2d at 679–80.

In dissent, Judge Bownes concluded that under Former 9–318(1)(a), "an assignee's rights to retain payments made to it under an assignment are subject to, or are exposed to, affirmative actions brought by the account debtor to recover payments mistakenly made."

This interpretation of section 9–318(1)(a), that the account debtor has rights of action against the assignee, is the fairest way to reconcile the rights of account debtors and secured creditors, particularly where, as here, credit is advanced through a line of credit. This case boils down to the question of whether the secured creditor or the account debtor should bear the cost of not finding out that JCC falsely claimed that it had paid its subcontractors. The secured creditor is in a better position than the account debtor to determine whether the assignor/borrower is complying with the terms of the contract in which the creditor has an interest. The reason is that the secured creditor can employ an effective sanction without having to initiate litigation and without risking any loss itself to ensure compliance; it can threaten to cut off credit unless it is satisfied with the borrower's performance. The other party, the account debtor, has no similar sanction. If he is not satisfied, he must litigate and bear the expense of litigation and the sure delay in completion of the contract. The creditor/assignee is not deterred from enforcing compliance by such costs. Obviously, either the secured creditor or the account debtor can make inquiries regarding compliance with the contract, but at some point both will have to rely on the representations of others, which creates opportunities for fraud, as occurred here. The secured creditor is accustomed to looking over the borrower's shoulder on an ongoing basis and can check compliance. By virtue of his control over credit, the creditor can ensure compliance with the contract. The account debtor can only investigate and if it holds up payments, it puts the contract in jeopardy.

666 F.2d at 684–85.

Which view do you find more persuasive? Had JCC negligently constructed the facility, do you suppose Judge Bownes would have permitted Michelin to recover compensatory damages from FNB? See Former 9–317, which is substantially identical to UCC 9–402 (mere existence of a security interest does not impose contract or tort liability upon the secured party for the debtor's acts or omissions).

Persons Obligated on a Promissory Note. We have seen that the right to enforce the obligation of a person to pay an instrument is subject to most claims and defenses. See UCC 3–305(a); Chapter 1, Section 4, supra.

However, a person who makes a negotiable instrument waives most claims and defenses as against a holder in due course. See UCC 3–305(b); Chapter 1, Section 4, supra. (Recall that a person cannot be a holder in due course of a note bearing the legend required by Federal Trade Commission Rule 433, 16 C.F.R. art 433. See UCC 3–104(d). Under a recent amendment to Article 3, a negotiable note lacking the legend would have the same effect as if it had included the legend, and the maker would be able to assert all claims and defenses that would have been available had the legend in fact been included. R3–305(e).)

On the question whether the maker of a negotiable promissory note may obtain affirmative recovery from an assignee, UCC Article 3 yields a result consistent with *Michelin Tires*, supra, and UCC 9–404(b): "[T]he claim of the obligor may be asserted against a transferee of the instrument only to reduce the amount owing on the instrument at the time the action is brought." UCC 3–305(a)(3). The claims and defenses available to the maker of a non-negotiable promissory note (other than one that is part of chattel paper) is governed by non-UCC law.

(5) Consumer Account Debtors. The account-debtor rules in UCC 9–403 through 9–406 are subject to non-Article 9 law that establishes a different rule for an account debtor who is an individual and who incurred the obligation primarily for personal, family, or household purposes. See, e.g., UCC 9–403(e); UCC 9–404(c); UCC 9–406(h). This non-Article 9 law includes not only federal law (which would preempt in any event) but also state statutes, judicial decisions, and administrative rules and regulations.

As we saw in Chapter 1, Section 4, Federal Trade Commission Rule 433, 16 C.F.R. art. 433, makes it an "unfair and deceptive trade practice" for the seller of goods to fail to incorporate in a contract of sale to a consumer a legend that will preserve the buyer's defenses against a financing agency to which the contract is assigned. In addition, if the seller receives the proceeds from a direct loan made to the buyer by a financing agency to which the seller "refers consumers" or with whom the seller "is affiliated . . . by common control, contract, or business arrangement," the loan contract must include a similar legend. 16 C.F.R. 433.1(d); 433.2. In both cases the legend must state also that the buyer's recovery against an assignee with respect to claims and defenses against the seller may not exceed amounts paid by the buyer under the contract. See 16 C.F.R. 433.2. We also saw in Chapter 1 that a substantial body of case law holds that FTC regulations do not ipso facto modify private rights. Thus, when a contract or note fails to include the required legend, the buyer may be unable to assert defenses against an assignee if other law, such as the UCC, so provides. Revised Article 9 changes this result: Under UCC 9–403(d) an assignee of such a contract takes subject to the consumer account debtor's claims and defenses to the same extent as it would have if the writing had contained the required notice. Similarly, a consumer account debtor has the same right to an affirmative recovery from an assignee of such a contract as the consumer would have had against the assignee had the record contained the required notice. See UCC 9–404(d).

SECTION 2. PURCHASERS OF CHATTEL PAPER, INSTRUMENTS, AND DOCUMENTS

INTRODUCTORY NOTE

Earlier in these materials we considered the rights of purchasers (including Article 9 secured parties) who obtain the status of a holder in due course of a negotiable instrument or a holder to whom a negotiable document of title has been duly negotiated. See Chapter 1, Sections 4 and 5, supra. As we saw, HDC's and HTWANDOTHBDN's take free of competing claims to negotiable instruments and negotiable documents. See UCC 3–306; UCC 7–502(1). Protected purchasers of investment securities acquire similar rights. See UCC 8–303.

UCC 9–331 provides expressly that the rules of Articles 3, 7, and 8, which allow certain purchasers to cut off earlier-in-time claims to negotiable instruments, documents of title, and investment securities, override any rule of Article 9 that otherwise would have given priority to an earlier-in-time security interest. UCC 9–331 merely refers and defers to other UCC Articles for applicable priority rules. Article 9 also provides supplementary priority rules that favor certain ordinary course purchasers of chattel paper and instruments. See UCC 9–330. The following Problems and Notes consider the roles of UCC 9–330 and UCC 9–331 in the Article 9 priority scheme.

Problem 6.2.1. A metals dealer ("Dealer") had a surplus stock of chromium, a valuable metal, in its own warehouse. Dealer needed additional working capital. On June 1 Dealer borrowed $50,000 from Firstbank. At the same time, Dealer signed a security agreement covering the chromium and a proper financing statement; Firstbank immediately filed the financing statement in the proper office.

On July 1 Dealer delivered the chromium to Warehouse. Warehouse issued and delivered to Dealer a written warehouse receipt calling for the delivery of the chromium to the order of Dealer.

On July 2 Dealer borrowed $50,000 from Secondbank. Dealer signed a security agreement covering the chromium and the warehouse receipt. Dealer indorsed and delivered the warehouse receipt to Secondbank. Secondbank did not search the UCC filing records and knew nothing about Firstbank's earlier security interest in the same chromium.

(a) Is each bank's security interest in the chromium a perfected security interest? See UCC 9–310(a); UCC 7–104; UCC 9–312(c), (a); UCC 9–313(a).

(b) Which bank has the senior security interest? On what basis? See UCC 9–312(c); UCC 9–331; UCC 7–501; UCC 7–502; UCC 7–503.

(c) What could the junior party have done differently to ensure its seniority?

(d) What are the policy justifications for the ranking of priorities in this case?

Problem 6.2.2. In the setting of the Prototype on receivables financing, Section 1(B), supra, Carguys created an "all-assets" security interest in favor of Eastinghome. Eastinghome perfected its security interest by filing. Carguys is the payee of a negotiable promissory note, payable "to the order of Carguys, Inc.," in the face amount of $25,000. The note becomes due and payable on May 15, 2003. Section 4.1 of the Security Agreement (Form 6.2) requires Carguys to deliver the note to Eastinghome. Nevertheless, faced with a "cash flow problem," on January 10, 2002, Carguys delivers the note to Redemption Bank to secure a loan for $18,000. Redemption Bank did not search the UCC filing records before making the purchase.

(a) Assume Carguys indorsed the note "to Redemption Bank" before delivering it. Does each lender hold a perfected security interest? See UCC 9–308(a); UCC 9–102(a)(47); UCC 9–203(b); UCC 9–312(a); UCC 9–313(a). Who has the better claim to the note, Eastinghome or Redemption Bank? See UCC 9–322(a), (f); UCC 9–331; UCC 3–306; UCC 3–302(a), (b); UCC 3–204(a); UCC 3–205(a); UCC 1–201(b)(21) [F1–201(20)] ; Note (1) on Purchasers of Instruments, infra. What could the losing party have done to protect itself?

(b) Assume Carguys did not indorse the note before delivering it to Redemption Bank. Who has the better claim to the note, Eastinghome or Redemption Bank? See UCC 9–322(a), (f); UCC 9–330(d) & Comment 7; UCC 9–102(a)(43); UCC 3–306; UCC 3–102(b); Note (1) on Purchasers of Instruments, infra. What could the losing party have done to protect itself?

(c) What result in parts (a) and (b) if the note were payable "to Carguys, Inc."? See UCC 9–102(a)(47); UCC 3–104(a).

Problem 6.2.3. In need of more money to lend to its young, professional clientele, Yuppie Finance Co. approached Firstbank. In a written agreement, Firstbank agreed to purchase at a discount, and Yuppie agreed to sell, Yuppie's entire portfolio of loans. The loans are evidenced by notes payable "to Yuppie Finance Co." To avoid administrative costs, Firstbank permitted Yuppie to retain possession of the sold notes and collect them on Firstbank's behalf as they came due. Firstbank also did not file a financing statement.

(a) Is Firstbank's interest in the notes subject to defeat by a lien creditor of Yuppie's? See UCC 9–317(a)(2); UCC 9–310(b)(2); UCC 9–309(4); 9-318.

(b) Shortly after the sale, in violation of its agreement with Firstbank, Yuppie purported to sell another one of Firstbank's notes to Secondbank, which promptly filed a financing statement covering the note upon paying for it. Which bank has the better claim to the note? See UCC 9–109(a)(3); UCC 9–102(a)(65); UCC 9–309(a)(4); UCC 9–318; UCC 9–203(b)(2); UCC 9–322(a), (g); UCC 9–330(d); Note (1) on Purchasers of Instruments, infra. What could the losing bank have done to protect itself?

(c) Shortly after the sale, in violation of its agreement with Firstbank, Yuppie purported to sell another one of Firstbank's notes to Thirdbank, which took possession of the note upon paying for it. Which bank has the better claim to the note? See UCC 9–109(a)(3); UCC 9–102(a)(65); UCC 9–309(a)(4); UCC 9–318; UCC 9–203(b)(2); UCC 9–322(a), (g); UCC 9–330(d); Note (1) on Purchasers of Instruments, infra. What could the losing bank have done to protect itself?

Problem 6.2.4. Dalrymple borrowed $100,000 from Secondbank on an unsecured basis. After suffering financial reversals, Dalrymple defaulted on the obligation to repay. As part of an effort to restructure its debts out of court, Dalrymple offers to bring interest current, make a $20,000 reduction in principal, and secure the $80,000 balance with one of its major assets, a $1,400,000 promissory note payable to Dalrymple's order. Firstbank holds a possessory security interest in the note to secure a claim of $750,000. Secondbank is content to take a junior security interest but wishes to insure that its security interest is perfected and its ability to turn the note into cash is protected.

Advise Secondbank. In particular, consider:

(i) How should Secondbank perfect its security interest while the note is held by Firstbank? See UCC 9–312(a); UCC 9–313(a), (c), (d), (f).

(ii) What will happen to the note when Dalrymple satisfies the debt to Firstbank?

(iii) How will Secondbank be able to enforce its security interest if Dalrymple defaults on the secured obligation? See UCC 9–607(a), (e); UCC 9–609; UCC 3–412; UCC 3–301; UCC 9–610; UCC 9–313(g).

(iv) Would it be necessary or helpful to obtain Firstbank's assistance in effectuating the transaction? Why might Firstbank be willing to cooperate? What concerns might it have? What might be done to alleviate those concerns?

NOTES ON PURCHASERS OF INSTRUMENTS

(1) Conflicting Priorities in Instruments under Article 9. Under Former Article 9, as under the common law, long-term perfection of a security interest in a note could be achieved only by the secured party's taking possession of the collateral. (Short-term perfection could be achieved under circumstances similar to those set forth in UCC 9–315 and UCC 9–312, which derive from similar provisions of Former Article 9.) Revised Article 9 makes a dramatic break from the past by permitting perfection in instruments, even negotiable instruments, to be achieved by filing a financing statement. It does so largely to enable transactions to proceed when the costs of the secured party's taking possession of large numbers of notes would be prohibitive. See UCC 9–312, Comment 2.

Under existing practices, those who buy or lend against a note typically take possession. The drafters of Revised Article 9 did not wish to upset these practices. If the note is negotiable is negotiated to the secured party under circumstances such that the secured party becomes a holder in due course ("HDC"), then the secured party will take free of all claims to the instrument, including competing security interests. See UCC 9–331(a); UCC 3–306. A purchaser who acquires a negotiable instrument with knowledge of an earlier security interest cannot be an HDC and, consequently, would not be entitled to priority under UCC 9–331. See UCC 3–302; UCC 3–306; UCC 9–331. Similarly, a purchaser who acquires a nonnegotiable instrument cannot become an HDC. Under UCC 9–330(d), however, the purchaser may obtain priority over the earlier security interest notwithstanding the purchaser's knowledge. See UCC 9–330, Comment 7.

In fact, UCC 9–330(d) provides strong protection for most purchasers of notes who take possession. Compare the requirements for priority under UCC 9–330(d) with those in UCC 3–302(a) for achieving HDC status and its attendant freedom from all claims to the instrument. In particular, compare the value and scienter requirements. With respect to the former, recall that the definition of "value" in Article 3 is narrower than the definition generally applicable under the UCC. Compare UCC 3–303(a) with UCC 1–204 [F1–201(44)]. The concept, in UCC 9–330(d), of "without knowledge that the purchase violates the rights of the secured party" derives from the analogous concept in the definition of "buyer in ordinary course of business" in UCC 1–201(9).

What accounts for the generous treatment UCC 9–330(d) affords to non-HDC's? Why does UCC 9–330(d) protect certain persons who take an instrument with actual knowledge of a conflicting claim to it? In considering these questions, compare the scope of protection that UCC 9–330(d) affords with that of UCC 3–306.

Unlike Former Article 9, Revised Article 9 governs the outright sale of certain instruments—specifically, "promissory notes" (as defined in UCC 9–102(a)(65)). See Section 1(D), supra. As with accounts and chattel paper, the buyer of promissory notes holds a security interest. See UCC 1–201(b)(35) [F1–201(37)]. But unlike the case of accounts or chattel paper, the security interest arising from a sale of promissory notes is automatically perfected upon attachment. See UCC 9–309(a)(4). The sale of property normally divests the seller of any interest in whatever the buyer bought. As we saw above in Section 1(D), however, if a buyer (B–1) of accounts or chattel paper fails to perfect its security interest, the seller retains the *power*, even if not the right, to resell the accounts or chattel paper to a third person (B–2) who can acquire good title to them. See UCC 9–318(b) & Comment 3; UCC 9–322(a). However, if B–1 perfects its security interest before the sale to B–2, then B–2 acquires no interest in the sold accounts or chattel paper. See UCC 9–318(a).

Problem 6.2.3 concerns double-dealing by the seller of a promissory note. Because the sale to Firstbank was perfected (automatically), Yuppie retained no interest in the sold notes. See UCC 9–318(a). Firstbank owned them free and clear of any interest that Yuppie had held. How, then, can Secondbank's security interest attach? UCC 9–203(b)(2) gives the answer: Although Yuppie retained no legal or equitable interest in the sold note, it did enjoy "the power to transfer rights in the collateral to a secured party." The fact that UCC 9–330(d) enables qualifying purchasers of instruments to take priority over earlier-perfected security interests necessarily means that the sellers of the instruments have power to transfer rights in the notes to the purchasers.

(2) "Transferable Records" under UETA. As we have just seen, an instrument differs from an account and payment intangible in that a second-in-time purchaser can achieve priority over an earlier-perfected security interest by taking possession of the paper under UCC 9–330(d) or, if the instrument is negotiable, by becoming an HDC under UCC 3–302. Businesses increasingly are using electronic, rather than paper, records to evidence transactions. Although electronic notes are uncommon today, they may well become more common in the future. Should those who finance this kind of intangible collateral have the opportunity to achieve non-temporal priority (i.e., priority not based on priority in the time) analogous to that afforded by UCC 9–330 and UCC 9–331 to purchasers of traditional notes?

The drafters of Revised Article 9 answered this question in the negative. A purchaser of a note cannot qualify for non-temporal priority under UCC 9–330 or take free of claims under UCC 9–331 and UCC 3–306 without taking possession. See UCC 1–201(b)(21) [F1–201(20)] (defining "holder"). An electronic note by its very nature is not susceptible of being possessed. Thus, a person financing electronic notes (other than notes that are part of electronic chattel paper) is subject to by the first-to-file-or-perfect rule, like those who finance other non-paper-based receivables (accounts and payment intangibles). The drafters of UETA disagreed with this result. As we saw in Chapter 1, Section 4, supra, "control" of a transferable record under UETA is the analogue to possession of a paper-based instrument: A person who takes control of a transferable record, like a person who takes possession of a tangible note, may qualify for priority over earlier-perfected security interests under UCC 9–330[1] and, if the requirements of UCC 3–302(a) are satisfied, take free of competing security interests and other claims as a holder in due course. See UETA 16(d); UCC 3–306; UCC 9–331(a). (Likewise, a person who has control of an electronic document of title may qualify for priority under UCC 9–331(a) if the requirements of UCC 7–501 for becoming a HTWANDOTHBDN are met.)

Recall that not every electronic note is a "transferable record." An electronic note can qualify as a transferable record only if the issuer agrees that it is to be considered a transferable record. See UETA 16(a)(2). Moreover, to meet the definition, an electronic record must be such that it would be a note under UCC Article 3 if it were in writing. See UETA 16(a)(1). Checks (even though negotiable) do not qualify; nor do nonnegotiable notes. (Nonnegotiable electronic notes that are part of chattel paper are discussed in Note (4) on Purchasers of Chattel Paper, infra.)

---

1.   At least we hope this will be the case. UETA 16(d) invites each legislature to insert a reference to its own enactment of "Section 3–302(a), 7–501, or 9–308" of the UCC. The last is the predecessor to UCC 9–330.

How should a transferable record be classified for purposes of attachment and perfection under Article 9? By definition a transferable record is not a writing. It would seem to follow that a transferable record cannot be an "instrument." See UCC 9–102(a)(47). Rather, a transferable record would appear to be an account, payment intangible, or part of electronic chattel paper. If this analysis is correct, then (depending on how Article 9 classifies a particular transferable record) even if a secured party has control of the transferable record, its security interest may be unperfected. See UETA 3(b)(2) (making UETA inapplicable to the extent a transaction is governed by Article 9) & Comment 6. Is this a sensible result?

(3) Electronic Documents. As with electronic notes, an electronic document of title will become a "transferable record," to which UETA applies, only if the issuer expressly agrees that it is to be considered a transferable record. See UETA 16(a)(2). However, Revised Article 7 applies to any document of title stored in an electronic medium.

"Control" of an electronic document under Revised Article 7 serves the function of indorsement and possession of a tangible document and so is a method of perfecting a security interest in an electronic document. See UCC 9–314(a) (2003). Filing is an alternative method of perfection. See UCC 9–310(a). R7–106 sets forth a general test for control of an electronic document: "A person has control of an electronic document of title if a system employed for evidencing the transfer of interests in the electronic document reliably establishes that person as the person to which the electronic document was issued or transferred." R7–106(a). It also provides a safe harbor, which derives from the definition of "control" in UETA. Compare R7–106(b) with UETA 16(c).

Negotiation of an electronic document is accomplished by "delivery," R7–501(b)(1), which is the voluntary transfer of control. UCC 1–201(b)(15). A person in control of an electronic document is its holder. R1–201(b)(21)(C). Like a tangible document of title, an electronic document may be duly negotiated to a HDWANDOTHBDN, who thereby acquires priority over most competing claims to the document and the goods it covers. R7–501(a)(5), (b)(3) (explaining when a document is "duly negotiated"); R7–502(a) (rights acquired by due negotiation); UCC 9–331 (nothing in Article 9 defeats the rights of a HDWANDOTHBDN, whose security interest normally has priority over other perfected security interests).

Problem 6.2.5. In the setting of the automobile financing Prototype (Chapter 3, Section 1, supra), Firstbank has a perfected (by filing) security interest in all of the existing and after-acquired inventory of Main Motors. As in the Prototype, (i) the security interest secures purchase-money advances made to enable Main to acquire its automobile inventory, and (ii) Main sold an automobile to Lee Abel, who signed the Instalment Sale Contract ("ISC") (Form 3.6) granting Main a security interest in the automobile to secure payment of the balance of its price and related charges. However, unlike the Prototype, the Dealer Inventory Security Agreement

(Form 3.2) signed by Main Motors covered only "inventory" (i.e., it did not contain subparagraphs 5(b), (c), and (d) of Form 3.2 in the Prototype).

Instead of assigning the ISC to Firstbank, Main assigned the ISC to a third party, Secondbank, which paid Main $18,380 and took possession of the ISC without having conducted a search of the UCC filing records and without knowledge of Firstbank's security interest. Firstbank gave no additional value in connection with the ISC.

(a) What type of collateral is the ISC? See UCC 9–102(a)(2), (11), (47), (61).

(b) Main enters bankruptcy six months after the assignment to Secondbank. As we shall see in Chapter 7, infra, security interests that are unperfected when the debtor enters bankruptcy can be avoided (nullified). Will Firstbank's security interest in the ISC be avoided in Main's bankruptcy? See BC 544(a); UCC 9–317(a)(2); UCC 9–315(c), (d); UCC 9–310(a); UCC 9–312(a); UCC 9–301(1); UCC 9–501(a). Is Secondbank's security interest avoidable? See BC 544(a); UCC 1–201(b)(35)] (2d sentence) [F1–201(37)]; UCC 9–109(a)(3); UCC 9–317(a)(2); UCC 9–310(a), (b)(6); UCC 9–313(a).

(c) In the Prototype, Firstbank (Main Motors' assignee) perfected its security interest in Abel's Chevrolet by a notation on the certificate of title. See UCC 9–311(a), (b); Form 3.8, supra. Would Firstbank's failure to perfect a security interest in the car affect your answers to part (b)? Would it have any other potential consequences for Firstbank or Secondbank?

(d) Who has priority in the ISC if Firstbank's security agreement does not mention collateral like the ISC? See UCC 9–330; PEB Commentary No. 8 (discussing the predecessor to UCC 9–330).

(e) Would the answer to part (d) be different if:

(i) Firstbank's security agreement explicitly covers such collateral (as in Form 3.2, ¶ 5(b), supra)?

(ii) Before taking the assignment, Secondbank searches the public records and discovers Firstbank's financing statement, which covers "inventory, accounts and chattel paper"?

(iii) Secondbank knows that Firstbank is financing Main's inventory? See UCC 1–202(b) [F1–201(25)] (definition of "knowledge"); UCC 9–102(a)(43).

(iv) Secondbank knows that Firstbank is financing Main's inventory and that Main is obligated to turn over all chattel paper to Firstbank? See UCC 1–202(b) [F1–201(25)] (definition of "knowledge"); UCC 9–102(a)(43).

(v) Secondbank has a first priority purchase-money security interest in the particular automobile sold by Main to Abel; Secondbank pays Main $18,380 for the ISC, $15,000 of which is applied toward Main's debt for the loan that Secondbank previously made to enable Main to acquire that automobile and $3,380 of which is credited to Main's checking account? See UCC 9–324(b); UCC 9–330(a), (b); UCC 9–102(a)(57); UCC 9–330(e).

(vi) Secondbank has a first priority purchase-money security interest in the particular automobile sold by Main to Abel and claims the ISC under an after-acquired property clause in its security agreement without advancing any additional funds against it? See UCC 9–324(b); UCC 9–330(a), (b); UCC 9–102(a)(57); UCC 9–330(e).

NOTES ON PURCHASERS OF CHATTEL PAPER

(1) Classification of Chattel Paper as a Separate Type of Collateral. Under Former Article 9, the categories of "account," "instrument," and "general intangible" were sufficiently broad to include all kinds of rights to payment that are taken as collateral. Nevertheless, the drafters created yet another, separate type of collateral, "chattel paper." See Former 9–105(1)(b) (definition of "chattel paper"). Why? The short answer may be that, at the time Former Article 9 was drafted, written payment obligations that were secured by (or represented leases of) specific goods received special treatment by professional providers of financing. Unlike unsecured accounts or general intangibles, which may not be evidenced by a writing, chattel paper frequently was (and still is) physically delivered to the purchaser. To accommodate those financing patterns in which the dealer (debtor) retained possession of the paper, the drafters thought it best that filing, as well as possession, be a permissible means of perfection. See F9–304(1) & Comment 1; Former 9–305. (Compare the treatment of instruments that are not part of chattel paper, as to which the filing of a financing statement was of no consequence under Former Article 9.) Finally, the drafters saw the need for special treatment to sort out priorities in certain situations on a basis other than the generally applicable first-to-file-or-perfect rule of Former 9–312(5). See Former 9–308.

For the same reasons, Revised Article 9 classifies chattel paper separately from other rights to payment. See UCC 9–102(a)(11) (definition of "chattel paper"). Perfection may be achieved by filing a financing statement or taking possession of the chattel paper. See UCC 9–312(a); UCC 9–313(a); Problem 3.3.23, p. 180, supra. And as discussed more fully in Note (3) below, Revised Article 9 provides a special rule that affords priority under certain circumstances to a person who is not the first to file or perfect. See UCC 9–330. Revised Article 9 also expands the definition of chattel paper to accommodate transactions dealing with both specific goods and software closely associated with the goods. See UCC 9–102(a)(11). It thereby expands the class of transactions eligible for the special priority rule.

(2) The Setting: Circumstances Leading to Purchase of Chattel Paper by a Person Other Than the Inventory Secured Party. Consider the setting of the automobile financing Prototype in Chapter 3, Section 1, supra. Firstbank has financed the purchase of automobile inventory delivered to Main Motors. Firstbank's perfected security interest will extend to all proceeds of the automobile inventory, such as the chattel paper (the Instalment Sale Contract, Form 3.6, supra) generated by the sale to Lee Abel. See UCC 9–315(a)(2), (c). In this setting, the parties often establish a course of business dealing (sometimes expressed in writing, but often resting on oral understanding) under which the provider of inventory financing (e.g., Firstbank) purchases the chattel paper and shares with the dealer (e.g., Main Motors) part of the handsome return from the buyers' finance charges.

In many cases the security agreement covering inventory prohibits the debtor from giving a security interest in any of the collateral (including chattel paper and other proceeds) to another lender. See Form 3.2, ¶¶ 11(c) and (d), supra. Nevertheless, debtors such as Main Motors sometimes may stray from this arrangement and assign chattel paper to another purchaser. What would lead Main Motors to do this? One possibility is that the other purchaser (Secondbank) offers Main a larger share of the finance charges to be paid by Lee Abel and the other account debtors. Although the assignment of Abel's Instalment Sale Contract to Secondbank violates Firstbank's security agreement, Firstbank probably would not be seriously concerned—as long as Main uses the funds received from Secondbank to repay the inventory loan made by Firstbank.

A second possibility is that Main Motors faces a financial crisis. Rent or payroll obligations must be met, but Main Motors is short of cash and its credit is exhausted; Main may face an immediate shutdown and bankruptcy unless it can get some extra cash to "tide it over." If Main assigns chattel paper to Firstbank, all or most what Main receives will be credited against Main's inventory loan debt to Firstbank, as in the Prototype. See Chapter 3, Section 1(G), supra. Assignments to Secondbank during this perceived emergency, however, produce *cash*. Main, of course, may hope that Firstbank does not check on which cars are on hand at Main's lot and discover that Main is "out of trust." Main well may believe that it soon can raise enough cash from other sources to meet its obligations to Firstbank.

It is impossible to know what portion of the deviations from arrangements to turn over the chattel paper to the inventory secured party springs from such financial crises. Certainly that factor seems to be present in the cases that lead to litigation. When a debtor receives a better deal from another secured party and uses the cash to repay the inventory secured party, the latter may be disappointed at losing the return on the chattel paper. And the latter may even refuse to deal further with the debtor. But that development is not likely to lead to litigation.

Bear in mind these two settings while considering the priority rules discussed in Note (3), which follows.

(3) Conflicting Priorities in Chattel Paper: Inventory Secured Party Claiming Chattel Paper as Proceeds versus Subsequent Purchasers of the Chattel Paper. UCC 9–330 provides strong protection for a purchaser who gives new value and takes possession of chattel paper in good faith and in the ordinary course of its business. Subsection (b) gives the purchaser seniority over an earlier-in-time, perfected security interest in chattel paper if the purchaser acts "without knowledge that the purchase violates the rights of the secured party." UCC 9–330(b). (This standard applies also to purchasers of instruments who seek special priority. See UCC 9–330(d); Note (1), p. 415, supra.) Recall that "knowledge" means "actual knowledge." UCC 1–202(b) [F1–201(25)] (definition of "knowledge"). UCC 9–330(f) contains a rule that imputes knowledge for purposes of subsection (b): if chattel paper indicates that it has been assigned to an identified secured party other than the purchaser, a purchaser of the chattel paper ipso facto has knowledge that the purchase violates the rights of the secured party. This rule reflects the common, longstanding practice whereby those who finance chattel paper and who wish to preserve the priority of their interest in chattel paper place a "legend" on the paper to indicate that it has been assigned. See UCC 9–330, Comment 5.[2]

What if a purchaser *did* know, at the time it gave value and took possession of the chattel paper, "that the purchase violates the rights of a secured party"? Or, what if the purchaser's knowledge is a disputed issue of fact? Subsection (a) of UCC 9–330 may give the purchaser yet another card to play. Notwithstanding the existence or assertion of knowledge, the purchaser can achieve priority over a competing security interest "which is claimed merely as proceeds of inventory subject to a security interest" if "the chattel paper does not indicate that it has been assigned to an identified assignee other than the purchaser." UCC 9–330(a).

The requirements for achieving priority as a purchaser of chattel paper under UCC 9–330(a) or (b) are different from and more stringent than the analogous requirements in UCC 9–330(d) for a purchaser of an instrument. A purchaser of an instrument need not take possession "in the ordinary course of the purchaser's business," nor need the purchaser give "new value"; for instruments, any value, even old value, will do. These differences reflect the perception that, unlike the purchase of notes, the financing of chattel paper is practiced only by specialized, professional financial institutions.

Some of the issues involved in the application of UCC 9–330 to purchases of chattel paper are considered in the remainder of this Note.

When Is a Security Interest "Claimed Merely as Proceeds"? As the Comments to UCC 9–330 explain:

Like former 9–308, this section does not elaborate upon the phrase "merely as proceeds." For an elaboration, see PEB Commentary No. 8.

Please study Issue I of Commentary No. 8 now. If, under the facts of the automobile financing Prototype, Main Motors had sold the car to Lee Abel without consulting Firstbank, Firstbank's security interest in the Abel's

---

2.   The presence of a legend on an instrument likewise will prevent a subsequent purchaser from acquiring priority over an earlier perfected security interest. See UCC 9–330(d), (f). However, perhaps because Former Article 9 did not contemplate long-term perfection of a security interest in an instrument without the secured party's taking possession, the practice of placing a "legend" on instruments has not developed.

chattel paper would appear to be one "claimed merely as proceeds." According to that Commentary, the fact that the security agreement covers chattel paper as original collateral (see Form 3.2, ¶ 5(b)) would not, alone, be sufficient to make the transaction more than a mere proceeds claim. However, in the actual Prototype transaction Firstbank did more; it made a specific advance of funds to Main Motors against the chattel paper. According to PEB Commentary No. 8, even less direct reliance on the chattel paper would permit an inventory lender to claim a security interest that is not a mere proceeds claim. (Because Firstbank itself provided the inventory financing in the Prototype, the assignment of the chattel paper to Firstbank did not implicate the priority contest envisioned by UCC 9–330.)

What Constitutes "Knowledge That the Purchase Violates the Rights of the Secured Party"? As mentioned above, one who purchases chattel paper or an instrument bearing an indication that the paper is subject to a security interest "has knowledge that the purchase violates the rights of the Secured Party" for purposes of the priority rules in UCC 9–330(b) and (d). UCC 9–330(f). Suppose that the purchaser knows of a security interest in the assignor's inventory and also knows of the legal rule that a security interest continues in proceeds (UCC 9–315(a)(2)). Would the purchaser have the requisite knowledge to disqualify it from priority under UCC 9–330 (b) or (d)? We seriously doubt it. Knowledge that the paper or instrument generally is subject to a security interest is a far cry from knowledge that the purchase violates the rights of the holder of that interest. Recall that questions of this kind do not arise in the normal priority contest between secured parties under the first-to-file-or-perfect rule of UCC 9–322(a), under which knowledge is not material. See Note (1), p. 244, supra. However, you also may recall that even though knowledge may be irrelevant to the application of the first-to-file-or-perfect rule, entering into a transaction with knowledge that it is *wrongful*—i.e., with knowledge that the taking of an interest in another party's collateral violates its agreement with the debtor—may give rise to adverse consequences: In appropriate cases the court may invoke one of several extra-UCC bases for rearranging priorities or may impose tort liability on the wrongdoer. See Note (5), p. 246, supra; UCC 1–103(b) [F1–103].

Consider the position of a purchaser who qualifies for priority over the inventory secured party under UCC 9–330(a) or (b), notwithstanding the purchaser's knowledge that the chattel paper is subject to a security interest. Is the purchaser's position impregnable? Is there any ground for an assault by the inventory secured party whose collateral gave rise to the chattel paper? It might be interesting to know whether second-in-time purchasers typically would consult with the inventory secured party in this situation, notwithstanding that these purchasers appear to enjoy priority under UCC 9–330. Is there an easy way for the purchaser to ensure that the cash will get to the inventory secured party? (What about a check made payable jointly to the assignor and the inventory secured party?) If consultation or joint payment were normal (or normal decent) practice, is there any basis for an attack by the inventory secured party if the purchaser fails to follow that practice? Is there so little substance for such an argument by the inventory secured party that you would advise the purchaser to purchase the paper without taking such steps? What would the purchaser gain if it follows your advice to purchase without consultation or joint payment? What would the purchaser lose if you are wrong?

To qualify under UCC 9–330(a) or (b) the purchaser must act "in good faith." In the setting of the preceding paragraph, is there an argument that, even in the absence of disqualifying "guilty" knowledge, a purchaser who fails to consult the inventory secured party or fails to undertake a UCC filing search acts in bad faith? Comment 6 to UCC 9–330 suggests a negative answer: "[A] purchaser of chattel paper under this section is not required as a matter of good faith to make a search in order to determine the existence of prior security interests."

Now consider the position of a purchaser who not only knows that the chattel paper is subject to a security interest but also knows "that the purchase violates the rights of the secured party." The purchaser would not qualify for priority over the inventory secured party under UCC 9–330(b), of course; but if the inventory secured party claims the chattel paper "merely as proceeds," would the purchaser with such wrongful knowledge nonetheless qualify for priority under UCC 9-330(a), which does not by its terms require the purchaser to be free of wrongful knowledge? We think not; such a purchaser surely would not be acting in good faith. If we are correct, then it essentially makes no difference whether subsection (a) or (b) applies to any given case.

Taking Possession: Multiple Signed Counterparts; Master Agreements and Schedules. Suppose that in the automobile financing Prototype transaction Lee Abel signed three identical counterparts of the Instalment Sale Contract and Main Motors received only two of them (Abel keeping the third). Main then delivered only one of the counterparts to Secondbank, which did not file, and Main retained the other counterpart. Is Secondbank's security interest perfected? Has Secondbank "take[n] possession" for purposes of UCC 9–330? In order to take possession for purposes of UCC 9–330 (and UCC 9–313), must a purchaser take possession of *all* signed originals of the writings comprising chattel paper?

These problems are compounded when parties to a chattel paper transaction enter into a **master agreement** (typical in the equipment leasing field) that contains general terms and conditions (inspections, maintenance and repairs, risk of loss, default, and the like) but makes no mention of any specific goods. The master agreement typically contemplates that the parties will enter into separate **schedules** from time to time. The schedules incorporate the terms of the master agreement and supplement the master agreement by specifying the goods that are to be leased or sold, the amount and timing of payments, and the like. What writing or writings comprise the chattel paper?

The court was forced to confront all of these questions in In re Funding Systems Asset Management Corp., 111 B.R. 500 (Bkrtcy.W.D.Pa.1990).

Although the court stated that chattel paper was comprised of both a master agreement and its schedules, it held that, under Former 9–305, perfection of a security interest could be achieved only by taking possession of a *signed original* of a *schedule*. "It was not the practice in the industry to require one seeking financing for the purchase of computer equipment identified in an equipment schedule to deliver the original master lease along with the equipment schedule." Another court has reached the same result on the perfection question. See In re ICS Cybernetics, Inc., 123 B.R. 467 (Bkrtcy.N.D.N.Y.1989) (master agreement did not constitute monetary obligation or lease of specific goods; intent of parties, as evidenced by language in documents, indicated that equipment schedule alone constituted chattel paper), affirmed without opinion 123 B.R. 480 (N.D.N.Y.1990).

Where multiple counterparts of signed original schedules were involved, however, the *Funding Systems Asset Management* court determined that the security interests were *un*perfected when the debtor retained possession of a signed original of a schedule, even though the secured party also had possession of such an original.

> What really mattered in determining whether or not [Secured Party] had perfected its security interests in all of the other challenged leases was whether or not Debtor possessed an original of the equipment schedules for that particular challenged lease. If Debtor possessed an original equipment schedule, then [Secured Party] had not perfected its security interest by virtue of its possession of the chattel paper which it retained. If, on the other hand, Debtor did not possess an original equipment schedule, then [Secured Party] had perfected its security interest by possession.

111 B.R. at 519. Presumably the court would have taken the same approach if the issue had arisen under Former 9–308.

There are good reasons why more than one party may wish to have an original, signed copy of writings comprising chattel paper (although in practice one *never* sees more than one signed promissory note, even if the note is non-negotiable). Does Revised Article 9 explain which of the originals the secured party must possess to perfect its security interest? Does it explain whether the master agreement, the schedules, or both constitute the chattel paper? If not, would you rely on *Funding Systems Asset Management*, even though it was decided under Former Article 9?

Suppose that you are charged with drafting documentation that will (i) avoid the problems just described; (ii) allow Abel, Main Motors, and Secondbank each to retain a signed original; and (iii) permit Secondbank to acquire a perfected security interest with priority under UCC 9–330. What would you write? Would each counterpart be identical? See UCC 9–330, Comment 4. See also the legend "ORIGINAL TO BANK" on the reverse side of the Instalment Sale Contract, Form 3.6, supra.

(4) Electronic Chattel Paper. As we have seen, UETA 16 enables a second-in-time purchaser of an electronic negotiable note ("transferable record") to achieve priority over an earlier-perfected security interest by taking control of the collateral. See Note (2), p. 417, supra. Revised Article 9 affords a similar possibility with respect to "electronic chattel paper"—the oxymoron with which the drafters named the electronic equivalent of chattel paper. See UCC 9–102(a)(31) (defining "electronic chattel paper"). (Revised Article 9 refers to paper chattel paper as "tangible chattel paper," which it defines in UCC 9–102(a)(78).)

Electronic installment sale contracts and electronic leases are uncommon. Nevertheless, the drafters of Revised Article 9 sought to minimize the differences in the legal consequences that otherwise would result from the parties' choice of the medium used for chattel paper. To that end Revised Article 9 introduced a new concept: "control" of electronic chattel paper. See UCC 9–105.[3] "Control" of electronic chattel paper serves the same functions as possession of tangible chattel paper. A person who takes control of electronic chattel paper, like a person who takes possession of tangible chattel paper, may qualify for priority over earlier-perfected security interests under UCC 9–330; control also can serve as a substitute for an authenticated security agreement and as a method of perfecting a security interest. See UCC 9–203(b); UCC 9–313(a); UCC 9–314(a). The definition of "control" is flexible, to accommodate future developments in the business practices surrounding electronic chattel paper.

Why should Article 9 treat electronic chattel paper differently from other rights to payment that are evidenced by electronic, rather than paper, records (e.g., accounts)? Why should a secured party who holds a perfected-by-filing security interest in electronic chattel paper be faced with the risk of having its security interest subordinated to a subsequent purchaser who has control? One explanation may be that, by enabling a later-in-time purchaser of chattel paper to take priority, the non-temporal priority rules in UCC 9–330 may make it more likely that dealers will find purchasers for their paper; the increased number of potential purchasers, in turn, probably increases the ability of dealers to offer purchase-money credit to buyers and lessees of goods.

As we have seen, the control provisions of UETA do not apply an electronic record unless the issuer expressly agrees that the record is to be considered a "transferable record." See UETA 16(a)(2). For this reason, a note issued in paper form cannot be converted into a transferable record; the issuer would not be the issuer of an electronic record. See id., Comment 2. In contrast, nothing in Article 9 prevents the conversion of tangible chattel paper into electronic chattel paper. Rather, the Comments expressly contemplate this possibility. See UCC 9–102, Comment 5.b.

---

3.   UCC 9–105 is the source of the "control" concept of both UETA and the federal E–SIGN act. The means for obtaining "control" of electronic chattel paper and transferable records are completely different from, and should not be confused with, the means for obtaining "control" of investment property or a deposit account. (Control of investment property and deposit accounts is discussed in Sections 3 and 4, infra.)

(5) Lease Chattel Paper. The foregoing focuses for the most part on chattel paper consisting of a record evidencing a payment obligation secured by specific goods. Yet the definition of "chattel paper" in UCC 9–102(a)(11) also includes *leases* of specific goods. One kind of recurring problem associated with assignments of personal property lease chattel paper—the problem associated with the practice of using master leases supplemented by schedules—is discussed above Note (3). See also UCC 9-330, Comment 11 (discussing the relationship between lease chattel paper and the lessor's residual interest in the leased goods). A more detailed consideration of issues relating to lease chattel paper appears in Chapter 8, Section 2, infra.

(6) Realty Paper. "Chattel paper" is limited to records relating to specific chattels (goods). A record or records evidencing a monetary obligation and a security interest in real property, e.g., a promissory note and mortgage, may serve as collateral under Article 9; however, the records would not be chattel paper. For a discussion of security interests in mortgage notes and similar obligations, see Chapter 8, Section 3(B), infra. Article 9 does not apply to a security interest in a lease of real property. See UCC 9–109(d)(11), discussed in Chapter 5, Section 4, supra.

————

UCC 9–330(a) and (b) address priority conflicts between a chattel paper purchaser and an inventory secured party as to the *chattel paper*. Priority conflicts also may arise between these two parties as to the *goods* that are the subject of the chattel paper. The following Problem raises a priority conflict of this kind. UCC 9–330(c)(2) resolves the conflict, and Comments 9, 10, and 11 explain the operation of that subsection.

Problem 6.2.6. In the setting of the Prototype, Main Motors sold Abel's chattel paper to Secondbank. Under UCC 9–330, Secondbank achieved priority over Firstbank's security interest in the chattel paper (whether as proceeds or as original collateral). Having perfected by possession, Secondbank did not file a financing statement against the chattel paper. Abel's new Chevrolet is a true "lemon." Abel revoked acceptance of the car, returned it to Main's lot, and walked away.[4]

(a) Does Firstbank have a security interest in the Chevrolet? If so, is the security interest perfected? See UCC 9–315(a)(2); UCC 9–102(a)(64); UCC 9–330, Comments 9 & 10.

(b) Does Secondbank have a security interest in the Chevrolet? See UCC 9–315(a)(2); UCC 9–102(a)(64); UCC 9–330, Comments 9 & 10.

(c) Which security interest is senior? See UCC 9–330(c) & Comments 9 & 10.

————

4.   Recall that in a consumer transaction the assignment of chattel paper must be *subject to* the buyer's defenses. See the discussion of the FTC's "holder in due course" rule in Section 1(F) and Chapter 1, Section 4, supra.

SECTION 3. SECURITY INTERESTS IN INVESTMENT PROPERTY

INTRODUCTORY NOTE

In this Section we consider security interests in stocks, bonds, and similar property. Our focus will be on financing at the "retail" level; we will not address the special rules that apply when the debtor is a broker or other securities intermediary.

The law governing security interests in investment property is particularly complex (even by Article 9 standards). Part of the complexity derives from the fact that investment property can be held in two different ways: directly, as where the debtor is the holder of a security (stock) certificate registered in the debtor's name, and indirectly, through a broker or other securities intermediary. (The patterns of holding investment property are described in greater detail in Notes (1) and (2) on p. 430, infra.) Where investment property is held through a broker, enforcement of a security interest is likely to implicate the broker; a secured party who relies on collateral of this kind would be remiss in failing to take into consideration not only the rules governing attachment, perfection, and priority but also the rules governing the broker's obligations with respect to the collateral. (We have seen related issues with respect to receivables. See Notes (3) and (4), p. 406, supra.) Finally, part of the complexity derives from the drafters' desire to afford flexibility to secured parties. A secured transaction in investment property—particularly investment property that is held through an intermediary—gives rise to a relatively large variety of risks; the governing law permits a secured party to decide which risks to protect against and which risks to accept. (Here, again, we have seen related issues. See Problem 3.3.21, p. 180, supra.)

Problem 6.3.1. Drahman is the owner of 1,000 shares of General Motors common stock. The stock certificates, in registered form (see UCC 8–102(a)(13)), are in Drahman's safe deposit box. On July 1 Drahman borrowed $10,000 from Lender and signed a security agreement granting Lender a security interest in "all my General Motors common stock." On July 15 Lean, one of Drahman's judgment creditors, acquired an execution lien on the stock (see UCC 8–112).

(a) Who has the superior claim to the stock? See UCC 9–317(a)(2); UCC 9–102(a)(49); UCC 8–102(a)(15), (a)(4), (a)(16); UCC 9–312(e); UCC 9–102(a)(57); Note (3) on Security Interests in Investment Property, infra.

(b) What result if the execution lien arose on August 1?

(c) What steps could Lender have taken to prevail in part (b)? See UCC 9–312(a); UCC 9–313(a); UCC 8–301(a); UCC 9–314(a); UCC 9–106(a); UCC 8–106(b); UCC 8–102(a)(11); Security Agreement § 4.3 (Form 6.2, supra). If more than one method of perfection is available, which method would you recommend? Include in your analysis the following considerations:

(i) the cost of perfection.

(ii) the risk of existing and future competing claims (including security interests and claims of future buyers). See UCC 9–328(1), (5); UCC 8–302; UCC 8–303; UCC 8–304(d); Note (3), p. 191, supra; Note (4) on Security Interests in Investment Property, infra.

(iii) the possibility that Drahman may default on the loan. See UCC 9–609; UCC 9–610; UCC 8–401(a)(2), (a)(3); UCC 8–304(d); UCC 8–307 & Comment 1; Note (3), p. 191, supra.

(iv) the possibility that General Motors might declare a dividend. See UCC 9–102(a)(64)(B); UCC 9–315(c), (d); Problem 3.5.6, p. 212, supra.

Problem 6.3.2. A stock certificate covering 50,000 shares of General Motors common stock was issued to and is registered in the name of the Depository Trust Company (actually, in the name of "Cede & Co.," DTC's nominee); the certificate is located in DTC's vault in New York City. DTC's books show that it is holding 7,000 of these shares for Broker and the remaining 43,000 shares for other brokers and banks who are participants in DTC. Broker's records show that it is "holding" 1,000 shares for Drabco, Inc., a Kentucky corporation, and 6,000 for other customers of Broker.

On May 1 Drabco borrowed $10,000 from Lender and signed a written security agreement describing the collateral as "1,000 shares of General Motors common stock in my account with Broker." At the time, Drabco's account contained only 1,000 shares. The loan was used to acquire business equipment. The same day Lender filed a proper financing statement covering the collateral. On June 1 Lean acquired a judicial lien on everything in the account.

(a) What UCC-defined type of collateral does the security agreement cover? See UCC 8–102(a)(17) & Comment 17; UCC 8–501; UCC 8–102(a)(9) & Comment 9, (a)(15), (a)(4); UCC 9–102(a)(49); Note (2) on Security Interests in Investment Property, infra.

(b) As between Lender and Lean, who has the superior claim to the stock? See UCC 9–317(a)(2); UCC 9–310(a); UCC 9–312(a). Which state's law governs this priority dispute? See UCC 9–305.

(c) In which office should the financing statement have been filed? See UCC 9–305(c)(1).

(d) What result in part (b) if the financing statement covered "securities"? (Assume that the filing was authorized.) See UCC 9–317(a)(2); UCC 9–310(a); UCC 9–504; UCC 9–108.

(e) What result in part (b) if the security agreement and financing statement covered "all securities accounts now or hereafter owned by me" and Drabco's account contained 1,000 shares of General Motors and 500 shares of AT & T on June 1? See UCC 9–203(b), (h); UCC 9–308(f); UCC 9–108. What result if the borrower were Drabco's president, D.D. Drabek, who created the security interest to secure a loan that was used to buy home furniture? See UCC 9–108(e); UCC 9–102(a)(26).

(f) Drabco, in violation of the security agreement, instructed Broker on May 5 to sell 600 shares of the General Motors stock. Broker dutifully followed Drabco's instructions and sold the shares through the stock exchange. Is Broker liable to Lender for having sold Lender's collateral? See UCC 8–507; UCC 8–102(a)(8); UCC 8–107(a); UCC 8–102(a)(7); UCC 8–107(b). What could Lender have done to protect itself? See Security Agreement § 4.3 (Form 6.2, supra).

(g) Drabco defaulted, and Lender instructed Broker to transfer 1,000 shares of General Motors common stock from Drabco's securities account to Lender's. What should Broker do? See UCC 8–507; UCC 8–107(a), (b). What could Lender have done to protect itself?

(h) Assume Lender did not file a financing statement. Instead, on May 1 Lender sent a copy of the signed security agreement by overnight courier to Broker. The following day Broker signed an acknowledgment indicating that it had received the envelope. As between Lender and Lean, who has the superior claim to the stock? See UCC 9–317(a)(2); UCC 9–310(a); UCC 9–312(a); UCC 9–310(b)(8); UCC 9–314(a); UCC 9–106(a); UCC 8–106; UCC 9–313(a), (c).

(i) Assume Lender filed a proper financing statement on May 1. On June 5 Drabco borrowed $5,000 from Broker under the "margin loan" provisions of Drabco's account agreement. Under that agreement, Drabco agreed that Broker would have a security interest in "all securities now or hereafter in my account with you" to secure any **margin loans**. Broker did not file a financing statement. Six months later, Lean acquired an execution lien on the securities account. As between Broker and Lean, who has the superior claim to the securities account? As between Broker and Lender? See UCC 9–317(a)(2); UCC 9–310(a), (b)(8); UCC 9–314(a); UCC 8–106(e); UCC 8–102(a)(7), (a)(14).

(j) The facts are as in part (i), except that on May 1 Broker agreed with Drabco and Lender that Broker would comply with Lender's instructions concerning the account without further consent of Drabco. As between Broker and Lender, who has the superior claim to the securities account? See UCC 8–106; UCC 9–328. What should the holder of the subordinate security interest have done to achieve priority? See UCC 9–339.

NOTES ON SECURITY INTERESTS IN INVESTMENT PROPERTY

(1) How Securities Are Held and Transferred. The rules governing the creation and perfection of security interests in stocks, bonds, and other investment property reflect the ways in which investment property is held and transferred. Traditionally, securities such as stocks and bonds were transferred by physically delivering the paper certificates that represented the equity or debt. The centralization of trading into markets, such as the New York Stock Exchange, facilitated this method of transfer. By the late 1960's, however, the volume and speed of transactions in the securities markets reached proportions that posed a crisis for the customary processes of transfer. This "paperwork crunch" generated important proposals to provide a legal framework for transactions in "certificateless" shares. These proposals and a supporting study were embodied in a Report issued on September 15, 1975, by the Committee on Stock Certificates of the ABA Section on Corporation, Banking and Business Law. The Report proposed amendments to the Model Business Corporation Act and also set forth proposed revisions of portions of the UCC—principally in Article 8 and related sections of Article 9.

The Report provided a thorough, 60–page analysis of then-current practices for transfer of certificates and of then-current problems that called for legislative solution. The Report identified the central problem as follows:

> In an era when electronic communication was unknown and buyers and sellers traded stock interests in face-to-face confrontations under a buttonwood tree, the physical delivery of a piece of paper from seller to buyer was a far quicker and safer means of transfer than the alternative—the seller's instruction to the corporation to make a transfer in its records and the corporation's subsequent acknowledgment to the buyer that the transfer had been made. Indeed, if the seller demanded contemporaneous consideration, perhaps only a journey by both parties to the corporation's office could have satisfied his objective.

> In today's securities markets, however, the world has been turned inside-out. In the typical market transaction, the buyer and seller are unknown to each other and may be geographically separated by thousands of miles. On the other hand, the marvels of electronic communication make it possible to transmit instructions and acknowledge their receipt in a matter of minutes. The physical delivery of a piece of paper has become the time-consuming unsafe process, passing, as it must, through the hands of intermediaries and spanning, as it might, an entire continent. Thus, the negotiable stock certificate, an instrument almost indispensable in the environment in which it grew, has become a serious impediment to the very transaction it was designed to promote.

> Notwithstanding the fact that the principal reason for its creation has ceased to exist, the negotiable stock certificate has become so firmly entrenched that an elaborate legal and operational structure has been built on its foundation. The relationships between buyers and sellers, donors and donees, corporations and their shareholders, fiduciaries and beneficiaries, taxing authorities and taxpayers have been delineated on the basic premise that a particular stock certificate uniquely represents every stock interest. The location of that certificate, the information noted thereon, in whose custody it reposes are all important and frequently crucial facts. As will be noted, these facts, in the current environment, often have little bearing on the solution of problems they were originally intended to resolve. In an environment without certificates, these facts will not exist and alternative solutions will have to be provided.

Report, ABA Stock Certificate Committee 2–3 (1975).

To address this situation, the scope of Article 8 was extended in 1977 to include securities that are not represented by a certificate, or "uncertificated" securities. The securities markets, however, could not wait for a legislative solution and developed a practical one. As a result, the "environment without certificates" that the ABA Committee envisioned in its 1975 report never appeared. Instead, stock certificates and bonds often are issued in the name of, and held in a warehouse by, a central depository. Each depository maintains records showing the person on whose behalf it holds each of the securities in its possession. In most cases, the depository holds for other institutional participants in the securities markets, such as stockbrokers and banks. Each of these persons, in turn, maintains records showing the person on whose behalf it "holds" each of securities.

Consider the "simple" case in which the debtor maintains a securities account with Broker A (a "securities intermediary," see UCC 8–102(a)(14)) and wishes to use the securities in the account as collateral for a loan from the bank. The bank will be unlikely to take possession of securities themselves, because they are not likely to be in Broker A's possession. Rather, the securities are likely to in the possession of a depository (a special kind of securities intermediary called a "clearing corporation," see UCC 8–102(a)(5)), and registered in the name of the depository (or its nominee) on the books of the issuer. The depository's books may show Broker B as the owner. Records maintained by Broker B (another "securities intermediary"), in turn, show Broker A as owner, and Broker A's records show the debtor as owner. In other words, the depository is holding for Broker B, which is "holding" for Broker A, which is "holding" for the debtor. The situation becomes even more complex when one takes into account the fact that this chain is likely to be different for each type of security, or even for different quantities of the same issue of stock. Not only might different depositories and securities intermediaries be involved, but some of the securities intermediaries might be in possession of some of the securities.

Despite the fact that, in many markets, ownership of securities was transferred without moving security certificates from hand to hand, the 1977 amendments to Former Article 8 reflected the importance traditionally attached to possession of security certificates. The amendments treated the tiers of relationships among the securities intermediaries and their customers as a series of bailments and sub-bailments. Applying the statutory rules to actual practices in the securities markets was awkward at best and uncertain and impractical at worst. For example, the proper method for taking and perfecting of a security interest in securities "in" a securities account whose contents are likely to change was not nearly so clear as both debtors and secured parties would have liked. The difficulties were compounded when the securities account, as often is the case, contained cash balances as well as financial instruments (e.g., **bankers'** acceptances[1]) that may not have been "securities" and therefore could not have been perfected by the methods available with respect to property covered by the 1977 version of Article 8. The uncertain application of the 1977 amendments was thought to have contributed to the severity of the "market break" of October, 1987,[2] which led to worldwide efforts to insure that the legal regime was adequate to support the ever-increasing volume of trades. One outgrowth of these efforts was the promulgation of Revised UCC Article 8 in 1994.

(2) The Structure of Revised UCC Article 8; Securities; Security Entitlements. The structure of Revised Article 8 reflects the two prevailing patterns of holding and transferring securities and other investment property. Although Part 1 of Revised Article 8 contains rules applicable to each pattern, each of the other parts of the Article applies only to one. Each pattern has not only its own rules but also its own terminology.

Parts 2, 3, and 4 of Revised Article 8 reflect the traditional pattern of securities holding, in which the owner of the security has a direct relationship with the issuer. In the case of a "certificated security," i.e., one that is represented by a certificate, the person usually is specified on the security itself. See UCC 8–102(a)(4) (defining "certificated security"). For example, in Problem 6.3.1, Drahman holds a certificated security and has a direct relationship with General Motors; General Motors' records show Drahman as the stockholder. Likewise, in Problem 6.3.2, DTC holds a certificated security and has a direct relationship with GM. In the case of an "uncertificated security," the person having the direct relationship with the issuer is shown as the registered owner in the records of the issuer, but no certificate is issued to represent the stock. See UCC 8–102(a)(18) (defining "uncertificated security").

The interest of a person who holds investment property indirectly, through an intermediary, is treated differently from the interest of one who holds directly. Consider the facts of Problem 6.3.2. Drabco is the owner of the General Motors stock; as the owner, Drabco enjoys the right to vote for the board of directors and the right to receive any dividends that General Motors may declare. Yet Drabco has only an indirect relationship with the issuer, General Motors. Drabco holds through a securities intermediary, Broker, which in turn holds through its own securities intermediary, DTC. Part 5 of Article 8 applies to the relationship between Drabco and Broker and the relationship between Broker and DTC. The rights that Drabco enjoys against Broker and that Broker enjoys against DTC with respect to

---

1. A bankers' acceptance begins as a negotiable time draft drawn on a bank (something like a check that the bank is instructed to pay at a specified time in the future). When the bank accepts the draft, the bank becomes obligated to pay it when it becomes due. See UCC 3–409; UCC 3–413. There is a market for these bank obligations.

2. On October 19, 1987, the Dow Jones Industrial Average closed down 22.6% for the day and 36.7% from its closing high less than two months earlier. The number of shares traded was nearly double the previous record, which had been set the preceding week.

the GM stock are called a "security entitlement," and Drabco and Broker are "entitlement holders." See UCC 8–102(a)(18) (defining "security entitlement"); UCC 8–102(a)(7) (defining "entitlement holder"). The General Motors stock itself is a "financial asset." See UCC 8–102(a)(9).

Unlike Broker and Drabco, DTC has a direct relationship with General Motors; it is the stockholder of record. For this reason, DTC's interest in the General Motors stock is classified as a "security," see UCC 8–102(a)(15), and *not* a security entitlement. The interest of DTC in the General Motors stock is a "certificated security," because the stock is represented by a certificate. See UCC 8–102(a)(4). If DTC's interest were registered on General Motors' books but no certificate had been issued, DTC would "hold" an uncertificated security. Whether DTC holds a certificated or uncertificated security does not affect the characterization of Broker's or Drabco's interest in the General Motors stock; in either case, each has a security entitlement, not a security.

(3) Creation and Perfection of a Security Interest in Investment Property. The rules governing the transfer of interests (including security interests) in investment property turn on the distinction between transfers by persons who hold directly (i.e., transfers of a security, whether certificated and uncertificated) and transfers by persons who hold indirectly (i.e., transfers of a security entitlement). The failure to understand the distinction and the terminology used to draw it is likely to lead to confusion and error.

Revised Article 9 adopts the terminology that appears in Revised Article 8 and adds the generic term, "investment property." This term includes securities (both certificated and uncertificated) and security entitlements, as well as securities accounts, commodity contracts, and commodity accounts. See UCC 9–102(a)(49). To a limited extent, Revised Article 9 protects secured parties who use the wrong terminology. For example, because a security entitlement may be described by describing the underlying financial asset, "all debtor's securities" adequately describes all debtor's security entitlements with respect to securities. See UCC 9–108(d)(2). Moreover, Revised Article 9 facilitates taking a security interest in all security entitlements carried in a securities account by eliminating any need to describe each particular security entitlement and by providing that perfection as to the securities account automatically perfects as to each security entitlement carried in the account. See UCC 9–203(h) (attachment); UCC 9–308(f) (perfection).

Revised Article 9 provides two principal methods for perfecting a security interest in investment property—filing and control.[3] See UCC 9–312(a); UCC 9–314(a). As one might suspect, the meaning of "control" differs depending on whether the collateral is a certificated security, an uncertificated security, or a security entitlement. See UCC 9–104(a); UCC

---

3.   A security interest in investment property may be perfected automatically under limited circumstances. See UCC 9–309(b)(9)–(11). Temporary perfection may be available with respect to certificated securities. See UCC 9–312(e), (g).

8–106. In addition, a security interest in a certificated security may be perfected by taking delivery. See UCC 9–313(a); UCC 8–301(a). In the case of a certificated security, "delivery" occurs when the secured party acquires possession of the security certificate. UCC 8–301(a)(1).

As with respect to instruments and chattel paper, not all methods of perfection with respect to investment property are equal. Although perfection by any method will achieve priority over a subsequent judicial lien creditor, perfection by control affords priority over more different types of competing claims than does perfection by filing. See UCC 9–317(a)(2) (competing lien creditor); UCC 9–328 (competing secured parties). Of particular importance for our purposes is that a security interest perfected by control has priority over a security interest perfected by filing. See UCC 9–328(1). Perfection by control affords other benefits, as well. See UCC 8–106, Comment 7 (control carries with it "the ability to have the securities sold or transferred without further action by the transferor").

"Control" has a specialized meaning when applied to investment property; in determining the rights of a secured party having control, one must not resort to the vernacular meaning of the term. In particular, do not assume that a secured party's control of a securities entitlement ipso facto prevents the securities intermediary (e.g., broker) from obeying entitlement orders (orders with respect to the transfer or redemption of a financial asset in a securities account) originated by the debtor. A securities intermediary is obligated to obey entitlement orders issued by the entitlement holder. UCC 8–107(b)(1), (a)(3). The securities intermediary's agreement that it will comply with entitlement orders originated by the secured party without further consent by the debtor (entitlement holder) gives the secured party control. UCC 8–106(d)(2). However, if the debtor remains the entitlement holder, the secured party's control is not inconsistent with the debtor's retention of the right to trade the security entitlements. A secured party who satisfies the requirements for control has control, even if the entitlement holder retains the right to make substitutions for the security entitlement, to originate entitlement orders to the securities intermediary, or otherwise to deal with the security entitlement. See UCC 8–106(f).

Also, the fact that the secured party has control, and thus "the *ability* to have the securities sold or transferred without further action by the transferor," UCC 8–106, Comment 7 (emphasis added), does not necessarily mean that the secured party has the *right*, as against the debtor, to issue entitlement orders. The circumstances under which a secured party enjoys the right to issue entitlement orders is determined by the agreement of the debtor and secured party. See, e.g., Security Agreement § 4.3, Section 1(B), supra.

Just as not all methods of perfection are equal, so not all forms of control are equal. If a security interest in a security entitlement is granted by the entitlement holder to the entitlement holder's own securities intermediary, the securities intermediary automatically has control the security entitlement. See UCC 8–106(e). Such a security interest has priority over all conflicting security interests, regardless of when or by what method they were perfected. See UCC 9–328(3). What justifies affording this non-temporal priority to securities intermediaries? The credit extended by a securities intermediary typically is a **margin loan**, i.e., a loan typically used to acquire the collateral (security entitlement). For this reason, a priority analogous to purchase-money priority may be appropriate.

(4) Good–Faith Purchase of Securities and Security Entitlements. The preceding Note and Note (3) on page 191, supra, suggest some reasons why a secured party may not be indifferent to the method by which its security interest in a security is perfected: certain methods of perfection (e.g., control) afford greater priority than do other methods (e.g., delivery or filing); certain methods (control and delivery) facilitate enforcement of the security interest. The doctrine of good-faith purchase, as applied to securities, may afford another reason to prefer control as a method of perfection. A secured party who qualifies as a "protected purchaser" of a security not only acquires the rights in the security that the debtor had or had power to transfer but also acquires its interest in the security free of any adverse claim. See UCC 8–303(b). The concept of "protected purchaser" is analogous to those of "holder in due course" in UCC Article 3 and "holder to whom a negotiable document of title has been duly negotiated" in UCC Article 7. See generally Chapter 1, Sections 4 and 5, supra. Observe, however, that a protected purchaser need not be a "holder." Indeed, one can be a protected purchaser of an uncertificated security. See UCC 8–303(a). Observe also that the phrase "good faith" does not appear with reference to protected purchasers. See UCC 8–303(a) & Comment 4. Although one cannot be a "protected purchaser" of a security entitlement, a purchaser for value of a security entitlement typically takes free of adverse claims. See UCC 8–502; UCC 8–510(a).

(5) Federal Book–Entry Securities. For many years United States Treasury securities have been "book-entry" (i.e., uncertificated) securities. Proposals for revisions to the federal regulations governing Treasury securities in the late 1980's attracted intense interest and substantial criticism. Indeed, the debates over the appropriate legal structure for the transfer of Treasury securities (including transfers of security interests) was the principal catalyst that gave rise to the project leading to the 1994 revisions of UCC Article 8. Representatives of the Department of the Treasury participated in and closely observed the Article 8 revision process. It is not surprising, then, that the Department effectively adopted Revised Article 8 for Treasury securities. See 31 C.F.R. pt. 357. To summarize briefly, Treasury and other federal agency book-entry securities are transferred in an indirect system in which the Federal Reserve Banks maintain books on behalf of the federal government, as issuer. Participating banks, in turn, claim securities through their accounts with a Federal Reserve Bank, and other intermediaries (e.g., broker-dealers), in turn, have accounts with participating banks. At the bottom of this "tiered" system are the ultimate entitlement holders (i.e., the beneficial owners of the securities), who have accounts with either participating banks or other intermediaries.

The following excerpt provides an overview of the method by which the Treasury Department has deferred to Revised Article 8 for federal securities.

> At the federal level, the Department of the Treasury promulgated the final TRADES [i.e., Treasury/Reserve Automated Debt Entry System] regulations, which became effective on January 1, 1997. Substantially identical regulations were adopted by federal agencies responsible for the various government sponsored enterprises (GSEs) that issue securities maintained on the Federal Reserve Bank (FRB) Book–Entry System. The GSE regulations also became effective in January 1997.

> The TRADES and GSE regulations apply federal substantive law to the rights and obligations of the United States or the issuing GSE and, subject to some exceptions, the rights and obligations of the FRBs. The regulations, however, defer to state law with respect to the remaining aspects of transactions between the FRBs and their participants [the participants generally are federally insured banks] and for all aspects of transactions on the books of lower-tier intermediaries [i.e., intermediaries that are not participants in the FRB system]. Thus, the rights and obligations of parties who hold federal book-entry securities through broker-dealers, custodian banks, clearing corporations, or other securities intermediaries (other than the FRBs) will be governed by state law.

Wittie, Review of Recent Developments in U.C.C. Article 8 and Investment Securities, 52 Bus. Law. 1575, 1576 (1997).

SECTION 4.   SECURITY INTERESTS IN DEPOSIT ACCOUNTS

INTRODUCTORY NOTE

This Section deals with security interests in checking, savings, and other deposit accounts. A deposit account is much like a securities account: each involves a claim against a regulated financial intermediary. It should come as no surprise that the rules governing security interests in deposit accounts are similar to those we explored in the preceding Section on investment property; in fact, the investment property rules were the source of the deposit account rules. The two sets of rules are not identical, however. When working through the following materials, please pay special attention to the differences. Can they be explained by differences between the two types of collateral? If not, what explains them?

Problem 6.4.1. Kinkco, Inc., maintains a checking account at Firstbank. To secure a $50,000 loan, Kinkco granted to Firstbank a security interest in all Kinkco's bank accounts, existing and after-acquired.

(a) What should Firstbank do to perfect its security interest? See UCC 9–102(a)(29); UCC 9–310(a); UCC 9–312(b); UCC 9–314(a); UCC 9–104; Note (3) on Security Interests in Deposit Accounts, infra.

(b) Would your advice in part (a) differ if the checking account belonged to Kinkco's president, Davies, who used the loan to buy home furniture? See 9–109(d)(13); 9–102(a)(26).

Problem 6.4.2. Secondbank would like to make a relatively small loan ($50,000) to Kinkco, Inc. Secondbank is unwilling to make the loan without taking a security interest in Kinkco's bank account at Firstbank.

(a) How can Secondbank perfect its security interest? See UCC 9–102(a)(29); UCC 9–310(a); UCC 9–312(b); UCC 9–314(a); UCC 9–104; UCC 9–102(b); UCC 4–104(a)(5); Note (3) on Security Interests in Deposit Accounts, infra; Security Agreement § 4.2 (Form 6.2, supra);

(b) If there is more than one option for perfection, which do you recommend? Include in your analysis the following considerations:

(i) the risk that Firstbank might be uncooperative. See UCC 9–342.

(ii) the cost.

(iii) the risk that Kinkco might create other security interests in the bank account. See UCC 9–327; UCC 9–339.

(iv) the risk that Kinkco might draw checks on the account to pay other creditors. See UCC 4–401; UCC 9–341; UCC 9–332(b).

(v) Secondbank's ability to enforce its security interest. See UCC 9–607(a)(4), (a)(5).

Problem 6.4.3. In the setting of the Prototype receivables financing transaction in Section 1(B), supra, Eastinghome obtained a security interest in Carguys' existing and after-arising accounts and filed a financing statement in the Delaware filing office. Thereafter, Carguys opened a deposit account with a branch of Firstbank in Los Angeles, near Carguys' corporate headquarters. The account agreement between Carguys and Firstbank provided that the deposit account secures all existing and future indebtedness of Carguys to Firstbank. As Carguys received payments from its account debtors, it deposited the payments into the deposit account at Firstbank. No other funds were deposited into the deposit account. In September Carguys borrowed $50,000 from Firstbank. A few months later Carguys defaults on its obligations to Eastinghome and Firstbank.

(a) Which state's law governs perfection and priority of the security interests? See UCC 9–304.

(b) Which security interest in the deposit account is senior, Eastinghome's or Firstbank's? See UCC 9–315(c), (d); UCC 9–322(a)(1), (b)(1), (f)(1); UCC 9–327. What could the holder of the junior security interest have done to protect itself? See Security Agreement § 4.2 (Form 6.2, supra).

Problem 6.4.4. Recall that in the *GECC* case, p. 215, supra, GECC held a security interest in certain of Machinery's inventory that GECC financed, and UPB held a "blanket lien" on all of Machinery's inventory and other assets. Machinery deposited proceeds of the GECC-financed inventory into a deposit account maintained with UPB. Assuming that the subordination agreement between GECC and Machinery did not affect priorities in the deposit account and that Revised Article 9 was in effect, would GECC have enjoyed first priority in the deposit account as proceeds of the collateral it financed? See UCC 9–324(b), (c); UCC 9–327(1).

NOTES ON SECURITY INTERESTS IN DEPOSIT ACCOUNTS

(1) **Background.** Security interests in checking, savings, and other deposit accounts give rise to special practical problems and policy issues. Comment 7 to Former 9–104 observed that "[r]ights under . . . deposit accounts, are often put up as collateral." Nevertheless, security interests in deposit accounts were excluded from Former Article 9, except insofar as they constituted proceeds of other collateral. See F9–104(g), (l); Chapter 3, Section 5, supra (discussing proceeds). As a consequence, Former Article 9 required a lender who took a consensual lien on (or "pledge" of) the debtor's bank account to consult non-UCC law to determine whether its lien attached and was protected against the competing claims of third parties. This non-UCC law may be both hard to find and unclear. In particular, it may include vaguely articulated requirements with respect to the secured party's dominion over the deposit account. Non–UCC law also regulated the enforcement of these liens.

One might question whether the exclusion of security interests in deposit accounts from Former Article 9 was justified, especially given the UCC's goals of simplifying, clarifying, and modernizing the law governing commercial transactions and of making uniform the law among the various jurisdictions. See UCC 1–103(a)(1), (3) [F1–102(2)(a), (c)]. Comment 7 to Former 9–104 explained that "[s]uch transactions are often quite special, do not fit easily under a general commercial statute and are adequately covered by existing law." Do you find that explanation persuasive? Others have not. See, e.g., Harris, Non–Negotiable Certificates of Deposit: An Article 9 Problem, 29 UCLA L. Rev. 330, 358–61 (1981); Phillips, Flawed Perfection: From Possession to Filing under Article 9 (pt. 1), 59 B.U.L. Rev. 1, 47–48 (1979).

(2) **Policy Issues.** The Article 9 Study Committee recommended that Revised Article 9 include deposit accounts as original collateral. See Permanent Editorial Board, Report of the Article 9 Study Committee, Recommendation 7.C., at 68 (Dec. 1, 1992). This recommendation proved to be one of the most controversial aspects of the Study Committee's Report.

From the outset of the drafting process that followed the publication of the Study Committee's Report, it was clear that a substantial minority of the Drafting Committee, including some members associated with the secured financing industry, had reservations about including deposit accounts as original collateral. Some thought the common law was adequate to deal with "blocked" accounts, to which the debtor is denied access, and they opposed making "transactional" accounts, which debtors use to pay their bills, easy to use as collateral. They argued that if a debtor enjoys unfettered access to the funds, then when the time comes to enforce its security interest, the secured party is likely to find that the deposit account has been depleted and the collateral is worthless. The Drafting Committee disagreed over whether, given this risk, lenders actually would extend additional credit in reliance on a deposit account to which the debtor had access.

The Drafting Committee also disagreed over whether obtaining a perfected security interest in all deposit accounts of a debtor would become the routine result in the vast run of secured transactions. It disagreed over the appropriate priority rule for resolving a conflict between a security interest in a deposit account as original collateral and a security interest in the deposit account claimed as proceeds of inventory, accounts, or other original collateral; it disagreed over the appropriate priority rule for resolving a conflict between a security interest in a deposit account and the bank's right of setoff; and it disagreed over whether the benefits of including deposit accounts as original collateral justified the many special provisions required to accomplish the task. The Federal Reserve Bank of New York expressed concern that security interests in deposit accounts would impede the free flow of funds through the payment system. Consumer-advocacy groups feared that individuals would inadvertently or unwisely encumber their bank accounts.

(3) Deposit Accounts under Revised Article 9. Ultimately, the Drafting Committee settled on an approach that appears to have satisfied (grudgingly, perhaps) all concerned. The basic principles of the approach are straightforward.

Free Flow of Funds. First, Revised Article 9 deals directly with the concern of the New York Fed by providing that transferees of funds from a deposit account take free of a security interest in the deposit account, even if they actually know of the security interest and even if they give no value. See UCC 9–332(b). The only exception is for a transferee who acts in collusion with the debtor in violating the rights of the secured party. (We have seen this rule before, in Problem 3.5.8, on page 214. It applies as well to security interests in money. See UCC 9–332(a).)

Consumer deposit accounts. Other than encountering some difficulties articulating the appropriate standard for the exception, the Drafting Committee had little difficulty settling on the "free-flow-of-funds" rule of UCC 9–332(b). The Drafting Committee had greater difficulty deciding what to do about consumer deposit accounts. Representatives of banks that extend consumer credit argued for including consumer deposit accounts as original collateral. They claimed that the applicable common-law requirements for an effective "pledge" of a deposit account were uncertain and costly to implement. Representatives of consumer-advocacy groups did not dispute this claim. Rather, they objected to eliminating the uncertainty and cost, lest the use of deposit accounts as original collateral become more widespread. Ultimately, the Drafting Committee agreed to exclude from

Revised Article 9 assignments of deposit accounts in consumer transactions. See UCC 9–109(d)(13). Is this rule a craven response to political pressure, or is the rule supported by a discernable policy? In answering this question, consider whether and the extent to which transactions with consumer debtors differ from those with business debtors, including sole proprietorships and "mom and pop" enterprises.

Perfection by Control. The third basic principle is that a security interest in a deposit account as *original* collateral may be perfected *only* by "control"; it may not be perfected by filing a financing statement. See UCC 9–312(b)(1); UCC 9–314(a). (A security interest in a deposit account that is *proceeds* of most other types of other collateral may be perfected by filing against the original collateral. See UCC 9–315(c), (d)(2).) "Control" of a deposit account is defined in much the same way as "control" of a security entitlement. One option is to use a three-party control agreement: A secured party has control of a deposit account if the debtor, secured party, and bank with which the deposit account is maintained agree in an authenticated record that the bank will comply with instructions originated by the secured party directing disposition of the funds in the deposit account without further consent by the debtor. See UCC 9–104(a)(2). Alternatively, a secured party has control if the secured party becomes the bank's customer with respect to the deposit account. See UCC 9–104(a)(3). If the secured party is the bank with which the deposit account is maintained, the secured party automatically has control. See UCC 9–104(a)(1).

A secured party having control of a deposit account normally has the power (even if not always the right) to appropriate the funds on deposit. For some participants in the drafting process, control served as a proxy for the secured party's having relied on the deposit account as collateral when deciding whether and to what extent to extend credit to the debtor. Perhaps more accurately, lack of control served as a proxy for lack of reliance. A secured party who does not even take the steps necessary to enable itself to reach the funds on the debtor's default is unlikely to rely on the deposit account as original collateral in any meaningful way. Its unperfected security interest is junior to the rights of the debtor's judicial lien creditors and trustee in bankruptcy.

Revised Article 9's control-only perfection rule is in part a response to those who argued that it should not be "too easy" to take a deposit account as original collateral. For third parties, the rule actually makes it more difficult to perfect a security interest in a deposit account as original collateral than under the nonuniform versions of Former Article 9 in force in some jurisdictions. See, e.g., Cal. Com. Code § 9302(1)(g) (perfection is achieved by giving written notice of the security interest to the bank at which the deposit account is maintained). On the other hand, the bank with which a deposit account is maintained obtains control by virtue of nothing more than its status. See UCC 9–104(a)(1). Does the control-as-proxy-for reliance argument apply to such a bank? Does the status-based method for obtaining control (and thus perfection) conflict with Revised Article 9's general insistence on giving public notice as a condition to achieving priority? Even if not, should something more than an oral security agreement (and the giving of value) be required as a condition to the bank's obtaining a perfected security interest?

Priority. Like the provisions defining "control," the rules governing priority of security interests in deposit accounts are analogous, but not identical, to those governing security entitlements. See UCC 9–327. In particular, the bank with which the deposit account is maintained enjoys priority over a third party who enters into a control agreement with respect to the deposit account. See UCC 9–327(3).

As indicated in Note (3), p. 433, supra, the credit extended by a broker or other securities intermediary typically is a margin loan used to acquire the collateral (security entitlement). For this reason, a priority analogous to purchase-money priority may be appropriate. Banks, on the other hand, do not typically extend credit that enables the borrower to acquire the funds in a deposit account. The proceeds of a loan may be disbursed by crediting the debtor's deposit account, but typically a loan is made with the intention that the debtor spend the funds, not keep them in the deposit account. Is there another reason why the bank's security interest should take priority?

With respect to security entitlements, we have seen that a third party who wishes to achieve priority over the security interest of the securities intermediary must induce the securities intermediary to enter into a subordination agreement. See UCC 9–328(3); Problem 6.3.2, p. 429, supra. In contrast, a secured party who has control by virtue of having becoming the bank's customer with respect to a deposit account obtains priority over the bank. See UCC 9–327(4). Can you explain this difference?

Enforcement. Because control of a deposit account gives a secured party the ability to direct the disposition of funds in the deposit account without further consent by the debtor, enforcement of a perfected-by-control security interest in a deposit account should be easy. If the secured party is the bank with which the deposit account is maintained, after default the bank may apply the balance of the deposit account to the obligation secured by the deposit account. See UCC 9–607(a)(4). A third-party secured party with control under UCC 9–104(a)(2) or (3) may instruct the bank to pay the balance of the deposit account to or for the benefit of the secured party. UCC 9–607(a)(5). Article 9 does not specifically address the enforcement rights of a secured party whose security interest in a deposit account is perfected by filing or unperfected. (Either of these situations might arise with respect to a deposit account that constitutes proceeds of other collateral.) As a general matter, after default, a secured party "may notify [a] person obligated on collateral to make payment . . . to or for the benefit of the secured party" and "may enforce the obligations of [a] person obligated on collateral and exercise the rights of the debtor with respect to the [person's] obligation . . . to make payment or otherwise render performance to the debtor." UCC 9–607(a)(1), (3). But UCC 9–607(e) makes clear that UCC 9–607 "does not determine whether [a] bank[] or other person obligated on collateral owes a duty to a secured party." UCC 9–607(e). Thus, unless non-UCC law otherwise provides (which it generally does not), a secured party who lacks control of a deposit account must resort to judicial process to obtain the funds on deposit.

Recoupment and Setoff. A bank may have a right of recoupment or setoff under the common law, as a matter of contract, or under a (non-UCC) statute. This right, when available, permits the bank to offset amounts it owes its customer (the depositor) on the deposit account against amounts that the debtor owes the bank. If the depositor creates a security interest in a deposit account, however, an obvious question arises as to the relationship between the security interest in the deposit account and the bank's right of setoff against the same deposit account. UCC 9–340 addresses this relationship. Under UCC 9–340(a), the bank "may exercise any right of recoupment or set-off against a secured party that holds a security interest in the deposit account." An exception is made in UCC 9–340(c), however; if the secured party has perfected its security interest by itself becoming the bank's customer on the deposit account (see UCC 9–104(a)(3)), then the bank may not effectively exercise setoff "based on a claim against the debtor."

A bank that holds a security interest in its debtor's (i.e., the bank's customer's) deposit account assumes an intriguing combination of roles—it is at once the assignee of the deposit account and the obligor on the deposit account. This situation also raises obvious questions about the relationship between the bank's right of setoff and its status as a secured party. UCC 9–340(b) provides that Revised Article 9 "does not affect a right of recoupment of set-off of the secured party as to a deposit account maintained with the secured party." Thus, Revised Article 9 generally leaves the bank's recoupment or setoff rights unimpaired. On the other hand, the secured party must look elsewhere for its right of recoupment or setoff, inasmuch as Revised Article 9 does not create any such right. See UCC 9–340, Official Comment 2.

Chapter 8, Section 4(D), addresses in more detail the relationship between security interests under Revised Article 9 and rights of recoupment and setoff.

(4) Classifying the Collateral. The line between a deposit account and a securities account, as to which an entitlement holder enjoys a security entitlement, is not always clear. The distinction can be important. For example, if a secured party has filed a financing statement against "debtor's account No. 12345, maintained with ABC Bank," the filing would be sufficient to perfect a security interest if the account is a securities account but would be ineffective if the account is a deposit account. See UCC 9–312(a) (security interest in investment property may be perfected by filing); (b)(1) (security interest in deposit account may be perfected *only* by control).

As to the conceptual distinctions between deposit accounts and securities accounts, consider the following excerpt from the Prefatory Note to Revised Article 8:

An ordinary bank deposit account would not fall within the definition of "security" in Section 8–102(a)(15), so the rules of Parts 2, 3, and 4 of Article 8 do not apply to deposit accounts. Nor would the relationship between a bank and its depositors be governed by the rules of Part 5 of Article 8. The Part 5 rules apply to "security entitlements.". . .. A person has a security entitlement governed by Part 5 only if the relationship in question falls within the definition of "securities account." The definition of securities account in Section 8–501(a) excludes deposit accounts from the Part 5 rules of Article 8. One of the basic elements of the relationship between a securities intermediary and an entitlement holder is that the securities intermediary has the duty to hold exactly the quantity of securities that it carries for the account of its customers. See Section 8–504. The assets that a securities intermediary holds for its entitlement holder are not assets that the securities intermediary can use in its own proprietary business. See Section 8–503. A deposit account is an entirely different arrangement. A bank is not required to hold in its vaults or in deposit accounts with other banks a sum of money equal to the claims of all of its depositors. Banks are permitted to use depositors' funds in their ordinary lending business; indeed, that is a primary function of banks. A deposit account, unlike a securities account, is simply a debtor-creditor relationship. Thus a bank or other financial institution maintaining deposit accounts is not covered by Part 5 of Article 8.

Today, it is common for brokers to maintain securities accounts for their customers which include arrangements for the customers to hold liquid "cash" assets in the form of money market mutual fund shares. Insofar as the broker is holding money market mutual fund shares for its customer, the customer has a security entitlement to the money market mutual fund shares. It is also common for brokers to offer their customers an arrangement in which the customer has access to those liquid assets via a deposit account with a bank, whereby shares of the money market fund are redeemed to cover checks drawn on the account. Article 8 applies only to the securities account; the linked bank account remains an account covered by other law. Thus the rights and duties of the customer and the bank are governed not by Article 8, but by the relevant payment system law, such as Article 4 or Article 4A.

SECTION 5.   NON–TEMPORAL PRIORITY IN PROCEEDS

INTRODUCTORY NOTE

Former Article 9 dealt with priorities in proceeds in substantially the same way that it dealt with priorities in original collateral. Under Former 9–312(6), for purposes of the first-to-file-or-perfect priority rule of Former

9–312(5), the date of filing or perfection for original collateral also was the date of filing or perfection for proceeds of the collateral. With one major exception—proceeds of collateral subject to a purchase-money security interest under Former 9–312(3) or (4)—the former Article otherwise was silent on the priority of security interests in proceeds. (A minor exception was Former 9–306(5), which dealt with returned and repossessed goods in the context of accounts and chattel paper financing.) The effect of this silence, however, was to make applicable the first-to-file-or-perfect rule.

We have seen that Revised Article 9 contains several non-temporal priority rules—*i.e.*, rules that award priority on a basis other than priority in time. The include priority rules for security interests in deposit accounts (UCC 9–327), investment property (UCC 9–328), chattel paper and instruments (UCC 9–330), and collateral subject to special priority rules under UCC Articles 3, 7, and 8 (UCC 9–331). During the drafting process, some people expressed concern that a secured party who enjoys non-temporal priority in original collateral would not enjoy priority in proceeds. Indeed, UCC 9–322(a) and (b) indicate that, in the absence of a contrary provision, the first-to-file-or-perfect rule, not the relevant non-temporal priority rule, would apply to proceeds. Moreover, inasmuch as filing is not a permissible method of perfection for certain types collateral covered by these non-temporal rules, the time of perfection would control priority. Because perfection is conditioned upon attachment, which is conditioned in turn upon the debtor's having rights in the collateral, perfection in proceeds of those types of collateral would not occur until (and thus priority under the first-to-file-or-perfect rule of UCC 9–322(a)(1) would date from when) the proceeds came into being as such. See UCC 9–203(b)(2); UCC 9–308(a).

In addition to concerns about the inapplicability of the non-temporal rules to proceeds, the prospect of fully extending the reach of the temporal priority rules to proceeds also generated concerns. For example, assume that on June 1 *SP–1* perfects its security interest in a debtor's deposit account by control, on July 1 *SP–2* perfects its security interest in the debtor's inventory by filing, and on August 1 *SP–1* files a financing statement covering inventory. The debtor then uses cash from the deposit account to purchase new inventory. Under the first-to-file-or-perfect rule (UCC 9-322(a)(1), (b)(1)), *SP–1*'s security interest in the inventory as proceeds of the deposit account would have priority over that of *SP–2*, even though *SP–2* filed first and a search failed to turn up *SP–1*'s filing (which had not yet been made). This effect arguably would undermine the filing system.

The statutory solution is an enormously complex and opaque set of priority rules found in subsections (c), (d), and (e) of UCC 9–322. The upshot is generally to extend the non-temporal priority to most proceeds, see UCC 9–322(c), but to apply a new first-to-file (*not* first-to-file-*or-perfect*) priority rule to proceeds consisting of the types of collateral for which filing is the typical means of perfection. See UCC 9–322(d), (e). The application of these new priority rules is illustrated in Comments 7, 8, and 9 to UCC 9-322, which contain eight examples. Please study these subsections and Comments now.

Only time and experience will reveal whether the benefits of the new rules on proceeds priorities outweigh the costs of complexity. If the rules were implicated only in the unusual case, the complexity might not be cause for concern. However, one must confront and understand this scheme to reach the conclusion that the first-to-file secured party claiming inventory or equipment will also have priority in after-acquired inventory or equipment purchased with cash proceeds of an encumbered deposit account—a scenario that may become very typical.

SECTION 6.   FINANCING OTHER INTANGIBLES

Intangibles other than those that we have encountered thus far (primarily accounts, chattel paper, deposit accounts, instruments (including promissory notes), investment property, and payment intangibles) also may be the subject of secured financing. Important examples are intellectual property consisting of interests in copyrights, patents, and trademarks, each of which is subject to regulation under a federal statute. In addition, the new Uniform Computer Information Transactions Act (1999) ("UCITA") promises to fill significant gaps in applicable state law, although it generally defers to Revised Article 9 as to secured transactions.

Intellectual property, such as copyrights, patents, and trademarks, is an enormously important–and valuable–commodity in today's economy and, no doubt, will be so increasingly in the future. Like other valuable property, intellectual property serves as collateral in a wide variety of transactional patterns. Be that as it may, law school courses in patent, copyright, and trademark law essentially ignore transfers of interests in intellectual property for security. Perhaps because many students in courses on secured transactions lack background on intellectual property law, those courses also generally do not address intellectual property as collateral. This book is no exception. Treatment of the financing of intellectual property, including the extent to which federal law may supersede provisions of the UCC, generally is beyond the scope of this book's coverage. However, this section identifies some provisions of Revised Article 9 that affect the financing of intellectual property and other intangibles.

We have seen already that software—computer programs—imbedded in goods (e.g., the software that runs the computer regulating the fuel system on an automobile) is treated as part of the goods under UCC 9–102(a)(44). See Problem 3.2.6, p. 133, supra. We also saw that software associated with specific goods in a transaction may, along with the goods, support chattel paper. See UCC 9–102(a)(11). See Note (1), p. 420, supra. Software (and many other types of intellectual property) typically is **licensed** by a **licensor**—the owner of the software (or a licensee that has the power to relicense the property)—to a **licensee**, the person who is authorized to use the software. The licensor's right to payment under the license arrangement is an "account." UCC 9–102(a)(2). Revised Article 9 also deals with the licensing of intellectual property in three additional contexts.

Licensee in Ordinary Course of Business. UCC 9–321(b) provides that a licensee in ordinary course of business of a general intangible under a nonexclusive license takes free of a security interest in the general intangible. The term "licensee in ordinary course of business" is defined in UCC 9–312(a). The rule contained in subsection (b) is, of course, analogous to the protection afforded to a buyer in ordinary course of business under UCC 9–320(a) and to a lessee in ordinary course of business in UCC 9–321(c). A typical example of the operation of subsection (b) would be the purchase at retail of word processing software. The purchaser (licensee) would take free of a security interest created by the licensor in the underlying intellectual property. The license is **nonexclusive** because licensor is free to enter into similar licenses with other licensees covering the same software.

Waiver of Defenses. Because Former 9–206 explicitly permitted waivers of defenses only in transactions relating to goods (sales and leases), it left open the question of how a licensee may effectively waive its defenses under a license as against its licensor's assignee. UCC 9–403 fills this gap; it validates waivers by any account debtor that complies with its terms.

Restrictions on Assignability. We have seen in Note (3), p. 406, supra, that, with the exception of property covered by UCC 9–406 through UCC 9–409, law other than Article 9 determines whether or not property is assignable. See UCC 9–401(a). However, UCC 9–408 goes quite far to facilitate the ability of a licensee of intellectual property to obtain financing secured by its rights under a license. It permits the creation and perfection of security interests in health-care-insurance receivables, promissory notes, or general intangibles notwithstanding otherwise effective contractual or legal restrictions on transfer. It renders these restrictions ineffective along with any provisions that would give rise to a default based on a violation of the restrictions. UCC 9–408(a), (c). By covering all general intangibles, the scope of UCC 9–408 is much broader than licenses of intellectual property; subsections (a) and (c) refer to: " . . . a general intangible, including a contract, permit, license, or franchise." Note that UCC 9–408 applies only to sales of promissory notes and payment intangibles (a type of general intangible). It does not apply to security interests in promissory notes or payment intangibles that secure obligations; those security interests are governed by UCC 9–406(f). As state law, UCC 9–408 cannot, of course, override any contrary federal law. See UCC 9–408, Official Comment 9.

Having facilitated the creation and perfection of certain security interests, UCC 9–408 balances this treatment with considerable protection for the other parties to the collateral that it affects (e.g., account debtors on general intangibles). Subsection (d) limits the ability of a secured party to enforce the collateral against the other party and provides several other protections; please review subsection (d) now. These limitations sharply distinguish UCC 9–408 from UCC 9–406(f); the latter renders legal restrictions "ineffective" in the case of collateral to which it applies. Why do you suppose the limitations in UCC 9–408 were thought necessary? See UCC 9–408, Official Comment 6.

Law other than Article 9 may temper the breadth of UCC 9-408 in yet another way. The collateral covered by the section—health-care-insurance receivables, promissory notes, or general intangibles—consists of *property* interests of a debtor. However, "[n]either this section nor any other provision of this Article determines whether a debtor has a property interest. . . . Other law determines whether a debtor has a property interest ("rights in the collateral") and the nature of that interest." UCC 9–408, Comment 3. A recent case squarely addressed this issue. Reversing the Bankruptcy Court, the District Court in In re Chris-Don, Inc. 367 F.Supp.2d 696 (D.N.J.2005), considered whether UCC 9-408 overrode a conflicting New Jersey statute regulating liquor licenses. It held that under a 1933 New Jersey statute as interpreted by the courts, the holder of a New Jersey liquor license does not have a property interest in the license (with limited exceptions). Consequently, the court held that the license was not a general intangible and thus was not covered by UCC 9–408.

The drafters of Revised Article 9 foresaw potential conflicts between the free-assignability provisions of UCC 9–408 and non-UCC law. To this end, UCC 9–408(e) affords each state the opportunity to list statutes, rules, and regulations that are trumped by UCC 9–408. New Jersey is among a number of states that adopted nonuniform provisions, under which the legislature listed those statutes that UCC 9–408 does *not* override. The secured party relied in part on New Jersey's nonuniform 9–408(e), which provides (with certain exceptions not relevant here) that UCC 9–408 "prevails over any inconsistent provisions of State statutes." The court rejected this argument on the ground that, inasmuch as a liquor licence is not available as collateral under Article 9 (because it is not property), UCC 9–408 cannot be inconsistent with the 1933 statute.

CHAPTER 7

SECURITY INTERESTS (INCLUDING THE "FLOATING LIEN") IN BANKRUPTCY

This Chapter discusses the rights of a secured party when the debtor enters bankruptcy. Although the debtor's insolvency is not a statutory prerequisite to the commencement of a bankruptcy case, the vast proportion of debtors who enter bankruptcy are insolvent. Unsecured creditors are likely to receive much less than the amount of their claims. Thus, bankruptcy is a time when a security interest may be of particular value.

SECTION 1.   OVERVIEW OF BANKRUPTCY

The Bankruptcy Process. As discussed above in Chapter 1, Section 1, the nonbankruptcy law of creditors' rights is a race of diligence: every creditor for itself. Bankruptcy substitutes a collective debt-collection procedure for individual collection activity. The filing of a bankruptcy petition puts an immediate halt to the race. See BC 362(a) (discussed infra). Instead, all creditors must satisfy their claims only through the bankruptcy.

The filing of a bankruptcy petition creates an estate. The property of the estate generally includes "all legal or equitable interests of the debtor in property as of the commencement of the case." BC 541.

Some bankruptcy cases are commenced for the purpose of liquidating the property of the estate and distributing the proceeds to creditors. In these cases, which are filed under Chapter 7 of the Bankruptcy Code, a trustee is appointed to "collect and reduce to money the property of the estate for which such trustee serves, and close the estate as expeditiously as is compatible with the best interests of the parties in interest." BC 704(a)(1). The bankruptcy court may authorize the trustee to operate the debtor's business, but only for a limited period and only if the operation is in the best interests of the estate and consistent with the orderly liquidation of the estate. See BC 721.

Cases filed under Chapter 11 (reorganization) contemplate that the debtor will continue to operate its business as debtor-in-possession ("DIP"). A trustee is not appointed in Chapter 11 cases, except in the relatively unusual circumstances set forth in BC 1104. Instead, the debtor-in-possession enjoys most of the rights and powers, and is charged with performing most of the functions and duties, of the trustee. See BC 1107; BC 1108; BC 1106(a). While the DIP operates the business, Chapter 11 affords creditors and the debtor (or, if the debtor is a corporation, its management) the opportunity to determine what should be done with the assets so as to maximize the return. Should some or all of the assets be sold? Used to continue one or more lines of the prebankruptcy business? Used to enter into a new line of business?[1]

Where corporate debtors are concerned, the principal purposes of bankruptcy are to maximize the value of the corporation and to allocate the value among various claimants. Substituting a collective remedy (bankruptcy) for individual remedies promotes the former purpose. Nonbankruptcy law subjects businesses to piecemeal dissolution: each creditor is free to levy upon and sell whatever assets it chooses. In contrast, bankruptcy enables the assets to be sold together. The sale of a business as a package is likely to yield more than individual sales of each of the assets; a buyer typically will be willing to pay an additional amount to reflect the cost savings in gathering together the different assets needed to operate the business. A business whose assets not only are maintained intact but also are up and running is likely to command an even larger ("going-concern") premium. Moreover, sales conducted to enforce judicial liens are distress sales. The seller (the sheriff) must sell quickly and so is in no position to hold out for a higher price. In contrast, bankruptcy liquidation puts the seller (the trustee, who represents the creditors) in a somewhat better bargaining position by affording the trustee a little more time.

Bankruptcy not only affects the size of the corporate pie but also its distribution. Allocating the value of the corporation requires both a determination of who is entitled to share and a ranking of the entitlements relative to one another. Potential claimants include not only the prebankruptcy creditors but also the postbankruptcy creditors and the shareholders. In a Chapter 7 case, the distribution is fixed by statute. See BC 726. The statute generally (but not always) respects the nonbankruptcy ranking of various claims. Thus, holders of secured claims ordinarily will be entitled to the value of their collateral, see BC 725; holders of unsecured claims may share in the collateral's value only to the extent it exceeds the secured debt. Unsecured creditors are entitled to be paid in full before shareholders receive any distribution. See BC 726(a).

Chapter 11 permits the interested parties to fix the distribution in a "plan." See generally BC 1123 (contents of plan). A Chapter 11 plan divides

---

1.   Chapters 13 (available only to individual debtors with "regular income") and 12 (available only to debtors who are "family farmer[s] with regular annual income") are similar to Chapter 11 in that the debtor remains in possession of the property of the estate and undertakes to pay prebankruptcy debts pursuant to a court-approved plan. But unlike in Chapter 11 cases, creditors in Chapters 12 and 13 cases do not vote on proposed plans. A trustee is appointed in every Chapter 12 and Chapter 13 case; however, the trustee's primary obligation is to serve as a disbursement agent for payments made pursuant to the plan.

creditors and holders of equity interests into classes and sets forth what (if anything) the members of each class will receive and when (if ever) they will receive it. See BC 1123(a). Most plans are **compositions** and **extensions**; that is, they provide (i) that the cash or other property (e.g., stock in the reorganized debtor) that creditors receive for their claims will be worth less than 100 cents on the dollar and (ii) that creditors will receive payment over time. The terms of any particular plan typically reflect extensive negotiations by representatives of shareholders and various creditor groups. Most claimants are afforded the opportunity to vote on the plan. Before their acceptances or rejections may be solicited, the court must approve a disclosure statement or summary of the plan as providing information sufficient to enable the voters to make an informed judgment about the plan. See BC 1125. Chapter 11 contains a number of protections for holders of claims in classes that reject the plan and for dissenting members of classes that approve the plan. See, e.g., BC 1129(a)(7), (a)(8); BC 1129(b).

Even when the debtor is an individual, bankruptcy may serve as a collective creditors' remedy. More often than not, however, there are few unencumbered assets available for distribution. For most individual debtors, bankruptcy affords a unique opportunity to begin financial life anew. This **fresh start** consists of three components. First, the individual debtor may keep certain prebankruptcy assets (**exempt** property) free of prepetition claims. See BC 522. Second, to the extent that the debtor's current, nonexempt assets do not suffice to pay prebankruptcy debts, the debts are **discharged**; that is, they no longer may be collected as personal liabilities of the debtor. The discharge has the effect of freeing the debtor's human capital (future earning potential) from the reach of prepetition creditors. See BC 727; BC 524; see also BC 541(a)(6) (property of the estate does not include earnings from services performed by individual debtors after commencement of bankruptcy case).[2] Third, employers and governmental units are prohibited from discriminating against the debtor *solely* because the debtor was insolvent, was in bankruptcy, or received a discharge. See BC 525. Moreover, BC 525(c) prohibits this type of discrimination in student loan programs, but it lacks the "solely" limitation.

What Will a Secured Party Recover From the Bankruptcy? As a first approximation, it is fair to say that bankruptcy respects the value of nonbankruptcy property rights, including security interests. Thus, a secured party is entitled to receive from the bankruptcy its collateral or the value of its collateral up to the amount of its claim. See BC 506(b); BC 725; BC 1129(a)(7). But see BC 1325(a) (entitling purchase-money secured party under specified circumstances to receive full amount of claim, even if claim

---

2.   In contrast, Chapter 13 contemplates that the debtor will use future income to pay prebankruptcy claims. Some individual debtors may enter Chapter 13 because their income net of expenses exceeds specified standards and precludes them from obtaining relief under Chapter 7. See BC 707(b). Chapter 13's discharge provisions are a little more generous to debtors than those applicable in a Chapter 7; for some debtors this can be an advantage.

exceeds value of collateral). As we explain below, the secured party may be compelled to wait quite some time before receiving this value; however, even with a substantial delay, a creditor usually is much better off to receive the value of its collateral than it would be if it were unsecured. Holders of general unsecured claims share pro rata in whatever unencumbered assets remain after payment of secured claims, expenses of administering the bankruptcy case, and unsecured claims entitled to priority of payment (priority claims include those for unpaid prebankruptcy wages and taxes). See generally BC 726(a); BC 507(a).

The following Problem demonstrates the desirability of having a security interest in bankruptcy.

Problem 7.1.1. Debtor files a petition under Chapter 7 and has two assets: (i) a piece of equipment worth $100,000, subject to a perfected security interest securing an $80,000 debt to Seller; and (ii) real property worth $500,000, subject to a recorded mortgage securing a $400,000 debt to Bank. In addition, Debtor owes $300,000 to other (unsecured) creditors.

(a) How will the assets be distributed? (The effect of Seller's having perfected its security interest is discussed infra, Section 2(A).)

(b) How would the assets be distributed if Debtor had purchased the equipment from Seller on an unsecured basis?

(c) How would the assets be distributed if the equipment is worth only $70,000 at the time Debtor enters bankruptcy? Note that BC 506(a) would divide Seller's $80,000 claim into two parts: Seller would have a secured claim in the amount of the value of its collateral ($70,000); the balance of its claim ($10,000) would be an unsecured claim.

The Automatic Stay. Bankruptcy cases can be complex and time-consuming. Even a relatively simple consumer bankruptcy can take several months: The debtor's assets must be gathered together, the claims against the debtor must be assessed, and the value of the assets must be distributed among the claimants. Chapter 11 cases typically take much longer. Months, even years, may elapse before a plan is proposed. Approval of the disclosure statement, solicitation of acceptances and rejections, and the confirmation hearing extend the process even further.

To effect the orderly administration of the bankruptcy estate, creditors must be prevented from continuing the nonbankruptcy race to the assets while the bankruptcy case is proceeding. If creditors were free to ignore the pendency of the bankruptcy case, then much of the value of a collective proceeding would be lost: creditors would incur duplicative costs of collection, and assets might be sold piecemeal at distress prices.

Under BC 362(a), the filing of a bankruptcy petition "operates as a stay, applicable to all entities," of all collection activity with respect to prebankruptcy claims.[3] The following Problems address the scope of the

---

3.   BC 362 sets forth several exceptions to the automatic stay. Discussion of these exceptions is best left to the Bankruptcy course.

automatic stay as it applies to secured parties. Note that any acts taken in violation of the automatic stay are void, and that parties who deliberately violate the stay may be held in contempt of court and fined.

Problem 7.1.2. Debtor is in the printing business. On November 1, Seller sold Debtor a press and retained a security interest in the press to secure its price. Debtor filed a Chapter 11 petition on November 25. Seller has yet to file a financing statement to perfect its security interest. May Seller do so? See BC 362(a)(4); BC 101(37) (defining "lien"); BC 541(a) (defining property of the estate). The consequences of having a security interest that is unperfected at the time the debtor enters bankruptcy are discussed infra, Section 2(A).

Problem 7.1.3. Assume that, in the immediately preceding Problem, Seller filed a financing statement on November 5.

(a) May Seller repossess the press? See BC 362(a)(3), (a)(4).

(b) May Debtor continue to use the press if Seller does not repossess it? See BC 363(c); BC 1108.

Problem 7.1.4. Seller is concerned that the case may last several years, and that the press will decline substantially in value during that time, whether because of depreciation caused by normal wear and tear, obsolescence resulting from technological improvements in presses, or unanticipated damage resulting from misuse or natural calamity. For these reasons, Seller would like to repossess the press and sell it now, rather than wait for a future distribution from the bankruptcy. What can Seller do? See BC 363(e); BC 362(d); BC 362(g); BC 361; Note on Relief from the Automatic Stay, infra.

NOTE ON RELIEF FROM THE AUTOMATIC STAY

BC 362(d) sets forth two circumstances under which the bankruptcy court "shall grant relief from the stay" as it affects security interests in personal property. Under subsection (d)(2), the court shall grant relief from the stay if the debtor "does not have an equity in [the] property" and the property is "not necessary to an effective reorganization." As used in BC 362(d)(2)(A), the debtor's "equity" is calculated by deducting from the value of the collateral the amount of debt that it secures. (When the property secures more than one debt, the cases tend to calculate the debtor's "equity" by deducting the aggregate amount of the secured obligations from the value of the collateral). See, e.g., In re Indian Palms Assocs., Ltd., 61 F.3d 197 (3d Cir. 1995). Accordingly, if Seller can prove that the press is worth $80,000 and secures a debt of $100,000, the first element of BC 362(d)(2) would be met. The court must grant relief from the stay unless the trustee (or DIP) proves that the property is "necessary to an effective reorganization." See BC 362(d)(2), (g)(2). According to a widely-cited dictum from the Supreme Court,

> [w]hat this requires is not merely a showing that if there is conceivably to be an effective reorganization, this property will be needed for it; but

that the property is essential for an effective reorganization *that is in prospect*. This means . . . that there must be "a reasonable possibility of a successful reorganization within a reasonable time."

United Savings Association v. Timbers of Inwood Forest Associates, Ltd., 484 U.S. 365, 375–76, 108 S.Ct. 626, 633, 98 L.Ed.2d 740, 751 (1988) (emphasis in original). Thus, the trustee will not succeed merely by proving that *if* Debtor is to continue in the printing business, continued use of the press would be essential.

The court also is required to lift the stay "for cause, including lack of adequate protection of an interest in property of [a] party in interest." BC 362(d)(1). BC 361 explains the term "adequate protection." To protect against an anticipated decline in the value of the press resulting from continued use by Debtor, the trustee might provide monthly payments to Seller in the amount of the anticipated decline. See BC 361(1). To protect against the risk of obsolescence, the trustee might secure Seller's claim with a lien on other property of the estate. See BC 361(2). Where there is a risk of destruction, the trustee might insure the collateral against loss. See BC 361(3).

But even if the trustee (or DIP) provides the described protection, Seller may be less than content. Seller has bargained for the right, upon Debtor's default, to repossess the collateral, sell it, and apply the proceeds toward its claim against Debtor. See UCC 9–609; UCC 9–610; UCC 9–615. Were the automatic stay not in place, Seller would receive the value of its collateral in a matter of weeks. Even if the trustee insures the press, makes periodic payments, and grants a supplemental lien, Seller will be worse off. Rather than have a certain $80,000 in the very near term, Seller has only part payment now and a promise of the balance when a distribution is made. Even if the promise is kept, Seller will receive the vast proportion of its claim in the future, perhaps years from now. Had the automatic stay been lifted, Seller would receive the money in a matter of weeks; by investing the money, Seller would have considerably more than $80,000 in a few years.

Consider the following statutory argument. Adequate protection of an interest of an entity in property (here, Seller's security interest) may be provided by "granting such other relief . . . as will result in the realization by such entity [Seller] of the indubitable equivalent of such entity's interest in such property." BC 361(3). Receipt of periodic cash payments and a secured promise to pay the balance at an indefinite time in the future is not the "indubitable equivalent" of receiving $80,000 today. If payment is to be deferred, Seller should be entitled to recover an amount equal to $80,000 plus interest on that amount, in order to put Seller in the same position it would have been in had the stay not been in effect. To support the argument, Seller might cite the legislative history of BC 361, which contains the statement that "[s]ecured creditors should not be deprived of the benefit of their bargain." H.R. Rep. No. 595, 95th Cong., 1st Sess. 339 (1977), reprinted in 1978 U.S.C.C.A.N. 5963, 6295; S. Rep. No. 989, 95th Cong., 2d Sess. 53 (1978), reprinted in 1978 U.S.C.C.A.N. 5787, 5839. The benefit of

Seller's bargain is to turn the collateral into cash promptly upon Debtor's default.

The Supreme Court considered and unanimously rejected this argument in United Savings Association v. Timbers of Inwood Forest Associates, Ltd., 484 U.S. 365, 108 S.Ct. 626, 98 L.Ed.2d 740 (1988). The Court concluded that the "interest in property" that BC 362(d)(1) protects does not include a secured party's right to foreclose on the collateral. Thus the "value of such entity's interest" in BC 361 means the dollar value of the collateral and not the present value of the secured party's right to use the collateral as a means to satisfy its claim. Accordingly, as long as the trustee takes appropriate steps to protect Seller's ultimate recovery of $80,000, Seller has received "adequate protection" for its security interest and is not entitled to relief from the stay on that ground.

In *Timbers*, the Supreme Court distinguished the undersecured creditor, whose collateral is worth less than its claim, from the oversecured creditor, whose collateral is worth more. In holding that undersecured creditors are not entitled to recover interest as part of the adequate protection required by BC 362, the Court relied in part on BC 502(b)(2) and BC 506(b). Under the former section, interest that is unmatured at the time of the filing of the petition is not part of the creditor's allowed secured claim; i.e., it ordinarily will not be paid from the bankruptcy. Under BC 506(b), to the extent that a claim is secured by collateral having a value in excess of the claim (i.e., to the extent that the secured creditor is oversecured), "there shall be allowed to the holder of such claim, interest on such claim." In other words, postpetition interest continues to accrue on oversecured claims. However, interest accruing postpetition becomes part of the allowed secured claim; nothing in the Bankruptcy Code requires that interest be paid as it accrues.

As you might expect from reading the foregoing, secured parties have incentives not to become enmeshed in a bankruptcy case. If they are undersecured, they ultimately will recover the value of their collateral but will lose the value of having received it promptly. Oversecured creditors will be entitled to recover accrued postpetition interest to the extent that the value of the collateral is large enough to cover it, but the rate at which interest accrues may be less than the rate to which the parties have agreed.[4] And even oversecured creditors must wait until the time of distribution before actually recovering interest that accrues postpetition.

Problem 7.1.5. Assume that, in Problem 7.1.3, Seller repossessed the press on November 10 (prior to bankruptcy) and scheduled a sale for December 10.

(a) May Seller conduct the sale? See BC 362(a)(4).

---

4. The courts generally agree that the contract rate is the appropriate rate at which interest accrues under BC 506(b); however, when the contract contains two rates, the higher of which comes into effect upon the debtor's default, courts sometimes consider the equities of the case in determining whether the higher rate applies under BC 506(b). Some courts also deny a default interest rate as an unreasonable "charge."

(b) Debtor's trustee demands that Seller return the press so that Debtor can use it during the bankruptcy case. Must Seller do so? See BC 542(a); BC 363(c)(1); BC 541(a)(1); United States v. Whiting Pools, Inc. 462 U.S. 198, 103 S.Ct. 2309, 76 L.Ed.2d 515 (1983) (turnover order was properly issued against IRS, which had seized property subject to federal tax lien before commencement of Chapter 11 case).

(c) Suppose Seller is concerned that, if Debtor uses the press, the value of its collateral will decline? See BC 363(e).

SECTION 2. THE BANKRUPTCY TRUSTEE'S AVOIDING POWERS

INTRODUCTORY NOTE

Generally speaking, the holder of a security interest will receive a secured claim in bankruptcy. As we discussed above, the holder of a secured claim is entitled to the value of its collateral (up to the amount of its claim) from the bankruptcy estate. However, not all security interests are valid in bankruptcy. The Bankruptcy Code affords the trustee (or DIP) the power to avoid (i.e., undo) certain otherwise valid prebankruptcy transfers, including transfers of security interests. This Section discusses the **avoiding powers** as they apply to security interests.

For the most part, BC 544–548 define the scope of the avoiding powers. BC 550 sets forth the consequence of avoidance: "to the extent that a transfer is avoided under [one of the enumerated sections of the Bankruptcy Code], the trustee may recover, for the benefit of the estate, the property transferred, or, if the court so orders, the value of such property." In other words, if the trustee succeeds in avoiding the transfer of a security interest, the trustee may recover the property transferred (i.e., the security interest) for the benefit of the estate. Any interest in property that the trustee recovers under BC 550 becomes property of the estate, see BC 541(a)(3), and is preserved automatically for the benefit of the estate. See BC 551. As a practical matter, this means that the avoided security interest no longer encumbers the collateral, and that whatever portion of the collateral it previously encumbered becomes available for distribution to creditors generally. Among those creditors will be the (former) secured party.

(A) UNPERFECTED SECURITY INTERESTS: THE STRONG ARM OF THE TRUSTEE

Problem 7.2.1. Debtor files a petition under Chapter 7 and has two assets: (i) a piece of equipment worth $100,000, subject to an unperfected security interest securing an $80,000 debt to Seller; and (ii) real property worth $500,000, subject to a recorded mortgage securing a $400,000 debt to Bank. In addition, Debtor owes $300,000 to other (unsecured) creditors. How will the assets be distributed? See UCC 9–203(b); BC 541(a)(1); BC

544(a)(1); UCC 9–317(a)(2); UCC 9–310(a); BC 541(a)(3); Notes on Bankruptcy Code Section 544(a), infra. (This Problem is identical to Problem 7.1.1, p. 452, supra, except that Seller's security interest is unperfected.)

Problem 7.2.2. On June 1 Devon bought a set of living-room furniture from Cellar Department Store and executed a security agreement, covering the furniture, to secure payment of the price. Cellar did not file a financing statement. On July 1 Devon went into bankruptcy. What are the rights of Cellar and the trustee? See UCC 9–309(1).

Problem 7.2.3. On June 1 Dramco purchased pharmaceutical equipment from Supplier. Supplier, who retained a security interest to secure payment of the price, filed a financing statement on June 9. In the interim, on June 7, Dramco filed a bankruptcy petition.

(a) What are the rights of Supplier and the trustee? See BC 544(a)(1); BC 546(b); UCC 9–317(e).

(b) Did Supplier violate the automatic stay? See BC 362(b)(3).

NOTES ON BANKRUPTCY CODE SECTION 544(A)

(1) The Operation of BC 544(a). The assets that will be available for distribution in the bankruptcy case are referred to as "property of the estate." Under BC 541(a)(1), property of the estate includes "all legal or equitable interests of the debtor in property as of the commencement of the case." When the bankruptcy case in Problem 7.2.1 was commenced, Debtor was the owner of the equipment, but its ownership interest was encumbered by Seller's security interest. As you know, Seller's failure to file or otherwise "perfect" its security interest does not impair Seller's rights to the collateral against Debtor. See UCC 9–203(b). Hence, at first blush, it would appear that the property of Debtor's estate would not include Seller's unperfected security interest, which would be effective in bankruptcy.

The bad news for Seller is BC 544(a). This section sometimes is called the "strong-arm" clause because of the formidable powers it confers on the bankruptcy trustee. BC 544(a)(1) affords to the trustee, as of the commencement of the case, the rights and powers of a creditor that extends credit to the debtor at the time of the commencement of the case, and that obtains, at that time and with respect to that credit, a judicial lien on all property on which a creditor on a simple contract could have obtained a judicial lien, whether or not such a creditor exists. In other words, BC 544(a)(1) asks us to *imagine* that a specified type of creditor has obtained a "judicial lien" on the property; it affords to the trustee the rights of that *hypothetical* lien creditor.

What is a "judicial lien"? Happily, the Bankruptcy Code gives us a definition that is short and relatively clear. The long list of definitions in BC 101 includes paragraph (36): "The term 'judicial lien' means lien obtained by judgment, levy, sequestration, or other legal or equitable process or proceeding." For personal property, the most significant illustration is a "lien obtained by . . . levy," e.g., seizure of the property by a sheriff under a writ of execution. Thus, if an imaginary levy, on an imaginary judgment of unlimited amount, would have established a lien in favor of an imaginary creditor, the rights and powers that the lien would have afforded to the imaginary creditor are taken over by the very real trustee in bankruptcy.

What are those rights and powers? Under a broad reading of the Commerce Clause of the Constitution, Congress might have established unified national rules on the relative rights of lien creditors and holders of security interests. However, Congress has not done so: the basic rules must be derived from state law. You are familiar with the applicable state law; it is UCC 9–317(a)(2), in the form enacted by the relevant state. Under UCC 9–317(a)(2), at the "commencement of the [bankruptcy] case"—i.e., the filing of the bankruptcy petition—would a judgment creditor of Debtor who obtained an execution lien on the equipment have acquired rights superior to Seller's unperfected security interest? If so, then the trustee likewise will do so and render Seller unsecured.

(2) The Policy Behind BC 544(a). Why does the Bankruptcy Code invalidate certain otherwise valid security interests in bankruptcy? Consider the following explanations:

BC 544(a)(1) Mirrors the Nonbankruptcy Result. Outside of bankruptcy, who would have been entitled to the value of Debtor's equipment? Although Seller retained a security interest effective against Debtor, Seller was not guaranteed "first dibs" on the equipment. Any creditor or group of creditors that acquired a judicial lien on the equipment before Seller perfected its security interest would have taken priority over Seller. In the nonbankruptcy race to this asset, Seller was leading, but had not yet won when bankruptcy occurred. When the ultimate nonbankruptcy outcome has yet to be determined, BC 544 has the effect of creating a "tie": Seller and the competing, unsecured creditors share equally in the value of the equipment. For a fuller explication of this argument, see T. Jackson, The Logic and Limits of Bankruptcy Law 70–75 (1986).

A variation on this argument is as follows: Traditionally, upon the commencement of a bankruptcy proceeding at the behest of creditors (i.e., an **involuntary bankruptcy**), a trustee took possession of the debtor's assets; the creditors represented by the trustee thereby acquired a lien on the debtor's property. Although most bankruptcy petitions now are filed by debtors rather than creditors (i.e., most bankruptcies are **voluntary**), the result should be the same: a judicial officer has taken control over the debtor's property and the creditors (or their representative) thereby should acquire a lien. Like any other lien that arises through the judicial process or through the exercise of a collective creditors' remedy, the lien that arises on bankruptcy should take priority over an unperfected security interest. See UCC 9–317(a)(2); UCC 9–102(a)(52).

BC 544(a)(1) Reflects a Bankruptcy Policy Against Secret Liens. Although phrased in general terms, the primary use of the strong-arm power historically has been the avoidance of unperfected security interests and other secret liens. As a normative matter, one might argue that bankruptcy distribution *should* mirror nonbankruptcy distribution; however, as a descriptive matter, BC 544(a) changes the distribution. Bankruptcy calls off the race to the assets. When the bankruptcy petition is filed, the secured party has an enforceable interest in the collateral; unsecured creditors do not. The secured party has won the race. BC 544(a) deprives the secured party of its victory because it has come at the expense of unsecured creditors, who may have been prejudiced by the secret lien. See McCoid, Bankruptcy, the Avoiding Powers, and Unperfected Security Interests, 59 Am. Bankr. L.J. 175 (1985).

(B) THE TRUSTEE'S POWER TO AVOID PREFERENCES

NOTE ON PREFERENCE LAW

Under nonbankruptcy law, each creditor is entitled to take all legal steps to be paid. If the debtor's assets do not suffice to pay all creditors, some creditors will succeed in obtaining payment; others will remain unpaid. The amount a particular creditor receives is likely to depend upon the leverage it enjoys. A trade creditor may threaten to withhold future supplies or services unless it is paid for past credit extensions. A secured creditor may threaten to repossess collateral unless it is paid. Collecting one's claims through persuasion or through the judicial process is perfectly appropriate conduct under nonbankruptcy law. Using unencumbered assets to pay some creditors rather than others typically does not violate any nonbankruptcy principle.

Consider the following scenario: Debtor is hopelessly insolvent, having incurred substantial trade debt as well as bank debt. Debtor has one remaining asset of value—a checking account containing $27,128.50. Debtor withdraws $25,000 and gives it to C, a favored creditor, in satisfaction of C's $25,000 claim. Although other, unpaid creditors may be chagrined to discover that C has beaten them to the assets, this fact alone is insufficient to enable them to cry "foul"; the other creditors ordinarily will have no right to deprive C of its payment.

Bankruptcy calls off the nonbankruptcy race to the assets. After bankruptcy has begun, payment of one creditor's claim at the expense of another creditor would violate the bankruptcy principle of pro rata distribution. Add to the foregoing scenario the additional fact that, immediately after paying $25,000 to C, Debtor files a bankruptcy petition. As before, C is overwhelmed with joy. Because Debtor preferred to pay C (for whatever reason or mix of reasons), C has been made whole. The other, unpaid creditors are not merely chagrined; they are outraged. Why, they ask, should C be paid in full when they receive a pittance? Had bankruptcy been filed 24 hours earlier, C would be sharing equally with them.

Preference law addresses prebankruptcy transfers that have the result of affording a particular creditor more than its pro rata share. BC 547 enables the bankruptcy trustee to avoid certain of these preferential transfers. Under BC 550, "the trustee may recover, for the benefit of the estate, the property transferred, or, if the court so orders, the value of [the] property." In the example, unless *C* has a defense to the preference action, see BC 547(c) (discussed infra), *C* would be required to return the property to the estate. *C*'s claim would be restored, and *C* would share pro rata with other holders of unsecured claims. See BC 502(h).

Traditional preference jurisprudence suggests that preference law is designed to promote equality of distribution among unsecured creditors: "the preference provisions facilitate the prime bankruptcy policy of equality of distribution among creditors of the debtor." H.R. Rep. No. 595, 95th Cong., 1st Sess. 177–78 (1977), reprinted in 1978 U.S.C.C.A.N. 5963, 6138. Without preference law, unsecured creditors would share pro rata in whatever property the debtor has when it enters bankruptcy. The pro rata shares would be based upon the actual size of the claims at the time of the commencement of the bankruptcy case. Avoiding preferential transfers puts the preferred creditor in the same position as the other creditors, who have not been preferred; all will share pro rata in the debtor's bankruptcy estate, which is enhanced by the preference recovery. Preference law thereby blunts the advantage that certain creditors otherwise would enjoy. It prevents some creditors from retaining payments and other transfers of property that otherwise would have been more widely shared.

Some argue that preference law ought to (and, at least to some extent, actually does) do more than protect the bankruptcy rule of pro rata sharing. They assert that preference law should deter creditors from obtaining payment whenever the debtor is approaching bankruptcy. In their view, preference law should be (and largely is) directed to "opt-out behavior"—acts by which creditors seek to remove themselves from an impending collective proceeding (bankruptcy) by "gun-jumping" and, in doing so, reduce the value of the property that is available for all creditors. See, e.g., T. Jackson, The Logic and Limits of Bankruptcy Law 123–138 (1986); Baird, Avoiding Powers Under the Bankruptcy Code, in The Williamsburg Conference on Bankruptcy 305 (1988).

The injurious effects of taking a preference are clearest when the creditor removes real property or goods prior to bankruptcy. Loss, for example, of a printer's presses may diminish the value of the printer's business by an amount greater than the value of the presses themselves. A complete printing business worth, say, $1,000,000 may be worth only $500,000 without the presses, even though the presses would fetch only $250,000 if sold separately. When a preferred creditor receives cash, however, the detrimental effects on the value of the assets available for distribution to creditors are considerably smaller.

As we shall see, preference law in fact does not distinguish among events (including payments) on the basis of their detrimental effect on the total return to creditors. Indeed, the repossession and sale of collateral—an event that is likely to be particularly destructive to the going concern value of the debtor's business—often will not constitute a preference. In contrast, the delayed filing of a financing statement—an event whose principal consequence is distributional—often will result in the secured party losing its collateral and becoming unsecured in bankruptcy.

BC 547(b) describes those prebankruptcy transfers that the trustee may avoid as preferences. Subsection (c) excepts from avoidance certain otherwise preferential transfers. The following Problems address "eve of bankruptcy" transfers.

Problem 7.2.4. On June 1 Debtor borrowed $12,000 from Firstbank and repaid the debt when due on September 1. On October 1 Debtor filed a bankruptcy petition. May the trustee recover the payment from Firstbank? See BC 547(b). (For now, do not worry about the exceptions in subsection (c).)

Problem 7.2.5. What result in the immediately preceding Problem if on September 1, instead of paying Firstbank, Debtor granted Firstbank a perfected security interest in a piece of equipment worth in excess of $12,000? Has there been a prebankruptcy "transfer" to Firstbank? See BC 101(54).

To answer the foregoing Problems, one must read BC 547 carefully. Has there been a "transfer of an interest of the debtor in property"? Is each of the other elements of BC 547(b) met? Observe that many of the terms used in BC 547(b) are defined in BC 101, among them "transfer," "debt," "creditor," and "insolvent." BC 547(g) imposes upon the trustee the burden of proving each element of BC 547(b). BC 547(f) gives the trustee a bit of help: For purposes of BC 547, the debtor is presumed to have been insolvent on and during the 90 days immediately preceding the filing of the bankruptcy petition.[1]

The most difficult element of BC 547(b) to comprehend is subsection (b)(5). This complex language is designed to capture only those transfers that have a preferential effect, i.e., that enable a creditor to receive more than its pro rata share of the property of the estate. BC 547(b)(5) requires one to compare (a) what the creditor would receive if (i) the transfer is allowed to stand and (ii) the creditor receives a distribution on any remaining claim in the bankruptcy, with (b) what the creditor would have received in a Chapter 7 case if the transfer had not been made.

Recall that Chapter 7 of the Bankruptcy Code provides for liquidation of the debtor's property and pro rata distribution of the proceeds to holders of unsecured claims. Suppose that, had the payment to Firstbank not been made, liquidation would have given general creditors (including Firstbank) 50 cents on the dollar. The prebankruptcy transfer in Problem 7.2.4 enabled

---

1. Under Federal Rule of Evidence 301, "a presumption imposes on the party against whom it is directed [in Problems 7.2.4 and 7.2.5, Firstbank] the burden of going forward with evidence to rebut or meet the presumption, but does not shift to such party the burden of proof in the sense of the risk of nonpersuasion, which remains throughout the trial upon the party on whom it was originally cast [in Problems 7.2.4 and 7.2.5, the trustee]." Nevertheless, the debtor's solvency is an issue in preference litigation only infrequently.

Firstbank to receive more than 50 cents on the dollar. Thus the requirement of subsection (b)(5) is satisfied. Would the same be true for the transfer of the security interest in Problem 7.2.5? How much would Firstbank receive if the transfer is not avoided? How much would Firstbank have received without the transfer in a Chapter 7 case? (Remember that holders of unavoided secured claims are entitled to receive the value of their collateral; general unsecured claims share pro rata in the unencumbered assets.)

Problem 7.2.6. On August 1 Debtor borrowed $12,000 from Firstbank and secured the loan with a piece of equipment worth in excess of that amount. Firstbank filed a financing statement covering the equipment shortly before the security agreement was signed. On October 1 Debtor filed a bankruptcy petition. May the trustee avoid the transfer of the security interest? Was there a transfer on account of an antecedent debt? See also BC 547(c)(1). What difference, if any, would it make if Firstbank took the security interest with knowledge that Debtor was insolvent?

Problem 7.2.7. What result in the immediately preceding Problem if Debtor repaid the debt when due on September 1? Did the payment enable Firstbank to receive more than it would have received had the payment not been made and Firstbank received a Chapter 7 distribution? See BC 547(b)(5); BC 547(c)(1); BC 547(a)(2); Note (1) on Prepetition Payments to Secured Parties, infra.

Problem 7.2.8. To alleviate Debtor's "cash flow" problem, Firstbank made a 90–day unsecured loan in the amount of $12,000 to Debtor on June 1. Debtor made no payment until September 20, when Debtor paid Firstbank only $8,000. The balance remained unpaid on October 1, when Debtor filed a bankruptcy petition.

(a) May the trustee recover the $8,000 payment?

(b) What result if Debtor had paid only $3,000? See BC 547(c)(8), (c)(9); BC 101(8).

Problem 7.2.9. On June 1 Debtor borrowed $12,000 from Firstbank and secured the loan with a piece of equipment worth only $7,000. Firstbank filed a financing statement covering the equipment shortly before the security agreement was signed. Debtor repaid the entire debt when due on August 1. On October 1 Debtor filed a bankruptcy petition. May the trustee recover the payment from Firstbank? See Note (1) on Prepetition Payments to Secured Parties, infra.

Problem 7.2.10. What result in the immediately preceding Problem if Debtor repaid only $5,000 when the debt was due? For purposes of BC 547(b) does it matter whether the $5,000 payment is applied to the $5,000 unsecured portion of Firstbank's claim or to the $7,000 secured portion? See BC 547(b)(2); BC 547(c)(1); BC 547(a)(2); Note (1) on Prepetition Payments to Secured Parties, infra.

Problem 7.2.11. On June 1 Firstbank made a one-year, unsecured installment loan in the amount of $120,000 to Debtor. Debtor was obligated to repay $10,000 in principal plus accrued interest on the first day of each month. Debtor made timely payments in July, August, and September.

Debtor filed a bankruptcy petition on October 1. May the trustee recover the three payments? See BC 547(c)(2); Note (2) on Prepetition Payments to Secured Parties, infra.

NOTES ON PREPETITION PAYMENTS TO SECURED PARTIES

(1) Allocating Payments Between the Secured and Unsecured Portions of Claims. BC 547 does not permit the trustee to avoid every prepetition payment to creditors. Rather, the trustee may avoid and recover only those payments that have the effect of enabling the creditor to receive more than it would have received in a Chapter 7 case had the transfer not been made. See BC 547(b)(5).

Whether a prepetition transfer will meet the test in BC 547(b)(5) may depend on whether, and the extent to which, the creditor's claim is secured. Payments to unsecured creditors almost invariably meet the test and are potentially preferential. An unsecured creditor who is permitted to keep a prepetition transfer receives 100 cents on the dollar for each dollar paid. Unless the creditor would have received 100 cents on the dollar in a Chapter 7 distribution (i.e., unless the bankruptcy debtor is solvent), the creditor always will do better by having received payment of even a portion of its claim prepetition.

On the other hand, perfected secured creditors are entitled to receive the value of their collateral from the bankruptcy estate. Theoretically, then, the claim of a fully secured creditor (i.e., one whose claim is less than or equal to the value of its collateral) will be paid in full from the bankruptcy. Accordingly, it appears that prepetition payments to fully secured creditors do not enable them to receive more than they would have received had no payment been made and had they received a Chapter 7 distribution. BC 547(c)(1) is consistent with this approach: to the extent that a fully secured creditor is paid, the creditor has given "new value" to the debtor; i.e., the value of its collateral is freed up for application to the payment of unsecured claims.[2] See BC 547(a)(2) ("new value" includes "release by a transferee of property previously transferred by such transferee in a transaction that is neither void nor voidable").

What about a payment to a creditor who, but for the payment, would have held two claims—one secured and one unsecured? This is the case presented by Problems 7.2.9 and 7.2.10. Problem 7.2.9 is the easier of the two. Did the payment meet the test in BC 547(b)(5)? Even if so, didn't Firstbank give "new value" in exchange for the payment?

---

2.   There is, however, a line of cases holding that for purposes of BC 547(b)(5) the collateral should be valued as of the date of the filing of the bankruptcy petition. Thus, if payments are made to a secured party whose collateral is declining in value, the payments may be preferential even though the value of the collateral exceeded the debt at the time the payments were made. However, this analysis fails to recognize that the "contemporaneous exchange" exception in BC 547(c)(1) would immunize this transaction from avoidance. See Carlson, Security Interests in the Crucible of Voidable Preference Law, 1995 U. Ill. L. Rev. 211, 265.

Problem 7.2.10 is a bit trickier. *In theory*, whether the $5,000 payment is treated as a payment of the secured portion of the claim or the unsecured portion should make no difference; the amount of Firstbank's secured claim can be adjusted to make sure that it receives no more than it would have received in a Chapter 7 case had the transfer not been made. Thus, the payment could be treated as if it were a payment on account of the secured portion of the claim. If so, the payment would be unavoidable; Firstbank would retain the payment and hold a $7,000 bankruptcy claim secured by $2,000 in collateral. Alternatively, the payment could be treated as if it were on account of the unsecured portion of the claim. If so, then the payment would be avoidable; after recovery, Firstbank would hold a $12,000 claim secured by $7,000 of collateral.

As you might have realized, the theory and the practice diverge. Neither Firstbank nor the trustee can be expected to be indifferent about whether Firstbank must return the $5,000 prepetition payment, even though under either scenario Firstbank ultimately would receive $7,000 plus a distribution on a $5,000 unsecured claim. "Ultimately"—there's the rub! To fully appreciate the import of the word, see Note on Relief from the Automatic Stay, Section 1, supra. Given the Supreme Court's decision in *Timbers of Inwood Forest* (discussed in the Note on Relief, supra), Firstbank would be likely to choose to keep the $5,000 prepetition payment so that the funds can generate income while the bankruptcy case is pending. Conversely, the trustee probably would choose to treat the payment as a preference, so that the estate could recover the funds and enjoy the use of $5,000 interest-free. (Recall from Section 1, supra, that postpetition interest on unsecured claims is not allowable.)

The reported preference cases generally treat prebankruptcy payments on partially secured claims as having been applied first to the unsecured portion. This approach, which treats Firstbank as having received payment of its $5,000 unsecured claim on August 1, is consistent with the position Firstbank probably would have taken had bankruptcy not been filed. (Suppose that, after paying Firstbank $5,000, Debtor had not entered bankruptcy. Instead, Firstbank repossessed the collateral and sold it for $7,000. Would Firstbank have applied only $2,000 to the debt and remitted the balance to Debtor or a junior lienor?) Under these cases, the payment to Firstbank in Problem 7.2.10 would be avoidable: Firstbank would be compelled to return $5,000 to the estate in exchange for a correspondingly larger secured claim.

(2) "Ordinary Course" Payments. BC 547(c)(2) contains an exception for certain "ordinary course" payments. As originally enacted, the exception shielded only those payments that were made within 45 days after the debt was incurred. The 1984 amendments to the Bankruptcy Code eliminated the 45–day limitation.

As originally written, the exception was of little use to secured parties; secured debts typically are outstanding for more than 45 days. Since the elimination of the 45–day limitation, secured parties who received timely payments on **term loans** and **revolvers** have argued that these payments qualify for BC 547(c)(2) even though they otherwise would be preferential. Some reported decisions took the view that the exception applies only to payments of trade debt and other current expenses, not to payment of longer-term debt. See, e.g., In re CHG International, Inc., 897 F.2d 1479 (9th Cir.1990) (timely interest payments on term loans held not to qualify for BC 547(c)(2)). But in Union Bank v. Wolas, 502 U.S. 151, 112 S.Ct. 527, 116 L.Ed.2d 514 (1991), the Supreme Court held that "payments on long-term debt, as well as payments on short-term debt, may qualify for the ordinary course of business exception." Unfortunately, the Court gave absolutely no guidance on the more difficult issues raised by BC 547(c)(2): What does it mean for a debt to be "incurred by the debtor in the ordinary course of business"? What are the characteristics of a payment "made in the ordinary course of business" or "according to ordinary business terms"?

(3) Payments on Revolving Credit Facilities. Assume the following, rather typical scenario: Bank agrees to make available to Debtor up to $1 million of credit under an unsecured, revolving **line of credit**. During the 90 days prior to bankruptcy, Debtor makes fifteen borrowings of $100,000 each and makes eleven payments of $100,000 each. Debtor's trustee seeks to recover $1,100,000 from Bank under BC 547(b). Bank is outraged, arguing that it never would have made all the advances unless Debtor had made the repayments; indeed, it took great care to insure that no more than $1 million was outstanding at any given time. Moreover, even though Bank has received $1,100,000 during the preference period, Bank has in effect replenished the bankruptcy estate by $1,500,000; accordingly, Bank argues that it should have no liability whatsoever under BC 547.

BC 547(c)(4) affords some relief to Bank under these circumstances, but sometimes not as much relief as Bank would wish. Under that section, the trustee may not avoid a transfer to the extent that, *after* the transfer, the creditor gave "new value" to or for the benefit of the debtor. Thus, to the extent that Bank can show that, after any one or more of the eleven payments, Bank extended additional credit to Debtor, Bank can use that additional credit to nullify the preference. It is as if Bank returned the preference to the estate. Bank may not, however, aggregate the new value and offset it against the aggregate amount of preferential payments. As in comedy, so with preferences: timing is everything!

Problem 7.2.12. On January 2 Creditor loaned $10,000 to Debtor. On that date, to secure the loan, Debtor executed a security agreement granting Creditor a security interest in a bulldozer that Debtor had previously purchased. Creditor did not file a financing statement until September 1. On September 2, Debtor filed a petition in bankruptcy. The trustee seeks to avoid the transfer of the security interest as a preference. What result? See BC 547(b); BC 547(e)(2); BC 547(e)(1); UCC 9–317(a)(2); UCC 9–201; UCC 9–203(b); Notes on Delayed Perfection, infra.

NOTES ON DELAYED PERFECTION

(1) The Application of BC 547 to Delayed Perfection. Problem 7.2.12 poses this question: *When* did Debtor transfer an interest in property to Creditor? Clearly, Debtor transferred a property interest to Creditor that was fully effective as between these two parties on January 2. See UCC 9–203(b). If the date of transfer is January 2 for purposes of BC 547(b), then the transfer cannot be avoided for two reasons: the transfer was made for a concurrent, rather than for an "antecedent," debt, and the transfer was made more than 90 days before the filing of the bankruptcy petition. On the other hand, if we deem that the transfer was not made until the financing statement was filed on September 1, then the "antecedent debt" requirement is satisfied and the remaining elements for avoidance probably can be established with ease.

BC 547(e) provides the way to date the transfer. The structure of subsection (e), unhappily, forces us to start with paragraph (2) and then back-track to paragraph (1). Paragraph (2) tells us that "a transfer is *made* . . . (B) at the time such transfer is *perfected*." (The exception in paragraph (2)(A) will be considered later.)

Having learned that the time when the transfer is "perfected" is the key, we move back to paragraph (1)(B), where we learn that a transfer of personal property is perfected "when a creditor on a simple contract cannot acquire a judicial lien that is superior to the interest of the transferee." We explored the meaning of "judicial lien" above in connection with the "strong-arm" clause, BC 544(a). For present purposes we may assume that the quoted language of BC 547(e)(1)(B) refers, inter alia, to the execution lien obtained by the holder of an ordinary contract claim.

Thus, instead of giving us the *answer*, the preference rules of BC 547 provide us with a hypothetical *question*. (In this regard, BC 547 is like the "strong-arm" clause of BC 544(a), discussed in Section 2(A) above.) In the setting of Problem 7.2.12, the question is this: *Suppose* a judgment creditor of Debtor had acquired a judicial lien on the bulldozer during the period leading up to September 1—the date on which Creditor filed the financing statement: Would this lien have been (in the language of BC 547(e)(1)(B)) "superior to the interest of the transferee" of the security interest? (Don't despair—we're almost home!)

Where can we find the answer to this hypothetical question that the Bankruptcy Code has thrown at us? Not in the Bankruptcy Code or in any other federal law! As in dealing with the strong-arm clause we must look to state law—more precisely, to the UCC as enacted in the relevant jurisdiction. Prior to the filing on September 1, could a creditor with a judicial lien have trumped the security interest? UCC 9–317(a)(2) and UCC 9–310(a) provide a clear answer.

Those who have followed the trail this far should be able to answer these questions: (1) In Problem 7.2.12, when was the transfer of the security interest made? (2) Can the trustee avoid the transfer? (If you have any doubts about how to answer these questions, keep going through the steps outlined above until the system is perfectly clear. You will soon need to use this system in solving problems that are much more difficult than Problem 7.2.12. As you probably now realize, Problem 7.2.12 was a sitting duck.)

(2) The Policy Behind Applying BC 547 to Delayed Perfection. On what basis might one argue in support of the result that the transfer occurred upon the filing of the financing statement and not earlier, when the transfer took effect between the debtor and the secured party? Some have argued that delayed perfection is a "false preference"—that preference law has been used to address indirectly an entirely different problem: that of secret liens that operate to the prejudice of unsecured creditors. See, e.g., R. Jordan, W. Warren & D. Bussel, Bankruptcy 376 (6th ed. 2002) ("There is no true preference . . . because the transfer of the security interest . . . is not on account of an antecedent debt. Rather, the problem of delayed perfection is the evil of the secret lien."). Of course, this argument assumes that bankruptcy law expresses a policy against secret liens that is more stringent than the anti-secret-lien policies of Article 9 and other state laws.

Others have argued that delayed perfection, at least in some cases, implicates the "anti-last-minute-grab" policy that they believe underlies preference law. As we have seen, a security interest that is unperfected at the time a bankruptcy petition is filed ordinarily will be avoidable by the bankruptcy trustee. A secured party who believes bankruptcy is imminent may review the loan files and discover that the security interest is unperfected. (Perhaps no financing statement ever was filed; perhaps the financing statement contained errors than made it ineffective; perhaps an effective financing statement became ineffective because the debtor changed its name or location). By perfecting before bankruptcy, an unperfected secured party improves its position relative to other creditors. Had no filing occurred, the secured party might have been rendered unsecured through the trustee's exercise of the strong-arm clause. By filing, the secured party immunizes the security interest from attack under BC 544(a). Is this not precisely the kind of opt-out behavior that preference law addresses? See Jackson, The Logic and Limits of Bankruptcy Law 138–46 (1986).

In assessing the explanations for using preference law to avoid security interests whose perfection has been delayed, one should consider the fact that the principal effect of delayed perfection is likely to be distributional. Delayed perfection is unlikely to affect the total value of the debtor's business; rather, it affects how the value of the business will be distributed among the creditors.

———

In working the following Problems, don't lose sight of the requirements of BC 547(b). In particular, be sure you can identify when the transfer was made and when the debt was incurred. You should also consider whether the outcome that the statute appears to compel is consistent with the policies that underlie preference law.

Problem 7.2.13. On January 2 Creditor loaned $10,000 to Debtor. On that date, to secure the loan, Debtor executed a security agreement granting Creditor a security interest in a bulldozer that Debtor had previously purchased. On September 2 Debtor filed a petition in bankruptcy. (These are the facts of Problem 7.2.12.) Creditor filed a financing statement on May 9. Is the transfer of the security interest avoidable? Would the result change if Debtor was a wholly-owned subsidiary of Creditor? See BC 547(b)(4); BC 101(31); BC 101(2).

Problem 7.2.14. What result in the immediately preceding Problem if Creditor filed the financing statement on January 9 and Debtor filed for bankruptcy on March 1? See BC 547(e)(2)(A). What is the reason for this refinement? Consider the technical attacks that might be made on security arrangements when there is a gap of one day (or one hour) between the loan and the filing. On the other hand, consider how much time normally elapses between the attachment of a security interest and the filing of a financing statement.

Problem 7.2.15. What result in Problem 7.2.13 if Creditor filed the financing statement on January 9 but bankruptcy fell on January 8? Note that, as in the other Problems in this set, Debtor owned the bulldozer before getting the loan from Creditor. Don't forget that the trustee is not confined to a preference attack but also enjoys the rights and powers of a judicial lien creditor under BC 544.

A quick glance at BC 546(b) may suggest that this provision gives effect to the postbankruptcy filing. Note, however, that BC 546(b) gives effect to such filing only when state law "permits perfection of an interest in property to be effective against an entity that acquires rights in such property *before* the date of such perfection." Does state law under the UCC protect a non-purchase-money security interest from a levy that occurs before perfection? See UCC 9–317(a)(2); cf. UCC 9–317(e).

What does the answer to this Problem suggest concerning the advisability of relying on the 30–day period in BC 547(e)(2)(A)?

Problem 7.2.16. Would the result in the immediately preceding Problem change if Creditor financed Debtor's purchase of a bulldozer that was delivered to Debtor on January 2? Recall Problem 7.2.3, p. 457, above. What is the relationship between the answer to Problem 7.2.3 and the powers of the trustee in bankruptcy? See BC 544(a); UCC 9–317(e); BC 546(b); BC 362(b)(3).

Problem 7.2.17. On June 1 Bank made a $100,000 term loan to Debtor. The loan was secured by "all Debtor's existing and after-acquired equipment." On June 1 Debtor owned equipment worth $90,000. Bank "prefiled" a financing statement on May 28. On July 1 Debtor purchased and took delivery of an additional piece of equipment worth $12,000. Debtor files a bankruptcy petition on August 1. The trustee seeks to avoid Bank's security interest in all the equipment. What result? See BC 547(e)(2)(A); BC 547(e)(3).

Problem 7.2.18. What result in the immediately preceding Problem if Bank and Debtor agreed that Debtor would use $12,000 of the loan proceeds to acquire an additional piece of equipment, and the proceeds were so used? See BC 547(c)(3).

Problem 7.2.19. On June 1 Creditor loaned $10,000 to Debtor and Debtor delivered to Creditor negotiable bonds in Company *A* worth $10,000. On September 1, at a time when Creditor knew Debtor to be insolvent, Creditor delivered the bonds in Company *A* to Debtor in exchange for bonds of the same value in Company *B*. The bonds of both companies continue to sell at par. On September 2 Debtor went into bankruptcy.

(a) May the trustee avoid the transfer of the Company *B* bonds as a preference? See BC 547(a)(2) & (c)(1).

(b) What difference, if any, would it make if on June 1 Debtor delivered bonds of Company *A* worth only $4,000, and on September 1 Debtor exchanged these bonds for bonds of Company *B* worth $10,000? What result if on September 1, instead of the exchange, Debtor delivered additional bonds in Company *A* worth $6,000?

(c) Would it make any practical difference if the bonds of Company *A* delivered on June 1 were worth $15,000 and these bonds were exchanged on September 1 for bonds in Company *B* worth $20,000? See BC 547(b)(5).

Problem 7.2.20. On June 1 Creditor loaned $100,000 to Debtor and at the same time, to secure the loan, Debtor delivered to Creditor stock in Company *X* worth $50,000. In July Company *X* announced the development of a new product; by the middle of August the stock had increased in value by 50 percent. On August 30 Debtor entered bankruptcy. The trustee argues that Creditor received a $25,000 preference. Do you agree? Was there more than one "transfer of an interest of the debtor in property"? If so, when did each transfer occur?

It is generally assumed that increases in the value of collateral shortly before bankruptcy do not constitute "transfers" giving rise to a voidable preferences. Is the conclusion that the "transfer" of the stock occurred on June 1 consistent with policies underlying the bankruptcy rules governing preferences? Does it violate the "anti-last-minute-grab" policy? Does it violate the "equality of distribution" policy? The latter arguably is directed toward recapturing transfers of the debtor's property that diminish the assets available for distribution to unsecured creditors. When, as in this Problem, the increase in the value of collateral is due to market forces, is the bankruptcy estate diminished within the preference period? See BC 101(54); BC 547(b)(5). As we shall see below, the answer is less clear-cut when the increase in value results from labor or other inputs supplied by the debtor.

NOTES ON THE "FLOATING LIEN" IN BANKRUPTCY

(1) Security Interests in After–Acquired Property. We now focus on the bankruptcy preference problems presented by the transitory character of some types of collateral, specifically inventory and receivables.

We begin by considering the way these assets are financed outside bankruptcy.

A merchant may think of inventory as a fairly constant unit. Inventory at the beginning of the year often is compared with inventory at the end without regard to whether any of the items is the same. But, from another point of view, there is a fairly constant process of exhaustion and replenishment, as inventory flows in through a merchant's stockroom and out over the counter or through the shipping room. Consider a hardware store: Each day there may be hundreds of sales (large and small) that convert inventory into cash or accounts. Situations of this kind arise in a wide range of retail, wholesale, and manufacturing settings. Accounts receivable go through a similar cycle: Each time a debtor contracts to sell goods or provide services, a new account is generated; upon payment the account disappears.

Over the past centuries, attempts to finance the flow of inventory and accounts, i.e., to create a security interest that "floats" over a debtor's inventory and accounts from the time the debtor acquires (or creates) them until the debtor disposes of (or collects) them, have generated serious and important legal problems, both within and outside of bankruptcy. Underlying the legal doctrines are conflicting values: the utility of added operating capital versus the desire to hold assets in reserve for last-ditch financing and to meet the claims of unsecured creditors.

Until the adoption of the UCC, secured parties found it difficult (and sometimes impossible) to maintain an effective security interest in collateral that was subject to a constant process of exhaustion and replenishment. However, Article 9 replaced the different common-law and statutory rules governing personal property security with a uniform legal regime that expressly validates the "floating lien." Comment 2 to Former 9–204 explained that Former Article 9 "decisively rejects" the "inarticulate premise" underlying pre-UCC hostility to the floating lien—that "a commercial borrower should not be allowed to encumber all his assets present and future, and that for the protection not only of the borrower but of his other creditors a cushion of free assets should be preserved"—"not on the ground that it was wrong in policy but on the ground that it was not effective." Like Former Article 9, UCC 9–204(a) provides explicitly that "a security agreement may create or provide for a security interest in after-acquired collateral." The filing of a single financing statement covering "inventory and accounts" is sufficient to perfect a security interest in inventory and accounts that the debtor acquires after the filing, even if the financing statement does not refer to after-acquired property. UCC 9–204, Comment 7. See Chapter 3, Section 3(A), supra.

Former Article 9 took another important step towards facilitating the "floating lien." Former 9–205 provided: "A security interest is not invalid or fraudulent against creditors by reason of liberty in the debtor . . . to use, commingle or dispose of proceeds, or by reason of the failure of the secured party to require the debtor to account for proceeds or replace collateral." This section, the substance of which now appears as UCC 9–205(a), was a frontal attack on the "doctrine of Benedict v. Ratner," under which a security arrangement was fraudulent if the debtor was given unfettered dominion and control over the collateral.[3]

For second thoughts about the UCC's validation of the floating lien and its rejection of the rule of Benedict v. Ratner, see Gilmore, The Good Faith Purchase Idea and the Uniform Commercial Code: Confessions of a Repentant Draftsman, 15 Ga.L.Rev. 605, 621–27 (1981).

(2) Acquisition of After–Acquired Property as a Preferential Transfer. Outside bankruptcy, a security interest in incoming collateral covered by an appropriate security agreement and financing statement will be senior to a judicial lien acquired by the debtor's other creditors. UCC 9–201(a); UCC 9–317(a)(2); Chapter 3, Section 3(A), supra. Does this mean that new collateral acquired shortly before bankruptcy will be immune from attack as a preference under BC 547?

In the floating lien, the loan is made, the security agreement is authenticated, and a financing statement is filed at the beginning of the arrangement. When bankruptcy falls, the debtor may hold little or none of the original collateral. The trustee's attack will center on collateral that the debtor acquired within the 90 days before bankruptcy: *When* was this collateral transferred to the creditor? If the transfer occurred only when the debtor acquired the collateral, then the trustee can assert that the new collateral was transferred to the creditor for an "antecedent debt." If so, the trustee is well on the way to proving a voidable preference under BC 547(b).

BC 547 contains special provisions that address potential preference attacks on floating liens. One of those provisions, BC 547(c)(5), is quite complicated and may be understood more easily in its historical context.

(3) The Historical Background of BC 547(c)(5). BC 547(c)(5) derives from a proposal put forward in a report of a committee of the National Bankruptcy Conference[4] known as the "Gilmore Committee." National Bankruptcy Conference, Report of the Committee on Coordination of the Bankruptcy Act and the Uniform Commercial Code (1970) ("Gilmore Committee Report"), reprinted in H.R. Rep. No. 595, 95th Cong., 1st Sess. 204 (1977), reprinted in 1978 U.S.C.C.A.N. 5963, 6164. The report explains:

---

3.   In Benedict v. Ratner, the Supreme Court found that, "[u]nder the law of New York a transfer of property as security which reserves to the transferor the right to dispose of the same, or to apply the proceeds thereof, for his own uses is, as to creditors, fraudulent in law and void." 268 U.S. at 360, 45 S.Ct. at 568, 69 L.Ed. at 997. The "doctrine of Benedict v. Ratner" was, with a few exceptions, followed in other states. 1 Gilmore, Security §§ 8.2–8.6, at 253–74. A substantial body of case law developed over how much "policing" by the lender of the debtor's accounting for proceeds was necessary to avoid the conclusion that the creditor lacked a property interest in the collateral that was effective against judicial liens obtained by competing creditors.

4.   The National Bankruptcy Conference is a nonprofit, unincorporated organization devoted to the improvement of bankruptcy law. Its members include bankruptcy judges, law professors, and practicing attorneys who specialize in bankruptcy and creditors' rights law.

In 1966 it appeared that security interests in personal property under Article 9 of the Uniform Commercial Code were in serious jeopardy in bankruptcy proceedings. At the time when the revision of [Bankruptcy Act] § 60 [governing preferences] which was enacted in 1950 was being prepared, the drafting of Article 9 was in its early stages. The § 60 revision, of necessity, was written in what we may call pre-Code language; it reflected the pre-Code structure of personal property security law. . . . . If the structure of security law had remained as it was, the compromise represented by the 1950 revision of § 60 would have worked perfectly well. With the general enactment of the Code, including Article 9, the situation was radically altered. Arguably, Article 9 contained little or nothing that was revolutionary, or even novel, as a matter of substance. The Article 9 terminology, on the other hand, represented a sharp break with the past. The difficulty of making the two statutes (§ 60 and Article 9) mesh or track with each other was immediately apparent. During the 1950's and continuing into the 1960's a quantitatively impressive amount of literature was devoted to the problem in the law reviews, specialized journals, and treatises. A considerable part of this literature seemed dedicated to the proposition that almost any Article 9 security interest could be turned into a voidable preference under § 60. The Article 9 security interest in after-acquired property (including inventory and receivables) was thought to be particularly vulnerable. . . . . This literature, it is true, was, to start with, merely literature; there were no cases. Nevertheless, the holders of Article 9 security interests became understandably concerned about their fate.

1978 U.S.C.C.A.N. at 6167.

In the late 1960's two circuit court opinions addressing the avoidability of security interests in after-acquired property gave comfort to secured lenders. The Ninth Circuit proclaimed the most sweeping theory for protecting the floating lien in DuBay v. Williams, 417 F.2d 1277 (9th Cir.1969). The *DuBay* opinion reached its result in two steps. The first step invoked the strong protection that Article 9 gives security arrangements that include a claim of after-acquired property. Under Former 9–301(1)(b), once the secured party filed a financing statement, the lien acquired by any creditor that levies on any property that might thereafter be acquired by the debtor would be junior to the perfected security interest. The second step integrated this rule of state law with section 60(a)(2) of the Bankruptcy Act, which governed the time when transfers shall be "deemed" to be made:

> a transfer of property . . . shall be deemed to have been made or suffered at the time when it became so far perfected that no subsequent lien upon such property obtainable by legal or equitable proceedings on a simple contract could become superior to the rights of the transferee.

As the Ninth Circuit applied the "levying-creditor" test, incoming property would be "deemed" to have been transferred to the debtor when it became immune from levy—the date of filing—even though at that time the debtor had no interest in the property; indeed, at the time of filing the property may not even have been in existence. (An admirer of "Man of La Mancha" has referred to this as the "impossible deem"; and Professor Countryman roundly condemned this approach as "The Abracadabra, or the Transfer Occurred before it Occurred, Theory." Countryman, Code Security Interests in Bankruptcy, 75 Com. L.J. 269, 277 (1970).) The sweeping theory of the *DuBay* case was as comforting to secured lenders as it was disturbing to others, for it set no controls over enlarging the protection given to the holder of the floating lien (at the expense of suppliers and other unsecured creditors) when the debtor purchased additional property shortly before bankruptcy.

During the same year, the Seventh Circuit applied preference law to a floating lien on accounts. In Grain Merchants of Indiana, Inc. v. Union Bank & Savings Co., 408 F.2d 209 (7th Cir.1969), cert. denied 396 U.S. 827, 90 S.Ct. 75, 24 L.Ed.2d 78 (1969), the court used three alternative theories to immunize the floating lien from preference attack. First, using an analysis similar to that of the Ninth Circuit in *DuBay*, the court found that accounts that were generated during the preference period had been transferred to the secured party a year before bankruptcy, when the financing statement was filed.

Second, the court suggested that one ought to consider all accounts, existing and future, as a single entity that was given as collateral at the outset of the transaction, in a contemporaneous exchange for the loan. It quoted Professor Hogan with favor:

> The secured creditor's interest is in the stream of accounts flowing through the debtor's business, not in any specific accounts. As with the Heraclitean river, although the accounts in the stream constantly change, we can say it is the same stream.

Hogan, Games Lawyers Play with the Bankruptcy Preference Challenge to Accounts and Inventory Financing, 53 Cornell L. Rev. 553, 560 (1968). Although the "entity theory" was inconsistent with Former 9–203(1) (UCC 9–203(b)), the court observed that a contrary result—one that would immunize only those accounts that were taken in exchange for a new loan—would jeopardize the flexible methods of financing that UCC 9–205 made possible by abrogating the requirement that a secured party must maintain dominion over collateral in order to protect its security interest.

The court's third theory was grounded in the long-standing "substitution of collateral" doctrine: a prebankruptcy transfer of collateral is not preferential when the collateral is taken in exchange for a release of other collateral. (Problem 7.2.19, supra, examines this doctrine.) Unlike other courts that had applied the doctrine, the Seventh Circuit found that "the newly arising accounts receivable may be considered as having been taken in exchange for the release of rights in earlier accounts and for a present consideration," without inquiring into either the timing of the supposed exchange (i.e., whether the release was substantially contemporaneous with or subsequent to the transfer of new collateral) or the relative value of the two items of collateral (i.e., whether the released collateral was worth at least as much as the new collateral). Rather, the court found that because the secured party no longer was required to assume dominion over individual accounts, "it is no longer appropriate to apply strict timing or value rules so long as at all relevant times the total pool of collateral, as here, exceeded the total debt."

The alternative grounds set forth in *Grain Merchants* were encouraging to lenders contemplating a floating lien but left nagging doubts as to the precise circumstances for protection. And, of course, one could not have safely predicted the approach of other federal courts. Nevertheless, as the Gilmore Committee reported, as of 1970:

> [T]he secured creditor bar (if there is such a thing) [was] basking happily in the warm glow of Judge Hufstedler's opinion in *DuBay* and, we may assume, [had] lost any interest it may once have had in reform of the Bankruptcy Act.

> What may be called the politics of the project of revising § 60 have thus come full circle during the past few years [ending in 1970]. What started out as a rescue mission for secured creditors may end up as a rescue mission for unsecured creditors.

1978 U.S.C.C.A.N. at 6168.

(4) The Bankruptcy Code and the Floating Lien. Drawing on the work of the Gilmore Committee, the drafters of the Bankruptcy Code addressed directly the problems raised by the floating lien, including the problem of determining the time when a transfer of a security interest in after-acquired property occurs. Section 547(e)(3) states that, for purposes of determining whether a transfer of a debtor's interest constitutes a preference, "a transfer is not made until the debtor has acquired rights in the property transferred." The avowed purpose of this provision was to overrule *DuBay* and *Grain Merchants*. S. Rep. No. 989, 95th Cong., 2d Sess. 89 (1978), reprinted in 1978 U.S.C.C.A.N. 5787, 5875. Certainly, this language leaves no room for either the "Heraclitean river" or "Abracadabra" ("impossible deem") approach.

The rule of BC 547(e)(3) is far from the end of the story. To meet the practical difficulties of maintaining security interests in inventory and receivables, the Bankruptcy Code provides an important exception from the general preference rules of 547(b). That exception is BC 547(c)(5).

Please look at BC 547(c)(5) now. As you can see, the subsection is somewhat forbidding. Its language is easier to understand if one starts with a general idea of what the drafters were trying to accomplish. Their central idea was that the floating lien should be subject to attack only to the extent that the acquisition of additional collateral in the aggregate resulted in an improvement in the secured creditor's position during the 90–day period preceding bankruptcy. More specifically, BC 547(c)(5) focuses on whether the aggregate of preferential transfers of security interests caused a reduction in the secured party's unsecured claim (what the statute calls the "amount by which the debt secured by such security interest exceeded the value of all security interests for such debt"). BC 547(c)(5) does not take into account day-to-day fluctuations in collateral levels; rather, one measures the actual unsecured claim as of the date of the bankruptcy petition and compares it to the secured party's unsecured position at the start of the preference period.[5]

The language of BC 547(c)(5) is difficult to penetrate. The following Problems are designed to facilitate your understanding.

Problem 7.2.21. Debtor filed a Chapter 11 petition on March 31, 2006. At that time, Debtor owed $70,000 to Creditor. This debt was secured by a security interest in all Debtor's existing and after-acquired inventory, then valued at $75,000.

At the end of 2005, Debtor's inventory had a value of $75,000 and secured a debt of $70,000. During the first quarter of 2006, Debtor's entire inventory turned over completely; that is, all the inventory that Debtor held at the start of the year was sold.

(a) How much, if any, of the security interest in the $75,000 of new inventory constitutes a preference under BC 547(b)?

(b) How much, if any, of the security interest in the $75,000 of new inventory can the trustee avoid? See BC 547(c)(5). On the ninetieth day prior to bankruptcy, what was the "amount by which the debt . . . *exceeded* the . . . security interest[ ] . . ."? Did subsequent transfers "cause[ ] a reduction" in that figure? Does the result surprise you?

Problem 7.2.22. Debtor filed a Chapter 11 petition on March 31, 2006. At that time, Debtor owed $70,000 to Creditor. This debt was secured by a security interest in all Debtor's existing and after-acquired inventory. At the end of 2005, Debtor's inventory had a value of $55,000 and secured a debt of $70,000. As of the time of the petition, Debtor's inventory is worth $60,000. During the first quarter of 2006, Debtor's entire inventory turned over completely.

(a) How much, if any, of the security interest in the $60,000 of new inventory can the trustee avoid?

(b) What result in part (a) if Creditor was owed $65,000 at the time of the filing of the petition? Of what relevance, if any, are the facts surrounding the reduction in the amount of the debt? Suppose the $5,000 payment came from unencumbered funds? Suppose it represented proceeds from the sale of inventory? Would it make any difference if the payment was one of a series of monthly payments required under the terms of the credit agreement? See Notes on Prepetition Payments to Secured Parties, supra.

Problem 7.2.23. Debtor filed a Chapter 11 petition on March 31, 2006. At that time, Debtor owed $70,000 to Creditor. This debt was secured by a security interest in all Debtor's existing and after-acquired inventory. At the

---

5.   In some cases, the secured party may not yet have extended any value to the debtor as of the start of the preference period. If so, then the secured party's actual unsecured claim as of the petition date must be compared to the secured party's unsecured position on the date on which new value was first given under the security agreement. See BC 547(c)(5)(B).

end of 2005, Debtor's inventory had a value of $55,000 and secured a debt of $70,000. During the first quarter of 2006, Debtor was unable to sell any inventory, but because of market shifts the inventory was worth $60,000 at the time of the filing of the petition.

How much, if any, of the security interest in the $60,000 of inventory can the trustee avoid? In what way, if any, does this Problem differ from Problem 7.2.22? Does this Problem implicate BC 547(c)(5)? If so, to what extent did *"transfers* to the transferee cause[ ] a reduction" in the unsecured portion of Creditor's claim?

Problem 7.2.24. Surf Advertising has a contract with Calvert Distillers, under which Calvert agreed to pay Surf $1,000 each month for two years, during which time Surf agreed to maintain certain advertising signs. Abrams made a loan to Surf and took a perfected security interest in Surf's rights under the unperformed contract with Calvert. During the 90 days prior to Surf's bankruptcy, Surf collected $3,000 from Calvert and paid those amounts to Abrams.

Did Abrams receive an avoidable preference? See BC 547(b); Rockmore v. Lehman, infra. Precisely what "transfer" would the trustee seek to avoid? How would the trustee distinguish this situation from that presented in Problem 7.2.23?

Rockmore v. Lehman[*]

United States Court of Appeals, Second Circuit, 1942.
129 F.2d 892 (1943).

[Proceedings were instituted for the reorganization of the Surf Advertising Corporation under Chapter X of the Bankruptcy Act. Abrams had advanced sums to Surf; in exchange, Surf assigned to Abrams Surf's rights to payment, still to be earned, under an existing contract to maintain advertising signs for Calvert Distillers Corporation. In an earlier opinion (here reversed on rehearing) the Court of Appeals had held that payment to Abrams of funds earned under these contracts constituted a preference.]

Augustus N. Hand, Circuit Judge. . . . In each of the cases before us, advances were made upon contracts whereby Surf in the first case and Fiegel Advertising Company in the second case were to furnish and maintain advertising signs for Calvert in return for which Calvert bound itself to pay fixed sums over a period of years for the furnishing and maintenance of the signs. The advances were not made upon a mere agreement to assign rights which might arise in the future and did not exist at the time contracts were made, but upon assignments of definite contractual obligations.

We are convinced that the New York Court of Appeals has differentiated assignments of existing contracts by way of pledge from agreements to assign rights that have not yet come into being, even as interests contingent

---

[*]   [Decided under the then-current version of the Bankruptcy Act of 1898.]

upon counter-performance. The most recent decision is Kniffin v. State, 283 N.Y. 317, 28 N.E.2d 853, where a building contractor assigned his contract with the State of New York to a subcontractor as security for a pre-existing indebtedness, and then became bankrupt. The State made payments under the contract to the assignor, but the assignee was allowed to recover the amount of its claim in spite of the fact that the assignment embraced moneys "to become due" under the contract.

We cannot agree with appellant's contention that Section 60, sub. a, of the present Bankruptcy Act, 11 U.S.C.A. § 96, sub. a, affects our decision, and that there would be an unlawful preference as to any sums paid or payable after knowledge of insolvency. On the contrary we hold that the date of the assignments governed the imposition of the liens on any sums due from Calvert. This is because the contracts, and not the moneys accruing under them, were the subjects of the assignments. Section 60, sub. a, provides that: "a transfer shall be deemed to have been made at the time when it became so far perfected that no bona-fide purchaser from the debtor and no creditor could thereafter have acquired any rights in the property so transferred superior to the rights of the transferee therein." It has long been the New York law that such an assignment is good against a bona fide purchaser, even though the bona fide purchaser is the first to give notice to the obligor. The same thing is true of an execution creditor or a trustee in bankruptcy. . . .

[The opinion also concluded that New York Lien Law § 230 did not require filing of the assignment.]

It follows from the foregoing that our former decision in this matter was erroneous and that the decision of the court below in both cases should have been affirmed.

Orders affirmed.

Problem 7.2.25. Suppose that, in order to perform the Calvert contract in Problem 7.2.24, Surf was required to hire Employee and purchase from Seller a piece of additional equipment. Surf's trustee makes the following argument: payments to Employee and Seller had the effect of exchanging Surf's unencumbered property for an increase in the value of Abrams's collateral, the Calvert account. Even if these payments were not transfers *to* a creditor (Abrams), they were transfers *for the benefit of a creditor* (Abrams) and thus potentially preferential under BC 547(b). See BC 547(b)(1). If the trustee can prove the other elements of BC 547(b), then BC 550(a)(1) enables the trustee to recover the property transferred (or its value) from "the entity for whose benefit such transfer was made." Thus, argues the trustee, Abrams is liable for payments made to Employee and Seller.

(a) Are you persuaded by the trustee's argument? As to the ability of the trustee to recover transfers that create preferences indirectly, see Note on Dean v. Davis, infra.

(b) Suppose Employee and Seller provided their services and goods to Surf on open credit and remained unpaid at the time of bankruptcy. Would the trustee's argument be stronger or weaker?

Problem 7.2.26. On June 1 Crystal Credit loaned $100,000 to the Dream Spinning Co. At the same time Dream granted Crystal a perfected security interest in bales of cotton then worth $60,000. The security interest also extended to after-acquired cotton and yarn. During June, July and August Dream processed this cotton into yarn. As a result of the processing, the yarn was worth $100,000 by August 30, when Dream went into bankruptcy. Can the trustee avoid Crystal's interest as a preference to the extent of the increase in value during the 90 days before bankruptcy? When did the "transfer" of the security interest in the yarn occur? See Note on "Prejudice of Other Creditors," infra.

NOTE ON "PREJUDICE OF OTHER CREDITORS"

At stake in Problems 7.2.24, 7.2.25, and 7.2.26 is nothing less than the continuing vitality of the leading case of Rockmore v. Lehman, supra. That decision rejected a trustee's attack on the secured party's receipt of amounts the debtor earned under a contract that had been assigned to the secured party, even though the debtor had earned those amounts by work performed shortly before bankruptcy.

Grappling with these Problems requires a bit of legislative history. As you know, the two-point test embodied in BC 547(c)(5) emerged from the work of the Gilmore Committee. The Gilmore Committee Report put a case where raw materials worth $10,000 are converted into finished products worth $20,000; the Gilmore Committee stated that under its proposal the $10,000 increase in value was not protected and would go to the trustee. It observed: "If the final holding in *Rockmore v. Lehman* [citation omitted] suggests the contrary conclusion, that holding is here overruled." 1978 U.S.C.C.A.N. at 6177–78.

This feature of the Gilmore Committee's recommendations encountered criticism. Professor Homer Kripke argued that any increase in the value of collateral due, e.g., to harvesting crops, completing work in progress, and sales of inventory, should redound to the benefit of the secured party "so long as it is not at the expense of other parties interested in the estate." H.R. Doc. No. 137, 93d Cong., 1st Sess. pt. 1, at 210 (1973) (quoting a letter from Professor Kripke to the Gilmore Committee). To implement this policy, Professor Kripke mentioned the formula used in Meinhard, Greeff & Co. v. Edens, 189 F.2d 792 (4th Cir.1951), which gave the secured creditor the entire value of the finished goods, less the costs expended in finishing them.

In response to this conflict in views, the provision that became BC 547(c)(5) was amended by inserting the qualifying phrase "and to the prejudice of other creditors holding unsecured claims." Does the meaning of this phrase become clear in the light of the legislative history? In Problem 7.2.26, what facts would show that Crystal's improvement in position resulted from "transfers to the transferee . . . to the prejudice of other creditors holding unsecured claims"?

Could this provision jeopardize construction loans, crop loans, and other types of complex financing in which the secured party gives value before the debtor does the work that creates value in the collateral? Can (and should) the Bankruptcy Code be interpreted to avoid such dangers?

One interpretation that would give some comfort to secured parties would be to focus on the requirement that the improvement in position results from "transfers" that otherwise would be avoidable under BC 547(b). The line between an increase in the value of a given item of collateral (which does not constitute a "transfer") and an exchange of one item of collateral for another (which does) may be difficult to discern. Consider, for example, an account receivable. What happens when the debtor earns a right to payment by performing its contractual obligation? Like Rockmore v. Lehman, both BC 547(a)(3) and UCC 9–102(a)(2) suggest that although the right to payment has increased in value, it is the same item of collateral. But under the pre–1972 version of Former 9–106, only earned rights to payment were accounts; unearned rights to payment were a different type of collateral, "contract rights." Should nonbankruptcy law's characterization of the collateral determine whether a preference has occurred?

NOTE ON *DEAN V. DAVIS*

A favorite aphorism of many first-year law students is "One cannot do indirectly what one cannot do directly." In Dean v. Davis, 242 U.S. 438, 37 S.Ct. 130, 61 L.Ed. 419 (1917), the Supreme Court applied this principle to preference law under the Bankruptcy Act of 1898. Fearing that Bank would have him arrested for fraud, Debtor borrowed $1,600 from his father-in-law, Dean, and secured the debt with a mortgage on substantially all his property. Shortly thereafter an involuntary bankruptcy petition was filed against Debtor. The trustee sought to set aside the mortgage and was successful. The district court held the mortgage constituted a fraudulent conveyance; the court of appeals held it also was a voidable preference.

In affirming the district court, the Supreme Court (Brandeis, J.) rejected the preference attack as follows:

> The mortgage was not voidable as a preference under § 60b. Preference implies paying or securing a preexisting debt of the person preferred. The mortgage was given to secure Dean for a substantially contemporary advance. *The bank, not Dean, was preferred.* The use of Dean's money to accomplish this purpose could not convert the transaction into a preferring of Dean, although he knew of the debtor's insolvency. Mere circuity of arrangement will not save a transfer which effects a preference from being invalid as such. But a transfer to a third person is invalid under this section as a preference, only where that person was acting on behalf of the creditor. . . .

242 U.S. at 443, 37 S.Ct. at 131 (emphasis added).

Inasmuch as the trustee did not proceed against Bank, the court's observation that the Bank was preferred is dictum. The recodification of preference law in the Bankruptcy Code is consistent with the notion that an otherwise nonpreferential transfer to one person may result in a preference to a creditor who received the benefit of the transfer. Thus, BC 547(b)(1) refers to transfers "to or *for the benefit of* a creditor" and BC 550(a)(1) permits recovery of an avoided transfer from "the initial transferee of such transfer *or the entity for whose benefit the transfer was made.*"

A number of reported cases are consistent with this aspect of Dean v. Davis. See, e.g., In re Air Conditioning, Inc. of Stuart, 845 F.2d 293 (11th Cir.1988), cert. denied 488 U.S. 993, 109 S.Ct. 557, 102 L.Ed.2d 584 (1988) (grant of security interest to issuer of letter of credit held preferential to beneficiary); In re Compton Corp., 831 F.2d 586 (5th Cir.1987) (same), rehearing granted per curiam 835 F.2d 584 (1988) (explaining what facts are to be considered on remand). A particularly interesting case is In re Prescott, 805 F.2d 719 (7th Cir.1986). In *Prescott,* transfers were made during the preference period to a partially secured senior creditor. Because the transfers had the effect of increasing the collateral available to a junior secured creditor (i.e., converting part of the unsecured portion of the claim into a secured claim), the court held that the transfers preferred the junior creditor.

Whether Dean v. Davis continues as a part of the fraudulent conveyance law applicable in bankruptcy is beyond the scope of this book.

NOTE ON VALUATION OF COLLATERAL

As should be apparent by now, most of the issues we have discussed in this Chapter implicate issues of valuing the collateral. For example, one cannot work the two-point test of BC 547(c)(5) without valuing the collateral at each of the two points. Nor can one determine whether the debtor has any "equity" in the collateral for purposes of BC 362(d)(2) unless one knows the collateral's value.

Depending on the circumstances, appraisers apply different standards of valuation to any given piece of property. Among the most common are going-concern value (what the property is worth as part of an ongoing business; this standard requires that the total value of the business be allocated among its various assets), fair market value (what the property would yield at a sale by a willing seller to a willing buyer), and forced-sale (or quick liquidation) value (what would the property yield at an immediate sale by a seller who was compelled to sell).

The Bankruptcy Code does not define the applicable standard. Under BC 506(a), the value of a security interest in property "shall be determined in light of the purpose of the valuation and of the proposed disposition or use of such property, and in conjunction with any hearing on such disposition or use or on a plan affecting such creditor's interest." The legislative history suggests that courts will have to determine value on a case-by-case basis and that a valuation at one time for one purpose (e.g., adequate protection) would not be binding at a later time for another purpose (e.g., distribution). See S. Rep. No. 989, 95th Cong., 2d Sess. 68 (1978), reprinted in 1987 U.S.C.C.A.N. 5787, 5854; H.R. Rep. No. 595, 95th Cong., 1st Sess. 356 (1977), reprinted in 1978 U.S.C.C.A.N. 5963, 6312.

In 1997 the Supreme Court considered the applicable standard for valuing collateral. Associates Commercial Corp. v. Rash, 520 U.S. 953, 117 S.Ct. 1879, 138 L.Ed.2d 148 (1997). In *Rash*, the Chapter 13 debtors proposed to retain the collateral (a truck) for use in a freight-hauling business. Their Chapter 13 plan proposed to "cram down" the secured party by paying the present value of the collateral in 58 monthly installments. The debtors argued that the standard for valuing the collateral should be foreclosure value, i.e., the amount the secured party would have received at a foreclosure disposition under Article 9. The Court rejected this argument and held that a replacement-value standard applied: "the value of property retained because the debtor has exercised the § 1325(a)(5)(B) 'cram down' option is the cost the debtor would incur to obtain a like asset for the same 'proposed . . . use.' " Elsewhere in the opinion, the Court referred to replacement value as "the price a willing buyer in the debtor's trade, business, or situation would pay a willing seller to obtain property of like age and condition." The valuation standard may well be different when the collateral is sold as part of a liquidation and not retained for use by the debtor.

In a footnote, the Supreme Court explained that:

Whether replacement value is the equivalent of retail value, wholesale value, or some other value will depend on the type of debtor and the nature of the property. . . . Where the proper measure of the replacement value of a vehicle is its retail value, an adjustment to that value may be necessary: A creditor should not receive portions of the retail price, if any, that reflect the value of items the debtor does not receive when he retains his vehicle, items such as warranties, inventory storage, and reconditioning. Nor should the creditor gain from modifications to the property—*e.g.*, the addition of accessories to a vehicle—to which a creditor's lien would not extend under state law.

Congress apparently was displeased with the result in *Rash*. In 2005 it added a new BC 506(a)(2), which changed the valuation standard, but only in Chapter 7 and Chapter 13 cases where the debtor is an individual. The value of personal property collateral in those cases "shall be determined based on the replacement value of such property as of the date of the filing of the [bankruptcy] petition without deduction for costs of sale or marketing." BC 506(a)(2). Also, with respect to property acquired for personal, family, or household purposes, replacement value now means "the price a retail merchant would charge for property of that kind considering the age and condition of the property at the time value is determined." Id.

Detailed discussion of valuation issues is best left to the Bankruptcy course.

Problem 7.2.27. On June 1 Castle Finance loaned $100,000 to Diggins Construction Company; Diggins executed an agreement granting Castle a security interest in "all of the construction equipment including bulldozers and other machinery, that Diggins now owns or may hereafter acquire." At the time of the agreement Diggins owned five bulldozers each worth $20,000. On June 9, Castle filed a financing statement, signed by Diggins, that referred to the collateral as "construction equipment."

On July 1, with Castle's approval, Diggins traded one of the bulldozers for a cement mixer that also was worth $20,000. On July 15 the construction business was slack, so Diggins sold two of its remaining four bulldozers for $40,000 and used these funds to pay workers and social security taxes. Castle was not informed of these sales. On August 1, Diggins received a $20,000 down payment from a new construction job and used this money to purchase a new $20,000 bulldozer.

On September 1 several creditors of Diggins threw Diggins into bankruptcy. Which assets of Diggins may Castle Finance claim against opposition by the trustee in bankruptcy? See Eisenberg, Bankruptcy Law in Perspective, 28 UCLA L. Rev. 953, 961–62 & n. 27 (1981) (discussing how BC 547(c)(5) distinguishes equipment from inventory and receivables).

NOTE ON PROCEEDS ARISING AFTER BANKRUPTCY

The filing of a bankruptcy petition does not necessarily coincide with the cessation of the debtor's business. Indeed, the debtor-in-possession may continue to operate the business in Chapter 11 unless the court orders otherwise. BC 1108. See also BC 721 (bankruptcy court may authorize Chapter 7 trustee to operate debtor's business).

In the course of operating the business, the DIP may acquire property that would be covered by an after-acquired property clause in a prepetition security agreement. Although the transfer of a security interest in property acquired postpetition ordinarily would not be avoidable under BC 547—the transfer would not have occurred *before* the date of the filing of the petition, see BC 547(b)(4)—a postpetition transfer of this kind might have the same effect as a voidable preference: the acquisition of additional collateral might improve the position of a secured creditor at the expense of other creditors.

BC 552 addresses this concern. The general rule, set forth in BC 552(a), is that property acquired by the bankruptcy estate after the commencement of the case is not subject to a security interest resulting from a prebankruptcy security agreement. In other words, BC 552(a) generally renders after-acquired property clauses ineffective as to property acquired after the commencement of a bankruptcy case.

Obviously, this rule is overbroad. It invalidates security interests not only in additional collateral but also in substitute collateral (e.g., an account that results from the postpetition sale of inventory collateral acquired by the debtor before bankruptcy). Subsection (b)(1) cuts back on the general rule when a prepetition security agreement "extends to property of the debtor acquired before the commencement of the case and to proceeds, products, offspring, or profits of such property." In that event, the security interest extends to such proceeds, etc., acquired by the estate after the commencement of the bankruptcy case to the extent provided by the security agreement and by applicable nonbankruptcy law. In other words, the filing of the bankruptcy petition does not invalidate a prepetition security agreement insofar as the secured party claims proceeds of prepetition collateral that the debtor acquires postpetition.

BC 552(b)(1) uses two important terms that the Bankruptcy Code leaves undefined: "extends to" and "proceeds." As discussed in Chapter 3, Section 5, supra, Article 9 gives every secured party a security interest in "proceeds" (as defined in UCC 9–102(a)(64)), even if the security agreement does not provide for one. See UCC 9–203(f), UCC 9–315(a)(2). The legislative history makes clear that a security agreement that is silent nevertheless "extends to" proceeds, as the term is used in BC 552(b)(1). See H.R.Rep. No. 595, 95th Cong., 1st Sess. 377 (1977), reprinted in 1978 U.S.C.C.A.N. 5963, 6333.

What constitutes "proceeds" within the meaning of BC 552(b)? In In re Bumper Sales, Inc., 907 F.2d 1430 (4th Cir.1990), the secured party claimed a security interest in inventory acquired by the debtor-in-possession during the bankruptcy case. The parties stipulated that the postpetition inventory was produced entirely with the proceeds of prepetition inventory. The Fourth Circuit held that "the UCC's definition and treatment of proceeds applies to Section 552 of the Bankruptcy Code" and covers "second generation proceeds" that are traceable to the prepetition collateral (e.g., inventory acquired with the proceeds of accounts generated postpetition from the sale of prepetition inventory).

The legislative history suggests that the term "proceeds" in BC 552 may encompass even more than the same term encompasses under the UCC. "The term 'proceeds' is not limited to the technical definition of that term in the U.C.C., but covers any property into which property subject to the security interest is converted." H.R.Rep. No. 595, 95th Cong., 1st Sess. 377 (1977). However, the Fourth Circuit "believe[s] that Section 552(b)'s express reference to 'nonbankruptcy law' should take priority over a vague and isolated piece of legislative history. We also note that the judicial creation of a definition for 'proceeds,' broader post-petition than pre-petition, would produce arbitrary and potentially inequitable results."

The definition of "proceeds" in UCC 9–102(a)(64) is somewhat broader than the definition of the term in Former Article 9, which was in effect when BC 552 was enacted. If a court follows the approach of the Fourth Circuit, will the meaning of "proceeds" in BC 552(b)(1) change to reflect changes in the Article 9 definition? One court recently failed to recognize that the expanded definition presents an issue under BC 552(b)(1). In re Skagit Pacific Corp., 316 B.R. 330 (9th Cir.BAP 2004). Citing Ninth Circuit authority that state law governs what constitutes proceeds for purposes of BC 552(b), the *Skagit Pacific* court quoted and applied Washington's UCC 9–102(a)(64). Although the court acknowledged that the revised definition differs from Former 9–306, it apparently disregarded the increased breadth of the new definition. (However, we doubt that the outcome of the case would have been different under the former definition.)

BC 552(b)(1) contains an important exception to the protection it affords to proceeds arising postpetition: the court may cut back on the security interest "based on the equities of the case." According to the legislative history, in the course of considering the equities, "the court may evaluate any expenditures by the estate relating to proceeds and any related improvement in position of the secured party." 124 Cong.Rec. 32400 (1978) (statement of Rep. Edwards); 124 Cong.Rec. 34000 (1978) (statement of Sen. DeConcini). See, e.g., In re Kain, 86 B.R. 506 (Bkrtcy.W.D.Mich.1988) (proceeds of sale postpetition offspring of prepetition livestock collateral "should be reduced by reasonable postpetition expenses validly and demonstrably paid or incurred by the Debtors to raise, preserve, enhance or market the livestock.") On the other hand, if production of the postpetition proceeds is achieved solely through the use of prepetition collateral or its proceeds, there is no basis for applying the "equities of the case" exception. See, e.g., *Bumper Sales*, supra. You should realize that the problem addressed by the "equities-of-the-case" exception to BC 552(b) also arises under BC 547(c)(5), where it is addressed from the perspective of "prejudice of other creditors." (The former deals with postpetition activity; the latter, prepetition.)

SECTION 3.   SELLER'S RIGHTS IN BUYER'S BANKRUPTCY

Problem 7.3.1. Buyer induced Seller to deliver goods on credit by fraudulently promising to pay for them in 30 days. (What is a "fraudulent promise"?) Shortly after delivering the goods, Seller discovered that, when Buyer promised to pay, Buyer was hopelessly insolvent. (These are the facts of Problem 1.2.4., p. 22, supra.)

(a) It is now one month after Seller delivered the goods to buyer; Seller learned that today Buyer filed a petition under Chapter 7 of the Bankruptcy Code. What are Seller's rights as to the goods? What advice would you give to Seller? See UCC 2–702(2) [R2-702(2)]; BC 546(c).

(b) Suppose it is now two months after Seller delivered the goods to Buyer and Buyer filed its bankruptcy petition today. Would your answers to part (a) change? If so, how?

(c) Suppose Seller delivered the goods to Buyer yesterday and Buyer filed its bankruptcy petition today. Would your answers to part (a) change? If so, how?

Problem 7.3.2. On June 1 Seller and Buyer tentatively agreed on a sale to Buyer of a load of cotton; the price was $4,000. Buyer then said, "I hope you can give me a week to pay." Seller replied, "I'm afraid I'll have to ask for cash." Buyer said, "I'll arrange for my driver to bring my check for the price tomorrow." The next day (June 2) Buyer's driver gave Seller a $4,000 check drawn by Buyer to Seller's order on Firstbank, and removed the cotton. Seller deposited the check in an account with Secondbank. Five days later

(June 7) Secondbank notified Seller that Buyer's check had been returned because of insufficient funds. (These are the facts of Problem 1.2.5., p. 22, supra.)

(a) It is now one month after Seller delivered the goods to buyer; Seller learned that today Buyer filed a petition under Chapter 7 of the Bankruptcy Code. What are Seller's rights as to the goods? What advice would you give to Seller? See UCC 2–507; UCC 2–511 [R2-507]; BC 546(c).

(b) Suppose it is now two months after Seller delivered the goods to Buyer and Buyer filed its bankruptcy petition today. Would your answers to part (a) change? If so, how?

(c) Suppose Seller delivered the goods to Buyer yesterday and Buyer filed its bankruptcy petition today. Would your answers to part (a) change? If so, how?

NOTES ON THE BANKRUPTCY RIGHTS OF UNPAID SELLERS

(1) Seller's Right to Payment in Bankruptcy. As we saw in Sections 1 and 2, supra, in bankruptcy, the difference between recognizing a secured party's *in rem* remedy against specific goods and its *in personam* claim for damages against the bankruptcy estate is crucial. Until the recent amendments to the Bankruptcy Code, the same could have been said for unpaid sellers. Where a seller did not enjoy a reclamation right—or where the trustee in bankruptcy avoided this right—the goods would remain in the estate, and their value ordinarily would have been distributed to unsecured creditors (including the unpaid sellers) pro rata according to the size of their claims; the debtor's liability for any unpaid portion of the debt normally would have been discharged. See BC 727; BC 1141; BC 524. In contrast, successful reclamation was likely to make the seller whole (or close to it).

For many unpaid sellers, however, new BC 503(b)(9) minimizes the difference between an *in rem* right to reclaim and an *in personam* claim for money damages. BC 503(a)(9), which applies to bankruptcy cases filed on or after October 17, 2005, entitles a seller to an **administrative expense** priority claim for the value of any goods received by the debtor within 20 days before the bankruptcy case is commenced, if the goods were sold to the debtor in the ordinary course of the debtor's business. Administrative expenses, which include also the trustee's fees and expenses and other costs of maintaining and preserving the estate, are paid from unencumbered assets ahead of nearly all other unsecured claims. See BC 507(a)(2). This means that sellers of goods normally will be paid in full for goods received by the debtor during the 20 days preceding the debtor's entry into bankruptcy, whether or not the seller would enjoy a right to reclaim the goods under nonbankruptcy law. As a result, a right to reclaim is likely to be most important in bankruptcy where the goods have been delivered to the debtor more than 20 days before the commencement of the bankruptcy case.[1]

(2) Seller's Right to Reclaim Goods Under BC 546(c). In addition to affording unpaid sellers a priority right to payment, the 2005 amendments to the Bankruptcy Code appear to create a federal bankruptcy right to reclaim certain goods. As amended, BC 546(c)(1) provides that several of the trustee's avoiding powers, including those in BC 544(a) and BC 547, are "subject to the right of a seller of goods that has sold goods to the debtor, in the ordinary course of such seller's business, to reclaim such goods if the debtor has received such goods while insolvent" and within 45 days before the commencement of the bankruptcy case. To qualify for this right, a seller must demand reclamation of the goods, in writing, not later than 45 days after the debtor received the goods, or (if the 45-day period expires after the commencement of the bankruptcy case) not later than 20 days after the commencement of the case.

A seller who fails to provide the required notice but who otherwise would be entitled to reclaim goods under BC 546(c) may be entitled instead to an administrative expense for the value of any goods received by the debtor within 20 days before the commencement of the bankruptcy case. See BC 546(c)(2); BC 503(a)(9); Note (1), supra.

Matters become more complex if the goods that are the subject of a right to reclaim under BC 546(c) also are encumbered by a security interest. BC 546(c)(1) provides that "subject to the prior rights of a holder of a security interest in such goods, [the trustee's avoiding powers are] subject to the right of a seller of goods . . . to reclaim such goods." Does this mean that a seller's right to reclaim is subject to a secured party's "prior rights"? If so, when are a secured party's rights "prior"? One meaning of "prior" is "at an earlier time." Under this reading, a secured party's rights are "prior" if they arise earlier in time than a seller's right to reclaim. What would be the relevant time from which to date a security interest for these purposes? When the security interest attaches? When it is perfected? When a financing statement is filed? And when does a right to reclaim under BC 546(c)(1) arise? At the commencement of the bankruptcy case? When the seller demands reclamation? When the goods are delivered to the buyer?

Another reading of BC 546(c)(1) is that a secured party's rights are "prior" to a reclamation right if the security interest would enjoy priority over (i.e., be senior to) a nonbankruptcy reclamation right. Under what circumstances, if any, would a secured party enjoy priority over a nonbankruptcy right to reclaim? See Chapter 1, Section 3, and Chapter 4, Section 4, supra.

---

1.   Even with respect to goods received within the 20-day period, a reclamation right will be valuable where the bankruptcy estate is or becomes **administratively insolvent**, i.e., where the aggregate amount of administrative expenses exceeds the value of the estate's unencumbered assets.

(3) Nonbankruptcy Reclamation Rights in Bankruptcy. Important questions remain notwithstanding (or perhaps because of) the recent revision of BC 546(c). Perhaps the most important is whether the section affects the bankruptcy treatment of reclamation rights arising under nonbankruptcy law. You may recall that the UCC contemplates two different rights to reclaim. The credit seller's right to reclaim goods arises when the seller discovers that the buyer has received goods on credit while insolvent. See UCC 2–702(2). The cash seller's right to reclaim goods arises when payment was due and demanded, but not received, upon delivery of the goods. See UCC 2–507(2). In addition, a seller may have a common-law right to recover goods by rescinding the sale for fraud. See Chapter 1, Sections 2 and 3, supra.

A seller may enjoy a nonbankruptcy right to reclaim but be ineligible to reclaim under BC 546(c). For example, the seller may have sold the goods on credit but not in the ordinary course of the seller's business; the seller may have delivered the goods on credit more than 45 days before the buyer's bankruptcy case began; or the seller may have delivered the goods to a solvent buyer who obtained them through active fraud or who purported to pay for them with a "rubber" check that "bounced." See generally Chapter 1, Section 2, supra.

Does BC 546(c) provide the exclusive remedy for a seller attempting to reclaim goods from a bankruptcy estate? In other words, does the inclusion of BC 546(c) mean that reclaiming sellers who do not fall within its scope automatically lose their nonbankruptcy reclamation rights in bankruptcy? Or does the section mean only that the trustee's right to avoid transfers of property under BC 544(a), BC 545, BC 547, and BC 549 does *not* apply if a seller qualifies for reclamation under BC 546(c)? The question is important, for under the latter reading one must first determine whether the trustee *has* the power to avoid the nonbankruptcy interest of an aggrieved seller under the sections of the Bankruptcy Code cited in BC 546(c).[2] If the trustee has no such power, then under this reading BC 546(c) becomes irrelevant and the seller may reclaim the goods (subject, of course, to the automatic stay).

Several courts had occasion to consider this issue under Former (pre-2005) BC 546(c). Unlike the new version, the former section specifically addressed nonbankruptcy reclamation rights. It provided that several of the trustee's avoiding powers, including those in BC 544(a) and BC 547, were "subject to any statutory or common-law right of a seller of goods that has sold goods to the debtor, in the ordinary course of such seller's business, to reclaim such goods if the debtor has received such goods while insolvent," if the seller demanded reclamation in writing within the time period specified in the Bankruptcy Code. We have seen that bankruptcy law

---

2.   For example, UCC 2–702(3) was amended in 1966 to delete the words "or lien creditor," thereby suggesting that the credit seller's reclamation right would prevail over a judicial lien creditor. In states that have adopted this amendment, the reclamation right would not be avoidable under BC 544(a).

generally respects nonbankruptcy property rights and other entitlements. A fair reading of Former BC 546(c) is that it afforded a safe harbor for certain nonbankruptcy reclamation rights and left to the trustee the burden avoiding other reclamation rights (e.g., those where the seller's demand satisfied the requirements of the UCC but not those of Former BC 546(c)) under other sections of the Bankruptcy Code. Nevertheless, most of the reported decisions have read Former BC 546(c) to be the exclusive mode of reclamation once the debtor enters bankruptcy. These courts permitted a defrauded seller to reclaim goods from the buyer's bankruptcy estate *only if* the seller enjoyed a nonbankruptcy right to reclaim *and* gave a written notice satisfying the requirements of Former BC 546(c). See, e.g., In re Contract Interiors, 14 B.R. 670 (Bkrtcy.E.D.Mich.1981).

What should courts make of the fact that BC 546(c) no longer applies to nonbankruptcy reclamation rights and instead creates a federal right to reclaim in bankruptcy? Does it evidence Congress's intention that a nonbankruptcy reclamation right be treated like other claims to property—i.e, it is recognized in bankruptcy, subject to the trustee's normal avoiding powers and the automatic stay? Or does new BC 546(c) evidence an intent to limit sellers' reclamation rights in bankruptcy to the right described in that section?

CHAPTER 8

COMPETING CLAIMS TO COLLATERAL: OTHER PRIORITY RULES

SECTION 1.   CHANGES IN BUSINESS STRUCTURE

INTRODUCTORY NOTE

X Corp merges into Y Corp; Y Corp survives and X Corp ceases to exist. As is typical, X Corp and Y Corp each has granted security interests: Each has a **working capital** lender, whose loan is secured with a **blanket lien** on all assets; other creditors hold purchase-money security interests in specific equipment and inventory. What are the consequences of the merger for the secured parties?

Quite probably, the merger constitutes a default under the loan agreements. If so, lawyers for X Corp and Y Corp are likely to have obtained consent to the merger from the secured parties. In the course of doing so, the various creditors of X Corp and Y Corp probably determined their rights (including the priority of their security interests) by contract. See UCC 9–339 (permitting subordination by agreement). If not, the parties will resort to Article 9 to resolve their differences.

Some changes in business structure are less likely to be lawyered—or, if lawyered, less likely to be well-lawyered—than are mergers of large corporations. For example, a sole proprietor or partnership whose inventory is subject to a security interest might incorporate the business (i.e., transfer the proprietor's business assets to a newly formed corporation) without taking into account the secured lender and the terms of the loan agreement. Similarly, the shareholders of a closely-held corporation might "reincorporate" in another state (i.e., transfer the closely-held corporation's business assets to a corporation newly formed in the other state) without giving a thought to the secured party's rights. In either case, the original secured party's claim to a security interest in property of the new corporation may come into conflict with a judicial lien or security interest claimed by another creditor of the corporation.

Resolution of the issues raised by changes in business structure has proven difficult for the courts under Former Article 9, whose provisions apparently were not drafted with these issues in mind. In contrast, Revised

Article 9 includes several provisions expressly addressing changes in business structure. This Section explores those provisions. Inasmuch as mergers, incorporations, and other changes in business structure typically include a transfer of collateral from one person to another, we begin with three Problems concerning transfer.

Problem 8.1.1. Oldcorp is a California corporation in the manufacturing business. *SP*–1 has a security interest in Oldcorp's existing and after-acquired inventory and equipment, all of which is located in Downey, California. *SP*–1 filed a proper financing statement against Oldcorp in 2006. On March 1, 2007, Oldcorp sells a used drill press to Buyer, a California corporation.

(a) Does *SP*–1's security interest in the drill press survive the sale? If so, does the security interest remain perfected? See UCC 9–315(a)(1); UCC 9–507(a).

(b) If *SP*–1's security interest survives the sale and remains perfected, for how long does *SP*–1's financing statement remain effective against the drill press? See UCC 9–515(a).

(c) Can *SP*–1 maintain the perfected status of its security interest in the drill press indefinitely? If so, how? See UCC 9–515(c), (d); UCC 9–509(c).

Problem 8.1.2. The facts are as in the immediately preceding Problem. In 2005 *SP*–2 acquired a security interest in Buyer's existing and after-acquired equipment and filed a proper financing statement covering the equipment.

(a) Is *SP*–1's security interest in the drill press senior or junior to *SP*–2's security interest? See UCC 9–325 & Comment 3; UCC 9–322(a); Note on "Double Debtor" Problems, infra. What could the losing party have done to prevent this result?

(b) Would the result in part (a) change if *SP*–2 financed Buyer's acquisition of the equipment from Oldcorp and filed a financing statement covering the equipment three days after Buyer took delivery? If so, how? What could the losing party have done to avoid the loss?

Problem 8.1.3. Would the answer to any of the questions in Problems 12.1.1 and 12.1.2, supra, change if Buyer is a Nevada corporation? If so, how? See UCC 9–316(a), (b); UCC 9–301; UCC 9–307; UCC 9–325; UCC 9–322(a)(2); Note (2), p. 276, supra.

NOTE ON "DOUBLE DEBTOR" PROBLEMS

Problem 8.1.2, supra, invites you to consider the appropriate solution for what has become known as the "double debtor" problem: the priority contest that arises when (i) a person acquires collateral subject to a security interest created by another and (ii) the person creates a security interest in the same collateral in favor of another secured party.

Consider how the "normal" priority rules would resolve the competing claims in the scenario presented by Problem 8.1.2: Buyer acquires goods subject to a perfected security interest. Once Buyer obtains "rights in the collateral," *SP–2*'s security interest attaches. In both parts (a) and (b), the "normal" rules would award priority to *SP–2*: In Problem 8.1.2(a), *SP–2* was the first to file under UCC 9–322(a)(1); in Problem 8.1.2(b), *SP–2*'s purchase-money security interest qualifies for priority under UCC 9–324(a). Do the "normal" rules yield the correct results in these cases, which concern security interests created by more than one debtor? Addressing the issue under Former Article 9, one commentator argued "no" in the following passage:

The first-to-file-or-perfect rule . . . is a variation of the "first in time, first in right" rule that pervades property law. The latter rule is a specific application of the basic principle of conveyancing: one cannot convey better title than he has. Once the debtor encumbers his interest in the goods with a security interest, any person whose interest derives from the debtor will take subject to the encumbrance. Thus, under a strict first-in-time rule, the first party to take a security interest in collateral would have priority over later secured parties. [The first-to-file-or-perfect rule] modifies the [first-in-time] rule to cure the ostensible ownership problem. . . .. For the first security interest to be effective against a subsequent secured party, the first creditor must publicize his interest, usually by filing. Among the penalties for failure to publicize is the loss of priority to subsequent creditors who may be disadvantaged by the absence of publicity.

Comment 1 to section 1–102 explains that "the proper construction of the [Code] requires that its interpretation and application be limited to its reason." In the case under consideration—[the buyer] acquires goods subject to *SP1*'s perfected security interest, *SP2*'s security interest attaches automatically to the after-acquired [property], and *SP2* has filed before *SP1*—the reason for [the first-to-file-or-perfect rule] is inapplicable. Prior to the contract of sale between the buyer and the seller, the buyer had no rights in the [property]. Accordingly, *SP2* had no interest in the goods and could not possibly have been disadvantaged by a secret security interest in favor of *SP1*. *SP1* publicized its interest by filing before *SP2*'s interest attached, and *SP2* could have discovered the encumbrance by checking the files. Having failed to discover *SP1*'s security interest, *SP2* should take subject to it. Conversely, having appropriately cured the ostensible ownership problem before *SP2* could have relied to its detriment on the seller's apparently unencumbered ownership, *SP1* should not suffer a penalty when its debtor, without authorization, later sells the collateral. . . .. If one does not impose the penalty of [the first-to-file-or-perfect rule], one must apply the ordinary rule of section 2–403(1), under which the purchaser (*SP2*) acquires no greater rights than his transferor (the buyer) had or had power to convey; that is, *SP2* takes his security interest subject to those encumbrances that are effective against the buyer, including *SP1*'s security interest.

Comment 5 to section 9–312 suggests a second justification for the first-to-file rule: "the necessity of protecting the filing system—that is, of allowing the secured party who has first filed to make subsequent advances without each time having, as a condition of protection, to check for filing later than his." [Compare UCC 9–322, Comment 4.] In the usual case, concerning only one debtor, the consequences of removing the search burden from the first to file and placing it on the second to file are not clearly undesirable. A potential creditor can check the filings, discover the first secured party's filing, and conduct himself accordingly. Ordinarily he will take second priority, but he can acquire first priority by taking a purchase money security interest and notifying the first secured party of that fact.

When two debtors are involved . . . the consequences of applying [the first-to-file-or-perfect rule] are clearly undesirable. When *SP1* takes a security interest in the seller's [property], it will not discover *SP2*'s security interest because it has no reason to investigate the title of goods owned by persons other than its debtor. If [the first-to-file-or-perfect rule] were applied to the case under consideration, then *SP1* may be completely unable to protect itself; whereas if *SP1* were afforded priority, then *SP2* would be able to discover that the [property] was encumbered and would refuse to make an advance against it. The Code generally affords the . . . lender considerable protection against third party claims to the collateral and so minimizes the need for a[ ] . . . lender to investigate the source of his collateral. Nevertheless, a[ ] . . . lender may become aware that his debtor has acquired [property subject to a security interest]. Placing the risk of loss on *SP2*, who can prevent the loss by refusing to lend, rather than on *SP1*, who may be unable to prevent it, seems reasonable. Thus, [in this context], I would read Article 9 to grant priority to *SP1* regardless of when each secured party filed.

Harris, The Interaction of Articles 6 and 9 of the Uniform Commercial Code: A Study in Conveyancing, Priorities, and Code Interpretation, 39 Vand.L.Rev. 179, 222–25 (1986).

Professor Harris argued that the buyer's purchase-money secured party likewise should not enjoy priority over a perfected security interest that encumbered the collateral before its debtor (the buyer) acquired rights in it:

The reason for the purchase-money priority is to aid a debtor in obtaining credit, without adversely affecting the interests of the original secured party. In a two-debtor case, *SP2* does not need a special priority rule as an incentive to finance the . . . purchase. If the buyer were to purchase unencumbered [goods], instead of goods subject to a security interest, *SP2* would be able easily to acquire a first-priority security interest. In that case, *SP2* should be willing to extend credit to the buyer for the acquisition of [collateral], even without a purchase-money priority over *SP1*. When there are two debtors, *SP2*'s need for the special priority arises not because the Code's ordinary priority rules favor the first to file, but because *SP2*'s debtor chooses to acquire encumbered goods. Moreover, in a two-debtor case, one cannot justify giving *SP2* priority on the ground that but for *SP2*'s enabling loan, *SP1* would not acquire any rights in the collateral. On the contrary, the award of priority to *SP2* would come at the expense of *SP1* and often would have the effect of depriving *SP1* of its collateral altogether. The buyer took subject to *SP1*'s security interest; *SP2*'s rights derive from the buyer; *SP2* can discover *SP1*'s perfected interest. In the absence of a good reason to prefer *SP2* at *SP1*'s expense, section 9–312(3) should not be read to apply to cases . . . that concern two debtors. Instead, the basic conveyancing principle—the transferee acquires no greater title than his transferor has—should apply.

39 Vand. L. Rev. at 229–30.

Revised Article 9 follows this approach in a new rule designed to deal with the "double-debtor" problem: When each security interest is created by a different debtor, UCC 9–325 protects *SP–1* both as against the holder of an earlier-filed non-PMSI and as against the holder of a PMSI that otherwise would qualify for purchase-money priority. Observe that *SP–1* does not get the benefit of this protection under all circumstances. Assume that, unlike in the Problems and the examples discussed by Professor Harris in the preceding excerpts, *SP–1*'s security interest is *un*perfected but the buyer's interest is *junior* to that of *SP–1* because the buyer has *knowledge* of *SP–1*'s interest. See UCC 9–317(b). In that case, Professor Harris's reasoning would work to give *SP–2* priority. Even if the buyer and *SP–2* had been careful to search against *SP–1*'s debtor, they could not have discovered *SP–1*'s interest in a search of the public records. Does Revised Article 9 adopt this reasoning? See UCC 9–325(a)(2) & Comment 4.

The "double debtor" issues raised in Problems 8.1.1 and 8.1.2 involved the transfer of collateral to a person who thereby becomes the debtor. Because Oldcorp and Buyer both were located in California for choice-of-law purposes, the law governing perfection and priority did not change; California law governed at all times. See UCC 9–301(1); UCC 9–307(e). Problem 8.1.3 is different, in that Buyer is located in Nevada. UCC 9–316 deals with the circumstances under which a security interest perfected under the law of one jurisdiction continues to be perfected following a change in the governing law. We saw in Chapter 3, Section 4, supra, that UCC 9–316(a)(3) provides for continued perfection for up to "one year after a transfer of collateral to a person that thereby becomes the debtor and is located in another jurisdiction." If the security interest is (re)perfected under the law of the new jurisdiction before the one-year period expires, then the security interest remains perfected thereafter. If it is not, then it not only becomes unperfected, but it is deemed never to have been perfected as against a purchaser of the collateral. See UCC 9–316(b).[1]

---

1.   Note that UCC 9–316(a) applies only to *perfected* security interests; perfection requires attachment. See UCC 9–308(a). Thus UCC 9–316(a) does not apply to a security interest that attaches after a change in governing law. To see how this limitation may

The following Problems address several variations on a theme: Before the transaction in question, a secured party held a security interest in the debtor's inventory; after the transaction, the debtor's business was being operated by a third party who acquired the collateral. Does Article 9 afford identical treatment to each of these transactions? If not, do the differences among the transactions justify any differences in treatment?

Problem 8.1.4. *SP*–1 has a security interest in all Oldcorp's existing and after-acquired inventory and equipment. *SP*–1 filed a proper financing statement against Oldcorp in 2006. Without *SP*–1's knowledge and in violation of the loan agreement, Oldcorp sold all its assets, including its inventory and equipment to Buyer, a competitor, whereupon Oldcorp promptly liquidated. Buyer continued to conduct Oldcorp's business. Both Oldcorp and Buyer are Maryland corporations.

(a) Is Buyer liable for Oldcorp's debts? What, if any, additional information do you need to answer this question? See Note (1) on Changes in Business Structure, infra.

(b) Does *SP*–1 retain a perfected security interest in the assets sold to Buyer? Assume alternatively that Buyer is and is not liable for Oldcorp's debts. See UCC 9–315(a); UCC 9–507(a); Problem 8.1.1, supra.

(c) Assume that *SP*–1's security interest survived the sale. In 2005 *SP*–2 acquired a security interest in Buyer's existing and after-acquired equipment and inventory and filed a proper financing statement. Is *SP*–1's security interest senior or junior to *SP*–2's security interest? See UCC 9–325; UCC 9–322(a); Note on "Double Debtor" Problems, supra; Problem 8.1.2(a), supra. What could the holder of the junior security interest have done to prevent this result?

(d) During the year following the purchase from Oldcorp, Buyer acquired additional inventory.

(i) Does *SP*–1 have a security interest in the additional inventory? (What, if any, additional facts do you need to answer this question?) See UCC 9–203(b), (d), (e); UCC 9–102(a)(56), (60); Note (1) on Changes in Business Structure, infra. If so, is the security interest perfected? See UCC 9–508; Note (2) on Changes in Business Structure, infra.

(ii) Who has a better claim to this inventory, *SP*–1 or *SP*–2? See UCC 9–326(a) & Comment 2; Note (3) on Changes in Business Structure, infra. What could the holder of the junior security interest have done to prevent this result?

Problem 8.1.5. Jack and Diane owned and operated a grocery store near their home in Brooklyn, New York. Home Bank provided inventory financing to the business. It properly perfected its security interest by filing. Jack and Diane decided to incorporate the business. On May 15, J/D Grocery, Inc., was chartered by the State of New York. In exchange for their

be significant, see UCC 9–316, Comment 2, Example 5; Problem 8.1.7, infra.

stock, Jack and Diane contributed all their business assets. J/D assumed all the business debts. The business continued to operate as before. One year later, J/D, Jack, and Diane filed Chapter 7 petitions. You represent the bankruptcy trustee. What arguments can you make to reduce the size of Home Bank's security interest in bankruptcy? To what extent do the arguments depend on when J/D acquired the inventory? What could Home Bank have done to avoid any loss? See UCC 9–315(a); UCC 9–203(d), (e); UCC 9–508; UCC 9–506(c), (d); UCC 9–509(b); BC 544(a); Notes on Changes in Business Structure, infra.

Problem 8.1.6. *SP*–1 has a perfected security interest in Oldcorp's existing and after-acquired inventory and equipment. *SP*–1 filed a proper financing statement against Oldcorp in 2006. Without *SP*–1's knowledge and in violation of the loan agreement, Oldcorp merged into Newcorp. Immediately upon the merger, the surviving corporation (Newcorp) changed its name to Oldcorp. Newcorp continued Oldcorp's business, acquiring more inventory in the ordinary course of business. Ten months after the merger, Newcorp filed a Chapter 11 petition.

Both Oldcorp and Newcorp are incorporated under the law of the same state. That state has adopted the Revised Model Business Corporation Act, which provides that, as a consequence of the merger, "'all liabilities of each corporation . . . that is merged into the survivor are vested in the survivor." Rev. M.B.C.A. § 11.06(a)(4).

(a) You represent the debtor in possession. What arguments can you make to reduce the size of *SP*–1's security interest in bankruptcy? See UCC 9–315(a); UCC 9–507; UCC 9–203(d), (e); UCC 9–508; UCC 9–506(c), (d); BC 544(a). To what extent do the arguments depend on when Newcorp acquired the inventory? What could *SP*–1 have done to avoid any loss?

(b) *Before* the merger, *Newcorp* granted *SP*–2 a security interest in its existing and after-acquired inventory to secure a line of credit. *SP*–2 perfected its security interest by filing a financing statement *before* the merger (but *after* *SP*–1 filed its financing statement). The financing statement named Newcorp as debtor. Which security interest, *SP*–1's or *SP*–2's, has priority in the surviving corporation's inventory? See UCC 9–315(a); UCC 9–507; UCC 9–325; UCC 9–326; UCC 9–508; UCC 9–322(a). Does it matter when the surviving corporation acquired the inventory? What could the losing party have done to avoid any loss?

(c) Shortly *after* the merger the surviving corporation granted Finance Company a security interest in its existing and after-acquired inventory to secure a line of credit. Finance Company immediately perfected its security interest by filing a financing statement naming the surviving corporation as debtor. Which security interest, *SP*–1's or Finance Company's, has priority? Does it matter when the surviving corporation acquired the inventory? What could the losing party have done to avoid any loss?

Problem 8.1.7. *SP*–1 has a perfected security interest in Oldcorp's existing and after-acquired inventory and equipment. *SP*–1 filed a proper financing statement against Oldcorp in 2006. Without *SP*–1's knowledge and in violation of the loan agreement, the shareholders of Oldcorp (a New York corporation) "reincorporated" Oldcorp in Delaware. That is, they established a new Delaware corporation (Newcorp) and caused Oldcorp to merge into Newcorp. Upon the merger, Oldcorp ceased to exist. Newcorp continued Oldcorp's business, acquiring more inventory in the ordinary course of business. Ten months after the merger, Newcorp filed a Chapter 11 petition. Applicable non-UCC law follows the Revised Model Business Corporation Act, which provides that, as a consequence of the merger, "all liabilities of each corporation . . . that is merged into the survivor are vested in the survivor." Rev. M.B.C.A. § 11.06(a)(4).

(a) You represent the debtor in possession. What arguments can you make to reduce the size of *SP*–1's security interest in bankruptcy? See UCC 9–315; UCC 9–507; UCC 9–203; UCC 9–316(a), (b); UCC 9–301; UCC 9–307; BC 544(a). To what extent do the arguments depend on when Newcorp acquired the inventory? What could *SP*–1 have done to avoid any loss? See UCC 9–509(c); BC 362(b)(3).

(b) Would the fact that, immediately upon the merger, the surviving corporation (Newcorp) changed its name to Oldcorp, affect your answer to part (a)? If so, how? What could *SP*–1 have done to avoid any loss?

NOTES ON CHANGES IN BUSINESS STRUCTURE

(1) Determining Whether a Third Party Is Bound by the Debtor's Security Agreement. Problems 8.1.4 through 8.1.7, supra, concern transactions in which one legal entity (the "new debtor") acquires collateral from, and takes over the business of, another legal entity (the "original debtor"). We already have examined the law governing security interests in collateral that a debtor sells or otherwise *transfers*. See Note on "Double Debtor" Problems, supra. The same principles apply to that aspect of Problems 8.1.4 through 8.1.7. Our focus here is on property that the *new debtor acquires* from sources *other than the original debtor*.

If the new debtor enters into a security agreement in favor of the old debtor's secured party (*SP*–1), then *SP*–1's security interest will attach to the collateral described in the agreement. But suppose the new debtor does not enter into such a security agreement. Is the security agreement entered into by the original debtor sufficient to bind the new debtor?

Nothing in all of Former Article 9 delineated the circumstances under which a third party becomes bound as debtor by a security agreement entered into by another person. Courts addressing this issue under Former Article 9 used a variety of statutory and common-law theories and reached a variety of results. Many of the courts that protected the original debtor's secured party appear to share the Ninth Circuit's concern that a debtor should not "be able to evade the obligations of a validly executed security agreement by the simple expedient of an alteration in its business structure." In re West Coast Food Sales, Inc., 637 F.2d 707 (9th Cir.1981). On the other hand, is a secured party who fails to discover that its debtor has gone out business—or no longer even exists—worthy of protection?

Revised Article 9 addresses this issue directly: UCC 9–203(d) sets out the circumstances under which a third party becomes bound as debtor by a security agreement; UCC 9–203(e) explains the consequences of the new debtor's having become bound. Observe that one may need to look to non-UCC law to determine whether a person becomes a new debtor. The answer may turn on whether the person becomes obligated for the debtor's obligations. A person who acquires another person's assets—even all the assets—generally does not ipso facto become obligated for the other person's obligations. However, there are exceptions to the general principle, and the scope of the exceptions may vary from state to state. Is the resulting nonuniformity in results, attributable to the diversity of existing non-UCC law on the point, inconsistent with the need for uniformity in secured transactions?

(2) Effectiveness of a Financing Statement Naming the Original Debtor With Respect to Collateral Acquired by the New Debtor. Assume now that a new debtor becomes bound by the security agreement of the original debtor under UCC 9–203(d). Under what circumstances, if any, is the financing statement filed against the original debtor effective to perfect a security interest in property acquired by the new debtor?

As with the attachment question, discussed in the preceding Note, Former Article 9 did not provide a clear answer, and the case law reveals a variety of judicial views on the subject. Here, again, Revised Article 9 addresses the issue directly. UCC 9–508 treats a transaction in which a new debtor becomes bound by the original debtor's security agreement in much the same way as UCC 9–507(c) treats a change in the debtor's name: As a general matter, a financing statement is not rendered ineffective unless the difference between the two names renders the financing statement seriously misleading; if the financing statement becomes seriously misleading, then the financing statement is effective only with respect to collateral acquired more than four months after the new debtor's becoming bound (or the debtor's name changes), unless the secured party files an initial financing statement against the new debtor (or an amendment reflecting the debtor's new name). See UCC 9–508; UCC 9–507(c); Note, p. 177, supra. No special authorization is needed for the filing of an initial financing statement (or amendment) under these circumstances. See UCC 9–509(b), (d).

Unlike a name change, which involves a single debtor, the changes in business structure under discussion involve two separate legal entities. How would you assess the decision to treat the two situations substantially the same way with respect to the continuing effectiveness of a filed financing statement? Consider the following argument: Ordinarily, a financing statement is ineffective against a debtor who did not authorize it to be filed. See UCC 9–510(a); UCC 9–509(a). Application of this principle would mean that a security interest in property acquired by a new debtor would be unperfected until the secured party files an otherwise effective financing statement whose filing is authorized by the new debtor.

This approach would result in distinctions between functionally similar transactions. For example, a financing statement would remain effective against a debtor into which a sister corporation is merged and which thereafter takes on the sister's name; however, if the debtor merges into the sister corporation and thereby loses its corporate existence, the financing statement would have no effect against the survivor. Does the difference between these two transactions justify distinguishing between them? In answering this question, keep in mind that this distinction would not be unique to Article 9; many existing loan agreements contain covenants drawing the same distinction (e.g., permitting only those mergers in which the debtor is the surviving corporation).

The foregoing approach has the virtue of being relatively clear cut: If the legal entity that was the original debtor survives but with a new name (a determination that one makes for a variety of other purposes), then UCC 9–507(c) would apply, as it does to simple name changes. If the legal entity does not survive, or if the legal entity survives but another legal entity becomes bound by the security agreement, then the case would be treated like Article 9 treats any other debtor.[2]

Notwithstanding its simplicity and relative ease of application, the forgoing approach may yield results that some find objectionable. We have mentioned the concern that some courts have expressed for secured parties whose debtors engage in a corporate or similar restructuring without the secured party's knowledge or consent. Changes in business structure may occur under circumstances such that even a diligent secured party would not discover them and so would be unaware of the need to refile against the new debtor to maintain the perfected status of its security interest in after-acquired property. The force of this argument becomes particularly strong when applied to individual debtors who incorporate their businesses into new debtors and large partnerships that become new debtors several times a year because a partner dies, retires, or otherwise leaves the partnership.

One response to this objection would be to have the status of a security interest—perfected or unperfected—turn on whether the secured party knew about the new debtor. Would a scienter-based rule of this kind be just? Would it be workable?

The approach that UCC 9–508 actually adopts—i.e., that a financing statement remains effective with respect to collateral acquired by the new debtor within four months after it becomes bound by the original debtor's security agreement—likewise is not without its problems. First, whenever the original debtor remains in existence, a single financing statement would be effective to perfect a security interest both in property acquired by the

---

2. Note that, although the rule may be clear, its application may present difficulties in some cases, particularly when corporate managers have not respected corporate forms.

original debtor and in property acquired by the new debtor.[3] Second, as discussed in the following Note, this approach has required the promulgation of a special priority rule.

(3) Priority of Competing Security Interests in Collateral Acquired by a New Debtor. Now consider this scenario: A new debtor (Newcorp) becomes bound by the original debtor's (Oldcorp's) security agreement in favor of its secured party (*SP–1*), and the financing statement filed against the original debtor remains effective to perfect a security interest in collateral in which the new debtor has or acquires rights. The new debtor has granted a security interest in the collateral to a competing secured party (*SP–2*), which has perfected its security interest by filing.

Who should have priority? As to collateral acquired by Newcorp subject to a security interest created by Oldcorp, we have seen that the basic conveyancing principle (*nemo dat*) and the rationale behind the Article 9 filing system support the award of priority to *SP–1*, regardless of which secured party was the first to file or perfect its security interest. See UCC 9–325; Note on "Double Debtor" Problems, supra. Does it follow that *SP–1* should enjoy first priority as to all other property acquired by Newcorp?

To the contrary, a strong case can be made for awarding priority to *SP–2*. *SP–2* gave value and took its security interest at a time when *SP–1* had no filing against *SP–2*'s debtor, Newcorp. Even if subsequent events somehow cause *SP–1*'s financing statement, naming Oldcorp, to become effective against Newcorp, should *SP–1*'s priority date from the time its financing statement became effective against Oldcorp? This result would prevent *SP–2* from relying on the fact that, when it filed against Newcorp, no other financing statements were of record. What justifies creating this uncertainty for *SP–2*? Would it not be more appropriate to give priority to *SP–2*, and thereby impose upon *SP–1* the risk that its debtor might merge into another entity and cease to exist?

This strong case persuaded the drafters. UCC 9–326(a) subordinates a security interest in collateral of a new debtor if the security interest is perfected *solely* under UCC 9–508. As Comment 2 explains, UCC 9–326(a) subordinates a security interest that is perfected solely by a financing statement filed against the original debtor that continues to be effective against the new debtor under Section 9–508.

As discussed above in Note (2), an alternative approach to perfection would require the original debtor's secured party (*SP–1*) to file against the new debtor in order to perfect against the new debtor's after-acquired collateral. Under this approach, the priority of the original debtor's secured party would date from the filing against the new debtor. If the new debtor has another secured party, that secured party's priority would date from its filing. UCC 9–322 contains appropriate rules to resolve the relative

---

3.   The statement in the text assumes that both the original debtor and the new debtor are located in the same jurisdiction for choice-of-law purposes. See Chapter 3, Section 4(A), supra; UCC 9–508, Comment 4.

priorities, inasmuch as both security interests were created in the first instance by the same debtor (the new debtor). There would be no "double debtor" problem, and there would be no need for a special priority rule. Another desirable feature of this approach would be that priorities would date from readily ascertainable events (the filing of financing statements) and not from a difficult to discover, secret event (a new debtor's becoming bound by another debtor's security agreement). Would this approach have been preferable to the one adopted by the drafters?

(4) Commingling of Transferred Goods. In Problem 8.1.6, supra, Newcorp acquired collateral subject to a security interest created by Oldcorp in favor of *SP*–1. Suppose the inventory acquired from Oldcorp was fungible and became "commingled goods," i.e., it was so commingled with Newcorp's other inventory that its identity was lost in the mass? See UCC 9–336(a) (defining "commingled goods"). *SP*–1's security interest would attach to the mass and would be perfected. See UCC 9–336(c), (d). If, as in Problem 8.1.6(b), *SP*–2 held a perfected security interest in Newcorp's existing and after-acquired inventory, then *SP*–1 and *SP*–2 each would hold a perfected security interest in the mass, and the security interests would rank equally in proportion to the value of the collateral at the time it became commingled goods. See UCC 9–336(f)(2).

SECTION 2.   LEASE CHATTEL PAPER

INTRODUCTORY NOTE

For the most part, our consideration of chattel paper in Chapter 5, Section 2, supra, addressed chattel paper consisting of a record of a payment obligation secured by specific goods. However, the definition of "chattel paper" in UCC 9–102(a)(11) also includes *leases* of specific goods. This Section deals with issues that spring from the inherent differences between leases and security interests. The following Problem and Note illustrate some special considerations affecting those who finance lease chattel paper.

Problem 8.2.1. Your client, Clearinghouse Credit Corp., is negotiating the terms of a prospective financing transaction with TV Shack Leasing Co. TV Shack is in the business of leasing small-to medium-priced electronic equipment and appliances to consumers and small businesses.

TV Shack proposes to sell (on a "non-recourse" basis) a pool of leases and the related goods to Clearinghouse for a price of approximately $25,000,000. Some of the leases contain purchase options. The parties contemplate that, after the sale, TV Shack would serve as a **servicing agent** for Clearinghouse; i.e., TV Shack would continue to collect the rentals and would remit them to Clearinghouse.

TV Shack's standard practice is to have three counterparts of each lease agreement signed by TV Shack and the lessee: the lessee gets one copy, TV

Shack's local office gets another, and TV Shack's regional office gets the third. These local and regional offices are located in 35 states.

Clearinghouse has asked you to advise it concerning the structure of the transaction and the precautions that should be taken to protect its interests against claims of TV Shack's creditors and the creditors of the lessees. You have been warned by Clearinghouse that any attempt to require physical delivery of the leases would be met with stiff objection (on cost and administrative grounds) by TV Shack and probably would cause the deal to "crater."

What advice do you give? In particular:

(a) How will you recommend that the interest of Clearinghouse in the leases be perfected? What are Clearinghouse's risks if it leaves TV Shack in possession of the leases? See UCC 9–102(a)(11); UCC 9–109(a)(3); UCC 9–312(a); UCC 9–313(a), (c); UCC 9–330; Notes, p. 420, supra; Note on *Leasing Consultants* and Lease Chattel Paper, infra. How could those risks be reduced while still structuring the transaction within the parameters set by your client?

(b) What body of law governs Clearinghouse's purchase of TV Shack's "ownership" or "residual" interest in the leased goods? See Note on *Leasing Consultants* and Lease Chattel Paper, infra. How will you recommend that Clearinghouse perfect its interest in the residuals?

(c) Would your answer to part (b) be different if the transaction were structured as a loan to TV Shack secured by the leases and the residual interests?

NOTE ON *LEASING CONSULTANTS* AND LEASE CHATTEL PAPER

By definition, both security-interest chattel paper (such as Lee Abel's Instalment Sale Contract (Form 3.6) in the Prototype on financing automobiles) and lease chattel paper embody two related property rights. See UCC 9–102(a)(11). One is the receivable—the right to be paid by the account debtor (i.e., the obligor). UCC 9–102(a)(11) refers to this as a "monetary obligation." The other is the right, upon default or under agreed circumstances, to apply the value of the specific goods involved (or the value of the lessee's leasehold interest in the goods) toward satisfaction of the monetary obligation.[1] A secured party enjoys this right under Article 9. See UCC 9–610; Chapter 9, Section 2, infra. And the remedies provisions of UCC Article 2A as well as the terms of many leases provide that, after a lessee's default, the lessor may dispose of the leased goods and credit a portion of the proceeds received against the lessee's obligation to pay damages. See UCC 2A–523 to–532 (lessor's remedies on lessee's default).

---

1.   Recall that the definition of "chattel paper" in UCC 9–102(a)(11) covers records evidencing interests in software associated with specific goods in addition to interests in the goods. This Section focuses solely on the interests in goods, however, because it is the nature of the interests in goods that distinguishes lease chattel paper from other chattel paper.

We saw in Chapter 5, Section 1(A), supra, that an essential attribute of a lease of goods is the existence of a meaningful residual (sometimes called a "reversion") for the lessor. Article 2A refers to this property interest as the "lessor's residual interest," which "means the lessor's interest in the goods after expiration, termination, or cancellation of the lease contract." UCC 2A–103(1)(q) [R2A–103(a)(w)]. Depending on the terms of the lease, the lessor's residual interest may be quite valuable; by definition it never is trivial.

In contrast, an Article 9 secured party does not enjoy a residual interest. Rather, in a secured transaction covering goods, the debtor is entitled to any collateral value remaining after the secured obligation is satisfied. See UCC 9–615(d) (discussed in Chapter 9, Section 2, infra). Stated otherwise, the only interest in goods that the assignor of security-interest chattel paper has to assign is the assignor's *security interest* in the goods. And that security interest is embodied in the chattel paper.

In *In re Leasing Consultants*, 486 F.2d 367 (2d Cir. 1973) (decided under the pre–1972 version of the UCC), the court had occasion to consider whether a lessor's residual interest, like a secured party's security interest, is embodied in the chattel paper. In *Leasing Consultants*, the Bank held a perfected security interest in Leasing's chattel paper, which included several leases of equipment to Plastimetrix. The dispute centered around which interests of the debtor (Leasing) were encompassed by the chattel paper. To the extent that a property interest of Leasing was embodied in the chattel paper, the Bank held a perfected security interest in that property interest. To the extent that a property interest was not so embodied and the Bank had not perfected separately as to it, Leasing's bankruptcy trustee could use its "strong-arm power" to avoid the Bank's unperfected security interest. Cf. BC 544(a); Chapter 7, Section 2(A), supra.

In *Leasing Consultants* the Bank argued that, by perfecting a security interest in Leasing's chattel paper, the Bank had perfected a security interest in any lessor's residual interest held by Leasing. The court rejected this argument. It concluded that a residual interest constitutes collateral—goods—that is distinct from the chattel paper. Any security interest in the residual thus must be analyzed separately to determine whether it is perfected. Because a "lease" that in fact is a secured transaction (e.g., the secured sale of goods from the debtor (Leasing) to a buyer (Plastimetrix)) does not leave the "lessor" with any residual interest, the court remanded the case for a determination whether the leases at issue in *Leasing Consultants* were true leases or disguised sales.[2]

---

2.   The leases provided that, following the lessee's default, all net proceeds of a disposition of the goods would be applied to unpaid rentals; provisions of this kind are strong indications that the leases are not true leases but, instead, create security interests. See Note (4), p. 324, supra. In addition, the Bank contended that there was no residual interest in the goods; if correct, this would be another indication that the chattel paper may not have consisted of true leases.

Both the reasoning and the result of *Leasing Consultants* have become a part of the accepted wisdom among those who finance lease chattel paper. Those secured parties not only take and perfect a security interest in the leases (chattel paper) but also normally take and perfect a security interest in the leased goods ("inventory," under UCC 9–102(a)(48)).[3] This practice is likely to continue; Comment 11 to UCC 9–330 cites *Leasing Consultants* with approval.

One final concern affecting those who finance lease chattel paper should be mentioned. The lessor's residual interest in goods that are leased to others is classified as "inventory." See UCC 9–102(48). Even if a prospective purchaser of lease chattel paper is satisfied that it will receive priority in the *paper* under UCC 9–330, it still must be concerned with the existence of an earlier-filed inventory secured party who might enjoy priority as to the *residual*.

SECTION 3. REAL PROPERTY–RELATED COLLATERAL: FIXTURES AND RECEIVABLES

(A) FIXTURES

NOTES ON SECURITY INTERESTS IN FIXTURES

(1) "Fixtures" in Article 9. Elevators, furnaces, kitchen stoves, refrigerators, air conditioners, "mobile" homes, printing presses, power lathes—these examples only suggest the wide range of goods that, when placed for use on land or in a building, generate problems associated with the concept of a "fixture."

"Fixtures" problems are interesting and challenging. A principal reason is that "fixtures" lie on the border between two legal worlds—real property and personalty. The following example sets the stage for consideration of the conflicting interests that are at stake: Dealer sells furnaces and retains purchase–money security interests to secure the purchase price. The furnaces are installed in homes, office buildings, and manufacturing plants. Upon installation the furnaces become part of the related real property: if the real property is sold, the furnace passes to the vendee under the deed; if the real property is subjected to a mortgage, the furnace becomes subject to that encumbrance.

Consider, first, what happens to Dealer's Article 9 security interest once the goods become real property. Article 9, for all its breadth, does not take

---

3.   Under Revised Article 9, a single filing covering both inventory and chattel paper will perfect against both types of collateral. See UCC 9–301(1). In contrast, the choice-of-law provisions of Former Article 9 may have required the filing against chattel paper to be in a different jurisdiction from the filing against inventory. See F9–103. In *Leasing Consultants*, the Bank's filed financing statement covered chattel paper but was not filed in the proper jurisdiction for inventory.

over the field of mortgages.[1] Recall that Article 9 generally does not apply to "the creation or transfer of an interest in or lien on real property, including a lease or rents thereunder." UCC 9–109(d)(11). Notwithstanding the general inapplicability of Article 9 to real property, Article 9 does apply "to the extent that provision is made for . . . fixtures in Section 9–334." Id.

An unforgettable classroom definition, still resonant with the frightening roar of Professor E. H. ("Bull") Warren, laid it down that a fixture is "realty, with a chattel past, and a hope of chattel future."[2] Article 9 contains its own definition, not unlike Professor Warren's: " 'Fixtures' means goods that have become so related to particular real property that an interest in them arises under real property law." UCC 9–102(a)(41). In other words, fixtures are realty with a chattel past. In addition, no Article 9 security interest exists in ordinary building materials incorporated into an improvement on land. See UCC 9–334(a). That is, even if realty with no hope of a chattel future (such as the concrete that forms the foundation of a building) might be a fixture, one cannot have an Article 9 security interest in it.

An Article 9 security interest may be created in goods that become fixtures or may continue in goods that become fixtures. See UCC 9–334(a). Accordingly, Dealer's Article 9 security interest remains in the furnaces, even after they are installed.

(2) Fixtures in Real Property Law: Affixation and the "Institutional" Approach. It may not have escaped your attention that reference to Article 9 alone is insufficient to enable one to determine whether particular goods have become fixtures. Rather, the definition of "fixtures" in UCC 9–102(a)(41) in effect poses a question that only applicable real property law can answer: have the goods "become so related to particular real property that an interest in them arises under real property law"?

The factors that work the change from personalty to realty are elusive; they vary from context to context, and from state to state. Writers, both judicial and academic, often discuss the issue in terms of whether a chattel has been "affixed" to the realty. This suggests that "affixing" is a physical process, accomplished with nails or bolts. "Affixation," however, is a conclusory word: the physical tie-in is relevant, but not decisive. In some states, production machinery in a factory provides a dramatic example.

Some courts (those in Pennsylvania and New Jersey are examples) have gone far to treat readily removable factory machinery as "fixtures." In an 1841 Pennsylvania case a judgment creditor levied on steel rollers for a

---

1.   The chattel mortgage having become an Article 9 security interest decades ago, we use the term "mortgage" to refer to a consensual lien on real property. See UCC 9–102(a)(55) (" 'Mortgage' means a consensual interest in real property, including fixtures, which secures payment or performance of an obligation.").

2.   Students of "the Bull" have no doubt that he was the model for the fictional Professor Kingsfield. See E. H. Warren, Spartan Education 20–28 (1942).

rolling mill; the rollers were not attached to the mill but were available for use when needed. The mortgagee successfully attacked this levy. Chief Justice Gibson proclaimed: "Whether fast or loose . . . all the machinery of a manufactory . . . without which it would not be a manufactory at all, must pass for a part of the freehold . . ." At stake was the factory's going-concern value that would be destroyed by dismemberment. In Gibson's graphic prose, "a cotton-spinner . . . whose capital is chiefly invested in loose machinery, might be suddenly broken up in the midst of a thriving business, by suffering a creditor to gut his mill of every thing which happened not to be spiked or riveted to the walls, and sell its bowels not only separately but piecemeal. A creditor might as well be allowed to sell the works of a clock, wheel by wheel." Voorhis v. Freeman, 2 Watts & Serg. 116 (1841). A century later, this view was applied to a security interest retained by the seller who provided new machinery for a candy factory; although the machinery could be removed with little or no damage to the physical structure, the seller could not enforce this security interest as against the mortgagee. The case was governed by a provision of the Uniform Conditional Sales Act that had been designed to strengthen purchase-money security in equipment that could be removed "without material injury to the freehold." But, the Pennsylvania court stubbornly insisted, physical injury was not the test; removal of the machinery would seriously injure "the operating plant." Central Lithograph Co. v. Eatmor Chocolate Co., 316 Pa. 300, 175 A. 697 (1934).

The "institutional" doctrine has not been followed in most states. However, an element of that approach may explain some widely-accepted and traditional "fixture" rules. For example, although the doors of a house can be readily removed, they are considered, as a matter of course, to be part of the realty; this legal conclusion must reflect the part they play in the use of the house as a dwelling.

The dichotomy between realty and personalty is drawn in many other settings; for example: the right of a tenant to remove, say, a stove or an air conditioner that the tenant has added to leased property; property taxes; recovery of possession upon a debtor's default. This dichotomy is used for many different purposes. The reason underlying the distinction, of course, may affect where the line is drawn. For example, the question whether a tenant forfeits to the landlord assets that the tenant has brought to the property is quite different from the question whether a sale of Blackacre includes removable things (like a kitchen stove) that usually "go with" the land. Unsophisticated handling of the realty-personalty distinction is common, and flirts with disaster.

(3) The Trouble With Fixtures: Source of the Problems. The conclusion that, in the example in Note (1), supra, Dealer retained an Article 9 security interest in furnaces that had been installed in buildings, provides little comfort. As we have seen, an unperfected security interest is subordinate to most competing claims to the collateral. See, e.g., UCC 9–317(a)(2); BC 544(a)(1). Transfers of interests in realty and personalty typically are governed by different legal rules. Transfers of real property, whether by deed, trust deed, or mortgage, typically are recorded in the county recorder's office; usually the document submitted for recording must be notarized and include a description of the real property that, even in simple cases, may be long and complex and call for the aid of a local real property lawyer. Financing statements for security interests in personal property subject to Article 9 need not comply with these formalities; they will almost always be filed in a different office—and even if filed in the county recorder's office, they may be indexed separately.

Will Dealer's filing of a financing statement in the personal property records operate to perfect its security interest once the goods have become real property? If the building is subject to a mortgage, will Dealer's security interest be entitled to priority? If the owner sells the building, will Dealer's security interest survive the sale? These are the kinds of questions that the following materials address.

Problem 8.3.1. Dowel Manufacturing Company, a Delaware corporation, owns and operates a large factory in Rantoul, Illinois. Production depends on a wide variety of machinery—power shafts built into the walls; heavy stamping presses held in place by their own weight; power lathes bolted to the floor; machinery on wheels. In 1999, when Dowel built the factory it obtained a $3,000,000 loan from Bank; payments were to be amortized over a period of twenty years. To secure the loan, Dowell executed and delivered to Bank a mortgage covering the land and buildings that comprise the factory, with the usual clauses bringing within the mortgage all "appurtenances and fixtures," then owned or thereafter acquired. Bank properly recorded the mortgage.

In 2006 Dowel Manufacturing obtained a loan from Finco; the borrowed funds were used to purchase a wide range of factory equipment: a stamping press built into the walls of the building, power lathes bolted to the floor, robotic electric carts that carry materials from one machine to another. Dowel executed and delivered to Finco a security agreement covering this equipment. Before the equipment arrived, Finco filed a "fixture filing" in the local office where mortgages are recorded. See UCC 9–102(a)(40); UCC 9–301(3)(A); UCC 9–502(b), (a); UCC 9–501(a)(1)(B). Dowel now is in default to Bank and Finco and has filed a petition under the Bankruptcy Code.

(a) Is Finco's security interest effective against the trustee in bankruptcy? See BC 544(a)(1); UCC 9–317(a)(2); UCC 9–310(a); UCC 9–102(a)(41); UCC 9–501(a); UCC 9–334(e)(3); Note on Perfection by Fixture Filings and Non–Fixture Filings, infra. Will the answer be the same (i) in the few states that follow the "institutional" approach, outlined above; and (ii) in states that reject that approach? In some of these states did Finco file in the wrong place? See Note on Perfection by Fixture Filings and Non–Fixture Filings, infra.

(b) Is Finco's security interest in the new equipment senior to any interest that Bank may claim? See UCC 9–334(c), (d). Which state's law governs this priority dispute? See UCC 9–301(3)(C).

(c) Suppose that in July 2001 Dowel granted a security interest in all its equipment, existing and after-acquired, to Lender, who properly perfected by filing in the Office of the Delaware Secretary of State.

(i) Which state's law governs the relative priority of Finco's security interest in the new equipment and Lender's?

(ii) Is Finco's security interest in the new equipment senior to Lender's? Does UCC 9–334 resolve this priority dispute? Does UCC 9–322? Does UCC 9–324?

(d) If you had acted as counsel for Finco at the time its loan was made, would you have advised it to take any additional precautions?

Problem 8.3.2. Bank is considering making a 20–year loan to a manufacturing company like Dowel; the loan would be secured by a first mortgage covering plant and equipment. Bank asks you (i) to evaluate the threat (if any) to its security posed by UCC 9–334, (ii) to consider what provisions should be included in the mortgage to minimize any problem you find, and (iii) to suggest operating procedures in the administration of the loan which might be useful to deal with the problem.

What is your advice?

Problem 8.3.3. In 2001 Dripps Faucet Company obtained from Bank a 20–year loan, secured by a mortgage covering the land, building, and appurtenances that comprise one of Dripps' two factories in the state. Bank promptly recorded the mortgage. In June 2006 Dripps purchased and paid cash for a new steam boiler and a power lathe; the power lathe is held to the concrete floor by large bolts. Applicable state law treats the steam boiler, but not the lathe, as having become part of the real property.

In September 2006 Dripps borrowed $100,000 from Finco and executed to Finco a security agreement covering the boiler and the lathe. Finco immediately filed a financing statement, in proper form, in the Office of the Secretary of State. See UCC 9–501(a). Thereafter Dripps defaulted on its obligations to Bank and Finco and filed a petition under the Bankruptcy Code.

(a) As among the trustee in bankruptcy, Bank, and Finco, what are the relative priorities as to the steam boiler? See UCC 9–334(c), (e)(3); Note on Perfection by Fixture Filings and Non–Fixture Filings, infra.

(b) What are the relative priorities as to the power lathe? Cf. UCC 9–334(e)(2).

(c) Would the results in parts (a) and (b) change if, instead of filing with the Secretary of State, Finco had made a fixture filing in the office where mortgages are recorded?

Problem 8.3.4. Darned Mills Co. obtained from Firstbank a 20–year loan, secured by a mortgage covering the land, building, and appurtenances that comprise Darned's sock factory. Firstbank promptly recorded the mortgage. In June 2006 Darned purchased and paid cash for a new furnace for the factory. Under applicable state law the furnace is considered a "fixture."

In September 2006 Darned borrowed $100,000 from Finco and executed to Finco a security agreement covering the furnace. Finco immediately made a fixture filing, in proper form, in the office where mortgages are recorded. In December 2006 Firstbank assigned to Secondbank all of Firstbank's interest in the note evidencing the Darned loan together with its interest in the mortgage securing the Darned note. Secondbank took possession of the note and recorded the assignment in the local real property records. Thereafter, following a Darned default to Secondbank and Finco, Darned filed a petition under the Bankruptcy Code.

As among the trustee in bankruptcy, Finco, and Secondbank, what are the relative priorities as to the Darned furnace? See UCC 9–334(e)(1) & Comment 6.

NOTE ON PERFECTION BY FIXTURE FILINGS AND NON–FIXTURE FILINGS

The rules of UCC 9–334 dealing with the priority of Article 9 security interests as against interests obtained through real property law lie at the heart of that section. (As among Article 9 secured parties claiming fixtures, priority would seem to be governed by UCC 9–322 and the other provisions generally applicable to competing Article 9 security interests.) The general priority rule is simple: A real property interest, whether that of an owner or encumbrancer, is senior to an Article 9 security interest in fixtures. See UCC 9–334(c). Other subsections provide exceptions, under which an Article 9 secured party may achieve priority. For some purposes—and in particular for PMSI's under UCC 9–334(d)—priority depends on the secured party's having "perfected by a fixture filing." See UCC 9–334(d), (e)(1). But UCC 9–334(e)(2) (certain "readily removable" goods) and (e)(3) ("lien on the real property obtained by legal or equitable proceedings"—e.g., an execution lien) award priority to a security interest that is "perfected by any method permitted by this article." This suggests that there is more than one method by which a security interest in fixtures can be perfected.

What are those methods? By definition, fixtures are goods. The most obvious method of perfection against goods is filing a financing statement. The other methods are either impractical (a secured party is most unlikely to take possession of fixtures), or unavailable (automatic perfection is available only for PMSI's in consumer goods). Does this mean that, as a practical matter, a secured party must make a fixture filing to achieve priority over a real property interest, even in those cases where UCC 9–334 provides that a security interest perfected by *any* perfection method can achieve priority?

A careful reading of UCC 9–501(a) reveals that a security interest in "goods that are or are to become fixtures" may be perfected *either* by filing a financing statement as a fixture filing *or* by filing a financing statement other than as a fixture filing. If the financing statement is filed as a fixture filing, it must be filed in the office in which a mortgage on the related real property would be recorded. See UCC 9–501(a)(1). However, if the financing statement is not filed as a fixture filing, the "regular" UCC filing office (e.g., the Office of the Secretary of State) is the proper place to file. See UCC 9–501(a)(2).[3]

With this in mind, consider again the priority rules. UCC 9–334(e)(2) and (3) award priority to certain security interests that are "perfected by any method permitted by this article." A fixture filing in the real property filing office is one such perfection method; a filing in the "regular" filing office is another. Either a fixture filing or a non-fixture filing would be sufficient to perfect and to qualify for priority under these rules. However, a security interest *perfected* by filing in the "regular" filing office would not be sufficient for *priority* under the PMSI rule in UCC 9–334(d) or the rule in UCC 9–334(e)(1); those rules condition priority on a fixture filing.

How does a "fixture filing" differ from an "ordinary" filing? In addition to being filed in a different filing office, a financing statement filed as a "fixture filing" must provide more information than an "ordinary" financing statement. See UCC 9–102(a)(40); UCC 9–502(a), (b). Please review the additional requirements in UCC 9–502(b). Can you explain the reason for each requirement? Now study the priority rules in UCC 9–334(d) and (e). Can you explain why the drafters thought that a fixture filing should be required for priority under some circumstances but not others? Consider, in this regard, the identity of the competing real property claimant as well as the nature of the goods constituting the fixtures.[4] See also the last paragraph of this Note.

Although both a non-fixture filing and a fixture filing can perfect a security interest in fixtures, a fixture filing *is not effective* to perfect a security interest in *non-fixtures*. In view of the difficulty of characterizing property as a fixture or non-fixture in many jurisdictions, it is not surprising that secured parties often file both a fixture filing and non-fixture filing as a precaution. The non-fixture filing may have two other advantages: it could eliminate any need to show that the goods "are to become fixtures" in the event that a competing interest in them arises before they are affixed to

3.   The treatment of fixtures differs in this regard from the treatment afforded other real property-related collateral. In the case of timber, minerals, and certain minerals-related accounts, the only proper place to file is in the real property records; the failure to file in those records means that a security interest is unperfected. In contrast, a filing covering fixtures need be filed in the real property records only if it is "filed as a fixture filing." UCC 9–501(a)(1).

4.   Under BC 544(a)(3) the "strong arm" of the bankruptcy trustee has the strength of a bona fide purchaser of real property instead of the weaker muscle of a hypothetical lien creditor available in the case of personal property. See BC 544(a)(1) (discussed in Chapter 7, Section 2(A), supra). The priority over a creditor with "a lien on the real property obtained by legal or equitable proceedings," given by UCC 9–334(e)(3), would be chimerical indeed if the security interest remained vulnerable to a trustee in bankruptcy. However, the trustee's bona fide purchaser powers under BC 544(a)(3) extend only to "real property, *other than fixtures*," BC 544(a)(3), leaving fixtures to the treatment afforded property other than real property. See BC 544(a)(1). See also BC 547(e)(1) (treating fixtures like personalty for preference purposes).

land, see UCC 9–501(a)(1)(B), and it could provide continued perfection should fixture collateral subsequently become unaffixed.

Not every secured party appreciates the subtleties in the law governing fixtures and makes both a fixture and non-fixture filing. A secured party may file in the UCC filing office, not realizing that the collateral is a fixture and that the security interest, while perfected, will be subordinate to many types of competing claims to the real property. See UCC 9–334(d), (e)(1). Likewise, having relied on the erroneous assumption that the collateral is a fixture and made a fixture filing, a secured party may be disappointed to learn that the collateral is not a fixture and the security interest is unperfected. Eliminating the concept of "fixture filing" would eliminate these complications: A filing in the UCC filing office would be sufficient to perfect as to both fixtures and non-fixtures; it would afford the same priority as does a fixture filing under UCC 9–334. Under this approach, a potential mortgagee who is concerned about a possible senior interest in fixtures would search not only the real property records but also the UCC records. If potential mortgagees routinely will conduct two searches in any event (because the possibility for subordination under UCC 9–334(e)(2) is perceived to be sufficiently great or because mortgagees are concerned about junior, as well as senior, security interests), then the elimination of fixture filings would achieve the benefit of simplicity without imposing additional costs in most transactions. This thinking led the New Jersey Law Revision Commission to recommended the elimination of fixture filings. See New Jersey Law Revision Commission, [untitled report on Revised Article 9] 4 http://www.lawrev.state.nj.us/rpts/ucc9.pdf (visited July 13, 2005). The recommendation failed to obtain the necessary support from county clerks, banks, and the real property bar and so was not enacted. Should Revised Article 9 have eliminated fixture filings? (Consider, in this regard, that filing in the real property records is the exclusive method of perfection for minerals and related accounts as well as timber to be cut. See UCC 9–501(a)(1)(A).)

Problem 8.3.5. On June 1 Realty and Builder made a contract for Builder to erect a $10,000,000 apartment building on Realty's lot. Realty was to make progress payments to Builder at defined stages of the construction. Realty made an arrangement with Bank to lend Realty the sums needed for the progress payments, and executed to Bank a mortgage covering its lot, any structures to be erected thereon, and any appurtenances thereto. Bank promptly recorded the mortgage.

The construction contract with Builder did not include installation of (a) the elevator; (b) stoves, refrigerators, dishwashers, and carpeting in the apartments; or (c) office furniture, computers, and other business equipment in the management office of the apartment building. Realty contracted directly with various appliance and furniture dealers for the delivery and installation of these items. Realty arranged for loans from Finco to pay the suppliers for these items. Realty executed and delivered to Finco a security agreement covering these items. The items were added when construction of the apartment building was nearly complete. Before the items were delivered, Finco filed a financing statement covering "equipment" in the Office of Secretary of State and made a "fixture filing" in the local office for the recording of mortgages. See UCC 9–102(a)(40); UCC 9–502(b), (a); UCC 9–501(a)(1)(B).

(a) Realty is in default to Finco. Finco has instituted proceedings to recover and remove the items ((a), (b), and (c), above) covered by its security agreement. Bank has intervened and asserted that it has a senior security interest. What result? See UCC 9–334(d), (h), (e), (f); Note on Purchase–Money Security Interests in New Equipment and the Construction Mortgage, infra.

(b) If you had acted as counsel for Finco at the time its loan was made, would you have advised it to take any additional precautions?

NOTE ON PURCHASE–MONEY SECURITY INTERESTS IN NEW EQUIPMENT AND THE CONSTRUCTION MORTGAGE

Proponents of purchase-money security interests argue for priority on the ground that this priority makes it possible for a debtor to acquire new assets. During the review of Article 9 that led to the 1972 amendments, lenders engaged in financing the erection of new buildings pointed out that a construction loan, extended through a series of progress payments, provides a stream of new value during the construction process. They urged that their claim to priority as to the structure should not be subordinated to purchase-money security interests of unpredictable and uncontrollable scope. In the words of one of the drafters, "A construction mortgagee who thought he was getting a lien on an operable apartment house has a right to be surprised to learn that his debtor has financed the elevators through another channel." Coogan, The New UCC Article 9, 86 Harv.L.Rev. 477, 498 (1973). This point of view is now reflected in UCC 9–334(h).

(B) REAL PROPERTY–RELATED RECEIVABLES

INTRODUCTORY NOTE

Real property transactions can spawn an enormous variety of rights to payment. Attempts to use real property-related receivables as collateral frequently give rise to some difficult problems under both Article 9 and applicable real property law. The general nonuniformity of real property law among the states exacerbates the difficulties. A full explication of the problems and issues would require in-depth treatment of real property recording systems and priority rules—a task beyond the scope of this book. The following materials nevertheless endeavor to scratch the surface, at least as it pertains to the relationship between Article 9 and real property law. We consider, here, three common types of real property-related receivables: promissory notes secured by mortgages or deeds of trust, rights to payment under installment land sale contracts, and rights to payment of rentals under leases of real property.

Problem 8.3.6. Gold Neckchain, Inc. (GNI), is a real property development concern. Needing additional cash for some front-burner, behind-schedule, over-budget, under-funded, in-trouble, and out-of-luck projects, GNI has approached your client, Firstbank, for additional financing in the amount of $2.5 million. GNI proposes to secure the loan with three receivables: (i) a promissory note secured by a duly recorded first mortgage on a choice piece of beachfront property, (ii) the remaining payments under a duly recorded installment land sale contract owed to GNI by the buyer of a tract of undeveloped land that GNI sold several years ago, and (iii) the remaining rental payments owed to GNI under a written and duly recorded lease of a warehouse (GNI also has offered to Firstbank a first mortgage on the leased real property).

Firstbank is satisfied with the aggregate amount of the streams of payments included in the proposed collateral, with the creditworthiness of the three obligors, and with the value of the real property interests involved. Because of some concerns about GNI's financial condition, however, Firstbank's credit policy committee is willing to proceed only if you can give "ironclad assurance that if GNI 'bites the dust' Firstbank will have a first priority security interest in the payment streams."

(a) Can you give that assurance to Firstbank? What steps would you take to ensure both perfection and priority with respect to each type of receivable? See UCC 9–109(b) & Comment 7; UCC 9–109(a)(1), (d)(11); UCC 9–203(g); UCC 9–308(e); Notes on Real Property–Related Receivables, infra.

(b) Are these steps sufficient to assure first priority in the payment streams if any of the three obligors goes "belly up"?

NOTES ON REAL PROPERTY–RELATED RECEIVABLES

(1) Notes Secured by Mortgages—"Realty Paper." Notwithstanding the fact that it applies to fixtures, as a general matter Article 9 is inapplicable to"the creation or transfer of an interest in or lien on real property." UCC 9–109(d)(11). Thus, if the owner of Blackacre borrows money and secures the debt with the real property, the rights of the owner-mortgagor (debtor) and the mortgagee (creditor) are determined entirely by non-UCC law.

Suppose, as sometimes is the case, a mortgagee becomes a debtor—it uses its interest in the note and mortgage to secure a loan. UCC 9–109(b) leaves little doubt that Article 9 applies to a security interest in the note (a UCC 9–102(a)(47) "instrument"), even though it is secured by real property collateral: "The application of this article to a security interest in a secured obligation is not affected by the fact that the obligation is itself secured by a transaction or interest to which this article does not apply."

Suppose a mortgagee grants a security interest in the mortgage. The secured party (Lender) takes possession of the note but does not record an assignment (for collateral purposes) of the mortgage in the real property records. Although UCC 9–109(b) seems straightforward enough, it is silent as to the relationship between a security interest in a secured note and the mortgage that secures the note.

Lender's primary concern is likely to be its priority over competing creditors of mortgagee. The prevailing common law view is that a mortgage is incident to any note it secures; rights in the mortgage follow ownership of the note. See, e.g., Carpenter v. Longan, 83 U.S. (16 Wall.) 271, 21 L.Ed. 313 (1872) ("An assignment of the note carries the mortgage with it, while an assignment of the latter alone is a nullity"); Epstein, Security Transfers by Secured Parties, 4 Ga. L. Rev. 527 (1970). We have seen that Article 9 adopts this principle with regard to security interests in notes secured by personalty (i.e., with regard to security interests in chattel paper): Attachment and perfection of a security interest in chattel paper is effective to create and perfect an enforceable security interest in the assignor's security interest in specific goods. See Chapter 5, Section 2, supra. The same result obtains with respect to what one might call "realty paper": Attachment of a security interest in the mortgage note or other secured obligation is also attachment of a security interest in the mortgage; perfection of the security interest in the obligation is also perfection of the security interest in the mortgage. See UCC 9–203(g) (attachment); UCC 9–308(e) (perfection).

The wisdom of this approach becomes apparent when one considers the consequences that may arise when the mortgage does not follow the note, i.e., when the mortgage is considered an interest in real property, separate from the note it secures. (This approach is reflected in the non-UCC law of some jurisdictions.) Under this approach, because Lender failed to record its interest in the real property records, Lender's priority in the note would not ensure its priority in the mortgage; rather, a competing creditor of the mortgagee (or the mortgagee's bankruptcy trustee) may have priority in the mortgage.

As a practical matter, what happens if Lender enjoys priority in the note but loses its interest in the mortgage by virtue of the bankruptcy trustee's power to avoid unrecorded transfers (BC 544(a))?[5] Can Lender reach only collections from the maker of the note (the owner-mortgagor) that are unrelated to the mortgage? Can a trustee who has avoided the assignment of the mortgage foreclose as against the defaulting mortgagor?

The flip side of this scenario appeared in In re Maryville Savings & Loan Corp., 743 F.2d 413 (6th Cir.1984), clarified on reconsideration 760 F.2d 119 (1985). In *Maryville Savings* the secured party *had recorded an assignment* of the mortgages (actually, deeds of trust) but *failed to take possession of the notes.* The court, relying in part on the pre–1966 version of Former 9–102, Comment 4, explained its holding as follows:

---

5.   If the mortgage is considered an interest in real property, then the trustee has the rights and powers of a bona fide purchaser of the mortgage and not merely those of a judicial lien creditor. Compare BC 544(a)(3) with BC 544(a)(1). See note 4, supra.

[W]e conclude that article nine applies to the plaintiff's security interest but only in the promissory notes themselves. Since plaintiff did not take possession of the notes, plaintiff's security interest in the notes was not perfected. See Tenn.Code Ann. § 47–9–304(1). On the other hand, we conclude that article nine does not apply to plaintiff's security interest in the deeds of trust. While defendant argues in his reply brief that plaintiff's security interest in the deeds of trust was not perfected even if article nine were held not to apply, he admits that he did not raise that issue below; plaintiff's security interest in the deeds of trust is therefore deemed to be a perfected interest.

743 F.2d at 416–17. What is the ultimate effect of having a perfected security interest in a mortgage and an unperfected security interest in the note that it secures? Wouldn't all collections received from enforcing the mortgage also be collections on the note? On reconsideration, the court attempted to clarify its opinion. Inasmuch as the security interest in non-foreclosure collections on the notes was unperfected, the trustee was entitled to them. As to funds that might be realized on foreclosure, "the result might be to the contrary."

UCC 9–203(g) and UCC 9–308(e) are intended to overrule cases like *Maryville Savings*, make clear that Article 9 and not real property law governs perfection of a security interest in both a mortgage obligation and the mortgage securing it, and prevent splitting the mortgage from the obligation it secures. UCC 9–109, Comment 7 explains:

It . . . follows from [UCC 9–109(b)] that an attempt to obtain or perfect a security interest in a secured obligation by complying with non-Article 9 law, as by an assignment of record of a real-property mortgage, would be ineffective. Finally, it is implicit from [UCC 9–109(b)] that one cannot obtain a security interest in a lien, such as a mortgage on real property, that is not also coupled with an equally effective security interest in the secured obligation. This Article rejects cases such as In re *Maryville Savings & Loan Corp.* . . . .

Of course, perfection is not a secured party's only concern. Consider again the case of Lender, who has a security interest in a mortgage note, takes possession of the note, but fails to record an assignment (for collateral purposes) of the mortgage. If the mortgage defaults, Lender may wish to enforce the mortgage by forcing a sale of the real property. Local real property law may limit the enforcement of the mortgage to the mortgagee of record. But recording can be expensive. When a transaction involves hundreds or thousands of mortgage-secured notes, as a securitization often does, see p. 83, supra, the cost of recording assignments may be prohibitive. To reduce the cost under these circumstances, secured parties sometimes obtain assignments at the outset of the transaction but record them on an "as needed" basis, i.e., only when necessary to enforce the mortgage.

A secured party who neglects to obtain an assignment of mortgage in recordable form at the outset of a transaction may find that the mortgagee-debtor is unwilling to provide one later, particularly if the mortgagee has defaulted on its obligation to the assignee. If local law permits the mortgage to be enforced nonjudicially, UCC 9–607(b) enables the secured party to become the mortgagee of record by recording in the applicable real property records the security agreement and an affidavit certifying that a default has occurred.

The failure to record an assignment of mortgage may have other consequences. Suppose the mortgagor (the owner of the real property and the maker of the secured note) sells the real property to a bona fide purchaser. Suppose also that, prior to the purchase, the mortgagee wrongfully executed and delivered a *release* of the assigned mortgage: Would the bona fide purchaser cut off Lender's rights? Yes, according to the Restatement. See Restatement (Third) of Property (Mortgages) § 5.4, Comment *b* (1997) (good faith purchaser for value "is entitled to rely on the record"). That scenario—protection against the assignor's wrongful (or mistaken) release of the mortgage—illustrates another reason why an assignee would prefer to have the assignment recorded.[6]

(2) Installment Land Sale Contracts. The principle that the collateral follows the secured obligation applies to **installment land contracts**. The most straightforward form of installment land sale contract (sometimes called a "**contract for deed**") is like a conditional sale agreement covering personal property. The seller agrees to sell, the buyer agrees to buy, and the seller agrees to convey title by delivering a deed to the real property when the buyer has made all of the required installment payments. Buyers typically insist that the installment land sale contracts be recorded in the real property records in order to protect their interests against bona fide purchasers from the seller and against the seller's trustee in bankruptcy.

These contracts are functionally equivalent to mortgages, and in many jurisdictions they are treated like mortgages for many purposes (such as protection for the buyer-debtor's equity of redemption upon a default). Unlike a mortgage secured by a note, however, there is unlikely to be an "instrument" in which a security interest could be perfected by possession. See UCC 9–102(a)(47); UCC 9–313(a). Rather, the rights to payment under installment land sale contracts are "accounts"; they are "right[s] to payment of a monetary obligation, whether or not earned by performance, . . . for property that has been or is to be sold." UCC 9–102(a)(2).

Under Article 9, attachment of a security interest in the obligation under the contract (an account) is attachment of a security interest in the real property securing the obligation. See UCC 9–203(g). Perfection of a security interest in the account perfects a security interest in the real

---

6.   The same risks exist with respect to assignments of Article 9 security interests, of course. But noting the assignment of a financing statement in the public record makes the assignee the "secured party of record," who has the power to amend the financing statement, e.g., by releasing collateral or by continuing or terminating the effectiveness of the financing statement. See UCC 9–514; UCC 9–511; UCC 9–510(a); UCC 9–509(d)(1).

property securing the obligation. See UCC 9–308(e). Article 9 rejects cases holding that recording an assignment of the contract in the real property records is necessary and sufficient to protect the assignee against competing claims. See UCC 9–109, Comment 7.

(3) Real Property Leases and Rents. Reading UCC 9–109(d)(11), standing alone, you may be hard put to see how Article 9 possibly could apply to a transaction in which a lessor assigns its rights to a rental stream under a lease of real property. Article 9 "does not apply . . . to the creation or transfer of an interest in or lien on real property, *including a lease or rents thereunder.*" UCC 9–109(d)(11). The potential for mischief arises, however, because under the law of some states a lessor's interest in a lease is considered *personal property* for some purposes. Does UCC 9–109(d)(11) exclude only leases that are treated as interests in real property under non-UCC real property law? Or, does it also exclude leases and rents that would be considered personal property under non-UCC law? This ambiguity aside, the overwhelming weight of authority is to the effect that an assignment of a lessor's interest under a lease of real property is not covered by Article 9. (Of course, this authority construes Former Article 9, which contains the exclusion now found in UCC 9–109(d)(11). See, e.g., In re Dorsey, 155 B.R. 263 (Bkrtcy.D.Me.1993).)

The most serious problems relating to assignments of leases as security arise under applicable real property law and under the Bankruptcy Code; these problems are largely outside the scope of this book.

(4) Mortgage Warehouse Lending; "Transferable Records." Mortgage lenders (**originators**) lend such substantial sums to their customers (buyers of real property) that they typically must borrow funds as they need them. The loans that banks and other financial institutions extend to originators typically are secured by the notes and mortgages. Because banks and other **warehouse lenders** obtain much of their funds from short-term deposits, they usually are content to make short-term mortgage warehouse loans. Towards this end, they enter into arrangements that permit the originator-borrower to sell the note in the secondary mortgage market, provided that the purchaser remit the proceeds of the sale to the warehouse lender.

The transfer of notes historically has been accomplished by delivering the note to the purchaser. A purchaser of a note has strong incentives to take possession of it. See UCC 3–203(b), (a); UCC 9–330; UCC 9–331; UCC 3–306; Chapter 1, Section 4, supra; Chapter 5, Section 2, supra. The administrative costs of transferring the paper and keeping it safe are not trivial; and despite their value, notes are lost with surprising frequency. See, e.g., Dennis Joslin Co. v. Robinson Broadcasting Corp., 977 F.Supp. 491 (D.D.C.1997) (action on lost note with principal amount in excess of $550,000). We have seen that section 16 of the UETA affords to a person having control of an electronic note ("transferable record") many of the same benefits afforded to the holder of a negotiable instrument, including eligibility for obtaining the rights of a holder in due course. See Chapter 1,

Section 4, supra; Chapter 5, Section 2, supra. Even in states in which UETA has not been enacted, a person in control of an electronic mortgage note may obtain these benefits. See E–SIGN § 201. Section 201 of E–SIGN generally tracks section 16 of UETA. However, it applies only to an electronic record that "relates to a loan secured by real property." Id. § 201(a)(1)(C).

Problem 8.3.7. The Dexters borrowed $200,000 from First Mortgage Lenders (FML) for the purchase of their new home. The debt is evidenced by a note secured by a mortgage on the home. FML borrowed the funds from Bank Two, in whose favor FML granted a security interest in the Dexters' note and mortgage. After the closing of the mortgage loan, FML indorsed the note in blank and forwarded the signed note and mortgage to Bank Two.

A past agreement between FML and Bank Two provides that FML will attempt to sell the note in the secondary mortgage market and use the sale proceeds to repay its obligation to Bank Two. To accomplish this result, Bank Two sent the original note and mortgage to the Mortgage Buyers Association ("MBA") for its consideration. The documents were accompanied by a **bailee letter** in which Bank Two informed MBA of its security interest, stated that the note and mortgage were to be held by MBA as a bailee for Bank Two, directed MBA to return the note and mortgage to Bank Two if MBA decided not to purchase them or to remit to Bank Two the proceeds of any sale, and agreed that its security interest terminates upon Bank Two's receipt of the proceeds.

(a) MBA holds the note and mortgage for 30 days without paying for it. Is Bank Two's security interest in the note perfected? See UCC 9–312(g); UCC 9–313(a), (g), (h).

(b) MBA purchases the note and mortgage but pays the proceeds to another creditor at FML's direction. What remedy for Bank Two? Assume alternatively that the mortgage note is negotiable and nonnegotiable. See UCC 9–102(a)(47); UCC 9–406(a); UCC 9–102(a)(3); UCC 9–609; UCC 9–330(d); UCC 9–331; UCC 3–306; UCC 3–302; UCC 9–315(a); UCC 9–332.

(c) Would you advise Bank Two to insist that FML use electronic notes that qualify as transferable records under UETA and E–SIGN?

SECTION 4.   NONCONSENSUAL LIENS

(A) LANDLORD'S LIENS

INTRODUCTORY NOTE

Household furnishings and other consumer goods sold on a secured instalment basis often will be kept in a rented apartment or home; industrial and farm equipment and growing crops also may be located in rented premises. Because a debtor in financial difficulty is likely to be delinquent in the payment of rent, the holder of a security interest must cope with the threat of a lien in favor of the landlord.

The landlord's powers stem from the ancient common-law remedy of distress. At common law, and still in some states, distress for rent is an interesting example of a self-help remedy with echoes of the powers of the feudal lord; for this remedy traditionally was effected, without legal process, by the landlord's seizure of goods on the premises.

Are state rules permitting seizure without a hearing subject to attacks based on constitutional guaranties of due process? There is good reason to believe that the Supreme Court would consider the "state action" component of a due process violation to be missing in the case of common-law or statutory landlord's liens. See Flagg Bros. v. Brooks, 436 U.S. 149, 98 S.Ct. 1729, 56 L.Ed.2d 185 (1978) (no state action is involved in enforcement of UCC 7–210 warehouseman's lien). The due process issue is considered in more detail in Chapter 9, Section 1, infra. At this point we are concerned with the substantive rules, still honored in many states, that expose a tenant's goods to distraint by the landlord, even if those goods are subject to an Article 9 security interest.

It is clear enough that Article 9 does not apply to a statutory or common-law landlord's lien, other than a statutory "agricultural lien" on farm products. See UCC 9–109(d)(1); UCC 9–102(a)(5) (defining "agricultural lien"); Section 4(C), infra (discussing agricultural liens). But that exclusion says nothing about the priority contest between a landlord and an Article 9 secured party. Some states have enacted statutes that give priority to the secured party when, for example, a security interest is perfected before the goods are brought to the rented premises or the secured party affords advance notice to the landlord. In the absence of such a statute, however, one must ask whether the adoption of the UCC eliminated any common-law threat of senior landlord's liens. And where the pre-UCC law protected only certain "types" of security interests from the landlord (e.g., conditional sales), what is the result under the UCC's unified approach to "security interests"? Each of these issues is encountered in the following case. Although the case was decided under Former Article 9, it remains relevant. Revised Article 9 contains statutory provisions that are similar to those that the court construes; in particular, UCC 9–109(d)(1) and (d)(2) follow Former 9–104(b) and (c), and UCC 9–333 (discussed in Section 4(B), infra) derives from Former 9–310.

Universal C.I.T. Credit Corp. v. Congressional Motors, Inc.[*]

Court of Appeals of Maryland, 1967.
246 Md. 380, 228 A.2d 463.

■ HAMMOND, CHIEF JUDGE.

At issue is the priority between a landlord's lien on automobiles of his tenant, a dealer, in the leased premises and the lien of a lender who had advanced the dealer the purchase price of the automobiles and prior to the

---

[*]   [The court's citations are to the applicable pre–1972 version of the UCC.]

levy under the warrant of distraint had perfected a security interest in them under the Uniform Commercial Code to cover his advances.

Congressional Motors, Inc. had leased premises in Montgomery County to Peter Palmer, Ltd., an automobile dealer. In early December 1965 Palmer owed rent to Congressional which directed the sheriff to levy upon seven automobiles owned by Palmer and located on the leased premises. The sheriff, having learned that Universal C.I.T. Credit Corporation was claiming a lien for its advances to Palmer superior to that of the landlord, refused to sell the automobiles as directed by Congressional, which then sought mandamus to compel the sale. Universal intervened, asserting its claimed prior lien. Judge Pugh ruled that the landlord had priority and ordered the sale of the automobiles.

The priority between the landlord's lien and Universal's lien must be determined by the state of the law in December 1965 when the levy under the distraint warrant was made. If the levy had been made on or after January 1, 1966, Universal's security interest would have been explicitly preferred to the landlord's lien under § 16 of Ch. 915 of the Laws of 1965, effective January 1 (Code, Art. 53, § 16), which completely revised and formalized the law of distress.

Universal, the lender, asserts, as it did below, that the provisions of the Uniform Commercial Code are applicable and controlling. In considering the contention we must examine the law of distress as it existed before 1966, including the extent to which it exempted property on the demised premises subject to security devices and the effect the passage of the Code had on the preexisting law.

Before 1966 distress was a mixture of rules of the common law (many stemming from feudal times), implementing and supplementing Maryland legislation, and long-standing practice.

In 1964 the Committee on Laws of the Maryland State Bar Association said in reporting on the bill which later became Ch. 915 of the Laws of 1965:

> "The present distraint law in Maryland is archaic in that a landlord's remedy of distress is exercised without supervision by any court in spite of the substantial rights, and important interests, of tenants and landlords which are involved. The sheriff or constable now acts merely as an agent of the landlord. No court record is made with respect to a distress proceeding including the levy and sale of goods on the leased premises."

Despite its somewhat amorphous structure, the Maryland law of distress prior to 1966 had definitely established rules and principles. A landlord had a "quasi-lien" for unpaid rent on the goods of his tenant subject to distress, even before the levy under the distraint warrant. Rhynhart, Law of Landlord and Tenant, 20 Md.L.Rev. 1, 36 . . . In Calvert Bldg. & Const. Co. v. Winakur, 154 Md. 519, 531, 141 A. 355, 359, Judge Parke, speaking for the Court said:

> "But a *quasi* lien in the sense used in Thomson v. Baltimore, etc., Co., supra, and the other cases cited, means nothing more than the

potential right of a landlord to subject to distress the goods and chattels on the demised premises for the rent in arrears."

The cases have held that the quasi lien of the landlord becomes a lien either upon levy . . . or upon assertion of the right, under the Statute of 8 Anne, Ch. 14, § 1, to be paid up to one year's rent in arrears by another creditor levying execution or attachment. . . . Rhynhart, op. cit., says (p. 36):

> "This quasi-lien may be converted to a lien, even without a distress under the Statute of 8 Anne, Ch. 14, and if the landlord's claim for rent is properly established it will take precedence over the debt on which an attachment issues and he is entitled to be first paid out of the proceeds of the property condemned."

In bankruptcy the landlord had a prior lien on the proceeds of sale of the bankrupt's asset sold by the trustee if the landlord had levied distress before the tenant's adjudication as a bankrupt, . . . and the lien acquired by such a levy within four months of a bankruptcy petition was not voidable as it was regarded as one secured other than through legal proceedings. In re Potee Brick Co. of Baltimore City, 179 F. 525, 530 (Rose, J., D.Md., 1910).

The landlord could distrain on any goods and chattels on the premises whether owned by the tenant or owned by another or subject to liens in favor of another, except as such goods were exempted by law. . . . The rule that the goods of a stranger were liable equally with those of the tenant had its origin in feudal times. This ancient privilege was regarded as an inseparable incident of the seigniory and as a remedy which was confined to the land out of which the rent issued. The tenant owed the rent but the remedy was enforced against the land as if it were the debtor.

Goods and chattels of strangers which at the times here pertinent were exempt from distress and liens which were then superior to the landlord's lien were set out in detail in § 18 of Art. 53, as it read in 1965. That section after exempting from distress a number of specified articles not the property of the tenant provided that, except in Prince George's County, if the landlord should distrain on any non-exempt goods or chattels covered by "a conditional contract of sale defined in § 66 of Article 21 or mortgaged by the tenant by a purchase money chattel mortgage under the terms of §§ 41 to 51, inclusive, of Article 21," he should either release such property from the distraint or pay the balance due "under such conditional contract of sale or mortgage."

Universal's lien was not a conditional contract of sale as defined in § 66 of Art. 21 of the Code as it read before its express repeal by the Uniform Commercial Code because title to the liened automobiles was never in Universal, the lender, nor was that lien a purchase money chattel mortgage within the terms of §§ 41–51 of Art. 21 and the contemplation of § 18 because the money it secured was not due from Palmer, the vendee, to the vendor of the automobiles for or on account of the purchase price, but was money advanced by a third person to provide the purchase price. The purchase money chattel mortgage exempted by § 18 was such a mortgage as it was defined by Maryland law prior to the enactment of the Uniform

Commercial Code, § 9–107. Thus under Maryland law as it existed before the enactment of the Uniform Commercial Code, the landlord's lien would have had priority over Universal's perfected interest since Universal did not have an interest of the types specifically excepted from distraint by § 18 of Art. 53.

We turn to whether the Uniform Commercial Code repealed § 18 of Art. 53 of the Code and enacted its own rules as to priority between a landlord's lien and a perfected Code security interest or amended that section to do this. It did not do either in terms. The lender explicitly concedes, as it must, that there was no complete repeal of § 18 of Art. 53 by virtue of Code . . . § 10–103, declaring that "all laws and parts of laws inconsistent with this article are hereby repealed." It really argues only that the Commercial Code impliedly amended § 18 of Art. 53 so as to add . . . chattels covered by security "financing statements" to [chattels exempted from distress] under conditional contracts of sale and purchase money chattel mortgages. We think Universal's concession is correct but that its contention of implied amendment is not. . . .

The matter of whether the Commercial Code impliedly amended § 18 of Art. 53 requires consideration of the purposes of that Code and the provisions enacted to accomplish those purposes.

The basic plan of Art. 95B [the Code] is to deal with the normal and ordinary aspects of a commercial transaction from start to finish by means of nine subtitles, eight of which are devoted to a specific phase or facet of commercial activity.

Subtitle 1 provides the general rules of construction and definitions applicable to all of the other subtitles. Section 1–103 . . . provides that "unless displaced by the particular provisions of this article, the principles of law and equity including the law merchant . . . shall supplement its provisions." . . .

Section 9–102(2) says:

"This subtitle applies to security interests created by contract including pledge, assignment, chattel mortgage, chattel trust, trust deed, factor's lien, equipment trust, conditional sale, trust receipt, other lien or title retention contract and lease or consignment intended as security. *This subtitle does not apply to statutory liens except as provided in § 9–310.*" (Emphasis supplied.)

The official comment states that the purpose of § 9–102 is to bring all consensual security interests in personal property, with exceptions specified in §§ 9–103 and 9–104, under subtitle 9. . . .

Section 9–310 gives those who furnish services or materials to goods subject to a security interest a prior lien over a perfected security interest, with specified exceptions. Section 9–312 defines priority among conflicting security interests in the same collateral, and §§ 9–401–406 and 9–501–507, respectively, establish the mechanics and effects of filing and procedures upon default.

The purposes and provisions of the Uniform Commercial Code lead us to believe that it did not impliedly amend § 18 of Art. 53 by exempting from distress security interests not previously exempted. We find persuasive indications to support that view. Bell v. State, 236 Md. 356, 365–367, 204 A.2d 54, recognized the theory of implied amendment as applicable in Maryland and delineated its controlling rules. An implied amendment is an act which does not state that it is amendatory but which in substance alters, modifies or adds to a prior act. Like repeals by implication, amendments by implication are not favored and will not be found unless there is a manifest repugnancy or irreconcilable conflict between the prior and the later act. If the two statutes can stand and be read together, there is no amendment of the first by the second, and the Code and § 18 of Art. 53 can be read together.

As we have noted subtitle 9 of the Commercial Code applies to all consensual security interests that are not specifically excluded by §§ 9–103 and 9–104, as § 9–102 makes plain. Section 9–104 lists a number of the "transactions excluded from subtitle" 9. The operative words here pertinent are:

> "This subtitle does not apply . . . (b) to a landlord's lien; or (c) to a lien given by statute or other rule of law for services or materials except as provided in § 9–310 on priority of such liens."

It appears that a landlord's lien and an artisan's lien were excluded from the applicability of subtitle 9 because they are nonconsensual. Comment 1 to § 9–102 says that " . . . the principal test whether a transaction comes under this Subtitle is: Is the transaction intended to have effect as security? For example, Section 9–104 excludes certain transactions where the security interest (such as an artisan's lien) arises under statute or common law by reason of status and not by consent of the parties." 2 Hawkland, A Transactional Guide to the Uniform Commercial Code, § 2.2201, p. 569, states:

> "The policy of Article 9 is to bring within its scope all transactions that are intended to create security interests in personal property or fixtures, and this policy, therefore, excludes real estate security, such as mortgages and landlord's liens, as well as personal property transactions that are not consensual in nature. Thus, artisan's liens generally are excluded from Article 9 because they are created not by agreement but by operation of positive law. Positive law creating nonconsensual liens often reflects local considerations and value judgments, and the draftsmen of the Code decided not to interfere with it."

We conclude that the flat and unqualified exclusion of landlord's liens from the application of the subtitle left the law on such liens as it was. The exclusion was not limited to ruling landlord's liens out as a Code security interest or to freeing them from procedural requirements applicable to such security interests; it provided in effect that no part, including rules as to priorities, of subtitle 9 controlled or governed them. This left their status and priority vis-a-vis those of security interests to the existing law. This was the view taken by the District Court for the Eastern District of Pennsylvania, In re Einhorn Bros., Inc., D.C., 171 F.Supp. 655, 660, and the Court of Appeals for the Third Circuit, which affirmed under the same name in 272 F.2d 434, 440–441. On the point here involved, the federal courts, in applying the law of Pennsylvania which adopted the Uniform Commercial Code in 1958 and which had a body of law on distress essentially the same as that of Maryland, held that as the Commercial Code in terms did not apply to a landlord's lien it did not deprive a landlord of the priority his perfected rent claim had under Pennsylvania law and therefore a landlord's lien continued to be superior to those consensual liens to which it was superior before the Code. See also 2 Anderson Uniform Commercial Code, § 9–104:3, pp. 480–481, and Schwartz, Pennsylvania Chattel Security and the Uniform Commercial Code, 98 U. of Pa.L.Rev. 530, 540–541, where the author in discussing whether a landlord's distraint for rent would take precedence over a Code security interest, pointed out that it had been held that the Pennsylvania exemption-from-distress statute did not exempt chattel mortgages, and suggested: "Should this decision be followed, form might retain importance even under the Commercial Code. To avoid such an unfortunate result, it is suggested that the exemption statutes be revised to protect any security interest in the designated types of collateral." Maryland as we have seen, did by Ch. 915 of the Laws of 1965, just what was suggested.

We think the intention to completely exclude a landlord's lien from every part of subtitle 9 is emphasized by the provision of § 9–104(c), immediately following that as to landlord's liens, which gives artisan's liens priority over perfected security interests as in § 9–310 provided. The comment to § 9–310 makes plain that the reason for giving priority expressly to artisan's liens is that "there was generally no specific statutory rule as to priority between security devices and liens for services or materials" since many decisions made the priority turn on whether the secured party did or did not have "title." A major Code purpose was to do away with differences and distinctions based on form (although allowing the retention of differences for other purposes, such as between the parties or for purposes of taxation) and the express rule of priority of § 9–310 accomplished this.

The lender argues that the landlord's lien which the Commercial Code excludes from the ambit of subtitle 9 must be a statutory lien. . . .

As has been noted, the landlord in Maryland had a lien by operation of law when the levy was made under the warrant of distraint. We conclude that this lien was "a landlord's lien" as that term is used in § 9–104(b) of the Commercial Code, and therefore is excluded from the operation of subtitle 9. . . . Liens of landlords arising by operation of law meet the test of being nonconsensual. . . .

Order affirmed, with costs.

NOTE ON THE PRIORITY OF LANDLORD'S LIENS

Most courts have concluded, as in *Congressional Motors*, that the priority contest between a landlord's lien and a security interest must be resolved by looking to law outside of Article 9. Depending on the jurisdiction, this law may be common law, statutory, or both. (The opinion in the *Congressional Motors* case noted that the dominance of the landlord's lien was reduced by Maryland legislation.) How can one best evaluate the relative merits of claims to priority by landlords and secured creditors? Is a landlord's claim as strong as that of service providers who repair or improve property subject to a security interest? See UCC 9–333 and Section 4(B), infra. Is the claim of either a landlord or a service provider comparable to that of a PMSI, which enjoys priority under UCC 9–324?

Why not determine priority by applying the *nemo dat* principle? See Chapter 1, Section 3(A), supra. Or would it be preferable to apply *nemo dat* as modified by the law's general distaste for "secret liens"? In many states, a landlord's lien arises only upon seizure of the goods but its priority relates back to the date of the lease. Should the unrecorded landlord's lien be subordinate to a security interest that is perfected before levy, or does recordation of the landlord's ownership of the real property give sufficient public notice of its potential lien?

––––––

To secure their obligation to pay rent, tenants sometimes grant a consensual security interest in personal property located on rented premises. Does this create a "landlord's lien," excluded under UCC 9–109(d)(1)? Consider the following Problem.

Problem 8.4.1. A lease of store facilities from Landlord to Tenant, a furniture retailer, provided: "To secure the payment of all rent due and to become due hereunder, Tenant hereby grants to Landlord a lien on all property, chattels or merchandise that Tenant may place on the leased premises." The lease was recorded in the real property records but not elsewhere. One year after Landlord and Tenant entered into the lease, Tenant obtained a line of credit from Bank, secured by all of Tenant's existing and after-acquired inventory. Bank properly perfected by filing. Under the law of the state, landlords have no right to distrain for rent.

Subsequently, Elsie, a judgment creditor of Tenant, levied on Tenant's inventory. Does Landlord have a lien on Tenant's inventory that is senior to Elsie's execution lien? Is Landlord's lien senior to Bank's security interest? See UCC 9–109(d)(1) & Comment 10; UCC 9–109(a)(1); *Shurlow v. Bonthuis*, 456 Mich. 730, 576 N.W.2d 159 (Mich.1998) (effectuating the clear intent of Former Article 9 to bring all consensual transactions within its scope, notwithstanding that a literal reading of F9–104(b) supports excluding consensual liens in favor of a landlord); *Butters v. Jackson*, 917 P.2d 87 (Utah Ct.App.1996) (lien created by contract is separate and distinct from lessor's statutory lien and is a security interest under Former Article 9).

(B) Liens in Favor of Providers of Services and Materials

The statutory and common law of each state recognizes a variety of liens in favor of various classes of persons who provide services and materials. For example, a mechanic who repairs an automobile may enjoy a statutory or common-law lien on the vehicle to secure the owner's obligation to pay the cost of repair. As a general matter, Article 9 does not apply to liens, other than agricultural liens, given by statute or other rule of law for services or materials; however, UCC 9–333 governs the priority of these liens. See UCC 9–109(d)(2). Liens of this kind sometimes are referred to as "artisan's liens"; UCC 9–333 refers to them as "possessory liens."

Problem 8.4.2. In the automobile financing Prototype in Chapter 3, Section 1, supra, Lee Abel purchased a Chevrolet from Main Motors. Main assigned Abel's Instalment Sale Contract (Form 3.6) to Firstbank, which perfected its security interest in the car by having its interest noted on the certificate of title (Form 3.8) in accordance with the applicable certificate of title act. Assume that the car was later damaged, and Abel took it to the Beater Body Shoppe for repairs. When the repairs were completed, Abel failed to pay for them or to reclaim the car. Applicable state law provides that a mechanic (such as Beater) who repairs a car may retain the car to secure payment of the costs of repair.

Abel's payments on the Instalment Sale Contract were in arrears, so Firstbank sought possession of the car from Beater. Beater is willing to turn over the car to Firstbank, but only on condition that someone first pay the $8,160.63 repair bill.

The following provisions of the certificate-of-title act are in effect:

Sec. 43. All liens on motor vehicles shall take priority according to the order of time the same are recorded on the certificate of title.

Sec. 46. Only liens noted on a certificate of title shall be valid as against creditors insofar as concerns the motor vehicle.

The statute providing for the mechanic's lien includes the following:

Nothing in this title shall be construed or considered as in any manner impairing or affecting the right of parties to create liens by special contract or agreement, nor shall it in any manner affect or impair other liens arising at common law or in equity, or by any statute of this State, or any other lien not treated of under this title.

Advise Firstbank. See UCC 9–333.

Problem 8.4.3. What result in the immediately preceding Problem if (i) the Instalment Sale Contract provided that Main Motors would retain title until Abel's payment in full thereunder (i.e., the transaction was documented as a "conditional sale"), and (ii) the statutory mechanic's lien arises only with respect to repair work that is authorized by the "owner" of the vehicle? See UCC 9–333; UCC 9–202; Note (1) on Non–UCC Liens for Suppliers of Materials and Services, infra.

NOTES ON NON–UCC LIENS FOR SUPPLIERS OF MATERIALS AND SERVICES

(1) Does Article 9 Affect Whether a Non–UCC Lien Attaches? Problem 8.4.3, supra, is based on Champa v. Consolidated Finance Corp., 231 Ind. 580, 110 N.E.2d 289 (1953). The principal opinion in the *Champa* case concluded that Champa, the mechanic, was not entitled to the benefit of a statutory mechanic's lien because the repair work was not authorized by the "owner." The court held that a conditional vendee (buyer) in a conditional sale is not an "owner" for purposes of that statute. Would the court decide the case differently today, given the unified approach to security interests under Article 9?

Indeed, would UCC 9–202 compel the court to decide the case differently? That section provides that "the provisions of this article with regard to rights and obligations apply whether title to collateral is in the secured party or the debtor." According to Comment 2:

> The rights and duties of parties to a secured transaction and affected third parties are provided in this Article without reference to the location of "title" to the collateral. For example, the characteristics of a security interest that secures the purchase price of goods are the same whether the secured party appears to have retained title or the debtor appears to have obtained title and then conveyed title or a lien to the secured party.

UCC 9–202, Comment 2. On the other hand, Comment 3.b. indicates that "Article [9] does not determine which line of interpretation (e.g., title theory or lien theory, retained title or conveyed title) should be followed in cases in which the applicability of another rule of law depends upon who has title." UCC 9–202, Comment 3.b. The Comment gives two examples of such rules of law: those imposing taxes on the legal "owner" of goods and those requiring shareholder consent for a corporation "giving" a security interest but not for a corporation acquiring property "subject to" a security interest. Is the statutory mechanic's lien a rule of law of this kind? Would the Indiana legislature have amended the mechanic's lien statute when enacting the UCC if someone had thought about this issue of "ownership"?

Consider, in this regard, the *Congressional Motors* case in Section 4(A), supra. The court concluded that the security interest was not a "conditional sale" or a "purchase money chattel mortgage" qualifying for preferred treatment under the Maryland landlord's lien statute. Should the court have looked to Former 9–202 (which is substantially the same as UCC 9–202)? Although Former 9–202 made title irrelevant with respect to "[e]ach provision of this Article," landlord's liens are wholly excluded from Article 9. See Former 9–104(b); UCC 9–109(d)(1). Moreover, inasmuch as it favors both purchase-money chattel mortgagees and conditional sellers, the Maryland statute seems to be directed to the character of a transaction—a purchase-money transaction in favor of a seller—and not the location of "title."

The principal opinion in *Champa* also concluded that Champa, the mechanic, did not qualify for any of the exceptions to the general rule in Indiana that artisans' claims are inferior to those of conditional vendors. In particular, the finance company did not know that the repairs were to be made, and the repairs were not of a real benefit to the finance company (although the car's engine had thrown a rod and the crankshaft was bent!).

The court reached a similar result in Associates Financial Services v. O'Dell, 491 Pa. 1, 417 A.2d 604 (1980). Reasoning that common-law possessory liens for improvement to personal property are based on actual or implied consent of the "owner," the court held that the absence of the secured party's consent to the improvement was fatal to the establishment of a lien. Although the court considered the secured party to be an "owner" for this purpose, it did not do so on the formalistic basis employed by the *Champa* court. Rather, it considered the secured party to have a significant property interest warranting "ownership" treatment for purposes of consent. Having found that the common-law lien never attached, the court did not reach the priority contest addressed by Former 9–310. Can the decision be squared with the letter of Former 9–310 or UCC 9–333? With the policy and spirit of Former 9–310 or UCC 9–333?

(2) Priority Rules When UCC 9–333 Does Not Apply. In many circumstances the priority rule of UCC 9–333 will not apply. One important circumstance is mentioned prominently in that section—"unless the lien is created by a statute that expressly provides otherwise." When that proviso applies, of course, the source of the governing priority rule is clear. But what if the priority given to a qualifying lien by UCC 9–333 does not apply because the lien is not a "possessory lien" as defined in UCC 9–333(a). Suppose, for example, that the lien remains effective under non-UCC law even if the claimant loses possession of the goods. Does UCC 9–333 create a negative implication that the lien then would be *junior* to the security interest? A negative answer seems appropriate. Remember that UCC 9–109(d)(2) makes Article 9 generally inapplicable to liens "for services or materials," with the exception of agricultural liens and the priority rule of UCC 9–333. When UCC 9–333 does not apply, then one must consult other law.

What priority rules apply when the non-UCC lien is not one "for services or materials" (a state tax lien, for example)? It is clear enough that such a nonconsensual, statutory lien would not be an Article 9 security interest. See UCC 9–109(a). But, unlike a landlord's lien or a lien for services or materials, a tax lien is not expressly excluded from the application of Article 9. See UCC 9-109(d). Does Article 9 determine priority when such a non-UCC lien conflicts with an Article 9 security interest? Arguably, UCC 9–201 provides a controlling priority rule—i.e., the security interest is always senior except as otherwise provided in the UCC. Is it likely that the drafters intended UCC 9–201 to have such a broad sweep? (The caption to the section reads "General Effectiveness of Security Agreement." Section captions are part of the Code. See UCC 1–107 [F1–109].) Is it more likely that the drafters intended to "interfere" with non-UCC lien priorities only in the limited context of UCC 9–333?

(C) AGRICULTURAL LIENS

Problem 8.4.4. Doobie grows corn on the family farm. Canopy sells seed to Doobie on unsecured credit. A state statute gives those who sell seed to farmers a lien on all crops grown from the seed. Doobie planted the seed, grew the corn, harvested the crop, and stored the corn in a silo.

(a) Elsie, a judgment creditor of Doobie's, causes the sheriff to levy on the corn. Which lien, Canopy's statutory lien or Elsie's execution lien, is senior? See UCC 9–109(a)(2); UCC 9–102(a)(5), (34), (35); UCC 9–317(a)(2); UCC 9–310(a); UCC 9–501(a); Note (2) on Agricultural Liens and Production–Money Security Interests, infra. Could the holder of the junior lien have achieved priority? If so, how?

(b) The preceding year, Doobie had obtained from Farmers Bank a line of credit, secured by Doobie's existing and after-acquired crops. Farmers Bank properly perfected by filing. Is Canopy's lien on the crops senior or junior to Bank's security interest? Could the holder of the junior claim have achieved priority? If so, how? See UCC 9–322(a), (g); Revised Article 9, Appendix II; Note (3) on Agricultural Liens and Production–Money Security Interests, infra.

NOTES ON AGRICULTURAL LIENS AND PRODUCTION–MONEY SECURITY INTERESTS

(1) The Problem. Statutory liens seem to be the rule, not the exception, in the agricultural industry. Consider the following excerpt:

[U]nlike security interests under Article 9 of the U.C.C., where uniformity between the states is quite extensive, agricultural statutory liens are noted for their lack of uniformity. Uniformity is lacking in two respects: as between states, and within a state.

First, each state has its own unique set of agricultural liens that reflects each state's own agricultural history. Many of these liens, on their face, reflect an agricultural history and past agricultural needs that seem quaint and old-fashioned, or possibly even anachronistic and detrimental when compared to today's agricultural realities. Just to hear the names of such agricultural liens makes one recall the times in which these agricultural liens arose: thresher's liens, horseshoer's liens, livery stable liens, moss gatherer's lien. Yet these liens cannot be easily dismissed as outmoded and unneeded. Naming other agricultural liens immediately makes their modern relevance clear: landlord's liens, seed supplier liens, fertilizer supplier liens, veterinarian's liens. . ..

Second, each state adopted its various agricultural liens at different times and under different pressures. As a state adopted an agricultural lien, no common pattern or organized approach was followed. Hence, within a particular state, agricultural liens may have different requirements as to how and when the lien is created, how and whether the lien is perfected through public notice, how and within what period of time the lien is enforced, or what priority the lien has vis-à-vis the claim of other creditors—whether they be other lienholders claiming the same crop, livestock, or farm equipment under a different agricultural lien or secured parties claiming a security interest.

Turner, Barnes, Kershen, Noble & Schumm, Agricultural Liens and the U.C.C.: A Report on Present Status and Proposals for Change, 44 Okla.L.Rev. 9, 12 (1991).

(2) The Solution. Revised Article 9 resolves many of the problems described in the preceding Note by expanding the scope of the Article to cover those statutory liens on farm products that fall within the definition of "agricultural lien." See UCC 9–102(a)(5) (defining "agricultural lien"); UCC 9–109(a)(2). The creditors eligible to hold an agricultural lien are those who in ordinary course of business furnished goods or services to the debtor, or who leased real property to the debtor, in connection with the debtor's farming operation. See UCC 9–102(a)(5)(B).

Although an agricultural lien is not a security interest, the affected farm products are "collateral," the owner of the collateral is a "debtor," and the holder of the agricultural lien is a "secured party." See UCC 9–102(a)(12), (a)(28), (a)(72). An agricultural lien is created by statute; no security agreement is required. An agricultural lien is perfected by filing a financing statement in the Article 9 filing office. See UCC 9–310(a); UCC 9–501(a). An unperfected agricultural lien is subordinate to the rights of a person who becomes a lien creditor before the agricultural lien is perfected. See UCC 9–317(a)(2). Priority between competing, perfected agricultural liens or between a perfected agricultural lien and a competing, perfected security interest is determined by the first-to-file-or-perfect rule of UCC 9–322(a). However, a perfected agricultural lien has priority over a competing security interest or agricultural lien if the statute creating the agricultural lien so provides. See UCC 9–322(g). The enforcement provisions of Article 9 generally apply to enforcement of agricultural liens. See UCC 9–601(a).

In short, Article 9 now affords a clear, easy, and uniform way for a holder of any one of the many, diverse agricultural liens to obtain priority over the debtor's judicial lien creditors and bankruptcy trustee, to ascertain the agricultural lien's priority as against conflicting security interests and agricultural liens in the same collateral, and to enforce the agricultural lien. At the same time, by subjecting agricultural liens to Article 9's filing requirements, Revised Article 9 enables potential secured lenders to ascertain with ease and at low cost, by searching the Article 9 filing records, whether farm products previously have been encumbered with an agricultural lien. This statutory approach proved so popular that some people questioned why it should be limited to agricultural liens on farm products. They urged the Drafting Committee to extend the perfection and priority provisions of Article 9 to cover all nonpossessory statutory liens on all kinds of collateral. The potential advantages of such an expansion of Article 9's scope are evident. Why do you suppose the Drafting Committee declined to proceed along these lines?

(3) Production–Money Priority. Suppliers often provide new value (e.g., seed or fertilizer) that is used in the production of crops. Some have argued that any security interest or agricultural lien on the crops in favor of a supplier should be afforded a special, PMSI-like priority over a competing security interest in the crops. As with both PMSI's and "possessory liens" under UCC 9–333, a claimant who files second would achieve priority nevertheless, on the theory that without the latecomer's new value, there would be no collateral as such.

Former 9–312(2) was intended to afford special priority to those who provide secured credit that enables a debtor to produce crops. However, it generally has been regarded as unworkable. Despite years of work, the Drafting Committee was unable to forge a consensus among themselves or among the interested groups on whether the section should be revised or removed from Article 9 entirely. Ultimately the Drafting Committee decided to present "model provisions" for a production-money security interest ("PrMSI") priority. These provisions appear in Appendix II to Revised Article 9. Only a few states have chosen to enact them. A quick look reveals that they track very closely the provisions governing purchase-money security interests in inventory. Observe also that the PrMSI provisions apply only to security interests; they do not afford a special priority to agricultural liens. See UCC 9–324A. If a secured party holds both an agricultural lien and an Article 9 production-money security interest in the same collateral, the priority rules applicable to agricultural liens govern. See UCC 9–324A(e). If the priority rules applicable to PrMSI's would be more favorable, the secured party can waive its agricultural lien. See UCC 9–324A, Comment 4.

(D) RIGHTS OF SETOFF

Problem 8.4.5. In the Prototype receivables financing transaction in Chapter 5, Section 1(B), supra, Eastinghome Credit Corporation has a perfected security interest in the inventory and accounts of Carguys. Section 13 of the Security Agreement (Form 6.2) reflects the fact that both Eastinghome and Carguys prefer that Carguys' customers remain ignorant of the transaction unless Carguys defaults. (Do you understand why?)

Assume that the Security Agreement requires Carguys to deposit all collections from its account debtors into a segregated, proceeds-only deposit account maintained with Firstbank. (As a finance company, Eastinghome is prohibited from taking the deposits itself.) On October 15, this account had a balance of $162,309, all of which constituted Eastinghome's proceeds.

Carguys owed Firstbank $50,000 on an unsecured loan on which Carguys defaulted. On October 15, Secondbank set off against the deposit account; that is, it applied $50,000 of the deposit account balance to the unpaid loan, leaving a balance of $112,309 in the deposit account and an unpaid balance of $0 on the loan.

Carguys defaults on its obligations to Eastinghome at a time when its debt under the Revolving Credit Agreement is in excess of $2,000,000. Eastinghome demands $162,309 from Firstbank, arguing that Firstbank misappropriated its collateral—the deposit account. What result? See UCC 9–109(d)(10); UCC 9–340; UCC 9–341; Notes (1) & (2) on the Conflict Between Security Interests and Setoff Rights, infra. What could the losing party have done to avoid the loss?

Problem 8.4.6. Drekko borrowed $50,000 from Banco Coolio and agreed to secure the loan with a $50,000 negotiable certificate of deposit issued by Issuer "to the order of Drekko." See UCC 3–104(j) (definition of "certificate of deposit"). Drekko indorsed the certificate in blank and delivered it to Banco Coolio.

Drekko defaulted on its obligations to Banco Coolio. When Banco Coolio makes demand upon Issuer, see UCC 9–607(a)(1), Issuer refuses to pay, asserting that its obligation under the certificate has been set off against an unpaid debt owed by Drekko.

(a) Does Issuer prevail against Banco Coolio? See UCC 9–109(d)(10); UCC 9–201; UCC 3–102; UCC 3–412; UCC 3–301; UCC 3–302; UCC 3–305; Note (3) on the Conflict Between Security Interests and Setoff Rights, infra; Problem 1.4.4, p. 49, supra; Note (2), p. 52, supra.

(b) Would the result in part (a) change if Banco Coolio took delivery of the certificate without obtaining Drekko's indorsement? See UCC 1–201(b)(21) [F1–201(20)]; UCC 3–412; UCC 3–301; UCC 3–203; UCC 3–305.

(c) Would the result in part (a) change if Banco Coolio took a security interest in the certificate without obtaining delivery? See UCC 9–312(a), (e); UCC 3–412; UCC 3–301; UCC 9–607(a), (e).

(d) Would the result in part (a) or (b) change if Issuer refused to pay because Drekko had purchased the certificate with a check that "bounced"? See UCC 3–305 & Comment 3.

(e) Would the result in part (a) change if the certificate ran "to Drekko"? See UCC 3–104 & Comment 2; Restatement (Second) of Contracts § 336(1) ("the assignee acquires a right against the obligor only to the extent that the obligor is under a duty to the assignor; and if the right of the assignor would be . . . unenforceable against [the assignor] if no assignment had been made, the right of the assignee is subject to the infirmity").

NOTES ON THE CONFLICT BETWEEN SECURITY INTERESTS AND SETOFF RIGHTS

(1) One Setting in Which the Conflict Arises. When each of two persons owes the other a money debt, each normally has the right to offset (subtract) the amount of one debt from the other and pay (or recover) only the difference. Although this right of setoff may arise in a variety of contexts, setoffs frequently are exercised by banks and other depositary institutions against funds on deposit. When these funds are encumbered by a security interest, a conflict arises between the bank and the secured party.

Problem 8.4.5, supra, presents a common fact pattern: The debtor disposes of collateral and deposits the proceeds in a deposit account maintained with the bank. The debtor defaults on an obligation to the bank, which attempts to satisfy its claim by setting off against the account. The secured party argues that the bank may not set off against an account in which the secured party claims a security interest.

Under what circumstances, if any, is the bank precluded from effectively setting off against a deposit account because the secured party holds a security interest in the account? The answer under Former Article 9 (or, indeed, whether Former Article 9 or non-UCC law provided the answer) was less than clear. Courts addressing conflict under Former Article 9 have applied a variety of common-law and statutory approaches to a variety of facts; however, the outcome generally has been the same: The courts have favored secured parties at the expense of banks seeking to exercise setoff rights.

Revised Article 9 provides to the contrary. Although the revised Article generally is inapplicable to a right of setoff, UCC 9–340 applies with respect to the effectiveness of a right of setoff against a deposit account. See UCC 9–109(d)(10). Under UCC 9–340 a bank may exercise its right of setoff against a secured party who holds a security interest in the deposit account. See UCC 9–340(a). However, if the secured party has control under UCC 9–104(a)(3) (i.e., if the secured party is the bank's customer with respect to the deposit account), then any setoff against a debt owed to the bank by the debtor (as opposed to a debt owed to the bank by the secured party) is ineffective against the secured party. See UCC 9–340(c).

What accounts for this dramatic rejection of the decided cases? A bank may hold both a security interest in, and a right of setoff against, the same deposit account. See UCC 9–340(b). The rules governing setoff yield the same results as would obtain if the bank with which a deposit account is maintained asserted a security interest in the deposit account. Specifically, a security interest held by the bank with which the deposit account is maintained has priority over a conflicting security interest. See UCC 9–327(3). However, a secured party who has control under UCC 9–104(a)(3) has priority even against the bank with which the deposit account is maintained. See UCC 9–327(4). This parallelism is not coincidental. What consequences would follow from a legal regime in which, say, a bank's security interest was senior to a competing security interest but its setoff right was junior (or vice versa)? (Consider, in this regard, the fact that enforcement of the security interest is accomplished in the same way as exercise of the setoff right, by applying the balance of the deposit account to the obligation secured by the deposit account. See UCC 9–607(a)(4).) Of course, the mere acknowledgment that the rules should be parallel does not dictate the substance of the rule. The decision to conform the setoff rules in UCC 9–340 to the priority rules in UCC 9–327 is sensible only if one is persuaded that the priority rules are appropriate. Are they? See Note (3), p. 440, supra.

If one were to undertake a resolution of the conflict between a security interest and a right of setoff from first principles, which rule should one adopt? One might construct a simple argument that favors the secured party: Every debtor has a bank account; it is a necessity of doing business. A bank into which proceeds are deposited (or that subsequently takes a security interest in a deposit account) should enjoy no greater rights than any other third party who deals with collateral. On the other hand, one might argue for the bank: The secured party should enjoy no greater rights than any other third party claiming an interest in another person's bank account. Any secured party concerned about the risk of setoff should take appropriate steps to protect the proceeds of its collateral by monitoring the debtor's behavior.

Alternatively, one might rely on the basic conveyancing principle (*nemo dat*), discussed in Chapter 1, Section 3, to resolve the conflict. The rights in collateral to which a security interest attaches generally extend no further than the debtor's rights. See Note (1), p. 137, supra. It follows that a secured party who claims a receivable as collateral generally does not acquire rights against an account debtor that are better than the those of the debtor. The deposit account is nothing more than the debtor's unsecured claim against the bank. Since there is no question that the bank is entitled to set off against the deposit account as between the bank and the debtor, on what conceptual basis can the secured party acquire its interest free of the bank's right of setoff? There is no "property" to which the secured party can lay claim. The issue is simply whether the bank must pay the secured party, the debtor's assignee, even though the bank is not obliged to pay the debtor. Are you persuaded by the foregoing analysis?

Yet another approach would draw on the general principle that, absent wrongdoing, those who are paid from a deposit account containing encumbered funds are entitled to keep the payment. See UCC 9–332. We considered this good-faith-purchase principle in Chapter 5, Section 4, supra. Recall that, in the *GECC* case, UPB "swept" the funds from Machinery's deposit account to pay down the balance owing on UPB's line of credit. The court observed that "UPB sufficiently established that the sweeps were payments" and held that the recipient, UPB, could keep the payment free of any security interest in the funds. If the "sweep" were considered a setoff, rather than a payment or transfer, would UPB have been protected under UCC 9–340(a) (assuming it was in effect)?

(2) The Bank's Right of Recoupment. UCC 9–340 addresses the bank's right of recoupment as well as its right of setoff. The two rights are quite similar; the exercise of each involves the offset of mutual claims. The principal difference is that recoupment concerns claims that arise from the same transaction, whereas setoff concerns claims that arise from different transactions. We have seen an example of recoupment in Chapter 1, Section 4, supra: If goods are delivered to and accepted by the buyer but do not conform to the contract of sale, the buyer has the right to deduct from its obligation for the price (UCC 2–709) its damages for breach of warranty (UCC 2–714). See UCC 2–717. With respect to a deposit account, the bank's claim in recoupment is unlikely to be substantial. It consists primarily of the right to payment for fees related to the deposit account.

(3) The Conflict in Another Setting. Problem 8.4.6, supra, poses the conflict between a security interest and a setoff right in another setting: The secured party has a security interest in a certificate of deposit; the issuer of the certificate of deposit seeks to set off against its obligation under the certificate.

The general exclusion of setoff rights from Article 9 would appear to leave the resolution of the priority contest to other law. See UCC 9–109(d)(10). If the certificate is negotiable, then UCC Article 3 would seem to govern the rights of the parties. See UCC 3–102(a). Thus, resolution of the conflict would turn on whether the issuer enjoyed the right to assert against the secured party the particular defense or claim in recoupment. This, in turn, might depend on whether the secured party had the rights of a holder in due course. See UCC 3–305(a), (b).

If, however, the certificate is not negotiable and thus outside the scope of Article 3, what law applies? Should a court apply UCC 3–305 by analogy? Should it apply UCC 9–404 in appropriate cases?[1] Should it look to the common law of contracts, which is similar to UCC 9–404? Or, should the court follow the approach taken by some courts under Former Article 9: read the exclusion in UCC 9–109(d)(10) narrowly (as if it means only that a right of setoff is not an Article 9 security interest), and automatically award priority to the secured party under UCC 9–201(a)?[2]

Interestingly, whereas the reported cases have tended to hold for the secured party when the dispute arises over proceeds in a deposit account, they have tended to award priority to the setting-off issuer in cases concerning a certificate of deposit. One might expect the same divergence were the courts to resolve the conflicts by applying the *nemo dat* principle.

---

1.   UCC 9–404(a) applies only when there is an "account debtor," i.e., a person obligated on an account, chattel paper, or a general intangible. See UCC 9–102(a)(3) (defining "account debtor"). A majority of cases have held that non-negotiable certificates of deposit—even those stamped "nontransferrable"—are Article 9 "instruments." See, e.g., McFarland v. Brier, 850 A.2d 965 (R.I.2004).

2.   The view that the exclusion in Former 9–104(i) means only that a right of setoff is not an Article 9 security interest and that, therefore, only the attachment and perfection provisions of Article 9 are irrelevant to setoffs has been attributed to Grant Gilmore, the principal drafter of Former Article 9. According to Professor Gilmore:

> This exclusion [of a right of setoff] is an apt example of the absurdities which result when draftsmen attempt to appease critics by putting into a statute something that is not in any sense wicked but is hopelessly irrelevant. Of course a right of set-off is not a security interest and has never been confused with one: the statute might as appropriately exclude fan dancing.

1 Gilmore, Security § 10.7, at 315-16.

(E) FEDERAL TAX LIENS

INTRODUCTORY NOTE

A debtor who defaults on obligations to the secured party is likely also to be indebted to others. We already have considered the competing claims of a variety of private creditors holding consensual, judicial, common-law, and statutory liens. We turn now to a special creditor—the United States government.

Although the government may become a creditor under a variety of circumstances, its most prominent role is that of tax collector: "[I]n this world nothing is certain but death and taxes."[3] Debtors in financial difficulty may be tempted to "borrow" from the government by wrongfully manipulating the tax system. Examples of this misconduct include understating tax liability and failing to remit sums withheld from workers for income and social security taxes. The accumulated liability to the government may be substantial; indeed, it may exceed the debtor's total assets.

In establishing the rights of the United States as a creditor for unpaid taxes, Congress has given the government a particularly strong set of entitlements. These are set forth in Chapter 64 (Collection) of the Internal Revenue Code (IRC). Of particular importance to secured parties is subchapter C, concerning the government's lien for taxes. 26 U.S.C. §§ 6321–27.[4]

The federal tax lien is pervasive. IRC § 6321, which creates the lien, provides as follows:

> If any person liable to pay any tax neglects or refuses to pay the same after demand, the amount (including any interest, additional amount, addition to tax, or assessable penalty, together with any costs that may accrue in addition thereto) shall be a lien in favor of the United States *upon all property and rights to property, whether real or personal,* belonging to such person.

---

3.   "Our constitution is in actual operation; everything appears to promise that it will last; but in this world nothing is certain but death and taxes." From Benjamin Franklin's letter to M. Leroy (1789), quoted in Bartlett, Familiar Quotations 348 (15th & 125th anniv. ed. 1980).

4.   The priority provisions of the Federal Tax Lien Act apply to liens for unpaid liabilities to the Pension Benefit Guaranty Corporation. See 29 U.S.C. § 1368(c)(1).

Generally, in the absence of a specific federal statute, the UCC as enacted by the appropriate jurisdiction applies to the government's rights as an extender of consensual credit. See Chapter 5, Section 4, supra. One federal statute of particular importance purports to grant priority in payment to *all* claims (whether secured or unsecured) of the federal government when, inter alia, a debtor is insolvent. 31 U.S.C. § 3713(a) (sometimes known as R.S. 3466). However, this statute does not apply when the taxpayer is a debtor under the Bankruptcy Code. And where 31 U.S.C. § 3713(a) conflicts with the Federal Tax Lien Act, the latter governs. See United States v. Estate of Romani, 523 U.S. 517, 118 S.Ct. 1478, 140 L.Ed.2d 710 (1998).

This lien arises "at the time the assessment is made." IRC § 6322. The assessment is an administrative act—a letter from the Internal Revenue Service to the taxpayer. Upon the occurrence of this private event, the government obtains a secret lien on *all* the taxpayer's property.

As you no doubt realize, such a secret lien would pose a severe threat to third persons who claimed an interest in the property subject to the tax lien, including secured lenders. Since 1928, however, a federal statute has protected many third persons against against a tax lien as to which the government had not filed a notice in a designated public office. The IRC currently provides that a federal tax lien imposed by IRC § 6321 is not "valid as against any purchaser, holder of a security interest, mechanic's lienor, or judgment lien creditor" until notice of the lien has been filed pursuant to section 6323(f). IRC § 6323(a).

Problem 8.4.7. Lender agreed to establish a line of credit in favor of Borcorp Brothers Manufacturing, a Delaware corporation engaged in the manufacture of automobile parts. Borcorp agreed to secure the line of credit with its existing and after-acquired equipment, inventory, and accounts.

Borcorp's manufacturing plants and warehouses are in Michigan, and its corporate offices are in California. After conducing a search of the UCC records in the appropriate state (see UCC 9–301(1); UCC 9–307) Lender filed a proper financing statement with Borcorp's permission on June 1, 2006. On June 10 Borcorp signed a loan and security agreement and Lender advanced $50,000 to Borcorp. (The loan agreement provides that all advances are discretionary on Lender's part.)

(a) On July 1—two months after assessing Borcorp for $20,000 in unpaid taxes—the IRS files a notice of tax lien. Who has priority in a $60,000 item of equipment that Borcorp acquired the previous January? See IRC § 6323(a); IRC § 6323(h)(1). Does your answer change if the issue is litigated in December? See IRC § 6323(a) (tax "lien . . . shall not be valid as against any . . . holder of a security interest . . . *until* notice thereof . . . has been filed.")

(b) What result in part (a) if Lender had failed to file a financing statement?

(c) What result in part (a) if the tax-lien filing occurred on May 29? What, if anything, could the junior party have done to achieve priority? See IRC § 6323(f); In re: Spearing Tool and Manufacturing Co., Inc., infra; Notes on Federal Tax-Lien filings, infra. Would the fact that, prior to 2001, Borcorp's corporate offices were located in Illinois affect your answer? See IRC § 6323(g).

(d) What result in part (a) if the tax-lien filing occurred on June 8? What, if anything, could the junior party have done to achieve priority?

In re: Spearing Tool and Manufacturing Co., Inc.

United States Court of Appeals, Sixth Circuit, 2005.
412 F.3d 653.

■ COOK, Circuit Judge.

In this case arising out of bankruptcy proceedings, the government appeals the district court's reversal of the bankruptcy court's grant of summary judgment for the government. For the following reasons, we reverse the district court, and affirm the bankruptcy court.

I. Background and Procedural History

In April 1998, Spearing Tool and Manufacturing Co. and appellee Crestmark entered into a lending agreement, which granted Crestmark a security interest in all of Spearing's assets. The bank perfected its security interest by filing a financing statement under the Uniform Commercial Code, identifying Spearing as "Spearing Tool and Manufacturing Co.," its precise name registered with the Michigan Secretary of State.

In April 2001, Spearing entered into a secured financing arrangement with Crestmark, under which Crestmark agreed to purchase accounts receivable from Spearing, and Spearing granted Crestmark a security interest in all its assets. Crestmark perfected its security interest by filing a UCC financing statement, again using Spearing's precise name registered with the Michigan Secretary of State.

Meanwhile, Spearing fell behind in its federal employment-tax payments. On October 15, 2001, the IRS filed two notices of federal tax lien against Spearing with the Michigan Secretary of State. Each lien identified Spearing as "SPEARING TOOL & MFG. COMPANY INC.," which varied from Spearing's precise Michigan-registered name, because it used an ampersand in place of "and," abbreviated "Manufacturing" as "Mfg.," and spelled out "Company" rather than use the abbreviation "Co." But the name on the IRS lien notices was the precise name Spearing gave on its quarterly federal tax return for the third quarter of 2001, as well as its return for fourth-quarter 1994, the first quarter for which it was delinquent. For most of the relevant tax periods, however, Spearing filed returns as "Spearing Tool & Manufacturing"—neither its precise Michigan-registered name, nor the name on the IRS tax liens.

Crestmark periodically submitted lien search requests to the Michigan Secretary of State, using Spearing's exact registered name. Because Michigan has limited electronic-search technology, searches disclose only liens matching the precise name searched—not liens such as the IRS's, filed under slightly different or abbreviated names.[2] Crestmark's February 2002 search results came back from the Secretary of State's office with a handwritten note stating: "You may wish to search using Spearing Tool & Mfg. Company Inc." But Crestmark did not search for that name at the time, and its exact-registered-name searches thus did not reveal the IRS

---

2.   The search engine ignores various "noise words" and their abbreviations, including "Incorporated" and "Company," but not "Manufacturing" or "and."

liens. So Crestmark, unaware of the tax liens, advanced more funds to Spearing between October 2001 and April 2002.

On April 16, 2002, Spearing filed a Chapter-11 bankruptcy petition. Only afterward did Crestmark finally search for "Spearing Tool & Mfg. Company Inc." and discover the tax-lien notices. Crestmark then filed the complaint in this case to determine lien priority. The bankruptcy court determined the government had priority; the district court reversed. The questions now before us are whether state or federal law determines the sufficiency of the IRS's tax-lien notices, and whether the IRS notices sufficed to give the IRS liens priority.

II. Federal law controls whether the IRS's lien notice sufficed.

Crestmark argues Michigan law should control the form and content of the IRS's tax lien with respect to taxpayer identification. The district court, though it decided in favor of Crestmark on other grounds, rightly disagreed.

When the IRS files a lien against a taxpayer's property, it must do so "in one office within the State . . . as designated by the laws of such State, in which the property subject to the lien is situated." 26 U.S.C. § 6323(f)(1)(A). The Internal Revenue Code provides that the form and content "shall be prescribed by the [U.S. Treasury] Secretary" and "be valid *notwithstanding any other provision of law regarding the form or content of a notice of lien.*" 26 U.S.C. § 6323(f)(3) (emphasis added). Regulations provide that the IRS must file tax-lien notices using IRS Form 668, which must "identify the taxpayer, the tax liability giving rise to the lien, and the date the assessment arose." 26 C.F.R. § 301.6323(f)-1(d)(2). Form-668 notice "is valid notwithstanding any other provision of law regarding the form or content of a notice of lien. For example, omission from the notice of lien of a description of the property subject to the lien does not affect the validity thereof even though State law may require that the notice contain a description of property subject to the lien." § 301.6323(f)-1(d)(1).

The plain text of the statute and regulations indicates Form-668 notice suffices, regardless of state law. We therefore need only consider how much specificity federal law requires for taxpayer identification on tax liens.

III. The notice here sufficed.

An IRS tax lien need not perfectly identify the taxpayer. See, e.g., Hudgins v. IRS (In re Hudgins), 967 F.2d 973, 976 (4th Cir. 1992); Tony Thornton Auction Serv., Inc. v. United States, 791 F.2d 635, 639 (8th Cir. 1986); Reid v. IRS (In re Reid), 182 B.R. 443, 446 (Bankr. E.D. Va. 1995). The question before us is whether the IRS's identification of Spearing was sufficient. We conclude it was.

The critical issue in determining whether an abbreviated or erroneous name sufficiently identifies a taxpayer is whether a "reasonable and diligent search would have revealed the existence of the notices of the federal tax liens under these names." *Tony Thornton,* 791 F.2d at 639. In *Tony Thornton,* for example, liens identifying the taxpayer as "Davis's Restaurant" and "Daviss (sic) Restaurant" sufficed to identify a business correctly known as "Davis Family Restaurant." In *Hudgins*, the IRS lien identified the taxpayer as "Hudgins Masonry, Inc." instead of by the taxpayer's personal name, Michael Steven Hudgins. This notice nonetheless sufficed, given that both names would be listed on the same page of the state's lien index.

Crestmark argues, and we agree, that those cases mean little here because in each, creditors could search a physical index and were likely to notice similar entries listed next to or near one another—an option which no longer exists under Michigan's electronic-search system. So the question for this case becomes whether Crestmark conducted a reasonable and diligent electronic search. It did not.

Crestmark should have searched here for "Spearing Tool & Mfg." as well as "Spearing Tool and Manufacturing." "Mfg." and the ampersand are, of course, most common abbreviations—so common that, for example, we use them as a rule in our case citations. Crestmark had notice that Spearing sometimes used these abbreviations, and the Michigan Secretary of State's office *recommended* a search using the abbreviations. Combined, these factors indicate that a reasonable, diligent search by Crestmark of the Michigan lien filings for this business would have disclosed Spearing's IRS tax liens.

Crestmark argues for the unreasonableness of requiring multiple searches by offering the extreme example of a name it claims could be abbreviated 288 different ways ("ABCD Christian Brothers Construction and Development Company of Michigan, Inc."). Here, however, only two relevant words could be, and commonly are, abbreviated: "Manufacturing" and "and"—and the Secretary of State specifically recommended searching for those abbreviations. We express no opinion about whether creditors have a general obligation to search name variations. Our holding is limited to these facts.

Finally, we note that policy considerations also support the IRS's position. A requirement that tax liens identify a taxpayer with absolute precision would be unduly burdensome to the government's tax-collection efforts. Indeed, such a requirement might burden the government at least as much as Crestmark claims it would be burdened by having to perform multiple lien searches. "The overriding purpose of the tax lien statute obviously is to ensure prompt revenue collection." United States v. Kimbell Foods, Inc., 440 U.S. 715, 734-35, 99 S.Ct. 1448, 59 L.Ed.2d 711 (1979). "[T]o attribute to Congress a purpose so to weaken the tax liens it has created would require very clear language," which we lack here. *Union Central,* 368 U.S. at 294, 82 S.Ct. 349. Further, to subject the federal government to different identification requirements—varying with each state's electronic-search technology—"would run counter to the principle of uniformity which has long been the accepted practice in the field of federal taxation."

Crestmark urges us to require IRS liens to meet the same precise-identification requirement other lien notices now must meet under

Uniform Commercial Code Article 9. *See* Mich. Comp. Laws § 440.9503(1) ("A financing statement sufficiently provides the name of [a] debtor [that is] a registered organization, only if the financing statement provides the name of the debtor indicated on the public record of the debtor's jurisdiction of organization which shows the debtor to have been organized."). We decline to do so. The UCC applies to transactions "that create[ ] a security interest in personal property or fixtures *by contract*." Mich. Comp. Laws § 440.9109(1)(a) (emphasis added). Thus, the IRS would be exempt from UCC requirements even without the strong federal policy favoring unfettered tax collection.

More importantly, the Supreme Court has noted that the United States, as an involuntary creditor of delinquent taxpayers, is entitled to special priority over voluntary creditors. *See, e.g., Kimbell Foods,* 440 U.S. at 734-35, 737-38, 99 S.Ct. 1448. Thus, while we understand that a requirement that the IRS comply with UCC Article 9 would spare banks considerable inconvenience, we conclude from Supreme-Court precedent that the federal government's interest in prompt, effective tax collection trumps the banks' convenience in loan collection.

IV. Conclusion

We reverse the district court and affirm the bankruptcy court's grant of summary judgment for the government.

NOTES ON FEDERAL TAX–LIEN FILINGS

(1) Where Is Notice of a Federal Tax Lien Filed? Congress could have provided that, once a federal tax lien arises, the lien enjoys priority even over pre-existing, perfected security interests. However, Congress chose to condition the priority of a tax lien on the filing of a public notice. See IRC § 6323(a). A filed notice is helpful only if secured parties and other claimants are able to find it. IRC § 6323(f)(1) provides that the notice should be filed "in one office within the State (or the county, or other political subdivision) . . . in which the property subject to the lien is situated." IRC § 6323(f)(2) explains where property is situated for purposes of tax lien filngs. Both tangible and intangible personal property are situated "at the residence of the taxpayer at the time the notice of lien is filed." IRC § 6323(f)(2)(b). Is a corporation's "residence" for federal tax lien purposes the same as its "location" for Article 9 choice-of-law purposes? Compare IRC § 6323(f)(2)(b) with UCC 9–307.

Having specified the state in which a notice of tax lien should be filed, Congress left it to each state to designate the filing office within that state. States have taken a variety of approaches to this task. Many states have adopted the Uniform Federal Lien Registration Act. Section 2 of the Act provides that notices of liens against real property are to be filed locally, where the property is located. Notices of liens against personal property are to be filed in the office of the Secretary of State, if the taxpayer is a corporation or partnership who principal executive office is in the state, and in the local recording office where the debtor resides, if the taxpayer is an individual. Even where tax lien notices are to be filed with the Secretary of State, in some states they are indexed separately (and searched separately) from the UCC filings.

(2) **Evaluating the *Spearing Tool* Opinion.** Needless to say, some Article 9 mavens find part III of the *Spearing Tool* opinion to be deeply flawed. Others think the case is correctly decided; they argue that any concern for secured lenders could (and should) be addressed by the adoption of more flexible standard search logic. What do you think? Among the questions you might consider are the following:

Should the court have adopted the "reasonable and diligent search" test? Even if so, did Crestmark conduct a reasonable, diligent search, given what UCC 9–506 requires when it comes to the debtor's name?

Would application of the rule of sufficiency in Michigan's UCC 9–506 be unduly burdensome to the IRS? How difficult would it have been for the IRS to have found the taxpayer's correct name? (One way to answer this question is to try to find the correct name yourself.) Is finding the correct name more difficult for the IRS than for a potential lender? Would application of each state's rule of sufficiency "subject the federal government to different identification requirements—varying with each state's electronic-search technology"?

Did the court correctly discern the underlying purpose of the Federal Tax Lien Act and, in particular, of IRC § 6323? Does the Act support the proposition that "the federal government's interest in prompt, effective tax collection trumps the banks' convenience in loan collection"?

How big a risk does the opinion really pose to secured parties? Would the tax-lien filing have been sufficient had the Michigan Secretary of State not suggested that Crestmark conduct additional searches? (The Michigan filing office is not unique in this regard.) If "Mfg." and "&" were not "most common abbreviations"? Although the court asserts that its "holding is limited to these facts," it authorized the opinion for publication. Which, if any, aspects of the opinion are of precedential value?

(3) **Life After *Spearing Tool*.** How should a cautious secured party respond to the opinion in *Spearing Tool*, short of searching for tax lien filings under every imaginable variation of the debtor's name? One possibility is to utilize the services of private firms that maintain "shadow" records of tax-lien filings. These records often can be searched with a broader search logic than the filing office's standard search logic. (Some filing offices also offer searches using a broader, nonstandard search logic.) Depending on the size of the transaction, before extending credit a secured party may wish to conduct an audit of the debtor's finances to determine whether the debtor has outstanding tax liability. A less costly approach is to file IRS Form 8821, in which the debtor (taxpayer) may authorize the secured party to inspect and receive both present and future confidential tax information.

_____

Problem 8.4.8. Cuspid, a dentist, owes $25,000 in back taxes to the IRS. On May 1 the IRS filed a proper notice of tax lien. On October 15 Cuspid took delivery of a new X–Ray machine from Manufacturer, who retained a security interest in the machine. Manufacturer had filed a proper financing statement on October 10.

(a) Who has priority? Was the security interest "in existence" before the tax-lien filing? See IRC § 6323(a); IRC § 6323(h)(1). The Treasury Regulations are silent concerning the priority of purchase-money security interests. Should a court be moved by the following passage from the legislative history:

> Although the so-called purchase money mortgages are not specifically referred to under present law, it has generally been held that these interests are protected whenever they arise. This is based upon the concept that the taxpayer has acquired property or a right to property only to the extent that the value of the whole property or right exceeds the amount of the purchase money mortgage. This concept is not affected by the bill.

S.Rep. No. 1708, 89th Cong., 2d Sess. 4 (1966), reprinted in 1966 U.S.C.C.A.N. 3722, 3725.

(b) What result in part (a) if Manufacturer filed on October 20? On November 15? See IRC § 6323(h)(1); UCC 9–323(b). Is the foregoing excerpt of any assistance to Manufacturer?

(c) What result in part (a) if, instead of obtaining financing from Manufacturer, Cuspid borrowed the funds from Bank, which paid Manufacturer the purchase price directly? Is the foregoing excerpt of any assistance to Bank?

_____

We have seen that the UCC's validation of the "floating lien" created difficult bankruptcy-avoidance issues that Congress ultimately addressed expressly in the Bankruptcy Code. See, e.g., BC 547(c)(5); Chapter 7, Section 2. Similar issues arose with respect to the relative priority of federal tax liens with respect to after-acquired property and future advances. The 1928 statute protecting security interests against unfiled tax liens appears to be a more generous concession than it turned out to be. Although the statute specifically protected a "mortgagee" from unfiled tax liens, courts construing the statute held that a recorded mortgage nevertheless was subordinate to the tax lien if the mortgage was "inchoate"—a mysterious concept of indefinite and elastic scope that, at the very least, threatened security interests based on an after-acquired property clause or a contractual provision contemplating future advances.

The threat of the federal tax lien was profoundly disturbing to the commercial community. The American Bar Association set up a Special

Committee on Federal Liens; years of drafting and persuasion led to the enactment in 1966 of important amendments to the law governing the federal tax lien. A member of and draftsman for the Committee, William T. Plumb, Jr., reported on the results of their labor.

Plumb, Legislative Revision of the Federal Tax Lien
22 Bus. Law. 271, 271–76 (1967).

> *"Now is the winter of our discontent*
> *Made glorious summer by this sun . . .."*

. . . [W]e have known 16 winters of growing discontent since the Supreme Court began the parade of decisions which expanded the priority of federal tax liens and eroded the protections on which the business and banking community rely for their security. The American Bar Association worked for many of those years to bring about an accommodation between the legitimate necessities of revenue collection and the practicalities of modern credit transactions. Now at last those efforts have borne fruit in the enactment of the first comprehensive revision of the law of federal tax liens in over half a century. Truly, the summer sun is shining!

What is this federal tax lien? It is a powerful collection tool, which serves the dual function of putting pressure on delinquent taxpayers to discharge their liabilities and of preserving the government's priority as against other claimants to their property. It attaches to "all property and rights to property, whether real or personal, belonging to" the taxpayer, including after-acquired property. It is a secret lien which arises automatically as of the moment a tax is assessed, if the taxpayer fails to make payment on demand. Originally, the secret lien prevailed even over a later bona fide purchaser; but for many years the law has protected mortgagees, pledgees, purchasers and judgment creditors against the tax lien unless notice thereof was filed in the office designated by state law. Other creditors were unprotected, not merely against pre-existing secret tax liens but also against those which arose *after* the other creditors had obtained statutory liens which were valid against everyone else.

The Supreme Court paid lip-service to the view that "the first in time is the first in right," but nullified that principle by prescribing that, in order to be "first in time," the competing lien must first have become "choate." That word (which, like "couth" and "ruly" and "sheveled," was not in most dictionaries until the Supreme Court gave it respectability) was not truly an antonym for "inchoate," but had its own peculiar meaning. A lien might be complete and perfected for every purpose of state law, and hence not "inchoate" as we understand that term. Yet it would also not be "choate," by federal tax standards, unless the identity of the lienor, the property subject to the lien, and the amount payable were fixed beyond possibility of change or dispute. Except for certain liens for state and local taxes and some possessory liens, it appeared that no statutory lien could qualify until the lienor's claim had been reduced to judgment. Furthermore, even mortgages and other contractual security, despite their specially favored position under the federal statute, were vulnerable to subsequently arising federal tax liens to the extent that the security embraced after-acquired property or involved disbursements later to be made.

Now at last the government has recognized that the "choateness" doctrine was inequitable and that it created risks and deterrents to business transactions generally which far outweighed the relatively few extra dollars of tax that might be collected in distress situations. Although the doctrine has not been wholly eliminated, the great bulk of business transactions have been freed from its effect by the adoption of express relief provisions. In the interest of equity, those provisions were, in general, made immediately and retroactively effective.

Secured Financing

Definition of "security interest"—The new law substitutes the term "holder of a security interest" for the terms "mortgagee" and "pledgee," among the classes which are protected from unfiled federal tax liens. This was a technical change, but a necessary one, because the government had argued that assignments of contracts and accounts receivable, and other forms of modern commercial financing, did not fit the conventional concept of either a mortgage or a pledge. "Security interest" is broadly defined [IRC 6323(a) & (h)(1)] as "any interest in property acquired by contract for the purpose of securing payment or performance of an obligation or indemnifying against loss or liability." Although the term is borrowed from the Commercial Code, the definition clearly embraces real estate mortgages and deeds of trust as well as all forms of commercial security.

Future advances and after-acquired property—The most serious deficiency of the former law, as it affected secured lenders, was that they could not safely make additional advances under an existing financing arrangement, or permit the substitution of security, without again searching for federal tax liens—a practical impossibility in many commercial finance situations. The new law deals with those problems by prescribing strict general rules and then carving out liberal exceptions to meet meritorious situations.

It is stated as a general rule [IRC 6323(h)(1)] that a security interest "exists" only "to the extent that, at such time [of filing a federal tax lien], the holder *has parted* with money or money's worth," and only if the property is "in existence"—no doubt meaning "owned by the taxpayer"—at such time. Therefore, unless one of the exceptions is applicable, the holder of an open-end real estate mortgage, for example, would be protected in making subsequent loans, without searching for intervening federal tax liens. And after-acquired property clauses in general mortgages and equipment trusts, even when they secure existing debts, would be ineffective, as against intervening federal tax liens, to give the lenders priority in the debtors' subsequent acquisitions.

All the exceptions to that general rule are subject to two conditions precedent. A written security agreement, which covers the subsequent advances or acquisitions, must have been entered into before notice of the federal tax lien was filed. And the security interest must be protected under local law (by recording, filing, taking possession, giving notice to the account debtor, or whatever such law requires) against a judgment lien arising, as of the time of tax lien filing, out of an unsecured obligation.

One of the exceptions is of general application. Any lender who meets the foregoing conditions is protected [IRC 6323(d)] with respect to disbursements made within *45 days after* a tax lien is filed, unless he sooner obtains *actual* (not merely constructive) notice or knowledge of such filing. This general exception, however, does not permit the addition or substitution of any property which was not owned by the borrower at the time the federal tax lien was filed. Its principal usefulness will be in making a new search for intervening federal tax liens unnecessary when there is a short delay between the perfecting of the security interest and the full disbursement of the loan. One such instance would arise in the case of an issue of mortgage bonds, which technically involves the making of optional advances by each original purchaser, at a date later than the search of the title and the execution of the mortgage.

Commercial financing—The first of several exceptions designed to meet special situations relates to loans on "commercial financing security," which is defined as inventory, accounts receivable, real estate mortgages, and "paper of a kind ordinarily arising in commercial transactions." Such security must have been acquired by the *borrower* in the ordinary course of his trade or business, and the loan must have been made in the course of the *lender's* trade or business. The lender need not be in the business of lending money, however; a business loan to a supplier or customer would qualify.

The exception for commercial financing is really a special case of the general exception last discussed, in that, . . . loans (or purchases) made as much as 45 days after the filing of a tax lien are protected, in the absence of actual notice or knowledge thereof. The added feature is that, when "commercial financing security" is involved, the protection is not confined to property owned by the borrower when the tax lien was filed, but may embrace property "acquired" by him within 45 days thereafter. This latter 45–day period is not cut short by earlier knowledge of the lien.

Some interesting questions may arise concerning when property is "acquired" for this purpose. Suppose the borrower assigns to the lender the expected proceeds of an executory contract, which is still not fully performed when the 45 days expire. Under earlier decisions, such expected proceeds were regarded as after-acquired property, and a security assignment thereof was deemed "inchoate" as against an intervening federal tax lien. However, the specific mention of "contract rights," as defined in the Commercial Code, among the items which qualify as "commercial financing security," suggests that the expected proceeds of an existing executory contract will now be considered as property already "acquired," since "contract rights" by definition are rights "not yet earned by performance." Similarly, the reference to "chattel paper," which under the Commercial Code embraces leases of tangible personal property, suggests that a security interest in the future rents from such a lease would be deemed to involve existing and not after-acquired property of the borrower.

The effect of the two 45–day rules is that a commercial lender or factor, having found no tax liens on file when he perfected his security interest, can now protect himself by making new searches for such liens at 45–day intervals, rather than before every advance. If he learns of a filed tax lien, and desires full priority, he must *immediately* cease new advances or purchases, and he must terminate the substitution of collateral 45 days from the date the tax lien was filed. . . .

A lender financing a manufacturing contract may not find it economically feasible to cut off his loans upon discovery of a tax lien, since he may be left with unfinished goods or the proceeds (if any) payable under an uncompleted contract as the only source of repayment of advances already made. The lender may then be able to work out an agreement with the tax collector, whereby the tax liens would be subordinated to the further loans necessary to complete the contract. Since completion would, in such circumstances, afford the only hope of recovery for the tax collector as well as for the lender, such a subordination agreement should be obtainable. . . .. If it is not, and the lender nevertheless feels he must continue, he may rely on a decision under prior law which viewed a manufacturing loan as analogous to a purchase money mortgage, and held that nothing but the *residue* of the contract proceeds, after satisfying the lender, ever became property "belonging to" the debtor, to which a pre-existing federal tax lien could attach. Nothing in the new law seems to detract from that principle.

———

Mr. Plumb's discussion was concerned primarily with IRC 6323(c) and (d). These sections are as important as they are difficult. Read them carefully as you work the following problems.

Problem 8.4.9. The facts are as in Problem 8.4.7(a), p. 536, supra: Lender filed a proper financing statement against Borcorp on June 1. On June 10 Borcorp signed a loan and security agreement covering all Borcorp's existing and after-acquired equipment, inventory, and accounts, and Lender made a $50,000 discretionary advance to Borcorp. The IRS filed a notice of tax lien on July 1.

Borcorp acquires raw materials and manufactures them into completed goods in the ordinary course of business.

(a) Who has priority in the raw materials acquired during the week of July 5? See IRC § 6323(c). What, if anything, could the junior party have done to achieve priority? Observe that the applicable rule of law, found in IRC § 6323(c)(1), contains several defined terms, including "security interest," "qualified property," and "commercial transactions financing agreement." The last two are defined in IRC § 6323(c)(2). The definition of "qualified property" itself contains another defined term, "commercial financing security," which is defined in IRC § 6323(c)(2)(C).

(b) What result in part (a) if Lender had seen the tax-lien filing on July 2? Does the notice provision of IRC § 6323(c)(2)(A) apply?

(c) Who has priority in the raw materials acquired during the last week of August? What, if anything, could the junior party have done to achieve priority?

(d) Would it make any difference in part (c) if Lender could show that Borcorp paid for the raw materials with a check drawn on its account at Firstbank and that the account contained only the proceeds of completed goods that were sold before August 10? Treasury Regulation § 301.6323(c)–1(d) (1976) provides as follows:

> Identifiable proceeds, which arise from the collection or disposition of qualified property by the taxpayer, are considered to be acquired at the time such qualified property is acquired if the secured party has a continuously perfected security interest in the proceeds under local law. The term "proceeds" includes whatever is received when collateral is sold, exchanged, or collected. For purposes of this paragraph, the term "identifiable proceeds" does not include money, checks and the like which have been commingled with other cash proceeds. Property acquired by the taxpayer after the 45th day following tax lien filing, by the expenditure of proceeds, is not qualified property.

(e) Who has priority in the completed goods manufactured in September? Would it make any difference if Lender could show that these goods were manufactured from raw materials acquired in July? Consider the approach of the Tenth Circuit in Donald v. Madison Industries, Inc., 483 F.2d 837, 844–45 (10th Cir. 1973):

> While we find it evident from the face of the statute that property not yet owned or "acquired" by the debtor-taxpayer by the 45th day after the tax lien filing, such as purchases of new raw materials or new equipment, would not be subject to the creditor's priority, we find it equally clear that where property owned by the debtor within the 45-day period subsequently undergoes transformations in character and form, such as the evolution of raw materials into final products and eventually into cash proceeds, as occurred herein, the creditor does not lose his security interest in the value of that property which was owned

on the 45th day. Implicit in this conclusion, however, is the fact that the creditor would have no rights to the "value-added" to the product after the 45th day by the addition of either labor or *parts subsequently acquired.*

Thus, the crucial fact which should have been determined in this case was an analysis of what portion of the finished products' value was attributable to the inclusion of property which was owned by the taxpayer before the 46th day after the tax lien filing. [The burden of proof on this issue is on the taxpayer.]

Problem 8.4.10. Under the facts of Problem 8.4.7(a), supra, Borcorp entered into a requirements contract with General Motors two months before the transaction with Lender. See UCC 2–306(1). The contract requires Borcorp to make deliveries of specified parts to GM upon 48 hours' notice; it requires GM to pay for the parts 30 days after delivery. On September 15 Borcorp receives notice of GM's need for parts; Borcorp makes a timely delivery.

Who has priority in Borcorp's right to payment from GM? Does it matter when the parts were manufactured? See IRC 6323(c); J.D. Court, Inc. v. United States, infra. See also Texas Oil & Gas Corp. v. United States, 466 F.2d 1040 (5th Cir.1972) (accounts receivable were not "acquired" by taxpayer until it performed the work). But see Pine Builders, Inc. v. United States, 413 F.Supp. 77 (E.D.Va.1976) (where taxpayer's right to receive weekly payments for services rendered arose under single contract and was subject to condition precedent, right to payment was "in existence" for purposes of IRC § 6323(h)(1) whether or not taxpayer had earned right to payment by performance). Cf. In re Ralls & Associates, Inc., 114 B.R. 744 (Bkrtcy.W.D.Okl.1990) (granting IRS priority over secured party in accounts *invoiced* more than 45 days after tax-lien filing).

Texas Oil & Gas, supra, was decided under the pre–1972 version of Article 9, which distinguished between a "contract right," which was not yet earned by performance, and an "account," which was earned. The Supreme Court has held that state law determines whether, and the extent to which, a taxpayer has property or rights to property to which a federal tax lien can attach. See Aquilino v. United States, 363 U.S. 509, 80 S.Ct. 1277, 4 L.Ed.2d 1365 (1960). Should the fact that the definition of "account" in Article 9 was amended to include a right to payment for goods sold, "whether or not [the right has been] earned by performance," change the outcome? UCC 9–102(a)(2). Does state law determine the meaning of "accounts receivable" in IRC § 6323(c)(2)(C)(ii)? Under the Treasury Regulations, a security interest in an account receivable is in existence "when, and to the extent, a right of payment is earned by performance." Treas. Reg. § 301.6323(h)–1(a)(1) (1976).

We have examined the issues posed by this Problem and the preceding one in another context, that of preference law. See Chapter 7, Section 2, supra. Is there any reason why the analysis should differ depending on the context?

Problem 8.4.11. Under the facts of Problem 8.4.7(a), supra, Lender advanced an additional $30,000 to Borcorp on July 15. (Recall that the loan agreement provides that all advances are discretionary on Lender's part.)

(a) On July 30 Borcorp's inventory is worth $60,000. Who has priority in the inventory? What, if anything, could the junior party have done to achieve priority? See IRC § 6323(d); UCC 9–323(b).

(b) What result in part (a) if Lender had seen the tax-lien filing on July 2? As to the meaning of "actual notice or knowledge," see IRC § 6323(i), which derives from Former 1–201(27) [UCC 1–202].

(c) What result in part (a) if Lender made the advance during the last week in August?

(d) Would the result in part (c) change if, in the credit agreement, Lender had undertaken to make advances upon Borcorp's demand, provided Borcorp met certain specified conditions precedent? See IRC § 6323(d); IRC § 6323(c)(1), (4).

J.D. Court, Inc. v. United States
United States Court of Appeals, Seventh Circuit, 1983.
712 F.2d 258.

■ COFFEY, CIRCUIT JUDGE.

This appeal involves a determination of the respective priority between a federal tax lien on a taxpayer's accounts receivable and a private individual's security interest in the same accounts receivable. The district court granted summary judgment in favor of the government finding that the federal tax lien was entitled to priority in all of the taxpayer's accounts receivable arising more than 45 days after the Internal Revenue Service first filed notice of its tax lien. We affirm.

I.

On June 20, 1977, the Director of the Illinois Department of Public Aid certified the taxpayer, Eventide Homes, Inc., to participate in the Title XIX Medicaid Program as a skilled and intermediate nursing care facility. Eventide Homes' initial certification for participation in the Medicaid Program was effective from March 1977 through March 1978, and was later extended through 1980. Under the certification agreement between Eventide Homes and the Illinois Department of Public Aid, Eventide Homes was under no obligation to provide medical and health care services to public aid recipients of the State of Illinois, but if they decided to provide such care, the Department agreed to reimburse Eventide Homes.

On May 10, 1979, Eventide Homes gave a $75,000 promissory note for value to Mervin Beil and executed a security agreement granting Beil a security interest in the taxpayer's "accounts receivable, and all goods, equipment, fixtures or inventory now or hereafter existing" to secure payment of the promissory note. Beil perfected his security interest . . . by filing a financing statement with the Illinois Secretary of State's office on

May 17, 1979. Beil later sold his security interest in Eventide Homes' accounts to the plaintiff J.D. Court. The assignment of that security interest was recorded with the Illinois Secretary of State on December 21, 1979.

During 1979 and 1980, the taxpayer Eventide Homes provided medical and health care services to Illinois public aid recipients entitling Eventide Homes to receive approximately $33,000 from the Illinois Department of Public Aid. Of this amount, $907.38 was for services rendered to Illinois public aid recipients by Eventide Homes prior to December 1, 1979, with the remainder representing amounts due for the services rendered after December 1, 1979.

Because of Eventide Homes' failure to pay its federal income taxes, the Internal Revenue Service assessed delinquent taxes against Eventide Homes and imposed a federal tax lien on Eventide Homes' property sometime prior to September 1979. On September 17, 1979, the Internal Revenue Service filed in the Kankakee County, Illinois Recorder's Office the first of four notices of tax liens against Eventide Homes' property, in the amount of $3,802.00. The three other notices of tax liens against Eventide Homes were filed in the Kankakee Recorder's Office on the following dates and for the following amounts: (1) October 10, 1979 for $11,084; (2) October 16, 1979 for $10,484; and (3) January 30, 1980 for $43,555.

On January 23, 1980, the Internal Revenue Service levied on the funds then due and owing to Eventide Homes from the Illinois Department of Public Aid for services rendered to public aid recipients. Approximately two weeks later, on February 15, 1980, Eventide Homes (the taxpayer) was placed in receivership. The plaintiff J.D. Court filed this action to enjoin the government from levying on the funds of the Illinois Department of Public Aid owed to Eventide Homes alleging that it is entitled to priority to all of the levied funds by virtue of its position as assignee of the security interest in Eventide Homes' "accounts receivable." The levied funds are presently being held in escrow pending resolution of this lawsuit.

In its summary judgment order, the trial court found that the plaintiff J.D. Court's security interest took priority in the taxpayer's accounts receivable which came into existence within forty-five days of the IRS's first filing of a notice of tax lien. The court further determined that the government had priority in the accounts receivable that came into existence after the forty-five days had expired from the filing of the first tax lien pursuant to 26 U.S.C. § 6323(c). The plaintiff J.D. Court appeals from the decision of the district court.

II.

Since one of the parties in this case is the United States holding a lien for unpaid taxes, federal law governs the priority of the conflicting liens on Eventide Homes' accounts receivable. Specifically, the Federal Tax Lien Act of 1966, 26 U.S.C. §§ 6321–6326 sets forth the rights of private creditors with respect to a federal tax lien.

The Tax Lien Act follows the general rule that a "lien first in time is first in right." In general, a federal tax lien arises (i.e., "attaches") "at the time the [tax] assessment is made," 26 U.S.C. § 6322, and therefore a tax lien normally takes priority over other liens arising subsequent to assessment of the delinquent tax. Section 6323(a) of the Act creates an exception to § 6322's rule that a federal tax lien generally attaches at the time the delinquent tax is assessed; under § 6323(a), when the "holder of a security interest" also claims an interest in property subject to a federal tax lien, the federal tax lien is deemed to have attached when the IRS files a notice of tax lien, rather than when the delinquent tax was first assessed. Thus, the holder of a security interest in a taxpayer's property will prevail against a government tax lien on the same property if the security interest "attaches" and is perfected before the government files its notice of tax lien, see Coogan, The Effect of the Federal Tax Lien Act of 1966 Upon Security Interests Created Under the Uniform Commercial Code, 81 Harv.L.Rev. 1369 (1968).

Therefore, to determine the priority between a federal tax lien and a security interest in the same property, it is necessary to determine (1) when the federal tax lien "attaches"; and (2) when the state law security interest "attaches." As we have noted above, § 6323(a) provides that a federal tax lien "attaches" in these circumstances when the notice of tax lien is filed in the appropriate place. However, the Act fails to expressly state when the competing state law security interest is deemed to have "attached." In answering this question, courts have long relied on the judicially created "choateness doctrine." Under the "choateness doctrine," where a security interest arising under state law (such as the plaintiff's) comes into conflict with a federal tax lien, the state law security interest "attaches" only when it becomes "choate." A state law security interest is deemed to be "choate" when all three of the following elements are satisfied: "the identity of the lienor, the property subject to the lien, and the amount of the lien are established." If this three-part "choateness" test is satisfied at the time the IRS files its notice of tax lien, *or within 45 days thereafter,* the state law security interest takes priority over the competing tax lien. 26 U.S.C. § 6323(c).

In the instant case, the district court applied the foregoing rules, including the "choateness doctrine," to determine the respective rights of the plaintiff and the United States in Eventide Homes' accounts receivable. The court found that the plaintiff's security interest in the Eventide Homes' accounts receivable did not satisfy the three-part "choateness" test until the property subject to the security interest (i.e., the accounts receivable) actually came into existence—namely, at the moment in time when the Illinois Department of Public Aid became indebted to Eventide Homes for the provision of health and medical services to Illinois public aid recipients. Applying this reasoning, the district court determined that the plaintiff's security interest was "choate" only with regard to the $907.38 of accounts receivable coming into existence within 45 days of the government's filing its first notice of tax lien and thus was only entitled to priority over the competing tax lien to that extent. The court further found that the IRS's tax liens were entitled to priority with regard to any accounts receivable coming into existence thereafter, totalling $31,965.34, since the plaintiff's security interest in those accounts receivable did not become "choate" until more than 45 days after the government filed notice of its tax liens.

In this appeal, the plaintiff first challenges the district court's reliance on the "choateness doctrine." The plaintiff states that the "choateness doctrine" was developed by the federal courts prior to enactment of the Tax Lien Act of 1966 and that the "choateness doctrine" is solely a tax lien concept not embodied in the Uniform Commercial Code. Since the Tax Lien Act was intended to "conform the lien provisions of the internal revenue laws to concepts developed in [the] Uniform Commercial Code," H.R.Rep. No. 1884, 89th Cong., 2d Sess., 35 (1966), the plaintiff concludes that the "choateness doctrine" was abrogated by the Tax Lien Act of 1966.

We disagree with the plaintiff's contention that the Tax Lien Act of 1966 abrogated the "choateness doctrine" since this court, as recently as 1979, recognized the continued viability of the "choateness doctrine" under the Tax Lien Act of 1966. In Sgro v. United States, 609 F.2d 1259 (7th Cir.1979) this court held that a government tax lien took priority over a state law security interest in a taxpayer's accounts receivable, and discussed the "choateness doctrine" as follows:

> "Notwithstanding the attachment of a tax lien upon assessment, [§ 6323(a)] provides that . . . holders of security interests, . . . will prevail if their interest attaches before the Government files appropriate notice. *Attachment occurs at the moment the interest becomes choate,* which is a question of federal law. . . .. If 'the identity of the lienor, the property subject to the lien, and the amount of the lien are established' before the Government files notice, those falling within the statutory class will prevail over a prior tax lien."

> . . .

> "[A] common way to secure a line of credit is to use one's accounts receivable as collateral. Such a loan may be secured by the outstanding balances in the debtor's accounts receivable at the time the loan is made and by further balances as they become due. . . .. Since a subsequently arising balance is not in existence at the time the loan is made, *the resulting lien remains inchoate until the underlying debt becomes due.* . . . [T]he resulting lien remains unprotected by [§ 6323(a)] until it becomes choate and *therefore would be subject to a tax lien filed in the interim."*

. . . [I]n determining priority between state law liens and federal tax liens under the Tax Lien Act of 1966, the "choateness doctrine" is recognized in this circuit as a valid legal principle, not abrogated by the Tax Lien Act.

Our conclusion that the "choateness doctrine" has continued validity under the Tax Lien Act is buttressed by the Supreme Court's opinion in United States v. Kimbell Foods, Inc., 440 U.S. 715, 99 S.Ct. 1448, 59 L.Ed.2d 711 (1979). In *Kimbell Foods,* the Court held that the "choateness doctrine" did not apply in determining priority between the government's *contractual* liens arising from federal loan programs and private liens.

Although the holding of *Kimbell Foods* does not directly affect our resolution of this case, the Court emphasized the critical distinction between a *contractual* lien arising from a government loan program and a government *tax* lien:

> "That collection of taxes is vital to the functioning, indeed existence, of government cannot be denied. . . .. Congress recognized as much over 100 years ago when it authorized creation of federal tax liens. . . .. *The importance of securing adequate revenues to discharge national obligations justifies the extraordinary priority accorded federal tax liens through the choateness and first-in-time doctrines.*"

Id. at 734, 99 S.Ct. at 1461 (emphasis added) (citations omitted).

We conclude that the "choateness doctrine" is a valid legal principle in determining the priority between the government's tax lien in Eventide Homes' accounts receivable and the plaintiff's security interest in the same accounts receivable. Having reached this conclusion, we consider only briefly the plaintiff's additional arguments. The plaintiff argues that its security interest in Eventide Homes' accounts receivable was in fact "choate" prior to September 17, 1979 when the government filed its first notice of tax lien. However, as we indicated in *Sgro*, a security interest in accounts receivable does not become "choate" until the accounts receivable actually come into existence, that is, at the time the services giving rise to the accounts receivable are performed. . . .

. . . The judgment of the district court is AFFIRMED.

SECTION 5.   IS SECURED CREDIT EFFICIENT?

INTRODUCTORY NOTE

Over the past twenty-five years or so, several legal scholars have debated whether the institution of secured credit is "efficient" (as that term is used by economists). Now that we have studied many of the effects of secured credit under current law—in particular, the priority rules and the favored treatment afforded to secured claims in bankruptcy—we can consider these effects in the context of this debate.

The question whether security interests are efficient is a positive, not a normative, inquiry. However, the literature reflects strong undercurrents of a normative debate as well. In particular, whether a legal regime that respects—indeed, fosters—secured transactions should be retained if it is found to be inefficient clearly is a normative question. And that question lies at (or just below) the surface in much of the commentary. (Not surprisingly, some of the participants demonstrate a normative preference for economically efficient legal rules.)

In concluding his important article on the security interest debate, Professor Paul Shupack wrote:

This Article has shown that there is a social gain from secured transactions, which must be set off against their social cost. Secured transactions have an economic function other than to act as conduits for the transfer of wealth from ignorant and involuntary creditors to shrewd debtors and creditors. Knowing whether that economic function outweighs the social harm that secured transactions can cause requires information, not only about the economy at large, but also about legal rules that have the effect of constraining secured creditors from taking full advantage of their capacity to use these normatively suspect transactions for their own benefit.

Solving the puzzle of secured transactions from the initial perspective of a perfect market does not tell us much about secured transactions. Identifying efficiency gains within the abstract model does not guarantee that those efficiency gains, though present in every secured transaction, are in reality the motivation for every secured transaction. This inability to move from the model to reality means that the explanation of how secured transactions are, and might be, efficient has little to say about the social structures built around secured transactions. Showing that secured transactions *can* be efficient justifies only that they *might* exist. The forms in which they exist depend upon a series of empirical claims, into which the model can give little insight. Solving the puzzle of secured transactions, therefore, offers surprisingly little help in answering the important public policy questions surrounding their creation and use in the real world.

Shupack, Solving the Puzzle of Secured Transactions, 41 Rutgers L. Rev. 1067, 1124 (1989).

The following excerpts from Dean Robert E. Scott's article illustrate much of the flavor and substance of the debate, in particular during the years following Professor Shupack's article.

Scott, The Truth About Secured Financing
82 Cornell L. Rev.1436, 1437, 1447–50, 1451,1453–61 (1997).

The debate over the social value of secured credit (and the appropriate priority for secured claims in bankruptcy) is entering its nineteenth year. Yet the continuing publication of succeeding generations of articles exploring the topic have yielded precious little in the way of an emerging scholarly consensus about the nature and function of secured credit. Put simply, we still do not have a theory of finance that explains why firms sometimes (but not always) issue secured debt rather than unsecured debt or equity. Moreover (and perhaps because of the lack of any plausible general theory), we lack any persuasive empirical data to predict whether, in any particular case, a later security-financed project will generate sufficient returns to offset any reduction in the value (i.e., the bankruptcy share) of prior unsecured claims.

. . .

II
WHAT WE DO (AND DO NOT) KNOW ABOUT SECURED DEBT

. . . The debate [concerning the social value of secured credit] persists with relatively small increments of progress largely because participants are asking fundamentally different questions. It is not that either side is wrong; rather it is that both sides are guilty of incomplete analyses. In truth, we cannot solve the puzzle of secured credit until we have both a coherent theory of finance that explains the welfare benefits of security and a database (derived from observation) that describes the patterns of security that actually exist in the world. Only then can we evaluate the regulatory regime of Article 9 and the Bankruptcy Code in order to make normative recommendations to policymakers. . . .

A. The Search for a Theory of Secured Finance

. . . The question at the core of the secured financing puzzle is not whether a given security-financed project is efficient for a firm to pursue. The answer to that question is quite clear: security-financed projects are efficient when the reduction in the expected bankruptcy share of prior creditors is less than the expected returns to the firm from the financed project. This question, however, is tangential to the security debate. Rather, the fundamental theoretical question requires a comparison between project financing with security and project financing without security. Thus the core question remains: why and when does the *method of financing* increase the net revenues from any positive value project the firm elects to pursue?

. . .

Thus, security solves a contracting problem for the parties by allowing them to "design verifiability" in the contract. Although the financer cannot verify that a subsequent investment is inefficient, it can observe such action. The ability to foreclose on the collateral once an inefficient investment decision is observed precludes the necessity of verifying that action to a court. In an important sense, the contract becomes self-enforcing.

. . .

2. Using Leverage to Reduce Underinvestment Conflicts

The risk alteration conflict is ubiquitous and occurs in all debt contracts. There is a final conflict that is peculiar to exclusive financing arrangements, and for which secured financing offers similar advantages over financing alternatives. The problem of underinvestment occurs when a debtor, having recouped a portion of its investment in a joint venture with a creditor, siphons off its resources to other projects from which it will reap more of the gain. The debtor will act in this manner even if further effort in the joint venture would enhance the firm's net worth. Once again, the leverage offered by a security interest in the debtor's assets gives a secured creditor the ability credibly to threaten sanctions if it discovers that the debtor is undertaking inadequate efforts to fully develop the financed project.

A wrap-around security interest (or "floating lien") offers several advantages to the creditor and debtor seeking to cement an exclusive financing relationship. The leverage of security has the effect of giving the creditor an economic hostage to ensure the debtor's faithful performance of the financed project. If the debtor defaults on any of the covenants in the financial contract, the creditor retains the power to foreclose and take operational control of the assets. The debtor agrees to this arrangement because there are significant costs to the creditor in exercising the power of foreclosure that deter frivolous or bad faith actions by the creditor. The effectiveness of the debtor's bond encourages the creditor, in turn, to provide financial management and counseling to enhance the general business prospects for the debtor. The creditor cannot provide these valuable services as cheaply unless it can structure the relationship so as to capture the returns from its efforts. Secured financing ensures that the debtor will heed the creditor's financial advice. Once again, however, the benefits of leverage are not cost-free. Debtors must submit to substantial administrative supervision that imposes significant burdens on the firms' decisionmaking processes.

Justifying secured financing as a uniquely effective means of controlling the conflicts of interest generated by risk alteration and underinvestment seems quite promising as a normative theory of finance. The theory claims that secured debt is able to reduce agency costs for firms financing positive value projects and thus returns benefits to the firm that other financing alternatives could not capture. The theory recognizes, however, that the leverage benefits of security carry offsetting costs. Thus, it does not predict that secured credit would be ubiquitous. Rather, it predicts that parties to financial contracts will choose this method of financing in those contexts where the expected benefits from leverage exceed the costs. To the extent, then, that the net returns inform value from this method of financing are greater than those obtainable from other methods of financing the project, and exceed any reduction in the bankruptcy share of unsecured creditors, secured credit is Kaldor–Hicks efficient.

3. Testing the Theory of Leverage Against the Rules of Article 9

The first test of any theory of secured financing requires that the theory be roughly congruent with the priority scheme that is institutionalized in Article 9. As Hideki Kanda and Saul Levmore have shown, we can rationalize many of the priority rules of Article 9 as attempts to balance the advantages and disadvantages of using security to ameliorate the agency costs of risk alteration. Specifically, we can understand the first-in-time priority granted to perfected secured creditors over prior-in-time unsecured creditors, and the superpriority granted to both subsequent purchase money security interests and subsequent purchasers of chattel paper over prior-in-time perfected secured creditors, as means of metering subsequent new money financing.

The first-in-time priority granted to secured claims by the terms of Article 9 can be explained as a cost-effective mechanism for preventing risk alterations that would disadvantage prior creditors.

. . .

Nevertheless, the first-in-time rule is something of a blunt instrument. Using security as a hostage may control the debtor's incentives, but it also sets in motion a parallel set of conflicts involving the creditor's incentives. Fully protected by the hostage of security, creditors are motivated to be excessively cautious in refusing to permit subsequent financing that would enhance total returns to the firm. Thus, the first-in-time rule must be tempered with a scheme of superpriorities that offer the debtor an escape hatch to guard against creditor myopia. Hence, purchase money security interests and subsequent purchasers of chattel paper are granted priority over prior-in-time secured creditors as a means of balancing the effects of using assets as hostages. As Kanda and Levmore suggest, therefore, one can explain the prominent contours of the priority system in Article 9 largely as a crude, but effective, compromise between the advantages and disadvantages of new money financing.

The Kanda and Levmore explanation leaves one salient feature of Article 9 unexplained: the institutionalization of the floating lien. Here, the underinvestment problem is a useful supplement. Some classes of debtors (the current estimate is twenty-six percent of secured claims) choose to enter into exclusive financing relationships with creditors. For certain classes of debtors, these long term relationships offer singular advantages in terms of providing financial counseling and general business guidance. For those firms that find exclusive financing optimal, the problem of underinvestment is peculiarly salient. Once the debtor and creditor enter into these kinds of joint ventures, the financing creditor is properly concerned about a further conflict: the motivation that the debtor may have to pursue other projects through which it can capture a greater share of the returns. The unique priority Article 9 grants to the floating lien general creditor in all the debtor's present and future assets appears to be a sensible method of using the same hostage device to solve the underinvestment problem that exclusive financing arrangements generate. In a world without secured credit, these arrangements might proceed only at greater cost, and some parties would not pursue otherwise beneficial exclusive financing arrangements.

For certain debtors, then, the blanket priority Article 9 gives to the floating lien secured creditor invites the creditor to become a joint venturer in the business opportunity. Thereafter, the creditor has an incentive to provide financial counseling and management advice to the debtor firm and, just as importantly, has the leverage to ensure that firm acts on the advice. These benefits accrue to all parties with claims against the firm to the extent that they enhance the returns from financed projects.

In sum, it is fair to conclude that a regime that privileges secured credit *may* enhance social welfare and that the scheme of priorities institutionalized in Article 9 is roughly congruent with plausible explanations of the comparative advantages of secured financing over other financing alternatives.

B. Theory v. Practice: Explaining Observed Patterns of Secured Debt

The central problem with this (and any other) theory of secured financing is the inconsistency between the predictions of the theory and observations of the actual patterns of secured financing that exist in the world. The leverage theory would predict that secured credit, although not ubiquitous (because it entails substantial costs), would nonetheless be observed in all segments of the credit market. This is because the agency problems upon which the theory rests are common to firms of all types, large and small, stable and volatile.

. . .

Even though secured debt is perceived as carrying the singular benefit of increasing the probability of repayment, financing parties understand it as an extremely crude device. Because providing assets as hostages imposes corresponding risks of creditor misbehavior, Mann reports that creditors and debtors are reluctant to use security except where significant reductions in nonpayment risks supplement its efficiency advantages. In other words, when the ex ante risk of nonpayment is significant, the redistributional benefits derived from leverage offer the additional advantages that justify the costs of using secured financing. Mann's analysis thus provides a coherent account for the persistent pattern of secured debt issued primarily by firms with unproven track records or firms that are financially volatile. For financially stable firms, secured debt remains unattractive presumably because the risk of nonpayment is trivial and the efficiency benefits of security are inadequate, standing alone, to justify the substantial costs.

C. Market Imperfections that Support the Redistributional Story: The Nonadjustment Phenomenon

It is dangerous, of course, to draw too many conclusions from observations by market participants. Perceptions by debtors and creditors that secured credit is cost-justified only when the redistributional benefits of leverage are substantial may not reflect the underlying economic reality. Thus, the related question recurs: if the market for credit is competitive, would not increases in the costs of extending credit experienced by unsecured creditors, whom secured debt disadvantages, be reflected in higher interest charges, and thus, in the debtor's total interest bill? Many have long recognized that nonconsensual creditors—such as warranty claimants and tort claimants—can recover only fixed-rate interest charges form debtors and would not be able to adjust to the presence of secured debt. But surely, this relatively small group of creditors cannot drive the institution of secured finance?

Lucian Bebchuk and Jesse Fried have offered the most promising explanation for why debtors do not internalize the redistributional effects of secured credit. Bebchuk and Fried explain the long term persistence of important classes of consensual creditors as "non-adjusting" creditors. They rely essentially on a transaction-costs argument to explain why prior-in-time consensual unsecured creditors (even those with large claims) and all consensual creditors with small claims would not rationally adjust to the increased risk occasioned by a particular debtor's decision to issue secured debt. If the cost of designing and enforcing adjustable rate provisions is too high, a rational creditor will assign an average value to the heightened risk of nonpayment, a value that is not sensitive to the lending patterns of the particular debtor. Any one of the classes of creditors Bebchuk and Fried identify may be insufficiently large to account for the redistributional effects of security. However, in combination, the presence of large numbers of creditors who either cannot or do not rationally choose to adjust to the increased risk of secured debt offers a strong market-based explanation for why debtors may systematically fail to internalize the redistributional costs of security.

Bebchuk and Fried emphasize the efficiency implications of nonadjustment. It may well be that nonadjusting consensual creditors who are repeat players are fully compensated for the increased risks of doing business in competition with secured debt. Nevertheless, the redistributional costs of security are independent of any fairness arguments that might be advanced in favor of involuntary or single-play participants in credit markets. The negative externalities that nonadjustment generates will skew the debtor's incentives in important respects. To the extent that debtors and secured creditors do not internalize the costs of secured credit, the debtor's investment decisions are skewed. Debtors will issue more secured debt than would be issued in a world where the contracting parties appreciated all the costs and benefits. This inefficiency leads to underutilization of other financing alternatives that might better enhance the returns from financing positive-value projects.

D. The "Discontinuity Assumption": Secured Debt as the Only Method of Financing Positive–Value Projects

Several commentators have mounted a strong defense of secured credit that posits a class of debtors with positive value financing projects that is unable to secure financing except by issuing secured debt. In other words, the claim goes, there is a discontinuity in the financing alternatives that are typically available to solvent debtors with positive-value projects. This claim was advanced some years ago by Homer Kripke and subsequently by Charles Mooney and Steve Harris. Most recently, Steven Schwarcz has argued that solvent debtors who confront a "liquidity crisis" are often unable to finance their projects or to fully realize the benefits from existing projects without new money that debtors can obtain on the market only by issuing secured debt. Schwarcz, along with Kripke and Harris and Mooney, support this "discontinuity assumption" by reference to experience and to (unsystematic) field studies.

The discontinuity assumption is the linchpin of the argument for preserving full priority for secured credit. From the assumption that for many debtors new money financing can be obtained only by offering security, it follows that the security-financed project that offers a greater return to the firm than any corresponding reduction in bankruptcy share to unsecured creditors is Kaldor–Hicks efficient. Indeed, the efficiency problem of nonadjusting creditors largely disappears. Because using security to finance these projects is efficient, it follows that the misinvestment and precaution concerns Bebchuk and Fried raise are nonexistent. A redistributional issue remains, of course, but even there one can advance the argument that most nonadjusting creditors are fully compensated in the enhanced returns from projects that creditors could not pursue but for security. Thus, given the assumption, the burden of proof on the empirical question should shift to those who wish to constrain the choices market actors would otherwise select. The normative implication follows: secured claims that facilitate positive value projects should be accorded full priority in bankruptcy.

But, of course, nothing is as easy as it seems. The discontinuity assumption is not a theoretical claim about the efficiency of secured debt. Rather, it is an empirical claim that, given a world with secured credit, and given the reasons why debtors and creditors choose to finance new money with security, whatever those reasons happen to be, some positive-value projects can be financed only with security. This is not to say that, in a world without secured credit (or a world that granted reduced priority to secured claims), unsecured debt or equity would not finance these positive-value projects. Nor does it suggest that all (or even most) of the security-financed projects currently undertaken are efficient. Indeed, it is perfectly consistent with the discontinuity assumption, and with the evidence from field studies of existing patterns of secured financing, to assert that these liquidity-crisis projects demand security primarily for its redistributional effects rather than its efficiencies. The most plausible reason why solvent, high-risk debtors can issue only secured debt is that the leverage security provides can substantially reduce the risk of nonpayment for the secured creditor. It is unlikely, after all, that new money secured financing of viable, high-risk debtors is primarily aimed at controlling risk alteration or underinvestment conflicts.

Thus, the discontinuity assumption merely begs the question. Even if true, it tells us what we already know from observation: secured credit is issued for a number of complex reasons that all center on the unique advantage of leverage to the secured creditor. To some extent, that leverage seems to be a singularly useful means of reducing conflicts of interest inherent in financial contracting relationships. These benefits are efficiency enhancing. To some degree, however, that leverage also appears to be a singularly useful means of enhancing the creditor's probability of repayment relative to other creditors. If, as seems plausible, some (or many) of these other creditors do not adjust to this reduction in bankruptcy share, there is a redistributional benefit to the creditor that the debtor does not fully internalize in assessing its total interest bill. This, then, would lead to some inefficient uses of security (as well as raise problems of distributional fairness). The question, in short, is simple: What are the relative values of these two offsetting effects? At this point we do not have a clue.

In a 1994 article, Professors Harris and Mooney raised fundamental questions about the utility and ground rules of the security interest debate. Consider the following:

The securing of debt is similar to a vast array of other voluntary transactions in which a debtor may dispose of its property. This Section compares two other transactions—the payment of debt and the sale of assets—to secured loans. As we shall see, payments and asset sales are like secured loans in that they may impose costs on unsecured creditors that exceed any attendant benefits. But, also like secured loans, these other transactions may redound to the net benefit of unsecured creditors. Many of the questions about secured transactions that the contributors to the Efficiency Literature and the adherents to Sympathetic Legal Studies have raised also might be raised with respect to payments and asset sales. Curiously, they have not been.

Consider the payment by a solvent debtor (. . . "D") of a debt owed to an unsecured creditor ("UC–1"), leaving another unsecured creditor ("UC–2") unpaid. Immediately after the payment (at T_0), holding other factors constant, UC–2's expected recovery actually will increase upon D's payment to UC–1 at T_0. This outcome merely recognizes that the incurrence of the debt to UC–1 itself exposed existing creditors (here, UC–2) to a risk of a lower distribution in the event of future insolvency; payment to UC–1 simply puts matters where they were just prior to UC–1's extension of credit. The same result would occur if, instead of paying UC–1, D secured UC–1's claim with collateral that did not decline in value or declined proportionately less than the unencumbered assets; that is, UC–2 would be better off if D secured UC–1's claim than if it did not.

Just as a debtor's receipt of new credit may work to the *advantage* of the debtor's existing creditors by reducing the risk of default, so D's loss of the use of the assets transferred to UC–1 may *disadvantage* UC–2 by increasing the risk of default. Securing, rather than paying, UC–1 would leave the assets available for D's use and would seem to be likely to increase the risk of default to a lesser extent than payment would (or perhaps not at all). Just as one needs additional information to determine whether UC–2 is better off if D pays UC–1 at T_0 rather than leave UC–1 unpaid, so one cannot determine whether UC–2 is better off if D secures UC–1's claim rather than pay it. Both determinations turn on facts that cannot be known in the abstract, including the extent to which any given transaction affects the risk of default and (in the case where D gives security) the extent to which UC–1's collateral declines in value relative to D's unencumbered assets.

Another useful means of considering how a payment to one unsecured creditor affects other unsecured creditors is to examine the consequences of D's decision to pay UC–1 *instead of* paying UC–2. By virtue of that decision, UC–1 received 100% of its claim at T_0, leaving UC–2 to receive only a fraction of its claim in liquidation at T_1. (A similar, but less pronounced, effect would result from D's decision to give security to SP for a new loan instead of paying or securing an existing creditor.) The law does, of course, respect payments by solvent debtors to their creditors even in the absence of pro rata payments to other creditors. As far as we know, no one has suggested that fraudulent transfer law should reach so far as to invalidate such payments.

Payment of an antecedent debt by an *insolvent* debtor is another matter. Any payment at T_0 clearly reduces the pool of assets available to the remaining unsecured creditors at that time and, if we hold constant the probability of default, thereby transfers wealth to the preferred creditor from the non-preferred creditors. Giving security for an antecedent debt has the same effect. At T_1 the remaining unsecured creditors will receive less than they would have received had the preferential transfer not been made. Both transactions are potentially vulnerable as preferences under Bankruptcy Code § 547, which generally does not distinguish between payments and transfers as security. But, because the grant of a security interest does not necessarily deplete the assets available for use by the debtor, a preferential transfer of security may well have a less deleterious effect on the expected recovery of other creditors than would a preferential payment.

The foregoing suggests that, from the perspective of UC–2, the consequences of D's making a payment to UC–1 are indeterminate. The expected value of UC–2's recovery might increase; it might decrease. The same would be true if D were to secure its debt to UC–1: One cannot ascertain the implications of the transaction for UC–2 *a priori*.

Now consider the consequences to existing creditors (UC–1 and UC–2) of D's selling an asset. Whether the expected return to creditors will increase or decrease depends on whether D makes more productive use of the cash received or of the asset sold. The grant of security for a new loan is quite similar to the sale of property; in both cases, D receives cash and parts with an asset. Of course, there are differences between a cash sale at T_0, on one hand, and giving security to SP for a new loan at T_0, on the other. One such difference arises from the possibility that at T_1 the unpaid and now undersecured SP may assert a deficiency claim that competes with the claims of UC–1 and UC–2 against a now insolvent D. Holding everything else constant, the secured transaction with SP reduces the expected return of the other creditors. In contrast, the cash seller to D is out of the picture at T_1 and does not hold a competing claim in an insolvency proceeding.

But, once again, the distributive effects in insolvency are only part of the story. In the cash sale D would lose the use of the asset sold, whereas in the secured loan D normally retains the use and possession of the collateral as well as the proceeds of the loan. D's retention of the use, possession, and control of collateral has value—value that would not be available if a buyer carries the collateral away. This additional value typically is reflected in the difference between the amount of the secured loan (which is the measure of the secured creditor's property interest in the collateral) and the (presumably greater) value of the collateral. Thus, unlike a seller, a debtor who grants a security interest enjoys more than the value represented by the cash it receives in the transaction. The debtor's retention of the additional value represented by the continued right to use, possess, and control the collateral may reduce the risk of default, perhaps enough to offset the reduction in the expected recovery of creditors' claims that otherwise would occur.

Cash payments, purchases, and sales, like secured loans, can result in wealth transfers from the unsecured creditors of a buyer or seller and can expose the unsecured creditors to additional risk, although these transactions do not necessarily do so. Thus, one cannot develop a plausible hypothesis for questioning the utility or equity of security interests on distributional grounds involving transfers of wealth, such as the reduction of the pool of assets remaining for unsecured creditors or the present value of remaining unsecured claims, unless one also questions, on similar grounds, other transactions such as payments, sales, and purchases. Consequently, one cannot view the creation of effective security interests with suspicion on those grounds unless one also questions the general effectiveness of these transactions.

Harris & Mooney, A Property–Based Theory of Security Interests: Taking Debtors' Choices Seriously, 80 Va. L. Rev. 2021, 2037–41 (1994).

NOTE ON THE EFFICIENCY DEBATE

In Chapter 6, Section 1, supra, we observed:

[F]actors such as disparities in bargaining power and information, profit margins of sellers of goods and providers of services on unsecured credit, the relative size and duration of credit extensions, the costs of creating secured financings, disparities among creditors in their ability to monitor the debtor's financial activities and use of collateral, and market competition all serve to explain current financing patterns, . . . which involve a mix of secured and unsecured credit.

. . . A positive explanation of why debtors sometimes give and creditors sometimes take secured credit under current law does not provide a normative justification for the advantages the current legal regime affords to secured claims.

Given what Professor Shupack calls the "transactional efficiency" of current law that facilitates the creation of effective security interests, is it difficult to understand why debtors sometimes give security in order to obtain credit and sometimes do not? Remember that the question whether there is an efficiency (or other) "normative" justification for our system of secured transactions underlies and drives the efficiency debate. That question is quite different from the question of why security is in fact given under the current regime. (Some of the participants in the debate have failed, at times, to keep this distinction in mind.) Professor Shupack systematically relaxed the economists' "perfect market" assumptions until he discovered examples of secured transactions that were "Kaldor–Hicks efficient"—i.e., the gains of the winners exceed in the aggregate the losses of the losers. Do examples of efficient secured lending under current rules necessarily mean that those rules should be retained intact?

Dean Scott concluded that "we do not have a clue" as to how to balance the "offsetting effects" of a legal regime (like Article 9) that facilitates secured credit. Scott, 82 Cornell L.Rev. at 1461. Assuming that he is correct, what lessons should lawmakers glean from the debate over security? In concluding his article, Dean Scott criticized the *process* employed by "private legislatures," such as The American Law Institute and the National Conference of Commissioners on Uniform State Laws (co-sponsors of the UCC). He argued that "admirably clear, bright-line rules so distinctively present in Article 9 . . . [are] strong evidence that a dominant interest group has influenced the process." Id. at 1463. In contrast, Dean Scott hails the benefits of "log-rolling" and hearings before state legislators to afford lawmakers better information, and he laments the "poor quality of information the voters in the private legislature possess." Id. at 1464. Does it seem likely to you that the members of 50 state legislatures would possess a better quality of information about secured credit than that presented to The American Law Institute and the National Conference of Commissioners on Uniform State Laws during the process of drafting and revising Article 9? As a thought experiment, consider whether a typical state legislator would be likely to grasp the analysis of secured financing presented in Dean Scott's article.

One might consider searching for any efficiency gains in moving from current law to a world that would not honor consensual security interests in personal property. Consider how that world would look. Would judicial liens be retained? Presumably *sales* and *exchanges* of property would be allowed. But would a sale for cash and a lease-back of equipment be honored (perhaps with a public notice requirement)? Would abolishing security interests put too much strain on already fuzzy lines between secured transactions and other kinds of dispositions of interests in property? Does this exercise suggest that respecting secured transactions can be seen as merely one genre of a more general principle of respect for the alienability of property? In thinking about how and where one might draw the line, consider the spectrum from a discrete sale of specifically identified receivables to a security interest in virtually all of a debtor's existing and after-acquired personal property securing all existing and future obligations to a secured party.

Do you find the indeterminacy of Shupack's, Scott's, and Harris & Mooney's conclusions unsatisfying? Assuming, as Professor Shupack concludes, that there can be no "general theory" of secured credit that consistently predicts behavior, does that mean that the participants in the debate have wasted their time (and ours)?

In an earlier article, Dean Scott recognized that "[i]t is unlikely that a single explanation can rationalize all of these various forms of security." Scott, A Relational Theory of Secured Financing, 86 Colum.L.Rev. 901, 912 (1986). However, theoretical explorations of legal institutions can accomplish much even if no general theory emerges. For example, the efficiency debate has served to identify areas in need of further empirical research and those where empirical research (even if "necessary") would be largely impossible. It has served to heighten sensitivities to the relationship between finance theory and the legal rules that regulate security interests and priorities in bankruptcy. And it has underscored the enormous variety of transactions (secured and unsecured) that are affected by Article 9.

CHAPTER 9

DEFAULT; ENFORCEMENT OF SECURITY INTERESTS

INTRODUCTORY NOTE

The preceding Chapters focused primarily on the acquisition and perfection of security interests and the priority of competing claims to collateral. For the most part, these issues become moot if the debtor pays the secured obligation.[1] Secured credit typically is extended with the expectation that the debtor *will* pay and that the secured party will not need to recover its claim from the collateral. A creditor's need to enforce its security interest typically is an indication that the credit transaction has failed.

Of course, transactions do fail and secured parties do find the need to turn their collateral into cash. This Chapter examines the rights and duties of a secured party who enforces a security interest. Section 1 deals with the scope of the secured party's right to take possession of collateral when the debtor is in default. Section 2 considers the right of a secured party to dispose of (e.g., sell) collateral and to apply the proceeds to the secured obligation. It also covers the effect of a secured party's noncompliance with its duties under Article 9. Section 3 addresses the implications of enforcement for certain third parties—secondary obligors (such as guarantors of the secured obligation), holders of competing security interests and other liens, and transferees from a secured party who disposes of collateral after default. Section 4, which deals with "redemption," examines the scope of the debtor's right to satisfy the secured obligation and recover the collateral before the secured party disposes of it. Section 5 then considers the enforcement of security interests in accounts and other rights to payment through "collections" from the account debtors or other enforcement of collateral. Finally, Section 6 deals with a secured party's acceptance of collateral in satisfaction of all or a portion of the secured obligation, sometimes called "strict foreclosure."

The term "foreclosure" is commonly used to refer to the process by which security interests are enforced against collateral, although the word appears only once in the text of Article 9. Under pre-UCC personal property security law (as well as current real property law), the term "foreclosure" embraces

---

1. Even if the debtor pays the secured obligation, questions of perfection and priority may be implicated if the debtor enters bankruptcy within the preference period. See BC 547; Chapter 7, Section 2, supra.

566

the process by which the debtor's right to "redeem" the encumbered property is "foreclosed." UCC 9–623 provides for the debtor's right to redeem collateral by paying in full the secured obligation at any time before the secured party has collected, disposed of, entered into a contract for the disposition of, or accepted collateral. Consistent with common parlance, these materials sometimes refer to "foreclosure," "foreclosure sale," and the like.

Most of the issues we have considered thus far involve three parties—the debtor, the secured party, and the holder of a competing claim to the collateral. Although the enforcement of a security interest sometimes affects the rights of third parties, more often only the debtor and secured party are involved. Questions of perfection and priority often are irrelevant; Part 6 of Article 9 (the 9–600's) takes center stage. And, as we shall see, important legislation intended to protect consumers often supplements and modifies the rules of the UCC.

As you work through the materials in this Chapter, you would do well to keep in mind what is at stake. A security interest, you will recall, is a limited "interest in . . . *property*." UCC 1–201(35) [F1-201(37)]. Unless the security interest has been perfected by possession or the debtor agrees otherwise, the secured party's right to exercise any dominion over collateral is contingent on the debtor's default. When the secured party does exercise dominion, it may do so only for the limited purpose of obtaining payment of the secured obligation. Indeed, the secured party's property interest is limited to the amount of the secured obligation (except in the cases of outright sales of accounts, chattel paper, payment intangibles, or promissory notes). These limitations on the interest that the secured party enjoys should not be overemphasized. Immediately upon the debtor's default, creditors who hold security interests can look to specific property to satisfy their claims; unsecured creditors cannot.

The debtor, too, holds a property interest, one that typically includes the right to possess, use, and otherwise exercise dominion over the collateral. The debtor also takes the risks and enjoys the benefits of changes in collateral value. Thus, enforcement implicates a delicate interplay of interests: Curtailing the secured party's dominion over the collateral can impair the security on which the transaction depends; taking the dominion over collateral away from the debtor can impair personal and economic well-being.

Perhaps for this reason, Part 6 of Article 9 departs from the UCC's general emphasis on freedom of contract. See UCC 1–302(a) [F1–102(3)] (the effect of UCC provisions generally may be varied by agreement). Part 6 contains a number of rules that cannot be waived or varied, even by sophisticated debtors who are represented by counsel. See UCC 9–602. As you study these rules, you should consider whether the departures from freedom-of-contract principles are justified.

This Chapter focuses primarily on the rights and remedies of debtors and secured parties under Part 6 of Revised Article 9. Its predecessor, Part 5 of Former Article 9, was an important and frequently litigated area of legal regulation. Although there is every reason to believe that this will continue to be so under Part 6, we have some optimism that the clarity offered by the revisions may reduce litigation. Keep in mind, however, that there is a large body of other, non-Article 9 law that features prominently in the relationship between creditors and debtors. Two aspects of this other law are particularly noteworthy. First, during the past twenty-five to thirty years a rapidly growing body of law, generally dubbed **lender liability**, has emerged. The courts have been developing myriad theories of liability, ranging from claims based on common-law fraud and duress to claims based on securities regulation statutes and claims based on the failure to observe duties of good faith and fair dealing.

Second, a secured creditor who engages in inequitable conduct in the course of enforcing its security interest runs the risk that its claim will be subordinated to claims of other creditors in bankruptcy. See BC 510(c). The doctrine of **equitable subordination** has developed through the case law since it appeared in 1939. The prevailing approach is that a creditor's claim will be equitably subordinated if the creditor has engaged in fraud or other inequitable conduct that resulted in an unfair advantage to the creditor or in harm to other creditors, provided that subordination would not be contrary to the principles of bankruptcy law. There are cases suggesting that secured creditors who act in accordance with their security agreements—albeit aggressively—are unlikely to have their claims subordinated.

As you work your way through the following materials, do not forget that much law other than the UCC regulates a creditor's behavior, as just noted. Before proceeding to the following Problems, cases and Notes, you may find it useful to peruse the brief overview of Article 9, Part 6, beginning on page 93, supra. Finally, please bear in mind that when a debtor enters bankruptcy *the rules change* (even if equitable subordination is not at issue). In particular, recall the broad sweep of the automatic stay under BC 362 and the bankruptcy trustee's turnover powers under BC 542, discussed in Chapter 7, Section 1, supra.

NOTE ON RIGHTS AND DUTIES AFTER DEFAULT

UCC 9–601 explains generally the rights and remedies of the secured party and the debtor. Subsections (a) and (d) make clear that the secured party may proceed without judicial process under Article 9, may exercise the rights and remedies agreed by the parties, and may enforce the security interest by any judicial procedure. Although the secured party's rights and remedies are cumulative under UCC 9–601(c), they are not entirely independent from one another. For example, UCC 9–601(e) and (f) explain the interplay between enforcement by judicial process and the secured party's rights under Article 9.

The rights and remedies of the debtor and secured party arise "after default." UCC 9–601(a), (d). The UCC neither defines the term nor explains the concept of "default." In common parlance, the primary meaning of the term is "to fail to perform a task or fulfill an obligation." We have seen in Chapter 5 that a security interest is "an interest in personal property or fixtures which secures payment or performance of an obligation." UCC 1–201(35) [F1–201(37)]. As to these security interests, a failure to perform a secured obligation clearly would constitute a default. Indeed, the most common default is the debtor's failure to make a required payment on a secured obligation when it becomes due. Most security agreements specify several other events of default as well. See Form 3.2, ¶ 12, and Form 3.6, ¶ 3.b.5, supra. As we shall see in Section 4, infra, determining whether a payment or other default has occurred sometimes can be difficult.

We have seen that some security interests do not secure an obligation: "[A]ny interest of a consignor and a buyer of accounts, chattel paper, a payment intangible, or a promissory note in a transaction that is subject to Article 9" is a security interest. UCC 1–201(35) [F1–201(37)]. Consignments and contracts to sell receivables typically create obligations on the part of the debtor (consignee or seller), but these obligations are not secured by the consigned goods or the sold receivables. The remedial provisions of Part 6 are not designed to address a default in these obligations. Accordingly, with one exception (discussed in Section 5, infra), Part 6 of Article 9 "imposes no duties upon a secured party that is a consignor or is a buyer of accounts, chattel paper, payment intangibles, or promissory notes." UCC 9–601(g).

SECTION 1.   TAKING POSSESSION OF COLLATERAL AFTER DEFAULT

(A) IN GENERAL

THEY'RE THE NIGHT STALKERS
On the prowl, silent and fast: Repo Men

By Edward Power
Inquirer Staff Writer

You are now entering Repo Reality:

Somewhere out on the dark side streets, or tucked away in the fringe neighborhoods of Philadelphia, there was a gold 1988 Hyundai Excel, parked by the curbside pretty as a trophy.

Two months ago, the car's owner had walked onto a dealer's lot and then signed a loan agreement with a Philadelphia bank. The value of the contract: $13,124.14.

Sixty days after driving away, the new owner had yet to make his first payment of $218.59 per month. "Never even got out of the gate," as Dick Harris put it.[*]

---

*   [Mr. Harris, who is quoted in this article, is not related to any of the authors of this book.]

That was when Harris, 58, and Jim Carden Jr., 25, got involved. They are repo men.

So there, motoring along the 1400 block of Fanshawe Street in Northeast Philadelphia, at 12:20 a.m. Friday, Carden and Harris let their eyes roam the taillights and license plates.

"You develop a feel, almost smell it," Harris said of the hunt for such cars.

"A sixth sense," Carden agreed, nodding.

And then Carden's sixth sense kicked like a turbocharger. There was the gold Excel, three cars ahead, a loan officer's dream.

"We've got to break into it and move it back so we can tow it," Harris said as Carden got out a long silver wire with a hook on one end. The street was dark, but suddenly a single porch light flicked on.

The two men ignored it. Within 30 seconds, Carden had the door open and was silently rolling the Hyundai back, just enough so he could get the tow boom from his truck under the fender.

Less than four minutes after spotting the car, Carden gunned the tow truck's engine, and he and Harris were rolling again.

"That's the name of that tune," Harris said, and on into the Philadelphia night he and Carden went, looking for more of the repossessions they call "deals."

Cruising the streets a little earlier, Harris had remarked on the reason he and Carden spend their nights fending off crack dealers, narrowly escaping irate car owners and looking for a prize $50,000 BMW owned by a drug dealer who is wanted by the police for stealing the car, not to mention executing his enemies.

"We're adrenalin freaks," Harris said smiling.

Inside the North Philadelphia warehouse where his repossession business is based, Jim Carden Sr., president of East Coast Recovery Inc., was readying the crews to go out one night last week; among them was his son, Jim.

. . .

"Because I'm a repossessor there's a stigma attached to me," Carden [Sr.] said. "It's difficult when you've always had acceptance and now you're looked at as a dirt bag or something."

"Picture yourself walking up somebody's driveway at 3 o'clock in the morning," the younger Carden said of the perils of the repo business.

"And King Kong comes out of the house," Harris added.

Find it. Hook it up. Hit the gas.

Repo man.

The Philadelphia Inquirer, Nov. 20, 1988, at 1–B, 3–B.

Problem 9.1.1. In the setting of the Prototype on automobile financing, Chapter 3, Section 1, supra, Lee Abel purchased a new Chevrolet and signed the Instalment Sale Contract. See Form 3.6, supra. As in the Prototype, Main Motors assigned the contract to Firstbank.

Abel made five monthly payments from August through December. Just after Christmas, Abel was laid off work and was unable to continue the payments. Two weeks after Abel missed the January 24 payment, an employee of Firstbank phoned to remind Abel that the payment was overdue. Firstbank wrote and phoned Abel several more times in February, and on February 20 Firstbank wrote to Abel stating that unless prompt payment was forthcoming, Firstbank would be required to repossess the car. Abel was still unable to find the money for the payments.

Abel kept the car at home, parked in the street. At around 11:00 P.M. on February 25, Abel saw a car stop in front of the house. Two people got out and approached Abel's car, inserted a key in the lock, and opened the door. Abel said to a friend who was visiting at the time: "Someone's messing around with my car. Call the police." Abel then rushed out the door. Before Abel got outside the two people had entered the Chevrolet and closed and locked the car doors. Abel ran up to the car and shouted: "Get out of my car." One of the people said: "Sorry, but we're repossessing the car for Firstbank." The other started the engine and they drove off with the car.

Before the car reached the corner, a patrol car arrived in response to a radio message that relayed the call from Abel's friend. Abel pointed to the departing Chevrolet; the patrol car caught up with the Chevrolet and stopped the car. The driver and passenger in the Chevrolet identified themselves as employees of a repossession firm retained by Firstbank, and showed the officers a copy of the Instalment Sales Contract and a copy of the February 20 letter to Abel giving notice that the payment was overdue. The officers then allowed the repo team to proceed with the Chevrolet.

(a) Abel sues Firstbank for conversion, for compensation for loss of the use of the car, and for punitive damages. What result? See UCC 9–609; UCC 9–625(b) & Comment 3, UCC 1–305(a) [F1–106]; UCC 9–625(c)(2); Stone Machinery Co. v. Kessler, infra; Thrash v. Credit Acceptance Corp., infra; Wade v. Ford Motor Credit Co., infra; Notes on Wrongful Repossession, infra.

(b) Suppose that Abel jumped into another car and gave chase, leading to traffic violations. What result? See Jordan v. Citizens & Southern National Bank, 278 S.C. 449, 298 S.E.2d 213 (1982) (high speed chase involving traffic violations following repossession was not a breach of the peace in the repossession; conduct at a distance from the place of repossession (plaintiff's home) was not "conduct at or near and/or incident to the seizure of the property"); Wallace v. Chrysler Credit Corp., 743 F.Supp. 1228, 1233 (W.D.Va.1990) (threatening to throw daughter and plaintiff in jail after repossession of property was not "incident to" the seizure of the property; "[o]nce a creditor has gained sufficient dominion over his collateral, objection by the debtor will be of no avail.").

(c) Now suppose that Abel rushed outside, confronted the repo team *before* they entered the car, and demanded that they leave the car where it was. Without responding, the repo team jumped in the Chevrolet and drove it away. What result?

(d) Suppose, instead, that, while still inside, Abel noticed that the repo team was armed with shotguns. Abel, being no fool, remained inside, did not confront the repo team, and watched as they drove away the Chevrolet. (You may assume that their possession of the shotguns was legal under applicable law.) What result? Is this scenario or the one presented in part (c) above more likely to result in actual violence?

(e) Suppose that the police had arrived before the repo team entered the car. Would their presence alone have affected the outcome? See *Stone Machinery*, infra; Note (2) on Wrongful Repossession, infra.

Problem 9.1.2. Misako Inaba bought a food freezer from Cellar Department Store pursuant to an installment sales contract that gave Cellar a security interest in the freezer. After making eight monthly payments, Inaba missed the next two installments. Cellar's employees phoned and sent written notices to Inaba; these messages warned Inaba that, unless payments were made, Cellar would be required to repossess the freezer. Inaba failed to pay. One afternoon two people knocked on Inaba's door. When Inaba opened the door, one of them said, "We've come to repossess the freezer," and then walked in. Inaba responded, "I think that's a terrible thing to do. I'll pay you as soon as I can." The other replied, "I'm awfully sorry, but we have our orders." Inaba spoke further, with considerable feeling, of the personal and family hardship of losing the freezer. But they picked up the freezer and carried it away.

Inaba sued Cellar for wrongful repossession. What result from the courts that decided the *Stone Machinery*, *Thrash*, and *Wade* cases, infra?

NOTE ON SELF–HELP REPOSSESSION UNDER FORMER AND REVISED ARTICLE 9

Both Former and Revised Article 9 entitle a secured party to take possession of collateral following a "default" (as noted above, "default" is an undefined term left to the agreement of the parties). See F9–503; UCC 9–609. Although Former 9–503 has given rise to a large number of reported cases, it remains essentially unchanged in UCC 9–609. The case law under Former 9–503 has been generally consistent as to certain issues relating to taking possession of collateral. For example, courts generally have attributed to the secured party noncompliance by an independent contractor who takes possession of collateral on the secured party's behalf. (This issue is discussed in Note (3) on Wrongful Repossession, infra.) Should Revised Article 9 have codified the results of the cases, addressed the issues in the comments, or been silent altogether? In general, Revised Article 9 treats these issues in the comments (see UCC 9–609, Comment 3) or is silent.

One of the most controversial and frequently litigated issues that arose under Former 9–503 was the meaning of that section's significant limitation on a secured party's right to take possession of collateral through nonjudicial self-help: A secured party may take possession nonjudicially only "without breach of the peace." F9–503. UCC 9–609 contains the same limitation. Comment 3 to UCC 9–609 states that the section follows Former 9–503 in that it "does not define or explain the conduct that will constitute a breach of the peace, leaving that matter for continuing development by the courts." The drafters resisted appeals to provide more explicit statutory guidance. See, e.g. Braucher, The Repo Code: A Study of Adjustment to Uncertainty in Commercial Law, 75 Wash. U. L.Q. 549 (1997) (hereinafter, "Braucher, Repo Code").

Professor Braucher argues that "breach of the peace" is a vague and unpredictable standard. Id. at 566–91. In consumer transactions, in particular, she believes that the lack of certainty based on case-by-case determinations provides inadequate deterrence. Id. at 614–15. In her article (published while Revised Article 9 was being drafted and debated), she urged the drafters to codify "a number of common types of repossession practices that are breaches of the peace," explaining that this approach "would likely lead to compliance by most repossessors." Id. at 615. As noted above, however, the drafters declined to adopt this suggestion; UCC 9–609 retains the general "breach of the peace" standard. As you read the following cases dealing with Former 9–503 and the related Problems and Notes, consider the relative merits of the broad standard retained by UCC 9–609 and a more specific listing of "common types of . . . breaches of the peace" urged by Professor Braucher.

Stone Machinery Co. v. Kessler[*]

Court of Appeals of Washington, 1 Wash.App. 750, 463 P.2d 651 (1970).
Review denied 77 Wn.2d 962 (1970).

■ EVANS, CHIEF JUDGE.

Plaintiff Stone Machinery brought this action in Asotin County to repossess a D–9 Caterpillar Tractor which plaintiff had sold to defendant Frank Kessler under conditional sales contract. Service of process was not made on the defendant but plaintiff located the tractor in Oregon and repossessed it. The defendant then filed an answer and cross-complaint in the Asotin County replevin action, alleging that the plaintiff wrongfully and maliciously repossessed the tractor, and sought compensatory and punitive damages under Oregon law. Trial was to the court without a jury and the court awarded defendant compensatory damages in the sum of $18,586.20, and punitive damages in the sum of $12,000 on defendant's cross-complaint.

The operative facts are not in serious dispute. Defendant Kessler purchased, by conditional sales contract, a used D–9 Caterpillar Tractor from the plaintiff Stone Machinery, for the sum of $23,500. The unpaid balance of $17,500 was to be paid in monthly installments, with skip

---

*   [The court's citations are to the applicable pre–1972 version of the UCC.]

payments.[**] The defendant's payment record was erratic and several payments were made late. However, payments of $3600 on March 29, 1966, and $1800 on July 18, 1966, put the contract payments on a current basis. The payment due on August 10, 1966 was not made and, on September 7, 1966, plaintiff's credit manager, Richard Kazanis, went to the defendant's ranch in Garfield, Washington, and demanded payment of the balance due on the contract or immediate possession of the tractor. At this time defendant had made payments on the purchase price totaling $17,200, including the trade-in. The defendant was unable to make full payment, or any payment at that time, and informed Mr. Kazanis that he would not relinquish possession of the tractor to him at that time, or at any time in the future, in the absence of proper judicial proceedings showing his right to repossess, and that "someone would get hurt" if an attempt was made to repossess without "proper papers." At that time the defendant informed Mr. Kazanis that he, the defendant, expected to be awarded a contract by the U.S. Bureau of Fisheries to do some work with the D–9 at their installation on the Grande Ronde River near Troy, Oregon, and that he would then be able to pay on the tractor.

On September 13, 1966, the plaintiff instituted this action in Asotin County, Washington, but the sheriff was unable to locate the tractor in that county. Thereafter, the plaintiff instituted another action in Garfield County, but the sheriff was unable to locate the tractor in that county. The evidence indicates that on September 24 Kessler took the tractor to Oregon to work the Bureau of Fisheries job.

On September 27, 1966, Mr. Kazanis, by use of an airplane, located the tractor on the Grande Ronde River, west of Troy, Wallowa County, Oregon. He then contacted the sheriff of Wallowa County and requested him to accompany them in the repossession of the tractor to prevent any violence by the defendant. The sheriff agreed to meet with Mr. Kazanis at Troy, Oregon, and on September 27, 1966, Mr. Kazanis in his private car, plaintiff's mechanic in a company pickup, and the plaintiff's truck driver in the company lo-boy truck, left Walla Walla, and the following morning met the Wallowa County Sheriff at Troy, where the sheriff was shown a copy of the conditional sales contract. The sheriff confirmed previous legal advice plaintiff had received that the plaintiff had the right to repossess the tractor (although not by the use of force) and thereupon the sheriff, in his official sheriff's car, followed by Mr. Kazanis in his private car, the mechanic in the pickup, and the truck driver in the lo-boy, proceeded to the scene where the defendant was operating the D–9 tractor in the Grande Ronde River approximately 7 miles west of Troy, pursuant to contract with the U.S. Bureau of Fisheries.

Upon arriving at the scene the sheriff, accompanied by Mr. Kazanis, walked to the edge of the river and motioned the defendant, who was

---

** [A "skip payment" arrangement allows the debtor to skip a certain number of payments each year; these arrangements are seen most often in transactions involving debtors in seasonal lines of business, such as agriculture and construction.]

working with the tractor in the river, to bring the tractor to shore. The sheriff was in uniform and wearing his badge and sidearms. The sheriff informed the defendant that the plaintiff Stone Machinery had a right to repossess the tractor, and stated, "We come to pick up the tractor." The defendant asked the sheriff if he had proper papers to take the tractor and the sheriff replied, "No." The defendant Kessler protested and objected to the taking of the tractor but offered no physical resistance because, as he testified, "he didn't think he had to disregard an order of the sheriff." The plaintiff's employee then loaded the tractor on the lo-boy and left for Walla Walla, Washington.

Within a few days the tractor was sold to a road contractor at Milton–Freewater, Oregon, for the sum of $7447.80 cash, on an "as is" basis. The sale price represented the balance due on the contract, plus the plaintiff's charges for repossession.

Plaintiff's first assignments of error are directed to the following findings of the trial court:

XII

That the plaintiffs actions in repossessing the defendant's tractor on September 28, 1966, and the actions of the Wallowa County Sheriff, in aid of the plaintiffs, amounted to constructive force, intimidation and oppression, constituting a breach of the peace and conversion of defendant's tractor.

XIV

That the plaintiffs failed to show just cause or excuse for the wrongful act of repossession of the defendant's tractor on September 28, 1966.

XV

That the wrongful act of repossession, done intentionally on September 28, 1966, was malicious and was so wanton and reckless as to show disregard for the rights of the defendant Frank Kessler.

Retaking possession of a chattel by a conditional seller, upon the default of the buyer, is governed by O.R.S. 79.5030 (U.C.C. 9–503):

Secured party's right to take possession after default. Unless otherwise agreed a secured party has on default the right to take possession of the collateral. In taking possession a secured party may proceed without judicial process *if this can be done without breach of the peace* or may proceed by action. * * *

(Italics ours.)

Defendant Kessler was admittedly in default for nonpayment of the August and September contract installments. By the terms of the above statute Stone Machinery had the right to take possession of the tractor without judicial process, but only if this could be done without a breach of the peace. The question is whether the method by which they proceeded constituted a breach of the peace.

No Oregon cases have been cited which define the term "breach of peace" so we must look to other authority. In 1 Restatement of Torts 2d, § 116 (1965), the term is defined as follows:

A breach of the peace is a public offense done by violence, or one causing or likely to cause an immediate disturbance of public order.

In the case of McKee v. State, 75 Okl.Cr. 390, 132 P.2d 173, breach of peace is defined (headnote 9, 132 P.2d 173), as follows:

To constitute a "breach of the peace" it is not necessary that the peace be actually broken, and if what is done is unjustifiable and unlawful, tending with sufficient directness to break the peace, no more is required, nor is actual personal violence an essential element of the offense. * * *

In the instant case it was the sheriff who said that he had no legal papers but that "we come over to pick up this tractor." Whereupon, the defendant Kessler stated, "I told him I was resisting this; there was an action started and I wanted to have a few days to get money together to pay them off." At this point defendant Kessler had a right to obstruct, by all lawful and reasonable means, any attempt by plaintiff to forcibly repossess the tractor. Had the defendant offered any physical resistance, there existed upon both the sheriff and plaintiff's agents a duty to retreat. However, confronted by the sheriff, who announced his intention to participate in the repossession, it was not necessary for Kessler to either threaten violence or offer physical resistance. As stated by the court in Roberts v. Speck, 169 Wash. 613, at 616, 14 P.2d 33 at 34 (1932), citing from Jones on Chattel Mortgages (4th ed.), § 705:

"The mortgagee becomes a trespasser by going upon the premises of the mortgagor, accompanied by a deputy sheriff who has no legal process, but claims to act *colore officii*, and taking possession without the active resistance of the mortgagor. To obtain possession under such a show and pretence of authority is to trifle with the obedience of citizens to the law and its officers."

Acts done by an officer which are of such a nature that the office gives him no authority to do them are "*colore officii*." See 7A Words & Phrases Perm.Ed. at 296.

In Burgin v. Universal Credit Co., supra, the conditional seller retook possession from the buyer, after default in payments, and in order to do so secured the presence of a police officer, without legal papers. The only act of the officer was to order the buyer to release the brakes and drive the car to the curb. The court said:

"Because a party to a contract violates his contract, and refuses to do what he agreed to do, is no reason why the other party to the contract should compel the performance of the contract by force. The adoption of such a rule would lead to a breach of the peace, and it is never the policy of the law to encourage a breach of the peace. The right to an enforcement of this part of the contract must, in the absence of a consent on the part of the mortgagor, be enforced by due process of law, the same as any other contract."

In the case of Firebaugh v. Gunther, 106 Okl. 131, 233 P. 460 (1925), the defendant secured the services of a deputy sheriff to take possession of the property. The deputy sheriff, not having legal papers, stated "he was going to take the property and did not want to make any trouble." It was held that his conduct constituted intimidation amounting to force.

In the instant case, when the sheriff of Wallowa County, having no authority to do so, told the defendant Kessler, "We come over to pick up this tractor," he was acting *colore officii* and became a participant in the repossession, regardless of the fact that he did not physically take part in the retaking. Plaintiff contends that its sole purpose in having the sheriff present was to prevent anticipated violence. The effect, however, was to prevent the defendant Kessler from exercising his right to resist by all lawful and reasonable means a nonjudicial take-over. To put the stamp of approval upon this method of repossession would be to completely circumvent the purpose and intent of the statute.

We hold there is substantial evidence to support the trial court's finding that the unauthorized actions of the sheriff in aid of the plaintiff amounted to constructive force, intimidation and oppression constituting a breach of the peace and conversion of the defendant's tractor.

Plaintiff's final assignment of error relates to the trial court's award of punitive damages. The Oregon law regarding punitive damages has recently been set forth in the case of Douglas v. Humble Oil & Refining Co., 445 P.2d 590 (Or.1968):

> As a general rule, punitive damages will be allowed only when the proof supports a finding that the defendant acted with improper motives or with willful, wanton, or reckless disregard for the rights of others. * * *

> We held recently that it is only in those instances where the violation of societal interests is sufficiently great and of a kind that sanctions would tend to prevent that the use of punitive damages is proper. "Regardless of the nomenclature by which a violation of these obligations is described (grossly negligent, willful, wanton, malicious, etc.), it is apparent that this court has decided that it is proper to use the sanction of punitive damages where there has been a particularly aggravated disregard * * * "of the rights of the victim. Noe v. Kaiser Foundation Hospitals, Or., 435 P.2d 306 (1967).

Defendant Kessler was in default of his contract and had announced his intention to resist any attempted nonjudicial repossession. The words used in announcing his intention, namely, "someone would get hurt," were of such a nature as to justify the presence of a sheriff during any attempt at peaceable repossession although, as we have already held, this did not justify participation by the sheriff in the process of repossession. However, the fact that the sheriff did undertake to act *colore officii* in the repossession was not, under the circumstances, sufficient to support a finding that the plaintiff thereby displayed a particularly aggravated disregard for the rights of Kessler, within the meaning of Douglas v. Humble Oil & Refining Co., supra.

Judgment for compensatory damages is affirmed. Judgment for punitive damages is reversed.

Thrash v. Credit Acceptance Corporation*
Supreme Court of Alabama, 2001.
821 So.2d 968.

■ WOODALL, JUSTICE.

The plaintiffs, Kenneth Thrash and Kathryn Thrash, appeal from a summary judgment in favor of a defendant, Credit Acceptance Corporation ("CAC"). We reverse and remand.

I.

On or about December 2, 1996, the Thrashes entered into a retail-installment contract and security agreement with CAC in connection with their purchase of a used automobile. The agreement required the Thrashes to make monthly payments, on a loan beginning on January 1, 1997, and the loan was secured by the 1989 Oldsmobile Cutlass Ciera automobile they purchased.

The agreement provided, in pertinent part:

"**Remedies**. . . . if you are in default on this Contract, we have all of the remedies provided by law and this Contract:

" . . .

"D. We may immediately take possession of the Property by legal process or self-help, but in doing so we may not breach the peace or unlawfully enter onto your premises. . . ."

(Emphasis added.)

The Thrashes made the payments required by the agreement on January 11, 1997, and on February 20, 1997, but made no payment in March or April. The Thrashes testified that CAC had agreed to allow the March and April payments to be made by the end of April.

CAC employed Gulf Coast Recovery Services & Storage, Inc. ("GCRS"), to repossess the Thrashes' automobile. During the early-morning hours of April 24, 1997, GCRS removed the automobile from the Thrashes' residence. GCRS did not contact the Thrashes before the repossession. Finding the automobile parked under a carport in a driveway, GCRS attached a winch to the rear of the vehicle to drag it to the street. Because the front wheels were locked, GCRS poured liquid dish-washing soap on the driveway, lubricating the driveway and making it easier to drag the vehicle to the street, where it could be towed from its front. GCRS did not tell anyone that it had placed the lubricant on the driveway.

---

*   [The court's citations are to Former Article 9.]

When the vehicle was being repossessed, Kenneth Thrash was at work. Kathryn, his wife, telephoned him from their residence, and informed him that the vehicle was being stolen. Kenneth told Kathryn to telephone the police, and he left work to return to their residence. When he arrived at their residence, Kenneth parked his vehicle in the driveway, got out of the vehicle, and ran toward the back door. In the carport, he stepped in the slippery dish-washing liquid and fell, allegedly suffering severe and disabling injuries.

II.

The Thrashes sued CAC and GCRS in the Mobile Circuit Court. Their complaint alleged that CAC and GCRS were negligent or wanton in leaving a clear liquid lubricant on the floor of their carport, allegedly causing Kenneth to slip and fall, injuring his back. They further alleged that CAC and GCRS's actions constituted a wrongful repossession and a trespass upon their real property and violated § 7-9-503, Ala. Code 1975.

CAC moved for a summary judgment, contending that it could not be vicariously liable for the alleged wrongdoing of GCRS, an independent contractor. Further, CAC argued that GCRS had not committed a breach of the peace for which CAC would be liable. The trial court entered a summary judgment in favor of CAC.

The case against GCRS proceeded to a jury trial. The Thrashes received a judgment in their favor, and later reached a pro tanto settlement with GCRS. The Thrashes appeal from the summary judgment in favor of CAC.

III.

CAC made a prima facie showing in support of its motion for a summary judgment that GCRS was an independent contractor and that in repossessing the vehicle GCRS had not committed a breach of the peace. Therefore, the burden shifted to the Thrashes to present "substantial evidence" creating a genuine issue of material fact. Bass v. SouthTrust Bank of Baldwin County, 538 So. 2d 794 (Ala. 1989); § 12-21-12(d), Ala. Code 1975. Evidence is "substantial" if it is "of such weight and quality that fair-minded persons in the exercise of impartial judgment can reasonably infer the existence of the fact to be proved." West v. Founders Life Assur. Co. of Florida, 547 So. 2d 870, 871 (Ala. 1989). This Court must review the record in a light most favorable to the Thrashes, and must resolve all reasonable doubts against CAC. Martin v. City of Linden, 667 So. 2d 732, 736 (Ala. 1995).

Applying these well-established principles, this Court must resolve two dispositive issues. First, did the Thrashes present substantial evidence that GCRS was acting as CAC's agent, and not as an independent contractor? Second, did the Thrashes present substantial evidence that in repossessing the vehicle GCRS committed a breach of the peace or an unlawful entry onto their premises? If both questions are answered in the affirmative, then the trial court erred in entering the summary judgment for CAC on all counts of the complaint.[1]

IV.

The Thrashes contend that GCRS was acting as CAC's agent in repossessing the automobile, and that, therefore, CAC is vicariously liable for GCRS's wrongdoing. This Court stated the controlling principles of agency law in Malmberg v. American Honda Motor Co., Inc., 644 So. 2d 888, 890 (Ala. 1994):

Agency is generally a question of fact to be determined by the trier of fact. See Oliver v. Taylor, 394 So. 2d 945 (Ala. 1981). When a defendant's liability is to be based on agency, agency may not be presumed; rather, when on a motion for summary judgment a defendant has made a prima facie showing that there was no agency relationship, the party asserting agency has the burden of presenting substantial evidence of the alleged agency. Carlton v. Alabama Dairy Queen, Inc., 529 So. 2d 921 (Ala. 1988); Wood v. Shell Oil Co., 495 So. 2d 1034 (Ala. 1986). The test to be applied in determining whether there existed an agency relationship based on actual authority is whether the alleged principal exercised a right of control over the manner of the alleged agent's performance. Control must be proven; and proof of control requires more than proof of a mere right to determine if the person claimed to be an agent is conforming to the requirements of a contract. Id." (Emphasis added.) The right-of-control test requires that the right be reserved, not that the right be actually exercised.

"The test for determining whether a person is an agent or employee of another, rather than an independent contractor with that other person, is whether that other person has reserved the right of control over the means and method by which the person's work will be performed, whether or not the right of control is actually exercised. Alabama Power Co. v. Beam, 472 So. 2d 619 (Ala. 1985). How the parties characterize the relationship is of no consequence; it is the facts of the relationship that control." Martin v. Goodies Distribution, 695 So. 2d 1175, 1177 (Ala. 1997).

The Thrashes contend that they presented substantial evidence indicating that CAC had reserved the right of control over the manner in which GCRS repossessed their automobile. We agree.

Terry McMillen, a representative of GCRS, testified by deposition that GCRS preferred to contact the debtor before repossessing a vehicle. However, CAC had instructed GCRS to make no contact with the debtor before a repossession, thus evidencing the actual exercise of a right of control over the manner of GCRS's performance. Following that instruction, GCRS did not advise the Thrashes that the vehicle was being repossessed. Consequently, Kathryn Thrash concluded that the vehicle was being stolen, and she so informed her husband.

---

1. CAC did not argue that there was no substantial evidence that GCRS had acted negligently in leaving the lubricant on the pavement of the carport.

There is evidence indicating that Kenneth Thrash fell when he stepped in slippery dish-washing liquid, which GCRS had used to lubricate the driveway and to facilitate the repossession. Randy Smirnoff, a representative of CAC, testified by deposition that once CAC learned that GCRS was using a lubricant, CAC had the authority to instruct GCRS to abandon its use, thus evidencing CAC's retained right of control over the manner of GCRS's performance.

V.

A creditor has a nondelegable duty to avoid a breach of the peace when repossessing a vehicle. General Fin. Corp. v. Smith, 505 So. 2d 1045 (Ala. 1987). In its retail-installment contract and security agreement with the Thrashes, CAC assumed another nondelegable duty -- the duty to avoid an unlawful entry onto the Thrashes' premises during the repossession of the automobile. The Thrashes contend that they presented substantial evidence indicating that GCRS committed a breach of the peace and that GCRS entered their premises unlawfully when it repossessed their automobile. We agree.

It is unlawful for a repossession to be accomplished in a manner that creates a substantial risk of injury to the secured parties or to any innocent bystanders.

"The applicable law regarding secured transactions and repossessions is well settled in Alabama. Ala. Code 1975, § 7-9-503, provides:

"'Unless otherwise agreed a secured party has on default the right to take possession of the collateral. In taking possession a secured party may proceed without judicial process if this can be done without breach of the peace. . ..'

"This section allows the secured party, after default, to take possession of collateral without judicial process if possession can be accomplished without risk of injury to the secured party or to any innocent bystanders. General Finance Corp. v. Smith, 505 So. 2d 1045 (Ala. 1987)."

Pleasant v. Warrick, 590 So. 2d 214, 216 (Ala. 1991) (emphasis added). The Thrashes offered substantial evidence indicating that GCRS created a hazard that posed a substantial risk of injury to them, when GCRS entered their premises under cover of darkness, poured a slippery substance onto the driveway, and then left the premises without removing the substance or warning the Thrashes of its presence.

The same evidence would also be sufficient to support a conclusion that GCRS had unlawfully entered onto the Thrashes' premises. One can be liable to another for trespass where "the person . . . intentionally causes some 'substance' or 'thing' to enter upon another's land." Born v. Exxon Corp., 388 So. 2d 933, 934 (Ala. 1980). The party who has a legal right to enter the land of another for a particular purpose becomes a trespasser when the party does some act that he has no legal right to do. See, e.g., Dixie Constr. Co. v. McCauley, 211 Ala. 683, 101 So. 601 (1924).

VI.

The trial court erred in entering the summary judgment for CAC. Therefore, the summary judgment is reversed, and the case is remanded for further proceedings consistent with this opinion.

REVERSED AND REMANDED.

■ JOHNSTONE, JUSTICE (concurring specially).

I concur. I add some observations of my own.

In the proceedings on the motion for summary judgment filed by CAC, the Thrashes, as the nonmovants, are entitled to the benefit of the versions of the evidence and the reasonable inferences from the evidence most favorable to their claims. Ex parte Kraatz, 775 So. 2d 801 (Ala. 2000), and System Dynamics Int'l, Inc. v. Boykin, 683 So. 2d 419 (Ala. 1996). I will summarize some critical facts supported by the record so considered.

In the contracts with the Thrashes, CAC promised them it would not commit a trespass or a breach of the peace in repossessing the car. After the Thrashes defaulted in their car payments, CAC notified them that it intended to repossess the vehicle. In a subsequent telephone discussion with Mr. Thrash, however, CAC agreed to allow him until the end of April to make the delinquent payments.

Nonetheless, about a week before the end of April, CAC sent the repossession agent GCRS to repossess the Thrashes' car. Unannounced, in the middle of the night, GCRS entered the Thrashes' premises and poured detergent under the front tires of the car in the carport and dragged the car away, but left the detergent. Matthew C. McBride, the next-door neighbor of the Thrashes, swore in an affidavit, in pertinent part:

"At some point at approximately midnight on April 24, 1997, I heard a loud screeching noise coming from the Thrash[es'] home which sounded like a chainsaw engine. At the time I heard this I was standing out on my carport smoking a cigarette. Upon hearing the noise, I walked towards the front of my home where I could view the front yard of the Thrash[es'] home. At this time I saw a pickup truck with a boom dragging a vehicle from the Thrash[es'] carport via some type of a winch which was on the boom. There was also an old model vehicle that looked like a Camaro with two men in it parked in the front of the Thrash[es'] home on Colonial Oaks Drive. The front end of the vehicle which was being dragged was pointing towards the Thrash[es'] carport. The pickup truck with the boom was backed into the drive and its front end faced the street. As the vehicle was being dragged down the Thrash[es'] driveway, it made a screeching sound because the front tires were locked and were not rolling as the car moved along the driveway.

"I saw the pickup truck with the Thrash[es'] vehicle hooked to it take a left out of the Thrash[es'] driveway and go down the street and take a left. The older model car followed the pickup truck. At some point I saw the pickup truck drop the Thrash[es'] vehicle then turn[] around to pick it up from the front end so that the Thrash[es'] vehicle had only the rear wheels on the ground. The pickup truck with the Thrash[es'] vehicle and the older car then proceeded back up Colonial Oaks Drive which required them to go past the Thrash[es'] home. At some point prior to this, I had moved into an area approximately in the front yard of the Thrash[es'] home and as the pickup truck drove by, I saw at least one man in the truck and several men in the older car. One of the men in the car yelled in a loud voice, 'Hey, there he is. Let's get him.' Another of the persons in the older car stated, 'No, that's not him.' At this point I became concerned from the words and actions of the persons involved in towing away the Thrash[es'] vehicle that they were going to get out and start a confrontation or fight or otherwise inflict physical damage upon me as I stood in the Thrash[es'] yard." (Emphasis added.)

Mrs. Thrash, awakened by McBride, called Mr. Thrash at his night-time job and told him the car had been stolen. Mr. Thrash rushed home and into his carport, where he suffered serious injury from slipping in the detergent.

The standing instructions of CAC to GCRS included the requirement that GCRS repossess each target vehicle "on sight," without any announcement to the debtor, even though the practice GCRS preferred was to knock on the debtor's door to tell the debtor that GCRS was about to repossess the collateral. Randy Smirnoff of CAC as much as admitted that using detergent to accomplish a repossession would constitute a breach of the peace. (C. 229, 232-33.)

By law and by contract with the Thrashes, CAC owed them a nondelegable duty not to commit trespass and not to injure them or to breach the peace in effecting a repossession. (C. 154.) § 7-9-503, Ala. Code 1975, and General Finance Corp. v. Smith, 505 So. 2d 1045 (Ala. 1987). Thus, CAC is liable for any trespass, injury, or breach of peace committed by GCRS in accomplishing CAC's repossession, even if GCRS be deemed an independent contractor. General Finance Corp., 505 So. 2d at 1048 ("'One who by statute or administrative regulation is under a duty to provide specified safeguards or precautions for the safety of others is subject to liability to the others for whose protection the duty is imposed for harm caused by the failure of a contractor employed by him to provide such safeguards or precautions.'" (quoting Restatement (Second) of Torts § 424 (1965)). See also Singer Sewing Mach. Co. v. Hayes, 22 Ala. App. 250, 114 So. 420 (1927). A repossession accomplished by a method likely to injure the debtor is, in and of itself, a breach of the peace. General Finance Corp., 505 So. 2d at 1048 (a repossession is peaceful only if it is done "without risk of injury to the secured party, the debtor, or any innocent bystanders"). "Whether the actions taken by a secured creditor to repossess collateral involves . . . an unreasonable likelihood of a breach of the peace in light of the time and manner in which the repossession occurred is ordinarily a question of fact to be determined by a jury." Madden v. Deere Credit Servs., Inc., 598 So. 2d 860, 867 (Ala. 1992). Moreover, a repossession accomplished by trick or deceit is wrongful and actionable. Big Three Motors, Inc. v. Rutherford, 432 So. 2d 483 (Ala. 1983), and Ford Motor Credit Co. v. Byrd, 351 So. 2d 557 (Ala. 1977).

The oral agreement by CAC to allow the Thrashes until the end of April to make their delinquent payments suspended the right of CAC to repossess the car until the end of April. Thus, the repossession of the car and the entry onto the Thrashes' property nearly a week before the end of April were without authority or right. See *Big Three Motors*, supra. The act of GCRS in pouring detergent in the Thrashes' carport was the means of the repossession, was a breach of the peace, and was the proximate cause of Mr. Thrash's injuries. Moreover, the acts of CAC in granting the Thrashes more time to pay and contemporaneously ordering the premature repossession of the car constituted deceit and trickery and rendered the repossession wrongful. *Big Three Motors*. Thus, the Thrashes are entitled to proceed against CAC for its own wrongful repossession and for the trespass, wantonness, and negligence by GCRS constituting a breach of the peace and a breach of a nondelegable duty. See *General Finance*, *Big Three Motors*, and *Ford Motor Credit*, supra.

■ MOORE, CHIEF JUSTICE (concurring in part and dissenting in part).

I concur with the majority's holding that Kenneth Thrash and Kathryn Thrash presented substantial evidence indicating that Credit Acceptance Corporation ("CAC") had reserved the right of control over the manner in which Gulf Coast Recovery Services & Storage, Inc. ("GCRS"), repossessed the Thrashes' vehicle.

I dissent from the majority's holding that the Thrashes presented substantial evidence indicating that GCRS committed a breach of the peace and entered the Thrashes' premises unlawfully when it repossessed the Thrashes' vehicle. GCRS placed liquid dish-washing soap on the Thrashes' driveway and carport because it could not tow the car from its position under the Thrashes' carport. While tearing down the Thrashes' carport to facilitate towing would certainly constitute a breach of the peace in this case, I do not believe that merely placing a water-soluble lubricant under the tires of the Thrashes' car constituted a breach of the peace.

To support the majority's holding that GCRS's actions in this case may constitute a breach of the peace, the majority quotes this Court's statement in Pleasant v. Warrick, 590 So. 2d 214 (Ala. 1991), that a secured party may repossess collateral "if possession can be accomplished without risk of injury to the secured party or to any innocent bystanders." 590 So. 2d at 216 (quoting General Finance Corp. v. Smith, 505 So. 2d 1045 (Ala. 1987)). In my opinion, the majority opinion places undue emphasis on this "risk-of-injury" language in Pleasant, to the exclusion of the plain meaning of the phrase "breach of the peace" and this Court's interpretations of that phrase.

Interestingly, the majority opinion does not cite the more recent case of Madden v. Deere Credit Servs., Inc., 598 So. 2d 860 (Ala. 1992), in which this Court discussed at length the meaning of the phrase "breach of the peace." In Madden, this Court turned to, inter alia, the Restatement (Second) of Torts § 183 (1965), for an explanation of a secured creditor's right of repossession:

"'Except as otherwise agreed, a conditional vendor ... of a thing who is entitled to immediate possession thereof . . . is privileged, at a reasonable time and in a reasonable manner, to enter land in the possession of the vendee ... for the purpose of taking possession of the thing and removing it from the land.'"

598 So. 2d at 865. Contrary to the implicit holding by the majority in this case, the slightest risk of injury to the secured party that may arise from a repossession tactic does not render such tactic unreasonable. I believe that GCRS's repossession tactics were entirely reasonable and, therefore, did not constitute a breach of the peace.

Wade v. Ford Motor Credit Co.[*]

Court of Appeals of Kansas, 1983.
8 Kan.App.2d 737, 668 P.2d 183.

■ SWINEHART, JUDGE:

This is an appeal by defendant Ford Motor Credit Company (Ford) from a judgment against it and in favor of plaintiff Norma J. Wade, awarding her damages for conversion, loss of credit reputation, punitive damages and attorney fees in an action arising out of Ford's alleged breach of the peace in the repossession of Wade's car.

Wade entered into an automobile retail installment contract on August 9, 1979, for the purchase of a 1979 Ford Thunderbird automobile. The contract was assigned to Ford which advanced $6,967.75 to enable her to purchase the car. Pursuant to the terms of the contract, Ford had a security interest in the car which had been fully perfected. Wade contracted to pay Ford forty-eight equal monthly installments of $194.52 commencing September 8, 1979. Wade was late with these payments right from the start. The following illustrates her payment record:

Payment Due:	Payment Made:
September 8, 1979	September 17, 1979
October 8, 1979	October 23, 1979
November 8, 1979	January 18, 1980
December 8, 1979	February 14, 1980
January 8, 1980	March 4, 1980

No other payments were made.

On December 6, 1979, Ford mailed Wade a notice of her default and of her right to cure the default. The notice was mailed to Wade pursuant to K.S.A. 16a–5–110 and 16a–1–201(6), and was sent by certified mail to the address listed in Ford's records from the information provided by Wade. [Kansas had adopted legislation based on the Uniform Consumer Credit Code (U3C); the section-numbers of the Kansas legislation conform to those of the U3C, quoted infra.] It was returned to Ford several days later marked

---

[*]   [The court's citations are to Former Article 9.]

"Return to sender, moved, left no address." Wade had moved and not notified Ford of a new address. K.S.A. 16a–1–201(6) provides:

"For the purposes of K.S.A. 16a–1–101 through 16a–9–102, and amendments thereto, the residence of a consumer is the address given by the consumer as the consumer's residence in any writing signed by the consumer in connection with a credit transaction. Until the consumer notifies the creditor of a new or different address, the given address is presumed to be unchanged."

The trial court found that Ford had complied with the statutory notice requirements precedent to repossession. That finding stands since Wade has not appealed from it.

Collection efforts continued after the mailing of the above notice. After communication with Wade, a payment was received and promises of additional payments were made. With the account still in arrears, Ford assigned it on February 4, 1980, to the Kansas Recovery Bureau, a subsidiary of Denver Recovery Bureau, as independent contractors to repossess the car.

On or about February 10, 1980, in the early afternoon, David Philhower, an employee of Kansas Recovery Bureau, located the car in the driveway of Wade's residence. He had a key for the car, so he unlocked the door, got in and started it. Philhower then noticed an apparent discrepancy between the serial number of the car and that listed in his papers. He shut the engine off, got out and locked the car door. At that time Wade appeared at the door of her house. Philhower told her that he had been sent there by Ford to repossess the car, and she replied that he was not going to take it because she had made the payments on it. She invited him in the house to prove her claim, but was unable to locate the cancelled checks and receipts for the payments made. Philhower told her of the serial number discrepancy, and stated that he was not going to take the car until he confirmed the number, and advised her to contact Ford to straighten out the problem.

Wade then told him that if he came back to get the car that she had a gun in the house, which she had obtained because of several burglaries in the area, and she would not hesitate to use it. She then called a representative of Ford and stated she had a gun and that if she caught anyone on her property again trying to take her car, that "I would leave him laying right where I saw him."

Ford then received two more payments, the last being received March 4, 1980. On March 5, 1980, Ford reassigned the account to Kansas Recovery Bureau for repossession. In the early morning hours of March 10, 1980, at around 2:00 a.m., Philhower made another attempt to repossess the car from the driveway of Wade's residence. This time he was successful. Wade heard a car "burning rubber" at around 2:00 a.m., looked out the window, and discovered her car missing. There was no confrontation between Wade and Philhower, since Wade was not even aware of the fact her car was being repossessed until after Philhower had safely left the area in the car. Upon calling the police, Wade was informed that her car had been repossessed.

Philhower had informed the police just prior to the repossession that he was going to recover the car in case they received reports of a prowler.

Wade subsequently brought an action against Ford for wrongful repossession, conversion and loss of credit, and sought both actual and punitive damages, along with attorney fees. Ford filed a counterclaim for breach of contract, seeking the deficiency of $2,953.44 remaining after the car was sold at public auction.

After a trial to the court, the trial court found Ford had breached the peace in repossessing the car and found in favor of Wade. The trial court also found for Ford on its counterclaim. Wade was awarded damages and attorney fees.

Ford appeals, raising the following two issues: (1) Did the trial court err in finding that Ford breached the peace on March 10, 1980, when it repossessed Wade's car? (2) Did the trial court err in assessing damages against Ford?

Defendant Ford contends that the trial court erred in finding that Ford breached the peace on March 10, 1980, when its agent repossessed Wade's car. The issue presented can be stated as follows: Does the repossession of a car, when there is no contact or confrontation between the repossessor and the debtor at the time and place of repossession, constitute a breach of the peace when there has been a prior threat of deadly violence if repossession is attempted? This particular set of facts has not been addressed by the courts before.

The trial court found that Ford had breached the peace in repossessing Wade's car. In its findings and conclusions made at the conclusion of the trial, the trial court emphasized Wade's lack of consent to the repossession and stated: "It's this Court's view that the Legislature, when it permitted self-help repossession, it was meant to cover amicable situations where there was no dispute as there apparently was in this particular case." At the hearing on defendant's motion to alter the judgment, the trial court stated:

"[I]n no way did she consent at no time did she consent to the peaceful recovery of the security, namely, one automobile that she kept and maintained on her private property, namely, that of her residence. The plaintiff, having threatened Mr. Philhower, the recovery agent, with bodily harm through the use of a lethal weapon known as a revolver, having informed Mr. Philhower never to enter her property again, otherwise she would shoot him. So, that being the last communication between Philhower and the plaintiff, at a later date when it was a month or so later, I don't recall since this hearing was seven months ago, Mr. Philhower, after that initial confrontation at 2:00 o'clock in the morning, 1:00 in the morning, quietly entered this private property, in effect, in this Court's opinion, taking the law in its own hands, come what may.

"Now, fortunately, no harm resulted from his entry on this private property. He was willing to assume that risk and that danger, knowing full-well that had he awakened the plaintiff, violence could very well have occurred and ensued. He knowingly and willfully brought that situation about in our community.

"I am reminded in some ways of the old frontier Wichita, Kansas in where firearms were used as a settlement of personal differences. Fortunately, the law and the courts have supplemented that mode or method of settling private differences.

"We have in this state the replevin action, which provides for an orderly process for the recovery of personal property held under a security for a debt and under oath, the parties are privileged to come into the court and expose through the witnesses and their evidence to the court, their claims such as in this case, the defendant claimed that the plaintiff was past due on her note involving the automobile involved here. Then, likewise, in that same hearing, the plaintiff in a replevin action would have had the right and the privilege to be heard by a judge or a jury to determine and make the finding as to whether or not she was in fact delinquent and in violation of her promise to pay thus providing for her being relieved of the security of the automobile in this case.

. . .

"These facts violate every principle of civilized procedures that is understood as to why we have the courts and why we have the law to avoid confrontations between parties to avoid dangers to life, limb, and property. It's an orderly process that we seek to serve in this case.

"The Court is very grateful that no violence did ensue, result from the ultimate repossession of the car by Mr. Philhower, but nevertheless, is of the view that such action as came out in this court, done by Mr. Philhower was a breach of the peace.

"The Court is convinced that the purpose of permitting creditors to obtain a peaceful repossession, recovery of their securities such as an automobile in this case, would apply to instances where the recovery is freely done without threats of violence with consent of the parties and in view of the facts, this Court feels that the threat of firearms that this was a breach of the peace and will affirm the decision made in October, 1981, after hearing the evidence. The motion of the defendant is denied."

It appears that the trial court put a great deal of emphasis on Wade's lack of consent and the great potential for violence involved in the second repossession attempt.

K.S.A. 16a–5–112 [U3C 5.112] provides:

"Upon default by a consumer, unless the consumer voluntarily surrenders possession of the collateral to the creditor, the creditor may take possession of the collateral without judicial process only if possession can be taken without entry into a dwelling and without the use of force or other breach of the peace."

K.S.A. 84–9–503 provides in part:

"Unless otherwise agreed a secured party has on default the right to take possession of the collateral. In taking possession a secured party may proceed without judicial process if this can be done without breach of the peace or may proceed by action."

The statutes do not define the term "breach of the peace." The courts are left with that job. There are few Kansas cases doing so, but numerous cases from other jurisdictions. The leading Kansas case is Benschoter v. First National Bank of Lawrence, 218 Kan. 144, 542 P.2d 1042 (1975), where the court found that the self-help repossession provisions of K.S.A. 84–9–503 do not violate constitutional due process. The court also held:

"A creditor may repossess collateral without judicial process if this can be done without breach of the peace. Standing alone, stealth, in the sense of a debtor's lack of knowledge of the creditor's repossession, does not constitute a breach of the peace." Syl. ¶ 2.

. . .

An extensive search of the cases in other jurisdictions does not reveal a case on point which involved an initial confrontation with a threat of future violence, an intervening period of time with communication between the parties, and a subsequent successful repossession without incident.

In Morris v. First Natl. Bank & Trust Co., 21 Ohio St.2d 25, 254 N.E.2d 683 (1970), the court considered a case involving a self-help repossession statute similar to Kansas'. The facts included a confrontation at the time of repossession. The court noted:

"While we leave the question of conversion to be determined in future proceedings below, we are constrained to hold that when appellee's agents were physically confronted by appellant's representative, disregarded his request to desist their efforts at repossession and refused to depart from the private premises upon which the collateral was kept, they committed a breach of the peace within the meaning of Section 1309.46, Revised Code, lost the protective application of that section, and thereafter stood as would any other person who unlawfully refuses to depart from the land of another." p. 30, 254 N.E.2d 683.

. . .

In Census Federal Credit Union v. Wann, Ind.App., 403 N.E.2d 348 (1980), the court also considered self-help repossession under U.C.C. 9–503 and what constitutes breach of the peace. There the creditor made demand on the debtor for possession of the secured car. The debtor refused to give possession of it to the creditor. Unlike the present case, there were no threats of future violence. Thereafter, the creditor, through its agents and without benefit of any judicial process, took possession of the car at approximately 12:30 a.m. by taking it from the parking lot of the apartment building where the debtor lived. During this second, successful, repossession attempt, no contact whatever was had by the creditor's agents with the debtor or any other person in the immediate control of the car. The court provided the following discussion on breach of the peace:

"In Deavers v. Standridge, (1978) 144 Ga.App. 673, 242 S.E.2d 331, the court held that blocking the movement of the defaulting debtor's automobile after his oral protest to the secured party's repossession attempt was a breach of the peace.

"Cases in other jurisdictions have held that absence of consent of the defaulting party to repossession is immaterial to the right of a secured party to repossess without judicial process. This, of course, is a necessary result, for contrary to the argument of plaintiff, Ind.Code 26–1–9–503, by its very existence, *presupposes that the defaulting party did not consent.* Should the defaulting party consent, no statutory authority would be required for a secured party to repossess, with or without judicial process. To hold otherwise would emasculate that statute."

We find it is clear from a survey of the cases dealing with self-help repossession that the consent of the debtor to the repossession is not required. K.S.A. 16a–5–112 even presupposes the lack of consent: "Upon default by a consumer, unless the consumer *voluntarily surrenders* possession. . . ." (Emphasis supplied.) The trial court's emphasis on the lack of consent by Wade in the present case and its view that "the Legislature, when it permitted self-help repossession . . . meant to cover amicable situations where there was no dispute. . . ." are not found in case law. Repossession, without the consent of the debtor, absent more, does not constitute a breach of the peace by the creditor.

The trial court also emphasized the potential for violence brought on by Wade's threats made during the first repossession attempt. A breach of the peace may be caused by an act likely to produce violence. The facts presented in this case do not, however, rise to that level. A period of one month elapsed between the repossession attempts. During that period, Wade and Ford were in communication and two payments were made. We find the potential for violence was substantially reduced by the passage of this time. Moreover, the actual repossession was effected without incident. The time of the repossession was such that in all likelihood no confrontation would materialize. In fact, Wade was totally unaware of the repossession until after Philhower had successfully left the premises with the car. We therefore find that as a matter of law there was no breach of the peace in the repossession of Wade's car.

The trial court's judgment finding a breach of the peace is reversed, and the case is remanded for a modification of the award of damages in accordance with this opinion.

Wade's motion for attorney fees on appeal is denied.

Reversed and remanded with directions.

NOTES ON WRONGFUL REPOSSESSION

(1) Measure of Damages for Wrongful Repossession. In the *Stone Machinery* case the court concluded that only "compensatory damages" would be awarded. How does one compute such damages for repossession by a secured party who (as in *Stone Machinery*) had a legal right to obtain possession by the use of appropriate procedures? (The *Stone Machinery* opinion does not explain how the trial court computed the "compensatory damages" of $18,586.20.) If damages are based on the interruption of the debtor's use of the collateral, should the relevant period of interruption be limited to the time that would have been required to repossess by judicial proceedings? In the *Stone Machinery* case, would it have been wrong for a judge to defer repossession of the tractor until Kessler, the debtor, could complete his current job—at least if Kessler would assign to the plaintiff the sums to become payable under the contract? Even if that approach would be sensible, how could a judge overcome the fact that Former 9–503 conferred upon Stone Machinery the unequivocal right to possession?

In *Stone Machinery* the court upheld the debtor's judgment for conversion. According to the Restatement (Second) of Torts, "[c]onversion is an intentional exercise of dominion or control over a chattel which so seriously interferes with the right of another to control it that the actor may justly be required to pay the other the full value of the chattel." Restatement (Second) of Torts § 222 A(1) (1965). Consider also Comment *c* to that section:

> The importance of the distinction between trespass to chattels and conversion . . . lies in the measure of damages. In trespass the plaintiff may recover for the diminished value of his chattel because of any damage to it, *or for the damage to his interest in its possession or use.* Usually, although not necessarily, such damages are less than the full value of the chattel itself. In conversion the measure of damages is the full value of the chattel, at the time and place of the tort. [Emphasis added.]

Is there any plausible justification for the debtor, who is in default, to recover the full value of the collateral from the secured party? Perhaps, but only if the secured party is entitled to set off the secured debt against the debtor's recovery. If a worthwhile compensatory measure of damages cannot be found (e.g., where the wrongful possession did not interrupt profitable use of the equipment), should further thought be given to the assessment of punitive damages?

Now consider *Stone Machinery* from another perspective. It was undisputed that Kessler, the debtor, was in default. It follows that, as between Kessler and Stone Machinery, the latter was entitled to possession under Former 9–503. Notwithstanding that Kessler was not (and did not claim to be) entitled to possession, Kessler refused to deliver the tractor to Stone Machinery and even made a threat of physical injury if a non-judicial repossession were to be attempted. Does it seem anomalous that it is Kessler, and not Stone Machinery, that is entitled to a judgment for conversion?

Section 272 of the Restatement (Second) of Torts provides that "[o]ne who is entitled to immediate possession of a chattel is not liable to another for dispossessing him of it." Relying in large part on Section 272 and the related comments, Professor Braucher has argued persuasively that a secured party's breach of the peace in connection with taking possession following default is *not* a conversion. See Braucher, Repo Code, supra, 74

Wash. U. L.Q. at 604–06. (Of course, if the secured party is not entitled to possession, e.g., because no default has occurred, then Section 272 would not apply.) Professor Braucher asserts, however, that even the measure of damages for conversion (i.e., the entire value of the collateral) with an offset for the unpaid secured debt provides an inadequate recovery for the non–converting secured party's breach of the peace:

> With breaches of the peace, the object of the remedy is not so much compensation of the debtor as putting a stop to a socially offensive practice, with the debtor's enforcement action serving the function of a private attorney general. In short, deterrence is the most important function of a breach-of-the-peace remedy, so the proper inquiry is what remedy will deter repossessors from offensive self-help.

Braucher, Repo Code, supra, 74 Wash. U. L.Q. at 613. Instead, she advocates the debtor's recovery of the *fair market value of the collateral plus a cancellation of the secured debt!* Id. at 613–14. Would that approach be consistent with the UCC's general approach of awarding compensatory, but not punitive, damages? See UCC 9–625(b), imposing liability for "any loss caused by a failure to comply with this article." See also UCC 1–305(a) [F 1–106(1)] (remedies are to be compensatory except as "specifically provided in this Act or by other rule of law"). And should the same measure of damages apply in cases of a breach of the peace by a secured party who is entitled to possession as in cases in which the secured party is not entitled to possession but takes possession nevertheless? Of course, if breach of the peace constitutes an independent tort (e.g., assault), nothing in Article 9 would restrict the debtor from obtaining an independent recovery in tort (assuming no double recovery). See UCC 9–625, Comment 3 (second paragraph).

(2) What is a Breach of the Peace? Procedural Aspects of the Breach–of–the–Peace Exception to Self–Help. Perhaps the results of cases like *Stone Machinery* can be understood best by viewing the breach of peace exception to self-help repossession as *procedural* in nature. The secured party is entitled to possession if, in fact, the debtor is in default. But the debtor can prevent self-help, and force the secured party to recover the collateral through judicial proceedings, *if* the debtor is able to control the circumstances so that self-help would constitute a breach of the peace. As illustrated by the *Wade* case (and to some extent the *Thrash* case), sometimes the debtor may find it difficult to challenge a successfully completed, self-help repossession on the basis that the secured party breached the peace.

Might this procedural conceptualization also explain why courts generally treat unauthorized involvement by law enforcement officials ("*colore officii*") as a breach of the peace? It seems highly unlikely that the involvement of a peace officer will result in an actual breach of the peace. But the appearance of authority that the officer conveys is likely to deprive the debtor of the opportunity to protest and to insist on a judicial recovery. Yet there is a fine but blurry line between a breach of the peace *colore officii* and the mere presence of a law enforcement official who acts only to prevent actual violence. See Barrett v. Harwood, 189 F.3d 297 (2d Cir. 1999), discussed below in Note (4).

This procedural conceptualization also is consistent with finding a breach of the peace when the secured party proceeds to take possession in the face of a contemporaneous objection by the debtor. Should the test for a breach of the peace focus on circumstances in which the *risk* of violence (i.e., an *actual* breach of the peace) is likely? This reasoning might explain cases in which a breach of the peace was based on circumstances such as breaking and entering the premises on which collateral is located (especially the debtor's residence), trickery, and the debtor's interruption of a repossession coupled with an objection.

(3) Liability for Acts of an Independent Contractor. Among the issues on which the case law under Former 9–503 has been generally consistent concerns a secured party's responsibility for the acts of an independent contractor who takes possession of collateral on the secured party's behalf but who fails to comply with Article 9 in doing so. Comment 3 to UCC 9–609 recommends that courts follow this case law and "hold the secured party responsible for the actions of others taken on the secured party's behalf, including independent contractors engaged by the secured party to take possession of collateral."

Is *Thrash* inconsistent with the line of independent contractor cases approved by Comment 3? The *Thrash* court remanded the case for consideration of whether the putative contractor (GCRS) was actually the secured party's agent; if so, the secured party would be vicariously liable for the torts GCRS committed in the course of the repossession. The court held that the plaintiffs adduced substantial evidence of agency. But the question of agency for purposes of vicarious tort liability is separate from the more narrow issue of the secured party's responsibility for noncompliance with Article 9 resulting from its contractor's behavior. The *Thrash* court appropriately recognized this distinction.

(4) Replevin, Due Process, and State Action. The traditional requirements for obtaining a writ of replevin (a procedure for recovering possession of personal property) were an *ex parte* application by the plaintiff, accompanied by an affidavit affirming the plaintiff's right to possession and a bond to assure compensation for the defendant if seizure under the writ was unjustified. The Supreme Court invalidated these procedures in Fuentes v. Shevin, 407 U.S. 67, 92 S.Ct. 1983, 32 L.Ed.2d 556 (1972). See also North Georgia Finishing, Inc. v. Di–Chem, 419 U.S. 601, 95 S.Ct. 719, 42 L.Ed.2d 751 (1975) (holding invalid the *ex parte* garnishment of an industrial corporation's bank account).[1]

---

1.   State procedural rules generally have been revised to require judicial supervision of replevin actions. These rules generally provide an opportunity for the defendant to be heard before seizure of property unless a court finds that emergency action is justified, in which case a hearing is held immediately after seizure.

Fuentes concerned the seizure of property by sheriffs who had acted pursuant to state legislative authority. The Supreme Court held that this procedure violated the following provision of the Fourteenth Amendment: "[N]or shall *any State* deprive any person of life, liberty, or property without due process of law." Does the *Fuentes* doctrine apply to *self-help* repossession of collateral by a private person? Does the *state* violate the Due Process Clause when, as in Former 9–503 and UCC 9–609, it authorizes repossession by the creditor?

The *Fuentes* decision led to widespread litigation challenging the constitutionality of self-help repossession by Article 9 secured parties. Several Courts of Appeals rejected Due Process attacks on self-help repossession. The prevailing view (in brief) has been that, although Former 9–503 permitted (just as UCC 9–609 permits) self-help in some circumstances, the creditor's action is based on the creditor's property right rather than on the "state action" contemplated by the Fourteenth Amendment. Consider, for example, the effects of a state's *repeal* of Former 9–503 or UCC 9–609. Nothing would seem to impair the effectiveness of a *contractual* right to self-help repossession. The prevailing view received support in the 1978 decision of the Supreme Court that a warehouse's sale of goods for unpaid storage fees, although permitted by UCC 7–210, was not "state action" in violation of the Due Process Clause. Flagg Brothers v. Brooks, 436 U.S. 149, 98 S.Ct. 1729, 56 L.Ed.2d 185 (1978) (Justices Stevens, White, and Marshall dissented). See Brest, State Action and Liberal Theory: A Casenote on Flagg Brothers v. Brooks, 130 U.Pa.L.Rev. 1296, 1330 (1982) ("The [state action] doctrine has seldom been used to shelter citizens from coercive federal or judicial power. More often, it has been employed to protect the autonomy of business enterprises against the claims of consumers, minorities, and other relatively powerless citizens.").

Unlike the typical self-help repossession, the participation of a sheriff *colore officii*, as in the *Stone Machinery* case, clearly seems to implicate state action. Does a debtor affected by that kind of state action have a *federal* claim against the secured party based on a violation of the debtor's constitutional rights? Cf. Lugar v. Edmondson Oil Co., 457 U.S. 922, 102 S.Ct. 2744, 73 L.Ed.2d 482 (1982) (a private creditor can be liable for use of unconstitutional state procedures as a "state actor" under 42 U.S.C. § 1983).[2] In Wyatt v. Cole, 504 U.S. 158, 112 S.Ct. 1827, 118 L.Ed.2d 504 (1992), the Court held that qualified *immunity from suit* is not available for private defendants faced with Section 1983 liability for having invoked a state replevin, garnishment or attachment statute that is declared unconstitutional. However, the court did not "foreclose the possibility that private defendants faced with § 1983 liability under *Lugar* . . . could be

---

2.   42 U.S.C. § 1983 provides in relevant part as follows:

Every person who, under color of any statute . . . of any State . . . subjects, or causes to be subjected, any citizen of the United States or any other person within the jurisdiction thereof to the deprivation of any rights, privileges, or immunities secured by the Constitution and laws, shall be liable to the party injured in an action at law, suit in equity, or other proper proceeding for redress.

entitled to an affirmative defense based on good faith and/or probable cause or that § 1983 suits against private, rather than governmental, parties could require plaintiffs to carry additional burdens." On remand, the Fifth Circuit accepted *Lugar*'s invitation and held that private defendants may be held liable for damages under Section 1983 only if they knew or should have known that the statute upon which they relied was unconstitutional. Wyatt v. Cole, 994 F.2d 1113 (5th Cir.1993). It might interest you to learn that, in *Wyatt,* the attorney who assisted his client in filing a replevin action was sued along with the client.

In a case somewhat reminiscent of *Stone Machinery*, the Second Circuit Court of Appeals held that the involvement of a police officer in a repossession did not constitute state action. Barrett v. Harwood, 189 F.3d 297 (2d Cir.1999). The court concluded that the police officer was merely exercising his duty to prevent violence and was not taking an active role to assist in the repossession or to intentionally intimidate the debtor from exercising the right to object.

(5) Is There a Better Way? As the foregoing suggests, repossession is not without its risks to the secured party. And, as we discuss in greater detail below, repossessed collateral sold at foreclosure ordinarily sells for less (sometimes substantially less) than comparable used goods sold at retail. For these reasons, a secured party may prefer to avoid actually repossessing the collateral and instead use the *threat* of repossession to encourage a debtor to pay the secured obligation.

Technological advances have given secured parties new means of encouraging payment. Consider the electronic device described in the following newspaper article. Does Article 9 regulate its use? If not, what remedy, if any, would a debtor have if the device is misused?

A red light flashes and a low-toned beep sounds every six seconds before the vehicle simply does not start.

It is one of the latest efforts of car dealerships to crack down on delinquent monthly payments.

And according to Dick Noble, owner of Affordable Autos in Elgin, the electronic device that disables a vehicle when a monthly payment is missed is the answer for customers with no credit or poor credit.

"The question is how to collect money from people who have thin credit credentials and this is how you do it. It is the technology of the day," Noble said.

"If you don't pay the bill you can't have the service. It's like anything else."

Developed in 1999 by California-based Payment Protection Systems, or PPS, the On Time system is an electronic device that monitors monthly car payments and aims to turn "credit-challenged prospects into paying customers," according to the company's Web site.

. . .

And during a time of mounting credit card debts, student loans and unemployment Noble said he wanted to offer customers with poor credit scores the opportunity to purchase a car even when banks and credit unions declined approval.

The On Time device does just that by providing the car dealer with what PPS called "payment protection."

Two days before a payment is due, a red light begins flashing on the On Time device as a reminder, according to Noble.

If the warnings are missed, one day after the due date drivers will hear a low-toned beep about every six seconds and after midnight, the vehicle simply will not start.

Noble emphasized that vehicles with delinquent payments do not shut down while they are running. They simply do not start after a missed payment.

Each customer at Affordable Autos is also allowed three "emergencies," during which they can punch in a special code and turn on their vehicle for an additional 24 hours after the payment's due date.

Nationally the devices have reduced delinquent car payments on average from 27 percent without the On Time system to 3 percent with the devices, according to data released by Mike Simon, president and chief executive officer of PPS.

. . .

Despite its alleged success, John Fenzel owner of Fenzel Motor Sales Inc., 206 S. State St., Hampshire said his dealership does not use the device and will not use it in the future.

However, he called it a good idea in metropolitan areas.

Fenzel said, "It wouldn't fly in Hampshire because it's a small town and a small dealership where a lot of your business is done on the past confidence between customer and dealer. . . . But in large metropolitan areas, yes it would work."

According to data released by Simon, president and chief executive officer of PPS, more than 1,500 dealerships nationwide use the On Time system and it is installed in nearly 200,000 vehicles.

. . .

Noble said, "When customer's cars are disabled they say 'Did you shut my car off?' I say, 'No you shut your car off.'"

Christine S. Moyer, Device eyes status of car payments, Elgin Courier-News, Aug. 9, 2005, at A1.

(B) Consumer Protection Legislation

Problem 9.1.3. In the setting of the Prototype on automobile financing, Lee Abel purchased a new Chevrolet and signed the Instalment Sale Contract. See Form 3.6, supra. As in the Prototype, Main Motors assigned the contract to Firstbank. Paragraph 1.b. (on the reverse side) of the contract provides, in part:

"You agree not to remove the vehicle from the U.S. or Canada, or to sell, rent, lease, or transfer any interest in the vehicle or this contract without our written permission."

Paragraph 3.b. (on the reverse side) of the contract provides, in part:

"If you break your promises (default), we may demand that you pay all you owe on this contract at once. Default means:

1. You do not pay any payment on time;

2. You start a proceeding in bankruptcy or one is started against you or your property; or

3. You break any agreements in this contract."

The monthly payments were due on the 24th of the month; Abel made the first seven payments (through February 24). On March 10 Abel was in desperate need of cash, took the Chevrolet to a used car dealer in another city, and offered it for sale. Dealer's manager asked to see the certificate of title; Abel said that the certificate was at home and that Dealer could have it as soon as Dealer bought the car. (In fact, Firstbank held the certificate, as in the Prototype, Chapter 3, Section 1, supra.) The manager indicated the price that Dealer would be willing to pay, but added that there could be no deal without a clean certificate of title. Abel agreed to bring in the car and certificate the next day in order to close the deal.

Dealer's manager took note of the number of the car's license and, as soon as Abel left, Dealer phoned the Bureau of Motor Vehicles to inquire about ownership and liens. Later that afternoon the Bureau reported by telephone that their records showed that Firstbank held a security interest in the Chevrolet. Dealer phoned Firstbank to inquire if the lien had been discharged. That night, employees of Firstbank found the Chevrolet parked at the curb three blocks from Abel's residence and towed it away.

(a) Abel sued Firstbank for compensatory and punitive damages. Does the Instalment Sale Contract authorize the repossession? If not, is Firstbank aided by UCC 1–303 [F1–208]? Does UCC 2–609 apply to the seller's *assignee* of a security interest, such as Firstbank? If so, are its provisions adequate for the current situation?

(b) Suppose that Abel (promising to bring in the certificate of title the next day) actually sold the Chevrolet to the out-of-town dealer on March 10. That clearly would be a default under the terms of the Instalment Sales Contract, and UCC 9–609 would permit repossession. The state has enacted the Uniform Consumer Credit Code (1974) (U3C). In this case, Firstbank has not given Abel the notice specified in U3C 5.110. Does the U3C bar repossession? See Notes (2) and (3) on Legislation Limiting Self–Help Repossession Against Consumers, infra. (Note (2) sets forth U3C 5.109(2), 5.110(1), and 5.111(1).)

(c) Now suppose that Abel failed to make the payments due on December, January, and February 24. The U3C remains applicable. Does the U3C bar repossession? If the court concludes that the repossession was improper under U3C, what judgment should be entered?

(d) On the morning after Firstbank's repossession of the Chevrolet (March 11), Firstbank concluded that its repossession was inconsistent with the provisions of the U3C. What can Firstbank do to extricate itself with a minimum of difficulty and liability?

NOTES ON LEGISLATION LIMITING SELF–HELP REPOSSESSION AGAINST CONSUMERS

(1) Article 9. As you know, the UCC contains only a few provisions that apply only to consumer transactions. A few of these concern enforcement of security interests. See, e.g., UCC 9–620(e) (discussed in Section 6, infra); UCC 9–625(c)(2) (discussed in Section 2, infra). Article 9 contains no special rules regulating repossession of collateral from consumers, despite the widespread belief that these repossessions may have particularly disruptive and destructive effects. In the face of Article 9's silence, regulation has come from other sources.

(2) The Uniform Consumer Credit Code. One of the UCC's sponsors, the National Conference of Commissioners on Uniform State Laws, has dealt with repossession in another of its products, the Uniform Consumer Credit Code. As initially promulgated in 1968, the U3C did not significantly restrict repossession. Experience with the 1968 version and pressure from consumer groups (including the National Consumer Law Center) led to the promulgation in 1974 of a second version that strengthens the rights of debtors.

Neither version of the U3C has been widely adopted. However, the U3C has been an influential model for states enacting legislation dealing with consumer credit.

Provisions of the U3C that relate to default and repossession follow.

UNIFORM CONSUMER CREDIT CODE (1974)

Section 5.109 [Default]

An agreement of the parties to a consumer credit transaction with respect to default on the part of the consumer is enforceable only to the extent that:

(1) the consumer fails to make a payment as required by agreement; or

(2) the prospect of payment, performance, or realization of collateral is significantly impaired; the burden of establishing the prospect of significant impairment is on the creditor.

Section 5.110 [Notice of Consumer's Right to Cure]

(1) With respect to a consumer credit transaction, after a consumer has been in default for ten days for failure to make a required payment and has not voluntarily surrendered possession of goods that are collateral, a creditor may give the consumer the notice described in this

section. A creditor gives notice to the consumer under this section when he delivers the notice to the consumer or mails the notice to him at his residence (subsection (6) of Section 1.201).

(2) Except as provided in subsection (3), the notice shall be in writing and conspicuously state: the name, address, and telephone number of the creditor to whom payment is to be made, a brief identification of the credit transaction, the consumer's right to cure the default, and the amount of payment and date by which payment must be made to cure the default. A notice in substantially the following form complies with this subsection:

_____

(name, address, and telephone number of creditor)

_____

(account number, if any)

_____

(brief identification of credit transaction)

_____ is the LAST DAY FOR PAYMENT
  (date)

_____ is the AMOUNT NOW DUE
  (amount)

You are late in making your payment(s). If you pay the AMOUNT NOW DUE (above) by the LAST DAY FOR PAYMENT (above), you may continue with the contract as though you were not late. If you do not pay by that date, we may exercise our rights under the law.

If you are late again in making your payments, we may exercise our rights without sending you another notice like this one. If you have questions, write or telephone the creditor promptly.

(3) If the consumer credit transaction is an insurance premium loan, the notice shall conform to the requirements of subsection (2) and a notice in substantially the form specified in that subsection complies with this subsection, except for the following:

(a) in lieu of a brief identification of the credit transaction, the notice shall identify the transaction as an insurance premium loan and each insurance policy or contract that may be cancelled;

(b) in lieu of the statement in the form of notice specified in subsection (2) that the creditor may exercise his rights under the law, the statement that each policy or contract identified in the notice may be cancelled; and

(c) the last paragraph of the form of notice specified in subsection (2) shall be omitted.

Section 5.111 [Cure of Default]

(1) With respect to a consumer credit transaction, except as provided in subsection (2), after a default consisting only of the consumer's failure to make a required payment, a creditor, because of that default, may neither accelerate maturity of the unpaid balance of the obligation, nor take possession of or otherwise enforce a security interest in goods that are collateral until 20 days after a notice of the consumer's right to cure (Section 5.110) is given, nor, with respect to an insurance premium loan, give notice of cancellation as provided in subsection (4) until 13 days after a notice of the consumer's right to cure (Section 5.110) is given. Until expiration of the minimum applicable period after the notice is given, the consumer may cure all defaults consisting of a failure to make the required payment by tendering the amount of all unpaid sums due at the time of the tender, without acceleration, plus any unpaid delinquency or deferral charges. Cure restores the consumer to his rights under the agreement as though the defaults had not occurred.

(2) With respect to defaults on the same obligation other than an insurance premium loan and subject to subsection (1), after a creditor has once given a notice of consumer's right to cure (Section 5.110), this section gives the consumer no right to cure and imposes no limitation on the creditor's right to proceed against the consumer or goods that are collateral. For the purpose of this section, in open-end credit, the obligation is the unpaid balance of the account and there is no right to cure and no limitation on the creditor's rights with respect to a default that occurs within 12 months after an earlier default as to which a creditor has given a notice of consumer's right to cure (Section 5.110).

(3) This section and the provisions on waiver, agreements to forego rights, and settlement of claims (Section 1.107) do not prohibit a consumer from voluntarily surrendering possession of goods which are collateral and the creditor from thereafter accelerating maturity of the obligation and enforcing the obligation and his security interest in the goods at any time after default.

[Subsection (4), dealing with insurance premium loans, is omitted.]

Section 5.112 [Creditor's Right to Take Possession After Default]

Upon default by a consumer with respect to a consumer credit transaction, unless the consumer voluntarily surrenders possession of the collateral to the creditor, the creditor may take possession of the collateral without judicial process only if possession can be taken without entry into a dwelling and without the use of force or other breach of the peace.

(3) Consequences of Violating the U3C's Default and Repossession Rules. What are the consequences of a creditor's noncompliance with the foregoing provisions of the U3C? A court may have some difficulty in finding the answer. U3C 5.201(1) lists 22 provisions of the U3C and states that if any of these provisions is violated the consumer may "recover actual damages and also a right in an action other than a class action, to recover from the person violating this Act a penalty in an amount determined by the court not less than $100 nor more than $1,000." The list of the 22 duties for which the U3C imposes a penalty does *not* include U3C 5.109–5.112.

Do U3C 5.109–5.112 specify legal consequences of failing to comply with the requirements set forth in these provisions? See U3C 5.111(1). Should one conclude that the *only* legal consequences of these provisions are those that are specified therein? U3C 1.103, in language closely comparable to UCC 1–103(b) [F1–103], states that "the principles of law and equity" and the UCC supplement the provisions of the U3C, unless displaced by its "particular provisions."

It should be noted that U3C 5.201, after a series of limited remedial provisions (including the listing in subsection (1) of the 22 provisions mentioned above), ends with the following subsection that seems to be of general applicability:

> (8) In an action in which it is found that a creditor has violated this Act, the court shall award to the consumer the costs of the action and to his attorneys their reasonable fees. In determining attorney's fees, the amount of the recovery on behalf of the consumer is not controlling.

(4) Other Approaches to the Problem. The Model Consumer Credit Act (1973) (MCCA), drafted by the National Consumer Law Center, gives short shrift to self-help repossession. Under Section 7.202 of the MCCA:

> No person shall take possession of collateral by other than legal process pursuant to this Part, notwithstanding any provision of law or term of a writing.

Wisconsin has taken a less extreme, but still restrictive, approach. Under the Wisconsin Consumer Act a secured creditor may repossess only after obtaining a court determination that the creditor is entitled to the collateral; following such a determination the creditor may repossess by self-help, provided there is no breach of the peace. Wis. Stat. Ann. §§ 425.203–.206. The effect of this Act, as evidenced by field studies, is analyzed in Whitford and Laufer, The Impact of Denying Self–Help Repossession of Automobiles: A Case Study of the Wisconsin Consumer Act, 1975 Wis.L.Rev. 607. The authors conclude that fears that the Act would cripple consumer finance are largely unfounded. While the cost of repossessions rose significantly and the volume of repossessions dropped, the principal impact on credit seemed to be confined to requiring larger down payments in the sale of used cars. Id. at 654.

SECTION 2. DISPOSITIONS OF COLLATERAL; DEFICIENCY AND SURPLUS; CONSEQUENCES OF NONCOMPLIANCE

INTRODUCTORY NOTE

Taking possession of collateral following a debtor's default only begins the process of enforcing a security interest in collateral. A secured party in possession of tangible collateral following a default typically wishes to sell the collateral and then to apply the net proceeds of the sale to the secured obligation. If the proceeds are insufficient to satisfy the secured obligation, the secured party may wish to pursue the debtor to collect the remaining, unsecured portion of the debt (the "deficiency"). If a disposition yields proceeds sufficient to satisfy the secured obligation, the secured party will pay over any excess funds (the "surplus") to the debtor (or, in some circumstances, to junior claimants).

UCC 9–610 through UCC 9–618 regulate dispositions of collateral after default. These sections deal with disposition itself (UCC 9–610), notification of a disposition (UCC 9–611 through UCC 9–614), application of the proceeds of a disposition (UCC 9–615), calculation and explanation of a surplus or a deficiency claim (UCC 9–615 and UCC 9–616), rights that a disposition transfers to a transferee of the collateral (UCC 9–617), and certain rights and duties of secondary obligors (UCC 9–618).

When a secured party opts to "sell, lease, license, or otherwise dispose of . . . collateral" under UCC 9–610, "[e]very aspect of . . . [the] disposition, including the method, manner, time, place, and other terms, must be commercially reasonable." UCC 9–610(a), (b). In addition, subject to narrow exceptions, a secured party is required to give a debtor, a secondary obligor (such as a guarantor), and certain other persons "a reasonable authenticated notification of disposition." UCC 9–611. This Section of the book deals with the strict, albeit (with a few exceptions) general, standards for dispositions of collateral after default. It also considers how the secured party's failure to comply with Part 6 when disposing of collateral affects the rights of the secured party and the debtor. See UCC 9–625 through UCC 9–627.

Before continuing on to the Problems, cases, and Notes that follow, please read carefully UCC 9–610 through UCC 9–618 and UCC 9–625 through UCC 9–627.

Problem 9.2.1. Schmelli Services, Inc., is an Arkansas-based personnel agency that provides temporary office employees to businesses. It has offices in twenty-four cities in several eastern and southeastern states. Schmelli owes your client, Atlanta Industrial Bank (AIB), approximately $4,500,000 under a **line of credit** facility, secured by a perfected, first priority security interest in Schmelli's accounts receivable and a first priority real property mortgage on Schmelli's home office building (located in Little Rock, Arkansas). The security agreement covering the accounts provides that the collateral secures not only Schmelli's $6,000,000 note executed pursuant to the line of credit facility, but also "all other obligations of Borrower to Bank now existing or hereafter incurred, whether (i) contingent or noncontingent, (ii) liquidated or unliquidated, (iii) disputed or undisputed, (iv) contemplated or uncontemplated, or (v) of the same or different type as the indebtedness evidenced by the Note."

Schmelli also owes AIB about $2,500,000, secured by a perfected, first priority security interest in a Learjet Model 35A–596. (Schmelli's flamboyant CEO, Telli Schmelli, uses the Learjet to fly from city to city while making monthly visits to each office.) There are about 1,500 hours on the airframe and engines, and Schmelli has maintained the aircraft in accordance with applicable Federal Aviation Administration regulations. The security agreement covering the Learjet provides that it secures the purchase-money loan (originally, $3,300,000) and also other obligations, using language identical to that in the line of credit security agreement, quoted above. Each security agreement provides that it is "governed by the law of the State of Georgia."

Schmelli is in default under both the line of credit facility and the aircraft loan. AIB has not yet "pulled the plug" on Schmelli; it continues to make discretionary advances against Schmelli's accounts receivable. However, yesterday a repo team retained by AIB peacefully took possession of the Learjet at the Pine Bluff, Arkansas, airport. AIB stored the aircraft with an aircraft dealer located at that airport.

The loan officer assigned to Schmelli wants to "turn the Learjet into cash as soon as possible." The officer, who has little experience with repossessions and enforcement, has asked you for advice on how to proceed.

(a) Which state's law governs a disposition of the Learjet by AIB? See UCC 1–301 [F1–105]; UCC 9–301; Note (12) on Commercially Reasonable Dispositions and Reasonable Notification, infra.

(b) Do you recommend a "public" or "private" disposition of the aircraft? What considerations bear on what approach to take? See Notes on Commercially Reasonable Dispositions and Reasonable Notification, infra. Will your recommendation be affected by whether AIB expects to sell the aircraft to a third person or expects (at least in the first instance) to buy the aircraft itself? See UCC 9–610 & Comment 7; UCC 9–626(a)(5); UCC 9–615(f); Vornado PS v. Primestone Investment Partners, infra; Note (2) on Commercially Reasonable Dispositions and Reasonable Notification, infra. Consider also that a secured party who buys at its own disposition normally pays itself for the collateral by "bidding in" its claim against the debtor, i.e., by giving the debtor credit against the obligation secured by the collateral.

(c) After settling on a general approach, what specific steps will you recommend? Assume, alternatively, that (i) Schmelli is very cooperative, being grateful for the continued financing, and (ii) shortly after the repossession AIB cut off Schmelli's financing, and now Schmelli and AIB are "not on speaking terms." (Telli Schmelli's ride in a crowded bus from Pine Bluff to Little Rock following the "surprise" repossession did not help matters!) You might begin your analysis with UCC 9–610(b) and UCC 9–611(b).

(d) Would you change any of your recommendations if AIB thinks Schmelli is extremely likely to contest AIB's deficiency claim by challenging AIB's compliance with Article 9? Would you consider taking any additional steps? See UCC 9–601(a), (f); UCC 9–627(c); Note (1) on Commercially Reasonable Dispositions and Reasonable Notification, infra.

(e) What provisions might the security agreement have included that would have made your advice, at the disposition stage, more definite and easier to give? See UCC 9–603; Note (5) on Commercially Reasonable Dispositions and Reasonable Notification, infra.

(f) Suppose that, three weeks after the repossession, while en route from Pine Bluff to Atlanta, the Learjet crashed and was destroyed. The loan officer has just told you that the insurer under Schmelli's policy (AIB is the loss payee on the policy) has denied AIB's claim for loss because the policy does not cover loss or damage incurred when the Learjet is flown by anyone other than an agent or employee of Schmelli. Are there any *additional* steps that you *wish* you had recommended in part (c) above? See UCC 9–603; UCC 9–207(a) & (b)(2); Note (13) on Commercially Reasonable Dispositions and Reasonable Notification, infra.

(g) Assume that the Learjet did not crash. AIB disposed of the Learjet at a public sale to an unrelated third person for $1,500,000 (net of expenses and attorney's fees) and sued Schmelli for a deficiency of $1,000,000. Schmelli's answer to the complaint asserted that AIB is not entitled to a recovery because (i) the notification of the sale failed to state that Schmelli is entitled to an accounting of the unpaid indebtedness, and (ii) a public disposition of a Learjet is not commercially reasonable. There is no doubt that the notification was as asserted. (The inexperienced loan officer prepared the notification based on a form that AIB had used under Former Article 9.) You think it is highly likely that Schmelli can establish the second assertion, as well, based on advice from several potential expert witnesses that (i) expensive aircraft are almost never sold at auctions and (ii) in a private, retail sale the Learjet would have brought between $2,500,000 and $3,000,000. What options are available to AIB? Which option would you recommend? See UCC 9–615(d); UCC 9–626(a); UCC 9–613(1)(D), (2); UCC 9–610(b); UCC 9–627(a); General Electric Capital Corp. v. Stelmach Construction Co., infra.

Problem 9.2.2. In the setting of the Prototype on automobile financing, Lee Abel purchased a new Chevrolet and signed the Instalment Sales Contract (Form 3.6, supra). As in the Prototype, Main Motors assigned the contract to Firstbank. Abel failed to make several payments required by the contract. After Firstbank properly repossessed the Chevrolet, Main paid Firstbank all amounts due under Abel's contract and received an assignment of the contract from Firstbank. See the Assignment and Repurchase Agreement (Form 3.5, supra). By virtue of its payment, Main acquired Firstbank's rights and duties as a secured party. See UCC 9–618. Main sold the Chevrolet to a retail customer in a commercially reasonable manner. However, Main inadvertently neglected to notify Abel before the sale.

Immediately after the sale, Main sues Abel in Philadelphia for $4,450.75, representing the unpaid time balance ($10,396.25) plus costs of repossession and sale ($400.00), less finance charge rebate ($1,345.50) and proceeds of the foreclosure sale ($5,000.00).

(a) What result? Assume that the Pennsylvania Supreme Court had applied the "rebuttable presumption" rule to both consumer and non-consumer transactions under Former Article 9. See UCC 9–611(b), (c); UCC 9–616; UCC 9–625; UCC 9–626; Form 3.6, supra; Notes (8) and (10) on Commercially Reasonable Dispositions and Reasonable Notification, infra.

(b) Assume instead that the Pennsylvania Supreme Court had applied the "absolute bar" rule to both consumer and non-consumer transactions under Former Article 9. What result?

(c) What result in part (a) if Main had notified Abel before the sale? See UCC 9–616; UCC 9–625; UCC 9–628.

General Electric Capital Corp. v. Stelmach Construction Co.*

United States District Court, District of Kansas, 2001.
2001 WL 969052.

■ MURGUIA, DISTRICT JUDGE.

This is an action brought by a creditor to recover a deficiency judgment against two debtors after the repossession and sale of collateral securing the loan at issue. Plaintiff General Electric Capital Corporation ("GECC") is the creditor in this action and defendants Stelmach Construction Company and Christopher S. Stelmach are the debtors. . . .

[P]ending before the court is plaintiff GECC's motion for summary judgment on damages. Plaintiff seeks to recover the full amount of its deficiency, including interest, attorneys' fees, and costs against defendant Stelmach Construction Company on a promissory note and against defendant Christopher S. Stelmach on his personal guaranty. As set forth in detail below, plaintiff's motion for summary judgment is granted.

I. Facts

Breach of Agreements

Plaintiff and defendant Stelmach Construction entered into a promissory note, a master security agreement, and several related agreements (the "Agreements") on or about June 30, 1998. Defendant Stelmach Construction signed the Agreements. Pursuant to the Agreements, defendant Stelmach Construction agreed to repay to plaintiff the principal sum of $ 400,000.00, plus interest at 9.32% in forty-two consecutive monthly installments to begin August 25, 1998. The Agreements also provide for interest at the rate of 18% per annum upon default and a 5% late payment charge on delinquent payments. Also, on or about June 30, 1998, defendant Christopher Stelmach

---

*   [The court's citations are to the applicable pre–1972 version of the UCC.]

executed an individual guaranty of the amount loaned to defendant Stelmach Construction.

As the term of the note progressed, Stelmach Construction failed to make the required principal and interest payments due under the Agreements. Accordingly, plaintiff and defendant Stelmach Construction entered into a modification agreement, thereby modifying the terms of payment. Defendant Stelmach Construction executed the modification agreement. Although defendants waived notice, presentment, and other defenses in the Agreements and the guaranty, on April 7 and June 9, 1999, plaintiff sent both defendants notices of default with respect to payments due by defendant Stelmach Construction.

Subsequently, on or about June 24, 1999, plaintiff and defendants entered into a voluntary surrender agreement, wherein defendant Stelmach Construction retained all of its rights as a debtor, including but not limited to the right to challenge the commercial reasonableness of the sale of the collateral.

Following plaintiff's motion for summary judgment on liability, on August 31, 2000 the court entered an order finding defendants breached the Agreements entered into between the parties and that amounts are due and owing by defendants to plaintiff as a result of such breach.

• Sale of Collateral

Pursuant to a voluntary surrender agreement, defendants voluntarily surrendered the collateral with the understanding that plaintiff would sell it. Plaintiff notified defendants that the sale of the collateral would occur on or after August 6, 1999.

Plaintiff hired Elcor, Inc to repossess, appraise and sell the collateral. Elcor inspected and evaluated the condition of each piece, and prepared a condition report and approximate value for each piece of equipment. When analyzing the collateral piece by piece, Elcor's approximate values totaled $ 258,200.00. In contrast, defendants present the report of Kenneth Fowler—their designated expert in the area of construction appraisal—who opines that the value of the collateral as of August 6, 1999 was $ 457,400.[**]

Plaintiff advertised the sale through publications in two nationally recognized trade magazines, and on two internet sites known by the trade. The advertisements gave a complete description of the make, model, and year of each piece of collateral, and identified where the collateral could be viewed. None of the advertisement specified whether the collateral would be sold by the lot or individually. GECC also advertised the sale of collateral through mass mailing, targeting potential purchasers.

The collateral was stored in the Lee's Summit, Missouri area during the advertisement period and was available for inspection by interested bidders. Plaintiff received six (6) bids for the collateral from third party bidders. All

---

**   [In an omitted part of this opinion, the court denied plaintiff's motion in limine and admitted the expert testimony offered by defendant.]

of the bids were made for the entire lot. The bids ranged in price from $ 225,000.00 to $ 311,000.00.

Plaintiff accepted the highest bid, selling the collateral for $ 311,000.00, with costs to plaintiff of $ 6,800.00 for obtaining possession of the collateral, evaluating the collateral and properly preparing the collateral for sale, and costs of $ 31,100.00 for commission expenses with respect to the sale. When the collateral was sold on August 24, 1999, the principal amount due by defendants was $ 389,710.68. Interest and delinquency charges at that time totaled $ 31,355.56. Additional interest accrued after August 24, 1999 at the contract rate of $ 54.91 per diem. Pursuant to the terms of the Agreements, defendants agreed to pay plaintiff's attorneys fees and costs incurred in collecting under the Agreements.

As of August 24, 1999 (the sale date of the collateral), the amount due and owing to plaintiff, after crediting all payments made and the proceeds from the sale of collateral, totaled:

- Remaining principal balance after sale of collateral ($ 389,710.68 (principal) less $ 311,000.00 (proceeds from sale of collateral)) $ 78,710.68
- Interest and delinquency charges (Additional interest accrued after August 24, 1999 at the contract rate of $ 54.91 per diem.) $ 31,355.56
- Costs to repossess/recondition collateral $ 6,800.00
- Commission expenses on sale $ 31,100.00
- Amount due and owing by defendants (attorneys' fees obligations not included) $ 147,966.24

The parties dispute the total amount due by defendants to plaintiff as a result of the breach. Plaintiff asserts the sale of the collateral was conducted in accordance with the Agreements between the parties and in accordance with Article 9 of the Uniform Commercial Code. Defendants, however, argue that the sale of collateral conducted by plaintiff was not commercially reasonable.

. . .

III. Motion for Summary Judgment

• Summary Judgment Standard

Summary judgment is appropriate if the moving party demonstrates that there is "no genuine issue as to any material fact" and that it is "entitled to a judgment as a matter of law." Fed. R. Civ. P. 56(c). In applying this standard, the court views the evidence and all reasonable inferences therefrom in the light most favorable to the nonmoving party.

• Commercially Reasonable

As liability in this case has been resolved, the issue that remains is whether the sale of the collateral securing the loan to defendants was conducted in a commercially reasonable manner. Determination of whether a sale has been held in a commercially reasonable manner is a question of fact to be determined by the trier of fact. Westgate State Bank v. Clark, 231 Kan. 81, 91, 642 P.2d 961, 969 (1982).

Plaintiff, as the secured creditor, has the burden to establish that the sale of the collateral at issue was conducted in a commercially reasonable manner. Id. ("in an action for a deficiency judgment, the secured creditor has the burden of proof to show that the disposition or sale of the collateral was made in a commercially reasonable manner"). Accordingly, to prevail on its summary judgment motion, plaintiff must set forth evidence demonstrating an absence of a genuine issue of material fact and entitlement to judgment as a matter of law in its favor in the amount of $ 147,966.24, for principal and interest through August 24, 1999, plus pre-judgment and post-judgment interest accruing after that time at a per diem rate of $ 54.91, plus reasonable attorneys fees and costs. Celotex, 477 U.S. at 331. Plaintiff must support its motion with uncontroverted evidence which would entitle it to a directed verdict at trial. Id.

The Kansas Uniform Commercial Code (UCC) provides that "every aspect of the disposition [of collateral] including the method, manner, time, place and terms must be commercially reasonable." Kan. Stat. Ann. § 84–9–504(3) (1996) [cf. UCC 9–610(b)]. When determining whether the sale of collateral was conducted in a commercially reasonable manner, "the trial court should consider all of the relevant factors together as part of a single transaction." Westgate, 231 Kan. at 91, 642 P.2d at 969. In Westgate, the Kansas Supreme Court identified nine factors relevant to determining whether a sale has been conducted in a commercially reasonable manner, including: (1) the duty to clean, fix up, and paint the collateral; (2) public or private disposition; (3) wholesale or retail disposition; (4) disposition by unit or in parcels; (5) the duty to publicize the sale; (6) length of time collateral held prior to sale; (7) duty to give notice of the sale to the debtor and competing secured parties; (8) the actual price received at the sale; and (9) other methods, including the number of bids received and the method employed in soliciting bids, the time and place of the sale. This list of factors is not exclusive and a court should consider other factors, where relevant in a particular case.

• Proper Notice

Defendants assert three separate arguments contending that the sale was not conducted in a commercially reasonable manner. First, defendants contend plaintiff did not provide proper notice of the sale. Prior to a sale or other disposition of repossessed collateral, a secured creditor is required to give the debtor notice of any proposed disposition. Kan. Stat. Ann. § 84–9–504(3) (1996) [UCC 9–611]. Generally, it is the secured party's decision whether to dispose of the collateral by public or private sale. See id. § 84–9–504(3) ("disposition of the collateral may be by public or private proceedings . . .") [cf. UCC 9–610(b)]. Under Kansas law, a public sale is "a sale by auction." Id. § 84–2–706, official UCC Comment, 4. In contrast, a private sale "may be effected by solicitation and negotiation conducted either directly or through a broker." Id.

The parties do not seem to dispute that the sale of the collateral here was by private sale, as it was not conducted by auction. Instead, defendants contend plaintiff did not properly notice the private sale. Pursuant to the Kansas UCC, any notice of sale must *state the time and place of any public sale or the time after which any private sale* or other intended disposition of the collateral will take place. Id. § 84–9–504(3) [cf. UCC 9–613(1)(E)].

The court finds plaintiff's notice of the private sale was sufficient under the Kansas UCC. The uncontroverted facts demonstrate that plaintiff notified defendants that the sale of the collateral would occur on or after August 6, 1999. The heading of plaintiff's notice indicated "NOTICE OF PRIVATE SALE OF COLLATERAL UNDER SECTION 9–504 OF THE UNIFORM COMMERCIAL CODE." The text of the notice provided "NOTICE is hereby given that on or after August 6, 1999, General Electric Capital Corporation ("GECC") will sell at a public or private sale the following property". . . the notice then listed each item of property to be sold.

Although it is clear under Kansas law that the notice of a public sale and subsequent holding of a private sale does not satisfy the statutory requirement of notice, Topeka Datsun Motor Co. v. Stratton, 12 Kan. App. 2d 95, 102, 736 P.2d 82, 88 (1987), defendants have not cited any precedent to the court demonstrating that the notice here is noncompliant. That is, defendants have not demonstrated that when a private sale is held following a notice: (1) including both public and private sale language, (2) not containing any indication that a public sale will take place at a specified time and place (as required for notice of a public sale), and (3) indicating the date after which a sale will take place (as required for notice of a private sale), that such sale is commercially unreasonable. Further, one of the primary reasons for the notice requirement is to allow the interest holder the opportunity to redeem the security by paying off the debt. Kan. Stat. Ann. § 84–9–506 [cf. UCC 9–623]. Here, the court finds the notice provided by plaintiff allowed defendants this opportunity, as the defendants were notified that the sale of the collateral would take place "on or after August 6, 1999." Accordingly, the court finds plaintiff's notice is compliant with the Kansas UCC and therefore, such notice does not render the sale of the collateral commercially unreasonable.

• Piecemeal Sale

Second, defendants contend that, in order for the sale to have been commercially reasonable, the collateral should have been disposed of on a piecemeal basis, rather than in bulk. Specifically, defendants argue the plaintiff's advertisements for the collateral implied that the collateral was offered only in bulk.

As noted above, the Kansas UCC allows that the "sale or other disposition [of repossessed collateral] may be as a unit or in parcels . . ." [cf. UCC 9–610(b)]. However, "the linchpin remains commercial reasonableness." Id. § 84–9–504, 1996 Kansas Comment, subsection (3). Accordingly, "the secured party may have a duty to dispose of collateral on a piecemeal basis if such a method would generate a higher price."

Reviewing plaintiff's advertisements, the court does not find that a reasonable fact finder could conclude that potential bidders were misled into believing that the collateral was available only as a lot, rather than individually. Plaintiff's advertisements for the sale of the collateral list each item of collateral and indicate that they are "accepting bids." The advertisements do not indicate the collateral may be purchased *only* in its entirety.

Defendants emphasize that each of the six bids received for the collateral was for the entire lot, rather than for a single item. However, an examination of the bids reveals that although each bidder did seek to purchase the entire lot, they did not use identical language, as may have been done where the advertisements limited purchase to the "entire lot." For example, the bidders placed bids on "your schedule of equipment," "entire package of equipment (16 pieces)," the "entire lot," the "total package," and the "package of equipment."

Moreover, although defendants' expert report places the fair market value of the collateral as a whole at $ 457,400, compared to the $ 311,000 received for the collateral by plaintiff, the expert did not opine that selling the collateral individually, rather than in bulk, would have been more likely to generate the fair market value of the collateral.

Accordingly, the court finds the plaintiff's advertisements and the plaintiff's acceptance of one of six bids for the entire lot, did not render the sale commercially unreasonable.

• Price Received for Collateral at Sale

Finally, defendants contend that the price received for the collateral indicates the sale was commercially unreasonable. Specifically, defendants argue the difference between defendants' expert's assessment of the fair market value of the collateral ($ 457,400) and the price plaintiff obtained from the sale ($ 311,000) demonstrates the commercial unreasonableness of the sale. That is, defendants argue the $ 146,400 difference makes the sale presumptively commercially unreasonable.

Although the court must examine the price obtained for the collateral in determining the commercial reasonableness of a sale, "the fact that a better price could have been obtained by a sale at a different time or in a different method from that selected by the secured party is not of itself sufficient to establish that the sale was not made in a commercially reasonable manner." Id. § 84–9–507(2) [cf. UCC 9–627(a)]. "If the secured party either sells the collateral in the usual manner in any recognized market therefor or if he sells at the price current in such market at the time of his sale or if he has otherwise sold in conformity with reasonable commercial practices among dealers in the type of property sold he has sold in a commercially reasonable manner." Id. [UCC 9–627(b)].

Defendants do not argue that the collateral was not sold in a recognized market for the equipment or that the collateral was not sold in the usual manner for the sale of such equipment. Nor do defendants contend that plaintiff did not follow reasonable commercial practices among dealers in the type of equipment sold when selling the collateral. Instead, defendants contend the price obtained for the collateral was not the current price in the market at the time of the sale.

"Courts will frown at a sale which yields a shockingly low price unless the secured creditor can offer a valid explanation . . . ." Id. § 84–9–504, 1996 Kansas Comment, subsection (3). Here, plaintiff's agent set forth a valuation of the collateral at the time of repossession of $ 258,200. In contrast, defendants' expert valued the collateral at the time of the sale at $ 457,400. Plaintiff obtained a price of $ 311,000 upon sale of the collateral. The difference between the price obtained and the presumptively correct valuation of the collateral by defendants' expert is large. However, as noted in the Kansas UCC and in Kansas case law, simply because a higher price could have been obtained does not establish a sale was not commercially reasonable. As noted herein, the court finds that each of the remaining factors regarding commercial reasonableness weigh in favor of plaintiff. Therefore, even though a low price was obtained from the sale, because the court has found all procedures regarding the sale of the collateral were handled in line with section 84–9–504 of the Kansas UCC, the court finds the low price, on its own, does not render the sale of the collateral commercially unreasonable. See id. § 84–9–504, 1996 Kansas Comment, subsection (3) ("However, if a low price is obtained in a sale for which all procedures were handles in line with this subsection [Kan. Stat. Ann. § 84–9–504], the creditor has a much stronger argument that the sale should not be considered commercially unreasonable.") [cf. UCC 9–627, Comment 2 ("While not itself sufficient to establish a violation of this Part, a low price suggests that a court should scrutinize carefully all aspects of a disposition to ensure that each aspect was commercially reasonable.")].

· Remaining Factors

Plaintiff argues that, in addition to the three factors discussed above, the five additional relevant factors set forth in *Westgate* demonstrate the commercial reasonableness of the sale of the collateral. First, plaintiff contends it satisfied its duty to prepare the collateral for sale by hiring Elcor, Inc. to assess, prepare and clean each piece of collateral prior to the sale. Plaintiff invested $ 6,800 preparing the collateral in order to maximize the ultimate sale price. Second, plaintiff contends it chose the method of disposition—a private sale—most likely to result in a higher return. See Westgate, 231 Kan. at 92, 642 P.2d at 970 (noting that a private sale should be used whenever such a disposition is likely to result in a higher return). Third, plaintiff advertised the sale in multiple national trade publications and on several internet sites commonly used by the construction industry. Plaintiff also conducted direct mail solicitations all over the country to likely purchasers. Plaintiff made the collateral available for inspection prior to any sale. Fourth, plaintiff held the collateral for approximately one month prior to agreeing to a sales price. And fifth, plaintiff received six bids from third party bidders prior to accepting the highest bid.

Defendants do not dispute the facts set forth by plaintiff supporting these five factors. Accordingly, the court finds plaintiff has set forth evidence sufficient to establish no genuine issue of material fact exists as to these five factors.

· Conclusion

Accordingly, given the above analysis, the court finds plaintiff has met its burden to establish entitlement to judgment as a matter of law on its damages claim. That is, plaintiff has met its burden to establish the commercial reasonableness of the sale of the collateral at issue. Therefore, plaintiff's motion for summary judgment on damages is granted. Plaintiff is granted judgment in the amount of $ 147,966.24, for principal and interest through August 24, 1999, plus pre-judgment and post-judgment interest accruing after that time at a per diem rate of $ 54.91, plus reasonable attorneys' fees and costs in an amount to be approved by the court.

. . .

Vornado PS, LLC v. Primestone Investment Partners, L.P.

Court of Chancery of Delaware, 2002.
821 A. 2d 296.

■ LAMB, VICE CHANCELLOR.

I.

This action arises out of two loans advanced to the defendant, a Delaware limited partnership engaged in the business of commercial real estate development, by the plaintiff, a Delaware limited liability company also engaged in the business of commercial real estate development. The loans were secured by units in a limited partnership. The borrower eventually defaulted on the loans, and the lender sought to dispose of the units in an open outcry auction. After a significant marketing process by the lender's financial advisor, the lender made the only bid at the auction and purchased the units.

The lender brought this action and now moves for summary judgment seeking a judicial determination that it is entitled to enforcement of its loans. The lender also seeks a declaration that its foreclosure auction was conducted in a commercially reasonable manner, and that it was the winner of the auction. The borrower opposes the summary judgment motion and also has counterclaimed on a variety of theories, including breach of contract, fraud, tortious interference, and breach of fiduciary duties.

. . .

II.

A. *The Units*

Primestone Investment Partners L.P. ("Primestone") is indebted to Vornado PS, L.L.C. for two loans: (1) a $62,000,000 loan made by Vornado on September 26, 2000 (the "Vornado Loan") and (2) a $40,000,000 loan originally made by Prudential Securities Corporation in 1997 (the

"Prudential Loan"). To secure this debt, Primestone pledged 7,944,893 limited partnership units (the "Units") of Prime Group Realty, L.P. ("PGRLP"). . . .

. . .

E. *Vornado's Purchase Of The Prudential Loan*

[Vornado and Prudential entered into an Intercreditor Agreement on September 26, 2000 to determine their respective rights in the Loans.] Under the Intercreditor Agreement, Vornado was required to obtain the consent of Prudential or purchase the Prudential Loan before enforcing its rights as a secured creditor. On October 31, 2001, after discussions with Prudential, Vornado purchased the Prudential Loan for the net amount then due, $37,978,479.97. The purchase of the Prudential Loan by Vornado terminated the Intercreditor Agreement.

. . .

H. *The Foreclosure Sale*

When Primestone failed to pay the two Loans, Vornado sought to sell the pledged Units in PGRLP in a commercially reasonable manner pursuant to Article 9 of New York's Uniform Commercial Code. It hired Goldman, Sachs & Co., a prominent investment banking firm, to assist it in developing a marketing process and identifying potential purchasers of the Units. Because the Units were not subject to an established trading market, Vornado believed Section 9–610(c) of the New York Uniform Commercial Code prohibited Vornado from buying the Units unless they were sold in a public sale. Vornado wanted an opportunity to purchase the Units and felt it might be the most willing and able potential purchaser of the Units. As a result, Vornado decided that Goldman Sachs's efforts to market the Units would culminate in a public auction.

On October 31, 2001, Vornado provided notice to Primestone and the Guarantors that it intended to sell the Units at a public auction scheduled for 4 p.m. on November 20, 2001. A licensed auctioneer was retained. Advertisements marketing the foreclosure sale were published in the *New York Times* on November 6 and 13, and in the *Chicago Tribune* on November 7.

In conjunction with Goldman Sachs's marketing efforts, Vornado sought assistance from Primestone and PGE to make the Units more marketable. As discussed above, no more than 9.9% of the Units may be converted into PGE common stock without the consent of the PGE Board. Vornado had obtained the Board's consent to convert all the Units into shares in a Consent and Agreement dated September 26, 2000 (the "9.9% Waiver"). [If such consent were given and all of the Units were converted, the Units would amount to 30.1% of PGE's common stock.] On October 31, 2001, Vornado wrote to Reschke [the chairman of PGE] to request that the PGE Board allow Vornado to assign the 9.9% Waiver to third parties. [This would enable a person who acquired the Units at a foreclosure disposition to convert all of them into stock.] Vornado also asked the PGE Board to release certain entities from certain standstill agreements with PGE so that they could acquire the Units.[*] By a letter dated November 7, 2001, PGE rejected both of these requests.

With the assistance of Vornado's counsel, Goldman Sachs assembled an Information Memorandum regarding PGRLP and the Units. The Information Memorandum only provided publicly available information to potential purchasers. This is due primarily to the fact that Vornado, a creditor, did not have access to much of PGE's or PGRLP's confidential information. The Information Memorandum stated that it "does not purport to be all-inclusive or to contain all of the information that prospective purchasers may desire." . . . Vornado, however, did possess some material non-public information regarding PGE and PGRLP. The Bidding Agreement, attached as Appendix A to the Information Memorandum, explicitly required potential bidders to acknowledge that, "Vornado may have received non-public information from PGE or its affiliates that has not been disclosed to the Bidder and which may be material to the Units and Shares."

In early November, Vornado and Goldman Sachs compiled a list of, and contacted, 51 potential purchasers, including public companies, opportunity funds, private investors, pension funds and advisors (including PGE and the Private Prime Parties).[**] An additional 8 potential purchasers were contacted either through referrals or by unsolicited calls from those bidders. Vornado also requested Primestone to provide a list of potential purchasers, but no response was ever received. Ultimately, copies of the Information Memorandum were sent to 33 potential purchasers, including PGE and the Private Prime Parties. . . .

Some of the potential purchasers of the Units contacted by Goldman Sachs stated that they were not interested because of the unavailability of confidential information. For example, Mark Reinisch of Klaff Realty, "explained that they are not interested in participating in the auction because they do not have access to private information." Similarly, Nick Rizzo of Westbrook Partners L.L.C. "did not feel comfortable with only having public information. He explained that they will not be participating in the auction."

. . .

In a November 8, 2001 letter to Vornado, Primestone objected to Vornado's auction process as "commercially unreasonable." It proposed an additional nine-week marketing process (including "management road shows" and property tours), which would culminate in a multi-round "private auction." Primestone was also concerned that the Units, which could amount to over a 31% stake in PGE, were not being marketed as a control block.

---

*   [In this context, a standstill agreement is an agreement in which a person who might otherwise acquire control of a corporation agrees to limit its holdings of the corporation's stock.]

** [Primetime and the five affiliates of Primetime that guaranteed the loans are the "Private Prime Parties."]

Primestone filed for bankruptcy on November 19, and Vornado was forced to cancel the foreclosure sale scheduled for the next day. Primestone's bankruptcy filing was subsequently dismissed as having been filed in bad faith, and Vornado rescheduled the auction for January 25, 2002. Goldman Sachs notified potential purchasers of the new date. Four of these potential purchasers, who had not been previously contacted by Goldman Sachs, were either referred to Goldman Sachs by entities it had previously contacted or were entities who contacted Goldman Sachs on an unsolicited basis. Two potential purchasers did not wish to bid any longer. Based on this information, beginning on or about December 22, Goldman Sachs distributed copies of the updated Information Memorandum to 33 potential purchasers . . .

The January 25 auction was canceled when Primestone obtained a stay pending appeal of the bankruptcy dismissal to the United States District Court. After that court affirmed the dismissal of the petition and vacated the stay, Vornado rescheduled the foreclosure sale for February 25, 2002. Beginning on or about February 11, 2002, Goldman Sachs contacted the potential purchasers to notify them that the foreclosure sale had again been rescheduled. . . . Vornado also retained its auctioneer again and published advertisements regarding the rescheduled auction in the *New York Times* and *Chicago Tribune* on February 14, 2002. Plans for the foreclosure were again canceled when the United States Court of Appeals granted a stay pending appeal on February 15.

On March 28, 2002, PGE filed a 10-K report with the Securities and Exchange Commission. That filing disclosed that Ernst & Young, PGE's auditor, included a "going concern" reservation in their audit report on PGE's financial statements based on short-term liquidity problems and the ability of PGE's Series A Preferred stockholders to require PGE to redeem the shares for $40 million. The audit report also disclosed that PGE's largest tenant was Arthur Anderson and that its failure to continue to pay rent would have an adverse effect on PGE. As a result of the 10-K filing, PGE's stock price fell significantly. On March 28, the stock closed at $7.66, down $1.49 from the previous day's close. On April 1, the stock fell to $4.05 in intraday trading, setting a new all-time low for the company.

On April 8, a group of stockholders wrote an open letter to the PGE Board calling for Reschke's resignation. Reschke resigned his post as chairman of PGE (although he remains a trustee), and Richard Curto resigned as PGE's chief executive officer. On April 12, PGE announced that it was cutting 13% of its workforce and that it was not paying dividends to its preferred stockholders. Because of this news, trading of PGE's shares was halted on the morning of April 12.

On April 12, the Court of Appeals conditioned the stay pending appeal on the posting of a $15 million bond by the end of business on April 17. Primestone did not post the bond and the stay was automatically lifted. In preparation for the possibility that the stay might be lifted, Goldman Sachs updated its Information Memorandum based on then-current publicly available information. Vornado, in consultation with Goldman Sachs, decided that if Primestone's stay was lifted on April 17, rescheduling the foreclosure sale for April 30, 2002 would provide sufficient time to remarket the Units.

On April 18, 2002, Vornado gave notice to Primestone and the Guarantors that the foreclosure sale would be held on April 30. Newspaper advertisements were again placed in the *New York Times* and the *Chicago Tribune* on April 22. A licensed auctioneer was again retained to conduct the auction. Goldman Sachs again approached all the potential purchasers it had contacted in February to notify them that the foreclosure auction had been rescheduled for 4 p.m. on April 30, 2002. Five additional potential purchasers were contacted, and Goldman Sachs ultimately distributed an updated Information Memorandum to 42 potential purchasers (including PGE and the Private Prime Parties).

By April 30, three prospective purchasers in addition to Vornado had expressed interest in bidding at the auction: (1) the Blackstone Group, (2) Friedman Billings & Ramsely ("FBR"), and (3) Cadim. On April 30, representatives of these entities attended the foreclosure sale at the offices of Sullivan & Cromwell.

The terms of the auction set forth in the final Information Memorandum provided that the sale to the winning bidder would be settled at a time selected by the purchaser up to 30 days after the auction. Because of the resulting exposure to the purchaser's credit, the terms required bidders to qualify by submitting a financing commitment or other satisfactory evidence of their ability to complete the purchase. Bidders were also required to sign a bidding agreement.

Primestone also expressed interest in bidding for the Units. At the auction, Reschke was asked to provide evidence of Primestone's financial ability to purchase the Units. Reschke produced a photocopy of [a memorandum of understanding with a third party,] which he claimed gave Primestone a firm commitment of $105 million . . . . Vornado notified Reschke that the [memorandum] was not a firm financing commitment and that Primestone, therefore, was not qualified to bid.

The auctioneer then read a description of the Units and began the auction. After he failed to attract any other bids, Vornado opened the bidding at $8.35 per Unit, which was the closing price of PGE's shares on the day of the foreclosure sale. No further bids were made. The Units were thus sold to Vornado for an aggregate price of $66,339,856.55.

I. *The Deficiency*

Primestone was indebted to Vornado on April 30, 2002 for $116,111,323. The indebtedness on the Vornado Loan included the $62,000,000 principal, an exit fee of $2,102,240 and accrued interest at an annual rate of 16% before maturity and 20% after maturity. All overdue amounts, including principal, interest, fees and reimbursable expenses, are subject to the 20% interest rate when an Event of Default has occurred. The Vornado Loan Agreement also requires Primestone to pay "all out-of-pocket costs and expenses incurred in connection with the enforcement or preservation of any rights under this Agreement" and related agreements. n19 As of April 30, Vornado had spent $2,499,573 in enforcing its rights under the Vornado Loan Agreement. Indebtedness on the Vornado Loan was reduced by $1,040,873 previously received pursuant to Vornado's security interest.

Primestone's indebtedness on the Prudential Loan includes the unpaid principal (net of cash received by Prudential pursuant to its security interest), late fees and accrued interest at the LIBOR rate plus 1.5% until maturity and LIBOR plus 7.5% after maturity. The result is remaining indebtedness under the Prudential Loan to Vornado by Primestone in the amount of $40,848,356. Thus after including the proceeds from the foreclosure sale, Primestone still remains indebted to Vornado for the net amount of $49,771,467.

III.

Vornado commenced this action on November 19, 2001.

. . .

After the stay pending appeal terminated on April 17, 2002, Primestone again tried to pursue its motion for a preliminary injunction on the ground that Vornado was not conducting a commercially reasonable foreclosure. When this court indicated that Primestone would have to post a substantial bond as a condition of any grant of injunction, Primestone chose to withdraw its motion for a preliminary injunction. Primestone subsequently filed an amended counterclaim on August 19, 2002.

Vornado currently seeks a judicial determination that it is entitled to enforce the terms of its loan agreements. Vornado also seeks a declaration that its foreclosure auction was conducted in a commercially reasonably manner, and that it was the winner of the auction. Finally, Vornado seeks summary judgment on all 14 of Primestone's counterclaims.

. . .

V.

A. *Vornado Is Entitled To The Enforcement Of Its Loans*

[The court rejected Primestone's arguments that the loans were not in default and that the maturities had been extended by Vornado.]

. . .

B. *Vornado's Foreclosure Auction Was Conducted In A Commercially Reasonable Manner*

Under New York law, a "secured party seeking a deficiency judgment from the debtor after sale of the collateral bears the burden of showing that the sale was made in a 'commercially reasonable' manner." Moreover, even when confronted with a "very close question of whether defendants have raised a question of fact" regarding commercial reasonableness, courts have followed the "rule that summary judgment should be denied" whenever "there is doubt as to the existence of a triable issue or when the issue is arguable." This stringent standard, however, has not precluded courts applying New York law from granting summary judgment when they found there was no genuine issue of material fact regarding the commercial reasonableness of a foreclosure sale.

Primestone complains the foreclosure auction was not performed in a commercially reasonable manner. New York U.C.C. Section 9–627 establishes guidelines for the determination of commercial reasonableness. Under subsection (a), the fact that a greater amount of money could have been "obtained by a collection, enforcement, disposition, or acceptance at a different time or in a different method from that selected by the secured party is not itself sufficient" to establish that the disposition was not made in a commercially reasonable manner. Subsection (b) provides that a "disposition of collateral is made in a commercially reasonable manner if the disposition is made . . . (2) at the price current in any recognized market at the time of disposition."

Primestone's first objection to Vornado's foreclosure auction was Vornado's belief that the Units needed to be sold at a public auction in order for it to make a bid for the Units. Although, such a requirement exists,[41] Primestone argues that Vornado should have sought a private sale anyway because the New York U.C.C. generally "encourages private dispositions on the assumption that they frequently will result in higher realization on collateral for the benefit of all concerned." Such a generalized policy must give way in this circumstance, however, because there can be little doubt that Vornado was one of the most interested and able potential purchasers of the Units. By conducting a private sale, and thus eliminating Vornado as a potential purchaser, the price for the Units had the potential to be much lower than the ultimate selling price.

Primestone also argues that the price attained for the Units was unreasonably low. At the auction, the Units sold at a price equivalent to the closing price of PGE shares on the New York Stock Exchange on the date of the foreclosure sale. Primestone admits that the Units were the economic equivalent of PGE shares. Their value, therefore, should be considered roughly equivalent to the PGE share price on that day. In fact, there can be little doubt that the Units' value was less than the value of PGE's publicly traded shares. Although the Units were the economic equivalent of PGE shares, they lacked significant voting rights. The Units only represented limited partnership interests and could not participate in the management of the partnership. PGE was still the General Partner of PGRLP. Thus, to obtain control of the PGRLP, one must obtain control of PGE. Absent a 9.9% Waiver, however, it was impossible to attain control of PGE. There is absolutely no indication such a waiver would have been given.

Primestone argues the Net Asset Value ("NAV") of the Units was $15 per Unit, which provides further evidence of the unreasonable price obtained in the auction. This argument is unpersuasive. NAV could only be realized, if

---

41.   . . . N.Y. U.C.C. § 9–610(c) provides that "a secured party may purchase collateral: (1) at a public disposition; or (2) at a private disposition only if the collateral is of a kind that is customarily sold on a recognized market or the subject of widely distributed standard price quotations".

at all, in a sale or disposition of PGRLP. There is no indication of any plans to liquidate PGRLP's assets or that the real estate in PGRLP's portfolio is easily liquidated. That is the reason market price in this case could diverge significantly from NAV.

It is also the case that the procedures employed by Vornado were reasonable. Goldman Sachs was hired to do the marketing, and the efforts undertaken by Goldman Sachs were "consistent in all material respects with actions it has taken in the past in connection with other marketing processes relating to real estate-related companies and equity interests therein." The only major flaw in the auction was the fact that only Vornado was privy to inside information relating to PGE. Primestone could certainly have chosen to provide such inside information to potential purchasers, yet it refused to do so. Vornado possessed some inside information, but it had no sense of how reliable it actually was. It also had no way to obtain any additional inside information.

For all these reasons, Vornado is entitled to a declaration that the foreclosure sale was conducted in a commercially reasonable manner . . . .

. . .

VI.

For the foregoing reasons, Vornado's motion for summary judgment as to Counts IV through IX of its amended complaint is **GRANTED**. Vornado's motion for summary judgment on Primestone's amended counterclaim is also **GRANTED. IT IS SO ORDERED.**

NOTES ON COMMERCIALLY REASONABLE DISPOSITIONS AND REASONABLE NOTIFICATION

(1) What Is a "Commercially Reasonable" Disposition? A secured party who is enforcing a security interest faces considerable uncertainty as to whether a proposed disposition will be "commercially reasonable," as required by UCC 9–610(b). How will a court or a jury view the circumstances in an after-the-fact examination? The serious consequences (and potentially disastrous consequences in a consumer transaction) of failing to dispose of collateral in a commercially reasonable manner underscore the importance of taking the proper approach. See Notes (7) and (8), infra (discussing the consequences of noncompliance with UCC 9–610).

It should be apparent that predicting what is "commercially reasonable" in a given context is an enormously subjective enterprise. What is "reasonable" leaves much to the imagination. A review of the case law and commentary often can leave a student or lawyer confused and uncertain about a given, specific set of facts. Might a more principled approach emerge from examining the *purpose* or *function* of the commercial reasonableness requirement?

Consider the following proposition: A commercially reasonable disposition is one in which all aspects of the disposition are reasonably calculated to bring a reasonable and fair price for the collateral. Although

UCC 9–627(a) seems to instruct that the failure to sell for the highest possible price does not ipso facto render the disposition commercially unreasonable, it is clear enough that whether the procedures followed in a disposition are commercially reasonable is a function of the price that those procedures could be expected to produce. (It is the price, of course, that will determine whether a debtor remains liable for a deficiency or entitled to a surplus under UCC 9–615.) Comment 10 to UCC 9–610 and Comment 2 to UCC 9–627 explain in identical words the relationship between the price for which collateral is disposed and the secured party's satisfaction of the commercial reasonableness requirement: "While not itself sufficient to establish a violation of this Part, a low price suggests that a court should scrutinize carefully all aspects of a disposition to ensure that each aspect was commercially reasonable." These comments reject the result in cases holding that a *really* low price is ipso facto sufficient to spell commercial unreasonableness under Former Article 9. Note (2), infra, discusses the background of this comment, as well as Revised Article 9's special treatment of certain low-price dispositions.

The commercial reasonableness of a disposition normally is a question of fact for the trier of fact. See, e.g., Dischner v. United Bank Alaska, 725 P.2d 488 (Alaska 1986). A secured party seeking a deficiency judgment bears the burden of proof as to compliance with Part 6, including the commercial reasonableness of a disposition and the reasonableness of a notification, once compliance is placed in issue. UCC 9–626(a)(1); Note (3), infra (discussing notification requirements). In a very real sense, however, the trial preparation begins during the process of disposing of collateral and before any challenge to commercial reasonableness has surfaced. Whether the proposed disposition involves unique or very expensive collateral (as in Problem 9.2.1, supra) or a routine disposition of an automobile (as in Problem 9.2.2, supra), secured creditors would do well to proceed on the assumption that the disposition will be challenged. Unless the case for commercial reasonableness is made and documented at the time of the disposition, an attack on the commercial reasonableness (or, indeed, any aspect of compliance with Part 6)—which could be asserted years in the future—may be difficult to withstand.

A secured party who desires enhanced certainty of compliance can obtain court approval (or certain other approvals) of the terms of a disposition, in which case the disposition "is commercially reasonable." UCC 9–627(c). UCC 9–627(b) offers useful guidance on what constitutes a commercially reasonable disposition, but hardly provides a sharply delineated "safe harbor." A secured party also could obtain a judgment on the secured debt, levy execution on the collateral, and have the collateral sold at a sheriff's sale, thereby obviating the need to comply with Part 6's notice and commercial reasonableness requirements. See UCC 9–601(f). Either route, however, is likely to be more expensive and time-consuming than non-judicial enforcement.

A secured party also may achieve a high level of comfort if the debtor is cooperative. Absent circumstances suggesting coercion or unfair advantage, a debtor's post-default agreement that particular procedures will constitute a commercially reasonable disposition can do much to reduce the risk of a contrary assertion by the debtor down the road. Even if the debtor is not cooperative, a secured party sometimes will be well-advised to communicate the proposed disposition procedures to the debtor; the debtor's failure to object or to make a reasonable counterproposal may weigh heavily in favor of the secured party in a later dispute concerning commercial reasonableness.

The requirement of a commercially reasonable disposition must be applied in a wide variety of circumstances. Smith v. Daniels, 634 S.W.2d 276 (Tenn.App.1982), provides useful guidance as to factors to consider. Among specific factors, such as adequate advertising and display, the court emphasized the relevance of customary commercial practices for selling a particular type of asset (the collateral, there, was amusement equipment). What will do for thoroughbred horses may not do for a Learjet aircraft and vice versa. Other factors considered by the courts have included (i) the circumstances under which the sale was conducted (e.g., collateral was not present, sale held during a snowstorm); (ii) appropriateness of the method of sale (i.e., either private or public); (iii) adequacy of the advertising; (iv) preparation of collateral prior to the sale; (v) passage of time between repossession and sale; and (vi) whether the collateral was sold as a unit or individually.

Some lenders and their counsel may develop substantial expertise concerning market practices for certain collateral—automobiles being a good example. But in many situations neither the staff of a secured creditor nor its lawyer will have sufficient expertise, and it will be necessary to retain or consult with experts. Nevertheless, the creditor and the lawyer responsible for conducting a commercially reasonable disposition must know the right questions to ask the experts.

(2) Low–Price Dispositions to Secured Party, Person Related to Secured Party, or Secondary Obligor. During the drafting of Revised Article 9, a controversy arose over whether the "price" received for collateral in a disposition following default was an "aspect" or "term" of the disposition that must be "commercially reasonable" under UCC 9–610(b). (The same issue had long been debated under Former 9–504(3).) Some argued that under the "plain meaning" of UCC 9–610(b) it was indisputable that the price was an "aspect" or "term"—indeed, probably the most important "aspect" or "term" imaginable. Others took the position that, properly read (together with UCC 9–627(a)), UCC 9–610(b) imposed only *procedural* requirements of reasonableness. Under that reading, if all of the steps taken were reasonable, the secured party could not be second-guessed by an attack on the price alone (although the price certainly would be relevant to an evaluation of the procedural reasonableness, as explained in Note (1), supra).

Eventually, a compromise emerged to deal with a specific class of dispositions that are procedurally commercially reasonable but nevertheless produce a very low price. The compromise is reflected in UCC 9–615(f). That provision applies only if the transferee in the disposition is "the secured party, a person related to the secured party, or a secondary obligor." UCC 9–615(f)(1). (Note that the terms "secured party," "person related to the secured party," and "secondary obligor" are defined in UCC 9–102(a).) Why were procedurally conforming dispositions to those classes of transferees thought to be suspect? Comment 6 to UCC 9–615 explains that in these cases the secured party may lack the incentive to maximize the proceeds of the disposition (i.e., the price). A disposition to the secured party itself or to a person related to the secured party are obvious examples of self-dealing. In the case of a disposition to a secondary obligor, the secured party may lack incentive because it is counting on being paid in full by the guarantor; it is indifferent as to how much derives from the collateral. And the less the guarantor pays for the collateral the larger will be *its* deficiency claim against the debtor. (More about secondary obligors follows in Section 3, infra.)

UCC 9–615(f) contains another condition to its application:

> (2) the amount of proceeds of the disposition is significantly below the range of proceeds that a complying disposition to a person other than the secured party, a person related to the secured party, or a secondary obligor would have brought.

In other words, subsection (f) applies when the proceeds are very low when compared to the proceeds that would have been received in a disposition to an unrelated third party. When subsection (f) applies, then, the surplus or deficiency is calculated not on the (very low) actual proceeds received but on the proceeds that *would have* been received in a complying disposition to an unrelated third party.

We think it unlikely that any trier of fact could feel confident about a determination of the highly speculative and hypothetical amount of proceeds that UCC 9–615(f) mandates that it determine. On the other hand, the compromise does permit a trier of fact to reduce the otherwise applicable deficiency (or increase the otherwise applicable surplus) when the proceeds are very low. That possibility pleased those who had advocated that price should be an "aspect" or a "term" of a disposition. But the compromise provision also accommodates a reduction of the deficiency (or increase in surplus) without the need to determine that the disposition itself did not comply with Part 6 (e.g., was not made in a commercially reasonable manner). That result pleased those who had advocated that price should not be an "aspect" or "term." Indeed, the fact that subsection (f) contemplates a commercially reasonable disposition that yields a very low price supports the inference that, at least under Revised Article 9 if not also under Former Article 9, the price for which collateral is disposed is not an "aspect" or "term" of the disposition. See UCC 9–610, Comment 10; UCC 9–627, Comment 2.

(3) "Reasonable Authenticated Notification of Disposition." UCC 9–611(b) provides that, with certain exceptions, a secured party undertaking a disposition of collateral under UCC 9–610 shall send "a reasonable authenticated notification" to the "persons specified in subsection (c)." Subsection (d) excepts from the notification requirement collateral that "is perishable or threatens to decline speedily in value or is of a type customarily sold on a recognized market."

To Whom Must a Notification be Sent? Why Require Notification? The secured party must send the notification required by UCC 9–611(b) to the persons specified in UCC 9–611(c): the debtor, any secondary obligor, and, in the case of collateral other than consumer goods, certain persons who may have competing claims to the collateral involved. This last category of competing claimants includes persons from whom the secured party has received an authenticated notification of a claim and, subject to somewhat complex timing rules, persons who have security interests in the collateral perfected by filing. The timing complexity, found in UCC 9–611(a), the definition of "notification date," and UCC 9–611(c)(3)(B) and (e), is designed to protect the enforcing secured party from long delays in receiving a report from a filing office as to financing statements filed against the debtor covering the collateral. See 9–611, Comment 4.

Why require that reasonable notification of a proposed disposition be given to these particular classes of persons? The short answer is that they all may have a stake in whether the secured party complies with Part 6 in connection with the disposition. (One exception may be competing claimants who have an interest *senior* to that of the enforcing secured party, but we shall hold that issue for Section 3, infra.) The debtor and junior claimants would prefer to see the secured party recover the maximum value from the collateral. They wish to enhance their chances of picking up any excess over the enforcing secured party's claim. The notification requirement is a procedural safeguard intended to aid the debtor and competing claimants in protecting their own interests.

How does a reasonable notification assist a notified person in protecting its interests? A person may wish to attend a public sale in order to observe, first-hand, the procedures that are followed. Knowing the time of a public sale and the time after which a private sale may take place (the contents of a reasonable notification are discussed below in this Note) also may permit a debtor to arrange for a third-party buyer who otherwise would not have been attracted to the collateral. Moreover, the act of disposition (or contracting for a disposition) cuts off the debtor's right to pay the secured obligation in full and thereby "redeem" the collateral. See UCC 9–623. Reasonable notification informs the debtor of the earliest date on which redemption rights could be lost. (Redemption is considered in Section 4, infra.) Moreover, particularly with respect to intangible collateral that has not been repossessed, the notification may alert the debtor to the need for a bankruptcy filing to stay the disposition. See BC 362(a) (discussed in Chapter 7, Section 1, supra). And it may induce a subordinate claimant to explore the possibility of an involuntary bankruptcy filing against the debtor so as to preserve the value of the collateral.

The exceptions to the notification requirement found in UCC 9–611(d) reflect the situation in which the benefits of notification are outweighed by other risks (i.e., that the collateral will quickly perish or decline in value) or in which the protection afforded by a notification is not necessary (disposition on recognized market).

Timeliness of Notification of Disposition. Implicit in UCC 9–611(b) is the idea that to be "reasonable" a notification must be sent within a reasonable time in advance of the date of the disposition. The question of timeliness is addressed more directly in UCC 9–612(a). See UCC 9–612, Comment 2 ("A notification that is sent so near to the disposition date that a notified person could not be expected to act or take account of the notification would be unreasonable.") How much time between giving a notification and a disposition is sufficient? Case law under Former 9–504(3) indicated that the secured party should feel reasonably safe in giving 10 days' notice. But this question of fact may turn on considerations such as the type, value, and location of the collateral; the knowledge and sophistication of the debtor; and general market conditions. Moreover, it should be answered in the context of the underlying purposes of the notification requirement, discussed above. The new 10–day "safe harbor" provided by UCC 9–612(b) for non-consumer transactions offers the prospect of greater certainty under Revised Article 9. However, questions as to whether a notification was *sent* in a reasonable manner will remain. See UCC 9–612, Comment 3.

Contents of a "Reasonable Authenticated Notification"; Authentication Requirement. The contents of a notification of disposition are specified in UCC 9–613(1) for transactions other than a consumer-goods transaction and in UCC 9–614(1) for a consumer-goods transaction. Each also contains a "safe-harbor" form of notification. In addition to information that serves to identify the relevant transaction, the most important requirements are found in UCC 9–613(1)(C) ("the method of intended disposition") and (1)(E) ("the *time and place* of a *public sale* or the *time after which* any *other disposition* is to be made") (emphasis added). The information required by UCC 9–613(1) is incorporated by reference in UCC 9–614(1); the latter provision also requires additional information thought to be particularly important in consumer-goods transactions. Note also the "plain English" formulation of the form of notification found in UCC 9–614(3).

Relying on the requirement in Former 9–504(3) that a notification be "sent" and the definition of "send" in Former 1–201(38) [UCC 1–201(36)], some cases applying Former Article 9 held oral notifications to be ineffective. Others upheld oral notification, especially when it was clear that the debtor had actual knowledge of all information that a written notification would have contained. Revised Article 9, as well, requires the Secured Party to "send" (now defined for Article 9 purposes in UCC 9–102(a)(74)) the notification of disposition. UCC 9–611(b). And it resolves the issue against the effectiveness of an oral notification by requiring the secured party to "send . . . a reasonable *authenticated* notification." UCC 9–611(b) (emphasis added); see UCC 9–102(a)(7) (defining "authenticate"), (69) (defining "record").

Send versus Receive; "Second Try." As just noted, UCC 9–611(b) does not require that a person to be notified actually *receive* a notice; it provides only that the secured party "send . . . a reasonable authenticated notification." Consider a secured party who sends a notification to a debtor's last known address, only to have the letter returned by the Postal Service: "Addressee unknown." Can the secured party comfortably proceed with a disposition? Must the secured party undertake at least "reasonable efforts" to locate the debtor's current address, taking into account whatever information is readily available to the secured party (e.g., telephone book, knowledge of the debtor's place of employment, etc.)? Some courts concluded under Former 9–504(3) that the secured party may need to "keep trying," at least for awhile. Comment 6 to UCC 9–611 observes that Revised Article 9 "leaves to judicial resolution, based upon the facts of each case," whether a "second try" may be necessary in order to effect a reasonable notification.

Confusion: Notification of Disposition versus Advertisement of Collateral. Courts sometimes have confused notification of disposition with the advertising that may be a necessary component of a commercially reasonable disposition. (We believe it likely that some courts may have been confused by confused briefs filed by confused lawyers who relied upon confused opinions by other confused courts!) Although an inadequate notification to the debtor could bear on the issue of commercial reasonableness, that relationship normally is quite attenuated. The notification requirement is separate and independent from the commercially reasonable disposition requirement. The requirement of commercial reasonableness encourages secured parties to dispose of collateral in a manner that is likely to bring a good price. As explained above, the notification requirement is a procedural safeguard intended to aid the debtor and other interested persons in protecting their own interests.

(4) Application of Proceeds of Disposition; Right to Surplus or Obligation for Deficiency. An enforcing secured party's duties with respect to application of cash proceeds are found in UCC 9–615(a). UCC 9–615(c) provides a framework for dealing with the application of noncash proceeds of a foreclosure disposition, such the buyer's promissory note. Comment 3 to that section provides an overview and an example. Section 3(B), infra, deals in more detail with the application of proceeds to junior interests.

A debtor's right to any surplus and an obligor's obligation for a deficiency following application of the proceeds of a disposition are established by UCC 9–615(d). Under subsection (e), however, these surplus and deficiency rules do not apply when the underlying transaction was a sale of accounts, chattel paper, payment intangibles, or promissory notes.

A secured party is required to send a written explanation of its calculation of a surplus or deficiency to a debtor in a consumer-goods transaction or to a consumer obligor in the circumstances described in UCC 9–616. Unlike much of Part 6, that provision had no predecessor under Former Article 9. Can you think of a reason why a secured party would object to the requirement? Can you think of a reason why the requirement should be limited to consumer-goods transactions?

(5) Pre– and Post–Default Debtor Waivers; Agreed Standards of Compliance. When the duties that a legal rule imposes are uncertain, the parties to a transaction may wish to eliminate the uncertainty through contract. For example, a secured party might seek the debtor's agreement that the secured party need not notify the debtor of a proposed disposition and need not dispose of the collateral in a commercially reasonable manner. Notwithstanding that the UCC generally promotes freedom of contract, see UCC 1–302(a) [F1–102(3)], Article 9 provides that the parties may not waive or vary the most significant rights or duties that it imposes. UCC 9–602 specifies the non-waivable rights and duties; please review these rights and duties now. For some narrow exceptions that permit certain post-default waivers, see UCC 9–624.

Subject to limitations of its scope, Article 9 permits a debtor to encumber *all* its assets simply by signing a single piece of paper; yet the statute prohibits the debtor from agreeing as part of the same transaction to waive the right, for example, to notification of a disposition upon default. What explains Article 9's solicitude for debtors? Professor Gilmore's treatise gives one the impression that the original drafters of the UCC did not examine this issue anew.

> Since the beginnings of mortgage law, *it has never been questioned* that the mortgagor's equity is entitled to absolute protection and cannot be frittered away. No agreement, we have long been told, will be allowed to "clog the equity of redemption." And not even the most drastic of pledge agreements has ever purported to free the pledgee from his inescapable duties of accounting to the pledgor for the value of the pledged property and of remitting any surplus. *Article 9, therefore, merely reflects history* when it provides that the debtor's rights and the secured party's correlative duties following default "may not be waived or varied."

2 Gilmore, Security § 44.4, at 1228–29 (emphasis added). The drafters of Revised Article 9 did not reexamine this hoary principle. Should they have?

Although UCC 9–602 is hostile to waivers, UCC 9–603(a) provides that "the parties may determine by agreement standards measuring the fulfillment of the rights of a debtor or obligor and the duties of a secured party under a rule stated in UCC 9–602 if the standards are not manifestly unreasonable." Security agreements that contain standards concerning the timeliness of notifications of disposition appear to be widely used, based on the reported cases.

Agreed standards concerning what constitutes a commercially reasonable disposition seem to be comparatively rare. One explanation for this phenomenon may be the widespread use of standard printed forms that normally are intended to cover many types of collateral. And in large business financings involving highly negotiated documentation, perhaps the anticipated result of a default is bankruptcy, not repossession; negotiating elaborate standards may not be considered worthwhile. On the other hand, might there be many kinds of repetitive transactions in which agreed standards may be advisable (e.g., secured financings of automobiles, trucks, farm equipment, horses)? Consider the types of standards that might be utilized (e.g., agreements as to the names and locations of publications where advertisements should be placed; the number of issues or days or weeks of advertising; whether the sale is to be public or private; specified auctioneer; maximum amount of sale-preparation expenses).

(6) Effect of Secured Party's Noncompliance Under Former Article 9: Three Approaches. As you know, to the extent that the proceeds of a disposition of collateral are insufficient to satisfy the secured obligation, the obligor (who usually is the debtor) is liable for the deficiency. See UCC 9–615(d). Suppose, however, that the secured party fails to dispose of collateral in a commercially reasonable manner under UCC 9–610(b), fails to send reasonable notification under UCC 9–611, or otherwise fails to comply with Part 6 of Article 9 in enforcing its security interest? (We have already considered in Section 1 the question of damages when a secured party creates a breach of the peace in using self help to take possession of collateral under UCC 9–609.) Article 9 deals with the effects of noncompliance in Subpart 2 of Part 6, UCC 9–625 through UCC 9–628. Before turning to the substance of the current rules, however, you should become familiar with the approaches to noncompliance taken by the courts under Former Article 9.

Former 9–507(1) provided that the debtor "has a right to recover from the secured party any loss caused by a failure to comply" with the enforcement provisions of Former Article 9.[1] (UCC 9–625(b) is to a similar effect concerning a failure to comply with any provision of Revised Article 9.) One might understand Former 9–507 to have limited a debtor's remedy for noncompliance to the assertion of a cause of action: If the noncomplying secured party does not claim a deficiency, then the aggrieved debtor would be entitled to an affirmative recovery; if the secured party does claim a deficiency, then the debtor would be entitled to set off its damages for noncompliance against the secured party's deficiency claim. Notwithstanding that the plain meaning of the text of Former Article 9 does not seem to support any other reading, most courts that considered the issue refused to adopt this "offset" rule. They adopted instead either the "rebuttable presumption" rule or the "absolute bar" ("loss of deficiency") rule. See Lloyd, The Absolute Bar Rule in UCC Foreclosure Sales: A Prescription for Waste, 40 UCLA L. Rev. 695 (1993) (indicating that 26 jurisdictions had adopted the rebuttable presumption rule, 11 the absolute bar rule, and 3 the offset rule).

As developed by the courts, the "rebuttable presumption" rule generally created a presumption that the value of the collateral was equal to the

---

1.   The third sentence of Former 9–507(1) afforded the debtor a minimum recovery for noncompliance where the collateral is consumer goods. UCC 9–625(c) is similar. See Note (10), infra.

secured obligation and that, therefore, the debtor was not obligated for a deficiency. However, the noncomplying secured party could recover a deficiency to the extent it rebutted the presumption by showing that the collateral in fact was worth less than the secured obligation. In contrast, the "absolute bar" rule barred a noncomplying secured party from recovering a deficiency altogether.

Thus, as the project to revise Article 9 began in 1993, the battle lines had been drawn. As described in the following Notes, the "battle" continued throughout the revision and enactment processes.

(7) Effect of Secured Party's Noncompliance Under Revised Article 9: Non–Consumer Transactions. Remarking upon the divergent case law concerning the consequences of noncompliance with Former Article 9's enforcement provisions, we predicted in a earlier edition of this book that "a statutory solution will emerge, whether in a revised Article 9 or in state-by-state nonuniform amendments." Our prediction proved only partially correct. For non-consumer transactions, UCC 9–626(a) contains a detailed, statutory, rebuttable presumption rule. For consumer transactions, however, Revised Article 9 is less forthcoming. It "leave[s] to the court the determination of the proper rules in consumer transactions." UCC 9–626(b). (Noncompliance in consumer transactions is discussed in Notes (8), (9), and (10), infra.)

The version of the rebuttable presumption rule codified in UCC 9–626(a) for non-consumer transactions is straightforward, but nonetheless worth a close reading along with the comments. Unlike some of the formulations in the case law, the statutory rule does not presume the *value* of the collateral to be equal to the secured obligation; instead, UCC 9–626(a) creates a rebuttable presumption that *compliance with Article 9* would have yielded an amount sufficient to satisfy the secured debt. More precisely, a noncomplying secured party has the burden of proving the amount that would have been recovered had the secured party complied with Article 9, and the secured party's deficiency recovery is limited to the difference between that amount and the amount of the secured debt. See UCC 9–626(a)(3)(B), (4), and Comment 3. In this way, the statutory rebuttable presumption rule ensures that a debtor is compensated for any loss caused by the secured party's noncompliance. UCC 9–625(d) and Comment 3 address and prevent the possibility of a debtor's obtaining double recovery or overcompensation.

(8) Effect of Secured Party's Noncompliance Under Revised Article 9: Consumer Transactions. Article 9's approach to noncompliance in consumer transactions differs dramatically from its approach to non-consumer transactions. In consumer transactions, rather than state a rule, Article 9 invites the court to fashion the rule governing the consequences of noncompliance with the Article. See UCC 9–626(b). You may find it odd for the legislature to prescribe statutory duties, such as the duty to conduct a commercially reasonable disposition of collateral, and yet leave the courts free to fashion the legal rules governing the consequences of noncompliance with those duties. Here is how this unusual state of affairs came about.

The Absolute Bar Rule: Arguments Pro and Con. During the drafting of Revised Article 9, advocates for consumer-credit providers sharply disagreed with advocates for consumer debtors and obligors about what the consequences of noncompliance with Article 9's enforcement provisions should be.[2] Consider the following scenario: Debtor gives Lender a security interest in collateral worth $10,000 to secure a loan of $100,000. On Debtor's default, Lender sells the collateral in a commercially unreasonable manner or without reasonable notification to Debtor. Application of the absolute bar rule would prohibit Lender from recovering the balance of the debt, even if Debtor were solvent and able to pay. Application of the rebuttable presumption rule would enable Lender to recover the entire unpaid amount of the loan, provided Lender could show that its noncompliance with Article 9 did not adversely affect the amount it recovered at the sale.

As the foregoing scenario suggests, the absolute bar rule is blatantly penal: any correlation between the harm done a debtor by the secured party's noncompliance and the sanction imposed on the secured party is entirely fortuitous. Why, creditors argued, should a secured party's noncompliance put a debtor in a better position than would have been the case had the secured party complied? Indeed, UCC 1–305(a) [F1–106(1)] makes clear that the UCC disapproves of such results.

The absolute bar rule has other potentially penal aspects. For example, under the facts set forth above, assume that Lender sold (again, employing defective procedures) only one item of collateral, worth $5,000; another item, also worth $5,000, remains unsold. Logically, having stripped Lender of its right to recover a deficiency (i.e., the remaining balance of the debt), the absolute bar rule would deprive Lender of any further right to recover from the remaining item, and even from any real property securing the obligation. Some secured parties actually have suffered this unfortunate fate under Former Article 9. At least one court, however, permitted a secured party to recover on an *in rem* claim against the remaining collateral in this context.[3]

A more finely-tuned absolute bar rule might reduce substantially its penal aspects. For example, one might craft a rule that applies only in contexts where some equivalence between the secured debt and the collateral might be expected, such as PMSI's in consumer goods. Or, one might apply the rule only to certain kinds of noncompliance and not others. (There is some judicial support for applying the absolute bar rule to the failure to give a required notification of disposition while applying the rebuttable presumption rule to noncompliance consisting of the failure to

2.   These advocates included representatives of the American Financial Services Association (a national trade organization of consumer finance companies), the finance companies of the "big three" domestic automobile manufacturers, the California Bankers Association, Consumers Union, and the National Consumer Law Center, as well as a few law professors and legal services lawyers.

3.   The same result would obtain if the secured debt were discharged in bankruptcy.

dispose of collateral in a commercially reasonable manner. There also is some authority for the converse: applying the rebuttable presumption rule to cases of improper (or missing) notification and the absolute bar rule to commercially unreasonable dispositions.) Do you see any reason to treat noncompliance consisting of defective notification differently from that consisting of a commercially unreasonable disposition?

Even acknowledging that the absolute bar rule is penal and that UCC remedies generally are compensatory, is there a case to be made for adopting the rule? Consider this argument: Noncompliance with Article 9 is difficult to discover and prove, and in many cases the damages likely to be recovered (or offset against a deficiency) are not sufficiently large to justify the cost of litigation. As a result, secured parties who fail to comply with the remedial provisions of Article 9 often suffer no adverse consequences. By increasing the stakes, the absolute bar rule increases the likelihood that a noncomplying secured party will be held to task. Moreover, when viewed in the aggregate, the rule is not penal. Many secured parties are repeat players. The total loss of deficiency in the few cases that are litigated is, arguably, a rough substitute for the many partial deficiencies that would have been lost had every case of noncompliance found its way into the judicial system. Do you find this argument persuasive? If so, does it apply equally to consumer transactions and non-consumer transactions?

The Statutory "Silent Treatment" for Noncompliance in Consumer Transactions. Recognizing that the disagreement at the drafting table would be likely to be reflected in debates before the state legislatures, the Drafting Committee decided that Revised Article 9 should offer statutory alternatives. Under a draft approved relatively late in the revision process, each legislature would have been invited to choose between (i) application of the rebuttable presumption rule (in substantially the form of UCC 9–626(a)) to all transactions and (ii) application of the absolute bar rule to consumer transactions and the rebuttable presumption rule to other transactions. The draft version of the absolute bar rule was tempered by providing that a secured party who is barred from a deficiency nonetheless could seek a recovery from any remaining collateral. The statutory alternatives were accompanied by a variety of other consumer-protection provisions. Considering that neither set of advocates was entirely satisfied by this approach to the effect of noncompliance (or by the consumer-protection provisions taken as a whole), the Drafting Committee realized that it probably had the balance about right. It was content with its centrist approach.

Long and intense discussions among consumer and creditor representatives followed. With few exceptions, neither the members of the Drafting Committee nor the Reporters participated in these discussions. Eventually, as part of a "compromise" on a variety of consumer issues, and over the objections of the Reporters, representatives of firms that provide consumer credit and representatives of consumer-advocacy groups settled upon language similar to that of UCC 9–626(b). The Drafting Committee and then the UCC's sponsors approved.[4] Assuming that nonuniformity on the consequences of noncompliance is inevitable, what reasons might there be for favoring judicial, as opposed to legislative, rulemaking in this context? Does anything other than political expediency justify the adoption of different rules for determining the consequences of noncompliance in commercial and consumer transactions?

With the background of UCC 9–626(b) in mind, we look forward. How will counsel for enforcing creditors and defaulting consumers be likely to respond to the "neutrality" of UCC 9–626(b)? Consider the Reporters' Comments to the March 10, 1998, draft of Revised Article 9 (the first draft to incorporate the "consumer compromise").

Reporters' Comments

Changes from Prior Draft:

A. This draft deletes Alternative A of Section 9–626,[5] which contemplated that a legislature might choose to adopt the absolute bar rule statutorily. Instead, Section 9–626 now codifies the rebuttable presumption rule for non-consumer-goods transactions. Except as to actual damages recoverable under Section 9–625(b), however, the draft is silent as to whether a secured party's noncompliance in a consumer-goods transaction affects a deficiency claim and, if so, the nature of the effect. Thus, if a jurisdiction is to adopt an absolute bar rule, it must do so judicially.

How the courts construe revised Article 9 will determine whether the status of consumer-goods transactions ultimately remains unchanged from that under former Article 9. Unlike this draft, former Article 9 contained no hint that deficiencies in consumer-and non-consumer transactions should receive differing treatment. This draft can be read to indicate that rebuttable presumption treatment should not (and certainly that it might not) be appropriate for consumer-goods transactions. Moreover, counsel for debtors in jurisdictions that have adopted the "actual damages" rule based on a straightforward reading of former Section 9–507 (in lieu or either absolute bar or rebuttable presumption) will be compelled to argue for absolute bar under revised Article 9. Courts may be loathe to embrace a rule that is *less* favorable for consumers (actual damages) than the rule applicable in non-consumer-goods transactions (rebuttable presumption). On the other hand, counsel for creditors in absolute-bar jurisdictions can be expected to argue that the legislative approval of the rebuttable presumption rule for non-consumer-goods transactions signals rejection of the absolute bar rule for all transactions, on the ground that all the

---

4.   Revised Article 9 distinguishes between consumer and non-consumer transactions not only with respect to the consequences of noncompliance but also in other aspects of enforcement. These provisions are listed in UCC 9–101, Comment 4.j., items (v) through (ix). See also Notes (3) and (4), supra; Note (1), p. 670, infra; Note (3), p. 671, infra.

5.   [The draft has been edited to reflect the current section numbers.]

policy reasons supporting the rebuttable presumption rule apply with equal force to consumer-goods transactions. Thus, the approach taken in the draft may lead to extensive litigation and relitigation under revised Article 9, even in jurisdictions where the law already had been settled under former Article 9. On the other hand, the Official Comments will indicate that the silence in this section with respect to consumer-goods transactions leaves courts free to continue to apply established law. See Comment y, below. If followed, this comment would leave the law where it was under former Article 9.

B. Alternative A of Section 9–626 also was intended to rationalize and clarify the law even in jurisdictions that may already have opted judicially for the absolute bar rule. For example, it dealt with the effect of noncompliance when other collateral securing the deficiency remains following a disposition. Section 9–626(c) also clarifies the application of the rebuttable presumption rule. Because subsection (c) does not apply to consumer-goods transactions, however, the benefits of the clarifications (e.g., allocation of the burden of proof) may be unavailable in those transactions. A court might be reluctant to apply the statutory rule embodied in Section 9–626 to consumer-goods transactions by analogy, inasmuch as it does not apply to those transactions by its terms. However, the Official Comments could attempt to negate any inferences that might otherwise be drawn from silence.

Subsequently, what is now UCC 9–626(b), the "no-inference" or "neutrality" provision was added to the draft. Do you think it will have the intended effects?

One thing is certain: UCC 9–626(b) will have no effect unless courts read it. When determining a deficiency under Revised Article 9, the court in In re Downing, 286 B.R. 900 (Bkrtcy.W.D.Mo.2002), failed even to mention the existence of UCC 9–626(b). Citing a case decided under Former Article 9, the court took as given that, "In Missouri, compliance with the notice provisions of Article 9 is a prerequisite to the recovery of a deficiency following the sale of repossessed collateral."

(9) Nonuniform Statutory Treatment of Consumer Transactions. Not every state legislature has been content to leave to the judiciary the consequences of noncompliance with Article 9 in consumer transactions. More than a dozen states have expanded the application of the rebuttable presumption rule of UCC 9–626(a) to include consumer transactions, thereby preventing their courts from imposing an absolute bar or offset rule.

Legislatures in other states have been more solicitous of defaulting consumer debtors. For example, California's enactment of Article 9 adopts a nonuniform UCC 9–626(b) that embraces for consumer transactions a version of the absolute bar rule along the lines of that found in California's nonuniform version of Former 9–504. See Cal. Com. Code § 9626(b) (effective July 1, 2001); Cal. Com. Code § 9504(2) (repealed 2001). Under California UCC 9–626(b), a debtor or secondary obligor is not liable for a deficiency unless, inter alia, notification was given in accordance with UCC 9–611 and the disposition or other enforcement was conducted in good faith and in a commercially reasonable manner. A secured party who loses a deficiency under UCC 9–626(b) or UCC 9–615(f) (dealing with "low price" dispositions to the secured party or a related person; see Note (2), supra) remains liable for any damages and also loses the benefits of any remaining collateral securing the deficiency: The secured party may not retain a security interest in any other collateral; and, if the secured party subsequently disposes of collateral that had secured the deficiency, the debtor may recover from the secured party the proceeds of the disposition.

Massachusetts has taken a different tack. Although it adopted UCC 9–626(b), the Massachusetts legislature made it subject to the following rules, which were in effect under its enactment of Former Article 9: In consumer credit transactions involving $2,000 or less that are secured by "a non-possessory security interest in consumer goods," the debtor is entirely excused from any deficiency liability once the secured party takes or accepts possession. In consumer credit transactions involving $2,000 or more (at the time of default), the deficiency is calculated by deducting from the outstanding secured obligation the "fair market value" of the collateral, *not* by deducting the net sale proceeds as provided by UCC 9–615(d). Mass. Ann. Laws ch. 255B, § 20B(d) & (e). (If the debt is *exactly* $2,000, *both* rules seem to apply!)

The Massachusetts legislation reflects an approach to deficiencies in consumer transactions that is a throwback to pre-UCC rules and that has gained some support nationally. In the classical conditional sale (in which "title" did not pass to the buyer until the buyer paid the purchase price in full), the conditional seller was required to elect between alternative remedies when the buyer defaulted: The seller could (i) repossess the goods sold *or* (ii) sue for the price (i.e., the remaining balance due). If the seller repossessed the goods, it had no further claim against the buyer. A claim for a "deficiency" was an attribute of a "mortgage" and not permitted in the setting of a conditional sale. See Gilmore, Security §§ 3.2, 43.1.

Before the UCC, most experts on the law of conditional sales concluded that the election doctrine was awkward and harsh; it generally was assumed that the Uniform Conditional Sales Act made a significant contribution to the law by permitting the seller, on repossession, to establish a deficiency (usually by a public sale) for which the buyer would be liable. See Uniform Conditional Sales Act § 22 (1918) (superseded).

With that background, one can appreciate the sensation of *deja vu* in encountering the election doctrine in the 1974 version of U3C 5.103, set out at the end of this Note. The 1968 version similarly restricted deficiency judgments with respect to consumer credit sales of goods or services. Although neither version of the U3C has been widely adopted, several states have adopted election-of-remedies statutes modeled, to a greater or lesser extent, on U3C 5.103.

Would Lee Abel, in the Prototype transaction (Chapter 3, Section 1, supra), and most other buyers of automobiles have protection from deficiency judgments under the U3C? What types of transactions and what buyers typically would receive protection under U3C 5.103? Would this provision provide some assistance when goods prove to be shoddy? Does it afford sufficient protection to the secured party when the goods are abused?

The denial of deficiency claims when the creditor repossesses has been characterized as self-defeating. Apart from cars, most consumer goods have little resale value; a creditor could avoid losing a claim for deficiency by not repossessing and pressing for collection of the debt. Perhaps the only consequence of this reform "is to leave the poor with the dissatisfaction of his merchandise." See Kripke, Gesture and Reality in Consumer Credit Reform, 44 N.Y.U.L.Rev. 1, 32–34 (1969). Professor Kripke suggests that a logical extension of the thinking behind the denial of deficiency judgments is a proposal to limit the creditor's recourse to the *collateral*. But such proposals to restrict the creditor's remedies, he suggested, could result in withdrawal of credit from the poorest credit risks, or in raising of the price level of merchandise "thus taxing the poor who struggle through their payment requirements with an added cost absorbing the losses of others who do not pay."

UNIFORM CONSUMER CREDIT CODE (1974)

Section 5.103 [Restrictions on Deficiency Judgments]

(1) This section applies to a deficiency on a consumer credit sale of goods or services and on a consumer loan in which the lender is subject to claims and defenses arising from sales and leases (Section 3.405). A consumer is not liable for a deficiency unless the creditor has disposed of the goods in good faith and in a commercially reasonable manner.

(2) If the seller repossesses or voluntarily accepts surrender of goods that were the subject of the sale and in which he has a security interest, the consumer is not personally liable to the seller for the unpaid balance of the debt arising from the sale of a commercial unit of goods of which the cash sale price was $1,750 or less, and the seller is not obligated to resell the collateral unless the consumer has paid 60 per cent or more of the cash price and has not signed after default a statement renouncing his rights in the collateral.

(3) If the seller repossesses or voluntarily accepts surrender of goods that were not the subject of the sale but in which he has a security interest to secure a debt arising from a sale of goods or services or a combined sale of goods and services[6] and the cash price of the sale was $1,750 or less, the consumer is not personally liable to the seller for the unpaid balance of the debt arising from the sale, and the seller's duty to dispose of the collateral is governed by the provisions on disposition of collateral (Part 5 of [Former] Article 9 [i.e., Part 6 of Revised Article 9]) of the Uniform Commercial Code.

---

6. [This provision would come into play only infrequently under current law, given the FTC's restrictions on nonpossessory, non-PMSI's. See 16 C.F.R. 444.2(a)(4) (it is an unfair practice for lenders or retail installment sellers to obtain from consumers nonpossessory security interests, other than PMSI's, in household goods).]

(4) If the lender takes possession or voluntarily accepts surrender of goods in which he has a purchase money security interest to secure a debt arising from a consumer loan in which the lender is subject to claims and defenses arising from sales and leases (Section 3.405) and the net proceeds of the loan paid to or for the benefit of the consumer were $1,750 or less, the consumer is not personally liable to the lender for the unpaid balance of the debt arising from that loan and the lender's duty to dispose of the collateral is governed by the provisions on disposition of collateral (Part 5 of Article 9) of the Uniform Commercial Code.

(5) For the purpose of determining the unpaid balance of consolidated debts or debts pursuant to open-end credit, the allocation of payments to a debt shall be determined in the same manner as provided for determining the amount of debt secured by various security interests (Section 3.303).

(6) The consumer may be held liable in damages to the creditor if the consumer has wrongfully damaged the collateral or if, after default and demand, the consumer has wrongfully failed to make the collateral available to the creditor.

(7) If the creditor elects to bring an action against the consumer for a debt arising from a consumer credit sale of goods or services or from a consumer loan in which the lender is subject to claims and defenses arising from sales and leases (Section 3.405), when under this section he would not be entitled to a deficiency judgment if he took possession of the collateral, and obtains judgment:

(a) he may not take possession of the collateral, and

(b) the collateral is not subject to levy or sale on execution or similar proceedings pursuant to the judgment.

(8) The amounts of $1,750 in subsections (2), (3) and (4) are subject to change pursuant to the provisions on adjustment of dollar amounts (Section 1.106).

(10) The Consumer Debtor's "Minimum Recovery." An injury caused by a secured party's noncompliance with Part 6 of Article 9 normally is limited by the monetary value of the collateral. Inasmuch as the value of most consumer goods is small and the cost of litigation often is high, one might expect that consumers often would be unwilling or unable to avail themselves of the remedy of damages under UCC 9–625(b). Perhaps for this reason, UCC 9–625(c)(2) affords what Comment 4 calls a "minimum recovery" as follows:

if the collateral is consumer goods, a person that was a debtor or a secondary obligor at the time a secured party failed to comply with this part may recover for that failure in any event an amount not less than the credit service charge plus ten per cent of the principal amount of the obligation or the time-price differential plus 10 per cent of the cash price.

Observe that, like the absolute bar rule, this remedy for noncompliance in the case of consumer goods need not bear any relationship to the injury resulting from the secured party's misconduct. Indeed, there may have been no injury at all. Isn't the "minimum recovery" more property called a "civil penalty"? At least one case has construed Former 9–507(1) to impose upon a noncomplying secured party *two* penalties—loss of deficiency *and* an adverse judgment. Does Revised Article 9 contemplate such a result? See UCC 1–305(a) [F1–106(1)]; UCC 9–625(c) & Comment 3 ("the statute is silent as to whether a double recovery or other over-compensation is possible in a consumer transaction").

(11) Consumer Advocacy. In discussing the special provisions for consumers in Part 6 we have referred to "advocates for consumer debtors" and "consumer-advocacy groups." Keep in mind, however, that in the context of default and remedies these advocates were speaking on behalf of consumers who *default* (presumably, a distinct minority of consumer debtors and obligors). Is it possible (probable?) that legal rules protecting and benefitting defaulting consumers do not necessarily benefit consumers generally? To the extent that "consumer-protection" provisions reduce the net recoveries of creditors, who bears the ultimate cost of those reductions? Do you suppose that the creditors' profit margins will decline correspondingly? Or, will the costs instead be passed on to other, non-defaulting consumers (e.g., in the form of increased finance charges)? Will the two groups, consumers and creditors, share the costs? (The vigor with which the advocates for consumer-credit providers fought against many of the consumer-protection provisions proposed for inclusion in Revised Article 9 suggests that they thought at least some of the costs would have come to rest with creditors.)

It may not be possible to answer these questions in the abstract; the answers may turn on facts such as the characteristics of the particular credit market and the size of the costs imposed by the particular consumer-protection provisions. For example, recall the reported effects of the Wisconsin Consumer Act, which permits repossession only after the secured party obtains a court determination that the creditor is entitled to the collateral: While the cost of repossessions rose significantly and the volume of repossessions dropped, the principal impact on credit seemed to be confined to requiring larger down payments in the sale of used cars. Whitford and Laufer, The Impact of Denying Self–Help Repossession of Automobiles: A Case Study of the Wisconsin Consumer Act, 1975 Wis.L.Rev. 607, 654. In his study of real property mortgagor-protection laws, Professor Schill concluded:

> In this Article I argue that the accepted wisdom regarding mortgagor protection laws requires substantial revision. I find, contrary to the results of other empirical studies, that it is unlikely that mortgagor protection laws substantially increase the costs of home credit. This empirical finding is consistent with the theory that when viewed from an ex ante perspective, mortgagor protections may promote, rather than impede, economic efficiency by functioning as a form of insurance against the adverse effects of default and foreclosure. Government intervention in mortgage markets to mandate protection, in the form of deficiency judgment prohibitions, statutory rights of redemption, or a

compulsory mortgage foreclosure insurance program, may be necessary to correct market failures attributable to imperfect information.

Schill, An Economic Analysis of Mortgagor Protection Laws, 77 Va. L. Rev. 489, 537–38 (1991).

Assume that statutory consumer-protection requirements impose costs on every consumer borrower, and that the requirements actually benefit only a very small proportion of consumer borrowers. Does it necessarily follow that the requirements are a bad idea? Or, can they be justified as a form of mandatory insurance against the risk of default? (That is, were the "consumer-advocacy groups" advocating not for every consumer who *does* default but rather for every consumer who *may* default?) Can statutorily-imposed mandatory insurance of this kind be justified only if all consumer borrowers would willingly pay for it? Most consumer borrowers?

(12) Applicable Law. It seems to be settled that an effective agreement as to the applicable law, under UCC 1–301(c) [F1–105(1)], will be controlling for purposes of enforcement under Article 9. See, e.g., Bancorp Leasing & Financial Corp. v. Burhoop, 749 F.2d 36, 39 U.C.C. Rep. Serv. 1426 (9th Cir.1984) (unpublished) (parties' choice of Colorado law, which follows rebuttable presumption rule for defective notification of disposition, controlled in California forum, notwithstanding California's adherence to absolute bar rule); Jones v. First National Bank of Pulaski, 505 So.2d 352 (Ala.1987) (parties' choice of Tennessee law controlled, in Alabama forum, as to adequacy of notification of disposition). As each state's approach to noncompliance in consumer transactions becomes clear, the parties in consumer transactions may wish to avail themselves of the opportunity to opt in or out of the absolute bar rule or rebuttable presumption rule (or other judicially created or statutory rule), particularly when a transaction is likely to bear a reasonable relation to more than one state. Note that consumer transactions may be subject to special legal restrictions on the selection of applicable law, thereby affording less flexibility than the UCC permits.

(13) Rights and Duties of Secured Parties Under UCC 9–207. When we considered perfection of security interests by possession we noted the rights and duties of secured parties under UCC 9–207. See Note (4), p. 193, supra. The most significant duty, of course, is the requirement to use "reasonable care in the custody and preservation of collateral" when it is in the secured party's possession. UCC 9–207(a). UCC 9–207 also applies when a secured party has taken possession after a debtor's default. UCC 9–601(b).

SECTION 3.   RIGHTS OF THIRD–PARTY CLAIMANTS

Sections 1 and 2 of this Chapter dealt with the enforcement rights of the secured party and the duties it owes to the debtor. This Section deals with the rights of certain third parties when a secured party enforces a security interest in collateral. Part (A) considers the rights of secondary obligors for secured obligations, such as guarantors of payment; Part (B) addresses competing secured parties and other lienholders, both senior and junior to the enforcing secured party, and the position of a transferee of collateral at a disposition conducted under UCC 9–610.

(A) SECONDARY OBLIGORS (INCLUDING GUARANTORS)

INTRODUCTORY NOTE: THE ELEMENTS OF SURETYSHIP

Secured lenders and sellers frequently bargain for (perhaps more accurately, insist on) a third-party **guaranty of payment**. Under a guaranty, a third party (the "guarantor") undertakes to pay an obligation of the debtor (the borrower or buyer). Most guaranties provide that the guarantor "unconditionally guarantees the punctual payment when due" of the debtor's obligations; they normally do not condition liability on the debtor's default. In practice, however, a guarantor usually will not be prepared to pay the guaranteed obligation unless it is informed that the debtor has failed to pay. Guaranties are given in transactions that span the spectrum of secured and unsecured credit. Examples abound: Large corporations guaranty payment of debts incurred by their subsidiaries; parents guaranty payment by young daughters and sons who do not have an established credit rating; principal shareholders of closely-held corporations guaranty the corporate borrowings, as in *Stelmach Construction*, Section 2, supra.

A lender may take a guaranty for many of the same reasons that the lender may take a security interest or mortgage. Like collateral, a guaranty provides an additional assurance to the person entitled to the payment that the payment will be made. And, as we observed in the Note on p. 226, supra, a guaranty can be an effective and persuasive mechanism to keep the guarantor interested in the debtor's continued performance and financial health.

A guaranty of payment is governed by the law of **suretyship**.[1] Before focusing specifically on our chief area of concern, the guaranty of payment in the context of secured credit, it will be useful to have a nodding acquaintance with the elements of suretyship law.

What Is "Suretyship"? Considerable (and unnecessary) confusion surrounds the exact meaning of "guaranty," "guarantor," and "surety." If there is any sense in attempting to dispel this confusion, the task is best left for another time and place. For our purposes, the Restatement (Third) of Suretyship and Guaranty (1996) ("Restatement") provides a satisfactory working definition using generic terms such as "secondary obligor" and "secondary obligation":

---

1.   There are many other kinds of suretyship contracts. A common example is the **performance bond**, under which an insurance company or other surety company agrees to complete the performance of a construction contract if the contractor fails to perform as agreed.

(1) This Restatement applies . . . and a secondary obligor has suretyship status whenever:

> (a) pursuant to contract (the "secondary obligation"), an obligee has recourse against a person (the "secondary obligor") or that person's property with respect to the obligation (the "underlying obligation") of another person (the "principal obligor"); and

> (b) to the extent that the underlying obligation or the secondary obligation is performed the obligee is not entitled to performance of the other obligation; and

> (c) as between the principal obligor and the secondary obligor, it is the principal obligor who ought to perform the underlying obligation or bear the cost of performance.

Restatement §1(1).

Take a simple example. Suppose that *P* wishes to borrow $50,000 from *O*. To induce *O* to make the loan, *P* has *S* join with *P* in promising to repay. As further security, *P* pledges $30,000 worth of corporate bonds to *O*. *S* has suretyship status under the Restatement because:

(a) Both *P* and *S* are under an obligation to *O*;

(b) *O* is entitled to but one performance; and

(c) as between *P* and *S*, *P* rather than *S* should perform.

In Restatement terms, *P* (the borrower) is the *principal obligor*; *S* (the guarantor) is the *secondary obligor*; *O* (the creditor) is the *obligee*.

The Obligee's Rights Against the Principal and Secondary Obligors. O's rights against *P* are governed basically by contract law: Absent a contract defense (e.g., *O's* fraud upon *P*; *P's* infancy), *O* will have the right to enforce the obligation against *P*.

In the alternative, *O* may proceed against *S*, the secondary obligor. If *P* defaults, generally *O* need not attempt to collect from *P* before enforcing *S's* liability; nor need *O* look first to the corporate bonds. Immediate recourse against *S* upon *P's* default was one of the advantages that *O* expected from *S's* suretyship contract. Even if *O's* lack of diligence in pursuing *P* causes loss, *S* is not discharged.[2] *S* may defend against *O* by raising any of *P's* contract defenses except *P's* bankruptcy discharge and *P's* capacity to

---

2.   See Restatement § 50(1). The Restatement recognizes exceptions to the rule preserving a dilatory obligee's right to recover from a secondary obligor, e.g., when a statute provides otherwise and when the obligee allows the statute of limitations to lapse on the underlying obligation. See id. Statutes adopted in a number of states provide that the obligee's failure to sue the principal obligor at the secondary obligor's request discharges the secondary obligor. (A few states follow this rule as a matter of common law.)

Of course, a surety may limit its engagement to a guaranty of *collection* of the principal's obligation. Such a **guarantor of collection** is, by the nature of the undertaking, discharged to the extent of any loss caused by the obligee's lack of diligence in proceeding against the principal. See Restatement § 50(2). Understandably, guaranties of collection are rare in the credit markets.

contract. See Restatement § 34. In addition, *S* may have the additional "suretyship defenses" discussed below.

The Secondary Obligor's Rights Against the Principal Obligor. *S*, who is subject to an action by *O* should *P* default, has in turn three major remedies against *P*: exoneration, subrogation, and reimbursement. **Exoneration** is an equitable remedy. Basically it allows *S*, upon *P*'s default, to compel *P* in a suit in equity to pay *O*. Restatement § 21(2) & comment *i*. It is reasoned that without this remedy *S* might undergo considerable hardship in raising the money to pay *O*, even though *S* could afterwards recover over from *P*. Secondary obligors rarely assert the right to exoneration, however, probably because most principal obligors who *do not* pay probably *cannot* pay. Moreover, the right to exoneration against *P* does not give *S* any right to delay paying *O*. Thus, a secondary obligor usually will pay the obligee and then attempt to recover from the principal under the right to subrogation or reimbursement.

A secondary obligor who pays in full the principal obligor's debt to the obligee is subrogated to the obligee's rights. See Restatement §§ 27–28. **Subrogation** may be viewed as equitable assignment. If *S* were to pay $50,000 to *O*, then, as by assignment, *S* would succeed to *O*'s rights (as holder of the secured debt and as pledgee of the corporate bonds) against *P* and to the priority of *O*'s security interest as against third parties. Because subrogation is an equitable remedy, it is subject to equitable limitations, particularly where the secondary obligor attempts to enforce a right that the obligee would have had against a third party. One such important limitation is that a surety ordinarily has no right of subrogation unless and until the obligee has received *full* payment of the debt. Thus, if *S* should pay *O* only $40,000, leaving $10,000 unpaid, usually *S* would not become entitled thereby to any part of *O*'s security interest in the bonds. This limitation insures that the benefits of *P*'s collateral remain available for the satisfaction of *P*'s remaining debt to *O*.

A surety who pays *any part* of the principal obligor's debt is, however, entitled to **reimbursement** (sometimes called **indemnification**) of the amount paid. See Restatement §§ 22–23. So, even if *S* pays only $40,000 of the $50,000 debt to *P*, *S* is entitled to reimbursement of that amount. Because *S* became bound as surety at *P*'s request, *S*'s right to reimbursement can be spelled out from *P*'s implied request to *S* to pay the debt at maturity and from *P*'s implied promise to reimburse *S* for any such payment. (Of course, well-drafted suretyship contracts explicitly provide for a right to reimbursement.) The right to reimbursement is only a right *in personam* against *P*. For this reason, it may be less satisfactory to *S* than subrogation, particularly if *S* must compete with other creditors of *P*.

The Secondary Obligor's Defenses. Exoneration, subrogation and reimbursement, then, are the three main remedies of a secondary obligor (here, *S*) against the principal obligor (*P*). An elementary understanding of them is necessary to answer the next question: How will an agreement between an obligee and the principal obligor to *modify* the principal's obligation affect the secondary obligor's obligation?[3] Suppose that O and P modified their original agreement so as to increase the interest rate from eight to nine per cent. Under traditional doctrine supported by much case law, S's obligation on the guaranty would be discharged; S would be "off the hook." Arguably, the modification has increased S's risk by increasing the burden of P's performance and making it more likely that P will default. Suppose, however, that the modification decreases the interest rate from eight to seven per cent. Because S would not be prejudiced, it is difficult to justify discharging S's obligation. Nevertheless, there is authority for the proposition that since a suretyship contract is *strictissimi juris* (i.e., to be interpreted in the strictest manner), the secondary obligor will be discharged whether the modification increases or decreases the burden of the principal's performance! Under the Restatement, however, the secondary obligor's obligation is discharged only to the extent that the modification imposes "fundamentally different" risks on the secondary obligor or causes the secondary obligor loss. Restatement § 41(b).

Consider two other common types of modification—O's release of P and O's extension of the time for P to perform. It is hardly surprising that, under traditional doctrine, *release* of the principal obligor generally discharges a secondary obligor. However, traditional doctrine provides an easy means by which O could release P but preserve S's liability nevertheless: O could merely reserve its rights against S at the time of P's release. One might question the fairness of this rule to P, who would be "released" but may not realize that it remains liable to S (via reimbursement or subrogation) for the full amount of the obligation. One might also question its fairness to S. S may not realize that P was released and instead assume that P had paid the underlying obligation. Had S been informed, S might have taken prompt action to protect its rights against P.

The Restatement takes an approach towards suretyship defenses that differs somewhat from the traditional doctrine. O's release of P's obligation to pay money is a type of "impairment of recourse" under the Restatement. See Restatement § 37(3)(a). Although in general the release would discharge S, the Restatement, like traditional doctrine, permits O to preserve S's liability. The Restatement replaces the "reservation of rights" doctrine with the doctrine of "preservation of the secondary obligor's recourse." Like its predecessor, the preservation-of-recourse doctrine enables O to release P while affecting no change in P's liability to S. See Restatement § 39(b). A release or extension effects a preservation of recourse if the *express terms* of the release or extension provide that (i) the obligee retains the right to seek performance from the secondary obligor and (ii) the secondary obligor's rights to recourse against the principal obligor continue as though the release or extension had not been granted. Restatement § 38(1).

Unlike a reservation of rights, a preservation of recourse does not necessarily prevent S from being discharged. Even if a secondary obligor's

---

3.   This discussion of discharge of a surety is premised upon the assumption that the obligee, O, has knowledge of the suretyship relationship of S. See Restatement § 32.

recourse has been preserved, the secondary obligor will be discharged to the extent that the release or extension would otherwise cause the secondary obligor a loss. Restatement § 39(c). The comments to the Restatement suggest that *O* can prevent the release or extension from causing a loss to *S* by informing *S* promptly of the release or extension and the fact that recourse has been preserved. Restatement § 38, comment *b*. Nevertheless, the comments indicate that even when *S* has been informed, "loss can still occur." Id. For example, the release may induce behavior on *P*'s part that lessens *P*'s ability to perform. In many cases, however, *S* will not suffer a loss because it would be unlikely that *S* could have had any recovery against an impecunious *P*. Restatement § 39, comment *f*.

A binding agreement between *O* and *P* *extending the time* for *P*'s performance is another type of "impairment of recourse" under the Restatement. Restatement § 37(3)(b). That impairment, as with a release of *P*'s payment obligation, will discharge *S* to the extent that the extension causes a loss, even if *O* has preserved *S*'s recourse against *P*. Restatement § 40(b). However, if *O* has preserved *S*'s recourse against *P* and *S* is not discharged, then *S* may avoid any prejudicial effect of the extension by paying at the original maturity and proceeding against *P* in spite of the extension. Restatement § 40(c).

Finally, a third type of impairment of recourse under the Restatement occurs if the obligee "*impair[s] the value of an interest in collateral* securing the underlying obligation." Restatement § 37(d). This impairment discharges *S* "to the extent that such impairment would otherwise increase the difference between the maximum amount recoverable by the secondary obligor pursuant to its subrogation rights . . . and the value of the secondary obligor's interest in the collateral." Restatement § 42(1). Thus, if *O* should release the security interest in the $30,000 worth of bonds securing *P*'s debt, then *S* would be discharged to the extent of $30,000. *O*'s failure to perfect the security interest also could constitute an impairment of collateral, if a buyer or other conflicting claimant were to prevent *S* from receiving the benefit of the collateral.

UCC 3–605 deals explicitly with issues of discharge of a secondary obligor who is an "accommodation party" to a negotiable instrument, i.e., who "signs the instrument for the purpose of incurring liability on the instrument without being a direct beneficiary of the value given for the instrument." UCC 3–419(a). (The "co-maker" of a negotiable note is an "accommodation party.") Extensions of time, other material modifications of terms, and impairment of collateral will discharge an accommodation party only to the extent that the accommodation party suffers loss thereby. UCC 3–605(c), (d), (f), & (g). (The 2002 amendments to Article 3 conform the rules governing accommodation parties to the rules found in the Restatement.) These UCC Article 3 provisions rarely come into play when the obligee is in the business of extending credit. Even if the obligation is evidenced by a negotiable note (which is uncommon), such obligees customarily obtain a separate guaranty.

Waiver of Suretyship Defenses; Consent by Secondary Obligor. Both Restatement § 48 and UCC 3–605(i) [R3–605(f)] give effect to a secondary obligor's consent to acts that otherwise would discharge the secondary obligor and to a secondary obligor's waiver of its suretyship defenses. Indeed, these consents and waivers almost universally appear in guaranties of payment used in financing transactions. On the other hand, good practice often dictates that a careful lender will request express and explicit consent from guarantor before pursuing a course of action that, absent effective consent or waiver, would cause a discharge (e.g., release of collateral). The relationship between the generally applicable ability of a secondary obligor to waive its suretyship defenses and the non-waivable rights and duties under UCC 9–602 is addressed in Note (2) on Rights of Guarantors of Secured Obligations, infra.

Secondary Obligor vs. Secured Party: A Brief Excursus. One additional aspect of the relationship between suretyship law and Article 9 should be mentioned. Assume that a contractor (*P*) has a contract to build a building for the owner of land (*O*). As is customary, *P* obtains a performance bond, under which a third-party secondary obligor (*S*) undertakes to complete the building if *P* should default in its performance. In addition, a secured party (*SP*) has a security interest in *P*'s accounts, including *P*'s right to payment from *O*. Following *P*'s default and *S*'s completion of the contract, both *S* and *SP* claim the remaining amounts owing by *O* to *P*. The source of *S*'s claim is the law of suretyship: Having completed the contract, *S* is subrogated to *P*'s rights against *O*, which include the right to be paid for a completed building. *S*'s claim may include the right to funds earned by *P*'s pre-default performance but withheld by *O* pursuant to the contract. This right is premised on the notion that *S* is subrogated to *O*'s rights.

Although *SP* has perfected its security interest by filing, *S* has not filed. Whose claim is senior? The law has become well-settled since the leading case of National Shawmut Bank v. New Amsterdam Casualty Co., 411 F.2d 843 (1st Cir.1969). *S* wins. *S*'s rights do not derive from a consensual security interest under Article 9, but instead are born of suretyship law. Accordingly, the priority rules of Article 9 are inapplicable.

As we have seen, Former 9–201 has been construed to award priority to a security interest over a conflicting non-Article 9 interest (the right of setoff). See Chapter 8, Section 4(D), supra. What accounts for the near unanimity of judicial opinion in favor of sureties? An intuitive approach might be to ask, what would the value of *SP*'s collateral have been had *S* not performed? Is it fair to pay *S* for the value its performance created? Alternatively, one might (but courts generally have not) rank the competing claims by reference to Former 9–318(1) (UCC 9–404(a)(1)). The secured party ordinarily takes its rights subject to "all the terms of the contract between the account debtor [*O*] and assignor [*P*] and any defense or claim arising therefrom." Wouldn't *P*'s breach have given *O* a defense to payment, or at least a partial setoff? *S*, having performed the contract, simply steps into *O*'s shoes as against *SP*. One can reach the same result by subrogating

S, who rendered performance to *O*, to *O*'s rights against *P* (including the right to retain amounts unpaid under the construction contract).

––––––––––

Problem 9.3.1. Under the facts of Problem 9.2.1, p. 602, supra, suppose that Telli Schmelli, the CEO, had executed in favor of the bank (AIB) an absolute, unconditional guaranty of payment, whereby Telli, individually, guaranteed to AIB the punctual payment when due of all existing and future indebtedness of Schmelli Services, Inc., to AIB. The guaranty thus covers the outstanding indebtedness on the line of credit facility as well as the Learjet indebtedness. Under the terms of the guaranty Telli waived all possible suretyship defenses and all rights (including rights to notice) relating to any collateral.

You are counsel for both Schmelli Services and Telli. The Learjet has been sold by AIB for an amount that left a substantial deficiency on the Learjet debt. AIB has accelerated the line of credit indebtedness and is in the process of collecting the accounts receivable, but Telli expects a deficiency on that loan as well.

Prior to selling the Learjet AIB sent a notification of private sale (by certified mail, return receipt requested) addressed to:

Schmelli Services, Inc.

1000½ E. Markham

Little Rock, Arkansas 72206

Attention: Telli Schmelli, Pres. & CEO

When the envelope containing the notice was delivered to Schmelli's headquarters, Telli's private secretary, Melli Vanelli, signed for it. Telli saw the notice the next day, while reading the mail, and immediately faxed a copy to you.

AIB has sued Telli on the personal guaranty of payment for an amount equal to the outstanding balance on all Schmelli corporate debt. What defenses, if any, will you raise? What is the likelihood of success? See UCC 9–611(b); UCC 9–102(a)(71); UCC 9–102(a)(74); UCC 9–602(7); UCC 9–624; UCC 9–626(a); Notes on Rights of Guarantors of Secured Obligations, infra.

NOTES ON RIGHTS OF GUARANTORS OF SECURED OBLIGATIONS

(1) Guarantors of Obligations Secured Under Article 9. There was considerable litigation under Former Article 9 as to whether a guarantor was a "debtor" who would be entitled to notification of a disposition of collateral and to whom various duties, e.g., to dispose of collateral in a commercially reasonable manner, would run. A substantial number of reported cases also addressed whether a guarantor who is entitled to notification nevertheless may make an effective pre-default waiver of the right to receive notice.

Revised Article 9 resolves these issues definitively. The key to understanding the resolution lies in large part in the distinction between a "debtor," who has an interest in the collateral, and an "obligor," who owes payment of the secured obligation. See UCC 9–102. In many transactions, the same person is both a debtor and an obligor. This would be the case, for example, as to the Prototype automobile financing transactions in Chapter 3, Section 1, supra: Main Motors is both debtor and obligor in the inventory financing transaction with Firstbank, and Lee Abel is both debtor and obligor in the Chevrolet transaction. A guarantor of the secured obligation, such as Abel's Aunt Bea in Problem 3.5.10, p. 226, is a "secondary obligor." See UCC 9–102(a)(71)(A) (explaining, most helpfully, that "secondary obligor" includes "an obligor to the extent that . . . the obligor's obligation is secondary") & Comment 2.a. The term also includes a "hypothecator," referred to below in Note (2). See UCC 9–102(a)(71)(B).

Even when a secondary obligor is not a debtor, the secondary obligor is entitled to notification of a disposition. See UCC 9–611(b), (c). In addition a secondary obligor who suffers loss as a result of the secured party's noncompliance with Article 9, e.g., from the secured party's failure to dispose of the collateral in a commercially reasonable manner, may obtain the benefit of the rebuttable presumption rule of UCC 9–626(a) or, in a consumer transaction, any deficiency-reducing rule the court may impose.

Having given rights to guarantors and other secondary obligors, Revised Article 9 restricts a secondary obligor's ability to waive those rights. See UCC 9–602; UCC 9–624. In other contexts, guarantors and other secondary obligors enjoy the virtually unrestricted ability to waive their rights. See, e.g., Restatement § 48. What policy supports restricting a guarantor's ability to waive rights under Article 9? Suppose that a secured party fails to comply with Part 6 and the noncompliance reduces its recovery from the collateral. Is a guarantor's liability for the resulting deficiency affected in the same way as that of the principal obligor?

(2) Security Interests in One Debtor's Collateral Securing Obligations of Another Debtor. There are means other than giving a guaranty by which a third party can lend support to an obligation of another. Sometimes a third party **(hypothecator)** will give a security interest in property that it owns to support another's obligation. For example, Telli's stock might be used to secure Schmelli Services' debt. Under these circumstances the hypothecator (Telli) is an "obligor." See UCC 9–102(a)(59)(ii). Because Telli's obligation is secondary (as between Schmelli and Telli, Schmelli should pay the debt to AIB), Telli is a "secondary obligor," regardless of whether Telli also guaranties the obligation. In addition, with respect to the stock, Telli is a "debtor." See UCC 9–102(a)(28)(A). However, inasmuch as Telli has no interest in the corporate Learjet and accounts, Telli is not a "debtor" with respect to that collateral. See UCC 9–102, Comment 2.a.

Suppose, in the example, AIB enforces its security interest in all the collateral (including Telli's stock) and remains unpaid in part. Is Telli, an obligor, liable for a deficiency? UCC 9–615(d)(2) says plainly that "the obligor is liable for any deficiency." But what is the deficiency? The answer depends on Telli's obligation, which is governed by Telli's agreement with AIB. If, for example, Telli hypothecated the stock but did not undertake personally to pay (i.e., did not guarantee) the corporate debt, there would be no deficiency with respect to Telli's obligation once AIB disposes of the stock; under these circumstances, Telli would not become liable for any deficiency. On the other hand, if Telli guaranteed Schmelli's debt, then Telli would be liable for any deficiency with respect to that obligation.

Similar care must be taken in determining who is entitled to a surplus. If the surplus arises from the disposition of Telli's stock, then Telli, as the debtor with respect to that collateral (and not as obligor), would be entitled to the surplus. See UCC 9–615(d)(1). Any surplus arising from the disposition of corporate assets would, of course, go to Schmelli, the debtor with respect to that collateral. Does this create undesirable incentives for Schmelli and Telli to compete in persuading AIB which collateral to look to first?

(B) COMPETING SECURED PARTIES AND LIENHOLDERS; TRANSFEREES OF COLLATERAL IN DISPOSITIONS UNDER UCC 9–610

We now leave (for a brief time) the paradigm of enforcement of security interests against obligors on secured indebtedness and owners of the collateral. The Problems and Notes in this part consider some of the difficulties and questions that can arise when collateral is subject to multiple security interests and other liens and one or more of the claimants seek to enforce a security interest. Most of the issues that have arisen over the duties that are or should be imposed upon an enforcing secured party in favor of a competing claimant concern (i) whether and under what circumstances the foreclosing secured party should be required to afford notice of a foreclosure sale to a competing claimant and (ii) the appropriate allocation of the proceeds of the sale.

Problem 9.3.2. Under the facts of Problem 9.2.1, supra, suppose that AIB's security agreement covering accounts also covers all equipment at any time owned by Schmelli Services. Suppose also that AIB has perfected its security interest by filing in Arkansas, Schmelli's state of incorporation.

You now represent Tuleight Co., one of Schmelli's trade creditors. Several months ago Tuleight's president was pressing Schmelli's treasurer for payment of past due invoices. To "buy some time," the treasurer offered Tuleight a security interest in all of Schmelli's office equipment located in Arkansas (where Tuleight's sole office is located). Tuleight agreed. To "save time and money," Tuleight did not consult you or any other lawyer. Tuleight's president bought a form security agreement and financing statement at a stationery store, completed the documents (properly, as luck would have it), obtained Schmelli's execution of the security agreement, and filed the financing statement in the Arkansas filing office. Also as luck would have it, Tuleight's president did not think to search the filings and was (and remains) ignorant of AIB's earlier filing and senior security interest.

Tuleight now asks for your advice about how to take possession of and sell the equipment. The outstanding balance that Schmelli owes Tuleight is $50,000.

(a) If Tuleight can recover possession of the equipment, to whom should Tuleight give notification of a disposition? Will you request a search of the UCC filing office in Arkansas? See UCC 9–611; Note (1) on Duties Owed by an Enforcing Secured Party to a Competing Secured Party or Lienholder and Rights of Transferees, infra.

(b) Assume, for the time being, that AIB has *no other collateral* for the Schmelli debt (i.e., assume that AIB already has liquidated the accounts, the equipment in other states, and the Learjet, and that a deficiency remains unpaid). Under which, if any, of the following scenarios will Tuleight be liable to AIB? See UCC 9–625(b), (c); Note (3) on Duties Owed by an Enforcing Secured Party to a Competing Secured Party or Lienholder and Rights of Transferees, infra.

(i) Tuleight takes possession of the equipment. See UCC 9–609 & Comment 5.

(ii) After Tuleight takes possession, AIB demands that Tuleight deliver the equipment to AIB and Tuleight refuses. Does it matter whether AIB's loan is in default?

(iii) After Tuleight takes possession, Tuleight sells the equipment. Does it matter whether the buyer at the sale disappears with the equipment? See UCC 9–610 & Comment 5.

(iv) Tuleight sells the equipment at a public sale following two days' advertising in a local "throw-away" newspaper.

(v) Tuleight sells the equipment at a commercially reasonable sale for $30,000 and keeps the money. Does it matter whether Tuleight gave reasonable notification of the disposition to AIB? See UCC 9–615; UCC 9–611 & Comment 4.

(vi) Tuleight sells the equipment at a commercially reasonable sale for $90,000, keeps $55,000 (including $5,000 costs of sale), and gives $35,000 to Schmelli.

Problem 9.3.3. How would the existence of the other collateral for the AIB debt affect any of the results in Problem 9.3.2(b)? See Note (4) on Duties Owed by an Enforcing Secured Party to a Competing Secured Party or Lienholder and Rights of Transferees, infra.

Problem 9.3.4. Under the facts of Problem 9.3.2, assume that Schmelli Services enters bankruptcy.

(a) If AIB wishes to satisfy its claim first from the Arkansas equipment, can Tuleight compel AIB to satisfy its claim first from the other collateral instead? See Note (4) on Duties Owed by an Enforcing Secured Party to a Competing Secured Party or Lienholder and Rights of Transferees, infra.

(b) If AIB wishes to satisfy its claim first from the other collateral, can the bankruptcy trustee compel AIB to satisfy its claim first from the Arkansas equipment instead?

Problem 9.3.5. Assume the facts of Problem 9.3.2. Assume also that Schmelli Services did not enter bankruptcy. You now represent Bonzo Co. Bonzo has reached tentative agreement with Tuleight to buy, in a private sale, various office equipment that Tuleight has repossessed from Schmelli. What steps do you take to protect Bonzo? See UCC 9–617; UCC 9–610(d)—(f) & Comment 5; UCC 2–312(1), (2) & Comment 5 [R2–312(1), (3) & Comment 6]; Note (3) on Duties Owed by an Enforcing Secured Party to a Competing Secured Party or Lienholder and Rights of Transferees, infra. What, if any, special provisions will you insist on in the sale agreement?

NOTES ON DUTIES OWED BY AN ENFORCING SECURED PARTY TO A COMPETING SECURED PARTY OR LIENHOLDER AND RIGHTS OF TRANSFEREES

(1) Duties of Senior Secured Parties to Junior Claimants: Notification Requirements. We have seen that UCC 9–610(b) requires an enforcing secured party to send "a reasonable authenticated notification of disposition." UCC 9–611(c) specifies the parties to be notified; they include "the debtor," "any secondary obligor," and certain other persons claiming an interest in the collateral, as specified in subsection (c)(3). Please read carefully UCC 9–611(a) (defining "notification date"), (c)(3), and (e).

As Comment 4 to UCC 9–611 explains in greater detail, since the 1962 Official Text of Article 9, the scope of a foreclosing secured party's duty to notify holders of conflicting security interests has been narrowed (in 1972) and then expanded (in Revised Article 9). The current approach reflects the view that "[m]any problems arising from dispositions of collateral encumbered by multiple security interests can be ameliorated or solved by informing all secured parties of an intended disposition and affording them the opportunity to work with one another." UCC 9–611, Comment 4. Requiring an enforcing secured party to give notice to others of record may delay a sale by the amount of time necessary to search the public record and determine whether other secured parties are on file. In an ideal world, this delay would be trivial; in the real world it may not be. Concerns about the potential for delay gave rise to UCC 9–611(e): If a secured party requests a search of the appropriate filing office between 20 and 30 days before the notification date, it need only give notice to the secured parties or other lienholders of record uncovered by that search. And if no response to the search request is received before the notification date, the secured party has complied with the notification requirement contained in UCC 9–611(c)(3)(B).

(2) Duties of Senior Secured Parties to Junior Claimants: Allocation of Proceeds. Revised Article 9 gives considerable guidance concerning the duties of a senior secured party with respect to proceeds of a disposition. See UCC 9–615. After payment of (i) the reasonable expenses of the disposition and (ii) any reasonable attorney's fees and legal expenses incurred by the secured party (to the extent provided for in the agreement and not prohibited by law), the proceeds are to be applied first to the satisfaction of the indebtedness secured by the security interest under which the disposition is made and, if any proceeds remain, then to "the satisfaction of obligations secured by any subordinate security interest or other lien the collateral." UCC 9–615(a)(3)(A). But the secured party must apply the proceeds to obligations secured by a subordinate interest only if the secured party has received an "authenticated demand for proceeds before distribution of the proceeds is completed." Id.[4] This rule has the effect of requiring a junior secured party who wishes to share in the proceeds of a senior's foreclosure sale to make written demand upon the senior.

The Drafting Committee decided early in the drafting process that it would not be wise to undertake a statutory resolution of every possible problem that might arise in connection with junior interests. For example, suppose that a junior secured party makes demand and receives payment from a senior, and the debtor claims that the junior's purported security interest is invalid (perhaps the security agreement contains a defective collateral description). Would the *senior* face liability to the debtor for having complied with the statute in good faith? Presumably not. Any recovery from the *junior* to which the debtor may be entitled would be governed by the law of restitution.

(3) Dispositions of Collateral by Junior Secured Parties Pursuant to UCC 9–610. By its terms, Part 6 of Article 9 applies to all security interests, regardless of priority. However, except for the adjustments to the notification rules in UCC 9–611 and the rules for application of proceeds in UCC 9–615 (see Notes (1) and (2), supra), UCC 9–610 and the accompanying provisions dealing with the disposition of collateral generally contemplate the paradigm in which the enforcing party will have the senior interest. Not surprisingly, questions abound concerning foreclosure sales conducted by juniors. For the most part, these questions are addressed, if at all, in the comments, particularly UCC 9–610, Comment 5.

Junior's Right to Take Possession of and Dispose of Collateral. Inasmuch as Article 9 recognizes junior security interests in collateral, it would be odd indeed if the Article did not permit a junior secured party to enforce its security interest by taking possession of and disposing of collateral. Nothing in Article 9 suggests that the holder of a junior security interest does not have the right to enforce its security interest. See UCC 9–609 and Comment 5; UCC 9–610 and Comment 5.

---

4.   Part 6 does not apply to the enforcement of a consignor's security interest. See UCC 9–601(g). However, when a non-consignor secured party enforces its security interest, special distribution rules apply to the proceeds of collateral that is the subject of a consignment. These rules take account of the fact that the consignor is the owner of the collateral. See UCC 9–615(a)(3)(B), (4), (d)(1), and Comment 2 (second paragraph).

Senior's Right to Take Possession From Junior. What are the rights of a senior secured party when a junior has taken possession of collateral after default? In most cases the debtor also will be in default as to the senior security interest, even if the debtor has not missed a payment on the senior secured obligation. Credit agreements often provide that the creation of a junior lien, the debtor's default under a junior secured obligation (a **cross-default**), and a junior's taking possession of collateral each constitutes a default. Is it a reasonable implication from a senior's senior status that its right to possession after default is superior to that of a junior? For an affirmative answer, see UCC 9–609, Comment 5.

Senior's Right to Control the Junior's Proposed Disposition. Assuming a senior secured party rightfully takes possession of collateral from a junior secured party, may the senior pick up where the junior left off? For example, may the senior avail itself of any advertisements concerning the proposed disposition and any notifications sent by the junior to the debtor and other secured parties? Or must the senior start the process all over again? On the other hand, is the senior necessarily *entitled* to begin anew? Perhaps the senior is concerned that the junior's planned procedures would not be commercially reasonable. But, could the debtor later argue successfully that the delay caused by the senior's starting all over again rendered the senior's (otherwise commercially reasonable) disposition commercially unreasonable? Neither the text of Revised Article 9 nor the comments undertake to provide specific answers to these questions.

Senior's Right to Notification From Junior. In specifying the class of secured parties entitled to notification of a disposition, UCC 9–611(c) does not distinguish between junior and senior creditors. Do you find it anomalous to require juniors to notify seniors of a disposition? If the notification is intended to afford parties an opportunity to protect their interests, arguably the senior does not need notification. Unlike a security interest that is junior to the interest being enforced, the senior's interest will not be cut off by the disposition. UCC 9–617(a)(3). Nevertheless, the disposition in fact may affect the senior adversely. In some cases, the senior may be unable to locate the collateral after sale and so in effect will have become unsecured. Even if the senior can locate the collateral, the senior will have incurred the costs of searching for it as well as the costs of repossessing it from the buyer, who may be less cooperative than the debtor would have been. (A buyer who did not take account of the senior's security interest when calculating the price is likely to be particularly ornery.) Moreover, when the senior has a security interest in all the assets of a debtor's business, the proceeds the senior will receive from the resale of a single item of collateral upon repossession from a buyer are likely to be less than the allocable portion of proceeds that the senior would have received upon a foreclosure sale of all the assets of the debtor's business.

Senior's Right to Recover Collateral From Transferee at Junior's Sale. Even if the senior has the right to control a disposition, in any given case it might not do so. Assume that the junior proceeds with its disposition of the collateral (because, for example, neither the junior nor the senior secured party is aware of the other's interest). One of the few issues, in this context, on which Article 9 does speak with clarity is the rights of a transferee in a disposition under UCC 9–610. As already mentioned, the transferee cuts off only "the security interest under which it is made and any security interest or lien *subordinate thereto.*" UCC 9–617(a)(3). If the senior did not authorize the disposition and if its security interest is perfected, the senior's security interest would continue notwithstanding the junior's disposition; the senior would be entitled to take possession of the collateral from the junior's transferee. See UCC 9–315(a)(1); UCC 9–317(b); Chapter 4, Section 2(A), supra.

What can a buyer do to protect itself against claims of a senior? As with any sale out of the ordinary course of business, the prudent buyer must undertake UCC searches and investigate the seller's source of title. As a practical matter, non-ordinary course buyers often fear little for hidden conflicting interests because they are satisfied with the creditworthiness of their seller and the seller's warranty of title. A disposition under UCC 9–610 is no exception. Unless the enforcing secured party disclaims its warranties, the transferee will have the benefit of any warranty obligations "which by operation of law accompany a voluntary disposition of property of the kind subject to the contract," e.g., a warranty of title under UCC 2–312. UCC 9–610(d). However, enforcing secured parties typically take advantage of the ease with which title warranties in a foreclosure disposition can be disclaimed. See UCC 9–610(e), (f). A disclaimer of warranties by an enforcing secured party should alert the prospective transferee to undertake appropriate due diligence. This approach is consistent with the overarching goal of encouraging all interested persons to find out about the others.

Rights to Proceeds Received Upon Junior's Disposition; Liability of Junior to Senior. Suppose that a junior secured party takes possession of collateral and sells it to a buyer pursuant to UCC 9–610; the buyer then flees with the collateral and cannot be found. The senior secured party then sues the junior, asserting that the junior converted the collateral by (alternatively) (i) taking possession of it in the first place, (ii) selling it, or (iii) failing to turn over the proceeds to the senior. What result?

The text of Article 9 addresses only the last of the three assertions. A junior secured party can retain cash proceeds without the duty to apply them to the senior's obligation or to account to or pay the senior, as long as the junior acts "in good faith and without knowledge that the receipt [of the proceeds] violates the rights of the holder of the" senior interest. UCC 9–615(g). Comment 5 to UCC 9–609 addresses the junior's having taken possession of the collateral, as follows:

> Non-UCC law governs whether a junior secured party in possession of collateral is liable to the senior in conversion. Normally, a junior who refuses to relinquish possession of collateral upon the demand of a secured party having a superior possessory right to the collateral would be liable in conversion.

And Comment 5 to UCC 9–610 explains that a junior's exercise of its right to dispose of collateral "does not of itself give rise to liability in favor of the holder of the senior security interest."

A Different Approach. Several commentators who addressed these issues under Former Article 9 recommended a different approach to protecting an enforcing junior and its transferee from claims of a senior secured party: If a notified senior fails to act by taking over the junior's disposition, the junior should be entitled to sell the collateral free of the senior interest. See Byrne, Murphy, & Vukowich, Junior Creditors' Realization on Debtors' Equity Under U.C.C. Section 9–311: An Appraisal and a Proposal, 77 Geo. L.J. 1905 (1989). See also Wechsler, Rights and Remedies of the Secured Party After an Unauthorized Transfer of Collateral: A Proposal for Balancing Competing Claims in Repossession, Resale, Proceeds, and Conversion Cases, 32 Buff.L.Rev. 373 (1983) (arguing for a similar result). Is this approach preferable to the one adopted by Revised Article 9?

(4) Determining Who Is Senior: Herein of Marshaling. In Problem 9.3.3, supra, both AIB and Tuleight held security interests in the Arkansas equipment. AIB's security interest was senior. AIB held a security interest in other collateral as well. Is AIB entitled to look to the Arkansas equipment, thereby leaving Tuleight with no collateral? Tuleight's counsel will, no doubt, invoke the doctrine of "marshaling of assets."

As explained by the Supreme Court, " [t]he equitable doctrine of marshalling rests upon the principle that a creditor having two funds to satisfy his debt, may not by his application of them to his demand, defeat another creditor, who may resort to only one of the funds.' " Meyer v. United States, 375 U.S. 233, 236, 84 S.Ct. 318, 321, 11 L.Ed.2d 293, 297 (1963), quoting Sowell v. Federal Reserve Bank, 268 U.S. 449, 456–57, 45 S.Ct. 528, 530–31, 69 L.Ed. 1041, 1049 (1925). The purpose of the doctrine is "to prevent the arbitrary action of a senior lienor from destroying the rights of a junior lienor or a creditor having less security." Id. at 237, 84 S.Ct. at 321, 11 L.Ed.2d at 297. Because it is an equitable doctrine, marshaling is applied only when it can be equitably fashioned as to all of the parties having an interest in the property. To invoke marshaling successfully, there must be two creditors of a common debtor and two separate assets or funds of that debtor. In addition, one of the creditors must have a lien on only one of the funds and the other a lien on both of the funds. Tuleight's situation presents a classic case for marshaling. And case law supports the availability of marshaling where an Article 9 security interest is involved. Comment 5 to UCC 9–610 approves of the foregoing analysis. (Indeed, if you notice the similarity between that comment and the foregoing, keep in mind that the foregoing passage appeared in a previous edition of this book, years before we wrote the Official Comments.) See also UCC 9–401, Comment 6, (suggesting, in a somewhat different factual setting, that marshaling "may be appropriate").

Now assume that all the collateral is sold in Schmelli's bankruptcy and that the proceeds of the other collateral is sufficient to repay AIB in full.

Which would be fairer to Tuleight: to pay AIB's claim, in part, from the proceeds of the Arkansas equipment and give Tuleight nothing, or to pay Tuleight's claim from the proceeds of the Arkansas equipment and pay AIB from the proceeds of the other collateral? Which approach would be fairer to AIB?

A number of cases have raised questions concerning the applicability of marshaling to secured claims in bankruptcy. Under the guise of marshaling, efforts have been made to require a secured party to seek recovery from sources other than the bankruptcy estate (e.g., from secured or unsecured guaranties). The cases are conflicting. Compare In re Jack Green's Fashions for Men—Big & Tall, Inc., 597 F.2d 130 (8th Cir. 1979) (upholding marshaling order that compelled secured party to look first to secured guaranties instead of collateral owned by debtor) with In re Computer Room, Inc., 24 B.R. 732 (Bkrtcy.N.D.Ala.1982) (rejecting *Jack Green* and declining to require secured creditor to look first to guarantor). In other cases, the bankruptcy trustee has attempted, with mixed success, to impose what may be called "reverse marshaling," i.e., to require a senior to look *first* to collateral in which a junior *has* a security interest, so as to reduce the size of secured claims against the bankruptcy estate. Compare In re Center Wholesale, Inc., 759 F.2d 1440 (9th Cir.1985) (denying junior secured party's request for marshaling order because the order would prejudice rights of trustee in bankruptcy, as hypothetical lien creditor under BC 544(a)(1), leaving less property in estate for general creditors) with *Computer Room*, supra (applying marshaling doctrine, senior secured creditor was required to look first to collateral not claimed by junior secured creditor).

SECTION 4.   REDEMPTION

INTRODUCTORY NOTE

UCC 9–623 gives "[a] debtor, any secondary obligor, or any other secured party or lienholder" a right to redeem collateral by "tender[ing] . . . fulfillment of all obligations secured by the collateral" together with related expenses incurred by the secured party. UCC 9–623(a) and (b).

> If the entire balance of a secured obligation has been accelerated, it would be necessary to tender the entire balance. A tender of fulfillment obviously means more than a new promise to perform an existing promise. It requires payment in full of all monetary obligations then due and performance in full of all other obligations then matured. If unmatured secured obligations remain, the security interest continues to secure them (i.e., as if there had been no default).

UCC 9–623, Comment 2. The right of redemption must be exercised before the secured party has collected on collateral (UCC 9–607), disposed of collateral or entered into a contract for disposition (UCC 9–610), or accepted the collateral in full or partial satisfaction of the secured obligations (UCC 9–622). Upon the occurrence of one of these events, the debtor's "equity of redemption" is *foreclosed*. Although UCC 9–602(11) generally prohibits waiver of redemption rights before default, UCC 9–624(c) explicitly permits waiver by agreement "entered into and authenticated after default."

Redemption is an ancient common law right. Professor Gilmore saw the right of redemption preserved by Former 9–506 as a "ghostly remnant of the seventeenth century right":

> Three centuries ago . . . the equity courts deduced the post-default right to redeem out of the mortgagor's pre-default equity. . ... To our ancestors the principal thing must have seemed to be not so much the fair resolution of a debtor-creditor relationship as it was the maintenance of stability in land tenure. Whatever could be done to keep the land in the ownership of the mortgagor and his family was a good thing.

2 Gilmore, Security § 44.2, at 1216.[1] As described by Mr. Clark, the right to redeem gives "the debtor one last opportunity to recover the collateral. The debtor may desire to scrape the redemption money together—perhaps through a refinancing—because it fears that the collateral will not be sold for a good price, or because there is sentimental attachment irrespective of price." Clark, Secured Transactions ¶ 4.11[1], at 4–314.2. It appears that debtors infrequently exercise the right of redemption—probably because defaulting debtors typically cannot, to repeat Mr. Clark's words, "scrape the redemption money together."

Problem 9.4.1. In the setting of the Prototype on automobile financing, Lee Abel purchased a new Chevrolet and signed the Instalment Sale Contract (Form 3.6, supra). As in the Prototype, Main Motors assigned the contract to Firstbank.

Abel made five monthly payments from August through December. Just after Christmas, Abel was laid off work and was unable to continue the payments. Two weeks after Abel missed the January 24 payment, an employee of Firstbank phoned to remind Abel that the payment was overdue. Firstbank wrote and phoned Abel several more times in February, and on February 20 Firstbank wrote to Abel stating that unless prompt payment was forthcoming, Firstbank would be required to repossess the car. Abel was still unable to find the money for the payments. On the night of February 25 the repo team repossessed the Chevrolet. (These are the facts of Problem 9.1.1, p. 570, supra, omitting the details of the repossession.)

On February 27 Firstbank sent Abel a Notice of Repossession (Form 3.9, supra). On March 2 Abel met with one of Firstbank's loan officers and offered to pay the January and February payments ($461.79 for each month) plus the default charges specified in the agreement (including the costs of repossession and storage). The loan officer pointed to provisions in paragraph 3.b. on the reverse of the Instalment Sales Contract that provide for acceleration of payments; the officer explained that the Chevrolet would

---

1.   UCC 9–623 follows Former 9–506 closely, except that the latter did not expressly extend redemption rights to secondary obligors or non-secured party lienholders. (However, some courts treated guarantors as "debtors." See Section 3(A), supra.) Accordingly, the *Williams* and *Dunn* cases, infra, dealing with Former 9–506, remain relevant under UCC 9–623.

be returned to Abel only on payment of the full unpaid balance and other charges specified in the Notice of Repossession.

Abel has sued Firstbank for recovery of the Chevrolet and for damages. The only applicable legislation is the UCC. What result? See UCC 9–623; Williams v. Ford Motor Credit Co., infra; Dunn v. General Equities of Iowa, Ltd., infra; Notes on Acceleration and Redemption of Collateral, infra.

Problem 9.4.2. The facts are the same as in the preceding Problem, except that the U3C is in force. See U3C 5.111(1) (quoted in Section 1, supra). What result?

Williams v. Ford Motor Credit Co.[*]

Supreme Court of Alabama, 1983.
435 So.2d 66.

■ MADDOX, JUSTICE.

Although several issues are presented for review, the issue which is dispositive of this appeal involves the question of whether a security agreement can be modified either orally or by waiver if the security agreement requires that all modifications be in writing. The directed verdict of the trial court is affirmed.

On November 1, 1976, Curtis Williams, plaintiff-appellant, entered into a contract to purchase a 1974 Oldsmobile from Joe Meyers Ford in Houston, Texas. The contract was financed through Ford Motor Credit Company (FMCC), the defendant-appellee. Thirty payments of $136.40 were to be made, commencing December 7, 1976, with subsequent payments to be made on the like day of each month thereafter.

The payment which was due on February 7, 1977, was not timely made, but on March 4, 1977, Mrs. Williams mailed two money orders to FMCC, one in the amount of $151.40 to include payment, plus late charges, for February, and another in the sum of $136.40 to be applied on the March 7, 1977, payment. On March 5, 1977, the vehicle was repossessed.

Mr. James Osbourn testified on behalf of FMCC that the two payments in question were received by FMCC on March 7, 1977, which was Monday after the unit was repossessed on Saturday. The deposition testimony of Samuel Wright, who was employed by the Houston West Branch of FMCC, indicated that as Customer Account Supervisor, he had custody and control of Williams's file. On March 4, 1977, Wright initiated action to repossess the car and accelerated the contract balance by means of a mailgram. He did so, he stated, after reviewing Williams's account and ascertaining that Williams was located in Mobile, and seeing that Williams was past due and that default in the March payment was imminent. FMCC had tried to contact Williams by phone, but his telephone was not in service. Williams stated that he had moved from Houston to Mobile on about the 11th or 12th of February, 1977, but he did not notify FMCC of his change in address. An independent contractor was employed by FMCC to repossess the vehicle.

---

[*]   [The court's citations are to the applicable pre–1972 version of the UCC.]

By affidavit and by deposition, Mrs. Williams stated that she made a long distance telephone call to FMCC on or about March 3 or 4. She stated that the substance of the call was that a representative of FMCC told her if the Williamses sent in two payments plus the $15.00 late charge, there would be no problem with the account. FMCC's motion in limine to suppress this evidence was granted over objection. The trial court sustained objection to Mrs. Williams's testifying that she made the call to FMCC.

After repossessing the automobile, FMCC, by letter dated March 11, 1977, sent Williams a notice of private sale. This notice informed Williams he had 10 days in which to redeem the automobile. It also stated that Williams would be liable for any deficiencies. Williams's attorney, on March 7, 1977, contacted FMCC by telephone and demanded return of the automobile because of the two payments submitted. FMCC denied that any employee of FMCC ever received a letter confirming the call.

Williams commenced this action against FMCC and other named defendants who were later dismissed from the case. The complaint, as amended, contained five counts seeking damages for the wrongful detention and conversion of a vehicle and the two money orders, and for fraud and misrepresentation. Williams sought $50,000 in damages under each of the first four counts, and $1,000,000 under the fifth count.

At the close of the plaintiff's evidence, FMCC submitted a written motion for directed verdict. After lengthy argument, this motion was later granted as to counts 3, 4, and 5. At the close of all the evidence, FMCC filed a further motion for directed verdict, which was granted as to the remaining two counts in the complaint. Williams's motion for J.N.O.V. or in the alternative a new trial was denied. This appeal followed.

We think our decision in Hale v. Ford Motor Credit Co., 374 So.2d 849 (Ala.1979), in which this Court delineated the rights and obligations of the parties under the terms of a security agreement containing both a non-waiver acceleration clause and a non-modification clause, is controlling here. In *Hale*, supra, this Court ruled that the secured party is not required to give notice to the debtor prior to repossession, even though past-due payments have been accepted on previous occasions. Further, this Court concluded that a security agreement is effective according to the terms expressed in the agreement and that the inadvertence of the debtor in failing to make timely payments cannot raise an estoppel against the contractual interest of the creditor under the express terms of the security agreement, when there has been no written modification as required by the terms of the agreement.

Assuming, *arguendo*, that Mrs. Williams's telephone conversation on March 3 or 4, 1977, was admissible to show that the contract between the Williamses and FMCC had been modified to extend the time for payment, that testimony would not change the outcome of this case since the security agreement expressly provided that any modification of its terms must be in writing. Likewise, the acceptance of the late payment could not, without a writing evidencing the modification, operate as a waiver of default. Thus, we need not decide whether the trial court erred by granting the motion in limine as to Mrs. Williams's testimony concerning the telephone call.

Mr. Wright testified that he exercised FMCC's right to accelerate the contract on March 4, 1977, by mailgram, because the appellant was in default on his February 7, 1977, payment. Paragraph 19 of the security agreement provides in pertinent part:

"Time is of the essence of this contract. In event [sic] Buyer defaults in any payment . . . Seller shall have the right to declare all amounts due or to become due hereunder to be immediately due and payable and Seller shall have the right to repossess the property wherever the same may be found with free right of entry, and to recondition and sell the same at public or private sale. Seller shall have the right to retain all payments made prior to repossession and Buyer shall remain liable for any deficiency. Buyer agrees to pay . . . expenses incurred by Seller in effecting collection, repossession or resale hereunder. Seller's remedies hereunder are in addition to any given by law and may be enforced successively and concurrently. Waiver by Seller of any default shall not be deemed waiver of any other default."

The evidence shows that FMCC received on March 7, 1977, subsequent to the acceleration and repossession, two money orders which, acceleration and repossession aside, would have made the appellant's account current through March 1977; however, in repossessing the automobile, FMCC incurred expenses of $323.50, which it was also entitled to recover.

We agree with FMCC that under the terms of the security agreement, its right to repossess the vehicle due to the default of the appellant existed independently of any right to accelerate the indebtedness due to that default. Consequently, the acceptance by FMCC of the late payment for February and the timely payment for March did not nullify the acceleration nor the remainder of the indebtedness; rather the payments received on March 7 must be considered as payments on the full indebtedness due on the appellant's account immediately after repossession on March 5. Had the appellant paid the entire contract balance, plus expenses incurred by FMCC in retaking the collateral, he would have been entitled to redeem the vehicle. The facts indicate, however, that the appellant did not redeem the automobile.

In a directed verdict case, such as the one here, the function of this Court is to view the evidence most favorably to the non-moving party; and if, by any interpretation, the evidence can support any inference supportive of a conclusion in favor of the non-moving party, we must reverse. After a review of the record, we conclude that there was no factual dispute requiring the trial court to submit the case to the jury; therefore, the trial court did not err in granting the directed verdict.

Affirmed.

Dunn v. General Equities of Iowa, Ltd.*
Supreme Court of Iowa, 1982.
319 N.W.2d 515.

■ McCormick, Judge.

The question here is whether the trial court erred in holding that the payees of two promissory notes waived their right to invoke acceleration clauses by accepting late payments on several prior occasions. We must decide if acceleration clauses can be waived by a previous course of dealing between the parties and, if so, whether the finding of waiver in this case is supported by substantial evidence. Because we give affirmative answers to each of these issues, we affirm the trial court.

Plaintiffs W.A. and Lola Dunn are payees on separate notes executed by defendant General Equities of Iowa, Inc., on March 31, 1974. The notes are identical except for the payees' names. Each provides for payment of $121,170 with seven percent annual interest. They are payable over a period of ten years, with annual installments due on or before March 31 of each year starting in 1975. Delinquent installments draw interest of nine percent. The acceleration clauses provide: "Upon default in payment of any interest, or any installment of principal, the whole amount then unpaid shall become due and payable forthwith, at the option of the holder without notice."

The parties agree that the 1979 payments were not made until April 10, 1979. Plaintiffs returned defendant's single check for both 1979 installments and demanded payment of the entire unpaid balance, with interest, in accordance with the acceleration clause. Defendant refused payment, and this suit resulted.

The determinative issue at trial was whether defendant established its defense that plaintiffs had waived their right to invoke the acceleration clause by accepting late payments in the past. The case was tried to the court at law, and the court found for defendant on the basis of its defense. This appeal followed.

I. *Waiver by course of dealing.* This court has not previously decided whether the right to enforce an acceleration clause can be waived by a course of dealing of accepting late payments on prior occasions. The issue is not affected by statute and therefore must be decided under common law principles.

The court has long held that acceleration clauses are subject to principles governing contracts generally:

> Stipulations such as are found in these notes and in the mortgage under consideration are not regarded in the nature of a penalty or forfeiture, and, for that reason, viewed with disfavor by the courts, but as agreements for bringing the notes to an earlier maturity than expressed on their face, and are to be construed and the intention of the parties ascertained by the same rules as other contracts.

* [The court's citations are to the applicable pre–1972 version of the UCC.]

Swearingen v. Lahner and Platt, 93 Iowa 147, 151, 61 N.W. 431, 433 (1894).

Contract rights, of course, can be waived, and an option to accelerate a debt is one such waivable right. Acceleration provisions are not self-executing, and "the holder of an instrument . . . must take some positive action to exercise his option to declare payments due under an acceleration clause. . . ." Weinrich v. Hawley, 236 Iowa 652, 656, 19 N.W.2d 665, 667 (1945). A failure to exercise the option or an acceptance of late payment will establish waiver:

> The notes did not become absolutely due on default in payment of the interest installment. Appellee had the right or "option" to so consider them, and to proceed at once to bring suit upon them, but was under no obligation so to do. It could waive the default and permit the notes to run without payment of any interest until they fell due on July 5, 1912, and the statute of limitations would not begin to run against the principal debt before that date. If, the interest installment being past due, its payment was tendered or offered by the defendant, and plaintiff received and accepted the same as interest, or if, knowing that defendant paid it, understanding that it was being received in satisfaction of the past-due interest, it will be held to have waived the default, and can not thereafter make it a ground for declaring the whole debt due.

Farmers' & Merchants' Bank v. Daiker, 153 Iowa 484, 487, 133 N.W. 705, 705–06 (1911).

Moreover, this court has recognized that one way to prove waiver of contract provisions is "by evidence of a general course of dealing between the parties." Livingston v. Stevens, 122 Iowa 62, 69, 94 N.W. 925, 927 (1903). The court has held, for example, that a prior "course of dealing," as defined in the Uniform Commercial Code, "may overcome express terms in [a] security agreement and translate into an authorization for sale free of lien." Citizens Savings Bank v. Sac City State Bank, 315 N.W.2d 20, 26 (Iowa 1982). As defined in the UCC, "course of dealing" means "a sequence of previous conduct between the parties to a particular transaction which is fairly to be regarded as establishing a common basis of understanding for interpreting their expressions and other conduct." § 554.1205(1), The Code. This definition is similar to the definition of course of dealing in Restatement (Second) of Contracts § 223 (1979):

> (1) A course of dealing is a sequence of previous conduct between the parties to an agreement which is fairly to be regarded as establishing a common basis of understanding for interpreting their expressions and other conduct.

> (2) Unless otherwise agreed, a course of dealing between the parties gives meaning to or supplements or qualifies their agreement.

It is obvious, therefore, that waiving an acceleration option on prior occasions may constitute a course of dealing sufficient to establish waiver of the right to exercise the option on a subsequent occasion. This court has previously applied the rule in the context of real estate contract forfeitures:

There is another reason why we think it should be held that appellees could make payment at the time the tender was made. The entire record shows a course of dealings between the buyer and the seller wherein the seller accepted payments made on dates other than those fixed by the contract. In so doing, we hold that the seller waived [its claim that payments could be made only at the time fixed in the contract].

Westercamp v. Smith, 239 Iowa 705, 717, 31 N.W.2d 347, 353 (1948). Because the rule is applicable to contract rights generally, the forfeiture context is not of controlling significance. Consequently we hold that the holder of an installment note who has engaged in a course of dealing of accepting late payments waives the right to accelerate the obligation upon a subsequent late payment unless the holder has notified the obligor that future late payments will not be accepted.

Other courts that have considered the issue have reached a similar conclusion.

The right to withdraw a waiver of time for performance upon reasonable notice to the other party has been recognized previously by this court.

The trial court was correct in holding that acceleration options in installment notes can be waived by a course of dealing of accepting late payments.

II. *Sufficiency of evidence.* Because the case was tried to the court at law, the court's findings of fact have the force of a jury's special verdict. They are binding on us if supported by substantial evidence. When reasonable minds could differ, a waiver issue is for the trier of fact.

The evidence here showed that plaintiff accepted late payments on at least three of the four prior occasions. The 1975 payments were made by a single check dated April 1, 1975. The 1976 payments were made in two installments, one on April 13 and the other on June 16 of that year. Although letters from plaintiffs following the partial payments in April demanded payment of the installment balance with interest, they did not invoke the acceleration clause or demand timely payment of future installments. The 1977 payments were made on April 11, 1977, and the 1978 payments were made by a check dated March 31, 1978.

This evidence provides a substantial basis for the trial court to find a course of dealing demonstrating waiver of timely payment of the 1979 installments. An issue of fact was presented. Therefore the trial court's finding of waiver has sufficient evidentiary support.

Affirmed.

NOTES ON ACCELERATION AND REDEMPTION OF COLLATERAL

(1) The Value of the Right of Redemption. One often hears of, or reads references to, the great value attributed to a debtor's right of redemption. As a practical matter, however, debtors infrequently are in a position to pay in full the secured obligation. Although the court in the

Williams case observed that "[h]ad the appellant paid the entire contract balance, plus expenses incurred by FMCC in retaking the collateral, he would have been entitled to redeem the vehicle[,]" neither that case nor the *Dunn* case directly involved an issue of redemption under Former 9–506. As the *Dunn* case illustrates, however, a debtor may have better luck by arguing that no default occurred or that the default was cured.

(2) Acceleration, Reinstatement, and Cure. The UCC does not regulate generally the powerful right of acceleration. For the most part it leaves to the parties' agreement both acceleration and the issue of curing defaults. It does contain limitations on the use of "at will" or "insecurity" acceleration clauses, however. UCC 1–309 [F1–208] limits the effectiveness of these provisions to situations where the accelerating party "in good faith believes that the prospect of payment or performance is impaired." Moreover, do not infer that the absence of specific regulation in the UCC is the end of the matter. See, e.g., Urdang v. Muse, 114 N.J.Super. 372, 276 A.2d 397 (Essex County Ct.1971) (secured party's refusal to return repossessed car to debtor upon debtor's credible offer to pay $900, when total amount of delinquent installment payments was $266.39 and expenses of repossession were $52.77, was a breach of secured party's duty of good faith under F1–203 [UCC 1–304]; equitable solution was to deny secured party's deficiency and leave parties as they were).

A debtor's right to cure a default prior to acceleration, a creditor's right to accelerate, and a debtor's right to reinstatement following acceleration are matters of considerable regulation in the area of consumer credit transactions. See, e.g., U3C 5.110; U3C 5.111 (quoted in Section 1, supra). Other statutes in effect in numerous states also provide a grace period following a default and a right to cure. In some states consumer debtors enjoy a right to "reinstate" the secured debt and obtain possession of collateral after repossession and acceleration. Reinstatement rights typically are conditioned upon the debtor's not only curing past defaults but also paying any required fees or charges and expenses of repossession.

(3) Who Is Entitled to Redeem Collateral? As noted in the Introductory Note, supra, Former 9–506 conferred the right to redeem collateral on the "debtor" and "any . . . secured party." UCC 9–623(a) now explicitly extends that right to "any secondary obligor." The right of redemption also extends to "any . . . lienholder." The latter extension addresses what Professor Gilmore considered a "drafting inadvertence." 2 Gilmore, Security § 44.2, at 1217–18.

Former 9–506 apparently did not provide a statutory right of redemption to a *buyer* of collateral subject to a senior security interest. Consider the potential plight of Bonzo Co. in Problem 9.3.5, p. 648, supra. Assume that Bonzo fails to discover AIB's senior security interest and buys the office equipment at Tuleight's foreclosure sale for $50,000. Even if Bonzo had a right to redeem the equipment, under Former 9–506, Bonzo would have been required to pay several million dollars to AIB because the equipment secures all Schmelli's indebtedness to AIB! But, would AIB have any incentive *not* to accept the fair value for the collateral instead? For an argument that a junior buyer should enjoy a statutory right to redeem collateral by paying to the senior secured party the fair market value of the collateral, *not* the entire amount of the secured debt, see Wechsler, Rights and Remedies of the Secured Party After an Unauthorized Transfer of Collateral: A Proposal for Balancing Competing Claims in Repossession, Resale, Proceeds, and Conversion Cases, 32 Buff. L. Rev. 373, 381–84 (1983). To what extent, if any, does Revised Article 9 adopt Professor Wechsler's proposal to afford a redemption right to the buyer of collateral subject to a security interest? See UCC 9–102(a)(28) & Comment 2.a. (2d paragraph).

(4) Notice of Redemption Rights. Former 9–506 did not, by its terms, require a secured party to notify the debtor or any other secured party of a right to redeem. Some states afford that protection to consumer debtors by statute other than the UCC. See, e.g., Pennsylvania Motor Vehicle Sales Finance Act, Pa. Stat. Ann., tit. 69 § 623D. In consumer-goods transactions, Revised Article 9 requires the notification of disposition to provide "a telephone number from which the amount that must be paid to the secured party to redeem the collateral under Section 9–623 is available." UCC 9–614(1)(C). The statutory "safe-harbor" form of notice includes the following: "You can get the property back at any time before we sell it by paying us the full amount you owe (not just the past due payments), including our expenses. To learn the exact amount you must pay, call us at [*telephone number*]." UCC 9–614(3). Should Article 9 require an enforcing secured party to give notice of redemption rights in all transactions?

What is the consequence of including an incorrect statement of the debtor's right to redeem? Suppose, for example, a debtor is notified that redemption of collateral by payment in full must be made earlier than the time specified in UCC 9–623, or may be made only by payment of a sum greater than that necessary to redeem. In consumer-goods transactions, the consequence depends on whether the secured party uses the statutory form. If the form is used, then the notice will be sufficient notwithstanding the error unless, as appears to be the case in the example, "the error is misleading with respect to rights arising under this article." UCC 9–614(5). If the notice is not in the statutory form, then law other than Article 9 "determines the effect of including information not required" in the notice. UCC 9–614(6). In consumer-goods transactions, the notice need not include the redemption amount, only a telephone number from which the amount can be obtained. Nor need the notice include information concerning the time before which the right must be exercised. See UCC 9–614(1). Assuming that the inclusion of this additional information precludes the notification from being in the safe-harbor form, then non-Article 9 law determines the consequence of including an incorrect statement of the debtor's right to redeem.

In other (non-consumer-goods) transactions, there is no requirement even to mention redemption in the notice. UCC 9–613(3) says that "The contents of a notification providing substantially the information specified in paragraph (1) are sufficient, even if the notification includes (A) information not specified by that paragraph; or (B) minor errors that are not seriously misleading." The notification probably would not qualify for the safe harbor in subparagraph (B), inasmuch as the errors appear to be seriously misleading. In addition, a notification containing incorrect information that pertains to important rights relating to the disposition of collateral would not seem to qualify as a "reasonable . . . notification" required by UCC 9–611(b).

SECTION 5. COLLECTIONS FROM AND ENFORCEMENT AGAINST ACCOUNT DEBTORS AND OTHER PERSONS OBLIGATED ON COLLATERAL

INTRODUCTORY NOTE

This book examines rights in and concerning receivables in many and varied contexts. For example, Chapter 1, Section 4, supra, introduces the basic principles governing the good faith purchase of rights to payment. Security interests in receivables and related priority contests are considered in several places. See, e.g., Chapter 3, Section 1, supra (Lee Abel's Instalment Sales Contract assigned to Firstbank, in the Prototype transaction); Chapter 3, Section 5, supra (collections of cash proceeds); Chapter 4, Section 2(B), supra (priority contests between buyers of accounts and general intangibles and unperfected security interests); Chapter 6, Section 1(B) (receivables financing Prototype); Chapter 6, Section 1(F), supra (collections of receivables and rights and duties of account debtors); Chapter 6, Section 2, supra (special priority rules for purchasers of chattel paper, instruments, and documents); Chapter 7, Section 2(B), supra (treatment of "floating lien" on receivables and inventory); Chapter 8, Section 3(B), supra (real property-related receivables); Chapter 8, Section 4(D), supra (account debtors' defenses and rights of setoff).

This Section deals with collections by secured parties from, and enforcement by secured parties against, account debtors and other persons obligated on collateral. As between a debtor and a secured party, the rights and duties of the secured party concerning collections and enforcement are governed by UCC 9–607. (The rights and duties of the account debtor are, of course, the subject of UCC 9–341 and UCC 9–403 through UCC 9–408. See UCC 9–607(e) and Comment 6; Chapter 6, Section 1(F), supra; Chapter 8, Section 4(D), supra.) UCC 9–607(a) entitles a secured party (again, vis-a-vis the debtor) to undertake direct collections from account debtors and other persons obligated on collateral and to enforce collateral against account debtors and other persons obligated on collateral "[i]f so agreed, and in any event after default[.]" The following materials focus primarily on the rights and duties of secured parties who elect to undertake collections or to enforce collateral following a debtor's default. As to the debtor's agreement to the assignee's collections on the collateral before default, recall Mr. Kupfer's discussion of the distinction between "notification" receivables financing, where account debtors are notified and instructed at the inception of the transaction to remit payments to the assignee, and "non-notification" financing, where the debtor is permitted to collect the receivables—at least until a default occurs. See Chapter 6, Section 1(A), supra. See also UCC 9–607, Comments 1 and 4.

Problem 9.5.1. Under the facts of Problem 9.2.1, p. 602, supra, you now represent AIB once again. AIB has ceased making new advances against Schmelli's accounts and has demanded payment of the $4,500,000 owed on the line of credit facility. The loan officer fears that the lagging economy and Schmelli's more aggressive collection efforts are combining to shrink Schmelli's pool of accounts receivable; the officer has asked you for advice on how to collect Schmelli's accounts as soon as possible.

(a) What alternatives are available? What do you recommend? Would your advice be different if AIB had bought the accounts from Schmelli "outright," on a non-recourse basis? See UCC 9–607(a), (c); R 9–608(b); Notes on Collections by Secured Parties, infra.

(b) After AIB notified Schmelli's account debtors, instructing them to remit all payments directly to AIB, a "funny" thing happened: the account debtors quit paying Schmelli and many of them *also* have not paid AIB. The loan officer has written letters to the delinquent account debtors. What else, if anything, should be done? See R 9–608(b); Note (1) on Collections by Secured Parties, infra.

(c) The loan officer has informed you that Fractured Factors, Inc. (FFI), has made an offer to buy all of Schmelli's accounts—on a non-recourse basis and at a very steep discount. However, considering how long it may take to collect the accounts, and considering the interest charges that continue to run (at the default rate) on Schmelli's loans, the officer thinks that selling to FFI "may be just about the best thing for us and for Schmelli as well." What advice do you give? What steps should be taken? See UCC 9–610; UCC 9–611; Note (4) on Collections by Secured Parties, infra.

(d) One of the largest accounts, about $50,000, is disputed. The account debtor, Gravilumps Corp. (GC), has demanded a credit of $18,000 because of "grossly unqualified personnel" supplied by Schmelli. (One of Schmelli's temps caused GC's computer to "eat" the payroll records.) GC refuses to pay anything until the matter is resolved. Schmelli adamantly denies GC's claims. The loan officer thinks that the matter could be settled by offering a $10,000 credit. What do you recommend? Would you give different advice if the amount involved were $180? $180,000? See Note (1) on Collections by Secured Parties, infra. What, if anything, might have been provided in the security agreement that would make your advice more certain? See UCC 9–602(3); UCC 9–603.

(e) Another of the largest accounts involves a financially troubled customer, Nodough Co. (NC). Last year Schmelli took a negotiable note from NC evidencing NC's two-year installment obligation; NC is current on the note and is willing and able to make this month's payment. Schmelli refuses to deliver the note to AIB. Is AIB entitled to collect the payment from NC?

See UCC 9–607(a), (e); UCC 3–412; UCC 3–301; Note (6) on Collections by Secured Parties, infra.

NOTES ON COLLECTIONS BY SECURED PARTIES

(1) **Commercially Reasonable Collections and Enforcement; Surplus and Deficiency.** A secured party who "undertakes to collect from or enforce an obligation of an account debtor or other person obligated on collateral" generally is required to "proceed in a commercially reasonable manner." UCC 9–607(c). This obligation is imposed only "if the secured party . . . is entitled to charge back uncollected collateral or otherwise to full or limited recourse against the debtor or a secondary obligor." Id. And if the "security interest secures payment or performance of an obligation," the debtor is entitled to any surplus and liable for any deficiency. UCC 9–608(a)(4). (These provisions recognize that a transaction could be a "true" sale but nonetheless impose *some* recourse against the debtor based on the amount recovered by the secured party from the receivable involved. See Note (2), infra. In such a transaction the secured party must act in a commercially reasonable manner.) Most of the factors and issues relating to commercially reasonable dispositions under UCC 9–610(b), considered in Section 2, supra, are equally applicable to the determination of whether a secured party's collections or enforcement efforts are commercially reasonable; the rules also share a common rationale. A secured party's failure to proceed in a commercially reasonable manner exposes the secured party to the same sanctions that can result from conducting a commercially unreasonable disposition. See Notes (7) and (8), p. 628, supra.

UCC 9–607(a)(1) and (2) afford a secured party the right to notify an account debtor or other person obligated on collateral to render performance to the secured party and to take any proceeds to which the secured party is entitled. UCC 9–607(a)(3) provides to the secured party a broader and more general right to "enforce" collateral. It recognizes that much collateral does not consist of a simple right to payment that the secured party could "collect." For example, if the collateral consists of the debtor's rights as a franchisee under a franchise agreement, the secured party might seek an injunction against the franchisor's termination of the agreement. Paragraphs (a)(4) and (5) provide special rules for security interests in deposit accounts that are perfected by control. See Chapter 6, Section 4, supra. Subsection (b) provides a means by which a secured party can become the assignee of record in order to utilize nonjudicial procedures to foreclose a real property mortgage that secures an obligation included in collateral. See Chapter 8, Section 3(A), supra.

The issue of whether collections are commercially reasonable has not been a frequent and major point of litigation, unlike the issue of commercially reasonable dispositions. Although foreclosure sales typically are out-of-the-ordinary transactions, collections normally are routine, whether undertaken by the debtor or an assignee. When an account debtor or other obligated person fails to pay, however, the reasonableness of the collecting assignee's response may be put to the test.

Note that UCC 9–607 differs in one important respect from its analogue for dispositions of collateral, UCC 9–611. There is no requirement in UCC 9–607 that notification be given to the debtor or any other interested persons. What justifications are there for the absence of a notification requirement? Is the interest of a debtor in commercially reasonable collections any less than in the case of dispositions? To take the most straightforward and typical example, perhaps the distinction results from the drafters' perception that a debtor is more likely to be able to increase the price that collateral fetches at a disposition (e.g., by finding potential buyers) than to increase the amount that an account debtor pays on a receivable.

Nothing in Article 9 would seem to impose a *duty* on an assignee of a receivable to undertake collection. The obligations in UCC 9–607(c) are triggered only when and if a secured party "undertakes to collect . . . or enforce. . . ." See F.D.I.C. v. Wrapwell Corp., 46 UCC Rep.Serv.2d 885 (S.D.N.Y.2002) (secured party who is not in "possession and control" of receivables and in exclusive control of collections is not subject to commercially reasonable standard unless debtor justifiably relies on secured party's collection efforts). If a secured party endeavors to collect one receivable, is it obliged to attempt collection of *all* receivables in which it has a security interest? What actions constitute an undertaking to collect or enforce that triggers UCC 9–607(c)? The statutory language is less than clear on these issues. See DeLay First National Bank & Trust Co. v. Jacobson Appliance Co., 196 Neb. 398, 243 N.W.2d 745 (1976) (secured creditor that took possession of all of debtor's records concerning its accounts, wrote two letters to some account debtors, and then took no further action failed to meet its burden of proof as to commercially reasonable collections under Former 9–502(2)).

(2) Sale versus Security for Obligation. The contours of UCC 9–607 and UCC 9–608 have been carefully crafted to take account of the scope of Article 9, which includes the sale of accounts, chattel paper, instruments, and payment intangibles. See Chapter 6, Section 1(D), supra. UCC 9–608(b) makes explicit what is implicit in UCC 9–608(a), dealing with application of proceeds (see Note (3), infra)—when there is a *sale* of a receivable the debtor (seller) is neither entitled to any surplus nor (absent agreement to the contrary) liable for a deficiency. With the exception of this provision and the corresponding provision in UCC 9–615(e), Part 6 provides identical treatment for secured transactions consisting of sales of accounts, chattel paper, payment intangibles, and promissory notes, and those where the receivables secure payment or performance of an obligation. Even if the transaction is a sale of receivables covered by Article 9, however, if the secured party has recourse against the debtor or a secondary obligor following the secured party's collection or enforcement efforts, the secured party is obliged to "proceed in a commercially reasonable manner." UCC 9–607(c).

When the right to a surplus or the liability for a deficiency is at stake under UCC 9–608(b), it will be necessary to distinguish a sale of accounts, chattel paper, payment intangibles, or promissory notes from a security interest that secures payment or performance of an obligation. At the extremes the distinction is easy to make. For example, a putative sale pursuant to terms that unconditionally require the assignor to repurchase the receivable upon default of the account debtor, for a price equal to the outstanding balance of the account, is the functional equivalent of a loan and would be treated as such. On the other hand, where the assignee has absolutely no recourse whatsoever against the assignor, regardless of whether the account debtor performs, characterization as an outright sale seems appropriate. Other arrangements may be much less clear.

Unlike its treatment of leases, the definition of "security interest" in UCC 1–201(35) [F1–201(37)] provides no explicit guidance as to when an assignment of receivables constitutes a "sale." "[T]he cases [dealing with the sale/secured loan dichotomy] are not easily harmonized, and different readers can argue as to which factors are relevant and which are entitled to the greater weight." S. Schwarcz, Structured Finance § 4:1, at 4-5 (3d ed. 2003 & Supp. 2005). Professor Schwarcz identifies the following factors, among others, as relevant: the existence and nature of recourse against the transferor, the extent to which the transferor retains rights (including the right to surplus collections), the nature of the pricing mechanism, and the arrangements for administration and collection.

(3) Application of Proceeds of Collection or Enforcement. UCC 9–608(a) contains provisions regulating a secured party's application of proceeds of collection or enforcement. These provisions are analogous to those contained in UCC 9–615(a) through (c) for the proceeds of dispositions of collateral.

(4) Dispositions of Receivables as an Alternative to Collection. Is a secured party entitled to sell a receivable in lieu of collection or enforcement under UCC 9–607? The references to accounts, chattel paper, payment intangibles, and promissory notes in UCC 9–615(e) clearly indicate that receivables can be the subject of a disposition under UCC 9–610. Of course, the disposition must itself be commercially reasonable, and one could imagine circumstances where the ease and certainty of collection would render unreasonable any disposition for a price less than the full present value of the receivable.

(5) "Lockbox" Arrangements. Collection of a debtor's receivables by a secured party following the debtor's default typically, and understandably, reflects poorly on the debtor's continued economic viability. Account debtors who fear that the debtor may be unable to perform future contracts may be tempted to withhold payments for goods or services that the debtor previously provided. Additionally, the account debtors' uncertainty about whether to pay a notifying secured party and their requests for evidence of the assignment (see UCC 9–406) frequently disrupt and delay the collection of the receivables.

To avoid these problems and to facilitate the secured party's collections following a default, the parties sometimes enter into a **lockbox** arrangement at the inception of a transaction. A typical lockbox arrangement involves a special **cash collateral deposit account** that is under the control of the secured party. The debtor is required to change its billing practices by instructing all account debtors to remit their payments to a particular post office box to which only the depository bank has access. The bank then deposits all receipts into the cash collateral account. The secured party typically agrees that the debtor may make withdrawals from the account, provided that no default has occurred. If a default does occur, collection efforts are facilitated and (unless the debtor wrongfully changes the payment instructions on its bills) the secured party need not disclose the fact of the default to the account debtors.

(6) Collections on Instruments. A secured party's collection and enforcement rights also extend to collections from persons obligated on instruments. See UCC 9–607(a) and (c) (collection and enforcement against "person obligated on collateral"); UCC 9–102(a)(3) (defining "account debtor" so as to exclude a person obligated to pay a negotiable instrument). Because the term "account debtor" includes only those persons obligated on an account, chattel paper, or general intangible, it also excludes a person obligated on a nonnegotiable instrument, unless the instrument in included in chattel paper. See UCC 9–102(a)(3) (defining "account debtor"), (a)(47) (defining "instrument"). However, with certain limited exceptions, a secured party cannot enforce an obligation evidenced by a negotiable instrument governed by UCC Article 3 unless the secured party is in possession of the instrument. See UCC 3–412; UCC 3–301; UCC 3–203; Chapter 1, Section 4, infra. This does not present a problem when the instruments involved are delivered to the secured party at the inception of a financing transaction. When this is not the case, the secured party must rely on the debtor's compliance with covenants to deliver them for the purpose of perfection (UCC 9–313), unless a financing statement has been filed, or the purpose of collection and enforcement in the event of a default. Non–UCC law determines whether possession is required to enforce a nonnegotiable instrument that is not part of chattel paper.

SECTION 6. ACCEPTANCE OF COLLATERAL IN SATISFACTION OF SECURED OBLIGATIONS: "STRICT FORECLOSURE"

INTRODUCTORY NOTE

After a debtor's default a secured party may agree with the debtor and other interested persons to accept collateral in satisfaction of the secured obligations. The procedures for the secured party's acceptance of collateral are set forth in a somewhat intricate statutory framework: UCC 9–620 through UCC 9–622. This remedy is commonly known as "strict foreclosure."

It is an alternative to the secured party's disposition of collateral or collection and enforcement of collateral. The conditions for an effective strict foreclosure are specified in UCC 9–620(a) and (b); please review those conditions.

The effect of a secured party's acceptance of collateral is equivalent to the secured party's acquisition of the collateral at its own private disposition: the secured party becomes the owner of the collateral, the secured obligations are discharged in whole or in part, and the debtor remains liable for any deficiency. As you may recall, UCC 9–610(c)(2) prohibits a secured party from acquiring collateral at a private disposition (except in limited circumstances), and Article 9 makes no provision for a debtor's waiver of this prohibition. See; UCC 9–624, Comment 2. Given this prohibition, why does UCC 9–620(a) explicitly permit acceptance of collateral in satisfaction of the secured obligations? The Drafting Committee thought that the benefits of encouraging strict foreclosure over dispositions of collateral outweighed any potential for overreaching.

Strict foreclosure can be advantageous to both secured parties and debtors. Section 9–620 "reflects the belief that strict foreclosure should be encouraged and often will produce better results than a disposition for all concerned." UCC 9–620, Comment 2. Through strict foreclosure, a secured party can avoid the time and expense of a disposition under UCC 9–610, can protect itself from later objections by the debtor to the commercial reasonableness of the disposition, and can eliminate the obligation to account to the debtor for any surplus. Because deficiencies arise much more often than surpluses, a debtor also may be advantaged by a strict foreclosure, especially one that satisfies the secured obligations in full.

In the case of collateral that is consumer goods, if an obligor has paid 60% or more of the principal amount of a secured loan or the cash price (i.e., the price of the goods, without taking into account finance charges and other amounts included in the secured obligations), UCC 9–620(e) prohibits strict foreclosure unless the debtor has signed after default a statement modifying or waiving the right to insist upon a disposition. UCC 9–624(b). The Notes on Acceptance of Collateral discuss other special provisions that apply in consumer transactions as well as the requirements for acceptance generally.

Problem 9.6.1. You continue to represent AIB under the facts of Problem 9.2.1, p. 602, supra. As in Problem 9.5.1, supra, AIB has ceased making new advances against Schmelli's accounts and has demanded payment of the $4,500,000 owed on the line of credit facility. So far AIB has not disposed of any of the collateral or collected any of the receivables.

The loan officer met today with Telli Schmelli. Although relationships remain strained, AIB and Schmelli have agreed in principle that the bank will accept ownership of the Learjet in full satisfaction of the $2,500,000 balance on the Learjet loan and in satisfaction of $600,000 of the line of credit debt. Both Schmelli and AIB recognize that the market for corporate aircraft is poor right now. Schmelli believes that it will receive a credit on the debts approximately equal to the fair market value of the Learjet. The loan officer is pleased not to be faced with the hassles and risks of a foreclosure sale.

(a) The loan officer has asked you to "draft the papers as soon as possible." How do you proceed? See UCC 9–620; Notes on Acceptance of Collateral, infra.

(b) Unbeknownst to AIB, in violation of the security agreement, and before AIB demanded payment of the $4,500,000, Schmelli created a junior security interest in the Learjet in favor of Hardluck Bank. Hardluck properly perfected its security interest under federal law by recording immediately with the Federal Aviation Administration. See UCC 9–109(c)(1); UCC 9–311. Two weeks after the papers referred to in part (a) are signed, AIB receives a letter from Hardluck demanding that AIB turn over the Learjet so that Hardluck can enforce its security interest. Advise AIB. (Assume that federal law defers to Article 9 on these issues.) See UCC 9–622; UCC 9–620(a), (c), (d); UCC 9–621.

NOTES ON ACCEPTANCE OF COLLATERAL

(1) Debtor's Consent to Acceptance. An obvious, and essential, condition to an effective acceptance is the debtor's consent. UCC 9–620(a)(1). For example, a disposition of the collateral might bring an amount many times the amount of the secured obligation. The debtor is entitled to the difference between the value of the collateral and the amount of the secured obligation. (This amount is often referred to as the **debtor's equity**.) Conditioning the secured party's acceptance of the collateral in satisfaction of the secured obligation enables the debtor to protect its equity. (The requirement of UCC 9–610(b) that a disposition be conducted in a commercially reasonable manner can perform the same equity-protecting function.)

UCC 9–620(c) specifies the elements of an effective consent by the debtor. This subsection contains two alternative methods for consent. First, the debtor may agree to the terms of the acceptance. Alternatively, the secured party may send a "proposal" to the debtor; if the secured party does not receive the debtor's authenticated objection within 20 days after sending the proposal, the debtor's consent is effective. See UCC 9–620(c)(2); UCC 9–102(a)(66) (defining "proposal"). Although UCC 9–620(a) provides that "a secured party may accept collateral in full or partial satisfaction of the obligation it secures," a *proposal* to a debtor will be the basis for an effective consent only if it is for *full* satisfaction of the secured obligations. For a partial satisfaction the debtor's actual agreement is required. Moreover, in consumer transactions, acceptances in partial satisfaction are not permitted under any circumstances. See UCC 9–620(g). Do you see any basis for these limitations?

(2) Objection to Acceptance by Claimants Other Than the Debtor; Notification Requirements. The second condition for an effective acceptance is specified in UCC 9–620(a)(2); it is a negative event: the secured party's failure to receive an objection to the acceptance from a specified person within the times provided in UCC 9–620(d). The persons specified include those to whom the secured party is required to send a proposal under UCC 9–621. These are the same persons who are to be given notification of disposition under UCC 9–611. Under UCC 9–621, however, there is no "safe harbor" to protect against filing office delays in responding to search requests. For an explanation, see UCC 9–621, Comment 2. Any other person who claims a subordinate interest in the collateral also may object and thereby prevent an effective acceptance from occurring. See UCC 9–620, Comment 3 (3d paragraph).

UCC 9–620(d) specifies the time within which an objection must be made in order to be effective. A person to whom a proposal is sent must object within 20 days after the notice was sent to that person. UCC 9–620(d)(1). A person to whom a proposal is required to be sent but is not sent (e.g., because the secured party does not know about that person) also has a right to object; the time for that person to make an effective objection expires within 20 days after the last notification of the proposal was sent pursuant to Section 9–621. If no proposal was sent to anyone, the time expires when the debtor consents to the acceptance under subsection (c). UCC 9–620(d)(2).

(3) Requirement That Collateral Be in Secured Party's Possession. Former 9–505(2) provided that a secured party must be "in possession" of collateral in order to propose a retention. UCC 9–621 generally eliminates that requirement. (Hence the concept is now called "acceptance" instead of "retention" of collateral.) This change makes clear that strict foreclosure is not limited to tangible collateral, such as goods. Not only can a secured party effect an acceptance of collateral without dispossessing a debtor, strict foreclosure is available for collateral such as accounts and other intangibles that *cannot* be possessed.

The possession requirement has been retained for consumer-goods collateral; the goods must not be in the debtor's possession when the debtor consents to the acceptance. UCC 9–621(a)(3). We suspect that the concerns about debtors in consumer-goods transactions arise from the fact that a debtor's consent can be achieved by sending a proposal followed by no timely objection. There is no requirement that the debtor actually *receive* the proposal. Compare UCC 9–620(c)(2)(A) with UCC 9–620(c)(2)(C). In the absence of the dispossession requirement for consumer goods, it would be possible for a secured party to become the *owner* of a debtor's consumer goods before the debtor had actual knowledge that an enforcement step was underway. At least when the secured party dispossesses the debtor of the collateral, the debtor normally would realize that an enforcement has begun.

(4) Effect of Acceptance of Collateral. Like a disposition of collateral, an acceptance of collateral discharges subordinate security interests and liens and terminates other subordinate interests. See UCC 9–622(a)(3) and (4). Moreover, under UCC 9–622(b) an acceptance discharges these subordinate interests and liens *"even if the secured party fails to comply with this article"* (emphasis added). The upshot of this provision is that the secured party's failure to send a proposal to the persons specified in UCC

9–621 does not render the acceptance ineffective. The acceptance nonetheless will discharge or terminate the lien or interest held by a person to whom the secured party was required to send, but did not send, a proposal. See 9–620(a)(2) (secured party's failure to receive an objection satisfies the condition for acceptance; actually sending a proposal under UCC 9–621 is not a condition). Of course, the secured party may be liable to a person to whom it fails to send a proposal. See UCC 9–625(b); UCC 9–622, Comment 2 (second paragraph).

(5) Acceptance of Collateral Followed by Immediate Sale; Good Faith. Nothing in Revised Article 9 prohibits a secured party from accepting collateral under UCC 9–620 and then selling it immediately. Former 9–505 likewise contained no such restriction. However, one court held a sale under these circumstances to be impermissible. In Reeves v. Foutz & Tanner, Inc., 94 N.M. 760, 617 P.2d 149 (1980), the secured party proposed to retain jewelry that was worth much more than the secured obligation. After the debtor (an individual) failed to make a timely objection, the secured party placed the jewelry in its inventory and promptly sold it. The court relied in part on Former 9–505, Statement of Reasons for 1972 Changes in Official Text: "Under subsection (2) of this section the secured party may in lieu of sale give notice to the debtor and certain other persons that he proposes to retain the collateral *in lieu of sale.*" (Emphasis added.) The court also relied on a Federal Trade Commission decision interpreting the cited Statement for the proposition that a waiver of surplus or deficiency rights is appropriate only when the creditor does not contemplate the prompt resale of the repossessed collateral in the ordinary course of business. See Reeves, 617 P.2d at 151 (citing and quoting In the Matter of Ford Motor Company, Ford Motor Credit Co., and Francis Ford, Inc., 94 F.T.C. Rep. 564, 3 Trade Reg. Rep. (CCH) 21756, 21767 (1979)). Mr. Clark argued that Reeves "puts the court in the position of repealing" Former 9–505 and, if that is the case, "the decision is obviously wrong." Clark, Secured Transactions ¶ 4.10[1], at 4–287.

Revised Article 9 suggests another approach to a proposal for an acceptance under which there is a substantial difference between the value of the collateral to be accepted and the (much lower) amount of the obligation to be satisfied. See UCC 9–620, Comment 11 (great disparity between value of collateral and obligation to be satisfied may constitute bad faith and render acceptance ineffective); UCC 1–304 [F1–203].

(6) "Constructive" Strict Foreclosure. Under Former Article 9 a number of courts held that a secured party's conduct in retaining possession of collateral without disposition for an unusually long period of time could constitute a retention in satisfaction within the scope of Former 9–505(2), whether or not the secured party intended to invoke that remedy. These decisions effectively denied the secured party any right to a deficiency judgment. Of course, courts were not likely to find an involuntary strict foreclosure when it was the creditor, instead of the debtor, who advanced the implied election argument.

There also existed a line of decisions under Former Article 9 that refused to find an involuntary strict foreclosure in cases of delay. Revised Article 9 follows these decisions and the recommendations of most commentators. Under UCC 9–620(b)(1), an acceptance is ineffective unless the secured party "consents in an authenticated record or sends a proposal to the debtor." Consequently, "constructive" strict foreclosures cannot occur under the revised Article; instead, a delay in collection or disposition of collateral is a factor relating to whether the secured party acted in a commercially reasonable manner for purposes of UCC 9–607 or UCC 9–610. See UCC 9–620, Comment 5.

INDEX

*